Distributed by Littlehampton Book Services, Ltd
Faraday Close, Durrington, Worthing, West Sussex, BN13 3RB
Copyright © Waitrose Ltd, 2015. Waitrose Ltd, Doncastle Road, Bracknell, Berkshire, RG12 8YA

Data management and export by AMA DataSet Ltd, Preston
Printed and bound in Italy by L.E.G.O. S.p.A.

A catalogue record for this book is available from the British Library
ISBN: 978 0 95379 833 9

Maps designed and produced by Cosmographics Ltd, www.cosmographics.co.uk
Mapping contains Ordnance Survey data © Crown copyright and database right 2015 UK digital
database © Cosmographics Ltd, 2015. Greater London map and North and South London maps
© Cosmographics Ltd, 2015. West, Central and East London map data © Cosmographics Ltd,
2015 used with kind permission of VisitBritain. Illustrations for features courtesy of Shutterstock.

Consultant Editor: Elizabeth Carter
Editor: Rochelle Venables
Editorial Assistant: Ria Martin

The Good Food Guide makes every effort to be as accurate and up to date as possible.
All inspections are anonymous, but Main Entries have been contacted separately for details. As
we are an annual Guide, we have strict guidelines for fact-checking information ahead of going
to press, so some restaurants were removed if they failed to provide the information we required.
The editors' decision on inclusion and scores in *The Good Food Guide* is final, and we will not
enter into any discussion on the matter with individual restaurants.

The publisher cannot be held responsible for any errors or omissions, or for changes in the
details given in this Guide. Restaurants may close, change chefs or adjust their opening
times and prices during the Guide's lifetime, and readers should always check with the restaurant.

We would like to extend special thanks to the following people: Iain Barker, Jackie Bates,
Ruth Coombs, Tom Fahey, Alan Grimwade, Joanne Murray, Alan Rainford, Emma Sturgess,
Mark Taylor, Steve Trayler, Andy Turvil, Stuart Walton, Jenny White, Lisa Whitehouse and
Shelley Wills. And thanks in particular to all of our hard-working inspectors.

www.thegoodfoodguide.co.uk

'You can corrupt one man.
You can't bribe an army.'

Raymond Postgate,
founder of The Good Food Guide, 1951

A message from Mark Price

Managing Director, Waitrose

I can remember as though it were only yesterday the well-worn and heavily thumbed copy of *The Good Food Guide* that would accompany my parents on all of our UK holidays. My brother, sister and I would then enter the heavy debate about which restaurant to choose; and it is safe to say we were never disappointed.

The Good Food Guide has also been my constant companion in thirty years of business, and I have come to value its impartial and authoritative guidance. I am delighted that such a national treasure is now under the care of Waitrose, especially in this, its 65th year. I wish it many more nourishing years to come.

Contents

Introduction

Elizabeth Carter, Consultant Editor

What you have in your hands is the UK's most trusted, best-loved food bible. It is 65 years since *The Good Food Guide* was first published, a hardback of 224 pages costing five shillings and listing '600 places throughout Britain where you can rely on a good meal at a reasonable price'. It became a post-war phenomenon. Guide founder Raymond Postgate's passionately held belief that if you shouted loud enough, the standard of restaurant food in Britain could and would be raised, inspired an army of like-minded people to report on places where the food was decent – and the rise of the consumer group as a force in the market place was born.

Postgate himself reserved his highest praise for the Guide's readers: 'This is your book. It could not exist if you ceased to communicate with us, advising, warning and praising. We only interpret, verify, co-ordinate, and evaluate.' The bare bones of Postgate's original Guide remain to this day: the book is still based on the huge volume of feedback received from readers throughout the year, inspections are carried out anonymously, and the Guide continues to be completely impartial, accepting neither industry sponsorship, payment for entry nor free meals.

The way we eat now

In the past decade, the UK's culinary reputation has grown dramatically. International chefs hail London as one of the world's most energetic and creative cities for new restaurants, and our celebrated chefs have established the capital as a global dining destination. But within the city-state that is London, with its bullish economy and vibrant restaurant scene, property premiums are changing the demographics of dining-out. This year and last, much of the buzz generated by new openings in central London has come from big, established operators with the finance to open second, third or more branches: Dishoom, Hawksmoor, Vinoteca, Corbin and King to name but a few. These places may no longer win any points for originality, but they have proved to be well-tested formulas for success.

So with lesser known, independent restaurateurs or chefs priced out of the city centre, should we be worrying about the strength of London's restaurant scene? The answer may well lie in the capital's suburbs. Central London property prices have forced restaurateurs to explore the possibilities to be found in residential areas in the capital's outer zones. Witness chefs like Robin Gill, who has hit the jackpot with his two hugely popular restaurants in Clapham: the Dairy and the Manor. In south London, chef Mike Davies' first solo venture, The Camberwell Arms, is beloved by locals, and Artusi in Peckham is fast becoming everyone's favourite Italian restaurant – a destination in its own right.

To the east, Charlotte and Michael Sager-Wilde's Mission, a wine bar with an ambitious kitchen, is proving a hit in Bethnal Green. The city-centre's stranglehold on a 'good meal out' looks to be on the wane as London's restaurateurs and residents vote with their feet; and increasingly eat local.

The good news...

Scan through the pages of this Guide and you will find many new names – and this year saw some of the more originally minded restaurants open outside of London. Throughout the UK, diners are now more interested in where ingredients come from, and the creative possibilities of how they are prepared, than in classic techniques. Above all, we are coming to value the simple formula of a kitchen that cooks fresh to order – the very principle on which this Guide was founded. One standout among such newcomers is Lake Road Kitchen in Ambleside, Cumbria, whose great achievement is that it is both highly ambitious and resolutely accessible: James Cross gathers, stores and preserves to create some truly memorable food. But honourable mention must also go to chefs Graham Squire at the Lickfold Inn in West Sussex, and to Tom Parker at the White Swan at Fence, Lancashire, both of whom do a superb job of taking a country pub pressed right up against tradition and tweaking it for modern taste.

...and the bad

Regular readers may have noticed that a larger number of restaurants than usual are missing from the Guide this year. There have been some surprising closures – among them Sienna in Dorset, and the British Larder in Suffolk – but a significant number have been jointly filtered out by readers and inspectors because they just do not make the grade. The comment 'I would not return' tells us all we need to know.

Getting into the Guide

Tapas, sharing plates, tasting menus, wine pairings, two-hour dining slots, no-reservations, high prices – these are all subjects on which *Good Food Guide* readers have voiced their opinions. Indeed, the strength of the Guide is that readers and reporters share their information for the benefit of others. But our main concern continues to be the food. We have often been asked by which criteria we reach our conclusions, and they are quite plain: quality of cooking is the criterion for entry. For this reason the Guide does not exclude restaurants on grounds of price. We recognise that our wide readership includes some people for whom £25 a head is pushing the boat out, others for whom £100 a head is no problem. The question 'is it value for money?' can and should be applied, and is as relevant at the top of the price spectrum as at the bottom. Good (and bad) value can be found throughout.

A point of view

Public interest in chefs and cooking, sourcing and production are at an all-time high, while the appetite to comment on how food gets to the plate is greater than ever. *The Good Food Guide* is your opportunity to have a say in whether you have been surprised or delighted, enchanted or let down, ripped-off or upset by what you have eaten. To everyone who has used our feedback system (thegoodfoodguide.co.uk) over the last year, many thanks, and please keep the reports coming in. By using this Guide you are supporting its aim to improve the quality of our meals out and the standards of restaurateuring – to the benefit of all with a genuine interest in the food on their plate.

Happy eating,
Elizabeth Carter
Consultant Editor

In casting my mind back over dishes I've eaten in the past year, I can recall a number that I would love to have again given the chance. Here are just a few that stick in my mind months after I tasted them.

Greedy Cow, Kent Quite simply the best burger for miles around.
Fresh from the Sea, Cornwall The freshest crab sandwich ever.
Ox, Belfast Cauliflower (every which way) with almond, nasturtium and maple.
Marcus, London White crab meat with new season's almonds, sweet peach and thin strips of raw courgette, the brown meat in croquettes flavoured with lemongrass.
Restaurant Sat Bains, Nottingham A single scallop draped with ponzu jelly on thin slices of pig's trotter.
Kitty Fisher's, London A pair of perfectly trimmed, char-grilled lamb cutlets topped with anchovy, mint and parsley.
The Dairy, London A dessert of blood-orange marmalade, brown butter ice cream and cubes of toast - posh buttered toast and marmalade.
Restaurant Nathan Outlaw, Cornwall Creamy Tunworth cheese with tangy celery - pickled and jelly - and crisp hazelnuts.
White Swan at Fence, Lancashire The beautifully explained board of British cheeses.

Top 50 Restaurants

The Top 50 recognises the very best talent in the country;
a place on the list represents a huge achievement, with each
position earned by its score in *The Good Food Guide*, editor
appraisal and strength of reader feedback.

1 L'Enclume, Cumbria (10)

2 Restaurant Gordon Ramsay, London (10)

3 Pollen Street Social, London (9)

4 Restaurant Nathan Outlaw, Cornwall (9)

5 Hibiscus, London (9)

6 Restaurant Sat Bains, Nottinghamshire (9)

7 Midsummer House, Cambridgeshire (8)

8 The Ledbury, London (8)

9 Fraiche, Merseyside (8)

10 Le Champignon Sauvage, Glos (8)

11 The Square, London (8)

12 Fera at Claridges, London (8)

13 Le Gavroche, London (8)

14 Andrew Fairlie at Gleneagles, Tayside (8)

15 Marcus, London (8)

16 Le Manoir aux Quat'Saisons, Oxfordshire (8)

17 The French, Manchester (8)

18 André Garrett at Cliveden, Berkshire (8)

19 Whatley Manor, The Dining Room, Wiltshire (8)

20 The Kitchin, Edinburgh (7)

21 Bohemia, Jersey (7)

22 The Waterside Inn, Berkshire (7)

23 Artichoke, Buckinghamshire (7)

24 Restaurant James Sommerin, Glamorgan (7)

25 Alain Ducasse at the Dorchester, London (7)

26 Dinner by Heston Blumenthal, London (7)

27 Paul Ainsworth at No. 6, Cornwall (7)

28 Casamia, Bristol (7)

29 Adam's, Birmingham (7)

30 Restaurant Martin Wishart, Edinburgh (7)

31 Pied à Terre, London (7)

32 Restaurant Story, London (7)

33 Murano, London (7)

34 Ynyshir Hall, Powys (7)

35 Sketch, London (7)

36 Llangoed Hall, Powys (7)

37 Hedone, London (7)

38 Hambleton Hall, Rutland (7)

39 The Peat Inn, Fife (7)

40 Gidleigh Park, Devon (7)

41 Fischer's Baslow Hall, Derbyshire (7)

42 Freemasons at Wiswell, Lancashire (7)

43 The Hand & Flowers, Buckinghamshire (6)

44 Yorke Arms, Ramsgill, Yorkshire (6)

45 The Dairy, London (6)

46 OX, Belfast (6)

47 The Raby Hunt, Durham (6)

48 Lake Road Kitchen, Cumbria (6)

49 The Sportsman, Kent (6)

50 Northcote, Lancashire (6)

Top 50 Pubs

The list below is unique in the UK: every pub has earned
its place through its score in *The Good Food Guide,* inspector
reports and strong reader feedback.

1 Freemasons at Wiswell, Lancashire
2 The Hand & Flowers, Buckinghamshire
3 The Sportsman, Kent
4 Red Lion, East Chisenbury, Wiltshire
5 The Pony & Trap, Chew Magna, Somerset
6 The Lickfold Inn, Sussex
7 The Woodspeen, Berkshire
8 The Ancrum Cross Keys, Borders, Scotland
9 The Pipe and Glass Inn, Yorkshire
10 The Royal Oak, Paley Street, Berkshire
11 The Coach, Marlow, Buckinghamshire
12 The Butcher's Arms, Eldersfield, Glos
13 The Treby Arms, Devon
14 The Cross at Kenilworth, Warwickshire
15 The White Oak, Cookham, Berkshire
16 The Hardwick, Abergavenny
17 The Star Inn, Harome, Yorkshire
18 The Stagg Inn, Titley, Herefordshire
19 The Harwood Arms, Fulham, London
20 The Plough, Bolnhurst, Bedfordshire
21 The Plough Inn, Longparish, Hampshire
22 The Hinds Head, Berkshire
23 The Nut Tree Inn, Oxfordshire
24 The Masons Arms, Knowstone, Devon
25 The Broad Chare, Tyne & Wear
26 The Miller of Mansfield, Berkshire
27 The Wellington Arms,
   Baughurst, Hampshire

28 The Falcon Inn, Withernwick, Yorkshire
29 The Lamb Inn, Crawley, Oxfordshire
30 The Springer Spaniel, Cornwall
31 The Star Inn, Sparsholt, Oxfordshire
32 The Felin Fach Griffin, Powys
33 The Duke of Cumberland Arms,
   West Sussex
34 The Purefoy Arms, Hampshire
35 The Duke of York Inn, Grindleton,
   Lancashire
36 The Kinmel Arms, Conwy
37 The Richmond Arms, West Ashling,
   West Sussex
38 The Five Alls, Oxfordshire
39 The New Inn, Great Limber, Lincolnshire
40 The General Tarleton, Yorkshire
41 The White Hart, Lydgate,
   Greater Manchester
42 The Sun Inn, Dedham, Essex
43 The Bay Horse, Hurworth-on-Tees, Durham
44 The Kingham Plough, Oxfordshire
45 The Square and Compasses, Essex
46 The Star at Sancton, Yorkshire
47 Bunch of Grapes, Glamorgan
48 Beckford Arms, Wiltshire
49 Wheatsheaf Inn, Northleach,
   Gloucestershire
50 The Camberwell Arms, London

Longest serving

The Good Food Guide was founded in 1951.
The following restaurants have appeared consistently
since their first entry in the Guide.

The Connaught, London, 63 years
Gravetye Manor, West Sussex, 59 years
Porth Tocyn Hotel, Gwynedd, 59 years
Le Gavroche, London, 46 years
Ubiquitous Chip, Glasgow, 44 years
Plumber Manor, Dorset, 43 years
The Druidstone, Pembrokeshire, 43 years
The Waterside Inn, Berkshire, 43 years
Airds Hotel, Argyll & Bute, 40 years
Farlam Hall, Cumbria, 39 years
Corse Lawn House Hotel, Glos, 37 years
Hambleton Hall, Rutland, 37 years
The Pier at Harwich, Essex, 37 years
Magpie Café, Whitby, North
    Yorkshire, 36 years
RSJ, London, 35 years
The Seafood Restaurant, Padstow,
    Cornwall, 35 years
The Sir Charles Napier, Oxfordshire, 35 years
Le Caprice, London, 34 years
Little Barwick House, Somerset, 34 years
Inverlochy Castle, Fort William, 33 years
Ostlers Close, Fife, 33 years
The Angel Inn, Hetton, 32 years
Brilliant, London, 31 years

Clarke's, London, 31 years
Le Manoir aux Quat'Saisons,
    Oxfordshire, 31 years
Blostin's, Somerset, 30 years
Read's, Kent, 30 years
The Castle at Taunton, Somerset, 30 years
The Three Chimneys, Isle of Skye, 30 years
Northcote, Lancashire, 29 years
The Old Vicarage, Ridgeway, 28 years
Cnapan, Pembrokeshire, 28 years
Kensington Place, London, 27 years
Le Champignon Sauvage, Glos, 27 years
Quince & Medlar, Cumbria, 27 years
Silver Darling, Aberdeen, 27 years
Harry's Place, Lincolnshire, 26 years
Plas Bodegroes, Gwynedd, 26 years
Bibendum, London, 26 years
The Great House, Suffolk, 26 years
Ynyshir Hall, Powys, 26 years
The Creel, Orkney, 26 years
Dylanwad Da, Gwynedd, 26 years
Crannog, Fort William, 26 years
Melton's, York, 25 years
Eslington Villa, Tyne & Wear, 25 years
Castle Cottage, Harlech, 24 years

Awards

The editors of *The Good Food Guide* are delighted to recognise the following restaurants and chefs who have shown excellence in their field.

Chef of the Year
Robin Gill
The Dairy and The Manor
Clapham, London

Restaurant of the Year
Ox
Belfast

Best New Restaurant Entry
Lake Road Kitchen
Ambleside, Cumbria

Best New Pub Entry
The Lickfold Inn
Lickfold, West Sussex

Local Gem of the Year
Flour & Ash
Bristol

Wine List of the Year
Tyddyn Llan
Llandrillo, Wales

Readers' Restaurant of the Year
The Miller of Mansfield
Goring, Berkshire

How to use The Good Food Guide

In our opinion, the restaurants included in *The Good Food Guide* are the very best in the UK; this means that simply getting an entry is an accomplishment to be proud of, and a Score 1 or above is a significant achievement.

The Good Food Guide is completely rewritten every year and compiled from scratch. Our research list is based on the huge volume of feedback we receive from readers, which, together with anonymous inspections by our experts, ensures that every entry is assessed afresh. Please keep the reports coming in: visit thegoodfoodguide.co.uk for details.

Symbols

We contact restaurants that we're considering for inclusion ahead of publication to check key information about opening times and facilities. They are also invited to participate in the £5 voucher scheme. The symbols against each entry are intended for at-a-glance identification and are based on the information given to us by each restaurant.

 Accommodation is available

 It is possible to have three courses, excluding wine, at the restaurant for less than £30.

£XX The average price of a three-course dinner, excluding wine.

 The restaurant is participating in our £5 voucher scheme. See vouchers for terms and conditions.

 The restaurant has a wine list that our experts have considered to be outstanding, either for strong by-the-glass options, an in-depth focus on a particular region, or attractive margins on fine wines.

V We will no longer display the V symbol; we will list 'v menu' in the details to indicate that the restaurant has a separate vegetarian menu.

Scoring

We add and reject many restaurants when we compile each guide. There are always subjective aspects to rating systems, but our inspectors are equipped with extensive scoring guidelines to ensure that restaurant bench-marking around the UK is accurate. As we take into account reader feedback on each restaurant, any given review is based on several meals.

'New chef' in place of a score indicates that the restaurant has had a recent change of chef and we have been unable to score it reliably; we particularly welcome reports on these restaurants.

Readers Recommend

These are direct quotes from our reader feedback and highlight places that have caught the attention of our loyal followers. Reports are particularly welcome on these entries also.

Local Gem

Local Gems highlight a range of brilliant neighbourhood venues, bringing you a wide choice at great value for money. Simple cafés, bistros and pubs, these are the places that sit happily on your doorstep, delivering good, freshly cooked food.

The Good Food Guide scoring system

1   Capable cooking with simple food combinations and clear flavours, but some inconsistencies.

2   Decent cooking, displaying good technical skills and interesting combinations and flavours. Occasional inconsistencies.

3   Good cooking, showing sound technical skills and using quality ingredients.

4   Dedicated, focused approach to cooking; good classical skills and high-quality ingredients.

5   Exact cooking techniques and a degree of ambition; showing balance and depth of flavour in dishes.

6   Exemplary cooking skills, innovative ideas, impeccable ingredients and an element of excitement.

7   High level of ambition and individuality, attention to the smallest detail, accurate and vibrant dishes.

8   A kitchen cooking close to or at the top of its game. Highly individual with impressive artistry. There is little room for disappointment here.

9   Cooking that has reached a pinnacle of achievement, making it a hugely memorable experience for the diner.

10 Just perfect dishes, showing faultless technique at every service; extremely rare, and the highest accolade the Guide can give.

London Explained

London is split into six regions. Restaurants within each region are listed alphabetically. Each main entry and local gem entry has a map reference. Here are the areas covered in each region.

London CENTRAL

Belgravia, Bloomsbury, Covent Garden, Fitzrovia, Green Park, Holborn, Hyde Park, Lancaster Gate, Leicester Square, Marble Arch, Marylebone, Mayfair, Oxford Circus, Piccadilly, Pimlico, Soho, Victoria, Westminster

London NORTH

Archway, Camden, Finsbury Park, Golders Green, Hampstead, Islington, Kensal Green, Kentish Town, King's Cross, Maida Vale, Muswell Hill, Neasden, Primrose Hill, Stoke Newington, Swiss Cottage, Willesden

London EAST

Barbican, Bethnal Green, Canary Wharf, City, Clerkenwell, Dalston, Farringdon, Hackney, Hoxton, St Paul's, Shoreditch, Spitalfields, Tower Hill, Whitechapel

London SOUTH

Balham, Battersea, Bermondsey, Blackheath, Borough, Brixton, Camberwell, Clapham, East Dulwich, Elephant & Castle, Forest Hill, Greenwich, Herne Hill, Peckham, Putney, South Bank, Southwark, Stockwell, Tooting, Wandsworth, Wimbledon

London WEST

Belgravia, Chelsea, Chiswick, Ealing, Earl's Court, Fulham, Gloucester Road, Hammersmith, Kensington, Knightsbridge, Ladbroke Grove, Notting Hill, Olympia, Parsons Green, Shepherd's Bush, South Kensington

London GREATER

Barnes, Croydon, Crystal Palace, East Sheen, Harrow-on-the-Hill, Kew, Richmond, Southall, Surbiton, Teddington, Twickenham, Walthamstow, Wood Green

LONDON

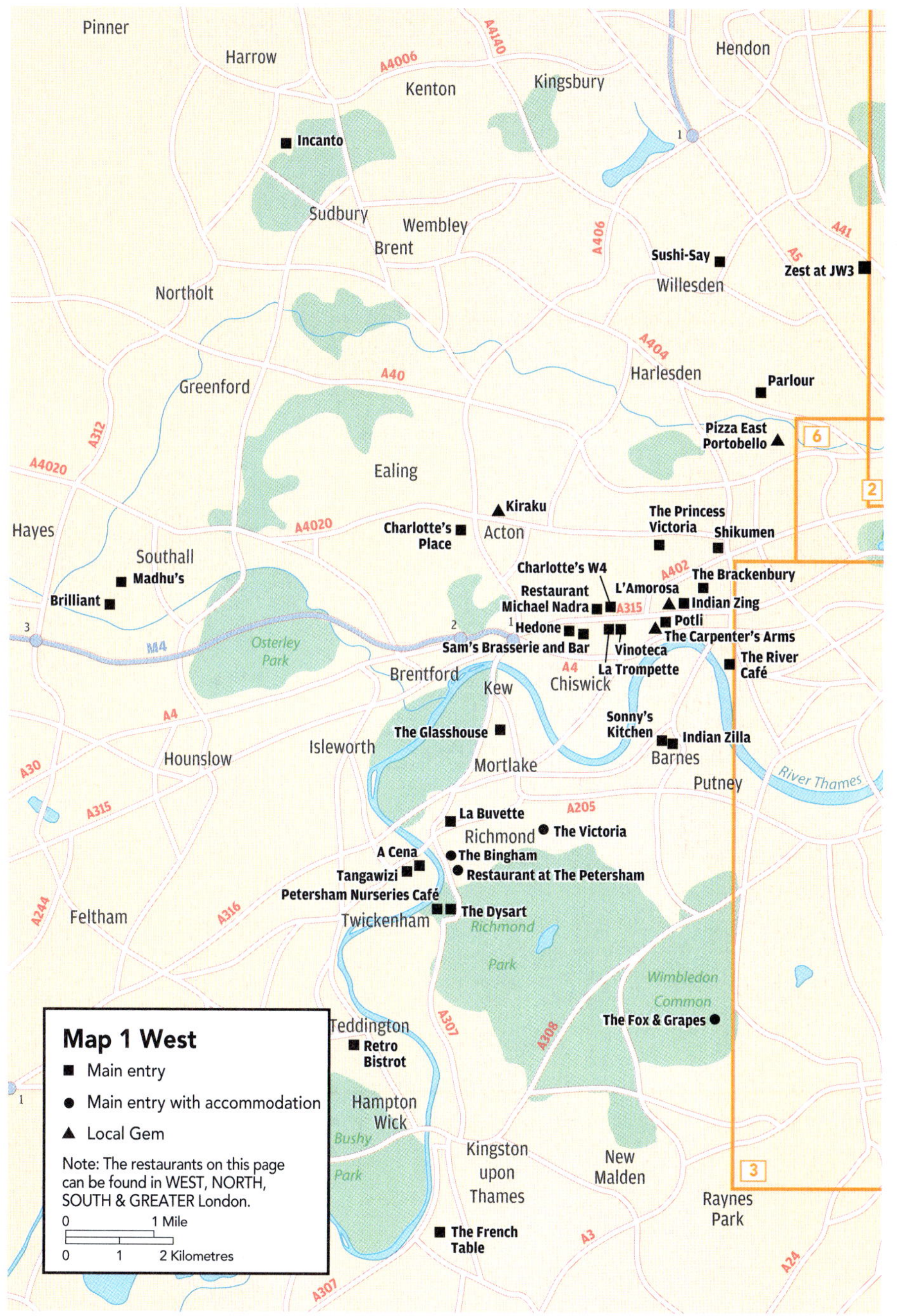

Map 1 West

■ Main entry

● Main entry with accommodation

▲ Local Gem

Note: The restaurants on this page can be found in WEST, NORTH, SOUTH & GREATER London.

0   1 Mile

0   1   2 Kilometres

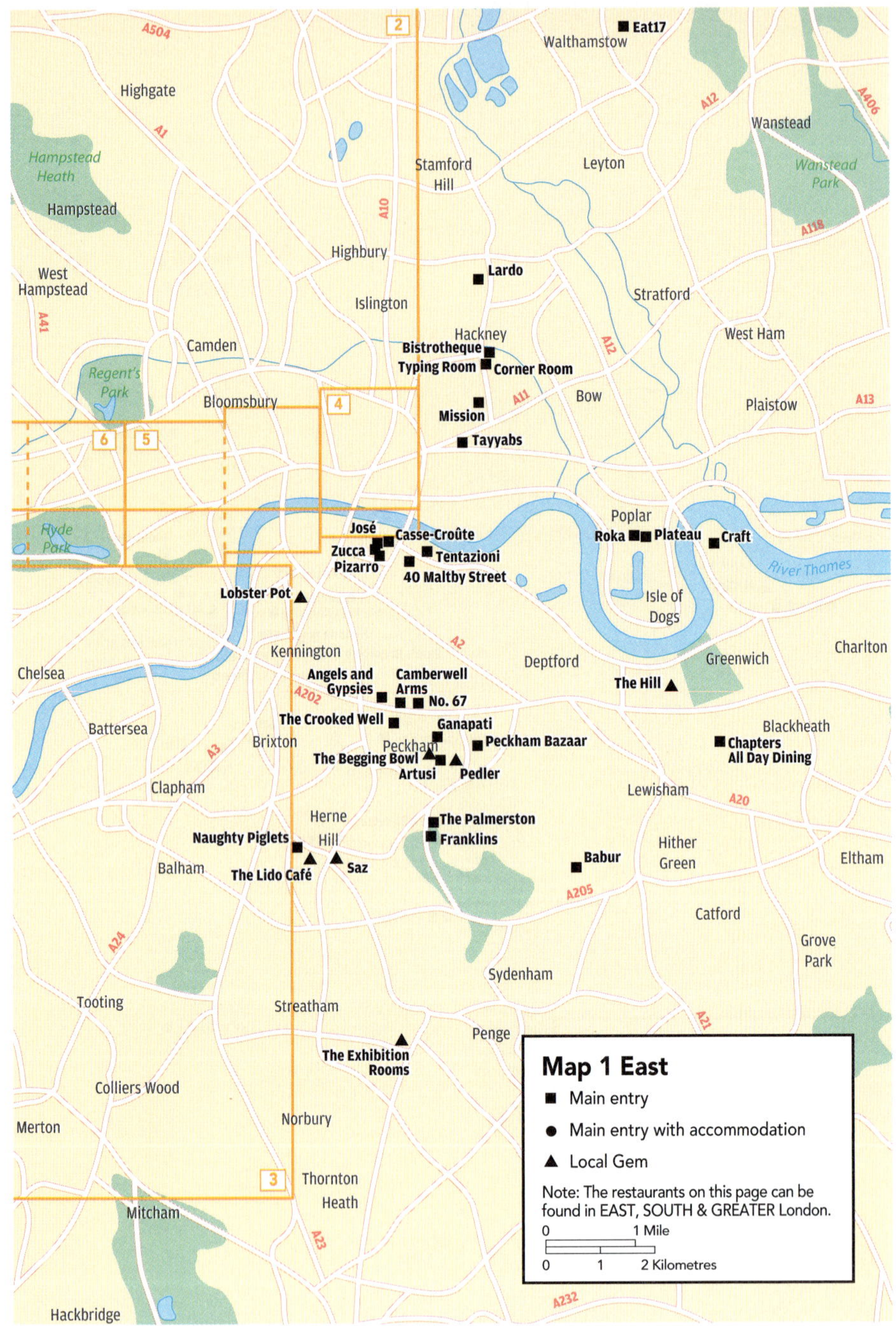

Join us at thegoodfoodguide.co.uk

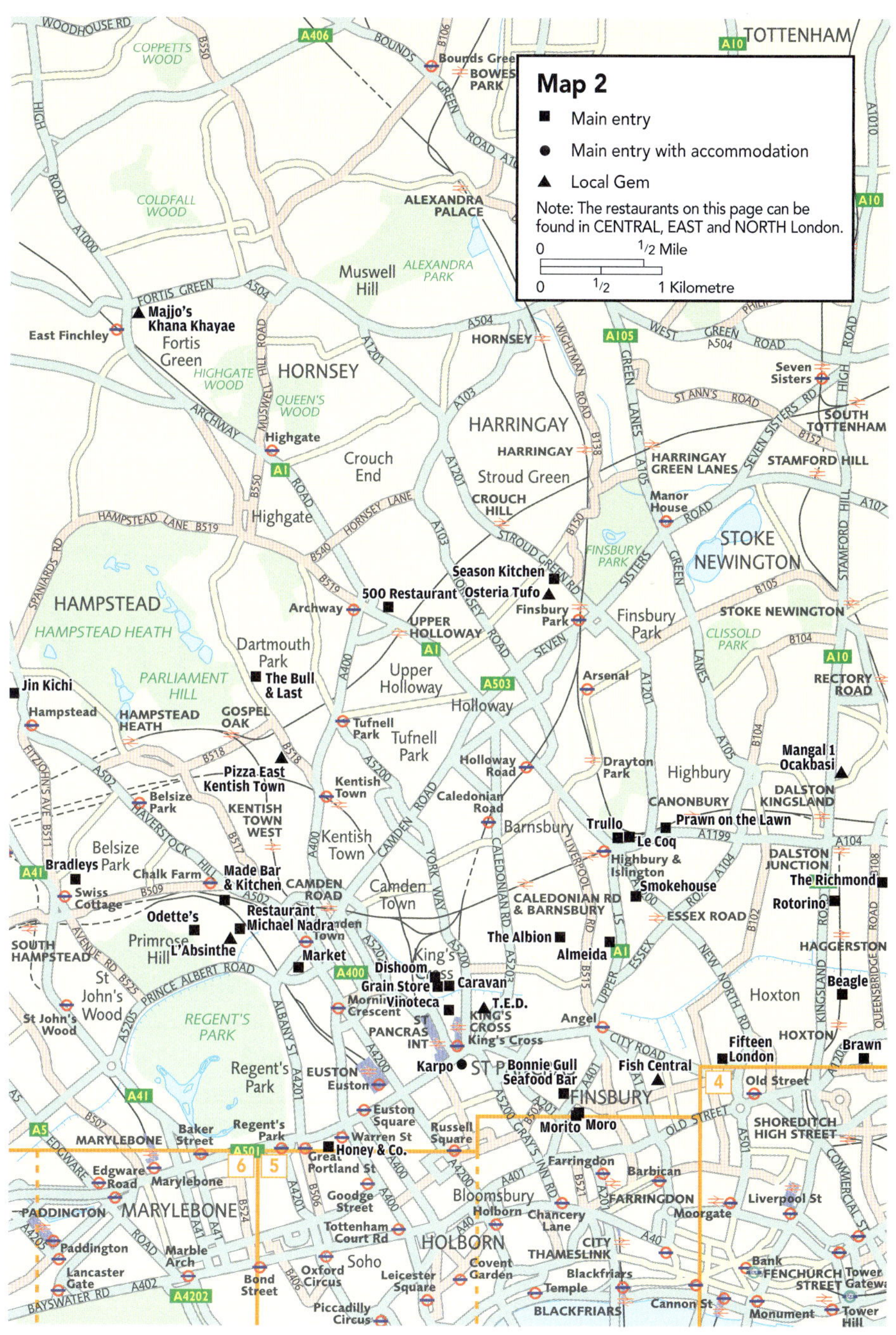
Map 2
Main entry
Main entry with accommodation
Local Gem
Note: The restaurants on this page can be found in CENTRAL, EAST and NORTH London.
0   1/2 Mile
0   1/2   1 Kilometre

TOTTENHAM
WOODHOUSE RD
COPPETTS WOOD
A406
BOUNDS GREEN ROAD
Bounds Green
BOWES PARK
A10
ALEXANDRA PALACE
COLDFALL WOOD
Muswell Hill
ALEXANDRA PARK
A1000
FORTIS GREEN
A504
Majjo's Khana Khayae
East Finchley
Fortis Green
HORNSEY
A504
HIGHGATE WOOD
Queen's Wood
WEST GREEN ROAD
WIGHTMAN ROAD
A105
A504
Seven Sisters
SOUTH TOTTENHAM
HORNSEY
ARCHWAY
Highgate
A1
HARRINGAY
HARRINGAY
Stroud Green
CROUCH HILL
ST ANN'S ROAD
B138
HARRINGAY GREEN LANES
SEVEN SISTERS RD
STAMFORD HILL
B152
HAMPSTEAD LANE B519
Highgate
B550
B540
B519
A103
A1201
STROUD GREEN RD
B150
Manor House
A105
STOKE NEWINGTON
A107
HAMPSTEAD
HAMPSTEAD HEATH
SPANIARDS RD
Season Kitchen
500 Restaurant
Osteria Tufo
Archway
UPPER HOLLOWAY
A1
FINSBURY PARK
Finsbury Park
Finsbury Park
STOKE NEWINGTON
CLISSOLD PARK
B104
A10
RECTORY ROAD
Jin Kichi
PARLIAMENT HILL
Dartmouth Park
The Bull & Last
Upper Holloway
A400
A503
Holloway
Arsenal
A1201
Highbury
Mangal 1 Ocakbasi
DALSTON KINGSLAND
B104
Hampstead
HAMPSTEAD HEATH
GOSPEL OAK
FITZJOHN'S AVE
B518
B518
Tufnell Park
Tufnell Park
A5200
Holloway Road
Drayton Park
CANONBURY
Prawn on the Lawn
A104
Pizza East Kentish Town
Kentish Town
Caledonian Road
Trullo
Le Coq
A1199
DALSTON JUNCTION
The Richmond
Belsize Park
A502
KENTISH TOWN WEST
A400
Kentish Town
Barnsbury
Highbury & Islington
Smokehouse
ESSEX ROAD
Rotorino
Belsize Park
HAVERSTOCK HILL
B517
Camden Town
York Way
CALEDONIAN RD
CALEDONIAN RD & BARNSBURY
B108
HAGGERSTON
Bradleys
A41
Chalk Farm
B509
Made Bar & Kitchen
CAMDEN ROAD
A5200
A1
Essex Rd
Beagle
Swiss Cottage
A502
Restaurant Michael Nadra
Camden Town
The Albion
Almeida
B515
Hoxton
HOXTON
Odette's
Primrose Hill
L'Absinthe
Market
A400
Dishoom
King's Cross
Caravan
T.E.D.
Angel
Fifteen London
Brawn
SOUTH HAMPSTEAD
AVENUE RD
B525
PRINCE ALBERT ROAD
Grain Store
Morning Crescent
Vinoteca
ST PANCRAS INT
KING'S CROSS
King's Cross
CITY ROAD
St John's Wood
St John's Wood
A5205
REGENT'S PARK
ALBANY ST
A4200
Karpo
ST P
Bonnie Gull Seafood Bar
Fish Central
Old Street
Regent's Park
EUSTON
Euston
Russell Square
FINSBURY
SHOREDITCH HIGH STREET
A41
A5
B507
Baker Street
Regent's Park
A501
Euston Square
Warren St
GRAY'S INN RD
Morito
Moro
A501
COMMERCIAL ST
MARYLEBONE
A5
Edgware Road
Marylebone
A501
Honey & Co.
Great Portland St
A4200
A400
Farringdon
Barbican
FARRINGDON
Liverpool St
EDGWARE ROAD
B524
B506
Goodge Street
A4201
Bloomsbury
Holborn
Chancery Lane
Moorgate
PADDINGTON
MARYLEBONE
Tottenham Court Rd
HOLBORN
CITY THAMESLINK
Paddington
Marble Arch
A402
Soho
Leicester Square
Covent Garden
Blackfriars
Temple
Bank
FENCHURCH STREET
Tower Gateway
Lancaster Gate
BAYSWATER RD
A4202
Bond Street
Oxford Circus
Piccadilly Circus
BLACKFRIARS
Cannon St
Monument
Tower Hill
A4205
A40

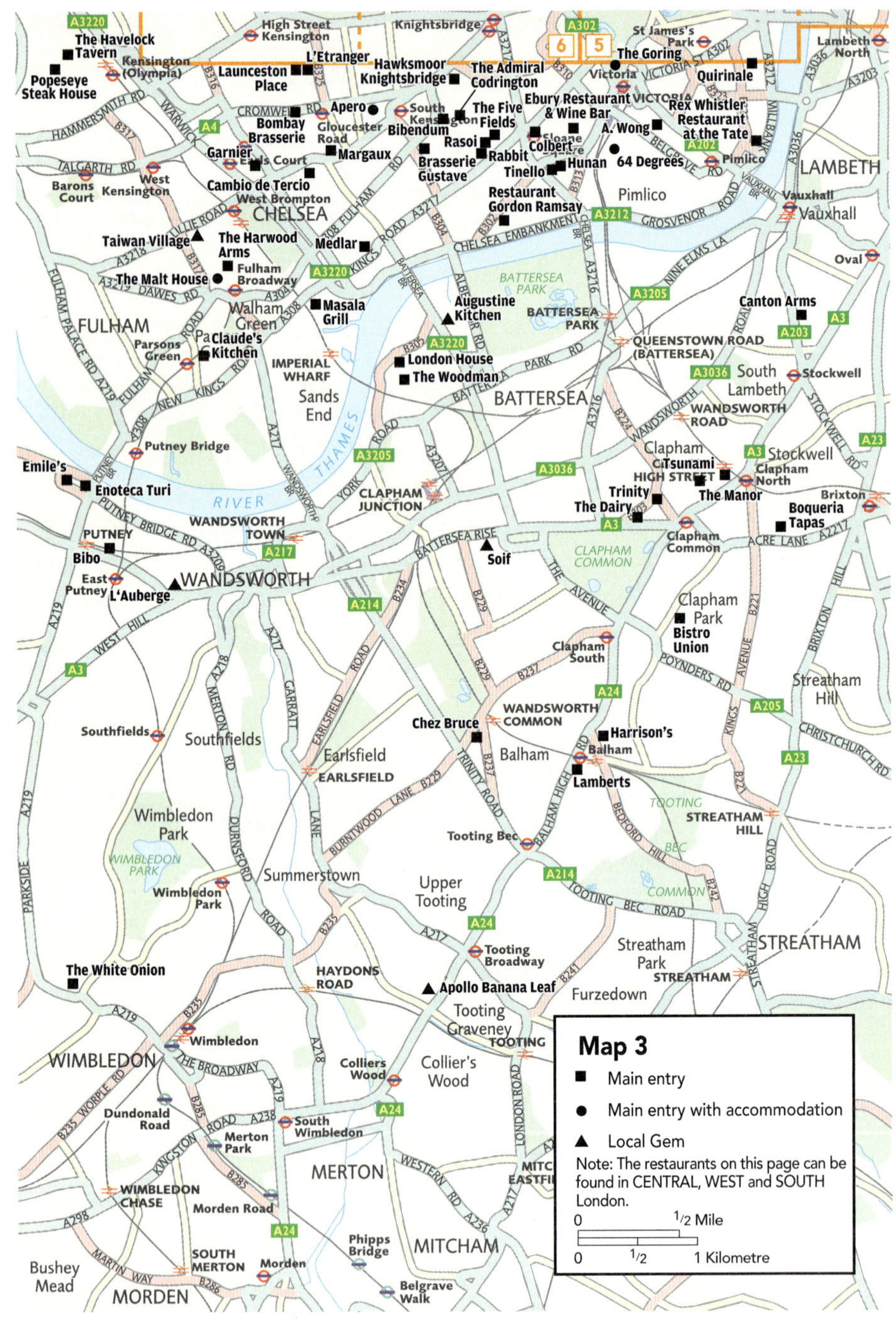

Map 3

- ■ Main entry
- ● Main entry with accommodation
- ▲ Local Gem

Note: The restaurants on this page can be found in CENTRAL, WEST and SOUTH London.

0 ⟶ ½ Mile

0 ½ 1 Kilometre

Join us at thegoodfoodguide.co.uk

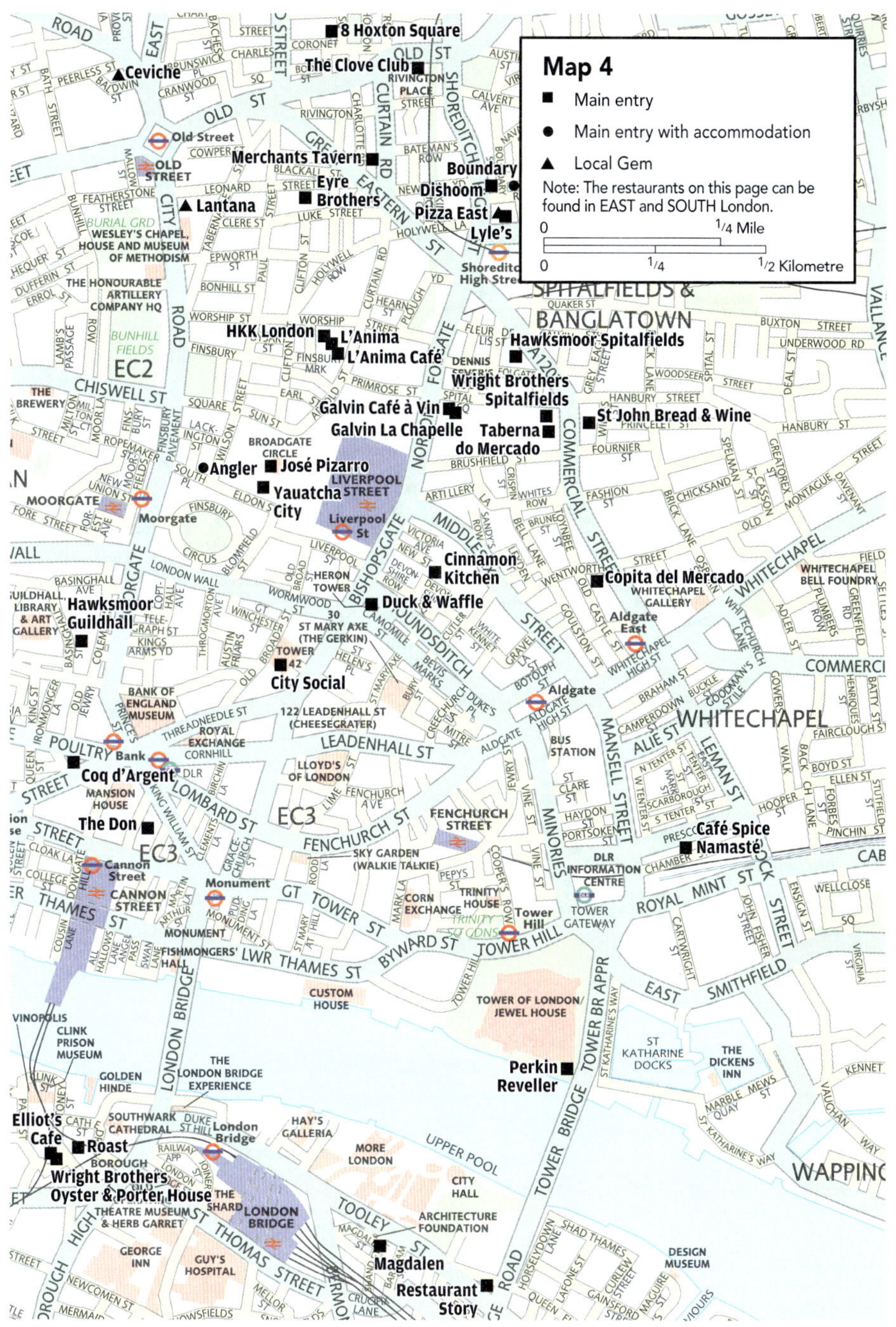

8 Hoxton Square
The Clove Club
Ceviche
Old Street
OLD STREET
Merchants Tavern
Boundary
Eyre Brothers
Dishoom
Pizza East
Lantana
Lyle's
Shoreditch High Street
Map 4
Main entry
Main entry with accommodation
Local Gem
Note: The restaurants on this page can be found in EAST and SOUTH London.
0   1/4 Mile
0   1/4   1/2 Kilometre
SPITALFIELDS & BANGLATOWN
HKK London
L'Anima
L'Anima Café
Hawksmoor Spitalfields
Wright Brothers Spitalfields
EC2
CHISWELL ST
THE BREWERY
Galvin Café à Vin
St John Bread & Wine
Galvin La Chapelle
Taberna do Mercado
Angler
José Pizarro
LIVERPOOL STREET
Yauatcha City
Liverpool St
MOORGATE
Moorgate
Cinnamon Kitchen
Copita del Mercado
WHITECHAPEL GALLERY
Hawksmoor Guildhall
Duck & Waffle
Aldgate East
TOWER 42
City Social
122 LEADENHALL ST (CHEESEGRATER)
Aldgate
WHITECHAPEL
Coq d'Argent
LEADENHALL ST
LLOYD'S OF LONDON
EC3
The Don
FENCHURCH STREET
FENCHURCH ST
Café Spice Namasté
Cannon Street
CANNON STREET
Monument
SKY GARDEN (WALKIE TALKIE)
CORN EXCHANGE
TRINITY HOUSE
Tower Hill
MONUMENT
THAMES ST
FISHMONGERS' HALL
LWR THAMES ST
BYWARD ST
TOWER HILL
CUSTOM HOUSE
TOWER OF LONDON JEWEL HOUSE
ST KATHARINE DOCKS
THE DICKENS INN
VINOPOLIS
CLINK PRISON MUSEUM
Perkin Reveller
GOLDEN HINDE
THE LONDON BRIDGE EXPERIENCE
Elliot's Cafe
Roast
London Bridge
HAY'S GALLERIA
WAPPING
Wright Brothers Oyster & Porter House
THE SHARD
LONDON BRIDGE
MORE LONDON
CITY HALL
GEORGE INN
GUY'S HOSPITAL
THOMAS STREET
TOOLEY ST
ARCHITECTURE FOUNDATION
DESIGN MUSEUM
Magdalen
Restaurant Story

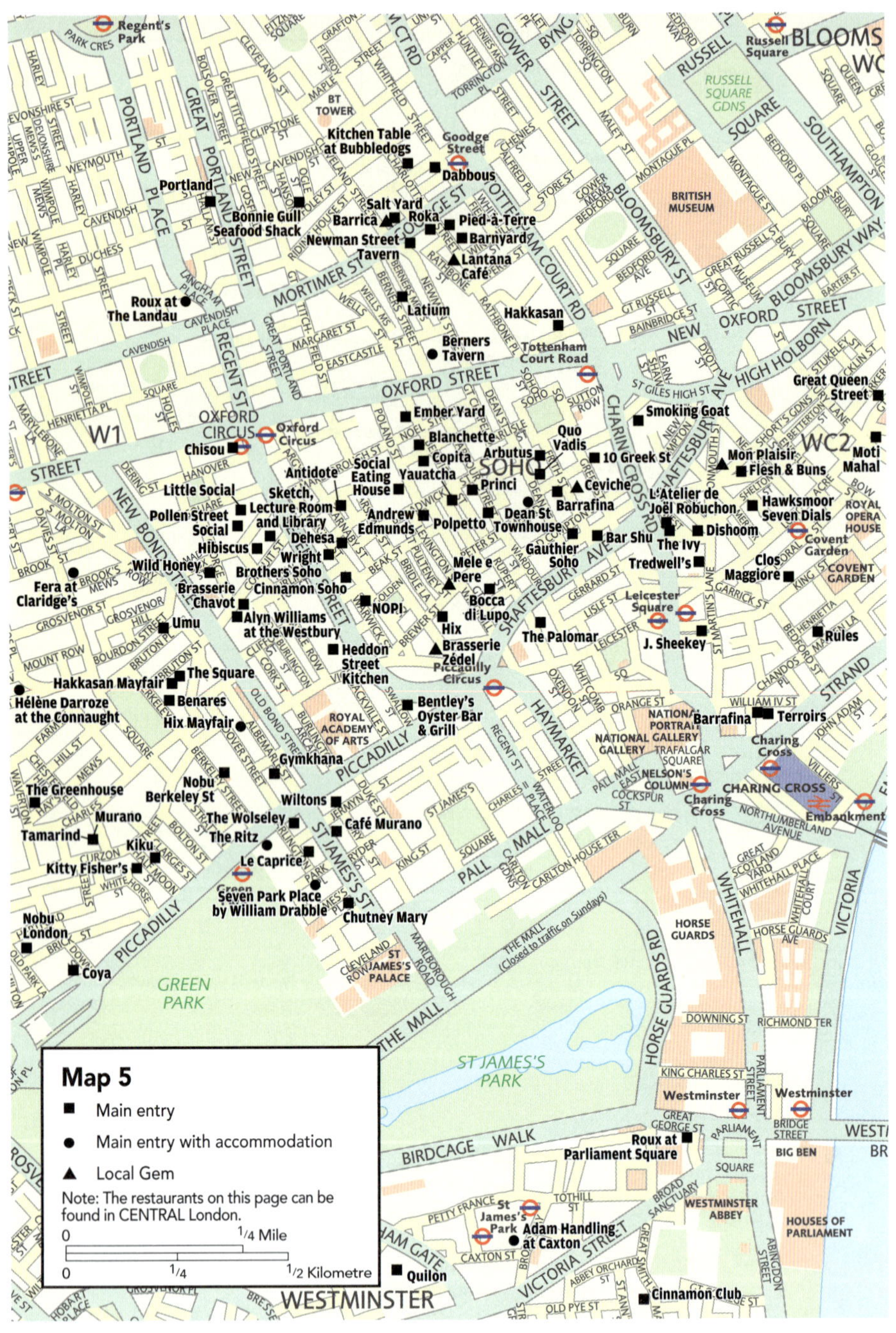

Join us at thegoodfoodguide.co.uk

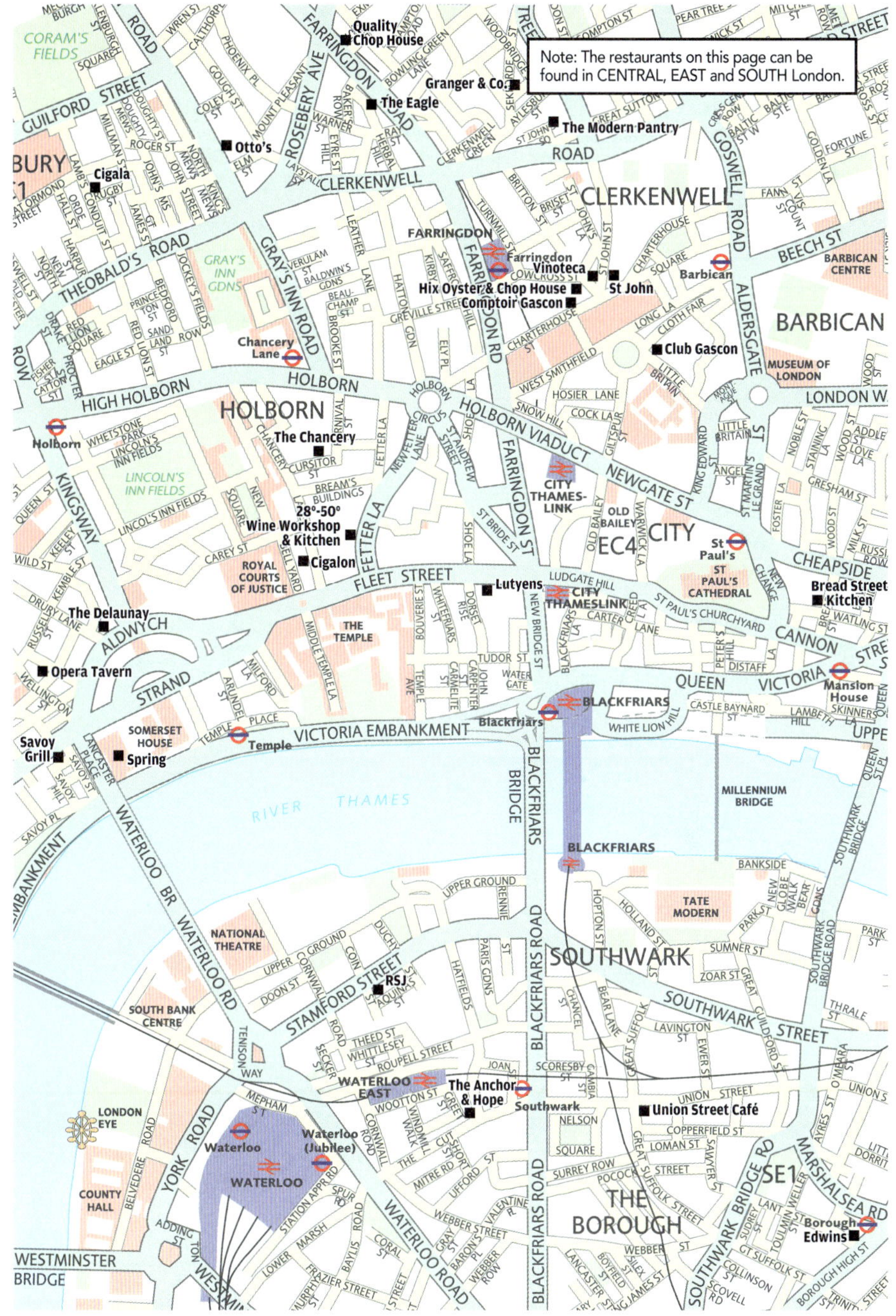

CORAM'S FIELDS
Quality Chop House
Granger & Co.
The Eagle
The Modern Pantry
Otto's
Cigala
CLERKENWELL
CLERKENWELL
FARRINGDON
Farringdon
Vinoteca
Barbican
BARBICAN CENTRE
BARBICAN
Hix Oyster & Chop House
St John
Comptoir Gascon
GUILFORD STREET
THEOBALD'S ROAD
GRAY'S INN GDNS
GRAY'S INN ROAD
BEECH ST
GOSWELL ROAD
ALDERSGATE
MUSEUM OF LONDON
Club Gascon
Chancery Lane
HOLBORN
LONDON W.
HIGH HOLBORN
HOLBORN
The Chancery
LINCOLN'S INN FIELDS
FETTER LA
HOLBORN VIADUCT
NEWGATE ST
CITY THAMES-LINK
LITTLE BRITAIN
OLD BAILEY
CITY
St Paul's
EC4
CHEAPSIDE
KINGSWAY
28°-50°
Wine Workshop & Kitchen
Cigalon
ROYAL COURTS OF JUSTICE
FLEET STREET
Lutyens
CITY THAMESLINK
ST PAUL'S CATHEDRAL
Bread Street Kitchen
CANNON
The Delaunay
ALDWYCH
THE TEMPLE
QUEEN VICTORIA
Mansion House
Opera Tavern
STRAND
MIDDLE TEMPLE LA
BLACKFRIARS
Blackfriars
WHITE LION HILL
Savoy Grill
SOMERSET HOUSE
Temple
VICTORIA EMBANKMENT
Blackfriars
Spring
BLACKFRIARS BRIDGE
MILLENNIUM BRIDGE
RIVER THAMES
WATERLOO BR
BLACKFRIARS
BLACKFRIARS ROAD
BANKSIDE
TATE MODERN
NATIONAL THEATRE
UPPER GROUND
SOUTHWARK
SOUTHWARK STREET
SOUTH BANK CENTRE
STAMFORD STREET
RSJ
WATERLOO EAST
The Anchor & Hope
Southwark
Union Street Café
LONDON EYE
Waterloo
Waterloo (Jubilee)
WATERLOO
SE1
COUNTY HALL
WESTMINSTER BRIDGE
THE BOROUGH
YORK ROAD
WATERLOO ROAD
SOUTHWARK BRIDGE RD
MARSHALSEA RD
Borough
Edwins
Note: The restaurants on this page can be found in CENTRAL, EAST and SOUTH London.

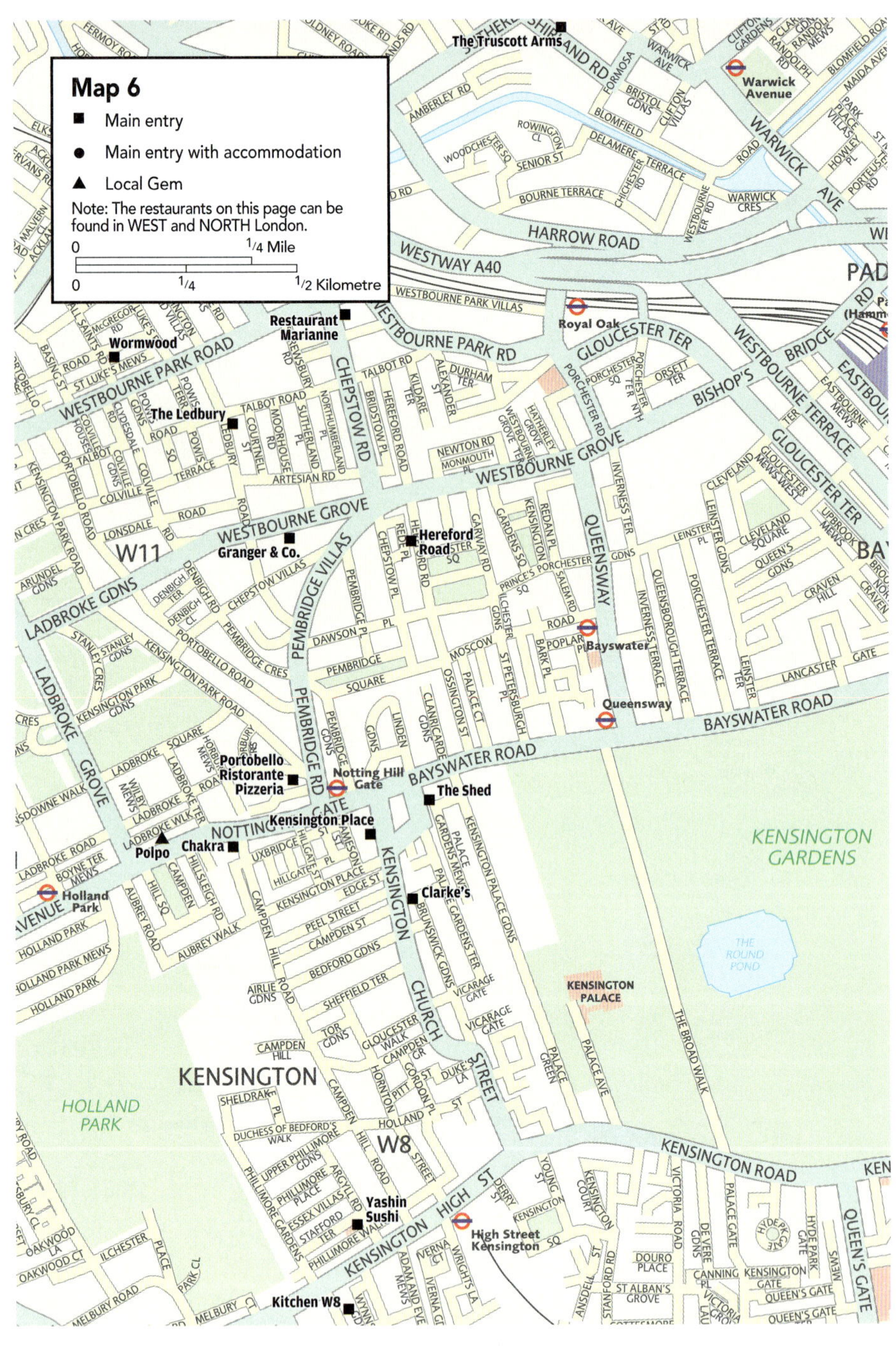

Join us at thegoodfoodguide.co.uk

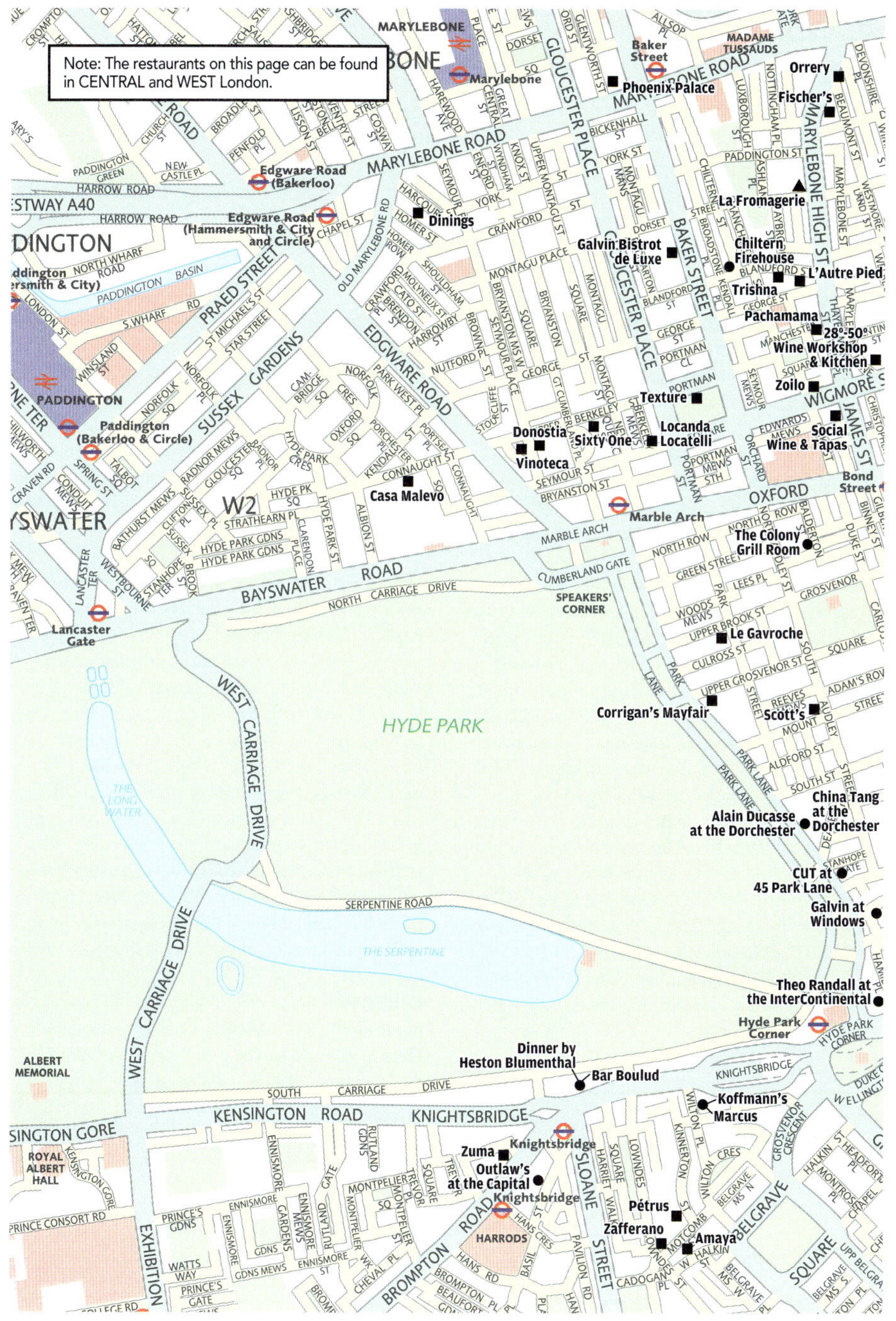

Note: The restaurants on this page can be found in CENTRAL and WEST London.
MARYLEBONE
Marylebone
Baker Street
MADAME TUSSAUDS
Orrery
Fischer's
Phoenix Palace
La Fromagerie
Edgware Road (Bakerloo)
Edgware Road (Hammersmith & City and Circle)
Dinings
Galvin Bistrot de Luxe
Chiltern Firehouse
L'Autre Pied
Trishna
Pachamama
28°-50°
Wine Workshop & Kitchen
Zoilo
Texture
Donostia
Sixty One
Vinoteca
Locanda Locatelli
Social Wine & Tapas
PADDINGTON
Paddington (Bakerloo & Circle)
Casa Malevo
Bond Street
Marble Arch
OXFORD
The Colony Grill Room
Lancaster Gate
SPEAKERS' CORNER
Le Gavroche
HYDE PARK
Corrigan's Mayfair
Scott's
China Tang at the Dorchester
Alain Ducasse at the Dorchester
CUT at 45 Park Lane
Galvin at Windows
THE LONG WATER
SERPENTINE ROAD
THE SERPENTINE
Theo Randall at the InterContinental
Hyde Park Corner
HYDE PARK CORNER
Dinner by Heston Blumenthal
Bar Boulud
KNIGHTSBRIDGE
Koffmann's
Marcus
ALBERT MEMORIAL
KENSINGTON ROAD
KNIGHTSBRIDGE
Zuma
Knightsbridge
ROYAL ALBERT HALL
Outlaw's at the Capital
Knightsbridge
Pétrus
Zafferano
Amaya
HARRODS

A. Wong

Chinese good fortune in Victoria
Cooking score: 4
⊖ Victoria, map 3
Chinese | £35
70-71 Wilton Road, Victoria, SW1V 1DE
Tel no: (020) 7828 8931
www.awong.co.uk

Andrew Wong's classy Chinese cooking far exceeds expectations, simply shining against a backdrop that can feel more like a café than a serious restaurant: polished floors, glinting copper lights and a visible kitchen add up to a fuss-free environment. For culinary thrills look to the full, multi-course Peking duck feast or an epic ten-course Taste of China menu (allow two and a half hours) where dishes could include a 63 degrees 'tea egg' with shredded filo and satay powder; poached Scottish razor clam with sea cucumber, pickled cucumber, vinegar tapioca and wind-dried sausage; a Shaanxi lamb 'burger' with Xinjiang pomegranate salad; and Yunnan seared beef with mint, chilli and lemongrass served with a truffle tofu crisp. A snowball meringue with lychee granita, mango purée and lime sorbet is a charming endnote. The lunchtime dim sum menu is also a must — offerings include a steamed duck-yolk custard bun, and a deep-fried prawn ball with abalone and chilli vinaigrette. Wines from £19.
Chef/s: Andrew Wong. **Open:** Tue to Sat L 12 to 2.30, Mon to Sat D 5.30 to 10.30. **Closed:** Sun, 23 Dec to 3 Jan. **Meals:** alc (main courses £8 to £23). Set L and D £13. Tasting menu £45 (10 courses).
Details: 50 seats. 16 seats outside. Bar. Wheelchair access. Music.

Adam Handling at Caxton

Rising young talent at Westminster hotel
Cooking score: 5
⊖ St James's Park, map 5
Modern British | £55
St Ermin's Hotel, 2 Caxton Street, Westminster, SW1H 0QW
Tel no: (0800) 6521498
www.caxtongrill.co.uk

Avid TV cookery programme viewers will recognise the name above the door at the grand St Ermin's Hotel's Caxton Grill…Adam Handling was runner-up in *Masterchef: The Professionals 2013*. Restaurants in city hotels are sometimes awkward, often corporate spaces, but this dining room succeeds with its light, unexpectedly relaxed modern touch of pale greys, splashes of colour from bold artworks and soft furnishings, wide floorboards and small bare tables. The menu comes in two parts; a 'Classic Grills' section (along the lines of Buccleuch ribeye) for the traditionalists, with 'Tastes & Textures' (grazing dishes for sharing) showcasing, along with the evening tasting option, the kitchen's real creative talent. Start with snacks like doughnuts with dressed crab, then explore pretty plates of black cod ('stunning quality') with sweet miso glaze and smoked leaves, and celeriac with truffle, green apple, sweet date, goats' cheese pearls and crème fraîche, all delivered to the table by chefs. The global wine list opens at £26, with plenty of choice by the glass and carafe.
Chef/s: Adam Handling. **Open:** Mon to Fri L 12 to 2, all week D 6 to 10. **Meals:** alc (main courses £15 to £39). Tasting menu £60 (7 courses). **Details:** 72 seats. V menu. Bar. Wheelchair access. Music.

Join us at thegoodfoodguide.co.uk

★ TOP 50 ★

Alain Ducasse at the Dorchester

A corner of France on Park Lane

Cooking score: 7
⊖ Hyde Park Corner, map 6
Modern French | £90
The Dorchester Hotel, 53 Park Lane, Hyde
Park, W1K 1QA
Tel no: (020) 7629 8866
www.alainducasse-dorchester.com

Monsieur Ducasse has been a *grand fromage* in
the world of French cuisine since the late 1980s
and these days his dominion covers the globe
from Tokyo to Las Vegas, via Doha, Tuscany,
Paris and London (to name but a few of the
locales). Arriving at the Dorchester in 2007,
Jocelyn Herland has been charged with
interpreting the Ducasse style in a dining
room that 'exudes luxury'. The service is
entirely in keeping: 'expert, seamless,
unobtrusive'. Overblown theatrics is not the
Ducasse way, so expect cultivated plates of
classically inspired food with supreme
technical prowess on show. Things get off to a
flyer with a pyramid of gougères done three
ways and whichever of the host of menus you
opt for (tasting, carte, seasonal, jardin or the
lunchtime 'flower'), luxury ingredients and
pretty plates await. Seared foie gras arrives
with white and green asparagus and morels
stuffed with lardo, Scottish langoustines are
dressed with a vinaigrette made from their
corals, and roasted Landaise chicken –
'boasting heavenly aromas' – is served with its
leg meat flavoured with lapsang souchong.
Every step of the way the central ingredients
are given room to shine. To finish, hazelnut
soufflé finds a perfect match with its
accomanying pink grapefruit sorbet. The wine
list is a feast of French stars with a good pick
from the rest of the world; prices start at £35.
It's part of the Sultan of Brunei's Dorchester
Collection; see entries for CUT at 45 Park
Lane and China Tang.

Chef/s: Jocelyn Herland. **Open:** Tue to Fri L 12 to
1.30, Tue to Sat D 6.30 to 9.30. **Closed:** Sun, Mon,
26 to 30 Dec, 1 to 6 Jan, 3 to 6 Apr, 9 Aug to 1 Sept.
Meals: Set L £65 (2 courses). Set D £90 (3 courses)
to £105 (4 courses). Tasting menu £125 (7 courses)
to £180. **Details:** 82 seats. V menu. Wheelchair
access. Music. Parking. Children over 10 yrs only.

Alyn Williams at the Westbury

Innovative tasting menus in a Mayfair hotel

Cooking score: 6
⊖ Oxford Circus, map 5
Modern European | £60
The Westbury Hotel, 37 Conduit Street,
Mayfair, W1S 2YF
Tel no: (020) 7078 9579
www.alynwilliams.co.uk

The Alyn Williams dining room is along the
main corridor off the Westbury lobby, an
expansive room with dark modern panelling,
plenty of space between tables and efficient
staff. Williams offers a seven-course tasting
menu at the weekends, with a carte running
through the week up to Friday lunch. Modern
European dishes of great innovative energy,
both in combining and presenting, use wild
seasonal and recherché ingredients to achieve
impact. Begin with marinated sea bream and
apple in whey dotted with malossol caviar,
before John Dory arrives in the earthy guise of
wild garlic, morels and broad beans. Beef
tartare made with barbecued Holstein,
garnished with an oyster and calçots, is a new
spin, while the main-course choice could be
between roast pigeon with alexanders and
sand carrots or Cornish hogget in white-
truffled soured milk. Textural dessert surprises
produce an aerated white chocolate creation
scented with candied fennel and lime. Top-
flight wines start at £27.
Chef/s: Alyn Williams. **Open:** Tue to Sat L 12 to
2.30, D 6 to 10.30. **Closed:** Sun, Mon, first 2 weeks
Jan, last 2 weeks Aug. **Meals:** Set L £30. Set D £60.
Tasting menu £70. **Details:** 55 seats. V menu. Bar.
Wheelchair access. Music. Parking.

Andrew Edmunds

Rustic European food and good-value wines
Cooking score: 2
Oxford Circus, Piccadilly Circus, map 5
Modern European | £30
46 Lexington Street, Soho, W1F 0LW
Tel no: (020) 7437 5708
www.andrewedmunds.com

Can Andrew Edmunds' place on its quiet street on the northern fringe of Soho really have been around for 30 years? Yes it can. When it started, it was a defiant antidote to the riptide of nouvelle cuisine that washed all around it, and look which survived. In the candlelit ambience of a Georgian town house, the place still deals in rustic European cooking of bracing simplicity, mixing Italian, Spanish and French modes to striking effect. There will be moments in life when nothing but a whole roast teal with pickled quince will do to start, and latest chef Bob Cairns may well oblige. Either that or a dressed crab. At mains, it's on to cod with cime di rapa and shrimps, or an Old Spot chop with breadcrumbs in burnt butter and a glob of aïoli. Popular fancies are tickled at pudding stage with the likes of white chocolate and maple cheesecake. The wine list does a thoroughly efficient job in sourcing inspired bottles at reasonable mark-ups, with bundles of French and California niche stuff for the big spenders. House wines are £18.50.
Chef/s: Bob Cairns. **Open:** all week L 12 to 3.30 (12.30 Sat, 1 to 4 Sun), D 5.30 to 10.45 (6 to 10.30 Sun). **Closed:** 23 to 31 Dec, Easter. **Meals:** alc (main courses £11 to £25). **Details:** 60 seats. 4 seats outside.

Antidote

Earthy food with fine-tuned technical flair
Cooking score: 5
Oxford Circus, map 5
Modern European | £42
12A Newburgh Street, Soho, W1F 7RR
Tel no: (020) 7287 8488
www.antidotewinebar.com

If the Holy Grail that a certain generation of London chefs is after is that mix of rumbustiously earthy dishes rendered with precision-tuned technical flair, Chris Johns can be numbered among the devout. In a place where the bareness of floorboards and lightbulbs is standard, there's a wine-and-nibbles entry level, with the restaurant itself upstairs. Efficient, unceremonious staff run the room well, and bring dishes that light up the day with joy. Monkfish in smoked anchovy cream with fried cavolo nero and torpedoes of pommes Anna are one possible main, but Middle White suckling pig with puréed broccoli, baked cauliflower and cider sauce is mesmerically satisfying, too. Starters, perhaps mackerel ceviche with seaweed and cucumber, or a chicken-and-egg raviolo in chive consommé, have less to say for themselves, as though not wishing to outshine the mains, and dessert might be a straight vanilla mille-feuille with rhubarb sorbet. Wines are mostly French, and firmly enlisted to the natural and biodynamic cause. Prices start at £20.
Chef/s: Chris Johns. **Open:** Mon to Sat L 12 to 2.30, D 6 to 10.30. **Closed:** Sun. **Meals:** alc (main courses £20 to £30). Set L £19 (2 courses) to £23. Tasting menu £40. **Details:** 75 seats. 16 seats outside. Bar. Music.

Arbutus

Groundbreaking Soho eatery
Cooking score: 5
⊖ Tottenham Court Road, map 5
Modern European | £45
63-64 Frith Street, Soho, W1D 3JW
Tel no: (020) 7734 4545
www.arbutusrestaurant.co.uk

Still playing to packed houses, this one-time trailblazer now feels much more mainstream than Soho radical. Launched back in 2006, Arbutus kick-started a mini movement towards fine dining without pomp, driven by affordability and daily changing menus built around lesser-used cuts. The décor fits the smart bistro bill with pastel walls, modern art and photographs, black leather banquettes, wooden floors and closely packed beech-wood tables – cool good looks without pretension – while a high-decibel bustle adds to that sense of in-place vitality. Though prices seem to have moved north, the switched-on kitchen still delivers sophistication via simplicity and flavour in well-dressed dishes. Though luxury ingredients such as main-course monkfish with plump Cornish mussels, crushed Jersey Royals, purple sprouting broccoli and sea greens take the spotlight these days, there's still room for some clever creativity with humbler ideas along the lines of pieds et paquets (lamb's tripe, shoulder and trotters). Excellent-value fixed-price lunch and pre-theatre deals are popular, while the compact global wines still offers almost everything by 250ml carafe (by glass on request), with bottles from £25.
Chef/s: Anthony Demetre and Patrick Leano. **Open:** all week L 12 to 2.30 (3 Sun), D 5 to 11 (11.30 Sat, 5.30 to 10.30 Sun). **Closed:** 25 and 26 Dec, 1 Jan. **Meals:** alc (main courses £19 to £31). Set L £20. Early D £21. **Details:** 70 seats.

L'Atelier de Joël Robuchon

An indulgent line-up
Cooking score: 6
⊖ Leicester Square, map 5
Modern French | £90
13-15 West Street, Covent Garden, WC2H 9NE
Tel no: (020) 7010 8600
www.joelrobuchon.co.uk

'Very styled, very cool and very dark', this three-storey venue caters for most eventualities: lone diners can settle at the bar facing the open kitchen on the clubby, red-and-black ground floor, where conversations are easily sparked with neighbours or the lovely waiting staff. For more traditional seating, try the next floor, which has more privacy, a slick black-and-white colour scheme and another open kitchen. After dinner, the top-floor bar with its rooftop terrace is the place to be. The food is as streamlined and stylish as the surroundings. Choose from internationally inspired small plates (three per person is recommended) or the regular à la carte. Stand-out choices have included seared, perfectly caramelised foie gras with marinated rhubarb and fresh pomegranate; crisp, juicy gyoza of braised veal shank with spinach and harissa; and a dessert of mango compote in white chocolate, topped by peanut-butter bavarois wrapped in intense, dark chocolate. It's a 'dazzling, theatrical experience' built on top-tier ingredients. An impressive wine list, covering France in detail, kicks off at £29.
Chef/s: Xavier Boyer. **Open:** all week L 12 to 3, D 5.30 to 11 (10.30 Sun). **Closed:** 25 Dec. **Meals:** alc (main courses £25 to £52). Set L £35 (2 courses) to £38. Sun L £55. Tasting menu £95 (5 courses). **Details:** 88 seats. V menu. Bar. Wheelchair access. Music.

L'Autre Pied

Classy little metropolitan eatery
Cooking score: 6
⊖ Bond Street, map 6
Modern European | £50
5-7 Blandford Street, Marylebone, W1U 3DB
Tel no: (020) 7486 9696
www.lautrepied.co.uk

£5
OFF

This petite Marylebone restaurant brims with charming, attentive staff. The simply styled interior is pretty and timeless, with red banquettes, green leather chairs and a floral feature wall. Andrew McFadden knows the ground well – he's been head chef since 2011, and was previously junior sous-chef at big brother Pied à Terre (see entry). McFadden's dishes are generous, contemporary and full of variety, 'as if his creativity can't quite be reined in'. This is good news for the greedy, interested diner: a 'magnificent' starter of Wye Valley asparagus, for instance, offers three different versions (wild, raw and cooked) plus Belper Knolle gratings, citrusy crab, sorrel, pea shoots and a kuzu crisp. The sourcing is faultless, as is the cooking: Roe deer shoulder comes rich and fall-apart tender, topped with rosy, juicy chunks of shoulder and backed by several different takes on beetroot, plus sprinklings of peanuts and cocoa nibs, their dark bitterness offset by sweet red grapes. A lengthy riff on rhubarb, vanilla and passion fruit delights at dessert, offering a calvacade of mousses, creams, gel and granita. The wine list is equally thorough, offering broad global reach, with French and Italian regions covered in detail. Prices start at £25.
Chef/s: Andrew McFadden. **Open:** all week L 12 to 2.30 (3.30 Sun), Mon to Sat D 6 to 10.30. **Closed:** 23 to 28 Dec. **Meals:** alc (main courses £28 to £30). Set L and D £24 (2 courses) to £29. Sun L £35. Tasting menu £75 (8 courses). **Details:** 48 seats. 12 seats outside. V menu. Music.

Bar Shu

Red-hot Szechuan lip-tingler
Cooking score: 4
⊖ Leicester Square, map 5
Chinese | £45
28 Frith Street, Soho, W1D 5LF
Tel no: (020) 7287 8822
www.barshurestaurant.co.uk

Szechuan, Sichuan, whichever spelling you choose (we go for the first one), this Chinese region, rich in history and with a fiery food culture, used to be called Ba-Shu, which suggests there's a bit of punning going on in the naming of this two-floor corner address. It looks like many another joint in Soho (it's on the fringes of Chinatown) with oriental details in the broadly neutral décor, while the menu itself stands apart, sticking loyally to the cuisine of the region. If you've heard they like to serve serve spicy food and want to test yourself, the 'fragrant chicken in a pile of chillies' is for you. Woof! Sweet-and-sour spare ribs and fragrant noodle dishes offer succour to those in fear of the heat, but it really isn't the place for chilliphobes. Twice-cooked pork, boiled sea bass with sizzling chilli oil and gong bao prawns with cashew nuts show the way. Wines start at £23.
Chef/s: Xiao Zhong Zhang. **Open:** all week 12 to 11 (11.30pm Fri and Sat). **Closed:** 24 and 25 Dec. **Meals:** alc (main courses £10 to £29). **Details:** 100 seats.

NEW ENTRY
Barnyard

Yankee curveball from a culinary wunderkind
Cooking score: 2
⊖ Goodge Street, Tottenham Court Road, map 5
British/American | £25
18 Charlotte Street, Fitzrovia, W1T 2LZ
Tel no: (020) 7580 3842
www.barnyard-london.com

£5 £30
OFF 

The *mise en scène* is unmistakably farm and fowl at this fun, faux-Americana 'shack'. Set behind a picket-fenced threshold, the

Join us at thegoodfoodguide.co.uk

corrugated metal-flanked interior with communal and stool seating ticks all the on-trend boxes (and the no-reservations one, too) and, come 7pm, throngs with local office workers. A Yankee curveball from culinary wunderkind Ollie Dabbous, Barnyard unabashedly touts simple, down-home pleasures rather than the dazzling finesse of Ollie's other joint (Dabbous – see entry). While you wait to sink your teeth into barbecued bavette, homemade dill pickle, mustard and black treacle or slow-roast chicken in a soft brioche bun from the meat-heavy menu of assured plates (staff suggest 2–3 dishes each) there are crowd-pleasing curtain-raisers to get things started – try warm cornbread or corn-on-the-cob with salted butter and meadowsweet. Addictive charred broccoli with vinaigrette hits the mark, as does sausage roll with piccalilli. The indulgent popcorn ice cream with smoked fudge sauce is a standout pud, and potent 'hard' shakes and shandies are all too easy to knock back. Wines from £20.

Chef/s: Ollie Dabbous. **Open:** all week 12 to 10.30 (11pm Fri and Thur, 11 to 11 Sat, 11 to 9 Sun). **Closed:** 25 and 26 Dec. **Meals:** alc (main courses £7 to £15). **Details:** Music.

Barrafina

Fast-paced, intriguing tapas
Cooking score: 4
⊖ Charing Cross, map 5
Spanish | £40
10 Adelaide Street, Covent Garden,
WC2N 4HZ
www.barrafina.co.uk

'It's a bright corner venue, all plate glass and everything on view – there's more space here, more staff'. So ran the notes of one reporter, delighted by this offshoot of Sam and Eddie Hart's second homage to Barcelona's Cal Pep. It offers the same modus operandi as the Soho original: no reservations, counter seating, fast-paced tapas that come as and when, chosen from a mix of chalked up specials and a printed menu dealing in classics and more unusual ideas. Of course, ingredients are everything; simple cooking methods – plancha, josper, grill – demand the freshest produce. Dishes are lively and as intriguing as ever: crab croquetas ('utterly moreish'); full of flavour Middle White pork loin; whole squid cooked on the plancha and served with puntarelle (a type of chicory); very good, garlicky pan con tomate; a deconstructed version of frito mallorquin (a Mallorcan classic of lamb's offal); doughnuts and chocolate sauce to finish. A list of sherries opens the likable, short list of Spanish wines, priced by the bottle (from £19) or glass (from £4).

Chef/s: Nieves Barragán Mohacho. **Open:** all week L 12 to 3 (1 to 3.30 Sun), D 5 to 11 (5.30 to 10 Sun). **Closed:** bank hols. **Meals:** alc (tapas £7 to £16). **Details:** 29 seats.

Barrafina

Crammed with good things
Cooking score: 5
⊖ Tottenham Court Road, map 5
Spanish | £40
54 Frith Street, Soho, W1D 4SL
Tel no: (020) 7813 8016
www.barrafina.co.uk

'The staff are great, the food delicious and although you have to sometimes queue for a while to get a space at the bar, it's always worth it,' is one appraisal of this warm-hearted purveyor of Spanish tapas 'that would be hard to beat even in Spain'. One of two restaurants of the same name (the latest opening is in Covent Garden, see entry), Barrafina is Sam and Eddie Hart's homage to Cal Pep in Barcelona, right down to the spare, narrow room with nothing but counter seating and space to queue. Pan con tomate, prawn and piquillo pepper tortilla, octopus with capers, milk-fed lamb – these are uncluttered, vibrant, produce-driven dishes. Some may be rooted in tradition (ham croquetas, plates of jamón de Bellota), while others are more new-fangled ideas (queen scallop empanadilla, pulpito tempura), but it's all top-drawer stuff. The dessert list takes in Santiago tart, Comice pears in red wine sauce and the popular crema catalana. Just about everything on the modern, all–Spanish list is available by the glass; bottles from £19.

Chef/s: Nieves Barragán Mohacho. **Open:** all week L 12 to 3 (1 to 3.30 Sun), D 5 to 11 (5.30 to 10 Sun). **Closed:** bank hols. **Meals:** alc (tapas £7 to £16). **Details:** 23 seats. 8 seats outside.

LOCAL GEM

Barrica

⊖ **Goodge Street, map 5**
Spanish | £21
62 Goodge Street, Fitzrovia, W1T 4NE
Tel no: (020) 7436 9481
www.barrica.co.uk

There's a busy buzz to this glossy, good-looking eatery where the front bar is good fun for a glass of sherry (from a choice of 16) before hitting the excellent Spanish wine list. The tapas menu is structured to include vegetarian, seafood and meat tapas, not only staples such as patatas bravas and grilled king prawns but also char-grilled aubergine with hazelnut and roasted vegetable sauce, gurnard with saffron, tomato and fennel sauce, and braised shank of kid with crushed potatoes. House wine is £23. Closed Sun.

Benares

Supercharged Indian high-roller
Cooking score: 5
⊖ **Green Park, map 5**
Indian | £60
12a Berkeley Square, Mayfair, W1J 6BS
Tel no: (020) 7629 8886
www.benaresrestaurant.com

Its location next to a Rolls-Royce showroom provides a clue to the pricing at Atul Kochhar's celebrated first-floor restaurant. Guests are guided upstairs, past a slinky bar and into a sizeable dining room with ochre or moulded white plaster walls, and brown leather banquettes. Multinational staff tend to the moneyed clientele. Kochhar's cooking often brings forth modern European shoots from Indian roots, and though spicing occasionally seems toned down – especially on the set menu (there's also a tasting menu and à la carte) – execution is impeccable. Sunday brunch offers a handy way of sampling the repertoire, providing a generous parade of dishes from dhokla lentil cake enlivened with a burst of coriander chutney, to four East meets West desserts (juicy-sweet rasmalai milk dumplings, and lemon cake included). Other highlights might include tangy pickled prawns with root vegetables (presented, on-trend, in a jam jar), a vegetable biryani singing with saffron, and exemplary traditional North Indian chicken curry (made from thigh meat, for peak flavour). Wine starts at £29, with spice-friendly grapes to the fore.

Chef/s: Atul Kochhar. **Open:** Mon to Sat L 12 to 2.30, D 5 to 11. **Closed:** Sun, 25 Dec, 1 Jan. **Meals:** alc (main courses £24 to £34). Set L and D £29 (2 courses) to £35. Tasting menu £82 (6 courses). **Details:** 90 seats. V menu. Bar. Wheelchair access. Music. No children after 7.

Bentley's Oyster Bar & Grill

Venerable seafood institution
Cooking score: 5
⊖ **Piccadilly Circus, map 5**
Seafood | £60
11-15 Swallow Street, Piccadilly, W1B 4DG
Tel no: (020) 7734 4756
www.bentleys.org

£5 OFF 🍷

Founded back in 1916 (watch for the upcoming centenary), Bentley's has the briny in its blood, and this venerable seafood institution has been rolling along with renewed vigour since Irish chef Richard Corrigan took the helm more than a decade ago. Inside, it's a place of two halves: the marble-hued oyster bar makes a lively rendezvous for those who fancy sipping fizz, slurping some bivalves and picking away at crustacean carapaces, while the upstairs grill room offers a more sedate prospect – a study in maritime blues and whites, with William Morris fabrics and piscine paintings on the walls – and tends to be favoured by tourists. Fastidiously sourced seafood is the main event and it receives exemplary treatment, whether you're after something classic (lobster bisque, dressed Cornish crab, Dover sole meunière) or something more modish – perhaps seafood ceviche or pan-seared scallops with red-spiced pork belly and 'sauce chutney'. If fish doesn't appeal, look to the wood-fired grill for truffled chicken or beef sirloin (Irish, of course) with salted bone marrow, before concluding with blood-orange and rhubarb trifle. Excellent sherries and dedicated 'wines of the sea' head up an expansive global list, which also has loads by the glass. Bottles from £28.

Chef/s: Richard Corrigan and Michael Lynch. **Open:** Sun to Fri L 12 to 2.30 (4 Sun), all week D 6 to 11. **Closed:** 25 Dec, bank hols. **Meals:** alc (main courses £19 to £46). Set L £26 (2 courses) to £29. Sun L £45. **Details:** 100 seats. 30 seats outside. Bar. Music.

Berners Tavern

Glitteringly opulent modern brasserie
Cooking score: 5
⊖ Tottenham Court Rd, Oxford Circus, map 5
Modern British | £45
10 Berners Street, Fitzrovia, W1T 3NP
Tel no: (020) 7908 7979
www.edition-hotels.marriott.com

When they say 'tavern', perhaps don't expect a round of darts after your dinner. This is a glitteringly opulent room at the heart of the London Edition hotel, overseen by Phil Carmichael on behalf of the man who gets everywhere, Jason Atherton. It's Atherton's stamp that's on the carefully worked modern brasserie food, where complex layers are built on classic foundations. A terrine constructed of braised rabbit, ham hock and foie gras comes with poached leek and apple and cider purée in a pickled hazelnut-mustard dressing to kick things off. Romney lamb rump and crisped breast are a cinch with peas, broad beans and wild garlic, while stone bass bourride with cockles and lemony garlic purée is the moderne alternative to straight Dover sole (the whole damn thing) in burnt caper butter. An apple caramel eclair with salt-caramel ice cream and Calvados cream is the covetable finale. The French-led wine list is classy and comprehensive, starting at £23 for Chilean Sauvignon.

Chef/s: Phil Carmichael. **Open:** all week L 12 to 3 (4 Sun), D 5 to 10.30 (6 Sun). **Meals:** alc (main courses £15 to £36). **Details:** 120 seats. Wheelchair access. Music.

Blanchette

French-style tapas in Soho
Cooking score: 1
⊖ Tottenham Court Rd, Oxford Circus, map 5
French | £30
9 D'Arblay Street, Soho, W1F 8DR
Tel no: (020) 7439 8100
www.blanchettesoho.co.uk

£5
OFF

This little area of north Soho, handy for Oxford Street, seems to be cornering the market in casual, tapas-style restaurants and this French example is worth exploring. Inside, it forgoes edgy statements in favour of a long stool-lined bar, exposed brick and rickety tables, with affable service that matches the easy-going vibe. Forget conventional courses – on offer is a line-up of classic bistro dishes designed for sharing, perhaps ox cheeks bourguignon, confit duck leg, mussels mouclade à la charentaise, or croque-monsieur. Enjoy plates of charcuterie and cheeses, too, as well as hot chocolate fondant with salted-caramel ice cream to finish. French wines from £18.

Chef/s: Tom Storrar. **Open:** Mon to Fri L 12 to 3, D 5 to 11. Sat 12 to 11, Sun 12 to 9. **Closed:** 25 and 26 Dec. **Meals:** alc (sharing plates £5 to £10). **Details:** 58 seats. 8 seats outside. V menu. Bar. Music.

Average price

The average price denotes the price of a three-course meal without wine.

Bocca di Lupo

Bustling Soho trattoria
Cooking score: 2
⊖ Piccadilly Circus, map 5
Italian | £35
12 Archer Street, Piccadilly, W1D 7BB
Tel no: (020) 7734 2223
www.boccadilupo.com

'No more need you settle for uninteresting pizza and pasta when eating Italian,' a reporter affirms. 'Bocca di Lupo blows boring out of the window.' Which seems a fair summation of what this brick-fronted Soho trattoria is all about. Visually stunning salads of radish, celeriac, pomegranate and pecorino in truffle dressing delight both eye and palate, while the carb repertoire takes in orecchiette with pungent cime di rapa, sea urchin tagliolini, and fortifying beef agnolotti with walnut sauce. Roasted and grilled items for nibbling at include scottadito (lamb chop cut long) and pork and foie gras sausage with faro and porcini, though more robust appetites will look to ox cheek braised in chocolate. Round things off with 'grandpa's balls' (no really, *le palle del nonno*), deep-fried globes of ricotta and chocolate, or a trio of Italian cheeses with pear mostarda. The classy but sternly inflated Italian wines start at £21.50.
Chef/s: Jacob Kenedy. **Open:** all week L 12.15 to 3, D 5.15 to 11 (9.30 Sun). **Closed:** 24 Dec to 2 Jan. **Meals:** alc (main courses £12 to £27). **Details:** 70 seats. Wheelchair access. Music.

Bonnie Gull Seafood Shack

A handy local asset
Cooking score: 2
⊖ Oxford Circus, Goodge Street, map 5
Seafood | £35
21A Foley Street, Fitzrovia, W1W 6DS
Tel no: (020) 7436 0921
www.bonniegull.com

£5
OFF

The name says it all, referring to both décor and food: a simple interior, deliberately short on comfort and frills (unless you count cloth-clad tables), offering a spot-on, no-nonsense seafood menu with the market determining each day's listings. Treatments range from traditional – Selsey crab bisque or beer-battered North Sea whiting with beef-dripping chunky chips – to the likes of Loch Duart salmon tartare with mustard, dill and pickles, and Falmouth cod with brown shrimp, buttered samphire, sea lettuce, cucumber and spinach velouté. Elsewhere, there are oysters, clams and cockles, salt cod brandade Scotch egg with smoked taramasalata, and variety in the shape of a more-than-just-token meat dish, say Lake District lamb (rump, crispy belly and consommé) with peas à la française, which supplements seafood choices. Desserts run to Yorkshire rhubarb and apple fool, service is pleasant and efficient, and the wine list does a good job, too, with prices starting at £18.
Chef/s: Christian Edwardson. **Open:** all week L 12 to 3 (4 Sat and Sun), D 6 to 10 (9 Sun). **Closed:** 25 Dec to 2 Jan. **Meals:** alc (main courses £15 to £30). **Details:** 24 seats. 10 seats outside. Bar. Music.

Brasserie Chavot

Boundlessly generous bourgeois food
Cooking score: 5
⊖ Oxford Circus, map 5
French | £40
41 Conduit Street, Mayfair, W1S 2YF
Tel no: (020) 7183 6425
www.brasseriechavot.com

Occupying a stunning room with gorgeous mosaic floors, soaring Corinthian columns, mirrored walls and decadent chandeliers, Eric Chavot's self-named brasserie feels like some extravagant fin-de-siècle Parisian fantasy – although red leather booths and close-packed tables are reminders of the more prosaic culinary theme. Sip a glass of Pineau de Charentes and imagine you're on the Boulevard Saint-Michel, before bracing yourself for some uncompromisingly bourgeois food with a hefty dollop of nostalgia on the side. Deep-fried soft-shell crab with whipped aïoli, rock oysters with crépinette, flavoursome daube of beef, cassoulet, garlicky roast poussin with lemon

Join us at thegoodfoodguide.co.uk

confit, roast cod with lentils – they're all present, correct and delivered with mouthwatering mastery of *la cuisine française*. Chavot's rich, elegantly fashioned dishes are backed up by classic desserts such as crème brûlée, profiteroles and lemon tart. Prices are relatively painless for this part of town, although the aristocratic French-led wine list invites big spending; house selections start at £25 (£7 a glass).

Chef/s: Eric Chavot. **Open:** Mon to Sat L 12 to 2.30 (12.30 Sat), D 6 to 10.30. **Closed:** Sun, 2 weeks Aug. **Meals:** alc (main courses £20 to £32). Set L £32 (2 courses) to £38. **Details:** 75 seats. Bar. Wheelchair access. Music.

Brasserie Zédel

⊖ **Piccadilly Circus, map 5**
French | £20
20 Sherwood Street, Soho, W1F 7ED
Tel no: (020) 7734 4888
www.brasseriezedel.com

Corbin and King's Zédel offers a concentrated dollop of 1930s Art Deco gorgeousness in the form of a restored hotel ballroom just off Piccadilly Circus. Pavilioned in soaring marble, you'll dine from a classic brasserie menu that bridges the chasm from no-brainer simplicity – endive and Roquefort salad – to *bon ton* luxuries like salt-baked sea bass or chicken in Champagne. If you prefer to keep things on the *paysan* level, consider andouillette in mustard sauce or a grilled onglet with shallots. The trundling chariot brings cheeses, and dessert a dramatic blood orange Romanoff, or less dramatic crème brûlée. Wines from £19.95. Open all week.

Café Murano

Smart-casual Mayfair hangout
Cooking score: 4
⊖ **Green Park, map 5**
Italian | £35
33 St James's Street, Green Park, SW1A 1HD
Tel no: (020) 3371 5559
www.cafemurano.co.uk

If you don't have the time or inclination for the full-dress Murano experience (see entry), this casual offshoot should fit the bill. Angela Hartnett's Café Murano has a reputation to uphold and it does the job, thanks to on-the-ball staff, a sleekly designed space and a simple, seasonal approach to north Italian cooking – a winning formula that has accrued a strong following. The kitchen concentrates its efforts on manageable, affordable items, ranging from excellent chichetti of fritto misto and truffle arancini and antipasti of, say, vitello tonnato, to squid-ink tagliolini with morels and peas, saffron risotto, and chicken milanese with rocket and Parmesan. Desserts include a salted-caramel custard tart, served with a milk sorbet. There's a good-value set deal at lunch and early/late evening and the all-Italian wine list (from £19.50) keeps everyone happy with its enticing carafe and by-the-glass selection and excellent regional goodies. Café Murano Covent Garden is at 34–36 Tavistock Street, London, WC2E 7PB.

Chef/s: Samantha Williams. **Open:** all week L 12 to 3 (11.30 to 4 Sun), Mon to Sat D 5.30 to 11. **Closed:** 25 to 28 Dec. **Meals:** alc (main courses £16 to £20). Set L and D £19 (2 courses) to £23. Sun L £30. **Details:** 75 seats. Bar. Music.

Le Caprice

Famous Mayfair brasserie with loyal fans
Cooking score: 4
⊖ **Green Park, map 5**
Modern British | £35
Arlington House, Arlington Street, Mayfair,
SW1A 1RJ
Tel no: (020) 7629 2239
www.le-caprice.co.uk

A restaurant as classic as the European brasserie food it serves, Le Caprice has been going strong for well over 30 years and has the timeless glamour of a Hermès handbag. The monochrome interior features gleaming mirrors and black-and-white portraits by David Bailey. It could be the late 80s again – yet it also feels surprisingly fresh, with no hint of faded glory. The menu has developed over time but is no slave to fashion: expect solid classics, perfectly executed and served – at the black marble bar or a linen-clad table – by a polished waiting team. Dressed Dorset crab is paired with a 'wonderfully mustardy' celeriac remoulade, watercress and wholesome slabs of toast; a vibrantly fresh fillet of hake sits on a punchy harissa fregola salsa brimming with broad beans, asparagus and peas; and a 'perfectly executed' dessert of rhubarb pannacotta came with 'a perfectly sweet-tangy confit rhubarb'. A decent, global selection of wines opens at £27.75.

Chef/s: Andrew McLay. **Open:** all week 12 to 12 (11.30 to 11 Sun). **Closed:** 25 and 26 Dec. **Meals:** alc (main courses £17 to £35). Set D £20 (2 courses) to £25. **Details:** 74 seats. 16 seats outside. V menu. Bar. Wheelchair access. Music. Parking.

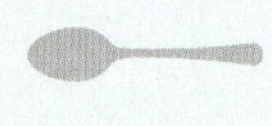

Please send us your feedback

To register your opinion about any restaurant listed in this guide, or a new restaurant that you wish to bring to our attention, please visit the web address at the bottom of the page. Your feedback informs the content of the book and will be used to compile next year's reviews.

Casa Malevo

Warm-hearted Argentinian dining
Cooking score: 2
⊖ **Marble Arch, map 6**
Argentinian | £40
23 Connaught Street, Marylebone, W2 2AY
Tel no: (020) 7402 1988
www.casamalevo.com

'We left contented and with a warm glow about this lovely place,' revealed a pair of reporters, smitten by the cheery vibes and welcoming staff at this sleek, cosy Argentinian restaurant on a quiet street in Connaught village. Diego Jacquet is praised for 'simply amazing' cooking. That might mean grilled chorizo on toast with onions and Malbec-braised ox cheeks, or grilled lamb's sweetbreads with criolla sauce (a South American version of salsa) and lemon to start, followed by grilled Patagonian lamb chops and anchovies salsa verde or a 'chimichurri' beef burger with smoked bacon, Provolone, tomato and caramelised onions. Casa Malevo regulars stick to their favourites – often beef empanadas, asado (slow-grilled flank steak with bone-marrow sauce), lemon and thyme chicken, and dulce de leche crème brûlée. Try as you might, you won't want to stick to the cheapest wine (£21.95) from an all-Argentinian wine list featuring more than the usual suspects.

Chef/s: Diego Jacquet. **Open:** all week L 12 to 2.30 (3 Sat and Sun), D 5.30 to 10.30 (10 Sun). **Meals:** alc (main courses £13 to £28). **Details:** 37 seats. 6 seats outside. Bar. Music.

Ceviche

⊖ **Tottenham Court Road, map 5**
Peruvian | £24
17 Frith Street, Soho, W1D 4RG
Tel no: (020) 7292 2040
www.cevicheuk.com

A pathfinder for London's Peruvian invasion, this jam-packed Soho joint brings some of that country's most bankable assets to the table in the shape of pisco sours (12 versions), grilled anticuchos skewers and, of course, the eponymous lime-marinated speciality in numerous forms – from king prawn, Jerusalem artichoke and superfood golden-berry to wild mushrooms with sweet potatoes. The real action is at the bar, but you can also squeeze on to a table for classics such as flame-cooked beef 'lomo' fillet with chips. Wines from £18. Open all week.

The Chancery

Packing a major punch in lawyerland
Cooking score: 6
⊖ Chancery Lane, map 5
Modern European | £47
9 Cursitor Street, Holborn, EC4A 1LL
Tel no: (020) 7831 4000
www.thechancery.co.uk

£5
OFF

'Excellent food, fantastic service…our favourite restaurant in London, at which we have held family celebrations and more intimate dinners,' sums up one visitor, catching the tone of this well-established and intimate restaurant that's been packing a major punch since the arrival of chef Graham Long in May 2014. Top-notch ingredients are Long's building blocks, the seasonally influenced menu changes often enough to keep regulars amused, and there have been good reports of marinated raw hand-dived scallops with cucumber jelly, avocado cream, sesame filo and shiso dressing (something of a signature dish) and monkfish tail roasted in onion cinders and served with butter lettuce, smoked anchovy, roasted and pickled onions. Elsewhere, there's been praise for ash-crusted venison with crapaudine beetroot (an heirloom variety) with dates, walnuts and dried goats' cheese – 'the flavours singing in close harmony' – and finely wrought desserts, say poached Yorkshire rhubarb with fromage blanc mousse, cranberries and gingerbread. The short wine list inspires confidence, with discerning selections from all over the world. Prices from £17.50.
Chef/s: Graham Long. **Open:** Mon to Fri L 12 to 3, Mon to Sat D 6 to 11. **Closed:** Sun, 23 Dec to 4 Jan, bank hols. **Meals:** Set L and D £40 (2 courses) to

£47. Tasting menu £68 (7 courses). **Details:** 55 seats. 4 seats outside. V menu. Bar. Wheelchair access. Music.

Chiltern Firehouse

Modern American brasserie food with stars
Cooking score: 6
⊖ Baker Street, Bond Street, map 6
Modern American | £70
1 Chiltern Street, Marylebone, W1U 7PA
Tel no: (020) 7073 7676
www.chilternfirehouse.com

The Firehouse has become so much the star-stuffed place to be seen since opening in 2014 that it's almost spilled into parody. What was the Marylebone fire station has been coaxed into the form of a contemporary boutique hotel, with an ingeniously laid-out eatery that's all half-moon banquette booths and exposed lighting, softened by hanging fronds. Service is reckoned superb ('really couldn't fault it'), and wily Nuno Mendes has concocted a repertoire of American brasserie food, overlaid with touches of on-the-spot modernism, to seduce the throngs. Crab-filled doughnuts with coral dusting, or fingers of cornbread with smoky chipotle-maple butter, are good things to nibble before starters arrive, perhaps roasted Jerusalem artichokes and hazelnuts on truffled stracciatella. Reports speak of outstanding salmon with beetroot risotto, the glorious char-grilled Ibérico pork with miso-dressed courgette and chard, and the signature dessert, frozen apple pannacotta with herb granité and burnt meringue. Wines start at £22, but soon hit prices that will set off the old fire alarms.
Chef/s: Nuno Mendes. **Open:** all week L 12 to 2.30 (3 Thur and Fri, 11 Sat and Sun), D 5.30 to 10 (6 Thur to Sun). **Meals:** alc (main courses £21 to £75). Set L £65. Set D £85. **Details:** 120 seats. 80 seats outside. V menu. Bar. Wheelchair access. Music.

China Tang at the Dorchester

Scintillating Shanghai glitz
Cooking score: 2
⊖ Hyde Park Corner, map 6
Chinese | £70
The Dorchester Hotel, 53 Park Lane, Hyde Park, W1K 1QA
Tel no: (020) 7629 9988
www.chinatanglondon.co.uk

Restaurant interiors don't come much more sumptuous than this: descend a broad flight of stairs into a dreamy vision of 1930s Shanghai, jewel-bright in reds and golds, brimming with Art Deco touches, ornate vases and chinoiserie. Diners are rather crammed in, but it adds to the buzz – and who knows what glamorous chitchat you might overhear? The menu gives an accessible snapshot of China, including some classic Cantonese and Szechuan dishes. Peking duck can be taken as two or three courses, and there are some high-end options (at high-end prices) including bird's nest soup. Don't expect too much spice here; dishes such as ma po tofu are toned down, presumably for Western tastes, but you can't go wrong with classics such as tender chicken satay or chicken in black bean sauce. A dessert of apple and banana with a caramelised sesame coating, coconut sorbet and a powerfully acidic kalamai cream was a pleasant, if not perfectly balanced, endnote. The wine list is a weighty tome, with prices starting at £29 and ending in the stratosphere.
Chef/s: Chun Chong Fong. **Open:** all week 11.30am to 11.30pm. **Closed:** 24 to 26 Dec. **Meals:** alc (main courses £14 to £45). Set L £28. **Details:** 130 seats. V menu. Bar. Wheelchair access. Music.

Chisou

Authentic, unobtrusive Japanese favourite
Cooking score: 4
⊖ Oxford Circus, map 5
Japanese | £40
4 Princes Street, Mayfair, W1B 2LE
Tel no: (020) 7629 3931
www.chisourestaurant.com

It may be only a stroll from Oxford Street, but there's something refreshingly calming about this unobtrusive, perfectly tuned Japanese restaurant where Japanese businessmen and aficionados of pure-bred traditional cuisine bag seats at the sushi bar for impeccably fresh nigiri and sashimi prepared with respectful razor-sharp technique. There's also plenty of space at tables in the understated wood-toned dining room if you fancy lingering over something more sophisticated from the carte or list of chef's recommendations. Little sharing plates of stir-fried pork belly with Chinese cabbage or a curious assemblage of pickled oyster mushrooms in rice bran with asparagus, spinach and sprinkling of Manchego cheese should pique the palate ahead of squid tempura, salted mackerel or teriyaki poussin from the robata grill. The set lunch menus are a bargain for the area, there's a quick-fix Sushi Counter next door and a full-on branch at 31 Beauchamp Place, Knightsbridge; tel: (020) 3155 0055. The saké list is a wonder to behold, and wines start at £24.50.
Chef/s: Dham Kodi. **Open:** Mon to Sat L 12 to 2.30 (12.30 to 3 Sat), D 6 to 10.30. Sun 1 to 9.30. **Closed:** 25 and 26 Dec, bank hols. **Meals:** alc (main courses £7 to £28). **Details:** 75 seats. V menu.

Join us at thegoodfoodguide.co.uk

NEW ENTRY

Chutney Mary

Glitzy Indian moves uptown
Cooking score: 5
Green Park, map 5
Indian | £45
73 St James's Street, Mayfair, SW1A 1PH
Tel no: (020) 7629 6688
www.chutneymary.com

After 25 years in Chelsea, Chutney Mary has moved to a new home in Mayfair and raised the design bar for Indian restaurants in London. The spacious interior has been sumptuously accessorised with expensive wallpaper, dark-wood panels, Indian artefacts, exotic paintings and seductive lighting, and it's all rounded off by 'smooth, well-mannered' service. Compared to some of its high-profile rivals in the capital, Chutney Mary feels refreshingly civilised. The menu is based around small plates, grills and slow-cooked dishes, and the kitchen can deliver some real treats: strawberry chutney is a snappy match for a kebab of guinea fowl infused with spices, and Calcutta wild prawn curry with coconut, tamarind and red chilli is delicately spiced. Even frequently encountered dishes such as bhindi nayantara (okra with tomato) are made with skill, and vintage basmati rice (aged for three years) is perfect. Finish with creative desserts such as strawberry jelly with pineberries and sorrel (gel and ice cream) or carrot and cardamom soufflé with salted pistachio ice cream. An exciting inventory of wines starts from £28 and is filled with imaginative choices to support the food.
Open: Mon to Sat L 12 to 2.15 (12.30 to 2.45 Sat), D 6 to 10.30. **Closed:** Sun. **Meals:** alc (main courses £16 to £38). **Details:** 110 seats. Bar. Music.

Symbols

 Accommodation is available
 Three courses for less than £30
 £5-off voucher scheme
 Notable wine list

Cigala

Tapas in Bloomsbury
Cooking score: 1
Holborn, Russell Square, map 5
Spanish | £30
54 Lamb's Conduit Street, Bloomsbury, WC1N 3LW
Tel no: (020) 7405 1717
www.cigala.co.uk

The corner site on the eastern fringe of bustling Bloomsbury is bright white on the inside, with big picture windows for views of the street life. It deals in Spanish tapas from the utterly traditional likes of pimientos de Padrón to more outgoing specials such as pigeon, pepper and onion empanada. Baked crab hot with cayenne and brandy is a signature, and bomba rice paellas stuffed with seafood or chicken and chorizo are popular. Grilled churrasco ribeye is the meaty way to go, and desserts get positively avant-garde for bitter chocolate mousse on saffron orange jelly with black bean ice cream. The Spanish wine list starts at £18.50, with sherry shots from £4.50.
Chef/s: Clayton Felizari. **Open:** all week 12 to 10.45 (12.30 Sat, 12.30 to 9.45 Sun). **Closed:** 25 and 26 Dec, 1 Jan. **Meals:** alc (main courses £14 to £20). Set L £20 (2 courses) to £23. Set D £25 (2 courses) to £28. Sun L £16. **Details:** 60 seats. 32 seats outside.

Cigalon

Provence on a plate
Cooking score: 2
Chancery Lane, map 5
French | £30
115 Chancery Lane, Holborn, WC2A 1PP
Tel no: (020) 7242 8373
www.cigalon.co.uk

Squarely in lawyerland, this homage to Provence is a classy joint, and does a roaring trade with the 'suited and booted' who work hereabouts. The room certainly has impact, most notable circular mauve velvet banquettes running down the centre of the room and a huge glass-lantern roof above, full of artfully arranged foliage – and it 'has an intimate feel…gentle lighting, good acoustics' noted one reporter approvingly. Classic south-eastern French dishes include niçoise salad or braised Carmague beef cannelloni with red wine and bone-marrow sauce to start, with grilled saddle of lamb with smoked anchovies to follow. Set lunch and dinner menus are good value, perhaps a delicately flavoured poached salmon with flavours of carrots – foam, purée, slivers, a Bugs Bunny-style miniature – and roasted pork loin with celeriac gratin and green apple. Elsewhere, bread arrives 'warm and scrumptious' with a pot of tapenade, service is 'skilful, but impersonal' and wine starts at £24.

Chef/s: Julien Carlon. **Open:** Mon to Fri L 12 to 2.15, D 5.45 to 10. **Closed:** Sat, Sun, 25 Dec to 1 Jan, bank hols. **Meals:** alc (main courses £14 to £22). Set L £22 (2 courses) to £27. Set D £30 (2 courses) to £35. **Details:** 68 seats. Bar. Music.

Cinnamon Club

Exhilarating new-wave Indian cuisine
Cooking score: 5
⊖ Westminster, map 5
Indian | £60
30-32 Great Smith Street, Westminster, SW1P 3BU
Tel no: (020) 7222 2555
www.cinnamonclub.com

At the forefront of the modern Indian food movement since 2001, Vivek Singh's handsome enterprise occupies the capacious confines of the former Westminster library; you can spot the odd MP at times. At its best, Singh's cuisine is a deliciously playful reworking of Anglo and Indian cookery: witness the chip-shop pastiche of a tandoori cod starter, with mango purée and pea relish – the fruity purée resembling an egg yolk, the relish (spiced with wasabi) like revved-up mushy peas. A pricey stew of sorpotel of Ibérico pork presa with Goan spiced pork dumplings wouldn't have suffered if cheaper meat had been used, and the accompanying rice cake seemed like two heavy idlis.

Nevertheless, the set lunch – chicken tikka of almost pâté-like softness, followed by equally light venison and prune kofta with black lentils and paratha, and completed by date and ginger pudding – is excellent value. Wine starts at £25 for a bottle buried in a voluminous list, with options by the glass and carafe.

Chef/s: Vivek Singh. **Open:** Mon to Sat L 12 to 2.30, D 6 to 10.30. **Closed:** Sun, 26 Dec, 1 Jan. **Meals:** alc (main courses £16 to £35). Set L and D £22 (2 courses) to £24. **Details:** 250 seats. Bar.

Cinnamon Soho

Harmonious Indian-based fusion food
Cooking score: 3
⊖ Oxford Circus, map 5
Indian | £25
5 Kingly Street, Soho, W1B 5PF
Tel no: (020) 7437 1664
www.cinnamonsoho.com

Indian food, as the world and her partner must have noticed by now, is on a dynamic upswing, and nowhere more so than in central London. Vivek Singh's Cinnamon group is a prime mover in the revolution, expressed here in the form of a low-lit, wood-toned room with something of the feel of a secret meeting place. Boundaries are cheerfully crossed for the likes of Indo-Chinese chicken with burnt chillies, and Anglo-Indian dishes such as rogan josh shepherd's pie and the Kerala version of seafood pie, while the more obviously authentic dishes, such as Lucknow chicken biryani and seared tilapia in garlic sauce, are singing with harmonious spice. Sprouted fenugreek salad or tandoori aubergine crush make wholesome side orders, there's potato paratha among the carbs, and it all ends on a fragrant note with something like saffron-poached pear in kheer rice pudding with cinnamon ice cream. Languedoc house wines are £19, and there are lassis and mocktails for the teetotal.

Chef/s: Vivek Singh. **Open:** all week L 12 to 5 (4 Sun), Mon to Fri D 5.30 to 11.15. **Meals:** alc (main courses £8 to £17). Set L £10 (2 courses) to £12. Set D £16 (2 courses) to £19. **Details:** 75 seats. 22 seats outside. Music.

Clos Maggiore

A seductive French experience
Cooking score: 3
⊖ Covent Garden, map 5
French | £40
33 King Street, Covent Garden, WC2E 8JD
Tel no: (020) 7379 9696
www.closmaggiore.com

Dubbed as one of London's most romantic eateries, Clos Maggiore hosts its fair share of Covent Garden tourists but is no slacker when it comes to quality and value. Quite how lashings of artificial blossom and privet can be romantic rather than tacky puzzled one reporter, who nonetheless agreed it is 'really rather lovely', especially if you sit in the main glass-roofed courtyard with branches and flowers rambling overhead. The rest of the restaurant has the demeanour of a gentlemen's club, with red banquettes, glossy floorboards and panelling and glass cabinets full of bottles. The cooking references the country inns of Provence and Tuscany, but the poise of the presentation suggests loftier ideals. That said, dishes are generally simple – as in a starter of Devon crab with celeriac remoulade, or a main course of oven-roasted chicken breast with thyme and garlic glaze, asparagus, roasted jus, confit lemon and potato gnocchi. Don't miss desserts such as the 'beautiful' milk chocolate and Frangelico verrine with peanut ice cream and a warm almond and raspberry financier. An impressive global wine list offers something for even the deepest pockets, and opens at £23.
Chef/s: Marcellin Marc. **Open:** all week L 12 to 2.30, D 5 to 11 (10 Sun). **Closed:** 24 and 25 Dec. **Meals:** alc (main courses £18 to £33). Set L and D £25 (2 courses) to £30. Sun L £30. Tasting menu £55 (6 courses). **Details:** 70 seats. V menu. Music. Children at L only.

The Colony Grill Room

A romp through American classics
Cooking score: 3
⊖ Bond Street, map 6
North American | £50
The Beaumont, 8 Balderton Street, Brown Hart Gardens, Mayfair, W1K 6TF
Tel no: (020) 7499 9499
www.colonygrillroom.com

Premier-league restaurateurs Chris Corbin and Jeremy King unveiled their first hotel in late 2014: a discreet model of understatement on a quiet Mayfair street, just a couple of hundred metres from Selfridges. The hotel's restaurant, the American-inspired Colony Grill – with a separate cocktail bar – may be windowless, but this is smoothed over by rich wood tones, deep-red leather banquettes, soft lighting, Deco-style murals by American artist John Mattos and black-and-white cartoons of famous actors, writers and musicians – 'very Manhatten', noted one American visitor approvingly. As is the menu. Open all day for breakfast and weekend brunch via lunch and dinner, the menu romps through classics such as chicken marengo, clam chowder, meatloaf, macaroni cheese and Corbin and King's greatest hits, from shepherd's pie to eggs Arlington. The chicken pot pie is a must, but there's also 'perfect' omelette Arnold Bennett and excellent hamburgers. Ice cream sundaes, made to your own specification, will have you purring with delight. Wines from £19.75.
Chef/s: Christian Turner. **Open:** all week 7am to midnight (11pm Sun). **Meals:** alc (main courses £8 to £40). **Details:** 100 seats. V menu. Bar. Wheelchair access.

Visit us online

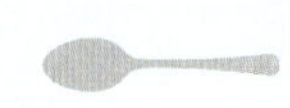

To find out more about The Good Food Guide, please visit thegoodfoodguide.co.uk

Copita

Big flavours in small packages
Cooking score: 3
⊖ Oxford Circus, Tottenham Court Rd, map 5
Spanish | £22
27 d'Arblay Street, Soho, W1F 8EP
Tel no: (020) 7287 7797
www.copita.co.uk

This confident tapas bar on the northern edge of Soho continues to thrive on accessibility, fair value and a stunning line-up of sharply executed small plates. It's from the same people behind Barrica (see entry), a vibrant, cramped space with high stools to perch on and a no-reservations policy at dinner (you're safe at lunch). The kitchen's regularly changing repertoire is a Spanish hybrid that runs all the way from jamón Ibérico and croqueta de champiñones to cured salmon with tarragon pear and confit duck leg and Brussels sprouts. There's thrifty use of all those overlooked bits of meat – ox tongue with red cabbage and mushroom sauce, for example, as well as pork jowl and lentil stew – and churros with chocolate make a popular finish. Modest prices extend to the illuminating list of regional Spanish wines, which opens with a superb selection by the glass and 375ml carafe. Bottles start at £20 and there are some dozen prestigious sherries.
Chef/s: Nacho Pinilla. **Open:** Mon to Sat L 12 to 4 (1 Sat), D 5.30 to 10.30. **Closed:** Sun, 25 and 26 Dec, 1 Jan, Easter Sun, bank hols. **Meals:** alc (tapas £6 to £15). **Details:** 40 seats. 8 seats outside. Music.

Corrigan's Mayfair

Gilded Mayfair flagship
Cooking score: 4
⊖ Marble Arch, map 6
Modern British | £50
28 Upper Grosvenor Street, Mayfair, W1K 7EH
Tel no: (020) 7499 9943
www.corrigansmayfair.com

If the dimly lit, moneyed, hunting-themed surrounds suggests effete culinary mannerisms, think again – there's not a wisp, foam or daub to be seen. Richard Corrigan knows all about seasonality and sourcing, so it's no surprise that his bold, uncluttered food resonates with ingredients-driven rusticity. As you might expect, seasonal game is a sure-fire success: a starter of pheasant sausage with artichoke and damson; loin of fallow deer with celeriac, chestnut and plum; the famous game pie; and a very well-reported roast saddle of rabbit with white asparagus and three-cornered garlic. This is also the place to come if your fancy turns to shellfish cocktail with tempura prawns (something of a signature) or lamb rump with wild mushrooms and salsify, and when it comes to dessert, the pistachio baked Alaska is hard to trump. Lunch is excellent value, but in general, lofty prices reflect the snazzy address, including the wine list (from £35).
Chef/s: Alan Barrins. **Open:** Sun to Fri L 12 to 3 (4 Sun), all week D 6 to 10.30 (9.30 Sun). **Closed:** bank hols. **Meals:** alc (main courses £18 to £38). Set L £25 (2 courses) to £29. Sunday L £29. **Details:** 80 seats. Bar. Wheelchair access. Music.

Coya

Slick, modern Peruvian cooking
Cooking score: 4
⊖ Hyde Park Corner, Green Park, map 5
Peruvian | £45
118 Piccadilly, Mayfair, W1J 7NW
Tel no: (020) 7042 7118
www.coyarestaurant.com

Coya's sister restaurants are in Miami and Dubai, which is perhaps a clue that this joint is aiming at the glam end of contemporary Peruvian cuisine rather than the humble street tucker you might find on your way to Machu Picchu. This is the new wave of Latin American food, where the classic preparations like ceviche, tiraditos and parrillada are sexed-up for our times. And damn, it's good. It all takes place in a rustic-chic setting with an open kitchen and Pisco Bar to confirm its street cred. Small plates lead the way: Cumbrae oysters, say, with an oyster emulsion and lime jelly, or Chilean Wagyu beef rib served on the bone. The ceviche such as

Join us at thegoodfoodguide.co.uk

corvina (a Pacific fish) with truffles, ponzu and chives are spot-on, while the charcoal grill turns out cracking anticuchos of chicken, ox heart and monkfish. The cost can rack up. The wine list opens at £28.
Chef/s: Sanjay Dwivedi. **Open:** all week L 12 to 2.45, D 6 to 10.45 (11 Thur to Sat). **Closed:** 25 Dec. **Meals:** alc (main courses £8 to £72). Set L £30 (2 courses) to £34. Sun L £36. Tasting menu £80. **Details:** 150 seats. V menu. Bar. Music.

CUT at 45 Park Lane

Glitzy all-American steakhouse
Cooking score: 4
⊖ Hyde Park Corner, map 6
North American | £75
45 Park Lane, Mayfair, W1K 1PN
Tel no: (020) 7493 4545
www.dorchestercollection.com

Madison Avenue comes to Park Lane at the Mayfair outpost of superstar chef Wolfgang Puck's US steakhouse chain. Of course, everything about this clubby hotel dining room is OTT, from the glitterball chandeliers, extravagant draped curtains and ritzy furnishings to the Damien Hirst artwork – not one, but the entire 16-print 'Psalm' collection. Likewise, the kitchen goes big on beef, deploying the char-grill/broiler double act for some seriously good (and seriously expensive) steaks – Black Angus, USDA Prime and, of course, gold-standard pure Japanese Wagyu, all accompanied by a motorcade of international sauces and sides ranging from chimichurri butter to wild mushrooms with shishito peppers. Fish fans could move from tuna tartare with wasabi aïoli to hand-cut linguine 'frutti di mare', and there are bountiful salads, too – perhaps Chinese chicken with pickled ginger and crispy won tons. If you still have room, 'sticky toffee' medjool date cake and Black Forest délice beckon. Part of the Sultan of Brunei's Dorchester Collection (see entries Alain Ducasse and China Tang at the Dorchester), CUT is also a hot ticket for stateside

breakfasts, while American stars pack a pricey punch on the jet-setting wine list, with bottles from £30.
Chef/s: David McIntyre. **Open:** all week L 12 to 2.30 (3.15 Sat, 11 to 3.15 Sun), D 6 to 10.30. **Meals:** alc (main courses £21 to £140). Set L £45 (2 courses). **Details:** 70 seats. V menu. Wheelchair access. Music. Parking.

Dabbous

Wild ingredients, modernist understatement
Cooking score: 6
⊖ Goodge Street, map 5
Modern European | £52
39 Whitfield Street, Fitzrovia, W1T 2SF
Tel no: (020) 7323 1544
www.dabbous.co.uk

If the relentlessly grim ground-floor dining room with its industrial ducting and naked lightbulbs has the air of an eastern European railway café, the bar downstairs feels like somewhere you might be taken for interrogation, the vodka, Curaçao, lemon and guava cocktails only lulling you into a sense of false security. And yet Ollie Dabbous is considered one of London's hot-ticket chefs. Amid this brutal urbanism, the seasonal notes of ingredients sourced from where the wild things are come as blessed paradox: a starter of peas and mint is 'three spoonfuls of intense green glory'. Mackerel and gooseberries are pulsatingly fresh, alliums repose in chilled pine broth, veal belly is pulled and topped with shaved white asparagus, and dessert might be barley sponge soaked in red tea with vanilla cream. The delicacy can sometimes feel like leg-pulling, as when cucumber sticks float pointlessly in a thin lemony fluid, but the understatement is otherwise enjoyed. Wines go from £25, or £4.50 a small glass.
Chef/s: Ollie Dabbous. **Open:** Mon to Sat L 12 to 2.30, D 6.30 to 9.30. **Closed:** Sun, 23 Dec to 5 Jan, Easter. **Meals:** Set L £32 (4 courses). Set D £52 (4 courses). Tasting menu £64 (7 courses). **Details:** 38 seats. V menu. Bar. Music.

Dean Street Townhouse

Glamorous Soho rendezvous
Cooking score: 3
 Tottenham Court Road, map 5
Modern British | £50
69-71 Dean Street, Soho, W1D 3SE
Tel no: (020) 7434 1775
www.deanstreettownhouse.com

If you're not a member of Nick Jones' Soho House over on Greek Street but rather fancy the idea of club life, head round to his Dean Street Townhouse for a taste of something similar without the need to find two nominees to put you forward. A couple of Georgian town houses make up a glamorous all-day restaurant (think wooden panelling, red leather and copious artworks by serious bods), luxe bedrooms and a trendy bar. The kitchen likes to inject a little modernity into traditional British preparations, so there might be Morecambe Bay potted shrimps alongside a terrine made with Gloucester Old Spot and haggis among starters, before a classic ribeye steak with béarnaise sauce or hake with fennel and cockles. Finish with a fashionable buttermilk pudding with pineapple. Just about every base is covered, from breakfast to afternoon tea and seductive cocktails. Wine prices start at £22.
Chef/s: Jason Loy. **Open:** all week 7am to 12am (8am Sat and Sun). **Meals:** alc (main courses £7 to £65). Set D £17 (2 courses) to £20. Sun L £25 to £28. **Details:** 120 seats. 22 seats outside. V menu. Bar. Wheelchair access. Music.

Please send us your feedback

To register your opinion about any restaurant listed in this guide, or a new restaurant that you wish to bring to our attention, please visit the web address at the bottom of the page. Your feedback informs the content of the book and will be used to compile next year's reviews.

Dehesa

Gregarious tapas pit-stop
Cooking score: 2
Oxford Circus, map 5
Tapas | £35
25 Ganton Street, Oxford Circus, W1F 9BP
Tel no: (020) 7494 4170
www.dehesa.co.uk

£5 OFF

Part of Simon Mullins' successful modern tapas empire (Salt Yard, Opera Tavern and Ember Yard – see entries), good things are crammed into this small Soho space. The lively tapas assortment is a Spanish/Italian hybrid that runs all the way from jamón Ibérico to pecorino sardo, and the repertoire extends beyond staples like salt cod croquetas, classic tortilla, patatas fritas and the never-off-the-menu courgette flower stuffed with goats' cheese and drizzled with honey. There could be Cornish crab and coriander brik partnered with fennel, watercress, chilli and radish, or slow-cooked lamb shoulder with warm silver onion, carrot and polenta crust. Sassy desserts put a brave new spin on the classics – Muscovado tart with a tangerine and date compote with vanilla custard, for instance. The modern wine list explores Spanish and Italian regional wines (from £19).
Chef/s: Ben Tish. **Open:** Mon to Fri L 12 to 3, D 5 to 11. Sat and Sun 12 to 11 (10 Sun). **Closed:** 25 and 26 Dec, 1 Jan. **Meals:** alc (tapas £4 to £10). Set L and D £35 to £40. **Details:** 54 seats. 42 seats outside. Bar. Music.

The Delaunay

All-day café dining, central Europe style
Cooking score: 3
Temple, map 5
Modern European | £40
55 Aldwych, Covent Garden, WC2B 4BB
Tel no: (020) 7499 8558
www.thedelaunay.com

Modelled on the kind of place where you might stop in for coffee and a cream cake while on holiday in central Europe, and soon decide to hang on for lunch, the Delaunay is an all-day café in the grand style. Camped on the corner of Aldwych and Drury Lane, it's all high gloss, from the patisserie counter to the afternoon cake stands, with an all-day à la carte menu worth getting bedded in for. Liverwurst with pickled walnuts and rye toast might precede one of the gloriously unreconstructed main dishes: schnitzels one way or another, sour cream goulash, stroganoff and a roll call of German würstchen. Fish offer one or two more modern shots – trout with leeks and girolles in thyme beurre blanc – among the goujons and kedgeree. Finish with a wodge of proper baked cheesecake redolent of vanilla. Wines from a serviceable list open at £19.75.

Chef/s: Malachi O'Gallagher. **Open:** all week 11.30am to midnight (11pm Sun). **Closed:** 25 Dec. **Meals:** alc (main courses £16 to £33). **Details:** 150 seats. V menu. Wheelchair access. Music.

Dinings

Teeny-weeny Japanese thriller
Cooking score: 3
Marylebone, map 6
Japanese | £50
22 Harcourt Street, Marylebone, W1H 4HH
Tel no: (020) 7723 0666
www.dinings.co.uk

Wedged into a dinky Marylebone town house, Dinings may be low on luxury but scores heavily with its captivating and intelligently off-piste take on contemporary Japanese cuisine. Fans of raw fish crowd the poky street-level counter for their sushi and sashimi fix, but most of the action takes place in the basement dining room – a brutalist concrete bunker with hard edges and equally hard seats. Despite a lack of creature comforts, you'll be rewarded with some immaculately assembled 'tapas-style' plates and more substantial offerings generously bestrewn with posh ingredients. Tokyo meets Barcelona as the kitchen delivers sea bass carpaccio with fresh truffle and ponzu jelly, Cornish crab croquetas with smoked paprika relish or crispy pork belly with apple salsa and cho-gochujang sauce. Otherwise, go for broke

with lobster miso bouillabaisse or Welsh Wagyu sukiyaki with foie gras and port-infused soy. Sumo-sized prices pay for serious skills in the kitchen, while wines (from £34) are simply expensive; better to explore the list of seasonal sakés, beers and aperitifs.

Chef/s: Masaki Sugisaki. **Open:** all week L 12 to 3 (12.30 to 3.30 Sat and Sun), D 6 to 10.30. **Closed:** 2 weeks Christmas and New Year. **Meals:** alc (main courses £11 to £28). **Details:** 28 seats. Music.

Dishoom

Funky all-day Indian café
Cooking score: 2
Leicester Square, Covent Garden, map 5
Indian | £30
12 Upper St Martin's Lane, Covent Garden, WC2H 9FB
Tel no: (020) 7420 9320
www.dishoom.com

Inspired by cafés opened by the Iranian Zoroastrian community that sprang up in Bombay in the early part of the 20th century, Dishoom provides Indian-inspired tucker all day long. The room looks like a cross between a French brasserie and a retro coffee shop, with lights dangling low over the tables, dark wooden panels on the walls and a mishmash of café-style chairs. It certainly doesn't look like an Indian restaurant. Start the day with akuri (spicy scrambled eggs), or if you're passing in the middle of the day go for an open-ended naan roll called a frankie. Stick around in the evening and dive into spicy lamb chops or sheekh kebab cooked on the grill, or a slow-cooked biryani such as one with chicken and cranberries. If you want it old school, go for the 'Ruby Murray' classic curry. Drink lassi, lager, IPA or wines from £20.

Chef/s: Naved Nasir and Arun Kumar. **Open:** all week 11.30 to 11 (midnight Fri, 12 to 12 Sat, 12 to 11 Sun). **Closed:** 25 and 26 Dec, 1 and 2 Jan. **Meals:** alc (main courses £5 to £17). **Details:** 140 seats. 18 seats outside. Bar. Wheelchair access. Music.

Donostia

Where to snack like the Basques
Cooking score: 3
⊖ **Marble Arch, map 6**
Spanish | £30
10 Seymour Place, Marylebone, W1H 7ND
Tel no: (020) 3620 1845
www.donostia.co.uk

'The tortilla was beautiful – still thinking about it days afterwards,' exclaimed one reporter, delighted by the dishes served at this smart but relaxed little Basque eatery. A perfect pit-stop for Oxford Street shoppers, it provides attentive service and an element of theatre: pintxos and tapas are handled with 'exquisite care' in the open kitchen and brought to you at the marble bar or simple white tables. The food is a riot of colour and flavour: take that tortilla 'liquid in the centre, lovely flakes of cod layered with the egg'; or a courgette flower 'stuffed with goats' cheese, crisp on the outside, fluffy inside'. Then there is pluma (Ibérico de Bellota pork shoulder), served with romesco sauce; piperrak (blistered Padrón peppers with sea salt); and maybe chocolate mousse to finish. The restaurant is an offshoot of the owners' wine import business, so expect an excellent, personally sourced selection of Spanish wines, including many from the Basque region, from £18.
Chef/s: Damian Surowiec. **Open:** Tue to Sun L 12.30 to 3 (1 to 4 Sun), all week D 6 to 10.30 (5 to 9 Sun). **Closed:** 25 to 30 Dec. **Meals:** alc (tapas £4 to £15). **Details:** 40 seats. 8 seats outside. Music.

Ember Yard

Small plates, big flavours in Soho
Cooking score: 4
⊖ **Tottenham Court Road, map 5**
Modern European | £25
60 Berwick Street, Soho, W1F 8SU
Tel no: (020) 7439 8057
www.emberyard.co.uk

Anyone hankering after the smoky aroma that only a charcoal grill can bring to the table will love Ember Yard. In deepest Soho, Simon Mullins and Ben Tish of Salt Yard, Dehesa and Opera Tavern fame (see entries) have created another hot spot where Spanish and Italian flavours come together in dynamic small plates to share or, better still, keep all to yourself. Expect dark-wood tables and bold artworks, and an atmospheric basement where you can sit at the counter close to the kitchen action. Bar snacks can be as creative as salt marsh lamb pintxos with peas and buttermilk, and when it comes to superb charcuterie plates, it's time to declare your allegiance: Italy or Spain? The grill works its magic in a dish of cuttlefish with honey-roasted butternut squash and gremolata, or another that partners Ibérico presa with whipped jamón butter. The excellent wine list covers the best ground in both countries starting at £20.
Chef/s: Jacques Fourie. **Open:** Mon to Fri L 12 to 3, D 5 to 11. Sat and Sun 12 to 11. **Meals:** alc (main courses £8 to £32). Set L and D £35 to £40. **Details:** 110 seats. V menu. Bar. Music.

Fera at Claridges

Phenomenally dynamic food
Cooking score: 8
⊖ **Bond Street, map 5**
Modern British | £61
49 Brook Street, Mayfair, W1K 4HR
Tel no: (020) 7107 8888
www.claridges.co.uk

Single-mindedness and a fiery determination to produce the best have landed Simon Rogan an enviable record. It is easy to slacken off once you get to the top, but the chef runs a tight ship and wows the customers: 'Simon Rogan has managed to encapsulate the ethos of l'Enclume in London's grand old lady stuck in the middle of Mayfair – no mean feat,' concluded one. The room is gracious with its Art Deco charm and wonderful glass ceiling panels, and one first-time visitor, noting that not everybody dresses up, was surprised at how down-to-earth the whole thing seemed – 'very professional and properly interactive staff' make you feel very welcome and the atmosphere is one of relaxed class. Copious praise continues to pour in from readers, whether singling out an earthy beetroot soup with freeze-dried yoghurt and contrasting oxalis leaf as a fitting climax to the first courses (of the ten-course tasting menu), or expressing delight at what sounded like a prosaic vegetarian dish – grilled salad smoked over embers, Isle of Mull, truffle custard and sunflower seeds – but was actually crispy smoky lettuce leaves in cheese sauce, truffled cauliflower and broccoli and 'just blew your mind'. Fabulous seasonal ingredients take centre stage. White asparagus, ramsons and allium teamed with *à point* Cornish lamb, sweetbread, sheep's milk yoghurt and emulsion, and a bravura dish of turbot with mussels, courgette and courgette flower, sea lettuce, fennel, rapeseed and 'an amazing tomato granola'. Dan Cox, who interprets the Rogan style on a day-to-day basis, keeps standards sky-high right to the end, sending out honeycomb and pear in a superb combination with lemon thyme, and perfect strawberries with cicely custard, sorrel and buttermilk crunch. A premier-league sommelier provides verbal notes for a wine list that ticks the boxes for serious intent and quality. Bottles from £34.

Chef/s: Simon Rogan and Dan Cox. **Open:** all week L 12 to 2, D 6.30 to 10. **Meals:** alc (main courses £20 to £36). Set L £30. Tasting menu £105. **Details:** 94 seats. V menu. Parking.

NEW ENTRY

Fischer's

A welcome newcomer to Marylebone
Cooking score: 2
⊖ **Baker Street, Regent's Park, map 6**
Austrian | £35
50 Marylebone High Street, Marylebone, W1U 5HN
Tel no: (020) 7466 5501
www.fischers.co.uk

An all-day neighbourhood café and *konditorei* (patisserie) evoking Vienna in the early 20th century, Fischer's is an enterprising addition to the Marylebone scene, although like

everything Messrs Corbin and King open (see entries for Wolseley, Delaunay et al), it looks like it has been in place for years. There's a stylish informality to the glossy, dark wood, tile-and-picture-lined room that embraces the plentiful service as much as the food – a formula that attracts a full house. A starter of käsespätzle (macaroni and cheese) and mains of berner würstel – bacon-wrapped pork and garlic sausage with Emmental – served with a potato salad, sauerkraut and caramelised onions, make for hearty choices, but there's also endive, Bavarian blue and walnut salad, spatchcocked chicken with a green herb dressing, and sea bream with beetroot and horseradish. Strudels, a vanilla and sweet cheese knödel, and scheiterhaufen (apple bread-and-butter pudding with Calvados anglaise) go down a treat. Wines from £19.75.

Chef/s: Ray Masson. **Open:** all week 8am to 10.30pm (10pm Sunday). **Closed:** 25 Dec, 1 Jan. **Meals:** alc (main courses £6 to £25). **Details:** 100 seats. 4 seats outside. V menu. Wheelchair access.

Flesh & Buns

Fast-food izakaya that's bang on target
Cooking score: 1
⊖ **Covent Garden, map 5**
Japanese | £28
41 Earlham Street, Covent Garden, WC2H 9LX
Tel no: (020) 7632 9500
www.fleshandbuns.com

Ross Shonhan's vibrant take on the Japanese fast-food izakaya is as endearingly unpretentious as its signature Taiwanese-style steamed hirata buns. With no frills or fripperies, the functional subterranean eatery achieves an easy informality that embraces the service as much as the food – a formula that attracts a full house. You may have to perch at the central communal table (there are normal ones, too) but who cares when there's a cavalcade of snacks and small plates (sashimi, chicken yakitori, soft-shell crab), and those delicious steamed buns to be stuffed with crispy piglet belly, ribeye steak or half a chicken with spicy citrus miso. Wines from £18.50.

Chef/s: Ross Shonhan. **Open:** Mon to Fri L 12 to 3, D 5 to 11. Sat and Sun 12 to 11 (9.30 Sun). **Closed:** 25 Dec. **Meals:** alc (main courses £10 to £27). Set L and D £19 (2 courses) to £22. Sun L £39. Tasting menu £35. **Details:** 150 seats. Bar. Wheelchair access. Music.

LOCAL GEM

La Fromagerie
Baker Street, Bond Street, map 6
Modern European | £33
2-6 Moxon Street, Marylebone, W1U 4EW
Tel no: (020) 7935 0341
www.lafromagerie.co.uk

It's nigh on 14 years since Patricia Michelson opened her cheese shop off Marylebone High Street and it's grown into an eye-catching oasis of good taste. The fabulous array of cheeses continue to take centre stage in what has become an upmarket delicatessen, with dining tables placed among the merchandise adding to the relaxed, friendly atmosphere. Simple dishes such as charcuterie or cheese plates, wild garlic and potato stew or round courgette stuffed with spiced lamb, put the spotlight on good-quality ingredients, and there are exceedingly good cakes. Wines from £23.15. Open all week.

Galvin at Windows
Precision-tuned food with a view
Cooking score: 6
Hyde Park Corner, Green Park, map 6
French | £70
Hilton Hotel, 22 Park Lane, Mayfair, W1K 1BE
Tel no: (020) 7208 4021
www.galvinatwindows.com

Chris Galvin's eyrie on the 28th floor of the London Hilton is not so much a room with a view, more a glamorous special-occasion window on the metropolis. Of course, the wraparound vistas are a regular conversation stopper, but there's plenty of distraction on the plate, too. France is the gastronomic reference point and in the kitchen Joo Won delivers precision-tuned cooking of a high order, with indulgent flavours and subtle contrasts in abundance – from silky white garlic velouté with native lobster, confit egg yolk and black garlic cream to an open lasagne of spring vegetables with morels, tofu, beurre noisette and Parmesan. There's ample evidence of scrupulous sourcing, too, be it roasted cutlet of Ibérico pork or Casterbridge beef fillet with seared foie gras and ox cheek. To finish, stupendous seasonal cheeses are well worth a sniff – or you could plump for warm chocolate fondant cleverly matched with praline, yoghurt and dill sorbet. The all-encompassing wine list oozes class, but you'll need a thick wallet to appreciate its treasures; bottles start at £25.

Chef/s: Joo Won. **Open:** Sun to Fri L 12 to 2.30 (11.45 to 3 Sun), Mon to Sat D 6 to 10 (10.30 Thur to Sat). **Meals:** Set L £26 (2 courses) to £30. Set D £70. Sun L £45. Tasting menu £99 (7 courses). **Details:** 109 seats. Bar. Wheelchair access. Parking.

Galvin Bistrot de Luxe
Big flavours and persuasive Gallic charm
Cooking score: 4
Baker Street, map 6
French | £39
66 Baker Street, Marylebone, W1U 7DJ
Tel no: (020) 7935 4007
www.galvinrestaurants.com

The Baker Street address was the very first outfit in the Galvin brothers' fraternal empire, which is based on their shared passion for French cuisine and their ability to deliver consistently high standards in every department. It's the sort of place you could visit every day, and one reader confessed to finding himself 'the last to leave'. They've certainly nailed the bistro de luxe look with all that leather and dark wood. The menu makes no bones about its Francophilia, while there are modern touches along the way and the quality of the source produce is outstanding. Venison Scotch egg with pommes neuf and celeriac remoulade is decidedly new wave,

with steak tartare with toasted sourdough a typically classic opener. Move on to risotto of wild mushrooms or a duck cassoulet, and finish with blood-orange soufflé with chocolate orange. The menu prix fixe is a good bet for lunch or early/late evening. Wines start at £21.50.
Chef/s: Tom Duffil. **Open:** all week L 12 to 2.30 (3 Sun), D 6 to 10.30 (11 Thur to Sat, 9.30 Sun). **Closed:** 25 and 26 Dec, 1 Jan. **Meals:** alc (main courses £18 to £28). Set L £22. Set D £24. **Details:** 122 seats. 26 seats outside. Bar. Music.

Gauthier Soho

French with a bold streak
Cooking score: 6
⊖ Leicester Square, map 5
Modern French | £40
21 Romilly Street, Soho, W1D 5AF
Tel no: (020) 7494 3111
www.gauthiersoho.co.uk

Alexis Gauthier's initial is embroidered in lipstick-red on pristine white napkins – a reminder that, though the town house setting is comfortable and the service old-fashionedly reticent, a bold streak runs through the food. The careful listing of calories in dishes such as roasted Orkney scallops with a pea emulsion, almonds and headily smoked pancetta is undercut, gloriously, by a procession of excellent bread and butter (try the salted brioche), Parmesan crisps and other welcome and well-judged folderols. Readers note that 'the deluxe menu is still an incredible bargain for this part of London', and praise the consistently 'warm welcome' that awaits those who ring the doorbell – the sound of which punctuates a meal in the ground-floor salon. Menus are vital and seasonal, with, for example, sweet baby Kentish carrots paired with creamy-crunchy sweetbreads and wild early summer mushrooms. At dessert, fruit soufflés provide an alternative showstopper to the well-loved chocolate Louis XV. A dynamic, French-led wine list starts at £25.

Chef/s: Alexis Gauthier and Gerard Virolle. **Open:** Tue to Sat L 12 to 2.30, Mon to Sat D 6.30 to 10.30. **Closed:** Sun. **Meals:** alc (main courses £10 to £13) Set L £18 (2 courses) to £25. Set D £40 (3 courses) to £60. Tasting menu £75 (8 courses). **Details:** 45 seats. V menu. Bar. Children over 8 yrs only.

Le Gavroche

A beacon of French excellence
Cooking score: 8
⊖ Marble Arch, map 6
French | £120
43 Upper Brook Street, Mayfair, W1K 7QR
Tel no: (020) 7408 0881
www.le-gavroche.co.uk

It is peripherally possible that we may all live long enough to see Le Gavroche given a contemporary makeover with exposed brickwork, bare tables and waiting staff in logoed hoodies, but let's hope not. It remains a beacon of eximious French taste, professional to its front-of-house fingertips, perfectionist in the culinary standards it expects of itself. If the menus evolve at glacial pace, who's complaining? These are the dishes that helped construct London's gastronomic standing: featherlight soufflé suissesse in its cheese bath; artichoke heart Lucullus, filled with truffled chicken mousse and foie gras; roast turbot in chive butter; the olive-crusted braised lamb shoulder. Every last note of intensity is expressed from the superfine ingredients, even in something as simple as marinated beef carpaccio with its pickled beetroot and horseradish dressing, while the first statement of each dish is its seductive aromas, rising as bewitchingly from stone bass in ras-el-hanout as from the terrific smoked pork cheek with its pork-rind cromesqui, ravioli of the belly and red cabbage purée. Nor are desserts lacking in truly memorable impact when spiced dark chocolate ganache turns up with various textures of orange, from genoise to ice cream and candied peel. Abandon all caution, and sign up for the Menu Exceptionnel for the access-all-areas experience. An encyclopedic list of fabulous wines awaits, not all French but with dozens of examples of superb Côte-Rôtie, Puligny-Montrachet, premier cru Bordeaux, the crème de la crème. Prices open at £32.

Chef/s: Rachel Humphrey. **Open:** Mon to Fri L 12 to 2, Mon to Sat D 6 to 10. **Closed:** Sun, 2 weeks Christmas and New Year, bank hols. **Meals:** alc (main courses £27 to £61). Set L £55. Tasting menu £126. **Details:** 100 seats. V menu. Bar.

Great Queen Street

Humming, no-frills eatery
Cooking score: 3
⊖ Covent Garden, map 5
Modern British | £28
32 Great Queen Street, Covent Garden, WC2B 5AA
Tel no: (020) 7242 0622
www.greatqueenstreetrestaurant.co.uk

As with elder sibling Anchor & Hope (see entry) this self-confident Covent Garden eatery is noted for Spartan surrounds and an easy-going atmosphere. The gutsy, no-frills British cooking puts the emphasis firmly on quality, but while the daily changing, seasonal dishes may seem relatively plain, they have a feel for rustic flavours. Start with excellent potted shrimps or a heap of warm duck heart and bacon salad, while for a main course kid goat ragù with white beans and chorizo or rabbit, bacon and mushroom pie are tempting choices, but there's also plaice, lemon and caper butter. Pace yourself if you are going to order dessert: the sour cherry, chocolate and almond pasty is highly recommended. Nine years on, Great Queen Street has become a local institution, so booking one of the close-packed tables is a must if you don't want to perch on a non-bookable stool at the long bar. Wines from £17.

Chef/s: Sam Hutchins. **Open:** all week L 12 to 2.30 (1 to 4 Sun), Mon to Sat D 5.30 to 10.30. **Closed:** 23 Dec to 1 Jan, bank hols. **Meals:** alc (main courses £15 to £20). Set L £18 (2 courses) to £20. **Details:** 60 seats. Bar. Wheelchair access.

The Greenhouse

Rarefied Mayfair oasis
Cooking score: 4
⊖ Green Park, map 5
Modern European | £95
27a Hay's Mews, Green Park, W1J 5NY
Tel no: (020) 7499 3331
www.greenhouserestaurant.co.uk

A discreet retreat from the pulsating big city, the Greenhouse greets guests with a leafy garden and canopied walkway adorned with stone sculptures. Inside, a rarefied calm descends as dutiful staff orchestrate proceedings in the serene dining room – a sober space done out in pale green and coffee hues, with a few vaguely sylvan design flourishes. Chef Arnaud Bignon's highly engineered cooking is driven by the latest trends and ingredients *du jour*: Orkney scallops with verbena, yuzu, green zebra tomato and samphire; wild turbot dressed with golden matcha tea; Limousin veal alongside prunes, Mexican tarragon, plum and kohlrabi. The emphasis on exclusive raw materials also extends to organic Rhug Estate lamb and presa Ibérico (perhaps served with aubergine, sobrasada, onion and smoked pimento). To finish, 'pick your fragrance' to go with the vanilla cream dessert or try Green Chartreuse soufflé with chestnut honey. There are rare vintage treasures on the imperious 90-page wine list, though you may shudder at prices that zoom skywards from £30.

Chef/s: Arnaud Bignon. **Open:** Mon to Fri L 12 to 2.30, Mon to Sat D 6.30 to 11. **Closed:** Sun, 2 weeks Christmas, bank hols. **Meals:** alc (main courses £45 to £55). Set L £35 (2 courses) to £40. Tasting menu £110 (6 courses). **Details:** 65 seats. Wheelchair access.

Join us at thegoodfoodguide.co.uk

Gymkhana

Top-notch modern Indian food
Cooking score: 5
⊖ Piccadilly Circus, Green Park, map 5
Indian | £65

42 Albermarle Street, Mayfair, W1S 4JH
Tel no: (020) 3011 5900
www.gymkhanalondon.com

The name may conjure up images of Thelwell cartoons of little girls on their fat ponies, but this Gymkhana is an Indian thoroughbred done out in the style of a Days of the Raj club – imagine rattan-trimmed booths, whirring ceiling fans, staff in Nehru-style tunics and walls emblazoned with photos of polo teams. It could be just another colonial-themed gimmick, but the food at this sibling of Karam Sethi's Trishna (see entry) is right up there with the best. There's excitement in every mouthful as the kitchen reinvents the curry-house classics and creates some genuinely original dishes based on top-notch ingredients. Quail kebabs are pointed up with pickled green chilli chutney, wild boar is given the vindaloo treatment, and there's a rich, sumptuous pilau with lotus root and jackfruit. The kitchen also gets full marks for its set-lunch deals, which might bring soft-shell crab with samphire and jhalmuri (puffed rice salad) or duck egg 'bhurji' with lobster. There's also plenty of interest in the drinks department – from Raj-style punches to thoughtfully chosen wines from £18.
Chef/s: Rohit Ghai. **Open:** Mon to Sat L 12 to 2.30, D 5.30 to 10.30. **Closed:** Sun, 25 to 27 Dec, 1 to 3 Jan. **Meals:** alc (main courses £14 to £48). Set L £25 (2 courses) to £30. Set D £35 (4 courses). Tasting menu £75 (7 courses). **Details:** 90 seats. V menu. Bar. Music. No children after 7.

Symbols

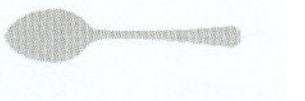

- Accommodation is available
- £30 Three courses for less than £30
- £5 OFF £5-off voucher scheme
- Notable wine list

Hakkasan

Thrillingly seductive Chinese jet-setter
Cooking score: 5
⊖ Tottenham Court Road, map 5
Chinese | £65

8 Hanway Place, Fitzrovia, W1T 1HD
Tel no: (020) 7927 7000
www.hakkasan.com

Still chilled, modern and seductive after all these years, the subterranean dining room casts its spell with fragrant aromas and pounding beats. But keep your head and there's some revelatory Chinese food to be had. Cantonese accents thread their way through the menu, but it's more about a fusion of East and West – even in the much-lauded dim sum. Nibble your way through scallop sui mai, char-siu cheung fun and fried mooli cakes or take a punt on the fried taro pear with chicken, black truffle dumplings or crispy smoked duck and pumpkin puffs. If time and money are no option, linger over larger plates of, say, roast silver cod with Champagne and honey (a Hakkasan classic), or stir-fried lobster in kombu soy with lily bulb and nameko mushrooms before alighting on one of the luscious crossover desserts. The fastidious food-friendly wine list is known for its quality (and stinging prices), from £29.
Chef/s: Tong Chee Hwee. **Open:** all week L 12 to 3 (4 Sat, 5 Sun), D 5.30 to 11 (12 Thur to Sat). **Closed:** 24 and 25 Dec. **Meals:** alc (main courses £19 to £61). Set L £35. Set D £65. Sun L £58 (6 courses). Tasting menu £118 (10 courses). **Details:** 210 seats. V menu. Wheelchair access. Music.

Hakkasan Mayfair

Slinky Chinese opulence
Cooking score: 4
⊖ Green Park, Bond Street, map 5
Chinese | £80

17 Bruton Street, Mayfair, W1J 6QB
Tel no: (020) 7907 1888
www.hakkasan.com

Occupying a prime slice of Mayfair real estate, though perhaps not as drop-dead cool as its big brother in grittier Hanway Place,

Hakkasan Mayfair aims to make a statement. Evenings get a noisy start as the adjoining bar is a high-decibel playground for hedge-fund managers and non-doms, who are unlikely to flinch at the prices, while the dining room, despite being on the ground floor (with windows), likes to pretend it's a basement in the evening, turning the lights down low to complement the slinky black-and-red décor. The star here is the first-rate contemporary Chinese cooking – nominally Cantonese, with impeccable ingredients. The kitchen copes impressively with classic specialities like its famed dim sum, the grilled Chilean sea bass in honey, sweet-and-sour Duke of Berkshire pork with pomegranate, and black truffle roast duck with tea plant mushroom. Western-style desserts are not a strong point, and drinking is expensive, with the illustrious list shooting up from £26.

Chef/s: Tan Tee Wei. **Open:** all week L 12 to 5.30 (6 Sat), D 6 to 11.30 (12.30 Thur to Sat). **Closed:** 24 and 25 Dec. **Meals:** alc (main courses £17 to £61). Set L £35 to £45. Set D £58 to £128. **Details:** 220 seats. Wheelchair access.

Hawksmoor Seven Dials

British beef at its best
Cooking score: 4
⊖ **Covent Garden, map 5**
British | £45
11 Langley Street, Covent Garden, WC2H 9JG
Tel no: (020) 7420 9390
www.thehawksmoor.com

One of the original of Will Beckett and Huw Gott's growing chain of eateries consecrated to the virtues of British beef is a sleek, pared-down basement that mixes brick, wood, leather, steel and industrial ducting to striking effect. This is the place for steak lovers with deep pockets and hearty appetites, with cuts ranging from affordable but richly flavoured rump, sirloin or ribeye to the butter-soft luxury of chateaubriand and fillet, all seared on the white-hot charcoal of a Josper grill. Saucing is minimal, perhaps béarnaise, peppercorn or anchovy hollandaise, with accompaniments including triple-cooked chips or creamed spinach. And just in case you're not in the mood for beef, there's lobster, whole sea bream with garlic, rosemary and chilli or grilled free-range chicken. Starters are equally enduring: shrimps on toast, steak tartare, bone marrow with onions. Portions are large so sherry trifle or pecan tart with clotted cream ice cream hardly seem necessary. Admirable wines from £21.

Chef/s: Karol Poniewaz. **Open:** Mon to Sat L 12 to 3, D 5 to 10.30 (11 Fri and Sat). Sun 12 to 9.30. **Closed:** 24 to 26 Dec. **Meals:** alc (main courses £13 to £50). Set L and D £24 (2 courses) to £27. Sun L £20. **Details:** 140 seats. Bar. Wheelchair access. Music.

NEW ENTRY

Heddon Street Kitchen

Assertive brasserie fare from Ramsay empire
Cooking score: 2
⊖ **Piccadilly Circus, map 5**
Modern European | £38
3-9 Heddon Street, Mayfair, W1B 4BN
Tel no: 020 7592 1212
www.gordonramsay.com/heddon-street

A hum of machismo permeates the contemporary steel and leather interior of Ramsay's latest outpost in Regent Street's self-proclaimed 'Food Quarter', following hot on the heels of Bread Street Kitchen. A one-size-fits-all modern European brasserie menu indulges the current vogue for all-day dining and largely succeeds. Reading like a greatest hits album for the nostalgic diner, expect lobster Thermidor, veal osso buco, chicken Caesar salad and slow-roast pork belly with spiced apple sauce, alongside hunks of smoky charred protein from the Josper charcoal grill. Lighter fare does sneak a look-in – perhaps a zingy salad of kale, red cabbage, fennel, carrots, pumpkin and sunflower seeds or delicate and spankingly fresh steamed bream with Jersey Royals, Wye Valley asparagus, rock samphire and girolles. Those seeking innovative cooking may be left wanting, but there's plenty to please, not least a sweet closing note of chocolate fondant with salted caramel. Potent cocktails draw in the suits after hours and house wine takes off at £22.

Chef/s: Maria Tampakis. **Open:** all week 12 to 11 (10 to 9 Sun). **Closed:** 25 Dec. **Meals:** alc (main courses £16 to £68). **Details:** 140 seats. 34 seats outside. Wheelchair access. Music.

Hélène Darroze at the Connaught

Ultra-refined, contemporary French cooking
Cooking score: 5
⊖ Bond Street, Green Park, map 5
Modern French | £92
16 Carlos Place, Mayfair, W1K 2AL
Tel no: (020) 3147 7200
www.the-connaught.co.uk

Oak-panelled splendour juxtaposed with a central display of raw produce under glass cloches cleverly dovetails late Victorian solidity with up-to-the-moment metropolitan ideas. As one of London's grand hotel dining rooms, it makes a fitting backdrop to Hélène Darroze's ultra-refined contemporary French cooking that weaves unusual pairings and constructions from a pick-and-mix of broadly European prime materials with culinary influences from east Asia. Darroze's dishes are not titled as such, but inventoried, as in lamb, turnip, carrot, 'navarin' (the latter turning out to be a rich, glossy sauce). At inspection, a finely pitched opener of foie gras parfait with wild strawberry, cherry, pistachio and elderflower delivered a standout juxtaposition of sweet and sour, while a brilliantly conceived savarin, flavoured with raspberries, Sawarak and Tasmanian peppers and Armagnac, was worthy of its signature dessert status (and £12 supplement); petits fours were superb, too. However, there are readers who wonder at the cost of it all. Individual items don't always deliver the hit rate the outlay seems to warrant, and the entry-level set lunch (also tried at inspection) does the kitchen few favours. The imposing wine list is the business, however, but mark-ups are sky-high; bottles from £39.

Chef/s: Hélène Darroze. **Open:** Tue to Fri L 12 to 2, Tue to Sat D 6.30 to 10. **Closed:** Sun, Mon, 2 weeks Jan, 2 weeks Aug. **Meals:** Set L £30 (2 courses) to £45. Tasting menus £92 (5 courses) to £155. **Details:** 62 seats. V menu. Wheelchair access. Music.

Hibiscus

On the serious gastronomic circuit
Cooking score: 9
⊖ Oxford Circus, map 5
Modern French | £90
29 Maddox Street, Mayfair, W1S 2PA
Tel no: (020) 7629 2999
www.hibiscusrestaurant.co.uk

'Confident service, well paced, good wine advice and the cooking made it all feel like a real treat,' began one reporter's notes. The small dining room with its oak floor, abstract paintings on pale walls and tables in full dress may present a rather formal face, but this is not a stuffy dining room, there is no obligation to whisper in hushed tones and in prospect is a smooth operation firing on all cylinders. Indeed, Claude Bosi's cooking is a must-do for anybody on the serious gastronomic circuit. The format can be a bit confusing: chose from an eight-course market menu, a short à la carte, or opt for three, six or eight courses and leave the rest up to the kitchen or choose your preferred main ingredients from a list. And the food excels. Single-mindedness, and a fiery determination to produce the best define Bosi's cooking and the chef is known for his freewheeling palate and nuanced instinct for building contrasts. He underscores the sweetness of crab, for example, by brightening it with elderflower and cucumber and giving texture with new-season almonds. Spring vegetable 'minestrone' sees delicate, wheat-free vegetable dumplings placed in a broth inflected with the intense sweetness of Obsiblue prawns. But it's fillet of sea bass that's the triumphant standout, delicate in texture and pure in flavour, dressed to excess with potato purée and inflected with the zip of caramel and capers – Bosi's take on grenobloise sauce. He knows his stuff and it shows. The set lunch is three courses, on one occasion cured mackerel with strawberry sauce vierge, confit chicken leg with Tropea onion, a tiny tart of peas and smoked eel with blood orange, and 'a pretty damned good' strawberries with honeycomb cream and whiskey ice cream. 'You won't beat this', maintained one reporter, 'and I doubt if there is much better value at the price.' The lengthy wine list (from £28) is a thoroughly modern tome that ventures well beyond the vineyards of France; sommelier Bastien Ferreri always has a glass or a bottle up his sleeve for any trick the kitchen might pull.

Chef/s: Claude Bosi. **Open:** Tue to Sat L 12 to 2.30, D 6.30 to 10.30 (6 Fri and Sat). **Closed:** Sun, Mon, 24 to 26 Dec, 1 Jan, 1 week Easter. **Meals:** Set L £50. Set D £90. Tasting menus £100 (6 courses) to £120. **Details:** 50 seats.

Hix

Über-cool Brit brasserie
Cooking score: 2
Piccadilly Circus, map 5
British | £35
66-70 Brewer Street, Soho, W1F 9UP
Tel no: (020) 7292 3518
www.hixsoho.co.uk

The Mark Hix empire extends to more than a half-dozen addresses including a converted tram shed in Shoreditch dishing out steak and chicken to a fishy place overlooking Lyme Regis's famous harbour, The Cobb. Exacting standards when it comes to sourcing British ingredients is the Hix way, and that's the case here in this throbbing all-day venue in Soho. The basement bar (Mark's Bar) is a cracker, while the main dining room with its own zinc-topped bar and mobile and neon artworks by British artists makes for a lively spot for comforting British grub. Steamed Wye Valley asparagus with hollandaise is simplicity itself, or warm your cockles with broad bean soup with Neal's Yard Dairy feta. Producers, farmers et al get name-checked on the menu. The burger is a classy rib steak version, lamb cutlets come with Isle of Barra cockles and sea aster, and desserts stick to the theme (rhubarb fool with shortbread). Wines start at £27.

Open: all week 12 to 11.30 (10.30 Sun). **Meals:** alc (main courses £15 to £38). Set L £20 (2 courses) to £25. Sun L £24. **Details:** 80 seats. V menu.

Hix Mayfair

Bulldog British cooking in Mayfair
Cooking score: 1
Green Park, map 5
British | £60
Brown's Hotel, 30 Albemarle Street, Mayfair, W1S 4BP
Tel no: (020) 7518 4004
www.roccofortehotels.com

Set in a true aristocrat of Mayfair hotels, Brown's dapper wood-panelled dining room has played host to Mark Hix's brand of modern British cooking for five years. Inside, works by Brit art royalty (Tracey Emin) hang over crisp linen tables, and there's a fervently patriotic streak to the menu too. Start off in the Welsh Marches with Wye Valley asparagus and hollandaise sauce, or else choose from a selection of 'raw' dishes: Manx scallops with ginger and ramsons impressed on inspection. Regulars swear by the Brown's fish and chips and mushy peas and desserts show a boozy bent – gin and lemon sherbet, white port trifle – as, of course, does the wine list, where prices start from £32 and quickly climb.

Chef/s: Lee Kebble. **Open:** all week L 12 to 3 (4 Sun), D 5.30 to 11 (7 to 10.30 Sun). **Meals:** alc (main courses £18 to £43). Set L £28. Set D £33. **Details:** 70 seats. V menu. Bar. Wheelchair access. Music.

Symbols

Accommodation is available
Three courses for less than £30
£5-off voucher scheme
Notable wine list

Honey & Co.

Unique, free-thinking cooking
Cooking score: 2
⊖ Warren Street, map 2
Middle Eastern | £28

25a Warren Street, Fitzrovia, W1T 5LZ
Tel no: (020) 7388 6175
www.honeyandco.co.uk

Nearly three years on, this tiny, cramped restaurant still buzzes, surprising and delighting visitors with lively and intriguing Middle Eastern-influenced dishes. Tables may be 'squeezed so tightly together that you're knocking elbows with your neighbours', but this adds to the cosy feel, and the cooking is as joyous as it is seasonal. The ever-innovative kitchen sends out terrific meze (rich labneh cut through by a chilli topping, falafels livened by red pepper, and a simple salad offset by earthy beetroot with sharp grapefruit, crunchy radishes, peppery dill and sweet pomegranate molasses). Seductively flavoured main courses follow, say slow-cooked chicken with chestnuts and golden raisins under a crisp kadaif topping (shredded filo pastry) served with a rocket and orange salad, or octopus with paprika and lemon with Tunisian bean stew. There's dense dark chocolate slice with blood orange and caramelised pecans for dessert, shakshuka (eggs in tomato sauce) for breakfast, and a short wine list, from £21.
Chef/s: Sarit Packer and Itamar Srulovich. **Open:** Mon to Sat 8am to 10pm (9.30am Sat). **Closed:** Sun. **Meals:** alc (main courses £13 to £15). Set L £16 (2 courses). Set D £27 (2 courses) to £30. **Details:** 25 seats. 4 seats outside. Music.

Sarit Packer and Itamar Srulovich

Honey & Co. London

What do you enjoy the most about being chefs?
We love feeding people and watching them enjoy their food.

What's your newest ingredient discovery?
We are more about old traditions and food that has been around for generations, but we are always discovering more of these foods from around the world. Pepper pastes from Turkey are a firm favourite currently.

What food trends are you spotting at the moment?
We cook Middle Eastern food, so to us it is the biggest trend at the moment.

What is your favourite time of year for food?
For us, it has to be summer; we come from a hot country and the sun gives produce a great flavour. Figs, peaches, tomatoes, baby cucumbers are all at their best in summertime.

What food could you not live without?
Chickpeas, they are the base of so many dishes that we love and serve all the time; falafel and hummus are just the starting point.

The Ivy

Ready for its centenary
Cooking score: 1
⊖ Leicester Square, map 5
Modern European | £39
1-5 West Street, Covent Garden, WC2H 9NQ
Tel no: (020) 7836 4751
www.the-ivy.co.uk

The trademark harlequin-stained glass windows, green leather banquettes and acres of wood are all present and correct, but a redesigned entrance, a splendid circular bar incorporated into the dining room and warmer lighting give notice that the Ivy is ready for its 100th birthday in 2017. Geared to cater for those bolting down a dressed Cornish crab before the show, as well as those hot-footing it, ravenous, from the curtain calls, 'something for everyone' might be a fair description of the menu – it is indeed possible to follow yellowfin and salmon sashimi or steak tartare with shepherd's pie, miso blackened salmon or chicken masala. Wines from £39.

Chef/s: Gary Lee. **Open:** all week 12 to 11.30 (10.30 Sun). **Closed:** 25 Dec. **Meals:** alc (main courses £14 to £39). Set L and pre/post-theatre D £22 (2 courses) to £27. **Details:** 120 seats. V menu. Wheelchair access. Music.

J. Sheekey

Theatreland's seafood star
Cooking score: 4
⊖ Leicester Square, map 5
Seafood | £37
28-35 St Martin's Court, Covent Garden, WC2N 4AL
Tel no: (020) 7240 2565
www.j-sheekey.co.uk

'I first visited this restaurant 40 years ago, and nothing has changed – except the prices!' observed an ardent supporter of this theatreland seafood star. The top-hatted doorman, frosted windows and masculine, wood-panelled dining room all look reassuringly familiar, while menus satisfy business brokers, tourists and theatre-goers alike. Bivalves and crustacea 'au naturel' are the kitchen's stock-in-trade, alongside excellent grilled Dover sole ('a must'), Cornish fish stew with celery hearts or smoked haddock with kale hash, poached egg and grain-mustard sauce. Sheekey's fish pie is legendary and there are always a few bright ideas such as razor clams with chorizo and broad beans. To finish, a plate of herring roes on toast is 'essential', according to one fish-loving native from Great Yarmouth. Attentive staff cope admirably, although the obligatory cover charge is a bit 'cheeky'. House wines from a well-spread international list start at £26 (£7 a glass). For similar seafood, but fewer bells and whistles, head next door to J. Sheekey's all-day Oyster Bar at 33-34 St Martin's Court; tel: (020) 7240 2565.

Chef/s: James Cornwall. **Open:** all week L 12 to 3 (3.30 Sat and Sun), D 5 to 12 (5.30 Sat and Sun). **Closed:** 25 and 26 Dec. **Meals:** alc (main courses £16 to £40). Set L £29 (3 courses, Sat and Sun). **Details:** 114 seats. 26 seats outside. V menu. Bar. Wheelchair access. Parking.

Kiku

Bastion of polished Japanese cuisine
Cooking score: 3
⊖ Green Park, map 5
Japanese | £30
17 Half Moon Street, Mayfair, W1J 7BE
Tel no: (020) 7499 4208
www.kikurestaurant.co.uk

Stone floors, clean lines, pale wood and oriental blinds create a mood of gentle Zen-like calm that no doubt soothes the Mayfair suits and Japanese salarymen who frequent this bastion of polished Japanese cuisine. On the upper level, an expansive sushi counter fills up quickly – especially at lunchtime, when plates of glistening fresh nigiri, maki rolls and sashimi are top calls. All-inclusive set menus also do the job, but those with more time (and money) should head to the main dining room for exquisitely formal kaiseki banquets or intricate meals from the carte: limpid zensai appetisers such as tsukimi natto (fermented soya beans served with quail's egg yolk) or nasu dengaku (deep-fried aubergine with sweet miso paste) could give way to something grilled (perhaps salted mackerel), a casserole (chicken with daikon, for example) or a plate of mixed tempura. Sukiyaki, shabu-shabu hotpots and noodle-based udonsuki are good for sharing, and there are dainty daifuku rice cakes to finish. Corney & Barrow house wines start at £16.50.

Chef/s: H Shiraishi and Y Hattori. **Open:** Mon to Sat L 12 to 2.30, all week D 6 to 10.15 (5.30 to 9.45 Sun). **Closed:** 24 to 27 Dec, 1 Jan. **Meals:** alc (main courses £15 to £45). Set L £24 (4 courses) to £34 (5 courses). Set D £59 (8 courses) to £82 (10 courses). **Details:** 99 seats. Wheelchair access.

Kitchen Table at Bubbledogs

The ultimate chef's table
Cooking score: 6
⊖ Goodge Street, map 5
Modern British | £88
70 Charlotte Street, Fitzrovia, W1T 4QG
Tel no: (020) 7637 7770
www.kitchentablelondon.co.uk

Here's the deal: pop behind a curtain in Bubbledogs (the Champagne and hot dog joint) and climb on to a stool at the counter around an open kitchen as a dozen or so new-wave courses cooked by James Knappet and his crew arrive in succession. It's at the vanguard of current culinary activity, with the likes of Noma and Per Se on James' CV, and a menu that takes brevity to the max (the chefs give you the low-down). Expect pin-sharp technique and ingredients that pack a punch. The real star of a plate heralded as 'burrata' is the Isle of Wight tomatoes, while 'duck' is 'fabulously flavoured' roasted breast with variations of beetroot and dried blackberries. The modern techniques don't overshadow the produce, quite the contrary in fact. 'Asparagus' is cooked over charcoal and arrives with cured egg yolks, the salty kick of aged Parmesan, puffed peal barley and stinging nettles (picked in Sherwood Forest). The kitchen is surprisingly calm, but the adjacent

Bubbledogs can generate quite a din. Wine flights can up the cost considerably; bottles from £35.

Chef/s: James Knappett. **Open:** Tue to Sat D only 6 to 10. **Closed:** Sun, Mon, 23 to 27 Dec, 2 weeks Jan. **Meals:** Tasting menu £88 (12+ courses). **Details:** 19 seats. V menu. Music.

Kitty Fisher's

Food you want to eat
Cooking score: 5
⊖ Green Park, map 5
Modern British | £40
10 Shepherd Market, Mayfair, W1J 7QF
Tel no: (020) 3302 1661
www.kittyfishers.com

'So simple, so friendly, so tiny, such delicious food' is how one reporter summed up the appeal of this doll's house of a restaurant in the heart of Shepherd Market. Perch on stools at the bar or window (reserved for walk-ins), or squeeze in at one of the four close-packed tables on the ground floor (there are more downstairs) if you're lucky enough to have secured a reservation. Then relish the sparkling fresh simplicities of whipped cod's roe on bread with fennel butter, a pair of perfectly trimmed, char-grilled lamb cutlets topped with anchovy, mint and parsley, a meaty piece of grilled lemon sole on the bone, served with soft, yielding pieces of fennel, a tangle of monk's beard and a blood-orange sauce, and creamy buttermilk rice pudding with nespoli (loquat) and toasted hazelnuts. This really is delicious food in all its seasonal glory. Service is charming. Do ask about the Bad Kitty cocktail, otherwise the short wine list opens with house bottles at £15.

Chef/s: Tomos Parry. **Open:** Tue to Fri L 12 to 2.30, Tue to Sat D 6.30 to 9.30. **Closed:** Sun, Mon. **Meals:** alc (main courses £18 to £30). **Details:** 35 seats. 8 seats outside. V menu. Bar. Wheelchair access. Music.

Lantana Café

⊖ Goodge Street, Tottenham Court Road,
map 5
Australian | £20
13 Charlotte Place, Fitzrovia, W1T 1SN
Tel no: (020) 7637 3347
www.lantanacafe.co.uk

Shelagh Ryan and Michael Homan opened this simple all-day eatery in 2008, bringing direct, unfussy Aussie food to a restaurant-rich slice of London. It's proved to be such a winning formula that folk frequently queue (no bookings) to get their fix of banana, bread, French toast, corn fritter stacks and excellent coffee. But there's more to Lantana than the breakfast/brunch menu. Lunch brings a tart of the day with green salad or duck burger with pickled cucumber, plum ketchup and Asian slaw and there's tapas for weekday dinners. Wine from £24. Open all week.

Latium

Gourmet Italian stalwart
Cooking score: 3
⊖ Goodge Street, Oxford Circus, map 5
Italian | £36
21 Berners Street, Fitzrovia, W1T 3LP
Tel no: (020) 7323 9123
www.latiumrestaurant.com

With an unremarkable exterior on an unremarkable street, you'd be forgiven for failing to notice this Italian restaurant. But Latium, just south of Fitzrovia's foodie strip, has been quietly delighting those in the know for 12 years with its upmarket and rigorously indigenous tour of Italy. The modern, fuss-free interior, replete with starched linen, bright artwork and 'ever so slightly obsequious service', conforms entirely with chef/patron Maurizio Morelli's picture-perfect dishes. His calling card is an extensive selection of homemade ravioli, to which he dedicates a separate menu, stuffed with the likes of veal and courgette or pea with cuttlefish sauce. Primi and secondi draw in wide-ranging regional influences, from which you might pick smoky roast Sicilian octopus, green

beans, red onions and chilli purée. Sweet ravioli make an appearance, too, though you may prefer a more traditional Neopolitan 'pastiera' with orange sorbet. An in-depth exploration of Italian viticulture starts at £16.
Chef/s: Maurizio Morelli. **Open:** Mon to Fri L 12 to 3, all week D 5.30 to 10.30 (11 Sat). **Meals:** Set L and early D £17 (2 courses) to £23. Set D £30 (2 courses) to £36. **Details:** 56 seats. Wheelchair access.

Little Social

Gregarious little blockbuster
Cooking score: 6
⊖ Oxford Circus, map 5
Modern European | £50
5 Pollen Street, Mayfair, W1S 1NE
Tel no: (020) 7870 3730
www.littlesocial.co.uk

This laid-back baby brother of Pollen Street Social across the road (see entry) is a useful place run with well-honed professionalism, not too dear if you come for the set lunch, and quite with-it in the kitchen department. The style is London-meets-Paris – dark wood, faux nicotine staining, red leather banquettes, French posters – and there's plenty to applaud on the menu. Indeed, regulars have a habit of reeling off their favourites: burrata, pear, truffled honey and pickled walnuts; steak tartare; aged-Scottish beef burger; and the Canadian chef Cary Docherty's version of poutine (Canada's national dish). The hallmark of the cooking is high flavour applied to first-class ingredients: say roasted cod with Asian-spiced cauliflower and aromatic duck broth or braised ox cheeks with roast marrow bone, sourdough crumb, carrot, and horseradish mash. Everyone loves the maple-glazed, apple-filled doughnuts, but you could have fresh-baked madeleines with hot chocolate and crème Chantilly. The modern wine list, which puts quality above showiness, starts at £28.
Chef/s: Cary Docherty. **Open:** Mon to Sat L 12 to 2.30, D 6 to 10.30. **Closed:** Sun, bank hols. **Meals:** alc (main courses £16 to £33). Set L £21 (2 courses) to £25. **Details:** 55 seats. V menu.

Join us at thegoodfoodguide.co.uk

Locanda Locatelli

Silky-smooth Italian flagship

Cooking score: 4

⊖ Marble Arch, map 6

Italian | £70

8 Seymour Street, Marylebone, W1H 7JZ

Tel no: (020) 7935 8390

www.locandalocatelli.com

Restored to its original glory following a gas explosion in 2014, Giorgio Locatelli's silky-smooth flagship looks almost freshly minted with its huge domed mirrors, cream leather banquettes and cleverly designed private spaces hidden by silver-beaded curtains. The result is 'completely reassuring, really elegant, a proper grown-up restaurant'. Locatelli's commitment to provenance, seasonal ingredients and regional specialities is as strong as ever, from the breads presented in an oversized box to the Amalfi lemons that go into his version of Eton mess. Few would dispute that his homemade pasta is as good as it gets – witness rich, buttery pappardelle with Parmesan, chives and mushrooms or egg-free spaghetti with stewed octopus and chilli. Elsewhere, antipasti and salads are zingily flavoursome (a combo of shredded heritage carrots, pea shoots and waxy strips of bottarga, for example), while mains such as salt-crusted sea bass or roast partridge with Swiss chard, grapes and chestnuts show Locatelli's mastery of genre. Matching the food is a majestic, deeply patriotic wine list extolling the virtues of Italian viticulture; bottles start at £17.

Chef/s: Giorgio Locatelli. **Open:** all week L 12 to 3 (3.30 Sat and Sun), D 6.45 to 11 (11.30 Fri and Sat, 10.30 Sun). **Closed:** 24 to 26 Dec, 1 Jan. **Meals:** alc (main courses £27 to £33). **Details:** 75 seats.

Mele e Pere

⊖ Piccadilly Circus, map 5

Italian | £33

46 Brewer Street, Soho, W1F 9TF

Tel no: (020) 7096 2096

www.meleepere.co.uk

Gregarious Mele e Pere is a cute fit for Soho with its dynamic offer of artisan Italian food and zingy drinks. Most of the action takes place in the pared-back basement, where British and imported ingredients sit together on a bright, seasonal menu of small plates, pastas and mains. Expect the likes of veal tripe alla romana, marinated Scottish scallops with roasted red pepper and buckwheat or Surrey ribeye with Barolo sauce. A tight list of Italian regional wines starts at £18, while the adjoining vermouth bar delivers boozy thrills. Open all week.

Mon Plaisir

⊖ Covent Garden, map 5

French | £35

21 Monmouth Street, Covent Garden, WC2H 9DD

Tel no: (020) 7836 7243

www.monplaisir.co.uk

The longest-running French eatery in London, the Plaisir is just up the road from Seven Dials and is a defiantly unfashionable redoubt of bistro food that harks back to the days of the Liberation. It's quite hard to find anywhere in the capital now where you dine on gratinée à l'oignon or coq au vin and find that none of them has been reinvented or deconstructed. True, there is cauliflower purée with the scallops these days, but the steak tartare and pommes allumettes haven't been foofed up, and there's no mention of salt in the caramel and chocolate moelleux. Wines from £19. Closed Sun.

Moti Mahal

Adventurous Indian regional cooking
Cooking score: 3
⊖ Covent Garden, map 5
Indian | £50
45 Great Queen Street, Covent Garden,
WC2B 5AA
Tel no: (020) 7240 9329
www.motimahal-uk.com

Spread over two floors, Moti Mahal is a sleek
and informal place to try Indian cooking based
on the Grand Trunk Road, a historical trade
route of over 2,500km. Indeed, eating here can
feel like an adventurous trek across the Subcontinent with good ingredients and subtle
spicing to the fore. At a test meal the open-to-
view kitchen showed a deft hand with a trio of
samosas filled with roasted guinea fowl and
pine nuts (served with chutney made with red
grapes), and, inspired by the cooking of Delhi,
sent out hake baked with tomato masala and
wild mushrooms that was 'pure spicy magic'.
Kashmir gets a look in with shredded spinach
cooked with cubes of kohlrabi subzi, while
desserts can cross continents: jamun brûlée
paired traditional sweet milk dumplings with
a lime and cardamom crème brûlée. Friendly
service is on hand to advise, and wines (from
£28) and an excellent whisky selection are
geared towards the spicy nature of the food.
Chef/s: Anirudh Arora. **Open:** Mon to Fri L 12 to 3,
Mon to Sat D 5.30 to 11. **Closed:** Sun, 24 to 27 Dec.
Meals: alc (main courses £9 to £26). Set L £16 (2
courses) to £30. Set D £23 (2 courses) to £55. Tasting
menu £58. **Details:** 105 seats. V menu. Bar.
Wheelchair access. Music.

Visit us online

To find out more about
The Good Food Guide, please
visit thegoodfoodguide.co.uk

Murano

Angela Hartnett's flawless flagship
Cooking score: 7
⊖ Green Park, map 5
Italian | £65
20-22 Queen Street, Mayfair, W1J 5PP
Tel no: (020) 7495 1127
www.muranolondon.com

Angela Hartnett has been pretty busy of late,
expanding her casual Café Murano brand (see
entry) and making her presence felt as far away
as Hampshire (see Hartnett Holder & Co), but
this plush Mayfair venue remains her flagship
– and a mighty impressive one too. Given that
Murano is named after a super-chic brand of
Venetian glassware, it's no surprise that suave
exclusivity is the theme with elegantly
sculpted chandeliers, frescoed panels and
mirrors adding a certain gravitas to
proceedings. But there are thrills, excitement
and panache on the plate as Hartnett's kitchen
delivers a highly distinguished and open-
minded take on contemporary Italian cuisine.
Lunch promises commendable value for W1,
while seasonal dinner menus offer the chance
to work your way through up to five stellar
courses: charred mackerel with clams, grapes,
lemon and ginger; wet polenta with kale,
Taleggio and trompette mushrooms; côte de
veau with sage, cavolo nero and macaroni…to
name but three. Homemade pasta is also a
must (perhaps beef anolini with broth, black
truffle and Parmesan), while desserts often
reprise the classics – blood-orange cake with
chocolate cream and bitter chocolate sorbet,
for example. Despite some steep mark-ups,
there is quality across the board on the
auspicious and international wine list; prices
start at £21.50 for a Sicilian Borgo Sasso.
Chef/s: Angela Hartnett and Pip Lacey. **Open:** Mon
to Sat L 12 to 3, D 6.30 to 11. **Closed:** Sun, 5 days
Christmas. **Meals:** Set L £28 (2 courses) to £33. Set
D £50 (2 courses) to £85 (5 courses). **Details:** 55
seats. Wheelchair access.

Newman Street Tavern

Seasonal bounty from the regional larder
Cooking score: 2
⊖ Goodge Street, map 5
British | £30
48 Newman Street, Fitzrovia, W1T 1QQ
Tel no: (020) 3667 1445
www.newmanstreettavern.co.uk

This modern-day Fitzrovia tavern has an unselfconscious ease, which lubricates lunch and dinner. It continues to draw praise for its now tried-and-tested formula of casual vibes, a worldwide wine list (with splendid tipples by the glass) and food that deals in traditional British ingredients and modern techniques. The tone is set immediately with quality seasonal ingredients seen in small plates of spiced brown crab on toast or cuttlefish à la plancha with ink sauce and wild garlic or grilled grass-fed quail with wilted spinach and chimichurri, and in main courses of monkfish fillet with new season's broad beans and peas and fennel broth, and roast chicken with St George mushrooms, celeriac purée and chicken and Maderia sauce. Desserts range from the traditional sticky toffee pudding to rhubarb ripple ice cream with ginger crumble, while the wine list ticks all the boxes for serious intent, quality and value, with prices from £24.
Chef/s: Peter Weeden. **Open:** all week 12 to 10.30 (4.30 Sun). **Closed:** 25 and 26 Dec. **Meals:** alc (main courses £14 to £21). **Details:** 140 seats. Music.

Nobu Berkeley St

High-gloss celebrity hangout
Cooking score: 4
⊖ Green Park, map 5
Japanese | £90
15 Berkeley Street, Mayfair, W1J 8DY
Tel no: (020) 7290 9222
www.noburestaurants.com

Judging by the mega-decibel mayhem in the permanently rammed bar, this high-gloss outpost of Nobu's glitzy global chain is still considered party central by many. But head up the staircase to the sparkling futuristic dining room and you'll be rewarded with a heady mix of fresh sushi, delicately astringent salads and top-end tempura, overlaid with big-money luxuries – Wagyu beef tataki or tuna tartare with caviar, say. Crisp scallop tacos, zingy lobster ceviche with quinoa and fiery anticuchos skewers add some Latin thrills, and the kitchen opens up 'new-style' possibilities with a range of 'dried miso' sashimi. There's also a wood oven for those who relish the smoky pleasures of roast duck breast with wasabi salsa or octopus with yuzu, lemon and garlic. Alternatively, perch at the counter with a lunchtime bento box if time and money are tight. Rare imported sakés are the fascinating stars on a wine list stuffed with super tipples at celebrity prices – there's precious little below £40.
Chef/s: Mark Edwards. **Open:** Mon to Sat L 12 to 2.30 (3 Sat), all week D 6 to 11 (12 Thur to Sat, 9.45 Sun). **Closed:** 25 Dec. **Meals:** alc (main courses £14 to £48). **Details:** 180 seats. V menu. Bar. Wheelchair access. Music. No children after 9.

Nobu London

Japanese fusion pioneer
Cooking score: 4
⊖ Hyde Park Corner, map 5
Japanese | £75
Metropolitan Hotel, 19 Old Park Lane, Mayfair, W1K 1LB
Tel no: (020) 7447 4747
www.noburestaurants.com

London's A-listers may get their kicks elsewhere these days, but this Japanese fusion pioneer remains a contender for those who like their black cod with a side order of Park Lane glamour. The rather severe white-walled dining room feels less rakish than before, although Nobu's food still has the power to excite – even if the approach now seems almost commonplace. A cavalcade of pristine old-style nigiri, exquisitely fashioned hand rolls and new-style sashimi share the limelight with sea urchin tempura, spicy sour shrimps and assorted South American sizzlers including blistering anticuchos skewers, boat-shaped tacos and tingling ceviches. Meanwhile, those craving new thrills should venture into the intriguing crossover world of 'osusume', where Padrón peppers, avocado salad and matsushisa sliders line up alongside seared o-toro with onion ponzu sauce and jalapeño dressing, crispy rice topped with spicy salmon or Wagyu and truffle gyoza with spicy ponzu. Lunchtime bento boxes provide a tempting sampler for first-timers, while the sexy wine and saké list promises depth, quality and pedigree with a celebrity price tag; bottles start at £30.

Chef/s: Mark Edwards. **Open:** all week L 12 to 2.15 (12.30 to 2.30 Sat and Sun), D 6 to 10.15 (11 Fri and Sat, 10 Sun). **Closed:** 25 Dec, 1 Jan. **Meals:** alc (main courses £10 to £42). Set L £24 (2 courses) to £30. Set D £35 (2 courses) to £75. **Details:** 150 seats. Bar. Wheelchair access. Music.

NOPI

Sunny ingredients and striking flavours
Cooking score: 3
⊖ Piccadilly Circus, map 5
Middle Eastern/Mediterranean | £50
21-22 Warwick Street, Soho, W1B 5NE
Tel no: (020) 7494 9584
www.nopi-restaurant.com

Yotam Ottolenghi's clean-lined, contemporary flagship restaurant is perched on the edge of Soho and benefits from the press of custom that an elevated reputation and some TV performances can provide. Eating options include breakfast seven days a week and a full à la carte menu that's anchored in the Med but takes a global view. Consistency and quality are never in doubt and dishes are taken way beyond the meat-and-two-veg approach – indeed, vegetables have a starring role. Ingredients are given centre-stage prominence in dish after dish trumpeting freshness and flavour, perhaps in a plate of burrata, blood orange, coriander seeds and lavender, or golden and candy beetroot with labneh and pistachio, and there's a kaleidoscope of world ingredients in dishes such as spiced gurnard wrapped in a banana leaf and served with pineapple sambal, and onglet with barley miso

and shiitake ketchup. For an indulgent finale, chocolate, orange oil and crème fraîche won't disappoint. There's a good cocktail selection and wines start at £24.

Chef/s: Yotam Ottolenghi. **Open:** all week 12 to 3 (5 Sat, 3.30 Sun), Mon to Sat D 5.30 to 10.15 (5 Sat). **Closed:** 25 and 27 Dec, 1 Jan. **Meals:** alc (main courses £20 to £25). **Details:** 108 seats. Bar. Music.

Opera Tavern

Creative tapas in theatreland
Cooking score: 4
⊖ Covent Garden, map 5
Tapas | £35
23 Catherine Street, Covent Garden, WC2B 5JS
Tel no: (020) 7836 3680
www.operatavern.co.uk

Forged from the same gastronomic DNA as Salt Yard, Dehesa and Ember Yard (see entries), this classy tapas hybrid gains additional kudos from its Covent Garden location and its setting within a handsomely transformed theatreland 'tavern'. Take pot luck in the gregarious ground-floor bar or book a table in the more sedate upstairs restaurant. Either way, expect a trademark mix of Spanish and Italian flavours grounded in excellent charcuterie and cheeses, but with a healthy streak of fired-up creativity that might yield char-grilled mackerel with piquillo and hazelnut sauce, roasted cauliflower and raisins or beef bavette with crispy tongue, wild garlic and confit mushrooms. Vegetables also wax strongly, from the signature stuffed courgette flowers drizzled with honey to roasted beetroot salad with radish and cumin dressing, while the sweet-toothed should seek out the cold chocolate fondant with salted PX caramel and espresso ice cream. To drink, tip-top sherries compete with a crackling list of well-annotated Iberian and Italian wines from £20.

Chef/s: James Thickett. **Open:** Mon to Fri L 12 to 3, D 5 to 11. Sat and Sun 12 to 11 (9.30 Sun). **Closed:** 25 Dec, 1 Jan. **Meals:** alc (small plates £5 to £10). **Details:** 59 seats. 4 seats outside. Bar. Music.

Join us at thegoodfoodguide.co.uk

Orrery

Slick professionalism at Marylebone grandee
Cooking score: 4
⊖ Baker Street, Regent's Park, map 6
French | £55
55 Marylebone High Street, Marylebone,
W1U 5RB
Tel no: (020) 7616 8000
www.orrery-restaurant.co.uk

It's a decade now since the D&D group took
over Conran's place above his eponymous
store on Marylebone High Street and it
remains a sybaritic refuge from all the five-star
shopping opportunities round here. Up on the
first floor, arched windows give views over St
Marylebone church gardens and the finish is
smart without being ostentatious. It's all very
tasteful. Cleverly positioned mirrors give even
those facing the wall a glimpse of the view.
The kitchen impresses with its contemporary
French output presented with a flourish. A
first-course terrine of duck foie gras has a
Riesling jelly and pear to cut through its
delicious richness, while main courses run to a
satisfyingly direct rump of lamb with seasonal
vegetables and rosemary jus, or pavé of salmon
with caramelised fennel and orange beurre
blanc. Among desserts, lime pannacotta comes
with hazelnuts and an orange sorbet. The first-
rate wine list has a top-drawer range by the
glass and carafe; bottles start at £25.
Chef/s: Igor Tymchyshyn. **Open:** all week L 12 to
2.30 (3 Sun), D 6.30 to 10 (10.30 Fri and Sat).
Meals: Set L £27 (2 courses) to £45. Set D £30 (2
courses) to £55. Sun L £33. Tasting menu £75.
Details: 80 seats. 20 seats outside. V menu. Bar.
Wheelchair access.

Otto's

Pressing on with French culinary tradition
Cooking score: 2
⊖ Chancery Lane, map 5
French | £50
182 Gray's Inn Road, Bloomsbury, WC1X 8EW
Tel no: (020) 7713 0107
www.ottos-restaurant.com

Eccentricity rules at Otto's, where beauty in
all its forms, from pouting retro poster girls to
intricately designed French silverware, is
celebrated. Otto's is known chiefly for the
things it presses in its mighty silver devices:
duck or lobster, squeezed, gussied up and
served in two spectacular courses. There's
Lyon-style poularde de Bresse, slowly
poached and served with truffles and morels,
too. These evocative show stoppers must be
pre-ordered, though there's still theatre to be
had via the regular à la carte thanks to high
levels of tableside activity. Enthusiasm rather
than perfectionism is the watchword in the
kitchen, so safe bets such as starters of grilled
French black pudding or lobster bisque,
followed by beef tartare or Limousin veal with
wild mushroom sauce, are wise. Fully live the
Otto's spirit with a shared tarte Tatin flamed
with Calvados. Wine, including a decent
selection of half-bottles, is predominantly
French and from £19.50.
Chef/s: Luca Puzzoli. **Open:** Mon to Fri L 12 to 2.15,
Mon to Sat D 6 to 9.45. **Closed:** Sun, 24 Dec to 7
Jan, bank hols. **Meals:** alc (main courses £18 to
£35). Set L £24 (2 courses) to £28. **Details:** 45 seats.
Bar. Children over 12 yrs only.

NEW ENTRY

Pachamama

Bold and original Peruvian flavours
Cooking score: 1
⊖ Bond Street, map 6
Peruvian | £40
18 Thayer Street, Marylebone, W1U 3JY
Tel no: (020) 7935 9393
www.pachamamalondon.com

£5 OFF

It's easy to miss Pachamama but it's worth venturing down into the eclectic basement space for a taste of Adam Rawson's bold Peruvian small plates. At inspection, his exciting but unpredictable cooking grabbed our attention from the first taste of a bright, firm sea bream tiradito with pink peppercorns and starfruit and wonderfully sticky miso lamb belly with jalapeño. Sadly, crab churros and pumpkin picarones (doughnuts), both from the fryer, missed the mark. Staff struggled with the menu and did a poor job of unlocking its mysteries. Drink a Pisco Negroni or wine, from £25 a bottle.
Chef/s: Adam Rawson. **Open:** all week L 11.30 to 3 (11 to 4 Sat and Sun), D 6 to 11 (10 Sun). **Closed:** 25 Dec. **Meals:** alc (main courses £8 to £25).
Details: 110 seats. V menu. Bar. Music.

The Palomar

Hot-ticket cooking from Jerusalem
Cooking score: 5
⊖ Piccadilly Circus, map 5
Middle Eastern | £35
34 Rupert Street, Soho, W1D 6DN
Tel no: (020) 7439 8777
www.thepalomar.co.uk

'If you only have one thing, make it the shakshukit,' writes one excited correspondent – in fact, this tiny Israeli eatery still seems to be on a roll, delivering lovely treats and unforgettable flavours. The set-up takes in a wood-panelled backroom where tables are 'a squeeze' but bookable; the main business still takes place at the front, at the 16 first-come, first-served kitchen-counter seats. Tomer Amedi's take on modern, non-kosher Israeli cooking is typified by the aforementioned shakshukit (a 'generous' deconstructed kebab, topped with tahini, yoghurt and a 'pesto-lemony sauce'), but his confident fusion of Middle Eastern and Mediterranean styles also yields an excellent corn-fed chicken cooked in buttermilk, and pork belly tagine with ras-el-hanout and Israeli couscous. Framing the main event is sensational kubaneh (pot-baked bread), kubenia (raw chopped beef) with tahini, pomegranate, olive oil, herbs and lemon juice, and desserts such as rose-scented milk pudding. Wines from £24.
Chef/s: Tomer Amedi. **Open:** all week L 12 to 2.30 (3.30 Sun), Mon to Sat D 5.30 to 11 (11.30 Thur to Sat). **Closed:** 25 and 26 Dec. **Meals:** alc (main courses £13 to £19). Tasting menu £55 (6 courses).
Details: 50 seats. Wheelchair access. Music.

Phoenix Palace

Superior dim sum
Cooking score: 2
⊖ Baker Street, map 6
Chinese | £35
3-5 Glentworth Street, Marylebone, NW1 5PG
Tel no: (020) 7486 3515
www.phoenixpalace.co.uk

Sprawling, flamboyant and gaudily decorated, the mighty Phoenix Palace brings some unexpected Hong Kong-style razzmatazz to the touristy environs close to Baker Street. Oriental dragon motifs, ornate lanterns, screens and antique carved furniture adorn the capacious dining room – a trademark mix of red, gold and black lacquered surfaces overseen by battalions of staff in flashy waistcoats. Daytime dim sum (12 to 5) is the big deal here and the kitchen sends out plates, bowls and bamboo baskets of superior stuff ranging from familiar morsels such as barbecued pork buns, silky shredded duck cheung fun and minced prawn dumplings to more esoteric items including sweet yam rolls with gingko nuts, fish balls with pork rind or preserved egg with pickled chilli. The full menu is a 200-dish tour through the main Chinese provinces, taking in the likes of shredded smoked chicken, grilled lobster with 'superior soy', steamed eel with black bean sauce and even Szechuan-style kangaroo. Wines start at £20.

Chef/s: Zhan Hong Yu. **Open:** all week 12 to 11.30 (11 to 10.30 Sun). **Closed:** 25 Dec. **Meals:** alc (main courses £10 to £54). Set D £33. **Details:** 250 seats. Wheelchair access.

Pied à Terre

Bijou Fitzrovia aristocrat
Cooking score: 7
⊖ Goodge Street, map 5
Modern French | £80
34 Charlotte Street, Fitzrovia, W1T 2NH
Tel no: (020) 7636 1178
www.pied-a-terre.co.uk

A lovely meal, agreeable surroundings and service that really knows how to make you comfortable is all many ask of a restaurant, and the bijou Pied à Terre – 'so intimate, so gently lit, so well served by its staff' – certainly delivers; eating here is all about being cherished. You know Marcus Eaves means to do things the right way when you taste the delicious bread and opening salvo (potato and truffle croquette and salmon tartare in squid-ink crisp at a winter test meal). His roasted saddle of Yorkshire hare is a perfect start, every ingredient cooked the way it should be – building flavour upon flavour with blackberries, quince, cavolo nero and wet walnuts. As a main course, very fresh poached and roasted lemon sole topped with delicate red prawns is made memorable by an amalgamation of fennel purée, black olive and pine nuts permeated by Meyer lemon. Elsewhere, copious praise continues to pour in from readers, whether singling out Cornish mackerel that's as 'fresh and tender as could be', or expressing delight at a 'simply top-class' partridge (poached breast with a subtle game flavour, a splendid, gamier confit leg). Desserts also hit the high notes, whether a strawberry, grape and elderflower trifle pre-dessert, or 'an amazing' chocolate mousse with caramel honeycomb, 'beautifully peanutty' ice cream topped with a PX jelly. To cap it all the hefty wine list is a real cracker – a knowledgeable, worldwide compendium (from £25) made navigable by the sommeliers' 'terrific double act' inspiring you to try something new.

Chef/s: Marcus Eaves. **Open:** Mon to Fri L 12 to 2.30, Mon to Sat D 6 to 11. **Closed:** Sun, last week Dec, first week Jan. **Meals:** Set L £28 (2 courses) to £34. Set D £65 (2 courses) to £80. Tasting menu £105 (10 courses) to £140. **Details:** 44 seats. V menu. Bar. Music.

Pollen Street Social

Utterly brilliant uptown eatery
Cooking score: 9
⊖ Oxford Circus, map 5
Modern British | £60
8-13 Pollen Street, Mayfair, W1S 1NQ
Tel no: (020) 7290 7600
www.pollenstreetsocial.com

'You know it's wonderful. We do too – that's why we went' is just one of many endorsements for the biggest jewel in Jason Atherton's very glittery crown. Tucked down a narrow Mayfair alleyway, it delivers exactly what its website promises, deformalised fine dining. Indeed, once settled at your table the convivial atmosphere means you may find yourself chatting to your neighbours. The look of the place is suave without ever feeling stiff: 'I could quite easily sit there all afternoon sipping a glass or three of the fine and rare and watching the world go by. It's that sort of place.' But the informality goes deeper than that, it is also about the food, which is sophisticated but also manages to feel generous, gutsy and sometimes even playful – witness a pine-smoked quail 'brunch' starter with cereals, toast and tea. The quality of the ingredients, and the amount of flavour that is coaxed out of them, are endlessly thrilling: 'I have never tasted guinea fowl like it. How do they do it?' While Cornish turbot with capers, brown butter, samphire, hazelnuts, grapes and caper gnocchi 'was as good a piece of fish as I

have ever eaten'. At the dessert stage, try goats' milk rice pudding with goats' cheese ice cream, oat and milk crumb and honeycomb. The wine list is as dazzling as you would hope, pulling together French classics, discoveries from lesser-known wine producing areas and artisan obscurities. Bottles start at £25.
Chef/s: Jason Atherton. **Open:** Mon to Sat L 12 to 2.30, D 6 to 10.30. **Closed:** Sun, bank hols. **Meals:** alc (main courses £30 to £37). Set L £29 (2 courses) to £34. Tasting menu £89 (8 courses). **Details:** 70 seats. V menu. Bar. Music.

Polpetto

Chic small-plates Italian eatery
Cooking score: 3
⊖ Oxford Circus, Piccadilly Circus, map 5
Italian | £30
11 Berwick Street, Soho, W1F 0PL
Tel no: (020) 7439 8627
www.polpo.co.uk

Born out of Russell Norman's populist Polpo concept, Polpetto is now a rather chic (if somewhat raucous) stand-alone eatery with a distinctive vibe created by tiled ceilings, deliberately worn linen, curved glass, old wallpaper and antique books. Chef Florence Knight is the undoubted star here, delivering a short, snappy seasonal menu of nominally Italian food for hungry folk who drop by for small plates of ale-battered Tropea onions, burrata with wild hops and preserved lemons, or mussels with wild fennel and crème fraîche. There are also gutsy servings of pasta (perhaps strozzapreti with beef shin), plus a handful of international desserts – anything from maple tart to rhubarb with shortbread and custard. Drink aperitifs, Aperol spritzs, cocktails or Italian regional wines (from £15 a carafe). Note that the original Polpo brand is now spreading its tentacles across the capital, with outlets currently in Soho, Covent Garden, Notting Hill and Smithfield – see website for details.

Chef/s: Florence Knight. **Open:** Mon to Fri L 12 to 3.30, D 5.30 to 11. Sat 12 to 11. **Closed:** Sun, 25 and 26 Dec, 1 Jan, bank hols. **Meals:** alc (tapas £7 to £10). **Details:** 60 seats. Bar. Wheelchair access. Music.

Portland

Short menu, bang-on flavours
Cooking score: 4
⊖ Great Portland St, Oxford Circus, map 5
Modern British | £35
113 Great Portland Street, Fitzrovia, W1W 6QQ
Tel no: (020) 7436 3261
www.portlandrestaurant.co.uk

Portland opened to a burst of enthusiasm in early 2015. The unfussy interior is understated and functional with perhaps 'too many hard surfaces', and there's no disputing the valiant intent behind this collaboration between chef Merlin Labron-Johnson (previously at In de Wulf, Belgium) and co-owners Will Lander (Quality Chop House) and Daniel Morgenthau (10 Greek Street) – it's all about new-Brit culinary cool. Dishes brim with stimulating, flavour-first gestures and flashes of brilliance – snacks of sticky lamb ribs with black sesame, and teriyaki quail with fermented turnip were star turns at a meal in May. The concise menu has a sense of seasonality, too, expressed in morels, ramson and slow-cooked duck egg, or a superb main course of Jersey Royals with asparagus and smoked egg emulsion. Otherwise, seek out the pleasures of onion with mussels, pig's head croquettes, and yearling hogget. Expect, too, a contemporary sheen to the presentation, pitch-perfect service and a savvy, offbeat wine list (from £21) with wonderful choice by the glass.

Chef/s: Merlin Labron-Johnson. **Open:** Mon to Sat L 12 to 2.30, D 6 to 11. **Closed:** Sun. **Meals:** alc (main courses £14 to £22). **Details:** 45 seats.

Princi

Good ingredients, good value, good buzz
Cooking score: 2
⊖ Tottenham Court Road, Piccadilly Circus, map 5
Italian | £20
135 Wardour Street, Soho, W1F 0UT
Tel no: (020) 7478 8888
www.princi.com

A useful address in Wardour Street, Princi is the real deal, an Italian bakery and pizzeria where style counts and there's an irresistible combination of charm and sociability. A long-time Soho favourite, it continues to win praise for its self-service café – pastries, salads, hot pasta dishes, stews – but folk really come for the 'practically perfect' wood-fired pizzas served in the adjoining pizzeria. But the open-to-view kitchen also pulls in bright ideas from across Italy, such as simple starters of artichoke and frisée salad or heritage tomatoes with buffalo mozzarella, and gnocchi with Sicilian Datterini tomatoes, anchovy and basil. There could also be tagliatelle with beef ragù, char-grilled baby chicken or braised octopus with polenta, and cannoncini (cream-filled pastry horn) to finish. With breakfast each day, brunch served at the weekends and plenty of snacking possibilities, it's all well suited to Princi's all-day opening and no-reservations policy. Wines from £22.
Chef/s: Matteo Cocchetti. **Open:** all week 8am to 11.30pm (8.30am to 10pm Sun). **Meals:** alc (main courses £8 to £12). **Details:** 46 seats.

Please send us your feedback

To register your opinion about any restaurant listed in this guide, or a new restaurant that you wish to bring to our attention, please visit the web address at the bottom of the page. Your feedback informs the content of the book and will be used to compile next year's reviews.

Quilon

Vibrant south west Indian cooking
Cooking score: 4
⊖ St James's Park, Victoria, map 5
Indian | £50
41 Buckingham Gate, Westminster, SW1E 6AF
Tel no: (020) 7821 1899
www.quilon.co.uk

Quilon may be located in a hotel, but the dining room with its elegant wooden lattice screens and modern art is far from being anonymous. Seafood is the cornerstone of an extensive menu, inspired by south west India (Goa, Kerala), although a starter of tender chicken breasts (coated with a little coconut cream) paired with a purée of chilli and cumin shows that meat dishes are equally pleasing. Vibrant colouring and delicate spicing lifted a fish curry at a recent meal, helping the chunks of halibut simmered in coconut, chilli and mango to deliver a subtle flavour hit. Paratha is particularly well made and vegetables are treated with care – spinach poriyal with mustard seeds can steal the show. To finish, try bebinca, a Goan layered pudding made from rice flour and served with vanilla ice cream. Wines (from £26) are assembled with care to match the spicy dishes and are augmented by an interesting, global selection of beers.
Chef/s: Sriram Aylur. **Open:** all week L 12 to 2.15 (12.30 to 3.15 Sat and Sun), D 6 to 10.30 (10 Sun). **Closed:** 25 Dec. **Meals:** alc (main courses £17 to £36). Set L £24 (2 courses). Set D £54. Sun L £24. **Details:** 82 seats. Bar. Wheelchair access. Music.

Quirinale

Majestic Italian dishes in a sunny basement
Cooking score: 3
⊖ Westminster, map 3
Italian | £35
1 Great Peter Street, Westminster, SW1P 3LL
Tel no: (020) 7222 7080
www.quirinale.co.uk

If the ambience seemed to have changed a little during the spring of 2015 at Quirinale, it's largely because a sizeable proportion of its regular clientele was out tramping the country canvassing for votes. The proximity to Westminster often fills this bright, airy basement room with MPs and journalists as well as sunshine, and efficient staff patrol the tables with authority. The Italian cooking isn't necessarily cutting edge, but dishes look majestic and are cooked with accuracy and flair. 'A simple but excellent lunch' isn't as easy to come by in these parts as it ought to be, but might consist of potato and leek ravioli with salsiccia ragù, followed by olive-crusted monkfish with courgette escabèche, or rack of tender lamb with aubergine and hazelnuts. To finish, there's a version of tiramisu that's as richly elaborate as a Puccini aria, or perhaps peach tortino and vanilla ice cream. The regionally classified Italian list opens at £21, or £5.50 a glass.

Chef/s: Stefano Savio. **Open:** Mon to Fri L 12 to 2.30, D 6 to 10.30. **Closed:** Sat, Sun. **Meals:** alc (main courses £17 to £24). Set L and early D £19 (2 courses) to £23. **Details:** 50 seats.

Quo Vadis

Born-again Soho legend
Cooking score: 4
⊖ Tottenham Court Road, map 5
Modern British | £45
26-29 Dean Street, Soho, W1D 3LL
Tel no: (020) 7437 9585
www.quovadissoho.co.uk

Karl Marx wrote much of *Das Kapital* in the room above, but Quo Vadis has come a very long way since then. Once a grandiose Italian for the old-school Soho crowd, it's now as sharply metro as can be — thanks to the savvy Hart brothers and their chef Jeremy Lee. Antique mirrors, Art Deco flourishes, glass panels and that famous revolving door are reminders of the past, but the kitchen now works to a jolly repertoire of born-again British food. The menu is a joy to behold — a mock-up broadsheet complete with Edwardian-style cartoons, woodblock prints, the weather forecast and little boxes advertising 'kickshaws'. Meanwhile, smartly groomed staff deliver generous, straight-

talking dishes ranging from marbled pork terrine with 'pickles and co' or brill with sea kale to mighty pies, pigeon with onions, sherry and 'sauce', or boiled beef and carrots with beetroot and horseradish. To finish, desserts trumpet steamed puddings, fruity tarts and meringues. Exemplary modern wines start at £21.

Chef/s: Jeremy Lee. **Open:** all week L 12 to 3 (1 to 3.30 Sun), Mon to Sat D 5.30 to 11. **Closed:** bank hols. **Meals:** alc (main courses £15 to £24). Set L and D £19 (2 courses) to £22. **Details:** 80 seats. 18 seats outside. Bar.

Rex Whistler at the Tate

Seasonal promise at a rejuvenated gallery
Cooking score: 2
⊖ Pimlico, map 3
British | £32
Millbank, Pimlico, SW1P 4RG
Tel no: (020) 7887 8825
www.tate.org.uk

Rex Whistler was in his early 20s when he got the commission in 1926 to paint a mural in the Tate's main dining space. He was killed in WWII. The room was revamped in 2013 and the pastoral scene with a hunting theme remains a compelling feature, along with pristine white columns and parquet flooring. It's timeless, and rather smart and ambitious for a lunchtime-only operation. There are contemporary elements to the modern British output, with botanical-cured smoked salmon served with gin and lime dressing, say, but there's also classical refinement in another starter that partners tender veal cheeks with parsnip cream and caramelised sweetbreads. Move onto Gressingham duck breast with its confit leg meat packed into a Savoy cabbage parcel, or roast brill with leeks and samphire, and finish with salted caramel chocolate pot. The wine list is a gem with good options by the glass; prices from £21.

Chef/s: Anthony Martin. **Open:** all week L only 12 to 3. **Closed:** 24 to 26 Dec. **Meals:** Set L £27 (2 courses) to £32. Sun L £27. **Details:** 80 seats. 20 seats outside. Wheelchair access.

The Ritz

One of the capital's great old dining rooms
Cooking score: 6
⊖ Green Park, map 5
French | £75
150 Piccadilly, Mayfair, W1J 9BR
Tel no: (020) 7300 2370
www.theritzlondon.com

Nothing quite prepares those unused to grand hotel dining rooms for the jaw-dropping magnificence of the Ritz. Rich and luxurious, it is marbled and chandeliered with an ornate painted ceiling and wall panels, gilded statues and legions of formally dressed staff. Despite all this, it is more relaxed than people may imagine, always providing that high prices don't make you feel jittery. It's definitely the place for an old-fashioned celebration and John Williams rises to the occasion, delivering a mix of classic and modern French dishes on a carte that deals in as many luxuries as it can lay its hands on (lobster, beetroot, bergamot and oscietra caviar, say, then Bresse duck with Savoy cabbage, duck liver and orange). Here's a tip, though: 'have the set lunch, it's great value, in fact better than afternoon tea'. Lovely bread, canapés and petits fours are all present and correct, as well as goose liver with spiced pineapple and gingerbread, then brill with brandade, watercress and bacon, and an exotic fruit soufflé with banana and rum ice cream to finish. Wine mark-ups are what one might expect; indeed, the list opens at £50.
Chef/s: John Williams. **Open:** all week L 12.30 to 2, D 5.30 to 10 (7 to 10 Sun). **Meals:** alc (main courses £36 to £48). Set L £34 (2 courses) to £49. Set D £36 (2 courses) to £59. Sun L £59. **Details:** 90 seats. V menu. Bar. Wheelchair access. Music. Parking.

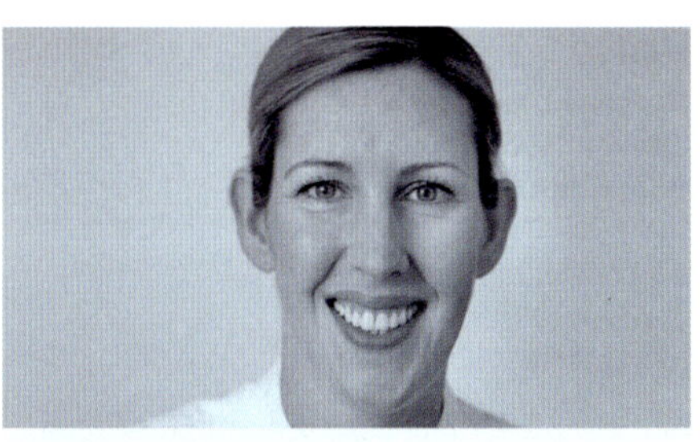

Clare Smyth

Restaurant Gordon Ramsay, Chelsea

What inspired you to become a chef?

I love working with food and have always had respect for nature; I have always been creative and love working in a team environment.

What would you be if you weren't a chef?

I would have been a professional show-jumper, I loved horse riding as a child and was pretty good at it!

What food trends are you spotting at the moment?

Lots of young chefs are setting up simple restaurants without massive overheads and they are cooking some of the best food.

Is there a particular dish that evokes strong memories for you?

Slow-cooked stews and soups always remind me of my mother's cooking – she would cook things overnight and I would wake up to the amazing smell.

Do you have a guilty foodie pleasure?

I love crisps!

Roka

Stylish urban Japanese eating
Cooking score: 4
⊖ Goodge Street, map 5
Japanese | £50
37 Charlotte Street, Fitzrovia, W1T 1RR
Tel no: (020) 7580 6464
www.rokarestaurant.com

Like Rainer Becker's other restaurant Zuma (see entry), the Roka phenomenon (there are branches at Canary Wharf, Mayfair and Aldwych) is still among the premier-league players on the contemporary Japanese restaurant scene. This plate-glass Charlotte Street venue attracts a lively crowd who are unlikely to flinch at the thumping soundtrack, bonsai portions or sumo-sized bills. Furniture is minimally plain – close-packed tables or counter seating at the robata grill – and the cooking gives a spin to trademark Japanese classics, fusing new-wave Japanese with pan-Asian undertones. Top-notch sushi and sashimi look the part, and the kitchen moves quickly from oysters with ponzu and chilli daikon, black cod, crab and crayfish dumplings, and tiger prawn tempura into the realms of smoked duck breast with barley miso and kumquats or Wagyu beef with pickled Japanese mushrooms. The Shochu Lounge downstairs is perfect for cocktails, there's an extensive list of sakés and wines are from £26.
Chef/s: Damon Griffith. **Open:** all week L 12 to 3.30 (4 Sat and Sun), D 5.30 to 11.30 (10.30 Sun). **Closed:** 25 Dec. **Meals:** alc (dishes from £13 to £36). Tasting menus £55 and £79. **Details:** 88 seats. 24 seats outside. Bar. Music.

Roux at Parliament Square

Inspired contemporary cooking
Cooking score: 4
⊖ Westminster, St James's Park, map 5
Modern British | £55
11 Great George Street, Parliament Square, Westminster, SW1P 3AD
Tel no: (020) 7334 3737
www.rouxatparliamentsquare.co.uk

A restaurant sited in the Royal Institution of Chartered Surveyors, not far from the Houses of Parliament, might sound like a recipe for stuffed-shirt establishmentarianism, but former *Masterchef Professionals* winner Steve Groves works against the grain to produce contemporary British food that illuminates the scene. The wide expansive room is run by punctiliously correct staff, bringing minutely detailed modern plates: Indian-spiced veal sweetbread with girolles and artichokes might presage the appearance of Brixham brill in a duo with brown crabmeat, alongside cauliflower textures and lemongrass. Or else a modern-classic partnering of roast scallop with pig's cheek and black pudding, apple and hazelnuts is the outrider for breast and heart of Gressingham duck with bergamot, cipollini onions and pink peppercorns. That determination to offer a welter of flavours in each mouthful continues into desserts such as gariguette strawberries with buttermilk, oats and lemon verbena. The wine list is compact in every section, opening at £33 and reaching for the stars.
Chef/s: Steve Groves. **Open:** Mon to Fri L 12 to 2, D 6.30 to 10. **Closed:** Sat, Sun, 24 Dec to 2 Jan, bank hols. **Meals:** alc (main courses £28 to £32). Set L £35 (3 courses). **Details:** 55 seats.

Join us at thegoodfoodguide.co.uk

Roux at the Landau

A paean to sumptuous luxury
Cooking score: 3
⊖ Oxford Circus, map 5
Modern European | £58
The Langham, 1c Portland Place, Oxford
Circus, W1B 1JA
Tel no: (020) 7965 0165
www.rouxatthelandau.com

The Langham celebrated its 150th anniversary
in 2015 – a dowager among London's grand-
hotel hierarchy – although it's business as
usual at the Landau. The Roux brothers'
restaurant in the hotel's reconfigured ballroom
comes complete with spindly modernist
chandeliers, high-toned detailing and lots of
elegant curves – a suitably swanky backdrop
for refined cooking in the modern European
idiom. Familiar and fanciful ideas sit side by
side, from Denham venison saucisson with
apple rémoulade or Dover Sole meunière to
quail with foie gras, hazelnuts, pickled raisins
and wilted escarole (curly endive) or monkfish
with black curry, saffron, pomegranate and
pistachio dressing. To finish, there are cheeses
from the trolley or cleverly crafted desserts
such as bitter chocolate mille-feuille with
maple ice cream and salted pecans. The food
comes across as gently luxurious, thanks to
clear concentrated flavours and some signature
Roux flourishes. Beyond the restaurant, a
bespoke 'corridor' gives a glimpse of the
aristocratic wines on offer, although there's
precious little under £35.
Chef/s: Chris King and Jamie Draper. **Open:** Mon
to Fri L 12 to 2.30, Mon to Sat D 5.30 to 10.30.
Closed: Sun, first week Jan. **Meals:** alc (main
courses £19 to £48). Set L and D £28 (2 courses) to
£35. **Details:** 91 seats. V menu. Bar. Wheelchair
access. Music.

Average price

The average price denotes the price
of a three-course meal without wine.

Rules

Bastion of traditional British cooking
Cooking score: 3
⊖ Covent Garden, Leicester Square, map 5
British | £48
35 Maiden Lane, Covent Garden, WC2E 7LB
Tel no: (020) 7836 5314
www.rules.co.uk

Old money may well feel at home among the
plump velvet booths, polished wood and
ornate carpets, but London's oldest restaurant
(circa 1798) on cobbled Maiden Lane attracts
its fair share of Covent Garden's tourists and
in-the-know foodies. Game is at the heart of
the operation, so visit during the winter game
season and you'll be rewarded with, among
other treats, a classic roast grouse from the
owner's Pennine estate. Otherwise you might
opt for potted shrimps or oysters to start
things off, followed by tender loin of venison
with red cabbage and roast celeriac, or one of
the restaurant's famed meaty pies or puddings
(expect top-class execution under head David
Stafford's watchful eye). Golden syrup sponge
pudding with custard befits the thorough
Englishness of this heritage-laden institution.
Wines – Old World dominated and mostly
red – start at a hefty £26, but over 20 are
available by the glass.
Chef/s: David Stafford. **Open:** all week 12 to 11.45
(10.45 Sun). **Closed:** 25 and 26 Dec. **Meals:** alc
(main courses £18 to £37). **Details:** 95 seats. V
menu. Bar.

Salt Yard

Versatile tapas hot spot
Cooking score: 2
⊖ Goodge Street, map 5
Tapas | £30
54 Goodge Street, Fitzrovia, W1T 4NA
Tel no: (020) 7637 0657
www.saltyard.co.uk

Salt Yard broke new ground when it gave us
Spanish and Italian-inspired tapas back in
2005, and now the idea just seems jolly
sensible. They've taken on new addresses, too,
with Ember Yard, Dehesa and Opera Tavern

doing much the same (see entries). Stick around the bar at ground-floor level if you want (or grab a pavement table), although it's best to head down to the main dining room with its smart leather banquettes and view into the kitchen. The charcuterie should not be missed – their own chilli and marjoram salami, maybe, top-drawer Serrano ham, or a trio of Italian classics. But creative highlights this year include confit Gloucester Old Spot with rosemary-scented cannellini beans ('very, very good') and a salad of golden beetroots and smoked ricotta with a stunning aged balsamic. Finish with ricotta dumplings with lemon curd and homemade jam. Sherry by the glass is a good bet, while house wine is £20.
Chef/s: Ben Tish and Dan Sherlock. **Open:** Mon to Fri L 12 to 3, D 5.30 to 11. Sat and Sun 12 to 11. **Closed:** 25 Dec, 1 Jan. **Meals:** alc (tapas £5 to £11). **Details:** 72 seats. 8 seats outside. Music.

Savoy Grill

An evocation of flavours past
Cooking score: 2
⊖ **Charing Cross, map 5**
Anglo-French | £40
The Savoy, Strand, Covent Garden, WC2R 0EU
Tel no: (020) 7592 1600
www.gordonramsay.com

The Savoy Grill has a headline-making new name behind the stoves. The hotel's original chef, Auguste Escoffier may have been dubbed 'king of chefs and chef of kings', but Kim Woodward is the first female head chef to run the stoves in its 126-year history. A Gordon Ramsay protégée, Woodward has remained faithful to the lengthy menu of Anglo-French brasserie staples served in the opulent wood-panelled Art Deco dining room with its creaking trolleys and table-side flambéeing: 'Most of my fellow diners appeared to be either tourists or people celebrating birthdays/anniversaries.' Comforting pies and charcoal-fired steaks and chops are still the main event here, but a starter of baked Hereford snails with sweet garlic purée and red wine sauce might be followed by roast new-season lamb loin with spring greens and its own braised lamb shoulder hotpot. Classily rendered desserts include an impressively light and puffy hazelnut soufflé with vanilla ice cream. The heavyweight wine list starts at £30.
Chef/s: Kim Woodward. **Open:** all week L 12 to 3 (4 Sun), D 5.30 to 11 (6 to 10.30 Sun). **Meals:** alc (main courses £18 to £42). Set L £26 (2 courses) to £30. Pre-theatre weekday D £24 (2 courses) to £28. **Details:** 100 seats. V menu. Wheelchair access.

Scott's

Single-minded dedication to seafood
Cooking score: 4
⊖ **Green Park, map 6**
Seafood | £45
20 Mount Street, Mayfair, W1K 2HE
Tel no: (020) 7495 7309
www.scotts-restaurant.com

Scott's is a sophisticated seafood venue that may be a long way from the sea in moneyed Mayfair, but lacks nothing in dedication to the cause. An outdoor terrace allows you to soak up the Mount Street sunshine, while inside, oak-panelled refinement reigns, with an oyster and Champagne bar for dropping in, or else starting as you mean to go on. A single fried bivalve in wasabi, cucumber and lime might open proceedings, before the cocktails, tartares and potted items take over. Bracingly marinated salmon with avocado in black pepper dressing is an effectively simple appetiser for main dishes such as seared sea bass in lemon and herb butter, or John Dory with artichokes, anchovies and capers. Simplicity is the watchword, and dishes gain in impact thereby. There are even some meat dishes, too, for the dissidents. Finish with chocolate and blood-orange fondant with vanilla crème fraîche. Wines start at £27.
Chef/s: David McCarthy. **Open:** all week 12 to 10.30 (10 Sun). **Closed:** 25 and 26 Dec. **Meals:** alc (main courses £19 to £30). **Details:** 120 seats. 20 seats outside. V menu. Bar. Wheelchair access.

Seven Park Place by William Drabble

Lustrous modern French food
Cooking score: 6
⊖ Green Park, map 5
Modern French | £61
St James's Hotel and Club, 7-8 Park Place,
Mayfair, SW1A 1LS
Tel no: (020) 7316 1615
www.stjameshotelandclub.com

Deep in historic St James's, this hotel is all concentrated elegance, and its dining room a sight for sore eyes. The restricted space leaps out of its confines with a fin-de-siècle decorative job featuring climbing tendrils on chocolate-brown walls, the argumentative patterning in carpets and upholstery overseen by a serene Klimt-ish lady in oils. William Drabble's production here is a continuation of the style he forged at Chelsea's Aubergine, with prime domestic ingredients alchemised into a prodigiously detailed French modernism. There is nothing on any plate that doesn't speak eloquently of itself, from the new season's asparagus that accompanies a butter-poached lobster tail in sauce maltaise to the marjoram crust on Lune Valley lamb saddle, its braised sweetbreads adding richness to a scatter of spring veg – peas, little onions, Jersey Royals. There are platefuls of the warm south, too, as for a first-course baked red mullet with courgette ribbons, black olive purée and sweet pepper sauce, and elements of the distantly domestic, chicken breast with creamed mushrooms. Lustrous desserts like mango cream and sorbet in passion fruit and mint syrup are the final flourish, while wines are a fabulous collection – mostly at St James's prices, but there are some at the more affordable end, starting at £28.
Chef/s: William Drabble. **Open:** Tue to Sat L 12 to 2, D 6.30 to 10. **Closed:** Sun, Mon, 21 to 29 Dec. **Meals:** Set L £26 (2 courses) to £30. Set D £55 (2 courses) to £61. **Details:** 30 seats. V menu. Wheelchair access.

64 Degrees

A tasty slice of retro cool
Cooking score: 3
⊖ Pimlico, map 3
Modern British | £30
Artist Residence Boutique Hotel, 52 Cambridge Street, Pimlico, SW1V 4QQ
Tel no: (020) 3262 0501
www.64degrees.co.uk

A tasty slice of retro/urban cool a few minutes' walk from Victoria Station, this is the London outpost of the successful Brighton venture of the same name (see entry). The interior makes a show of the building's bones, from weathered bricks to nut-brown floorboards. At the heart of it all is a long copper bar with the kitchen behind it. Sit here and get your food directly from the chefs or opt for a table and well-informed service. Dishes are small and priced accordingly: the recommended three won't break the bank. Asparagus spears on kelp with a confit egg yolk and potato espuma is typical of the simple, trendy style. 'Beautiful ingredients' shine in a crisp-skinned fillet of sea trout with butter and whey emulsion and fennel slaw, while a juicy, rosy hunk of lamb chump with golden beetroot, preserved lemon and a rich, dark jus is a 'perfectly cooked' meat course. Expect zingy flavours throughout – not least in a dessert of citrus curd, Italian meringue and crumble. A modest but interesting wine list begins at £14.25
Chef/s: Michael Bremner. **Open:** all week L 12 to 3 (5 Sat and Sun), Mon to Sat D 6 to 9.45 (10 Fri and Sat). **Closed:** 25 Dec. **Meals:** alc (main courses £12 to £18). Set L £15 (2 courses). Sun L £25. **Details:** 42 seats. 12 seats outside. Bar. Wheelchair access. Music.

Sixty One

Precisely cooked, creative food

Cooking score: 4

⊖ Marble Arch, map 6

Modern British | £41

61 Upper Berkeley Street, Marylebone, W1H 7PP

Tel no: (020) 7958 3222

www.sixtyonerestaurant.co.uk

'This is just not somewhere you'd expect to find a restaurant, let alone a very smart restaurant offering precisely cooked, pleasantly creative food at extremely fair prices,' is praise indeed for this hotel dining room in a Marylebone side street near Marble Arch. The room is slick and smart but not overly dressy, one that supports special occasions as much as quick business lunches, and chef Arnaud Stevens is clearly talented. A spring dinner showed immense promise: from the excellent bread, via a generous chunk of beef fillet, roasted pink, with some beautifully sweet and savoury little aubergines glazed with miso, an exceptionally smooth parsnip purée, a light but intense sauce 'that showed real craftsmanship' with buds of young punterelle cutting through all the richness, to a chocolate fondant flavoured with praline, 'one of the best I can recall trying'. Formal service comes 'with a smile and a lot of pride', and wines start at £19.50 .

Chef/s: Arnaud Stevens. **Open:** all week L 12 to 2.30 (5 Sun), Mon to Sat D 5.30 to 10.30. **Closed:** 25 and 26 Dec. **Meals:** alc (main courses £16 to £28). Set L and D £18 (2 courses) to £22. Sun L £18.
Details: 70 seats. V menu. Bar. Wheelchair access. Music.

Average price

The average price denotes the price of a three-course meal without wine.

Sketch, Lecture Room & Library

An extravagant pleasure palace

Cooking score: 7

⊖ Oxford Circus, map 5

Modern European | £95

9 Conduit Street, Mayfair, W1S 2XG

Tel no: (020) 7659 4500

www.sketch.uk.com

There's a lot going on in this seemingly unassuming 18th-century town house. Inside it feels like an exclusive club with its wildly contemporary art installations and dining rooms and bars that pop up all over the various levels, and it goes without saying that the Swarovski-encrusted bathrooms are not to be missed. The Lecture Room sets the silky smooth tone with its cosseting surrounds, tailor made for Mayfair and for cooking that relies on top ingredients and meticulous craftsmanship – the ideas of Pierre Gagnaire (one of France's most lauded chefs) are given free reign under the charge of head chef Johannes Nuding. As for the menu – it's complicated. You chose a theme, and with each theme you get an assemblage of little dishes – 'all fabulous'. 'Spring' brings rich, buttery morels in vin jaune, Palomas gambas bouillon with mustard (a sort of prawn bisque), green pea soup with broad beans, gnocchi à la parisienne and red tuna tartare and much more besides. At main course the 'Lake District' offering ('because they've found a fabulous supplier in Cumbria') is fillet of wild rainbow trout meunière with verbena and gratinated cabbage with Gruyère, and side dishes of 'lovely, fresh-tasting' crayfish tails, and 'zam zam' of zander with Mac vin (a sweet white wine from the Jura). To finish there's a cavalcade of desserts. The set lunch is considered a very good deal, while the list of thoroughbred wines teems with quality at wallet-denting prices, though there are a few bottles between £30 and £40.

Chef/s: Pierre Gagnaire and Johannes Nuding.
Open: Tue to Fri L 12 to 2.30, Tue to Sat D 6.30 to 11. **Closed:** Sun, Mon, 23 to 30 Dec, 1 Jan, 18 to 29

Aug. **Meals:** alc (main courses £49 to £55). Set L £35 (2 courses) to £40. **Details:** 48 seats. V menu. Music. Children over 6 yrs only

Smoking Goat
Brilliantly inventive, lip-smacking food
Cooking score: 4
⊖ Tottenham Court Road, map 5
Thai | £27
7 Denmark Street, Soho, WC2H 8LZ
Tel no: (020) 7999 9999
www.smokinggoatsoho.com

'I've now been to Smoking Goat about five times. Why? Well, it's certainly not for the tables packed so close together you can't walk between them without knocking a beer over. No, I come for brilliantly inventive food that you simply cannot get anywhere else.' This sparklingly idiosyncratic restaurant is a bold, brilliant oddball. Seb Holmes'cooking is new-wave modern British, yet it tastes like Thai food: 'the limey, palm-sugary, fish-saucy, blazingly chilli-hot and salty combinations are as good or better than anything I've tried in Thailand.' But Holmes is 100% a product of the modern London restaurant scene, and the queues at the door speak volumes. 'Supremely affordable', gutsy, surprisingly simple dishes include oysters brought to life with lime and a touch of chilli; smoked lamb ribs with fermented shrimp and som tam; and whole Devon chilli crab with aromatic herbs, roasted chilli, palm sugar and fresh coconut cream with fresh mint and salted curry leaves. A snappy European wine list opens at £16.
Chef/s: Seb Holmes. **Open:** Mon to Sat L 12 to 3, D 5 to 12. Sun 12 to 9. **Closed:** 25 and 26 Dec. **Meals:** alc (main courses £15 to £20). **Details:** 30 seats. Music.

Social Eating House
Modern mood food
Cooking score: 6
⊖ Oxford Circus, map 5
Modern British | £49
58 Poland Street, Soho, W1F 7NR
Tel no: (020) 7993 3251
www.socialeatinghouse.com

Buried in Soho, the Eating House is the roughest and readiest of Jason Atherton's Social chain, at least in appearances. The scuffed and distressed look, with worn leather banquettes and brickwork, suits the district, and what Paul Hood sends out from the kitchen is modern mood food with deep roots in home cooking. Ham, egg and chips offers smoked duck ham with triple-cooked chips and a breaded duck egg slashed with truffle oil, served, naturally, on a roof tile. Wild mushrooms turn up in a bag with cep purée on toast, while the pick of the mains may be the lamb neck fillet with goats' curd risotto, unexpectedly luscious and offset by the textural counterpoint of roasted hazelnuts, or there may be seaweed-glazed sea bass with spelt and puréed parsley root in mushroom tea. Jars of scoff such as shrimp and grits with green chilli slaw provide the drinkers with bulk, and sweet-tooths will hanker for blackberry jelly with rum ice cream, tarragon and quince. Witty, imaginative cocktails supplement a list of confidently chosen wines, with plenty available by the glass from £4. Bottles from £19.50.
Chef/s: Paul Hood. **Open:** Mon to Sat L 12 to 2.30, D 6 to 10.30. **Closed:** Sun, bank hols. **Meals:** alc (main courses) £18 to £29. Set L £21 (2 courses) to £25. Tasting menu £55. **Details:** 70 seats. V menu. Bar. Music.

Social Wine & Tapas

Vivacious Aladdin's wine cave
Cooking score: 3
◉ Bond Street, map 6
Modern British | £28
39 James Street, Marylebone, W1U 1DL
Tel no: (020) 7993 3257
www.socialwineandtapas.com

The fifth addition to Jason Atherton's London-based Social portfolio is a smart-fronted, two-tiered wine and tapas bar. The cool, stylish décor mixes exposed ducting with variations on old gold, wood, copper and leather, moody lighting picks out rack upon rack of wines, and it possesses that essential bit of modern restaurant kit: an open-to-view kitchen (with a spare in the basement). Wine takes centre stage – Laure Patry, Atherton's charismatic chief sommelier, manages the place – the food is a freewheeling take on tapas: ballsy yet subtle, lots of chilli, garlic, spice and citrus, but with a Spanish backbone. Brilliant hams and charcuterie set the tone, seafood and rabbit Spanish rice delivers big, pugnacious flavours, a pair of rose veal, foie gras and pulled pork burgers are rich and comforting, while heirloom tomato salad with truffle burrata and basil is almost too good to share. And wine? It's a fabulous list with many desirable bottles (from £28), small, interesting producers galore and good choice by the glass. Note, no reservations.
Chef/s: Frankie Van Loo. **Open:** all week 12 to 10.30 (9.30 Sun). **Meals:** alc (tapas £2.50 to £17).
Details: 70 seats. Bar.

Spring

Attractive Italian-inspired food
Cooking score: 5
◉ Temple, Waterloo, map 5
Modern European | £55
Somerset House, Lancaster Place, Strand, WC2R 1LA
Tel no: (020) 3011 0116
www.springrestaurant.co.uk

This light-filled, classically proportioned room at Somerset House was wasted on the Inland Revenue until October 2014, when it opened to the public as Spring. And how beautiful it looks! Every last detail has been attended to from the ceramic flowers on the walls to the Amalfi lemons at every table. Visually, it's perfect: theatrical, inspiring and made for 'special occasions' (it's very expensive). Skye Gyngell's (ex-Petersham Nurseries, see entry) Italianate food is beautiful, too – rustically so. Vitello tonnato was a casual assembly of soft pink veal, pickled agretti, early tomatoes and olives, in perfect harmony. We were impressed also by sea bass, a generous tranche, with braised peas and fregola in a rich lemony broth. Here is a kitchen that clearly tastes its food. Rhubarb and rye tart to finish was, however, a bit pedestrian. The less wallet-pounding option would be the set lunch or small plates in the adjacent 'Salon'. Drink seasonal Bellinis or elegant wines (from £25).
Chef/s: Skye Gyngell. **Open:** all week 12 to 11 (5 Sun). **Closed:** 25 to 29 Dec. **Meals:** alc (main courses £16 to £34). Set L £26 (2 courses) to £30.
Details: 100 seats. 30 seats outside. Bar. Wheelchair access.

The Square

Flawless, elegant cooking
Cooking score: 8
⊖ Green Park, map 5
Modern French | £90
6-10 Bruton Street, Mayfair, W1J 6PU
Tel no: (020) 7495 7100
www.squarerestaurant.com

It's worthwhile to be reminded occasionally of the culinary cornerstones on which the capital has built its world-class gastronomical pedigree. Phil Howard's London standard-bearer is doubtlessly one of these, and it quietly continues to dazzle and deliver, 24 years on, despite the frenetic contemporary dining scene and dizzying roll call of trendy newcomers forging new frontiers. Howard and his current incumbent at the pass, Gary Foulkes, flaunt The Square's fine-dining heritage in a spacious room with an appropriately old-school-glamour Mayfair backdrop, the muted tones and fine napery adding up to a pleasing place to linger. And linger you must, for the flawless, elegant modern French cooking, with roots embedded firmly in French culinary tradition, is a delight in conception and delivery. The 'seriously good dining experience', enhanced by the calm composure of the front-of-house team, kicks off with titillating amuse-bouches, and segues into an aesthete's dream: soft-boiled black-headed gull's egg with a remoulade of St Austell Bay mussels, cultured cream, sea grasses, lovage and oscietra caviar is simply exquisite, and though breaking new ground is not Howard's game, there is clearly an innovative edge to the output of late. A tasting of Lavinton lamb with purple garlic, thyme gnocchetti and Italian artichokes, augmented by the tang of sheep's curd (accoutrements are no afterthought), shows off superlative produce and flawless technique, and the glorification of prime British produce continues, be it with the slow-cooked Cornish cod with creamed potato, morels, white asparagus, spring garlic

and red wine or breast of corn-fed guinea hen with new season's mousserons. The Square's long-standing signature soufflé and tarte fine of GoldRush apple with almonds or the 'generous and classy' cheese plate are winning finales. Prestige wines starting at £32 inevitably take precedence on the pedigree French-leaning list, though wines by the glass are notably good and superlative wine pairings get special recognition from one reader.
Chef/s: Phil Howard. **Open:** Mon to Sat L 12 to 2.45, all week D 6.30 to 10 (10.30 Fri and Sat, 9.30 Sun). **Closed:** 24 to 27 Dec, L bank hols. **Meals:** Set L £33 (2 courses) to £38. Set D £70 (2 courses) to £90. **Details:** 70 seats. V menu. Bar. Wheelchair access.

Tamarind

Moghul cuisine, Mayfair-style
Cooking score: 4
⊖ Green Park, map 5
Indian | £60
20 Queen Street, Mayfair, W1J 5PR
Tel no: (020) 7629 3561
www.tamarindrestaurant.com

Long lauded as one of Britain's finest Indian restaurants, Tamarind now faces the future without Alfred Prasad, who headed the kitchen for over a decade. The premises remain stylish: a spacious Mayfair basement, with burnished gold pillars and carefully tarnished mirrors. Waiters are polite and amenable. The kitchen gained renown for producing ultra-refined versions of northern Indian dishes boosted by innovative tweaks. Culinary skills remain high, but at inspection, a set meal lacked inspiration. Expertly battered cod resembled two exalted fish fingers, though needed more of the accompanying mint chutney. A main-course highlight was a superbly spiced tarka dhal, crunchy with cumin seeds and zinging with garlic. However, the other side – lightly cooked cauliflower and peas in a tomato-based masala – seemed one-paced, and the centrepiece keema aloo was dominated by a welter of spiced mince. Perhaps the concise, expensive carte (featuring luxury ingredients such as lobster) shows more panache. Wine from £29.

Chef/s: Peter Joseph. **Open:** all week L 12 to 2.45, D 5.30 to 10.45. **Closed:** 1 Jan. **Meals:** alc (main courses £20 to £40). Set L £22 (2 courses) to £25. Sun L £32. Tasting menu £75. **Details:** 84 seats. Music. No children under 5 yrs after 7.

10 Greek Street

Nice vibes, sharp cooking, no reservations
Cooking score: 4
⊖ Tottenham Court Road, map 5
Modern European | £32
10 Greek Street, Soho, W1D 4DH
Tel no: (020) 7734 4677
www.10greekstreet.com

The tiny space, basic décor and tightly packed tables reflect the owners' aim to provide great food and drink without breaking the bank while the fashionably straightforward cooking is based on a zealous enthusiasm for entirely fresh ingredients. Greek Street was a mould breaker when it opened in 2012, the consistent flow has not been interrupted, despite the inevitable queues – reservations are for lunch only – and the crowds keep returning for plates of veal carpaccio with tuna mayonnaise, scurvy grass and fried capers, Dorset crab with blood orange and fennel, and wild stone bass with cime di rape and salsa verde. The kitchen shows its mettle, too, with an amazing piece of Longhorn beef (for two) served with kale, Gorgonzola potato gratin and horseradish. Desserts might include Seville orange and poppy seed marmalade cake, and almost everything on the short, modern wine list is available by the glass or carafe; bottles from £17.

Chef/s: Todd Higgs. **Open:** Mon to Sat L 12 to 2.30, D 5.30 to 10.45. **Closed:** Sun, 25 and 26 Dec, 1 Jan. **Meals:** alc (main courses £14 to £22). **Details:** 30 seats. 2 seats outside. Bar. Music.

Terroirs

Crowd-pulling bistro with great wines
Cooking score: 3
⊖ Charing Cross, map 5
French | £32
5 William IV Street, Covent Garden, WC2N 4DW
Tel no: (020) 7036 0660
www.terroirswinebar.com

Arguably, the biggest draw of this self-confident, upbeat and invariably crowded wine bar on the edge of theatreland is the extensive natural wine list, though the kitchen also puts up a good fight. Visit with friends to put the menu of small plates, cheese and charcuterie through its paces. There's nothing fancy about a dish of cuttlefish, 'nduja and samphire, but the combination of lip-tingling spicy sausage and salty samphire really rev up this underrated seafood. The *plats du jour*, including a superb boudin noir produced in the Basque Country by chef Christian Parra, are on the small side. Add a glass of 'skin-macerated white' or a juicy Beaujolais and the bill can easily mount. Though there's a cavernous basement dining room, the best seats in the house are at the zinc-topped bar where helpful waiters will guide you through the thought-provoking and brilliantly written wine list. House wine by the 500ml carafe is £13.

Chef/s: Dale Osbourne. **Open:** Mon to Sat L 12 to 3, D 5.30 to 11. **Closed:** Sun, 24 to 28 Dec, 1 Jan, bank hols. **Meals:** alc (main courses £16 to £19). **Details:** 125 seats. 6 seats outside. Bar. Music.

Join us at thegoodfoodguide.co.uk

Texture

Innovative Icelandic cuisine
Cooking score: 4
⊖ Marble Arch, map 6
Modern French/Nordic | £65
34 Portman Street, Marylebone, W1H 7BY
Tel no: (020) 7224 0028
www.texture-restaurant.co.uk

The new Scandinavian cuisine has been one of the prime drivers of international food innovation in the past decade and more, and Icelandic-born Agnar Sverrisson brings its creative alchemy to central London. Little leaves abound, as do what look like beds of dark soil, along with clouds of processed dairy product, crisp shards, bubbly foams and hunks of pure fresh fish. The take on gravadlax has all the expected ingredients, yet looks freshly coined, while a snow of Parmesan brings a counterintuitive hint of winter to new-season Wye Valley asparagus. Lightly salted Iceland cod with brandade, avocado and chorizo is a balancing act brought off with panache, and there's an almost traditional offering of best end and shoulder of Elwy spring lamb with baby carrots. The fish-based taster menu is a strong draw, and meals end with skyr – Icelandic cultured yoghurt – textured with rye breadcrumbs and Muscatel grapes and scented with vanilla. Well-heeled lovers of Riesling and Pinot Noir are in for a treat with the wine list. Prices open at £35, with small glasses from £6.

Chef/s: Agnar Sverrisson. **Open:** Tue to Sat L 12 to 2.30, D 6.30 to 10.30. **Closed:** Sun, Mon. **Meals:** alc (main courses £29 to £40). Set L £25 (2 courses) to £30. Tasting menu £79 (7 courses). **Details:** 50 seats. V menu. Bar.

Theo Randall at the InterContinental

Top-flight Italian dining
Cooking score: 6
⊖ Hyde Park Corner, map 6
Italian | £72
InterContinental London Hotel, 1 Hamilton Place, Mayfair, W1J 7QY
Tel no: (020) 7318 8747
www.theorandall.com

Theo Randall's education in Italian food began in the back of his parents' Citroën on childhood gastro-trips, the next best apprenticeship to a hardscrabble upbringing in Calabria. It's paid off in his present residency at the five-star InterContinental, where in an elegant mirrored room with mint-green and caramel upholstery, he performs the modern miracle of transporting you convincingly to southern Europe. There is some innovation, but the foundation of solid simplicity by which the appeal of Italian food abides is never far away. Kick off with fried squid on Castelluccio lentils seasoned with anchovies and chilli, prior to a primo of hop-shoot risotto dressed in Parmesan and butter. Wood-fired mains boost the umami quotient: perhaps turbot with braised fennel, spinach and capers, or pink rack of lamb with roasted artichokes, a clump of fresh veg and salsa d'erbe. Finish with Amalfi lemon tart or a vanilla-speckled pannacotta draped with poached rhubarb strands. Now's the time to explore some unfamiliar Italian varietals – Teroldego, Pecorino, Arneis. Prices open stiffly at £41.

Chef/s: Theo Randall. **Open:** Mon to Fri L 12 to 3, Mon to Sat D 6 to 11. **Closed:** Sun, 25 and 26 Dec, bank hols. **Meals:** alc (main courses £25 to £38). Set L £27 (2 courses) to £33. **Details:** 125 seats. V menu. Bar. Wheelchair access. Music. Parking.

NEW ENTRY

Tredwell's

Casual eatery for switched-on urbanites

Cooking score: 2

Leicester Square, map 5

Modern British | £32

4A Upper St Martin's Lane, Covent Garden,
WC2H 9NY

Tel no: (020) 3764 0840

www.tredwells.com

Tredwell was the butler in Agatha Christie's novel *The Seven Dials Mystery*, but there's nothing puzzling about this casual mid-price eatery from high-flying Marcus Wareing. Inside, it's a straight-up blend of green-and-white tiling, copper work and Edison light bulbs, with 'far too many' overeager young staff in Victorian-style waistcoats hovering around – 'slightly Steampunk', noted one visitor. The food is a mixed bag of populist offerings: a 'taste of Tredwell's' brings sliders, charred bread with chorizo jam and sticky glazed chicken wings to share, or you might go for pickled beetroot with goats' cheese and walnut pesto. Steaks and burgers made from Lake District beef are a popular call, while other mains are fancily plated up – perhaps corn-fed chicken breast with leg croquette, broad beans and girolles or sea bass with cashews, carrots and coriander. For afters, an 'uncooked-style' cheesecake laced with G&T has gone down handsomely. Cocktails, craft beers and global wines (from £26) complete a sociable offer.

Chef/s: Chantelle Nicholson. **Open:** Mon to Wed L 12 to 3, D 5 to 10.30. Thur to Sun 12 to 11 (9 Sun). **Meals:** alc (main courses £13 to £29). **Details:** 130 seats.

Trishna

Classy Indian seafood

Cooking score: 4

Marylebone, Bond Street, map 6

Indian/Seafood | £65

15-17 Blandford Street, Marylebone,
W1U 3DG

Tel no: (020) 7935 5624

www.trishnalondon.com

Leaving younger sister Gymkhana (see entry) to grab most of the headlines, dining at Trishna is a more discreet affair. The interior has a relaxing feel and casual vibe: think bricked walls painted white and complemented by shades of grey, antique mirrors, wood floor, pendant lighting, marble-topped tables, big band jazz music. The seafood-centric menu is buffed up by a variety of tasting options, and the output from Karam Sethi's kitchen is classy. Materials and treatments are varied, ranging from quail fried with black pepper and Keralan spices and teamed with French beans and softened onions via a creamy caldine jheenga curry of tiger prawns with poppy seeds to duck breasts cooked in the tandoor oven. An everyday dish of sag aloo is given a lift by deep-fried onions, and beetroot and fennel brûlée, paired with mandarin sorbet and candied ginger, is a pleasant way to end. Attentive staff keep everything on track. A page of premium labels heads the noteworthy wine list (from £26).

Chef/s: Karam Sethi. **Open:** all week L 12 to 2.30 (3 Sun), D 6 to 10.30 (5.30 Sat, 5.30 to 9.45 Sun). **Closed:** 25 to 27 Dec, 1 to 3 Jan. **Meals:** alc (main courses £16 to £24). Set L £19 (2 courses) to £24. Set D £28. Tasting menu £55. **Details:** 60 seats. 5 seats outside. V menu. Wheelchair access. Music. No children after 8 in restaurant.

28°-50°

Wine-centric bistro
Cooking score: 4
◉ Bond Street, map 6
French | £32
15-17 Marylebone Lane, Marylebone,
W1U 2NE
Tel no: (020) 7486 7922
www.2850.co.uk

Putting food and wine on an equal footing,
Agnar Sverrisson's 28°-50° concept of lively
bistro/wine bars has reached three outlets in
the capital (the other two are in Mayfair and
the City) and he also runs Texture (see entry),
which is a high-powered joint off Oxford
Street. Far hipper than your average wine bar,
expect an urban finish here on Marylebone
Lane, with exposed ducting, lots of natural
wood and a zinc-topped horseshoe bar where
hanging glasses shimmer like chandeliers. The
menu deals in 'above average offerings at
reasonable prices', modern bistro dishes that
deliver feel-good flavours, perhaps scallops
with pea purée, pancetta and lemon confit,
onglet cooked rare with a simple béarnaise
sauce and some skinny fries, even a fish pie and
cheese burger. Over 30 different wines are
offered by the 75ml, 125ml, or 250ml glass, so
finding something to your taste is very easy:
'we had 75ml glasses of eight different wines,
which gave us a lovely representation of what
the wine list could offer.' Bottles from £21.
The Mayfair branch houses the group's first
Champagne bar: 17-19 Maddox Street, W1S
2QH; tel: (020) 7495 1505.
Chef/s: Ben Meuor. **Open:** Mon to Sat L 12 to 2.30,
D 6 to 10 (10.30 Thur to Sat). **Closed:** Sun, 25 Dec, 1
Jan. **Meals:** alc (main courses £21 to £45). Set L £17
(2 courses) to £20. **Details:** 59 seats. 16 seats
outside. Wheelchair access. Music.

Umu

Britain's only Kyoto-style restaurant
Cooking score: 5
◉ Green Park, Bond Street, map 5
Japanese | £100
14-16 Bruton Place, Mayfair, W1J 6LX
Tel no: (020) 7499 8881
www.umurestaurant.com

In the heart of well-upholstered Mayfair,
Umu's claim to be the only Kyoto-inspired
restaurant in the UK is a fair enough USP. The
sliding wood door with its touch-panel effects
a *Star Trek*-style entry to a world of tranquil
courtesy, with traditional wood screens and
knowledgable waiting staff. Exquisitely
presented Japanese dishes, informed by ancient
technique (Yoshinori Ishii teaches meticulous
practice to the Cornish fishermen who supply
much of the catch for sashimi) are the order of
the day, and there are flourishes of palate-
priming innovation too. Spider crab with
celeriac purée in ginger tosazu sauce may be
among the market specials, while a cool £95
will get you a serving of Grade II charcoal-
grilled Wagyu in ponzu. Pair the sushi options
with morsels such as langoustine and ginger,
or red mullet with pesto and bottarga, and
finish with a poached clementine with
chestnut-tofu purée. A splendid saké list is
bolstered by a list of world-class wines
from £35.
Chef/s: Yoshinori Ishii. **Open:** Mon to Fri L 12 to 2,
Mon to Sat D 6 to 10. **Closed:** Sun, 25 Dec to 5 Jan,
bank hols. **Meals:** alc (main courses £22 to £95). Set
L £35. Kaiseki menu £125 (8 courses). **Details:** 55
seats. Wheelchair access.

Vinoteca

Welcoming, buzzy, bibulous brasserie
Cooking score: 2
⊖ Marble Arch, map 6
Modern European | £28
15 Seymour Place, Marylebone, W1H 5BD
Tel no: (020) 7724 7288
www.vinoteca.co.uk

 £30

The growing Vinoteca group has made a big impact on London since opening in Farringdon six years ago, and everybody has a good word to say about this Marylebone branch. The all-embracing European-influenced menus scream seasonal credentials, offering everything from sautéed Mersea octopus with gem lettuce, samphire and cocoa beans or house-made venison chorizo with pickled chanterelles and bruschetta, to cod fillet with Tokyo turnip, tomato and wild garlic. If you can resist the never-off-the-menu grilled, marinated bavette steak, try the grilled Middle White pork chop with chickpeas, spinach and aïoli. Desserts such as cinnamon-dusted doughnuts with dark chocolate sauce hit all the right spots, but there are exemplary British cheeses from Neal's Yard Dairy, too. On the wine front, the ever-evolving list of nearly 300 bins offers an excellent choice by the glass – it pays to turn up early (or pray your guest is late) and perhaps knock back that sneaky first glass. Bottles from £16.50.
Chef/s: William Lauder. **Open:** all week L 12 to 2.45, Mon to Sat D 6 to 10.30. **Closed:** 24 Dec to 1 Jan. **Meals:** alc (main courses £13 to £17). **Details:** 55 seats. Music.

Wild Honey

Grown-up food in an upbeat setting
Cooking score: 5
⊖ Oxford Circus, Bond Street, map 5
Modern European | £60
12 St George Street, Mayfair, W1S 2FB
Tel no: (020) 7758 9160
www.wildhoneyrestaurant.co.uk

There's nothing wild about this smart Mayfair address, though the operation is as slick and silky as honey. Sadly for some, Wild Honey is not the steal it once was, when it brought Soho dining and prices to Mayfair (off the back of the success of its big brother, Arbutus, see entry). The main distinction between the two now is in its suave sophistication, both in looks and calm demeanour. Clubby wood panelling, curving low-slung red leather banquettes and funky yellow chairs cut a sharp look, and there's a marble-topped counter for fashionable bar dining. The cooking is likewise modern, light and seasonally aware. Luxury ingredients dominate the roster of skilfully balanced, neatly dressed plates, in dishes such as wild turbot, perhaps teamed with asparagus, Jersey Royals, Cornish shellfish and sea greens, while a signature offering of roasted rabbit saddle comes with slow-cooked shoulder cottage pie, gnocchi, morels, peas and lime. The equally slick global wine list delivers a good two dozen by glass and carafe (with bottles from £35).
Chef/s: Anthony Demetre and Jamie McCallum. **Open:** Mon to Sat L 12 to 2.30 (3 Sun), D 6 to 10.30. **Closed:** Sun, 25 and 26 Dec, bank hols. **Meals:** alc (main courses £24 to £38). Set L £30. Set early D £40. **Details:** 50 seats.

Wiltons

Upholding the best of British traditions
Cooking score: 4
⊖ Green Park, map 5
British | £90
55 Jermyn Street, Mayfair, SW1Y 6LX
Tel no: (020) 7629 9955
www.wiltons.co.uk

Reassuringly old fashioned, Wiltons welcomes with velvet-lined, wood-panelled comfort and this is a large part of its charm. What is also clear is that the cooking doesn't seek to astound or amaze; rather it focuses on simple, high-quality ingredients – fish and shellfish have always been a speciality – and if you start with the best possible ingredients and don't overcomplicate matters, then you can hardly go wrong. From this perspective the food is well judged and precisely rendered, if pricey. As one fan put it: 'the lobster and crab omelette at £32 was the most expensive we have ever had, but was terrific'. Those on a budget should look to the seasonal set menu, say delicate smoked mackerel with a refreshing, crunchy radish salad and tangy rhubarb compote, and rainbow trout, crushed new potatoes and a perfectly buttery sauce 'with just a hint of sweetness', making a wonderful follow-on. Proper puddings, though, may not be quite up to the same standard. On the wine front, prices are not cheap, with bottles from £30.
Chef/s: Daniel Kent. **Open:** Mon to Fri L 12 to 2.30, Mon to Sat D 5.30 to 10.30. **Closed:** Sun, 24 Dec to 3 Jan, bank hols. **Meals:** alc (main courses £18 to £60). Set L and D £30 (2 courses) to £38.
Details: 120 seats. Bar. Wheelchair access.

Symbols

🛏 Accommodation is available
£30 Three courses for less than £30
£5 OFF £5-off voucher scheme
🍾 Notable wine list

The Wolseley

The mother of all grand cafés
Cooking score: 2
⊖ Green Park, map 5
Modern European | £40
160 Piccadilly, Mayfair, W1J 9EB
Tel no: (020) 7499 6996
www.thewolseley.com

Conceived by serial restaurateurs Chris Corbin and Jeremy King (see the Delaunay, the Colbert et al), the Wolseley is the mother of all grand cafés – a monumental, almost cinematic space with towering black columns, dramatic arches, marble floors and sparkling chandeliers. The Wolseley's day kicks off as one of the most sought-after breakfast spaces in town, then the huge transcontinental menu rumbles its way through caviar and crustacea, chopped liver and steak tartare, schnitzels and soufflé suisse. There's also room for burgers, salade niçoise, kedgeree and choucroute alsacienne, before the inevitable stop-off for some gorgeously calorific Viennese patisserie – think Black Forest gâteau, chocolate eclairs, strudels, sachertorte and suchlike. Delectable ice cream coupes and three-tiered afternoon teas are yet more reasons to scramble for a table. The ample wine list starts at £19.95.
Chef/s: Lawrence Keogh. **Open:** all week 7am to midnight (8am Sat, 8am to 11pm Sun). **Meals:** alc (main courses £12 to £45). **Details:** 140 seats. V menu. Bar. Wheelchair access.

Wright Brothers Soho

Oysters and zingy Asian flavours
Cooking score: 2
⊖ Oxford Circus, map 5
Seafood | £35
13 Kingly Street, Soho, W1B 5PW
Tel no: (020) 7434 3611
www.thewrightbrothers.co.uk

As seafood specialists, Wright Brothers are making their presence felt right across the capital, but this Soho outlet remains a firm favourite. Spread over three floors, the space looks in great shape following its 2014 makeover, with a custom-built 'raw bar' at street level and blood-red banquettes in the smart upstairs dining room. Oysters from near and far are still the mainstays, but the kitchen now adds some Asian spice, fire and zing to many of its small plates – think seared swordfish with pearl barley miso, tuna tartare with avocado and ponzu or tempura of soft-shell crab with jalapeño dressing. Elsewhere, larger dishes might see skate wing with chilli jam as well as whole plaice with salsa verde or grilled native lobster with chips and garlic butter. Affluent meat eaters can treat themselves to slabs of Australian Wagyu, while puds might bring palate-cleansing lychee granita. The fish-loving wine list starts at £21.

Chef/s: Sasha Ziverts. **Open:** all week L 12 to 3, D 5 to 11 (9 Sun). **Closed:** bank hols. **Meals:** alc (main courses £14 to £48). Set L £19 (2 courses) to £22. **Details:** 78 seats. 32 seats outside. Bar. Music.

Yauatcha

Marvellous dim sum with a dash of style
Cooking score: 4
⊖ Tottenham Court Road, map 5
Chinese | £40
15-17 Broadwick Street, Soho, W1F 0DL
Tel no: (020) 7494 8888
www.yauatcha.com

Yauatcha continues to draw the crowds after more than a decade, its distinctive electric blue tint marking out its corner plot. There's a choice of two floors: the stylish ground floor is great for people-watching, but downstairs, moody illumination makes the room feel like a mysterious subterranean world. 'Excellent' dim sum is the calling card here, and 'they are marvellous': whether king crab Shanghai siew long bun 'that popped in the mouth' or prawn and crispy bean curd cheung fun, as well as Wagyu beef puffs, they all set the bar high. Larger plates are equally delicious, stir-fried scallops and prawns are accorded due respect by asparagus with black pepper and chilli, while desserts 'look like edible works of art' with a layered cake of passion fruit, mango, coconut and pandan 'worthy of the catwalk'.

An extensive selection of teas and a wine list, starting from £29, complements the style of food.

Chef/s: Tong Chee Hwee. **Open:** all week 12 to 11.30 (10.30 Sun). **Closed:** 25 and 26 Dec. **Meals:** alc (main courses £12 to £30). **Details:** 191 seats. V menu.

Zoilo

Dynamic Argentinian food
Cooking score: 2
⊖ Bond Street, map 6
Argentinian | £30
9 Duke Street, Marylebone, W1U 3EG
Tel no: (020) 7486 9699
www.zoilo.co.uk

Stray into the hinterland north of Oxford Street's cacophony and civilisation dawns once more, not least in the form of Diego Jacquet's lively Argentinian bistro, which features a ground-floor room centred on a long bar, with kitchen-counter seating downstairs. The atmosphere is as racy and authentic as tango, and the food full of brightly spiced, eclectic appeal. Empanadas filled with chicken, peppers, shallots and cumin, and snacking items such as Provoleta cheese with almonds and oregano honey, establish the mood. Ceviche is a dependable feature, made with sea bass, while mussel escabèche may be the bracing accompaniment to grilled octopus and Jerusalem artichokes, and it wouldn't be Argentina without substantial cuts of thoroughbred beef, or perhaps a chimichurri burger with smoked bacon, Provolone and pickles. Finish with the signature crème brûlée made with dulce de leche, served with banana ice cream. The all-Argentinian wine list offers rose-fragrant Torrontes, beefy Malbecs and many other varietals, from £21.95.

Chef/s: Diego Jacquet. **Open:** Mon to Sat L 12 to 2.30, D 5.30 to 10.30. **Closed:** Sun, 2 days Christmas. **Meals:** alc (tapas £7 to £24). Set L £10 (2 courses). **Details:** 48 seats. Wheelchair access. Music.

Join us at thegoodfoodguide.co.uk

L'Absinthe

⊖ Chalk Farm, map 2
French | £24
40 Chalcot Road, Primrose Hill, NW1 8LS
Tel no: (020) 7483 4848
www.labsinthe.co.uk

There's a real feeling of Gallic bonhomie about this bourgeois bistro-deli-cum-bar that's just a stone's throw from Regent's Park in Primrose Hill. Visitors are drawn by the warmth of the service and the menu of honestly crafted French classics. There's plenty of good stuff on offer: leeks vinaigrette with poached egg; beef bourguignon; duck confit; chocolate mousse; apple tarte Tatin with clotted cream ice cream. House wine is £18.75, or buy a bottle in the shop and add £10 corkage. Closed Mon D.

The Albion

Lively local with no-frills Brit food
Cooking score: 2
⊖ Angel, Highbury & Islington, map 2
British | £35
10 Thornhill Road, Islington, N1 1HW
Tel no: (020) 7607 7450
www.the-albion.co.uk

Once upon a time the Albion had a rural outlook, but that was in the 18th century. A covering of wisteria on the Georgian façade brings a bit of rustic charm to the urban setting, while the walled garden out back is positively idyllic for a good part of the year. The interior has been left well alone – save for a lick of heritage paint – with a smattering of armchairs and real fire. The service doesn't always match the happy mood of the customers. The kitchen team set the tone with appealing partnerships taking a British and European perspective; slow-roasted smoked pork shoulder, say, among the 'small plates', served with trotters, butter beans and toast, or a 'large plate' of corn-fed chicken with confit wing and a 'slaw' made with pine nuts and spring onion. Steaks cooked on the grill,

Sunday roasts and weekend brunches entrench it further in the community. Wines start at £18.
Chef/s: Philip Kain. **Open:** Mon to Sat L 12 to 3 (4 Sat), D 6 to 10. Sun 12 to 9. **Closed:** 1 Jan. **Meals:** alc (main courses £12 to £24). **Details:** 80 seats. 90 seats outside. Bar. Wheelchair access. Music.

Almeida

Attractive brasserie food at an old favourite
Cooking score: 2
⊖ Angel, Highbury & Islington, map 2
French | £40
30 Almeida Street, Islington, N1 1AD
Tel no: (020) 7354 4777
www.almeida-restaurant.co.uk

The good old Almeida has finally enjoyed a refurb, and looks all the better for it, with dark-wood elements closing in what could often feel a rather oceanic space, and a wine wall to tempt you to get stuck in. A semi-open kitchen invites peeps from the nosiest, and the place is still flooded with natural light from full-drop windows, a particular lure on light evenings when the pre-theatre crowds flock in. Tommy Boland's attractive Anglo-French brasserie menus take in roast foie gras with pear textures, almonds and honeycomb, followed by halibut and mussels with creamed watercress and ricotta gnocchi, or black-leg chicken with an onion tart and spinach. Finish with baked vanilla cheesecake and citrus fruits, or prune and Earl Grey soufflé with milk ice. House French is £21.50, or £5.50 a glass, on a list that vaults with compact agility up to the heady realms of *grand cru* Burgundy.
Chef/s: Tommy Boland. **Open:** Tue to Sun L 12 to 2.30 (3.30 Sun), Mon to Sat D 5.30 to 10.30. **Closed:** 26 Dec, 1 Jan. **Meals:** alc (main meals £18 to £27). Set L and D £19 (2 courses) to £22. Sun L £20 (2 courses) to £25. Tasting menu £45. **Details:** 120 seats. 15 seats outside. Bar. Wheelchair access.

Anima e Cuore

Italian

129 Kentish Town Road, Kentish Town,
NW1 8PB
Tel no: (020) 7267 2410

'A really convivial, warm Italian. The pasta is
phenomenal, authentic and delicious. I had
salt-cod ravioli with sardines and polenta.'

Bradleys

Long-running French favourite
Cooking score: 3
⊖ Swiss Cottage, map 2
French | £40

25 Winchester Road, Swiss Cottage, NW3 3NR
Tel no: (020) 7722 3457
www.bradleysnw3.co.uk

Simon Bradley's self-named restaurant has
been feeding the denizens of Swiss Cottage
and showtimers from the nearby Hampstead
Theatre since 1993, and is still packing them
in. It has also kept its good looks, with a
soothing mix of pastel shades, dark
woodwork and contemporary artwork
reflecting the kitchen's fondness for modern
Anglo-French flavours. Ingredients are spot-
on, and fish from the Brixham day boats is
always a good call – perhaps grilled fillet of
turbot with leeks, cauliflower and mushroom
duxelle or sea bass with ceps, celery, basil and
salsify. Elsewhere, there is craftsmanship and
creativity in abundance, whether you fancy
salt-baked beetroot with mâche, goats' milk
purée, burnt apple and walnuts or a Med-
inspired plate of Barbary duck breast with a
leg-meat croustillant, crushed turnips, cavolo
nero and Seville orange. To conclude, fine
British and Gallic cheeses vie with tiramisu or
hot prune and Armagnac soufflé. A
thoroughly commendable, French-led wine
list does the place proud, with bottles
from £19.
Chef/s: Simon Bradley. **Open:** all week L 12 to 3,
Mon to Sat D 5.30 to 10.30. **Meals:** alc (main
courses £17 to £23). Set L £17 (2 courses) to £21. Set
D £28. Sun L £26. **Details:** 60 seats. V menu.

The Bull & Last

Tried-and-true modern Brit dishes
Cooking score: 3
⊖ Tufnell Park, Kentish Town, map 2
Modern British | £36

168 Highgate Road, Hampstead, NW5 1QS
Tel no: (020) 7267 3641
www.thebullandlast.co.uk

'Even though it has been open for many years,
still feels as popular as ever,' noted one visitor
to this welcoming pub and restaurant that
offers an ideal refueling spot after a bracing
walk on nearby Hampstead Heath. You can eat
downstairs in the bar or in the upstairs dining
area at busier times. The ever-changing menu
mixes inventive rustic creations alongside
traditional classics, with one reporter giving
the thumbs-up to a meal that opened with
oxtail tortellini, French snails, garlic butter
and herbs, and went on to a main course of
confit of rabbit leg, with wild garlic, ratte
potatoes and wild mushrooms. 'Do leave room
for dessert' is sound advice, as alongside
traditional favourites such as blueberry
cheesecake or apple crumble, there's a selection
of homemade ice creams and some good
artisan cheeses. There's an interesting slate of
real ales and a balanced wine list (from £18).
Chef/s: Oliver Pudney. **Open:** all week L 12 to 3
(12.30 to 4 Sat and Sun), D 6.30 to 10 (9 Sun).
Closed: 24 to 26 Dec. **Meals:** alc (main courses £15
to £25), Set D £38. Sun L £38. **Details:** 40 seats. 25
seats outside. Bar. Music.

Caravan

Buzzing, laid-back brunch spot
Cooking score: 2
⊖ King's Cross, map 2
Global | £28

Granary Building, 1 Granary Square, King's
Cross, N1C 4AA
Tel no: (020) 7101 7661
www.caravankingscross.co.uk

This cavernous hangout on Granary Square,
in the revitalised King's Cross area, draws in a
perpetual stream of hipsters, fashion students

and other creative young things to gorge on its Antipodean-style fare. Caravan's pick-and-mix menu and laid-back setting are tailored to all-day grazing (though breakfast-brunch is a major draw). Full-throttle flavours hold forth throughout: expect to see eggs every which way and chilli-spiked cornbread, along with courgette and corn fritters, chilli jam, herbed feta and rocket, or a 'Caravan fry' with St John bakery bread. The judicious addition of bright, fresh herbs and spices lifts every dish a few decibels. Try, perhaps, crispy soft-shell crab, red lentil dhal, tomato kasundi and yoghurt and – to finish – affogato with Caravan's own-blend espresso (coffee connoisseurs can rest assured that they are well served by excellent house-roasted brews). But be prepared to queue and jostle – weekend brunch is a first come, first served affair. Wines from £18.

Chef/s: Miles Kirby. **Open:** Mon to Fri 8am to 10.30pm. Sat and Sun 10 to 4, Sat D 5 to 10.30. **Closed:** 25, 26 and 31 Dec, 1 Jan. **Meals:** alc (main courses £15 to £23). **Details:** 120 seats. 70 seats outside. Bar. Wheelchair access. Music.

Le Coq

Buzzy neighbourhood rotisserie
Cooking score: 2
⊖ Highbury & Islington, map 2
Modern European | £22
292-294 St Paul's Road, Islington, N1 2LH
Tel no: (020) 7359 5055
www.le-coq.co.uk

The chickens had a free-range life in Sutton Hoo in Suffolk, the bread comes from a social enterprise bakery, charcuterie is cured down the road and the ice cream is from Gelupo in Soho – suffice to say the good people at Le Coq haven't gone into the chicken business half-cocked. The room is a no-frills space with white walls and tightly packed tables and the vibe is suitably breezy and unpretentious. The chicken arrives hot off the rotisserie in generous portions in the company of kohlrabi and cabbage slaw sexed up with cashews and pomegranate, or creamed chard and mustard,

while on Sundays the likes of wild salmon and shoulder of lamb get a turn. Start with apple, burrata and honey salad, or deep-fried squid with smoked garlic mayo, and end on a sweet note with those ice creams or ginger and treacle tart. Wines start at £22.

Chef/s: Adam Middleton. **Open:** Thur to Sat L 12 to 3, all week D 5 to 10.30. Sun 12 to 9. **Closed:** 24 Dec to 2 Jan. **Meals:** Set L and D £17 (2 courses) to £22. Sun L £21 (2 courses) to £25. **Details:** 40 seats. Music.

NEW ENTRY

Dishoom

Chip off the old Bombay block
Cooking score: 2
⊖ King's Cross, map 2
Indian | £30
5 Stable Street, King's Cross, N1C 4AB
Tel no: (020) 7420 9321
www.dishoom.com

Described by one reporter as the 'the lovechild of a Bombay brasserie and a 19th-century factory', this lively, cavernous chip off the old Bombay block (in St Martin's Lane and Shoreditch, see entries) is proving a hit, complete with reports of queues even on wintry evenings: '45 minutes and an aromatic cocktail later, we'd all but forgotten the night outside'. Look past the faux industrial clichés of brick, wood, ducting and scaffolding to the kitchen and there's the same studied craft that has earned its siblings legions of fans. Opening early enough for breakfast, there's a casual approach to eating. From a selection of dishes ordered across the table and arriving in a seemingly haphazard way – 'somehow, amid the crazy bustle, it works' – could come a standout creamy black house dhal, sheekh kebab, chicken biryani, muttar paneer, wafer-thin roomali roti, and a satin-smooth sweet mango kulfi on a stick. Lovely service, too, and wines from £19.90.

Chef/s: Naved Nasir. **Open:** all week 8am to 11pm (9am Sat and Sun, midnight Thur to Sat). **Closed:** 25 and 26 Dec, 1 and 2 Jan. **Meals:** alc (main courses from £5 to £21). **Details:** 250 seats. 20 seats outside. Bar. Wheelchair access. Music.

500 Restaurant

Genuine, reliable neighbourhood Italian
Cooking score: 2
⊖ Archway, map 2
Italian | £28
782 Holloway Road, Archway, N19 3JH
Tel no: (020) 7272 3406
www.500restaurant.co.uk

'Consistently excellent, we have eaten here regularly since it opened in 2008. Dishes are seasonal, with truffles in autumn, and fritto misto in summer.' It's good to note that Mario Magli and Giorgio Pili's 'Cinquecento' continues to be a reliable favourite in Archway. Casual, unpretentious and noted for honest regional cooking, expect to start with sweet sardines or lasagnette di pane (layers of Sardinian crisp bread) with crabmeat and diced tomatoes, although the tagliere 500 is worth considering 'but only to share': a long platter with small portions of most of the starters. Elsewhere, there could be taglierini with funghi, char-grilled T-bone veal with roasted baby carrots and dry Martini and herbs, or a regular special of controfiletto with Dijon mustard, and lavender-flavoured pannacotta with pear and cinnamon compote. Italian wines start at £14.50.
Chef/s: Mario Magli. **Open:** Fri and Sat L 12 to 3, Mon to Sat D 6 to 10.30. Sun 12 to 9.30. **Closed:** Christmas, 2 weeks Aug, bank hols. **Meals:** alc (main courses £12 to £17). **Details:** 37 seats. Music.

Grain Store

Putting vegetables in the spotlight
Cooking score: 4
⊖ King's Cross, map 2
Global | £25
Granary Square, 1-3 Stable Street, King's Cross, N1C 4AB
Tel no: (020) 7324 4466
www.grainstore.com

A warehouse conversion on the magnificently regenerated Granary Square provides the dramatic setting for this sociable eatery from chef Bruno Loubet – imagine a cavernous and versatile space mixing high-spec industrial chic and touches of gentrified rusticity, with an 'exploded kitchen' at the heart of things. The cooking is clever, enlightened and versatile too, ushering vegetables and greenery into the spotlight, consigning meat and fish to supporting roles, and plundering the world larder for ideas – witness roast endives in kimchee butter with courgette spaghetti and hot-smoked sea trout or ginger and cardamom heritage carrots with Swiss chard and freekeh-stuffed quail. Vegetarians are particularly well served here – in fact, the Grain Store really does 'cater for everyone', whether your penchant is for pickled Tokyo turnips and cucumber with radish, borage, oyster leaves and XO sauce or tapioca 'caviar' with fermented corn brioche, seaweed butter and crème fraîche. In short, this is refreshingly incisive food 'of the highest quality' – just add a gregarious Italianate piazza, seasonal cocktails and a forward-thinking list of organic wines from £22.
Chef/s: Bruno Loubet. **Open:** Mon to Sat 10am to 11.30pm (midnight Thur to Sat). Sun 11 to 4.
Meals: alc (main courses £8 to £16). **Details:** 140 seats. 75 seats outside. V menu. Wheelchair access. Music.

Jin Kichi

Japanese local worth travelling for
Cooking score: 2
⊖ Hampstead, map 2
Japanese | £35
73 Heath Street, Hampstead, NW3 6UG
Tel no: (020) 7794 6158
www.jinkichi.com

In the heart of Hampstead, Jin Kichi delights with its range of accomplished Japanese dishes and exceptionally friendly staff. With only a small number of seats, it's worth making a reservation if you plan to go at busy times as queues can quickly develop, and do try for a seat at the bar if possible, to watch the chef work the open robata grill. Grilled skewers are a speciality with yakitori (chicken and onion) and kamonegi (duck and spring onion) the highlights. At a test meal, we were impressed by the quality of the freshly prepared sushi but less so by the hour-long wait for its arrival – however, the very long wait was mitigated by trying other dishes; the delicately fried tempura and butashoga (pan-fried pork with ginger sauce) were further highlights. To accompany the food, saké is a popular choice, but for those who prefer wine, a very limited selection starts at a toppy £28.

Chef/s: Rei Shimazu. **Open:** Tue to Sun L 12.30 to 2, D 6 to 11 (10 Sun). **Closed:** Mon, 25 and 26 Dec. **Meals:** alc (main courses £8 to £17). **Details:** 44 seats.

Karpo

A King's Cross asset
Cooking score: 1
⊖ King's Cross, map 2
Modern European | £35
23 Euston Road, King's Cross, NW1 2SD
Tel no: (020) 7843 2221
www.karpo.co.uk

Opposite King's Cross-St Pancras (and part of the Megaro Hotel), Karpo's concept appeals to a broader age range than the zany graffiti-covered frontage and pseudo-industrial theme within might suggest. Good service and relaxed formality are part of the appeal, as is the all-day opening offering breakfast, weekend brunch and modern European brasserie dishes (with coffee and pastries to fill in the gaps). Dishes are straightforward, as in a classic Caesar salad, confit pork belly with prunes and mashed potato, or Josper-grilled Herdwick lamb chops with mint béarnaise and watercress, and there is a good burger and seafood pappardelle, too. Finish with Bramley apple crumble. Wines from £20.

Chef/s: Kimmo Makkonen. **Open:** Mon to Fri 7am to 10pm. Sat and Sun 8am to 10pm (9pm Sun). **Meals:** alc (main courses £13 to £25). Set L £15 (2 courses) to £18. **Details:** 84 seats. Bar. Wheelchair access. Music.

Made Bar & Kitchen

Spirited food in garrulous surroundings
Cooking score: 3
⊖ Chalk Farm, map 2
Modern European | £28
Roundhouse, Chalk Farm Road, Camden, NW1 8EH
Tel no: (020) 7424 8495
www.roundhouse.org.uk

With gig posters plastered on the wall, a long bar and a generally garrulous cacophony filling the air, this casual glass-fronted joint attached to the iconic Roundhouse feels a bit like a grown-up take on a students' union, with the bonus of some spirited modern food. Mediterranean influences abound, from starters of monkfish carpaccio with deep-fried lovage leaves to mains such as a duo of guinea fowl with girolles, samphire and gnocchi or halibut with crushed new potatoes, broad beans, rhubarb and Prosecco dressing. There are also steaks and burgers from the grill, cut-price fish lunches on Fridays and a handful of desserts including a summery take on tiramisu involving verbena and strawberries. Breakfast and weekend brunch are added attractions for the early crowd. Alternatively, hang out at the bar with some duck croquettes and BBQ chicken wings plus a pint of ale from the locally based Camden Brewery. Drinkers can also invest in cocktails, and there are plenty of wines from £18.

Chef/s: Jean-Baptiste Barbosa. **Open:** Tue to Sun L 12 to 3, D 5 to 9. **Closed:** Mon. **Meals:** alc (main courses £12 to £17). **Details:** 54 seats. Bar.

LOCAL GEMS

Majjo's Khana Khayae

⊖ East Finchley, map 2
Indian | £18
7 Fortis Green, East Finchley, N2 9JR
Tel no: (020) 8883 4357
www.majjos.com

The family-run, deli-style takeaway has been an East Finchley favourite for more than 30 years, so loyal supporters are delighted there's now a restaurant next door, offering authentic north Indian/Pakistani cuisine based on family recipes and fresh ingredients. The cooking is consistently good, varied in flavour and very good value. Samosas are light and crisp, and there is good papri chaat as well as tender char-grilled lamb chops, chicken ginger, sag aloo and excellent dhal. It's 'unpretentious, unexpected' and unlicensed, so you can BYO corkage free. Open Tue to Sat D only.

Mangal 1 Ocakbasi

⊖ **Dalston Kingsland, map 2**
Turkish | £18
10 Arcola Street, Stoke Newington, E8 2DJ
Tel no: (020) 7275 8981
www.mangal1.com

In a postcode where there are almost as many kebab shops as residents, Mangal 1 Ocakbasi still reigns as the heavyweight champion of Stoke Newington grills. Hummus, lahmacun (Turkish-style pizza) and salads are the support acts inside the spartan, whitewashed dining room, but the star of the show will always be the mangal itself – a sizzling steel barbecue that's a production line for tender kebabs. Expect big, muscular flavours in favourites like cop sis and adana kofte – along with more unusual options like bildircin (grilled quails). Turkish beers and wines are available, though most bring their own. Open all week.

Market

Camden's best neighbourhood restaurant
Cooking score: 2
⊖ **Camden Town, map 2**
Modern British | £30
43 Parkway, Camden, NW1 7PN
Tel no: (020) 7267 9700
www.marketrestaurant.co.uk

'Market' to most people in Camden conjures up images of thumping music, questionable tattoos and clouds of exotic tobacco smoke. By contrast, Market the restaurant looks a study in understatement – a dining room with timber floors, exposed brick walls and tall windows looking out to the hubbub of Parkway. The kitchen follows the same no-nonsense philosophy, its modern British dishes assembled with a zealous insistence on seasonality. A scan through the starters might yield beetroot-cured salmon, with cucumber, dill and rye bread – or else something as simple and satisfying as Dorset brown crab spread over toast. The meat-heavy main selection showcases gutsy flavours: our inspection took in a deftly cooked Lake District lamb topside – worthy of a Wordsworth sonnet in its tenderness – served alongside spring vegetables, and a delicate main of skate on a bed of tomatoes, capers, basil and shallots. Sign off with the likes of citrus cheesecake and blood-orange sorbet. Wines are affordable, starting at £18.

Chef/s: Richard Teague. **Open:** all week L 12 to 2.30 (11 to 3 Sun), Mon to Sat D 6 to 10.30. **Closed:** 24 Dec to 2 Jan. **Meals:** alc (main courses £14 to £26). Set L £10 (2 courses). Set D £18 (2 courses) to £20. **Details:** 48 seats. 4 seats outside. Music.

Odette's

Letting quality ingredients do the talking
Cooking score: 5
⊖ **Chalk Farm, map 2**
Modern British | £42
130 Regent's Park Road, Primrose Hill, NW1 8XL
Tel no: (020) 7586 8569
www.odettesprimrosehill.com

'For modern British cooking and a pleasant dining experience in north London that won't break the bank, Odette's fits the bill,' pronounced one reader, and such praise is echoed in many reports for chef/proprietor Bryn Williams' contemporary restaurant. People love the way the place strikes just the right note for a neighbourhood eatery. They applaud pleasant service ('considerate and unhurried') and the 'imaginative and well-executed' cooking with its emphasis on good-quality, seasonal ingredients. An admirably short menu of five choices per course (plus tasting-menu option) piques the interest immediately with openers such as crab lasagne with mushroom, ham and parsley and, to follow, Goosnargh duck breast with tarte fine, blood orange and crushed turnips. Dessert may see a pistachio cake teamed with apple terrine and green apple sorbet. The compact wine list (from £19.75) is vigorously marked-up, but there is reasonably priced choice by the glass or carafe.

Chef/s: Bryn Williams and Jamie Randall. **Open:** Tue to Sun L 12 to 2.30 (3 Sat and Sun), D 6 to 10 (10.30 Sat, 9.30 Sun). **Closed:** Mon, first week Jan. **Meals:** alc (main courses £17 to £23). Set L £13 (2 courses) to £15. Set D £17 (2 courses) to £20. Sun L £32. Tasting menu £52. **Details:** 56 seats. 24 seats outside. V menu. Music.

LOCAL GEM

Osteria Tufo

⊖ Finsbury Park, map 2
Italian | £25
67 Fonthill Road, Finsbury Park, N4 3HZ
Tel no: (020) 7272 2911
www.osteriatufo.co.uk

From its menu of Italian classics to its ebullient hosts, this place is every inch a neighbourhood osteria – crammed, buzzy and a lot of fun. Pasta is made in-house, every wine (Italian, naturally) is available by the glass, and a table on the little terrace is the place to be when the mercury rises. Scottish beef carpaccio with caponata, ricotta and spinach ravioli, whole sea bass, and duck breast with porcini risotto – all good, unpretentious stuff. Wines from £16. Open Tue to Sun D, and Sun L in summer.

Parlour

All-day comfort food pit-stop
Cooking score: 2
⊖ Kensal Green, map 1
British | £30
5 Regent Street, Kensal Green, NW10 5LG
Tel no: (020) 8969 2184
www.parlourkensal.com

In a part of town where 'frankly there's not a great deal going on food-wise', Parlour is a hugely popular place with bare boards and

scuffed wooden furniture helping to crank up the volume. But long before opening this all-day eatery and bar, Jesse Dunford-Wood had made a success of providing sensible dishes in that no-frills British style. The simple menu opens with breakfast, say 'Back Door' smoked salmon and 'that' soda bread with scrambled eggs; after that, regular big-flavoured fixtures that continue to please include popcorn chicken nuggets and the signature cow pie, but there's also steamed sea trout with broccoli, peppers and almonds, and duck breast with rhubarb and Swedish potatoes. Dishes are substantial enough that finishing with sticky toffee apple pudding and butterscotch or a toasted marshmallow Wagon Wheel can seem like self-indulgence. Informal service contributes to a laid-back feel and modest prices extend to the global wine list, which opens at £16.50.

Chef/s: Jesse Dunford-Wood and Ryan Lowery. **Open:** Tue to Sun 10am to 10pm. **Closed:** Mon, 2 weeks Christmas, 1 week Aug. **Meals:** alc (main courses £10 to £23). Set L £10 (2 courses) to £13. Set D £18 (2 courses) to £20. Sun L £18. **Details:** 110 seats. 60 seats outside. Bar. Wheelchair access. Music.

LOCAL GEM

Pizza East Kentish Town

⊖ Kentish Town, map 2
Italian-American | £22
79 Highgate Road, Kentish Town, NW5 1TL
Tel no: (020) 3310 2000
www.pizzaeast.com

Authentic, filling and fun, a meal at Pizza East is everything that mid-range dining out should be. This Kentish Town version, part of a trio from the Soho House empire – also in Notting Hill and Shoreditch, see entries – mixes a low-key industrial finish with American-style sourdough pizzas puffed and charred from the wood oven. Toppings include pork belly, yellow pepper and spring onion, or veal meatballs with prosciutto, cream and sage, while mac 'n' cheese and short rib with rosemary gremolata are great alternatives. Wines from £20.

Prawn on the Lawn

Fishmonger dabbling in dining
Cooking score: 3
⊖ Highbury & Islington, map 2
Seafood | £25
220 St Paul's Road, Highbury, N1 2LL
Tel no: (020) 3302 8668
www.prawnonthelawn.com

'Look for the black shop with the pink circle, it's guiding you to the prawns,' advises a fan of this modest fishmonger-cum-seafood bar. Wherever you sit – in the intimate cellar dining room or atop stools in the white-tiled shop – you can expect carefully sourced and very fresh fish from Cornwall and Devon in tapas-sized portions. The recommendation is for three dishes each with the daily changing menu offering up plenty of culinary zest and imagination. Consider small plates of scallop ceviche with chilli, coriander, passion fruit and Hendrick's gin, or seared tuna with chilli, spring onion, soy and mirin. A few hot dishes are served, say monkfish and chorizo stew, otherwise, seek out the sharing pleasures of a whole Brixham crab, half-lobster or seafood platter. Staff are really good-natured. Wines start at £22.50.
Chef/s: Rick Toogood. **Open:** Tue to Sat 12 to 10. **Closed:** Sun, Mon, 25 Dec to 8 Jan, last 2 weeks Aug. **Meals:** alc (main courses £8 to £33). **Details:** 32 seats. Music.

Restaurant Michael Nadra

Lively canal-side cooking
Cooking score: 4
⊖ Chalk Farm, map 2
Modern European | £37
42 Gloucester Avenue, Primrose Hill, NW1 8JD
Tel no: (020) 7722 2800
www.restaurant-michaelnadra.co.uk

Aside from the fact that it occupies the only Grade II-listed horse tunnel on the Regent's Canal, this offshoot of Michael Nadra's restaurant in Chiswick (see entry) is an altogether more ambitious proposition with assets including a dedicated Martini bar, a conservatory and an expansive terrace/outdoor space – as well as a chic, low-lit dining room done out with caramel leather banquettes. Value for money is a big plus as the kitchen delivers an assortment of eclectic modern dishes with pin-sharp flavours: a duo of tuna tartare and salmon ceviche is gilded with chilli-pickled cucumber, shiso leaves and salmon 'crackling', while sautéed baby squid is given the Spanish treatment with Padrón peppers, tomato and sherry dressing. Nadra's team also knows its way round the classics – as in roast lamb rump, braised neck and sautéed sweetbreads with kale, shallot purée and rosemary jus. Rice pudding, treacle tart and chocolate fondant are staples of the comforting dessert menu. A well-travelled wine list starts at £20.
Chef/s: Michael Nadra. **Open:** all week L 12 to 2.30 (4 Sat and Sun), D 6 to 10 (10.30 Fri and Sat, 9 Sun). **Closed:** 24 and 28 Dec, 1 Jan. **Meals:** Set L £21 (2 courses) to £26. Set D £31 (2 courses) to £37. Tasting menu L £48, D £59 (6 courses). **Details:** 75 seats. 35 seats outside. V menu. Bar. Wheelchair access. Music.

Season Kitchen

Confident neighbourhood cooking
Cooking score: 3
⊖ Finsbury Park, map 2
Modern British | £25
53 Stroud Green Road, Finsbury Park, N4 3EF
Tel no: (020) 7263 5500
www.seasonkitchen.co.uk

You know the grow-your-own revolution in British restaurateuring has reached a peak when even a neighbourhood spot in Finsbury Park has its own vegetable garden out back. It helps supply a weekly changing menu in a lilac-painted bistro that puts on no airs and graces, but has gained a strong local following for Ben Wooles' confident, attractive cooking. Modern ideas are neatly incorporated in the essentially simple dishes, adding wasabi parfait to scallop ceviche, and pairing potted rabbit and ham hock with blood-orange marmalade and Poilâne toast. Hearty stews featuring the likes of oxtail with parsnip purée – 'all dark mounds of flesh' – sit alongside earthy veggie dishes like spelt risotto with girolles and tarragon for main, and then it's on to savoury-seasoned desserts such as rosemary chocolate pot with 'tongue-pricking' black pepper biscotti, or poached pear with brown-bread ice cream and salted-caramel hazelnuts. A tiny wine list opens with Languedoc white and Spanish red at £15.50 (£5.75 a glass).

Chef/s: Ben Wooles. **Open:** Tue to Fri D 5.30 to 10.30. Sat and Sun 12 to 10.30 (10 Sun). **Closed:** Mon, 25 and 26 Dec, 1 Jan, bank hols. **Meals:** alc (main courses £13 to £20). Set D £16 (2 courses) to £20. Sun L £16. **Details:** 35 seats. 6 seats outside. Music.

Smokehouse

Smoky meats and world beers
Cooking score: 3
⊖ Highbury & Islington, map 2
Modern British | £33
63-69 Canonbury Road, Islington, N1 2DG
Tel no: (020) 7354 1144
www.smokehouseislington.co.uk

'I absolutely loved this and can't wait to go back. It's a bit unassuming from the outside, but inside it's the dream of a relaxed, country pub,' enthused one recent visitor. Great portions of 'man food' cooked with an 'abundance of passion' call the shots at the Smokehouse – a deceptively refined and accommodating boozer set up by chef Neil Rankin. Inside it's a hotchpotch of exposed brickwork, wooden pews, blackboards and curios – with the prospect of a delightful cottage garden irresistible on fine days. Either way, the foodie action takes place in a semi-open kitchen, where chefs roll out their seriously punchy wares: goat tacos; smoked pork belly with brown shrimps, udon noodles and pear miso; Highland 'cow burgers' with Korean pulled pork; duck heart on toast. If that sounds too meaty, veer off-piste with a plate of blackened pumpkin, tahini, flatbread and dill, before getting your sweet fix from

the Double D chocolate tart. To drink, there are scores of bottled and draught beers from around the world, plus a serviceable list of European wines from £17.95. A second branch is at 12 Sutton Lane North, Chiswick, W4 4LD; tel: (020) 7354 1144.

Chef/s: Neil Rankin. **Open:** Sat L 11 to 4, Mon and Thur to Sat D 6 to 10. Sun 12 to 9. **Closed:** Tue, Wed, 25 to 27 Dec. **Meals:** alc (main courses £14 to £19). **Details:** 90 seats. 60 seats outside. Wheelchair access. Music.

Sushi-Say

Japanese delicacies from a sushi master
Cooking score: 3
⊖ Willesden Green, map 1
Japanese | £30
33b Walm Lane, Willesden, NW2 5SH
Tel no: (020) 8459 7512

Sushi-Say doesn't have a website. Sushi-Say is off the beaten track (apologies to the residents of Willesden). It doesn't look all that from the outside either, but punters come again and again for the cracking sushi made by Katsuharu Shimizu. The no-frills décor matters not a jot (simple wooden tables, white walls and a counter where you can perch and watch the knife action), and the cost is fair if not cheap. Superbly fresh seafood is a given in the likes of saba battera (marinated mackerel with kelp) or tekka don toro (fatty tuna), and grilled options such as black cod with teriyaki sauce. Tempura and noodle dishes are spot-on, too, with soft-shell crab and soba or udon up for grabs respectively, and you might start with jellyfish in vinegar sauce or turbot with sticky fermented soya beans. Drink saké, shochu (spirits made from rice or potatoes) or wines from £22.

Chef/s: Katsuharu Shimizu. **Open:** Sat and Sun L 12 to 3, Wed to Sun D 6.30 to 10 (10.30 Sat, 6 to 9.30 Sun). **Closed:** Mon, Tue, 1 week Christmas, 2 weeks Sept, bank hols. **Meals:** alc (main courses £11 to £29). Set L £16 to £24. Set D £29 (6 courses) to £48. **Details:** 41 seats. Wheelchair access.

LOCAL GEM

T.E.D.

⊖ **King's Cross, map 2**
Modern British | £32
47-51 Caledonian Road, King's Cross, N1 9BU
Tel no: (020) 3763 2080
www.tedrestaurants.co.uk

Think. Eat. Drink. is the eco-friendly creation of Jamie Grainger-Smith and John Todd. It's a cheerfully informal and fiercely seasonal eatery and a useful addition to the vibrant King's Cross scene – a more bijou alternative to the behemoth eateries found at Pancras and Granary Squares. Expect lunchtime salads, devilled Cornish lamb kidneys on toast or Somerset beef burger with fried Lincolnshire potatoes, while dinner brings Oxfordshire wood pigeon with caramlised cep tart and monkfish cheeks with red lentil dahl and toasted coconut and carrot oil. Wines from £18. Closed Sun.

Trullo

An all-Italian local diamond
Cooking score: 3
⊖ **Highbury & Islington, map 2**
Italian | £35
300-302 St Paul's Road, Islington, N1 2LH
Tel no: (020) 7226 2733
www.trullorestaurant.com

The low-key blue-black frontage doesn't give much away, but Trullo is truly a local diamond amid the hurly-burly of Highbury Corner. Inside, it looks and feels sparsely contemporary (think bare floorboards, dangling metal lamps, etc.), with a cheery bistro mood on the ground floor and a cooler, more urban vibe in the bare-brick basement. Coming from Jamie Oliver's Fifteen and the River Café (see entries), the two owners know all about artisan Italian food, and it shows in a short daily menu that leans heavily on the char-grill and pasta-roller. Here you will find big flavours on small plates (braised cuttlefish with 'nduja, baby gem and peas, for example) ahead of, say, tagliatelle with violetta artichokes and larger items straight out of the oven – perhaps red-leg chicken with

Castelluccio lentils and salsa rossa. To finish, try the caramel and vanilla pannacotta. Cheeses are from the Italian regions, likewise a spirited collection of wines with plenty by the glass or carafe; bottles from £20.
Chef/s: Conor Gadd. **Open:** all week L 12.30 to 3, Mon to Sat D 6 to 10.30. **Closed:** Christmas.
Meals: alc (main courses £15 to £22). **Details:** 88 seats. Music.

The Truscott Arms

A neighbourhood gem that aims high
Cooking score: 3
⊖ **Warwick Avenue, map 6**
British | £34
55 Shirland Road, Maida Vale, W9 2JD
Tel no: (020) 7266 9198
www.thetruscottarms.com

£5 OFF 🍷

Five minutes' walk from Warwick Avenue tube, on the first floor of a chatty, bustling neighbourhood pub, is a dining room that takes its food seriously. There's a commitment to seasonal and sustainable produce and the kitchen delivers rustic modern British cooking of a high standard. A dinner in late winter was 'a very enjoyable evening', getting off to a good start with duck in an Earl Grey sauce (served with beetroot, pomegranate and smoked duck hearts), going on to South Downs lamb (neck and tongue) with baby leeks, broad beans, potatoes and heirloom tomatoes (pronounced 'gorgeous') and finishing with a Kentish Well apple pudding and a fine selection of English and Irish cheeses ('which would benefit from more narrative on the cheeses and producers'). All this comes with a reasonably modest price tag, and that policy extends to the extensive, carefully curated wine list, where prices start at £19, with plenty in the £20 to £30 range.
Chef/s: Aidan McGee. **Open:** dining room Wed to Sat D only 6 to 10. **Meals:** Set L £22 (2 courses) to £27. Set D £29 (2 courses) to £34. Sun L £18.
Details: 52 seats. 24 seats outside. Bar.

Vinoteca

Mega wine bar with good food

Cooking score: 1

⊖ King's Cross, map 2

Modern British | £28

One Pancras Square, King's Cross, N1C 4AG

Tel no: (020) 3793 7210

www.vinoteca.co.uk

With six tube lines, two mainline stations and Eurostar on the doorstep, it's no wonder that the biggest branch of Vinoteca is super-busy. Occupying the ground floor of the high-impact Gridiron building, it's a grand scale, faux-industrial venue consecrated to the enjoyment of wine. There's some food, too, (including breakfast) and the all-day menu has a seasonal slant, grazing feel and modern European flavour: Italian-cured meats or British cheeses to share, grilled Bideford squid with aubergine and harissa salad or a more substantial new-season Barnsley chop with Provençal vegetables – all with their own by-the-glass wine matches. Reasonable pricing extends to the exemplary global list with bottles from £16.50.

Chef/s: Kieren Steinborn. **Open:** all week 7.30am to 11pm (10am Sat and Sun). **Closed:** 24 to 26 Dec, 31 Dec. **Meals:** alc (main courses £12 to £17). Set L £13 (2 courses) to £16. **Details:** 90 seats. 40 seats outside. Wheelchair access. Music.

Zest at JW3

Boldly flavoured, sunny food

Cooking score: 3

⊖ Finchley Road, map 1

Jewish | £35

341-351 Finchley Road, Swiss Cottage, NW3 6ET

Tel no: (020) 7433 8955

www.zestatjw3.co.uk

In the past, any kosher restaurants featuring in the Guide were Ashkenazi, delivering heavy eastern European-style dishes. But while chefs like Yotam Ottolenghi and the Clarks at Moro have made vibrant Middle Eastern flavours familiar over the years, a good Sephardic kosher restaurant is quite new to the London dining scene. Indeed Zest, on the lower-ground floor of the Jewish Community Centre, is a welcome breath of fresh air. Eran Tibi's meat-free modern cooking delivers a line-up of wildly delicious flavours, seen in mezze of labneh with hazelnut dukkah paste and garlic oil, in raw and cooked beetroot salsa, and in pistachio hummus cream with hand-picked girolles salsa. Mains take in charred mackerel fillets with mixed herbs and radish salad, plums, falafel and fennel and almond dukkah, as well as cod with ptitim (Israeli couscous) with okra, aubergine, tomato braise and crème fraîche, while tahini parfait with coffee sauce is a perfect finale. Wines from £15.95.

Chef/s: Eran Tibi. **Open:** Sun to Thur L 12 to 3 (10.30am Sun), Sat to Thur D 6 to 10 (8 to 10 Sat). **Closed:** Fri. **Meals:** alc (main courses £14 to £25). **Details:** 70 seats. 24 seats outside. V menu. Wheelchair access. Music. Parking.

Angler

City high-flyer with classy seafood
Cooking score: 4
◉ Moorgate, map 4
Seafood | £50
South Place Hotel, 3 South Place, Moorgate,
EC2M 2AF
Tel no: (020) 3215 1260
www.anglerrestaurant.com

The logo – a fish with a top hat – tells you all you need to know about this glitzy City destination perched on the seventh floor of the South Place Hotel. Voguishly fitted out with shiny surfaces, mirrored ceilings and striped upholstery, the narrow glass-walled dining room provides its regulars with expansive views over their territory. Seafood is the culinary theme, and the kitchen has forged links with fishermen across the country in its search for seasonal supplies. Caviar and crustacea are a given, but the menu also wends its way from Dorset crab Waldorf salad with pickled cucumber and crab cakes via Dover sole meunière to roast turbot with squid ragoût, fennel purée and sea purslane – precise dishes with big, strong flavours and bags of oomph. Meat isn't ignored (think roast guinea fowl with seared foie gras and Périgord truffle sauce), while desserts are classy classics such as chocolate fondant with pistachio ice cream. Well chosen, fish-friendly wines start at £21.
Chef/s: Tony Fleming. **Open:** Mon to Fri L 12 to 2.30, Mon to Sat D 6 to 10. **Closed:** Sun, 24 to 26 Dec, 1 week Jan. **Meals:** alc (main courses £25 to £36). Set L and D £35. Tasting menu £75 (6 courses).
Details: 80 seats. 40 seats outside. Bar. Wheelchair access. Music.

L'Anima

Gorgeous modern Italian food
Cooking score: 5
◉ Liverpool Street, map 4
Italian | £55
1 Snowden Street, City, EC2A 2DQ
Tel no: (020) 7422 7000
www.lanima.co.uk

Glossy L'Anima remains a premium address for modern Italian dining in the capital despite the departure of its founding chef/patron, Francesco Mazzei, in the first quarter of 2015. It still looks like a room prepped for a photo-shoot in a fashion mag – white leather chairs and a luxe bar separated from the restaurant by a wall of glass, and southern Italy and the islands still guide the culinary direction. The food certainly has the promised *anima* (or soul, to translate), with the quality of the ingredients impressing from start to finish. An antipasti such as scallops with air-dried cod sets the tone, followed by a pasta option (wild boar ragù with maltagliati from Emilia-Romagna, flavoured with juniper and pistachios), and then secondi such as cod marinated in liquorice or oven-roasted black pig with black pudding sauce. Rhubarb soufflé with chocolate ice cream is a classy finish. Italians wines start at £22 and rise steeply.
Chef/s: Antonio Favuzzi. **Open:** Mon to Fri L 11.45 to 3, Mon to Sat D 5.30 to 11 (11.30 Sat). **Closed:** Sun, bank hols. **Meals:** alc (main courses £17 to £38). **Details:** 120 seats. Bar. Wheelchair access. Music.

Join us at thegoodfoodguide.co.uk

L'Anima Café

Slick Italian in the City
Cooking score: 2
⊖ Shoreditch High Street, map 4
Italian | £40
10 Appold Street, Shoreditch, EC2A 2AP
Tel no: (020) 7422 7080
www.lanimacafe.co.uk

Don't be fooled by the name, this vast glass-walled Italian is no mere café. It's the 'casual' sibling of high-achieving L'Anima, and though one can grab a filled ciabatta at the deli, most diners come for a better class of business lunch. The pan-Italian menu retains Calabrian influences from Francesco Mazzei's days but the rest is geared towards City eating habits from spicy 'nduja pizza to lighter tonno crudo and steak tagliata. Cured mackerel and agrodolce vegetables with quinoa felt virtuous rather than delicious. Far better was risotto primavera, creamy with firm rice and young vegetables. 'Fatto qui' is the motto, and certainly the homemade pasta (e.g. lamb ragù paccheri) and the really beautiful selection of bread are excellent. Desserts such as light tiramisu from the trolley are old-school Italian. Steep prices buy professionalism rather than passion; it can feel a little corporate. Wines start at £20.
Chef/s: Luca Terraneo. **Open:** Mon to Sat 11.30 to 10 (Sat 4 to 10). **Closed:** Sun, bank hols. **Meals:** alc (main courses £11 to £24). **Details:** 120 seats. Wheelchair access. Music.

Beagle

Vaulted and vaunted Brit-Med hangout
Cooking score: 3
⊖ Hoxton, map 2
British | £35
397-399 Geffrye Street, Hoxton, E2 8HZ
Tel no: (020) 7613 2967
www.beaglelondon.co.uk

Turning a trio of derelict railway arches into a thriving restaurant, bar and coffee shop is no mean feat. Two years on, in the spruced up cavernous space under Hoxton station, replete with industrial-lite décor and open kitchen, chef James Ferguson still mans the stove. Seasonal, pared back British fare is the deal here, with Med accents running throughout; perhaps elegant Cornish mussels, celery and 'nduja or mallard and partridge terrine with spiced pear chutney to start off proceedings. A refreshing lack of novelty concepts lets the food do the talking, and a wood grill gets the juices flowing, adding a seductive char to the likes of grilled octopus, Pink Fir potatoes and coriander, or spit-roast Sutton Hoo chicken, lemon potatoes and aïoli. A chocolate and salted-caramel pot finishes things off nicely. The express lunch menu is a steal, and wine starts at £19.
Chef/s: James Ferguson. **Open:** Wed to Sun L 12 to 3 (11 Sat, 11 to 5 Sun), Mon to Sat D 6.30 to 10.30. **Closed:** 24 to 29 Dec. **Meals:** alc (main courses £12 to £22). Set L £15 (2 courses) to £18 (Mon to Fri). **Details:** 60 seats. 36 seats outside. Bar. Wheelchair access. Music.

Bistrotheque

Cool east London pioneer
Cooking score: 2
⊖ Bethnal Green, map 1
Modern British | £40
23-27 Wadeson Street, Bethnal Green, E2 9DR
Tel no: (020) 8983 7900
www.bistrotheque.com

Hard-edged vibes and a clamorous buzz may come with the territory in this cool, capacious and light-filled warehouse restaurant, but there's no doubt it has been delighting the good folk of Bethnal Green for more than ten years – and has lost none of its allure. Dinner offers simple, clean-cut bistro-style assemblies, blending no-nonsense home-grown classics such as asparagus with smoked shallots and Lincolnshire Poacher cheese or cod and chips with pea purée and tartare sauce with more wide-ranging options, say smoked lamb shoulder with tumeric chicory and duck-fat toast or whole mackerel with kohlrabi and walnuts. Desserts hit the crème brûlée/chocolate pudding with milk ice cream comfort zone, while brunch is a weekend treat of crab rarebit, pancakes, eggs Florentine, burgers and roast chicken. The wine list has a global spread, with bottles from £19, or opt for the distinctive Bethnal Green-brewed bottled beers from the Redchurch Brewery.

Chef/s: Jackson Berg. **Open:** Sat and Sun L 11 to 4, all week D 6 to 10.30 (11 Fri and Sat). **Meals:** alc (main courses £11 to £30). Set D £20 (3 courses). **Details:** 100 seats. Music.

NEW ENTRY

Bonnie Gull Seafood Bar

The British seaside caff gets a makeover

Cooking score: 1

⊖ Farringdon, map 2

Seafood | £25

55-57 Exmouth Market, Clerkenwell, EC1R 4QL

Tel no: (020) 3122 0047

www.bonniegull.com

Bonnie Gull's second outpost speaks to the landlocked Londoner's seaside cravings. Its gingham-topped tables and maritime colour palette conjur up images of fish and chips on wind-whipped beaches, not so much the trendy small plates served here. There's a strong seasonal bent to the (confusingly over-designed) menu, that manifested itself at inspection in a dish of Manx queenies that let its tomato, asparagus and pea garnish shine at the expense of the seafood. Ox heart and Hispi cabbage was less attractive but more purposeful. Soft-serve ice cream is a fittingly 'beachy' finish. The £10 set lunch is popular. Wine from £17.50.

Chef/s: Luke Robinson. **Open:** Mon to Sat L 12 to 3 (4 Sat), D 5.30 to 10. **Closed:** 25 and 26 Dec, 1 Jan. **Meals:** alc (main courses £15 to 18). Set L £10. **Details:** 60 seats. 25 seats outside. Bar. Wheelchair access. Music.

Boundary

French pedigree in Shoreditch

Cooking score: 3

⊖ Shoreditch, Old Street, map 4

Modern French | £40

2-4 Boundary Street (entrance in Redchurch Street), Shoreditch, E2 7DD

Tel no: (020) 7729 1051

www.theboundary.co.uk

A high-class offer from Messrs Conran and Prestcott, Boundary is probably as posh and old-school as it gets in Shoreditch – and it's quite a package, comprising boutique accommodation, a rooftop café and three main eating spaces including a suave dining room in the basement of this expansive warehouse conversion. Once you're seated, take note of the details: the ceiling painted with constellations of the zodiac; the comfortable banquettes; the well-groomed staff carving roast meats from the trolley or wheeling the cheese chariot from table to table. The open kitchen focuses on French cooking in the modern mode, although it also knows how to please traditionalists with steak tartare, fois gras terrine, cassoulet, herb-crusted rack of lamb and peach tarte Tatin. Signature plates of braised beef and roast fillet with celeriac purée and red wine sauce tell their own story, but also look for sprightly seasonal fish dishes such as poached monkfish with cockles, samphire and broad beans. Drinkers have an all-encompassing, Euro-accented list of serious wines, including 35 selections under £35.

Chef/s: Frederick Forster. **Open:** Sun L 12 to 3.30, Mon to Sat D 6.30 to 10.30. **Closed:** 25 Dec to 1 Jan, bank hols. **Meals:** alc (main courses £18 to £50). Set D £22 (2 courses) to £26. Sun L £26. **Details:** 100 seats. Bar. Wheelchair access.

Brawn

Unbuttoned neighbourhood eatery
Cooking score: 4
◉ Shoreditch, map 2
Modern European | £28
49 Columbia Road, Shoreditch, E2 7RG
Tel no: (020) 7729 5692
www.brawn.co

'I was at Brawn today (very good as always)', was the verdict of one fan of this easy-going eatery, which occupies the ground floor of a former furniture warehouse. It has heaps of character. Oak floors, big windows, rustic furniture and cheery staff all encourage a sense of bonhomie, but it's the down-to-earth cooking and seasonal British produce that has everyone competing for space in the two dining rooms. The kitchen is scrupulously seasonal and deserves credit for its lack of ostentation, there are no pretensions or unnecessary garnish – flavours are direct and enjoyable, whether a classic pork rillette, outstanding grilled duck hearts with soft polenta and gremolata, or hake à la grenobloise with ratte potatoes. Desserts will tempt, even if you didn't think you needed one. Vanilla cheesecake or chocolate ganache, hazelnut cream and meringue are highly recommended. The reasonable prices extend to the stash of fascinating modern wines, mainly French and Italian (from £18), with a good selection by the glass or pichet.
Chef/s: Ed Wilson. **Open:** Tue to Sun L 12 to 3 (4 Sun), Mon to Sat D 6 to 10.30 (11 Fri and Sat). **Closed:** 24 Dec to 2 Jan. **Meals:** alc (main courses £11 to £15). **Details:** 70 seats.

Bread Street Kitchen

Industrial Art Deco New York canteen dining
Cooking score: 2
◉ St Paul's, map 5
Modern British | £39
One New Change, 10 Bread Street, St Paul's, EC4M 9AJ
Tel no: (020) 3030 4050
www.gordonramsay.com/breadstreet

Imagine a New York loft space with Art Deco pillars and light fittings, equipped with lemon-yellow banquettes, overseen by an industrial canteen kitchen, and you're there. The Ramsay Group's outpost near St Paul's is dedicated to informal city brasserie dining, with a lengthy menu of modern classics to prove it. Baked scallops with puréed carrot and treacled bacon should set you up nicely for a Josper-grilled speciality such as Herdwick lamb cutlets or a Dingley Dell pork chop, while the main menu offers steamed bream with shrimps and sea purslane in shellfish dressing, or forthrightly flavoured duck breast with boulangère potatoes, cabbage purée and a sauce stippled with mulled berries. Chocolate fondant with salted caramel and mint choc chip ice cream is the self-indulgent way to finish, or be virtuous and order an iced yoghurt with your choice of topping. The wine list covers a lot of fertile ground from £22.
Chef/s: Erion Karaj. **Open:** all week 11 to 11 (11 to 8 Sun). **Closed:** 25 and 26 Dec. **Meals:** alc (main courses £13 to £37). **Details:** 220 seats. 12 seats outside. Bar. Wheelchair access. Music.

Café Spice Namasté
Long-running innovative Indian
Cooking score: 2
 Tower Hill, map 4
Indian | £30
16 Prescot Street, Tower Hill, E1 8AZ
Tel no: (020) 7488 9242
www.cafespice.co.uk

In 2015, Cyrus and Pervin Todiwala celebrated the twentieth anniversary of their original venue near the Tower of London, bringing Goan, Hyderabadi and Kashmiri food to a London overdue an update on the ancient curry-house formula. The results have been impressive, both in terms of the unfailing congeniality with which the place is run, and the colourful, attention-grabbing freshness and precision of the food. Menus painstakingly explain each dish with several lines of text, guiding you from beetroot and coconut samosas sizzled in mustard seeds and curry leaves, through lamb frankie sandwiches (original Mumbai street food), to richly satisfying mains such as Goan prawn curry on red rice, and the textbook preparation of dhansak, made with puréed lentils and veg, brown onion rice, a lamb kebab and kachumber onion salad. Finish with Bombay caramel custard for that all-important sweet hit. Carefully chosen wines start at £22.95.
Chef/s: Cyrus Todiwala. **Open:** Mon to Fri L 12 to 3, Mon to Sat D 6.15 to 10.30 (6.30 Sat). **Closed:** Sun, 25 Dec to 1 Jan, bank hols. **Meals:** alc (main courses £15 to £20). Set L and D £30 (2 courses) to £35. Tasting menu £70. **Details:** 130 seats. Wheelchair access. Music.

Symbols

🛏 Accommodation is available
£30 Three courses for less than £30
£5 OFF £5-off voucher scheme
🍾 Notable wine list

Ceviche
 Old Street, map 4
Peruvian | £24
2 Baldwin Street, Old Street, EC1V 9NU
Tel no: (020) 3327 9463
www.cevicheuk.com

London took to Peruvian restaurant Ceviche just as warmly as it welcomed Paddington Bear, leading to the opening of this new second outpost in Old Street. Ceviche is of course the headline act on the menu: the Peruvian national dish of citrus-cured raw fish: among the excellent riffs on the theme you'll find chinguirito: dried stockfish with tiger's milk marinade, coriander, limo chilli and red onion. Be warned: staff recommend four dishes per person, which can quickly make for a rapidly snowballing bill. House wines start at £20. Open all week.

Cinnamon Kitchen
Stylish modern Indian in the City
Cooking score: 3
⊖ Liverpool Street, map 4
Modern Indian | £45
9 Devonshire Square, City, EC2M 4YL
Tel no: (020) 7626 5000
www.cinnamon-kitchen.com

Tucked into the rear of a warehouse dating from 1768 and once owned by the East India Company, Cinnamon Kitchen juxtaposes the heritage surroundings with modern design (exposed piping, counter seating, grey leather) to create a high-octane and stylish space, capped off by sprightly service. When it comes to the food, the kitchen utilises British produce to deliver exciting dishes, such as tender pieces of grilled lamb escalopes infused with black stone flower and paired with mint purée and diced celery. Fresh and vivid flavours linger in the memory, especially four Tanjore-spiced king prawns that glistened in a rich curry sauce and shared the plate with a spinach and coconut poriyal. Desserts are as well curated as the rest of the menu – kulfi

made from buffalo's milk was paired with vermicelli and rounded off with mango coulis. The perky wine list, starting from £22.50, is a suitable match for spicy food.
Chef/s: Vivek Singh. **Open:** Mon to Fri L 12 to 2.45, Mon to Sat D 6 to 10.45. **Closed:** Sun, 28 Dec, bank hols. **Meals:** alc (main courses £15 to £29). Set L £15 (2 courses) to £18. Set D £14 (2 courses) to £21. Tasting menu £57 (7 courses). **Details:** 130 seats. 55 seats outside. Bar. Wheelchair access. Music.

City Social

Room with a view
Cooking score: 6
Ⓔ Liverpool Street, map 4
Modern British | £54
Tower 42, 25 Old Broad Street, City, EC2N 1HQ
Tel no: (020) 7877 7703
www.citysociallondon.com

Man of the moment Jason Atherton is spreading his gastronomic largesse across the capital, and this wonderful City humdinger on the 24th floor of Tower 42 is a dream ticket. With its own entrance and a dedicated lift to whisk you skywards, it offers fabulous wraparound views and a bar and restaurant in brown wood, leather, shiny metallic ceilings and horseshoe banquettes – how could you not fall in love with this place? Most importantly, Paul Walsh's cooking rises to the occasion with intelligence and confident craftsmanship. The menu takes in reworked Atherton classics and modish oriental riffs as well as pasta and grills for the City's old guard. Picking a winner is tricky, but you might go for a plate of violet artichoke and black truffle with chervil root, sweet cicely and celeriac juice, a sensational risotto of ceps dotted with crispy sweetbreads or 'perfectly glossy' Middle White pork loin and braised belly with cavolo nero, black pudding and cider gel – it's all about clear flavours, freshness and intensity. To finish, try a textbook pillowy soufflé. The wine list from group sommelier Laure Patry is

another 'Social' corker, stuffed with classy names and curious finds; house selections from £24.
Chef/s: Paul Walsh. **Open:** Mon to Sat L 12 to 2.30, D 6 to 10.30. **Closed:** Sun, 25 and 26 Dec, bank hols. **Meals:** alc (main courses £18 to £38).
Details: 105 seats. Bar. Wheelchair access. Music.

The Clove Club

Fashion-forward roots
Cooking score: 6
Ⓔ Old Street, Shoreditch High Street, map 4
Modern European | £55
Shoreditch Town Hall, 380 Old Street, Shoreditch, EC1V 9LT
Tel no: (020) 7729 6496
www.thecloveclub.com

The ultimate Shoreditch trendsetter, the Clove Club packs a major punch in a grand but seen-better-days Victorian town hall. There's no real décor – just high ceilings, clattering wood floors, rustic wood tables, but hams hanging in the window and a kitchen that's part of the dining room – with chefs ambling out to serve diners – signal a down-to-earth restaurant that only makes a show of itself where it matters – on the plate. Indeed, it's the devotion, enthusiasm and skill of Isaac McHale and his brigade and innate sense of hospitality from front-of-house staff that makes the place memorable. The opening salvo of the evening tasting menu is terrific – flavoursome nuggets of buttermilk-fried chicken, wood pigeon sausage with greengage chutney, oak-smoked cod's roe with fennel and rye crackers – while at the finale, Amalfi lemonade and Sarawak pepper ice cream has become something of a signature. Elsewhere, larger plates show minimum posturing but big flavours, whether 100-day Lincolnshire chicken with spinach and South Indian spices or the Cornish Thornback ray with pear, spring onions and langoustine bisque that so impressed one couple trying out the good-value set lunch. The modern wine list starts at £24.

Chef/s: Isaac McHale. **Open:** Tue to Sat L 12 to 2.30, Mon to Sat D 6 to 10.30. **Closed:** Sun, 2 weeks Christmas. **Meals:** alc (main courses £16 to £24). Set L £35. Tasting menu £55 (8 courses). **Details:** 65 seats. V menu. Bar. Music.

Club Gascon

Celebrating south-west France
Cooking score: 5
⊖ Barbican, Farringdon, map 5
Modern French | £60
57 West Smithfield, City, EC1A 9DS
Tel no: (020) 7600 6144
www.clubgascon.com

Is it really 18 years since Pascal Aussignac and Vincent Labeyrie opened Club Gascon and threw new light on the rich culinary heritage of south-west France? Sited between Smithfield Market and St Bartholomew's Hospital, the square room with its marble walls, wood floor and small, close-packed tables was among the very first to serve everything in small portions, via a menu divided into half a dozen sections with a handful of dishes in each – including six ways with foie gras. Strong but well-balanced flavours are characteristic of Aussignac's style – say seared and braised hare with tulip, green quinoa and watercress. Results have been variable this year, but praise has been heaped on an impressive mousse of Catalane spring cress with sea urchin jus and some charcoal shallots adding texture, and an exemplary roast guinea fowl served with elderflower-glazed chicory, mustard and wild garlic. Breads and smoked butter get a special mention and well-trained staff deliver smooth, non-intrusive service. The all-French wine list (from £22) is a veritable treasure trove of south-western appellations but also reaches out to the Midi, Provence and Corsica. Classic varietals also shine and there's a fine slate of 'vins au verre'.
Chef/s: Pascal Aussignac. **Open:** Mon to Fri L 12 to 2, Mon to Sat D 6.30 to 10 (10.30 Fri and Sat). **Closed:** Sun, 24 Dec to 5 Jan, bank hols. **Meals:** alc

(main courses £13 to £29). Set L and £29 (2 courses) to £39. Set D £39. Tasting Menu (5 courses) £65.
Details: 42 seats. V menu. Bar. Music.

Comptoir Gascon

Rustic regional pleasures
Cooking score: 4
⊖ Farringdon, Barbican, map 5
French | £26
61-63 Charterhouse Street, Clerkenwell, EC1M 6HJ
Tel no: (020) 7608 0851
www.comptoirgascon.com

Playing the understudy to nearby Club Gascon (see entry) doesn't seem to have affected this charming bistro one jot – in fact, it relishes the chance of upping the ante when it comes to earthy peasant richness. Gascony is the menu's compass point, with 'the best of duck' at the very heart of things: moist rillettes, impeccable confit and garbure, classic cassoulet Toulousain, burgers layered with foie gras and fries 'so full of fat they would have burned all afternoon as a tallow candle'. Alternatively, soak up the rustic pleasures of 'piggy treats', roast capon with braised Swiss chard and barigoule or éclade of mussels, asparagus and confit lentils before tackling the calorific creaminess of a Gascon mess (a boozy variant on the Eton original). Comptoir Gascon also functions as a deli, selling wine, cheese, charcuterie and chocolates, while the all-French wine list is dominated by iconic names from the south – Gaillac, Corbières, Languedoc, Irouléguy etc. Wine from £17.90.
Chef/s: Pascal Aussignac. **Open:** Tue to Sat L 12 to 2.30, D 6.30 to 10 (10.30 Fri and Sat). **Closed:** Sun, Mon, 24 Dec to 5 Jan, bank hols. **Meals:** alc (main courses £10 to £16). **Details:** 40 seats. 6 seats outside. Wheelchair access. Music.

Join us at thegoodfoodguide.co.uk

Copita del Mercado

A Spanish armada welcomed in Whitechapel
Cooking score: 3
⊖ Aldgate East, map 4
Spanish | £25
60 Wentworth Street, Whitechapel, E1 7AL
Tel no: (020) 7426 0218
www.copitadelmercado.com

A new counterpart to pint-sized Copita of Soho (see entry), this new Whitechapel restaurant takes the best elements of its little sibling and makes everything, well, much bigger. Not only is this the case with the spacious dining space – all tiled walls and light fittings cleverly fashioned from old gramophones – but also with the tapas, more generous in portion size and evenly split between meat, veg and seafood. The meat selection naturally shows a porky prevalence – delicious acorn-fed Ibérico presa, offset with piquant moruna salsa, for instance – though an inspection dish of lamb with pistachio and apricot was especially impressive. Dive into the seafood selection for the likes of grilled octopus tentacle, swimming in a sea of arrocina beans and sobrasada – while vegetarians are not neglected: opt for a lively medley of squash, duck egg yolk, truffled Hispi cabbage and chestnuts. Churros con chocolate would be an appropriately Spanish finale. A sensational, all-Iberian wine list, with plenty by the glass, starts at £23.
Chef/s: Ignacio Pinilla. **Open:** all week L 12 to 3.30, Mon to Sat 5.30 to 10.30. **Closed:** 24 Dec to 1 Jan, Easter bank hol. **Meals:** alc (main courses £6 to £14). **Details:** 70 seats. 35 seats outside. Wheelchair access. Music.

Visit us online

To find out more about The Good Food Guide, please visit thegoodfoodguide.co.uk

Coq d'Argent

City slicker with spectacular views
Cooking score: 2
⊖ Bank, map 4
Modern French | £40
1 Poultry, City, EC2R 8EJ
Tel no: (020) 7395 5000
www.coqdargent.co.uk

There's a neatly trimmed grassy lawn on top of 1 Poultry – part of the terrace garden – that adds an unexpected splash of colour to the grey city skyline. The terrace is at its best when the sun is out, of course, but there's reason enough to visit Coq d'Argent all year round. That reason is the French-focused food offered up by Damien Rigollet and his 'friendly' service team. The bilingual menu doesn't attempt to shake the foundations of the city, with the simple things done well and no shortage of interesting options. Scallop ceviche with vanilla and yuzu dressing shows its not all escargots de Bourgogne, with main courses running to braised rabbit leg with Dijon mustard sauce and yellowfin tuna with mini ratatouille. Williams pear and rhubarb combine in a crumble for dessert. Global wines start at £22.50.
Chef/s: Damien Rigollet. **Open:** all week L 11.30 to 3 (12 to 3.45 Sat, 12 Sun), Mon to Sat D 5.30 to 10. **Closed:** 25 and 26 Dec, bank hols. **Meals:** alc (main courses £26 to £44). Set L £26 (2 courses) to £29. Sun L £26. **Details:** 140 seats. 100 seats outside. V menu. Bar. Wheelchair access. Music.

Corner Room

A hidden bistro with bright ideas
Cooking score: 2
⊖ Bethnal Green, map 1
Modern European | £30
Town Hall Hotel, Patriot Square, Bethnal Green, E2 9NF
Tel no: (020) 7871 0460
www.townhallhotel.com

The small second restaurant at Bethnal Green's Town Hall Hotel doesn't get the attention of Typing Room, its showier rival at the front of the property, but it would be a mistake to overlook this hidden bistro's affordable offering. Chef Ben Gallier magics up a short, chic menu of seasonal dishes whose sharp looks and trendy techniques turn humble into hip. A cured mackerel and cucumber starter didn't need the texture of crunchy quinoa but smoked passion fruit butter was a nifty idea. To follow, lamb neck with braised swede with 'mussel emulsion' and turnip discs looked very 'now', but was secretly pretty conventional. To finish, tangy goats' cheese parfait with rhubarb was light and refreshing. Few venture here at lunch (in spite of the good-value set menu) but things pick up at dinner, when diners can have a tasting menu paired with wines from the interesting, if minimalist, list.

Chef/s: Ben Gallier. **Open:** all week L 12 to 3 (4 Fri to Sun), D 6 to 10 (10.30 Thur to Sat). **Meals:** alc (main courses £10 to £14). Set L £19 (2 courses) to £23. Tasting menu £45. **Details:** 30 seats.

Dishoom

Buzzy all-day Bombay café

Cooking score: 2

⊖ Old Street, Liverpool Street, map 4

Indian | £30

7 Boundary Street, Shoreditch, E2 7JE

Tel no: (020) 7420 9324

www.dishoom.com

The Irani cafés in Bombay that provided the inspiration for Dishoom (and its siblings in Covent Garden and King's Cross; see entries) have pretty much disappeared in the old country, but there is clearly an appetite for them in London. Open all day for a bacon naan roll at breakfast to a late-night 'Ruby Murray' (a proper chicken curry with a silky sauce), it's the kind of place where you might find yourself queueing for a table at peak times. The industrial shabby-chic interior is more akin to a trendy bar than a curry house. Tuck into small plates of lamb samosas – 'if there are better lamb samosas in London, I haven't had them' – or prawn koliwada, or try the sheekh kebab or superb chicken tikka.

Spicing is effective and subtle in curries such as lamb raan and a black daal side dish. Drink lager, lassi, chai or wines from £19.90.

Chef/s: Naved Nasir. **Open:** all week 11.30 to 11 (midnight Fri, 12 to 12 Sat, 12 to 11 Sun). **Closed:** 25 and 26 Dec, 1 and 2 Jan. **Meals:** alc (main courses £5 to £23). **Details:** 235 seats. Bar. Music.

The Don

Fine wines and enterprising cooking

Cooking score: 2

⊖ Bank, Cannon Street, map 4

Modern European | £35

The Courtyard, 20 St Swithin's Lane, City, EC4N 8AD

Tel no: (020) 7626 2606

www.thedonrestaurant.co.uk

This striking, modern ground-floor restaurant, with paintings by John Hoyland, is housed in an 18th-century building tucked round the back of the Mansion House and is valued for its aristocratic wine list and reliable modern cooking. You only get a sense of the building's history if you venture down to the brick-lined basement bistro (which has its own menu), for these were once Sandeman's bottling cellars. Considered a venerable City institution, the Don's menu deals in refreshingly robust and uncomplicated combinations, starting perhaps with ballotine of foie gras with gingerbread crumb and Conference pear, and finishing with lemon tart or crème brûlée. In between, there might be pot-roast lamb, grilled whole Dover sole or haunch of venison with spiced red cabbage, chestnut and celeriac purée and pommes cocotte. The wine list deals in top names from classic regions in France and around the globe, but there are plenty of surprises, too, from £22, and the list culminates in a range of ports and sherries.

Chef/s: Matt Burns. **Open:** Mon to Fri L 12 to 3, D 6 to 10. **Closed:** Sat, Sun, bank hols. **Meals:** alc (main courses £17 to £33). Set L £29. **Details:** 65 seats. Bar.

Join us at thegoodfoodguide.co.uk

Duck & Waffle

High-flyer with a bird's-eye view of the City
Cooking score: 3
⊖ Liverpool Street, map 4
International | £40
Heron Tower, 40th floor, 110 Bishopsgate,
City, EC2N 4AY
Tel no: (020) 3640 7310
www.duckandwaffle.com

There is nothing else quite like this energetic 24-hour venue. Once the super-fast glass lift to the 40th floor has been negotiated, diners are relieved to find that the designer of the high-flying Duck has sensibly decided not to compete with the floor-to-ceiling view over London; apart from the open kitchen, there's nothing to detract from the city spread below. You might think Dan Doherty had his work cut out to match the cooking to these rarefied surroundings, but his finger is firmly on the pulse of today's tastes for robust combinations. The chef's dishes are designed for sampling and sharing, and in his international box of tricks he has cumin, garlic and sumac yoghurt to go with coal-charred aubergine; apricot jam and paprika sugar to accompany a spicy ox cheek doughnut; marmite hollandaise to be paired with Longhorn rib eye; and desserts include dark chocolate brownie sundae with peanut crunch. Wines from £26.
Chef/s: Daniel Doherty. **Open:** all week 24-hour opening. **Meals:** alc (main courses £17 to £40).
Details: 120 seats. Bar. Wheelchair access. Music.

The Eagle

The pub that launched 1,000 imitations
Cooking score: 2
⊖ Farringdon, map 5
Modern European | £25
159 Farringdon Road, Clerkenwell, EC1R 3AL
Tel no: (020) 7837 1353
theeaglefarringdon.co.uk

Celebrating 25 years in January 2016, the Eagle remains a hugely popular local rendezvous and has never strayed from its avowed aim – which is why drinkers jostle with diners in the spacious ground-floor bar, enjoying real ales and pub vibes. Indeed, very little changes: there have been just three head chefs in all those years, and proprietor Michael Belben only got around to setting up a website in 2014. A scuffed wooden floor, battered tables and mismatched chairs create just the right utilitarian mood for a chalked-up menu of fairly priced, robust British-Mediterranean dishes cooked in a tiny corner of the bar. Come here for plates of spaghetti with roasted fennel, lemon and chilli, Catalan fish stew, piri-piri quail with pomegranate couscous and tzatziki, and the famed steak sandwich. Note there's no standing on ceremony – you order and pay at the bar and share a table if necessary. Wines from £14.70.
Chef/s: Ed Mottershaw. **Open:** all week L 12 to 3 (3.30 Sat, 4 Sun), Mon to Sat D 6.30 to 10.30.
Closed: 1 week Christmas, bank hols. **Meals:** alc (main meals £8 to £19). **Details:** 65 seats. 16 seats outside. Music.

8 Hoxton Square

Impressive newcomer in hipsterland
Cooking score: 4
⊖ Old Street, map 4
Modern European | £32
8-9 Hoxton Square, Hoxton, N1 6NU
Tel no: (020) 7729 4232
www.8hoxtonsquare.com

It may look like any other small restaurant with its stripped-back brick, scrubbed floor and close-packed tables, but the basic décor reflects the aim of the folk behind 10 Greek Street (see entry) to provide great food and drink without breaking the bank. The kitchen majors on broad-shouldered seasonal dishes with emphatic Mediterranean overtones and modern techniques. Light and colourful plates are driven by flavour in 'fresh, clean and simple' mussels and clams teamed with chorizo and fino, or when kale, Jerusalem artichokes and quince partner Gressingham duck. Characteristic, too, is the admirable balance to be found in a dish of sea bream with chilli, coriander and spiced yoghurt. To conclude, there's brown-sugar meringue with blood orange, mascarpone and pistachio or pear and walnut tart. Enthusiastic staff have been praised and the short, global wine list (from £15) is intelligent, gently priced and offers a good selection by the glass.

Chef/s: Cameron Emirali. **Open:** all week L 12 to 3 (1 Sat, 1 to 4 Sun), Mon to Sat D 6 to 10.30. **Closed:** 25 Dec, 1 Jan, bank hols. **Meals:** alc (main courses £16 to £21). **Details:** 60 seats. 16 seats outside. Bar. Wheelchair access. Music.

Eyre Brothers

Gutsy Iberian cooking
Cooking score: 4
⊖ Old Street, map 4
Spanish-Portuguese | £36
68-70 Leonard Street, Shoreditch, EC2A 4QX
Tel no: (020) 7613 5346
www.eyrebrothers.co.uk

The Iberian Peninsula sits on Europe's south-western perimeter and its cuisine has been influenced by everything from unwanted invasions to the colonisation of vast tracts of faraway continents. The result is one of the world's most compelling culinary melting pots, and if you want a taste of Spain and Portugal in London, no one is doing it with more conviction than David Eyre. This is Shoreditch, so the setting is urban, slick and trendy, with a sprinkling of Iberian pizazz. Tapas and petiscos (Portuguese tapas pretty much) such as fried duck livers, deep-fried baby cuttlefish and the classic Portuguese steak sandwich, o prego, arrive done just right, while the main menu spreads its wings from region to region to deliver Malaga-style salt cod salad, or feijoada de pato (black beans with duck, toucinho bacon and chouriço). The acorn-fed Ibérico pork is hard to ignore, while, to finish, tarta de Santiago hits the spot. The wine list is an inspirational journey across the peninsula; from £19.

Chef/s: David Eyre and João Cleto. **Open:** Mon to Fri L 12 to 3, Mon to Sat D 6.30 to 10.30 (7 Sat). **Closed:** Sun, 22 Dec to 3 Jan, bank hols. **Meals:** alc (main courses £14 to £23). **Details:** 84 seats. Bar. Wheelchair access. Music.

Fifteen London

Jamie O's remodelled flagship
Cooking score: 3
⊖ Old Street, map 2
Modern British | £40
15 Westland Place, Shoreditch, N1 7LP
Tel no: (020) 3375 1515
www.fifteen.net

After cruising around Italy for more than a decade, Jamie Oliver's philanthropic flagship changed tack dramatically in 2013 and headed for 21st-century Britain – gastronomically speaking. As a charitable venture, Fifteen is still in the business of training up a crew of disadvantaged youngsters, but the kitchen is now focused on daily menus bursting with home-grown flavours – plus the odd detour to the Med and the Far East for, say, cured pork loin with violet artichokes, heritage carrots and mustard leaves or white and green asparagus with tamari and nettles. Sharing is a given here, and bigger plates also fit the bill, from Cornish hake with wild garlic, Jersey Royals and smoked crème fraîche to Middle White pork chop complemented by celeriac purée and purple sprouting broccoli. Williamsburg meets Shoreditch in the laid-back basement dining room with its red banquettes and exposed brickwork, while the ground-floor bar serves craft beers and 'spirituous' cocktails. Wines start at £19.

Chef/s: Robbin Holmgren. **Open:** Mon to Sat L 12 to 3, D 6 to 11. Sun 12 to 9. **Meals:** alc (main courses £16 to £36). **Details:** 140 seats. Bar. Wheelchair access. Music.

LOCAL GEM

Fish Central

⊖ Old Street, map 2
Seafood | £15
149-155 Central Street, King Square, Old Street, EC1V 8AP
Tel no: (020) 72534 970
www.fishcentral.co.uk

'Quite amazing,' remarked a visitor to this ex-cabbies haunt found north of Old Street tube in a 1960s municipal square at the grittier end of the City Road. Inside it's utilitarian (but with white tablecloths) and with plenty of room – more or less what you would expect from a place that specialises in fish and chips (very good, very fresh, both battered and matzo meal, with 'real' chips). 'Reasonably priced' langoustine is 'as fresh as could be', turbot is 'beautifully cooked', and treacle pudding is 'just like mother used to make'. Wine from £12.45. Closed Sun.

Galvin Café à Vin

Café-bar dining
Cooking score: 3
⊖ Liverpool Street, map 4
French | £30
35 Spital Square, Spitalfields, E1 6DY
Tel no: (020) 7299 0404
www.galvinrestaurants.com

The happily ubiquitous Galvin brothers' portfolio covers a range of eclectic dining options, this café and wine-bar venue being sited next to Galvin La Chapelle (see entry), joined to it by an umbilical glass link, a long bar with counter seating running through the middle. What's on offer here is French bistro food of engaging simplicity, with a wood-fired oven turning out tartes flambées, as well as flatbreads topped with white asparagus, duck egg and Ossau Iraty sheep's cheese from the Pays Basque, as preludes to principals like lamb leg steak with Jersey Royals and mint, or char-grilled monkfish with shallots and piquillo peppers. The prix fixe offers exemplary value for a three-course roundup of pea and mint soup, red mullet escabèche and lemon tart. Cheeses from Androuet supplement the likes of rum baba, crème brûlée and rhubarb fool. Despite the prevailing tone, wines are not all French, but open at £18.50 for Languedoc house white.
Chef/s: Jack Boast. **Open:** all week 11.30 to 10.30. **Closed:** 25 and 26 Dec, 1 Jan. **Meals:** alc (main courses £14 to £19). Set L and D £17 (2 courses) to £20. Sun L £20. **Details:** 65 seats. 80 seats outside. Bar. Wheelchair access. Music.

Galvin La Chapelle

Polished French cuisine
Cooking score: 6
⊖ Liverpool Street, map 4
Modern French | £49
35 Spital Square, Spitalfields, E1 6DY
Tel no: (020) 7299 0400
www.galvinrestaurants.com

What was once St Botolph's church hall, following its previous incarnation as a Victorian girls' school, makes one of the more arresting venues in the East End, and one that sits regally in the expanding Galvin brothers' portfolio. When the place is all a-glisten beneath its vaulted ceiling, with a mezzanine gallery for private functions, it's a magical setting for the polished French cuisine on offer, which steers a course between traditional technique and modern ideas. Crab lasagne in shellfish emulsion with sea purslane is a light but stimulating opener, if you can be prised away from ham hock and foie gras terrine wrapped in Bayonne ham with leek vinaigrette. Feathered French game, Landes guinea fowl and Bresse pigeon – the latter in Moroccan suiting with couscous, preserved lemon and harissa – are the meatier alternatives to cod with capers and brandade on samphire. A classic Tatin with Normandy crème fraîche is worth getting stuck into. The wine list is naturally very strong in France, including a run of Jaboulet's Hermitage La Chapelle back to 1952, with shorter but still interesting shrift elsewhere. Bottles open at £21.50.
Chef/s: Jeff Galvin and Eric Jolibois. **Open:** all week L 12 to 2.30 (3 Sun), D 6 to 10.30 (9.30 Sun). **Closed:** 25 and 26 Dec, 1 Jan. **Meals:** alc (main courses £27 to £33). Set L and early D £24 (2 courses) to £29. Sun L £29. Tasting menu £70 (7 courses). **Details:** 110 seats. 25 seats outside. V menu. Wheelchair access.

Granger & Co.

Lovely, zingy, cross-cultural cooking
Cooking score: 2
⊖Farringdon, map 5
Australian | £35
50 Sekforde Street, Clerkenwell, EC1R 0HA
Tel no: (020) 7251 9032
www.grangerandco.com

This is what is meant by a local restaurant: a convivial, friendly place that has a good, regular following and where value for money is a big plus. Indeed, nowhere better exemplifies how Londoners eat and drink today than Bill Granger's group of restaurants (including venues in Westbourne Grove and King's Cross). The flexible, all-day menu works hard, going from cross-cultural breakfasts where just about every dish begs to be ordered (ricotta hotcakes, chilli fried egg and bacon brioche roll, or shrimp, chorizo and kim chee fried brown rice) to indulgent lunches and dinners, where excellent burgers, salads and pizzas vie for attention with the likes of Parmesan-crumbed chicken schnitzel or crispy duck with mandarin, star anise and jasmine rice. The spacious, light-filled surroundings – all neutral colours, blond wood, big windows – fit the all-day ethos very well. Cocktails fit the bill, too, and the short, global wine list starts at £19.50.
Chef/s: Tom Cajone. **Open:** Mon to Sat 8am to 11pm (9am Sat). Sun 10 to 6. **Closed:** 25 and 26 Dec. **Meals:** alc (main courses £9 to £24). **Details:** 90 seats. Bar. Wheelchair access. Music.

Hawksmoor Guildhall

A sizzling advert for British beef
Cooking score: 4
⊖Bank, map 4
British | £45
10-12 Basinghall Street, City, EC2V 5BQ
Tel no: (020) 7397 8120
www.thehawksmoor.com

There's an almost sepulchral glow to this tremendous subterranean dining and drinking venue. Steak is king here (as at all of Will Beckett and Huw Gott's Hawksmoor group), but this City branch has always been considered the most beef-obsessed – a temple to the delights of porterhouse, chateaubriand, fillet, ribeye and sirloin. While still a place of pilgrimage for lovers of beef at premium prices (and its sides of triple-cooked chips and béarnaise sauce), there have been some changes to the menu, which is now equally weighted between steaks and seafood, with the kitchen showing its mettle with octopus carpaccio, Poole clams and braised pig's trotters or char-grilled monkfish. Elsewhere, bone marrow and onions remains a popular starter and there's peanut-butter shortbread with salted caramel ice cream to finish. Staff are painstakingly helpful, and whether you are eating seafood or steak, the wine list has an array of indulgent choices from £21.
Chef/s: Phillip Branch. **Open:** Mon to Fri L 12 to 3, D 5 to 10.30. **Closed:** Sat, Sun, 24 Dec to 2 Jan, bank hols. **Meals:** alc (main courses £13 to £50). Set D £24 (2 courses) to £27. **Details:** 160 seats. Bar. Wheelchair access. Music.

Hawksmoor Spitalfields

Prime British steakhouse
Cooking score: 3
⊖Liverpool Street, Aldgate East, map 4
British | £45
157a Commercial Street, City, E1 6BJ
Tel no: (020) 7426 4850
www.thehawksmoor.co.uk

The Hawksmoor boys (Will Beckett and Huw Gott) got off to a flyer here on Commercial Street and have since expanded to several addresses across the capital and a northern outpost in Manchester. Give the people prime steaks and they will come. The basement bar fuels the punters with cocktails, while the restaurant, with its broodingly dark demeanour, offers up 'tender and delicious' porterhouse, T-bone, ribeye and the gang, cooked how you like (most of the time) and served with whichever sides you fancy paying extra for (triple-cooked chips, buttered broccoli, macaroni cheese et al). It's busy, loud and fun, all facilitated by 'amazing service'. Start with Brixham crab on toast, or more of

the red stuff in tartare form, with baked lemon sole and grilled lobster alternatives to the prime protein among main courses. There's an express menu at lunch and early evenings, and Sunday lunch is a cracker. The wine list prioritises beefy reds; prices start at £21.
Chef/s: Pav Costa. **Open:** all week L 12 to 2.30 (4.30 Sun), Mon to Sat D 5 to 10.30. **Meals:** alc (main courses £12 to £50). Set L and D £24 (2 courses) to £27. Sun L £20. **Details:** 116 seats. Bar. Wheelchair access. Music.

Hix Oyster & Chop House

Bivalves and meat on the bone
Cooking score: 2
◉ Farringdon, map 5
British | £40
35-37 Greenhill Rents, Cowcross Street, Clerkenwell, EC1M 6BN
Tel no: (020) 7017 1930
www.hixoysterandchophouse.co.uk

Mark Hix's intensive restaurant network is in operation everywhere you look these days, but here, hard by Smithfield meat market, is where it began. The interior is at once stripped-down and fancy, with tiled walls and wood floor offset by a marble oyster bar and table linen. From the bar flow forth rock natives, fried in scrumpy, paired with spicy sausages, or just au naturel. The chop side of things is covered by mighty steaks cooked on the bone, cutlets of lamb Reform, and veal chop in sage butter, or perhaps a thundering great assiette of seasonal cuts for sharing. Otherwise, go for Torbay monkfish curry, or John Dory gently roasted in rosemary, and finish with white port jelly and saffron ice cream, garnished with raspberries. The drinks list carries the proprietor's imprimatur in the form of 'what Mark's drinking' (oyster ale, since you ask) and 'Mark's favourites', a slate of cocktail inventions. Wines open at £23.
Chef/s: Jamie Guy. **Open:** all week 12 to 11 (5 to 11 Sat, 10pm Sun). **Meals:** alc (main courses £18 to £60). Set L £20 (2 courses) to £25. **Details:** 65 seats. 6 seats outside. Wheelchair access. Music.

HKK London

Revelatory Chinese cuisine
Cooking score: 6
◉ Liverpool Street, map 4
Chinese | £65
Broadgate West, Worship Street, City, EC2A 2BF
Tel no: (020) 3535 1888
www.hkklondon.com

In contrast to its sultry Hakkasan cousins (see entries), HKK looks rather subdued with only some white baubles breaking up the serene dining room's muted grey tones. The setting may be low-key, but the food emanating from Tong Chee Hwee's kitchen is way beyond expectations – a revelatory exploration of Chinese cuisine refracted through an occidental prism. Ingenious tasting menus are the deal, and it's worth going for broke with the 15-course version if you want to experience the full breadth and depth of the food here. Everyone mentions the stunning dim sum 'trilogy', but also look for exclusive British ingredients including cumin-spiced organic Rhug Farm lamb and marinated Duke of Berkshire pork with osmanthus wine jelly. Otherwise, the undisputed show stopper is a matchless version of Peking duck, dramatically roasted over cherry wood and presented in different forms – a mini pancake roll, shards of crispy skin, slivers of breast meat, and so on. Finally, wallow in the fragrant crossover delights of jasmine pannacotta with rhubarb sorbet. As befits HKK's Hakkasan lineage, the wine list is a wallet-challenging global blockbuster with bottles from £29.
Chef/s: Tong Chee Hwee. **Open:** Mon to Sat L 12 to 2.30, D 6 to 9.45. **Closed:** Sun, 24 and 25 Dec, 1 Jan, bank hols. **Meals:** alc (main courses £10 to £29). Set L £35. Tasting menus £78 (10 courses) to £98 (15 courses). **Details:** 77 seats. V menu. Wheelchair access. Music.

José Pizarro

Staples of the tapas repertoire and more
Cooking score: 2
⊖ Liverpool Street, map 4
Spanish | £28
36 Broadgate Circle, City, EC2M 1QS
www.josepizarro.com

When José Pizarro opened on gritty Bermondsey Street he earned a reputation for delivering two of the most authentic Spanish venues in town (José and Pizarro, see entries). This Broadgate Circle offshoot may be an odd choice of location but it's no different. The small, intimate dining room sports a faux-industrial look with trademark hams hanging above the bar, and there's the luxury of outside tables. On the all-day food front, things kick off with breakfast, then move on to snacks such as pan con tomate or really excellent prawn fritters and plates of charcuterie or cheese. Other staples of the tapas repertoire include pan-fried chicken livers with garlic, shallots and dry sherry or there could be grilled baby gem with big fat fillets of anchovy, Pico de Europa cheese, piquillo and PX honey dressing and larger plates of, say, bacalao a la riojana with garlic chips. Crema catalana features among simple desserts. Spanish wines from £22. Note: no telephone number, book online.
Chef/s: José Pizarro. **Open:** Mon to Sat 8am to 11pm (11am Sat). **Closed:** Sun. **Meals:** alc (main courses £12 to £14). **Details:** 60 seats.

Lantana

⊖ Old Street, map 4
Australian | £20
Unit 2, 1 Oliver's Yard, 55 City Road, Shoreditch, EC1Y 1HQ
Tel no: (020) 7253 5273
www.lantanacafe.co.uk

A change of name (from Salvation Jane) has emphasised the relationship of this Shoreditch eatery to the popular Lantana Café in Fitzrovia (see entry). It delivers the same Aussie-style breakfasts (corn fritters stacked with streaky bacon and fresh spinach, French toast with grilled bananas and toasted pecans) that cause such long queues at the mothership, but there's a more spacious feel here, and evening opening (Tue to Fri), when a short menu brings duck burger with pickled cucumber, plum ketchup and Asian slaw, say, or hake with kale, chilli, tahini and toasted pumpkin seeds. Wines from £24. Open all week.

Lardo

Hip neighbourhood pizzeria
Cooking score: 2
⊖ Hackney Central, map 1
Italian | £26
205 Richmond Road, Hackney, E8 3NJ
Tel no: (020) 8985 2683
www.lardo.co.uk

New restaurants come and go each week in hipster Hackney but Lardo – ever rammed – is a keeper. In fact, its growing into a mini Italian chain now with its offshoot Lardo Bébé now open in Hackney Downs (158 Sandringham Rd, E8 2HS) and its salumeria, Lonzo, near London Fields (5 Helmsley Place, E8 3SB). Lardo's primary selling point is pizza (charcuterie comes a close second), which is wood-fired in the Neapolitan style but with jazzier toppings than is traditional – think squash, broccoli and goats' curd or radicchio, speck and Gorgonzola. The delectable chewiness we expected of Lardo pizza crust wasn't there on a recent visit; we found the seasonal antipasti and primi better. Marinda tomato, chickpea and ricotta salata on a vintage plate was an effective assembly; casarecce with pesto, potatoes and beans was authentically rustic. Finish with tiramisu or gelato. The contemporary European wine list (from £20.40) has plenty of smart choices by the glass.
Chef/s: Matthew Cranston. **Open:** all week 12 to 10.30 (11am Sat and Sun). **Closed:** 10 days Christmas. **Meals:** alc (main courses £8 to £18). **Details:** 60 seats. 50 seats outside. Bar. Wheelchair access. Music.

Join us at thegoodfoodguide.co.uk

Lutyens

Classy, confident Conran classic
Cooking score: 4
♁ Chancery Lane, St Paul's, Temple, map 5
Anglo-European | £60
85 Fleet Street, City, EC4Y 1AE
Tel no: (020) 7583 8385
www.lutyens-restaurant.com

Conceived by architectural grandee Sir Edwin Lutyens and now adopted by design supremo Sir Terence Conran, this high-end behemoth is a boon for the crowd of City and Inns of Court suits who relish its many and varied assets – from power breakfasts and bistro lunch deals to clubby encounters and dinners in the restaurant. The flatteringly lit, eau-de-nil dining room purrs contentedly with the murmurs of money well spent, while impeccably choreographed service attends to every detail. The food is also custom-built for City appetites, whether it's a delicate tartare from the 'raw bar' or some unadulterated richness in the shape of foie gras and duck liver parfait, ox cheek with veal tongue and monk's beard, or monkfish with charred leeks, salsify, black truffle and hazelnuts. To conclude, Neal's Yard cheeses are an alternative to Euro-accented desserts such as passion fruit soufflé with lime ice cream. The wine list is a pedigree international showcase aimed at big spenders, although entry-level selections start at £20.
Chef/s: Henrik Ritzen. **Open:** Mon to Fri L 12 to 3, D 6 to 10. **Closed:** Sat, Sun, 2 weeks Christmas and New Year. **Meals:** alc (main courses £14 to £39). Set L £24 (2 courses) to £28. Set D £30. **Details:** 120 seats. 14 seats outside. Bar. Wheelchair access. Music.

NEW ENTRY

Lyle's

Great British ingredients stand out
Cooking score: 5
♁ Shoreditch High Street, map 4
Modern British | £39
Tea Building, 56 Shoreditch High Street, Shoreditch, E1 6JJ
Tel no: (020) 3011 1547
www.lyleslondon.com

The refurbished 1930s Tea Building is a Shoreditch landmark and home to Lyle's, James Lowe's modern British restaurant that goes about its business with gusto, proud of its wares. The light-filled ground-floor room is hugely welcoming despite the barest of fittings and little decoration save for an open-plan kitchen, and the food is as plain and unadulterated as the dining room. The tersely written menu (à la carte lunch, tasting menu at dinner) promises the likes of raw Dexter rib with mussel emulsion and land cress, and while the cooking can appear deceptively simple, it works because of the quality of the fiercely seasonal ingredients. Cods' tongues on a slick of silky mash and an intensely green, pungent ramson (wild garlic) sauce, for example, has an earthiness that echoes the surroundings, while the freshness of mackerel is perfectly accented by apple and horseradish, and Highland flank teamed with new season's onions and wild garlic. For dessert, look no further than a light treacle tart with raw milk ice cream. Gentle pricing extends to the short, modern wine list, which opens at £21.
Chef/s: James Lowe. **Open:** Mon to Fri L 12 to 2.30, Mon to Sat D 6 to 10. **Closed:** Sun, 2 weeks Christmas, bank hols. **Meals:** alc (main courses £12 to £17). Tasting menu £39 (5 courses). **Details:** 48 seats. V menu. Bar. Wheelchair access.

Merchants Tavern

A grown-up restaurant of serious intent
Cooking score: 5
⊖ Old Street, map 4
Modern European | £41
36 Charlotte Road, Shoreditch, EC2A 3PG
Tel no: (020) 7060 5335
www.merchantstavern.co.uk

This collaboration between Angela Hartnett, Neil Borthwick and the founders of the Canteen chain is a merry affair, alive with the sound of people having a good time. The Victorian warehouse and former apothecary is a cavernous, brick-lined space, divided into a front bar where you can feast on toasted sandwiches, charcuterie and classy snacks such as deep-fried oysters or crispy pork with Asian pickles, and the back dining room with its open kitchen giving grandstand views of Neil Borthwick and his team toiling away to produce fresh, vibrant dishes with vivid flavours. There is much to fall in love with here: rosemary duck-heart skewers; quail with hazelnut pesto, remoulade and foie gras; Barbary duck breast with garlic, orange and endive; a shared côte de boeuf with béarnaise; and Muscovado tart with fromage frais and black pepper ice cream. Wines from £20.
Chef/s: Neil Borthwick. **Open:** all week L 12 to 3 (4 Sun), D 6 to 11 (9 Sun). **Closed:** 24 to 27 Dec, 1 Jan. **Meals:** alc (main courses £16 to £22). Set L £16 (2 courses) to £21. Sun L £20 (2 courses) to £25. **Details:** 85 seats. Wheelchair access. Music.

NEW ENTRY

Mission

Local wine bar with an ambitious kitchen
Cooking score: 2
⊖ Bethnal Green, map 1
Modern European | £35
250 Paradise Row, Bethnal Green, E2 9LE
Tel no: (020) 7613 0478
www.missione2.com

£5 OFF 🍾

Bringing a ray of Napa Valley sunshine to a Victorian railway arch in Bethnal Green, Mission is a new wine bar-plus-kitchen taking its inspiration (and its bottles) from the shady vineyards of northern California. Said vintages are stacked high behind the bar in the cavernous dining space (rattling as trains pass overhead), while tables are tightly packed beneath a slightly incongruous palm tree. No such peculiarities on the succinct, well-considered Modern European menu, divided between small and large plates – our inspection started well with exquisitely cooked octopus tentacle, lying on a bed of winter tomatoes and ramson aïoli. Larger offerings are similarly elemental in their construction: tender rabbit leg, lentils and wild garlic, for instance, or monkfish, lardo and white sprouting broccoli. Desserts might include the likes of crème caramel or moreish pistachio cake – but the headline attraction is of course the wine list, which reads like a Great American Novel; wines by the glass from £6.
Chef/s: James De Jong. **Open:** all week L 12 to 3 (10 to 4 Sat and Sun), D 6 to 10.30 (11 Thur to Sat). **Closed:** 24 to 26 Dec. **Meals:** alc (main meals £7 to £38). Set L £35 (3 courses). **Details:** 62 seats. 50 seats outside. Bar. Wheelchair access. Music.

The Modern Pantry

Flexible fusion in Clerkenwell
Cooking score: 3
⊖ Farringdon, map 5
Fusion | £35
47-48 St John's Square, Clerkenwell, EC1V 4JJ
Tel no: (020) 7553 9210
www.themodernpantry.co.uk

£5 OFF 🍾

Readers often wonder how Anna Hansen can take ordinary ingredients and turn them into something to be fought over, but then the Canadian-born and New Zealand-raised chef is known for her culinary inventiveness and excursions into odd corners of fusion cooking. The surroundings, a casual and relaxed Georgian town house incorporating a ground-floor café and pair of first-floor dining rooms, embody minimalist style and fit the all-day ethos very well. Sugar-cured prawn omelette with smoked chilli sambal, green chilli, spring onion and coriander speaks of Hansen's signature style. Grilled tamarind-marinated Tamworth pork chop could follow, served with Persian spice roast butternut squash, braised red cabbage, sour cherry and a hijiki (seaweed) and onion relish. A rum, raisin and wattleseed parfait with caramelised banana and coconut sponge is on hand to fill any remaining gaps. Organic and biodynamic wines appear on a well-annotated wine list with prices from £21.

Chef/s: Anna Hansen. **Open:** Sat and Sun 9 to 4 (10 Sun), D 6 to 10.30 (6.30 to 10 Sun). **Closed:** 25 and 26 Dec, Aug bank hol. **Meals:** alc (main courses £17 to £21). Set L £23 (2 courses) to £28. **Details:** 100 seats. 32 seats outside. Music.

Morito

Pint-sized paragon of Moorish tapas
Cooking score: 4
⊖ Farringdon, map 2
Tapas | £20
32 Exmouth Market, Clerkenwell, EC1R 4QE
Tel no: (020) 7278 7007
www.morito.co.uk

This popular tapas and meze bar may be tiny, but Morito more than makes up for its diminutive size with the bold Iberian-eastern Med plates it sends out. The scramble for a stool at this playful sibling of Moro (next door) can be avoided by taking advantage of a lunch booking – evenings are a frenetic free-for-all; a bar seat gives you an enviable view of kitchen theatrics. Morito majors on punchy snacks and small plates for sharing, enticing maximum flavour from humble ingredients, with a talent for culinary alchemy, particularly with vegetables: fried chickpeas are dangerously addictive, and an intense Iranian beetroot borani is enlivened with feta, dill and walnuts. Alongside tapas classics, excellent breads and plancha specials, moreish spiced lamb, aubergine, yoghurt and pine nuts hits a high note. If you haven't let greed get the better of you, save room for affogato or Malaga raisin ice cream. Spanish wines start at £18, though you may prefer to sample their extensive, well-thought-out sherry list.

Chef/s: Henry Russell. **Open:** all week L 12 to 4, Mon to Sat D 5 to 11. **Closed:** 24 Dec to 2 Jan, bank hols. **Meals:** alc (tapas £2 to £10). **Details:** 36 seats. 6 seats outside. Wheelchair access. Music.

Moro

Moorish-Spanish charmer
Cooking score: 5
⊖ Farringdon, map 2
Spanish-North African | £37
34-36 Exmouth Market, Clerkenwell, EC1R 4QE
Tel no: (020) 7833 8336
www.moro.co.uk

Twenty years in the business and Moro still looks the sunny-natured, unruffled customer it always was. You can rock up on a summer evening and find every outdoor seat and berth at the bar taken, and yet the place runs on rails, the staff impressively unfrazzled, the same easy-going amiability pervading as ever. The Moorish and Spanish dishes helped establish a London trend back in the day, and still delight: barbecued quail with labneh, pistachio dukkah, broad beans and radish is right on the map, though other offerings stray creatively off-piste, perhaps for seared mackerel with pickled rhubarb, walnuts and tarragon. At main, bulgur pilaff adds bulk to a wing of skate, while wood-roasted lamb is tenderly pink, offset with creamy white beans and tomato and almond salsa. Finish with cardamom and rosewater ice cream, or yoghurt cake with pistachios and jewels of pomegranate. Cava laced with blood orange and vanilla, or something from the sherry list, might presage a delve through the pedigree Iberian wines, starting at £19.50.

Chef/s: Sam and Samantha Clark. **Open:** all week L 12 to 2.30 (12.30 to 3.30 Sun), Mon to Sat D 6 to 10.30. **Closed:** Christmas, New Year, bank hols. **Meals:** alc (main courses £19 to £22). **Details:** 90 seats. 20 seats outside. Wheelchair access.

Perkin Reveller

Tipples and tuck by the Tower

Cooking score: 2

Tower Hill, map 4

British | £28

East Gate, Tower of London, St Katherine's Way, Tower Hill, EC3N 4AB

Tel no: (020) 3166 6949

www.perkinreveller.co.uk

A modern building squeezed between the Tower and the Thames, Perkin Reveller is all clean lines and big windows. With Tower Bridge next door, it's a tourist's dream – yet it feels a world removed from the back-packed crowds on the wharf outside. Much of the seating is at long tables, nurturing a feasting spirit befitting a restaurant named after a Chaucerian character. There's more than a hint of heritage to the menu, where potted shrimps, fish and chips and apple crumble all make a showing, and instead of crème brûlée you get burnt Cambridge cream. This is the place for a fulsome chicken, ham and mushroom pie or a fresh ham hock and egg salad with Jersey Royals – yet Italian-accented crab and lobster linguine or broccoli risotto also make a showing. A global wine list kicks off at £21, and there are plenty of interesting cocktails in the bar.
Chef/s: Tony Schwartz. **Open:** all week L 12 to 3 (4 Sun), Mon to Sat D 6 to 9. **Closed:** 25 and 26 Dec, 1 Jan. **Meals:** alc (main courses £14 to £18). Set L and D £18 (2 courses) to £22. Sun L £22. **Details:** 110 seats. 60 seats outside. Bar. Wheelchair access. Music.

Pizza East

Liverpool Street, Old Street, map 4

Italian-American | £25

56 Shoreditch High Street, Shoreditch, E1 6JJ

Tel no: (020) 3310 2000

www.pizzaeast.com

Laid-back, canteen-style and with the hip industrial-meets-utilitarian vibe you expect in Shoreditch, this Californian-inspired pizzeria occupies the ground floor of the area's landmark Tea Building. The wood oven is the workhorse of the kitchen, with authentic pizzas topped with such combinations as asparagus, speck and fontina or veal meatballs, prosciutto and cream. Don't fancy pizza? Try the crispy pork belly with salsa verde or chicken cacciatore. Wines from £20. Open all week. Also has branches in Portobello and Kentish Town.

Plateau

Lofty cooking in high-rise setting

Cooking score: 4

Canary Wharf, map 1

Modern European | £45

4th Floor, Canada Place, Canary Wharf, E14 5ER

Tel no: (020) 7715 7100

www.plateau-restaurant.co.uk

Perched on the fourth floor of a steel and glass building in the heart of Canary Wharf, Plateau is great place from which to enjoy the gleaming skyline of the city's financial district. The light-washed dining room is decked out with marble-topped tables and contemporary white furnishings, the covered terrace is 'an ideal spot in which to chill out' and service is 'well-drilled and attentive'. When it comes to the food, the repertoire is modern, the kitchen advocating freshness – witness a ceviche of Orkney scallops paired with green apple and fennel. Technique is also a strength, helping to bring harmony to the various components (goats' cheese polenta, black truffles and lovage), which share a plate with a roasted squab pigeon. For the final act, mille-feuille arrives with Cognac jelly and cherry coulis and hits all the right notes. The praiseworthy wine list (from £21.50) has three pages of wines by the glass and is pitched at every taste and budget.
Chef/s: Daniel McGarey. **Open:** Mon to Fri L 12 to 3, Mon to Sat D 6 to 10.30. **Closed:** Sun, 25 Dec, 1 Jan. **Meals:** alc (main courses £19 to £36). Set L £25 (2 courses) to £28. **Details:** 190 seats. 46 seats outside. V menu. Bar. Wheelchair access. Music. Parking.

Quality Chop House

A reinvented Victorian classic

Cooking score: 3

⊖ Farringdon, map 5

Modern British | £35

94 Farringdon Road, Clerkenwell, EC1R 3EA

Tel no: (020) 7278 1452

www.thequalitychophouse.com

Once a humble 19th-century canteen, billed as 'Progressive Working Class Caterers', the Quality Chophouse is now a fun piece of reinvented Victoriana feeding Clerkenwell creatives. Eat in the wine bar or repair to the gloriously preserved, Grade II-listed dining room with its original booths, tiled floors and famous bench seating. On the food front expect breaded bone marrow with a dose of trendy kimchee, mackerel with kale pesto or hare with celeriac, pear and onions – all fashioned daily from fine ingredients. Generous helpings of Galloway mince with dripping toast and venison with mushroom ketchup summon up a few ghosts of yesteryear, while puds might bring rhubarb and vanilla tart or apple and pear crumble – modishly served with malted barley custard. Bottles of Kernel beer and French 'cidre' are alternatives to wines from a weighty international list (priced from £21). Don't forget to check out the butcher's and food shop next door.
Chef/s: Shaun Searley. **Open:** all week L 12 to 3 (4 Sun), Mon to Sat D 6 to 11. **Closed:** 1 week Christmas and New Year. **Meals:** alc (main courses £13 to £25). Set D £39. Sun L £18. Tasting menu £60.
Details: 66 seats. 6 seats outside. Music.

Symbols

🛏 Accommodation is available

💷30 Three courses for less than £30

£5 OFF £5-off voucher scheme

🍾 Notable wine list

The Richmond

Former boozer with raw bar and cocktails

Cooking score: 2

⊖ Dalston Junction, map 2

Modern British | £30

316 Queensbridge Road, Hackney, E8 3NH

Tel no: (020) 7241 1638

www.therichmondhackney.com

Brett Redman's north-of-the-river follow-up to Elliot's is in edgy Dalston. Redman has converted this once-grotty corner pub into a handsome bistro-cum-cocktail-and-raw-bar, a concept fit for the fashionable and increasingly well-heeled locals. It's a little rough around the edges (scratched pub chairs, splintery but fabulous painted wooden floor), but it works. At the raw bar along one side, a menu of excellent oysters (including Maldon kumamotos and Menai rocks), ceviches, carpaccios et al is served; a full carte is available in the dining area. As an opener, an English muffin, little larger than a pocket watch but brimful of buttery white crab with espelette pepper, was a resounding success; far stronger than a Moroccan-inspired tuna tartare, overpowered by intrusive cumin. The spicy 'nduja in fish stew to follow was better judged. Finish with banana tart, cheese, or simply get stuck into the natural wines.
Chef/s: Jon Atashroo. **Open:** Mon to Sat D 6 to 12 (5 Sat). Sat L 12 to 3. Sun 12 to 8. **Meals:** alc (main courses £14 to £17). **Details:** Bar.

Roka Canary Wharf

Striking contemporary Japanese

Cooking score: 2

⊖ Canary Wharf, map 1

Japanese | £50

4 Park Pavilion, Canary Wharf, E14 5FW

Tel no: (020) 7636 5228

www.rokarestaurant.com

On the first floor of a glass and steel building with an abundance of pale wood and a central open-grill kitchen manned by an army of chefs, this offshoot of Roka in Charlotte Street (see entry) catches the eye and the crowds. Although underpinned by Japanese influences, the cooking has a distinct cross-cultural slant. Snacks of beef, ginger and sesame gyoza, and steamed edamame with sea salt, are a sensible way to kick things off, then there's an enticing variety of sushi, sashimi and maki rolls, assorted vegetable tempura, black cod marinated in yuzu miso, beef fillet with chilli, ginger and spring onion, rice hot pot with king crab and wasabi tobiko, and salads such as spinach leaves and sesame dressing. Prices can mount up, but the weekend brunch makes a good introduction with menus priced at £42, £54 and £66, including unlimited wine. Service is pleasant and helpful. Wine from £26.

Chef/s: Hamish Brown. **Open:** Mon to Sat L 11.45 to 3, D 5.30 to 11. Sun 11.30 to 8.30. **Closed:** 25 Dec. **Meals:** alc (dishes from £13 to £36). Tasting menus £55 and £79. **Details:** 89 seats. 40 seats outside. Bar. Wheelchair access. Music.

NEW ENTRY

Rotorino

Inclusive Italian in hipster heartland
Cooking score: 3
⊖ **Haggerston, Dalston Junction, map 2**
Italian | £30
434 Kingsland Road, Dalston, E8 4AA
Tel no: (020) 7249 9081
www.rotorino.com

Nestled among Kingsland Road's kebab shops, Stevie Parle's Rotorino is a diamond in the rough. There's little sign, inside or out, to suggest that good food's on offer: the vintage furniture, loud music and dim lighting feel more 'hipster drinking den' than high-end Italian. But then the carta di musica arrives, heavily spiked with salt and rosemary, and a strong, distinctively East London dining experience starts to take shape. The menu's structured and priced to allow one to dip in or take four courses. We did the latter, beginning disappointingly with greasy fried pumpkin and anchovy sauce and an underpowered, though fresh and crunchy brown shrimp, apple and kohlrabi salad. Casarecce pasta alla Norma to follow was a nonna-style knockout

success, however, and a shared veal T-bone was excellent. Cleanly fried cannoli are the signature dessert. Wines are exciting, contemporary Italians, from £20; different ones are served by the glass daily.

Chef/s: Stevie Parle and James Knight. **Open:** Mon to Fri D only 6 to 10. Sat and Sun 12 to 12. **Meals:** alc (main courses £9 to £20). **Details:** 60 seats. Bar. Music.

READERS RECOMMEND

Sager and Wilde

European
193 Hackney Road, Hackney, E2 8JL
Tel no: (020) 8127 7330
www.sagerandwilde.com
'The type of intimate neighbourhood wine bar and restaurant you wished you lived a few doors from. The pièce de résistance is their famous grilled cheese: molten Comté and soft onion ooze temptingly between toasted slices of satisfyingly chewy sourdough.'

St John

Nose-to-tail pioneer
Cooking score: 5
⊖ **Farringdon, map 5**
British | £40
26 St John Street, Clerkenwell, EC1M 4AY
Tel no: (020) 7251 0848
www.stjohngroup.uk.com/smithfield

This former Smithfield smokehouse was a game-changer in the 1990s when Fergus Henderson and Trevor Gulliver set up shop, creating a shrine to nose-to-tail eating, regional curiosities and hedgerow finds. These concepts are no longer groundbreaking, but the place is as fresh as a daisy – and while everything from offal to foraging has found its way on to the country's more forward-thinking menus, the food here is defiantly old-school. 'I love the almost monastic feel of the dining space – white, white, white with simple crockery and glassware,' noted one customer who relished crispy pig's ears with dandelion salad followed by tender pig's tongue with alexanders and radishes and a 'lovely broth'. Others praise the 'true and

Join us at thegoodfoodguide.co.uk

uncomplicated' flavours of both braised veal with fennel and the grouse with bread sauce. The vintage feel extends to desserts of tapioca and crab apple jelly or date loaf and butterscotch sauce. Wash it down with interesting French wines, priced from £25. **Chef/s:** Jonathon Woodway. **Open:** Sun to Fri L 12 to 3 (1 to 3 Sun), Mon to Sat D 6 to 11. **Closed:** 25 Dec to 1 Jan, bank hols. **Meals:** alc (main courses £13 to £33). **Details:** 85 seats. Bar.

St John Bread & Wine

Untainted British victuals
Cooking score: 3
⊖ Liverpool Street, map 4
British | £35
94-96 Commercial Street, Spitalfields, E1 6LZ
Tel no: (020) 7251 0848
www.stjohngroup.uk.com

This laid-back offshoot of nose-to-tail trailblazer St John (see entry) delivers 'a whole lot of flavour' in canteen-style surroundings that reflect the kitchen's single-minded approach — whitewashed walls, bare tables, noisy acoustics…you know the score. Artisan breads and cakes from their own bakery make the place a hit for breakfast or elevenses, while the daily menu is a roll call of brassy seasonal dishes that bang the drum for untainted British victuals. It's the kind of patriotic stuff that delights readers: 'absolutely perfect' duck ham with quince and cobnuts; 'rich, dark, full in-your-face' ox cheek; 'voluptuously sensual' roast grouse with proper accompaniments. Fans of fish and greenery might veer towards salt hake with white cabbage and chervil or purple sprouting broccoli with duck egg and anchovy, while everyone orders the Eccles cake with a hunk of Lancashire cheese. By contrast, the wine list majors on 'very drinkable' French country wines from £25. **Chef/s:** Tristram Bowden. **Open:** all week L 12 to 3 (4 Sat and Sun), D 6 to 11 (9 Mon). **Closed:** 25 and 26 Dec, 1 Jan. **Meals:** alc (main courses £15 to £18). **Details:** 64 seats.

Taberna do Mercado

Portuguese tapas from world-class chef
Cooking score: 4
⊖ Liverpool Street, Aldgate East, map 4
Portuguese | £35
Old Spitalfields Market, 107b Commercial Street, Spitalfields, E1 6BG
Tel no: (020) 7375 0649
www.tabernamercado.co.uk

When chef *do dia* Nuno Mendes (exec-chef Chiltern Firehouse — see entry) opens a Portuguese tapas place in Spitalfields market, people sit up and take notice. That this stripped-back dining room with its white-washed walls and clutch of marble-topped tables serves inventive, flavour-packed dishes comes as no surprise to Mendes' many followers. Take a snack of runner bean fritters, for example, in which the light, crunchy batter encasing the squeaky fresh beans soaks into a lemon and coriander broth to be slurped at the end. Or tiny roe-on scallops, served in a tin, and swimming in brown butter to be mopped up with chewy sourdough bread. Don't miss the tartare of Bísaro pork, its smoky hit offset by sweet paprika and a meaty cozido broth. Knowledgeable staff are happy to explain the menu and advise on the all-Portuguese wine list that includes plenty of selections by the glass, with bottles starting at £20. Note that dinner, served from 6 to 9.30, is not bookable. **Chef/s:** Nuno Mendes. **Open:** all week 12 to 9.30 (5 Sun). **Meals:** alc (tapas £5 to £15)

Tayyabs

Punjabi canteen with wicked spicing
Cooking score: 2
⊖ Whitechapel, Aldgate East, map 1
Pakistani | £20
83-89 Fieldgate Street, Whitechapel, E1 1JU
Tel no: (020) 7247 6400/9543
www.tayyabs.co.uk

People have been beating a path to Tayyabs' door since 1972 and it's been in the same family all that time; the three sons of the founding

father now carrying on the good work. It's tucked out of the way, but it's easy enough to find if you just follow the crowds, and as it seats around 350 people you definitely won't be alone! It's so vast it takes up several shopfronts. The atmosphere is rarely less than 'incredible', or at least incredibly lively. Punjabi-style grilled meats are the mainstay of the menu, with the lamb chops still getting rave reviews, and the seekh kebab praised for its 'remarkable combination of herbs and spices'. There are classic curries, too, like the veggie tinda masala (baby pumpkin) and karahi chicken keema served in the traditional cooking pot. The BYO policy helps make what is already a relatively cheap night out even cheaper.
Chef/s: Wasim Tayyab. **Open:** all week 12 to 11.30. **Meals:** alc (main courses £5 to £12). **Details:** 350 seats. V menu. Wheelchair access. Music.

28°-50°

Dedicated to the fruit of the vine
Cooking score: 4
♌ Chancery Lane, map 5
French | £32
140 Fetter Lane, City, EC4A 1BT
Tel no: (020) 7242 8877
www.2850.co.uk

With its reasonable prices, simple food and informal atmosphere, this original branch of the 28°-50° group feels so right. It operates as a French-influenced bistro with fantastic wines, but folk also come here for a menu that puts a modern spin on the core French repertoire. Crème soubise (white onion soup), foie gras terrine, ribeye steak with béarnaise sauce and lemon sole with sauce vierge represent the old-guard, while scallops with char-grilled cucumber, fennel salad and lemon purée, and duck breast with leek and onion tartlet, morels and duck jus strike a contemporary note. To finish, pistachio crème brûlée is typical of the desserts on offer. The wine list is a wonderful example of how to pour a quart of quality into a pint pot. There's intelligent choosing written all over it (not an

Australian Chardonnay or New Zealand Sauvignon among them) and real choice by the glass. Prices open at £21.
Chef/s: Julien Baris. **Open:** Mon to Sat L 12 to 2.30, D 6 to 10 (10.30 Thur to Sat). **Closed:** Sun. **Meals:** alc (main courses £14 to £17). Set L £17 (2 courses) to £20. **Details:** 60 seats.

Typing Room

Astonishing cooking in the admin room
Cooking score: 6
♌ Bethnal Green, map 1
Modern European | £60
Patriot Square, Town Hall Hotel, Bethnal Green, E2 9NF
Tel no: (020) 7871 0461
www.typingroom.com

If there's a more unusual eating venue in Bethnal Green – it's in what was the admin room of the former east London town hall, where council memos were once hammered out on manual typewriters – we've never heard of it. Diversion from the mostly bare white walls comes in the form of views into the bustling kitchen, and in Lee Westcott's vigorously inventive modern cooking. The seven-course taster covers a lot of ground (and sea), from eel with red cabbage and oranged duck, and spiced halibut with mussels and brassicas, to the unabashed traditionalism of a lump of Cumbrian shorthorn beef with watercress and garlic. Should gasps of astonishment have begun to fade, dessert will evoke them anew, with smoked apple in Jack Daniel's and dill, or rhubarb, blood orange and wild rice. The preamble 'snacks' are not worth forgoing either: smoked cod and fish skin, pig trotter with brown sauce jam. Wines are strongest in western Europe, with prices from £23.
Chef/s: Lee Westcott. **Open:** Wed to Sat L 12 to 2.30, Tue to Sat D 6 to 10. **Closed:** Sun, Mon, 24 to 26 Dec. **Meals:** Set L £24 (2 courses) to £29. Tasting menu £60 (5 courses) to £75. **Details:** 35 seats. Bar. Wheelchair access. Music.

Vinoteca

Just good food and wine
Cooking score: 2
⊖ Farringdon, Barbican, map 5
Modern European | £28
7 St John Street, Farringdon, EC1M 4AA
Tel no: (020) 7724 7288
www.vinoteca.co.uk

The original Vinoteca (see also Marylebone, Chiswick and King's Cross) comes with an incontrovertible buzz – 'the din was as much a feature as the good food and wine' – while the clientele make it 'just an all-round fun place to spend an hour or two'. Readers consider it has the Holy Trinity of what makes a good café/ restaurant: food, service and atmosphere. The set-up delivers the same char-grilled bavette with chips and tremendous collection of modern wines as the other branches, but then takes its own path, delivering hearty, Med-inspired dishes such as wild Somerset hare ragù with fresh pappardelle, red wine and Parmesan or the grilled chorizo, Puy lentil and roasted red onion salad that so impressed one reporter. Finish with a generous portion of prune and frangipane tart. The wine list, a constant work in progress, offers exemplary choice by the glass. Bottles from £16.50.
Chef/s: John Cook. **Open:** Mon to Sat L 12 to 2.45, D 6 to 10.30. **Closed:** Sun. **Meals:** alc (main courses £12 to £17). **Details:** 35 seats. Music.

NEW ENTRY
Wright Brothers Spitalfields

Seafood-sourcing specialists
Cooking score: 3
⊖ Liverpool Street, map 4
Seafood | £35
8-9 Lamb Street, Old Spitalfields Market, Spitalfields, E1 6EA
Tel no: (020) 7377 8706
www.thewrightbrothers.co.uk

A new addition to a mini-empire that includes oyster houses in Borough and Soho, Wright Brothers recently laid anchor in Smithfield Market in what might be their smartest venture yet. A spacious, bare-brick interior is presided over by a hefty marble bar, plus tanks full of snapping claws and nervous beady eyes from which customers can pick their meal if they choose. Wondrously fresh whole Dorset crab justifiably gets recommended by staff – served either garlic-roasted or chilled with lemon and mayonnaise – along with a support act of distinguished oysters hailing from France to Ireland. Simple but precise preparation extends to more conventional courses on the menu, too – a starter of yellowfin tuna tartare with aïoli and quail's egg for instance, or a main of skrei cod with fennel and dill purée. House wines start from £21, but there's also a commendable selection of porters and stouts to be glugged.
Chef/s: Richard Kirkwood. **Open:** all week L 12 to 4.30 (11 to 3 Sat and Sun), D 5 to 10.30 (4 Sat, 4 to 9 Sun). **Closed:** bank hols. **Meals:** alc (main courses £17 to £29). **Details:** 62 seats. 27 seats outside.

NEW ENTRY
Yauatcha City

Chic Chinese for the salaryman
Cooking score: 1
⊖ Liverpool Street, map 4
Chinese | £40
Broadgate Circle, City, EC2M 2QS
Tel no: (020) 3817 9888
www.yauatcha.com

It's an odd move from edgy Soho to a salaryman part of the City, but this Yauatcha offshoot has gone down well in EC2. It sweeps across the entire upper tier of Broadgate Circle – a narrow, window-hugging restaurant of restrained décor – offering a menu that applies the same combination of experimentation and familiarity as the Soho original. Dim sum moves quickly from reworked versions of Chinatown staples to edamame truffle dumpling and venison puff; larger plates deliver steamed halibut with homemade chilli and salted radish, crispy aromatic duck, and chicken pot with chestnut. Wines from £28.
Chef/s: Tong Chee Hwee. **Open:** Mon to Sat 12 to 11.30. **Closed:** Sun. **Meals:** alc (main courses £12 to £30). **Details:** 198 seats. Bar.

The Anchor & Hope

Big-hearted food with no frills
Cooking score: 3
⊖ Waterloo, Southwark, map 5
Modern European | £30
36 The Cut, South Bank, SE1 8LP
Tel no: (020) 7928 9898
www.anchorandhopepub.co.uk

There are no airs and graces here, so don't even think of calling to make a booking. You turns up and tries your luck. The charcoal-grey frontage and aubergine interior form the roughest and readiest setting for peasant cooking that's full of big-hearted flavour. Deal of the day is the 'worker's lunch', worth a cheeky hour away from the keyboard. Look to blackboard menus for the likes of snail and bacon salad, or plates of winter vegetables in hot anchovy sauce with toasted hazelnuts, but leave room for the sturdily fortifying main dishes such as roast mallard with grilled semolina, braised chicory and damson jelly. The kitchen beavers away industriously in the background, and a happy babble fills the air. A slinky wedge of pear and almond tart with clotted cream should seal the deal. A few dozen rustic wines start at £17.
Chef/s: Jonathan Jones. **Open:** Tue to Sun L 12 to 2.30 (3.15 Sun), Mon to Sat D 6 to 10.30. **Closed:** Christmas, bank hols. **Meals:** alc (main courses £11 to £25). Set L £15 (2 courses) to £17. **Details:** 70 seats. 25 seats outside. Wheelchair access. Music.

Angels and Gypsies

Home-style tapas and churros
Cooking score: 2
map 1
Spanish | £25
33 Camberwell Church Street, Camberwell, SE5 8TR
Tel no: (020) 7703 5984
www.angelsandgypsies.com

The singular approach to modern tapas, set within a Latin American-themed hotel in Camberwell, takes place against a backdrop of arched windows and stained glass, whereon a gypsy caravan is surrounded by a flight of angels. 'It's an asset to the area,' reckons a local. On the other hand, the little dishes are perfectly formed homages to the food that mamá and her mamá used to make, whether they hailed from north-western Galicia or the broiling shores of the Med. Nibble a few marinated olives with a sherry to start, before setting about cuttlefish and tomato stew, salt cod fritters, gigantes butter beans in cep oil, stuffed courgette flowers with ricotta and honey, or the ritzy 45-day aged Longhorn beef rump with black beans, horseradish allioli and a fried quail's egg. Finish classically with churros dusted in cinnamon and unrefined rapadura sugar and dipped in thick chocolate. The predominantly Spanish wines start at £17.95, or £4.75 a glass.
Chef/s: Mel Raido. **Open:** all week L 12 to 3 (3.30 Sat, 4 Sun), D 6 to 10.30 (11 Fri and Sat). **Meals:** alc (tapas £5 to £13). **Details:** 45 seats.

LOCAL GEM

Apollo Banana Leaf

⊖ Tooting Broadway, map 3
Sri Lankan | £20
190 Tooting High Street, Tooting, SW17 0SF
Tel no: (020) 8696 1423

Behind plate-glass windows giving ample views of the busy A24, Apollo's rudimentary interior sports crimson chairs and tablecloths, and huge photos of mountain scenery. South Indian and Sri Lankan food dominates the menu (alongside curry-house staples), including various dosas and uthappam pancakes – and fiery devilled dishes. Freshly fried green banana bhaji makes a good opener (best shared), though needed a tangier foil than its creamy yoghurt-mint dip. To follow, seafood string hopper fry (a biryani-like dish of chopped rice noodles with squid and shrimps) was well spiced and flavoursome, if slightly dry, and aubergine curry was unusually creamy. Unlicensed: BYO. Open all week.

NEW ENTRY

Artusi

Everyone's favourite Italian

Cooking score: 3

⊖ Peckham Rye, map 1

Italian | £25

161 Bellenden Road, Peckham, SE15 4DH

Tel no: (020) 3302 8200

www.artusi.co.uk

In recent years, this quaint part of Peckham has adopted the moniker 'Bellenden Village'. As with any urban village worth its salt, this one boasts an artisan deli, an independent butcher's, several gourmet coffee shops and some genuinely impressive neighbourhood restaurants. But this intimate, pared-back haunt is more than just a place for locals. Food lovers from across the capital flock here on account of its growing reputation as one of south London's best restaurants. Its popularity is not surprising: Artusi's daily changing menu of rustic Italian dishes is exceptional. Sublimely creamy burrata is paired with braised radicchio and tomatoes, al dente homemade tagliatelle comes with a gorgeous ox cheek ragû and a beautifully cooked leg of lamb is served with beetroots and cavolo nero. As for pudding, it's a hard choice between homemade ice cream (no cutting of corners here) and olive oil cake with blood orange. The impressive but exclusively Italian wine list opens at £20.

Chef/s: Jack Beer. **Open:** Tue to Sun L 12 to 2.30 (3 Sun), Mon to Sat D 6 to 10. **Closed:** 2 weeks Christmas, 1 week Aug. **Meals:** alc (main courses £11 to £20). Sun L £20. **Details:** 36 seats. Music.

LOCAL GEMS

L'Auberge

⊖ East Putney, map 3

French | £30

22 Upper Richmond Road, Putney, SW15 2RX

Tel no: (020) 8874 3593

www.ardillys.com

The discreet black-and-white frontage on the long stretch of Upper Richmond Road might easily be missed, were it not for the fact that Pascal Ardilly's neighbourhood restaurant has become a firm local favourite. In an ambience of properly clothed tables and rough-textured walls, gently modernised French bistro cooking is one of the delights of Putney, arriving in the shape of scallops with crispy ham and pine-nuts, and mains such as veal kidneys in mustard and honey, or sesame-crusted salmon in lemongrass beurre blanc. Sweet-spiced dessert specialities include apple and dried fruit tart with ginger ice-cream. Wines from £15.95. Tue to Sat D only.

Augustine Kitchen

map 3

French | £30

63 Battersea Bridge Road, Battersea, SW11 3AU

Tel no: (020) 7978 7085

www.augustine-kitchen.co.uk

Produce from Franck Raymond's native Evian region is the focus of this relaxed French bistro that offers a 'lovely welcome and happy atmosphere'. Inside, it's light and modern with luxurious touches (a twinkling chandelier, golden swags) hinting at the warmth and generosity of the cooking. Reblochon tart with herb salad is a good way to start, followed up by roast cod, orange and rosemary reduction and black quinoa. A coconut floating island or rhum baba are typical of the classical thrust of the desserts. French wines from £19. Closed Mon.

Babur

Creative Indian cooking
Cooking score: 2
map 1
Indian | £28
119 Brockley Rise, Forest Hill, SE23 1JP
Tel no: (020) 8291 2400
www.babur.info

From the moment you step through the door, you'll realise that Babur isn't your average suburban curry house. A big hand-painted kalamkari horoscope covers one wall of the foyer, while the dining room is a creative mix of exposed brickwork and veneered timbers. The restaurant celebrated its 30th anniversary in 2015, but the food continues to evolve – witness a dish of pan-seared stone bass with fennel chutney, green beans, channa dhal and fennel pollen. Forget lamb vindaloo and chicken tikka masala, this is the world of crispy sago-coated beetroot cutlets with papaya chutney, dry-fried goat patties and twice-marinated jumbo prawns with a prawn lattice and pickle purée – creative ideas bursting with complex flavours, textures and colour. There's an authoritative wine list, too, with fascinating spice-friendly recommendations from £20.25.
Chef/s: Jiwan Lal. **Open:** all week L 12 to 2.30 (4 Sun), D 6 to 11.30. **Closed:** 25 to 27 Dec. **Meals:** alc (main courses £14 to £18). Sun L £14 (buffet).
Details: 72 seats. Music.

The Begging Bowl

Tiptop Thai street food
Cooking score: 2
⊖ Peckham Rye, map 1
Thai | £25
168 Bellenden Road, Peckham, SE15 4BW
Tel no: (020) 7635 2627
www.thebeggingbowl.co.uk

Beat the evening rush for New Zealander Jane Alty's vibrant, informal Thai spot, and you'll bypass the queue that inevitably snakes around the premises as night falls (or you can always put your name on the list and sit it out in a nearby pub). On a plum corner plot in leafy Peckham, Begging Bowl's colourful, light interior and communal seating plays host to Alty's refreshing take on Thai street food. Bland has no place here: a David Thompson alumnus – she spent three years working with the renowned authority on Thai food – her bowls of fragrant, umami-laden Siamese cuisine have locals hooked, and those from further afield making a beeline for the likes of charcoal-grilled long aubergine salad with salted minced crispy prawns and soft duck egg or deep-fried free-range pork belly with a sour chilli sauce and gravy. The dishes, designed for sharing, arrive as and when, and everything comes with rice. Set lunch offers great bang for your buck, and wines, with helpful descriptions, start at £16.90.
Chef/s: Jane Alty. **Open:** Tue to Sun L 12 to 2.30 (3.30 Sun), Mon to Sat D 6 to 10. **Closed:** 24 to 27 Dec. **Meals:** alc (sharing plates £6 to £15).
Details: 50 seats. 30 seats outside. Music.

Bibo

A refreshingly independent Italian local
Cooking score: 3
⊖ East Putney, map 3
Italian | £32
146 Upper Richmond Road, Putney, SW15 2SW
Tel no: (020) 8780 0592
www.biborestaurant.com

Bibo's concept suits the way Putney wants to eat and drink these days: an atmosphere of warm informality, menus that allow for nibbling as much as three-coursing it and a wine list that encourages exploration. The décor evokes a big French brasserie, but the dining experience is quintessentially Italian, offering a simple, straightforward approach and reasonable prices. From the powerful punch of fiery 'nduja crocchette and truffle arancini to the delicate flavours of broad bean and new-season asparagus risotto with Gorgonzola, it is the immediacy and quality that is the main appeal. Pappardelle with slow-cooked pork ragù, marjoram and lemon, cod atop spinach, mint, braised chickpeas and chilli, organic salmon with agretti, ratte potatoes, Marinda tomatoes and Amalfi lemon aïoli, and cannoli stuffed with ricotta, candied citrus and chocolate: the list may be predictable, but they are still done well. Weekday lunch specials are a real deal and the all-Italian wine list (from £17.50) covers all the wine-growing areas, plus a few Italians abroad.

Chef/s: Sanji Thommadura. **Open:** all week L 12 to 2.30 (3 Sat and Sun), D 6 to 10 (11 Fri and Sat, 9 Sun). **Closed:** bank hols. **Meals:** alc (main courses £13 to £17). Weekday L £10 (1 course). Sun L £25. **Details:** 70 seats. 12 seats outside. Bar. Wheelchair access.

Bistro Union

Straight-talking British bistro
Cooking score: 2
⊖ Clapham South, map 3
British | £35
40 Abbeville Road, Clapham, SW4 9NG
Tel no: (020) 7042 6400
www.bistrounion.co.uk

Given the spike in house prices in recent years you're already pretty lucky if you live in this part of town (unless you're renting!), and doubly so since Adam Byatt of Trinity fame (see entry) opened up on Abbeville Road. It's a neighbourhood bistro that aims to provoke memories of a British childhood (if that's what you had) and delivers gutsy ingredients in feel-good combinations. With its awning and cheerfully tiled counter at the front, there's a Continental vibe to the interior. Kick-start the day with a fry-up or wait a while and tuck into smoked trout with kohlrabi, cucumber and sweet mustard, followed by ribeye steak cooked over charcoal, roast chicken to share, or squid with parsley salad and aïoli. Cap it all off with rhubarb and ginger fool. There's a kids' menu, bar snacks and a Sunday supper club to which you can bring your own booze for no charge. Wines start at £20.

Chef/s: Karl Goward. **Open:** all week L 12 to 3, Mon to Sat D 6 to 10. **Closed:** 24 to 27 Dec, 1 and 2 Jan. **Meals:** alc (main courses £11 to £26). Sunday supper £26. **Details:** 39 seats. 10 seats outside.

Boqueria Tapas

Sparklingly fresh, authentic tapas
Cooking score: 3
⊖ Clapham North, Brixton, map 3
Spanish | £20
192 Acre Lane, Brixton, SW2 5UL
Tel no: (020) 7733 4408
www.boqueriatapas.com

A hit with Clapham and Brixton residents, this unpretentious tapas bar has earned a reputation for running one of the most authentic venues in town. There's a stab at interior design with a stylish stool-lined bar and light, wood-floored dining area, and there's 'a great atmosphere and very friendly staff', according to one 'pleasantly surprised' reporter from San Sebastián who declared the tapas 'exquisite'. On the food front things kick off simply, with a plate of acorn-fed jamón Ibérico before going on to other staples of the tapas repertoire such as tortilla, croquetas with Iberian ham and chicken, and pork, beef and chicken meatballs in tomato sauce. More unusual is sea bass with wheat risotto with Parmesan and scallops cream, or beef tenderloin with foie and Pedro Ximénez on toasted bread. Manchego and goats' cheeses make a fine alternative to desserts such as triple chocolate tart. A compact list of Spanish wines starts at £18. A futher branch is at 278 Queenstown Road, SW8 4LT; tel: (020) 7498 8427.

Chef/s: Julian Gil. **Open:** all week D only 5 to 11 (12 Fri and Sat). **Closed:** 25 Dec. **Meals:** alc (tapas £6 to £10). **Details:** 110 seats. Bar. Wheelchair access. Music.

Camberwell Arms

Under-the-radar with great potential
Cooking score: 3
map 1
Modern British | £27
65 Camberwell Church Street, Camberwell,
SE5 8TR
Tel no: (020) 7358 4364
www.thecamberwellarms.co.uk

This 19th-century building was formerly a dancehall but has been dusted down and reconfigured as a proper foodie pub for our times: exposed brick, wallpaper, wood, leather, chandeliers and mismatched tables. Indeed, the crew behind this agreeable local certainly know what's what when it comes to feeding and watering Camberwell's residents, but then chef/proprietor Michael Davies used to work at the Anchor & Hope and the Canton Arms (see entries). Davies treats visitors to a mix of home-grown and European flavours for a raft of thoroughly modern dishes. Perhaps a little crispy smoked lamb's tongue kebab or a simple dish of devilled lemon sole fillet with tartare sauce to start, then barbecued partridge with mash, choucroute and house-cured lardo or roast brill with Pink Fir potatoes, monk's beard and spiced butter. The global wine list provides admirable drinking, from £17.50.
Chef/s: Michael Davies. **Open:** Tue to Sun L 12 to 2.30 (4 Sun), Mon to Sat D 6 to 10. **Meals:** alc (main courses £14 to £15). **Details:** 70 seats. Bar. Music.

Canton Arms

Revitalised local boozer
Cooking score: 1
⊖ Stockwell, map 3
Modern British | £30
177 South Lambeth Road, Stockwell, SW8 1XP
Tel no: (020) 7582 8710
www.cantonarms.com

Located between tube stops on one of south London's busiest thoroughfares, the Canton Arms can feel oddly isolated – unless you're a fast walker. And yet this upmarket dining boozer continues to draw in customers from far and wide. A big part of its charm is its reluctance to pander to the ever-changing needs of London's in-crowd. Exposed bulbs are shunned in favour of stuffy lampshades. Hoppy craft beers are trumped by draught pints of proper bitter and the food focus is decidedly Mediterranean: a salad of feta, Datterini tomatoes, mint and crumbs; 'Tuscan style' braised Hampshire pork cheeks with polenta; Seville marmalade ice cream and baked vanilla custard with raspberries. The French and Italian wine list starts at 17.50.
Chef/s: Rory Shannon. **Open:** Tue to Sun L 12 to 2.30 (4 Sun), Mon to Sat D 6 to 10. **Closed:** 24 Dec to 2 Jan. **Meals:** alc (main courses £15 to £17). **Details:** 70 seats. Bar. Music.

Casse-Croûte

French from beginning to end
Cooking score: 4
⊖ London Bridge, Borough, map 1
French | £30
109 Bermondsey Street, Bermondsey,
SE1 3XB
Tel no: (020) 7407 2140
www.cassecroute.co.uk

It seems intimate 25-seater Casse-Croûte has settled into a very nice groove since opening in July 2013. With a bar down one side, line of tight-packed, red-checked tables down the other, black-and-white floor and walls covered in French posters, and with hospitable French staff, a lot of effort has gone into creating a mood that is warm and unpretentious. The daily changing blackboard menu consists of just three starters, mains and dessert, all reasonably priced when you consider the quality of the cooking. Come here if you want straight-talking French brasserie classics, say ragoût d'escargots with crêpe vonnassienne (potato blini) or terrine de foie de volaille, then lapin à la moutarde or sole grenobloise with pommes vapeur, and soufflé au chocolat or Paris-Brest to finish. 'It's more French than places I've been to in France,' confided one reporter. French wines from £20. Booking is essential.

Chef/s: Sylvain Soulard. **Open:** Sun L 12 to 4. Mon to Sat 12 to 10. **Closed:** 24 to 28 Dec. **Meals:** alc (main courses £16 to £20). **Details:** 25 seats. 2 seats outside. Wheelchair access. Music.

Chapters All Day Dining

User-friendly neighbourhood brasserie
Cooking score: 3
map 1
Modern British | £27
43-45 Montpelier Vale, Blackheath, SE3 0TJ
Tel no: (020) 8333 2666
www.chaptersrestaurants.com

A generous wide-fronted place on the edge of the heath, Chapters is bright, airy and smartly designed without being over the top. Clean lines, polished surfaces and exposed brickwork ramp up the brasserie aesthetic, and the menu toes the line nicely. It makes much of its Josper oven, which turns out weighty options such as a venison burger with Roquefort and 'Aussie frites' or spatchcock chicken with lemon and thyme. Elsewhere, fusion flavours shines through – witness a starter of crisp pork belly, quails' eggs, kimchee and miso dressing. A main of hake with wild asparagus and pommes mousseline hit the spot for one diner, while a dessert of salted-caramel tart with apple sorbet apple crumble and an apple crisp proved 'flawless, with some of the thinnest pastry I have seen in a while'. 'Fantastically friendly' staff manage to be attentive but not intrusive, while the wine list offers much by the glass and opens at £16.95 a bottle.

Chef/s: Nick Simmons. **Open:** all week L 12 to 3 (5 Sat and Sun), D 6 to 11 (9 Sun). **Closed:** 2 and 3 Jan. **Meals:** alc (main courses £11 to £17). Set L £13 (2 courses) to £15. Set D £15 (2 courses) to £18. **Details:** 100 seats. 20 seats outside. Bar. Wheelchair access. Music.

Chez Bruce

Rewarding, top-notch cooking
Cooking score: 6
⊖ Balham, map 3
Modern British | £50
2 Bellevue Road, Wandsworth, SW17 7EG
Tel no: (020) 8672 0114
www.chezbruce.co.uk

Striding confidently into its 21st year, Bruce Poole's restaurant shows no sign of slowing down, and is as popular as ever. The modest, mauve-coloured frontage is set among a parade of shops overlooking Wandsworth Common, while inside it's relaxing and informal, the bright space with wood flooring, modern art, simple dark-wood chairs and white linen-clad tables is 'filled with good-natured clamour'. 'No foams, no froths, just excellent contemporary food' is the deal here, offered on a daily changing menu that is an appealing mix of broadly based European dishes, and the kitchen rewards with well balanced cooking. Start, perhaps, with fillet of Cornish mackerel served with wafer-thin courgettes, spicy harissa, couscous, preserved lemon and mint, then go on to succulent Anjou pigeon breasts teamed with foie gras, a white onion stuffed with pearl barley and a poivrade sauce. To finish there's a tiptop cheeseboard, unless you fancy bowing out with a rum baba with blood-orange compote. Friendly but not overfamiliar staff deserve a lot of credit, too. The superb wine list (from £22) is a veritable treasure trove.

Chef/s: Matt Christmas. **Open:** all week L 12 to 2.30 (3 Sat and Sun), D 6.30 to 10 (10.30 Fri and Sat, 9.30 Sun). **Closed:** 24 to 26 Dec, 1 Jan. **Meals:** Set L £25 (2 courses) to £30. Set D £38 (2 courses) to £50. Sun L £35. **Details:** 80 seats. Wheelchair access.

Craft
Clever cooking in an unexpected location
Cooking score: 3
⊖ North Greenwich, map 1
Modern British | £42
Peninsula Square, Greenwich, SE10 0SQ
Tel no: (020) 8465 5910
www.craft-london.co.uk

'A brilliant addition to an area where all other options are limited to ubiquitous chains,' noted a reporter, mightily impressed by this three-storey bar and restaurant opposite the O2. With floor-to-ceiling curved glass, a balcony running all the way around the top-floor bar (panoramic views, obvs), rich colours and 'a lovely warm, golden light' in the dining room on the floor below, this is 'a place with personality'. Expect very seasonal, very fresh, uncomplicated dishes where the high quality of the raw materials speaks for itself – 'hence the punchy prices'. But the expense is forgiven when there's hot, crisp flatbread, three fat, juicy, wood-grilled scallops, the roe pan-fried separately and giving off a delicious salty richness, served with puffy anchovy fritters, and a clever dessert of chocolate, coffee and burnt ice cream. Service is 'friendly and knowledgeable'. Wines from £20.
Chef/s: Stevie Parle and Craig Johnson. **Open:** Wed to Sat L 11.30 to 2.30, Mon to Sat D 5.30 to 10.30. **Closed:** Sun. **Meals:** alc (main courses £18 to £32). Set L £28 (3 courses). **Details:** 90 seats. Bar. Parking.

The Crooked Well
More gastro than pub
Cooking score: 3
⊖ Oval, map 1
Modern British | £30
16 Grove Lane, Camberwell, SE5 8SY
Tel no: (020) 7252 7798
www.thecrookedwell.com

£5 OFF

With its ambitious menu, rustic-chic décor and impressive roster of cocktails, the Crooked Well is more dining pub than boozer – a place for people who want to experience quality food without the formalities of a fine-dining restaurant. The focus here is seasonal and British, with the odd foray to Mediterranean shores. As such, you'll find starters like crisp salt-and-pepper squid rubbing shoulders with pan-fried quail and bubble and squeak. To follow, whole plaice is paired with king prawns, capers and garlic butter, while marinated haloumi comes with a chickpea ragoût and spiced couscous. Just as memorable are the restaurant's hearty sharing plates, which may include a whole roast leg of lamb or a huge rabbit and bacon pie. It's worth finding space for desserts such as pannacotta with lemon curd or a warm prune and Armagnac tart. Wines from £16.
Chef/s: Matt Green-Armytage and Erica Hines. **Open:** Tue to Sun L 12.30 to 3 (4 Sun), all week D 6.30 to 10 (10.30 Fri and Sat, 7 to 9 Sun). **Closed:** 24 to 26 Dec, bank hols. **Meals:** alc (main courses £13 to £20). Set L £10 (2 courses). **Details:** 56 seats. 30 seats outside. Music.

The Dairy
Ingredient-driven foodie hot spot
Cooking score: 6
⊖ Clapham Common, map 3
Modern British | £35
15 The Pavement, Clapham, SW4 0HY
Tel no: (020) 7622 4165
www.the-dairy.co.uk

'What a fabulous place,' observed a first-timer to Robin and Sarah Gill's determinedly low-key restaurant, impressed by the 'really exciting dishes and lovely flourishes'. A delicatessen has opened next door and there's a second restaurant, The Manor (see entry) nearby, but style-wise the long, narrow dining room remains artfully distressed, full of action and close-packed tables. The well-organised small-plates menu, divided into 'snacks', 'garden', 'sea', 'land' and 'sweet', showcases fiercely seasonal British produce, while the cooking is home-grown gastronomy with a vengeance that on a springtime visit yielded terrific results: an oh-so-simple plate of sweet

Cornish crabmeat with thinly shaved, raw Wye Valley asparagus and hazelnuts; own-smoked trout with tiny Jersey pearl potatoes, sorrel and radish; chicken oyster with crispy skin, kim-chee and burnt kale; and, in an inspired riff on toast and marmalade, blood-orange marmalade, brown-butter ice cream and cubes of toast. Malty-tasting sourdough is 'fabulous', service is 'friendly and engaged' and the wine list offers a good choice of mainly European wines from £22.50.

Chef/s: Robin Gill and Richie Falk. **Open:** Wed to Sun L 12 to 3 (4 Sun), Tue to Sat D 6 to 10. **Closed:** Mon, 25 Dec to 1 Jan. **Meals:** alc (small plates £9 to £11). Set L weekdays £25 (4 courses). Tasting menu £45 (7 courses). **Details:** 60 seats. V menu. Bar. Music.

NEW ENTRY

Edwins

A handy local asset and cosy oasis

Cooking score: 1

Borough, map 5

Modern British | £30

202-206 Borough High Street, Borough, SE1 1JX

Tel no: (020) 7403 9913

www.edwinsborough.co.uk

£5 OFF

This quirky gem of a restaurant is a cosy oasis above noise-ridden Borough High Street. The unassuming dining room is done out in shoestring contemporary style – bare boards, polished tables, dangling lights, junk-shop finds – while the modern British kitchen champions seasonal produce, delivering a menu that bristles with down-to-earth ingredients. Expect small plates of ox cheek pudding, pork belly and cauliflower or beetroot, pomegranate and organic goats' curd, while large plates bring grilled whole lemon sole or a classic partridge with bread sauce, bacon and turnip. Wines from £16.50.

Chef/s: Salim Massouf. **Open:** all week L 12 to 2.30 (10 to 3 Sat, 10 to 4 Sun), Mon to Sat D 6 to 10. **Meals:** alc (main courses £13 to £28). Set L £20 (2 courses) to £25. **Details:** 40 seats. Bar. Music.

Elliot's Café

On-trend foodie canteen

Cooking score: 3

London Bridge, map 4

Modern European | £26

12 Stoney Street, Borough, SE1 9AD

Tel no: (020) 7403 7436

www.elliotscafe.com

 £30

A likeable eatery beneath the arches opposite Borough Market, Elliot's follows the dress code for the well-appointed café hereabouts: exposed brick walls, wood-burner, a central communal table, hard seats. There's plenty to applaud, from the charming, engaged service to a daily menu that places butch British steaks alongside dishes where the Mediterranean and the seasons are at play, say small plates of baby artichokes with butter beans and lemon mayonnaise or black tomatoes with white crab and monk's beard. Larger plates are similarly simple but spirited: cod with creamed wild garlic, almonds and Jersey Royals, or rose veal schnitzel with fennel, apple and wine white mayo. To finish, it's hard to ignore the salted-caramel tart with reduced milk ice cream and strawberries. Drinks run from craft beers to an interesting if pricey selection of organic and biodynamic wines (from £26.50).

Chef/s: Adam Sellar. **Open:** Mon to Sat L 12 to 3 (4 Sat), D 6 to 10. **Closed:** Sun, bank hols. **Meals:** alc (large plates £12 to £16). **Details:** 35 seats. 12 seats outside. Bar. Music.

Emile's

Long-serving Putney favourite

Cooking score: 1

Putney Bridge, map 3

Anglo-French | £32

96-98 Felsham Road, Putney, SW15 1DQ

Tel no: (020) 8789 3323

www.emilesrestaurant.co.uk

 £5 OFF

A fixture of the Putney scene since 1990, Emil Fahmy and Andrew Sherlock's popular neighbourhood restaurant occupies a pair of Victorian houses and offers a keenly priced menu crammed with Gallic favourites and simple modern British classics. Individual fillet of beef Wellington still reigns supreme as the house dish, but there's also roast lamb marinated in rosemary and juniper berries with potato and chorizo croquettes, and slow-braised five-spice Gloucester Old Spot pork cheeks in Shaoxing wine. Start with scallops, haggis fritter and roast cauliflower purée, and finish with a rather distinctive sticky ginger and date pudding with toffee sauce. Wines start at £16.90.

Chef/s: Andrew Sherlock and Jonathan Higgonson. **Open:** Mon to Sat D only 7.30 to 11. **Closed:** Sun, 24 to 30 Dec, 2 Jan, Easter Sat, bank hols. **Meals:** Set D £28 (2 courses) to £32. **Details:** 90 seats. Music.

Enoteca Turi

Italian oenophile heaven
Cooking score: 3
⊖ Putney Bridge, map 3
Italian | £39
28 Putney High Street, Putney, SW15 1SQ
Tel no: (020) 8785 4449
www.enotecaturi.com

A stalwart of the Putney dining scene, this reliable Italian has been serving regional Italian cooking for 15 years now, and still knows how to please its customers. Slightly faceless from the outside, once across the threshold it's a pleasant enough room and the genial Giuseppe Turi and his wife are there to greet regulars and welcome newcomers. An excellent bread basket 'reassures diners that the kitchen is entirely competent', and the likes of grilled squid with broad bean purée, risotto with burrata and cime di rapa, and slow-cooked veal shoulder served with crespolini are 'of a high standard' and beautifully served. What makes this restaurant truly exceptional, however, is the wine list. Turi's passion is wine and his 300-strong list is carefully sourced, well kept and eruditely but readably annotated, with recommendations for food and wine pairings on the list and menu alike. The budget-conscious need not worry,

however – carafes of house wine are inexpensive and, happily, better than expected – while bottles open at £20.

Chef/s: Michele Blasi. **Open:** Mon to Sat L 12 to 2.30, D 7 to 10.30 (11 Fri and Sat). **Closed:** Sun, 25 and 26 Dec, 1 Jan. **Meals:** alc (main courses £14 to £27). Set L £19 (2 courses) to £22. Set D £30 (2 courses) to £35. **Details:** 85 seats. Wheelchair access. Music.

NEW ENTRY

40 Maltby Street

Fabulous wines and seasonal British produce
Cooking score: 2
⊖ Bermondsey, map 1
Modern British | £28
40 Maltby Street, Bermondsey, SE1 3PA
Tel no: (020) 7237 9247
www.40maltbystreet.com

Five minutes south of Bermondsey Street is a little foodie enclave – railway arches with trains thundering overhead – in which are housed a series of increasingly high-profile eateries and coffee shops; these include 40 Maltby Street, home to Gergovie Wines and its shop/bar upfront. This wine bar, with its inevitable rough-and-ready industrial décor (stacks of wooden pallets serve as tables), is known not only for its interesting organic wines, which you can buy to take home or drink in, but also for its zealous enthusiasm for seasonal British produce, belted out from a tiny, rather makeshift kitchen levered in beside the bar. In spring, expect raw asparagus, pea shoots and mint, or cod, Jersey Royals, anchovy and lettuce ('like eating super-posh fish and chips'), while summer brings a salad of oyster, cucumber and elderflower. There is undeniable care in what's coming out of the kitchen, and the economy of the place is laudable. There's just one 'proper' dessert, for example, say a lemon curd and hazelnut tart, which sits temptingly on the bar and 'when it's gone, it's gone'. On our visit, four fantastic wines were offered by the glass, from £5.60, or you can choose from one of the Gergovie wines from £25.

Chef/s: Steve Williams. **Open:** Fri and Sat L 12.30 to 2 (11 to 3.30 Sat), Wed to Sat D 6 to 9.30. **Closed:** Sun, Mon, Tue. **Meals:** alc (main courses £11 to £15). **Details:** 40 seats. Bar.

The Fox & Grapes
Fancy food in relaxed surroundings
Cooking score: 2
⊖ Wimbledon, map 1
British | £33
9 Camp Road, Wimbledon, SW19 4UN
Tel no: (020) 8619 1300
www.foxandgrapeswimbledon.co.uk

'Very family- and dog-friendly' is the verdict of one visitor to this lovely wood-framed pub close to Wimbledon Common. It's modishly rustic in a 21st-century fashion (light with high ceilings, but original lead windows, wood panelling and an open fire) and is a 'good dining option after a walk on the common'. Steaks are a speciality, but the food straddles both traditional and contemporary – prawn cocktail or salmon tikka with pickled cucumber, yoghurt and peshwari (naan); burger with caramelised onions, mustard mayo, Ogelshield cheese and triple-cooked chips or ras-el-hanout chicken breast with quinoa, apricot and feta. For dessert there's treacle tart with stem ginger ice cream or lime posset with mango chilli salsa and coconut biscuits. One minor quibble is service, trundling along at glacial pace. But on the whole, this place has been through a few incarnations and has settled into 'a very nice pub'. Wines from £19.
Chef/s: Yann East. **Open:** Mon to Sat L 12 to 3, D 6 to 9.30. Sun 12 to 8.30. **Closed:** 25 Dec. **Meals:** alc (main courses £13 to £19). **Details:** 90 seats.

Franklins

Strong on seasonal British produce
Cooking score: 2
map 1
British | £28
157 Lordship Lane, East Dulwich, SE22 8HX
Tel no: (020) 8299 9598
www.franklinsrestaurant.com

Set in a handsome Victorian building on ever-buzzing Lordship Lane, this patriotic pub has made a name for itself as a champion of seasonal, organic and local produce. Seemingly taking its cue from a corpulent 17th-century still life, the menu is a boisterous feast of hearty British produce with a distinctly meaty bent. As you'd expect, starters are robust: West Mersea oysters, potted shrimps on toast, smoked quail and coleslaw, and a generous serving of duck liver pâté with cornichons. A terse selection of main courses, meanwhile, further ramps up the brawn-factor: calf's faggots with white cabbage and black pudding, pork chops with lentils and chorizo, and a sturdy slab of sirloin steak with horseradish. For afters, it's a choice between classic sweets (butterscotch tart, coffee ice cream and orange and almond cake) or eccentric post-main savouries like black pudding on toast and Scotch woodcock. There's a good selection of hand-pulled ales and wines start at £16.
Chef/s: Ralf Wittig. **Open:** all week 12 to 10.30 (10am Sat, 10pm Sun). **Closed:** 25 and 26 Dec, 1 Jan. **Meals:** alc (main courses £13 to £21). Set L £14 (2 courses) to £17. **Details:** 72 seats. 20 seats outside. Bar. Wheelchair access. Music.

NEW ENTRY

Ganapati

Authentic South Indian cooking

Cooking score: 3
⊖ Peckham Rye, map 1
Indian | £30
38 Holly Grove, Peckham, SE15 5DF
Tel no: (020) 7277 2928
www.ganapatirestaurant.com

This tiny Peckham stalwart avoids all the trappings of your typical Indian restaurant. Housed in what looks to be a former corner shop, the atmosphere is airy, inviting and decidedly laid-back, with a big emphasis on bold, primary colours and shabby-chic furniture. The menu, meanwhile, draws on a unique brand of South Indian street food from the regions of Tamil Nadu, Kerala and Kanataka. In essence, this is food brimming with seasonal vegetables, delicate spices and homemade pickles, poppadoms and chutneys – all of it easy on the oil. Quirky appetisers include spicy potato balls fried in chickpea batter and mackerel fillets marinated in chilli and ginger. Mains take in dishes like roasted aubergine masala with coconut rice, and swordfish steak cooked in onion, tomato, garlic and smoked tamarind. Be sure to book ahead, the restaurant has a large local following. Wines start at £22.
Chef/s: Aboobacker Koya. **Open:** Tue to Fri L 12 to 2.45, D 6 to 10.30. Sat and Sun 12 to 10.30 (10pm Sun). **Closed:** Mon, 1 week Christmas. **Meals:** alc (main courses £11 to £15). **Details:** 38 seats. 10 seats outside. Wheelchair access. Music.

Harrison's

Swaggering neighbourhood brasserie

Cooking score: 1
⊖ Balham, map 3
Modern British | £30
15-19 Bedford Hill, Balham, SW12 9EX
Tel no: (020) 8675 6900
www.harrisonsbalham.co.uk

This sibling of Sam's Brasserie in Chiswick (see entry) is full of renewed vigour following its 2014 refit: a clubby cocktail bar downstairs keeps the crowd in high spirits, while the ground-floor dining room goes for style as well as substance with its orange banquettes, copper lights, concrete floors and open kitchen. Harrison's reasonably priced offer begins with breakfast (from 9am) before drifting into eclectic brasserie mode for the likes of wild mushroom arancini, crab bruschetta with shaved fennel, smoked aubergine curry and pan-seared swordfish with caponata. Wines from £18.50.
Chef/s: Mark Bains. **Open:** all week L 12 to 4, D 6 to 10.30 (10 Sun). **Closed:** 24 to 26 Dec. **Meals:** alc (main courses £10 to £24). Set L and D £14 (2 courses) to £17. Sun L £22. **Details:** 90 seats. 12 seats outside. Bar. Wheelchair access. Music.

LOCAL GEM

The Hill

⊖ Greenwich, map 1
Mediterranean | £30
89 Royal Hill, Greenwich, SE10 8SE
Tel no: (020) 8691 3626
www.thehillgreenwich.com

On a corner site in a residential area of Greenwich, the Hill contrasts its dark interior with a delightful terraced garden. Classic Italian and Spanish tapas draw the locals, perhaps a 'soft and smoky' grilled octopus with paprika and lemon, and 'spot-on and generous' ham croquetas. Try Ecuadorian ceviche and empanadas – the owners are South American. Churros with dulce de leche is 'lovely, classic for the sweet toothed'.

José

Custom-built for grazing and sipping

Cooking score: 3
⊖ London Bridge, Borough, map 1
Spanish | £20
104 Bermondsey Street, Bermondsey, SE1 3UB
Tel no: (020) 7403 4902
www.josepizarro.com

You can't book and must choose between standing or perching (on high stools) while you eat and drink, but this laid-back sibling of

Pizarro (further down Bermondsey Street – see entry), has won legions of fans with its appealing tapas and compact list of well-chosen Spanish wines and sherry. There's plenty to applaud here, and regulars have a habit of reeling off their favourites: plates of 100% acorn-fed jamón Iberico; pisto with duck egg; chorizo al vino; tortilla; mackerel with mussels and tomato sauce; calamares fritos; Iberico pork fillet…and so forth. As one regular noted, 'no matter what José puts on – whether oddity or cliché – as long as it's done well, London will provide willing diners'. In other words, it gets very busy. To finish, there's chocolate with sea salt and olive oil or turron mousse. Staff are happy to recommend sherry and tapas pairings and wines start at £19.50. **Chef/s:** José Pizarro. **Open:** all week 12 to 10.30 (12 to 5.30 Sun). **Closed:** 24 to 26 Dec, 1 Jan. **Meals:** alc (tapas £7 to £11). **Details:** 40 seats.

Lamberts

Good-natured local asset
Cooking score: 2
⊖ Balham, map 3
Modern British | £30
2 Station Parade, Balham High Road, Balham, SW12 9AZ
Tel no: (020) 8675 2233
www.lambertsrestaurant.com

£5
OFF

With fierce seasonality underpinning the cooking at Joe Lambert's modern British dining room – a smart cream, banquette and wood affair – there's little chance of tiring of the ever-changing market menu, divided into 'field', 'sea' and 'farm'. 'Field' delivers purple sprouting broccoli with mustard and crispy shallots, while salt-baked celeriac is teamed with hen's egg and rosemary oil. 'Sea' brings lemon sole with spinach, caper and shallot butter, while 'farm' offers 'super-simple', beautifully soft rump of Herdwick lamb with roasted Jerusalem artichoke, rich jus and the mineral, salty crunch of monk's beard, or char-grilled ox heart with dandelion leaves and pickled mushrooms. Desserts are no slouch either, perhaps cream-cheese ice cream with

forced rhubarb and meringue, and there's baked Tunworth cheese with toasted sourdough and candied walnuts. Sharpen up with a seasonal cocktail (we loved the rhubarb Collins with gin, honey and soda), while wines are defined by style and start at £19. **Chef/s:** Matthew Harris. **Open:** Tue to Sun L 12.30 to 2.30 (12 to 5 Sun), Tue to Sat D 6 to 10. **Closed:** Mon, bank hols. **Meals:** alc (main courses £13 to £20). Set L 15 (2 courses) to £18. Set D £17 (2 courses) to £20. Sun L £20. **Details:** 53 seats. 8 seats outside. Music.

The Lido Cafe

⊖ Brixton, map 1
Modern British | £28
Brockwell Park, Dulwich Road, Herne Hill, SE24 0PA
Tel no: (020) 7737 8183
www.thelidocafe.co.uk

For sheer oomph, this laid-back café in the grounds of the listed Brockwell Lido knocks spots off catering at most swimming pools. Breakfast is the top deal, ranging from baps filled with free-range Gloucester Old Spot sausage or bacon to smoked salmon with scrambled eggs. Come lunch (or dinner), the emphasis shifts to charcuterie, smoked haddock risotto, dry-aged Longhorn beef burger or rump steak (with peppercorn sauce), with cardamom pannacotta to finish. Wines from £17.25. Open all week.

Lobster Pot

⊖ Kennington, map 1
Seafood | £44
3 Kennington Lane, Elephant and Castle, SE11 4RG
Tel no: (020) 7582 5556
www.lobsterpotrestaurant.co.uk

Old-fashioned but still fun, Hervé Régent's nautically themed and delightfully traditional French restaurant, now in its 25th year, continues to delight with its maritime sound effects, an interior resembling a trawler cabin and house specialities of homemade fish soup and big platters of fruits de mer. For something more inventive, try grilled sea bass fillets with tomato and coconut cream sauce. Head next door to sister venue Toulouse Lautrec for live music after your dinner. Wine from £19.50. Closed Sun and Mon.

London House

Glam Ramsay venue
Cooking score: 3
⊖ **Clapham Junction, map 3**
Modern European | £40
8-9 Battersea Square, Battersea, SW11 3RA
Tel no: (020) 7592 8545
www.gordonramsay.com/londonhouse

This whacking great construction on the corner of picturesque Battersea Square, put up to help meet Georgian London's insatiable desire for oysters, got a makeover by team Gordon Ramsay in 2014, and is looking spruce. There's a swish bar where posh snacks run to polenta fingers with salt cod purée and cocktails are the order of the day, and a series of dashing dining rooms with neutral walls and splashes of colour from modern artworks. It's all very smart. Anna Haugh leads the line in the kitchen and is turning out pin-sharp plates of food steeped in British and European tradition that show a measured appreciation of contemporary techniques. Crab tortellini with black radish and shellfish broth shows real know-how, while main course Dingley Dell pork chop with pommes purée and mustard sauce is old-school done just right. Among desserts, Jerusalem artichoke ice cream makes a compelling partner for a chocolate tart. Wines start at £25.
Chef/s: Anna Haugh. **Open:** Thur to Sun L 12 to 3, Tue to Sun D 6 to 10. **Closed:** Mon. **Meals:** alc (main courses £16 to £25). Set L and D £23 (2 courses) to £28. **Details:** 70 seats. 25 seats outside. Bar. Wheelchair access. Music.

Magdalen

Intelligently crafted seasonal food
Cooking score: 4
⊖ **London Bridge, map 4**
Modern British | £35
152 Tooley Street, Southwark, SE1 2TU
Tel no: (020) 7403 1342
www.magdalenrestaurant.co.uk

The astonishingly good-value set lunch at James Faulks' handsome corner restaurant makes it a hit with local suits. Book ahead for the likes of chilled artichoke soup, fish stew and lemon pot, all for £20 for three courses. The simplicity of the presentation belies the complexity of some dishes: the fish stew combines Cornish hake, black bream and clams, all cooked separately and brought together in a fragrant saffron-enriched broth with a punchy aïoli. Ingredients are always top-notch so an à la carte dish of roast quail comprises two small, plump birds served with super-fresh broad beans and a hit of marjoram. Puddings are particularly noteworthy, so save room for lemon curd baked Alaska or cocoa-dusted salted-caramel chocolates – essentially, grown-up Rolos. The French-focused wine list includes interesting house and glass selections like a Languedoc Marsanne or a Ploussard from Jura, a welcome change from Sauvignon Blanc or Merlot. Wine from £20.
Chef/s: James Faulks. **Open:** Mon to Fri L 12 to 2.30, Mon to Sat D 6.30 to 10. **Closed:** Sun, 23 Dec to 4 Jan, 16 Aug to 1 Sept, bank hols. **Meals:** alc (main courses £16 to £23). Set L £17 (2 courses) to £20. **Details:** 90 seats. Wheelchair access.

NEW ENTRY
The Manor
Simple, obsessively seasonal, full of flavour
Cooking score: 5
Clapham Common, Clapham North, map 3
Modern British | £30
148 Clapham Manor Street, Clapham,
SW4 6BX
Tel no: (020) 7720 4662
www.themanorclapham.co.uk

With its good-time mix of buzz, bonhomie and fairly priced food and drink, the team behind the Manor have kept it all very inclusive, matching the style of nearby big brother the Dairy (see entry). As for décor, the house style is, shall we say, unpolished, a characteristic that defines the bohemian (bordering on basic) interior. What dazzles is the simple, well-prepared food with its penchant for simplicity and flavour and a keen eye for the seasons. Excellent bread arrives in a hessian bag and the menu is a refreshingly eclectic assortment of small plates with the kind of rustic British combos that make foodies go weak at the knees: smoked Kentish venison tartare with burnt apple and walnuts, Cornish crab with charred celeriac, hazelnuts and buttermilk, smoked cod with cultured cream, new potatoes and sorrel…great stuff. But the kitchen also applies its skills to wonderful, unusual desserts such as peas, mint sorbet and smashed buttermilk. Genuinely committed staff are much appreciated, likewise the excellent advice given on a modern wine list that opens at £24.
Chef/s: Robin Gill and Dean Parker. **Open:** Wed to Sun L 12 to 2.45 (4 Sun), Tue to Sat D 6 to 10. **Closed:** Mon, 1 week Christmas, 1 Jan. **Meals:** alc (main courses £10 to £13). Set L Wed to Fri £25. **Details:** 50 seats. V menu. Bar. Wheelchair access. Music.

NEW ENTRY
Naughty Piglets
Warm, welcoming, buzzy and personal
Cooking score: 2
Brixton, map 1
Modern British | £28
28 Brixton Water Lane, Brixton, SW2 1PE
Tel no: (020) 7274 7796
www.naughtypiglets.co.uk

Halfway between Brixton and Herne Hill you'll find this 'brilliant local' in the middle of a parade of shops. It looks like an upmarket café, is warmly welcoming and the bar feels intimate with its cookbook clutter, pig paraphernalia and low-hanging filament light bulbs. Joe Sharratt is ex Trinity (see entry) and his short blackboard menu delivers the likes of burrata, peas and broad beans that are so fresh he sends a message that only tiptop produce is used. Six fat prawns grilled with chilli and garlic are 'really plump and juicy with finger-licking juices', and a full-flavoured leg of lamb ('generous pink slices') atop a rough-cut salsa verde, Cornish new potatoes and cabbage is 'deeply satisfying'. 'Chocolate, milk, almond' is 'sinfully delicious': chocolate mousse on a heap of buttery biscuit crumb scattered with flaked almonds, dulce de leche shards and a swipe of thick caramel around the outer edge of the bowl. A terrific modern wine list, bursting with organic and natural options, opens at £22.
Chef/s: Joe Sharratt. **Open:** Thur to Sun L 12 to 3 (2.30 Thur, 4 Sun), Tue to Sat D 6 to 10. **Closed:** Mon. **Meals:** alc (main courses £9 to £16). **Details:** 30 seats. Bar.

No. 67
Laid-back gallery restaurant
Cooking score: 2
◉ Peckham Rye, map 1
Modern European | £23
South London Gallery, 67 Peckham Road,
Peckham, SE5 8UH
Tel no: (020) 7252 7649
www.number67.co.uk

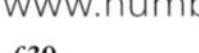

This popular café-cum-bistro is housed in one of London's edgiest contemporary art spaces. But don't let the uber-hip location put you off, or the fact that it's not particularly close to any train stations. Beyond the clean lines, exposed light bulbs and chic furniture, it has all the hallmarks of a trusted neighbourhood restaurant: warm welcoming service, intimate but informal atmosphere and a snappy but ambitious menu of seasonal dishes. By day, 67 serves as a popular breakfast, brunch and lunch spot, serving up freshly made cakes, pastries, tarts, salads and soups. By night, however, lights are dimmed, candles are lit and a menu of more substantial food comes into play: fiery devilled chicken livers on toast; guinea fowl ballotine with soft root polenta; and a gorgeous rhubarb and pear crumble with custard. There's a good selection of British cheeses, too, and all meals kick off with a generous portion of warm and waxy sourdough bread. Wines from £17.
Chef/s: Raul Cruz. **Open:** Tue to Sun L 12 to 3.30 (10.30am Sat and Sun), Wed to Sat D 6.30 to 10.
Closed: Mon, 22 Dec to 1 Jan. **Meals:** alc (main courses £12 to £14). **Details:** 45 seats. 30 seats outside. Wheelchair access. Music. Parking.

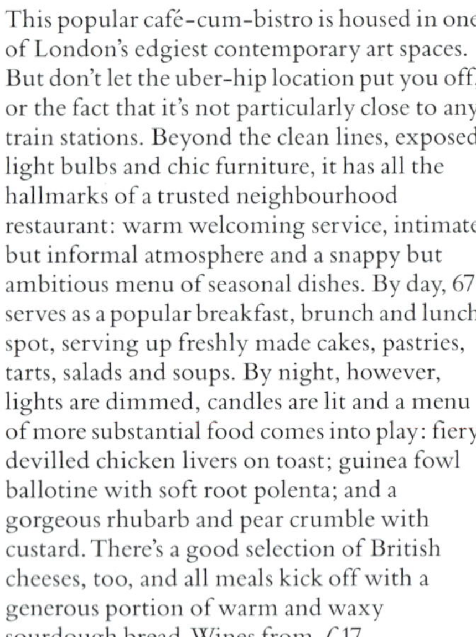

Symbols

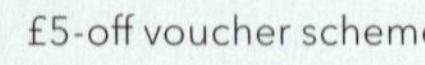

Accommodation is available
Three courses for less than £30
£5-off voucher scheme
Notable wine list

The Palmerston
Solid Dulwich performer
Cooking score: 1
map 1
Modern British | £37
91 Lordship Lane, East Dulwich, SE22 8EP
Tel no: (020) 8693 1629
www.thepalmerston.co.uk

The 'Dining Room' tag is a reminder that this solid Dulwich performer is more about food than booze – although you can still drop by for a pint of ale at the bar. Otherwise, most of the space in the handsome, wood-panelled Palmerston is taken up with neatly laid tables. Locals appreciate the warm feel of the place and the trendy modern menu – a sparky mix of influences from far and wide. Grilled piri-piri duck hearts with marinated cauliflower, Cornish mussels in green masala sauce, and rabbit leg with braised Catalan ganxet beans, chorizo, kale and salt-baked celeriac are the kind of dishes to expect. Wines kick off with 30 by the glass or carafe (from £12.40).
Chef/s: Robert Willcox. **Open:** all week L 12 to 2.30 (3 Sat and Sun), D 7 to 10 (9.30 Sun). **Closed:** 25 and 26 Dec, 1 Jan. **Meals:** alc (main courses £15 to £22). Set L £14 (2 courses) to £17. Sun L £16. **Details:** 70 seats. 24 seats outside. Music.

NEW ENTRY
Peckham Bazaar
A destination for creative Balkan cooking
Cooking score: 2
◉ Peckham Rye, map 1
Middle Eastern | £28
119 Consort Road, Peckham, SE15 3RU
Tel no: (020) 7732 2525
www.peckhambazaar.com

Prior to becoming one of south-east London's more exciting restaurants, Peckham Bazaar was a pop-up meze and grill spot, replete with colossal outdoor barbecue and a BYO wine policy. Despite being a little off the beaten track, it garnered glowing support from critics and punters and morphed into this bona fide restaurant centred around an open charcoal grill. The menu of seasonal dishes from the Balkans, eastern Mediterranean and Middle East continues to astound: perfectly char-grilled octopus, served with capers, braised pearl onions and delightfully creamy Greek fava (yellow split pea purée); juicy imam bayaldi (stuffed aubergine) with rice, pine nuts and a side of zingy labneh (a type of strained yoghurt); and there's succulent lamb leg fillet with artichoke and avgolemono (a classic Greek sauce of lemon juice and egg yolks). The pan-Balkan theme extends to dessert, with walnut baklava, kaymak ice cream and rhubarb a standout dish. The wine list, from £20, features producers from Greece, Israel, Crete and Bulgaria.

Chef/s: John Gionleka. **Open:** Sat and Sun L 12.30 to 3, Tue to Sun D 6 to 10. **Closed:** Mon. **Meals:** alc (main courses £13 to £17). **Details:** 58 seats. Music.

Pedler

⊖ Peckham Rye, map 1
Modern British | £25
58 Peckham Rye, Peckham, SE15 4JR
Tel no: (020) 3030 5015
www.pedlerpeckhamrye.com

Rammed to the rafters most weekends and evenings, this compact all-day eatery combines 'incredible', seamless service with comfort food classics and a killer cocktail list, like a slice of Brooklyn in Peckham. Expect artery-clogging 'frizzle chicken', or brunch favourites (house-made baked beans; burgers) combined with the flavours of the American south (creamed corn toastie; duck-fat scone). Wines from £18. Open Fri to Sun L and Tue to Sun D.

Local Gem

Local Gems are the perfect neighbourhood venues, delivering good, freshly cooked food at great value for money.

Pizarro

Thrilling fare from a Spanish food hero
Cooking score: 4
⊖ London Bridge, Borough, map 1
Spanish | £30
194 Bermondsey Street, Southwark, SE1 3TQ
Tel no: (020) 7378 9455
www.pizarrorestaurant.com

The competition is fierce down Bermondsey Street, but José Pizarro's laid-back venue is still holding its own. Spanish cooking in Britain is on an exciting trajectory these days with Pizarro at the forefront, offering 'more of a meal' than its nearby sibling José (the go-to place for tapas and sherry – see entry). Here the tapas formula has been ditched in favour of greater culinary integrity, regional definition and a range of less familiar ingredients. Expect some clever ideas, from starters of artichoke three ways (pudding, soup and crisps) or stuffed squid with butifarra, jamón and Vizcaina sauce (a rich red pepper and tomato sauce from the Basque Country), to main courses of chuletón (a large beef chop), which comes with Manchego froth and piquillo peppers. Gin and tonic 'on the plate' makes the perfect finish. The all-Spanish wine list starts at £22.

Chef/s: José Pizarro and Dani Molero. **Open:** all week 12 to 10.45 (9.45 Sun). **Closed:** 24 to 26 Dec. **Meals:** alc (main courses £12 to £29). **Details:** 80 seats. Wheelchair access.

Restaurant Story

A story of spirited individuality
Cooking score: 7
⊖ London Bridge, map 4
Modern British | £75
201 Tooley Street, Bermondsey, SE1 2UE
Tel no: (020) 7183 2117
www.restaurantstory.co.uk

Looking like a drop-in centre for designers (Architects Anonymous maybe), this modern construction of wood and glass is an appropriate setting for the new-wave work of

Tom Sellers – the context is minimalist (concrete floor, glassed-in kitchen), the attitude passionate (see the glint in the server's eye), and the food is creative, inspired and personal. The 'story' is Tom's, but it was experiences gained with the likes of René Redzepi that unleashed the prodigious talent within. Make sure you've got over three hours to spare and be prepared for an onslaught of little 'snacks' from the off. An 'insanely gorgeous' oyster with lemon thyme snow and crispy pearl barley, and tomato bruschetta (elevated to classic status with its crystal-clear vanilla-infused consommé) might just be the pick of the early courses. Technique is used to enhance, not overwhelm ingredients, such as when scallops are cured for four minutes in elderflower vinegar, or the dash of the same vinegar that elevates mashed potato to an inspirational level (served with asparagus and coal oil). The full array of contemporary techniques are brought to bear on various cuts of Herdwick lamb, while the cheese course comes in a picnic hamper with a zesty local ale. Almond and dill prove to be sweet bedfellows in a masterstroke of texture and flavour. The drinks list offers carafe options, London ales and cocktails. Wines start at £24.

Chef/s: Tom Sellers. **Open:** Tue to Sat L 12 to 2, D 6.30 to 9.30. **Closed:** Sun, Mon, 21 Dec to 6 Jan, 3 to 8 Apr, 24 Aug to 2 Sept. **Meals:** Set L £35. Tasting menus £75 (6 courses), £95 (10 courses). **Details:** 40 seats. V menu. Bar. Wheelchair access.

Roast

Valiant British foodie patriot
Cooking score: 2
⊖ London Bridge, map 4
British | £60
Floral Hall, Stoney Street, Southwark, SE1 1TL
Tel no: (020) 3006 6111
www.roast-restaurant.com

For more than a decade this popular restaurant with commanding views over Borough Market has been a champion of British food. Regulars love the high-decibel conversational mood of the place, but it's the sensible dishes of seasonal British food that brings them back, whether for breakfast, which takes in anything from grilled Orkney kippers to eggs every which way, or lunch/dinner of straight-taking staples such as beer-battered cod and chips and daily specials along the lines of roast leg of lamb with mint relish (Monday) and roast sirloin of beef and Yorkshire pudding (Friday). For those with eyes trained forwards, not back, the kitchen offers some more modern-tasting dishes such as mixed beetroot, orange and wild herb salad with deep-fried Ragstone goats' cheese, and roast monkfish tail with wild boar bacon, cockles and laverbread. Dessert might bring boozy baked Conference pear with cinnamon ice cream. There's a good kids' menu, too. Wines start at £23.

Chef/s: Marcus Verberne. **Open:** Mon to Sat L 12 to 3.45, D 6 to 10.45. Sun 11.30 to 6.30. **Closed:** 25 and 26 Dec, 1 Jan. **Meals:** alc (main courses £13 to £35). Set L and D £28 (2 courses) to £30. Sun L £38. **Details:** 110 seats. V menu. Bar. Wheelchair access. Music.

RSJ

South Bank old-stager with fabulous wines
Cooking score: 2
⊖ Waterloo, Southwark, map 5
Modern European | £32
33 Coin Street, Southwark, SE1 9NR
Tel no: (020) 7928 4554
www.rsj.uk.com

It served as stables for the Duchy of Cornwall back in Victorian times, but there's no pomp or circumstance about RSJ – a well-liked fixture of the restaurant scene down Waterloo way since 1980. Inside, its studiously understated mix of cool grey walls and light wood is equally appealing to loyal locals and visitors to the South Bank. The kitchen mines a vein of Euro-accented cuisine with lots of Mediterranean overtones, from rabbit ravioli with beurre noisette, crispy sage and Parmesan or confit lamb shank with butter beans and steamed leeks to toasted polenta cake with fig compote. Sadly, the cooking is starting to seem less reliable than the sturdy rolled steel joists (RSJs) after which the restaurant is named, with reports of disappointments across the board. Service is pleasant enough, but can 'stutter badly' at peak times. Thankfully, the restaurant's fabulous list of Loire wines shines as brightly as ever; organic producers are well supported, with appellations ranging from Anjou-Saumur and Touraine to the Layon and Aubance (noted for their sweet wines). Prices start at £19.75.

Chef/s: Matthew Pepperell. **Open:** Mon to Fri L 12 to 2.30, Mon to Sat D 5 to 11. **Closed:** Sun, 24 to 26 Dec, bank hols. **Meals:** alc (main courses £15 to £23). Set L and D £17 (2 courses) to £20. **Details:** 95 seats. 12 seats outside. V menu. Bar.

LOCAL GEMS

Saz

map 1
Turkish | £15
23 Norwood Road, Herne Hill, SE24 9AA
Tel no: (020) 8671 3772
www.saz-hernehill.co.uk

£5
OFF

A bright spark on Norwood Road, this well-run Turkish eatery comes with an open kitchen and turns out meze and hearty char-grilled meats. The former is an ideal way to explore the range of cold dips, stuffed vine leaves and salads, plus some cooked options – arnavut cigeri (diced lamb's liver) and sigara boregi (deep-fried feta cheese and parsley in filo). Main courses are mostly variations of kebabs, with good-quality meat served with rice or cracked wheat and salad. Wines from £11.50. Open all week.

Soif

Clapham South, map 3
Modern European | £30
27 Battersea Rise, Battersea, SW11 1HG
Tel no: (020) 7223 1112
www.soif.co

'A super little place,' notes a regular of this lively Battersea hangout where décor is upmarket café (rustic wood tables, terracotta tiles) matched by a menu of straightforward

French-accented food. Flavour is everything in dishes such as snails, parsnip and garlic butter, bone marrow on toast with pickled beetroot and shallots, or pork tenderloin with mash, lentils, bacon and salsa verde. There's also steak haché, peppercorn sauce and chips, and crème brûlée to finish. France claims the lion's share on the impeccable wine list, though the rest picks out interesting wines from around the globe; prices from £19.50.

Tentazioni

Popular Italian cooking with a Sardinian tang
Cooking score: 3
Bermondsey, London Bridge, map 1
Italian | £38
Lloyds Wharf, 2 Mill Street, Bermondsey, SE1 2BD
Tel no: (020) 7237 1100
www.tentazioni.co.uk

Famed for its longevity, Tentazioni ('temptation' in Italian) has occupied this former warehouse close to Tower Bridge for almost two decades. A warm, inviting place with a long, narrow dining room, polished wood floor, warm red walls hung with bold modern art and white-clad tables, it comes across as a good, honest local. And while it may not be the most of-the-moment place, the kitchen gets the key things right – good ingredients and truly welcoming service. The appeal is cooking that is a contemporary take on traditional Italian cuisine: a starter of creamy Roman broccoli soup with a sheep's cheese raviolini, say, followed by pan-fried cod steak and Venus clam stew with chestnuts, white cabbage and caviar timbale. Pasta might take in a splendid dish of orecchiette with lamb ragù and ricotta cheese, while desserts run to Mont Blanc with creamy, caramelised chestnut cream. Prices on the short, all-Italian wine list start at £17.

Chef/s: Alessandro Cattani. **Open:** Sun to Fri L 12 to 2.45, all week D 6 to 10.45 (9 Sun). **Closed:** 24 to 26 Dec, last week Aug, bank hols. **Meals:** alc (main courses £7 to £26). Set L £12 (2 courses) to £15. Tasting menu £50 (7 courses). **Details:** 60 seats. Music.

Trinity

Brilliant bistro food
Cooking score: 5
⊖ Clapham Common, map 3
Modern British | £46
4 The Polygon, Clapham, SW4 0JG
Tel no: (020) 7622 1199
www.trinityrestaurant.co.uk

It's nearly a decade now since Adam Byatt opened a neighbourhood restaurant in the environs of Clapham Common, and the continuing press of business speaks for itself. If it's splashes of colour you're after in a determinedly monochrome room, you'll have to bring them yourself, but they're all there where they belong: on the plate. Byatt has an unerring feel for what a modern London audience wants to eat, which turns out to be go-ahead bistro food cooked with guts and flair. Crispy trotters with sauce gribiche, cider mayonnaise and crackling is a twenty-teens dish if ever there was, its earthiness followed without missing a beat by the unexpected delicacy of lemon sole with mussels, charred leeks and cucumber. There's a hint of rough country sustenance in pot-roast veal rump with turnips and thyme, except that it comes with truffled macaroni cheese, and proceedings could end on a note of ethereal sophistication with prune and Armagnac soufflé. An enjoyably democratic wine list (including 'the best bottle of Muscat I can remember drinking') gives fair shakes around the world, at prices that show restraint, from £19.
Chef/s: Adam Byatt. **Open:** Tue to Sun L 12 to 2.30 (3 Sun), Mon to Sat D 6.30 to 10. **Closed:** 24 to 27 Dec, 1 Jan. **Meals:** alc (main courses £24 to £30). Set L £22 (2 courses) to £27. Sun L £32. **Details:** 72 seats. V menu. Wheelchair access.

Average price

The average price denotes the price of a three-course meal without wine.

Tsunami

Sleek Japanese fusion favourite
Cooking score: 3
⊖ Clapham North, map 3
Japanese | £28
5-7 Voltaire Road, Clapham, SW4 6DQ
Tel no: (020) 7978 1610
www.tsunamirestaurant.co.uk

Fans of the Bond film franchise might feel they've wandered on to set. The moodily lit space done out in dark shades, with designer furniture and flashes of colour from behind wall screens and the bar (which is a vivid beam of yellow light), is evidently modern Japanese territory. The menu doesn't let the side down, serving up classic sushi and sashimi alongside lots of new-wave numbers. Get revved up with suzuki sashimi (sea bass) or octopus nigiri, but don't ignore the likes of a black cod tempura or steamed dumpling filled with snow crab and prawns. Sharing works a treat. Bigger plates include 'dynamite beef', which is chillied up Scottish Angus ribeye, and steamed sea bass with saké and ponzu. Drink cocktails, saké or wines from £22. There's a sister restaurant in Charlotte Street, W1T 4PY.
Chef/s: SW Cheung. **Open:** Sat and Sun L 12.30 to 4, all week D 5.30 to 10.30 (11 Fri and Sat). **Closed:** 24 to 26 Dec. **Meals:** alc (main courses £8 to £28). Set L £15 (2 courses). Set D £37 to £42. **Details:** 86 seats. 22 seats outside.

Union Street Café

Ramsay does neighbourhood Italian
Cooking score: 3
⊖ Southwark, map 5
Italian | £37
47-51 Great Suffolk Street, Southwark, SE1 0BS
Tel no: (020) 7592 7977
www.gordonramsay.com

It's been noted with relief that the 'celebrity chef thing' is not overdone at this Ramsay-does-neighbourhood Italian. Instead of Gordon Ramsay references you get a vast dining room brimming with style and combining faux-industrial fittings with glam touches including polished wood, leather banquettes and oversized statement art. Tuck into antipasti such as beef tartare with peas, Sarawak pepper and lemon or smoked baby carrots with ricotta, lemon and peanut, then move on to primi and secondi brimming with freshness and flavour: maybe spaghetti with monk's beard, anchovies lemon and bottarga, then sea bass with peppers, olives and clams. Desserts range from simple homemade gelato through to Earl Grey pannacotta with Yorkshire rhubarb, or look to the cheeseboard – there's a superb selection, specially imported. The wine list focuses on Italy – although the rest of the world does get a look-in. Bottles start at £15.

Chef/s: Davide Degiovanni. **Open:** Mon to Sun L 12 to 3 (4 Sat, 5 Sun), D 6 to 11 (10.30 Sat). **Closed:** 25 to 28 Dec. **Meals:** alc (main courses £19 to £25). Set L £19 (2 courses) to £25. Sun L £29. **Details:** 100 seats. Bar. Wheelchair access. Music.

The White Onion

Sleek high-street performer
Cooking score: 3
⊖ Wimbledon, map 3
Modern French | £40
67 High Street, Wimbledon Village,
Wimbledon, SW19 5EE
Tel no: (020) 8947 8278
www.thewhiteonion.co.uk

A spruce-up at this Wimbledon Village restaurant (formerly the Lawn Bistro) has resulted in this smart-casual new venture from Eric and Sarah Guignard of the French Table in Surbiton (see entry). Heading up the kitchen is Frederic Duval who reads from a largely European script with a distinct French accent. He recognises the appeal of familiar ideas and seems at home with dishes such as a duo of foie gras (excellent brûlée and pan-fried liver), and cannelloni of Dorset crab with a julienne of vegetables, lime leaf and a foamy crab sauce. Pan-fried stone bass with Wye Valley green and purple asparagus, an intense French watercress purée and tarragon sauce packs

flavour, while an assiette of Herdwick lamb is teamed with smoked aubergine purée, garlic emulsion, saffron panisse and lavender and lamb jus. The bread selection is very good, and desserts, perhaps hazelnut and coffee pavé with Kahlua ice cream, are more than a cut above. Wines from £19.

Chef/s: Frederic Duval. **Open:** Fri to Sun L 12 to 2.30, Tue to Sat D 7 to 10.30 (6.30 Fri and Sat). **Closed:** Mon. **Meals:** alc (main courses £20 to £29). Set L £17 (2 courses) to £20. **Details:** 70 seats.

The Woodman

Unpretentious pub with civilised dining room
Cooking score: 2
⊖ Clapham Junction, map 3
British | £30
60 Battersea High Street, Battersea,
SW11 3HW
Tel no: (020) 7228 2968
www.woodman-battersea.co.uk

£5
OFF

The Rogers have breathed new life into this Battersea High Street boozer, its gentrified rural-chic interior striking a rare balance between food and drink. The front bar attracts drinkers, while diners head further back to the dining room for bold, no-frills British cooking built around a commitment to seasonality and careful sourcing. James Rogers may keep prices on a tight rein but there's no shortage of confidence or quality on the plate. To start, you might fancy the Woodman's signature venison Scotch egg or Suffolk duck and chicken liver pâté with marmalade toast, while big-hearted mains could stretch from Hampshire Angus sirloin steak with peppercorn sauce to Scottish sea trout with cream, dill and white wine sauce with braised vegetables, capers and potato. Finish with generous desserts, perhaps a classic sticky toffee pudding or chocolate, orange and brandy torte. The sheltered patio is worth knowing about. Wines from £15.95.

Chef/s: James Rogers. **Open:** Mon to Sat 12 to 10, Sun L 12 to 6. **Meals:** alc (main meals £10 to £19). Sun L £13. **Details:** 70 seats. 35 seats outside. Bar. Music.

Wright Brothers Oyster & Porter House

Straightforward fish cookery
Cooking score: 2
London Bridge, map 4
Seafood | £40
11 Stoney Street, Southwark, SE1 9AD
Tel no: (020) 7403 9554
www.thewrightbrothers.co.uk

The original begetter of the little Wright Brothers fish and seafood empire (see also entries in Soho and Spitalfields) is in the heart of clamorous Borough Market, which landlocked location suits it improbably well. Rob Malyon took over at the end of 2014, maintaining the emphasis on straightforward fish cookery done with confidence and respect for the prime materials. The oysters are best Duchy of Cornwall natives, and make a good appetiser for the likes of classic fish soup with rouille and shredded Gruyère, crispy squid with mayo, devilled whitebait, dressed crab, and a majestic whole plaice scattered with brown shrimps and slivered leek. Oysters naturally find their way into the beef and Guinness pie, and the simple bistro desserts encompass tarte Tatin with vanilla ice cream, or a crème brûlée entirely innocent of any extraneous lily-gilding. Bottled porters, ales and stouts, modern cocktails, and well-chosen wines from £20 (£4.90 a glass) should keep everybody happy.
Chef/s: Rob Malyon. **Open:** Mon to Wed L 12 to 3, D 6 to 10. Thur to Sun 12 to 9. **Closed:** 25 to 28 Dec, 1 Jan, Easter, bank hols. **Meals:** alc (main courses £16 to £24). **Details:** 35 seats. 6 seats outside. Bar. Wheelchair access.

Zucca

Get-stuck-in Italian cooking
Cooking score: 3
London Bridge, Borough, map 1
Italian | £40
184 Bermondsey Street, Bermondsey, SE1 3TQ
Tel no: (020) 7378 6809
www.zuccalondon.com

Competition is fierce in this bustling south London street but Sam Harris's lively neighbourhood Italian more than holds its own. It's a pleasant, down-to-earth dining room, full of pale, muted colours and plain tables, and there's plenty of action from the open-to-view kitchen, which delivers some real treats. Passion for quality runs through every aspect, from antipasti of prosciutto with cavolo nero and Parmesan or baby peppers with smoked eel and crostini, and from mains of veal chop with spinach and lemon or osso buco with yellow polenta and gremolata – each dish owing everything to superb ingredients. Pasta remains a strength with praise for bigoli with cuttlefish, and taglierini with tomato, spinach and salted ricotta. Seafood is also pitch-perfect, perhaps roast cod with borlotti, speck and herbs. Chocolate semifreddo is a good way to finish. The well-curated wine list does a whirlwind rip through the Italian regions. Prices open at £28.
Chef/s: Sam Harris and Megan Rogers. **Open:** Tue to Sun L 12 to 3 (3.30 Sat, 4 Sun), Tue to Sat D 6 to 10. **Closed:** Mon, Christmas, New Year, Easter. **Meals:** alc (main courses £12 to £19). **Details:** 55 seats. V menu. Wheelchair access.

The Admiral Codrington

All-purpose Chelsea bolt-hole
Cooking score: 2
⊖ South Kensington, map 3
Modern British | £28
17 Mossop Street, Chelsea, SW3 2LY
Tel no: (020) 7581 0005
www.theadmiralcodrington.co.uk

Every pub worth its salt has a nickname used by the locals, so welcome to the 'Cod'. It's moved with the times has the Cod. Back in the day the south-west London crowd could get a little tasty, but these days its more of a foodie joint. The front bar can still offer succour to seasoned drinkers, although the main business takes place in the L-shaped dining room to the rear. It's a genteel, sky-lit space with a contemporary finish and an informality that suits the feel-good modern British menu. Kick off with salt-and-pepper squid or ham hock terrine with prune and brandy purée, before tucking into a steak cooked on the grill (35-day aged Black Angus ribeye, maybe). There's the likes of Portland crab linguine, too, and when it comes to desserts, expect some old faves such as sticky toffee pudding and a crumble. House wine is £19.
Chef/s: Orett Hoilett. **Open:** Mon to Sat L 12 to 3 (4 Sat), D 6 to 10 (11 Thur to Sat). Sun 12 to 9. **Closed:** 24 to 26 Dec. **Meals:** alc (main courses £12 to £28). Set L and D £17 to £20. **Details:** 50 seats. 20 seats outside. Bar. Music.

Amaya

Indian grazing-food served with style
Cooking score: 4
⊖ Knightsbridge, map 6
Indian | £55
15 Halkin Arcade, Motcomb Street, Knightsbridge, SW1X 8JT
Tel no: (020) 7823 1166
www.amaya.biz

The design job at Belgravia's Amaya provides a jolt to the visual sense, with fabrics in purple and gold shimmering in a dimly lit interior, a complementary adjunct to the fragrant intensity of the Indian-based fusion cooking. Grilling is a favoured technique, retaining the clarity of flavour of prime materials, and there is plenty of inventive verve to the fashionable small plates that are the menu's stock-in-trade. Expect tamarind-glazed tandoori foie gras, and Punjabi chicken wing lollipops char-grilled in chilli, cinnamon and lime, as preludes to monkfish tikka, pungent with fenugreek and turmeric, and lamb slow-cooked osso buco-style with dried lemon. Vegetable dishes are equally inspired, as in spinach and fig tikki, or griddled asparagus with mango chutney, and it all ends with desserts variously based on fruit or chocolate, with Indian seasonings adding lustre. A large selection of wines by the glass, from around £7, complements the food admirably.
Chef/s: Karunesh Khanna. **Open:** all week L 12.30 to 2.15 (12.45 to 2.45 Sun), D 6.30 to 11.30 (10.30 Sun). **Meals:** alc (sharing plates £12 to £30). **Details:** 100 seats. V menu. Bar. No children after 8.

LOCAL GEM

L'Amorosa

⊖ Ravenscourt Park, Stamford Brook, map 1
Italian | £30
278 King Street, Ravenscourt Park, W6 0SP
Tel no: (020) 8563 0300
www.lamorosa.co.uk

When Andy Needham moved from his decade-long post at Zafferano (see entry) and set up a neighbourhood restaurant in Hammersmith, the locals couldn't believe their luck. But while this is not the grand special-occasion dining that they may have been used to at Needham's alma mater, this is proper everyday Italian food and 'great for the neighbourhood'. Lamb ragù on homemade pasta, veal escalope with tomato sauce and Needham's own version of tiramisu, all washed down with Italian-led cocktails and an all-Italian wine list (from £14), is what brings the customers back. As does consistency, friendly service and a sensibly sized bill.

Apero

Stylish Italian all-day dining
Cooking score: 3
⊖ South Kensington, map 3
Mediterranean | £28
The Ampersand Hotel, 2-10 Harrington Road,
South Kensington, SW7 3ER
Tel no: (020) 7591 4410
www.aperorestaurantandbar.com

Open-minded versatility is the key to this charming bar and restaurant hidden in the basement of the Ampersand Hotel. Very handy for South Kensington tube, the décor evokes the Mediterranean with its mix of exposed whitewashed brick and shiny white tiles, wood floors and turquoise leather chairs. The food follows suit, sending out a terrific array of sharing plates revelling in sunny Mediterranean flavours. And what a zesty assortment they are: buttermilk chicken burger on a saffron bun with avocado, chilli mayo and 'nduja; oxtail gougères with white onion and truffle formagella (cheese); soft-shell crab fried in semolina with kale and aïoli; and braised pig's cheek with beetroot risotto and Dorset snails. Afterwards, there are good cheeses, or a Sicilian lemon curd with hazelnut crumble and meringue should provide a sweet hit. Lubrication comes from predominantly French and Italian wines, from £18.75.
Open: all week L 12 to 2.30, D 6 to 10.30. **Meals:** alc (main courses £7 to £19). Set L £12 (2 courses) to £15. **Details:** 40 seats. V menu. Wheelchair access.

Bar Boulud

Razzle-dazzle brasserie, New York style
Cooking score: 4
⊖ Knightsbridge, map 6
French | £42
Mandarin Oriental Hyde Park, 66
Knightsbridge, Knightsbridge, SW1X 7LA
Tel no: (020) 7201 3899
www.barboulud.com

The enduringly popular Bar Boulud continues to draw well-heeled crowds, attracted by the accessible location underneath the Mandarin Oriental hotel, the warmly lit, brasserie de luxe-style of the high-cover operation, the 'absolutely brilliant' service and the vibrant atmosphere. The cooking here waves the French flag with pride and is not afraid to do things in straightforward fashion. Nor does it flinch at good ingredients, which may go some way to explaining the prices. It is this immediacy and quality that is the main appeal: oysters, steak tartare, charcuterie, salade lyonnaise, boudin blanc, moules à la crème, coq au vin, cheeses, tarte aux pommes; the list may be predictable, but they are still done well. It's all very appealing, even more so when you factor in New York-based chef Daniel Boulud's famous beef burgers – a guaranteed treat. The exhaustive wine collection has plenty by the glass (from £4.25), but forbidding prices. House wine is £24.50.
Chef/s: Thomas Piat. **Open:** all week 12 to 11 (10 Sun). **Closed:** 2 weeks Aug. **Meals:** alc (main courses £17 to £40). Set L £17 (2 courses) to £19. **Details:** 169 seats. V menu. Wheelchair access. Music.

Bibendum

Aristocratic South Ken landmark
Cooking score: 4
⊖ South Kensington, map 3
French | £40
Michelin House, 81 Fulham Road, South
Kensington, SW3 6RD
Tel no: (020) 7581 5817
www.bibendum.co.uk

It opened in the 1980s and remains one of the capitals most atmospheric and enduring restaurants. Found on the first floor of a landmark Edwardian building, formerly the Michelin Tyre Company's HQ, and named after Michelin's portly mascot, Bibendum continues to draw well-heeled locals and culinary tourists. A gentle refurbishment of the Art Deco dining room has coincided with the arrival of Peter Robinson, the first new head chef for two decades, although the Simon Hopkinson-curated menus stick to the timeless French classics and unfussy modern British favourites, say rabbit and pancetta ravioli with chicken consommé and wild garlic or creamed morels on toasted brioche. Main courses offer ham hock, parsley sauce and broad beans alongside braised duck leg with peas, bacon and turnips. Finish with apple and sultana crumble with Calvados custard or, perhaps, passion fruit bavarois. A revamped wine list with strong house choices remains a delight, both in price and range. Bottles start at £24.50, and there are around 20 offered by the glass.

Chef/s: Peter Robinson. **Open:** all week L 12 to 2.30 (3 Sat and Sun), D 7 to 11 (10.30 Sun). **Closed:** 25 and 26 Dec, 1 Jan. **Meals:** alc (main courses £17 to £35). Sun L and D £34. **Details:** 80 seats.

Bombay Brasserie

Born-again Indian veteran
Cooking score: 3
⊖ **Gloucester Road, map 3**
Indian | £50
Courtfield Road, South Kensington, SW7 4QH
Tel no: (020) 7370 4040
www.bombayb.co.uk

The long-standing Bombay Brasserie has been rebooted, brought up to date with an opulent and comfortable interior – crystal chandeliers, dark wood, exotic ornaments, modish grey banquettes, very well-spaced tables – with the conservatory considered 'a particularly lovely spot'. The menu, on the other hand, sticks to familiar classics but there are a few surprises – lemon sole steamed in a banana leaf, for example. Spicy duck cakes stuffed with red onions neatly offset by a mint and yoghurt chutney shows the kitchen's pedigree, while the tandoor oven is put to good use with a kasundi monkfish given zing by a marinade of coriander, lime leaves and mustard. Vegetarian dishes stood out at a test meal, especially baby jackfruit and spinach masala with deep-fried garlic. Malai kulfi or rice pudding served with saffron, pistachio and a rose cream biscuit are familiar desserts. The youthful service tries hard to please, and the wide-ranging wine list starts at £24.

Chef/s: Prahlad Hegde. **Open:** Tue to Sun L 12 to 2.30 (3.30 Sat and Sun), Mon to Sun D 6 to 11.30 (10.30 Sun). **Closed:** 25 Dec. **Meals:** alc (main courses £16 to £25). Sat and Sun L £31. **Details:** 200 seats. V menu. Bar. Wheelchair access. Music.

The Brackenbury

Vivid Mediterranean flavours
Cooking score: 2
⊖ **Hammersmith, map 1**
Mediterranean | £29
129-131 Brackenbury Road, Hammersmith, W6 0BQ
Tel no: (020) 8741 4928
www.brackenburyrestaurant.co.uk

Reinvented, resurrected and reconstituted by three well-connected new owners in 2014, this one-time bastion of Brackenbury 'village' is now back in the high life, serving dressed-up seasonal ingredients for savvy Hammersmith foodies. Split into two halves, the rather spare-looking, beige-toned dining room provides a risk-free, understated backdrop for Humphrey Fletcher's vivid, Med-influenced cooking – perhaps twice-baked Gruyère soufflé with winter leaf and lentil salad, baked cod with potatoes, fennel 'al forno' and salsa verde or spatchcock partridge accompanied by a veritable Italian cornucopia of polenta, treviso, porcini, Parma ham and sage. A plate of green romanesco with ricotta, chilli, olives and pangrattato ('grated bread') delivers a colourful opening salvo, while desserts take a trip down memory lane for rhubarb fool, chocolate marquise or Yorkshire ginger pudding with butterscotch sauce. Alternatively, fans of obscure British cheeses can nibble on a wedge of Bermondsey Hard Pressed with pear chutney and Orkney oatcakes. Around 30 reasonably priced global wines start at £14.20 a carafe.

Chef/s: Humphrey Fletcher. **Open:** Tue to Sun L 12 to 3 (3.30 Sun), Tue to Sat D 7 to 10. **Closed:** Mon, Easter, Christmas. **Meals:** alc (main courses £13 to £24). Set L £16 (2 courses) to £18. **Details:** 52 seats. 20 seats outside. Bar. Music.

NEW ENTRY

Brasserie Gustave

Nostalgia and classic French cuisine
Cooking score: 2
⊖ South Kensington, map 3
French | £32
4 Sydney Street, Chelsea, SW3 6PP
Tel no: (020) 7352 1712
www.brasserie-gustave.com

£5 OFF

Time was when all London restaurants aspired to be like Brasserie Gustave – serving classic French cuisine to a French-led international clientele. The truth is that though the flavours are remarkably familiar, part of our collective culinary psyche, it's surprisingly hard to get the cooking and the service 'comme il faut' – but they manage it here. A goats' cheese soufflé, chosen from a selection that includes frogs' legs, moules marinières and asparagus with hollandaise, is light and well risen, the accompanying honey and pine nuts making it easy on the palate. Main courses veer towards classical meat dishes – veal kidney rubs shoulders with duck breast with orange, and there's an impressive tartare prepared at the table – but there's Dover sole and truffle risotto, too. Desserts tend towards 1970s show stoppers: crêpes suzette and crème brûlée. Match it with a classic French wine list (from £18) and a Parisian interior circa 1920 and you've a nostalgic winner.

Chef/s: Laurence Glayzer. **Open:** Wed to Sun L 12 to 2.30 (11 to 3 Sat and Sun), Tue to Sun D 6 to 10.30 (11 Fri and Sat). **Closed:** Mon. **Meals:** alc (main courses £16 to £39). Set L and D £20 (2 courses) to £23. Sun L £24. Tasting menu £39 (5 courses). **Details:** 50 seats. Bar. Music.

Cambio de Tercio

Ambitious and striking Spanish
Cooking score: 5
⊖ Gloucester Road, map 3
Spanish | £45
163 Old Brompton Road, Earl's Court, SW5 0LJ
Tel no: (020) 7244 8970
www.cambiodetercio.co.uk

Cambio de Tercio is a South Kensington institution, home to some dynamically creative Spanish cuisine for two decades – and chef Alberto Criado remains restlessly inventive. In a warmly decorated space with close-packed, white-clad tables and an atmosphere that positively throbs with activity, a conceptual approach is taken to Spanish food, with small dishes very much the thing here. Some compositions sound almost straightforward, as in prawns cooked 'a la plancha' or a succulent piece of roasted suckling pig from Salamanca, which is served with roasted parsnips and pickled kumquats, while others head for the wilder shores, as when a foie gras parfait (with a hint of Pedro Ximénez) arrives shaped like an apple set atop apple purée and accompanied by a sweet pear coloured with beetroot. A finale of an edible Oyster card next to chocolate ganache paired with coconut and yuzu cream nestling on a map of the London Underground made from rice paper has also garnered praise. The well-curated wine list opens with a magnificent range of sherries and there are plenty of Spanish gems from £23.

Chef/s: Alberto Criado. **Open:** all week L 12 to 2.30 (3 Sat and Sun), D 6.30 to 11.30 (11 Sun). **Closed:** 17 to 31 Aug, 21 to 31 Dec. **Meals:** alc (main courses £20 to £28). Sun L £24. Tasting menu £45. **Details:** 80 seats. 8 seats outside. V menu. Bar. Music.

The Carpenter's Arms
⊖ Stamford Brook, Ravenscourt Park, map 1
Modern European | £25
89-91 Black Lion Lane, Hammersmith,
W6 9BG
Tel no: (020) 8741 8386
www.carpentersarmsw6.co.uk

A well-regarded local asset famed for its
enviably pretty beer garden, cosy winter fires
and general air of lazy Hammersmith
bonhomie, the Carpenter's Arms keeps things
affable for drinkers and those after a bite to eat.
Burgers, steaks and fish pie rub shoulders with
bistro standbys including charcuterie platters,
lamb shank with mash and garlic jus or a
fricassee of pork belly with Jerusalem
artichokes, fried plantain and kale. Chocolate
and cashew brownie is a typical pud. Wines
from £17.70. Open all week.

Chakra
Luxurious Indian with a hint of mystery
Cooking score: 3
⊖ Notting Hill Gate, map 6
Indian | £40
157-159 Notting Hill Gate, Notting Hill,
W11 3LF
Tel no: (020) 7229 2115
www.chakralondon.com

The interior is luxurious – lots of large
mirrors, crystal chandeliers and walls lined
with white leather – to match this big-league
Indian kitchen's food. There's 'some fine
cooking indeed', based on mystic Vedic
principles and the banquets of the Maharajahs.
Indeed, 'dishes taste distinctively different and
spicing is well handled' thought one reporter.
Delicate spices are used to lift a masala-
flavoured lamb seekh kebab grilled on the
chulha (indoor cooking stove) and offset with
a mint sauce. Then, 'taste-buds are put into a
pleasant tail spin' with surkhi jingha – a trio of
tiger prawns marinated with ginger and
lemon juice before being seared in the
tandoor. Elsewhere, baby asparagus, broccoli

and mangetout sautéed with herbs are cooked
with care. Desserts reveal a Western influence,
in a nutmeg and cinnamon-flavoured apple
sponge paired with elderflower mousse.
Service is provided by a polished crew and an
international wine list starts at £23.
Chef/s: Andy Varma. **Open:** all week L 12 to 3, D 6
to 11 (10.30 Sun). **Closed:** 25 and 26 Dec, 1 Jan.
Meals: alc (main courses £5 to £19). Set L £10 (2
courses) to £15. Set D £15 (2 courses) to £20. Sun L
£15. Tasting menu £45 to £60. **Details:** 75 seats. 12
seats outside. V menu. Bar. Music.

Charlotte's Place
Stellar output from much-loved local
Cooking score: 4
⊖ Ealing Broadway, Ealing Common, map 1
Modern European | £33
16 St Matthew's Road, Ealing, W5 3JT
Tel no: (020) 8567 7541
www.charlottes.co.uk

The forerunner to its baby sister in Chiswick,
Charlotte's Place makes the art of retaining
customer loyalty appear effortless. The cosy
yet light dining room looks on to Ealing
Common, and there's extra room to dine
downstairs, but it's the smart, considered food
that grabs the attention. Sustainability is to the
fore and, taking pride in the best of British,
the menu is a glorious roll-call of top-notch
seasonal ingredients, handled with precision.
You might start with excellent black pudding
ravioli with cauliflower and shellfish cream
and capers, then move on to Middlewhite
pork belly with Dorset snails, garlic milk and
parsley. Puddings – perhaps apple
dauphinoise with vanilla and cinnamon
doughnut – delight, and there's stellar roast
beef on Sundays. If you expect all of this to
come at quite a hefty price, you'll be pleasantly
surprised. A fine, predominantly French wine
list starts at £18.
Chef/s: Lee Cadden. **Open:** Mon to Sat L 12 to 2.30,
D 6 to 10. Sun 12 to 9. **Meals:** Set L £20 (2 courses)
to £24. Set D £30 (2 courses) to £35. Sun L £23 (2
courses) to £27. **Details:** 54 seats. 16 seats outside.
Music.

Charlotte's W4

Slick neighbourhood eatery
Cooking score: 3
⊖ Turnham Green, map 1
Modern European | £30
6 Turnham Green Terrace, Chiswick, W4 1QP
Tel no: (020) 8742 3590
www.charlottes.co.uk

At the Chiswick High Road end of posh, pretty Turnham Green Terrace, this is a sparky offshoot of Charlotte's Place in Ealing. A 'gorgeous neighbourhood gem', it's 'everything you could want at the end of your road' – smart and special enough to feel like a treat but relaxed and friendly, too. You'll be bowled over by the genuine welcome from the staff, and the food echoes this warmth and generosity. Settle in the dark bar overlooking an open kitchen or in the 'lovely, light-filled dining room' with its bright glass ceiling. Beetroot-cured mackerel with horseradish and chive potato salad typifies the wholehearted, classy bistro cooking, followed perhaps by slow-cooked lamb rump with braised shoulder, red cabbage and sprouts. A chocolate pot with Irish cream mousse and candied hazelnuts rounds things off nicely. Almost everything on the chatty, global wine list is available by the glass or carafe. Bottles start at £18.
Chef/s: Roxanne Gough. **Open:** all week 12 to 10 (10.30 Fri and Sat, 9 Sun). **Closed:** 26 Dec, 1 Jan. **Meals:** alc (main courses £13 to £24). **Details:** 56 seats. Bar. Music.

Clarke's

Pioneering Notting Hill favourite
Cooking score: 3
⊖ Notting Hill Gate, map 6
Modern British | £37
124 Kensington Church Street, Notting Hill, W8 4BH
Tel no: (020) 7221 9225
www.sallyclarke.com

More than three decades since Sally Clarke set up shop here, she remains a hands-on presence and a key part of the 'friendly, welcoming' atmosphere that keeps guests coming back for more. A year or so ago she moved her café-bakery-deli to a new home over the road, allowing expansion of the restaurant, which now includes a new kitchen and private dining room below. 'Slightly chaotic' on busy nights, but with staff always 'doing their best', it continues to turn out classically-inspired dishes with gentle modern touches. Handmade spinach and potato gnocchi with crisp sage, pea leaves and aged Parmesan typifies the fresh, lively flavour, followed perhaps by char-grilled veal chop with pine nut, raisin and parsley pesto and parsnip chips. To finish, maybe spring rhubarb and pistachio trifle with vanilla cream. An interesting global selection of wines starts at £20.
Chef/s: Sally Clarke. **Open:** Mon to Sat L 12.30 to 2 (12 to 2.30 Sat), D 6.30 to 10. **Closed:** Sun, 10 days Christmas, 2 weeks Aug. **Meals:** alc (main courses £20 to £29). Set L £25 (2 courses) to £30. Set D £39.
Details: 90 seats. Bar. Wheelchair access.

Claude's Kitchen

Neighbourhood eatery with big ideas
Cooking score: 4
⊖ Parsons Green, map 3
Modern British | £31
51 Parsons Green Lane, Parsons Green, SW6 4JA
Tel no: (020) 7371 8517
www.amusebouchelondon.com

One-time street-food vendor and former chef at Petersham Nurseries (see entry), Claude Compton turned up the heat in Parsons Green when he launched this self-named, evenings-only eatery above the Amuse Bouche Champagne bar. What was a function room has morphed into a bijou space tailor-made for a taut menu of cleverly assembled seasonal ingredients. Scuffed surfaces, vintage tables and framed posters create a stripped-back look. Dish descriptions tell it like it is: 'smoked herring, blood orange, popcorn, sauce, lovage oil'; 'beef cheek, date and Earl Grey, parsley root, popped wild rice, sage'; 'grilled cornbread, pumpkin ice, red onion ceviche, beetroot, coal, black garlic'. Welcome to the

Join us at thegoodfoodguide.co.uk

maverick world of 21st-century London cuisine. Turn the dial to 'sweet' and you might be offered peanut-butter parfait with pretzels, salted toffee and sour vanilla, while the cheese course is a real eye-opener. Hilarious tasting notes and left-field selections (from £19) typify the kindly priced but intelligent wine list. A two-minute walk away is the Tommy Tucker, Claude Compton's lively, laid-back pub (22 Waterford Road, SW6 2DR; tel: 020 7736 1023).

Chef/s: Claude Compton. **Open:** Mon to Sat D only 6 to 10.30. **Closed:** Sun. **Meals:** alc (main courses £15 to £19). **Details:** 44 seats. Bar. Music. No children.

Colbert

Popular Parisian brasserie fare
Cooking score: 2
⊖ Sloane Square, map 3
French | £38
50-52 Sloane Square, Chelsea, SW1W 8AX
Tel no: (020) 7730 2804
www.colbertchelsea.com

Messrs Corbin and King know a thing or two about putting together a restaurant (from the Wolseley to the Colony Grill – see entries) and they hit the nail on the head with this Sloane Square venture. There's more than a touch of the Parisian brasserie about the place, from the black-and-white tiled floor, red leather banquettes, white-clad tables, wood panelling and walls covered in posters and monochrome photographs from the 1930s, and the menu reinforces the impression: soupe à l'oignon; steak tartare; salade niçoise; moules marinières; chicken paillard; rognons de veau à la moutarde; rum baba – the list goes on. The day is a long one, starting at 8am for breakfast, and there is a lot of pressure on tables, but, as one reporter put it: 'it is refined and civilised and feels like a lovely treat'. Service is slick and efficient and the all-French wine list opens at £19.95.

Chef/s: Maarten Geschwindt. **Open:** 8am to 11pm (11.30pm Fri and Sat, 10.30pm Sun). **Meals:** alc (main courses £8 to £35). **Details:** 142 seats. 23 seats outside. V menu. Bar. Wheelchair access.

Dinner by Heston Blumenthal

A taste of history
Cooking score: 7
⊖ Knightsbridge, map 6
British | £70
Mandarin Oriental Hyde Park, 66 Knightsbridge, Knightsbridge, SW1X 7LA
Tel no: (020) 7201 3833
www.dinnerbyheston.com

The Mandarin Oriental is a behemoth of a hotel with a five-star finish and liveried doormen who usher you inside to nowhere in particular – good luck finding Dinner (it's in there somewhere, towards the back). It's a pleasant, typically refined space with views over Hyde Park and a glassed-in kitchen showcasing the renowned spit-roasting pulley system where pineapples take the brunt of the heat. Ashley Palmer-Watts has been Heston's right-hand man since the early days and delivers a menu inspired by the past that is 'exciting to read'. Luckily it's exciting to eat, too. The meticulous research and development required to create the menu means it doesn't change all that much, but new dishes do arrive, and the most popular ones (and most written about) are permanent fixtures. The long-running meat fruit (c. 1720), spiced pigeon (c. 1780) and tipsy cake (c. 1810) are hard to ignore. The ingredients are seldom less than exceptional, such as the tender grilled octopus that arrives with smoked tea broth (inspired by a recipe from the 1400s), and roast Ibérico pork chop with ham hock and spelt risotto of which, one reader recalled, 'no words can do justice'. Finish with sambocade (c. 1390), a goats' milk cheesecake flavoured with elderflower and apple. The pricey wine list kicks off at £35.

Chef/s: Ashley Palmer-Watts. **Open:** all week L 12 to 2.30, D 6.30 to 10.30. **Meals:** alc (main courses £28 to £42). Set L Mon to Fri £38. **Details:** 102 seats. Bar. Wheelchair access. Parking.

Ebury Restaurant & Wine Bar

Steadfast commitment to enjoyment
Cooking score: 2
✆ Victoria, map 3
Modern European | £38
139 Ebury Street, Belgravia, SW1W 9QU
Tel no: (020) 7730 5447
www.eburyrestaurant.co.uk

This well-established wine bar (it opened in 1959) is in a seriously expensive part of Belgravia but fears of scary prices are soon dispelled. Nigel Windridge has been serving the needs of drinkers and diners since 1973 and for many it remains a faithful and reliable old friend. The setting is old-school (trompe l'oeil walls, close-packed tables, floral displays), the style unchanging, scoring well on atmosphere, and to mix a metaphor, the kitchen goes about its task in a freewheeling way without going overboard. Pigeon breast with pickled mushrooms, candied walnuts and celeriac purée, followed by chorizo-crusted cod with courgette and saffron fondue or guinea fowl breast with Savoy cabbage, white onion purée and thyme jus and indulgent desserts, say chocolate marquise, are typical choices. As you might expect, the wine list is full of Bacchic delights from around the world – modestly priced (from £19.50) with plenty of choice by the glass.
Chef/s: Bernard du Monteil. **Open:** all week L 12 to 2.45, D 6 to 10.15. **Closed:** 24 Dec to 2 Jan.
Meals: alc (main courses £15 to £34). Set L and D £23 (2 courses) to £29. **Details:** 70 seats. Bar. Music.

L'Etranger

Idiosyncratic Franco-Japanese alliance
Cooking score: 4
✆ Gloucester Road, South Kensington, map 3
Modern French | £50
36 Gloucester Road, South Kensington, SW7 4QT
Tel no: (020) 7584 1118
www.etranger.co.uk

Well established on the Kensington dining scene, this smart Franco-Japanese venue is distinguished by its astonishing wine list ('heaven to oenophiles'), which opens at £22. The sexy, if slightly passé modern Japanese look, does however embrace the marriage of East and West, with its soothing shades of silver-grey and black and sparkling beaded curtains. Low-slung leather banquettes, shiny black lacquer tables and mirror-lined walls set an intimate low-lit tone. Matched by 'suited and booted' formal service and a 'quite hushed tone', the kitchen's serious French credentials and flirtation with Japan rides in harmony. Smoked Landes duck (a succulent pink breast and rich leg meat croquette) with sweet pomegranate, asparagus and melting, buttery seared foie gras, is delivered with a cloche-lifting flourish, although the chopsticks come out for a high-rolling caramelised Alaskan black cod with miso and sushi rice. The huge wine list is a bit attraction; from £22. In the basement is the more casual spin-off Meursault.
Chef/s: Jérôme Tauvron. **Open:** all week L 12 to 3, D 5.30 to 11. **Meals:** alc (main courses £13 to £36). Set L £25 (3 courses). Tasting menu £75. **Details:** 65 seats. Bar. Music.

Join us at thegoodfoodguide.co.uk

The Five Fields

Upping the ante in Chelsea
Cooking score: 5
⊖ Sloane Square, map 3
Modern British | £50

8-9 Blacklands Terrace, Chelsea, SW3 2SP
Tel no: (020) 7838 1082
www.fivefieldsrestaurant.com

Discreet elegance is the Five Fields stock-in-trade, perceptible from the moment you step into the bijou dining room. There is a sense of luxury and ease and the menu backs it up with appropriate ingredients with visuals accorded maximum priority. Taylor Bonnyman cooks with a featherlight touch. A jewel-like sphere of foie gras encased in beetroot jelly with shimeji mushrooms and more beetroot is a signature dish, or consider the contrasting textures and temperatures that make 'Rock Pool' such a bravura opener: a slate of raw tuna, sea urchin and smoked eel strewn with purées, gel, yuzu meringue and flowers, herbs and green buds, alongside a raw langoustine atop its own little rock and oyster tartare topped with Bloody Mary granita. A just-cooked, translucent piece of cod garnished with fresh peas and asparagus, purées of pea and almond shows admirable judgement, while mango with peanut (crumbs), celery and apple granita, buttermilk (pannacotta-style) and mango (sorbet and fruit) is a studiously assembled masterpiece. Service is attentive, and 'slightly formal, but nice with it'. Wines from £25.
Chef/s: Taylor Bonnyman and Marguerite Keogh.
Open: Tue to Sat D only 6 to 10. **Closed:** Sun, Mon, Christmas, first 2 weeks Jan, 2 weeks Aug.
Meals: Set D £50. Tasting menu £75. **Details:** 40 seats. V menu. Bar. Wheelchair access. Music.

Symbols

- 🛏 Accommodation is available
- £30 Three courses for less than £30
- £5 OFF £5-off voucher scheme
- 🍾 Notable wine list

Garnier

As French as they come
Cooking score: 2
⊖ Earl's Court, map 3
French | £40

314 Earl's Court Road, Earl's Court, SW5 9BQ
Tel no: (020) 7370 4536
www.garnier-restaurant-london.co.uk

A neighbourhood restaurant that looks likes its neighbourhood is the 7th arrondissement rather than Earl's Court, Garnier delivers the sort of classic French cuisine that has universal appeal. The red seats, cream walls, mirrors and prints all add to the cross-Channel impression. Didier Garnier has history when it comes to serving up brasserie-style fare to demanding Londoners and here he offers a bilingual menu that covers familiar and comforting ground. Pan-fried calf's brain with capers and lemon butter sauce doesn't pull any punches, or you might start with the more contemporary sounding seared tuna with oregano and soya dressing. Dover sole comes grilled or à la meunière, confit duck leg with braised lentils and Savoy cabbage, and filet de boeuf au poivre speaks for itself. Desserts are as old-school as crêpes suzette. The wine list sticks unashamedly to the old country; bottles start at £18.50.
Open: all week L 12 to 3, D 6 to 10.30 (10 Sun).
Meals: alc (main courses £19 to £34). Set L £18 (2 courses). Set D £22 (2 courses). Sun L £18.
Details: 45 seats. Wheelchair access.

The Goring

Old and new British food near the Palace
Cooking score: 4
⊖ Victoria, map 3
Modern British | £50

15 Beeston Place, Belgravia, SW1W 0JW
Tel no: (020) 7396 9000
www.thegoring.com

🛏

Tea on the lawn may seem a little counter-intuitive in a central London hotel, but this one is only a short hop from the Palace. Family-owned for over a century, it has eased into the modern era with a new dining approach under Shay Cooper. Swagged drapes and immaculate table settings establish a refined tone, and the modern British thinking of the menus is in tune with the times, including nostalgic nods to Brit tradition, as celebrated in chicken and mushroom soup adorned with egg yolk and sausage roll. Eggs Drumkilbo, a seafood cocktail in egg mayonnaise, was a firm favourite of the late Queen Mother. New territory is mapped for truffled halibut with celeriac purée, artichokes and hazelnuts, but then again a properly regal beef Wellington won't lack for support. Desserts span the range too, from rice pudding with oat clusters to chestnut parfait with cranberry gel, rum mousse and vanilla meringue. The £28 launchpad for wines is soon a vanishing dot.

Chef/s: Shay Cooper. **Open:** Sun to Fri L 12 to 2.30, all week D 6 to 10. **Meals:** Set L £43. Set D £53. **Details:** 70 seats. 40 seats outside. V menu. Bar. Wheelchair access. Parking.

Granger & Co.

All-day Australian of international repute
Cooking score: 2
Notting Hill Gate, map 6
Australian | £30
175 Westbourne Grove, Notting Hill, W11 2SB
Tel no: (020) 7229 9111
www.grangerandco.com

TV chef Bill Granger began the London arm of his international operation here in Notting Hill, where the cosmopolitan heart has always beaten strongly. Bright yellow awnings announce the sunny disposition of a place that specialises in all-day, kick-back Australian no-worries relaxation, with pretty much any level and style of appetite catered for. Breakfast runs till noon, including Bill's legendary scrambled eggs on sourdough toast, renowned on four continents, but later the menus kick into gear with small plates such as raw tuna and avocado poke with brown rice, cherry tomatoes and samphire, and bigger ones bearing a shrimp burger slathered in jalapeño mayo, or beef shin mole with cauliflower rice and tomatillo salsa.

Sweets offer the chance to cop a load of something exotic, perhaps pistachio pavlova with passion fruit, or pandan rice pudding with poached fruits. Cocktails and real beers supplement a wine list that kicks off with Languedoc varietals, Grenache Blanc and Syrah, at £19.50.

Chef/s: Nick Grundy. **Open:** all week L 12 to 5, D 5 to 10.30 (9.30 Sun). **Meals:** alc (main courses £13 to £24). **Details:** 68 seats. 6 seats outside. Bar. Wheelchair access. Music.

The Harwood Arms

Gastronomic excellence in handsome pub
Cooking score: 5
Fulham Broadway, map 3
British | £40
Walham Grove, Fulham, SW6 1QP
Tel no: (020) 7386 1847
www.harwoodarms.com

'I would return to the Harwood in a heartbeat; its dishes feel both like a treat and like something thoroughly British, that you should be eating every day,' volunteered one reporter of this city pub with a country edge in the 'posh bit of Fulham'. Robust and handsome with its room-length bar, green-panelled walls and mismatched furniture, it feels like a pub, but really 'this place is all about the food'. The cooking creates an impression of sophistication and flair, while remaining down-to-earth and wholesome-sounding. Salt-baked Hereford snails with oxtail braised in stout and parsley and a little Welsh rarebit toast, and a 'rich and pungent' new-season garlic and potato soup with poached egg, asparagus and lardo are typical of the to-the-point, seasonally aware approach, as are slow-cooked shoulder of Herdwick lamb with black garlic, artichokes and creamed spinach, and fillet of Cornish turbot with tenderstem broccoli, fennel and brown shrimp. Wines are an intelligent, decent, well-priced selection from £20.

Chef/s: Alex Harper. **Open:** Tue to Sun L 12 to 3 (4 Sun), all week D 6.15 to 9.30 (7 to 9 Sun). **Closed:** 24 to 27 Dec, 1 Jan. **Meals:** Set L £34 (2 courses) to £40. Set L weekdays £20 (2 courses) to £25. **Details:** 50 seats. V menu. Music.

The Havelock Tavern
Good cooking, good drinking
Cooking score: 1
⊖ Shepherd's Bush, Olympia, map 3
Modern British | £30
57 Masbro Road, Shepherd's Bush, W14 0LS
Tel no: (020) 7603 5374
www.havelocktavern.com

Behind the distinctive blue-and-white tiled exterior, The Havelock is much as it has been for nearly 20 years – much to everyone's delight. There's plenty of room for drinkers supping a rotating selection of cask ales, head chef James Howarth's food is 'well thought out', and the sight of fresh loaves cooling on racks hints at the amount of cooking done in-house: the menu changes daily. Try crispy sardines with marinated beetroot, shaved fennel and hazelnut pesto followed by char-grilled bavette steak with flavoured butter – perhaps tomato and tarragon, or green peppercorn, herb and shallot. Banana bread with toffee sauce ratchets up the feel-good factor. Wines from £17.95.
Chef/s: James Howarth. **Open:** all week L 12.30 to 3 (4 Sat and Sun), D 7 to 10 (9.30 Sun). **Closed:** 25 and 26 Dec. **Meals:** alc (main courses £12 to £17). **Details:** 95 seats. 60 seats outside. Bar.

NEW ENTRY
Hawksmoor Knightsbridge
Meaty magnificence in Knightsbridge
Cooking score: 4
⊖ Knightsbridge, South Kensington, map 3
British | £45
3 Yeoman's Row, Knightsbridge, SW3 2AL
Tel no: (020) 7590 9290
www.thehawksmoor.com

A temple to the glories of steak, this fifth restaurant in the Hawksmoor group follows the winning formula of its counterparts: a subterranean dining room with leather banquettes, dark-wood surfaces, unfussy service and a boisterous bar for afterwards. That said, this branch will suit the weighty wallets of Knightsbridge, who will appreciate the greater emphasis on glitzy seafood – there's Brixham lobster, alongside an assortment of oysters and Finnish caviar. Among the more conventional dishes, starters show undeniable craft: try exquisitely textured raw sea bass with chilli and ginger. The inner sanctum of the menu is still, however, faultlessly cooked and divinely juicy slabs of British beef. Choose between ribeye, fillet and 55-day aged D-rump – knowledgeable staff evangelise about the optimum combination of sides and sauces to go with it. Puddings, as you'd expect, are indulgent affairs: try sticky toffee pudding or passion fruit crème brûlée. House wines from £22.
Chef/s: Richard Sandiford. **Open:** Mon to Sat L 12 to 3, D 5 to 10.30. Sun 12 to 9.30. **Closed:** 24 to 26 Dec. **Meals:** alc (main courses £20 to £45). Set L and D £24 (2 courses) to £27. Sun L £20. **Details:** 130 seats. Bar. Music.

★ TOP 50 ★

Hedone
Sublime exploratory cooking
Cooking score: 7
⊖ Chiswick Park, map 1
Modern European | £75
301-303 Chiswick High Road, Chiswick, W4 4HH
Tel no: (020) 8747 0377
www.hedonerestaurant.com

Mikael Jonsson's Hedone is a boundlessly creative, attention-gripping star player. The building's exposed brick innards are very much the mood of the design moment, and the pre-designed menus (the carte is long gone) offer an exploratory tour of what's best in modern European innovation, with many of the ingredients selected from among what's best in Europe. The asparagus this year is from the Wye Valley, its vernal intensity emphasised with a velouté of lettuce and hay hollandaise, while the *de rigueur* scallop arrives from Mull, to be very slowly warmed, then grilled and dressed in amontillado. The ravioli of liquid Parmesan continue to be a squirty delight, while main course brings on either venison loin of ineffable tenderness, fragrant with basil and cinnamon, or Bourbonnais spring lamb with artichoke, puréed dates and black garlic. Incomparable gariguette strawberries are scented with hibiscus and partnered with coconut and lime sorbet, before the famously delicate final construction of a powdered raspberry biscuit topped with vanilla ice cream, balanced on warm chocolate mousse and passion fruit jelly, makes its evanescent appearance. In full flow, Jonsson's food is sublime, an extended exhibition that wins over sceptics about contemporary cuisine. The framework in which it's served still needs fine-tuning. Why not leave the menu on the table for those ordering the wine flight? 'While they obviously expected us to be interested, and gave good explanations, trying to hear and remember what the waiters said is hard in a noisy restaurant.' The Classic wine pairing is £59 for the six-course taster, £79 for Prestige wines.

Chef/s: Mikael Jonsson. **Open:** Thur to Sat L 12 to 2.30, Tue to Sat D 6.30 to 9.30. **Closed:** Sun, Mon. **Meals:** Set L £45 (4 courses). Tasting menus L and D £75 to £125. **Details:** 40 seats.

Hereford Road

Heritage cooking from a local champion
Cooking score: 2
◉ Bayswater, map 6
British | £28
3 Hereford Road, Notting Hill, W2 4AB
Tel no: (020) 7727 1144
www.herefordroad.org

Something of a local hot spot when it comes to British heritage cooking, this cannily converted Victorian butcher's shop still packs an earthy punch: 'the quality is as high as ever,' noted one returning regular. A quick glance at the terse menu will tell you that main man Tom Pemberton earned his spurs with nose-

to-tail guru Fergus Henderson at St John (see entry): this is the heroically seasonal world of grilled leeks with cow's curd, braised hare leg and lentils or skate with salsify and parsley. The cooking shows 'an intelligent understanding of ingredients and flavours' – witness the 'simple delights' of beetroot with sorrel and boiled egg or perfectly timed lemon sole with roast cauliflower and capers. After that, apple crumble or brown-bread and marmalade ice cream guarantee a satisfying finale. Regulars swoop on the booths by the open kitchen, while 'professional, friendly staff' add to the hospitable mood. Wines from £19.50.

Chef/s: Tom Pemberton. **Open:** all week L 12 to 3 (4 Sun), D 6 to 10.30 (10 Sun). **Closed:** 24 Dec to 3 Jan, last weekend Aug. **Meals:** alc (main courses £12 to £17). Set L £14 (2 courses) to £16. **Details:** 66 seats. 6 seats outside. Wheelchair access. Parking.

Hunan

Regional Chinese surprises
Cooking score: 3
◉ Sloane Square, map 3
Chinese | £56
51 Pimlico Road, Chelsea, SW1W 8NE
Tel no: (020) 7730 5712
www.hunanlondon.com

'Leave it to us' is the mantra behind Chinese veteran Hunan – an idiosyncratic one-off run with tremendous glee and enthusiasm by chef/patron Michael Peng. There's no menu: simply spell out your preferences and any vetoed ingredients before going with the flow and allowing the kitchen to do its thing. What follows is a bespoke feast of up to 18 little courses arranged in clusters: the legendary steamed bamboo cup soup; pot-sticker dumplings; pickled ear fungus with chicken; crispy breast of lamb; braised ox tongue served cold; sesame spinach rolls. There's sweetness, too, in the shape of toffee apples or red-bean pancakes. The cramped, utilitarian dining room isn't much to look at, but service is cheery and clued-up, with Michael regularly popping out of the kitchen to check that's all

Join us at thegoodfoodguide.co.uk

well. Hunan also springs plenty of surprises on the wine front: the authoritative list has pedigree growers and vinous treasures in abundance to match the kitchen's cavalcade of complex, cleverly balanced flavours – and prices (from £20) are rarely excessive.
Chef/s: Michael Peng. **Open:** Mon to Sat L 12.30 to 2, D 6.30 to 10.30. **Closed:** Sun, 24 Dec to 7 Jan, 2 weeks Aug, bank hols. **Meals:** Set L £36. Set D £56. **Details:** 50 seats. 4 seats outside. V menu.

Indian Zing

Interesting Indian flavours
Cooking score: 2
⊖ Ravenscourt Park, map 1
Indian | £30
236 King Street, Hammersmith, W6 0RF
Tel no: (020) 8748 5959
www.indianzing.co.uk

£5
OFF

Behind Indian Zing's smart, modern frontage is a homely restaurant with simple modern furnishings and pale walls bearing Indian artwork. While the setting will win no awards for fancy styling, the food is enough to entice plenty of regulars, who say it is 'consistently good', with 'flavours that are much more complex and interesting than a standard curry house'. After poppadoms and khakara with tangy chutney and cooling yoghurt, try a fat pea and potato samosa with chickpea curry, yoghurt and a sauce of coriander, mint and jaggery. You can stay on familiar ground with lamb rogan josh or dhansak, or explore lesser-known regional dishes such as the bananaflower and colocasia leaves kofta – a Mumbai dish in a rich and rounded spiced pumpkin gravy. Portions can be 'sparing' but at least that leaves room for dessert: an impressive selection might include rasmalai – milk dumplings poached in saffron – and then traditional paan (betel leaf) to cleanse your palate. A short wine list opens at £16.
Chef/s: Manoj Vasaikar. **Open:** all week L 12 to 3 (1 to 4 Sun), D 6 to 11 (10 Sun). **Meals:** alc (main courses £9 to £22). Set L £12 (2 courses) to £15. Sun L £12 (2 courses) to £15. **Details:** 51 seats. 32 seats outside. V menu.

Kensington Place

Long-running brasserie icon
Cooking score: 2
⊖ Notting Hill Gate, map 6
Modern British | £32
201-209 Kensington Church Street, Notting Hill, W8 7LX
Tel no: (020) 7727 3184
www.kensingtonplace-restaurant.co.uk

When it opened nearly 30 years ago, KP was right at the top of any self-respecting foodie's list of must-visit destinations, and although the place doesn't have the same buzz about it these days, there's still good reason to visit. Old-timers will recall the noise generated when it's full (that's the same), while the finish in the glass-fronted space has kept up with the times. A few olive trees and banquettes add a softer edge. The kitchen focuses on seafood these days, sourced from the on-site fishmongers, with brasserie-inspired plates that aim to please. Spiced Devon crab with grilled chapati shows the world is their oyster, or go old-school and plump for the prawn cocktail. Follow on with roast fillet of hake with smoked haddock fishcake and garlic sausage, or go meaty with 28-day aged ribeye steak, and finish with dark chocolate mousse with peanut praline and milk ice cream. Wines start at £24.
Chef/s: Daniel Loftin. **Open:** Tue to Sun L 12 to 2.30 (3.30 Sun), Mon to Sat D 6.30 to 10.30. **Closed:** 24 to 26 Dec, 1 and 2 Jan, bank hols. **Meals:** alc (main courses £14 to £28). Set L and D £20 (2 courses) to £25. **Details:** 90 seats. Wheelchair access. Music.

LOCAL GEM

Kiraku

⊖ Ealing Common, map 1
Japanese | £25
8 Station Parade, Ealing, W5 3LD
Tel no: (020) 8992 2848
www.kiraku.co.uk

£5
OFF

A cheerful drop-in for Ealing commuters who enjoy Japanese delicacies. Take a seat at the bar for some flamboyantly decorated futomaki rolls (a house special) or bag one of the functional tables if you fancy a bigger spread – perhaps chilled beancurd with bonito flakes, spicy octopus with cucumber and grilled salted salmon. There are also generous bowls of udon noodles with various toppings – including wild vegetables. Wines start at £16, but beer and saké are better bets. Closed Mon.

Kitchen W8

Big-city brio and neighbourhood glitz
Cooking score: 6
◉ High Street Kensington, map 6
Modern European | £44
11-13 Abingdon Road, Kensington, W8 6AH
Tel no: (020) 7937 0120
www.kitchenw8.com

With its family-friendly mix of neighbourly vibes and big-city brio, Kitchen W8 is now part of Kensington's gastronomic DNA – a feeling reinforced by the smartly turned out, grown-up dining room with its soft lighting, satin-style wallpaper and striking modern prints. The influence of co-owners Phil Howard and Rebecca Mascarenhas is everywhere, although the resident brigade is keen to make its own mark, delivering a raft of fine-tuned, sure-footed dishes with a suitably deft touch. BBQ glazed quail comes with Yorkshire rhubarb, spiced bread, pickled turnips and foie gras, while an Ibérico pork chop is embellished with smoked celeriac, charred pear, bacon dauphinoise and sherry reduction – it's a very busy approach and there's always a lot happening on the plate, although the results never seem cluttered. To finish, a 'perfect' poached Comice pear with malted barley, gingerbread and spiced wafer blew one reader away, although chocolate pavé with peanut ice cream, caramelised popcorn and lime sounds like fun. The cosmopolitan wine list is a spot-on match for the food, with prices from £22.
Chef/s: Mark Kempson. **Open:** all week L 12 to 2.30 (12.30 to 3 Sun), D 6 to 10.30 (6.30 to 9.30 Sun).
Closed: 24 to 26 Dec, bank hols. **Meals:** alc (main courses £20 to £28). Set L £20 (2 courses) to £23. Set D £22 (2 courses) to £25. Sun L £33. **Details:** 75 seats. Wheelchair access.

Koffmann's

The old master rides on
Cooking score: 5
◉ Knightsbridge, Hyde Park Corner, map 6
French | £70
The Berkeley, Wilton Place, Belgravia, SW1X 7RL
Tel no: (020) 7235 1010
www.the-berkeley.co.uk

Koffmann's certainly pleases our more long-standing contributors, and it is one of a handful of places favoured by off-duty inspectors, who agree that the rating is well justified. The appeal lies not in fashionable ingredients, global dishes and in-your-face flavours, but rather in materials that are well sourced and intelligently handled. Ideas rarely break new ground. Stuffed pig's trotter with sweetbreads and morels, for example, has been mentioned on and off in the Guide since the days of La Tante Claire in the late 1970s. Here you can expect to eat foie gras chaud, endive et sauce Sauternes, go on to carré d'agneau en croûte d'herbes, and finish with a pistachio soufflé that was 'something of a masterpiece and worth every penny of the £15' – handsome prices come with the five-star luxury hotel location. More accessible, indeed 'a bit of a bargain', are the set lunch and pre-theatre menus, which this year produced a country terrine with 'deep, rich flavours', 'posh' duck cassoulet, 'delectable' beef Wellington, and a 'gorgeous' apple tart. A wine lovers' tour of the French regions opens at £30, but 500ml carafes start at £20.
Chef/s: Pierre Koffmann. **Open:** all week L 12 to 2.30, D 6 to 10.30. **Meals:** alc (main courses £22 to £29). Set L £23 (2 courses) to £26. Pre-theatre D £24 (2 courses) to £28. Tasting menu £80 to £100.
Details: 120 seats. Bar. Music.

Average price

The average price denotes the price of a three-course meal without wine.

Launceston Place

Fashionable food without frivolity
Cooking score: 6
 Gloucester Road, map 3
Modern European | £55
1a Launceston Place, South Kensington, W8 5RL
Tel no: (020) 7937 6912
www.launcestonplace-restaurant.co.uk

You can't miss the curved frontage of Launceston Place, which fills the corner of a smart South Kensington side street. Looking like a posh pub, its doors open on to a series of 'very sophisticated and refined' rooms where bursts of fresh flowers, modern art and gleaming mirrors enliven the urbane, slate grey colour scheme. Chef Timothy Allen arrived a few years ago from Whatley Manor in the Cotswolds, and has really hit his stride here, turning out refined Modern European cooking that's as easy on the eye as it is on the palate. There is no superfluous fuss and frippery: just beautiful ingredients and an emphasis on full flavours and interesting textures. A crisp and creamy white polenta bonbon with barbecued asparagus and pata negra lardo was a 'flawless' starter, while John Dory with linguine, brown shrimp and crab sauce infused with tomato and sea purslane proved to be 'another belter', tiny morsels of tomato perfectly cutting through the creamy sauce. A dessert of GoldRush apple with caramelised custard ice cream was a charming twist on tarte Tatin and apple crumble. A connoisseur's wine list offers plenty of classics and new discoveries, starting at £25.
Chef/s: Tim Allen. **Open:** Wed to Sun L 12 to 2.30, Tue to Sun D 6 to 10 (6.30 to 9.30 Sun). **Closed:** Mon, 1 week Dec, 1 Jan. **Meals:** Set L £29 (2 courses) to £34. Set D £55. Sun L £35. Tasting menu £70 (6 courses). **Details:** 50 seats. Wheelchair access. Music.

The Ledbury

A decade of sustained excellence
Cooking score: 8
 Notting Hill Gate, Westbourne Park, map 6
Modern British | £95
127 Ledbury Road, Notting Hill, W11 2AQ
Tel no: (020) 7792 9090
www.theledbury.com

In 2015, Brett Graham celebrated a decade at the helm of the Ledbury, a period of sustained excellence that has seen the place catapulted into the first division of London dining. Being away from the competitive bustle of the West End has its advantages, although once inside the former pub, you could as easily be cocooned in Mayfair, given the mirrored and linened ambience of refinement, and the unquestionable professionalism of staff. Graham's stock-in-trade has been modernist cooking of great technical proficiency that never loses sight of the principle of striking, positive flavour. Baking white beetroot in clay teases out all its assertive sweetness, which is then offset with smoked and dried eel and caviar salt. Another starter, refusing to rest on the obvious beguilement of foie gras, adds violet artichoke, duck ham, hazelnuts and grapes for harmonious layering. An intermediate course might supply shoulder of rabbit with lentil cream and chanterelles as a precursor to the bracing tang of sea bass with brassicas and seaweed in saké, or reverse the order by taking shiitake-wrapped langoustine with pumpkin, mandarin and ginger, ahead of gamily mature pigeon with beetroot, olives and pickled wild rose. Distinctiveness in presentation backs up the compositional ingenuity of dishes, through to the signature brown-sugar tart, which is dusted in cocoa and coffee, and served with dried grapes and ginger ice cream. The wine list strides through each of the headline regions with inspiring confidence, finding hotshot young growers as well as ancestral names. Italian selections are particularly commendable, and if you thought

German Rieslings had gone forever, prepare to be delighted. Bottles open at £32, standard glasses at £9.

Chef/s: Brett Graham. **Open:** Tue to Sun L 12 to 2, all week D 6.30 to 9.45 (6.45 Sun). **Closed:** 25 and 26 Dec, Aug bank hol. **Meals:** Set L £50. Set D £95. Tasting menu £115 (9 courses). **Details:** 58 seats. V menu. Wheelchair access.

The Malt House

Upmarket boozer with inviting food
Cooking score: 2
⊖ Fulham Broadway, map 3
British | £30
17 Vanston Place, Fulham, SW6 1AY
Tel no: (020) 7084 6888
www.malthousefulham.co.uk

Farrow & Ball paintwork, green leather dimpled banquettes, a grey-coloured bar and plenty of light flooding through large windows make this smart Georgian boozer a pleasant place to enjoy a drink or a casual meal; there's even a terrace for when the sun shines. A casual vibe and service that 'keeps well on track even during busy periods' are matched by good-value pub classics: fish and triple-cooked chips, good burgers and monthly pies with matching beer or wine. Elsewhere, the kitchen shows its creative side with seasonal specials, perhaps a pair of golden-brown smoked chilli fishcakes, given zing by a piquant lime and coriander mayonnaise, and fillet of hake paired with seaweed crushed potato, monk's beard and beetroot butter. Sticky toffee pudding with honeycomb ice cream is a pleasant way to end. Well-crafted wines from Berry Bros kick off from £21.

Chef/s: Oliver Tobias. **Open:** all week L 12 to 3, D 6 to 10 (4 to 9 Sun). **Closed:** 25 Dec. **Meals:** alc (main courses £13 to £23). **Details:** 62 seats. 42 seats outside. Wheelchair access. Music.

The Ledbury

The Good Food Guide welcomes Joanna Clifford, winner of our Restaurant Critic Competition, with an excerpt from her review of the Ledbury. Read the full story at thegoodfoodguide.co.uk

The Ledbury sets a luxurious scene, with pristine linen tablecloths and golden chandeliers twinkling in the light that pours through floor-to-ceiling windows.

The curtain rises to beignets topped with a lip-tingling dash of mustard fruit that cuts through the richness of hearty pigeon morsels concealed within. They arrive on a bed of pine needles, setting the tone for a series of seasonal ingredients treated gently to preserve their character. Complex methods are used, but only to allow diners to experience familiar flavours anew, as with grated foie gras that resembles a crumble but melts to buttery pâté in the mouth.

The star performance is given by a warm pheasant's egg with glazed amber yolk, whose attendant Arbois sauce, Ibérico ham, shaved celeriac and summer truffles are choreographed to perform a harmonious dance of nutty flavours on the tongue. The menu also showcases several excellent understudies, including a tender jowl of pork accompanied by slivers of pear to draw out its sweet notes, before being brought into focus by the assertive aniseed of fennel.

The dénouement belongs to a dainty tartlet of wafer-thin pastry bursting with vanilla custard and crowned with wild strawberries, berry sorbet and a violet cream that whispers of floral. This is food that plays to the crowd and, from me, it earned a standing ovation.

Marcus

Consummate special-occasion dining
Cooking score: 8
⊖ Hyde Park Corner, Knightsbridge, map 6
Modern British | £85

The Berkeley, Wilton Place, Belgravia,
SW1X 7RL
Tel no: (020) 7235 1200
www.marcus-wareing.com

These days Marcus Wareing may not sweat much at the stoves, but his restaurant in the Berkeley Hotel remains close to his heart and those who have been delegated to run the show on his behalf go about their duties with consummate skill – service is relaxed, expert, meticulous and accommodating. And in Mark Froydenlund, Wareing has a chef who interprets his style with confidence – classic techniques and flavour combinations rather than novelty being the keynotes here. Look no further than an astonishing dish of Dorset crab, the white meat served in a tangle of new season's almonds, sweet peach and thin strips of raw courgette, the brown meat served on the side as a pair of croquettes gently flavoured with lemongrass. Perfect. Another starter of veal sweetbreads is set off by the punchy sweetness of artichoke, peas and pea shoots and just bursts with savoury intensity. Or there's salmon that has 'the unctuousness of smoked and the freshness of just cooked', which arrives with a couple of langoustines, a few chunks of pickled cucumber 'giving a sharp crunchiness' and a buttermilk and lime dressing that 'worked surprisingly well'. Rhug Estate chicken is a star dish – 'a booming savoury hit' full of textures and contrasts – a happy marriage of breast, crisp skin, black garlic purée, carrots and chopped peanuts. To finish, toffee, peanut and milk chocolate nougat (Wareing's famed take on a Snickers bar) is the rich classic. The fixed-price format means bills are predictable, just as long as you don't get lost in the excellent wine list – aimed at those prepared to pay for quality. Bottles from £35.

Chef/s: Mark Froydenlund. **Open:** Mon to Sat L 12 to 2.45, D 6 to 10.45. **Closed:** Sun. **Meals:** Set L £49 (3 courses). Set D £85 (3 courses). Tasting menu £120. **Details:** 75 seats. V menu. Bar. Wheelchair access. Children over 12 yrs only at D.

Margaux

Cracking wines and Euro-accented food
Cooking score: 1
⊖ Gloucester Road, map 3
Modern European | £35

152 Old Brompton Road, South Kensington,
SW5 0BE
Tel no: (020) 7373 5753
www.barmargaux.co.uk

Despite its Gallic moniker, this wine-loving venue (formerly Bar Margaux) feels more Brooklyn than Bordeaux with its deliberately pared-back urban interiors. The kitchen pleases all-comers with its clean-cut Euro-accented cooking. Pork terrine with grape reduction or grilled aubergine salad with burrata and asparagus could precede pappardelle with rabbit ragù, beef bourguignon with creamy polenta or roast stone bass with sour cream mousseline and sautéed cauliflower. Fifteen selections by the glass or carafe kick off the knowledgeably chosen 150-bin wine list (note the inviting 75ml 'tasting' options). Bottles start at £25.
Chef/s: Xavier Castella. **Open:** all week L 12 to 2.30 (4 Sat and Sun), D 6 to 10.30 (11 Sat, 10 Sun). **Closed:** 24 to 26 Dec, 1 Jan. **Meals:** alc (main courses £15 to £29). Set L £16 (2 courses) to £20. Sun L £35. **Details:** 80 seats. Bar. Music.

Please send us your feedback

To register your opinion about any restaurant listed in this guide, or a new restaurant that you wish to bring to our attention, please visit the web address at the bottom of the page. Your feedback informs the content of the book and will be used to compile next year's reviews.

Masala Grill

Worthy successor to a Chelsea legend
Cooking score: 2
⊖ Fulham Broadway, map 3
Indian | £32
535 King's Road, Chelsea, SW10 0SZ
Tel no: (020) 7351 7788
www.masalagrill.co

After 25 years in Chelsea, Chutney Mary has moved to Mayfair (see entry) and been replaced by Masala Grill – 'a worthy successor' from the same owners. The dining room has been given more than a face-lift to create an informal yet sophisticated space, warmly dressed in shades of red, and buffed up with Indian tapestries and artefacts; the plant-filled conservatory is decorated with bunting and is an especially convivial spot. When it comes to the food, prices have been lowered and the style simplified with street snacks, tandoor grills and curries taking centre stage. At inspection, a pair of griddled scallops served with a creamy coconut sauce was pronounced 'delicious', spicy lamb shish kebab came with good mint sauce, and lasuni saag (spinach with burnt garlic) was faultless. Bebinca with orange sorbet is a pleasant way to end. Service 'could not be more friendly'. The compact wine list, starting at £23, is sensibly priced.
Open: all week D 6.30 to 11.15 (10.30 Sun). Sun L 12.30 to 3. **Meals:** alc (main courses £15 to £20). **Details:** 108 seats. Bar. Music.

Medlar

Bold flavours and culinary skill
Cooking score: 5
⊖ Sloane Square, Fulham Broadway, map 3
Modern European | £46
438 King's Road, Chelsea, SW10 0LJ
Tel no: (020) 7349 1900
www.medlarrestaurant.co.uk

'What a treasure,' said one reader of this confident neighbourhood restaurant that continues to thrive on accessibility, fair value and seriously considered cooking. Inside, it forgoes edgy statements in favour of a long, narrow dining room of muted hues and splashes of green, edged with dressed tables, with 'keen, knowledgeable but unfussy' service that matches the easy-going vibes. From here, turn your attention to the colourful, innovative cuisine that Joe Mercer Nairne has made his signature. Stone bass ceviche with avocado, red and yellow peppers, cucumber and puffed corn is a starter to make you sit up and take notice; mains might offer a superb grilled ox tongue with a truffled gratin of macaroni, cauliflower, walnuts and a glazed shallot. Bow out with a tarte Tatin for two or passion fruit curd beignets with coconut ice cream and lime. Grand French vintages dominate the global wine list, but there's good drinking to be had from £26.
Chef/s: Joe Mercer Nairne. **Open:** all week L 12 to 3, D 6.30 to 10.30. **Closed:** 24 to 26 Dec, 1 Jan. **Meals:** Set L Mon to Fri £23 (2 courses) to £28. Set L Sat £30. Set D £38 (2 courses) to £46. Sun L and D £35. **Details:** 75 seats. 8 seats outside.

Outlaw's at the Capital

Flat-out excellent seafood
Cooking score: 6
⊖ Knightsbridge, map 6
Seafood | £55
Capital Hotel, 22-24 Basil Street, Knightsbridge, SW3 1AT
Tel no: (020) 7591 1255
www.capitalhotel.co.uk

Possibly one of London's most understated hotels, the Capital does as much as it can to make eating in a posh Knightsbridge hotel a pleasurable experience. Service is attentive and helpful without being obtrusive and everything seems to happen at a relaxed pace. The menu is classic Nathan Outlaw, interpreted by Peter Biggs who runs a classy, confident kitchen. Seasonality is characteristic of the output, supremely fresh seafood a hallmark, taking in paprika-cured brill with dill yoghurt, smoked almonds and peppers, and chunky bass with smoked leeks and mash and enlivened by a roast chicken dressing. This is simple, ingredient-led cooking of a high order. The succinct menu also finds room for a 'first-class' barbecued quail with cider and onion tart, apple and tarragon, and lamb neck and sweetbreads served with kohlrabi, seaweed and mint, while treacle tart (baked to order) and served with orange marmalade ice cream could head up desserts. There's a decent selection of wines by the glass on a global list that opens at £22.

Chef/s: Nathan Outlaw and Peter Biggs. **Open:** Mon to Sat L 12 to 2, D 6.30 to 9.15. **Closed:** Sun. **Meals:** Set L £22 (2 courses) to £27. Set D £45 (2 courses) to £55. Tasting menu £75 (5 courses). **Details:** 33 seats. V menu. Bar. Wheelchair access. Music. Parking.

Pétrus

Blue-blooded Ramsay outpost
Cooking score: 6
⊖ **Knightsbridge, map 6**
Modern French | £75
1 Kinnerton Street, Knightsbridge, SW1X 8EA
Tel no: (020) 7592 1609
www.gordonramsay.com

At the polished end of the Gordon Ramsay restaurant group, Pétrus is known for its modern French food and a sophisticated neighbourhood vibe. It's sleek and comfortable, all pastel shades, slashes of claret, leather chairs, linen-draped tables and imposing flower arrangements all set around a centrepiece glass walk-in wine cellar. Chef Neil Snowball has carried on seamlessly where Sean Burbidge left off, delivering high-end modern European cooking 'that's as stylish and well-honed as the surroundings', built around luxury ingredients and eye-catching presentation. Witness dishes such as 'succulently pink' best end of Herdwick lamb with a herb crust, artichokes, ceps and smoked tapenade, and a 'fabulous' vanilla mousse with poached Kentish rhubarb, lemon balm and black sesame granola. The lunch menu is 'something of a steal at this level', and might feature Cornish hake rolled in courgette ribbons, served with braised potato and a striking red pepper bisque that shows 'clean flavours, balance and light touch'. The wine list has France as its main focus and is a roll call of starry names and top vintages (including a raft of namesake Pétrus vintages). It also accommodates the wider world, with bottles from £24.

Chef/s: Neil Snowball. **Open:** Mon to Sat L 12 to 2.30, D 6.30 to 10.30. **Closed:** Sun, 21 and 27 Dec. **Meals:** Set L £38. Set D £75. Tasting menu £95. **Details:** 50 seats. V menu. Wheelchair access.

Pizza East Portobello

⊖ **Ladbroke Grove, map 1**
Italian-American | £25
310 Portobello Road, Ladbroke Grove, W10 5TA
Tel no: (020) 8969 4500
www.pizzaeastportobello.com

In the heart of Portobello, this branch of Pizza East (see also Pizza East Shoreditch, Pizza East Kentish Town) is a dependable, busy, buzzy place on two floors. The open-to-view kitchen on the ground floor is a hive of activity, producing not just pizzas (crispy pork belly with tomato and mushroom, perhaps) but some appealing modern brasserie dishes at kind prices. Bone-marrow bruschetta or lamb meatballs with tomato sauce and Parmesan, or mac 'n' cheese or roast chicken aïoli from the wood oven are popular calls. Wines from £19.50. Open all week.

Pizzicotto

Italian
267 Kensington High Street, Kensington, W8 6NA
Tel no: (020) 7602 6777
www.pizzicotto.co.uk
'I've developed a longing for pasta, so last night I popped into Pizzicotto to seek some out and it was amazing. The menu changes each month and I can't wait to to back and try their pizza.'

LOCAL GEM

Polpo

⊖ **Notting Hill Gate, map 6**
Italian | £25
126-128 Notting Hill Gate, Notting Hill,
W11 3QG
Tel no: (020) 7229 3283
www.polpo.co.uk

The Notting Hill Polpo extends a warm tentacular embrace over the Gate, with Italian sharing plates of chichetti and pizzette served to tables with stools for connoisseurs of the brick-wall approach to anti-design. Its informality intends to echo the little backstreet bars of Venice, down to the meatballs and spaghettini, cod cheeks in lentils, lamb neck with white beans and rosemary, and anchovy and mozzarella mini-pizzas. It's easy to run away with the ordering, but leave room for a wodge of flourless lemon and almond cake. Bitter up a Gin Fizz with Cynar artichoke liqueur, then look to the Italian wines (from £18). Open all week.

Popeseye Steak House

A red-blooded steak-fest
Cooking score: 1
⊖ **Olympia, map 3**
Steaks | £25
108 Blythe Road, Olympia, W14 0HD
Tel no: (020) 7610 4578
www.popeseye.com

This friendly neighbourhood spot has lost none of its charm since opening some 20 years ago. It's a dimly lit evening venue, snug and intimate, that fills with hungry locals from around 8pm, when the atmosphere 'perks up'. A no-frills menu offers excellent 28-day hung Aberdeen Angus steak such as rump (or popeseye as its known in Scotland), T-bone or sirloin, cooked on an open grill and served alongside 'moreish' hand-cut chips and a side salad. For dessert, the homemade white chocolate cheesecake 'is worth saving room for'. The predominantly red wine list starts at

£19. There's another branch at 277 Upper Richmond Road, Putney; tel: (020) 8788 7733.
Chef/s: Ian Hutchinson. **Open:** Mon to Sat D only 6 to 10. **Closed:** Sun, bank hols. **Meals:** alc (steaks £12 to £66). **Details:** 34 seats.

Portobello Ristorante Pizzeria

Eat-me pizza and more
Cooking score: 2
⊖ **Notting Hill Gate, map 6**
Italian | £27
7 Ladbroke Road, Notting Hill, W11 3PA
Tel no: (020) 7221 1373
www.portobellolondon.co.uk

Maybe it's the outside terrace, perhaps it's the Neapolitan wood-fired oven or the fact that the ingredients are flown over from Italy, whatever the reason, as one fan put it, 'I'm seduced by somewhere making me feel like I'm on holiday.' It could also be that the pizzas are really, really good – the sourdough is left to rise for 48 hours (72 hours for the excellent bread) and the toppings are fresh and vibrant. The pavement terrace is surprisingly big, covered by a canopy (this is W11 after all, not Sorrento), and a prime spot in warm weather, but it's perfectly jolly and smart inside, too. The kitchen – and that oven – are open to view out back and offer up much more than just pizza: beef carpaccio adorned with truffles, penne with aubergines, tomato sauce and Sicilian ricotta cheese, or charcoal-grilled rack of lamb. Regional Italian wines start at £19.50.
Chef/s: Gaz Tefia. **Open:** all week 12 to 11.30 (10.30pm Sun). **Closed:** 25 and 26 Dec, 1 Jan, Easter Sun. **Meals:** alc (main courses £9 to £23). **Details:** 60 seats. 30 seats outside. Music.

Potli

Authentic Indian street food
Cooking score: 3
⊖ Ravenscourt Park, Stamford Brook, map 1
Indian | £27
319-321 King Street, Ravenscourt Park,
W6 9NH
Tel no: (020) 8741 4328
www.potli.co.uk

Widely regarded as the real deal, this modest west London eatery has entranced scores of followers with its faithful take on Indian market food, with one regular even admitting 'I love this place so much I get a bit emotional thinking about it.' A homely modern space combining spice-coloured walls, Indian knick-knacks and simple wooden furniture, it's a place to kick back and relax while basking in the vivid flavours and 'super-friendly, informed' service. Chicken 65 is 'a must-try', a traditional battered chicken dish with pepper and curry leaves. Other choices include paneer in an Indo-Chinese influenced sauce of chilli and garlic, served with peppers and spring onion; dhaba murgh, a roadside speciality of tandoori-grilled chicken on the bone simmered in aromatic rich sauce; and shrikhand, a sweet strained yoghurt dish. The substantial wine list offers helpful advice on wine and food pairings; bottles start at £18.
Chef/s: Jay Ghosh. **Open:** Mon to Sat L 12 to 2.45, D 6 to 10.30 (11 Fri and Sat). Sun 12 to 10.30.
Meals: alc (main courses £10 to £15). Set L £10 (2 courses). Sun L £15. **Details:** 80 seats. 20 seats outside. V menu. Bar. Wheelchair access. Music.

The Princess Victoria

Superior pub food and glorious wines
Cooking score: 2
⊖ Shepherd's Bush Market, map 1
British | £30
217 Uxbridge Road, Shepherd's Bush,
W12 9DH
Tel no: (020) 8749 5886
www.princessvictoria.co.uk

Found in an unlikely spot on the gritty Uxbridge Road, this rebooted Victorian gin palace offers polished décor with ornate fixtures, a gracefully curving bar and a dining room that is illuminated by a central skylight. Readers report favourably on the quality of the 'confident and creative' food: Roquefort, walnut and endive salad is 'a perfect balance of sour and salty flavours', for example, while 'tasty' toasted sourdough is topped prettily with piquillo peppers and squid. For mains, a succulent Tamworth pork is served with potato gnocchi, and a smoked haddock risotto with fried hake. To finish, a clotted cream pannacotta is particularly impressive, with its lemongrass and lime granita delicately offset against fresh basil. Service has been described as 'fantastic, couldn't do enough to recommend dishes from personal experience'. The Princess Victoria is well known for its superbly comprehensive drinks list offering some 400 bins of Old and New World wines (from £16.90), home-blended gins and classic cocktails.
Chef/s: Matt Reuther. **Open:** all week L 12 to 3 (4.30 Sun), D 6.30 to 10.30 (9.30 Sun). **Closed:** 24 to 28 Dec. **Meals:** alc (main courses £11 to £26). Set L £13. **Details:** 60 seats. 30 seats outside. Bar. Music. Parking.

Rabbit

A celebration of British food

Cooking score: 1

⊖ Sloane Square, map 3

Modern British | £30

172 King's Road, Chelsea, SW3 4UP

Tel no: (020) 3750 0172

www.rabbit-restaurant.com

Success with the Shed in Notting Hill (see entry) has inspired the Gladwin brothers to truck their celebration of wild British food over to Chelsea. The L-shaped dining room works the bucolic theme – wood floors, brick walls or large wooden planks 'used to good effect', metal tractor seats (not comfy), brown leather banquettes (better). The menu is split into nibbles, say choux pastry filled with mushroom duxelle infused with truffle oil; 'slow-cooked', which brings lamb chips, 'a twist on fish fingers vamped up by parsley and harissa'; and 'fast cooking' delivering roasted hake with salsify, mussels and sea spinach. The wine list (from £22) includes organic or biodynamic wines.

Chef/s: Oliver Gladwin. **Open:** Sun L 12 to 4, Mon D 6 to 11. Tue to Sat 12 to 12. **Meals:** alc (small plates £8 to £14). **Details:** 48 seats. Bar. Wheelchair access. Music.

Rasoi

Modern highbrow Indian

Cooking score: 4

⊖ Sloane Square, map 3

Indian | £66

10 Lincoln Street, Chelsea, SW3 2TS

Tel no: (020) 7225 1881

www.rasoirestaurant.co.uk

Ring the doorbell and walk into a dark and exotic Chelsea town house, intimate and dimly lit, the air scented with incense, the décor making much of ancient masks, Indian antiquities, soft velvet and silk fabrics. The cooking, however, is modern with skill and invention evident in an opening dish that saw two small prawns cooked in the tandoor arrive with Gilafi lamb seekh kebab and a piece of chicken tikka infused with mustard-curry leaf, with roasted tomato sauce adding a surprising and subtle lift to the flavours. Elsewhere, grilled duck breast is teamed with confit of the leg, coconut tandoori pineapple chaat and finished off with a duck jus. At dessert stage the kitchen seeks to astound: orange-flavoured gulab jamun is reinvented as a cheesecake and paired with orange shrikhand (yoghurt), orange spaghetti and chocolate soil. The wine list is dominated by the Old World and starts at £30.

Chef/s: Vineet Bhatia. **Open:** Tue to Fri and Sun L 12 to 2.30, Tue to Sun D 6 to 10.30 (9.45 Sun). **Closed:** Mon, 25 and 26 Dec, 1 and 2 Jan. **Meals:** alc (main courses £33 to £51). Set L £24 (2 courses) to £30. Set D £54 (2 courses) to £66. Sun L £24. Tasting menu £89 (7 courses). **Details:** 55 seats. V menu.

Restaurant Gordon Ramsay

Scaling the pinnacles of formal French dining

Cooking score: 10

⊖ Sloane Square, map 3

Modern French | £95

68-69 Royal Hospital Road, Chelsea, SW3 4HP

Tel no: (020) 7352 4441

www.gordonramsay.com

Recent years may have proved that there is still an inextinguishable hankering in London for unreconstructed French bistro food, but perhaps we've paid less attention to the appetite for formal French dining at the upper end – where the pinnacles are scaled – which remains quite as keen. Nobody would describe the food here as anything other than modern, and yet this is thrown into relief by the surrounding context, and the sheer commitment, in both the craft of cooking and its aesthetic presentation, to excellence. If it's modern, it's because it has moved with the times, not devoted weeks in the laboratory to devising eighteen new ways of denaturing a carrot. The whole approach matters: 'what turns this wonderful experience into brilliance is the superlative service, all working as a team, all willing to engage, led so well by Jean-Claude Breton'. As to the kitchen, it long ago ceased to be Gordon Ramsay's fiefdom, and the free rein that Clare Smyth enjoys is why the place is London's premier-league champion. There is nerveless accuracy and artfulness in combinations such as the opening smoked mackerel with its salt-baked beetroot salad, buttermilk, horseradish and pink grapefruit, and waves of complex fragrance in the following roast pigeon with sautéed foie gras, fennel, lavender, honey and orange, and the overall balance is close to perfection. Even dishes that look more obviously like bids for haute-cuisine seduction – the glorious lobster, langoustine and salmon ravioli poached in light seafood bisque with sorrel velouté and a garnish of oscietra – ring honest and true, and the anatomical guide to pork (crisped belly, roast loin, spiced shoulder boudin), served with chou farci, crushed potatoes and spring onions, is an authoritative demonstration. The tarte Tatin for two receives rave reviews, but there are more exploratory dessert options – the witty gag of a smoked chocolate cigar, carrot cake with bee pollen ice cream, lemonade parfait with bergamot. Incidentals, from the golden eggshell appetiser to petits fours in swirling dry ice, are all sublime, as is the splendid wine list, which has all the classical French gear your overdraft will handle, but much imaginative choosing in the less trodden byways. Prices ascend dizzily from £28, glasses from £6.

Chef/s: Clare Smyth. **Open:** Mon to Fri L 12 to 2.15, D 6.30 to 10.15. **Closed:** Sat, Sun, 1 week Dec. **Meals:** Set L £55. Set D £95. Tasting menu £135 to £195. **Details:** 44 seats. V menu. Music.

Restaurant Marianne

Modern European cooking, bijou setting
Cooking score: 5
⊖ Royal Oak, map 6
Modern European | £85
104 Chepstow Road, Notting Hill, W2 5QS
Tel no: (020) 3675 7750
www.mariannerestaurant.com

'We are tiny and we do not turn tables,' declares Marianne Lumb of her pocket-sized venue in Westbourne Park. Full at fourteen covers, it's an undeniably winning formula that lends itself now, as many have, to an exclusive tasting menu format of six courses at dinner, five at lunch, plus all the usual little extras. Choice comes only at main course, when the agony of deciding between sea bass with celeriac, salsify and sea veg or loin and pressed shoulder of venison with braised red cabbage, parsley root purée and rainbow kale must be faced. There's a French inclination to much of the output, matching foie gras with Passe Crassane pear and pecans, but other European traditions have their say in truffled gnocchi with Parmesan foam, and scallop ceviche with Sicilian blood orange. Allow room for cheeses, which precede a gentle coming to rest with prune and vanilla soufflé and Armagnac ice cream. The wine list is as dinky as the surroundings, with strong selections but nothing below £39.

Chef/s: Marianne Lumb. **Open:** Fri to Sun L 12 to 3, Tue to Sun D 6 to 11. **Closed:** Mon, 21 Dec to 5 Jan, 28 Aug to 1 Sept. **Meals:** Tasting menu L £65 (5 courses), D £85 (6 courses). **Details:** 14 seats. V menu. Music. Children over 12 yrs only.

Restaurant Michael Nadra

Finely considered combinations
Cooking score: 4
⊖ Turnham Green, map 1
Modern European | £37
6-8 Elliott Road, Chiswick, W4 1PE
Tel no: (020) 8742 0766
www.restaurant-michaelnadra.co.uk

£5
OFF

Chiswick is the elder sibling of Michael Nadra's two London venues (the other is Primrose Hill, north London – see entry) is a defiantly unadorned brasserie-style room, with slate-tiled floor and grey banquette seating at mostly tiny tables. His stock-in-trade is technically complex European dishes with overlays of sharp east Asian seasoning, full of finely etched flavours and considered combinations. Soft-shell crab tempura is a menu stalwart, its daikon and carrot salad and ginger-chilli sauce enhancing its bracing freshness, while main courses might bring on roast rump, braised neck and breaded sweetbreads of lamb with root dauphinois in rosemary jus, or perhaps Chinese-themed sea bass with a prawn dumpling, pak choi and gingery carrot purée in lemongrass-scented crab bisque. The gooey richness of treacle tart and clotted cream is offset with raspberry sorbet to finish, or there are thoroughbred cheeses from La Fromagerie. A wine list arranged by grape opens at £20, or £4 for small glasses, of house Languedoc blends.

Chef/s: Michael Nadra. **Open:** all week L 12 to 2.30 (3.30 Sat and Sun), Mon to Sat D 6 to 10 (10.30 Fri and Sat). **Closed:** 24 to 27 Dec, 1 Jan. **Meals:** alc (main courses £16 to £21). Set L £21 (2 courses) to £26. Set D £31 (2 courses) to £37. Tasting menu L £48, D £59 (6 courses). **Details:** 50 seats. Wheelchair access. Music.

The River Café

Italian icon by the river
Cooking score: 5
⊖ **Hammersmith, map 1**
Italian | £80
Thames Wharf, Rainville Road, Hammersmith, W6 9HA
Tel no: (020) 7386 4200
www.rivercafe.co.uk

A reporter, visiting the River Café for the first time, found it hard to pinpoint its appeal. On the one hand, it seems such an old smoothie – hard to imagine a lovelier spot than the capacious terrace on a sultry summer's evening with waiters 'greeting everyone as if they knew them intimately'. Then again, it has never been stuck in a culinary time warp. At heart, it is a highly successful and largely consistent local restaurant, with a vast silver bar dominating one side of the dining room, the open kitchen at the end showing Ruth Rogers at work and that famous projected clock on the far wall still ticking away. Prices may not be for the faint hearted, but the modern Italian food is flawlessly of the moment, delivering at inspection a pretty plateful of clams cooked in Terlano Pinot Bianco and dressed with courgette flowers with parsley, sliced courgettes, croutons and

chilli, and a huge piece of chargrilled turbot with a zingy salsa verde, cubes of crunchy pan-fried potatoes, Amalfi lemon 'al forno' and black olives. The wine list is an Italian treasure trove with bottles from £30.

Chef/s: Ruth Rogers. **Open:** all week L 12.30 to 2.15 (2.30 Sat, 12 to 3 Sun), Mon to Sat D 7 to 9 (9.15 Fri and Sat). **Closed:** 25 Dec to 1 Jan, bank hols. **Meals:** alc (main courses £35 to £45). **Details:** 120 seats. 80 seats outside. Bar. Wheelchair access.

Sam's Brasserie & Bar

Busy, buzzy neighbourhood brasserie
Cooking score: 2
⊖ **Chiswick Park, map 1**
Modern European | £28
11 Barley Mow Passage, Chiswick, W4 4PH
Tel no: (020) 8987 0555
www.samsbrasserie.co.uk

'Our old faithful' is how a couple of regulars describe Sam Harrison's brasserie and bar, which he's been running with commendable reliability for a decade. It's squirreled away in an old paper factory – there's the odd rough finish and ducting – and it's an infectiously buzzy place on two levels with an open kitchen that keeps an eye on the calendar, changes its menu each day and overlays British produce with vibrant Mediterranean flourishes. Cornish crab is served on toast with rocket and fennel and aïoli, Dingly Dell pork belly comes with Puy lentils and pancetta stew, and Welsh lamb rump is served with smoked celeriac purée, cavolo nero and green olive tapenade. British cheeses are an alternative to the likes of passion fruit pannacotta or milk chocolate and chilli mousse with black cherries. Wines from £18.50.

Open: all week L 12 to 3 (4 Sat and Sun), D 6.30 to 10.30 (9.30 Sun). **Closed:** 24 to 26 Dec. **Meals:** alc (main courses £12 to £24). Set L and D (6.30 to 7.30) £14 (2 courses) to £17. Sun L £22 (2 courses) to £24. **Details:** 105 seats. Bar. Wheelchair access. Music.

The Shed

Quirky farm-to-table experience
Cooking score: 3
⊖ Notting Hill Gate, map 6
Modern British | £30
122 Palace Gardens Terrace, Notting Hill,
W8 4RT
Tel no: (020) 7229 4024
www.theshed-restaurant.com

The Gladwin brothers' tiny restaurant is
considered a quirky place. Fronted by a small
terrace, it has a worn, rustic look within (think
wagon wheel, stuffed boar's head and metal
drums used for the base of dining tables).
While some readers have found the Shed 'a
little too low on creature comforts', there's
general approval for the sound sourcing of
ingredients, for the 'fresh and lively' dishes on
the 'wonderful creative menu', and the good,
cheerful service. Dishes may be small in size
but are big on impact: mouthfuls of hake
rillettes with lemon marmalade or mushroom
marmite egg confit, perhaps, or a rainbow
beetroot salad (from the Gladwins' farm)
served with feta, sunflower seeds and star
anise. Equally satisfying this year has been
grilled veal with purple sprouting broccoli,
celeriac and almonds, and pan-fried goats'
cheese with hazelnut and honey with a hint of
thyme. Conclude with a superb rhubarb baba
with marjoram and vanilla cream. Wines start
from £22 for a bottle from the family vines.
Chef/s: Oliver Gladwin. **Open:** Tue to Sat L 12 to 3
(4.30 Sat), Mon to Sat D 6 to 11. **Closed:** Sun, 25
Dec to 1 Jan, Easter Sun and Mon, 1 week Aug.
Meals: alc (small plates £9 to £13). Set L £25. Set D
£37. **Details:** 48 seats. 12 seats outside. Bar. Music.

NEW ENTRY

Shikumen

Chinese classics in sleek surroundings
Cooking score: 3
⊖ Shepherd's Bush Market, map 1
Chinese | £33
Dorsett Hotel, 58 Shepherd's Bush Green,
Shepherd's Bush, W12 8QE
Tel no: (020) 8749 9978
www.shikumen.co.uk

A 'sleek, minimalist take on oriental styling',
Shikumen's slate-grey floors, high ceilings
and Shanghai-style screens have an almost
temple-like grandeur. The look and the name
reference an East-meets-West architectural
style that first appeared in Shanghai in the
1860s. There are fusion influences on the menu
– notably a 'very enjoyable' green tea pudding
that is essentially a crème brûlée, but mostly
you'll get faithful renditions of Chinese
classics: Peking duck carved at the table;
exquisite dim sum; congee; salt-and-pepper
squid – the list goes on. To sample as much as
possible, the various set menus are a good way
to go. Highlights of one meal in May included
a salad of warm, crispy duck with tangy hoisin
sauce; a 'vivid, fresh' stir-fry of asparagus, lotus
root, mushroom and pumpkin, with gingko,
pak choi and a sprinkling of toasted nuts; and
fat, sticky, 'compellingly moreish' prawns with
pumpkin and salted egg yolk, served with
radish and melon. Drinks include saké, or a
modest selection of wines, starting at £17 a
bottle. If you like this, there is another branch
at the Hotel Xanadu, 26–42 Bond Street,
Ealing, W5 5AA; tel: (020) 8567 2770.
Chef/s: Mr Kam Choon Lai. **Open:** all week 12 to 11
(11.30am Sun). **Closed:** 25 Dec. **Meals:** alc (main
meals £10 to £20). Set L and D £27 (3 courses).
Details: 160 seats. V menu. Bar. Wheelchair access.
Music.

LOCAL GEM
Taiwan Village
✈ West Brompton, map 3
Chinese | £20
85 Lillie Road, Earl's Court, SW6 1UD
Tel no: (020) 7381 2900
www.taiwanvillage.com

Tucked away in a parade of shops, Taiwan Village showcases a number of dishes from Taiwan, Hunan and Szechuan in a room buffed up by faux plants and elaborate wood carvings. 'Nest of imperial jewels' – a lettuce wrap of wok-fried prawns with mustard greens – makes for an exotic start, followed, perhaps by General Tso's stir-fried chicken with red chillies and rice vinegar (a dish popularised in the USA and not actually originating from China or Taiwan) while dry-fried French beans can steal the show. Wines from £15.20. Open all week D, Sat and Sun L.

Tinello
The Italians' Italian
Cooking score: 4
✈ Sloane Square, map 3
Italian | £40
87 Pimlico Road, Chelsea, SW1W 8PH
Tel no: (020) 7730 3663
www.tinello.co.uk

A few minutes' walk from Sloane Square is this smart but informal Italian restaurant, its interior a low-key study in exposed brickwork and moody lighting. Owned by Giorgio Locatelli (with protégé Frederico Sali in the kitchen) it's no surprise that the place has built a steady following – Tinello's sophisticated take on Italian cooking hits just the right notes. The sheer quality of ingredients stands out on a menu that's neatly divided into antipasti (stuffed squid with fish tomato sauce) and small plates (traditional Tuscan chicken liver crostini), before going on to excellent pasta – pasta ribbons with lamb ragù has been praised – while a main course veal cutlet, served with potato purée and braised artichokes, has yielded satisfying results too. Dolci such as fig tart with yoghurt ice cream conclude things perfectly. It's a formula that,

together with on-the-ball service, attracts a full house. The mainly Italian wine list starts at £17.50.
Chef/s: Federico Sali. **Open:** Mon to Sat L 12 to 2.30, D 6.15 to 10.30. **Closed:** Sun, 24 to 28 Dec, 1 Jan, bank hols. **Meals:** alc (main courses £19 to £25). **Details:** 74 seats. 6 seats outside. Bar.

La Trompette
European food, enlivening combinations
Cooking score: 5
✈ Turnham Green, map 1
Modern European | £40
3-7 Devonshire Road, Chiswick, W4 2EU
Tel no: (020) 8747 1836
www.latrompette.co.uk

The Platts-Martin and Poole group is a small, perfectly formed amalgam of Chez Bruce, the Glasshouse (see entries) and this broad, commodious room in Chiswick, with its spaciously disposed tables, abstract artworks and expansive views of neighbourhood street-life. There are affinities among the group's menus, but Rob Weston stamps his own discreet authority on matters here with modernised European classic dishes and enlivening combinations. Buttermilk-simmered chicken wings come in hand-rolled macaroni with Vacherin and truffle for a starter celebration of the dairy arts, or there could be roast foie gras with turnip, quince and pain d'épices. At main, the principal components are given their due, the guinea fowl accompanied by spätzle, Jerusalems and chanterelles, or the John Dory with brown shrimps and pearl barley. Finish up with a simple crème fraîche tart topped with clementine and dates, or a selection from the glorious French cheese array. The geographical reach of the wine list is astonishing, with New York State and Japan in the running, as well as an enterprising pair from Syria. It's all good, and not grabbingly priced at all for Chiswick. Start at £22.
Chef/s: Rob Weston. **Open:** all week L 12 to 2.30 (12.30 to 3 Sun), D 6.30 to 10.30 (7 to 9.30 Sun).
Closed: 24 to 26 Dec, 1 Jan. **Meals:** Set L £25 (2

courses) to £30. Set D £43 (2 courses) to £48. Sun L £33 (2 courses). **Details:** 88 seats. 12 seats outside. Wheelchair access.

Vinoteca

Perfect neighbourhood restaurant

Cooking score: 2
Turnham Green, map 1
Modern British | £28
18 Devonshire Road, Chiswick, W4 2HD
Tel no: (020) 3701 8822
www.vinoteca.co.uk

'Surely the epitome of the perfect neighbourhood restaurant,' thought one visitor, who went on to praise 'the warmest of welcomes, peals of contented laughter, trencherman portions with seasonality and quality produce at the heart of the every dish.' The growing Vinoteca group has made a big impact on London since opening their first venue in Farringdon six years ago. This Chiswick venue may deliver the same pared-back, functional style as its siblings, and list the same char-grilled bavette (with chips, watercress and horseradish) and tremendous collection of well-chosen modern wines, but goes its own way when it comes to regularly changing, calendar-correct menus. In spring that means lovely, creamy Venetian salt cod bruschetta with grumolo (a salad leaf), fennel and raw peas, a spatchcock Suffolk wood pigeon ('rose pink and tender') with dandelion, pancetta and balsamic, and the 'buttery gorgeousness' of lemon sole, brown shrimp and Umbrian lentils. On the wine front, there's excellent choice by the glass, and bottles from £16.50.
Chef/s: James Robson. **Open:** all week L 12 to 3, D 6 to 10.30. **Closed:** 24 to 26 Dec, 31 Dec, 1 Jan. **Meals:** alc (main courses £12 to £17). **Details:** 45 seats. Music.

Wormwood

Cooking with heart and generosity

Cooking score: 4
Ladbroke Grove, Westbourne Park, map 4
Mediterranean | £35
16 All Saints Road, Notting Hill, W11 1HH
Tel no: (020) 7854 1808
www.wormwoodrestaurant.com

Round the corner from Portobello Road, down posh-boho All Saints Road, is one of those sunny, special neighbourhood restaurants that radiate warmth. Two whitewashed, white-furnished rooms mix Moroccan tiling, a Moorish patterned ceiling and lots of interesting artefacts with an attention to detail that carries through to the food. The ambitious kitchen delivers unique, freethinking cooking with 'some whacky touches', and while not all the dishes work, it is not at the expense of enjoyment. Flavours are strikingly vivid: in the silky richness of sweet port jelly, smooth foie gras mousse and black olive layered in a miniature kilner jar; in the brilliant spicing and fantastic textural contrasts of lobster couscous (studded with almonds and prunes) with a 'thick, deep, lemony bisque' poured at the table; in an aromatic hummus topped with full-flavoured lamb; and in a zingy, sweet-sour yuzu sorbet, with lemon mousse and ice cream. Service is 'delightful'. Wines from £27.
Chef/s: Rabah Ourrad. **Open:** Tue to Sat L 12 to 2, Mon to Sat D 6 to 10. **Closed:** Sun. **Meals:** alc (main courses £9 to £21). Set L £35 (3 courses). **Details:** 44 seats. Music.

Yashin Sushi

Sushi with an original twist

Cooking score: 3
High Street Kensington, map 6
Japanese | £50
1a Argyll Road, Kensington, W8 7DB
Tel no: (020) 7938 1536
www.yashinsushi.com

A neon sign proclaiming 'without soy sauce – but if you want to' puts down an emphatic marker at this innovative sushi joint run by two guys who trained at Nobu London (see entry). Dangling lights, green tiles and dark-wood surfaces set the scene for some original forays into the world of contemporary fusion – although the chefs are well versed in the founding principles of traditional sushi. The menu is all about hot and cold 'tapas' plates designed for sharing: some items are shown the blowtorch, others are dressed with anything from truffle-infused ponzu jelly to salted kombu seaweed. Try your luck with, say, Scottish smoked salmon, Hibiki whiskey jelly and chocolate 'amer' or hot sugar snaps and cauliflower with ginger and lime salt. Also expect creative salads and a few bigger plates including char-grilled Chilean sea bass with sour miso. Omakase tasting menus are 'a must', service is all smiles and there are some premium sakés, too; otherwise, wines start at £22. An offshoot 'nose-to-tail' seafood restaurant, Yashin Ocean House, can be found at 117-119 Old Brompton Road, SW7 3RN.

Chef/s: Yasuhiro Mineno and Shinya Ikeda. **Open:** all week L 12 to 3, D 6 to 11. **Closed:** 24 to 26 and 31 Dec, 1 Jan. **Meals:** alc (main courses £8 to £26). Set L £13 to £25. **Details:** 37 seats. Music.

Zafferano

Accomplished Italian cooking
Cooking score: 4
Knightsbridge, map 6
Italian | £55
15 Lowndes Street, Belgravia, SW1X 9EY
Tel no: (020) 7235 5800
www.atozrestaurants.com

For the past two decades this Knightsbridge restaurant has been something of a landmark for fans of Italian food. It's divided into three sections, an intimate room at the rear, a more informal bar area and a larger front room, while a mix of stone floors, exposed brick walls, banquettes and large floral displays set the tone. The kitchen understands the subtleties of Italian food, and the output is accomplished, although the menu holds few surprises: a salad of cuttlefish with croûtons and pesto (which impressed with its freshness and flavour at inspection); pappardelle with

wild mushrooms cooked with pin-point accuracy; pan-fried brill teamed with purple sprouting broccoli and a red pepper and carrot escabèche. Desserts such as tiramisu aim for comfort rather than creativity. Service is attentive, and the wine list (from £28) delves deep into the Italian regions, along with some prestige labels from France.

Chef/s: Daniele Camera. **Open:** all week 12 to 11.30 (11 Sun). **Meals:** alc (main courses £22 to £38). **Details:** 150 seats. 25 seats outside. Bar. Music.

Zuma

Stylish Japanese dining
Cooking score: 5
Knightsbridge, map 6
Japanese | £75
5 Raphael Street, Knightsbridge, SW7 1DL
Tel no: (020) 7584 1010
www.zumarestaurant.com

Rainer Becker's international chain of Zumas extends from Hong Kong Island through the Arab Emirates and eastern Med to New York, via this splendidly cool and relaxing venue in Knightsbridge. Book the semi-private tosho table for a true taste of the high life, or else get bedded in at the sushi counter or the robata grill. Latticed wood screens and textured stone are the setting for Japanese food that has some modern flourishes, but is essentially deeply traditional. Nigiri sushi, maki rolls and tempura morsels are the foundation of the menus, which offer impeccable raw materials for seared tuna with chilli daikon in ponzu sauce, Wagyu beef with aïoli, and signature specialities like roast lobster with green chilli and garlic hojiso (shiso flower) butter. Finish with green tea banana cake, served with coconut ice cream and toffee peanut sauce. Wines from £22 will add enthusiastically to the bill, and there is a comprehensive range of saké in all styles.

Chef/s: Oliver Lange. **Open:** all week L 12 to 2.30 (12.30 to 3.30 Sat and Sun), D 6 to 11 (10.30 Sun). **Closed:** 25 Dec. **Meals:** alc (sharing plates £10 to £60). Tasting menu £124. **Details:** 175 seats. Bar. Wheelchair access. Music.

A Cena

Attractive local Italian with reliable food
Cooking score: 2
⊖ Richmond, map 1
Italian | £45
418 Richmond Road, Twickenham, TW1 2EB
Tel no: (020) 8288 0108
www.acena.co.uk

£5 OFF

A long-term feature in East Twickenham, this locally owned and run eatery deserves its loyal following. 'A reasonably austere looking place' with monochrome walls adorned with black and white photos, it's the chatter and laughter of regulars that lend the necessary colour and ambience. Following the well-established principle of modern Italian cooking, namely taking great ingredients and allowing them to speak for themselves, first courses might involve mozzarella served with warm lentils or asparagus with fried egg and Parmesan. Good pastas – ravioli filled with sea bass served with lemon oil; spaghetti with spicy pork and fennel balls – follow the likes of calf's liver with grilled polenta, with affogato or almond tart to follow. The all-Italian wine list is reasonably priced, around £6.00 a glass, and £19 a bottle.
Chef/s: Nicola Parsons. **Open:** Tue to Sun L 12 to 2, Tue to Sat D 6 to 10. **Closed:** Mon, 24 to 27 Dec, 2 weeks Aug, bank hols. **Meals:** alc (main courses £13 to £24). Sun L £21 (2 courses) to £25. **Details:** 55 seats. Bar. Music.

Albert's Table

Neighbourhood bistro with culinary clout
Cooking score: 3
Modern British | £35
49b/c Southend, Croydon, CR0 1BF
Tel no: (020) 8680 2010
www.albertstable.co.uk

£5 OFF

With its gentle prices, enterprising food and outgoing vibe, Albert's Table ticks all the boxes as a confident neighbourhood bistro, and – thanks to chef/proprietor Joby Wells – it injects some culinary clout into the suburban enclaves of South Croydon. With stints at big hitters such as The Square and La Trompette (see entries) on his CV, Joby brings plenty of swagger to the party – although he's not one for idle showboating. Instead, expect sound ingredients, true flavours and lots of appetising ideas – from grilled Devon scallops with gnocchi, curry butter and black onion purée to pressed Old Spot pork belly with crispy skin, glazed turnips, greens and sherry vinegar. A few simpler offerings such as beef and ale pie or chicken and red wine casserole crop up on the lunch menu, while desserts span everything from steamed treacle sponge to pine nut and lemon thyme cake with lemon curd and almond milk. Wines from £18.
Chef/s: Joby Wells. **Open:** Tue to Sun L 12 to 2.30 (3.30 Sun), Tue to Sat D 6.30 to 10.30. **Closed:** Mon. **Meals:** Set L £21 (2 courses) to £24. Set D £28 (2 courses) to £35. Sun L £24. **Details:** 60 seats. Bar. Wheelchair access. Music. Parking.

The Bingham

Accomplished cooking by the Thames
Cooking score: 4
⊖ Richmond, map 1
Modern British | £45
61-63 Petersham Road, Richmond, TW10 6UT
Tel no: (020) 8940 0902
www.thebingham.co.uk

£5 OFF 

The urban frontage of this Georgian town house hotel hides the views afforded by the public rooms at the back, which overlook the well-kept garden with the Thames flowing just beyond. Here, the restaurant has built up a loyal local following over the years and the kitchen has evolved to suit its clientele – gone is the heavily wrought haute cuisine and 'it's more fun now, a real buzz with everyone enjoying themselves'. The kitchen delivers vibrant flavours and colours in a fresh, modern British style mixed with influences from further afield. A lively starter of sea bream tartare, dressed with lime and avocado, and a tender, punch-packing smoky roast haunch of venison lifted by the brilliant magenta of a beetroot gratin are typical choices. Puddings

include brûlées, crumbles and tarts with a twist. Prices start at £24 on a wine list that offers something for all occasions.
Chef/s: Andrew Cole. **Open:** all week L 12 to 2.30 (4 Sun), Mon to Sat D 6.30 to 10 (10.30 Thur to Sat). **Meals:** alc (main courses £13 to £25). Set L £15 (2 courses) to £20. Set D £25 (2 courses) to £35. Sun L £38. **Details:** 55 seats. 27 seats outside. Bar. Wheelchair access. Music. Parking.

Brilliant

Long-lived and lustrous north Indian star
Cooking score: 4
Hounslow West, map 1
Indian | £25
72-76 Western Road, Southall, UB2 5DZ
Tel no: (020) 8574 1928
www.brilliantrestaurant.com

In 1975, the Anand family, newly arrived from Kenya, opened their renowned Punjabi restaurant. Visits by Prince Charles and latterly Gordon Ramsay followed, along with various refurbishments, the latest of which has produced a large, nattily-attired interior with burnished-copper bar, TVs and a first-floor banqueting suite. A joyous hubbub of multicultural diners (including Sikh families and Chinese tourists on our visit) pay homage. The menu has few innovations, yet the north Indian cooking is rarely surpassed. A handsomely presented inspection meal showed Brilliant at its most lustrous – from own-made relishes with poppadoms (don't miss the lemon pickle or fresh mint chutney) via perfectly battered fish pakora and exemplary papri chaat (chickpeas and crisp sev in yoghurt and tamarind relish) to deeply savoury chicken methi, tender lamb biryani, and creamy, not-too-sweet ras malai dessert. Salt lassi, crunchy with cumin seeds, makes the ideal accompaniment, though wine starts at just £11.
Chef/s: Jasvindersit Singh. **Open:** Tue to Fri L 12 to 3, Tue to Sun D 6 to 11.30 (12 Fri and Sat). **Closed:** Mon, 25 Dec, bank hols. **Meals:** alc (main courses £15 to £32). Set L and D £20. **Details:** 230 seats. V menu. Music. Parking.

La Buvette

Dyed-in-the-wool French bistro
Cooking score: 3
Richmond, map 1
French | £29
6 Church Walk, Richmond, TW9 1SN
Tel no: (020) 8940 6264
www.labuvette.co.uk

It may be housed in a former municipal tea room attached to a church hall, but there's no doubting that La Buvette is a dyed-in-the-wool French bistro – just look at the chequered tablecloths, big blackboards and bentwood chairs, not forgetting the pretty walled garden outside. The menu also tells its own story, with a stoic line-up taking in bourgeois classics from charcuterie with cornichons to poule au pot, mussels with aïoli and sea bass en papillote, and beetroot and parsnip bourguignon for the vegetarians. Desserts include the much-talked-about warm waffles with poached pear, hot chocolate sauce and Chantilly cream as well as a croustillant of spiced orange and citrus zest with pistachio ice cream. As befits a neighbourhood bistro, there are excellent-value prix-fixe deals, an ever-changing roster of chalked-up specials and a patriotic wine list with plenty by the glass and carafe. Bottles start at £17.50, but also note the tempting 100ml white flights (£15.75 for three).
Chef/s: Buck Carter. **Open:** all week L 12 to 3, D 5.45 to 10. **Closed:** 25 and 26 Dec, Good Fri, Easter Sun. **Meals:** alc (main courses £14 to £18). Set L and D £18. **Details:** 50 seats. 35 seats outside.

Please send us your feedback

To register your opinion about any restaurant listed in this guide, or a new restaurant that you wish to bring to our attention, please visit the web address at the bottom of the page. Your feedback informs the content of the book and will be used to compile next year's reviews.

Join us at thegoodfoodguide.co.uk

The Dysart

Precision and invention in bucolic surrounds
Cooking score: 6
Richmond, map 1
Modern British | £42
135 Petersham Road, Richmond, TW10 7AA
Tel no: (020) 8940 8005
www.thedysartpetersham.co.uk

Time has been called on the mock-Tudor Dysart's era as a public house. It is a restaurant. End of. And the sort of restaurant that is worth ten dodgy boozers. Built on an impressive scale with generous internal proportions complete with a grand piano and Arts and Crafts features, not to mention an enviable position overlooking Richmond Park, the modern-day Dysart is a blisteringly fine place to eat. Kenneth Culhane offers up a vision of contemporary dining with plates (or planks or elegant bowls) of well-crafted dishes that combine good sense with present-day cooking techniques and a pretty rusticity (think scattered wild flowers). Charred mackerel with kombu-braised daikon, ginger and Champagne might precede wild Cornish sea bass with Gewürztraminer and lobster sauce, or English woodcock with Cevenne onion and Muscat sauce, with the first two also starring on the tasting menu. Finish with Petersham damson granita with fresh chestnuts and start planning your return visit. Wines start at £19
Chef/s: Kenneth Culhane. **Open:** all week L 12 to 3 (3.30 Sat, 4 Sun), Mon to Sat D 6 to 9.30. **Meals:** alc (main courses £16 to £29). Set L and D £19 (2 courses) to £23. Sun L £34. Tasting menu £60.
Details: 50 seats. 40 seats outside. V menu. Wheelchair access. Music. Parking. No children under 12 yrs after 7.30.

Average price

The average price denotes the price of a three-course meal without wine.

Eat17

Abidingly popular neighbourhood eatery
Cooking score: 1
Walthamstow Central, map 1
British | £25
28-30 Orford Road, Walthamstow, E17 9NJ
Tel no: (020) 8521 5279
www.eat17.co.uk

EAT17 is the one-stop shop for all things gastronomical in the E17 postcode – be it lazy weekend brunches that are 'worth getting out of bed for', dinner dates or craft-beer-fuelled nights out. The dining room is trendy without being aggressively hipster – with leather banquettes that invite hours of dawdling – and a menu that takes a few detours from its comfort food heartland. Start out with a refreshing starter of crispy rabbit with lime citrus cabbage and pomegranate, before piling into something heartier – wild boar sausage, Parmesan and wondrously rich truffle mash, perhaps. Puds comprise crowd-pleasers like crumbles and cheesecakes, with bottles from £17.
Chef/s: Chris O'Connor. **Open:** all week L 12 to 3 (4 Sun), Mon to Sat D 6 to 10. **Meals:** alc (main courses £12 to £18). **Details:** 50 seats. Bar. Wheelchair access. Music.

LOCAL GEM

The Exhibition Rooms

map 1
Modern British | £26
69-71 Westow Hill, Crystal Palace, SE19 1TX
Tel no: (020) 8761 1175
www.theexhibitionrooms.com

A neighbourly vibe and flexible menus make an appealing package at this popular restaurant and cocktail lounge (with heated terrace). Locals love it, service is charm personified and the menu promises plates of mozzarella with ratatouille, basil and pine nut salad, full-flavoured braised lamb shank with Moroccan spices, chickpeas and rosemary jus or cod fillet with mussel and cockle chowder, and hot chocolate fondant with ice cream to finish. Wines from £17.50. Open Fri to Sun L, all week D.

The French Table

Fantastic neighbourhood restaurant
Cooking score: 4
map 1
French | £35
85 Maple Road, Surbiton, KT6 4AW
Tel no: (020) 8399 2365
www.thefrenchtable.co.uk

'This is a brilliant, ever-changing local restaurant with a great welcome and consistently delicious food,' observes a Surrey reporter. Since opening 15 years ago, Eric and Sarah Guignard have made the French Table a destination for fans of Mediterranean cooking with a French accent. The cooking may not keep up with the whims of current stove-top practice, but the menu is peppered with impressive, high-end ingredients – many of them British – conjured into industrious dishes displaying plenty of technique. The short carte might start with ham hock and rabbit terrine with 'a good robust flavour', move on to Cornish stone bass served with olive oil mash, Swiss chard, crispy Jerusalem artichoke and herb cream, and finish with a trio of rhubarb or chocolate fondant with honeycomb and salted-caramel ice cream. The predominantly European wine list begins at £17.95 for a regional French red and white, with ten served by the glass and carafe.

Chef/s: Eric and Sarah Guignard. **Open:** Tue to Sat L 12 to 2.30, D 7 to 10.30 (6.30 Fri and Sat). **Closed:** Sun, Mon, 25 to 27 Dec. **Meals:** alc (main courses £20 to £29). Set L £20 (2 courses) to £25. Tasting menu £45. **Details:** 87 seats. V menu. Music.

The Glasshouse

Low-key high achiever
Cooking score: 5
⊖ Kew Gardens, map 1
Modern European | £45
14 Station Parade, Kew, TW9 3PZ
Tel no: (020) 8940 6777
www.glasshouserestaurant.co.uk

Out of the same stable as neighbourhood stars La Trompette and Chez Bruce (see entries), this neighbourhood local by a parade of shops outside Kew station is quite the high achiever. The surroundings may be low-key, the location suburban, but peep inside and you'll see a happy throng in the classily lit, beige-toned dining room. On offer is a daily menu of forthright seasonal creations, delivered with confidence, flair and an open mind when it comes to influences and ingredients. France and Italy claim most of the honours, from pig's head terrine with endive salad, clementine and honey mustard dressing to Gigha halibut with langoustines, linguine, roasted salsify and shellfish sauce – big ideas with big, gutsy flavours to boot. Desserts plunder the same geographical territory, witness stracciatella ice cream or warm hazelnut financier with candied lemons, blood orange and crème fraîche. By contrast, the democratically priced wine list offers mouthwatering distractions from across the viticultural globe, with half-bottles and by-the-glass selections galore; bottles start at £22.

Chef/s: Berwyn Davies. **Open:** all week L 12 to 2.30 (12.30 to 3 Sun), D 6.30 to 10.30 (7 to 10 Sun). **Closed:** 24 to 26 Dec, 1 Jan. **Meals:** Set L £25 (2 courses) to £30. Set D £40 (2 courses) to £45. Sun L £33. **Details:** 60 seats.

Join us at thegoodfoodguide.co.uk

Incanto

Creative Italian food and fascinating wines
Cooking score: 5
 Harrow-on-the-Hill, map 1
Italian | £35
41 High Street, Harrow-on-the-Hill, HA1 3HT
Tel no: (020) 8426 6767
www.incanto.co.uk

£5 OFF

There's enchantment indeed atop Harrow Hill (where Harrow School stood in for Hogwarts in the Harry Potter movies), for an easily missed café frontage hides something special – an old post office turned smart dining room that's drawing in not just visiting parents but muggles from '20 miles away'. 'Very easy and engaged service' eases you into comfy booths, a fun amuse-bouche of, say, mini pulled pork hot dog with sweetcorn velouté sets the tone for food that is 'exceptional' and 'exciting' and 'one of the best meals in years'. Charred mackerel with cucumber, apple tapioca, horseradish and dill or pork belly with croquettes, piccalilli and puff crackling are 'beautifully presented, very artistic', while main courses of olive oil-poached cod with spinach salsify, and roasted chicken with potato hash, salt-baked carrot and golden enoki mushroom are 'first class'. With mango and passion fruit délice 'as beautifully done as the other dishes', some readers are at a loss to explain why Incanto 'doesn't have a three-month waiting list'. Wines start at £18.
Chef/s: Peter Howarth. **Open:** Tue to Sun L 12 to 2.30 (12.30 to 4 Sun), Tue to Sat D 6.30 to 10.30. **Closed:** Mon, 24 to 26 Dec, 1 Jan, Easter Sun, bank hols. **Meals:** alc (main courses £16 to £22). Set L £22 (2 courses) to £24. Set D £23 (2 courses) to £25. Tasting menu £65 (7 courses). **Details:** 64 seats. Wheelchair access. Music.

Indian Zilla

Style, creativity and Indian pizazz
Cooking score: 3
map 1
Indian | £27
2-3 Rocks Lane, Barnes, SW13 0DB
Tel no: (020) 8878 3989
www.indianzilla.co.uk

£5 OFF 

Just round the corner from the main streets of Barnes is this welcoming, friendly and surprisingly good Indian restaurant. Manoj Vasaikar, who honed his skills under the Oberoi hotels group in India as well as London's Chutney Mary (see entry), has distilled his vision of good Indian cooking to a simple, manageable menu with enough to make it interesting and enticing, but not too much to frighten the timid. From the zingy dips for the poppadoms, bursting with flavour, and the earthy lentil soup amuse, the kitchen woos its clientele. While traditionalists will be happy with the sweet, soothing chicken makhani, the more adventurous should try the karawari fish curry, which demonstrates Manoj's adept management of spices, giving plenty of depth of flavour without searing heat, though if it's a proper burn you're after they'll happily accommodate. Beautiful presentation, polite and helpful staff and a decent wine list with a surprisingly good Indian house wine all help to keep the place busy, particularly at weekends. Wines from £16.
Chef/s: Manoj Vasaikar. **Open:** Sat and Sun L 12 to 3, all week D 6 to 11 (10 Sun). **Closed:** 25 Dec. **Meals:** alc (main courses £9 to £22). Set L £12 (2 courses) to £15. **Details:** 75 seats. 4 seats outside. Music.

Madhu's

Flashy Punjabi specialist
Cooking score: 3
map 1
Indian | £25
39 South Road, Southall, UB1 1SW
Tel no: (020) 8574 1897
www.madhus.co.uk

A Southall stalwart since 1980, Madhu's is a serious player in a neighbourhood renowned for its Indian eateries. With its designer staircase, mirrors and glossy black surfaces, the flashy interior might suggest a clubby hangout, but the kitchen is true to its roots – no modish East/West crossovers here. Instead, expect a line-up of ultra-traditional tandooris and curries with a strong Punjabi accent and a few 'Kenyan twists', all based on top-drawer ingredients. Fresh, vivid spicing is the hallmark, whether you're sampling the signature butter chicken, keema mattar (mince and peas) or the entertainingly titled 'boozi bafu' – spring lamb chops on the bone in a spicy onion and tomato sauce. Wines from £16.
Chef/s: Rakesh Verma. **Open:** Mon and Wed to Fri L 12.30 to 3, Wed to Mon D 6 to 11.30 (12 Fri to Sun). **Closed:** Tue, 25 Dec. **Meals:** alc (main courses £6 to £13). Set L and D £25. **Details:** 110 seats. V menu. Wheelchair access. Music. Parking.

Petersham Nurseries Café

Glorious Italian-influenced menus
Cooking score: 3
⊖ Richmond, map 1
Modern European | £45
Church Lane, off Petersham Road, Richmond, TW10 7AG
Tel no: (020) 8940 5230
www.petershamnurseries.com

Greenhouse dining doesn't come much lovelier, or more upmarket, than this: it's a 'beautiful' setting, the shop replete with posh bric-à-brac, little plants prettying the tables and the diners in smart casuals with smatterings of fur and jewels. As of late 2014 there's a new chef in the kitchen, but rest assured that Damian Clisby comes (like, one suspects, everything here) with a good pedigree, having notched up time as head chef at Hix Soho (see entry). He works under the guidance of long-time gardener, food writer and culinary director Lucy Boyd, and between them they conjure glorious Italian-influenced menus bursting with home-grown ingredients and finds from small-scale producers. Wild garlic and potato gnocchi with pecorino romano points the way, followed perhaps by Black Mountain chicken breast with rainbow erbette and pulses from British producer Hodmedod. Finish with Yorkshire rhubarb, almond and ginger tart and rhubarb ice cream. Italian wines start at £24 and rise quickly.
Chef/s: Damian Clisby. **Open:** Tue to Sun L only 12 to 2 (2.30 Fri, 3 Sat, 3.30 Sun). **Closed:** Mon, 21 to 28 Dec. **Meals:** alc (main courses £19 to £30). Set L £23 (2 courses) to £28. **Details:** 120 seats. 100 seats outside. Wheelchair access.

Restaurant at The Petersham

River views and reinvigorated food
Cooking score: 5
⊖ Richmond, map 1
Modern European | £42
Nightingale Lane, Richmond, TW10 6UZ
Tel no: (020) 8939 1084
www.petershamhotel.co.uk

The Petersham hotel seems somewhat off the beaten track, but it's worth seeking out for two reasons. Firstly, there's the mesmeric pastoral view. Ignore the staid beige carpets and the slightly dated décor and look out of the window instead, to where the Thames ribbons past, a herd of Belted Galloways (in the summer) grazing in the watermeadows alongside. The second reason is the food. Adebola Adeshina has taken over the kitchen and breathed fresh energy into something that was already good. There are dishes to suit the old-timers – Dover sole with brown caper butter, grilled fillet with bordelaise sauce –

but Adeshina's flare shows in his own inventions. Steak tartare is served on a sweet-sour aubergine base, with fermented black quinoa for added texture and piquancy, a dark escabeche of yellowfin tuna arrives seared and then rolled in herbs, and a rack of lamb, the fat cooked to a crunch, is perfectly pink within, served with dainty new season peas and beans and a savoury thwack of new season garlic. Staff are enthusiastic, and a really well priced, far reaching wine list starts at around £20. **Chef/s:** Adebola Adeshina. **Open:** all week L 12.15 to 2.15 (12.30 to 3.30 Sun), D 7 to 9.45 (9.15 Sun). **Closed:** 25 and 26 Dec, 1 Jan. **Meals:** alc (main courses £17 to £34). Set L and D £23 (2 courses) to £27. Sun L £35. **Details:** 60 seats. V menu.

Retro Bistrot

Warm, buzzy French bistro
Cooking score: 3
map 1
French | £35
114-116 High Street, Teddington, TW11 8JB
Tel no: (020) 8977 2239
www.retrobistrot.co.uk

£5 OFF

There's much to praise about Vincent Gerbeau's flamboyant neighbourhood bistro on Teddington's high street: the excellent service, the warm and elegant atmosphere, the reassuringly classic French dishes. The cooking more than lives up to expectations in every detail – pitched exactly right, with no messing and no nonsense, whether it's a flavourful foie gras terrine with Pink Lady apple chutney and Muscat jelly, steak tartare with quails' eggs and capers, poached lemon sole with pomme purée, wild mushroom cream, poppy seed pastry and parsley cress or slow-roast pork belly with spicy red cabbage, parsnip purée, garlic and cider jus. Among straightforward posh comfort desserts, an apple and cinnamon soufflé with cinnamon ice cream and apple coulis and a lemon crumble parfait with a poppy seed tuile and lemon pie ice cream stand out. The

straightforward wine list favours France but has good choice by the glass among the decent international selection. Bottles from £17.90. **Chef/s:** François Fayd'Herbe de Maudave. **Open:** all week L 12 to 3.30, Mon to Sat D 6.30 to 11. **Closed:** 25 and 26 Dec, first week Jan, first 2 weeks Aug. **Meals:** alc (main courses £14 to £29). Set L £13 (2 courses) to £16. Set D £20 (2 courses) to £23. Sun L £23. **Details:** 110 seats. V menu. Bar. Music.

Sonny's Kitchen

An old Barnes favourite
Cooking score: 2
map 1
Modern European | £33
94 Church Road, Barnes, SW13 0DQ
Tel no: (020) 8748 0393
www.sonnyskitchen.co.uk

£5 OFF

Running since 1986, and with Philip Howard of The Square (see entry) on board as consultant since 2012, Sonny's is a veritable Barnes institution. The walls are covered in prints and drawings by some of the conjurable names of 20th-century art – Stanley Spencer, Elisabeth Frink, Jim Dine – and the terrazzo fireplace isn't just decorative, but plays its part in the cold season. Brasserie cooking of precision and vigour pours forth, much of it founded on classic French principles. Parsley and garlic velouté with morels and truffle oil is a good start in that cold weather, while asparagus with shallots and a quail's egg in Cheddar cream greet the spring sun. Classic mains take in calf's liver veneziana, sirloin on the bone in smoked butter, and sparkling-fresh grilled lemon sole with squid, leeks and an oyster. At the end come lemon posset or rhubarb crumble soufflé. Wines open at £17.25, or £4.45 a glass. **Chef/s:** James Holah. **Open:** all week L 12 to 2.30 (3.30 Sat and Sun), D 6.30 to 10 (11 Fri and Sat, 9.30 Sun). **Closed:** 25 Dec to 1 Jan, bank hols. **Meals:** alc (main courses £13 to £30). Set L and D £18 (2 courses) to £20. Sun L £25. **Details:** 90 seats. Music.

Tangawizi

Modern Indian food not far from the stadium
Cooking score: 2
⊖ Richmond, map 1
Indian | £28
406 Richmond Road, Twickenham, TW1 2EB
Tel no: (020) 8891 3737
www.tangawizi.co.uk

The smart mirrored interior and purple seating make a refreshing change from the decorative style of old-school Indian restaurants. Not far from the Thames and the home of English rugby (lunchtime openings on big International days make early booking a must), it offers an inspired take on Subcontinental food with modern thinking to the fore. Strips of tilapia fried in chilli, garlic and pepper, or cauliflower florets in curry leaves and green chilli, get the taste-buds properly primed for generous main dishes such as madafi tiger prawns cooked in coconut and coriander, chicken liptey with spring onions and peppers in a mild creamy sauce, and lamb with chickpeas. A long slate of vegetarian mains keeps non-omnivores happy, and the crisp filo samosas of chocolate are the sort of thing you could happily scram by the half-dozen during a match. Large glasses come as standard for wines, from £5.50 for French and Portuguese house blends, with bottles from £15.95.

Chef/s: Surat Singh Rana. **Open:** all week D only 6 to 11 (10.30 Sun). **Closed:** 25 and 26 Dec, 1 and 2 Jan. **Meals:** alc (main courses £7 to £15). Set D £26 (3 courses) to £31. **Details:** 60 seats. Music.

The Victoria

Appealing, family-friendly all-rounder
Cooking score: 3
⊖ Richmond, map 1
Modern British | £35
10 West Temple Sheen, East Sheen, SW14 7RT
Tel no: (020) 8876 4238
www.thevictoria.net

This suburban pub-with-rooms has the feel of a country pub, its warm and cosy atmosphere just the thing after a morning stroll in nearby Richmond Park. There's deep leather seating, real ales on tap in the wood-panelled bar and a suntrap conservatory and south-facing garden, making the place extremely popular for long, lazy lunches and family gatherings (it's very family friendly). Chef Paul Merrett is a well-known advocate of sustainable produce, and his cooking make those ingredients sing. Starters might yield a homemade Scotch egg with fresh green beans, or a tart goats' curd sweetened by honey and thyme-roasted butternut squash, and main courses of roasted hake or a Richmond Park risotto. The Gloucester Old Spot pork roast is a particular favourite on Sundays. Bar staff are 'all very friendly and accommodating'. The wine list offers a carefully selected range of both Old and New World wines with bottles from £19.

Chef/s: Paul Merrett. **Open:** all week L 12 to 2.30 (11 to 3 Sat, 4 Sun), Mon to Sat D 6 to 10. **Closed:** 1 Jan. **Meals:** alc (main courses £13 to £21). Set L and D £17. Sun L £24 (2 courses) to £28. **Details:** 100 seats. 50 seats outside. Bar. Music. Parking.

ENGLAND

Bedfordshire, Berkshire, Buckinghamshire,
Cambridgeshire, Cheshire, Cornwall,
Cumbria, Derbyshire, Devon, Dorset,
Durham, Essex, Gloucestershire & Bristol,
Greater Manchester,
Hampshire (inc. Isle of Wight),
Herefordshire, Hertfordshire, Kent,
Lancashire, Leicestershire and Rutland,
Lincolnshire, Merseyside, Norfolk,
Northamptonshire, Northumberland,
Nottinghamshire, Oxfordshire, Shropshire,
Somerset, Staffordshire, Suffolk, Surrey,
Sussex – East, Sussex – West, Tyne & Wear,
Warwickshire, West Midlands, Wiltshire,
Worcestershire, Yorkshire

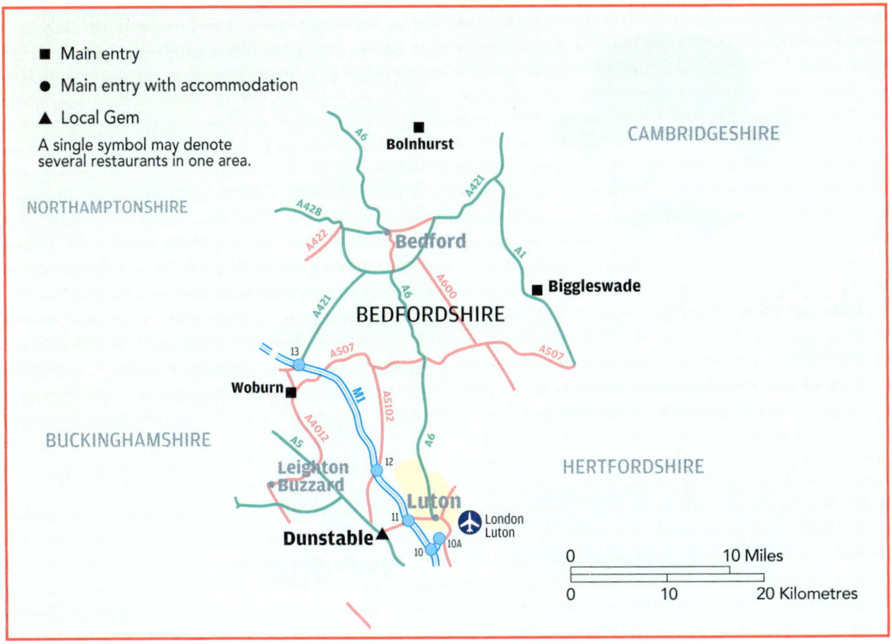

Bedford

Nazar

Turkish

17 High Street, Bedford, MK40 1RN
Tel no: (01234) 954147
nazarturkishrestaurant.co.uk
'Nazar delivered a dining experience that
many high street restaurants get wrong:
simple food cooked just right, presented with
relaxed flair, served with a smile.'

Readers recommend

A 'readers recommend' review is a
genuine quote from a report sent in by
one of our readers. We intend to follow
up these suggestions throughout the year
to come.

Biggleswade

The Croft Kitchen

Simple, refined, precise
Cooking score: 5
Modern British | £45
28 Palace Street, Biggleswade, SG18 8DP
Tel no: (01767) 601502
www.thecroftbiggleswade.com

£5
OFF

The Croft Kitchen's two adjoining, low-
ceilinged cottages sit between a corrugated-
iron barn and a patchwork of brick and iron
walls – not the most obvious place to find
accomplished, refined cooking. But the two
brothers who own this 'diamond in the rough'
have succeeded, hands down. Black beams,
beech-effect floors and white walls dotted
with framed vintage advertising posters add
up to a 'smart but softened dining room' that's
comfortable and relaxing. The cooking is
simple, refined and precise with an emphasis
on – but not obsession with – bringing clever

Undercover Eats

One of our anonymous inspectors gives us the low-down on their menu highlights from this year.

Lamb fat brioche at Freemasons at Wiswell. This little roll is the single most mesmerising recipe I have encountered all year. How lamb fat and flour can become so ethereally light and fluffy is a mystery known only to the Freemasons.

Chicken wings at the Smoking Goat, Soho. It's hard to imagine the size of the chicken these gargantuan wings must come from; the contrast of a sticky, crispy, fish sauce-packed exterior against slippery, silky flesh beneath is what gourmet junk-food was supposed to be all about.

Rib of beef at the Magdalen Arms, Oxford. These giant slabs of long-aged Dexter or Longhorn, carved pink alongside their crusty, Flintstones-sized bones (for gnawing) are by some margin my beef pick of the year.

Coffee and Cigar at Elderflower, Lymington. I'm not one for gimmickry, but even if the various tuiles, ice creams, and parfaits of coffee, chocolate and whisky that create this visually-arresting pudding didn't look exactly like a coffee and a Cuban, they'd still be worth the trip.

technique to bear on local ingredients. It's rooted in great British ingredients but overlaid with international influences. Stand out dishes have included a mellow wild garlic soup topped with a wafer-thin croûte bearing quenelles of whipped goats' cheese; a crisp-skinned fillet of wild bream with a light stew of sweet roasted peppers and onions, tapenade, and a 'brilliant' crab croquette; and a slice of rich banana cake with perfectly ripe banana, a powder of peanut oil and a 'superbly light' peanut-butter ice cream. The wine list is short but covers most bases, starting at £17.50.
Chef/s: Michael Singh. **Open:** Fri to Sun L 12 to 2, Wed to Sat D 6.30 to 9. **Closed:** Mon, Tue, 26 Dec, 1 week Aug. **Meals:** alc (main courses £20 to £25). Set L and D £28 (2 courses) to £31. Sun L £31. Tasting menu £50 (5 courses) to £70. **Details:** 30 seats. Music. No children after 6.30.

Bolnhurst

★ TOP 50 PUB ★

The Plough
Big, true flavours and cracking wines
Cooking score: 5
Modern British | £38
Kimbolton Road, Bolnhurst, MK44 2EX
Tel no: (01234) 376274
www.bolnhurst.com

Away from it all in rural Bedfordshire, Martin and Jayne Lee's singular venue is a fully functioning top-end restaurant in the setting of a village pub – complete with thick stone walls, tiny windows and low beams everywhere. Much of the available space may be taken up with tables, but there's nothing prissy about this set-up. The food has real immediacy and big, true flavours, with superb ingredients gleaned from near and far: 'limited edition' Bellota jamón is offered as an opener, the fabulous home-baked bread comes with Sicilian olive oil, and Cornish lamb finds its way on to the Josper grill. Otherwise, there are Orkney scallops with Puy lentils, smoked pancetta and thyme, or loin of Denham Estate venison or roast sea

Join us at thegoodfoodguide.co.uk

bass with cavolo nero, fennel and cardamom sauce. 'Traceable' well-hung steaks also have their moment, the artisan cheese selections get rave reviews, and dessert might bring butterscotch soufflé. The authoritative wine list offers oenophile thrills from sought-after names at prices that never offend. House selections start at £16.95 (£4.75 a glass). **Chef/s:** Martin Lee. **Open:** Tue to Sun L 12 to 2, Tue to Sat D 6.30 to 9 (9.30 Sat). **Closed:** Mon, 31 Dec, first 2 weeks Jan. **Meals:** alc (main courses £16 to £30). Set L £18 (2 courses) to £22. Sun L £22 (2 courses) to £28. **Details:** 90 seats. 30 seats outside. Bar. Wheelchair access. Parking.

Dunstable

LOCAL GEM
Chez Jerome

French | £35
26 Church Street, Dunstable, LU5 4RU
Tel no: (01582) 603310
www.chezjerome.co.uk

£5
OFF

Occupying a 15th-century timber-framed building just off Dunstable's main shopping drag, Jerome and Lina Dehoux's neighbourly bistro is a spirited antidote to the town's fast-food joints. Inside, the cheery, sociable vibe is matched by no-nonsense bourgeois cooking with a strong provincial slant: expect generous helpings of soupe à l'oignon or rabbit 'en gelée' with green lentils followed by herb-crusted lamb fillet with rosemary or an assiette of seafood with capers and butter sauce. Duck is always a hit, while desserts are old faithfuls such as warm apple tart. House French is £14.25. Closed Sun D.

Local Gem 

Local Gems are the perfect neighbourhood venues, delivering good, freshly cooked food at great value for money.

Woburn
Paris House

Risk-taking global food
Cooking score: 6
Modern European | £75
London Road, Woburn Park, Woburn, MK17 9QP
Tel no: (01525) 290692
www.parishouse.co.uk

£5
OFF

Paris House always looks dressed to impress, a gorgeous prospect that positively gleams in the sunshine while herds of muntjacs frolic around the verdant expanses of Woburn Park. It's a cocooned world of civility and decorum, although the place never takes itself too seriously – just look at the cheeky prints, voguish red chandelier and kooky modern sculptures. Since taking over the show in 2014, executive chef Phil Fanning has upped his game, ditching the deconstructed retro gimmicks in favour of a risk-taking global style that borrows liberally from South-East Asia: expect the unexpected as the kitchen fashions pretty plates of carrot and red miso with coriander, sesame and saké, cod cheek with wakame seaweed, hazelnut and brown onion juice or Japanese peach with black bean and mandarin. Fanning also knows how to do orthodox high-end cuisine – witness partridge with chanterelles, chestnuts and crème fraîche. Meals are built around a bewildering array of multi-course tasting menus, with support from myriad 'micro' wine flights if required; otherwise, the well-rounded list offers serious drinking from £28. **Chef/s:** Phil Fanning and Paul Lobban. **Open:** Wed to Sun L 12 to 1.30 (2 Sun), Wed to Sat D 7 to 8.30. **Closed:** Mon, Tue, 24 Dec to 3 Jan. **Meals:** Set L £39 (6 courses). Set D £75 (8 courses) to £99 (10 courses). Sun L £55. **Details:** 25 seats. Bar. Music. Parking.

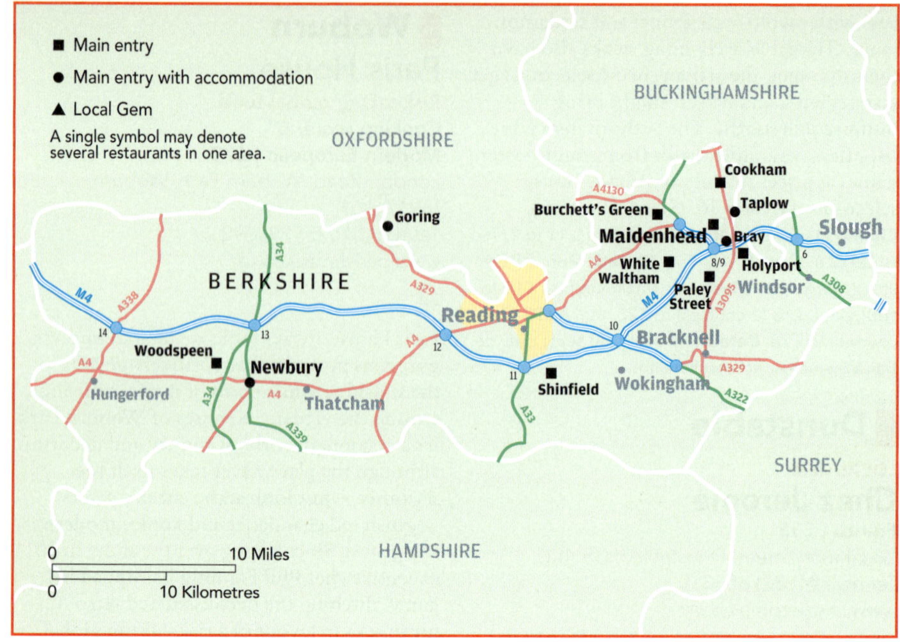

Bray
The Fat Duck

The wizard of Bray is back
Modern British | £220
1 High Street, Bray, SL6 2AQ
Tel no: (01628) 580333
www.thefatduck.co.uk

After a six-month closure for extensive refurbishment (and a spectacular 20th-anniversary sojourn at the Crown Melbourne Resort in Australia), Heston Blumenthal's Fat Duck will re-open in the latter part of 2015. We have no opening details (please see the restaurant's website) but a change of culinary direction is not expected. Eating here is a one-off, a unique dining experience that takes you on a journey of nostalgia and history through iconic creations such as snail porridge, 'Sounds of the Sea', and the Mad Hatter's tea party, built around mock turtle soup, a gilded pocket watch and toast sandwiches. Inventive, clever, idiosyncratic, a Good Food Guide perfect 10

from 2011 to 2015, we are sure the Fat Duck will continue to be the prize most restaurant hunters want to bag.
Meals: Tasting menu L and D £220. **Details:** 40 seats. V menu.

The Hinds Head

The English country pub, Blumenthal-style
Cooking score: 5
British | £40
High Street, Bray, SL6 2AB
Tel no: (01628) 626151
www.hindsheadbray.com

Heston Blumenthal's 15th-century pub pulls in a decidedly upmarket, international crowd, but it's still a good spot for a pint. Try for a table in the original part of the pub – it's intricately done with parquet floor, wood panelling, a fire and fine furniture – but wherever you sit, good service makes this feel special. There's a sprinkling of the old Blumenthal magic in starters such as waxy,

Join us at thegoodfoodguide.co.uk

powdered duck 'ham' with soft-cooked quail's egg salad, and tea-smoked salmon with sour cream butter, pickled cucumber and dill. Triple-cooked chips are the perfect accompaniment to Hereford prime steaks with bone marrow or Reform club sauce, while desserts have fun with the culinary history that Blumenthal enjoys – the accompanying note to chocolate wine 'slush' explains it as a 17th-century aphrodisiac tonic. Wines from £22.50.

Chef/s: Janos Veres. **Open:** all week L 12 to 2.30 (4 Sun), Mon to Sat D 6.15 to 9.30. **Meals:** alc (main courses £17 to £35). Set L £18 (2 courses) to £22. **Details:** 90 seats. Parking.

The Waterside Inn

A perfect package
Cooking score: 7
French | £140
Ferry Road, Bray, SL6 2AT
Tel no: (01628) 620691
www.waterside-inn.co.uk

The impressive Thames-side location, 'marvellous even in the winter', tends to inspire a succession of superlatives in first-time visitors. But this is a small corner of England that will be forever France – the Waterside exists to show just how good refined French cooking can be. The tone of Alain Roux's 'near perfect' cuisine barely alters from one year to another, and he offers a highly efficient demonstration of the culinary arts. 'One feels in safe hands when eating here,' observed one visitor, summing up the combination of first-rate ingredients and a rare harmony that stems from sound culinary judgement and a respect for the classics. This is grand dining in old-fashioned style, producing escalopes of foie gras with a thin slice of 'brilliant' gingerbread, apple and quince compote and mulled wine sauce, pan-fried medallion of 'excellent, tender, tasty' lobster with a white port sauce and ginger-flavoured vegetable julienne, spit-roasted poulet de Bresse flavoured with truffle, potato mousseline and a jus thickened

with foie gras butter, or the duo of game enjoyed by a pair dining in December – 'good, strong partridge was a great partner for the excellent venison, but the star turn here was the sensational pumpkin subric, backed up by a Brussels purée and magic wild mushrooms'. French cheeses are kept in prime condition and desserts always seem to impress. Soufflés, such as a warm orange and lingonberry soufflé, are the business – 'without question one of the best ever'. It's best not to eat here if counting the pennies for prices are high, an effect to which the wines contribute. The list is as resolutely French as the rest of the operation, with prices starting at £29.

Chef/s: Alain Roux. **Open:** Wed to Sun L 12 to 2 (2.30 Sun), D 7 to 10. **Closed:** Mon, Tue, 26 Dec to 28 Jan. **Meals:** alc (main courses £52 to £60). Set L £50 (2 courses) to £62 (Mon to Fri) £70 (Sat). Sun L £80. Tasting menu £160 (6 courses). **Details:** 70 seats. Bar. Parking. Children over 9 yrs only.

The Crown at Bray

British | £30
High Street, Bray, SL6 2AH
Tel no: (01628) 621936
www.thecrownatbray.com

This bustling village local has a full quota of beams, an open fire and a beer garden for fine weather. It not only pulls in drinkers attracted by well-kept ales, but also diners lured by reasonably priced menus that stay firmly in pub classics territory (much to one reader's relief, as the owner is Heston Blumenthal). Reports praise the generous prawn cocktail, potted confit duck, the cheeseburger 'with proper French fries', good old fish and chips, and a 'huge' banana Eton mess. Wines from £21.50. No food Sun D.

Local Gem

Local Gems are the perfect neighbourhood venues, delivering good, freshly cooked food at great value for money.

Brightwalton

READERS RECOMMEND

Saddleback Tea Room

British

California Farm, Brightwalton, RG20 7HR
Tel no: (01488) 638806
www.saddlebackfarmshop.co.uk

'The Saddleback burger is made from their home-bred, matured beef, local bacon and cheese, and is more than enough for a healthy appetite. We've never had room for a pudding, but my grandchildren recommend the cakes.'

Burchett's Green

The Crown

Gutsy bourgeois flavours
Cooking score: 3
French | £28
Burchett's Green, SL6 6QZ
Tel no: (01628) 824079
www.thecrownburchettsgreen.com

£30

'I was warmly welcomed by some of life's most beautiful people,' noted a reader who stumbled upon this diminutive pub deep in the Berkshire countryside. It may have been decorated on a shoestring, but the whole place feels cool, light and refreshing, with lovely views of the village green outside. Simon Bonwick is an endearingly eccentric chef who runs the kitchen single-handed and takes his cue from the gutsy flavours of bourgeois French cuisine, while respecting the British seasonal larder. The result is 'refined domestic' cooking of a high order, and the blackboard menu says it all: artichokes in the style of Provence; torchon of duck liver; rabbit stuffed with boudin noir; Cornish monkfish with black mustard and hazelnuts, etc. His fish soup is as 'rich, sweet and deep as anything served in St Tropez', according to one fan, who also loved the 'dark and dangerous' Rocky Road chocolate pudding. Wines start at £18, but also check the 'haggle board' of vintage French heavyweights.

Chef/s: Simon Bonwick. **Open:** Sun L 12 to 2, Tue to Sat D 6 to 9. **Closed:** Mon, 2 weeks Dec/Jan, 2 weeks Jul/Aug. **Meals:** alc (main courses £13 to £19). **Details:** 28 seats. 18 seats outside. Bar. Wheelchair access. Parking. No children.

Cookham

★ TOP 50 PUB ★

The White Oak

Village pub that follows the seasons
Cooking score: 5
British | £30
The Pound, Cookham, SL6 9QE
Tel no: (01628) 523043
www.thewhiteoak.co.uk

 £5 OFF

Now given free rein at the White Oak after the departure of Clive Dixon, Adam Hague is proving himself to be a reactive, produce-driven cook, his creations chiming with the smart country-pub setting. Yes, this is homely, often traditional food but it also has breathtaking polish and precision, and more sophistication than the dishes' familiar names might suggest. Try roast chicken ravioli with roast chicken juices, then Cornish lamb shepherd's pie with crisp lamb breast, sweetbreads and pickled red cabbage. In line with the pub setting there are also burgers and steaks, and even a mighty 30oz Boston rib for two. Cosy puds include chocolate tiramisu or 'lovey' hot brioche doughnuts with raspberry purée and vanilla sauce. There are decent ales at the bar, but wine is also a serious option, with a crammed page of international finds starting at £17.

Chef/s: Adam Hague. **Open:** all week L 12 to 2.30 (3 Fri and Sat, 5 Sun), Mon to Sat D 6 to 10. **Meals:** alc (main courses £12 to £19). Set L £12 (2 courses) to £15. Set D £15 (2 courses) to £19. Sun L £25. **Details:** 85 seats. 45 seats outside. Bar. Wheelchair access. Music. Parking.

▌Goring

★ TOP 50 PUB ★

READERS' RESTAURANT OF THE YEAR

NEW ENTRY

The Miller of Mansfield

Cracking inn with serious food
Cooking score: 4
British | £30
High Street, Goring, RG8 9AW
Tel no: (01491) 872829
www.millerofmansfield.com

The arrival in 2014 of Nick Galer, following stints with Heston Blumenthal and other luminaries, breathed new life into this handsome 18th-century coaching inn, where Nick and partner Mary have since attracted loyal local custom and created a 'perfect' ambience. Stripped-back décor and informality belie the ambition behind the pass, where Galer's commanding grasp of classic and modern techniques results in everything not just being cooked as it should be, but taken up a notch. Take the 'nibbles': no clichéd 'stuff on toast' – instead, fat sausage rolls and a deft improvement on HP sauce. Intricate, accomplished dishes vary seasonally and daily, and a starter of honey-glazed quail, quail's egg, slow-cooked leg, truffle risotto and Parmesan sets the bar high. Favouring a smaller-plate-smaller-price approach, mains aren't gutsy pub grub, but they still pack a punch: try slow-cooked Gigha halibut with charred leeks, Jerusalem artichokes, smoked bacon and red wine sauce, or confit and poached corn-fed chicken, layered potato cake, asparagus, morel mushrooms and Madeira sauce. For pudding try, perhaps, the excellent rhubarb sundae. Wines from £19.
Chef/s: Nick Galer. **Open:** all week L 12.30 to 2.30 (3.30 Sun), D 6.30 to 9.30. **Meals:** alc (main courses £14 to £23). Set L £13 (2 courses) to £15. **Details:** 80 seats. 50 seats outside. Bar. Music.

▌Holyport

The Belgian Arms

Good pub food at exactly the right price
Cooking score: 3
British | £28
Holyport, SL6 2JR
Tel no: (01628) 634468
www.thebelgianarms.com

'A terrifically tranquil spot on the green and in the garden willow trees laze over the village duck pond,' enthused a visitor to this pleasant village local owned by Nick Parkinson of the Royal Oak Paley Street (see entry). Inside, the uncomplicated, comfortably decorated interior is packed with sporting memorabilia – there are regular 'sportsman's dinners' with visiting luminaries, and the food plays it with a straight bat. There are the usual pub classics, but it's worth exploring the more captivating dishes, starters such as smoked salmon with blood orange, radish, black olives and herb croûtons or crispy duck egg with English asparagus and brioche soldiers. Elsewhere, readers have reported favourably on the likes of pan-fried hake with mini crab cake, grilled cucumber and tomatoes, served with a crunchy fennel salad cut with the sharp tang of lemon vinaigrette, and desserts reinvent British classics – pineapple crumble with iced ginger and lime crème fraîche, perhaps. In a pricey area, the Belgian Arms offers good value. Wine is from £16.
Chef/s: Graham Kirk. **Open:** all week L 12 to 2.30 (4 Sun), Tue to Sun D 6.30 to 9.30 (10 Fri and Sat, 9 Sun). **Meals:** alc (main courses £13 to £19). Sun L £23 (2 courses) to £27. **Details:** 60 seats. 40 seats outside. Bar. Music. Parking. Children over 3 yrs only at D.

Maidenhead
Boulters Riverside Brasserie

Brasserie fare with captivating views
Cooking score: 2
Modern British | £35
Boulters Lock Island, Maidenhead, SL6 8PE
Tel no: (01628) 621291
www.boultersrestaurant.co.uk

£5 OFF

The River Thames and its wooded banks make for a captivating view from Boulters Brasserie, which sits on an island lock as if floating on the water. It would be remiss not to make the most of the spectacular setting, and it is rightfully served up via floor-to-ceiling windows (or from the terrace bar above). Settle into the unremarkable contemporary interior and expect modern brasserie cooking and big-hearted flavours. Kick off with grilled Cornish mackerel with saffron escabèche and bouillabaisse dressing or leek and potato soup enriched with smoked haddock and a poached egg, before a steak cooked on the grill. Herb and garlic risotto gets a lift from its accompanying truffle cream, and, among desserts, treacle tart with forced rhubarb and an ice cream made from oats and golden syrup catches the eye. The wine list favours France but embraces the rest of the world; bottle prices from £15.95.
Chef/s: Daniel Woodhouse. **Open:** Sun L 12 to 3.30. Tue to Sat 12 to 9.30. **Closed:** Mon. **Meals:** alc (main courses £13 to £19). Set L £16 (2 courses) to £20. **Details:** 80 seats. Bar. Music. Parking.

Newbury
Brebis

Shrinking violet worthy of attention
Cooking score: 2
French | £31
16 Bartholomew Street, Newbury, RG14 5LL
Tel no: (01635) 40527
www.brebis.co.uk

To find such an understated little place in Newbury town centre, with its stripped-wood interior, whitewashed walls, French-style accordion music and well-chalked blackboards, came as a surprise to one reporter. More surprising was to find it virtually empty, but 'is Newbury ready for £20 wood pigeon breasts on vanilla-heavy cauliflower purée with roasted spring onions and fingerling potatoes beneath a slab of seared foie gras?' A shame, as Brebis is a fine modern take on French bistro cooking, and there is evident skill at play – in simple two-tone Wye Valley and French white asparagus dressed with well-made gribiche vinaigrette or the aforementioned pigeon just pink, the foie gras properly cooked, the sauce deep with meaty flavour. Quirky desserts – perhaps a cup of salted caramel ice cream with warm chocolate mousse squirted from a foam gun – add a bit of fun. The set-lunch deal offers the best bang for your buck. Wines, with a generous by-the-glass selection, start at £18.
Chef/s: Samuel Mansfield. **Open:** Wed to Sat L 12.30 to 3, D 6.30 to 11. **Closed:** Sun, Mon, Tue, 25 Dec to 6 Jan, 26 to 29 Aug. **Meals:** alc (main courses £17 to £22). **Details:** Wheelchair access. Music.

The Vineyard

Haute cuisine and epic wines
Cooking score: 5
Modern French | £65
Stockcross, Newbury, RG20 8JU
Tel no: (01635) 528770
www.the-vineyard.co.uk

£5 OFF

California meets Berkshire at the Vineyard – a restaurant-with-rooms on a grandiose scale, designed like a West Coast hacienda and named in honour of owner Sir Peter Michael's US winery. With over 500 pieces of art on show, this place is all about opulence, right down to the split-level restaurant at the centre of things. Here, visitors can sample a cavalcade of highly worked specialities presented with real élan and razor-sharp detailing. Pick four or five dishes (rather than fixed courses) from the flexible menu: pumpkin velouté with Cornish cock crab tortellini; Norwegian 'skrei' cod with ratte potato, chorizo and anchovy; corn-fed duck breast with

Cheltenham beetroot and blackberry; rhubarb and vanilla parfait with rhubarb roulade and tarragon dressing. While the food has its moments, the Vineyard is ultimately all about the stupendous contents of the glass-floored wine vault. The numbers are astonishing: 800 bins drawn from a cellar holding 30,000 bottles, with 100 available by the glass. You could spend a fortune here, but ease in gently with the mini list headed 'everyday drinking under £30'.

Chef/s: Daniel Galmiche. **Open:** all week L 12 to 2, D 7 to 9. **Meals:** Set L £29. Set D £65 (4 courses) to £75 (5 courses). Sun L £39. **Details:** 90 seats. 60 seats outside. V menu. Bar. Wheelchair access. Music. Parking.

▮ Paley Street

★ TOP 10 PUB ★

The Royal Oak

Civilised pub with top-tier food
Cooking score: 5
Modern British | £35
Littlefield Green, Paley Street, SL6 3JN
Tel no: (01628) 620541
www.theroyaloakpaleystreet.com

From the off, this cleverly reimagined and highly civilised Berkshire hostelry shows its pedigree. Chic creature comforts and real ales on tap are topped by food that is way beyond anything you're likely to find in your average boozer. Who wouldn't want to order Wye Valley asparagus, crispy pheasant egg and hollandaise or try wood pigeon with ham, pickled mushrooms and dandelion and almonds? Even the obligatory steak comes with a bit of highly seasonal fun in the form of baby onions, bone-marrow crumb, wild garlic leaves and St George's mushrooms. A 'flavour explosion' of barbecued squid on silky red pepper purée with grilled fingerling potatoes, cubes of crisp and fatty chorizo and massive, juicy caper berries, and crisp-skinned chicken breast with a grilled cep, a chunk of salt-baked celeriac infused with ample butter, a flawless caramelised cauliflower purée and

two fat spring onions grilled to just-tender, have also impressed. The 300-bin wine list is a superb match for the food, with French big hitters, New World contenders and a 'quality' selection by the glass; bottles from £19.50.

Chef/s: Michael Chapman. **Open:** all week L 12 to 2.30 (3.30 Sun), Mon to Sat D 6.30 to 9.30 (10 Fri and Sat). **Meals:** alc (main courses £16 to £27). Set L £20 (2 courses) to £25. **Details:** 80 seats. Bar. Music. Parking.

▮ Shinfield

L'Ortolan

Prosperous Berkshire destination
Cooking score: 5
Modern French | £65
Church Lane, Shinfield, RG2 9BY
Tel no: (0118) 9888500
www.lortolan.com

At first glance, Alan Murchison's departure hasn't ruffled L'Ortolan's feathers one jot. This converted Berkshire vicarage surrounded by gorgeous gardens still feels rather stiff with its deep-pile carpets and legions of compliant staff delivering formal service, while the kitchen is now fronted by Tom Clarke who deputised as head chef during Murchison's final months. The format is also much as before, with clever canapés, a complimentary 'thimble of soup' and pre-dessert shots fleshing out the offer. Despite the occasional slip, Clarke has brought some welcome freshness, invention and 'focused flavours' to proceedings – as in silky confit sea trout with daikon spirals, marinated cucumber, dots of lemon curd and mild horseradish mousse or 'blushing pink' lamb loin alongside crispy sweetbreads, semi-dried cherry tomatoes, sheep's curd, wild garlic leaves and olive crumb ('a delicious smart plate of food'). Highly worked desserts such as a dome of smooth buttermilk parfait with poached rhubarb and rosemary ice cream also aim for innovation. The aristocratic wine list blends vintage class with fine examples of organic viticulture; 24 house recommendations start at £29.

Chef/s: Tom Clarke. **Open:** Tue to Sat L 12 to 2, D 7 to 9 (9.30 Fri and Sat). **Closed:** Sun, Mon, 25 Dec to 2 Jan. **Meals:** Set L £28 (2 courses) to £32. Set D £58 (2 courses) to £65. Tasting menu £75 (7 courses). **Details:** 60 seats. V menu. Bar. Music. Parking. Children over 3 yrs only.

▌Taplow

★ TOP 50 ★

André Garrett at Cliveden

Harmonious balance in a celebrated setting
Cooking score: 8
Modern European | £65
Cliveden House, Taplow, SL6 0JF
Tel no: (01628) 607100
www.clivedenhouse.co.uk

'It's our special place,' confided one reader. 'The best restaurant I have been to in a long time,' trumpeted another, adding 'the service, the food, the ambience, the setting is absolutely first class'. Pedigree, poise and harmony are the unifying principles behind this aristocratic Italianate country house where 'a gloriously sunny day at a window seat in the grand dining room overlooking the parterre with the Thames in the distance, is the perfect setting for a delicious lunch'. There's no doubt that André Garrett is really on song – everything about his cooking dazzles. Classic technique and flavour combinations rather than novelty are his keynotes, with the signature Dover sole véronique (with verjus butter sauce, salted grapes, grilled lettuce and chicken juices) considered by many to be 'the best dish I have ever eaten'. But there are other dishes that effortlessly proclaim the kitchen's class, among them 'a wonderful' game consommé, ballotine of rabbit and foie gras with candied carrots, celery and vanilla brioche, and saddle of Salisbury venison with braised shoulder boulangère, pickled red cabbage, quince and cardamom. Desserts are a high point judging by praise for various soufflés, for a caramelised blood-orange curd tart, and for the first rate 'bonbons' served with coffee. And wine? It's a fascinating, widely spread list with many expected treasures and small interesting producers, too. There's an interesting by-the-glass choice; bottles from £28.

Chef/s: André Garrett. **Open:** all week L 12.30 to 2.45, D 7 to 9.45. **Meals:** Set L £28. Set D £70. Sun L £50. Tasting menu £95. **Details:** 68 seats. Bar. Parking.

▌White Waltham

NEW ENTRY
The Beehive

Straightforward, flawless cooking
Cooking score: 3
British | £25
Waltham Road, White Waltham, SL6 3SH
Tel no: (01628) 822877
www.thebeehivewhitewaltham.com

Sheep graze among the oak trees and there are views over the cricket ground, but visitors can enjoy similarly pastoral eating at this refurbished pub, the first solo venture from chef Dominic Chapman (ex Royal Oak Paley Street, see entry). When not out front greeting locals, he's in the kitchen producing what reporters confirm as 'flawless but simple, straightforward cooking'. Bar snacks include rabbit on toast, or rollmops, with more pickling to be seen in a starter of ('very good') pickled local trout (caught a few hundred metres away), teamed with ratte potato salad, horseradish cream, beetroot salad and watercress, or there could be Dorset snails with garlic butter, Gorgonzola and grilled sourdough. Main courses are no less accomplished, with a Black Angus cottage pie with spring greens packing both the requisite richness and a pleasing tomato-ey tang. Dessert might be Eton mess or a Cox's apple tart with vanilla ice cream. Wine from £17 a bottle.

Chef/s: Dominic Chapman. **Open:** all week L 12 to 2.30 (3 Sat, 4 Sun), D 6 to 9.30 (10 Sat, 8.30 Sun). **Closed:** 25 and 26 Dec. **Meals:** alc (main courses £13 to £23). Set L £16 (2 courses) to £20. Set D £20 (2 courses) to £25. **Details:** 70 seats. 50 seats outside. Bar. Wheelchair access. Music. Parking.

John Campbell

The Woodspeen, Berkshire

What food could you not live without?
Salt - it teases out flavour, used well it's a conductor that brings balance to dishes.

What is your favourite time of year for food?
Spring. Britain's larder comes alive after six months of hibernation - the berries, shoots, peas - such an exciting time of the year for the chef and the diner.

Do you have a guilty foodie pleasure?
Chopped tinned tomatoes with a beef OXO cube sprinkled in, with poached eggs - my kids and I have it every Sunday morning. It reminds me of my grandmother.

Is there a particular dish that evokes strong memories for you?
Red-lentil soup with bacon ribs. Every Saturday we would eat it with my grandmother after my grandad and I came back from watching the football! It was amazing.

Tell us something about yourself that might surprise your diners.
I am fascinated by ancient cultures and how they fed themselves.

Woodspeen
★ TOP 10 PUB ★

NEW ENTRY

The Woodspeen
Cooking with an eye to polished city fashion
Cooking score: 6
British | £38
Lambourn Road, Woodspeen, RG20 8BN
Tel no: (01635) 265070
www.thewoodspeen.com

£5 OFF

Country chic, Scandi-style – call it what you will, this is a place where classy, contemporary design collides joyfully with a country pub. Looks aren't everything though, and chef John Campbell is in bullish mood, cosseting with a modern British menu that's as on-trend as it is truly, deeply rooted in the location. The food ('an unadulterated joy') hits you with assertive flavours and the confidence is palpable. Simple classics have a please-all quality: for example, the well-reported wild mushroom risotto with aged Parmesan, and Berkshire partridge with lentil and mushroom pie and bread sauce. The kitchen is also happy to give pub-grub throwbacks a shake-up, applying some canny modern touches here and there – witness a cottage pie made with chopped, shredded chunks of lamb with horseradish and onion and excellent pickled red cabbage, or a dish of braised beef cheek with onion and parsley gratin, creamed potato and bacon cabbage. Desserts might feature a delicate, wobbly egg custard tart with clementine sorbet. Wines from £19.
Chef/s: John Campbell. **Open:** Tue to Sun L 12 to 2.30 (4 Sun), Tue to Sat D 6.30 to 9.30. **Closed:** Mon, 25 and 26 Dec, 1 Jan. **Meals:** alc (main courses £15 to £25). Set L £18 (2 courses) to £24. **Details:** 66 seats. 32 seats outside. Bar. Wheelchair access. Music. Parking.

Amersham

★ TOP 50 ★

Artichoke

Technical panache and creativity
Cooking score: 7
Modern British | £48
9 Market Square, Amersham, HP7 0DF
Tel no: (01494) 726611
www.artichokerestaurant.co.uk

Deep in the medieval heart of Amersham, the
Artichoke has taken root in a 16th-century
house that if anything looks a little prosaic
from outside, but has been given a touch of
sleek Scandinavian chic indoors, with a muted
palette of wintry grey and walnut. Any sense
of northern chill is banished by the appreciable
warmth with which Laurie and Jacqueline
Gear run the place. 'That we consider it worth
driving 70 miles to return here is a tribute to
the superlative cooking,' declares a reader for
whom the price of fuel is a mere bagatelle in
light of the assured technical refinement and
creativity on display, courtesy of Laurie Gear
and head chef Ben Jenkins. Ingredients are
combined with panache and sensitivity for an
opener of hop-smoked sea trout with malted
grains and beetroot sorbet in a terrific dill
sauce. Lime-pickled mooli and seaweed jelly
illuminate a plump Skye scallop, while game
cookery shows bundles of confidence when
locally shot partridge turns up with curly kale,
puréed parsnip, chestnuts and an
unforgettable charred pear. Desserts keep the
engine firing with a top-notch Brillat-Savarin
cheesecake, served with poire William sorbet,
pickled pear, sweet cicely and nutty granola.
Intermediate courses, petits fours and breads
all maintain the elevated standard in a
production where, as our correspondent puts
it, 'the wow-factor is the norm'. Much the
same could be said of the intelligent and
imaginative approach to wine, where there is
exciting quality in abundance. Listings in two
glass sizes, from £7, and half-bottles are
especially inspired. Bottles start at £27.50.

Chef/s: Laurie Gear and Ben Jenkins. **Open:** Tue to Sat L 12 to 3, D 6.30 to 11 (6 Fri and Sat). **Closed:** Sun, Mon, 1 week Christmas, 1 week Easter, 2 weeks Aug. **Meals:** alc (main courses £23 to £25). Set L £24 (2 courses) to £28. Set D £42 (2 courses) to £48. Tasting menu L £38 (5 courses), D £68 (7 courses). **Details:** 48 seats. 2 seats outside. V menu. Music.

LOCAL GEM
Gilbey's
Modern British | £35
1 Market Square, Amersham, HP7 0DF
Tel no: (01494) 727242
www.gilbeygroup.com

A durable and well-liked fixture of the Amersham scene, this amenable neighbourhood bistro occupies what was Dr Challoner's grammar school – complete with a suntrap courtyard. The kitchen dresses up its dishes with modish embellishments, from ginger and lemongrass gel, pickled beets and radish with treacle-cured salmon to chervil root, black cabbage and truffle-braised potato alongside noisette and slow-roasted shoulder of lamb. Generous Sunday lunches too. The Gilbeys are also wine importers, so expect a sound French contingent (from £17.50) on the well-rounded list. Closed Sun D.

Aylesbury
Hartwell House
Luxurious dining at a magnificent mansion
Cooking score: 2
Modern British | £52
Oxford Road, Aylesbury, HP17 8NR
Tel no: (01296) 747444
www.hartwell-house.com

Hartwell is a 17th-century manor house in a meticulously landscaped park, with rococo interior styling added in the Georgian era and its occupants over the years including a luminous quota of deposed monarchs, scientists and parliamentarians. It may sound intimidatingly grand, but is run with comfortable hospitality, the staff as sunny-natured in their approach as the primrose-yellow dining room. A couple of winter lunchers felt properly set up for the festive season after gingerbread-crumbed pigeon breast with carrot and orange, char-grilled lamb shoulder with its sweetbread, puréed butternut squash and rosemary jus, and a first-rate blond chocolate délice with vanilla cream. Fixed-price dinners pull out the stops for sea bream and samphire in liquorice sauce, or braised bourguignonne brisket with Delmonico potatoes and Savoy cabbage. Dessert could be fashioned from Hartwell's own orchard, in the form of apple mousse and jelly, served with cinnamon ice cream and honeycomb. A huge wine list opens at £27.50, with small glasses from £6.50.
Chef/s: Daniel Richardson. **Open:** all week L 12.30 to 1.45, D 7.30 to 9.30. **Meals:** alc (main courses £18 to £38). Set L £25 (2 courses) to £32. Set D £25 (2 courses) to £62. Sun L £36. **Details:** 90 seats. Bar. Wheelchair access. Parking.

Buckingham

LOCAL GEM
Nelson Street Restaurant
Modern British | £27
53/54 Nelson Street, Buckingham, MK18 1BT
Tel no: (01280) 815556
www.nelsonstreetrestaurant.co.uk

On a pretty residential street in Buckingham's Old Quarter, this converted period house is a 'brilliant local asset', offering great bistro dishes in an ill-served area. The menu is a please-all affair – honey mustard sausages, fishcakes and stuffed pork belly – with a few ambitious plates thrown in, say tea-roasted cod with sea vegetables, or grilled mackerel with champ, leek fondue, beetroot and tomato salsa. A chocolate and lime fondant with smooth ice cream topped with toasted coconut rounds things off nicely. Wines from £14.59. Closed Sun and Mon.

Dinton

LOCAL GEM

La Chouette
Belgian | £40
High Street, Dinton, HP17 8UW
Tel no: (01296) 747422
www.lachouette.co.uk

Frédéric Desmette's loyal fan base keeps his Belgian bistro in a sixteenth-century low-beamed building on the village green enduringly popular. What they return for is hearty traditional fare with a few modern frills: brown shrimp croquettes followed by wild duck with woodland mushrooms, or chicken livers flamed in Cognac, with sole fillet in crayfish and Chardonnay sauce up next. This being Belgium, you'll want something chocolatey to finish, perhaps a soufflé. If you've got your smartphone with you, look up our host's website of wildlife photography. The substantial French wine list is a connoisseurial dream, starting with IGP country wines at £18.50. Closed Sat L and Sun.

Easington
The Mole & Chicken
Sympathetically gentrified pub-with-rooms
Cooking score: 1
Modern British | £35
Easington Terrace, Easington, HP18 9EY
Tel no: (01844) 208387
www.themoleandchicken.co.uk

£5
OFF

Incredible views of the Buckinghamshire countryside are a big selling point at this sympathetically gentrified pub-with-rooms – no wonder alfresco tables are at a premium on fine days. Otherwise, the refurbished interior promises designer fabrics, comfy sofas and country-chic trappings in a warren of little rooms – plus open fires come winter. Food-wise, the kitchen majors on steaks with classic sauces and trendy sides (polenta chips, roast bone marrow, mac 'n' cheese), but its broad remit also takes in everything from salt-and-pepper squid or seared scallops with bacon jam and artichoke purée to braised ox cheek with horseradish mash or pappardelle with rabbit ragù and wild mushrooms. Wines from £20.
Chef/s: Steve Bush. **Open:** all week L 12 to 2.30 (4 Sun), D 6.30 to 9.30 (6 to 9 Sun). **Closed:** 25 Dec. **Meals:** alc (main courses £12 to £22). **Details:** 62 seats. 60 seats outside. Bar. Wheelchair access. Music. Parking.

Great Missenden
La Petite Auberge
Long-running classical French bistro
Cooking score: 2
French | £37
107 High Street, Great Missenden, HP16 0BB
Tel no: (01494) 865370
www.lapetiteauberge.co.uk

£5
OFF

Not far from the Roald Dahl Museum, Hubert Martel's classical French bistro retains the same comfortingly domestic feel that has kept it popular since opening in 1989. You pretty much have to head out into the sticks these days to find honest, unreconstructed cuisine of the old school, and it's well worth the journey for what one pair of reporters called 'three courses of careful perfection'. Seared scallops dressed in soy sauce offer a welcome respite from cauliflower purée, or start with a slab of duck foie gras terrine with onion relish. Mains aim to fill you up with precisely cooked, often fruitily dressed proteins – calf's liver with a lime-tinged sauce, duck in blackcurrant – or with full-flavoured fish such as turbot and anchovies in caper sauce. Overlooked French classics such as nougatine glacé, or apple chaudfroid with cinnamon ice cream, compete with caramelised lemon tart for afters. The short French wine list opens at £21.80 (white) and £23.80 (red).
Chef/s: Hubert Martel. **Open:** Mon to Sat D only 7 to 10. **Closed:** Sun, 2 weeks Christmas, 2 weeks Easter. **Meals:** alc (main courses £18 to £23). **Details:** 30 seats. Wheelchair access.

Marlow

★ TOP 50 PUB ★

NEW ENTRY

The Coach

Glossy new venture from the pub king
Cooking score: 5
British | £30
3 West Street, Marlow, SL7 2LS
www.thecoachmarlow.co.uk

'Not only pretty brilliant, it's also unusual', summed up one reporter, for Tom Kerridge's glossy new venture is hard to pigeonhole. Pub-wise, you can come in for a drink, but you must occupy a designated armchair-style barstool or table – no standing at the bar with a pint – and with a no booking policy, the Coach is not your typical small-town restaurant. Service, too, is an unfamiliar but warm, efficient affair shared between chefs and bar staff. The best way to imagine the style (and menu) is as Barrafina (see entries, London) gone British. We enjoyed a thick slice of 'stunning' belly bacon 'full of crisp, gooey fat' with a perfectly fried egg and a lick of parsley sauce; 'lovely' crispy pig's head, also on the Hand & Flowers menu, but served here for half the price with a kind of deconstructed piccalilli, a thin stick of crackling and an intense jus; venison chilli, flavoured with red wine and chocolate; chips 'worthy of serving as a course on their own'; and banana custard topped with honeycomb, pistachios, dried banana and a few chopped dates. There's a good range of ales, some interesting bottled beer and a modest wine list (with plenty by the glass) starting at £22.
Chef/s: Nick Beardshaw. **Open:** all week L 12 to 2.30, D 6 to 10.30 (9 Sun). **Closed:** 25 Dec. **Meals:** alc (main courses £4 to £18). **Details:** 45 seats. Music.

TOP 50 ★ TOP 10 PUB

The Hand & Flowers

Big-hearted, resourceful cooking
Cooking score: 6
Modern British | £56
126 West Street, Marlow, SL7 2BP
Tel no: (01628) 482277
www.thehandandflowers.co.uk

May we presume you've heard of Tom Kerridge? You'll have seen him on the telly over the past year or so, or maybe you've bought one of his books. He also runs the most famous pub in Britain (and has just added another – the nearby Coach, see entry). That being said, trying to get a booking is a character-building challenge, in which you'll find that the next available table is a year from now. Is it worth the hassle? Opinions are mixed. Some reporters have objected to the two-hour turnaround of tables and the prices (and it is certainly pricey), but on the whole this is a 'charming little pub restaurant' with 'excellent' service. Some dishes are pure magic: 'a smooth and subtle' duck liver parfait enlivened with port and Madeira, good toast and orange chutney; salt cod Scotch egg with deep-fried chorizo making a good contrast with the red pepper sauce; 'light, fresh and delicious' roast English onion tart with étuvé alliums, smoked butter and salt-cured pork; slow-cooked duck breast with duck confit hidden in a tiny pot of Savoy cabbage and 'the chips done in duck fat just to die for'. Also good is the 'quite simply delicious' Bramley sorbet served with an apple custard slice, and tonka bean pannacotta with chunks of honeycomb and rhubarb jelly providing an interesting contrast. Wines from £28.
Chef/s: Tom Kerridge. **Open:** all week L 12 to 2.45 (3.15 Sun), Mon to Sat D 6.30 to 9.45. **Closed:** 24 to 26 Dec. **Meals:** alc (main courses £27 to £39). Set L Mon to Sat £15 (2 courses) to £20. **Details:** 45 seats. Bar. Wheelchair access. Music. Parking.

NEW ENTRY
Sindhu
Indian mastery by the Thames
Cooking score: 6
Indian | £45
Compleat Angler, Marlow Bridge, Marlow,
SL7 1RG
Tel no: (01628) 405405
www.macdonaldhotels.co.uk

Top-class Indian venues are rare outside cities, so Atul Kochhar's opening of Sindhu, in Marlow's Compleat Angler riverside hotel, should thrill locals. Thrilling, too, is the panoramic view of the foaming-water weir from plentiful windows in the plush dining room. Kochhar helped develop London's modern Indian restaurant scene and many of his innovations introduced to Mayfair – at Tamarind and then Benares – are discernible in the 'palate-provoking flavours' here. Try the curry-leaf-flavoured Sindhu Martini before embarking on an exquisitely presented meal, which might start with an amuse of delicate steamed rice and lentil cake with tomato chutney and conclude with featherlight cardamom shortbread among the petits fours. In between there could be expertly deep-fried pomfret in spicy batter; pink, perfect duck breast on a bed of spiced pulses; then deconstructed rose-yoghurt cheesecake boosted by freeze-dried raspberries. Occasionally, dishes veer into Italianate territory, and spicing can be meek, but immaculately executed peripherals (moreish bread, fluffy rice) show the kitchen has mastered the essentials. Wine from a voluminous list starts at £21, with ample spice-friendly options by the glass.
Chef/s: Atul Kochhar. **Open:** Wed to Sun L 12 to 2.45 (3.15 Sun), Tue to Sat D 6 to 10. **Closed:** Mon. **Meals:** alc (main courses £16 to £32). Set L £19 (2 courses) to £22. **Details:** 58 seats. V menu. Bar. Wheelchair access. Parking.

The Vanilla Pod
Sure-footed food and neighbourly civility
Cooking score: 5
Modern European | £45
31 West Street, Marlow, SL7 2LS
Tel no: (01628) 898101
www.thevanillapod.co.uk

Occupying an intimate two-storey town house that was once home to poet TS Eliot, Michael Macdonald's eminently likeable little restaurant is happy to keep it low-key in foodie-centric Marlow. Inside, the unstuffy soft-toned dining room positively encourages neighbourly civility, while the chef plays out his one-man culinary show in the kitchen, delivering technically astute, sure-footed dishes rather than high-risk gastronomic pyrotechnics. Consistency is the watchword, from a deceptively simple salad of goats' cheese with beetroot mousse or gin- and juniper-cured salmon with pepper vinaigrette to Parmesan-roasted brill with creamed lentils or deeply flavoured sirloin of beef with mushrooms, confit shallots and port sauce. Local ingredients also get a namecheck, as in Loomswood duck breast served with endive tarte Tatin. Thankfully the kitchen doesn't overplay the 'vanilla' theme, although the eponymous pod does crop up here and there – particularly in precise desserts such as butter-roasted pear with vanilla sponge and buttermilk cream. The commendable French-led wine list has house selections from £22 (£5 a glass).
Chef/s: Michael Macdonald. **Open:** Tue to Sat L 12 to 3, D 7 to 10. **Closed:** Sun, Mon, 24 Dec to 5 Jan, 25 May to 3 Jun, 24 Aug to 3 Sep. **Meals:** Set L £16 (2 courses) to £20. Set D £45. Tasting menu £60 (7 courses). **Details:** 38 seats. 10 seats outside. V menu.

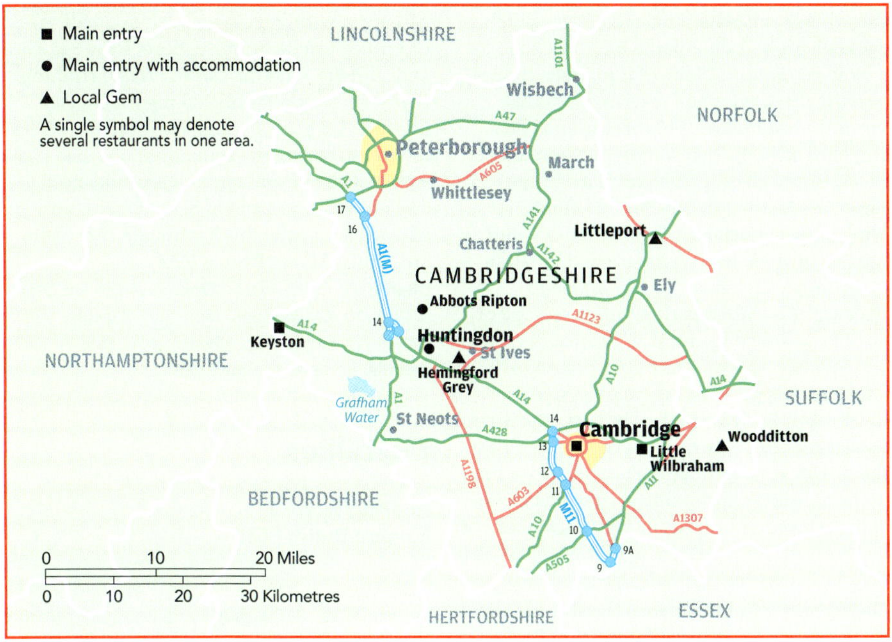

Abbots Ripton

NEW ENTRY

The Abbot's Elm

Practically perfect thatched inn
Cooking score: 2
British | £30
Abbots Ripton, PE28 2PA
Tel no: (01487) 773773
www.theabbotselm.co.uk

'Just pubby enough' is how one diner summed up this pretty thatched inn and restaurant. Despite first appearances, this is 'no crumbling page out of history'; these days you can pick from the restaurant ('all white cloths and brightly coloured banquettes'), or the dining area in the pub, which has a stunning, towering beamed ceiling centred around a vast stone chimney. The food is 'generous and extremely tasty', from a fat, crisp and juicy Scotch egg to a halibut and crab risotto with lobster butter, and the kitchen really hits its stride at dessert: witness a textbook lemon tart with a 'film of crisp, brûléed sugar'. The wine list offers at least four own-label wines made specifically for the pub in Chablis, and there are some 40 by the glass. Bottles start at £18.50.

Chef/s: Julia Abbey. **Open:** all week L 12 to 2 (2.30 Sun), Mon to Sat D 6 to 9. **Meals:** alc (main courses £9 to £23). Set L £14 (2 courses) to £18. Set D £18 (2 courses) to £23. **Details:** 75 seats. 50 seats outside. Wheelchair access. Music. Parking.

Cambridge

Alimentum

Hot ticket with high-impact food
Cooking score: 6
Modern European | £53
152-154 Hills Road, Cambridge, CB2 8PB
Tel no: (01223) 413000
www.restaurantalimentum.co.uk

For the uninitiated, Alimentum packs a few surprises. There's the unlikely location on the ground floor of a modern block of flats, and then there's the black-and-red décor, which evokes a nightclub or piano bar more than a serious restaurant. None of it matters, though, because the service and cooking 'are both seriously impressive'. This operation is slick and hard to fault. Take a starter of smoked eel slices, for instance, grilled until gushing juices, with silky, lightly charred chicken wings, grilled petals of Roscoff onion, and squares of apple in a crystal-clear dashi-like consommé. Or a main of wood pigeon 'Rossini' – a chilled parfait with a sausage of heavily seasoned leg meat, a 'gloriously rich and savoury' mushroom purée, potato balls, lardons, wild garlic, a big, juicy oyster mushroom and two pigeon breasts – 'brilliant cooking with every element complementing the others yet standing up completely on their own'. Desserts play on nursery favourites, so expect clever riffs on Arctic roll, Battenberg or lemon curd. Wines start at £19, with plenty by the glass and some cheering bargains.

Chef/s: Mark Poynton. **Open:** all week L 12 to 2.30 (2 Sun), D 6 to 10 (9 Sun). **Closed:** 23 to 31 Dec. **Meals:** alc (main courses £28 to £33). Set L and D £21 (2 courses) to £27. Tasting menu £72 (7 courses) to £92. **Details:** 62 seats. Bar. Wheelchair access. Music.

Cotto

Hard-to-fault sourcing and flavours
Cooking score: 3
Modern European | £55
183 East Road, Cambridge, CB1 1BG
Tel no: (01223) 302010
www.cottocambridge.co.uk

This is an intimate venue on Cambridge's busy East Road, the sort of place to cherish, for the kitchen here is not short of ambition. Hans Schweitzer's contemporary French-inspired repertoire, based on fine, often local materials, is loyal to some classic combinations: fillets of Dover sole with mussels, Chardonnay and baby artichokes, and sautéed veal kidneys and sweetbreads with wholegrain mustard sauce. Despite a few minor excursions – into Loch Duart salmon served as lapsang tea smoked, as tartare with pickled cucumber, and as

carpaccio with yuzu coriander, and ballotine of guinea fowl with miso glaze, baby pak choi and shiitake – it's the classic French cooking that seems to keep the cooking on course. Desserts are good enough to put many places to shame, taking in caramelised poached pear with warm almond tart and Manuka honey and rosemary ice, and as Schweitzer is an expert chocolatier, his handmade chocolates are a must. Wines from £22.

Chef/s: Hans Schweitzer. **Open:** Wed to Sat D only 6.30 to 10. **Closed:** Sun, Mon, Tue, 2 weeks Christmas, Easter, Aug. **Meals:** Set D £55. **Details:** 50 seats. V menu. Music.

Fitzbillies

Revived city tea room with fresh ideas
Cooking score: 2
Modern British | £30
51-52 Trumpington Street, Cambridge, CB2 1RG
Tel no: (01223) 352500
www.fitzbillies.com

From behind its Art Nouveau façade, this bakery/tea room has been a Cambridge institution since 1921. Following a change of ownership and sympathetic transformation in 2011 that stuck to the original aesthetic, but paired teacup nostalgia with utilitarian, urban touches, Fitzbillies has regained its loyal following. By day, sustaining sandwiches and snacks are the fallback if you're not in the mood for something sweet, but three times a week dinner is served. From the Brit-meets-Med menu, stone bass fillet comes with smoky bell peppers and basil faro risotto, and the cooking can be very good, from a starter of long-braised, pink-fleshed Jacob's Ladder in a deeply-flavoured but not overwhelmingly rich jus, via a homely chicken, leek and mushroom 'porter's pie' with fondant potatoes. The main attraction is the justifiably renowned Chelsea buns (available by mail order). Wines from £17.

Chef/s: Calum Maclean. **Open:** all week L 12 to 3, Thur to Sat D 6 to 9.30. **Closed:** Aug and early Sept. **Meals:** alc (main courses £15 to £20). **Details:** 70 seats. V menu.

Midsummer House

Ingenuity, precision and skill on the Common
Cooking score: 8
Modern British | £83
Midsummer Common, Cambridge, CB4 1HA
Tel no: (01223) 369299
www.midsummerhouse.co.uk

Daniel Clifford's restaurant, aloof on Midsummer Common by the murmuring River Cam, where university rowing teams plough by, is a beautifully situated place to eat. Refurbishments continue apace, making the place ever lovelier, and there are other diversions too: 'Maître d' Jean-François Imbert opened his big green egg and pulled out the beetroots. Charred black like lumpwood, they were sliced in two and turned for us to see. They were deep red like rare fillet, the cross-section sleek and vivid against the carbonised skin. He hollowed out a nugget of flesh from each, aranging it on the garnished plates with their goat's cheese, quinoa and mizuna, before dropping the blistered husks into a hole in the trolley. "For our pigs," he explained.' The beetroot baked on open coals is one of the early signature moments in a 10-course performance that puts the magnum into Midsummer's opus. Following it might be braised pork cheek with carrots, ginger and yoghurt, a truffled scallop with puréed Jerusalems, and then a succession of astonishing courses each vying for the idea of main – quail with grapes and celery, monkfish with salsify and bacon, the almost prosaic-sounding chicken with leeks and mushrooms. Nothing is prosaic at all of course, the level of ingenuity, precision and flat-out skill in each presentation evoking raptures. 'The meal culminated in an exciting showpiece dessert involving a hot coffee sauce poured over a chocolate dome, which melted to reveal an assortment of treasures, among them almonds and mascarpone.' The wine list is an excitement in itself, but marked up with intimidating vigour. Prices open at £28.

Chef/s: Daniel Clifford. **Open:** Wed to Sat L 12 to 1.30, Tue to Sat D 7 to 9.30 (6.30 Sat). **Closed:** Sun, Mon, 2 weeks Christmas. **Meals:** Tasting menus £48 (5 courses) to £83 (7 courses) to £105 (10 courses). **Details:** 45 seats. V menu. Bar.

The Dumpling Tree

Chinese | £20
8 Homerton Street, Cambridge, CB2 8NX
Tel no: (01223) 247715
www.thedumplingtree.com

Step inside this unpretentious, friendly newcomer to have your taste-buds awakened and preconceived notions of Chinese food binned. Choose the Dirty Dozen for a pot-luck mix of the freshest, lightest dumplings generously filled with prawn, pork and chives, or lamb and coriander. Graze on mineral-rich seaweed salad or just-steamed pak choi, fresh foils to fluffy pork buns and hearty Yunnan chicken noodles. Finish with what else but the tantalisingly titled 'Purr Louder', a sweet concoction of coconut milk and tapioca pearls. Wine from £17. Closed Mon.

Pint Shop

British | £25
10 Peas Hill, Cambridge, CB2 3PN
Tel no: (01223) 352293
www.pintshop.co.uk

The craft beer revolution continues apace and the Pint Shop's mantra 'Meat. Bread. Beer' makes perfectly plain what provisions are on offer at this listed building in central Cambridge. The main draw is the ever-changing craft kegs and draught ales, all from small, mostly British brewers, chalked up in the old-school panelled dining room and the stripped and painted wood bar, but food is no afterthought. There's deep-fried pork belly with homemade brown sauce, perhaps, or gutsy fare from the charcoal grill (ribeye or flank steak…you get the picture). Wines start at £18. Open all week.

■ Hemingford Grey

LOCAL GEM
The Cock
Modern British | £27
47 High Street, Hemingford Grey, PE28 9BJ
Tel no: (01480) 463609
www.thecockhemingford.co.uk

A village hostelry of two halves: enter through the door marked 'pub' for real ales; pick the entrance marked 'restaurant' if you're after well-crafted food in rustic-chic surroundings. Blackboards listing homemade sausages and fresh fish catch the eye, but the rolling menu also promises the likes of walnut-crusted goats' cheese mousse with beetroot 'three ways' or venison haunch with braised red cabbage, chestnut purée and caramelised pear. The 'beautifully light' pistachio and sea-salt cake has drawn high praise. Tuesday night is steak and chop night. Fascinating Languedoc wines from £19 (£13.20 a carafe). Open all week.

■ Huntingdon
The Old Bridge Hotel
Eat, drink and enjoy
Cooking score: 2
Modern British | £33
1 High Street, Huntingdon, PE29 3TQ
Tel no: (01480) 424300
www.huntsbridge.com

The Old Bridge is a boutique hotel and inn with a serious attitude to food and wine, its handsome ivy-clad exterior hiding smart-casual eating and drinking areas and a wine shop with 24 bottles open for tasting at any one time – owner John Hoskins is a Master of Wine, so you're in good hands. The cooking taps British and European classics, with occasional flavours from further afield: a lobster salad might feature mango, chilli and lime, but the main focus is on homely comforts such as slow-cooked pork belly with crackling, sage and onion mash, wilted spinach and apple sauce, or venison Wellington with garlic mash and creamed Savoy cabbage. Finish in a similar vein with raspberry Bakewell tart and Chantilly cream. The hefty wine list is as interesting as you would hope as well as bargain-packed (from £17.95) with dozens by the glass.

Chef/s: Jack Woolner. **Open:** all week L 12 to 2 (2.30 Sun), D 6.30 to 10. **Meals:** alc (main courses £16 to £30). Set L and D £19 (2 courses) to £24. Sun L £25 (2 courses) to £30. **Details:** 80 seats. 30 seats outside. Bar. Parking.

■ Keyston
The Pheasant
Traditional and modern country-pub cooking
Cooking score: 2
Modern British | £25
Loop Road, Keyston, PE28 0RE
Tel no: (01832) 710241
www.thepheasant-keyston.co.uk

The low-slung, gleaming-white thatched country inn is a good 12 miles out of Huntingdon, and comes with its own kitchen garden, as is the modern preference. A touchingly old-fashioned look with hunting-scene wallpaper in the dining room makes a nice change from the stripped-down look favoured by many pub makeovers, but Simon Cadge's cooking is in the unmistakably modern global idiom. Thai-style beef salad, crab linguine with chilli, and smoked haddock with spinach and a poached egg make up a tempting preliminary roll call. Then trad pub classics such as fish pie offset the on-trend likes of char-grilled Scotch beef with Wagyu oxtail croquette, horseradish mash, confit swede, sprout tops and pancetta in a truffled green peppercorn sauce. After that little lot, a dish of homemade cinnamon ice cream might suffice, if you can resist the lure of almond tart with Armagnac-steeped prunes and crème fraîche sorbet. John Hoskins MW, whose family has deep roots in the place, oversees an authoritative wine list that offers quality and value all over the show, from Reynaud's white Crozes-Hermitage to

Grosset's Gaia, a blend of Cabernets from Australia's Clare Valley. Bottles start at £17, standard glasses £4.75.

Chef/s: Simon Cadge. **Open:** Tue to Sun L 12 to 2 (2.30 Fri and Sat, 3.30 Sun), Tue to Sat D 6.30 to 9.30. **Closed:** Mon, 2 to 15 Jan. **Meals:** alc (main courses £12 to £22). Set L and D £15 (2 courses) to £20. Sun L £25. **Details:** 80 seats. 25 seats outside. Bar. Parking.

Little Wilbraham
The Hole in the Wall

Ardently modern food in an old pub
Cooking score: 3
Modern British | £30
Primrose Farm Road, Little Wilbraham, CB21 5JY
Tel no: (01223) 812282
www.holeinthewallcambridge.com

'This place gets better every time we visit,' declared a fan of this 17th-century pub that's been in the hands of former MasterChef finalist Alex Rushmer since 2011. Indeed, the place has come a long way since the days it dispensed beer to thirsty farm workers through a hole in the wall. It still looks and feels like an old tavern, but the culinary output has been sharpened up to include a tasting menu, and a focused fixed-price à la carte that's creative, contemporary and delivers the likes of bourbon-cured salmon with vanilla sauce and orange jelly, followed by shoulder and rump of lamb with potato dumplings and charred lettuce. The set lunch is a winner, too, 'absolutely outstanding value for food of this quality', when you consider rabbit and bacon terrine with sweet carrot chutney, a pastry-topped fish pie 'packed with perfectly seasoned fish', and vanilla cheesecake served with a beautiful poached pear. Wines start at £18.

Chef/s: Alex Rushmer. **Open:** Wed to Sun L 12 to 2 (3 Sun), Tue to Sat D 7 to 10. **Closed:** Mon, 2 weeks Christmas. **Meals:** alc (main courses £15 to £28). Set L £18 (2 courses) to £20. Set D £26 (2 courses) to £30. Tasting menu £45. **Details:** 50 seats. 25 seats outside. Bar. Music.

Littleport

LOCAL GEM
The Fen House
Modern British | £40
2 Lynn Road, Littleport, CB6 1QG
Tel no: (01353) 860645
www.fen-house.com

David and Gaynor Warne have been running this small-scale restaurant for almost 30 years. With just 18 seats and limited opening times, booking is essential but the four-course, seasonally attuned dinner menu is a pleasure and indicates Mr Warne's high standards. A typical meal would take in a tartlet of chicken livers tossed with grapes, tarragon and dry sherry, go on to roasted saddle of lamb with red onion polenta and caper sauce, a cheese course, and apricot sorbet with meringues and raspberries. Meals are slowly paced, but service is good. Wines from £17. Open Fri and Sat D.

Woodditton

LOCAL GEM
The Three Blackbirds
Modern British | £27
36 Ditton Green, Woodditton, CB8 9SQ
Tel no: (01638) 731100
www.thethreeblackbirds.co.uk

£5 OFF

James Barber plunders Suffolk's larder for his unpretentious menu in this pretty 17th-century pub. It has cracked the village-local-or-restaurant identity crisis, so choose a lunchtime pint and proper sandwich at the cosy bar, or head to the dining area where black pudding and caramelised apple are the salty-sweet foil to a locally smoked duck breast starter. Braised lamb shoulder is textbook soft and the memory of dull polenta is erased thanks to meatily rich gravy and tiptop vegetables. To finish, nutty, jammy Bakewell tart works better than overly rosewatered pannacotta. Wine from £17. Closed Tue and D Sun.

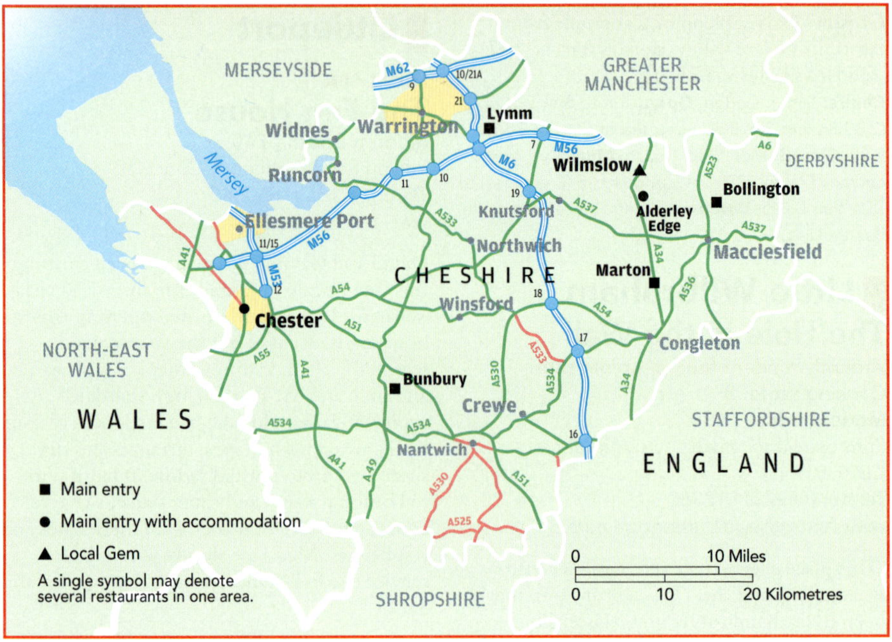

■ Alderley Edge
Alderley Edge Hotel

Cheshire favourite with serious food
Cooking score: 3
Modern British | £46
Macclesfield Road, Alderley Edge, SK9 7BJ
Tel no: (01625) 583033
www.alderleyedgehotel.com

The wooded slopes above Cheshire's most desirable village make a luscious setting for this handsome Victorian Gothic-style building. It's suitably swanky inside, setting out its stall as a venue for special occasions: 'It's the sort of place you might come for a birthday or anniversary,' opines one regular. That said, it recently acquired a trendy, metropolitan-style brasserie for less formal steak-and-chips-style dining. For the full caboodle, though, look to the conservatory restaurant, which capitalises on the luxuriant views. The kitchen is performing well under the guidance of newly promoted head chef Sean Sutton (here since 2005). He's turning out cunningly crafted dishes with real ambition. Sous-vide cooking and foams are very much in evidence, and there's a commendable engagement with the local landscape: foraged elderberries accompany Goosnargh duck with smoked beetroot juice and tarragon emulsion, while Cheshire lamb cutlets are served with stuffing, pressed shoulder croquette, confit tomatoes and basil emulsion. Set Cluizel chocolate with cherries, toasted chocolate powder and pistachio ice cream is a ritzy end-note. Wines from £24.50.
Chef/s: Sean Sutton. **Open:** all week L 12 to 2 (4 Sun), Mon to Sat D 7 to 10. **Meals:** alc (main courses £23 to £24). Sun L £28. **Details:** 64 seats. Wheelchair access. Music. Parking.

Visit us online

To find out more about The Good Food Guide, please visit thegoodfoodguide.co.uk

Join us at thegoodfoodguide.co.uk

■ Bollington
The Lord Clyde

A country pub pushing the boundaries
Cooking score: 3
Modern British | £37
36 Clarke Lane, Kerridge, Bollington,
SK10 5AH
Tel no: (01625) 562123
www.thelordclyde.co.uk

£5 OFF

Ambition reigns in rural Cheshire, and not just among the local footballers. This converted 19th-century mill is where chef Ernst Van Zyl gives his considerable creativity a run-out, with more consistent results than at previous locations. The pub (and drinkers do come) has a neat but easy-going air and complex dishes are served without fussiness – unless you count the little sacks the bread comes in, or the smoked butter alongside. Signature dishes have multiple elements and demonstrate bags of technique; a scallop and celeriac starter features the star ingredient in seared, dried and tartare form with a scallop roe crisp, warm celeriac foam and smoked bacon dashi. It makes sense together, as does a lamb and cauliflower dish with a spiced lamb sausage. Dessert could be rhubarb and gingerbread with white chocolate and coriander. Tasting menus are available (the 10-course complete with a 'crossover' savoury-to-sweet dish); wine starts at £16.50.
Chef/s: Ernst Van Zyl. **Open:** Tue to Fri L 12 to 2.30, Mon to Sat D 6.30 to 9.30. **Meals:** alc (main courses £14 to £25). **Details:** 28 seats. 20 seats outside. Music. Parking. No children Fri and Sat D.

LOCAL GEM
The Lime Tree

Modern British | £28
18-20 High Street, Bollington, SK10 5PH
Tel no: (01625) 578182
www.limetreebollington.co.uk

The younger sibling of the Lime Tree in West Didsbury (see entry), this has the better looks. It's in a 'great setting' on Bollington Green,

with a modern rustic style that nods to the area's cotton-rich history. Favourites from the mothership are served alongside wild mushroom bruschetta with spinach and cream, or plaice with gremolata and fennel dauphinois. If service could be sharper, it's a reasonable price to pay for a vibrant statement of confidence in this small Cheshire town. Wines from £21. Closed Mon and D Sun.

■ Bunbury
The Yew Tree Inn

Village pub with a modern twist
Cooking score: 1
Modern British | £25
Long Lane, Spurstow, Bunbury, CW6 9RD
Tel no: (01829) 260274
www.theyewtreebunbury.com

 £5 OFF £30

'Country pub meets contemporary styling' is an apt description of this 19th-century country pub where real ales and craft beers emphasise old-fashioned pubby virtues, but a wine list with plenty by the glass says 21st century. Settle in to one of the many nooks and crannies to enjoy traditional favourites, say steak and ale pie, fish and chips or gammon with pineapple salsa. Dishes in two portion sizes are helpful for mixing and matching – among them smoked chicken Caesar salad, or a salad of marinated feta, roasted squash, spinach, hazelnuts and preserved lemon. Chocolate and hazelnut pavlova 'won't disappoint'. Wines start at £15.50.
Chef/s: Rob McDiarmid. **Open:** all week 12 to 9.30 (10 Fri and Sat, 9 Sun). **Closed:** 25 Dec. **Meals:** alc (main courses £10 to £18). **Details:** 65 seats. 65 seats outside. Bar. Music. Parking.

Symbols

🔲 Accommodation is available
£30 Three courses for less than £30
£5 OFF £5-off voucher scheme
🍾 Notable wine list

▌Chester
Joseph Benjamin
Lively food and cracking wines
Cooking score: 2
Modern European | £29
134-140 Northgate Street, Chester, CH1 2HT
Tel no: (01244) 344295
www.josephbenjamin.co.uk

Brothers Joe and Ben Wright lent their first names to this easy-going deli-restaurant by Chester's historic city walls, and they try to keep things personal in surroundings that are conducive to having a good time. Drop by for a bacon sandwich early doors, share a plate of charcuterie at lunchtime or go for something more substantial – perhaps a pig's head fritter with rhubarb and ginger followed by hare bourguignon or cod cheeks with shrimps, curried cauliflower, spinach and raisin purée. It's a lively compendium of attractive ideas gleaned from near and far, although there's also room for a smattering of no-nonsense brasserie staples such as chicken Caesar salad and char-grilled bavette steaks, plus wholesome desserts including coconut rice pudding with mango. The wine list is a cracking collection of astutely chosen bottles at drinker-friendly prices; from £18.50.
Chef/s: Joe Wright. **Open:** Tue to Sun L 12 to 3 (4 Sun), Thur to Sat D 6 to 9.30. **Closed:** Mon. **Meals:** alc (main courses £11 to £19). Sun L £20. **Details:** 36 seats. Wheelchair access. Music.

Michael Caines at ABode Chester
Good food with a view
Cooking score: 4
Modern British | £40
Grosvenor Road, Chester, CH1 2DJ
Tel no: (01244) 347000
www.michaelcaines.com

Located on the fifth floor, this refreshingly airy restaurant come with fantastic views over the River Dee and Chester racecourse and occupies 'the most attractive position of all the ABode hotel group restaurants', according to one well-travelled visitor. Ian Hird is now executive head chef, overseeing seasonal menus that interpret Michael Caines' innovative feel and wide ranging approach perfectly – from an 'Amazing Graze' lunch menu to tasting and à la carte. A test meal opened with a silky, intensely flavoured chilled asparagus velouté with spring salad, went on to perfectly timed sea bream with fennel, orzo pasta and a slick of langoustine bisque, then a 'savoury and moreish' polenta topped with broad bean and mushroom fricassee with a thyme beurre noisette, and finished with a melting dark chocolate fondant with bitter-sweet poached cherries. The wine list (from £22) is organised by grape, with plenty by the glass.
Chef/s: Ian Hird. **Open:** all week L 12 to 2.30, D 6 to 9.45 (9 Sun). **Meals:** alc (main courses £11 to £26). Set L £10 (2 courses) to £15. Set D £17 (2 courses) to £23. **Details:** 76 seats. 10 seats outside. V menu. Bar. Wheelchair access. Music. Parking.

Simon Radley at the Chester Grosvenor
The smartest address in town
Cooking score: 6
Modern European | £75
Eastgate, Chester, CH1 1LT
Tel no: (01244) 324024
www.chestergrosvenor.com

The smartest address in town has a restaurant to match, and Simon Radley's reputation for luxurious but inventive food is well established. The eponymous dining room, with its golden lightwell, portraiture, polished marble and unusually comfortable chairs, is absolutely fit for purpose: to cosset and soothe, without the slightest suggestion that dinner here is an everyday affair. In such classic surroundings, the food must look lively, and it does; a main course of squab with coffee, dates and Israeli couscous takes the bird east, while a starter of brick-red Devon crab custard, strewn with seaweed and topped with

prawn toast and langoustine, has a tiny but enlivening dot of yellow yuzu curd at its centre. Puddings lack fireworks, and on our vist a vanilla-poached peach with golden apricots and basil sorbet could have been more yielding. Service is knowledgeable and twinkly, there are some excellent breads on the trolley, and the lengthy wine list, which includes a by-the-glass Coravin selection, is impeccably chosen with bottles from £25.
Chef/s: Simon Radley. **Open:** Tue to Sat D only 6.30 to 9. **Closed:** Sun, Mon, 25 Dec, first week Jan. **Meals:** alc (main courses £75). Set D £50. Tasting menu £99 (8 courses). **Details:** 40 seats. V menu. Bar. Wheelchair access. Parking. Children over 12 yrs only.

Sticky Walnut

Unstuffy food, sharply executed
Cooking score: 4
Modern European | £31
11 Charles Street, Chester, CH2 3AZ
Tel no: (01244) 400400
www.stickywalnut.com

'In terms of British bistros in the 21st century this is a genre-defining template,' noted one visitor to Gary Usher's 'brilliant local bistro'. It's a simple setting with pale walls, crammed bookshelves, bare-wood floors and a mishmash of wooden furniture. If you want to experience the full force of its camaraderie and warmth, opt for a downstairs table; those seated upstairs have felt 'left out of the fun'. Staff don't always toe the line in terms of bonhomie, but there's nothing half-hearted about the cooking – while no new ground is broken here, it's all about simple, approachable, everyday eating at a fair price. Thus a rolled piece of lightly cured salmon with pickled carrot, a crispy egg and a swipe of romesco, then grilled lamb rump on buttery roast potatoes with capers and a single grilled spring onion, and lime cheesecake with pecan butter biscuit and chocolate sorbet proved to be an 'enjoyable, well-cooked meal'. The wine list opens at £15 and stays below £50, with plenty of by-the-glass options.

Chef/s: Gary Usher. **Open:** all week L 12 to 2.30, Mon to Sat D 6 to 9 (10 Fri and Sat). **Closed:** 25 and 26 Dec. **Meals:** alc (main courses £14 to £22). Sun L £16 (2 courses) to £20. **Details:** 48 seats. Music.

■ Lymm
The Church Green
Pub food with frills and grills
Cooking score: 2
Modern British | £35
Higher Lane, Lymm, WA13 0AP
Tel no: (01925) 752068
www.aidenbyrne.co.uk

Billed as a 'British grill', this pubby venture from chef Aiden Byrne (see Manchester House) stands right next to the beautiful Lymm dam and village church – a rather quaint setting for food that adds some thrills and frills to the old classics. Black pudding Scotch eggs involve morcilla, Manchego cheese and pickled red pepper, cottage pie is topped with garlic mash, and bowls of mussels come with beef-dripping fries. Otherwise, the main event is rare-breed British meat from Cheshire farms, cooked on an Inka grill over 'coconut husk' charcoal and served with various sauces and accompaniments. The kitchen also shows its fancier side by offering the likes of pheasant breast with charred kale, smoked foie gras and hazelnut risotto, while desserts span everything from sticky toffee pudding to caramel parfait with fig sorbet. Tasting menus, weekend breakfasts, Sunday roasts and kids' deals complete the foodie picture, with wines kicking off at £18.
Chef/s: Aiden Byrne. **Open:** all week 12 to 9 (10 Sat, 7 Sun). **Closed:** 25 Dec. **Meals:** alc (main courses £10 to £34). Sun L £25. Tasting menu £60 (5 courses). **Details:** 70 seats. 100 seats outside. Wheelchair access. Music. Parking.

Average price

The average price denotes the price of a three-course meal without wine.

■ Marton

La Popote

French classics in friendly setting
Cooking score: 1
French | £40
Manchester Road (A34), Marton, SK11 9HF
Tel no: (01260) 224785
www.la-popote.co.uk

What's cooking (the colloquial meaning of La Popote) at this cosy bistro-style venue is classic French in the main, from seared scallops with beurre blanc to a confit of duck leg salad. Take a trip down memory lane and have your tournedos of beef flambéed at table or perhaps stick to less ostentatious mains in the form of queue de boeuf – oxtail in red wine – or sea bass bordelaise. Desserts range from a 'delicately flavoured' lavender pannacotta to crème brûlée and tarte Tatin with calvados. The wine list is predominantly French with a smattering from everywhere else and is good value; bottles from £18.50.

Chef/s: Victor Janssen. **Open:** Wed to Sun L 12 to 2.30 (3.30 Sun), Wed to Sat D 6 to 10. **Closed:** Mon, Tue, 26 Dec to 9 Jan. **Meals:** alc (main courses £11 to £27). Set L £15 to £18. **Details:** 36 seats. 24 seats outside. V menu. Wheelchair access. Music. Parking.

■ Sandbach

READERS RECOMMEND

Park Lane Deli and Eatery

Armenian
175 Crewe Road, Sandbach, CW11 4PA
Tel no: (01270) 761732
'The Armenian inspired menu ranges from slow-cooked ox cheek to traditional falafel to pasta stuffed with melting pork hock, and the portions are generous. The only quibble…is that it is impossible not to over order.'

■ Wilmslow

LOCAL GEM

Stolen Lamb

Greek | £28
70a Grove Street, Wilmslow, SK9 1DS
Tel no: (01625) 419571
www.stolenlamb.com

The restaurant's name is a reference to the kleftiko that is slow-cooked in a wood-fired oven for four hours. George Yannis is a Greek Cypriot and his rather contemporary first-floor joint (neutral colours, modern art, dark-wood tables) offers a progressive take on traditional dishes. Saganaki of tiger prawns and feta is fired up with ouzo, while char-grilled sea bream comes in true Med-style with red peppers and capers. Drink Greek wines such as something from the excellent Alpha Estate; house wine from £16.95. Closed Mon.

Join us at thegoodfoodguide.co.uk

■ Carlyon Bay

Austell's

Metropolitan flavours in a parade of shops

Cooking score: 3
Modern British | £30
10 Beach Road, Carlyon Bay, PL25 3PH
Tel no: (01726) 813888
www.austells.co.uk

'From the outside it could be mistaken as another fish and chip shop,' thought one visitor to this 'superb' restaurant found 'in a 1970-ish parade of suburban shops'. The interior gives more of a measure of things: the shining steel of the open kitchen, the cool slate and dove greys of the décor, the friendly efficiency of the staff – it's 'a very special discovery'. 'Excellent' onion bread with herb butter is a fitting prelude to an exuberant modern British menu brimming with prime ingredients. Cornish crab, for instance, comes in fat tortellini with cauliflower cheese purée and a rich crab bisque. An asparagus menu tried at inspection included a 'textbook'

asparagus risotto and a 'superb, but salty' asparagus and Brie tart with dauphinois potatoes and sautéed asparagus. Chocolate orange ice cream sandwich with cinnamon doughnuts, chocolate mascarpone and marinated oranges makes a faultless, charismatic dessert. Wines from £16.95.
Chef/s: Brett Camborne-Paynter. **Open:** Sun L 12 to 2, Tue to Sun D 6 to 9. **Closed:** Mon. **Meals:** alc (main courses £17 to £20). Set L £15 (2 courses) to £20. Set D £22 (2 courses) to £28. **Details:** 50 seats.

■ Falmouth

Oliver's

Cute, down-to-earth bistro

Cooking score: 3
Modern British | £30
33 High Street, Falmouth, TR11 2AD
Tel no: (01326) 218138
www.oliversfalmouth.com

A cute little café-like restaurant set at the quieter end of Falmouth's town centre among boho music, coffee, surf gear and clothing shops, Oliver's is proof positive that small is not only beautiful but highly effective too. It's owned and run by Ken and Wendy Symons: he cooks, she takes care of front-of-house. Inside, it's all about unstuffy informality with a bare-wood floor and tables, white-painted walls, and not much else in between; everything revolves around the food. Carefully sourced ingredients come from local, named producers and the well-executed dishes (listed on an orange plastic board) are not without their sophistication – note a starter of warm ham hock, served with a confit duck yolk, pickles, watercress gel and mustard. Mains bring roast fillet of beef with ox cheek ravioli, mash, wild mushrooms and shallot and to conclude, a magnificent lemon tart with curd jelly, lime sorbet and lemon verbena. Expect, too, imaginative vegetarian dishes and appealingly modest prices, both for food and the concise wine list, which starts at £15.95.

Chef/s: Ken Symons. **Open:** Tue to Sat L 12 to 2, D 7 to 10. **Closed:** Sun, Mon, 3 weeks Nov. **Meals:** alc (main courses £16 to £24). Set L £15 (2 courses) to £22. **Details:** 28 seats. V menu. Music.

Rick Stein's Fish

Seafood | £27
Discovery Quay, Falmouth, TR11 3XA
Tel no: (01326) 330050
www.rickstein.com

You can't book at this Falmouth outpost of Rick Stein's seafood empire, but it's worth taking pot luck if you fancy a taste of the TV chef's zesty global repertoire. Inside it's light, modern and casual, with a menu that runs all the way from Thai fishcakes and mussels masala to gloriously messy whole chilli crab or hake fillet with Pardina lentils, Serrano ham and persillade butter. Fish and chips cooked in beef dripping is a bestseller, and there's a handy takeaway counter too. Wines from £17.95. Open all week.

Gulval

The Coldstreamer Inn

Village local with fresh flavours
Cooking score: 2
Modern British | £25
Gulval, TR18 3BB
Tel no: (01736) 362072
www.coldstreamer-penzance.co.uk

From the outside this Victorian pub-with-rooms exudes a real sense of tradition with its mock-Tudor façade and piles of logs. It is still very much a village pub, with Cornish ales for those wanting a drink in the beamed bar, but the dining room moves things up a notch or two. Here, eager diners are drawn by a commitment to local and regional suppliers, and by a menu of updated pub classics (slow-cooked beef brisket and mash, fish and chips), plus more ambitious ideas. Expect starters such as home-cured venison bresaola with pickled walnuts, smoked apple and chestnut, and mains of pulled lamb bun with pomegranate raita, cucumber salad and hand-cut chips or a simple dish of Newlyn-landed hake with herb-crushed potatoes. Finish with Cornish cheeses or a homely sticky toffee pudding with butterscotch and clotted cream. Wines from £16.

Chef/s: Derren Broom. **Open:** all week L 12 to 3, D 6 to 9. **Closed:** 25 Dec. **Meals:** alc (main courses £11 to £19). Set L £15 (2 courses) to £17. **Details:** 56 seats. 12 seats outside. Bar. Music.

Halsetown

Halsetown Inn

Fastidious sourcing and keen prices
Cooking score: 2
Modern British | £26
Halsetown, TR26 3NA
Tel no: (01736) 795583
www.halsetowninn.co.uk

The owners behind indie burger joint Blas Burgerworks in St Ives (see entry) have applied the same green thinking and uncompromising eco-friendly approach to this big-hearted granite-walled boozer in the nearby village of Halsetown. 'Real pub, thoughtful food' is no empty promise, with fastidious local sourcing and keen prices ticking all the necessary boxes. The kitchen stirs the global pot, assembling plates of grilled carrots, Parmesan custard, burnt honey syrup, sesame and almonds, offsetting a red curry of tea-smoked duck with green mango and pear salad, and pairing crispy mackerel with black olive and black bean dressing. Burgers and grills are available (obviously), while pudding might be crema catalana or Halsetown's take on the Jaffa cake. Good-value 'pub lunches' and menus for 'little people' complete a rousing foodie package, with drinks ranging from Sharp's locally brewed ales to a dozen wines from £16 (including a Cornish sparkler).

Chef/s: Angela Baxter. **Open:** all week L 12 to 2 (3.30 Sun), Mon to Sat D 6 to 9. **Closed:** 5 Jan to 6 Feb. **Meals:** alc (main courses £12 to £20). Set L £12 (2 courses) to £15. **Details:** 70 seats. 30 seats outside. Bar. Wheelchair access. Music. Parking.

Helford Passage
Ferryboat Inn

Bivalves, booze and brilliant views
Cooking score: 2
Seafood | £20
Helford Passage, TR11 5LB
Tel no: (01326) 250625
www.thewrightbrothers.co.uk

Whether you arrive by road or ferry, you can't fault the brilliant views from this 300-year-old hostelry set back from the beach on the Helford estuary. Revamped and reinvented by seafood specialists the Wright Brothers (see entries, London), it now majors on bivalves from the Duchy Oyster Farm on the Helford River – although there's much more on the daily menu. Stay with the maritime theme by ordering Cornish crab rarebit with pickled vegetables, a bowl of garlicky Fowey mussels or whole plaice with green beans and new potatoes; otherwise, look inland for parsley-crusted macaroni cheese, a Ferryboat cheeseburger or Kernow bratwurst sausages with sauerkraut and mustard mash. Desserts promise anything from affogato to a wicked chocolate and stout pudding with double cream. Sup St Austell ales or pick from a snappy list of international wines from £17.

Chef/s: Robert Bunny. **Open:** all week L 12 to 3, D 6 to 9 (10 Fri and Sat). **Meals:** alc (main courses £8 to £16). Set L and D £20. **Details:** 92 seats. 140 seats outside. Wheelchair access. Music. Parking.

Marazion
Ben's Cornish Kitchen

Understated bistro making big waves
Cooking score: 5
Modern British | £30
West End, Marazion, TR17 0EL
Tel no: (01736) 719200
www.benscornishkitchen.com

Since opening in 2009, Ben Prior continues to do what he does best: serving up straight-to-the-point, calendar-friendly dishes that make the most of the West Country's fantastic produce. An easy-going approach is just the ticket, too; the understated bistro-style dining room on Marazion's main street delivers an intimacy that endears it to visitors. Humble cuts such as pork cheek or slow-braised blade of beef help keep prices in check, but there's no shortage of determination, style or classy technique in the kitchen – whether pan-frying duck livers and serving them with pancetta, sherry cream and salsa verde, or grilling a fillet of brill and teaming it with crushed celeriac, chard, samphire and mussel sauce. Desserts show skill in every department from a rich duck egg crème brûlée with new-season rhubarb, blood orange and shortbread to warm griotte cherry and hazelnut financier. The wine list (from £17) offers plenty of choice at eminently fair prices.

Chef/s: Ben Prior. **Open:** Tue to Sat L 12 to 2, D 7 to 8.45. **Closed:** Sun, Mon, 25 and 26 Dec, 1 Jan. **Meals:** alc (main courses £14 to £20). Set L £17 (2 courses) to £20. **Details:** 36 seats. Wheelchair access. Music.

Mawgan
New Yard Restaurant
A kitchen with its money on local produce
Cooking score: 3
Modern British | £30
Trelowarren Estate, Mawgan, TR12 6AF
Tel no: (01326) 221595
www.newyardrestaurant.co.uk

It's in a quiet and picturesque corner of Cornwall and, as you head down a single-track road to the heart of the Trelowarren Estate, seemingly miles from anywhere, yet the New Yard pulls in the punters with its good, unpretentious cooking and informal but efficient service. The converted coach house set in an old cobbled stable yard makes an elegant, contemporary country restaurant, one where trouble is taken over sourcing raw materials (including estate game, fish from day boats and locally grown fruit and vegetables), and the kitchen distinguishes itself with enthusiasm and honest effort. The menus centre on appetising combinations: local Ruby Red beef carpaccio served with rocket and Parmesan, John Dory véronique comes with samphire and spinach, while sweet potato, baby carrots and spiced yoghurt accompany Cornish lamb rump. A selection of West Country artisan cheeses makes a fine alternative to desserts such as dark chocolate tart with mandarin sorbet. Wines from £16.
Chef/s: Chris Philliskirk. **Open:** all week L 12 to 2.15, D 6.30 to 9. **Closed:** 3 weeks Jan. **Meals:** alc (main courses £11 to £17). **Details:** 50 seats. 20 seats outside. V menu. Bar. Wheelchair access. Music. Parking.

Millbrook
The View
Outstanding clifftop package
Cooking score: 3
Modern British | £34
Treninnow Cliff, Millbrook, PL10 1JY
Tel no: (01752) 822345
www.theview-restaurant.co.uk

The view that gives this friendly little restaurant its name is a dizzying slide down to the sea, across which you can see Rame Head, where watchmen warned of the Spanish Armada in 1588. A simple, shiplapped building with windows running the length of the narrow dining room, its wood floors, pale-wood furniture and white walls suggest that nothing should detract from the experience of being on one of Cornwall's rockiest and most beautiful coastlines. The food is as uncluttered and honest as the surroundings: expect cracking local ingredients, treated with respect, accuracy and a hunger for flavour. Plump, ruby-hued wood pigeon with caramelised pear and crispy ham is a case in point. Local sea bass also shines, served with a pleasant juxtaposition of sweet raisin purée and rich Vermouth cream. A runny lemon posset with a brûlée-style caramelised top and raspberry sorbet also pleased at inspection with its 'lively, fresh flavours'. Several pages of international wines kicks off at £17.95.
Chef/s: Matt Corner. **Open:** Wed to Sun L 12 to 2, D 7 to 9. **Closed:** Mon, Tue, Feb. **Meals:** alc (main courses £17 to £22). Set L £14 (2 courses) to £16. **Details:** 45 seats. 20 seats outside. Music. Parking.

Join us at thegoodfoodguide.co.uk

 Mousehole
The Old Coastguard
Coastal inn with confident local food
Cooking score: 3
Modern British | £27
The Parade, Mousehole, TR19 6PR
Tel no: (01736) 731222
www.oldcoastguardhotel.co.uk

The impossibly picturesque coastal village of Mousehole (pronounced 'mowze-all') is home to the third venue in Charles and Edmund Inkin's group of food-focused inns (check out the entries for the nearby Gurnard's Head and Felin Fach Griffin, Wales). The location on the edge of the village gives far-reaching views across the sea to St Michael's Mount and the Lizard Peninsula, and the hard-working kitchen provides a degree of local flavour in its appealing modern British output. The place is relaxed, unpretentious and full of beans. Tuck into artichoke, apple and cider soup, or salt-baked beetroot with blue cheese, salsa verde and crispy egg, and move on to a rich fishy stew with fennel and aïoli or megrim sole with sea vegetables and brown caper butter. They're appealing contemporary combinations grounded in culinary good sense. A meaty main might be braised lamb shoulder with crisp sweetbreads, and 'puddings' run to chocolate fondant with marmalade ice cream. Wines start at £17.50.
Chef/s: Matthew Smith. **Open:** all week L 12.30 to 2.30, D 6 to 9 (9.30 Fri and Sat). **Closed:** 25 Dec, 4 days Jan. **Meals:** alc (main courses £13 to £18). Set L £14 (2 courses) to £18. Sun L £15 (2 course) to £25.
Details: 70 seats. 70 seats outside. Bar. Wheelchair access. Music. Parking.

Symbols

 Accommodation is available
 Three courses for less than £30
   £5-off voucher scheme
   Notable wine list

2 Fore Street
Unpretentious Cornish bistro
Cooking score: 3
Modern British | £28
2 Fore Street, Mousehole, TR19 6PF
Tel no: (01736) 731164
www.2forestreet.co.uk

With its prime position close to the harbour, Joe Wardell's easy-going restaurant is an especially captivating spot on a sunny day, what with its large windows looking on to the action out front and a little terrace garden out back complete with palm trees, but it's no fair-weather friend – it's open all year (apart from a few weeks in deepest winter). The décor is simple and contemporary. Seafood gets a good outing on a menu that focuses on local stuff first and foremost. A starter of seared scallops with hog's pudding, pear and perry beurre blanc reveals a steady hand on the tiller, while there's evident Med inspiration in a sexed-up sardines on toast (with roasted tomatoes and tapenade). Move on to monkfish with curried mussels or a meaty option such as corn-fed Cornish chicken with Puy lentils and smoked bacon. Lunch has some slightly simpler options. Wines start at £15.95.
Chef/s: Joe Wardell. **Open:** all week L 12 to 3.30, D 5 to 9.30. **Closed:** Mon, 25 and 26 Dec, 4 Jan to 12 Feb. **Meals:** alc (main courses £14 to £18).
Details: 36 seats. 24 seats outside. Music.

■ Newlyn
NEW ENTRY
The Tolcarne Inn
Exemplary Cornish produce in a proper pub
Cooking score: 2
Seafood | £29
Newlyn, TR18 5PR
Tel no: (01736) 363074
www.tolcarneinn.co.uk

Only the seawall separates the Tolcarne Inn from the elements and its harbourside position next to Newlyn's fish market ensures that the day's catch is used to good effect. It dates from around 1717 and has almost 300 years of maritime history etched into its weather-beaten, whitewashed walls. Ben Tunnicliffe has been one of Cornwall's more capable chefs for the past two decades – his previous establishments have all been restaurants, and although bookings are pretty much essential, this is still very much a pub 'where salty sea dogs supping pints of locally brewed Betty Stoggs ale prop up the bar'; it's all very informal. Cornish produce, including exemplary seafood, dictates the uncompromisingly concise blackboard menu, ranging from a starter of seared scallops, cauliflower purée, capers and raisins to a main of pan-fried brill, Jerusalem artichokes, lemon-glazed salsify, purple sprouting broccoli and herb cream. Rhubarb, saffron and mascarpone trifle makes a good finale. Wines from £14.95.

Chef/s: Ben Tunnicliffe. **Open:** all week L 12 to 2.15 (3 Sun), D 7 to 10. **Meals:** alc (main courses £16 to £19). **Details:** 40 seats. 20 seats outside. Parking.

■ Padstow

Paul Ainsworth at No. 6

Padstow's premier gastronomic address
Cooking score: 7
Modern British | £51
6 Middle Street, Padstow, PL28 8AP
Tel no: (01841) 532093
www.number6inpadstow.co.uk

No. 6's quirky, intimate appeal is a distinct plus. The tiny Georgian town house in the centre of Padstow offers an engaging mix of small but light dining rooms set over two floors, bought up to date with modern touches – from huge ceiling lampshades to plain tables. Judging by glowing comments from reporters this year, Paul Ainsworth's combination of classical cooking techniques with bold, ultra-modern touches is a winning one, too – 'he has that ability to transform ingredients into those eye-shutting taste

moments'. What gives Mr Ainsworth's food its vitality, indeed its identity and character, is his use of sharp flavours to point up the main item: for example, an inspired combination of translucent smoked haddock on a bed of pearl barley and parsley with lemon and aged Parmesan. Or take a disarmingly simple and fresh-tasting torched mackerel with celeriac remoulade, Coppa ham and cucumber, or a 'noteworthy' roast Galloway beef, 'beautifully pink', with Montgomery potato, onion and mushroom duxelle, and a great piece of cod, perfectly timed, with 'sublime' crab mayonnaise, fenugreek and grilled leeks, these are dishes full of vibrancy and bold strokes. Reporters agree that desserts are a high point – everyone commends the bread-and-butter pudding 'like no ordinary b-and-b pudding' – and the set lunch has been praised for value and performance. Staff are charming and the confident, well-spread wine list is teeming with imaginative choices, from £26.

Chef/s: Paul Ainsworth. **Open:** Tue to Sat L 12 to 2.30, D 6 to 10. **Closed:** Sun, Mon, 24 to 26 Dec, 3 weeks Jan. **Meals:** alc (main courses £28 to £38). Set L £19 (2 courses) to £25. **Details:** 45 seats. 6 seats outside. V menu. Music. Children over 4 yrs only.

The Seafood Restaurant

Rick Stein's seafood original
Cooking score: 5
Seafood | £55
Riverside, Padstow, PL28 8BY
Tel no: (01841) 532700
www.rickstein.com

When the Seafood Restaurant opened, Harold Wilson was still PM – Rick Stein's place celebrated 40 years of service in 2015. The Stein brand grew out of Padstow and into living rooms via the TV and printed page, and continues to grow (with restaurants opening in Porthleven and Winchester in 2014). Back where it all began, the whitewashed dining room with vast contemporary canvases and focal seafood counter presents an upmarket straightforwardness that matches the food. Prices are steep (15 quid or so for starters), but quality and freshness remain the watchwords. There are classic ideas from Europe and Asia – lobster and fennel risotto, or crisp smoked mackerel with Thai-inspired flavours – and the confidence to keep things simple. Singapore chilli crab is a hands-on main course, or go for the comfort of fish and chips. Desserts include rice pudding with salted caramel and caramelised toasted nuts. Despite the good vibes, there are reports of inconsistent service. Wines start at £24.

Chef/s: Stephane Delourme. **Open:** all week L 12 to 2.30, D 6.30 to 10. **Closed:** 25 and 26 Dec. **Meals:** alc (main courses £16 to £55). Set L £31 (winter), £40 (summer). **Details:** 120 seats. 20 seats outside. V menu. Bar. Wheelchair access. Music. Children over 3 yrs only.

Rick Stein's Café

Seafood | £29
10 Middle Street, Padstow, PL28 8AP
Tel no: (01841) 532700
www.rickstein.com

It's all quite close-packed, which encourages chatting to your neighbours, at this light, cheery all-day café offering a relatively inexpensive shot at the Stein seafood experience. The menu is short, with dishes hopping from one part of the globe to another, the main bias being towards India (masala mussels, cod curry from Pondicherry), but there's also grilled miso salmon with rice noodles, goujons of plaice, or rump steak for those not in the mood for fish. At busy times, join the swifter queue at Stein's Fish and Chips by the harbour. Wines from £18. Accommodation. Open all week.

Penzance
Bakehouse and Steakhouse

Locally reared steaks and more
Cooking score: 2
Modern European | £25
Old Bakehouse Lane, Chapel Street, Penzance, TR18 4AE
Tel no: (01736) 331331
www.bakehouserestaurant.co.uk

Spread over two floors of an old bakery – complete with the original bread ovens and walls hung with exhibits by Cornish artists – Andy and Rachel Carr's eatery peddles its wares in a small courtyard off Penzance's main drag. As you might guess from the name, locally reared Angus steaks from the butcher up the road are one of the prime attractions (served with a choice of sauces, rubs and butters), although other ingredients from the region also shine out on the menu. Fish from the West Country boats might yield Newlyn crab salad, roast monkfish with romesco sauce or hake fillet atop a Tuscan-style stew loaded with tomatoes, olives and capers, while produce form nearby farms goes into the char-grilled vegetables with roasted beetroot and haloumi. Elsewhere, falafels with yoghurt and harissa or slow-cooked Moroccan-style lamb with merguez sausage strike an exotic note, before puds such as lemon tart with Cornish ice cream add the final flourish. Wines from £13.95.

Chef/s: Andy Carr. **Open:** Tue to Sat D 6 to 9. **Closed:** Sun, Mon, first 2 weeks Jan. **Meals:** alc (main courses £9 to £40). Early D £13 (2 courses). **Details:** 56 seats. 6 seats outside. Bar. Music.

The Bay

Arty brasserie with stunning views
Cooking score: 3
Modern British | £34
Hotel Penzance, Britons Hill, Penzance,
TR18 3AE
Tel no: (01736) 366890
www.thebaypenzance.co.uk

Occupying an extension of the Hotel Penzance, this appropriately named brasserie has views over Mount's Bay and offers regular art exhibitions. Take advantage of the decked balcony if the weather is clement, although there are excellent vistas from the windows of the conservatory-style dining room with its well-spaced tables and black wicker chairs. Given the location, it's no surprise that the menu veers towards fish, be it pan-fried scallops with apple purée, sherry dressing and meaty hog's pudding, or roast cod fillet with squid, vegetable compote and seaweed salsa. Lobsters and fruits de mer merit special attention, but the kitchen also shows its flair, finesse and invention in other areas – witness roast West Country beef fillet paired with beetroot, chicken livers, Serrano ham and shallot jus, or crispy polenta cake with Jerusalem artichokes, wild mushrooms, orange and cardamom reduction. To finish, the West Country cheeses are worth a punt. Wines from £17.50.
Chef/s: Ben Reeve. **Open:** all week L 12 to 2.30, D 5 to 9.30. **Closed:** first 2 weeks Jan. **Meals:** alc (main courses £14 to £24). Sun L £14. **Details:** 60 seats. 15 seats outside. Music. Parking.

Harris's

Veteran bistro with big Cornish flavours
Cooking score: 2
Modern European | £32
46 New Street, Penzance, TR18 2LZ
Tel no: (01736) 364408
www.harrissrestaurant.co.uk

Roger and Anne Harris have run this small side-street restaurant for the past 43 years – the building itself has been associated with the catering business since 1860 – and it's considered a Penzance institution. After so many years, the Harrises have their customers pretty well weighed up and their fiercely loyal regulars return time and again for palate-pleasing Anglo-French classics. Solid technical skills and fresh local and regional produce are the foundations of Roger's uncomplicated, seasonally aware cooking and seafood dishes continue to be a strong suit. The kitchen takes full advantage of its close proximity to Newlyn fish market: cornets of smoked salmon with fresh white crabmeat might precede roasted turbot with hollandaise, with medallions of venison loin with beetroot and caraway seed, glazed pear and red wine sauce for those not in the mood for fish. Finish with chocolate torte served with a vanilla and Amaretto sauce and blackcurrant sorbet. Wines from £22.
Chef/s: Roger Harris. **Open:** Tue to Sat L 12 to 2, Tue to Sat D 6.30 to 9. **Closed:** Sun, Mon, 2 weeks Feb, 2 weeks Nov. **Meals:** alc (main courses £8 to £30). **Details:** 36 seats. Bar. Music. Children over 5 yrs only.

▉ Port Isaac
Outlaw's Fish Kitchen

Impressive seafood at the harbour's edge
Cooking score: 4
Seafood | £35
1 Middle Street, Port Isaac, PL29 3RH
Tel no: (01208) 880237
www.outlaws.co.uk

What better setting for a seafood restaurant than this charming building at the harbour's edge – now a restaurant in Nathan Outlaw's group. The ancient, heavily beamed premises were transformed into a bright yet modest space in 2014 – whitewashed throughout with tight-packed tables and wicker chairs. While dishes are small plates, they are 'not always designed for sharing', according to many reporters, and dishes turn up 'rather quickly', which does mess up the pace of the meal. But while there's no standing on ceremony, the food can impress. Recent highlights have been

Join us at thegoodfoodguide.co.uk

excellent English asparagus with brown shrimps on butter-soaked toast, breaded plaice with a zingy cucumber tartare salad and dill mayonnaise and, from the specials board, thin slices of raw turbot dressed with mint and coriander and delicious smoked anchovies. Staff are a delight, booking for dinner is essential (no booking at lunch means you can get in – if early) and the house white (£20) matches the food perfectly.
Chef/s: Simon Davies. **Open:** all week L 12 to 3, D 6 to 9.30. **Closed:** 1 week Christmas, Jan. **Meals:** alc (small plates £7 to £22). Set L £20 (5 courses, min 2 pers). Set D £40 (10 courses, min 2 pers). **Details:** 25 seats. Music.

★ TOP 10 ★

Restaurant Nathan Outlaw

Starring perfect fish and seafood
Cooking score: 9
Seafood | £99
6 New Road, Port Isaac, PL29 3SB
Tel no: 01208 880896
www.nathan-outlaw.com

The move to new premises has taken place. The new restaurant is his, nobody else's, and this seems to have provided Nathan Outlaw with a further motivation to demonstrate his enormous talent. The restaurant itself is simple, strikingly contemporary and comes with wonderful sea views but with a limited number of tables. And in this period marked by change, the view of reporters familiar with the old restaurant is that Outlaw and his team have not missed a beat. The kitchen wheels out a procession of dishes of such clarity and cohesion, starring perfect fish and seafood with a supporting cast of local and seasonal vegetables, that one old hand wondered 'does it get any better than this?' Scallop tartare surprises with its delicacy and sweetness offset by a subtle acidity from slivers of apple and radish. Equally deft is the umami hit of slow-cooked onion and the subtle chilli notes in a dish of cured monkfish with preserved herring. Consideration is given to texture: tiny, delicate strips of lemon sole arrive with a light oyster tempura and seaweed hollandaise; the sweetest, freshest crab meat is given acidity by the tiniest diced apple and complemented by a delicate asparagus mousse and raw shaved asparagus; and creamy Tunworth cheese is baked with fennel crackers and served with tangy celery – pickled and jelly – and crisp hazelnuts. The centrepiece of this meal was turbot sprinkled with bacon crumb, backed up by watercress, cauliflower and broad beans and served with an intense, sweet chicken and red wine stock – 'a wonderful interplay of tastes and textures'. Desserts are clever and innovative – strawberry (fruit, jelly, granita) with a tiny ball of rich, thick yoghurt, and a raspberry and vanilla crème brûlée on the side, served at the same time as a tiny, warm passion fruit, pineapple and coconut tart, proved a complete winner at inspection. Controlling front-of-house is Stephanie Little, who chats amiably and sets people at ease ('a perfect level of sociability and expertise') while her husband Damon can be relied upon to get the best out of the fascinating wine list ('as usual, the wines were a perfect match for all the courses'). Bottles from £20.
Chef/s: Nathan Outlaw and Christopher Simpson. **Open:** Fri and Sat L 12 to 2, Wed to Sat D 7 to 9. **Closed:** Sun, Mon, Tue, Jan. **Meals:** Set L £49 (4 courses). Tasting menu £99 (8 courses). **Details:** 24 seats. V menu. Music. No children under 12 yrs.

LOCAL GEM

Fresh from the Sea

Seafood | £15
18 New Road, Port Isaac, PL29 3SB
Tel no: (01208) 880849
www.freshfromthesea.co.uk

Everyone seems to enjoy Calum and Tracey Greenhalgh's tiny, easy-going café. They offer a simple menu, the stars of the show being crab and lobster caught sustainably by Calum on his boat *Mary D*, and served in either a sandwich or salad, although there's support from crab soup, prawns with Marie Rose sauce, homemade smoked mackerel pâté, Porthilly oysters and homemade cakes. Take away or sit at one of the small tables inside or out. Glass of white wine £3.50. Open daytime all week.

▌**Porthleven**

Kota

All about seasonality, balance and flavours
Cooking score: 4
Fusion-Modern European | £32
Harbour Head, Porthleven, TR13 9JA
Tel no: (01326) 562407
www.kotarestaurant.co.uk

A skip and a jump from the harbour, cheery Kota looks and feels like a converted pub: knobbly whitewashed walls, a wood-burner, traditional wooden furniture and mellow Art Deco-style lighting give it a lovably artless warmth. The staff seal the deal with a genuine welcome and friendly, well-paced service. The menu speaks of a chef getting creative with the best ingredients he can find each day, and the result is a gutsy, occasionally spicy, riff on European themes: fat oysters might be tempura-battered and topped with wasabi tartare sauce; mussels are enlivened by a chorizo, chilli, orange and coriander broth; and homemade gnocchi is tumbled together with spinach, grilled haloumi, pungent Parmesan, purple sprouting broccoli and landcress in a verdant hedgerow sauce of nettles and wild garlic. Desserts are a must: a tarte Tatin with spiced rum and pink peppercorn caramel, passion fruit sorbet and vanilla bean Chantilly cream elevates a classic to new levels of delight and complexity. Several pages of international wines kick off at £15.95.
Chef/s: Jude Kereama. **Open:** Mon to Sat D only 6 to 9. **Closed:** Sun, 1 Jan to 13 Feb. **Meals:** alc (main courses £14 to £21). Set D £18 (2 courses) to £22. **Details:** 40 seats. Bar. Wheelchair access. Music.

▌**Portscatho**

Driftwood

Elegant clifftop hotel with stylish food
Cooking score: 5
Modern European | £55
Rosevine, Portscatho, TR2 5EW
Tel no: (01872) 580644
www.driftwoodhotel.co.uk

It's a picture-perfect piece of Cornwall: pretty pastel paintwork, subtle 'boutique' styling, broad sea views; surely the south west at its best? Especially when the hotel has its own private beach and cove, plus acres of gardens and a sheltered sun terrace. Chef Chris Eden takes the Cornish theme and runs with it, seeking out the best produce from the surrounding land and sea and treating it with respect and imagination. Jerusalem artichoke mousse with cured duck ham, liver parfait, hazelnut and orange is a typically multi-faceted starter, followed, perhaps, by steamed cod with taramasalata, kale crisps, St Austell Bay mussels and broccoli or hay-baked Cabrito kid with goats' curd, homemade sausage, turnip and spiced granola. To finish, maybe lemon verbena sorbet with white chocolate and macadamia nuts or the 'Driftwood chocolate bar' with salted peanut, honeycomb and milk sorbet. The global wine list includes decent options by the glass or half-bottle, and opens at £20.
Chef/s: Chris Eden. **Open:** all week D only 6.30 to 9.30. **Closed:** 7 Dec to 4 Feb. **Meals:** Set D £55 (3 courses). Tasting menu £80. **Details:** 36 seats. Bar. Wheelchair access. Music. Parking. Children over 5 yrs only.

Rosevine
Modern British | £29
Rosevine, Portscatho, TR2 5EW
Tel no: (01872) 580206
www.rosevine.co.uk

Subtle boutique styling, with big windows and the palest blue-green rattan furniture underscoring the sea-and-palm-tree view, sets the tone for fresh, honest cooking that does the simple things best. Flavour and seasoning can be understated but technical skill is evident in a beautiful piece of sea bass, which arrives with perfect crisp, salty skin and plump coriander and coconut dumplings, while a hefty, juicy beef burger and fries are handled perfectly. A dessert of ginger and coconut rice pudding with Champagne rhubarb makes a mild but hearty dessert. Wines start at £18.

■ Rock

The Mariners
Classy modern pub serving honest food
Cooking score: 1
British | £30
Rock, PL27 6LD
Tel no: (01208) 863679
www.themarinersrock.com

Rock is an estuary village perfect for a waterfront walk and a pub meal. The latest addition to Nathan Outlaw's Cornish empire, the Mariners fits the bill nicely. Overlooking the water, it's a modern Cornish pub selling local ales in tiptop condition. The under-stated first-floor restaurant combines white walls, slate floors and rustic stonework with Parisian bistro chairs and rustic wooden tables and deals in simple, wholehearted dishes such as steak and chips, local smoked salmon with horseradish yoghurt and beetroot, or cod with lentils and a caper, anchovy and gherkin sauce, with lemon posset with honeycomb and blood orange to finish. A modest selection of wine (from £14.85) offers great value.

Chef/s: Zack Hawke. **Open:** all week L 12 to 3 (4.30 Sun), D 6 to 9. **Meals:** alc (main courses £10 to £20). Set L £13 (2 courses) to £15. Sun L £13. **Details:** 70 seats. 30 seats outside. Bar. Music.

Outlaw's
Fantastic fish and more in seaside hotel
Cooking score: 4
Seafood | £45
St Enodoc Hotel, Rock Road, Rock, PL27 6LA
Tel no: (01208) 862737
www.nathan-outlaw.com

There has been much going on behind the scenes at this lovely seaside hotel. Restaurant Nathan Outlaw relocated to Port Isaac in March 2015 (see entry) making the more casual Outlaw's the St Enodoc Hotel's sole restaurant; the chef has also taken over the Mariners, a Sharp's Brewery pub down the road (see entry). Tom Brown heads the kitchen, interpreting the straightforward Outlaw style perfectly, taking his cue from land and estuary (on view from the outdoor terrace and smart, informal dining room) and exploiting ample local resources. There is a strong seafood bent, though not to the exclusion of meat (readers have enjoyed pork faggots with bubble and squeak and apple sauce). There's praise, too, for marinated sole with grapes and pickled shallots, for a perfectly calibrated main of hake with bacon and hazelnut dressing and St Enodoc asparagus, and for vanilla and passion fruit cheesecake with coconut and yoghurt sorbet. There's also professional 'but never snooty' service, and a short wine list with every bottle (from £20) available by the glass or carafe.

Chef/s: Tom Brown. **Open:** all week L 12 to 2.30, D 6 to 9.30. **Closed:** 20 Dec to 29 Jan. **Meals:** Set L and D £35 (2 courses) to £45. **Details:** 46 seats. 30 seats outside. Wheelchair access. Music. Parking. Children over 10 yrs only at D.

■ St Agnes
No.4 Peterville
Good-humoured neighbourhood eatery
Cooking score: 3
Modern British | £30
Peterville Square, St Agnes, TR5 0QU
Tel no: (01872) 554245
www.no4peterville.co.uk

£5 OFF

Next door to the local pub in a pretty Cornish fishing village, No.4 Peterville is the very model of a modern neighbourhood eatery – a good-humoured, big-hearted kind of place noted for its 'lovely warm atmosphere', cheery welcome and retro chic vibe (think ceramic tiles, whitewashed panelling and industrial lighting). 'Foams belong in the bath tub,' say the owners, who have no truck with the fancy-pants gewgaws of modern gastronomy. Instead, they buy wisely and treat native ingredients with the respect they deserve: the result is a short roster of surprisingly imaginative seasonal dishes that might see slow-braised rabbit paired with celeriac, crispy sage and Old Winchester cheese or cod with crispy squid, heritage carrots, romesco and spiced almonds. Quail pops up in a Caesar salad, while dessert might bring a colourful plate of lemon meringue, roasted rhubarb and pistachios. The no-frills 18-bin wine list kicks off at £15.50 but 'you must start with one of the house cocktails,' insists a fan.

Chef/s: Adam Vasey. **Open:** Sat and Sun 10 to 1 (2 Sun), Tue to Sat D 7 to 10.30. **Closed:** Mon (exc Aug), Tue and Wed (winter only), 23 to 27 Dec, 1 Jan to 14 Feb, bank hols. **Meals:** alc (main courses £14 to £22). **Details:** 30 seats. 4 seats outside. Wheelchair access. Music.

■ St Ives
Alba
Ex-lifeboat house that lifts the spirits
Cooking score: 3
Modern European | £30
Old Lifeboat House, Wharf Road, St Ives, TR26 1LF
Tel no: (01736) 797222
www.thealbarestaurant.com

£5 OFF

A veritable veteran of the St Ives restaurant scene, this glass-fronted former lifeboat house on the harbour front continues to be one of the town's most consistent places. The décor is light, bright and minimalist with the ground floor given over to the bustle of an open kitchen; upstairs secures spectacular views over the harbour. The menu showcases local produce, particularly locally landed fish and seafood. Ingredients are handled with care and respect – grey mullet is teamed with pearl barley, cauliflower couscous and Jerusalem artichoke purée; plaice appears with smoked haddock, pea, mint and mussel butter sauce. Elsewhere, croustade of pheasant and foie gras makes a good start, followed perhaps by a satisfying beef and red wine stew with mash and greens. Pudding might be a perfect duck egg custard tart with roasted rhubarb and peach sorbet, although a south west cheeseboard is a perfect alternative. Wines from £14.95.

Chef/s: Grant Nethercott. **Open:** all week L 12 to 2, D 6 to 9.30. **Closed:** Sun and Tue L (Nov to Mar), 25 and 26 Dec. **Meals:** alc (main courses £12 to £24). Set L and D £17 (2 courses) to £20. **Details:** 60 seats. Music.

Join us at thegoodfoodguide.co.uk

The Black Rock

Imaginative cooking from friendly local gem
Cooking score: 2
Modern British | £26
Market Place, St Ives, TR26 1RZ
Tel no: (01736) 791911
www.theblackrockstives.co.uk

'Already planning to go back when next in St Ives with the family,' remarked a delighted first-timer to David Symons' modest family restaurant. In a town where most eating places have sea views, Black Rock's side street location could be seen as a disadvantage, but it is a big hit with the locals who appreciate the serving of well-sourced ingredients in a perky space, and the fact that bare white tables, slate floors and splashes of colour from local art allow little distraction from cooking that is distinguished by honesty, simplicity and full-on flavours. From the hard-working kitchen come homemade bread with Cornish rapeseed oil, a well-reported crab gratin, mussels in Cornish cider, a Sri Lankan seafood curry served with aubergine pickle, basmati rice and coconut flatbread, pork belly with a braise of butter beans, tomato, chilli and peppers, and an excellent cardamom pannacotta with rhubarb and ginger and a cinnamon biscuit. Wines from £14.95.
Chef/s: David Symons. **Open:** Mon to Sat D only 6 to 10.30. **Closed:** Sun, Nov to Feb. **Meals:** alc (main courses £13 to £21). Set D £17 (2 courses) to £20.
Details: 36 seats. Bar. Music.

Blas Burgerworks

Feel-good eco-friendly burger bar
Cooking score: 1
Burgers | £15
The Warren, St Ives, TR26 2EA
Tel no: (01736) 797272
www.blasburgerworks.co.uk

Concealed down a narrow street behind the harbour, this granite storehouse – once a net loft used by fishermen – is now a eco-friendly burger bar that reels in locals and tourists with a range of top-notch patties. Char-grilled burgers are made from beef reared at a nearby farm or from free-range chicken, with day-boat mackerel arriving from the bay visible from the front door. Tuck into a burger topped with Primrose Herd bacon and Davidstow Cheddar and wash it down with Cornish beer or cider. There's locally made ice cream to finish, and a bottle of house wine is £16.
Chef/s: Marie Dixon. **Open:** all week D only 5.30 to 9.30 (12 to 9.30 school hols). **Closed:** 1 Nov to 13 Feb. **Meals:** alc (main courses £9 to £12).
Details: 30 seats. Music.

Porthgwidden Beach Café

An idyllic setting to sample local seafood
Cooking score: 1
Modern British | £22
Porthgwidden Beach, The Island, St Ives, TR26 1PL
Tel no: (01736) 796791
www.porthgwiddencafe.co.uk

This sister to the Porthminster Beach Café (see entry) is located on a secluded beach overlooking St Ives Bay and has real charm – the atmosphere on the outside tables on a sunny day is a joy. Like the simple décor, there's nothing cluttered or fancy about the food, which aims to please with local seafood and casual bistro favourites such as fish and chips and moules marinère. Otherwise, crispy calamari or smoked haddock chowder followed by sea bass fillets with shellfish bouillabaisse are typical choices. Lunchtime baguettes, steaks, burgers and laid-back breakfasts (to 11am) are also part of the excellent package. Wines from £15.25.
Chef/s: Robert Michael. **Open:** all week L 12 to 3, D 6 to 9. **Closed:** 6 to 19 Dec. **Meals:** alc (main courses £9 to £16). **Details:** 34 seats. 38 seats outside. Music. Parking.

Average price

The average price denotes the price of a three-course meal without wine.

Porthmeor Beach Café

Tapas and stunning St Ives sunsets
Cooking score: 1
Tapas | £20
Porthmeor, St Ives, TR26 1JZ
Tel no: (01736) 793366
www.porthmeor-beach.co.uk

There's certainly no arguing with the 'terrific location' of this fast-moving beachside café below Tate St Ives. Relaxed, jolly and very popular, this is where you can drop in during the morning for scrambled eggs on toast or buttermilk pancakes. By lunchtime the place has moved up a gear, sending out contemporary tapas such as cauliflower, corn and ricotta fritters, hake croquettes with pickled tarragon aïoli, and crispy pork belly with Asian slaw and Japanese mayo, as well as local crab sandwiches and Cornish beef brisket slider. The likes of Thai red prawn curry or Moroccan-marinated chicken breast expand choice in the evening. Wines from £15.50.
Chef/s: Nathan Madden. **Open:** all week L 12 to 4.30, D 5.30 to 9. **Closed:** late Oct to mid Mar. **Meals:** alc (tapas and main courses £3 to £18). **Details:** 31 seats. 70 seats outside. V menu. Bar.

Porthminster Beach Café

Beach hangout with enticing global dishes
Cooking score: 3
Seafood | £35
Porthminster Beach, St Ives, TR26 2EB
Tel no: (01736) 795352
www.porthminstercafe.co.uk

'Stunning location with food to match,' enthused one visitor to this popular eatery located on one of Cornwall's finest beaches and open from breakfast to dinner. The big draw is the sundeck, which is well equipped with background heaters and blankets if it gets too chilly. But plenty of the luminous seaside glow finds its way inside, so book ahead to bag one of the coveted window tables overlooking the sea if the weather isn't cooperating. The kitchen ranges far and wide for culinary influences, turning out good Cornish hen crab with almond gazpacho, sweetcorn custard and caviar, and 'deliciously fresh' battered fish and 'awesome' chips, while a boneless Dover sole paired with braised shin beef gives notice that the menu is not just a paean to seafood; expect, too, dishes such as massaman-style Thai duck curry. Prices are high, but the quality is good and a good-natured team and keenly priced wines from £16.95 help soften the blow.
Chef/s: Michael Smith and Ryan Venning. **Open:** all week L 12 to 4, D 6 to 10. **Closed:** 25 Dec, Jan. **Meals:** alc (main courses £6 to £27). **Details:** 60 seats. 70 seats outside. V menu. Music.

St Kew

St Kew Inn

Ancient charm with locally rooted cooking
Cooking score: 2
Modern British | £27
St Kew, PL30 3HB
Tel no: (01208) 841259
www.stkewinn.co.uk

This ancient rural Cornish pub with its huge wood-burning range, exposed stone, flag floors, beams, well-kept real ale and informal, relaxed atmosphere pleases drinkers and hungry diners in equal measure. Indeed, the convivial way the place is run is a great draw, as is the lovely garden with views of the 15th-century church and river, which comes into its own in fine weather. A starter of home-smoked salmon pâté with toasted carrot bread is typical of the simple, no-nonsense style, and the kitchen generally makes a good fist of mainstream dishes such as fish and chips or sausage, mustard mash and onion gravy. Otherwise there's grilled sand sole with brown shrimp and caper butter, new potatoes and salad, or pheasant, bacon and mushroom pie with sauté potatoes. Among desserts an old-fashioned marmalade sponge and custard stands out. Drink St Austell Brewery ales or wine from £16.
Chef/s: Martin Perkins. **Open:** all week L 12 to 2, D 6 to 9. **Closed:** 25 Dec. **Meals:** alc (main courses £13 to £18). Sun L £12.50 (1 course) to £21.50. **Details:** 70 seats. 100 seats outside. Bar. Parking.

St Mawes
Hotel Tresanton
Stylish seaside bolt-hole
Cooking score: 3
Modern European | £50
27 Lower Castle Road, St Mawes, TR2 5DR
Tel no: (01326) 270055
www.tresanton.com

It may lack the obvious nautical clichés but there's a maritime flavour to the bright, elevated dining room of this sleek boutique hotel. Off-white wood-panelled walls, white mosaic floors and blue-and-white furniture echo the tones of the heavenly view, which takes in harbour, boats, distant hills and a broad expanse of sky. In warm weather there's the option to dine outside on the terrace. The menu borrows greedily from sea and land, steering a classical course with minimal fussy flourishes. A starter of crab, avocado, quail's egg, confit tomato and pea shoots is simple and true, the ingredients fresh and the flavours balanced. A main course of peachy sea trout with new potatoes, perfectly cooked asparagus and hollandaise sauce is equally beguiling – this menu won't win prizes for innovation but for classic, competent handling of prime ingredients you won't go wrong. Pear tarte Tatin (a whole pear half encased in pastry) is a handsome, generous endnote. Several pages of wines from around the globe start at £20.
Chef/s: Paul Wadham. **Open:** all week L 12.30 to 2.30, D 7 to 9.30. **Closed:** 3 weeks Jan. **Meals:** alc (main courses £18 to £32). Set L £23 (2 courses) to £27. **Details:** 55 seats. 70 seats outside. Bar. Wheelchair access. Parking. Children over 6 yrs only at D.

St Merryn
The Cornish Arms
Stein's take on a proper pub
Cooking score: 2
British | £25
Churchtown, St Merryn, PL28 8ND
Tel no: (01841) 532700
www.rickstein.com

Like just about every big-name chef these days, Cornish hero Rick Stein wanted a pub in his portfolio, and has done a good job here – maintaining most of the Cornish Arms' natural assets, while resisting the temptation to go gastro on the food front. Raw stonework, weathered beams and a wood-burning stove set the scene for a proper pub menu that isn't afraid to advertise ploughman's, burgers, sandwiches or scampi 'in a basket'. But this is the Stein brand, so expect diligent local sourcing, fresh fish and real quality – even in the simplest things: bowls of mussels with bread and butter; grilled hake and chips; sausages and mash; rump steaks; blue cheese tart with tomato salad. A few specials such as salt cod fritters keep customers on their toes, while homely desserts might include chocolate torte or apple and blackberry pie. Rick Stein's fingerprints are all over the sharp 24-bin wine list, which starts at £15.95 (£10.90 a carafe).
Chef/s: Alex Clark. **Open:** Mon to Sat L 12 to 3, D 5.30 to 9.30. Sun 12 to 7. **Closed:** 25 Dec.
Meals: alc (main courses £10 to £18). **Details:** 140 seats. 130 seats outside. Bar. Wheelchair access. Music. Parking.

NEW ENTRY
Rafferty's
Buzzy country tapas bar and restaurant
Cooking score: 3
Modern British | £30
St Merryn, PL28 8NF
Tel no: (01841) 521561
www.raffertyscafewinebar.co.uk

It's wise to book at this restaurant-cum-wine bar: its charismatic mix of great drinks, tapas and more substantial main courses has made it deservedly popular. The interior is exactly how a country wine bar should be, with modern-retro touches and lots of natural materials. Owner Ed Rafferty used to manage The Seafood Restaurant in Padstow (see entry) and is very much at home in his first solo venture – the atmosphere is friendly, informal, and the service excellent. Among the tapas, 'deeply flavoured' venison sliders, goats' cheese fritters with honey, and 'superb' squid in soy, ginger and spring onion have impressed, and a main of pan-fried hake with tartare sauce, sautéed potatoes and pea purée is a classy, perfectly executed take on fish and chips. The sunken chocolate cake is soft, sticky, 'melt-in-the-mouth perfection'. The global wine list offers plenty of choice, from £16.50.
Chef/s: Craig Jeffery. **Open:** all week D 5 to 11. **Meals:** alc (main courses £15 to £20). **Details:** 36 seats. 20 seats outside. Bar. Music.

■ Sennen Cove

NEW ENTRY
Ben Tunnicliffe
A real find for food and views
Cooking score: 1
Modern British | £27
Sennen Cove, TR19 7BT
Tel no: (01736) 871191
www.benatsennen.com

The former Beach Restaurant, a wood-framed building with terrace occupying a fabulous spot at Sennen Cove is, as the name change indicates, now run by chef Ben Tunnicliffe, who splits his time between here and the Tolcarne Inn (see entry). Inside, it's all slate floors, wooden beams, surfboards and bikes hanging from the ceiling, while staff in dark blue-and-white Breton tops complete the seaside vibe. Relaxed, familiar and kid-friendly, this is a seriously busy place in season, a real honeypot for tourists during the day (calmer in the evening), with its fish and chips and burgers, but there's also very fresh Newlyn crab on toast and excellent roast monkfish with peperonata, grilled polenta and parsley pesto. Wines from £15.50.
Chef/s: Ben Tunnicliffe and Adam Ashworth. **Open:** all week 11.30 to 9.30. **Closed:** 2 Jan. **Meals:** alc (main courses £9 to £19). **Details:** 80 seats. 80 seats outside. Wheelchair access. Music.

■ Treburley

★ TOP 50 PUB ★
The Springer Spaniel
Smart pub with pitch-perfect food
Cooking score: 4
Modern British | £30
Treburley, PL15 9NS
Tel no: (01579) 370424
www.thespringerspaniel.org.uk

Former Masterchef winner Anton Piotrowski wowed us with the Treby Arms in Devon (see entry) and is doing the same with this homely roadside inn. The approach echoes the Treby's mix of rustic informality and upmarket yet often gutsy British cooking – indeed, some of the dishes are the same. Piotrowski's long-time sous chef Ali Fraiser steers the kitchen, turning out patriotic Scotch eggs and fish and chips alongside classy but unfussy dishes such as cocoa-marinated venison with colcannon and a roast portobello mushroom or pan-fried sea bass with celeriac and sea spaghetti. For dessert, 'Treby's gone carrots' a dish imported from the Treby Arms – is a successful bit of fun comprising warm carrot cake in a plant pot topped with crunchy, malty 'soil' and planted with a single carrot. There's a real commitment to sourcing great local ingredients, and presentation reflects the

country setting – perhaps with too much reliance on wooden serving platters. A respectable global wine list includes plenty by the glass, with bottles starting at £16.50.
Chef/s: Ali Fraiser. **Open:** Tue to Sun L 12 to 3 (2.30 Sun), D 6 to 9 (7.30 Sun). **Closed:** Mon. **Meals:** alc (main courses £14 to £23). Set L £16 (2 courses) to £20. Sun L £16. **Details:** 70 seats. 30 seats outside. Music. Parking.

Treen
The Gurnard's Head
Clifftop pub with a local flavour
Cooking score: 3
British | £30
Treen, TR26 3DE
Tel no: (01736) 796928
www.gurnardshead.co.uk

This remote inn is found on the Atlantic coast between St Ives and St Just, reached via a winding road – but it's worth the effort. Posh frocks are not required, though: it's a relaxed, unstuffy dining pub-with-rooms, a slightly offbeat place with a sophisticated modern edge. There's a proper bar with real ales, but the main interest is in the cooking, which has a feel for combining diverse flavours with a commitment to local produce, especially fish, everything from Newlyn mackerel escabèche with pickled cucumber and radish to pan-fried ray with crushed potatoes, chard, samphire, lemon butter and brown shrimps. Or consider ox tongue with pickled shallot, Parmesan and salsa verde, and Primrose Herd pork belly with brawn, date and five-spice, butternut and charred leeks. Puddings may be fairly traditional in range, but very good – perhaps dark chocolate brownie with praline ice cream. A global wine list opens at £18.
Chef/s: Jack Clayton. **Open:** all week L 12 to 2.30, D 6 to 9.30 (6.30 Sun). **Closed:** 5 days Dec. **Meals:** alc (main courses £13 to £18). Set L £16 (2 courses) to £19. Sun L £18 (2 courses) to £23. **Details:** 80 seats. 20 seats outside. Bar. Music. Parking.

Truro
Tabb's
Gently evolving, sensitive food
Cooking score: 5
Modern British | £35
85 Kenwyn Street, Truro, TR1 3BZ
Tel no: (01872) 262110
www.tabbs.co.uk

The interior of Nigel Tabb's smart little restaurant (formerly a pub) is prettily painted in lilac, its crisp linen-clad tables sporting Riedel glasses and classy tableware. It's an intimate, peaceful setting for Nigel's ever-evolving cooking, which combines excellent ingredients, wide-ranging flavours and classical techniques in a host of interesting dishes. Homemade bread comes highly recommended, as does a 'beautifully cooked and flavoured' starter of scallops with hog's pudding. Glazed goats' cheese with carrot and dukkah salad, radish and mooli, tapenade dressing and couscous crumbs is a smart spin on your average goats' cheese starter, while a main course of seared fillet of beef and braised shin keeps things classic with accompaniments of mushrooms, green peppercorns, celeriac, red pepper hash and horseradish cream. To finish, chocolate marquise is 'elegantly presented and extremely moreish' – and a parting shot of coffee with elderflower-flavoured chocolates delighted one diner. The wine list includes plenty under £25, with prices from £16.95.
Chef/s: Nigel Tabb. **Open:** Tue to Fri L 12 to 2, Tue to Sat D 5.30 to 9 (Sat 6.30). **Closed:** Sun, Mon. **Meals:** alc (main courses £16 to £21). Set L and D £20 (2 courses) to £25. Tapas L £12. **Details:** 28 seats. Bar. Music.

Visit us online

To find out more about The Good Food Guide, please visit thegoodfoodguide.co.uk

Wadebridge
Little Plates

Stylish sharing plates in a relaxed setting
Cooking score: 3
Mediterranean | £19
Polmorla Road, Wadebridge, PL27 7ND
Tel no: (01208) 816377
www.littleplatesbar.co.uk

'Funkily functional', is how one reporter described the lovingly eccentric riot of bright colours, scuffed wood, industrial fittings, vintage plates and open kitchen that makes up this modern tapas bar in the town centre. Owners Rupert and Sarah Wilson have put their heart and soul into the place and take a dressed down, casual approach to things. 'Great plates of food to share with very friendly service' is immediately appealing, and the Mediterranean-orientated cooking delivers grilled aubergine with chickpeas in a tomato, chilli and cumin sauce, arancini with rocket and Parmesan, and Moorish minced lamb on spiced flatbread, all in either small or large portions. One reporter, who 'sat at the bar and sampled most of the menu', singled out pork belly with chorizo and cannellini beans as a standout. Crema catalana makes a smooth, sweet finish. The short wine list starts at £16.75.
Chef/s: Rob Brinham. **Open:** Tue to Sat L 12 to 2, D 6 to 9. **Closed:** Sun, Mon, 25 and 26 Dec. **Meals:** alc (main courses £8 to £13). **Details:** 32 seats. Music.

Watergate Bay
Fifteen Cornwall

Unpretentious Italian cooking, Jamie O style
Cooking score: 4
Italian | £48
On the beach, Watergate Bay, TR8 4AA
Tel no: (01637) 861000
www.fifteencornwall.co.uk

'A joy to visit again,' confirmed one reader of Jamie Oliver's Cornish outpost, which sits above the surf on Watergate Bay. 'The restaurant was almost full,' he went on, 'with half-term children all behaving beautifully' – for which relief, much thanks. Andy Appleton's food can take a large slice of the credit for that, in its vividly flavoured, fresh, attention-capturing way. Buffalo mozzarella with something fruity – perhaps orange, or char-grilled pear – is always a winner, and sets the stage for a pasta in-betweenie such as taglierini with mussels, 'nduja sausage and gremolata, and then precisely timed dry-aged longhorn ribeye with rocket and horseradish, or maybe sea bass in aïoli with baked potato and chard. The directness and lack of pretension are warmly appreciated by regulars, through to finishers like rosewater pannacotta with rhubarb and biscotti, or plum frangipane tart with a splot of clotted cream. Wines listed by grape start at £21.50 for house white from the Veneto.
Chef/s: Andy Appleton. **Open:** all week L 12 to 2.30, D 6.15 to 9.15. **Closed:** 4 to 14 Jan. **Meals:** alc (main courses £19 to £32). Set L £32. Tasting menu £65 (5 courses). **Details:** 121 seats. Bar. Wheelchair access. Music. Parking. Children over 12 yrs only at D.

LOCAL GEM
The Beach Hut

Modern British | £25
Watergate Bay Hotel, Watergate Bay, TR8 4AA
Tel no: (01637) 860877
www.watergatebay.co.uk

'Feel the wind on your face and relish the coolest hangout in Cornwall,' exhorts a fan of this vibrant, laid-back café 'carved out of driftwood in the cliffs'. When the tide is in it feels like you're floating on the waves, but the 'hut' looks good in any weather and the menu takes a something-for-everyone approach – Cornish crab bisque served in a huge Le Creuset pot, Goan fish curry with fluffy lemon rice, lamb meatballs, pulled pork sandwiches, and crème brûlée. Wines from £19. Open all week.

Ambleside

The Drunken Duck Inn

Glorious old inn with modern tucker

Cooking score: 2

Modern British | £35

Barngates, Ambleside, LA22 0NG
Tel no: (015394) 36347
www.drunkenduckinn.co.uk

This old white-painted Lakeland property stands out against the raw, wild landscape, acting like a beacon to passing travellers. And the Drunken Duck truly does have a sense of place. There are smart bedrooms in which to rest weary limbs (those hills can get to you), a proper bar stocked with real ales, including from their own on-site Barngates Brewery, and a menu that packs a punch. During the day it's a case of ordering at the bar – pork shoulder sandwich with guacamole and chipotle mayo, say – while in the evening the restaurant makes for a soothing setting. There's care taken to seek out the best local ingredients: lamb's sweetbreads come with goats' curd, pea and mint, followed by stone bass in a cockle and lemongrass broth, with a creative combination of lemon curd, fennel and olive oil to finish. Wines start at £21.

Chef/s: Jonny Watson. **Open:** all week L 12 to 4, D 6.30 to 9. **Closed:** 25 and 26 Dec. **Meals:** alc (main courses £15 to £22). Sun L £16. **Details:** 60 seats. 60 seats outside. Bar. Parking.

★ TOP 50 ★

BEST NEW RESTAURANT ENTRY

NEW ENTRY

Lake Road Kitchen

A young chef, passionate about his craft

Cooking score: 6

Modern European | £40

Lake Road, Ambleside, LA22 0AD
Tel no: (015394) 22012
www.lakeroadkitchen.co.uk

This little restaurant on Ambleside's main drag is a 'brilliant addition to the area'. James Cross is an inventive, inspired chef, as can be seen in his approach to foraging (gathering, storing and preserving in a very narrow season), his self-imposed restriction of sourcing only northern European ingredients, and his deployment of unusual creative techniques to put 'something unique and delicious in front of his customers'. But it wouldn't work without sure-footed support from his front-of-house team or, indeed, his loyal regulars who are voluble in their support, the detail of dishes lingering passionately in their memories. For one, it was a fat octopus tentacle cooked for three days at 63c, then roasted to produce 'a unique crispy-gooey contrast and a huge amount of toasty, savoury flavour', with dots of fermented wild garlic purée adding a gentle acidic punch, and three great slabs of 'aged' pork shortloin cooked just-pink and 'almost gamey in flavour', served with a salted, roasted turnip, juicy braised gem lettuce, and lots of garlic bud capers delivering zing to a glossy and intense sauce. For another, the highlight was 'stunning' guinea fowl, the skin impossibly crisp, the breast supremely juicy and succulent, the thighs turned into little balls of posh KFC popcorn ('think Clove Club') with the counterpoint of homemade macaroni with dried ceps, a few slices of warm, sharply pickled onions and a sauce 'that was at least 50% beurre noisette'. Good bread, and every wine on the short list available by the fairly priced glass or carafe complete the picture. Bottles from £23.

Chef/s: James Cross. **Open:** Wed to Sun D only 6 to 10. **Closed:** Mon, Tue, 22 to 28 Dec. **Meals:** alc (main courses £19 to £30). Tasting Menu £65. **Details:** 30 seats. Music.

Old Stamp House

Ambitious regional modern cooking
Cooking score: 4
Modern British | £39
Church Street, Ambleside, LA22 0BU
Tel no: (015394) 32775
www.oldstamphouse.com

Although he went on to become Poet Laureate, Wordsworth also had an illustrious 30-year career as distributor of stamps for Westmorland, and this is where he worked. Ryan Blackburn's keen eye for a venue with potential led to his opening this basement dining room in early 2014, bringing contemporary regional food to a county still often stuck on country-house autopilot. The local accent is strong. Herdwick hogget from a local farm comes in Westmorland tatie-pot (think hotpot), roe deer is from the Cartmel valley, served with parsnip purée, braised chicory and salsify. Fish has a longer journey, but one that's worth it for a starter of Loch Duart salmon with brown shrimps in spiced mead velouté. Enthusiastic spring reporters enjoyed rabbit with wild garlic, pickled mushrooms and lobster mayonnaise ('the flavours were a delight'), and brill with spring veg and Jersey Royals. Dessert might be Cumbrian gingerbread parfait with rhubarb in poached, purée and sorbet manifestations. An exhaustively annotated wine list opens with Languedoc house blends at £19.90.

Chef/s: Ryan Blackburn. **Open:** Tue to Sat L 12.30 to 2, D 6 to 9. **Closed:** Sun, Mon, 25 and 26 Dec, 2 weeks Jan. **Meals:** alc (main courses £18 to £25). Set L £19 (2 courses) to £23. **Details:** 30 seats. V menu. Music.

Bowland Bridge

LOCAL GEM
Hare & Hounds
British | £25
Bowland Bridge, LA11 6NN
Tel no: (015395) 68333
www.hareandhoundsbowlandbridge.co.uk

'A very welcoming place on a miserable March weekend,' thought a visitor to this 17th-century inn-with-rooms in the heart of the South Lakes. Whether you're in need of sustenance after a ramble or a cosy evening meal next to a log fire, you will get tasty honest food. The traditional menu shows off local produce: beef and ale pie made with Hare of the Dog ale; lamb hotpot with Fell House Farm lamb; a very good ribeye steak 'cooked perfectly' or hearty ploughman's with

Cumbrian smoked meats and cheeses. Wines start from £14.95. Accommodation. Open all week.

Bowness-on-Windermere
Linthwaite House

Quality cooking at a delightful hotel
Cooking score: 5
Modern British | £52
Crook Road, Bowness-on-Windermere, LA23 3JA
Tel no: (015394) 88600
www.linthwaite.com

£5 OFF 🍷 🛏

Judging by its wooded vantage point looking down to Lake Windermere, Linthwaite was built for an Edwardian gentleman who evidently had a keen eye for a view. Today it's the guests of the hotel who get to benefit, and to linger awhile in its stylish conservatory lounge, retro-looking bar, and the three dining rooms that make up the smart, Regency-esque restaurant. Chris O'Callaghan cooks in the modern British vein, using prime regional ingredients and showing adroit technical abilities. There are decidedly contemporary ideas in play with scallop ceviche with pressed leek, peanut and lime, and octopus carpaccio with the sweet/sharp hit of blood orange. Move on to roasted sirloin of beef, which avoids any hint of traditionalism by the company it keeps – cavolo nero purée, sarladaise potato and snail bonbon. Roasted halibut is a dynamic fishy number, with meaty merguez sausage, and desserts might include rhubarb (poached and parfait) with yoghurt sorbet and toasted oats. The wine list makes good reading and good drinking; bottles from £20.50.
Chef/s: Chris O'Callaghan. **Open:** all week L 12 to 2, D 7 to 9. **Meals:** Set L £15 (2 courses) to £20. Set D £52 (4 courses). Sun L £25. **Details:** 60 seats. Bar. Wheelchair access. Music. Parking. Children over 7 yrs only.

Braithwaite
The Cottage in the Wood

Bold cooking and breathtaking views
Cooking score: 4
Modern British | £45
Magic Hill, Whinlatter Forest, Braithwaite, CA12 5TW
Tel no: (01768) 778409
www.thecottageinthewood.co.uk

£5 OFF 🛏

The 'Wood' of the title actually refers to the rugged, mountainous reaches of Whinlatter Forest – a favourite with Lakeland fell-walking legend and author AW Wainwright. Nowadays, however, this boutique 17th-century inn stakes its claim as a kind-hearted foodie destination rather than a hiker's refuelling point, with an attractive semi-circular dining room at the heart of things. Soak up the arboreal vistas and the prospect of mighty Skiddaw while considering a concise seasonal menu peppered with clipped, pithy dish descriptions: 'chestnut-morcilla-truffle'; 'scallop-satay-radish-lime', 'chocolate-cherry-Kirsch', and so on. Diligently sourced regional ingredients take centre stage here, from Cartmel duck with apricot and vanilla or Whitehaven turbot with mussels, cauliflower and Guinness to Cumbrian lamb with crispy hogget, broccoli and artichoke. This is bold, carefully considered cooking with just enough risky business to keep diners on their toes – how about a wild-sounding dessert involving Arctic roll, fig, pistachio and green tea. There's also a simplified no-choice set menu for residents, while the 60-bin wine list offers reasonably priced drinking from £19.95 (£4.75 a glass).
Chef/s: Chris Archer. **Open:** Tue to Sat L 12.30 to 2, D 6 to 9. **Closed:** Sun, Mon, Jan. **Meals:** Set L £21 (2 courses) to £25. Set D £45. Tasting menu £50 (5 courses) to £65 (7 courses). **Details:** 20 seats. 40 seats outside. V menu. Wheelchair access. Parking. Children over 10 yrs only at D.

Brampton
Farlam Hall
Charming country house hotel
Cooking score: 3
Modern British | £48
Brampton, CA8 2NG
Tel no: (016977) 46234
www.farlamhall.co.uk

Overlooking the landscaped gardens and ornamental lake, Farlam Hall is a charming country house hotel of the old school. It's been in the Quinion family for 40 years and offers just the sort of finely tuned hospitality that both visitors and locals appreciate. The dining room has an air of refined elegance with its antiques, white napery and polished silverware, while Barry Quinion's concise set-price menu follows the country house tradition of a single sitting for dinner at 8pm. The cooking is based on classic technique and an abundance of regional ingredients. Parsnip and ginger soup might be one of the three starters, whilst Cumbrian pork, Lancashire guinea fowl and Gressingham duckling could all make appearances among main courses, the last perhaps turning up pan-roasted with apple and sultana risotto, cranberry and port wine sauce. For dessert, perhaps lemon, honey and pistachio mousse with fruit coulis. A short, global wine list opens at £22.

Chef/s: Barry Quinion. **Open:** all week D only 8 for 8.30 (1 sitting). **Closed:** 25 to 30 Dec, 4 to 21 Jan. **Meals:** Set D £48 (4 courses). **Details:** 40 seats. Parking. Children over 5 yrs only.

Please send us your feedback

To register your opinion about any restaurant listed in this guide, or a new restaurant that you wish to bring to our attention, please visit the web address at the bottom of the page. Your feedback informs the content of the book and will be used to compile next year's reviews.

Cartmel

L'Enclume
One of the world's greatest restaurants
Cooking score: 10
Modern British | £120
Cavendish Street, Cartmel, LA11 6PZ
Tel no: (015395) 36362
www.lenclume.co.uk

Even in high season, Cartmel doesn't get flustered. There's not much to fluster – a few tearooms and souvenir shops to browse around, as well as the partly 12th-century Priory that stood fast against the gale of the Dissolution. And the UK's greatest restaurant. The stone-built forge, for such it was, next to the tiny River Eea, is the unassuming location for an undoubted pinnacle of the new British cooking. It achieves its apogee in Simon Rogan's repertoire, now divided among various locations, including nearby Rogan & Company (see entry) and pooling out towards Manchester and London. Tom Barnes is the virtuoso performer here, producing a lengthy menu of singular creations sourced from the venue's own expanding farmland – the cooking being of its landscape as well as of its time. Many dishes have become long-running masterpieces, in particular the Cartmel valley venison tartare infused in charcoal oil with 'a gorgeous boule of fennel and a local mustard cream', while Holker milk-fed lamb (loin and belly) with onions cooked off in whey, ramson leaves and flowers and potato, and 'a juicy, flavourful pack of three artichokes' (Japanese, Jerusalem and globe) enclosed in a wonderful Jerusalem crisp with excellent local goats' cheese and perched on a stout vinegar smear, reveal a rusticity of their components balanced with airy delicacy of construction and infectious playfulness. Desserts, too, are shot through with seasonal fragrances: a 'really special' apple tart with gingerbread ice cream with birch sap, oat granola and muscovado caramel tuile, and a spectacular sheeps' milk ice cream with granita and chunks of lovely

Join us at thegoodfoodguide.co.uk

rhubarb, sweet wafers and 'delightful sorrel leaf and smear'. The service tempo for 'six amuses, six starters and mains and five palate cleansers and desserts' is just right. Prearranged wine flights are the obvious way to sort out the drinking. One reporter felt that wine advice was not as freely forthcoming as it might be, which seems a shame when there is a magisterial list to celebrate, at prices that are by no means silly for the pedigree. Bottles start at £33.

Chef/s: Simon Rogan and Tom Barnes. **Open:** Wed to Sun L 12 to 1.30, all week D 6.30 to 8.30. **Closed:** 7 to 13, 25 and 26 Dec, 1 week Jan. **Meals:** Set L £45. Set D £120. **Details:** 55 seats. V menu. Wheelchair access. Parking. Children over 12 yrs only.

Rogan & Company

Imaginative brasserie cooking
Cooking score: 5
Modern British | £37
The Square, Cartmel, LA11 6QD
Tel no: (015395) 35917
www.roganandcompany.co.uk

Joined at the hip to the legendary Enclume in the edibly lovely village of Cartmel, Simon Rogan's second venue adopts a winning brasserie formula, with a neat mix of interior style points, sleek steel pillars supporting the ancient beamed ceiling. Service is endearing and relaxed in equal measure, and new chef Ashley Bennett maintains the cracking pace set by predecessors with finely conceived, gutsily seasoned dishes of distinct imagination. Start gently with a slab of duck terrine, dressed with plum compote and pickled ginger, before proceeding to well-judged main dishes like crisp-skinned bream fillets on a rollicking cassoulet of shrimps, chorizo, kohrabi and beans, or tender lamb rump chafed in cumin and bedded on wilted spring greens and smoked tomato in a zinging lime dressing. Refreshing lightness is the hallmark of a dessert that matches slices and gel cubes of blood orange with tonka ice

cream and a dribble of butterscotched miso. A short page of wines is perfectly serviceable, from £20.

Chef/s: Ashley Bennett. **Open:** Tue to Sat L 12 to 2, Mon to Sat D 6.30 to 9. **Closed:** Sun. **Meals:** alc (main courses £13 to £25). **Details:** 40 seats. Wheelchair access. Music.

▮ Clifton

George & Dragon

Lakeland pub with serious local connections
Cooking score: 3
Modern British | £30
Clifton, CA10 2ER
Tel no: (01768) 865381
www.georgeanddragonclifton.co.uk

When local estate owner Charles Lowther took on the George & Dragon back in 2008, he set about transforming this 18th-century coaching inn into a forward-thinking pub with serious regional connections. The interior is now a thoughtful and confident blend of slate, oak, coir and other natural materials, while the food is big on provenance. Organically reared rare-breed meats, free-range chickens and seasonal gleanings from nearby pastures and hedgerows are teamed up with ingredients from top Lakeland producers for a menu full of imaginative ideas and assertive flavours. Shorthorn beef from the estate appears in the form of steaks, burgers and twice-cooked rissoles (served with wild mushrooms, spring onions and port sauce), but there's much more besides – from venison liver accompanied by truffle-scented braised potatoes, caramelised sprouts and juniper jus to Saddleback pork (perhaps served 'osso buco' with saffron tagliatelle). Fish also gets a look-in, while desserts could include Askham apple and treacle toffee crumble – a neat twist on a Lakeland classic. A well-annotated global wine list starts at £16.50.

Chef/s: Ian Jackson. **Open:** all week L 12 to 2.30, D 6 to 9. **Closed:** 26 Dec. **Meals:** alc (main courses £13 to £18). Set L and D £15 (2 courses) to £19. **Details:** 104 seats. 60 seats outside. Bar. Music. Parking.

Cockermouth
Quince & Medlar

Long-serving Lakeland veggie
Cooking score: 2
Vegetarian | £27
11-13 Castlegate, Cockermouth, CA13 9EU
Tel no: (01900) 823579
www.quinceandmedlar.co.uk

Banish any preconceptions of what a vegetarian restaurant should look like, for the Q&M occupies a delicious Georgian property with a rather handsome interior. Colin and Louisa Le Voi arrived way back in 1989, steeped in the traditions of Lakeland hospitality (at Sharrow Bay no less), and set about creating a vegetarian restaurant of ambition and integrity. Passion for the local landscape is reflected in the artworks on the walls and the ingredients that arrive in the kitchen, with vegan and wheat-free options listed as such on the menu. The wine list is entirely organic and vegetarian (and mostly vegan). Mini millet muffins enriched with cheese and sun-dried tomatoes come in a first course with Kalamata olive tapenade and dressed leaves, which could be followed by a complex construction of leeks cooked in red wine, watercress soufflé, poached pear and red pepper sauce. Finish with rhubarb pannacotta or the decidely un-vegan cheeseboard. Wines from £17.

Chef/s: Colin Le Voi. **Open:** Tue to Sat D only 6.30 to 9.30. **Closed:** Sun, Mon, 24 to 26 Dec. **Meals:** alc (main courses £15). **Details:** 26 seats. V menu. Music. Children over 5 yrs only.

Crosthwaite
The Punch Bowl Inn

Smartly reinvented Lakeland inn
Cooking score: 3
Modern British | £32
Lyth Valley, Crosthwaite, LA8 8HR
Tel no: (015395) 68237
www.the-punchbowl.co.uk

The 'unspoilt pastoral delights' of the Lyth Valley provide a lovely backdrop to this smartly reinvented stone-built Lakeland inn, which creates quite an impression with its slate floors, framed prints and elegant *Country Living* accoutrements. Regional ingredients are given some creative oomph on a thoughtfully crafted menu that might range from venison tartare with blue cheese, capers and smoked egg yolk purée to Morecambe Bay shrimps brightened up with pickled cucumber, lemon and radish salad. Elsewhere, roast cod loin is dressed with cider, mussels, leeks and smoked bacon, while pork fillet and black pudding are partnered by salt-baked celeriac, cabbage and the Lyth Valley's famous damsons. These plump beauties are also transformed into soufflés, ice creams, chutneys and vinegars, while roast local beef is the juicy star of the show on Sundays. Warm-hearted service, reasonable prices and locally brewed ales at the bar suit the Punch Bowl's boozy roots. Carefully chosen wines start at £21.95.

Chef/s: Scott Fairweather. **Open:** all week L 12 to 5.30 (4 Sat and Sun), D 5.30 to 8.30. **Meals:** alc (main courses £15 to £20). **Details:** 85 seats. 48 seats outside. Bar. Music. Parking.

Join us at thegoodfoodguide.co.uk

Culgaith
Mrs Miller's
Unpretentious, classy cooking
Cooking score: 3
British | £27
Hazel Dene Garden Centre, Culgaith,
CA10 1QF
Tel no: (01768) 882520
www.mrsmillersculgaith.co.uk

It seems that chef-proprietor James Cowin and his team are building quite a reputation at this café-cum-restaurant housed in a 'higgledy-piggledy' garden centre. There are no plush furnishings or fancy crockery but it doesn't matter, 'the food is what counts'. Whether weekday lunches or weekend dinners there is an emphasis on the local and home-grown from breads and hearty soups, say leek and celeriac, to the more elaborate pork and pistachio terrine, sea bass on prawn risotto and grilled Low Howgill Farm shorthorn beef sirloin steak with red wine and shallot sauce, a little Stilton salad and proper home-cut chips. At inspection, 'superb quality and perfectly cooked' hake came with excellent cauliflower purée, toasted almonds and saffron cream sauce, while honey and whiskey crème brûlée made a superb final. Prices, too, are very reasonable for cooking of this quality, and there's a limited wine list, which starts at £12.50.
Chef/s: James Cowin. **Open:** all week L 11.30 to 3, Fri and Sat D 7 to 9. **Closed:** 25 and 26 Dec, Easter Sun. **Meals:** alc (main courses £14 to £18). Set L £14 (2 courses) to £16. Set D £20 (2 courses) to £25. Sun L £14. **Details:** 54 seats. 20 seats outside. V menu. Wheelchair access. Music. Parking.

Visit us online

To find out more about
The Good Food Guide, please
visit thegoodfoodguide.co.uk

Grasmere
The Jumble Room
Global cooking in the heart of Lakeland
Cooking score: 1
Global | £40
Langdale Road, Grasmere, LA22 9SU
Tel no: (015394) 35188
www.thejumbleroom.co.uk

Andy and Chrissy Hill have run this cheerful restaurant for nigh on 20 years and it's still just the ticket for Grasmere visitors looking for evening sustenance – just make sure you bag a ground-floor table to make the most of the lively atmosphere. Giant cow paintings, black-and-white photos of jazz artists and a music-fuelled atmosphere form the backdrop to colourful cooking that roams round the globe, mixing European ways, Asian flavours and local produce. Expect curried cauliflower and spring onion bhajias, braised shoulder of lamb with a root vegetable and pearl barley casserole or halibut with lightly curried mussel and seasonal vegetable chowder. Wines from £15.99.
Chef/s: Simon Boden and Darren McGuigan.
Open: all week D only 5.30 to 9.30. **Closed:** 12 to 27 Dec. **Meals:** alc (main courses £17 to £24).
Details: 50 seats. Music.

Oak Bank Hotel
Simple surroundings, seriously good cooking
Cooking score: 3
Modern British | £40
Broadgate, Grasmere, LA22 9TA
Tel no: (015394) 35217
www.lakedistricthotel.co.uk

Darren Cornish's cooking, judging by reports, is fast putting this modest Grasmere hotel on the foodie destination map. A pleasant dining room overlooking a lovely garden is the setting for some 'really ambitious' cooking. A local lad, Darren likes to use local ingredients so expect starters of goats' cheese and baby leek terrine with Grasmere gingerbread, beetroot sorbet and pickled vegetables or hand-picked crab, onion seed and lime doughnut with brown crab pannacotta, citrus and confit egg yolk. The local theme continues with main of Herdwick lamb (served with potato terrine, courgette and basil purée) or wild brill with Morecambe Bay shrimps (and herb gnocchi, asparagus and hazelnut velouté). Desserts show a sense of fun and nostalgia – Arctic roll being in this case mango-flavoured with pistachio sponge, coconut sorbet, macaroon and passion fruit gel, or there could be BFG, a Black Forest gâteau with cherry sorbet and cherry gel. Wine prices start at £16.95.

Chef/s: Darren Cornish. **Open:** all week L 12.30 to 1.30, D 6.30 to 8.30. **Closed:** Christmas, 3 weeks Jan, 1 week May and Aug. **Meals:** Set L £23 (2 courses) to £26. Set D £40. Sun L £23. **Details:** 30 seats. 12 seats outside. V menu. Music. Parking. Children over 10 yrs only in restaurant.

Great Urswick
The General Burgoyne

Hospitable Lakeland pub
Cooking score: 2
Modern British | £29
Church Road, Great Urswick, LA12 0SZ
Tel no: (01229) 586394
www.generalburgoyne.com

Pitched midway between Dalton and Ulverston, this spruced-up 17th-century boozer remains generous with its hospitality and hasn't forgotten those inestimable pubby virtues – real ales, lingering Sunday roasts with live music, afternoon teas, steaks and pies, all served by 'relaxed, enthusiastic staff'. That's the deal for walkers, hikers and tourists in the beamed and fire-warmed snugs, but there's more culinary action in the contemporary Orangery restaurant, where chef Craig Sherrington has plenty of surprises in store. A jokey starter called 'East meets Westmorland' involves spring onion bhaji, local smoked cheese, coriander cress and curry oil, while mains span everything from classic roast rump of Duddon Valley lamb with dauphinois potatoes, Savoy cabbage and

rosemary jus to baked salmon fillet with curly kale, carrot and cardamom butter sauce. The specials menu generally features some more inventive ideas, and there's toffee, vodka and praline profiteroles for afters, or sticky toffee pudding for the traditionalists. Wines from £14.

Chef/s: Craig Sherrington. **Open:** Tue to Sat L 12 to 2, D 5 to 9. Sun 12 to 8. **Closed:** Mon, 26 Dec, first week Jan. **Meals:** alc (main courses £11 to £25). Set L and D £10 (2 courses). Sun L £18. **Details:** 50 seats. 12 seats outside. Bar. Music. Parking.

Kirkby Lonsdale
Carter at the Sun Inn

Olde-worlde charm, modern cooking
Cooking score: 2
Modern British | £32
6 Market Street, Kirkby Lonsdale, LA6 2AU
Tel no: (015242) 71965
www.sun-inn.info

Kirkby Lonsdale is a charming historic market town in a beautiful spot. At its heart is Lucy and Mark Fuller's well-heeled, stone-built 17th-century inn, a popular operation run as a proper local (a rustic beamed bar, real fire, real ales) and dining destination (rich colours, polished wood, soft lighting). It's beloved by regulars who praise the courteous service and attention to detail, which extends to Sam Carter's 'careful but innovative' food that is an interesting mix of seasonal produce, sound cooking and wide-ranging influences. Come for lunch and there could be game samosa with masala chickpeas, and roast chicken and leek puff pastry pie. More adventurous ideas appear at dinner, say 'extremely good' scallops with morteau sausage to start, followed by gurnard teamed with a thick-sauced bouillabaisse, smoked mussels and red pepper rouille, and a 'large and quite delicious' rhubarb crème brûlée to finish. Wines from £17.50.

Chef/s: Sam Carter. **Open:** Tue to Sun L 12 to 3, Mon to Sun D 6.30 to 9 (9.30 Fri and Sat). **Meals:** alc (main courses £15 to £28). Set L £22 (2 courses) to

£28. Set D £27 (2 courses). Sun L £14 (1 course) to £23. **Details:** 42 seats. V menu. Bar. Wheelchair access. Music.

 Lupton

LOCAL GEM
The Plough
British | £27
Cow Brow, Lupton, LA6 1PJ
Tel no: (015395) 67700
www.theploughatlupton.co.uk

£5 OFF

Handy for junction 36 of the M6, travellers call into this smartly refurbished roadside inn for good value, hospitality and food that shows plenty of flair. Free-range chicken with fondant potato, wild mushrooms and baby leeks, Cumberland Ale battered haddock with chunky chips, and slow-cooked pheasant breast with Puy lentils, streaky bacon and red wine jus fly the flag for local produce, with desserts such as stem ginger and black treacle parkin bringing up the rear. Wines from £16.95. Open all week. Accommodation.

 Ulverston
The Bay Horse
Romantic charm and breathtaking views
Cooking score: 3
Modern British | £37
Canal Foot, Ulverston, LA12 9EL
Tel no: (01229) 583972
www.thebayhorsehotel.co.uk

From the foot of the Ulverston Canal, the views across the bracing expanses of Morecambe Bay will take your breath away – especially when the sun goes down. No wonder this former coaching inn enthrals visitors with its romantic charms, dreamy vistas and finely honed hospitality. Lunch revolves around soup, sandwiches and 'light bites' in the bar, while dinner at 8pm in the green-toned conservatory-style restaurant is the main event – seascapes included. The kitchen shows its pedigree with a succession of skilfully wrought Anglo-European dishes ranging from toasted goats' cheese with celery, grape and rocket salad to home-cured corned beef with white pudding mash or pot-roast guinea fowl with mushrooms and rosemary. Aberdeen Angus steaks are a top seller and there are a few South African intrusions from the likes of bobotie and malva pudding (a sticky, syrupy apricot number). Meanwhile, Cape vineyards have a big say on the global wine list; bottles from £17.
Chef/s: Robert Lyons. **Open:** Tue to Sun L 12 to 2, all week D 7.30 for 8. **Meals:** alc (main courses £16 to £27). **Details:** 40 seats. 20 seats outside. V menu. Bar. Music. Parking. Children over 10 yrs only at D.

 Watermillock
Rampsbeck Country House Hotel
Gracious comforts and fine modern food
Cooking score: 5
Anglo-French | £51
Watermillock, CA11 0LP
Tel no: (017684) 86442
www.rampsbeck.co.uk

A classic country house with immaculate grounds on the shores of Ullswater, this is a setting fit for an Agatha Christie mystery. Expect oil paintings, oak panelling and flock wallpaper aplenty, along with gleaming antiques and big sofas by crackling fires. The menu promises a 'taste of Cumbria' and it doesn't disappoint: Ben Wilkinson's classic but clever four-to-five course menus might offer salad of West Coast Cumbrian crab with watercress, brown crab custard, paprika bread sticks and saffron mayonnaise, then seared hare loin with salt baked turnip, quince, soused turnips, kale, chard and sherry cream dressing or roast loin of Herdwick hogget with haggis, turnips, burnt leeks, braised Herdwick shoulder and mash with toasted oats and thyme infused sauce. A dark chocolate delice with salted caramel truffle and a feuilletine crisp is a stylish way to finish. The

substantial wine list covers classic and lesser-known wine producing areas and offers plenty by the glass. Bottles start at £19.50.
Chef/s: Ben Wilkinson. **Open:** all week L 12 to 2, D 6.30 to 9. **Closed:** 5 days Jan. **Meals:** Set L £32. Set D £51 (3 courses) to £69. Sun L £32. **Details:** 40 seats. 12 seats outside. V menu. Bar. Wheelchair access. Music. Parking. Children over 10 yrs only.

Windermere

Gilpin Hotel & Lake House

TV winner in an Edwardian Lakeland lodge
Cooking score: 5
Modern British | £58
Crook Road, Windermere, LA23 3NE
Tel no: (015394) 88818
www.thegilpin.co.uk

The Edwardian lodge is securely hidden along a B-road a few miles from Bowness, once the perfect bolt-hole for an owner whose lungs had been ravaged in the Great War. Set amid delightful country gardens, it opens up in a succession of gorgeously appointed lounges and dining rooms inside. *Chefs on Trial* winner Hrishikesh Desai arrived in late winter 2014, and brings exquisite modern culinary sensibility to the regionally based prix-fixe menus. Salt cod in red wine with cockles, smoked garlic, almonds and shimejis might be the prelude to rolled Old Spot belly with caramelised apple in five-spice sauce, and then blackberry soufflé with gin-and-tonic sorbet to conclude. Lunch takes a different tack for a refined country-pub repertoire: grilled brill with chips in their skins, rogan josh with cumin rice, lovely lemon posset with pink grapefruit jelly. A masterful wine list accompanies, with concise but inspired selections from each region. Wines by the glass could use an overhaul; six-month-old St-Chinian twanging with new-ferment acidity is a bit of a turn-off. Bottles start at £28.
Chef/s: Hrishikesh Desai. **Open:** all week L 12 to 2, D 6 to 9. **Meals:** Set L £30. Set D £58 (4 courses). Sun L £35. Tasting menu £85. **Details:** 58 seats. 26 seats outside. V menu. Bar. Parking. Children over 7 yrs only.

Holbeck Ghyll

The straight and narrow road to excellence
Cooking score: 6
Modern British | £75
Holbeck Lane, Windermere, LA23 1LU
Tel no: (015394) 32375
www.holbeckghyll.com

We do tend to go on a bit about the setting of Holbeck Ghyll, but seeing is believing. The opulent lounge and oak-panelled interlinked dining rooms look out over Windermere, the lake a burnished mirror on a serene evening, with cloud-topped peaks rising behind it. Staff do their level best from greeting to farewell to make all feel welcome in these grandiose surroundings, and David McLaughlin's cooking is once more on the straight and narrow course to excellence. Menus don't do anything to make the dishes sound as spectacular as they are, but the evidence comes thick and fast, from superlative crab tian with pellets of pink grapefruit jelly and avocado purée, or marinated salmon on granola with apple sorbet, to brilliant treatments of thoroughbred meats. Aberdeen Angus turns up with wasabi mash and fondant celeriac, venison loin with juniper berries, beetroot sticks and wilted spinach. Desserts seal the deal with impressive complex assemblages like Cointreau parfait wrapped in pistachio sponge with pistachio ice cream, cranberry jelly, crunchy bits of meringue and piles of sherbet. A wine list to suit the occasion offers plenty of mature bottles to go at, from £29.
Chef/s: David McLaughlin. **Open:** all week L 12.30 to 1.30, D 6.30 to 9.30. **Closed:** first 2 weeks Jan. **Meals:** Set L £35 (2 courses) to £45. Set D £75. Sun L £35. Gourmet menu £95. **Details:** 46 seats. V menu. Bar. Wheelchair access. Music. Parking. Children over 8 yrs only.

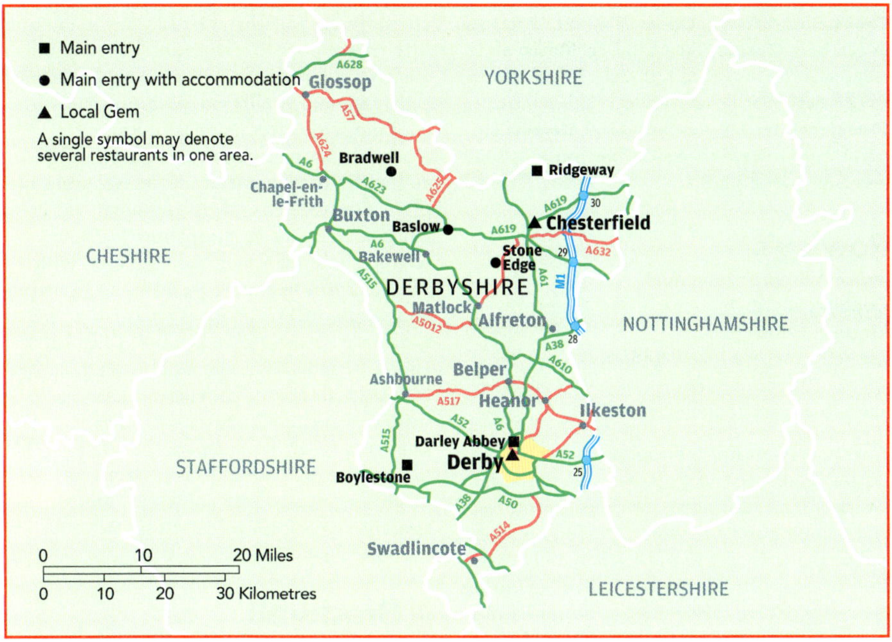

Baslow

Fischer's Baslow Hall

Modernist menus in a faux-Jacobean setting
Cooking score: 7
Modern European | £72
Calver Road, Baslow, DE45 1RR
Tel no: (01246) 583259
www.fischers-baslowhall.co.uk

If you're new to the Peak District, Baslow Hall makes a pretty good start. Perched at the edge of the Chatsworth estate, with Bakewell only four miles distant, it's a peach of a place, a stone-built Edwardian impression of a Jacobean manor house in five acres of gardens. A kitchen garden supplies much of Rupert Rowley's production, beehives included, and dining options extend from the swagged and mullioned tradition of the dining room to the kitchen bench, where 'it was fascinating to see five chefs prepare our tasting menu, as well as everybody else's lunches'. The cooking is thoroughgoing British modernism, the sort of style that delivers much gratification to those attuned to it. Scallops dressed in ponzu with a sesame rice cracker seem almost ordinary when there's sea bass with radicchio and sea herbs alongside Parmesan and mascarpone risotto to go at. Presentations can be intriguing, as when lemon sole appears tightly rolled amid an allium storm of leeks, crispy onions and green onion sauce, and prime materials are reliably excellent, such as the White Peak lamb that includes pinkly roasted best end and crisply pané sweetbread on lemon purée with chickpeas and Hispi. The pre-dessert that involved a rip-roaring gooseberry granita was 'certainly a wake-up call', and raspberry soufflé is of awesome intensity, even outshouting its accompanying pistachio ice cream. There have been reports of the odd dish lacking impact, but not many. An authoritative wine list offers some of the brightest and the best of five continents at a democratic range of prices, starting at £22, or £5.50 a glass.

Chef/s: Rupert Rowley. **Open:** all week L 12 to 1.30, D 7 to 8.30. **Closed:** 25 and 26 Dec. **Meals:** alc L only (main courses £25 to £30). Set L £20 (2 courses) to £27. Set D £55 (2 courses) to £72. Sun L £32. Tasting menu £60 (8 courses) to £80. **Details:** 60 seats. V menu. Bar. Parking. Children over 5 yrs at L (exc Sun); over 8 yrs at D.

Rowley's

Stylish all-purpose venue
Cooking score: 1
Modern British | £32
Church Lane, Baslow, DE45 1RY
Tel no: (01246) 583880
www.rowleysrestaurant.co.uk

A cool, easy-rolling sibling of Fischer's at Baslow Hall (see entry), Rowley's has a certain swagger with its modish interiors, purple hues and contemporary artwork. The food is spot-on for the setting, and the kitchen delivers a line-up of appetising brasserie dishes spanning everything from crispy duck spring rolls and smoked haddock risotto with a poached egg to ox cheek bourguignon and pan-fried hake with chorizo, mussels, saffron potatoes and haricot beans. 'One of the very best traditional Sunday roasts ever' completes a fine package, while service 'can't be bettered'. Wines from £17.45.
Chef/s: Jason Kendra. **Open:** Tue to Sun L 12 to 2.30 (3 Sun), Tue to Sat D 5.30 to 9 (6 to 9.30 Sat). **Closed:** Mon, 25 Dec, bank hols. **Meals:** alc (main courses £16 to £21). Set L £16 (2 courses) to £20. Sun L £23 to £28. **Details:** 84 seats. Bar. Wheelchair access. Music. Parking.

■ Boylestone
The Lighthouse Restaurant

Shining bright in Derbyshire
Cooking score: 3
Modern British | £40
New Road, Boylestone, DE6 5AA
Tel no: (01335) 330658
www.the-lighthouse-restaurant.co.uk

The Lighthouse couldn't be much less coastal, but as a foodie beacon in Derbyshire, it shines. Customers are 'extremely happy' with the food

and service at Jonathan Hardy's airy restaurant, offbeat due both to its location behind a pub and its limited opening hours. Catch it at the right time and you'll find solid modern British cooking with a fresh, appealing touch, alongside less patriotic dishes like miso black cod with a duck wonton and orange and soy glaze. Details such as the toffee apple and crisp chicken skin used to complement Orkney scallops, and the sea vegetables served with wild Cornish halibut, help both the à la carte and tasting menu (which is reasonably priced) keep pace with culinary fashion. To finish, the chocolate sphere with peanut butter ganache, candied walnuts and salted caramel sauce is a reader favourite. Wines start at £14.95.
Chef/s: Jonathan Hardy. **Open:** Sun L 12 to 4, Thur to Sat D 7 to 12. **Closed:** Mon to Wed, 1 to 14 Jan. **Meals:** alc (main courses £24 to £25). **Details:** 36 seats. Bar. Wheelchair access. Music. Parking. Children at Sun L only.

■ Bradwell
The Samuel Fox Inn

Cut-above country pub
Cooking score: 3
British | £27
Stretfield Road, Bradwell, S33 9JT
Tel no: (01433) 621562
www.samuelfox.co.uk

This smartly refurbished Peak District inn on the edge of the village is 'a beacon for good food' according to one reader. It's also valued for its comfortable, contemporary feel, for friendly and welcoming service and for chef/proprietor James Duckett's sharply focused seasonal flavours. Pheasant could feature in winter, perhaps a roast breast with braised leg, with cabbage, Madeira and parsnips, alongside the likes of beef cheeks braised in red wine with violet potatoes, roasted leeks and ox tongue croquette. Tortello of goats' cheese with basil, beetroot and pecan nuts, and a cauliflower and chorizo soup have been show-stopping starters, and there's been praise for the homemade bread. Desserts, meanwhile, have ranged from a pitch-perfect white chocolate cheesecake with raspberry to a fruity ensemble of fig roll, Amaretto, banana bread and caramel ice cream. Plenty of affordable wines line up on the thoughtful global list, with bottles from £17.50.

Chef/s: James Duckett. **Open:** Thur to Sat L 12 to 2, Wed to Sat D 6 to 9. Sun 1 to 8. **Closed:** Mon, Tue, first 2 weeks Jan. **Meals:** alc (main courses £14 to £19). Set D £15 (2 courses) to £20. **Details:** 40 seats. 40 seats outside. Wheelchair access. Music. Parking.

 Chesterfield

Calabria

Italian | £30

30 Glumangate, Chesterfield, S40 1TX
Tel no: (01246) 559944
www.calabriacucina.co.uk

This punchy little Italian eatery on the cobbled and marvellously named named Glumangate caters for all comers: you can drop by for breakfast, coffee or a full meal. The menu is written in Italian as well as English, and the kitchen has a modern outlook. Roast breast of wood pigeon with roasted potatoes, celeriac textures and jus is a typical starter – followed, perhaps, by rack of lamb with rosemary potato terrine, garlic and parsley purée and purple sprouting broccoli. To finish, try the 'deconstructed tiramisu'. An almost exclusively Italian wine list opens at £16.50.

Darley Abbey

Darleys

Tourist hot spot with ambitious cooking
Cooking score: 3
Modern British | £38
Darley Abbey Mills, Haslams Lane, Darley Abbey, DE22 1DZ
Tel no: (01332) 364987
www.darleys.com

Occupying a converted cotton mill by the River Derwent, with a World Heritage site all around, Darleys is tailor-made for tourists and family gatherings. The kitchen rises to the challenge with a repertoire of ambitious and 'faultlessly executed' dishes in the contemporary British mould – from pastrami of wood pigeon with pickled red cabbage and onion popcorn to Icelandic cod fillet with smoked bacon polenta and clam sauce. Readers have singled out the nori-wrapped salmon with ginger and soy dip and a shard of crispy salmon skin, while traditionalists should appreciate the pleasures provided by a rich, slow-cooked daube of Derbyshire beef with thyme dumplings. For afters, who could resist the 'snowball trifle' or a mini lemon cake with Swiss meringue and red lollipop parfait. Unfortunately, not everyone is sold on the décor – a mix of mosaic mirrors, floral curtains and jewelled light fittings that jars a little with the restaurant's photogenic location. Wines from £17.75.

Chef/s: Jonathan Hobson and Mark Hadfield. **Open:** all week L 12 to 2, Mon to Sat D 7 to 9.30. **Closed:** 25 Dec to 10 Jan. **Meals:** alc (main courses £20 to £25). Set L £20 (2 courses) to £23. Sun L £25. Tasting menu £50 (7 courses). **Details:** 60 seats. 26 seats outside. V menu. Bar. Music. Parking.

 Derby

Masa

Modern European | £32
The Old Wesleyan Chapel, Brook Street, Derby, DE1 3PF
Tel no: (01332) 203345
www.masarestaurantwinebar.com

The original pews, pulpit and memorial tablets in this converted Wesleyan chapel add greatly to its personality as a venue. European classic bistro dishes overlaid with the modernist touch, served with great aplomb on unconventional plates, are what to expect, starting perhaps with seared scallops in white chocolate with asparagus, Parmesan and truffle oil, before moving on to beef fillet and cheek with wild mushrooms and pancetta in green peppercorn jus, or sea trout with vegetables à la grecque in Dijon hollandaise.

Finish with Pimm's jelly, served with the expected accoutrements of cucumber, basil, elderflower and lemonade. Wines from £18. Open all week.

■ Ridgeway
The Old Vicarage

A temple of natural-born cooking
Cooking score: 6
Modern British | £75
Ridgeway Moor, Ridgeway, S12 3XW
Tel no: (0114) 2475814
www.theoldvicarage.co.uk

£5 OFF

A 'lovely old building' full of 'character and quirks', the Old Vicarage sits at the end of a sweeping drive in two acres of lush lawns and shady copses. The grounds were laid out in the 1840s and overlook the Moss Valley conservation area, giving a suitably bucolic backdrop for a lazy lunch or dinner. Chef/ owner Tessa Bramley has run the show since 1987, and has made her name using local produce to create beautiful, sophisticated dishes befitting the smart country-house setting. Baked Whitby cod with tomato, mussel and star anise broth, saffron potatoes and garlic croûtons is a typically classy starter, while Bramley's penchant for game is evident in a main of roast local partridge with braised red cabbage, parsnips, crab apple jelly and elderberries. For a fresh finish, try Champagne rhubarb jelly with poached rhubarb, rhubarb and ginger sorbet with brandy-snap, vanilla parfait and a rhubarb tuille. A lengthy, eclectic wine list divided by style starts at £24.
Chef/s: Tessa Bramley and Nathan Smith. **Open:** Tue to Fri L 12 to 2, Tue to Sat D 6.30 to 9.30 (10 Sat). **Closed:** Sun, Mon, 26 Dec to 5 Jan, 2 weeks Jul/ Aug, bank hols. **Meals:** Set L £40 (3 courses). Set D £75 (4 courses). Tasting menu £85. **Details:** 48 seats. 20 seats outside. Parking. Children over 6 yrs only at D.

■ Stone Edge
Red Lion Pub & Bistro

Seriously scrubbed-up rural package
Cooking score: 2
Modern British | £35
Peak Edge Hotel, Darley Road, Stone Edge, S45 0LW
Tel no: (01246) 566142
www.peakedgehotel.co.uk

£5 OFF

'We have eaten here before and this visit confirmed the good impression from last time,' enthused one fan of Damien Dugdale's self-styled pub and bistro (with modern hotel attached) in the moorland fringes of the Peak District. Exposed stone, beams, open fires and leather sofas give the place oodles of traditional character. The menu is a jumble of all-day dining options (pub classics, lunchtime sandwiches, afternoon tea), alongside fancier ideas laid out in set-meal deals and a tasting menu, but dishes are skilfully made using good ingredients. The kitchen mixes influences in true modern British style: venison bresaola served with Manchego, membrillo and cured duck egg might rub shoulders with crab and curried pumpkin soup, while rabbit loin and confit leg bonbon with peas and carrots lines up alongside sea bass with artichoke, black olive, anchovy and crab. To finish, there are sweet hits from tarts, brûlées and chocolate desserts. Wines from £18.95.
Chef/s: Oliver Parnell. **Open:** all week 12 to 9 (9.30 Fri and Sat). **Meals:** Set L £19 (2 courses) to £23. Set D £24 (2 courses) to £28. Sun L £20. Tasting menu £45 to £70. **Details:** 80 seats. 40 seats outside. V menu. Bar. Wheelchair access. Music. Parking.

■ Ashwater

Blagdon Manor

Hospitable West Country retreat
Cooking score: 2
Modern British | £40
Ashwater, EX21 5DF
Tel no: (01409) 211224
www.blagdon.com

Don't be surprised if you're greeted by a pair of lolloping chocolate Labradors when you arrive at Steve and Liz Morey's Grade II-listed manor house on the fringes of Dartmoor – it's a reminder that this place is all about family hospitality. With lush Devon pastures all around, Blagdon is an instantly appealing prospect – especially if you're enjoying dinner in the conservatory-style restaurant. Steve's cooking takes its cue from West Country produce but looks further afield for inspiration – perhaps goats' cheese pannacotta with apples, celeriac, grapes and sugared walnuts or pan-fried hake with char-grilled potatoes, tiger prawns, lentils and curried cauliflower. Elsewhere, fillet of Devon beef comes with corned beef fritters, guinea fowl is paired with local hog's pudding, and crispy confit duck is given the bourgeois Gallic treatment alongside Savoy cabbage, parsnip purée and wild mushrooms. To finish, look for the seasonal fruit 'tasting' plates or hot chocolate soufflé with a peanut-butter doughnut. Wines start at £17.

Chef/s: Steve Morey. **Open:** Thur to Sun L 12 to 1.30, Wed to Sun D 7 to 9. **Closed:** Mon, Tue, 2 weeks Jan. **Meals:** Set L £17 (2 courses) to £20. Set D £35 (2 courses) to £40. Sun L £22 (2 courses) to £28. **Details:** 26 seats. V menu. Bar. Wheelchair access. Parking. Children over 12 yrs only.

Symbols

Accommodation is available
Three courses for less than £30
£5-off voucher scheme
Notable wine list

Bigbury-on-Sea

LOCAL GEM
The Oyster Shack
Seafood | £38
Milburn Orchard Farm, Stakes Hill, Bigbury-
on-Sea, TQ7 4BE
Tel no: (01548) 810876
www.oystershack.co.uk

'It has the atmosphere of a Greek taverna and even when the sun doesn't shine, the staff do,' noted one reporter of this accommodating seafooder above the River Avon. No frills, no fuss, just fresh seafood and locally landed fish 'always perfectly cooked'. Eat in the spruce dining room or outside, under a giant sail-covered deck where oysters, mussels, seafood chowder, line-caught wild sea bass all tempt, but sometimes 'you just want to get stuck into one of their whole lobsters or crabs with a side of fries'. House wine £16. Closed Sun D.

Chagford

★ TOP 50 ★

Gidleigh Park
Spiritual home of Michael Caines' cooking
Cooking score: 7
Modern European | £118
Chagford, TQ13 8HH
Tel no: (01647) 432367
www.gidleigh.com

Gidleigh is more above Chagford than in it, standing proud on its isolated hillside. 'As you drive up what seems an endless network of narrow lanes, you do wonder why so many people make the effort,' grumped a first-timer. 'When you drive back down, you don't.' Built in virtually the last era (the 1920s) in which an overseas shipping magnate might build himself a stately home, the house is decorated and run with a sense of unarguable civility and grace, looking out across Dartmoor from over 100 acres of its own land. The style of cooking is pitched in perfect equilibrium between British modernity and country-house opulence, courtesy of Michael Caines, who has considered Gidleigh his spiritual home for the past 20 years. However, the chef has announced he will be moving on in early 2016, but it seems likely that the style of food will continue in the same vein. Start with the signature Loch Duart salmon in courgette tagliatelle with wasabi and salmon jelly, or the sublime tartlet piled with quail and its eggs, smoked bacon and onion confit. Main courses get creative with the likes of Cornish salt cod partnered with crab, chorizo and samphire and a razor-sharp lemon purée, while ever-popular duck appears in almost domestic guise with roast garlic, cabbage and turnips in a superb spiced jus. At close of play, there may be a wicked chocolate orange confit mousse with orange sorbet, which was 'pleasantly redolent of orange peel' and 'left us very satisfied'. A pity, then, that for one couple, the level of service was not quite the equal of the food: 'we found it hesitant and slightly standoffish, at least to begin with'. However, a wine list of indubitable pedigree suits the mood. Quality growers and mature vintages abound, with prices from £26.
Chef/s: Michael Caines MBE. **Open:** all week L 12 to 2.30, D 7 to 9.30. **Meals:** Set L £46 (2 courses) to £59. Set D £118. Signature menu £143. **Details:** 50 seats. V menu. Bar. Wheelchair access. Parking. Children over 8 yrs only.

Clyst Hydon
The Five Bells Inn
Inventive cooking in a remote thatched pub
Cooking score: 1
British | £31
Main Street, Clyst Hydon, EX15 2NT
Tel no: (01884) 277288
www.fivebells.uk.com

The thatched village inn, lost among winding Devon lanes, is owned by the same team who have the Jack in the Green at Rockbeare. In an ambience of gnarled oak columns and slate-tiled floor, the modernised country-pub food scores many hits for mussels in local cider, or scallops with mushrooms and parsley roots, with sinew-stiffening main courses like

Dartmoor lamb, charred leeks and pickled garlic in a sauce of Somerset Rambler sheep's cheese and tarragon. An inventive spin is put on desserts such as caramel tart, which comes with smoked salt and spiced apple. House wines from the Ardèche are £15.50.
Chef/s: Ian Webber. **Open:** all week L 12 to 2 (5 Sun), D 6 to 9 (9.30 Fri and Sat). **Closed:** 25 and 26 Dec. **Meals:** alc (main courses £16 to £23). Set L £15. Sun L £23. **Details:** 70 seats. 70 seats outside. Wheelchair access. Music. Parking.

▮ Dartmouth
Rockfish Seafood and Chips

Proper seaside fish and chips

Cooking score: 1
Seafood | £25
8 South Embankment, Dartmouth, TQ6 9BH
Tel no: (01803) 832800
www.therockfish.co.uk

'A perfect light lunch at 3pm on a sunny Monday, accurately cooked brill with a fresh green salad.' So ran one reporter's notes on Mitch Tonk's seafood haven overlooking the River Dart. It's the kind of place everyone loves, and all are agreed that it has 'good standards for an all day operation'. Part of a small group (other branches are in Dartmouth, Plymouth, Torquay), Rockfish is on the money when it comes to local and sustainable sourcing and fresh and forthright flavours. Come for first-class fish and chips, dressed south Devon crab with mayonnaise, seafood rolls, even a steak and oyster burger. Wines from around £18.
Chef/s: Kirk Gosden and Joshua Carter. **Open:** all week 12 to 9. **Meals:** alc (main courses £7 to £15). **Details:** 60 seats.

Average price

The average price denotes the price of a three-course meal without wine.

The Seahorse

Enlightened seafood eatery

Cooking score: 5
Seafood | £45
5 South Embankment, Dartmouth, TQ6 9BH
Tel no: (01803) 835147
www.seahorserestaurant.co.uk

On the quayside overlooking Dartmouth marina, Mitch Tonks and Mat Prowse have created something quite special. Art Deco lamps, wooden parquet floor and comfortable leather banquettes give the Seahorse a timeless quality. A wood-burning oven is the main focal point of the open-view kitchen. Fish from nearby Brixham market is served in a variety of classic ways (brill fillet with sauce béarnaise, perhaps, or fritto misto of local seafood with a glossy, garlicky aïoli) but the owners' culinary adventures around the Mediterranean add a sunny influence to a starter of octopus carpaccio with salad niçoise, and to a dish of hake with sweet garlic and sauce romesco. Meat eaters are not neglected; look for grilled lamb cutlets with aubergine, broad beans and mint. The imaginatively chosen Old World wine list is packed with interesting bottles, opening at £19.
Chef/s: Mitch Tonks and Mat Prowse. **Open:** Tue to Sat L 12 to 2.30, Tue to Sat D 6 to 9.30. **Closed:** Sun, Mon, 22 to 26 Dec. **Meals:** alc (main courses £20 to £33). Set L and early D £20 (2 courses). **Details:** 40 seats. 4 seats outside. V menu. Music.

▮ Dittisham
Anchorstone Café

Seafood lovers' paradise

Cooking score: 3
Seafood | £23
Manor Street, Dittisham, TQ6 0EX
Tel no: (01803) 722365
www.anchorstonecafe.co.uk

With a 'heart-stopping view of woodland and estuary', you'd be hard-pressed to find a nicer place to have lunch on a summer's day than on the terrace of this brightly painted clapperboard café on the banks of the River Dart. It may be hard to get to (boat from Dartmouth is the best way) and the interior is basic and rustic, but Clare Harvey's ringingly fresh seafood-led menu fits the setting perfectly. Many return just for the hand-picked Brixham crab sandwich or local mussels with fries, but the straightforward preparations of Caesar salad with roasted scallops, salade niçoise with fresh mackerel, free-range eggs and olives, and whole wild black bream baked with fresh herbs and chilli are equally typical of a simple formula that works well. There are meat dishes for non-participants and tempting puddings such as a zesty lemon tart served with a huge dollop of local clotted cream. Wines from £16.95. Note, there's now a second Anchorstone at Sharpham Vineyard, tel: (01803) 732178.

Chef/s: Clare Harvey. **Open:** all week L 12 to 4. **Closed:** Nov to Mar. **Meals:** alc (main courses £12 to £15). Set L £20 (2 courses) to £35. **Details:** 30 seats. 75 seats outside. V menu. Bar.

▌ Drewsteignton
The Old Inn

Exclusive little restaurant-with-rooms
Cooking score: 3
Modern European | £49
Drewsteignton, EX6 6QR
Tel no: (01647) 281276
www.old-inn.co.uk

'Just what you need when you walk off Dartmoor,' approved one worn-out soul, who was warmly greeted with a glass of beer and the promise of a roaring fire in this exclusive little restaurant-with-rooms. The aptly named Old Inn is a grown-up kind of place run with quiet professionalism by chef/proprietor Duncan Walker and his team, who also treat guests to an 'impressively short' menu of carefully crafted dishes in the Franco-European mould. A well-liked starter of sautéed calf's sweetbreads with olive potato cake, brown butter and capers shows that the kitchen cares about flavour as well as technical

nous – likewise a combo of grilled red mullet with anchovies, parsley, lemon and garlic. Dartmoor lamb and Devon-reared duck also step into the spotlight – the latter in luxurious company with sautéed foie gras and celeriac chips. After that, take your pick from just three desserts, perhaps hot blackcurrant soufflé or warm plum tart with cinnamon ice cream. Around 40 international wines start at £23.

Chef/s: Duncan Walker. **Open:** Fri and Sat L 12 to 2, Wed to Sat D 7 to 10. **Closed:** Sun, Mon, Tue, 2 weeks Jan. **Meals:** Set L £30. Set D £43 (2 courses) to £49. **Details:** 18 seats. V menu. No children.

▌ Exeter
The Magdalen Chapter

Good ingredients, good value, good buzz
Cooking score: 3
Modern British | £30
Magdalen Street, Exeter, EX2 4HY
Tel no: (01392) 281000
www.themagdalenchapter.com

The stylish and individual conversion of this imposing Edwardian eye hospital into a boutique hotel includes a striking, glass-fronted marquee-style restaurant with an open-theatre kitchen and dramatic lighting. Here, 'really good food' strikes a balance between classical and contemporary; nothing is outlandish or challenging. South Devon crab with samphire, for example, is 'nicely shredded and full of flavour'. One of the kitchen's strengths is that they don't pile on the extras, knowing when to stop and keep things simple, as in a dish of roast duck breast with radicchio, polenta and prunes, or roast whole lemon sole with chilli and tomato salsa and crisp chickpeas. There's been praise, too, for 'top-class' desserts such as plum and almond tart with local cream. Booming music has not been appreciated. The wine list on an iPad ('an educational novelty' for some readers) is a drinker-friendly collection with plenty by the glass or 500ml pichet. Prices from £19.50.

Chef/s: Matt Downing. **Open:** all week L 12 to 2.30 (12.30 to 3 Sun), D 6 to 10 (9.30 Sun). **Meals:** alc (main courses £11 to £28). Set L and D £15 (2

Join us at thegoodfoodguide.co.uk

courses) to £17. Sun L £17 (2 courses) to £20.
Details: 75 seats. 40 seats outside. Bar. Wheelchair access. Music. Parking.

Michael Caines at ABode Exeter

A polished set-up
Cooking score: 4
Modern European | £34
Cathedral Yard, Exeter, EX1 1HD
Tel no: (01392) 223638
www.abodeexeter.co.uk

Hard by Exeter's gothic cathedral, in what was the historic Royal Clarence Hotel (now ABode Exeter), this outpost of Michael Caines' culinary empire occupies a swish, contemporary-style room done out in shades of cream and grey with lots of mirrors and natural woodwork. It's a polished set-up and the mood is matched by cooking that has all those familiar MC trademarks – from the exemplary use of seasonal West Country ingredients to the fine detailing applied to dishes with strong French overtones. Head chef Nick Topham is in tune with his master's voice, fashioning clever plates of goats' cheese mousse with jasmine raisins, walnuts and apple ahead of, say, roast venison with wintry quartet of braised pork belly, red cabbage, chestnut purée and fig. Fish from the Devon boats also gets a good airing, from lime-infused mackerel tartare with soused turnip and beetroot to poached hake with roasted scallop, leek fondue and red wine sauce. To conclude, consider salted-caramel tart with praline macaroon and gingerbread ice cream. The 150-bin wine list offers classy drinking from £21.25.
Chef/s: Nick Topham. **Open:** Mon to Sat L 12 to 2.30, D 5.30 to 9.30 (6 to 10 Fri and Sat). **Closed:** Sun, 26 Dec. **Meals:** alc (main courses £9 to £24). Set L £15 (2 courses) to £20. Set D £18 (2 courses) to £23. **Details:** 70 seats. Bar. Wheelchair access. Music.

Exmouth
Les Saveurs

French flavours and Devon seafood
Cooking score: 2
French | £35
9 Tower Street, Exmouth, EX8 1NT
Tel no: (01395) 269459
www.lessaveurs.co.uk

Regular hauls of Devon seafood are one of the big selling points at this amenable neighbourhood bistro – a rough-and-ready mix of bare floorboards, bare brick walls and smartly laid tables. Familiar Gallic flavours loom large, from bowls of garlicky Exmouth mussels to whole tiger prawns flamed in Pernod, but the kitchen also likes to sprinkle some exotic spices here and there – cumin velouté and ras-el-hanout caramel with pan-fried local scallops, for example. There's room for chicken liver parfait and goats' cheese crostini, too, although mains are in the time-honoured bourgeois mould of fillet steak with green peppercorn sauce or roast rump of lamb with a Dijon mustard and herb crust. Dishes generally arrive with ample servings of seasonal vegetables. Dessert is a romp through Gallic staples such as tarte Tatin, crème brûlée and oeufs à la neige, while cheeses are artisan Devon yokels. Regional French wines pepper the cosmopolitan list, with vins de pays de l'Ardèche from £19.
Chef/s: Olivier Guyard-Mulkerrin. **Open:** Tue to Sat D only 7 to 10.30. **Closed:** Sun, Mon, Jan. **Meals:** alc (main courses £18 to £25). **Details:** 54 seats. Music. Children over 10 yrs only.

Visit us online

To find out more about The Good Food Guide, please visit thegoodfoodguide.co.uk

Gulworthy
The Horn of Plenty
Ravishing views and confident cooking
Cooking score: 5
Modern British | £50
Gulworthy, PL19 8JD
Tel no: (01822) 832528
www.thehornofplenty.co.uk

With its ravishing views of the wooded Tamar Valley, bountiful orchards and gardens ablaze with seasonal blooms, this aptly named cornucopia of delights boasts the kind of location that wedding planners dream about. Inside, the Horn of Plenty is a paragon of civilised comforts and cosseting – although there's also some 'seriously good dining' to be had, according to one reader. Meals are served in a conservatory, and the kitchen works to a monthly changing menu that accommodates top-notch ingredients from near and far: 'succulent' Devon lamb gets rave reviews, while 'excellent fish' might range from hand-dived scallops with celeriac fondant, soy and truffle vinaigrette to pan-roasted turbot with Thai-scented purée, crispy kale, crab and ginger tortellini. Dartmoor venison has its seasonal moment in the limelight (perhaps accompanied by honey-roast beetroots and winter greens), while 'mouthwatering puds' could include a signature riff on 'milk and chocolate', as well as rhubarb meringue tart with gingerbread ice cream. The wine list opens with 11 house selections from £19.50. **Chef/s:** Scott Paton. **Open:** all week L 12 to 2, D 7 to 9.30. **Meals:** Set L £19 (2 courses) to £25. Set D £50. Sun L £25. **Details:** 60 seats. 20 seats outside. Wheelchair access. Music. Parking.

Symbols

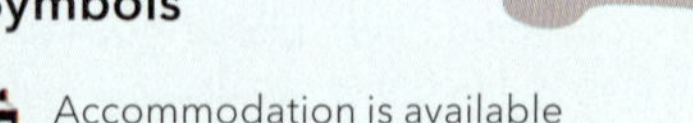

	Accommodation is available
	Three courses for less than £30
	£5-off voucher scheme
	Notable wine list

Honiton
The Holt
Enterprising foodie pub
Cooking score: 1
Modern British | £26
178 High Street, Honiton, EX14 1LA
Tel no: (01404) 47707
www.theholt-honiton.com

Brothers Joe and Angus McCaig are the dynamic duo behind this enterprising pub by the banks of the River Gissage: they put on live music events, hold cookery classes and even find time to keep a smokehouse fired up – don't miss their apple-smoked venison haunch with roasted beetroot. Otherwise, the menu mixes doughty British fodder with global forays – from pork and duck terrine with preserved plums or pan-fried lamb rump with thyme-roasted potatoes to crispy five-spice beef with sweet-and-sour roots or grilled sea bream with shrimp fritters and Asian dressing. Tapas plates are available in the bar. Wines from £16.50. **Chef/s:** Angus McCaig. **Open:** Tue to Sat L 12 to 2, D 6.30 to 9 (9.30 Fri and Sat). **Closed:** Sun, Mon, 25 and 26 Dec. **Meals:** alc (main courses £14 to £18). **Details:** 75 seats. Bar. Wheelchair access. Music.

Kings Nympton
The Grove Inn
Proper country inn with local food
Cooking score: 2
British | £22
Kings Nympton, EX37 9ST
Tel no: (01769) 580406
www.thegroveinn.co.uk

Set in a pretty north Devon village surrounded by lush, beautiful countryside, this listed 17th-century thatched building lives up to most people's idea of a model country inn. It won't disappoint inside either, the Globe's beamed ceilings, walls of rough stone and two open fires are matched by Deborah Smallbone's deceptively simple-

Join us at thegoodfoodguide.co.uk

sounding and homely menu based on regionally sourced produce. There could be a duo of smoked north Devon trout with horseradish cream or a grilled West Country goats' cheese salad, while mains include free-range chicken breast stuffed with Devon Blue cheese, Parma ham and thyme (own-grown of course), Devon hog's pudding with onion gravy and buttered mash or locally shot pheasant burger topped with Devon Cheddar and served with chunky chips. With sticky toffee pudding to finish, this may be unashamedly populist stuff, but it is refreshing to find somewhere serving straightforward, unpretentious food without ceremony and with willing, smiley service. Wines from £15.

Chef/s: Deborah Smallbone. **Open:** Tue to Sun L 12 to 2 (2.30 Sun), Tue to Sat D 6.45 to 9 (6.30 to 8.30 Tue). **Closed:** Mon, 25 Dec. **Meals:** alc (main courses £8 to £18). **Details:** 28 seats. 24 seats outside. V menu. Bar.

Kingsbridge

LOCAL GEM

Beachhouse
Seafood | £30
South Milton Sands, Kingsbridge, TQ7 3JY
Tel no: (01548) 561144
www.beachhousedevon.com

£5
OFF

Bang on the beach overlooking South Milton Sands, this aptly named all-day eatery is a godsend for holidaymakers and locals alike with its offer of West Country seafood and bracing views. Expect anything from herby Salcombe crab salad and bowls of Exmouth mussels to fishcakes, seared scallops with capers and sage or sizzling garlic prawns with chilli – plus the odd burger and pasta dish too. Breakfast, lunchtime sandwiches, kids' food and takeaways complete a cracking seaside package. Wines from £17.50. Open all week.

Knowstone

★ **TOP 50 PUB** ★

The Masons Arms
Fancy cooking in a medieval pub
Cooking score: 5
Modern British | £40
Knowstone, EX36 4RY
Tel no: (01398) 341231
www.masonsarmsdevon.co.uk

It's a long way from the haute cuisine finery of the Waterside Inn (see entry) to the bucolic backwaters of Exmoor, but since upping sticks a decade ago, Mark Dodson and his wife have made this dreamy-looking medieval thatched inn very much their own. Inside, the Masons Arms is a pub of two halves, with a roaring fire and Devon ales in the darkly rustic bar, plus a separate beamed dining room for those who want to sample Mark's sure-footed, satisfying food. His cooking has all the silky panache, technical know-how and fondness for fancy embellishments you would expect from a Roux-trained chef – although ideas and influences are gleaned from far and wide: breast of wood pigeon is audaciously married with curried Brussels sprout purée and stuffing, smoked chicken sits on a Thai-style salad, and fillet of beef arrives with oxtail cannelloni, salsify and red wine jus. There's some splendid Devon fish too – perhaps mustard-crusted sea bass with white beans and carrot ketchup or John Dory with crab risotto and mangetout tempura. Afterwards, you might consider Amaretto mousse with poached plums. House wines start at £15.50.

Chef/s: Mark Dodson. **Open:** Tue to Sun L 12 to 2, Tue to Sat D 7 to 9. **Closed:** Mon, first week Jan, Feb half term, last week Aug. **Meals:** alc (main courses £19 to £27). Set L £20 (2 courses) to £25. Sun L £37. **Details:** 28 seats. 16 seats outside. Bar. Music. Parking. Children over 5 yrs only at D.

◼ **Lewdown**
Lewtrenchard Manor
Cosy, welcoming Jacobean manor
Cooking score: 5
Modern British | £50
Lewdown, EX20 4PN
Tel no: (01566) 783222
www.lewtrenchard.co.uk

The house does date back to the Jacobean era, but it was the Victorian poet and hymnist Sabine Baring-Gould, whose ancestors are preserved in oil on the dining room walls, who gave it the refit job that suits it. Mullioned windows and age-deep oak panelling make for a cosily enfolding atmosphere, rather than alienating grandeur, and the extensive gardens are the last word in pretty. West Devon unfolds all around, providing Matthew Peryer with the nuts and bolts of his modern country-house repertoire. Herbed gnocchi with sautéed wild mushrooms in Parmesan foam might be the prelude to local estate venison with braised salsify and Savoy in chocolate-boosted jus, or citrus-roasted pollack fillet with garden leeks in shellfish consommé. Desserts are also ambitious, to judge from a délice of bitter chocolate and salt caramel with caramelised banana and matching ice cream. Wines are confined to short but good selections from each region, with bottles from £25, or £6.50 a standard glass.
Chef/s: Matthew Peryer. **Open:** all week L 12 to 2, D 7 to 9. **Meals:** Set L £20 (2 courses) to £24. Set D £50. Sun L £25. **Details:** 50 seats. 15 seats outside. V menu. Bar. Wheelchair access. Parking. Children over 8 yrs only at D.

◼ **Lifton**
The Arundell Arms
Family-owned village inn
Cooking score: 3
Modern British | £45
Fore Street, Lifton, PL16 0AA
Tel no: (01566) 784666
www.arundellarms.com

It may look like a standard village pub from the road, but the 350-year-old coaching inn feels more like a swish country house hotel on the inside. Family-run since 1961, it's a tribute to the care and dedication of its owners, the dining room done in light sandy tones, with fresh flowers and crisp linen to add refinement. Steven Pidgeon maintains a firm hand on the kitchen tiller, producing seasonal English food that acknowledges modern currents without being carried away by them. Grilled John Dory on creamed lentils with brown shrimps in saffron and tomato dressing makes a delicate opener to local venison mignon with spiced red cabbage and onion and beer purée in peppercorn sauce, or brioche-crusted best end of lamb in white wine gravy. Puddings warm the cockles of traditionalists with apple, rhubarb and ginger crumble and custard, or sticky toffee with butterscotch. Wines start at £20, or £5 a glass.
Chef/s: Steven Pidgeon. **Open:** all week L 12 to 2, D 6 to 10. **Meals:** Set L £20 (2 courses) to £27. Set D £42 (2 courses) to £47. Sun L £23. **Details:** 80 seats. 30 seats outside. V menu.

Join us at thegoodfoodguide.co.uk

■ Newton Poppleford
Moores'

Likeable neighbourhood eatery
Cooking score: 1
Modern British | £26
6 Greenbank, Newton Poppleford, EX10 0EB
Tel no: (01395) 568100
www.mooresrestaurant.co.uk

Jonathan and Kate Moore are now into their second decade as custodians of this likeable neighbourhood eatery housed in what was once Newton Poppleford's village shop. These days, seasonal provisions from West Country producers are the venue's stock-in-trade, with Devon-reared meats, day-boat fish, farmhouse cheeses and suchlike finding their way on to the plate. Menus change with the markets and the seasons, which might mean crab, fennel and leek thermidor followed by ginger and orange marinated duck breast with pearl barley and bacon broth in winter. For afters, bread-and-butter pudding with clotted cream should warm the cockles. House wine is £13.95.
Chef/s: Jonathan Moore. **Open:** Tue to Sun L 12 to 1.30, Tue to Sat D 7 to 9.30. **Closed:** Mon, first 2 weeks Jan. **Meals:** Set L £17 (2 courses) to £23. Set D £20 (2 courses) to £26. Sun L £17. **Details:** 32 seats. V menu. Wheelchair access. Music.

■ Plymouth
The Greedy Goose

Thrilling food and a slice of history
Cooking score: 4
Modern British | £32
Finewell Street, Plymouth, PL1 2AE
Tel no: (01752) 252001
www.thegreedygoose.co.uk

Formerly Tanners, the oldest – and one of the prettiest – slices of Plymouth's history started a new life in late 2014 when chef/proprietor Ben Palmer created the Greedy Goose. Behind those leaded, mullioned windows is a snaking series of stone-walled rooms, one of which houses an original freshwater well. The interior design lets this former merchant's house speak for itself, with just a smattering of goose-themed artwork for adornment. Palmer's ambition is plain to see: the service is faultless, and the modern European cooking feels lively and original (the closest comparison is Glazebrook House, see entry, where Palmer is also involved). Crisp Porthilly oysters with citrus mayonnaise, pickled fennel, orange and jewel-like flying-fish eggs get things off to a thrilling starter. 'Fresh-as-it-gets' stone bass with monkfish 'scampi', sea beet, samphire, pickled cucumber, a creamy seafood sauce and potato terrine is another 'sophisticated delight'. Desserts such as banana bread with chocolate sorbet are not quite as sparkling, but still deserve greedy attention. It's all deemed 'excellent value' – including international wines, priced from £16.
Chef/s: Ben Palmer. **Open:** Tue to Sat L 12 to 2.30, D 6 to 9.30 (10 Fri and Sat). **Closed:** Sun, Mon. **Meals:** alc (main courses £14 to £28). Set L £17. Set D £20. **Details:** 45 seats. 40 seats outside. Bar. Wheelchair access. Music.

Rock Salt

Accommodating all-day eatery
Cooking score: 2
Modern British | £28
31 Stonehouse Street, Plymouth, PL1 3PE
Tel no: (01752) 225522
www.rocksaltcafe.co.uk

On the fringes of the city centre, unassuming Rock Salt is a paragon of flexible dining, open all day, every day, with a bar and dining areas spread casually over one floor. Dinner covers a variety of culinary styles (sometimes within a single dish), typically taking in starters such as black pudding Scotch egg with apple and crisp ham, then mains of stone bass with bouillabaisse nage, soft-shell crab fritter and braised fennel or crisp duck confit with shrimp noodles and Asian salad, while mango and rambutan crumble, macadamia, and cardamom ice cream is an original finish. Light lunches include a choice of burgers, fish and chips and the like, while a café menu delivers an all-day breakfast, sandwiches and nibbles. It's a 'homely environment', with 'pleasant, unobtrusive service' and a short wine list that focuses on good-value drinking, bottle prices starting at £14.95.

Chef/s: David Jenkins and Joe Turner. **Open:** all week from 10am (8am Sat), L 11 to 2.30, D 5 to 10. **Closed:** 24 to 26 Dec, 1 to 7 Jan. **Meals:** alc (main courses £11 to £22). Set D £22 (2 courses) to £28. Sun L £14. **Details:** 60 seats. Music.

LOCAL GEM

Lemon Tree Café & Bistro

Modern European | £20

2 Haye Road South, Elburton, Plymouth, PL9 8HJ

Tel no: (01752) 481117

www.lemontreecafe.co.uk

An enterprising family-run set-up, the Lemon Tree brings a breath of fresh air and some terrific bistro-style food to the outskirts of Plymouth. Deli sandwiches, croques, omelettes and hot paninis are the staples, but the really interesting stuff is on the daily blackboard: look forward to the likes of roast duck and orange salad with pomegranate dressing or linguine with locally caught crab followed by lemon syllabub with raspberry coulis. House wine is £14.95. Open Tue to Sat for breakfast, coffee, snacks and lunch. Note: cash only.

 Salcombe

South Sands Beachside Restaurant

Local seafood beside the seaside

Cooking score: 2

Seafood | £35

Bolt Head, Salcombe, TQ8 8LL

Tel no: (01548) 845900

www.beachsidesalcombe.co.uk

Perfectly positioned on a secluded inlet and reached via a series of twisting single-track roads, this charming boutique bolt-hole commands fantastic views of the beach and estuary. The big, wide-windowed dining room is coolly stylish with muted colours, lots of blond wood and the option of the terrace if the weather is fine. The cooking ranges far and wide for culinary influence but stays close to home for supplies, particularly ozone-fresh seafood, perhaps crab risotto or charred mackerel fillet with rhubarb, quinoa and chicory salad to start, followed by lemon sole with brown shrimps, capers and samphire. If meat is on your mind, you might veer towards pan-fried pigeon with shallot Tatin, candied granola and corn mayo before considering herb-crusted lamb rack with fondant potato and gooseberry compote, and desserts are right on the money – witness a clean-tasting rhubarb pannacotta with poached rhubarb, elderflower jelly and orange meringue. Wines from £19.50.

Chef/s: Lee Morgan. **Open:** all week L 12 to 3, D 6.30 to 9 (9.30 Sat and Sun). **Meals:** alc (main courses £14 to £75). **Details:** 80 seats. 70 seats outside. Bar. Wheelchair access. Music. Parking.

 Shaldon

ODE Dining

Creative ideas from an organic champion

Cooking score: 5

Modern British | £43

21 Fore Street, Shaldon, TQ14 0DE

Tel no: (01626) 873977

www.odetruefood.co.uk

£5 OFF

Take one three-storey Georgian town house, fit it out according to eco-friendly principles and name the resulting restaurant after its postcode – welcome to ODE, Tim and Clare Bouget's crusading eatery in a Devon fishing village. Every 'green' detail rings true here, from the fixtures and fittings, heating and lighting to the ingredients for Tim's seasonally creative dinner menus. Organic, local and sustainable are the strictly observed keywords, be it Eversfield pig's cheek braised in red wine with crackling, carrot and cumin or steamed fillet of wild sea bass with south Devon brown crab agnolotti, lemon purée and watercress.

Join us at thegoodfoodguide.co.uk

Inspiration comes from far and wide, although artisan cheeses sit closer to home – likewise desserts such as a Cox Royal apple crumble tart with cinnamon doughnut and warm clove custard. Teas and coffees wear the Fairtrade stamp, while the wine list is an exemplary collection from organic and biodynamic champions, with bottles from £18.50. The Bougets also run family-friendly Café ODE and the Two Beach Brewing Company at nearby Ness Cove; tel: (01626) 873427.

Chef/s: Tim Bouget. **Open:** Wed to Sat D only 7 to 9.30. **Closed:** Sun, Mon, Tue, Oct half term. **Meals:** Set D £38 (2 courses) to £43. **Details:** 24 seats. V menu. Music. No children under 7 yrs after 8.

▮ Sidford
The Salty Monk

Industrious cooking and personal hospitality
Cooking score: 2
Modern British | £45
Church Street, Sidford, EX10 9QP
Tel no: (01395) 513174
www.saltymonk.co.uk

£5 OFF

Andy and Annette Witheridge's 16th-century building opposite St Peter's Church (formerly a salt store for Benedictine monks) continues to delight visitors. It glides along as a polished restaurant-with-rooms, the kitchen's output dependent on seasonal and local supplies. A few easy dining options are offered in the bar/bistro area at lunchtime, but the main focus of the operation is dinner, served in the attractive dining room looking over the garden at the back. Here, Andy's repertoire moves along gently with plenty of original ideas, but the focus is on sound culinary principles and traditional cooking methods. You might start with a trio of own-smoked fish (salmon, soft-poached beetroot-cured pollack, ling with a caper dressing), move on to roast breast of Greedy Carver duck on an onion and shallot purée with fondant potatoes and a sweet-spicy duck jus, and finish with Devon apple sponge with toffee sauce and clotted cream. Wines start at £18.50.

▮ South Brent

NEW ENTRY
Glazebrook House

Luscious country-house dining
Cooking score: 4
Modern British | £32
South Brent, TQ10 9JE
Tel no: (01364) 73322
www.glazebrookhouse.com

£5 OFF

Chef/s: Andy Witheridge. **Open:** Thur to Sun L 12 to 1.30, all week D 6.30 to 9. **Closed:** Jan, 2 weeks Nov. **Meals:** Set L £25 (2 courses) to £30. Set D £39 (2 courses) to £45. Sun L £30. **Details:** 32 seats. 22 seats outside. Bar. Wheelchair access. Music. Parking.

The interior designers have been let loose on this little country house hotel, and the results are stunning. Expect a quirky, clubby take on heritage chic, incorporating everything from apothecary jars to an ostrich skeleton. Silver tea trays and blue-and-white china adorn the walls in the restaurant, which sports chandelier sparkles, trendy furniture and chequered floors. Executive chef Ben Palmer lives up to the gloss, pulling together global influences and superb fresh ingredients with confidence and flair. A amuse of smoked trout and pickled shallot points the way with 'deep, punchy flavours', followed perhaps by smoked ham hock and Cheddar terrine with remoulade – 'possibly the best version of this dish I've tasted,' thought one reporter. A generous portion of sea bass with basil pomme purée, crab bisque and langoustine scampi also delighted with its superb ingredients and balanced flavours, while a simple bread-and-butter pudding provided a comfortable finish. The wine list opens at £18.50.

Chef/s: Ben Palmer. **Open:** all week L 12 to 3, Mon to Sat D 6 to 9. **Closed:** 2 weeks Jan. **Meals:** alc (main courses £13 to £30). Sun L £15. **Details:** 45 seats. 24 seats outside. Bar. Wheelchair access. Music. Parking.

South Pool
The Millbrook Inn

French food in a proper village pub
Cooking score: 2
French | £32
South Pool, TQ7 2RW
Tel no: (01548) 531581
www.millbrookinnsouthpool.co.uk

£5
OFF

It may be tiny, but what this quaint 17th-century village pub lacks in size it makes up for in character. Inside are low, crooked beams and exposed brick walls, a real fire and rustic mahogany furnishings. Located right on the Salcombe estuary, local food and drink are at its heart. Devon-brewed beers are updated daily while dishes are built around local and regional produce. Chef Jean-Philippe Bidart delivers smart classical French cooking, from an excellent, 'perfectly spiced' bouillabaisse to a thick cut of onglet steak and frites, served alongside more modern ideas such as chipirones on a crisp salad with a tangy dressing, chilli and ginger pork belly, and fresh 'ceviched' mackerel with sweet crab quenelles – all dishes that worked surprisingly well at inspection. Desserts also surpass pub grub expectations, too; crowd-pleasers include a crumbly white chocolate meringue cake and a nostalgic rice pudding. Service is homely and warm. Wines begin at £18.
Chef/s: Jean-Philippe Bidart. **Open:** all week L 12 to 5 (3 Sun), D 7 to 9. **Meals:** alc (main courses £13 to £20). Set L £12. Set D £15. Sun L £17. **Details:** 40 seats. 50 seats outside. Wheelchair access.

Sparkwell

The Treby Arms

It doesn't get much better...
Cooking score: 5
Modern British | £40
Sparkwell, PL7 5DD
Tel no: (01752) 837363
www.thetrebyarms.co.uk

Despite outward appearances, this is one village pub where food definitely takes precedence over pints of beer. Make no mistake, Anton Piotrowski (the 2012 winner of *MasterChef: The Professionals*) can deliver the goods and he has made the Treby Arms a serious contender in the Devon food stakes since his arrival some four years ago. Mr Piotrowski's strength lies in the quality of his suppliers – he is dedicated to sourcing the finest seasonal ingredients, with vegetables from the pub's own garden in season. His menus are all about vivid modern British combinations: pork-crackling-coated king prawn served with a black pudding Scotch egg, cucumber and pickled onion, say. Hay-baked poussin might follow, teamed with sage and onion croquettes and celeriac purée, while desserts confidently push the right buttons with lemon curd mille-feuille, citrus mascarpone and raspberry sorbet or a warm chocolate mousse with mint ice cream. There's also a mainly West Country cheeseboard and well-spread global wines from £18.50.
Chef/s: Anton Piotrowski. **Open:** Tue to Thur L 12 to 2, D 6 to 9. Fri to Sun 12 to 9. **Closed:** Mon, 25 and 26 Dec, 1 and 2 Jan. **Meals:** alc (main courses £15 to £30). Set L £20 (2 courses) to £25. **Details:** 70 seats. 20 seats outside. Bar. Wheelchair access. Music. Parking.

◼ Topsham
La Petite Maison

Engaging 'auberge' with assured cooking
Cooking score: 4
Modern European | £32
35 Fore Street, Topsham, EX3 0HR
Tel no: (01392) 873660
www.lapetitemaison.co.uk

£5
OFF

'They have always been consistently excellent,' notes one reader, a visitor to this pint-sized charmer for some 14 years. A former grocer's shop on a bend in Topsham's hair-raising Fore Street, it comprises a couple of pretty rooms that blend original brickwork with smart monochrome styling. Elizabeth Pestell oversees front-of-house, 'making everyone feel welcome', while husband Douglas is in the kitchen. The results balance modernity with European traditions. Blue cheese, poached pear, pecan nuts and proscuitto salad with lemon dressing points the way, followed perhaps by fillet of Dover sole, king prawn and scallop with spinach potato cake, spaghetti of vegetables and a white wine beurre blanc or a medallion of outdoor-reared Somerset pork in a breadcrumb crust with slow-roasted belly of pork and black pudding on creamy leeks with dauphinois, caramelised apple and cider jus. Pear tarte Tatin with butterscotch sauce and vanilla ice cream is typical of the classically-inflected desserts. A decent global selection of wines opens at £18.75.
Chef/s: Douglas Pestell and Sara Bright. **Open:** Wed to Sat L 12.30 to 2, Tue to Sat D 7 to 10. **Closed:** Sun, Mon, 24 Dec. **Meals:** Set L and D £33 (2 courses) to £39. **Details:** 28 seats.

Visit us online

To find out more about The Good Food Guide, please visit thegoodfoodguide.co.uk

◼ Torquay
The Elephant

Torquay's classiest destination
Cooking score: 5
Modern British | £55
3-4 Beacon Terrace, Torquay, TQ1 2BH
Tel no: (01803) 200044
www.elephantrestaurant.co.uk

If the very thought of eating out in Torquay conjures up *Fawlty Towers*, then you're in for a surprise at Simon Hulstone's Elephant. Located on the waterfront, this is a big, classy destination of two halves: a year-round brasserie deals in stimulating cosmopolitan dishes such as boneless skate with spiced chickpeas, squid and sprouting broccoli, but the really smart money is on the seasonal tasting menus served in the evenings-only Room upstairs. Against a backdrop of big mirrors, polished floorboards and antique lights, Hulstone fashions some highly original dishes from a stockpile of West Country produce. Plates of Brixham crab with turnip, samphire and lovage could precede, say, fallow deer with beetroots, blueberries and truffle. Artisan local cheeses come next, before a pair of desserts, often pointed up with fresh herbs – perhaps chocolate, olive oil, blackberry and pistachio with wood sorrel. Wines are equal to the food, with bottles from £19.50. Note that the details below are for The Room only.
Chef/s: Simon Hulstone. **Open:** Tue to Sat D only 6.30 to 9. **Closed:** Sun, Mon, Oct to Mar. **Meals:** Tasting menu £55 (8 courses). **Details:** 36 seats. V menu. Bar. Music.

The Orange Tree

Local food with candlelight and charm
Cooking score: 2
Modern European | £34
14-16 Parkhill Road, Torquay, TQ1 2AL
Tel no: (01803) 213936
www.orangetreerestaurant.co.uk

Sharon and Bernd Wolf have built up a head of steam since opening on a quiet backstreet in the centre of town. The place radiates encouraging warmth and bonhomie, catering to the numerous occasions when only starched linen and candlelight will do. Brixham seafood and locally reared meats are the strong suits on menus that run from precisely grilled fillet of gilthead bream on a slew of brown shrimps with green leek in saffron vinaigrette to satisfying hunks of south Devon tournedos with foie gras in truffle-oiled morel jus. Vegetarian dishes show evidence of care too, as in the building of a potato rösti construction with creamed ceps, vine tomatoes and pistou, and desserts show their paces with Amaretto-laced rhubarb cheesecake garnished with white chocolate and almond meringues. Homemade breads are pretty nifty, too. Wines on a list that could do with a bit more pizazz open at £17.50 for Languedoc Sauvignon and Merlot.

Chef/s: Bernd Wolf. **Open:** Tue to Sat D only 7 to 9. **Closed:** Sun, Mon, 26 Dec, 1 week Jan, 2 weeks Oct. **Meals:** alc (main courses £15 to £26). **Details:** 42 seats. Music.

 Totnes
Rumour

All-day high-street venue with personality
Cooking score: 1
International | £29
30 High Street, Totnes, TQ9 5RY
Tel no: (01803) 864682
www.rumourtotnes.com

£30

Totnes as a community has no truck with corporate gigantism, and Rumour is the kind of venue it intends to preserve, a garrulous high-street all-dayer of singular personality. Blackboard menus offer up-to-date bistro food at mealtimes, with fried haloumi bruschetta in lime and caper vinaigrette, followed by roast hake with mussels in aïoli broth, or pork belly braised in balsamic with garlic mash, caramelised shallots and greens. Finish with lemon posset, served with spiced prunes and a ginger snap. House Italian on the new wine list is £15.95, or £4 a standard glass.

Chef/s: Lee Hegerty. **Open:** Mon to Sat L 12 to 3, all week D 6 to 10 (9 Sun). **Closed:** 25 and 26 Dec, 1 Jan. **Meals:** alc (main courses £14 to £18). **Details:** 70 seats. Music.

 Yelverton
Prince Hall Hotel

Pretty views and beautiful ingredients
Cooking score: 3
British | £48
Yelverton, PL20 6SA
Tel no: (01822) 890403
www.princehall.co.uk

£5 OFF

This modestly proportioned, buttercup yellow country house stands out amid the rugged greens of Dartmoor, looking out over 'rumpled, tussock fields to a pretty little humpback bridge that really ought to have a troll living under it'. The fire-warmed lounge is a harmonious hotchpotch of influences: timeworn country-house furnishings, original artwork plus Middle Eastern and modern touches. In contrast, the restaurant has a breezy simplicity, pairing stripped floors with palest blue walls. Warmed sourdough and garlic and herb breads get things off to a flying start, and a starter of Parmesan pannacotta with wild asparagus and a focaccia crisp impressed with its 'glossy freshness and textural contrasts'. Roast loin venison, braised red cabbage, dauphinois and red wine and horseradish jus showcased 'beautiful ingredients and balanced flavours', while a dessert of treacle tart was a delightful mix of crisp pastry and sticky filling. A decent wine list, including organic options, opens at £22. Expect an enthusiastic canine welcome, too, as the hotel is fervently dog friendly.

Chef/s: Chris Daly. **Open:** all week L 12 to 3, D 7 to 10. **Meals:** Set L £26 (2 courses) to £30. Set D £40 (2 courses) to £48. Sun L £25. **Details:** 20 seats. 30 seats outside. V menu. Bar. Wheelchair access. Music. Parking. Children over 10 yrs only.

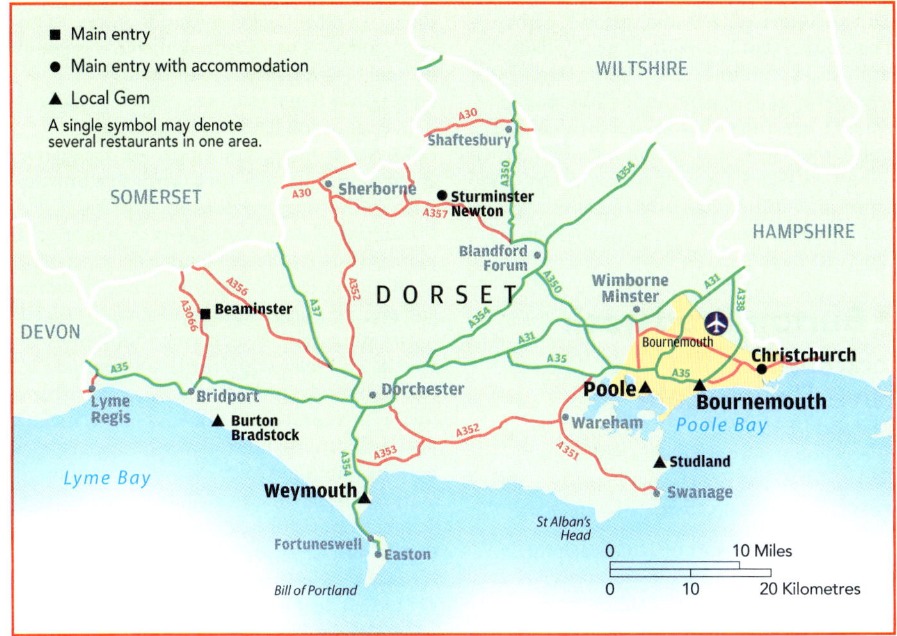

Beaminster

NEW ENTRY

Brassica

Just great ingredients...
Cooking score: 4
Modern British | £30
4 The Square, Beaminster, DT8 3AS
Tel no: (01308) 538100
www.brassicarestaurant.co.uk

'Simple, smart and high quality, but with just enough tasteful, quirky detail to never be dull', is how one visitor summed up Cass Titcombe and Louise Chidgey's reworking of the old Wild Garlic site. Cass is known for bang-on flavours and for using first-rate British ingredients, and in this first solo venture his short menu is pretty much that: led by West Country produce and simple enough to support brilliant execution, say buttermilk-fried pheasant with aïoli and pickles or grilled Wye Valley asparagus that's teamed with toasted focaccia, wild garlic dressing and a virtually translucent lardo rapidly melting into the smoky, salty seasoning. Elsewhere, a huge grilled skate wing arrives with lots of capers, butter and lemon or there's hogget with tomato ragù and polenta, and a 'remarkably light' Bakewell tart made with Seville orange marmalade to finish. Service is 'incredibly engaging' and good-value prices extend to wines — a small, fun list, from £19.
Chef/s: Cass Titcombe. **Open:** Wed to Sun L 12 to 2.30, Tue to Sat D 6.30 to 9.30. **Closed:** Mon. **Meals:** alc (main courses £13 to £19). Set L £14 (2 courses) to £17. **Details:** 35 seats. Music.

Bournemouth

LOCAL GEM

WestBeach

Seafood | £35
Pier Approach, Bournemouth, BH2 5AA
Tel no: (01202) 587785
www.west-beach.co.uk

Slap-bang on Bournemouth's West Beach, this glass-fronted seaside favourite naturally attracts its share of punters, the main draw being ozone-fresh fish and seafood; perhaps Thai mussels cooked with ginger, coriander, chilli and kaffir lime leaves; Poole Bay lobster with garlic and herb butter; or Weymouth wild sea bass fillet with mixed shellfish and crab bisque. It's not all seafood, though. Fillet of beef will do the trick if you are in the mood for meat, but there's also the likes of red pesto and tarragon risotto. Wines from £17.50. Open all week.

◼ Burton Bradstock

LOCAL GEM
Hive Beach Café
Seafood | £30
Beach Road, Burton Bradstock, DT6 4RF
Tel no: (01308) 897070
www.hivebeachcafe.co.uk

With a 'fabulous location…the beach finely ground shingle and a wide-open vista of the sea', this gem of a café is open for breakfasts and lunches, plus Tuesday to Friday evenings from June to September. It gets rammed, even with marquee-style awnings expanding the seating, and you have to queue to order, but everyone seems to have a good time. Tuck into fresh local seafood: bowls of mussels and prawns; brill or lemon sole with garlic and lemon butter; turbot with samphire, saffron aïoli and chips. Wines from £15. Open all week.

◼ Christchurch
The Jetty
Slick harbourside restaurant
Cooking score: 4
Modern British | £35
Christchurch Harbour Hotel & Spa, 95 Mudeford, Christchurch, BH23 3NT
Tel no: (01202) 400950
www.thejetty.co.uk

Cool and chic, with swathes of glass and a sprawling decked terrace making the most of jaw-dropping views, the aptly named Jetty stands right by the water's edge on Mudeford Quay – a dream ticket for sundowners. Main man (and local hero) Alex Aitken has applied a sustainable green ethos to the place – especially when it comes to sourcing: daily deliveries of fish from the local boats are bolstered by foraged pickings, seasonal game and regional produce for a menu that bristles with clean-cut contemporary flavours. Prodigious plates of fruits de mer (hot or cold) vie with bowls of Jetty bouillabaisse and smart ideas such as seared tuna with seaweed, radish and pickled ginger salad, or you could take the meaty route with steak tartare followed by seared calf's liver with truffle sausage and caramelised shallots. Otherwise, mix surf and turf with a combo of pork tenderloin, sticky pork belly and squid stuffed with haggis before sampling Aitken's signature passion fruit soufflé. Wines (from £18.95) are a suitably cosmopolitan bunch.
Chef/s: Alex Aitken. **Open:** Mon to Sat L 12 to 2.30, D 6 to 9.45. Sun 12 to 9. **Meals:** alc (main courses £17 to £34). Set L and D £19 (2 courses) to £23. Sun L £30. **Details:** 70 seats. 30 seats outside. V menu. Bar. Wheelchair access. Music. Parking.

◼ Poole
LOCAL GEM
Guildhall Tavern
French | £35
15 Market Street, Poole, BH15 1NB
Tel no: (01202) 671717
www.guildhalltavern.co.uk

Frederic Seweryn's restaurant, opened in Poole's Old Town in 2000, ticks all the boxes when it comes to recreating the sort of French seafood joint that is common across the Channel, but sadly lacking in the UK. It's only a short walk to the quay. Expect locally caught fish and shellfish in traditional preparations; moules marinière, bouillabaisse, skate wing with capers, and sea bass flambéed at the table. Meat and veggie options broaden its appeal, as does the patio out back. Wines start at £17. Closed Sun and Mon.

Join us at thegoodfoodguide.co.uk

Studland

LOCAL GEM
Pig on the Beach
Modern British | £35
Manor House, Manor Road, Studland,
BH19 3AU
Tel no: (01929) 450288
www.thepighotel.com

Overlooking stunning Studland Bay, this elegant 18th-century villa has been given the familiar chi-chi treatment by the fast-growing Pig hotel chain. In the glasshouse-themed restaurant, the focus is produce grown in the kitchen garden as well as just-caught seafood from the Dorset coast. A typical meal might start with char-grilled cuttlefish and Hampshire chorizo with pickled sea kale and white bean purée followed by Poole Bay mackerel with confit beetroot and pickled rock samphire. Wines from £16. Open all week.

Sturminster Newton
Plumber Manor
What eating out in England should be
Cooking score: 2
British | £38
Sturminster Newton, DT10 2AF
Tel no: (01258) 472507
www.plumbermanor.com

Inhabiting a world of its own, overlooking beautiful gardens, historic Plumber Manor is certainly the genuine article, sporting family portraits and antiques, home to the same family since it was built in the 17th century. It has been a hotel for more than 40 years now, with the Prideaux-Brunes still doling out old-fashioned English hospitality in a sedate, genteel and polite atmosphere. The food remains comfortingly familiar. Brian Pideaux-Brune's cooking doesn't aim to be daring or flirt with fashion, but deploys good judgment allied to sound technical skills, producing, perhaps, crab mousseline with a light curry sauce ahead of partridge breast with black pudding and bubble and squeak. Scallops on minted pea purée, then beef Wellington with béarnaise sauce have been well reported this year, and the pudding trolley pleases everyone with its generously proffered medley of desserts. Wines touch on many countries and are attuned to modest pockets, starting with house French at £18.50. **Chef/s:** Brian Prideaux-Brune. **Open:** Sun L 12.30 to 1.30, all week D 7.30 to 9. **Closed:** Feb. **Meals:** Set D £30 (2 courses) to £38. Sun L £30. **Details:** 65 seats. Bar. Parking.

Weymouth

LOCAL GEM
Crab House Café
Seafood | £32
Ferryman's Way, Portland Road, Weymouth,
DT4 9YU
Tel no: (01305) 788867
www.crabhousecafe.co.uk

It may well be a humble wooden cabin, but with the owner's oyster beds just out front and views over Chesil Beach, the Crab House Café is a waterside hot ticket. Sit outside under a pink parasol or indoors (which is actually perfectly fine) and expect fish and shellfish from local waters. The oysters – Portland Royals – are spot-on, crabs are just waiting to be cracked and fishy options might include grey mullet with citrus fruits and coriander butter. Wines start at £14.95. Closed Tue and early Dec to early Feb.

Durham

Bistro 21

Appealing modern bistro cooking

Cooking score: 3

Modern British | £28

Aykley Heads House, Aykley Heads, Durham,
DH1 5TS

Tel no: (0191) 3844354

www.bistrotwentyone.co.uk

Out in the Aykley district to the north of the
city, not far from the University Hospital,
Bistro 21 is another gem from Terry
Laybourne's jewellery box. The ambience is
fresh and bright, with wicker chairs on a
pitch-pine floor the setting for confident
modern bistro cooking with immediate and
obvious appeal. Smoked salmon with all the
up-to-date accoutrements of beetroot, fennel,
blood orange and a quail's egg might compete
with ham, mushroom and Gruyère soufflé to
start, before the main business brings on
butter-poached smoked haddock with mash
and celeriac cream, or slow-cooked smoked
pork belly with char-grilled cabbage, black
pudding and apple purée. Finish with toasted
blackberry marshmallows, blackberry sorbet
and spiced pear. Wines from £17.40.

Chef/s: Ruari McKay. **Open:** all week L 12 to 2 (3
Sun), Mon to Sat D 5.30 to 10. **Closed:** 25 and 26
Dec. **Meals:** alc (main courses £8 to £18). Set L £16.
Set D £20. Sun L £22. **Details:** 59 seats. 23 seats
outside. V menu. Bar. Music. Parking.

Restaurant DH1

Classy cooking with a playful wink

Cooking score: 3

Modern British | £40

The Avenue, Durham, DH1 4DX

Tel no: (0191) 3846655

www.restaurantdh1.co.uk

Previously the Gourmet Spot, Restaurant
DH1 was undergoing 'adjustments' at the time
of reviewing, and all hopes are that the new
look will reflect the smooth styling of the

Join us at thegoodfoodguide.co.uk

cooking. Chef Stephen Hardy took over the restaurant in March 2014 – a building full of Victorian swagger and stern charm – and his efforts continue to ensure its position as one of the area's more ambitious dining venues. Pan-fried halibut with cauliflower, mussels and fennel is a typical starter, while 50-day-aged sirloin with oyster emulsion, shallot, wakame and fresh wasabi reflects a penchant for classy ingredients and imaginative flourishes. Wasabi notwith-standing, most flavours are resolutely European – such as rump of hogget cooked with hay, garlic, sprouting broccoli and ewes' milk cheese. There's the occasional playful wink from the kitchen – as in the 'Aero' dessert featuring aerated chocolate, salted caramel and popcorn. A nicely annotated international wine list kicks off at £17.

Chef/s: Stephen Hardy. **Open:** Tue to Sat D only 6 to 10. **Closed:** Sun, Mon, 25 and 26 Dec, 1 week Jan, 1 week May. **Meals:** Set D £32 (2 courses) to £40. Tasting menu £60 (8 Courses). **Details:** 22 seats. V menu. Bar. Music. Parking.

Hurworth-on-Tees

★ TOP 50 PUB ★

The Bay Horse

Cut-above village pub
Cooking score: 4
Modern British | £35
45 The Green, Hurworth-on-Tees, DL2 2AA
Tel no: (01325) 720663
www.thebayhorsehurworth.com

Set in an attractive village on the banks of the Tees, the Bay Horse is a 15th-century hostelry with a 21st-century soul. Beams, a real fire, polished antique tables, local ales, lunchtime sandwiches and roast joints on a Sunday tell one side of the story, while a menu of exemplary food with a strong seasonal accent completes an affable, contemporary package. In Marcus Bennett's hands, diverse elements such as king scallops, herb garlic purée, fondant potato, herb crumb, pancetta lardons, king scallop ketchup and mustard cream pull together into one glorious whole. Roasted chicken breast with crisp skin, breaded drum

sticks, confit ratte potatoes, creamed leeks and Madeira jus, and pressed, salted pork belly with mini pork pies, caramelised apples, shallot rings and cinnamon crumb typifies his flexible approach to British and classical themes. To finish, there's raspberry mousse and purée with vanilla sponge and blackberry ice cream. Wines from £17.85.

Chef/s: Marcus Bennett. **Open:** all week L 12 to 2.30 (4 Sun), D 6 to 9.30 (8.30 Sun). **Closed:** 25 and 26 Dec. **Meals:** alc (main courses £17 to £28). Set L £14 (2 courses) to £17. Set D £21 (2 courses) to £26. Sun L £24. **Details:** 40 seats. 40 seats outside. V menu. Bar. Wheelchair access. Music. Parking.

Hutton Magna

The Oak Tree Inn

Immensely appealing gastronomic oasis
Cooking score: 3
Modern British | £38
Hutton Magna, DL11 7HH
Tel no: (01833) 627371
www.theoaktreehutton.co.uk

Is it a pub? Is it a restaurant? In truth, the Oak Tree Inn is a bit of both – although you'll need to book ahead to sample the food served in the smart green-upholstered dining room. In the rugged North Pennines, close to the Yorkshire border, this spruced-up hostelry still rolls out the barrel for local drinkers, but it's also an immensely appealing gastronomic oasis famed for its judicious local sourcing and pin-sharp cooking. Landlord/chef Alastair Ross knows how to extract precise flavours from his seasonal ingredients, while delivering picture-pretty creations for an appreciative local crowd: signature plates of seared sea bream with leeks, curry and mussels or loin of Middle White pork with sticky red cabbage, apple and smoked sausage are typical of his short, daily menu. Dessert might bring ginger-beer-poached rhubarb with poppy seed meringue, beer jelly and blood-orange sorbet. Wines from £16.

Chef/s: Alastair Ross. **Open:** Tue to Sun D only 6 to 9. **Closed:** Mon, 24 to 27 Dec, 31 Dec to 2 Jan. **Meals:** alc (main courses £20 to £25). **Details:** 20 seats. Bar. Music. Parking.

Summerhouse

★ TOP 50 ★

The Raby Hunt

Remarkable cooking of subtle power

Cooking score: 6
Modern British | £55
Summerhouse, DL2 3UD
Tel no: (01325) 374237
www.rabyhuntrestaurant.co.uk

'It's not flashy but it is crisp and immaculately looked after,' noted one reporter, charmed by the 'aura of elegant calm' at this ambitious country restaurant. In former times the RabyHunt was an inn, but in James Close's hands it has become a fine destination restaurant offering a high-definition version of modern food, underpinned by a mastery of sous-vide and low-temperature cooking techniques. To get a glimpse, the five-course tasting menu is a good intro; otherwise it's nine courses beginning with a salvo of intensely flavoured bites, among them a light, crisp cod skin dotted with aïoli and fronds of fennel and a meaty Lindisfarne oyster cooked at 62 degrees. The technique is 'seriously impressive' in a mesmerising combination of eel, beetroot several ways and cherry, but what astounds is the balance. Among meat dishes quail is taken apart, the leg confited, the breast roasted and the offal chopped into a rich stew with stunning depth of flavour, while a liquorice crossover dish plays with sweet and savoury tastes. This is top-drawer cooking, one where the 'free-thinking, ever-evolving but always confident approach represents everything one hopes to find in a chef likely to go places'. A pedigree wine list inspires confidence, too. Prices start at £29.
Chef/s: James Close. **Open:** Wed to Sat L 12 to 2.30, D 6 to 10. **Closed:** Sun, Mon, Tue, 1 week Christmas, 1 week spring, 2 weeks summer.
Meals: Set L £35 (5 courses) to £70 (9 courses). Set D £70 (5 courses) to £80 (9 courses). **Details:** 30 seats. V menu. Bar. Wheelchair access. Music. Parking.

Winston

The Bridgewater Arms

Character, warmth and local ingredients
Cooking score: 1
British | £40
Winston, DL2 3RN
Tel no: (01325) 730302
www.thebridgewaterarms.com

This deeply agreeable village pub is found in a listed 19th-century building that was once a school. An agreeable feeling of pastoral prosperity characterises both the fire-warmed bar and dining room and chef/proprietor Paul Grundy's menu fits the bill, listing the kind of food everybody likes to eat, whether a Lincolnshire Poacher mature Cheddar and spinach soufflé or the famed seafood pancake thermidor, to confit duck leg with garlic mashed potato and red wine sauce, and pan-fried wild turbot fillet on a lemon, scallop and pancetta risotto. Finish with saffron and cardamom poached pear with ginger ice cream. Wines from £15.50.
Chef/s: Paul Grundy. **Open:** Tue to Sat L 12 to 2, D 6 to 9. **Closed:** Sun, Mon, 25 and 26 Dec, 1 Jan.
Meals: alc (main courses £15 to £32). **Details:** 54 seats. V menu. Wheelchair access. Music. Parking.

Dedham

★ TOP 50 PUB ★

The Sun Inn

Classic inn with an Italian heart
Cooking score: 4
Italian | £25
High Street, Dedham, CO7 6DF
Tel no: (01206) 323351
www.thesuninndedham.com

£5 OFF

'Dedham is pretty idyllic to start with, but this pub had me checking the local estate agent windows and dreaming of moving there.' Such are the charms of Piers Baker's charming 15th-century village inn, which has 'a whole dedicated wood-panelled sitting room with open fire and no other use than to hang out…a few dogs lazing around, plus large stepped-down dining room'. Italian-accented cooking with locally sourced ingredients is the successful formula here – from antipasti of spiced duck salad, salami, speck or hake and wild garlic aïoli via starters of venison carpaccio with watercress, ricotta and hazelnut sauce, through to tagliatelle with chicken livers, sage and Marsala, and Saffron Walden duck breast with porcini polenta, Parmesan and spinach. Finish with vanilla pannacotta, with Lawford strawberries, grappa and meringue. Of particular note is the exceptional wine list, a blend of Old World and New, with good choice in each section in the £16 to £18 bracket, ensuring its accessibility, even for those on a tight budget.
Chef/s: Jack Levine. **Open:** all week L 12 to 2.30 (3 Sat and Sun), D 6 to 9.30 (10 Fri and Sat). **Closed:** 25 and 26 Dec. **Meals:** alc (main courses £9 to £25). Set L and D £12 (2 courses) to £18. Sun L £21.
Details: 70 seats. 100 seats outside. V menu. Bar. Music. Parking.

Average price

The average price denotes the price of a three-course meal without wine.

Le Talbooth

Classy food, classy location
Cooking score: 4
Modern British | £47
Gun Hill, Dedham, CO7 6HP
Tel no: (01206) 323150
www.milsomhotels.com

The waters of the Stour lap gently past this many-gabled and heavily beamed Essex evergreen – once a 'toll booth' for horse-drawn traffic across the river. Since 1952, this has been the Milsom family's domain, and it remains a wonderfully discreet 'special-occasion' treat noted for its country comforts, exceptional service and modern cooking. The kitchen knows its clientele, offering a warm pavé of home-smoked salmon, grilled Dover sole and chateaubriand with dauphinois potatoes alongside a roster of more contemporary ideas – from pan-roast wing of Cornish skate with razor clams, smoked shallots and lardo to saddle of Norfolk venison with thyme-infused polenta, blackberries, kale and red wine jus. The Anglo-French cheeseboard is a must, as are cleverly wrought desserts, such as butter-roast pear with Poire William, cashew nut and cinnamon. Wines from £19.25.

Please send us your feedback

To register your opinion about any restaurant listed in this guide, or a new restaurant that you wish to bring to our attention, please visit the web address at the bottom of the page. Your feedback informs the content of the book and will be used to compile next year's reviews.

Chef/s: Andrew Hirst. **Open:** all week L 12 to 2 (3 Sun), Mon to Sat D 7 to 9.30. **Meals:** alc (main courses £20 to £33). Set L £25 (2 courses) to £31. Sun L £36. **Details:** 80 seats. 80 seats outside. V menu. Bar. Wheelchair access. Parking.

Fuller Street

★ TOP 50 PUB ★

The Square and Compasses

Inspired cooking – an absolute treat
Cooking score: 4
British | £26
Fuller Street, CM3 2BB
Tel no: (01245) 361477
www.thesquareandcompasses.co.uk

Hard to find and with a deceptively modern exterior, it's tempting to give this 17th-century rural pub a miss, but 'that would be a shame' cautions one first-time visitor who persevered. He found the Square and Compasses 'absolutely lovely inside' with the wooden ribs of a delightful old building, lovely cosy spaces and dining alcoves and an open fire. Ignore the laminated pub classics menu of standard burgers, ham, egg and chips – the real action is chalked up on daily specials boards: pan-fried pigeon breast with a haggis and potato croquette, a 'delicious' wild rabbit and basil-spinach tortellini with smoked bacon risotto and rosemary cream sauce, and roasted turbot with lightly curried barley pilau – all evidence of rich, classically inspired cooking that feels like an absolute treat. It is best to book as the place seems to be 'a perpetually busy spot'. Wines start at £18.75.
Chef/s: Clint Arnold. **Open:** all week L 12 to 2 (2.30 Sat, 6 Sun), Mon to Sat D 6.30 to 9.30. **Meals:** alc (main courses £11 to £20). **Details:** 56 seats. 36 seats outside. Bar. Wheelchair access. Music. Parking.

Gestingthorpe
The Pheasant
Delightful inn with generous grub
Cooking score: 1
Modern British | £25
Church Street, Gestingthorpe, CO9 3AU
Tel no: (01787) 465010
www.thepheasant.net

Hidden in an Essex backwater overlooking the Stour Valley, this lovingly run hostelry is an absolute delight, with low-beamed rooms and a cosy home-from-home appeal. Green-fingered landlord/chef James Donoghue lives the good life here, cultivating a vegetable garden, keeping bees, raising chickens and smoking his own fish, as well as doing his bit to support the local food network. The result is honest pub grub with bags of generosity – witness ham hock terrine with homemade relish, slow-roast shoulder of lamb with Jerusalem artichoke and potato dauphinois or beer-battered haddock with hand-cut chips. Pies, steaks and crumbles complete the picture. East Anglian ales and good-value wines (from £15.95), too.
Chef/s: James Donoghue. **Open:** all week L 12 to 2 (2.30 Sun), D 6.30 to 8.30. **Closed:** Mon (winter), 25 and 26 Dec, first 2 weeks Jan. **Meals:** alc (main courses £13 to £20). **Details:** 40 seats. 20 seats outside. Bar. Music. Parking.

Harwich
The Pier at Harwich, Harbourside Restaurant
Fine seafood and estuary views
Cooking score: 2
Seafood | £37
The Quay, Harwich, CO12 3HH
Tel no: (01255) 241212
www.milsomhotels.com

'This is the nicest place in Harwich. Its tables are well positioned for a pretty good view across the sea/estuary, although it's a bit blocked by the actual *Boat that Rocked*, which is now a museum ship.' So ran the notes of one visitor to this spaciously appointed and smart seafood restaurant. While some come for posh fish and chips – deep-fried turbot with minted peas and gribiche sauce, perhaps – there's fancier cooking, too, from starters such as local crab and lobster salad with mango and coriander to main courses that stay admirably close to the idea of keeping fine ingredients simple, say pan-fried brill with spinach and hollandaise, or whole grilled lemon sole with beurre noisette, French beans and new potatoes. For a special occasion there's lobster (from their own saltwater tank), simply grilled or thermidor, and finish with a honey pannacotta with poached rhubarb and ginger shortbread. Wines start at £19.25.
Chef/s: John Goff. **Open:** Wed to Sat L 12 to 2, D 6 to 9.30. Sun 12 to 8. **Closed:** Mon, Tue. **Meals:** alc (main courses £19 to £30). Set L £20 (2 courses) to £26. **Details:** 80 seats. 30 seats outside. Bar. Music. Parking.

Horndon on the Hill
The Bell Inn
Medieval pub with a modern menu
Cooking score: 2
Modern European | £32
High Road, Horndon on the Hill, SS17 8LD
Tel no: (01375) 642463
www.bell-inn.co.uk

The Verekers' good-natured gem of a 15th-century coaching inn is run with genuine enthusiasm but then the family has clocked up some 75 years of experience here. It's still run very much as a free house, dispensing real ales and genuine hospitality, but it also successfully bridges the hard-to-achieve divide between village pub and stylish restaurant-with-rooms. The kitchen is not trying to reinvent the culinary wheel, but the carefully sourced produce is precisely cooked and thoughtfully presented. In the bar there's honey-roast confit pork belly or minute steak with tomato jam and fried duck egg, while in the dining room choice ranges from treacle-

cured salmon gravadlax with mustard and dill mayonnaise to sous-vide lamb saddle stuffed with chicken mousse and mushrooms and confit shoulder with minted pea purée. Wines from £15.95.

Chef/s: Stuart Fay. **Open:** all week L 12 to 2 (2.30 Sun), D 6.30 to 10 (6 Sat, 7 Sun). **Closed:** 25 and 26 Dec, bank hols. **Meals:** alc (main courses £12 to £29). **Details:** 80 seats. 50 seats outside. Bar. Wheelchair access. Parking.

▋ Mistley
The Mistley Thorn

Vibrant cooking and tiptop seafood
Cooking score: 2
Modern European | £25
High Street, Mistley, CO11 1HE
Tel no: (01206) 392821
www.mistleythorn.co.uk

Tiptop seafood is the main attraction at this sturdy 18th-century coaching inn, and Sherri Singleton takes full advantage of the catch from the Mersea day boats for her regularly changing repertoire. Local oysters and mussels are always in demand, but readers have also singled out scallops with minted pea purée and 'succulent, beautifully cooked' whole lemon sole with tarragon and anchovy butter. Otherwise, there are plenty of vibrant, Mediterranean flavours in the shape of, say, home-smoked chicken with panzanella, tomato, capers and basil, wild mushroom and pearl barley risotto or char-grilled venison steak with cavolo nero, vegetable crisps and béarnaise sauce. To finish, expect anything from apple and cinnamon crumble to chocolate terrine with malt ice cream. Wines start at £15.95.

Chef/s: Sherri Singleton and Karl Burnside. **Open:** all week L 12 to 2.30 (4.30 Sat, 5 Sun), D 6.30 to 9.30 (6 Fri to Sun). **Meals:** alc (main courses £11 to £22). Set L and D £13 (2 courses) to £15. Sun L £19. **Details:** 86 seats. 12 seats outside. Music. Parking.

▋ Stock
The Oak Room at the Hoop

Enthusiastically run local asset
Cooking score: 1
Modern British | £35
21 High Street, Stock, CM4 9BD
Tel no: (01277) 841137
www.thehoop.co.uk

They've been dishing out ales at the Hoop for 450 years and the white weatherboarded pub is an Essex gem in a pretty village. Head upstairs, though, and you'll discover the Oak Room restaurant, where linen tablecloths and some serious tucker await. Potted rabbit with Waldorf salad and toasted sourdough is a heartfelt little number, or go for an assiette of salmon. Creedy Carver duck comes with chicory Tatin, and 30-day aged beef with béarnaise and fat chips. Wines from £14.

Chef/s: Phil Utz. **Open:** Tue to Fri and Sun L 12 to 2.30 (3 Sun), Tue to Sat D 6 to 9. **Closed:** Mon, first week Jan, 1 week May. **Meals:** alc (main courses £12 to £27). Sun L £25. **Details:** 40 seats. 60 seats outside. Bar. Music.

▋ West Mersea

LOCAL GEM
West Mersea Oyster Bar

Seafood | £20
Coast Road, West Mersea, CO5 8LT
Tel no: (01206) 381600
www.westmerseaoysterbar.co.uk

Folk flock from far afield to eat at this basic wooden shed set among the hulks of the estuary's shipyard, packing the place 'to the rafters' for the very best in fresh local fish and shellfish. Simple tables are shoehorned in and cheerful staff dish up Colchester native oysters, 'spectacular' seafood platters loaded with silky smoked salmon, crab, lightly Thai-spiced tiger prawns, rollmops, cockles, mussels and more, and daily specials like crab linguine or five gigantic seared king scallops with bacon and salad. Wines from £13.95.

Join us at thegoodfoodguide.co.uk

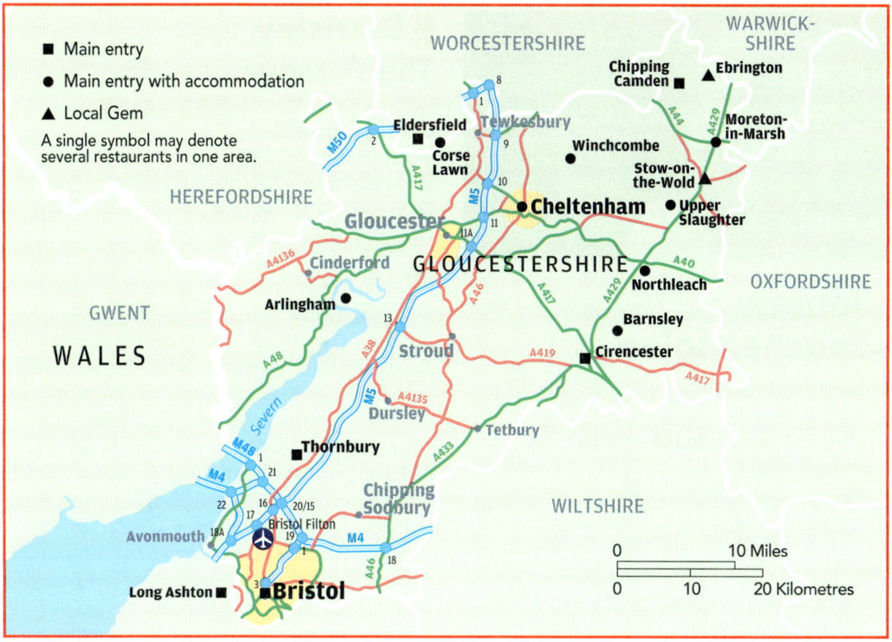

Arlingham
The Old Passage

Spanking fresh seafood and enviable views
Cooking score: 3
Seafood | £35
Passage Road, Arlingham, GL2 7JR
Tel no: (01452) 740547
www.theoldpassage.com

'Super place, river views, walks, lovely people and fabulous breakfasts too,' enthused one couple after staying over at this converted Georgian farmhouse down by the banks of the Severn. Gaze across the water to Newnham and the Forest of Dean before eyeing up the local art on the walls of the light-filled dining room, where spanking fresh seafood is the order of the day. Despite the odd gripe from readers about high prices, there is much to enjoy on the food front – from crispy Porthilly oysters and 'rather beautiful' razor clams to lobsters from the seawater tanks and colossal fruits de mer. Otherwise, consider a Salcombe crab 'club sandwich' with confit tomato, fennel purée and avocado cream followed by roast wild halibut with braised pak choi, celeriac purée, girolles and oxtail. Meat eaters might veer towards pheasant with braised red cabbage, while dessert could offer milk chocolate bavarois with salt caramel. White wines (from £19.80) naturally get top billing on the well-spread list.
Chef/s: Mark Redwood. **Open:** Tue to Sun L 12 to 2 (2.30 Sun), Tue to Sat D 7 to 9. **Closed:** Mon, 25 and 26 Dec. **Meals:** alc (main courses £18 to £48). Set L £15 (2 courses) to £20. **Details:** 40 seats. 24 seats outside. Wheelchair access. Music. Parking. Children at L only.

Symbols

Accommodation is available
£30 Three courses for less than £30
£5 OFF £5-off voucher scheme
Notable wine list

Jonray Sanchez-Iglesias

Casamia, Bristol

What do you enjoy the most about being a chef?
I love working in a creative environment and being able to work with my hands. I feel really lucky to work with so many people who share my passion and inspire me. The ultimate thing about being a chef is being able to see your guests enjoy the food you have created for them.

What inspired you to become a chef?
My family, in particular my dad and brother. When my brother Peter and I were younger our parents opened Casamia. Peter was the first to jump into the kitchen, but after seeing him and my dad at work, I was desperate to join them.

What food could you not live without?
I couldn't live without Indian food. I find it so exciting to eat. The interesting flavours and spices are so intriguing, yet comforting to me. I'm always in a good mood after a great curry.

At the end of a long day, what do you like to cook?
A full English breakfast. Mornings are normally very busy in my house so I don't often get to enjoy a leisurely breakfast. So, after a long day there's nothing better.

▌Barnsley
The Potager
Rich pickings from a famous garden
Cooking score: 3
Modern British | £38
Barnsley House, Barnsley, GL7 5EE
Tel no: (01285) 740000
www.barnsleyhouse.com

Swarms of enthusiasts (green-fingered or otherwise) regularly descend on boutique Barnsley House to marvel at its world-famous gardens – the enduring legacy of horticultural doyenne Rosemary Verey. The hotel's productive acres also provide trug-loads of seasonal produce for the appropriately named Potager restaurant – a long dining room done out in refreshing light tones. Casual lunches and more serious dinners make the most of the day's pickings, and the result is a roster of bright, peppy dishes with strong Mediterranean overtones: grilled polenta with pheasant, chestnut and cavolo nero sits alongside the signature vincisgrassi (a luxurious 18th-century take on lasagne), but the menu also accommodates small plates of, say, potted duck with celeriac rémoulade and quince. After that, go large with Brixham crab, Cox's apple and cress or confit duck with cauliflower cheese, sauté potatoes and sprout flowers. To finish, tangy Sicilian lemon tart with lime and yoghurt sorbet hits all the right notes. A substantial wine list opens with numerous house selections from £25.75.
Chef/s: Graham Grafton. **Open:** all week L 12 to 2 (2.30 Sat and Sun), D 7 to 9.30 (10 Fri and Sat, 9 Sun). **Meals:** alc (main courses £14 to £28). Set L £24 (2 courses) to £28. **Details:** 70 seats. 25 seats outside. Bar. Music. Parking. Children over 12 yrs only.

LOCAL GEM

The Village Pub

Modern British | £28

Barnsley, GL7 5EF

Tel no: (01285) 740421

www.thevillagepub.co.uk

It's a pub all right, but quite a posh one, with a gentrified rusticity that works a treat in the Cotswolds. Owned by the Barnsley House people (see entry for its Potager restaurant), expect real ales, real fires and a British-inspired menu that aims to deliver the feel-good factor. The pork pie is a posh Gloucester Old Spot version, Fowey mussels are simmered in Cotswold cider, and the fish and chips and burger are a cut above. Wines start at £18.75. Accommodation. Open all week.

■ Bristol

Bell's Diner

Robust eclectic flavours

Cooking score: 5

Mediterranean | £30

1-3 York Road, Montpelier, Bristol, BS6 5QB

Tel no: (0117) 9240357

www.bellsdiner.com

A one-time grocer's shop in the city's graffiti-strewn bohemian quarter, Bell's Diner has been a Bristol institution since 1976. As a quirky bistro and bar it's so informal that customers even take over turntable duties, happy to choose from an eclectic range of old vinyl LPs; staff also keep emergency supplies of cigars and spectacles for diners who have misplaced their own. In the kitchen, Sam Sohn-Rethel looks to the Mediterranean, the Middle East and North Africa for inspiration, using impeccable ingredients in robust, unfussy dishes that are big on flavour, say salt cod, avocado and blood-orange salad. Following on might be a main course of ricotta ravioli with ox cheek and red wine ragù, then a selection of outstanding homemade ices (hazelnut praline is a favourite), although rosewater poached pear with saffron ice cream also catches the eye. A carefully constructed, lively wine list starts at £18.

Chef/s: Sam Sohn-Rethel. **Open:** Tue to Sat L 12 to 3, Mon to Sat D 6 to 10. **Closed:** Sun, 25 to 26 Dec. **Meals:** alc (small plates £5 to £16). **Details:** 60 seats. Bar. Music.

Birch

Earthy and astute British cooking

Cooking score: 4

Modern British | £27

47 Raleigh Road, Bristol, BS3 1QS

Tel no: (0117) 9028326

www.birchbristol.co

Before Birch, Sam Leach and Beccy Massey ran supper clubs from their home, but a spell learning their craft in notable London establishments such as St John (see entry) armed them with enough know-how to follow their dream and go it alone. Since it opened in May 2014, this small neighbourhood restaurant has become one of Bristol's hottest culinary tickets. The white, minimalist room is as unpretentious and unshowy as the robust food, which demonstrates an almost puritanical commitment to seasonality and local produce, much of it grown in the owners' abundant market garden on the outskirts of the city. In spring, for example, dinner might start with lamb's sweetbreads, celeriac, wild garlic and jack-by-the-hedge and continue with roast Dexter beef paired with parsnip, anchovy, turnip and chard. For dessert, there could be rhubarb and hazelnut mess. The conscientiously sourced European-only wine list opens at £19 and showcases small producers, many of whom the owners have visited personally.

Chef/s: Sam Leach. **Open:** Wed to Sat D only 6 to 10. **Closed:** Sun, Mon, Tue, 2 weeks Christmas, 2 weeks Aug. **Meals:** alc (main courses £12 to £17). **Details:** 24 seats. Music.

Peter Sanchez-Iglesias

Casamia, Bristol

What do you enjoy the most about being a chef?

I love creating an experience for someone that they will remember for a long time. For me, the best thing about being a chef is the creative freedom I have, it's so exciting to be part of an industry that has no boundaries.

What's your newest ingredient discovery?

Recently I've discovered some new varieties of seaweed and sea herbs growing on our doorstep in Portishead. We've been working with these in the restaurant and we're currently using them on our lamb dish.

Is there a particular dish that evokes strong memories for you?

Food is very emotive for me. If I had to pick just one I would say my dad's Spanish stew. Just the smell of roasted garlic and chickpeas evokes happy memories of my family all together enjoying my dad's delicious food.

At the end of a long day, what do you like to cook?

Definitely something simple, quick and tasty. Pasta with garlic and olive oil normally hits the spot.

Bravas

Atmospheric and effervescent tapas bar
Cooking score: 2
Spanish | £15
7 Cotham Hill, Bristol, BS6 6LD
Tel no: (0117) 3296887
www.bravas.co.uk

£5 OFF £30

What started out as a secret underground supper club run from Kieran and Imogen Waite's Bristol home has become one of the city's most in-demand eateries. Small, cramped and buzzing, Bravas has the genuine feel of a lively Barcelona tapas joint as diners and drinkers sit cheek by jowl at tables at the back or grab high stools at the elmwood bar. From the tiny open kitchen behind the bar, the daily changing seasonal menu may include mussels in crab broth; venison and oyster mushroom in garlic chilli oil or pepper, courgette and harissa salad. The sizzling plancha grill is the lynchpin of the kitchen and comes into its own when wild red prawns or Ibérico pork are available. Too full for dessert? Then order the salted chocolate truffles or share a plate of goats' cheese topped with honey, thyme and walnuts. A conscientiously sourced all-Spanish wine list starts at £16.95.
Chef/s: Imogen Waite. **Open:** Tue to Thur D only 5 to 11. Fri and Sat 12 to 11. **Closed:** Sun, Mon, 24 to 26 Dec, first week Jan. **Meals:** alc (tapas £3 to £7). **Details:** 38 seats. Music.

★ TOP 50 ★

Casamia

Proud, vital, destination dining
Cooking score: 7
Modern British | £68
38 High Street, Westbury on Trym, Bristol, BS9 3DZ
Tel no: (0117) 9592884
www.casamiarestaurant.co.uk

£5 OFF

Don't be deceived by the name or the suburban Bristol location: this is a cutting-edge restaurant, understated and relaxed, one of the unsung heroes of the British restaurant scene. Indeed, a first meal here can feel like stumbling across a well-kept secret, though with booking advised even early in the week, Casamia obviously has a considerable number of fans. Peter and Jonray Sanchez-Iglesias's cooking has pursued an interesting trajectory in recent years. They are chefs who have journeyed out to the wilder shores, picked up some ideas and then headed back to safe harbour again, combining modern juxtapositions with classical technique. What they deliver is a (one per season) tasting menu that gives a totally up-to-date perspective on the best ingredients. Not rich, not fussy, just simple ingredients perfectly cooked. There's some theatre, which is all good fun, with the junior chefs nipping out from the open-to-view kitchen to deliver and explain dishes. Consider these highlights from the winter menu: a superb winter salad with carrot and goats'curd ('a masterpiece'), a top-flight risotto of mushroom and spelt, brown trout with variations of cabbage, a 'sensational' fallow deer with parsnip, and a 'fabulous' transitional dish of celery rice pudding, a mix of 'hot-cold, sweet-savoury'. The likeable modern wine list (from £26) explores an interesting range of varietals from around the globe and there's a good selection by the glass. **Chef/s:** Jonray and Peter Sanchez-Iglesias. **Open:** Tue to Sat L 12 to 2, D 6 to 9.30. **Closed:** Sun, Mon, 24 Dec to 5 Jan. **Meals:** Tasting menu L £38 (5 courses) to £68 (10 courses). Tasting menu D £68 (Tue to Thur) to £88 (Fri and Sat). **Details:** 40 seats. V menu. Bar. Music.

Flinty Red

Vibrant Med menu and cracking wine list
Cooking score: 4
Modern European | £25
34 Cotham Hill, Bristol, BS6 6LA
Tel no: (0117) 9238755
www.flintyred.co.uk

The term 'wine bar' doesn't have the same kudos it did in, say, the 1980s, and Flinty Red describes itself as a wine-tasting venue and restaurant. It's not as catchy. But when there is good drinking and eating to be had, what's in a name? With its bare-brick walls, dark-wood tables and buoyant service, it's a fun place to be. Food and wine play equal parts in the package – it's part-owned by the owners of a wine shop a few doors down – with a Med-inspired menu of tapas-style plates (with larger versions of some allowing for three-course convention) and plenty of options by the glass and carafe on the European-focused wine list. Dive into cuttlefish and ink croquetas with aïoli, roast suckling pork belly with black pudding and rhubarb, ricotta gnocchi with braised lentils, and end on a sweet note with tonka bean crème brûlée. Sherry, vermouth and global beers are tempting alternatives to wines (from £16). **Chef/s:** Matthew Williamson. **Open:** Tue to Sat L 12 to 3, Mon to Sat D 6.30 to 10. **Closed:** Sun, first week Jan, bank hols. **Meals:** alc (main courses £12 to £24). Set L £10. **Details:** 36 seats. Wheelchair access. Music.

Greens

Welcoming bistro with wonderful food
Cooking score: 3
Modern European | £27
25 Zetland Road, Bristol, BS6 7AH
Tel no: (0117) 9246437
www.greensbristol.co.uk

Just off the main drag, hidden down a quiet and leafy side street, this contemporary bistro continues to impress locals with the quality of its cooking and value-for-money menus. The setting is relaxed, comfortable and welcoming, with Martin Laurentowicz's modern European cooking low on frills but big on flavour. A well-balanced smoked salmon and tarragon tart with celeriac rémoulade is one of the notable starters, followed, perhaps, by an equally impressive rabbit ragù with pappardelle pasta, spinach and purple sprouting broccoli. Chamomile pannacotta with citrus compote and shortbread makes for a refreshing and interesting finale. The two-course lunch deal remains a popular option, as does the separate vegetarian menu, which might include celeriac and apple soup with blue cheese and dukkah, followed by butternut squash and leek roulade with fennel and watercress salad. The concise, interesting wine list starts at £15.50 with ten offered by the glass.

Chef/s: Martin Laurentowicz. **Open:** Tue to Sat L 12 to 2.30, Mon to Sat D 6 to 10, Sun 12 to 10. **Closed:** 24 to 30 Dec. **Meals:** alc (main courses £12 to £20). Set L £11 (2 courses) to £15. Set D £16 (2 courses) to £21. Sun L £16. **Details:** 37 seats. 8 seats outside. V menu. Music.

Lido

Aromatic food in awesome setting
Cooking score: 3
Mediterranean | £35
Oakfield Place, Clifton, Bristol, BS8 2BJ
Tel no: (0117) 9339530
www.lidobristol.com

If you think the heyday of the lido is long gone, check out this one in Bristol's Clifton to see a bright and vibrant vision of the present and future. The old Victorian premises is still an actual lido – swim in the heated, low-chlorinated open-air pool – but the old viewing gallery is a thrustingly contemporary eatery with a wood-fired oven, and there's an outdoor terrace and poolside bar if you want to soak up the rays like the bathers. Freddy Bird takes inspiration from Spain, the Middle East and the broader Mediterranean to deliver inspiring stuff such as double-sucker octopus slow-cooked with harissa, and scallops roasted in the wood oven and matched with sweet herbs and garlic butter. Veggies fare well (wood-baked pumpkin and feta fatayer), while meat courses run to slow-cooked Ibérico pig's cheek perked up with Pedro Ximénez. A set menu, Freddy's tasting option ('Birdfood') and a wine list that sticks to the brief complete a compelling picture. Wines start at £18.

Chef/s: Freddy Bird. **Open:** all week L 12 to 2.45, Mon to Sat D 6 to 9.45. **Closed:** 25 and 26 Dec. **Meals:** alc (main courses £16 to £25). Set L and D £16 (2 courses) to £20. **Details:** 160 seats. 24 seats outside. Bar. Music.

Manna

Flavours from around the Med
Cooking score: 2
Modern European | £26
2B North View, Bristol, BS6 7QB
Tel no: (0117) 9706276
www.mannabar.co.uk

It may have started life as the unbuttoned offspring of Prego over the road, but Manna rips up the familial Italian blueprint, throwing Spanish and Middle Eastern flavours into a menu that's as easy-going as the warm, wood-rich interior. The tapas concept that once defined it still holds sway, but the menu has evolved into a charmer that satisfies both tapas/meze nibblers at the window bar and those who want a full, sit-down meal. Try Valencian home-fried almonds or Ibérico morcón to whet your appetite, then dive into eight-hour roast mutton shoulder with green beans and harissa (all the starters double as tapas-style small plates). If you fancy a main course, the 'creative and original' stuffed Cornish squid on 'proper baked beans' is 'terrific: rich and warming'. Desserts range from British classics (Eton mess) to the continental zing of blood-orange polenta cake with blueberry compote and crème fraîche. A short but interesting choice of European wines kicks off at £14.50.

Chef/s: Olly Gallery. **Open:** all week D only 6 to 10. **Closed:** 1 week Christmas. **Meals:** alc (main courses £12 to £14). Set D £15 (2 courses) to £20. **Details:** 40 seats. Bar. Wheelchair access. Music.

The Ox

Locally sourced steaks and cool cocktails
Cooking score: 3
British | £33
The Basement, 43 Corn Street, Bristol,
BS1 1HT
Tel no: (0117) 9221001
www.theoxbristol.com

Descend the flight of curving marble steps and you find yourself in the former vaults of the Ocean Safe Deposit deep beneath Bristol's old banking district. Now a steakhouse and cocktail bar run by the same team responsible for Pata Negra tapas bar (see entry), the Ox attracts a cool Bristol crowd. The wood-panelled dining room has a genuine wow factor with its polished parquet floor, frosted grape-cluster lamps and vintage mirrors. A range of impeccably sourced local steaks cooked over charcoal is the main attraction here but that's not to say the rest of the menu doesn't warrant closer inspection. A starter of charred squid, rosemary, garlic and chilli might be followed by BBQ pork loin chop served with ham and onion gratin and charcuterie sauce. End with chocolate délice, praline cream and poached pear or choose from several homemade ice creams and sorbets. Wines from £20.
Chef/s: Todd Francis. **Open:** Thur, Fri and Sun L 12 to 2.30 (4 Sun), Mon to Sat D 5 to 10.30. **Closed:** 25 to 28 Dec. **Meals:** alc (main courses £13 to £28). Set L £13 (2 courses) to £15. Early D £13. Sun L £17. **Details:** 80 seats. Music.

Prego

Tiptop local Italian
Cooking score: 3
Italian | £26
7 North View, Bristol, BS6 7PT
Tel no: (0117) 9730496
www.pregobar.co.uk

In an affluent part of the city previously starved of good restaurants, Prego quickly won over the locals when it opened in this former shop some six years ago. The Italian roots of chef/proprietors Olly Gallery and Julian Faiello mean rustic regional dishes of that country steer the menu, although the kitchen uses as much seasonal local produce as it does specialist Italian imports. The handmade pizzas are highly recommended, although the appealing carte and eye-catching daily specials board are just as enticing. A starter of fresh crab bruschetta topped with wild prawns and slow-roast cherry tomatoes might be followed by English rose veal loin with wild mushrooms, potato and cream ragù, greens and Marsala. All puddings are made on the premises; a zesty blood-orange cake with clementines and pomegranate being one highlight of a late winter visit. A commendably affordable all-Italian wine list starts at £14.50.
Chef/s: Julian Faiello. **Open:** Tue to Sat L 12 to 2, Mon to Sat D 5.30 to 10 (9 Mon). **Closed:** Sun, 1 week Christmas. **Meals:** alc (main courses £9 to £20). Set L £10 (2 courses) to £14. **Details:** 55 seats. 20 seats outside. Wheelchair access. Music.

The Pump House

Waterfront venue with bold seasonal food
Cooking score: 3
Modern British | £28
Merchants Road, Hotwells, Bristol, BS8 4PZ
Tel no: (0117) 9272229
www.the-pumphouse.com

Now a waterside pub with its own mezzanine restaurant upstairs, this converted Victorian pumping station is perched on the waterfront where Bristol's city docks meet the river Avon. Chef/patron Toby Gritten concentrates on bold, uncompromising seasonal flavours and he is also a keen forager, as can be seen from the wooden dresser lined with jars of pickles and preserves. Grab one of the scrubbed pine tables or relax on squishy sofas with bar snacks and 'nibbles' such as apple and black pudding Scotch egg or scampi monkfish tails with curry sauce. Alternatively, the carte might bring seared Bath chap with apple, celeriac and fried quail's egg, followed by brown butter hake with leeks, white beans and chorizo, then steamed Seville orange marmalade pudding. Regional ales in the bar are supplemented by interesting wines, from £18, and a phenomenal range of more than 450 gins. **Chef/s:** Toby Gritten. **Open:** all week L 12 to 3 (4 Sun), D 6.30 to 9.30. **Closed:** 25 Dec. **Meals:** alc (main courses £13 to £23). Set L and D £15 (2 courses) to £18. **Details:** 100 seats. 60 seats outside. Bar. Music. No children in restaurant.

riverstation
Confident cooking at this waterfront veteran
Cooking score: 3
Modern European | £30
The Grove, Bristol, BS1 4RB
Tel no: (0117) 9144434
www.riverstation.co.uk

£5
OFF

'This is still one of the go-to restaurants in Bristol,' is the considered opinion of one who has been eating at this harbourside veteran since it opened in late 1997. In days gone by the modernist building was a river-police station but inhabits a very different world now as a downstairs bar and café and first-floor restaurant – both making the best of river views. Chef Toru Yanada favours a predominantly European approach on his daily changing restaurant menu and has the good sense to keep things simple and seasonal. Quality ingredients make up a cracking starter of caramelised chicory, ewes' curd, walnuts, Red Meat radish and blood orange, while mains could run to Cornish wild sea bass with three-seed freekeh (lightly toasted wheat), spinach and romesco or a dry-aged English ribeye steak with peppercorn sauce and 'super' chunky chips. Desserts range from a 'very hearty' bread-and-butter pudding to bergamot orange crème brûlée. Service is 'prompt and friendly', and the wide-ranging wine list starts at £16.50.
Chef/s: Toru Yanada. **Open:** all week L 12 to 2.30 (3 Sun), Mon to Sat D 6 to 10.30 (11 Fri and Sat). **Closed:** 24 to 26 Dec. **Meals:** alc (main courses £16 to £20). Set L £13 (2 courses) to £16. Set D £15 (2 courses) to £19. Sun L £21. **Details:** 120 seats. 30 seats outside. Bar.

The Rummer
Inventive modern cooking in historic hostelry
Cooking score: 3
British | £30
All Saints Lane, Bristol, BS1 1JH
Tel no: (0117) 9294243
www.therummer.net

There may be a Nordic influence to Andrew Clatworthy's foraged and wild produce-driven menu but the setting is wholeheartedly Bristolian: the Rummer is tucked down one of the historic alleyways in the Old City, located in a medieval cellar beneath St Nicholas Market. It's a one-time Georgian coaching inn, the location of the first Berni Inn half a century ago. Not that Clatworthy's dishes are backward-looking in any way. Imaginative and resourceful flavour marriages and contrasting textures can be seen in a starter billed as 'burnt forest floor', which turns out to be an inventive pairing of wild mushrooms, truffles and leaves. It might precede a main course of braised Wagyu brisket, charred onion, black cabbage and star anise. For dessert, look no further than popcorn custard, nutmeg crumble, salt caramel and shoots. More straightforward and good-value lunch dishes include venison stew and toasted roast beef sandwiches. Wines from £18.
Chef/s: Andrew Clatworthy. **Open:** all week L 10 to 5 (11 Sat, 12.30 to 5 Sun), Mon to Sat D 6 to 10. **Closed:** 25 and 26 Dec, 1 Jan. **Meals:** alc (main courses £14 to £20). Set L £12 (2 courses) to £15. Sun L £22 (3 courses). Tasting menu £44 (7 courses). **Details:** 24 seats. Bar. Music. No children.

The Spiny Lobster
Quality seafood brasserie
Cooking score: 4
Seafood | £35
128-130 Whiteladies Road, Bristol, BS8 2RS
Tel no: (0117) 9737384
www.rockfishgrill.co.uk

£5
OFF

The name may have changed but it's still pretty much business as usual at the former Rockfish Grill. Owner Mitch Tonks wanted

this Bristol sibling of his Seahorse in Dartmouth (see entry) to establish a separate identity from his Devon collection of Rockfish seafood cafés. During the modest refurbishment, the fishmongers at the side has returned and diners now enter through a new curtained entrance on the main road. Sea-green leather banquettes and pictures of family and fishermen set the scene for skilfully cooked dishes that change daily depending on seafood deliveries from Brixham fish market, and much of it is destined for the charcoal grill. Start with crab baked in the Basque style with sherry and pimentón, go on to hake with sherry and capers (or bavette with rosemary and red wine sauce if you're not in the mood for fish), and finish with blood-orange jelly and Prosecco jelly. Wines from £18.
Chef/s: James Davidson. **Open:** Tue to Sat L 12 to 2.30, D 6 to 10 (10.30 Fri and Sat). **Closed:** Sun, Mon, 24 Dec to 5 Jan. **Meals:** alc (main courses £18 to £25). Set L and D £15 (2 courses) to £18. **Details:** 45 seats. Music.

Wallfish Bistro
Seasonal cooking from the heart
Cooking score: 4
British | £30
112 Princess Victoria Street, Bristol, BS8 4DB
Tel no: (0117) 9735435
www.wallfishbistro.co.uk

'The variety and quality of this great local doesn't seem to fail' was the verdict of one visitor to this intimate restaurant on the site of the late Keith Floyd's original bistro. Owners Seldon Curry and Liberty Wenham learnt their craft under the likes of Mark Hix and Rowley Leigh and Wallfish Bistro has become a treasured hangout for Bristol foodies since it opened in 2013. With caramel leather banquettes and lampshades fashioned out of metal colanders, and set over two floors, it's a quirky and unpretentious place. Curry's unwavering seasonal cooking looks to the south west larder, whether for a starter of Portland crab with asparagus, pea shoots and soft-boiled egg or a main course of grilled Weymouth squid served with veal cheek,

cauliflower and almond. The quality remains high to the end: apple and scrumpy bread pudding with toffee sauce and clotted cream being one persuasive dessert. Wines from £17.
Chef/s: Seldon Curry. **Open:** Wed to Sun L 12 to 3 (10am Sat and Sun), D 6 to 10 (9 Sun). **Closed:** Mon, Tue, 23 Dec to 2 Jan, 2 weeks Jan, 2 weeks Jul. **Meals:** alc (main courses £10 to £20). **Details:** 38 seats. Music.

Wilks
Local favourite with top-class cooking
Cooking score: 4
Modern European | £44
1-3 Chandos Road, Bristol, BS6 6PG
Tel no: (0117) 9737999
www.wilksrestaurant.co.uk

£5 OFF

Prior to opening Wilks in 2012, James Wilkins and Christine Vayssade honed their skills in a number of notable restaurants around the world, James working closely with the highly acclaimed Michel Bras in France and the Galvin brothers in London. With its slate-grey walls, black enamel lamps and seagrass-style table coverings, this modish backstreet restaurant oozes class, and Christine's razor-sharp service has been described by one reporter as 'immaculate throughout'. In the kitchen, James uses classic techniques and the best available local produce to create dishes that pack a punch when it comes to flavour: a light and delicate tian of Dartmouth crab teamed with quinoa, mango and wild sorrel, say, followed by a haunch of local roe deer with sprouting kale, sweet potato, chestnut purée and sautéed fresh chanterelles. Yorkshire rhubarb compote, walnut crunch and vanilla and cardamom ice cream makes a good finish. The meticulously sourced, French-leaning wine list opens at £19.50.
Chef/s: James Wilkins. **Open:** Wed to Sun L 12 to 2 (3 Sun), D 6.30 to 10 (9 Sun). **Closed:** Mon, Tue, 1 week Dec, 2 weeks Jan, 3 weeks Aug. **Meals:** alc (main courses £19 to £26). Set L £19 (2 courses) to £23. Tasting menu £70. **Details:** 34 seats. 6 seats outside. V menu. Wheelchair access. Children over 6 yrs only at D.

LOCAL GEMS

LOCAL GEM OF THE YEAR
Flour & Ash

Italian | £20
203b Cheltenham Road, Bristol, BS6 5QX
Tel no: (0117) 9083228
www.flourandash.co.uk

Owner Steve Gale used to be a high-flying banker, but he gave it all up to follow his passion for cooking. The result is a modest one-room pizza and ice cream joint in a former Indian takeaway that's been a hit since it opened, the go-to family-friendly place for locals, and a unique and well-deserved winner of our Local Gem of the Year Award for 2016. The wood-fired oven is the workhorse of this kitchen, whether it's for a starter of harissa lamb kebabs or one of the dozen sourdough pizzas with toppings such as aged fillet of beef, Old Winchester, rosemary oil and watercress. With eight flavours of ice cream changing daily, that's about it, apart from a short, lively wine list (from £16) and a few local beers. Open all week.

Pata Negra

Spanish | £25
Corn Street, Bristol, BS1 1YH
Tel no: (0117) 9276762
www.patanegrabristol.com

From the same team behind the Ox (see entry), this lively Spanish bar is ideal for a good-value plate of tapas and a glass of fino. Bag a stool at the counter or grab one of the armchairs beneath the vintage bullfight posters and sherry casks; either way, you'll find yourself overwhelmed with options – simple, no-frills tapas, albeit seasonal and featuring quality ingredients, whether a charcuterie tasting platter, salt cod brandade or pan-fried pigeon, blood orange, fennel and chicory. The Spanish-heavy wine list starts at £19. Closed Sun.

READERS RECOMMEND

Bosco Pizzeria

Italian-American
96 Whiteladies Road, Bristol, BS8 2QX
Tel no: (01179) 737978
www.boscopizzeria.co.uk
'I always grab one of the tables next to the open kitchen to watch the chefs throwing the dough and using the wood fired oven. The Venetian pizzas topped with salted Calabrian anchovies, mozzarella, marinara sauce, capers and black olives are to die for.'

New Moon Café

International
9 The Mall, Bristol, BS8 4DP
Tel no: (0117) 2393858
www.newmooncafe.co.uk
'The tapas is delicious…the baked quail with figs was delightfully cooked and the venison meatballs were braised to perfection. It makes a perfect lunch out and very reasonably priced.'

Cheltenham

★ TOP 10 ★
Le Champignon Sauvage

If heaven be a restaurant...
Cooking score: 8
Modern French | £59
24-26 Suffolk Road, Cheltenham, GL50 2AQ
Tel no: (01242) 573449
www.lechampignonsauvage.co.uk

'If heaven be a restaurant, let it be called Le Champignon Sauvage,' a reader rhapsodises, and it's hard to believe there's any 'if' about it when you contemplate the impressive form of the Everett-Matthiases' long-running Cheltenham thoroughbred. Decorated these days in warm coffee-and-cream tones, the place is enhanced by well-selected modern artworks, and the assured, serene tone of a front-of-house led by Helen. For a place that's been around since 1987, the Champignon does a knockout job of always feeling fresh, David's menus being alert to current trends while nonetheless mining their own rich seam of singular innovation. Respecting the integrity of top-drawer ingredients is one of the secrets, as can be seen in a starter that voguishly pairs scallops with stickily glazed confit chicken wing and baby parsnips, scented with woodruff, or there may be miso-glazed hake to start, in a Japanese medium of sea vegetables in dashi stock with chrysanthemum and seaweed. Those aromatising foraged components of dishes lend individuality to main courses such as lamb with caramelised bitter dandelion and baby turnips, and nerveless balancing of sweet-and-sour elements sees pickled butternut, black pudding and chocolate ganache form an eloquent backing chorus to roast partridge. Desserts have reporters reaching for sex metaphors (always a good sign) to encapsulate the likes of bergamot parfait with liquorice cream and orange jelly. The wine list conscientiously cherry-picks reliable producers in each of its concise sections, with house wines from a Burgundy négociant at £22.

Chef/s: David Everitt-Matthias. **Open:** Tue to Sat L 12.30 to 1.15, D 7.30 to 8.30. **Closed:** Sun, Mon, 2 weeks Christmas, 3 weeks Jun. **Meals:** Set L £26 (2 courses) to £32. Set D £48 (2 courses) to £59. **Details:** 38 seats.

The Daffodil

Pleasing food in stunning Art Deco venue
Cooking score: 3
Modern British | £34
18-20 Suffolk Parade, Cheltenham, GL50 2AE
Tel no: (01242) 700055
www.thedaffodil.com

A 'fab Art Deco restaurant mecca' is how one reader summed up this restored cinema – Cheltenham's first picture house back in the 'silent' era. These days, it's a very different prospect with a sweeping staircase up to the bar, 'kissing seats' in the mosaic-lined foyer, movie memorabilia everywhere and an 'open theatre' kitchen where the screen used to be. 'Perfectly executed' Anglo-European cooking is the main attraction, and the menu aims to please, whether you're after deep-fried cod with chips, crushed peas and tartare sauce or slow-cooked pork belly with crackling, cauliflower purée, buttered cabbage and star anise sauce. There are dry-aged steaks and lobsters from the Josper grill, the British artisan cheeses are worth a go, and the list of puddings might run to popcorn pannacotta with chocolate macarons and popcorn ice cream or iced rhubarb parfait with crunchy meringue, orange and ginger syrup. Service is 'second to none' and readers also applaud the well-chosen wine list, which starts at £23.50.

Chef/s: Tom Rains. **Open:** Mon to Sat L 12 to 2.30, D 6 to 10. **Closed:** Sun. **Meals:** alc (main courses £15 to £25). Set L and early D £14 (2 courses) to £16. Tasting menu £50. **Details:** 80 seats.

Lumière

Inventive modern dishes
Cooking score: 5
Modern British | £55
Clarence Parade, Cheltenham, GL50 3PA
Tel no: (01242) 222200
www.lumiere.cc

£5
OFF

Jon and Helen Howe's mid-terrace address near the town centre is handily placed to cope with custom from the nearby Ladies' College. It may look ordinary enough from outside, but indoors is a stylishly understated room adorned with abstract artworks, in which Jon's vigorously inventive British food feels entirely at home. Dishes make great aromatic as well as visual impact, scents of truffle and black garlic rising from butternut risotto with chanterelles and lardo, or star anise and cumin to perfume a classic pairing of scallops and pork belly with carrot and orange. At main, thoroughbred meats are wheeled forth, perhaps venison from the Badminton estate, with celeriac, sprouts, chocolate and pear, or there may be a robustly meaty treatment for fish, when oxtail, salsify and girolles turn up with stone bass. Vegetarian dishes show the same imagination, and dessert creations have included a white chocolate snowball fired up with whisky and exoticised with matcha green tea. Helpfully annotated wines start at £19.

Chef/s: Jon Howe. **Open:** Fri and Sat L 12 to 1.30, Tue to Sat D 7 to 9. **Closed:** Sun, Mon, 2 weeks winter, 2 weeks summer. **Meals:** Set L £28. Set D £55. Tasting menu £60 (7 courses) to £75. **Details:** 25 seats. V menu. Music. Children over 8 yrs only.

No. 131

Cool styling and big-hearted cooking
Cooking score: 3
British | £40
131 Promenade, Cheltenham, GL50 1NW
Tel no: (01242) 822939
www.no131.com

A stylish town-centre hotel with a cool basement cocktail bar populated by Cotswold hipsters, No.131 effortlessly blends contemporary style with old-school charm. After reports of inconsistencies, things have appeared to settle down in the kitchen since the arrival of Michael Bedford. In a former life, Bedford worked under Pierre Koffmann and Gary Rhodes and won acclaim for his own ventures in the Cotswolds. His no-frills, robust cooking is typified in starters of 'clearly very fresh and wonderfully light' devilled crab on a thick slice of toast or black truffle risotto with thyme and Parmesan. As well as steaks and shellfish, main courses follow a similarly classic theme, as shown in an early summer dish of turbot with asparagus, Jersey Royals and 'exemplary' hollandaise. Only three desserts were available at inspection, but a well-made tiramisu pushed all the right buttons. The French-heavy wine list opens at £17, with plenty by the glass.
Chef/s: Michael Bedford. **Open:** all week L 12 to 3 (11 to 4 Sat and Sun), D 6 to 10.30. **Meals:** alc (main courses £16 to £36). Sun L £18. **Details:** 128 seats. 48 seats outside. Bar. Music.

Purslane

Brilliantly conceived neighbourhood eatery
Cooking score: 6
Modern British | £35
16 Rodney Road, Cheltenham, GL50 1JJ
Tel no: (01242) 321639
www.purslane-restaurant.co.uk

'It was grey, cold and wet outside, but the welcome was warm in this little restaurant brightened by splashes of yellow.' So wrote one delighted visitor to this brilliantly conceived neighbourhood eatery run by 'smiling, knowledgeable and thoughtful staff', where Gareth Fulford delivers really creative food with bags of enthusiasm and expertise. His menu makes a big splash with deliveries of fish from Cornwall and elsewhere – hence 'truly exceptional' hand-dived Oban scallop with braised leeks, Mayan Gold potato and black pudding crumble, or lemon sole with wild garlic gnocchi, brown shrimps, grilled onions and parsley pesto. Seasonal produce from nearer home is also given eye-catching imaginative treatment, as in slow-cooked Cotswold hare with roasted parsnips, dates, chanterelles and hare consommé or a startlingly original twice-baked carrot soufflé accompanied by spring greens, smoked rainbow carrots and buttermilk dressing. Light lunches get rave reviews, while dessert might bring a fascinating assemblage of pistachio and olive oil sponge with lemon curd, goats' yoghurt sorbet and limoncello jelly. The wine list keeps it short, with bottles from £19.
Chef/s: Gareth Fulford. **Open:** Tue to Sat L 12 to 2.30, D 6.30 to 9.30. **Closed:** Sun, Mon, 2 weeks Jan, 2 weeks Aug. **Meals:** alc (main courses £18). Set D £35. **Details:** 34 seats. 4 seats outside. Music.

LOCAL GEM
The Tavern
International | £25
5 Royal Well Place, Cheltenham, GL50 3DN
Tel no: (01242) 221212
www.thetaverncheltenham.com

Spam fritters meet sticky chicken wings at this rebranded Cheltenham boozer – now a funky Anglo-American diner/drinking joint done out with reclaimed vintage furnishings, enamel lamps and other faux-industrial essentials. Typewritten brown-paper menus promise a transatlantic mash-up involving the likes of blackened salmon on noodles, Cobb salad, piri-piri poussin and 'beer can' chicken, plus a contingent of burgers, sliders and dogs. To finish, don't miss the baked peanut-butter and jelly sandwich. Booze is taken seriously, too, with over 20 bottled beers on show, plus real ales, cocktails and global wines from £17. Open all week.

◼ Chipping Campden

NEW ENTRY
The Chef's Dozen
Class, creativity and greedy enjoyment
Cooking score: 3
British | £38
Island House, High Street, Chipping Campden, GL55 6AL
Tel no: (01386) 840598
www.thechefsdozen.co.uk

In a big stone-built house in the heart of exquisitely pretty Chipping Campden, the Chef's Dozen feels a world apart from the street below, its first-floor dining room fronting on to a terrace shaded by a weeping willow. The interior combines heritage features (stonework, floorboards, beams and a stone fireplace) with smart contemporary furniture, and the kitchen keeps pace with British ingredients and a modern outlook. Black pudding might be a filling for ravioli, served with fresh pea velouté and horseradish foam, or mushrooms could arrive in a risotto

with pickled walnuts and an egg yolk. This is confident, ingredient-led cooking with assertive flavours and a focus on greedy enjoyment: bread is almost a course in itself, arriving as a whole fresh-baked loaf with churned butter, smoked pork dripping and a side of radishes with smoked cod roe dip. The native flavours continue with desserts such as layered meringue, custard and rhubarb jelly, with cooked rhubarb and rhubarb sorbet. Wines from £19.
Chef/s: Richard Craven. **Open:** Wed to Sat L 12 to 2, Tue to Sat D 6.30 to 9. **Closed:** Sun, Mon, 25 and 26 Dec, 12 to 26 Jan. **Meals:** alc (4 courses £38). Set L and D £16 (2 courses) to £19. **Details:** 26 seats. 20 seats outside. V menu. Music.

◼ Cirencester
Jesse's
Cute bistro with big ideas
Cooking score: 1
Modern British | £35
The Stableyard, Black Jack Street, Cirencester, GL7 2AA
Tel no: (01285) 641497
www.jessesbistro.co.uk

£5
OFF

Discovering this cute little Cotswold bistro among the low passages and climbing plants of an old brick stableyard is part of the fun, but don't be fooled by its cosy interiors, greystone walls, oak beams and polished tiled floors. The food coming out of Jesse's open kitchen is all about big ideas and busy combos – think dill-cured salmon with hot-smoked salmon roulade, beetroot and horseradish jus or hazelnut-crusted loin of pork partnered by a black pudding and apple bonbon, choucroute and grain-mustard sauce. Simpler dishes from the set menu also cut the mustard, the home-baked bread is a treat and the British cheeseboard is worth a go. Wines from £22.
Chef/s: David Witnall and Andrew Parffrey. **Open:** Mon to Sat L 12 to 2.30 (3 Sat), Tue to Sat D 7 to 9.30. **Closed:** Sun, 25 and 26 Dec, 1 and 2 Jan. **Meals:** alc (main courses £16 to £33). Set L and D £20 (2 courses) to £25. **Details:** 47 seats. 25 seats outside. Wheelchair access. Music.

Made by Bob

Deli-dining in a Cotswold town
Cooking score: 3
Modern British | £30
The Corn Hall, 26 Market Place, Cirencester,
GL7 2NY
Tel no: (01285) 641818
www.foodmadebybob.com

You can't get much closer to the action than this: Made by Bob's fresh, cool interior includes a large open kitchen – a feast of busy chefs and stainless steel – edged by a bar for those who want to watch. The rest of the seating, at simple, unclothed tables, channels the same deli vibe as the rest of the place (which includes a shop full of rare treats to take home). Chef-owner Bob Parkinson conjures a snappy Euro-slanted menu that covers everything from breakfast to afternoon snacks most days and runs into the evening on Fridays. Smoked haddock brandade with poached egg and mustard dressing is a typical starter, while linguine with fresh black truffle and Parmesan typifies the Italian flavour of much of the cooking. Be sure to try sweet treats such as salted-caramel and chocolate tart with pistachio brittle. A snappy and interesting selection of wines starts at £16.
Chef/s: Bob Parkinson. **Open:** Mon to Sat L 12 to 3, Fri D 7 to 9. **Closed:** Sun. **Meals:** alc (main courses £11 to £21). **Details:** 70 seats. Wheelchair access.

Corse Lawn
Corse Lawn House Hotel

Old-school elegance and classic cooking
Cooking score: 3
Anglo-French | £35
Corse Lawn, GL19 4LZ
Tel no: (01452) 780771
www.corselawn.com

Since 1978, this gracious Queen Anne mansion has been dutifully tended by Baba Hine and other family members, who have imbued the place with bags of old-school elegance. Framed prints on peach-toned walls, thick red carpets and period furnishings set the tone in the dining room, where well-drilled staff go about their business in very proper fashion. Appropriately, the kitchen keeps things familiar, overlaying bourgeois Anglo-French themes with the odd contemporary riff – although its heart is in the world of fish soup, slow-cooked beef cheeks with mushrooms or pheasant with Savoy cabbage and cranberry sauce. Otherwise, oxtail terrine and Chinese-spiced pork belly with lime, ginger and honey add some spice to proceedings, while desserts stay in the mainstream for caramelised rice pudding or rhubarb and custard mille-feuille. Simpler food is available in the adjoining bistro. The lovingly curated wine list is true to the family's vinous pedigree, with exhaustive coverage of the French regions and beyond. Bottles from £20.50.
Chef/s: Martin Kinahan. **Open:** all week L 12 to 2, D 7 to 9.30. **Closed:** 24 to 26 Dec. **Meals:** alc (main courses £15 to £23). Set L £23 (2 courses) to £26. Set D £34. Sun L £26. **Details:** 80 seats. 40 seats outside. Bar. Wheelchair access. Parking.

Ebrington

LOCAL GEM
The Ebrington Arms
Modern British | £30
Ebrington, GL55 6NH
Tel no: (01386) 593223
www.theebringtonarms.co.uk

A stone-built 17th-century Cotswold inn, all beams and log-burners within, is the textbook setting for modern Anglo-French pub food with a definite edge of ambition. How else to explain the blowtorching of salmon for a starter that adds buttermilk, gazpacho, tomatoes and sea purslane to the mix? Next up could be breast and leg of Tiddenham duck given the à l'orange treatment, as well as confit carrots and a seasoning of ras-el-hanout, and then proceedings conclude satisfyingly with a dark chocolate délice, accompanied by the essential salt caramel and an ice cream flavoured with mead. An impressive wine list starts at £19.50. Open all week.

Eldersfield

The Butchers Arms

Proper pub, confident cooking
Cooking score: 5
Modern British | £45
Lime Street, Eldersfield, GL19 4NX
Tel no: (01452) 840381
www.thebutchersarms.net

James and Elizabeth Winter's unalloyed rural idyll elicits delighted reactions from many readers. That's thanks in part to a careful balance of pubby approachability, genuine civility and warmth, and James' simple but alluring cooking. When a meal can open with faggot and onions with black pudding and oxtail pie, it is clear that cooking is taken seriously. Everybody seems to find everything 'delicious', and reporters have applauded 'beautifully cooked' turbot, roasted on the bone and served, on one occasion, with a Fowey mussel sauce, mashed potato and brown shrimp croquette, on another with lobster tortellini, pea purée and a fish sauce. Elsewhere, there could be pork chop teamed with almond and rhubarb tart, lentils and bacon and buttered spinach. Desserts have been a particular highlight for many, and peach and pistachio macaroons with raspberry sorbet and pistachio ice cream garners as much praise as dark chocolate fondant with white chocolate and strawberry ice cream. Local ales are tapped from the cask and the short, well-chosen wine list opens at £21.50.
Chef/s: James Winter. **Open:** Fri to Sun L 12 to 1 (bookings only), Tue to Sat D 7 to 9. **Closed:** Mon, 2 weeks Christmas, 2 weeks Aug. **Meals:** alc (main courses £20 to £26). **Details:** 25 seats. 3 seats outside. Bar. Parking. No children under 10 yrs.

Long Ashton

The Bird in Hand

Handsome village pub on the up
Cooking score: 2
British | £27
17 Weston Road, Long Ashton, BS41 9LA
Tel no: (01275) 395222
www.bird-in-hand.co.uk

Run by the team behind the Bristol's Pump House (see entry), this much improved village pub takes its food seriously, right down to walls plastered with pages ripped from old Mrs Beeton cookbooks. Shelves lined with homemade chutneys and preserves are another indicator that the kitchen means business and chefs favour the wild and foraged approach for many of the seasonal ingredients on the menu. Dishes are simple and produce-driven: from the bar menu could come hot Scotch egg, Cheddar and ale rarebit, or rare onglet with horseradish butter and watercress salad. In winter, the carte has delivered confit hake, fennel and blood orange, then beef cheek and sirloin with onions, kale, salsify and marrow crumbs, with puddings running from lemon meringue parfait to warm gingerbread with stout ice cream. The well-judged wine list has been intelligently tailored to complement the food, with bottles from £16.
Chef/s: Jack Williams. **Open:** all week L 12 to 3 (4 Sun), D 6 to 9 (6.30 Sun). **Closed:** 25 Dec. **Meals:** alc (main courses £13 to £19). **Details:** 48 seats. 45 seats outside. Bar. Music.

It seemed a good idea at the time...

Barely a month goes by without somebody dreaming up a new restaurant concept, and the urge to push the boundaries is leading diners into strange new territory.

Concept restaurants and cafés can broadly be divided into two types: those whose theme relates to the food and those built around a non-food-related concept: step forward Lady Dinah's Cat Emporium, where your cup of tea comes with a side order of eleven purring felines!

The food-led contenders range from wacky novelties to destinations for a proper hot meal – London's snappy Bubbledogs (Champagne and hot dogs) and Bristol's Flour and Ash (sourdough pizza) are good examples of the latter.

For novelty, look to Brick Lane's Cereal Killer, where you can have whatever you want – as long as it's cereal.

Other mono-line players include the Poached Egg Bar on Stoke Newington Road – and at the time of going to print, Britain's first insect restaurant, Grub Kitchen, is set to open in Pembrokeshire. It's all great fun – but only time will separate the sublime from the ridiculous.

Moreton in Marsh
Horse & Groom

Consistently satisfying hilltop inn
Cooking score: 2
Modern British | £27
Bourton on the Hill, Moreton in Marsh, GL56 9AQ
Tel no: (01386) 700413
www.horseandgroom.info

£5 OFF 🛏 £30

Panoramic Cotswold views are just one of the assets at this honey-coloured stone inn perched on a hill. Brothers Will and Tom Greenstock have preserved the pub's original virtues by dispensing real ale for the locals and reeling in long-distance diners with a seasonal menu and daily blackboards. Local sourcing is close to the kitchen's heart and the frequently changing menu makes its point with dishes such as a satisfying starter of pressed Tamworth pork and chicken terrine with piccalilli, rocket and toast. One reporter, who enjoyed a 'terrific' main course of griddled Longhorn ribeye steak with green peppercorn, rocket, horseradish and shallot butter, appreciated the precise cooking of the meat as much as the 'super' homemade chips. When it comes to desserts, consider the steamed marmalade pudding with marmalade sauce and Jersey cream. Starting at £15, the concise wine list offers an interesting spread of contemporary-meets-Old World styles.
Chef/s: Will Greenstock. **Open:** all week L 12 to 2 (2.30 Sun), Mon to Sat D 7 to 9 (9.30 Fri and Sat). **Closed:** 25 Dec, 31 Dec, 1 week Jan. **Meals:** alc (main courses £12 to £22). **Details:** 75 seats. 54 seats outside. Bar. Parking.

Northleach

The Wheatsheaf Inn

Captivating Cotswold coaching inn
Cooking score: 3
Modern British | £35
West End, Northleach, GL54 3EZ
Tel no: (01451) 860244
www.cotswoldswheatsheaf.com

The Pearmans' lovingly renovated 18th-century coaching inn is an agreeable blend of country boozer and upper-crust inn. The succession of rooms is bright, airy and sophisticated and done largely in heritage colours, accessorised by flagstones, scuffed boards, polished tables and auction-house finds. A no-nonsense menu offering appealing and flexible ideas completes the sense of easy-going sophistication, taking in devilled kidneys on toast or pollack crudo with fennel, orange and dill salad. Indeed, the kitchen knows how to press all the right crowd-pleasing buttons while conveying a sense that this is more than just ordinary pub food. It offers beer-battered whiting with fries, crushed peas and tartare sauce, wild boar ragù with handmade pappardelle pasta, or pigeon pie with January King cabbage and creamed potato. Desserts hit the comfort zone with either sticky toffee or marathon pudding and an apple tarte Tatin for two. The wide-ranging wine list opens at £17.
Chef/s: Ethan Rogers. **Open:** all week L 12 to 3 (3.30 Sun), D 6 to 10 (10.30 Fri and Sat, 9.30 Sun). **Meals:** alc (main courses £11 to £25). Set L £10 (2 courses) to £13 (Mon to Fri). **Details:** 90 seats. 60 seats outside. Bar. Wheelchair access. Music. Parking.

Visit us online

To find out more about The Good Food Guide, please visit thegoodfoodguide.co.uk

Stow-on-the-Wold

LOCAL GEM

The Old Butchers

Modern European | £30
7 Park Street, Stow-on-the-Wold, GL54 1AQ
Tel no: (01451) 831700
www.theoldbutchers.com

After a spell at the Fox at Oddington, the Robinsons are back in Stow (though with Peter in an executive role as he is now head chef at Bibendum, London – see entry). It seems only fitting for a restaurant in a former butcher's shop that homage should be paid to nose-to-tail eating: Bath chap and scotched quail's egg, game in season, perhaps a well-seasoned game pithiviers with smooth pomme purée. Cornish Lemon sole with brown shrimp, caper and lemon is a piscine alternative. Service, led by Louise, is 'super'. Wines from £17. Open all week.

Thornbury

Ronnies

Low-key gem
Cooking score: 3
Modern European | £32
11 St Mary Street, Thornbury, BS35 2AB
Tel no: (01454) 411137
www.ronnies-restaurant.co.uk

Happily straddling the roles of casual bar and more formal dining room, this modernised 450-year-old stone building in a pedestrianised area of Thornbury is now something of an all-rounder. The food on offer reflects this. Bag an armchair or sofa in the inviting, ground-floor Atwells Bar for keenly priced small plates such as duck hash salad with poached raisins, or venison, Sharpham and cranberry slider. Otherwise, head upstairs to Ronnies, for a menu of seasonal, produce-driven modern European food. Here you'll find langoustine bisque with a warm salad of langoustine and lime gel, followed by pollack with fennel salad and Jerusalem artichoke velouté, or fillet of beef with shallot purée, beef risotto cake and olive jus. The look is predictably cool, even if the surroundings are a bit stark – but service is cheerful and the international selection of wines (from £15) is good value.

Chef/s: Ronnie Faulkner. **Open:** all week L 12 to 2.30 (2 Mon), Mon to Sat D 6 to 10. **Closed:** 25 and 26 Dec, 1 to 8 Jan. **Meals:** alc (main courses £14 to £23). Set L £10 (2 courses) to £13. Sun L £21 (2 courses) to £25. **Details:** 42 seats. 20 seats outside. Bar. Music.

LOCAL GEM

Romy's Kitchen

Indian | £25
2 Castle Street, Thornbury, BS35 1HB
Tel no: (01454) 416728
www.romyskitchen.co.uk

Romy's Kitchen is one of a rare breed – an Indian restaurant run by a female chef/patron. Romy Gill started out by hosting local dinner parties and pop-ups before opening her first restaurant in a building that might easily be mistaken for a quaint tea room. There are no poppadoms, the menu is concise with very few of the Anglicised curry-house staples, and the authentic Indian home cooking is reflected in robust and aromatic dishes such as spicy Bengali-style goat with potatoes, onions, ginger and garlic, and chicken in pomegranate paste. Wines from £21. Closed Sun and Mon.

█ Upper Slaughter
Lords of the Manor

Cooking with technical gloss
Cooking score: 4
Modern British | £73
Upper Slaughter, GL54 2JD
Tel no: (01451) 820243
www.lordsofthemanor.com

Built in the warm tones of Cotswold stone and surrounded by impeccable grounds, this 17th-century former rectory coddles from the word go, delivering superlative service and

'faultless' French-inspired food. Guests love the 'fresh, original and inventive, without being experimental' menu, which might include a starter of port-marinated foie gras with apples with sweet wine jelly (a 'serious foodie moment' for one diner), or a main of loin and ragoût of Salisbury Plain venison with pickled red cabbage purée and crosnes. A 'stunning' deconstructed tiramisu makes a memorable finale, though an utterly classic hazelnut dacquoise with chocolate mousse and refreshing bitter orange sorbet could fit the bill too. Care is taken to match dishes with wines by the glass, and the serious list – it opens at £26 – deserves plaudits for its mix of distinguished bottles from well-known domaines and finds from, for example, Russia and Slovenia.

Chef/s: Richard Picard-Edwards. **Open:** all week L 12 to 2 (1.45 Sun), D 6.45 to 9.15. **Meals:** alc (Mon to Sat L only, main courses £16 to £32). Set D £73. Sun L £40. **Details:** 40 seats. 20 seats outside. Bar. Parking. Children over 7 yrs only at D.

█ Winchcombe
5 North Street

Classical cooking in a 500-year-old house
Cooking score: 6
Modern European | £45
5 North Street, Winchcombe, GL54 5LH
Tel no: (01242) 604566
www.5northstreetrestaurant.co.uk

The Ashenfords are well into their second decade at number 5, a stone-built, endearingly wonky-looking old house that's 500 years old. Catering for just 26 covers at capacity keeps things manageable, and contributes to the sense of taut control that Marcus – or Gus, as he prefers – brings to his classically based, European-influenced cooking. There are various set menus at different prices, which may be mixed and matched, supplemented by vegetarian alternatives such as cep gnocchi with sweet-sour peppers, shallot purée, baby leeks and sage. Plotting a course through the principal options might produce truffled smoked haddock risotto with quail's eggs and borage, then roast breast and spiced leg of duck with salt-baked celeriac in a reduction sauce enriched with caramelised orange. Thought-provoking finales include rice pudding pannacotta with bay leaf and lemon meringue, or a Banbury cake bursting with dried fruits, served with Roquefort ice cream and port syrup. Wines from a concise list open at £22.

Chef/s: Marcus Ashenford. **Open:** Wed to Sun L 12.30 to 1.30, Tue to Sat D 7 to 9. **Closed:** Mon, 1 week Jan, 2 weeks Aug. **Meals:** alc (main courses £18 to £25). Set L £24 (2 courses) to £28. Set D £35 (2 courses) to £48. Sun L £34. **Details:** 26 seats. V menu. Music.

The Lion Inn

Revamped inn with eclectic food
Cooking score: 1
Modern British | £30
37 North Street, Winchcombe, GL54 5PS
Tel no: (01242) 603300
www.thelionwinchcombe.co.uk

A godsend for tourists looking to explore the Cotswolds, this seriously revamped 15th-century coaching inn is also a boon for Winchcombe locals with its real ales, real fires and brushed-up rustic vibe – think heritage colours, warm rugs and polished floorboards. The kitchen delivers upmarket brasserie-style food with an eclectic slant, from pigeon breast with pearl barley and chorizo ragù or white crab frittata with black bean dressing to lobster and scallop linguine with lemongrass sauce or braised lamb kleftiko with Puy lentil stew. For afters, consider pumpkin pie with custard and honeycomb ice cream. Wines from £18.

Chef/s: Alex Dumitrache. **Open:** all week L 12 to 3, D 6 to 9. **Meals:** alc (main courses £14 to £25). **Details:** 35 seats. 50 seats outside. Bar. Music.

Wesley House

Modern dishes in a medieval house
Cooking score: 2
Modern European | £35
High Street, Winchcombe, GL54 5LJ
Tel no: (01242) 602366
www.wesleyhouse.co.uk

One of our more venerable listings, Wesley House has been around since the 1400s, a half-timbered merchant's house in an Anglo-Saxon town at the heart of old England. It all looks a sight more modern inside, with zebra-print bar-stools in the wine bar and grill, and neatly dressed tables against exposed stone and cream walls in the dining room. The kitchen produces a creditable version of modern European food, offering seared scallops with carrot and leek julienne in coconut cream to begin, or perhaps herb-crusted goats' cheese with red onion marmalade, before finely balanced main dishes that might partner lemon sole with rainbow chard and leek fondue in caper butter, or add potted cabbage and mustard mash to grilled pork tenderloin in sage jus. Poor old Black Forest gâteau gets taken apart again at dessert, or there may be fragrant orange and rosewater pannacotta with fig granola and pistachio sponge. Wines are grouped by style, opening at £19.

Chef/s: Cedrik Rullier. **Open:** Tue to Sun L 12 to 2, Tue to Sat D 7 to 9.30. **Closed:** Mon, 26 Dec. **Meals:** alc (main courses £16 to £22). Set L £15 (2 courses) to £19. Set D £22 (2 courses) to £28. Sun L £14 (1 course) to £25. **Details:** 60 seats. Bar. Music.

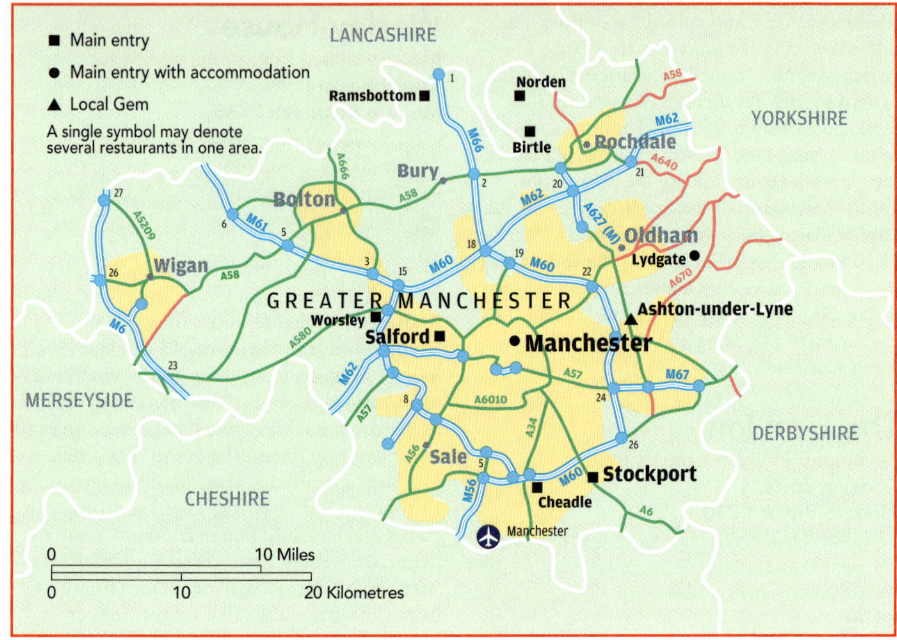

Ashton-under-Lyne

LOCAL GEM
Lily's Vegetarian Indian Cuisine

Indian vegetarian | £10
75-83 Oldham Road, Ashton-under-Lyne,
OL6 7DF
Tel no: (0161) 339 4774

'Well worth a visit if in the area. And worth a small detour if not in the immediate area.' So ran the notes of one reporter of this small, basic, all-day Indian vegetarian attached to the Asian ASM supermarket. The menu has a good mix of dishes from both North and South India, including a fine bhel puri, an 'absolute belter' of a crisp masala dosa, the potato filling well spiced with mustard seeds and chilli and teamed with a superb coconut chutney, and Punjabi aloo gobi, a well-rounded dish of potatoes and cauliflower with a zingy sauce. Unlicensed. Closed Tue.

Birtle

The Waggon at Birtle

Traditional and modern thinking
Cooking score: 2
Modern British | £30
131 Bury and Rochdale Old Road, Birtle,
BL9 6UE
Tel no: (01706) 622955
www.thewaggonatbirtle.co.uk

£5
OFF

The transformation from dilapidated pub to spanking-modern eatery put new wheels on the old Waggon over a decade ago, and there's a real feeling of something for everyone in David Watson's kitchen approach. You'll find staples such as mushroom soup, grilled haddock in parsley butter, and ribeye and chips in tarragon cream sauce on the Market Menu, but there's also room for some modern British thinking on the main carte. With Bury so near, expect benchmark black pudding, tempuraed up and served with Lancashire cheese, bacon and apple in mustard vinaigrette, before a modish lamb trio – rack, shoulder and shepherd's – with garlicky white bean purée in redcurrant and rosemary jus. Puddings span the range, too, from ginger sponge and custard to plum, pear and peanut tart with liquorice and blackcurrant ice cream. Five house wines at £15.95 (£4.25 a glass) head up a decent, fully annotated list.

Chef/s: David Watson. **Open:** Thur and Fri L 12 to 2, Wed to Sat D 6 to 9.30. Sun 12.30 to 7. **Closed:** Mon, Tue, first week Jan, 2 weeks summer. **Meals:** alc (main courses £11 to £24). Set L and D £16 (2 courses) to £18. **Details:** 45 seats. Bar. Wheelchair access. Music. Parking.

▊ Cheadle

NEW ENTRY
Indian Tiffin Room
Indian street food that rightly packs 'em in
Cooking score: 3
Indian | £23
Chapel Street, Cheadle, SK8 1BR
Tel no: 0161 (4912020)
www.indiantiffinroom.com

One local observes that ITR, as this suburban street-food specialist styles itself, is 'always busy' – and it deserves to be. Sure spicing, brilliant textural contrasts and the masterly application of hot hot heat characterise the best Indian street food, and the chefs cloistered in Indian Tiffin Room's modest semi-open kitchen can do the lot. The dining room is close-packed and the staff relaxed and knowledgeable. Hits include goat keema pav, the delicately minced and spiced meat mined with green peas and ready to pile into a buttered bun, perfect tandoor-cooked lamb chops, and the crunchy pastry globes of dahi puri drizzled with tamarind-sour yoghurt. Dosas are vast and crisp and, should you get to them, main courses include the house ITR chicken in a clingy, nutty sauce with a rich complexity that's rather wasted on inevitably dry chicken breast. It's all (including desserts like carrot halva at around £3) cheap at the price. Wine is from £16.

Open: Tue to Sun 5 to 10. **Closed:** Mon. **Meals:** alc (main courses £7 to £12). **Details:** 40 seats.

LOCAL GEM
Aamchi Mumbai
Indian | £20
2A Gatley Road, Cheadle, SK8 1PY
Tel no: (0161) 4283848
www.aamchimumbai.co.uk

The food of Mumbai – from the streets as well as the domestic kitchen – is celebrated at this boldly-designed Cheadle newcomer, where any colour goes as long as it's orange. Hits include the bhel puri, pav bhaji and mixed vegetables Kolhapuri, and 'cauliflower, potato, chickpea and paneer, in a well made sauce with a good spice kick'. Vada pav ('or spicy potato barmcake, as we'd say in these parts') works too, and there are Indo-Chinese and even Mumbai pizza options. Open all week.

▊ Lydgate

★ TOP 50 PUB ★
The White Hart
Hilltop inn with some stellar food
Cooking score: 4
Modern British | £33
51 Stockport Road, Lydgate, OL4 4JJ
Tel no: (01457) 872566
www.thewhitehart.co.uk

Over the last two decades the White Hart has fared well under the stewardship of Charles Brierley, who has transformed it from a top-of-the-Pennines village pub into a well-bred and handsome destination on every level (including weddings). It generates a mood of understated elegance and down-to-earth bonhomie where everyone feels at home. There's no standing on ceremony and no false posturing: what you see is what you get when it comes to service and food. The rustic brasserie offers an upbeat take on pub classics – Cumberland sausage and mash, crispy haddock and hand-cut chips – but upgrade to the more modern restaurant for young pigeon with date, pistachio and orange, and John Dory with tenderstem broccoli and brown shrimp butter or, should you be in the mood, one of the chef's tasting menus. Meals may end with six British and French cheeses, otherwise there's tarte Tatin with vanilla ice cream. Wines from £18.50.

Chef/s: Michael Shaw. **Open:** Mon to Sat L 12 to 2.30, D 6 to 9. Sun 12 to 8. **Closed:** 26 Dec, 1 Jan. **Meals:** alc (main courses £12 to £26). Set L £14 (2 courses) to £17. Sun L £23. **Details:** 100 seats. 50 seats outside. V menu. Bar. Wheelchair access. Music. Parking.

Manchester
Albert Square Chop House

Boldly British chophouse
Cooking score: 2
British | £29
The Memorial Hall, Albert Square, Manchester, M2 5PF
Tel no: (0161) 8341866
www.albertsquarechophouse.com

Local spies tell us that Albert Square Chop House is the pick of Roger Ward's revivalist chophouse mini-chain. Housed in the splendidly restored Victorian Memorial Hall, the bar and dining room mix dark wood, leather and brick with industrial-chic paraphernalia, lashings of conviviality and a hearty, tub-thumping approach to quality British meat. Tuck into richly flavoured 28-day aged rump or ribeye steak, served with chips and terrific sauces, a dry-cure bacon chop or a first-class steak and kidney pudding – considered a tempting option. The rest of the menu covers all bases, from Cornish fish soup, corned beef hash cake topped with a soft-poached egg, via whole lemon sole, and Goosnargh duck breast with smoked garlic mash, to golden syrup sponge with vanilla custard. Albert Square also scores with its lively street-level bar, and well-chosen, up-to-the-minute wine list. An extensive by-the-glass selection provides wonderful value and choice and bottles start at £18.95.

Chef/s: Jacques Hilton. **Open:** Mon to Fri L 12 to 3, D 5 to 9.45. Sat and Sun 12 to 9.45 (8.30 Sun). **Closed:** 25 Dec. **Meals:** alc (main courses £12 to £29). Set L and D £14 (2 courses) to £17. **Details:** 80 seats. 30 seats outside. Bar. Wheelchair access. Music.

Australasia

Pan-Asian fusion down under
Cooking score: 2
Pan-Asian | £32
1 The Avenue, Spinningfields, Manchester, M3 3AP
Tel no: (0161) 8310288
www.australasia.uk.com

Down under Deansgate, Manchester's airiest basement restaurant has kept its looks better than any Aussie soap star. The breezy beach-house interior still feels pristine, while staff seem fresh-minted from a source of positivity, knowledge and easy-going appeal. At lunch it's a calm, cool space (nights are livelier, especially at the swish bar), with a menu of small plates offering decent value. Sharing the smaller pan-Asian offerings makes sense at any time of day, with serviceable sushi available in pure and more offbeat (watermelon, beetroot and feta) variants. Hits at inspection included a sweet duck and crab broth with tapioca pearls and crisp shallots, and steaming pork and jasmine rice balls in crisp tempura jackets. Mango or chocolate soufflés are the house specials, but orange-inflected buttermilk pannacotta, buried beneath a riotous fruit 'garden' and served in a wooden box, is good fun for those who can tolerate a distinct lack of plate. Wine is from £18.

Chef/s: Jamie Smith. **Open:** all week 12 to 12. **Closed:** 25 and 26 Dec, 1 Jan. **Meals:** alc (main courses £14 to £20). Set L £12 (2 small plates) to £21. **Details:** 150 seats. Bar. Wheelchair access. Music.

Bollywood Masala

Punjabi with pizazz

Cooking score: 3

Indian | £15

15-25 Liverpool Road, Manchester, M3 4NW

Tel no: (0161) 8321290

www.bollywoodmasalauk.com

Vivacious and highly popular, this large restaurant handy for the Museum of Science and Industry injects Bollywood pizazz into Liverpool Road's gastronomic mix. Coloured lighting, psychedelic wallpaper and plate-glass windows showing the bustling street outside create an upbeat vibe, and a battalion of prompt staff maintains the pace. The expansive menu is a catch-all assembly that might first sound warning bells with its chicken and mash options, but examine closer and you'll find genuine Punjabi cooking executed to high standards. Look to the 'apna-style' list for authentic recipes such as on-the-bone lamb karahi, or magaz: lamb's brain of pâté-like consistency in a wonderfully fierce-flavoured masala. Fish tikka and a vast 'family' naan arriving on a hook show the kitchen's tandoori skills are sound, while momo (Nepalese dumplings) and southern Indian masala dosas indicate the geographic spread. A visiting Bollywood star might even consider the lobster masala. Wine from £12.50.

Chef/s: Mohammad Nawaz. **Open:** all week 3 to 11.30 (1am Fri and Sat). **Meals:** alc (main courses £9 to £15). Set D £14 to £19. **Details:** 150 seats. V menu. Bar. Wheelchair access. Music.

Please send us your feedback

To register your opinion about any restaurant listed in this guide, or a new restaurant that you wish to bring to our attention, please visit the web address at the bottom of the page. Your feedback informs the content of the book and will be used to compile next year's reviews.

The French by Simon Rogan

Bang on for seasonality

Cooking score: 8

Modern British | £65

16 Peter Street, Manchester, M60 2DS

Tel no: (0161) 2363333

www.the-french.co.uk

Like its older sibling L'Enclume (see entry), the French is in the front line of British gastronomy's new order and is driven by Simon Rogan's guiding principles: cooking that is bang on for freshness and seasonality. And recent meals suggest the cooking is 'getting better and better as time goes on'. The six- or ten-course tasting menus, overseen by Adam Reid, are built around little platefuls of confident, intelligent and skilfully crafted food, including the signature raw ox in coal oil, with crunchy kohlrabi, pumpkin seed and mustard leaf. Then there are dishes where vegetables form the centrepiece: yellow turnip dumplings and dice of marrow and fresh horseradish with a powerful beef and onion broth, for example, or sweet, earthy pickled red cabbage with a 'sharpish' Beenleigh Blue cream and sweet and spicy violet mustard with a scattering of linseed and walnut giving texture. Equally deft is the way barbecued purple sprouting, chicken-fat potatoes and briny cockles highlight the delicacy of a butter-poached brill that's 'just about cooked through'. Desserts continue the theme of exploring particular ingredients and extracting contrasting textures – as in poached forced Yorkshire rhubarb topped with toasted ginger oats and sheep's milk. No one has a bad word to say about service, it's 'pretty much perfect'. As for wine, it's hard to choose when the menu is so varied, so if your budget allows, go for the set wine pairings; if not, go for expert by-the-glass guidance (from £7); bottles from £22. And there's good news for those who find the historic inner room off the hotel lobby – now with greeny colours, woody carpet floor and two big shiny

chandeliers – 'not an instant winner'. Various 'design and space improvements' are planned to take place after the Guide goes to press.
Chef/s: Adam Reid and Simon Rogan. **Open:** Wed to Sat L 12 to 1.30, Tue to Sat D 6.30 to 9. **Closed:** Sun, Mon, 2 weeks Christmas, 2 weeks Aug,.
Meals: Set L and D £65 (6 courses) to £85.
Details: 58 seats. V menu. Bar. Wheelchair access. Children over 8 yrs only.

Greens
Iconic Mancunian veggie
Cooking score: 2
Vegetarian | £25
43 Lapwing Lane, West Didsbury, Manchester, M20 2NT
Tel no: (0161) 4344259
www.greensdidsbury.co.uk

Since opening in 1990, Simon Rimmer's meat-free Didsbury eatery has gone up in the world, morphing from down-home café to spirited foodie destination with dapper interiors to match – dark-wood panelling, dangling lights, posh floral wallpaper and olive-green banquettes. Dishes such as Rimmer's take on the classic Chinese shredded duck and pancake – here deep-fried oyster mushrooms with pancakes and plum sauce – and a 'belter' of a chickpea and veggie black pudding burger that comes on decent brioche and is topped with melted Cheddar regularly turn heads, but the kitchen is equally adept in other departments. Witness a 'lovely light salad' of charred and slightly wilted Little Gem with artichokes, broad beans, peas and a lemony dressing, and a couple of 'full of flavour' Lancashire cheese sausages with proper mash and beer gravy that so delighted one reporter. Desserts, however, are not a strong suit. Wines start at £16.
Chef/s: Simon Rimmer and Tom Pattinson. **Open:** Tue to Sat L 12 to 2 (2.30 Sat), Mon to Sat D 5.30 to 9.30 (10 Thur to Sat). Sun 12.30 to 9.30. **Closed:** 25 and 26 Dec, 1 Jan. **Meals:** alc (main courses £13 to £14). Set L and D £12 (2 courses). Sun L £15.
Details: 75 seats. 8 seats outside. V menu. Music.

NEW ENTRY
Hawksmoor
Beckett and Gott's steak in the north
Cooking score: 3
British | £45
184-186 Deansgate, Manchester, M3 3WB
Tel no: (0161) 8636980
www.thehawksmoor.com

The perfect fit for Manchester, where simplicity, warmth, meat and potatoes remain popular, this is Will Beckett and Huw Gott's first venture outside the capital. Hawksmoor brings 'really, really good' premium British beef, solid-but-opulent design features and high service standards to the old probate court on Deansgate. The bar is dark and moody, the main restaurant much brighter, with flashes of fire visible from an in-between space alongside the open kitchen. Daintiness is left at the door – potted beef with Yorkshires is a 'vast' starter serving of puddings, shredded meat and onion gravy, and the smoky house hamburger releases bone-marrow-rich juices that run down the unwary diner's arm. Steak, priced per 100g, might be impeccably charred 55-day aged D-rump with 'proper, perfectly fried chip-sized chips', or the rump and chips lunch special. Signature puds improve on nostalgia with salted caramel Rolos. Wine is from £20.
Chef/s: William Kirwan. **Open:** Mon to Sat L 12 to 3, D 5 to 10 (10.30 Fri and Sat). Sun 12 to 9.30. **Closed:** 24 to 26 Dec. **Meals:** alc (main courses £12 to £34).
Details: 137 seats. Bar. Wheelchair access. Music.

The Lime Tree
Long-serving local trouper
Cooking score: 3
Modern British | £30
8 Lapwing Lane, West Didsbury, Manchester, M20 2WS
Tel no: (0161) 4451217
www.thelimetree.co.uk

To be 'pretty much everything you want from a neighbourhood gaff' is praise indeed in these demanding times. The Lime Tree, as full now as when it opened almost 30 years ago, champions (very) local supply, turning to its own 20-acre smallholding for eggs, beef, rare-breed pork and lamb. Well-rehearsed combinations open the menu with the likes of a pan-fried duck egg with Bury black pudding hash and crispy bacon, or pork and game terrine with piccalilli, while mains might include slow-cooked shoulder of lamb from the farm with garlic mash and wilted greens. Wine is taken particularly seriously here. A glass of something sweet is recommended for each pudding – a mouthful of Monbazillac with an iced praline parfait and rich chocolate mousse, for example – and there's a selection of bottles, from £16, that delves into the cellars of small winemakers as readily as it plunders the big names.

Chef/s: Jason Parker and Gary Hinchcliffe. **Open:** Tue to Fri L 12 to 2.30, Mon to Sat D 5.30 to 10. Sun 12 to 9. **Meals:** alc (main courses £13 to £25). Set L and D £15 (2 courses) to £18. **Details:** 75 seats. 20 seats outside. Music.

Manchester House

Aiden Byrne's biggest stage yet
Cooking score: 5
Modern British | £55
Tower 12, 18-22 Bridge Street, Manchester, M3 3BZ
Tel no: (0161) 8352557
www.manchesterhouse.uk.com

As seen on TV (BBC Two's *The Restaurant Wars: The Battle for Manchester*), Aiden Byrne's high-flying joint opened in the spotlight, and for some it's 'improving all the time'. The lounge bar on the 12th floor of an unassuming office block gives views over the the city, but the restaurant (on level two) is no slouch either, with its vast open kitchen and décor that brings a bit of bling to the urban landscape. It's big, it's theatrical and it's even a little audacious. That sense of theatre extends to the compellingly modern food that arrives dressed to impress (some say 'fussy'), with a dish of cured duck and foie gras mousse served in the cross-section of a tree. But fears of style over substance are mostly allayed; 'the greatest

scallops ever tasted' arrive with a mist of dry ice and accompanying wakame mousse and pig's trotter. Desserts such as chocolate and violet mille-feuille are no less creative. Drink flashy cocktails, or wines starting at £25.

Chef/s: Aiden Byrne. **Open:** Tue to Sat L 12 to 2.30, D 7 to 9.30 (6 to 10 Fri and Sat). **Closed:** Sun, Mon, 2 weeks Jan, 2 weeks Aug. **Meals:** alc (main courses £25 to £45). Set L £28 (2 courses) to £33. Tasting menu £95 (12 courses). **Details:** 78 seats. V menu. Bar. Wheelchair access. Music.

Michael Caines at ABode Manchester

Classy city-centre dining
Cooking score: 5
Modern European | £40
107 Piccadilly, Manchester, M1 2DB
Tel no: (0161) 2477744
www.michaelcaines.com

The rather grandiose surrounds of a Victorian cotton warehouse provide an apposite setting for this Mancunian outpost of the ABode Hotels group, with Michael Caines' restaurant and swanky Champagne bar occupying a rather sleek but sedate space in the basement. Reporters relish the 'opportunities for bargain dining' here, and there's plenty to applaud when it comes to the self-styled 'amazing graze' lunches. Modest fixed-price dinner menus also 'demonstrate real skill in getting the best out of cheap ingredients', from shallot tarte fine embellished with mushroom duxelles to rolled breast of lamb, 'braised to unctuous tenderness' and served atop a truffle-tinged risotto. Elsewhere, head chef Robert Cox delivers plates of technically impressive food inspired by top-notch raw materials: consider glazed lamb's sweetbreads with roasted white asparagus, wild garlic and hazelnuts or pan-fried cod with Jerusalem artichoke, curly kale, brown shrimps and meunière sauce. Desserts such as green apple parfait or Valrhona Dulcey pannacotta with Sauternes jelly and Yorkshire rhubarb are in similar vein. Knowledgeably chosen wines cover all bases from big-name French vintages to New World young bloods, with prices from £25.

Chef/s: Robert Cox. **Open:** Tue to Sat L 12 to 2.30, D 6 to 10. **Closed:** Sun, Mon, 26 to 31 Dec. **Meals:** alc (main courses £16 to £22). Set L £15 to £20 (4 courses). Set D £18 (2 courses) to £23. Tasting menu £60 (7 courses). **Details:** 70 seats. V menu. Bar. Wheelchair access. Music.

The Northern Quarter

Well-established Mancunian brasserie
Cooking score: 2
Modern British | £29
108 High Street, Manchester, M4 1HQ
Tel no: (0161) 8327115
www.tnq.co.uk

Known locally as TNQ, this vibrant and buzzing brasserie is now in its tenth year and it remains 'one of those places that, as you walk through the door, there's a welcome and you just feel that everything's going to be OK'. The floor-to-ceiling windows of the Victorian corner site provide fine views of the city's old Smithfield markets, as does the sunny terrace, while the utilitarian, shabby-chic interior makes a perfect backdrop for satisfying dishes created from seasonal north west produce. It's all cooked with confidence and a lack of pretence, from a starter of pickled herring and chicory with new potatoes, carrots and horseradish dressing to mains of long-cooked Cheshire blade beef with wild mushrooms, pancetta, baby onions and glazed carrots, and roast fillet of Middle White pork with chorizo, beans and crispy sage gnocchi. Desserts such as sticky toffee pudding with 'a very rich and generous serving of toffee sauce' and apple and berry crumble will satisfy traditionalists. Wine from £18.

Chef/s: Anthony Fielden. **Open:** all week 12 to 10.30 (7 Sun). **Closed:** 24 to 26 Dec, 1 Jan. **Meals:** alc (main courses £10 to £23). Set L £14 (2 courses) to £17. Set D £30 (3 courses). Sun L £18. **Details:** 60 seats. 70 seats outside. Wheelchair access. Music.

The Rose Garden

Keeping it quirky on Burton Road
Cooking score: 1
Modern British | £32
218 Burton Road, West Didsbury, Manchester, M20 2LW
Tel no: (0161) 4780747
www.therosegardendidsbury.com

The inhabitants of Didsbury look kindly on William Mills' small, modern eatery and it's easy to see why. A neighbourly vibe is one of its attributes, although there is much to be said for the carefully crafted seasonal food, too. Drop by in winter and you might be treated to a taste of mackerel (fillet, ceviche, pâté) with radish and cucumber, then cod chowder or a medium-rare hanger steak served alongside fillet tartare and an oxtail croquette, with rhubarb, rhubarb sorbet, ginger crumble, ginger-beer jelly and vanilla pannacotta making a fine finish. Service is 'excellent', prices reasonable and wines start at £17.50.

Chef/s: William Mills. **Open:** Mon to Sat D only 6 to 10.30 (11 Sat). Sun 1 to 7.30. **Closed:** 25 and 26 Jan, 1 Jan. **Meals:** alc (main courses £15 to £20). Set D £18 (2 courses) to £21. **Details:** 58 seats. Music.

Second Floor

A room with a view
Cooking score: 3
Modern European | £30
Harvey Nichols, 21 New Cathedral Street, Manchester, M1 1AD
Tel no: (0161) 8288898
www.harveynichols.com

First opening in London in 1831, it was well over a century before a Harveys Nichols appeared elsewhere, but now the group is happily ensconced in many of the UK's major cities. Up on the second floor in New Cathedral Street, expect a Manchester skyline exploited by floor-to-ceiling windows and a shiny, buff décor. The room really does fit the bill for just about any occasion (the brasserie being the more relaxed option), and that goes

Join us at thegoodfoodguide.co.uk

for the menu, too, which matches seared mackerel with pickled turnip among starters, and brings Yorkshire venison to the table in the company of choucroute and chocolate oil. The brasserie's all-day dining options include sardines grilled in the Josper oven, or tandoori monkfish with sticky mango rice. It's got to be Manchester tart with coconut ice cream and banana jelly for pud. Wines from £20.
Chef/s: Matthew Horsfield. **Open:** all week 12 to 10 (7 Mon, 5 Sun). **Closed:** 25 Dec, 1 Jan, Easter Sun. **Meals:** alc (main courses £11 to £21). Set D £21 (3 courses). Sun L £13. **Details:** 100 seats. Bar. Wheelchair access. Music.

Solita

Satisfying a primal need
Cooking score: 1
Italian-American | £23
Turner Street, Manchester, M4 1DW
Tel no: (0161) 8392200
www.solita.co.uk

Solita is loud, brash and a lot of fun. If you hanker after US-style wings, burgers and hot dogs, it's definitely the place for you. They've got a trendy Inka grill, which they put to good use by putting prime protein over the hot coals – the signature 40-day aged bone-in prime rib for example. Salads run to a buttermilk-fried chicken version and the ice cream doughnut sandwich sounds like something from *The Simpsons*. Needless to say, there's a lot of youthful energy to the place (eat at ground-floor level if you can). Drink beer or a keenly priced cocktail, with wines starting at £17.90. Another branch of Solita can be found in Didsbury; tel: (0161) 4344884.
Chef/s: Marcin Bialoskorski. **Open:** all week 12 to 10 (11pm Sat, 11am Sat and Sun). **Closed:** 25 Dec. **Meals:** alc (main meals £9 to £23). **Details:** 120 seats. 60 seats outside. Music.

Volta

Small plates and easy-going cool
Cooking score: 2
International | £25
167 Burton Road, West Didsbury, Manchester, M20 2LN
Tel no: (0161) 4488887
www.voltafoodanddrink.co.uk

Owned by dance-floor heroes the Unabombers, who now combine the operation of catering-size coffee machines with their DJing duties, Volta embodies easy-going cool. It's a flexible space, with drinkers (they're big on beer) just as likely to occupy a formica-topped table or spot on the Burton Road pavement as those ordering from a selection of small plates. Deep-fried Monte Enebro is crisp, oozing and drenched in honey, grounded by the crisp earthiness of raw white beetroot, while chorizo grilled with piquillo peppers is a luscious, smoky tangle. At lunch, a limited selection of large plates includes middleweight gnocchi in a cream sauce with tomato tang, or lamb 'shawarma', spiced, pulled and crisped up, with a plain bread, yoghurt and salad. Later on, there are more small plates, exemplary char-grilled hanger steak and desserts including pecan and orange pudding with toffee sauce. In music terms, it's more killer than filler. Wines are from £15.50.
Chef/s: Alex Shaw. **Open:** Tue to Sun L 12 to 4, D 5 to 9.30. **Closed:** Mon. **Meals:** alc (small plates £5 to £8). **Details:** 30 seats. 25 seats outside. Music.

Wing's
Reliable Cantonese favourite
Cooking score: 3
Chinese | £30
Heron House, 1 Lincoln Square, Manchester,
M2 5LN
Tel no: (0161) 8349000
www.wingsrestaurant.co.uk

In a city flattered by the flirtatious advances of the big restaurant brands, Wing's isn't exactly hot. But this venerable Cantonese doesn't need to show too much leg; it secured its admirers long ago, attracting shoppers, the local office crowd and Sunday diners with an extensive menu and reliable take on old standards galore. The interior offers privacy rather than glamour with booths, partitions and strategically placed greenery, and service is friendly and efficient, with the senior team on hand to smooth the way. Commence navigation of the menu with lettuce-wrapped chilli duck or minced chicken with nuts, or simply steamed shell-on king prawns with garlic and soy. From there, the choices are mind-boggling, with regional dishes including Shanghai-style hot chilli sliced lamb, ma po tofu, Singapore vermicelli and Hakka clay pot yams with pork belly. Dim sum addicts and vegetarians are catered for with equal consideration, and wine is from £17.90.
Chef/s: Mr Chi Wing Lam. **Open:** all week 12 to 12 (4 to 12 Sat, 1 to 11 Sun). **Meals:** alc (main meals £12 to £55). Set D £45 (4 courses). **Details:** 85 seats. V menu.

Yuzu
No-frills Japanese eatery
Cooking score: 3
Japanese | £20
39 Faulkner Street, Manchester, M1 4EE
Tel no: (0161) 2364159
www.yuzumanchester.co.uk

Pitched defiantly on the fringes of Manchester's Chinatown, this independently run Japanese eatery sets out its stall with origami figures, multi-coloured saké bottles, plain wooden furnishings and some deftly executed traditional cooking – although you won't find any sushi on the menu (they don't have a specialist chef). Instead, fans of raw fish can get their fix from mixed sashimi sets and various donburi rice bowls topped with, say, organic salmon, tuna or scallops. Browse the modest line-up and you'll also see a smattering of popular classics, from chicken and spring onion yakitori skewers, silken agedashi tofu and breaded prawn katsu to assorted tempura and bowls of udon noodles – including a version with 'curry soup'. At lunchtime, tourists, students and office workers are lured here by the promise of reasonably priced 'teisyoku' set deals, with rice and miso soup included. Yuzu doesn't serve desserts and there's no wine list either, but drinkers can sip Japanese beer, potent shochu spirits or classy saké (from £6.50 a shot) – if something stronger than a pot of green tea is required.
Chef/s: David Leong. **Open:** Tue to Sat L 12 to 2 (2.30 Sat), D 5.30 to 10. **Closed:** Sun, Mon, 2 weeks Christmas. **Meals:** alc (main courses £11 to £17). Set L £9 (2 courses). **Details:** 26 seats. Music.

Fazenda
South American | £34
The Avenue, Spinningfields, Manchester,
M3 3AP
Tel no: (0161) 8341219
www.fazenda.co.uk

Rodizio might get a bad rap, but Fazenda's strolling meat-slicers are a cut above – as are the serious wine list, backlit marble décor, pro service and 'salad' bar loaded with crisp chicharrónes, feijoada, sautéed spring greens and wholegrain-based sides. Start with delicate but moreish cheese-stuffed pastries and look out for the man with the signature picanha: beef rump cut to retain its cap of flavour-giving fat. Sausages, black pudding and chicken hearts feature alongside the premium cuts. Wine is from £18.70. Open all week.

Siam Smiles
Thai | £18
48a George Street, Manchester, M1 4HF
Tel no: (0161) 2371555

The definition of basic (and none the worse for it), this family-run café occupies one side of a Thai supermarket. It's light and bright despite its below-ground location, and delivers thrills without frills courtesy of a menu of well-balanced, street-food-inspired salads, noodle soups and curries. The on-site shop means there's no compromise on ingredients, resulting in earthy, deeply flavoured dishes. Try the laab moo minced pork salad, loaded with fresh herbs. Open all week.

Teacup Kitchen
Modern British | £20
55 Thomas Street, Manchester, M4 1NA
Tel no: (0161) 8323233
www.teacupandcakes.com

Weekend queues snake out of Teacup's door for all-day breakfast, lunch, tea and cake, cake, cake, all served under the aegis of local DJ and loose leaf brew enthusiast Mr Scruff. There's sunny service, a welcoming vibe and uncomplicated food; try a Longhorn beef pie or 'Moorish' wrap stuffed with creamy-light falafel. Cakes can seem designed to survive a stint on the tempting display, giving naturally dense bakes like mocha layer cake the edge. Wine from £16.50. Closed Sun.

◼ Norden
Nutters
Wacky indulgence and serious purpose
Cooking score: 2
Modern British | £34
Edenfield Road, Norden, OL12 7TT
Tel no: (01706) 650167
www.nuttersrestaurant.co.uk

Occupying an 18th-century manor set in six acres of groomed parkland not far from Rochdale, this offbeat set-up may smack of wacky indulgence and eccentricity, but there is serious purpose when it comes to the food on the plate. Local and regional produce is at the heart of things, from the Bury black pudding used for Andrew Nutter's signature won tons to the stock of more than 50 artisan cheeses in the larder, and the chef is 'bang on for seasonality'. His crispy fritters are also famous (try the 'ploughman's lunch' version or the lobster riff with quinoa salad), but he applies nous and skill in other departments, too – witness loin of Harefield lamb with globe artichoke, pickled onions and basil mash or satsuma and Grand Marnier crème brûlée with orange curd. Nutters is not without critics, however, especially when it comes to service, which could be sharper, more on the ball. The hefty, eclectic wine list starts at £16.
Chef/s: Andrew Nutter. **Open:** Tue to Sun L 12 to 2 (4 Sun), D 6.30 to 9.30 (8 Sun). **Closed:** Mon, 1 or 2 days after Christmas and New Year, bank hols.
Meals: alc (main courses £16 to £24). Set L £17 (2 courses) to £20. Set D £42 (6 courses). Sun L £24.
Details: 146 seats. V menu. Bar. Wheelchair access. Music. Parking.

◼ Ramsbottom
Hearth of the Ram
Classy food in relaxed surroundings
Cooking score: 3
Modern British | £27
13 Peel Brow, Ramsbottom, BL0 0AA
Tel no: (01706) 828681
www.hearthoftheram.com

All is joyfully warm and welcoming inside the Heart of the Ram, thanks in part to crackling fires, enthusiastic staff and ever-present chef Naz Naseem. It's a well-bred and handsome place on every level, with lots of pubby attributes but also a serious side. There's a pleasing flexibility about the menus, which offer well-rendered pub food (homemade corned beef hash, shepherd's pie, slow-cooked pork shoulder in a homemade muffin), alongside considerably more involved (and pricier) dishes such as black cod with black garlic confit, crayfish and wild rocket dumplings, baby leeks and lemon velouté. A starter of seared breast of Bowland partridge with confit leg bonbon, Puy lentils, baby turnip, date purée and pancetta confirms the kitchen's seasonal intentions, while custard and nutmeg tart with rhubarb (carpaccio and sorbet) and ginger biscuits is a favoured finale, if the excellent British cheeseboard hasn't caught your eye. Wines from £14.95.

Chef/s: Abdullah Naseem. **Open:** all week 12 to 10.30 (11.30 Fri and Sat, 10 Sun). **Meals:** alc (main courses £9 to £21). Sun L £21 (2 courses). **Details:** 90 seats. 50 seats outside. Bar. Wheelchair access. Music. Parking.

Sanmini's

Family-run Indian with pitch-perfect flavours
Cooking score: 3
Indian | £27
7 Carrbank Lodge, Ramsbottom Lane, Ramsbottom, BL0 9DJ
Tel no: (01706) 821831
www.sanminis.com

Serving southern Indian food that's 'very much up to scratch', Sanmini's is a family affair (with some some of the idiosyncrasies that implies) in increasingly foodie Ramsbottom. A 19th-century gatehouse has been converted to accommodate a series of quiet, nondescript rooms where the newest addition is weekend breakfasts of masala dosai, idli and sambar, and simple lunch dishes served in two sittings. Vegetarian cooking gets a prominent billing, thanks to unusual dishes such as mung bean sundal with brown mustard and red chillies. At dinner, readers rate the lentil, cashew nut and spinach pakora with coconut chutney, and 'elegantly plated' kari dosa enclosing spiced lamb and egg. Chicken Chettinad is cooked dry, and Chennai potato masala has assertive chilli and cumin flavours. Excellent lemon rice and chapatis seal the deal, and a traditional dessert selection is more extensive than most. The wine list, from £13.95, includes some Indian bottles.

Chef/s: Dr Padmini Sankar. **Open:** Sat and Sun L 10 to 2.30, Wed, Fri and Sat D 6 to 10. **Closed:** Mon, Tue, Thur, 2 weeks Jan. **Meals:** alc (main courses £9 to £16). Sun L £9. **Details:** 40 seats. V menu. Bar. Wheelchair access. Music.

■ Salford

Damson

Bold seasonal flavours and a plum location
Cooking score: 2
Modern British | £40
MediaCity, Broadway, Salford, M50 2HF
Tel no: (0161) 7517020
www.damsonrestaurant.co.uk

More business-like and metropolitan than the original in Stockport (see entry), this branch of Damson draws much of its trade from the nearby Lowry Theatre, the MediaCity UK complex and the populace of re-energised Salford Quays. Floor-to-ceiling windows make the most of stunning waterfront views from the first-floor dining room and the interiors are pointed up with signature plummy tones, while the menu promotes big-city flavours and on-trend combos – all based on soundly sourced ingredients. A salad of poached quinces, artichokes, walnuts and foie gras or tuna tartare with avocado purée, soy and lime jelly might open proceedings, while mains are all about bold seasonal impact – think roast cod with truffled Puy lentils and winter cabbage or slow-cooked Middle White pork belly and sticky ginger-braised cheek with crushed pumpkin, spiced plums and kale. Elsewhere, slow-cooked duck egg, trencherman helpings of well-timed lamb rump and grilled plaice with cauliflower and hazelnut purée have found favour with readers. Wines start at £16.95.

Chef/s: Simon Stanley. **Open:** all week L 12 to 2.45 (5.30 Sun), Mon to Sat D 5 to 9.30 (10 Fri and Sat). **Closed:** bank hols. **Meals:** alc (mains £15 to £25). Set L and D £17 (2 courses) to £20. Sun L £17. **Details:** 130 seats. 16 seats outside. Bar. Wheelchair access. Music.

■ Stockport
Damson

Colourful neighbourhood restaurant
Cooking score: 2
Modern British | £40
113-115 Heaton Moor Road, Stockport,
SK4 4HY
Tel no: (0161) 4324666
www.damsonrestaurant.co.uk

£5 OFF

Since opening in 2009, the suitably purple-
painted Damson has served Heaton Moor well
– straightforward, well organised, with an
unfussy attitude and accessible food. The
menu is a familiar run through the modern
British catalogue, although there are a few
unexpected twists and turns along the way.
Duck leg confit and foie gras ballotine comes
with grapefruit purée and citrus brioche,
while monkfish is poached in black olive oil
and served with roasted garlic and rosemary
gnocchi, confit lemon, capers and spring
greens, and lemon sabayon. Vegetarians also
get a good look in with mushroom parfait
with pickled mushroom and beetroot salad,
and risotto of spring vegetables. Cheesecakes
(perhaps goats' cheese with strawberries and
pistachio) are skilfully crafted, and walnut
milk parfait with carrot cake and carrot and
apple sorbet has been well received. Readers
agree that this is cooking that is well served by
fresh ingredients, proper skills and by keenly
priced lunch and evening deals. Wines
from £18.95.
Chef/s: Jake Buchan. **Open:** Tue to Fri L 12 to 2.30,
Mon to Sat D 5.30 to 9.30 (10 Sun). Sun 12 to 7.30.
Closed: 26 Dec, 1 Jan. **Meals:** alc (main courses
£19 to £28). Set L and D £17 (2 courses) to £20. Sun
L £17. **Details:** 75 seats. 25 seats outside. V menu.
Bar. Wheelchair access. Music.

■ Worsley
Grenache

Intimate neighbourhood bistro
Cooking score: 2
Modern British | £38
15 Bridgewater Road, Walkden, Worsley,
M28 3JE
Tel no: (0161) 7998181
www.grenacherestaurant.co.uk

£5 OFF

Chef Mike Jennings has settled into his new
role as proprietor of this abidingly popular
local bistro – although he isn't about to
neglect his cooking duties. Bare tables, gentle
lighting and an upstairs bar create an intimate,
laid-back vibe, while the food shows just the
right amount of ambition for an understated
neighbourhood haunt. Menus change
monthly and the kitchen isn't afraid to cherry-
pick ideas – from twice-baked Lancashire
cheese soufflé with Waldorf salad to spiced
monkfish with coconut and coriander dhal,
crispy mussels and pickled carrots. There are
big meaty flavours, too – witness dry-aged
fillet steak with ox cheek and sweet onion
tarte Tatin or a dish of slow-cooked pork belly
with smoked mash and toffee apple. The well-
documented Anglo-French cheeseboard is
worth a sniff, and there are some intriguing
desserts – how about cinnamon-dusted deep-
fried plums with clotted cream and damson
jam? Surprisingly, the eponymous Grenache
grape plays only a minor role on the revamped
wine list, with bottles from £16.
Chef/s: Mike Jennings. **Open:** Thur to Sun L 12 to
2.30 (5 Sun), Wed to Sat D 5.30 to 9.30 (10 Fri and
Sat). **Closed:** Mon, Tue, 25 and 26 Dec, 1 Jan.
Meals: alc (main courses £17 to £25). Set L £16 (2
courses) to £20. Set D £20 (2 courses) to £24. Sun L
£24. **Details:** 55 seats. Bar. Music. No children after
7 Fri and Sat.

Alresford

NEW ENTRY

Pulpo Negro

A standard-bearer for quality tapas
Cooking score: 3
Spanish | £25
28 Broad Street, Alresford, SO24 9AQ
Tel no: (01962) 732262
www.pulponegro.co.uk

This second venture from Andres Alemany (the Purefoy Arms, see entry) is a smart tapas bar that couldn't be further removed from the usually tired, provincial formula – where the average punter's idea of tapas is rooted largely in La Tasca. Indeed, Pulpo Negro's repertoire is something of a masterstroke, combining traditional favourites with more innovative ideas, with everything built around good local produce. Classic grilled Catalan tomato bread, drenched in good olive oil with well-flavoured tomato pulp may well be served alongside three little discs of 'crisp-to-gooey' pig's trotter in a very rich romesco-style sauce or fat, juicy, crisp-skinned chicken thighs buried in almonds, capers, butter and parsley, and thin slices of Secreto Ibérico, 'charred to just pink', with more romesco. Service is excellent – 'interested, efficient, knowledge-able' – and the all-Spanish wine list is great, opening at £19.50, with a broad spread and at least 75% by the glass and carafe.

Chef/s: Andres Alemany. **Open:** Tue to Sat L 12 to 3, D 6 to 10. **Closed:** Sun, Mon, 25 and 26 Dec, 1 Jan. **Meals:** alc (tapas £3 to £18). **Details:** 40 seats. 12 seats outside. Wheelchair access. Music. Children over 5 yrs only.

Symbols

Accommodation is available
Three courses for less than £30
£5-off voucher scheme
Notable wine list

Join us at thegoodfoodguide.co.uk

Barton on Sea
Pebble Beach

Clifftop views and sparkling seafood
Cooking score: 3
French | £35
Marine Drive, Barton on Sea, BH25 7DZ
Tel no: (01425) 627777
www.pebblebeach-uk.com

Perched high on the cliffs above Barton on Sea's pebble-strewn beach, this bright and breezy, split-level restaurant-with-rooms comes with alfresco terraces and full-length windows for those who want to soak up the unrivalled views of the Needles and the Isle of Wight. The kitchen casts its net wide, although fresh seafood is the main attraction on Pierre Chevillard's seasonal menus. Plates of local shellfish are always in demand, but also look for zippy French-inspired ideas ranging from scallops and crisp potato with Jerusalem artichoke velouté to cod thermidor or croûton-crusted turbot with a lentil, bacon and mushroom casserole. Kids love the plates of fish and chips. Steaks and juicy cuts are dealt with on the char-grill, although meat eaters can also get their fix from duck burgers or honey-braised lamb shank with prune and apricot semolina. Desserts are mostly Gallic classics, and the carefully sourced wine list is bolstered by appetising seasonal specials. Prices from £18.65.
Chef/s: Pierre Chevillard. **Open:** all week L 12 to 2 (2.30 Sat and Sun), D 6.30 to 9.30 (10 Sat and Sun).
Closed: 25 Dec, 1 Jan. **Meals:** alc (main courses £14 to £37). **Details:** 112 seats. 55 seats outside. Bar. Wheelchair access. Music. Parking.

Baughurst

The Wellington Arms
Good times at this perpetual crowd-pleaser
Cooking score: 4
British | £28
Baughurst Road, Baughurst, RG26 5LP
Tel no: (0118) 9820110
www.thewellingtonarms.com

The polished-but-cluttered, posh country-cottage décor and the beautifully tended garden look like something plucked from the pages of *House & Garden*, and everyone seems to be having a jolly good time. No wonder, given that the Wellington Arms' simple dishes offer superior produce and greater culinary skill than the pub-with-grub norm, thanks to Simon Page and Jason King, who rear livestock on site and whose garden supplies produce. Start, perhaps, with twice-baked Cheddar soufflé or country-style chicken liver parfait with leaves, shoots and radish from the garden. Mains bring the likes of lemon sole with crispy capers and brown butter, and there's always steak from Grange Farm and always a pot pie with mash (sometimes lamb, more usually venison). The individual-sized treacle tart with homemade custard or ice cream is a little piece of perfection: thin, light and buttery pastry and a warm filling, which hits crunchy on top but gooey in the middle, that avoids being cloying while remaining indulgent – just one illustration of why this 'warm and welcoming' restaurant-with-rooms is so popular. The lunch menu is an absolute steal, the wine list (from £18) a balanced affair with good tasting notes.
Chef/s: Jason King. **Open:** all week L 12 to 1.30 (3 Sun), Mon to Sat D 6 to 8.30 (9 Fri and Sat).
Meals: alc (main courses £12 to £24). Set L £16 (2 courses) to £19. **Details:** 35 seats. 30 seats outside. Wheelchair access. Music. Parking.

Beaulieu
The Terrace Restaurant
Fine-tuned cooking in a country retreat
Cooking score: 5
Modern European | £75
Montagu Arms Hotel, Palace Lane, Beaulieu,
SO42 7ZL
Tel no: (01590) 612324
www.montaguarmshotel.co.uk

Named after the local lords of the manor, this gentrified Georgian inn sits proud in a charming New Forest village, directly opposite Lord Montagu of Beaulieu's grandiose pile. From the outside, the Montagu looks like your archetypal wisteria-clad country retreat, but it also cuts quite a dash on the food front – thanks to Matthew Tomkinson's fine-tuned modern cooking. With its oak-panelled walls, gilt-framed mirrors and French windows overlooking the garden, the capably run Terrace Restaurant is formal without seeming sniffy, while the food shows bags of contemporary panache. Seasonal ingredients are cleverly deployed for a roster of intricate dishes ranging from crispy pig's trotter croquettes with smoked eel, pickled beetroot and apple to grilled rump of Dorset rose veal with roasted garlic gnocchi, romaine lettuce and confit lemon. The New Forest contributes game and wild fungi, while South Coast fish might include Lymington sea bass with watercress, Jerusalem artichoke purée, ham and red wine sauce. To finish, try the reworked lemon meringue pie with poached oranges and basil sorbet. Organic and biodynamic wines get top billing on the auspicious terroir-led wine list, which also boasts some notable Rieslings, kosher and 'orange' tipples. House selections start at £28.
Chef/s: Matthew Tomkinson. **Open:** Wed to Sun L 12 to 2, Tue to Sun D 6.30 to 9. **Closed:** Mon.
Meals: Set L £25 (2 courses) to £30. Set D £55 (2courses) to £75. Sun L £35. Tasting menu £95.
Details: 60 seats. 40 seats outside. Bar. Wheelchair access. Music. Parking. Children over 11 yrs only.

Brockenhurst
LOCAL GEM
The Pig
Modern British | £35
Beaulieu Road, Brockenhurst, SO42 7QL
Tel no: (01590) 622354
www.thepighotel.com

The recreation of a Victorian glasshouse for the dining room makes a lovely setting, and everything from glasses to bone-handled cutlery is determinedly mismatched. Ingredient sourcing begins in the kitchen garden, but doesn't stray more than 25 miles. Pickled beetroot salad, red kale, shallots and tarragon dressing accompany hot-smoked trout, while 'Piggy bits' – 'very crackly pork crackling, soft pig's ears, salami and chorizo sticks' – are the obvious way to pique the appetite. A ginger sponge with pear hits the spot. Wines from £16.50. Open all week.

Droxford
The Bakers Arms
Scenic charms and admirable pub food
Cooking score: 3
Modern British | £26
High Street, Droxford, SO32 3PA
Tel no: (01489) 877533
www.thebakersarmsdroxford.com

With the South Downs Way nearby, the River Meon just a stroll away and the green expanses of the region's own National Park all around, this beguiling pub has scenic charms galore. It also boasts terrific hosts who have maintained the place as a proper watering hole dedicated to serving its resident populace (note the village shop tacked on to the side of the building). Chef/landlord Adam Cordery is also bang on the money when it comes to food, buying locally and offering an admirable mix of pub grub alongside clever ideas for inquisitive palates. Daily pies, burgers, sausages and steaks are the mainstays, but he can also conjure up authentic salt-cured duck confit, slow-cooked neck of lamb with

Join us at thegoodfoodguide.co.uk

pappardelle or fillet of grey mullet with Gruyère potatoes, spinach, leeks and saffron sauce. The surrounding countryside provides hot-smoked 'chalk stream' trout, Dorset snails and farmhouse cheeses, too, while dessert might bring apple and berry crumble with custard. Ales from the nearby Bowman micro-brewery stake their claim alongside a handy list of wines from £15.50.
Chef/s: Adam Cordery. **Open:** all week L 12 to 2 (2.30 Sat, 3 Sun), Mon to Sat D 7 to 9 (6.30 to 9.30 Fri and Sat). **Meals:** alc (main courses £13 to £20). Set L and D £15 (2 courses). Sun L £15. **Details:** 45 seats. 20 seats outside. Bar. Parking.

▌Emsworth
36 On The Quay

Destination restaurant-with-rooms
Cooking score: 5
Modern European | £58
47 South Street, Emsworth, PO10 7EG
Tel no: (01243) 375592
www.36onthequay.co.uk

Take one cottagey listed building by a photogenic quayside, add desirable letting rooms and finish off with some meticulous, picture-pretty food – no wonder this charming restaurant-with-rooms is a dream ticket for out-of-towners. Bow windows, period charms and pristine tables set the tone in the soothing dining room, where guests are treated to the full panoply of dainty extras as they savour Ramon Farthing's fixed-price menus. Fish from the quay obviously plays its part, as in fresh crab encased in light apple jelly with artichokes, crisp apple and foraged leaves or brill fillet with ceps, herb quinoa, onion marmalade and delicate mushroom broth. Meat and game are given similar treatment – witness an elaborate assemblage of rabbit loin with rillette of leg, salt-baked turnip, honey and mead gel, mustard crumbs and broad beans. And there's no let-up when it comes to intricate desserts such as granola parfait with pear terrine, crisp spiced biscuits, damson

cream and pear liqueur foam. The idiosyncratic wine list has seasonal selections from £21.50.
Chef/s: Ramon Farthing and Gary Pearce. **Open:** Tue to Sat L 12 to 1.45, D 6.30 to 9.30. **Closed:** Sun, Mon, 24 to 26 Dec, first 2 weeks Jan, first 2 weeks Jun. **Meals:** Set L £24 (2 courses) to £29. Set D £48 (2 courses) to £58. **Details:** 50 seats. 10 seats outside. Bar. Wheelchair access.

▌Isle of Wight
Hillside Bistro

Refurbished café strong on island produce
Cooking score: 2
French | £25
30 Pier Street, Ventnor, Isle of Wight, PO38 1SX
Tel no: (01983) 852271
www.hillsideventnor.co.uk

An outpost of the hotel of the same name, this attractive refurbished café is close to the sea, with an open kitchen providing customers with some alternative sightseeing. It opens for breakfast, brunch and lunch, turning IoW produce (some grown in its own gardens) into simple but well-thought-out dishes, then jazzes things up slightly in the evening. Try island-smoked salmon with rye blini, Hillside beetroot and chive crème fraîche, followed by pot-roast chicken or confit of duck leg with chorizo and butter beans. The local catch comes simply served or as a risotto of Ventnor Bay crab with island tomatoes. Puddings include a take on apple strudel with spiced apple ice cream, or, in another homage to the locality, îles flottantes. Day-tripping families should note that children under 12 are not allowed. Wine is from £21 – most is under £25 – and includes a handful of bottles imported directly from the Languedoc.
Chef/s: Gerald Fruitier. **Open:** all week 9 to 3, D 6 to 9. **Meals:** alc (main meals £12 to £16). **Details:** 30 seats. 4 seats outside. Wheelchair access. Music. Children over 12 yrs only.

The Crab Shed

Seafood | £15

Tamarisk, Love Lane, Steephill Cove, Isle of Wight, PO38 1AF
Tel no: (01983) 855819
www.steephillcove-isleofwight.co.uk

If you are looking for no frills, no fuss and the weather is fine (everything takes place outdoors at rustic tables), head to the simple Crab Shed right by the water's edge at Steephill Cove – which lives up to its name. The freshest fish from the café's own boat *Endeavour* is the draw, with fresh-picked crab, homemade crab pasties and mackerel ciabattas the stars of the show, served alongside homegrown salads and daily specials. Wines from £16. Closed Oct to Easter. Cash only.

Dan's Kitchen

Modern British | £35

Lower Green Road, St Helens, Isle of Wight, PO33 1TS
Tel no: (01983) 872303
www.danskitcheniow.com

There's a sense of true dedication at Dan Maskell's unassuming restaurant overlooking the village green. Noted for mellow vibes and good food, menus are packed with sharp, seasonal dishes built around local ingredients, although Dan mixes robust tradition (a lunchtime shepherd's pie, say) with techniques from further afield. So you could start with confit duck leg 'burger' with pickled vegetables, move on to beef fillet with caramelised shallot tart, and finish with 'bourbon biscuit' with salted peanut caramel and Horlicks ice cream. Wines from £15. Closed Sun and Mon.

The Hut

Modern British | £30

Colwell Bay, Colwell Chine Road, Isle of Wight, PO40 9NP
Tel no: (01983) 898637
www.thehutcolwell.co.uk

Beachside at Colwell, with stripped boards, sanded tables and old school chairs, the Hut brings a bit of sophistication to west Wight. The big attraction is the ample outside seating and decking areas, plus the panoramic view from the dining room – all sea and boats. Fish of the day is the star turn, perhaps 'a lovely bream caught in Yarmouth that morning', but there's also beetroot carpaccio with feta, pine nuts and cider vinaigrette, steak tartare, and fillet of ling on orzo pasta, broad and green beans and Parmesan. Pair it all with a modest but well-chosen wine list (from £16.50). Open all week Mar to Sept.

The Pond Café

Italian | £28

Bonchurch Village Road, Bonchurch, Isle of Wight, PO38 1RG
Tel no: (01983) 855666
www.thehambrough.com

The Italian-inspired Pond Café sticks to the promise of the café premise with coffee, cake and light lunches during the day (tagliatelle pomodoro or pizza), then offers a little more oomph in the evening. Start with hand-dived scallops (fried in truffle oil) with celeriac purée and crispy pancetta, then pork chops with girolles or local sea bass with crab mayonnaise. There are duck-pond views and seats on the terrace. Wines from £23. Closed Mon and Tue.

Longparish

★ TOP 50 PUB ★

The Plough Inn

A proper foodie pub
Cooking score: 5
Modern British | £36
Longparish, SP11 6PB
Tel no: (01264) 720358
www.theploughinn.info

Jason Atherton protégé James Durrant has certainly found his niche since decamping to this family-friendly hostelry in the Test Valley. Various 'jars', 'bags' and grills will keep you nourished if you fancy a pint by the fire in the beamed bar, but most people are here for the seasonal carte and tasting menus. Prices are reckoned to be 'unbeatable' for food that shows real finesse, style and imagination – from 'sublime' warm smoked salmon with chopped duck egg and caviar to a 'celestial combination' involving English burnt cream, rhubarb jam, 'cheek-tingling' blood-orange jelly and almond crumbs. Other dishes also have readers reaching for the superlatives: a 'thoroughly ravishing' take on mac 'n' cheese; Cornish cod with kohlrabi, cider, burnt apple purée and cabbage; confit hogget belly with baked onion, fried kale and smoked mash. Durrant's triple-cooked chips go down a storm too. While the cooking is 'consistently exceptional', service can fall short of the mark and the 'bleak' toilets are a reminder that this is still an old village boozer. Decently priced wines start at £18.

Chef/s: James Durrant and James Salkeld. **Open:** Tue to Sun L 12 to 2.30 (3.30 Sun), Tue to Sat D 6 to 9.30. **Closed:** Mon. **Meals:** alc (main courses £18 to £24). Tasting menu £55 (6 courses). **Details:** 50 seats. 44 seats outside. V menu. Bar. Wheelchair access. Music. Parking.

Lymington

The Elderflower

Modern cooking with high ambitions
Cooking score: 2
Modern French | £30
4-5 Quay Street, Lymington, SO41 3AS
Tel no: (01590) 676908
www.elderflowerrestaurant.co.uk

An asset to Lymington, Andrew and Marjolaine du Bourg's restaurant-with-rooms just about gets away with its chintzy décor (think lime green upholstery and fake plants), the saving grace being low, beamed ceilings and an appealing glass frontage looking out on to Lymington's pretty cobbled backstreets. Alongside the succinct modern British carte there's a tasting menu and 'market tapas' menu, a simpler affair that featured, on inspection, mackerel tartare and confit goose leg. Rich, braised and roasted rose veal from the carte sits beneath confit egg yolk, blobs of béchamel, shards of crispy anchovy, Dorset snails and kale. Du Bourg has an estimable resume (Club Gascon, The Square – see entries), and there is unquestionable talent on show, although dishes can verge on the overly complicated. Desserts, although 'gimmicky on occasion', can be truly remarkable – 'cup of coffee' and chocolate 'cigar' wowed one reporter. The Elderflower exudes effortless charm and is clearly eager to please. The extensive French-leaning wine list starts at £17.

Chef/s: Andrew du Bourg. **Open:** Tue to Sun L 12 to 2.30 (4 Sun), Tue to Sat D 6.30 to 9.30 (10 Fri and Sat). **Closed:** Mon, 1 to 14 Jan. **Meals:** alc (main courses £16 to £25). **Details:** 40 seats. Music.

Egan's
Modern British | £31
24 Gosport Street, Lymington, SO41 9BE
Tel no: (01590) 676165
www.eganslymington.co.uk

The setting, halfway between Lymington harbour and the station, 'is a gift', thought a visitor to this 'genuine local' where the staff 'clearly know most customers' and there's a 'lovely little courtyard area at the back for when the sun shines'. A generous serving of 'pink and silky' ham hock terrine, salmon fillet with spinach, crayfish tails, toasted almonds, lots of butter and a top-drawer dauphinois (creamy yet light with a decent garlic punch) are typical choices. Lunch is good value, as is the wine list (from £18.95).

The Mill at Gordleton
Silver Street, Lymington, SO41 6DJ
Tel no: (01590) 682219
www.themillatgordleton.co.uk
'Now back as a jewel in the New Forest. I ate crab with a well-executed gazpacho jelly; finished with Pimm's ice cream; and had a starter of goat's-cheese soufflé with rocket and pine nuts.'

Lyndhurst
Hartnett Holder & Co.
Foods of the forest, Italian-style
Cooking score: 3
British-Italian | £55
Lime Wood Hotel, Beaulieu Road, Lyndhurst, SO43 7FZ
Tel no: (02380) 287167
www.limewoodhotel.co.uk

In a 'stunning' New Forest bolt-hole with serious contemporary appeal, Hartnett Holder & Co. leads readers to 'expect good things'. The Italian-inflected menu is a collaboration between Angela Hartnett, the big name and major influence, and chef Luke Holder. The third player is the rustic backdrop, with cured meat and salmon prepared in the hotel's smokehouse and abundant game and forest flavours; with the polenta agnolotti with truffle and artichoke, a donation is made to the New Forest Trust. Readers have enjoyed slow-cooked beef cheek swathed in a meaty reduction and served with risotto milanese, and linguine with hare ragù. Impressions of service range from 'variable' to 'discreet and friendly', and a little more balance and consistency would also, for some, be welcome in the food. To finish, good bets are tiramisu with chocolate sorbet or a raspberry tart crammed with fruit and served with salted oat ice cream. Wine is from £24.

Chef/s: Angela Hartnett and Luke Holder. **Open:** all week 12 to 11. **Meals:** alc (main courses £18 to £50). Set L £20 (2 courses) to £25. Sun L £38. **Details:** 62 seats. 40 seats outside. Bar. Wheelchair access. Music. Parking.

New Milton
The Dining Room
Modern themes in an aristocratic retreat
Cooking score: 4
Modern British | £60
Chewton Glen, Christchurch Road, New Milton, BH25 6QS
Tel no: (01425) 275341
www.chewtonglen.com

From the pillared portico entrance to the vast dining room, this aristocratic old-money playground exudes classiness. With a pleasing outlook over the manicured gardens, there is an undeniably sophisticated air to this country retreat, but it's refreshingly unstuffy, though readers have reported inconsistent service this year. Underpinned by classic themes, the kitchen has a contemporary outlook although influences happily embrace West and East. Hand-dived scallops are teamed with confit pork belly, broad bean and mint purée and extravagantly garnished with summer truffle, although Vietnamese crispy chilli beef salad is another way to start a meal. Mains bring assertive fish dishes such as white miso cod,

Chinese greens and black sesame or glazed Quantock duck breast, carrot and orange, braised chicory. An inspection meal was let down at the final hurdle by a rhubarb and raspberry soufflé that failed to rise to the challenge. A Bible-thick wine list aimed at diners with well-padded wallets starts at £29.
Chef/s: Luke Matthews. **Open:** all week L 12 to 2 (2.30 Sun), D 6 to 9.30 (10 Fri and Sat). **Meals:** alc (main courses £21 to £39). Set L £25. Sun L £40. Tasting menu £70 (6 courses). **Details:** 186 seats. 50 seats outside. V menu. Bar. Wheelchair access. Music. Parking. No children after 8.

▌Old Basing
The Crown

Classy retro pub classics
Cooking score: 3
British | £30
The Street, Old Basing, RG24 7BW
Tel no: (01256) 321424
www.thecrownoldbasing.com

With its unreconstructed décor and retro vibe, the Crown might look like your common-or-garden local boozer but when it comes to food it's a genuine find. The kitchen here is run by chefs with a background in some serious establishments and their pedigree shines through in well-executed, unpretentious versions of pub classics. Starters may deliver a warm organic Stockbridge mushroom tart with Rosary goats' cheese and pickled red onion, which might precede slow-cooked collar of pork with duck-fat roast potatoes, crispy black pudding and creamed Savoy cabbage. The Cornish haddock in beer batter with triple-cooked chips, homemade tartare sauce and crushed peas was 'the best fish and chips meal I've ever eaten' according to one reporter. The ante is well and truly upped with the desserts, Earl Grey tea pannacotta accompanied by poached pears, toasted almonds and shortbread. The bar stocks real ales and wines start at £18.
Chef/s: Tom Wilson. **Open:** all week L 12 to 2 (2.30 Fri to Sun), Mon to Sat D 6 to 9 (9.30 Fri and Sat). **Closed:** 26 and 31 Dec. **Meals:** alc (main courses

£10 to £23). Tasting menu £35 (4 courses).
Details: 55 seats. 40 seats outside. Bar. Music. Parking.

▌Petersfield
Annie Jones

Amiable local restaurant and tapas joint
Cooking score: 2
Modern British | £40
Lavant Street, Petersfield, GU32 3EW
Tel no: (01730) 262728
www.anniejones.co.uk

£5 OFF

A splendid local asset that plies its trade as a daytime coffee-and-cake drop-in, garden bar, 'undercover' tapas joint and full-blown neighbourhood restaurant, Annie Jones occupies chic boho premises bang in the middle of Petersfield. The interior received a major refurb in 2015, but Steve Ranson's kitchen is still in the business of delivering vibrant contemporary flavours and bags of satisfaction, whether you're in the market for some Iberian nibbles or a three-course meal. Grazers might fancy a plate of charcuterie or some lamb merguez meatballs, while others could opt for beef tartare with pickles and wasabi mayo followed by cod, chorizo and clams with squid ink-linguine and textures of cauliflower. It's surprisingly inventive stuff (check out the smoked fillet of beef with hay ash and celeriac), and Steve tops things off with some intriguing Mediterranean-style desserts such as almond and rhubarb cake with mascarpone ice cream, cider apple and pine tree oil. House wines from £17.
Chef/s: Steven Ranson. **Open:** Wed to Sun L 12 to 2, Tue to Sat D 6 to 10. **Closed:** Mon, 25 and 26 Dec, first week Jan. **Meals:** Set L £28 (2 courses) to £35. Set D £30 (2 courses) to £40. Sun L £28 (2 courses) to £35. **Details:** 22 seats. 30 seats outside. Bar. Music.

JSW

Uncluttered cooking with tricksy touches
Cooking score: 6
Modern British | £50
20 Dragon Street, Petersfield, GU31 4JJ
Tel no: (01730) 262030
www.jswrestaurant.com

The personal acronym JSW says a lot about chef/proprietor Jake Saul Watkins' understated approach to running his restaurant. Inhabiting what was an oak-beamed 17th-century coaching inn, the dining room doesn't puff itself up (despite some refurbishment) and there's something refreshingly uncluttered about his cooking – clarity is the key, although brief dish descriptions conceal quite a few tricksy touches. Duck with hay-baked turnips, salted orange purée and sea beet or turbot with a ratatouille tart and coriander play it straight, but there's mischief too: 'truffling' suckling pig served with 'what it eats'; scallops with Japanese dashi stock, shiitake ravioli and ice lettuce; lamb 'spag bol' with slow-cooked tomato and basil. Tasting menus are the default setting for special occasions, complete with creative, bar-raising desserts such as milk chocolate ganache with lime, salted caramel and peanut praline or a boozy amalgam of 'get smashed' stout, G&T and Pimm's. Gentle mark-ups are a feature of the passionately curated wine list, with lesser-known 'terroir' names among the big boys, a cracking choice of half-bottles and house selections from £19.50.
Chef/s: Jake Saul Watkins. **Open:** Wed to Sun L 12 to 1.30, Wed to Sat D 7 to 9. **Closed:** Mon, Tue, 26 Dec to 8 Jan, first 2 weeks Apr, last 2 weeks Aug.
Meals: Set L £33 (2 courses) to £40. Set D £40 (2 courses) to £50. Tasting menu £95 (9 courses).
Details: 50 seats. 28 seats outside. V menu. Wheelchair access. Parking.

Andres Alemany

Purefoy Arms/Pulpo Negro, Hampshire

What inspired you to become a chef?

My father Javier was a pâtissier and a chocolatier and had his own business in Barcelona, so I think it's always been in my blood, that's certainly where I get my work ethic from. I always used to be in the kitchen with my mother, Gillian, helping out. Even at a very young age I cooked dinner for the family although it wasn't very good! A bit too creative, shall we say.

What food could you not live without?

Almonds and lemons – I love every form they come in, I use them everyday, they are always on my menu!

Is there a particular dish that evokes strong memories for you?

Making picada (toasted stale bread, almonds, garlic and chopped parsley), which is normally used to thicken stews. It has a wonderful aroma; if I close my eyes I could be back in my mother's kichen.

Tell us something about yourself that will surprise your diners.

I failed my GCSE home economics, I got an F. I was told by the teacher not to pursue a career that involved cooking.

Portsmouth

LOCAL GEM

Abarbistro

Modern British | £23
58 White Hart Road, Portsmouth, PO1 2JA
Tel no: (023) 9281 1585
www.abarbistro.co.uk

A former pub and hotel with a history stretching back several hundred years, the modern-day incarnation of this corner site in the old town is bright and contemporary, with some outdoor tables and only a short stroll from Gunwharf Quays. The kitchen's unfussy output runs to a burger, ribeye steak with peppercorn sauce and fat chips and moules marinière in two portion sizes. As a wine merchant, too, there are good options starting at £14.50. Open all week.

Preston Candover

★ TOP 50 PUB ★

The Purefoy Arms

Spanish flavours in a Hampshire hostelry
Cooking score: 4
Modern European | £28
Alresford Road, Preston Candover, RG25 2EJ
Tel no: (01256) 389777
www.thepurefoyarms.co.uk

 £30

'It's hardly cheap but excellent value, warmly welcoming, polished and smart with no hint of tack or formula.' This is the Purefoy Arms, a really quite skilful balancing act that adds up to a 'brilliant local dining pub'. The interior blends classic stripped floors and mismatched furniture with bright colours. And the food? One of the owners is from Catalonia, hence the occasional Spanish accent: Catalan tomato bread; salt cod croquettes with wild garlic aïoli and chorizo; confit Middle White with rhubarb and beetroot compote, morcilla and watercress. Otherwise, 'stunning, chunky' slices of hogget loin and belly with charred shallots and Little Gem, steamed carrots, wild garlic purée and an intense meat sauce hit the spot at inspection. To finish, try a 'light, spongy hazelnut financier with dots of salted-caramel mousse and chocolate ganache, a few pieces of caramel popcorn, and a scoop of wonderfully dense, almost chewy turrón ice cream'. The wine list (from £16), offers plenty of bargains and lots by the glass.
Chef/s: Andy Yates. **Open:** Tue to Sun L 12 to 3 (4 Sun), Tue to Sat D 6 to 10. **Closed:** Mon, 26 Dec, 1 Jan. **Meals:** alc (main courses £14 to £22). Set L £15 (2 courses) to £18. **Details:** 54 seats. 50 seats outside. Music. Parking.

Romsey

The Three Tuns

Local with updated pub classics
Cooking score: 2
Modern British | £24
58 Middlebridge Street, Romsey, SO51 8HL
Tel no: (01794) 512639
www.the3tunsromsey.co.uk

 £30

Mere minutes from Romsey's market square, the Three Tuns is a whitewashed 300-year-old inn that has a distinct countryside feel to it, what with the River Test burbling by just along the street. Oak beams, flagstones and winter fires cheer the senses, and the menu of creatively retooled pub classics eschews pretension in favour of big hearty flavours. Ham hock and parsley terrine with egg mayonnaise and pineapple pickle is a stout way to kick the ball into play, and main dishes do their bit too, perhaps with a sturdy beef and mushroom pie, hot with horseradish, cushioned with mash, or else smoked haddock and leek risotto topped with a poached egg (that's if you can resist the fish and chips with mushies and tartare). The white chocolate cheesecake to finish somehow finds itself 'upside down', or fortify yourself against the elements with rice pudding strewn with raisins soaked in Sailor Jerry's spiced rum. Wines start at £16.

Chef/s: Damian Brown and Declan Bungay. **Open:** all week L 12 to 2.30 (3 Fri and Sat, 4 Sun), D 6 to 9 (9.30 Fri and Sat, 8.30 Sun). **Meals:** alc (main courses £10 to £13). **Details:** 50 seats. 30 seats outside. Bar. Music. Parking.

■ Southsea
Restaurant 27

Intricate modern cooking
Cooking score: 4
Modern French | £44
Burgoyne Road, Southsea, PO5 2JF
Tel no: (023) 9287 6272
www.restaurant27.com

'It's surprisingly large and quite expansive,' noted a visitor to the Binghams' bright modern restaurant with its double-height ceiling, neutral colours and plain furniture. Inspection found the experience 'far more formal than it really needs to be', but concluded 'this does not stop the kitchen from serving up some enjoyable food'. Kevin Bingham's intricate modern cooking fashions dishes that dovetail British ingredients with complex, contemporary European technique. Highlights of our test meal were rose veal ribeye, a lovely, juicy piece of meat grilled in a super savoury burnt onion butter with 'good mash, spinach, two rings of pickled shallot, a few little girolles, a glazed carrot and – bafflingly – a single baby corn', and a 'fabulous' crème brûlée, so luscious and evenly studded with vanilla that it really didn't need the addition of vanilla 'rocks' and marshmallow, 'the several swipes of thickened milk, and – the oddest detail – a vanilla olive oil'. Excellent bread and wines from £20 complete the picture.
Chef/s: Kevin Bingham. **Open:** Sun L 12 to 2.30, Wed to Sat D 7 to 9.30. **Closed:** Mon, Tue, 25 and 26 Dec, 1 Jan. **Meals:** Set L £29. Set D £44. Sun L £29. Tasting menu £39 to £50. **Details:** 36 seats. V menu. Music.

■ Sparsholt
The Avenue

Modernist aims in a manor house
Cooking score: 5
Modern British | £55
Lainston House Hotel, Woodman Lane, Sparsholt, SO21 2LT
Tel no: (01962) 776088
www.lainstonhouse.com

The 17th-century red-brick manor house stands at the end of an avenue of lime trees in over 60 acres of gentle parkland. Not far from the main building is a ruined chapel that's another 500 years older again. It adds up to a magical setting for an ambitious country-house restaurant pursuing modernist aims in an atmosphere of leather upholstery and panelled walls. An opening pairing of octopus and chorizo dressed in pine nuts, green olives and basil sounds an Iberian note, as an overture to robust main dishes such as venison in red wine and white balsamic with Jerusalem artichokes and salsify. Seafood is a strong suit, as in turbot with crab, clams and red pepper, all scented with ginger, while the winning dessert involves coconut parfait and chocolate mousse with adornments of caramel, banana and passion fruit. An eight-course tasting menu leaves no stone unturned. The wine list ranges enterprisingly across the board, with bottles from £24.50. House sparkler is Sussex's reference-point Nyetimber blanc de blancs.
Chef/s: Olly Rouse. **Open:** Sun to Fri L 12 to 2, all week D 7 to 9.30 (10 Sat). **Meals:** Set L £22 (2 courses) to £33. Set D £45 (2 courses) to £55. Sun L £35. Tasting menu £75. **Details:** 60 seats. 50 seats outside. V menu. Bar. Wheelchair access. Parking. Children at 6pm sitting only for D.

Join us at thegoodfoodguide.co.uk

Stockbridge

The Greyhound on the Test

Rustic-chic pub with a local flavour
Cooking score: 2
Modern British | £30
31 High Street, Stockbridge, SO20 6EY
Tel no: (01264) 810833
www.thegreyhoundonthetest.co.uk

A good-looking inn in picture-perfect Stockbridge, the Greyhound does rustic chic with breezy flair. It's a captivating destination favoured by locals and tourists, thanks to a telling blend of upmarket pubby virtues and more genteel, contemporary attributes. In the bar the obligatory wood-burner, an extremely low-beamed ceiling and real ales tells one side of the story; smart bedrooms and a light, pleasant dining room with scrubbed tables and a crowd-pleasing menu of modern British cooking complete an affable, cosmopolitan package. Welsh rarebit, carpaccio of beef with celeriac remoulade, char-grilled tuna niçoise or char-grilled squid with curried chickpeas and chorizo, and ribeye steak, is food that comforts rather than challenges. An excellent set lunch could bring ham hock terrine ahead of plaice, green beans, sautéed potatoes and caper butter, then chocolate brownie with vanilla ice cream. Service from smart young staff is on the ball, homemade sourdough is excellent and the wine list opens at £19.95.
Chef/s: Chris Heather. **Open:** all week L 12 to 3 (4 Fri to Sun), D 6 to 9.30. **Closed:** 24 to 26 and 31 Dec, 1 Jan. **Meals:** alc (main courses £13 to £30). Set L £15 (2 courses) to £20. Sun L £28. **Details:** 60 seats. 40 seats outside. Bar. Music. Parking.

Symbols

 Accommodation is available
Three courses for less than £30
£5-off voucher scheme
Notable wine list

Woodfire

Mediterranean deli dining
Cooking score: 1
Mediterranean | £20
High Street, Stockbridge, SO20 6EX
Tel no: (01264) 810248
www.woodfirestockbridge.co.uk

Three cheers for Woodfire, a relaxed, all-day, Med-inspired eatery from the team behind Stockbridge's Thyme & Tides deli. Staff are efficient and sunny, matching the cheerful yellow, white and wood aesthetic. Pizzas from the titular brick oven are first-rate, sporting a chewy charred crust, zippy fresh tomato sauce and generous toppings (try the Italian fennel sausage). Burgers, too, are a cut above – note pulled lamb, hummus and apricot. But it's the little extra garnishes that delight: proper, chunky baba ganoush flecked with pomegranates; ribbony, just-grated slaw sprinkled with coriander seeds; a touch of sumac here, a splash of rosewater there. Wines from £18.
Chef/s: Alex Thomelin. **Open:** Sun, Mon and Wed 9 to 5.30 (10 to 4 Sun). Thur to Sat 9am to 11pm. **Closed:** Tue. **Meals:** alc (main courses £9 to £12). **Details:** 36 seats. 25 seats outside. Wheelchair access. Music.

Stuckton

The Three Lions

Old-fashioned English auberge
Cooking score: 3
Anglo-French | £45
Stuckton, SP6 2HF
Tel no: (01425) 652489
www.thethreelionsrestaurant.co.uk

Not everyone favours the pared-back neutrality that is the default setting of today's restaurant designers, and anyone hankering after swirly patterned carpets and country-style furniture will love the Three Lions. It has the feel of a French auberge (circa 1990), with simple bedrooms and a neat garden. 'Not quite sure what to make of it,' mused one reader. Whatever your take on the ambience, the fact is Mike Womersley turns out wholly satisfying French-inflected food that is rooted in classical ways. Start with a ravioli of artichoke and ceps, say, or a galette of smoked haddock, before moving on to trimmed loin of lamb with 'crispy bits', or baked sea bream with white wine and saffron sauce. There's evident passion for the old ways and no tricks or affectations, but that's not to say there isn't a creative touch here and there – verbena ice cream with the butterscotch tarte Tatin, for example. House wine is £15.75.

Chef/s: Mike Womersley. **Open:** Tue to Sun L 12 to 2, Tue to Sat D 7 to 9. **Closed:** Mon, last 2 weeks Feb. **Meals:** alc (main courses £19 to £27). Set L £24. Set D £30. **Details:** 60 seats. 10 seats outside. Bar. Wheelchair access. Music. Parking.

▮ West Meon
The Thomas Lord

Modern village pub fare
Cooking score: 2
British | £27
High Street, West Meon, GU32 1LN
Tel no: (01730) 829244
www.thethomaslord.co.uk

The whitewashed pub in a postcard-pretty village near Petersfield is named in honour of the same luminary as is the north London cricket ground. It still looks a proper pub inside, with half-panelling and framed excerpts from the cricket almanacs, while vegetables are grown and eggs laid in the back garden. Fran Joyce cooks in the modern idiom, with plenty of detail and big belting flavour in dishes that keep one foot firmly on British soil. A sausage roll filled with chicken, black pudding and artichoke is as certain to catch on as the venison variant on Scotch egg with tarragon mayonnaise. Sturdy butternut barley risotto dressed in truffle oil and Parmesan comes in two sizes, and a hefty veal chop is given all the accoutrements it could wish for – pickled squash, treacled carrots and rösti, with

a consommé of mushrooms and bone marrow. Finish with star anise pannacotta, gingerbread and apple jelly. Wines are priced from £17.50.

Chef/s: Fran Joyce. **Open:** all week L 12 to 2.30 (3 Sat, 4 Sun), D 6 to 9.30 (10 Fri and Sat, 9 Sun). **Meals:** alc (main meals £12 to £18). Set L £16 (2 courses) to £20. Set D £20. Sun L £16. **Details:** 65 seats. 50 seats outside. Bar. Wheelchair access. Music. Parking.

▮ Winchester
The Black Rat

Ambitious cooking and polished service
Cooking score: 6
Modern British | £45
88 Chesil Street, Winchester, SO23 0HX
Tel no: (01962) 844465
www.theblackrat.co.uk

'Deliciously eccentric' is probably the best way to describe this city pub-turned-restaurant that is both completely unexpected ('kooky, almost ramshackle looks') and a godsend to anyone in Winchester who enjoys ambitious cooking and polished service. The upstairs bar shares the dining room's taste for rug-strewn floorboards and oddity artefacts and ornaments, while in the kitchen Ollie Moore is all about smart technique and quality ingredients. Silky monkfish cheeks, perhaps, paired with a nest of crisp potato, a swipe of jam-like egg yolk, a tartare-inspired dressing of capers and gherkins and some blanched potato, before 'delicious' lamb-fat gnocchi that's served with a rolled cylinder of braised lamb neck, leeks and plenty of buttery girolles, and a black cardamom pannacotta 'balanced precisely between collapse and wobble', with tender poached plums and plum sorbet. The weekend set lunch has been praised, in warmer months you can eat in one of three wicker huts in the back garden, while the limited wine list is very French and starts at £22.

Chef/s: Ollie Moore. **Open:** Sat and Sun L 12 to 2.15, all week D 7 to 9.30. **Closed:** 2 weeks Christmas, 2 weeks Easter, 2 weeks Sept. **Meals:** alc (main courses £20 to £26). Set L £25 (2 courses) to £29. **Details:** 40 seats. 16 seats outside. Bar. Music. Children over 12 yrs only at D.

The Chesil Rectory
Half-timbered heritage and modern food
Cooking score: 4
Modern British | £34
1 Chesil Street, Winchester, SO23 0HU
Tel no: (01962) 851555
www.chesilrectory.co.uk

'With its history and quirky original features, this restaurant is unique, and I always recommend it,' says one fan of this half-timbered piece of Winchester's history. Dating back 600 years, Chesil Rectory has all the wonky beams, weathered floorboards and pretty brickwork you could wish for. A real fire, a touch of taxidermy and other curios complete the look, yet there is nothing backward-looking about the menu. A warm salad of chicken livers with sweetcorn purée, watercress and pancetta crumb typifies the bright, contemporary style, followed perhaps by lemon sole with crispy oyster, blood orange, confit potatoes and chicory marmalade. Vegetarian dishes such as a whole roast cauliflower with truffled purée, pickled walnuts, crisp shallots, hazelnut and pistachio romesco are clearly more than an afterthought. To finish, maybe white chocolate cheesecake with ginger brittle and rhubarb. Carefully chosen wines, ranging from classics to rising stars, start at £19.95.
Chef/s: Damian Brown. **Open:** all week L 12 to 2.20 (3 Sun), D 6 to 9.30 (9 Sun). **Closed:** 25 and 26 Dec. **Meals:** alc (main courses £14 to £21). Set L and D £16 (2 courses) to £20. Sun L £22 (3 courses). **Details:** 75 seats. Bar. Music. Children at L only.

Woodlands
Hotel TerraVina
Wine-focused foodie destination
Cooking score: 4
Modern European | £43
174 Woodlands Road, Woodlands, SO40 7GL
Tel no: (023) 8029 3784
www.hotelterravina.co.uk

Set up by world-beating sommelier Gerard Basset OBE, this striking contemporary hotel sits snug in a woodland hamlet on the fringes of the New Forest. At its heart is a clean-lined dining room with big picture windows, light woodwork, high-backed banquettes and an open kitchen, inspired by Basset's love of all things Californian. Local, organic and free-range ingredients are deftly deployed across the board – from a salad of Hampshire beetroot with goats' cheese, eight-year balsamic and horseradish sorbet to roast New Forest venison and braised shoulder with garlic kale and chestnuts. Elsewhere, modern influences and Mediterranean themes crop up in, say, potted mackerel with tomato jelly or an intricate dish of slow-roast pork belly with pumpkin purée, cavolo nero, spiced plums and honey granola. After that, it's worth waiting 15 minutes for the apple and vanilla soufflé with blueberry sorbet. Given Basset's pedigree, it's no surprise that the wine list is a suitably expansive tome with quality in every department and excellent monthly selections from £18.25.
Chef/s: Gavin Barnes. **Open:** all week L 12 to 2 (3.15 Sun), D 7 to 9.30 (9.45 Sat). **Meals:** alc (main courses £18 to £28). Set L £22 (2 courses) to £27. Sun L £24 (2 courses) to £30. Tasting menu £65 (6 courses). **Details:** 56 seats. 26 seats outside. V menu. Bar. Wheelchair access. Parking.

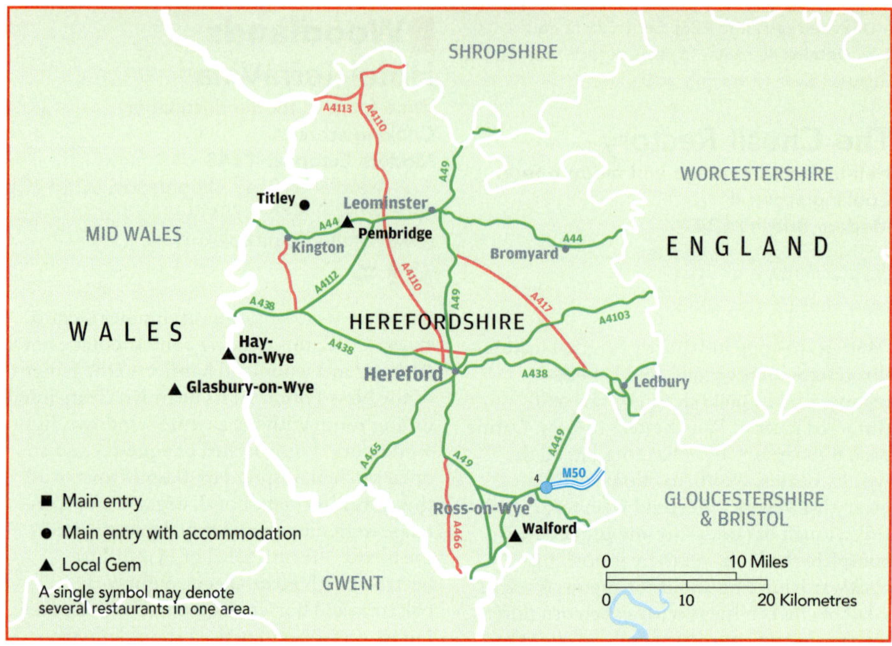

Glasbury-On-Wye

LOCAL GEM

The River Café

Italian | £22
Glasbury-On-Wye, HR3 5NP
Tel no: (01497) 847007
www.wyevalleycanoes.co.uk

The eating option at the Wye Valley Canoe Centre sits as close to the river as you can get without hiring a boat. A crisp, white, modern space with rustic furniture, it majors in breezy, vivid cooking, often with an Italian flavour. Try clam chowder with samphire and pancetta ahead of crab pappardelle or a beef burger with chilli and coriander jam, mustard mayo, fennel slaw and chives. Besides full restaurant meals it offers hearty breakfast and afternoon coffees and pastries. A modest, international selection of wines opens at £14.95. Closed Sun D.

Hay-on-Wye

LOCAL GEM

Richard Booth's Bookshop Café

Modern British | £18
44 Lion Street, Hay-on-Wye, HR3 5AA
Tel no: (01497) 820322
www.boothbooks.co.uk

Cultural hub during the Hay Literary Festival and year-round bibliophile's paradise, Richard Booth's legendary bookshop also accommodates a cinema, 'wellness' studio and this splendidly rustic, stone-walled café festooned with artwork. Come here for comforting breakfasts, tea and cake, snacks and vibrant savoury dishes ranging from sweet pepper frittata to pan-fried hake on crushed new potatoes and red chard with green herb sauce or marinated pork belly on mango and carrot salad with pastis dressing. Wines from £19. Open Tue to Sun, with suppers on Fri and Sat.

Pembridge

LOCAL GEM
The Cider Barn
Modern British | £30
Dunkertons Cider Mill, Pembridge, HR6 9ED
Tel no: (01544) 388161
www.the-cider-barn.co.uk

The redundant barn at Dunkertons Cider makes a charming setting for a restaurant. With classic exposed beams, mismatched furnishings, country views, local beers and ciders and chalked-up specials boards, it has all the hallmarks of a pub, but this is a much more rooted place, run by a Herefordshire couple and glorying in local produce. Though Hereford steaks feature, the kitchen's strengths lie in the quirkier dishes: chicken rillette with deep-fried crisp poached egg; a huge slab of goats' cheese rolled in almonds and baked, served with a light basil-led salad; custard cheesecake with roast rhubarb and rhubarb granita. Wines from £17. Closed Tue, L Mon to Wed and D Sun.

Titley

★ TOP 50 PUB ★

The Stagg Inn
Herefordshire pub star
Cooking score: 5
Modern British | £35
Titley, HR5 3RL
Tel no: (01544) 230221
www.thestagg.co.uk

£5 OFF

Things started to look up for the British pub when a new wave of rejuvenated and vital places hit the headlines in the 1990s, none more so than the Stagg Inn. Steve and Nicola Reynolds got the keys in 1998 and got off to a flyer. The pretty old inn (part medieval, part Victorian, part…erm…1970s) has charming rooms, a diminutive bar filled with locals and a restaurant that delivers Steve's pin-sharp food. Local supply lines run deep. With an output that combines refinement with

rusticity and integrity, kick off with campfire trout with horseradish and potato, or smoked breast of pheasant with beetroot and leaves. Main courses might see partridge matched with sweet-and-sour parsnips and smoked mash, and sea bass with fennel and apple. Herefordshire steaks and a cracking Sunday roast show customer satisfaction is to the fore. Finish with three crème brûlées (vanilla, coffee and cardamom). The impressive wine list is keenly priced and starts at £15.90.
Chef/s: Steve Reynolds and Matthew Handley.
Open: Wed to Sun L 12 to 2 (2.30 Sun), D 6.30 to 9 (8.30 Sun). **Closed:** Mon, Tue, 25 and 26 Dec, 1 Jan, 1 week Jan/Feb, first 2 weeks Nov. **Meals:** alc (main courses £17 to £25). **Details:** 70 seats. 16 seats outside. V menu. Bar. Parking.

Walford

LOCAL GEM
The Mill Race
Modern British | £28
Walford, HR9 5QS
Tel no: (01989) 562891
www.millrace.info

'This isn't our local, but we make it our local' was one emphatic endorsement of this pub-restaurant three miles from Ross-on-Wye. The owners own a neighbouring farm, which supplies much of the meat, poultry and game on the produce-driven menu so expect seasonal treats such as wood pigeon pasty, followed by rotolo of Wye Valley asparagus with roast garlic and butternut squash. Local rump steak sandwiches, rarebit and 'posh' cheesy chips keep pub grub fans happy. Wine from £15.50. Open all week.

Local Gem

Local Gems are the perfect neighbourhood venues, delivering good, freshly cooked food at great value for money.

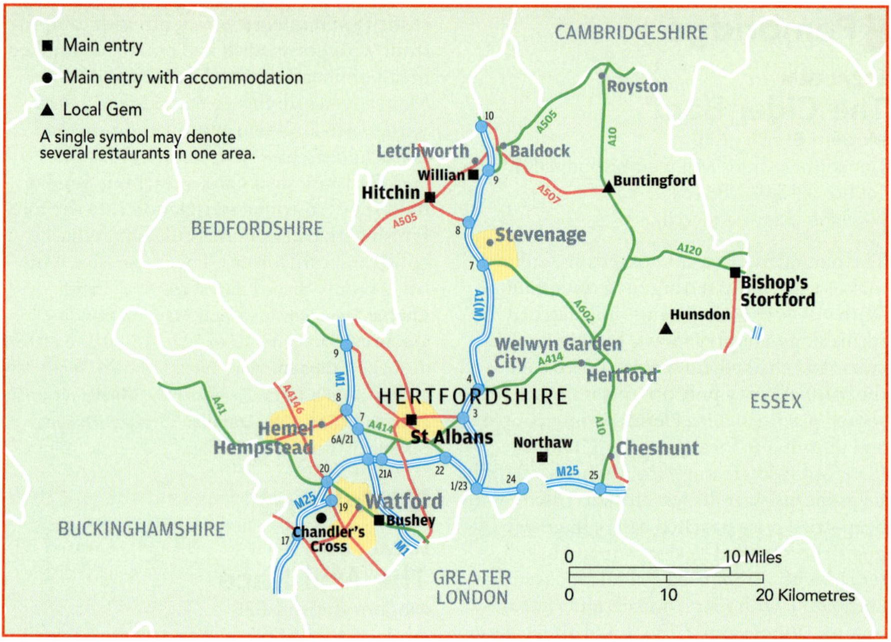

Bishops Stortford
Water Lane

Lively, solid crowd-pleaser
Cooking score: 1
Modern British | £27
31 Water Lane, Bishops Stortford, CM23 2JZ
Tel no: (01279) 211888
www.waterlane.co

£30

This high-decibel bolt-hole with its stark, urban look and lively relaxed atmosphere occupies a spacious former brewery and delivers a modestly priced menu that's diverse enough for a knowledgeable palate and familiar enough for the novice. Small plates (smoked haddock Scotch egg; wild mushrooms on toast), mains of roast sea trout with tomato, mussel and tiger prawn bisque, grills of bourbon-glazed pork belly or an excellent oxtail burger are its stock in trade. A handy local asset, it's part of the Nye family's Anglian Country Inns, and shares DNA with the group's popular Hermitage Rd, Hitchin (see entry). Wines from £17.50.
Chef/s: Will Ingarfill. **Open:** Tue to Sun 12 to 10 (12 to 4 Sun). **Closed:** 25 Dec. **Meals:** alc (main courses £12 to £16). **Details:** 100 seats. Bar. Wheelchair access. Music.

Buntingford

LOCAL GEM
Pearce's Farmshop and Café

Modern European | £22
Hamels Mead, Buntingford, SG9 9ND
Tel no: (01920) 821246
www.pearcesfarmshop.com

Charming service and panoramic views over the Hertfordshire countryside are reason enough to visit this well-bred farm shop-cum-café on the south carriageway of the A10, but the food also demands attention. Reporters have enjoyed informal meals in the green-oak-framed dining room where you

Join us at thegoodfoodguide.co.uk

can eat a little or a lot (afternoon tea is also served here). Warm salad of ham hock, and stuffed chicken with rosemary and lemon and Moroccan roasted vegetables are praised, along with apple and sultana strudel. Wines from £14.95. Open daytime all week.

Bushey
St James
A boon for Bushey
Cooking score: 1
Modern European | £40
30 High Street, Bushey, WD23 3HL
Tel no: (020) 8950 2480
www.stjamesrestaurant.co.uk

It's been doing Bushey proud since 1997, and this hard-grafting local asset opposite St James' Church keeps on spreading the gospel, with garrulous host Alfonso La Cava as the life and soul of the place. In the kitchen, long-serving Matt Cook conjures up generous plates of dependable food with strong Anglo-European leanings – from grilled scallops with pea purée, crispy Parma ham and chive butter sauce to roast loin of venison with truffle oil mash, red cabbage, parsnips, port and redcurrant jus. Set menus are a big plus for the locals, while desserts include the signature Toblerone cheesecake with black cherry compote. House wines are £15.95.
Chef/s: Matt Cook. **Open:** all week L 12 to 3, Mon to Sat D 6.30 to 10. **Closed:** 25 and 26 Dec, bank hols. **Meals:** alc (main courses £15 to £23). Set L £17 (2 courses) to £22. Set D £19 (2 courses) to £24. Sun L £21 (2 courses) to £26. **Details:** 100 seats. 20 seats outside. V menu. Bar. Wheelchair access. Music.

Chandler's Cross
The Grove, Colette's
Great British modernism
Cooking score: 6
Modern British | £65
Chandler's Cross, WD3 4TG
Tel no: (01923) 296010
www.thegrove.co.uk

It often comes as a surprise to find how close the rolling acres of the Home Counties are to sprawling London, and the Grove bids fair to consider itself 'London's country estate'. In this extended Georgian mansion, Queen Victoria once threw house parties, courtesy of its owners, successive Earls of Clarendon. Expect mudbaths and golf these days, but also a pleasantly understated, elegant dining room, Colette's, where Russell Bateman brings in the provender of kitchen-garden Hertfordshire and points south to fashion a British modernism worthy of the name. A scallop is hardly lonely when it turns up with its best mate, the oyster, along with salt-baked celeriac, apple and seaside herbs, as a possible preamble to Wiltshire venison with pumpkin, chanterelles, Brussels and walnuts in mulled wine, or perhaps cod with its smoked roe and the indecorously termed 'crab scraps'. The dessert to go for is a Moroccan-inspired blood orange affair with cardamom pannacotta and white chocolate granita. An illustrious wine list opens at £29, with glasses from £7.50.
Chef/s: Russell Bateman. **Open:** Tue to Sat D only 6.30 to 9.30. **Closed:** Sun, Mon, Tue after bank hols. **Meals:** Set D £75 (6 courses) to £85 (8 courses). **Details:** 40 seats. 20 seats outside. V menu. Bar. Wheelchair access. Music. Parking. No children.

André Garrett

André Garrett at Cliveden, Berkshire

What do you enjoy the most about being a chef?
The creativity, the diversity, travel and getting to meet great people.

What inspired you to become a chef?
My grandmother was maître d' at the Pump Room in Bath. We used to visit the kitchens and I would watch the chefs at work. The more I learned, the more I wanted to be a part of this fantastic trade.

What would you be if you weren't a chef?
I cannot imagine doing anything else.

At the end of a long day, what do you like to cook?
Linguine, olive oil, garlic and Italian tomatoes. My partner is Italian and we always have great produce at home.

What food could you not live without?
Cheese, I can't imagine not being able to eat it, there are so many wonderful flavours.

Tell us something about yourself that might surprise your diners.
I don't live on the Cliveden estate!

▌Hitchin

Hermitage Rd
Sparky food and feel-good vibes
Cooking score: 2
Modern British | £26
20-21 Hermitage Road, Hitchin, SG5 1BT
Tel no: (01462) 433603
www.hermitagerd.co.uk

Lots of brick and industrial ducting, huge windows, wood floors, quirky artefacts – welcome to Hermitage Rd, an edgy, urban eatery carved out of a first-floor former dance hall. Matching the food to this 'fabulous' funky vibe – the bar is all-day and the brasserie can be equally high-decibel – is a tricky matter, but the guys in the open-plan kitchen do their best with a crowd-pleasing menu of 'exceptional' brasserie dishes. Pulled pork and chorizo croquettes with Hermitage smoked beans sounds typically left-field, while mains move into more orthodox territory for the likes of a pot of Norfolk mussels, calf's liver with truffle mash, greens and crispy bacon and red wine jus, burgers, and various steaks with a choice of sauces. After that, consider burnt Cambridge cream with homemade Oreo or a Snickers sundae with peanut-butter ice cream. Service is 'spot on'. The global wine list starts at £17.50.
Chef/s: Kumour Uddin. **Open:** Mon to Fri L 12 to 2.30, D 6.30 to 10. Sat and Sun 12 to 10 (12 to 6 Sun). **Closed:** 25 Dec. **Meals:** alc (main courses £12 to £18). **Details:** 150 seats. Bar. Wheelchair access. Music.

▌Hunsdon

Fox & Hounds
Modern British | £30
2 High Street, Hunsdon, SG12 8NH
Tel no: (01279) 843999
www.foxandhounds-hunsdon.co.uk

'Excellent' hand-rolled pasta and prime pickings from the Josper oven are major talking points at this easy-going roadside pub,

Join us at thegoodfoodguide.co.uk

but there's much more to enjoy – from lamb rump with sautéed sweetbreads, parsnip purée and sprouting broccoli to spot-on roast cod with spinach and a 'delightful' mussel and saffron sauce. For afters, try apple tarte fine with caramel sauce. The Fox & Hounds also earns bonus points for its summertime terrace, child-friendly garden, smart dining room and local ales – plus its very decent wine list (from £16.50). No food Sun D and Mon.

▮ Northaw
The Sun at Northaw

English rose of a pub
Cooking score: 2
British | £29
1 Judges Hill, Northaw, EN6 4NL
Tel no: (01707) 655507
www.thesunatnorthaw.co.uk

This sturdy 16th-century pub offers the complete package when it comes to the world of country pubs. Whether you're relaxing by the open fire or taking advantage of alfresco tables in the garden, it all sets the scene for straightforward seasonal cooking. Oliver Smith is something of a local hero when it comes to supporting local food and his network of suppliers is at the heart of the operation; the kitchen makes the most of the exceptional bounty for some terrific dishes. Beetroot, goats' cheese and pickled walnuts or beer-battered cod cheeks with tartare sauce make good openers. After that, big seasonal flavours prevail, from roast witch sole with watercress, shrimps, lemon and capers to roast venison loin with braised red cabbage and salsify. To finish, try the banana, caramel and walnut Eton mess. Service has been found erratic at times, which has lead to not a few grumps. Wines from £17.

Chef/s: Oliver Smith. **Open:** Tue to Sun L 12 to 3 (4 Sun), Tue to Sat D 6 to 10. **Closed:** Mon. **Meals:** alc (main courses £13 to £25). Sun L £30 (2 courses) to £37. **Details:** 80 seats. 60 seats outside. Bar. Music. Parking.

▮ St Albans
Lussmanns

Independent ethical brasserie
Cooking score: 1
Modern European | £27
Waxhouse Gate, off High Street, St Albans, AL3 4EW
Tel no: (01727) 851941
www.lussmanns.com

The name sums up the confidently-simple offerings at this 'wonderful' neighbourhood brasserie, which has had readers waxing lyrical since its inception a decade ago. The first of a burgeoning chain, Lussmanns – with its modern feel and sensibly-priced menu – is a boon for locals, in an area with arguably little epicurean excitement. Proudly vocal about its support for welfare-driven producers, expect attributions aplenty on the crowd-pleasing menu: Woodland bruschetta with Cotswold wild boar chorizo, wild rabbit and wild mushrooms to start might appeal, with MSC fish and chips or Sussex free-range pork loin from the grill to follow. Spiced treacle and citrus pudding with cinnamon ice cream makes for a decadent conclusion. Wines from £15.95.

Chef/s: Bogdan Comza. **Open:** all week 12 to 10 (9.30 Mon, 10.30 Fri and Sat, 9 Sun). **Closed:** 25 and 26 Dec. **Meals:** alc (main courses £12 to £22). Set L and early D £12 (2 courses) to £15. **Details:** 100 seats. Wheelchair access. Music.

Thompson at Darcy's

Big modernist ideas in a posh bistro
Cooking score: 5
Modern British | £45
2 Hatfield Road, St Albans, AL1 3RP
Tel no: (01727) 730777
www.thompsonatdarcys.co.uk

Posh but popular, casual but plush…that's the thinking behind chef Phil Thompson's self-named venture in what was Darcy's – a local hot ticket housed in a weatherboarded cottage conversion and one-time ironwork shop.

Inside, it's a step up from bistro chic with stripped-wood floors, floral artwork and grey-green walls, while the cooking is fancy, modern and 'tight' without overgilding the lily. Flavours are sharply judged, ingredients are à la mode and the menu reads well: roast garlic-dressed squid with burnt cauliflower, sea vegetables and confit lemon; confit Dingley Dell pork belly with seared scallops, carrot, morteau sausage and quinoa; smoked rib and Wagyu beef rump with Roscoff onions, spinach and king oyster. For afters, yuzu and lime parfait with verbena, passion fruit, blood orange and sesame sounds suitably cosmopolitan. Reasonably priced weekday lunches, a kids' menu, excellent vegetarian deals and 'lobster and steak' suppers on Sundays broaden the venue's all-round appeal, with a delightfully relaxed team out front and back-up from an eminently accessible wine list – including 16 house selections from £17.95. **Chef/s:** Phil Thompson. **Open:** all week L 12 to 2 (3 Sun), D 6 to 9 (9.30 Fri and Sat). **Meals:** alc (main courses £17 to £32). Set L £17 (2 courses) to £21. Set D £19 (2 courses) to £23. Sun L £25 (2 courses) to £30. **Details:** 90 seats. 18 seats outside. V menu. Bar. Wheelchair access. Music.

The Foragers
Modern British | £30
The Verulam Arms, 41 Lower Dagnall Street, St Albans, AL3 4QE
Tel no: (01727) 836004
www.the-foragers.com

£5
OFF

The Foragers at the Verulam Arms trumpets its green message in the shadow of St Albans cathedral, its crusading, eco-friendly ethos taking in foraging walks, a micro-brewery brewing ales from foraged ingredients, a wild (in the natural sense) cocktail menu, and cooking that is seasonally and locally attuned. The flavours of winter, for example, feature home-smoked salmon with slow gin gel, locally shot pheasant and wood pigeon, or

pulled venison and hedgerow BBQ burger, and a spiced pear jelly to finish. Wines £16.95. No food Sun D.

Willian
The Fox
Niftily converted village boozer
Cooking score: 2
Modern British | £28
Willian, SG6 2AE
Tel no: (01462) 480233
www.foxatwillian.co.uk

£30

Hard by Willian village green, this niftily converted 18th-century boozer is now a smart cookie with two strings to its bow. You can slurp oysters and pints of real ale in the bar, although most people repair to the more formal dining room for modish assemblages served on wooden boards and stylish plates. Given that the Fox is owned by the Nye family from the White Horse, Brancaster Staithe (see entry), it's no surprise that Norfolk seafood is a strong suit – from pots of Brancaster mussels to fillet of sea bass with grilled new potatoes, celeriac purée and sautéed wild mushrooms. Otherwise, meat eaters and vegetrians can consider home-cured corned beef with an ox cheek croquette, slow-roast collar of pork with bubble 'n' squeak or chestnut gnocchi with roasted squash, Stilton purée and toasted pine nuts. To finish, Anglo-Irish cheeses compete with puds such as cornmeal and almond cake with honey ice cream. Wines from £17.50. **Chef/s:** Sherwin Jacobs. **Open:** all week L 12 to 2 (3 Sun), Mon to Sat D 6.30 to 9.15. **Meals:** alc (main courses £13 to £20). **Details:** 120 seats. 80 seats outside. Bar. Wheelchair access. Music. Parking.

Biddenden
The West House

Innovative cooking in laid-back surroundings
Cooking score: 5
Modern European | £40
28 High Street, Biddenden, TN27 8AH
Tel no: (01580) 291341
www.thewesthouserestaurant.co.uk

A low-key but enviably consistent performer on Biddenden's high street, West House occupies a rather lovely Kentish weaver's cottage so discreetly signed 'we drove past and missed it the first time'. Inside, the half-timbered dining room is relatively spacious and smart, and with undressed tables and high-backed leather chairs makes an unobtrusive setting for Graham Garrett's sure-footed and technically astute food. It's the kind of cooking that has the confidence to do the simple things with supreme panache, as evidenced by a report of a 'deeply delicious' February dinner starring a beetroot cheesecake as an 'avante garde curtain-raiser' and where a pre-dessert of sweet risotto with rhubarb and white chocolate was described as 'banishing forever our loathing of rice pudding'. In between there could be steamed hare brioche bun with chocolate sauce and horseradish, followed by suckling pig belly served with cauliflower, prunes and Earl Grey, with banana cake and sorbet, date purée and candied walnut as the grand finale. The wine list is a treasure trove, ticking all the boxes for serious intent, quality and value (from £18), and rewards experimentation.
Chef/s: Graham Garrett. **Open:** Tue to Fri and Sun L 12 to 2 (2.30 Sun), Tue to Sat D 7 to 9 (9.30 Fri and Sat). **Closed:** Mon, 24 to 26 Dec, 1 Jan. **Meals:** Set L £25. Set D £40. Tasting menu £60 (6 courses). **Details:** 35 seats. V menu. Parking.

Average price

The average price denotes the price of a three-course meal without wine.

 Broadstairs
Albariño
Assured neighbourhood tapas joint
Cooking score: 3
Tapas | £19
29 Albion Street, Broadstairs, CT10 1LX
Tel no: (01843) 600991
www.albarinorestaurant.co.uk

£30

Four years on, Steven Dray's unpretentious little restaurant continues to enjoy faithful support. It's a tiny, cramped dining room and bar where tightly packed tables sit perfectly with the versatile menu of Spanish tapas. High-quality raw materials are apparent in straightforward dishes: say Ibérico pork and lamb meatballs, local crab on toast with pancetta and apple, or grilled butifarra, morcilla and chorizo. There's a pleasing mix of the familiar (patatas bravas, smoked haddock croquetas) and more unusual items, perhaps crispy duck with creamed celeriac, wild mushrooms and plum, or ox cheek with cauliflower, liquorice and fried breadcrumbs (now something of a signature dish). Still hungry? Order the deep-fried Catalan custard with spiced pear. A good selection of sherries by the glass and wines from the Albariño region head the short, Iberian list. Bottles from £16.
Chef/s: Steven Dray. **Open:** Sat L 12 to 3, Mon to Sat D 6 to 10. **Closed:** Sun, 19 Dec to 1 Jan. **Meals:** alc (tapas £5 to £9). **Details:** 26 seats. Bar. Wheelchair access. Music.

Wyatt & Jones
Confident harbourside British fare
Cooking score: 2
British | £29
23-27 Harbour Street, Broadstairs, CT10 1EU
Tel no: (01843) 865126
www.wyattandjones.co.uk

 £5 OFF £30

The inhabitants of Broadstairs look kindly on Jan Wyatt and Katherine Hughes Jones' good-natured all-day eatery located just up from the beach by York Gate. It's easy to see why. An edgy, modern look and a neighbourly vibe are major attributes, although there is much to be said for the carefully crafted food, too. The open-to-view kitchen runs with the seasons, shows a steadfast commitment to British produce and pleases with the likes of 'fabulous' oysters, potted crab or mackerel tart with horseradish cream and radish salad. Mains are similarly simple but spirited: barbecued pork belly with smoked mash, broccoli and apple, or perhaps opt for Dover sole with fried garlic potatoes, wild mushroom and truffle oil. Lemon posset with fennel shortbread makes a great finish. It's a handy spot for breakfast, too, but getting in, especially at weekends, can be a headache, so do book. Wines from £17.
Chef/s: Jessica Leah. **Open:** Thur to Sun L 12 to 3 (12.30 to 5 Sun), Thur to Sat D 6 to 10. **Closed:** Mon, Tue, Wed. **Meals:** alc (main courses £16 to £20). Set L £14 (2 courses) to £18. Set D £19 (2 courses) to £24. Sun L £16. **Details:** 60 seats. Bar. Music.

 Canterbury
County Restaurant at ABode Canterbury
Hotel dining room with upbeat food
Cooking score: 3
Modern European | £45
High Street, Canterbury, CT1 2RX
Tel no: (01227) 766266
www.abodehotels.co.uk

Once known as the County Hotel, ABode Canterbury sits at the heart of the city on a high street dominated by pizza and pasta joints. With its bland façade, it may not leap out as somewhere to eat well – but be prepared to change your mind. Michael Caines is no longer involved with the restaurant but Jaunca Catalin has worked with the chef previously and delivers an à la carte of intricately worked dishes (inexpensive at lunch, pricier at dinner). The sedate dining room can feel rather anonymous but the front-of-house staff put on a friendly face, and lunch could bring salmon rillettes with compressed cucumber, wasabi yogurt and honey and soy vinaigrette to start, followed by braised feather-blade of beef with spinach, pearl barley and red wine jus or steamed hake atop fennel risotto with fennel cream sauce, and rhubarb and ginger cheesecake with poached rhubarb and sorbet, and ginger biscuit to finish. Wines from £21.50.

Chef/s: Jaunca Catalin. **Open:** all week L 12 to 2.30, Mon to Sat D 5.30 to 9.30. **Meals:** alc L (main courses £9 to £11); alc D (main courses £17 to £22). Early D £13 (2 courses) to £18. Tasting menu £55. **Details:** 70 seats. V menu. Bar.

The Goods Shed

Shedloads of good things
Cooking score: 2
Modern British | £32
Station Road West, Canterbury, CT2 8AN
Tel no: (01227) 459153
www.thegoodsshed.co.uk

'We love coming here – great atmosphere in unique environment overlooking the food market,' enthused a pair of regulars to this informal restaurant in the cavernous Goods Shed. What powers the kitchen is impeccable local produce from the neighbouring stalls, the resulting dishes scrawled up on a blackboard. Good for everyday dining as well as easy celebrations, this is the place to come for grouse in season, 'with the customary vegetables which you can tell are fresh from the market stalls', Kentish Ranger chicken with leeks and chorizo, and wild halibut with mussels, garlic and cream. As for dessert, treacle tart has proved 'irresistible'. Staff are 'always friendly and welcoming' and wines start at £15.75. Elsewhere in the market, readers can't say enough about the 'brilliant' Wild Goose bar and counter, which deals in small plates of market produce and cocktails made with their own herb-infused spirits.

Chef/s: Rafael Lopez. **Open:** Tue to Sun L 12 to 2.30 (3 Sat and Sun), Tue to Sat D 6 to 9.30. **Closed:** Mon, 25 to 27 Dec, 1 and 2 Jan. **Meals:** alc (main courses £14 to £24). **Details:** 60 seats. Parking.

 Crundale
The Compasses Inn

Lost in the Garden of England
Cooking score: 3
British | £27
Sole Street, Crundale, CT4 7ES
Tel no: (01227) 700300
www.thecompassescrundale.co.uk

Robert and Donna Taylor are splendid custodians of this beguilingly unassuming 15th-century country inn. Set in a pretty part of Kent within driving distance of Canterbury, it's a real pub with real ales (from local brewers Shepherd Neame), a cosy vibe and a short, to-the-point menu that reveals plenty of seasonality and local sourcing. It's all delivered in an unfussy manner, with good, full flavours coming through in a dish of confit lamb with roast garlic butter beans and a simple main course of roast loin of cod with champ potatoes, greens and cockle butter. Braised ox cheek with red cabbage and mustard clotted cream is worth considering, and desserts are in keeping – especially ginger parkin with poached rhubarb and vanilla ice cream. In addition, there are sandwiches at lunchtime when pub classics such as fish and chips or treacle-cured bacon, duck egg and chips are available. Wines from £14.50.

Chef/s: Robert Taylor. **Open:** Tue to Sun L 12 to 3 (4 Sun), Tue to Sat D 6 to 10. **Closed:** Mon. **Meals:** alc (main courses £11 to £17). **Details:** 50 seats. 40 seats outside. Bar. Wheelchair access. Music. Parking.

Please send us your feedback

To register your opinion about any restaurant listed in this guide, or a new restaurant that you wish to bring to our attention, please visit the web address at the bottom of the page. Your feedback informs the content of the book and will be used to compile next year's reviews.

Deal

NEW ENTRY

Victuals & Co.

Local asset with big ideas
Cooking score: 2
Modern British | £33
2-3 St George's Passage, Deal, CT14 6TA
Tel no: (01304) 374389
www.victualsandco.com

£5 OFF

Pronounced 'vittals', Andy and Suzy Kirkwood's bijou slate-grey eatery in the quaint backstreets of Deal has, despite its selective opening hours and discreet presence, proved quite a hit. From the moment its doors opened in 2012, head chef Derek Bond has been turning out imaginative, smart interpretations of the Kirkwoods' aspirations for cosmopolitan, globally influenced fare, with a starter of 'ham, egg and chips' as dainty as you like, fun and technically spot-on, comprising shredded ham hock, string potato chips, piccalilli and soft-boiled quail's egg. The rather extravagantly priced main courses take you on a tour of the Med but also cover bistro classics, perhaps cannelloni with mixed mushroom, shaved fennel, garlic cheese croûton and truffle dust, or a fillet steak with dauphinois potatoes. Fruit soufflés make for an indulgent finish, and obliging and enthusiastic service hits all the right notes. Wines from £17.50. Note: opening hours can change seasonally.
Chef/s: Derek Bond. **Open:** Wed to Sun L 12 to 2.30 (3 Sun), D 6 to 9 (8.30 Sun). **Closed:** Mon, Tue, and seasonal closures. **Meals:** alc (main courses £15 to £23). Set L £16 (2 courses) to £19. Sun L £16 (2 courses) to £19. **Details:** 40 seats. 10 seats outside. Bar. Music. Children over 9 yrs only at D.

Visit us online

To find out more about
The Good Food Guide, please
visit thegoodfoodguide.co.uk

Dover
The Allotment

Welcoming port of call
Cooking score: 1
Modern British | £23
9 High Street, Dover, CT16 1DP
Tel no: (01304) 214467
www.theallotmentdover.com

£5 OFF

Offering refuge from the busy thoroughfare it inhabits, this reputable local eatery has the laudable aim of serving only the best Kentish produce it can get its hands on, including ingredients from their own plot of land. Beyond Allotment's ornate glass frontage lies a warm welcome, and once ensconced in the tongue-and-groove-panelled, bistro-style interior with open-plan kitchen, the day's blackboard menu is presented. A succinct list of seasonally biased fare conveys modest ambition – good, hearty food is where green-fingered owner and chef Dave Flynn's strength lies. Strong offerings include Trevélez ham and celeriac remoulade, spankingly fresh whiting with pipérade, pork goulash and the signature Allotment burger. Finish, perhaps, with a homemade cake. Wines from £16.
Chef/s: David Flynn. **Open:** Tue to Sat 8.30am to 11pm. **Closed:** Sun, Mon, 24 Dec to 12 Jan. **Meals:** alc (main courses £9 to £16). **Details:** 26 seats. 24 seats outside. Wheelchair access.

Faversham
Read's

Elevated dining at a Georgian manor house
Cooking score: 6
Modern British | £60
Macknade Manor, Canterbury Road, Faversham, ME13 8XE
Tel no: (01795) 535344
www.reads.com

£5 OFF

'A dinner and night at Read's is always a treat,' enthused one visitor, while a local wondered where this part of Kent would be without it. In the smartly appointed Georgian manor house, décor is agreeable, tables are well spaced and there is evident skill and enthusiasm in the kitchen. David Pitchford's cooking stands out from the crowd not least because he starts with high-quality raw materials, from own-grown vegetables to English orchard fruit-fed pork. His style is at once classical yet contemporary, embracing terrine of slow-braised ham hocks with homemade piccalilli alongside a less usual partnership of vodka-cured organic Loch Duart salmon with pickled cucumber, crème fraîche and satsuma purée or, at main-course stage, breast of Gressingham duckling with a beetroot tarte Tatin, roast carrot purée and a Seville orange marmalade sauce. Both cherry and rhubarb soufflés have pleased, there's a well-kept selection of British cheeses and the set lunch is excellent value. The extensive wine list offers a cannily selected range from around the world, quality is consistent and for those on a budget, there's the condensed list of Best Buys from £24.

Chef/s: David Pitchford. **Open:** Tue to Sat L 12 to 2, D 7 to 9. **Closed:** Sun, Mon, 25 to 27 Dec, first week Jan, first 2 weeks Sept. **Meals:** Set L £26. Set D £50 (2 courses) to £60. **Details:** 50 seats. 24 seats outside. V menu. Bar. Wheelchair access. Parking.

Folkestone

Rocksalt
Seafood | £28
4-5 Fishmarket Road, Folkestone, CT19 6AA
Tel no: (01303) 212070
www.rocksaltfolkestone.co.uk

The ultra modern restaurant by the fishing harbour comes as a surprise – and everyone enjoys the view of boats bobbing on the water. On the food front due attention is paid to local produce (marinated Folkestone whelks on bone marrow toast, potted Dungeness shrimps, hay-baked rump of Romney Marsh lamb in a salt crust). Elsewhere, devilled duck hearts and roe deer bresola have been highlights, fish, bought mainly from local day boats, is 'done really well', and there are

enjoyable puddings along the lines of Kentish gypsy tart and baked egg custard. Wines from £16.50. Closed Sun D.

Hythe

La Salamandre
French | £15
30 High Street, Hythe, CT21 5AT
Tel no: (01303) 239853

This French-owned and run patisserie and simple café has become a badly kept secret among local food lovers who pack the place for pâtissier Alain Ronez's exceedingly good cakes. Ogling the display of beautifully worked pastries is a joy, not to mention a simple snack menu that's astonishingly good value. Breakfast takes in light, fluffy scrambled eggs on homemade brioche or a perfect almond croissant, while lunch brings soup (French onion, say), an omelette or delicate quiche (perhaps broccoli and blue cheese). Closed D, Sun and Mon. Unlicensed. Cash only.

Locksbottom
Chapter One
Big-city cooking at local prices
Cooking score: 6
Modern European | £40
Farnborough Common, Locksbottom, BR6 8NF
Tel no: (01689) 854848
www.chaptersrestaurants.com

'We are so lucky to have such a fabulous restaurant on our doorstep, and at local prices too,' is praise indeed, and there's no shortage of vocal support for this local eatery of the best sort – just off the A21 with welcome parking and a smart, separate bar. The spacious, comfortably appointed surroundings are tailored to conversational get-togethers, and Andrew McLeish's cooking pleases, excites and soothes in equal measure – witness a beautifully composed starter of quail Kiev

with its roasted leg, herb mayonnaise, dandelion leaf and Gruyère cheese or compression of pig's head and crispy pork jowl with chestnuts and honey mustard dressing. Consider, too, well-timed hake with good potato gnocchi, lovely buttered leeks and Périgord truffle, and a haunch of venison served sliced atop a superb shallot tarte fine, the plate decorated with dabs of intense spinach purée, a deeply flavoured cumin-roasted carrot and venison jus, while a hot, molten Valrhona chocolate fondant, served with chocolate soil and griottine cherries, is 'sheer delight'. The agreeably priced wine list (from £18) encourages guests to discover something new.
Chef/s: Andrew McLeish. **Open:** all week L 12 to 2.30 (3 Sun), D 6.30 to 10.30 (9 Sun). **Closed:** 2 to 4 Jan. **Meals:** alc (main courses £17 to £22). Set L £20. Sun L £23. Tasting menu £59. **Details:** 90 seats. 20 seats outside. V menu. Bar. Wheelchair access. Music. Parking.

▮ Lower Hardres
The Granville

A great local asset
Cooking score: 3
Modern European | £30
Street End, Lower Hardres, CT4 7AL
Tel no: (01227) 700402
www.thegranvillecanterbury.com

A decade on and this younger sibling of the Sportsman in nearby Whitstable (see entry) has worn in very nicely. The roadside pub a few miles outside Canterbury is modishly rustic in a 21st-century fashion, a relaxed, casual place with scrubbed pine tables, winter fire and ales from local brewer Shepherd Neame. The cooking is bang-up-to-date and the food is driven by well-sourced local and regional produce. Reporters have praised mulligatawny soup, buttery potted shrimps, crispy brawn with mustard mayonnaise, and plump mussels in white wine, garlic and parsley. For main course, pork belly is a perennial favourite, perhaps teamed with cabbage, mashed potato, apple sauce and crisp crackling, as is the crispy duck leg with sour

cream and smoked chilli salsa, and everyone loves the homemade soda bread and crusty white. A big hit, too, has been ginger cake with banana ice cream. Wines from £16.
Chef/s: Dave Hart. **Open:** all week L 12 to 2.30 (2 Mon, 3 Sun), Tue to Sat D 6.30 to 9. **Closed:** 25 and 26 Dec. **Meals:** alc (main courses £14 to £22). Set L £16 (2 courses) to £18. **Details:** 55 seats. 40 seats outside. Bar. Wheelchair access. Parking.

▮ Margate

LOCAL GEMS
GB Pizza Co
Italian | £16
14a Marine Drive, Margate, CT9 1DH
Tel no: (01843) 297700
www.greatbritishpizzacompany.com

'Amazing pizza – amazing service – amazing atmosphere – amazing location.' It seems readers love this unassuming little place that's currently packing a major punch on Margate's seafront. Done out in sparse, contemporary style, it is something of a badly kept secret among the town's devotees. Choose from a small selection of thin-crust wood-fired pizzas – favourites include British chorizo, chilli, tomato, mozzarella, and the Margate-rita (tomato, basil, mozzarella) – but there's also salted-caramel tart, Kentish ales and wines from £13. Open all week.

Greedy Cow
British | £15
3 Market Place, Old Town, Margate, CT9 1ER
Tel no: (01843) 447557
www.thegreedycow.com

Rachel and Peter Hunt's characterful, quirky café in the heart of Margate's old town is a convivial, welcoming place. The flexible all-day menu works hard, going from breakfasts of full English or Turkish eggs to big-on-flavour lunch dishes of spicy slow-roasted pork on freshly baked flatbread, open sandwiches of beef or haloumi and apple, and the reason most people pile in here – the best burgers for miles around, served with homemade coleslaw but no chips. Expect careful sourcing and locally made cakes too. Wines by the glass from £3. Closed Mon.

Minster

LOCAL GEM
The Corner House
British | £29
42 Station Road, Minster, CT12 4BZ
Tel no: (01843) 823000
www.thecornerhouseminster.co.uk

A simple, shoestring look that mixes low beams, bare brick, wood tables and candles, creates a mood of easy reassurance at this restaurant-with-rooms opposite Minster church. Matt Sworder is an accomplished cook who knows his customers: he employs quality seasonal ingredients and, menu-wise, there's nothing to frighten the horses. Popular stuff – mussels, chicken liver parfait, pork belly and mash, flat-iron steak and triple-cooked chips – is served in generous portions and treatments are simple. Treacle tart or British cheeses could bring up the rear and wines start at £14.50. Closed Mon, Tue L and Sun D. Accommodation.

Oare
The Three Mariners
The full country-pub package
Cooking score: 2
Modern British | £28
2 Church Road, Oare, ME13 0QA
Tel no: (01795) 533633
www.thethreemarinersoare.co.uk

John O'Riordan's archetypal country pub has the full complement of heart-warming features: bare beams and floorboards, real ales (from local brewer Shepherd Neame) and a roaring winter fire, plus a summer terrace looking towards Oare Creek. What really sets it apart, however, is O'Riordan's straight-talking cooking. British and European classics underpin a menu full of feisty flavours and fresh ingredients. Fish makes a strong showing – as in fish soup with aïoli and croûtons, or a fillet of wild sea bass with harissa, Greek herb yoghurt and sablée potatoes. Meat lovers could try Iberian pork pluma with patatas bravas. To finish, classic sticky toffee pudding with homemade ice cream is a good way to go. Bargain hunters should look to the walkers' or business lunch set menus, available most lunchtimes, but at any time of day this pub offers solid value – as evidenced by the decent wine list, which offers plenty by the glass, with bottles from £14.70.
Chef/s: John O'Riordan. **Open:** all week L 12 to 2.30 (3 Sat and Sun), D 6.30 to 9 (9.30 Fri and Sat, 7 to 9 Sun). **Meals:** alc (main courses £14 to £20). Set L £13 to £18 (3 courses). Set D £18 to £21 (3 courses). Sun L £18 to £23. **Details:** 65 seats. 34 seats outside. Music. Parking.

Stalisfield Green
The Plough
A convivial oasis
Cooking score: 1
British | £25
Stalisfield Green, ME13 0HY
Tel no: (01795) 890256
www.stalisfieldgreen.co.uk

Marianne and Richard Baker are the driving force behind this amenable, off-the-beaten-track country inn – a medieval 'hall house' with open fires and great character. Real ales on tap mean drinkers are still welcome, while diners are drawn by a commitment to local, seasonal produce and good pricing. The regularly changing menu is peppered with ideas that attempt to please all palates: homespun pub diehards (fish and chips, a sea salt-and-black pepper burger) sit happily beside more up-to-date ideas – pavé of halibut served with Norfolk brown shrimps and buttered leek risotto or roast rack of Kentish lamb with dauphinoise potatoes and ratatouille. Wines from £14.50.
Chef/s: Richard Baker. **Open:** Tue to Sun L 12 to 2 (3 Sat, 4 Sun), Tue to Sat D 6 to 9. **Closed:** Mon, first week Jan. **Meals:** alc (main courses £11 to £19). Set

L and D £14 (2 courses) to £17. Sun L £18 (2 courses). **Details:** 70 seats. 40 seats outside. Bar. Music. Parking.

Tunbridge Wells
Thackeray's
Classy French food
Cooking score: 5
Modern French | £55
85 London Road, Tunbridge Wells, TN1 1EA
Tel no: (01892) 511921
www.thackerays-restaurant.co.uk

Right in the heart of Tunbridge Wells, this long-established bastion of the Kent dining scene offers clever lighting and bold wallpaper to give the former home of the Victorian novelist William Makepeace Thackeray a chic, metropolitan air, offset by a quirky English feel. The menu keeps regulars returning with a repertoire that straddles classic French and modern British cooking. The set-up continues to deliver well-rehearsed dishes in which prime ingredients (breast of wood pigeon, perhaps, served with a warm salad of quails' eggs, smoked tomato, mushroom and salt-baked beetroot) produce seductive results. 'The kitchen clearly knows how to cook wonderful food,' noted one reporter after enjoying an assiette of aged beef 'bourguignon' (coal-grilled sirloin, sweetbreads, slow-cooked Jacob's ladder), which was served with braised celery, watercress purée and braising liquor. To finish, the raspberry soufflé (and sorbet) with Tahitian vanilla sauce is a masterpiece. Lunch is good value and the global wine list starts at £21.
Chef/s: Shane Hughes. **Open:** Tue to Sun L 12 to 2.30 (3 Sun), Tue to Sat D 6.30 to 10.30. **Closed:** Mon. **Meals:** alc (main courses £26 to £30). Set L £18 (2 courses) to £20. Sun L £30. **Details:** 40 seats. 30 seats outside. Bar. Music.

Whitstable
East Coast Dining Room
Good food in up-and-coming Tankerton
Cooking score: 2
Modern British | £33
101 Tankerton Road, Whitstable, CT5 2AJ
Tel no: (01227) 281180
www.eastcoastdiningroom.co.uk

£5
OFF

Despite a low-key, suburban location, East Coast Dining Room doesn't need to flaunt its charms or puff itself up. A quick peek through the glass-paned frontage at the happy company of locals and visitors is usually enough to do the trick. Everything on the regularly changing menu arrives in an unfussy style, which perfectly matches the pared-back look of slate grey and white, and crisp-clothed tables. A dedication to seasonal ingredients sets the tone, and among intriguing possibilities could be sautéed chicken livers with oat crumble, watercress and parsnip purée, coq au vin, an ox cheek and oyster pie, and local cod with bacon, brown shrimp and squash risotto. Puddings, perhaps buttermilk pudding with blood-orange syrup and mango ice cream, and homemade bread draw praise, too. Claire Houlihan (who ran the Three Mariners at Oare for several years) presides over this 'lovely neighbourhood restaurant', where service is charming and wines start at £16.
Chef/s: Ryan Smith. **Open:** Wed to Sun L 12 to 2.30 (3 Sat, 4 Sun), Wed to Sat D 6.30 to 9 (9.30 Fri and Sat). **Closed:** Mon, Tue, 25 and 26 Dec. **Meals:** alc (main courses £15 to £20). Set L £13 (2 courses) to £16. Sun L £18 (2 courses) to £22. **Details:** 36 seats. 16 seats outside. Wheelchair access. Music.

JoJo's

Top-notch tapas by the sea
Cooking score: 4
Tapas | £25
2 Herne Bay Road, Whitstable, CT5 2LQ
Tel no: (01227) 274591
www.jojosrestaurant.co.uk

The light, open-plan dining room overlooking the North Sea is easy-going, lively and committed – a simple setting for good food cooked without fuss. Nikki Billington puts the focus on the careful sourcing of ingredients and reporters feel they get fair value for money on a wide-ranging, zingily fresh tapas menu that runs from a mixed mezze of meats, cheese, salads and dips via 'delicious' mutton and feta kormas to char-grilled sardines or patatas bravas. Deep-frying is a favoured technique: calamari in a 'beautifully light and crispy' batter, say, or haddock goujons with tartare mayo, and pea and mint risotto balls. Thinly sliced lamb cannon with mint jelly and a blackboard special of 'lovely pink venison' have also been praised, as has a blood-orange sorbet, and the chocolate tart with salt caramel. Some reporters have grumbled about the ending of the BYO policy, but JoJo's is now licensed and offers a short, reasonably priced wine list (from £15). Note: cash only.

Chef/s: Nikki Billington, Sam Clowes, Nick Cane and Buddy Rowden. **Open:** Thur to Sun L 12.30 to 2, Wed to Sat D 6.30 to 9.30. **Closed:** Mon, Tue. **Meals:** alc (tapas £5 to £11). **Details:** Cash only. 60 seats. Wheelchair access. Music.

More Undercover Eats

Another of our anonymous restaurant inspectors tips us off about their highlights this year.

Pre-dinner nibbles at The Chef's Dozen, Chipping Campden. A whole fresh granary loaf between two; churned butter and smoked pork dripping; and fat radishes with a dish of smoked cod roe.

Asparagus and hollandaise at Spire, Liverpool, served with pea purée, broad beans, quail's eggs and a silky shallot hollandaise sauce – a perfect twist on a classic.

Veal gyoza at L'Atelier de Joël Robuchon. Tender, flavoursome braised veal shank, harissa warmth, and a crisp casing.

Creedy Carver duck breast at Goldstone Hall, Market Drayton. Possibly the biggest, most delicious piece of duck I have ever eaten: crisp skin, melt-in-the mouth tender, juicy and full of flavour.

Baked Alaska at the Art School, Liverpool. Retro brilliance, teamed with crumbled heather honey cake, yoghurt pannacotta and golden dribbles of honey.

★ TOP 50/TOP 10 PUB ★

The Sportsman

Refined pub food that's Kentish to the core
Cooking score: 6
Modern British | £38
Faversham Road, Seasalter, Whitstable,
CT5 4BP
Tel no: (01227) 273370
www.thesportsmanseasalter.co.uk

'There's a reason why the chefs from Noma travel to the UK to eat here. Stephen Harris was using their scavenging concepts long before they were, right down to the seaweed he collects from the beach 50 yards away.' So ran the notes of one reporter who 'was transported to heaven' by slip sole with seaweed butter and local Monkshill Farm lamb. Indeed, its doorstep larder keeps the Sportsman abundantly supplied: oysters and fish from the Thames estuary, meat from the salt marshland, and some produce from the kitchen garden and polytunnels. Mr Harris's country inn is Kentish to its fingertips, a light and pleasant place with local artworks for sale. Three rooms furnished with tables of reclaimed wood are the setting for blackboard menus (order at the bar) of food that inclines more to the refined than the rustic, even for a bowl of mussel and bacon chowder. Roast gurnard with green tapenade in shellfish sauce, or breast and confit leg of duck in spiced jus, are main courses to satisfy, and the pick of the desserts may well be the intensely flavoured apple soufflé with salt caramel ice cream, unless you feel you could murder a jasmine tea junket with rosehip syrup and breakfast crunch. A short wine list opens at £16.95 for Languedoc Viognier.
Chef/s: Steve Harris. **Open:** Tue to Sun L 12 to 2 (12.30 to 2.30 Sun), Tue to Sat D 7 to 9. **Closed:** Mon, 25 and 26 Dec, 1 Jan. **Meals:** alc (main courses £20 to £24). **Details:** 50 seats. Music. Parking. Children over 10 yrs only at D.

Wheelers Oyster Bar

British seaside through and through
Cooking score: 4
Seafood | £36
8 High Street, Whitstable, CT5 1BQ
Tel no: (01227) 273311
www.wheelersoysterbar.com

Wheelers has been in business for 160 years and with its striking candyfloss-pink-and-blue frontage is a Whitstable institution. Snagging one of the few table gets harder and harder (booking is essential), but if you're lucky enough to bag a counter stool in the front oyster bar or be squeezed into the back parlour, you can look forward to some incredibly fresh fish. Mark Stubbs' big-hearted foray into the world of fish cookery is generous, full-flavoured stuff, from flamed mackerel served with cucumber and yoghurt gazpacho, horseradish sorbet, smoked beetroot and mackerel cannelloni, cucumber and dill tartare to a main course lasagne of whole Kentish lobster, which arrives with leek ragoût, lobster bisque, wild mushrooms, tenderstem broccoli and shavings of aged Parmesan. Good things for dessert, too, if a hot apple and strudel soufflé with cinnamon ice cream and apple crumble trifle is anything to go by. Note: no licence means BYO (no corkage) and it's cash only.
Chef/s: Mark Stubbs. **Open:** Thur to Tue 1 to 7.30. **Closed:** Wed, 2 to 3 weeks Jan. **Meals:** alc (main courses £20 to £32). **Details:** Cash only. 18 seats.

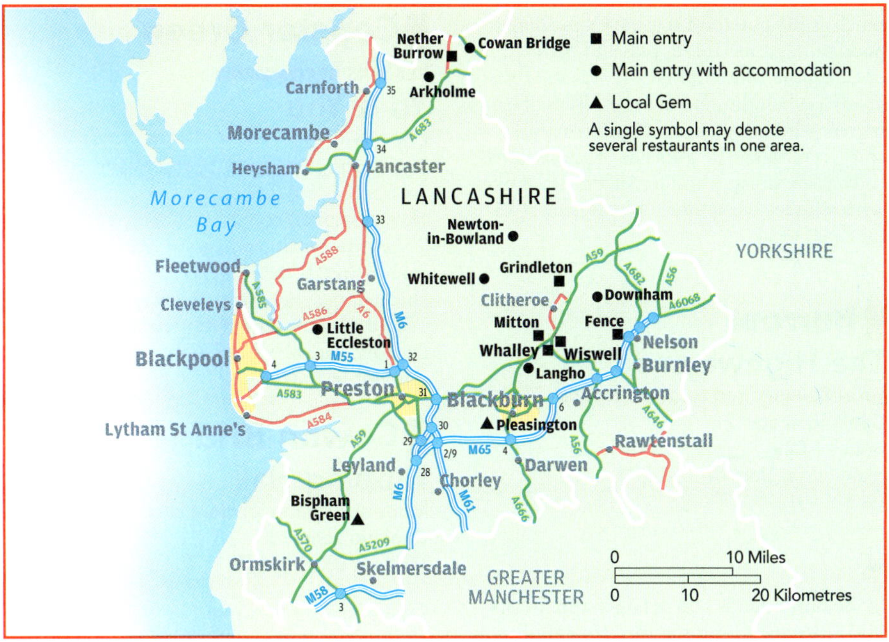

Arkholme

The Red Well

Modern flavours in a traditional setting
Cooking score: 2
Modern British | £27
Kirkby Lonsdale Road, Arkholme, LA6 1BQ
Tel no: (01524) 221240
www.redwellcountryinn.co.uk

The building dates from the 1640s and has seen many incarnations, from courthouse to auction room, but is now an immaculate hostelry noted for traditional comforts and hearty food. Lounge on leather sofas by the blazing wood-burner, then settle in the restaurant for chef/proprietor Rob Talbot's satisfying take on British and European classics. The pub incorporates its own smokehouse and shop, so a glazed omelette of own-smoked haddock with a micro-herb salad is a typical opener. After that, maybe slow-roasted Gloucester Old Spot pork belly with Anya potatoes, morels and garlic, and then a dessert of gariguette strawberries with burnt cream, black pepper honeycomb and sorbet. Meat-free options could include four-cheese pancake cannelloni. The nicely annotated wine list includes a good number by the glass. Bottles start at £18.95.
Chef/s: Rob Talbot. **Open:** all week 12 to 8.30 (8 Sun). **Meals:** alc (main courses £15 to £22). Sun L £23. **Details:** 80 seats. 30 seats outside. Bar. Wheelchair access. Music. Parking.

Bispham Green

LOCAL GEM

The Eagle & Child

British | £25
Malt Kiln Lane, Bispham Green, L40 3SG
Tel no: (01257) 462297
www.eagleandchildbispham.co.uk

This very welcoming pub has been feeding the locals of West Lancashire for many years and they enjoy the traditional setting (flag floors, a mishmash of antique furniture) as much as the pub food staples. Come here for good sausage and mash, pies and battered fish or go for the contemporary twists and turns of the daily changing menu for the likes of haggis fritters with sweet piccalilli, Goosnargh chicken with truffle gnocchi or pan-roasted cod, crispy mussels and Jerusalem artichokes with white wine velouté. Wines from £15. Open all week.

Burrow
The Highwayman
Local flavours and local enterprise
Cooking score: 2
British | £29
Main Road, Burrow, LA6 2RJ
Tel no: (01524) 273338
www.highwaymaninn.co.uk

In the borderlands where Lancashire meets Yorkshire and Cumbria, this stone-built country inn feels English to a T. It's a big, sprawling place, done out in restrained colours and cool fittings and plays to regular full houses who applaud the convivial way the pub is run. One of Nigel Haworth's Ribble Valley Inns, it follows the group's policy of drawing on local and regional supply lines to great effect with the menu name-checking many of the producers. A bowl of ham hock broth with a poached egg and homemade bread is a good wintry way to start, following which there may be fish pie with leek and herb sauce and cheesy mash or a regionally unimpeachable dish of braised shoulder of Kitridding lamb with a herb-oatcake crust. A fortifying finish sees sticky toffee pudding with banana ice cream and butterscotch sauce. Outside tables are a great draw in summer, and there are regional ales alongside a well-chosen wine list (from £16).

Chef/s: Bruno Birkbeck. **Open:** Mon to Fri L 12 to 2, D 5.30 to 9 (9.30 Fri). Sat and Sun 12 to 9.30 (9 Sun). **Meals:** alc (main courses £12 to £26). Set L and D £13 (2 courses) to £15 (Mon to Fri). Sun L £18 (2 course) to £21. **Details:** 110 seats. 45 seats outside. Bar. Wheelchair access. Music. Parking.

Copster Green

Yu & You
Chinese
500 Longsight Road, Copster Green, BB1 9EU
Tel no: (01254) 247111
www.yuandyou.com
'Everything was really good. We had steamed sea bass (really delicate flavour), crispy chilli chicken (very moreish) and stir-fried fillet of beef (delicious). The staff were attentive and friendly, and we would definitely recommend it to our friends.'

Cowan Bridge
Hipping Hall
Modern cooking, ancient setting
Cooking score: 5
Modern British | £55
Cowan Bridge, LA6 2JJ
Tel no: (01524) 271187
www.hippinghall.com

'I returned to stay at Hipping Hall…after a few years and found the same tranquillity, friendliness and quiet professional efficiency as before,' is the firm endorsement of one visitor to this small but distinguished 17th-century country house hotel. It's in a beautiful spot, sitting on the borders of Lancashire, Cumbria and Yorkshire, with a lush, well-tended garden and a dining room that occupies a 15th-century hall complete with polished oak floorboards, well-spaced, white-clad tables, a log fire and minstrels' gallery. In the kitchen, former sous-chef Oli Martin has been promoted and the consensus is that his cooking is on song. His modern approach teams up prime regional ingredients with a resourceful range of techniques. In among the excellent canapés, amuse-bouches and pre-desserts, there might be fresh mackerel with rhubarb, smoked eel and nettles, prior to 'super' stone sea bass, local Morecambe Bay shrimps and salt-baked celeriac or Lakeland beef with wild garlic and pear barley. A well-chosen list of wines is a model of informative concision and starts at £22.

Chef/s: Oli Martin. **Open:** Sat and Sun L 12 to 2, all week D 7 to 9. **Meals:** Set L £30. Set D £55. Tasting menu £40 (6 courses) to £65. **Details:** 32 seats. V menu. Wheelchair access. Music. Parking. Children over 12 yrs only at D.

Downham

The Assheton Arms

Fresh seafood in a revitalised pub
Cooking score: 2
Modern British | £27
Downham, BB7 4BJ
Tel no: (01200) 441227
www.asshetonarms.com

Once a run-down local boozer in a conservation village at the foot of Pendle Hill, the Grade II-listed Assheton Arms has been revitalised by Chris and Joycelyn Neve as part of their Seafood Pub Company – Chris, a former Grimsby trawlerman, now oversees daily supplies of fresh fish for the kitchen. Against a tasteful background of rich fabrics and muted colours, diners can nibble on mixed platters of home-smoked salmon, devilled crab, brown shrimp fritters and haddock goujons or fill up on seafood specials, piggy treats from the robata grill and various 'world pies'. Other items also plunder the global cookbook, from BBQ baby back ribs or steamed Korean buns stuffed with crispy duck to monkfish tikka with dhal, king prawn pakoras and mint raita. One-dish weekday lunches are a steal, kids have their own menu and there's steamed marmalade pudding with 'proper' custard for afters. The wine list naturally favours well-chosen fish-loving whites, with prices from £15.50.

Chef/s: Antony Shirley. **Open:** Mon to Sat L 12 to 3, D 5 to 9 (10 Fri and Sat). Sun 12 to 8. **Meals:** alc (main courses £11 to £24). **Details:** 80 seats. 60 seats outside. Bar. Wheelchair access. Music. Parking.

Fence

White Swan

Village pub in a class of its own
Cooking score: 5
British | £25
300 Wheatley Lane Road, Fence, BB12 9QA
Tel no: (01282) 611773
www.whiteswanatfence.co.uk

Fence is in farming country, a quiet village within easy reach of the M65, its pub solid and traditional-looking, dispensing Timothy Taylor's ales. But here, too, is a talented young chef who is doing magical things in the kitchen. Tom Parker sensibly doesn't set himself over ambitious targets, his daily changing menus offer just three choices per course, enabling him to exploit ample local resources and deliver the finest materials at their seasonal best. A meal in spring could bring an intense wild garlic soup with curd cheese and morels or a delicate dish of English asparagus with 'delicious' lardo and tarragon, as well as spot-on Cornish brill with cucumber spirals and dill, and lovely, meaty corn-fed chicken breast with a perfectly crisped skin and more asparagus and morels. Fine British cheeses should be a banker, if you're not in the market for a carefully wrought dish of coconut pannacotta with honey mango and lime leaf. Service is friendly and well informed, fair prices are a plus and this extends to the well-considered wine list that opens at £17.

Chef/s: Tom Parker. **Open:** Tue to Sat L 12 to 2.30, D 5.30 to 8.30 (9 Fri and Sat). Sun 12 to 7.30. **Closed:** Mon. **Meals:** Set L and D £20 (2 courses) to £25. **Details:** 35 seats. Bar.

Grindleton

The Duke of York Inn

Pub that punches above its weight
Cooking score: 4
Modern British | £28
Brow Top, Grindleton, BB7 4QR
Tel no: (01200) 441266
www.dukeofyorkgrindleton.com

The Ribble Valley boasts many traditional pub restaurants but Michael Heathcote continues to raise the bar for informal eating. Whether eating in the cosy bar or the comfortable restaurant, the menu offers 'simply delicious' food that celebrates local and regional produce. Start with Heathcote's excellent soufflé of Kirkham's Lancashire cheese, caramelised onion and apple, or his West Coast Scottish scallops with pork belly croquette, cauliflower purée 'with a hint of curry' and homemade pickled onions, considered 'the best dish of the night' at inspection. Mains show off Fleetwood-landed fish, say a thick slab of 'perfectly cooked' cod with a superb brandade-style cod cake, wilted pak choi and a 'great' mustard cream sauce, or opt for three perfectly pink slices of Lancashire-farmed beef rump with 'gorgeous roasted vegetables and an excellent red wine reduction'. Puddings, too, show flare, perhaps a 'silky smooth' Earl Grey pannacotta and poached prunes. Lovely young waiting staff know their stuff, there's a good range of local beers and a carefully thought out wine list from £16.50.
Chef/s: Michael Heathcote. **Open:** Tue to Sun L 12 to 2, D 6 to 9 (5 to 7.30 Sun). **Closed:** Mon.
Meals: alc (main courses £14 to £28). Set L and D £15 (2 courses) to £17. Sun L £18. **Details:** 70 seats. 25 seats outside. V menu. Bar. Wheelchair access. Parking.

Langho

Northcote

A smartly revitalised, timeless retreat
Cooking score: 6
Modern British | £60
Northcote Road, Langho, BB6 8BE
Tel no: (01254) 240555
www.northcote.com

Northcote continues to be 'a real gem of the North' for many readers. Celebrating 35 years in 2016, this regal, 'almost castle-like building' has been reinvigorated with a bold and no-expense spared makeover, producing a contemporary bar and new look restaurant with full height glass doors looking out over a pretty terrace and vegetable garden. Menus continue to be laid out as tasting, gourmet and à la carte, with the seasonal lunch an undoubted bargain, and Nigel Haworth's trademark Lancastrian gutsiness shining through in some very fine cooking. Innovative combinations, thoughtful presentation and clearly defined flavours can be seen in a lovely seared Angus beef with 'sensational' roasted marrow-bone toast and salsify (pickled, deep-fried, puréed), and in a sheep's milk ricotta with a gazpacho-style garlic and bread soup and acidulated tomatoes, which covers the whole range of tastes from sweet to sharp. Others have praised Cumbrian milk-fed lamb (including excellent lamb belly), which arrives with good Hispi cabbage and spring vegetables, and a 'super' coconut ice cream accompanying a dessert of mango, blueberries and basil cream. Co-owner Craig Bancroft has produced a weighty wine list (from £25.50), a deftly selective range of classics and new-wave wines chosen for quality and value.
Chef/s: Nigel Haworth. **Open:** all week L 12 to 2, D 7 to 9.30 (6.30 to 10 Fri and Sat, 9 Sun). **Meals:** alc (main courses £25 to £55). Set L £21 (2 courses) to £27. Set D £50 (2 courses) to £65. Sun L £40. Tasting menu £85 (8 courses). **Details:** 60 seats. V menu. Bar. Wheelchair access. Music. Parking.

Little Eccleston
The Cartford Inn

Revamped inn with personality
Cooking score: 2
Modern British | £28
Cartford Lane, Little Eccleston, PR3 0YP
Tel no: (01995) 670166
www.thecartfordinn.co.uk

The Cartford Inn has come a long way since its days as a refuelling point by a historic ford over the River Wyre. Following some serious refurbishment, it's now a boutique country hotel and restaurant with a new private facility and exhibition space in a converted barn. Drinkers can still sup at the bar or out on the terrace, but the Cartford's main business is food, with Fleetwood fish and local supplies showing up across the board. The kitchen does a decent job, delivering everything from French onion soup, burgers and beef bourguignon to ham hock and crispy egg with barley, mustard crème fraîche and pea purée, or pulled lamb wrapped in caul fat with sweet potato mash and masala lentils. Grills, fruits de mer and comfort puds complete the picture. House wine is £15.
Chef/s: Ian Manning. **Open:** Tue to Sat L 12 to 2, Mon to Sat D 5.30 to 9 (10 Fri and Sat). Sun 12 to 8.30. **Closed:** 25 Dec. **Meals:** alc (main courses £12 to £16). **Details:** 85 seats. 26 seats outside. Bar. Wheelchair access. Music. Parking.

Mitton
The Three Fishes

Flying the flag for regional food
Cooking score: 2
British | £25
Mitton Road, Mitton, BB7 9PQ
Tel no: (01254) 826888
www.thethreefishes.com

It seems everyone falls in love with this lovingly nurtured village hostelry, where the 'welcome is warm, the food exceptional and the service splendid'. The flagship of Nigel

Haworth's Ribble Valley Inns may seat 130, but eating areas are divided into cosy sections and the place perfectly marries the country pub ethos of exposed stone, flag-stone floors and wood-burners with modern tweaks. A network of trusted local suppliers provides much of the produce for the seasonally changing menus and the food delivers plenty of flavour without pretension. Venison Scotch egg comes with Lythe Valley pickled damsons, there's warm Morecambe Bay shrimps, Lancashire hotpot made with local lamb and served with pickled cabbage, and Goosnargh corn-fed chicken from the charcoal grill. Lemon curd doughnuts with ginger yoghurt make a luscious finish, but the 'fantastic local cheeseboard' is a winner, too. There are local cask ales, and wines from £16.50.
Chef/s: Ian Moss. **Open:** Mon to Fri L 12 to 2, D 5.30 to 9 (9.30 Fri). Sat and Sun 12 to 9.30. **Meals:** alc (main courses £11 to £23). Sun L £18 (2 courses) to £21. **Details:** 130 seats. 40 seats outside. Wheelchair access. Music. Parking.

Newton-in-Bowland
The Parkers Arms

Revitalised village pub with fascinating food
Cooking score: 2
Modern British | £28
Hallgate Hill, Newton-in-Bowland, BB7 3DY
Tel no: (01200) 446236
www.parkersarms.co.uk

Kathy Smith and chef Stosie Madi have done a grand job revitalising this village hostelry in the beautiful Hodder Valley, while maintaining its status as a thoroughgoing local boozer – complete with flagstones, log fires and North Country ales in the bar. However, the Parkers Arms is also an aspiring foodie destination, so repair to the understated dining room for some fascinating and unexpected pub food in the modern mould: small plates of potted Manx kippers or locally grown purple sprouting broccoli with watercress, potatoes, wild garlic and mayonnaise set the tone, ahead of ample servings of oat-crumbed cod tongues with air-dried ham or roast leg of Bowland hogget and crispy breast with creamed mash, spring greens and minted gravy. Also look for 'perennials' including char-grilled steaks, bangers and the pub's renowned hand-raised pies, perhaps served with triple-cooked chips and red cabbage pickled in damson vinegar. For afters, the Portuguese-style custard tarts with Seville orange marmalade come highly recommended. House wine is £18.

Chef/s: Stosie Madi. **Open:** Tue to Fri L 12 to 2.30, D 6 to 8.30. Sat and Sun 12 to 9 (6 Sun). **Closed:** Mon. **Meals:** alc (main courses £13 to £22). **Details:** 100 seats. 200 seats outside. Bar. Parking.

Pleasington

The Clog & Billycock

British | £29

Billinge End Road, Pleasington, BB2 6QB
Tel no: (01254) 201163
www.theclogandbillycock.com

An attractive Lancashire village, a stylishly converted pub with alfresco dining in the summer, log fires in winter and bags of unforced charm: it's most people's idea of a quality day out. Part of the Ribble Valley Inns group, the Clog works along comfortingly familiar lines – the array of starters such as warm Morecambe Bay shrimps, sandwiches, steaks and classics like Lancashire hotpot tell of a relationship with the farmer, not the freezer. And it's hard to go wrong with 'chippy tea Fridays' and homemade jam roly-poly. Wines from £16. Open all week.

Whalley
Food by Breda Murphy

An urban-minded eatery
Cooking score: 2
Modern British | £25
Abbots Court, 41 Station Road, Whalley, BB7 9RH
Tel no: (01254) 823446
www.foodbybredamurphy.com

£30

It opened a decade ago, but Breda Murphy's modern café-deli occupying the ground floor of a converted suburban house opposite Whalley railway station continues to be very much in tune with the current times: simple, affordable, flexible. An all-day drop-in that's equally handy for coffee with the papers or something more filling, it's an urban-minded eatery with pitch-perfect service and attractive, big-on-flavour food. Breakfast (say char-grilled smoked salmon with scrambled eggs on granary toast) and a counter loaded with cakes sets the tone, but after that it's a free-ranging tribute to good regional produce with a healthy balance between familiarity and innovation: open sandwiches, salads along the lines of roast breast of Goosnargh chicken with pink grapefruit, toasted cashews and maple chilli dressing, hot dishes such as fish pie with champ potatoes and Lancashire cheese or marinated lamb cutlets with chickpea couscous, tagine crust and preserved lemon purée. Wines from £15.95.

Chef/s: Gareth Bevan. **Open:** Tue to Sat 10 to 6, occasional evenings 7 to 9.30. **Closed:** Sun, Mon, 24 Dec to 6 Jan. **Meals:** alc (main courses £12 to £17). **Details:** 46 seats. 20 seats outside. V menu. Wheelchair access. Music. Parking.

 Whitewell
The Inn at Whitewell
A Lancashire hostelry for all seasons
Cooking score: 3
British | £35
Whitewell, BB7 3AT
Tel no: (01200) 448222
www.innatwhitewell.com

'What a delight!' exclaimed one couple who stumbled upon this greatly extended 14th-century manor while driving through the Forest of Bowland. With views of the River Hodder and sylvan vistas all around, 'The Whitewell' is big on Lancashire hospitality and unfussy food. Visitors congregate in the splendid rambling bars for pub-style lunches and suppers of fish pie, Cumberland bangers and champ or char-grilled sirloin of beef with hand-cut chips, while the restaurant stakes its claim for dinner. Here you can expect generous helpings of North Country produce given a lift by long-serving chef Jamie Cadman: Nidderdale spring lamb is as tender as can be, but also look for the homemade black pudding with fried egg, potatoes and mustard emulsion or whole roast Goosnargh poussin flavoured with lemon and thyme. After that, keep it traditional with sticky toffee pudding. The inn is also home to Bowland Forest Vintners, whose extensive global list offers dependable drinking from £16.90.

Chef/s: Jamie Cadman. **Open:** all week L 12 to 2, D 7.30 to 9.30. **Meals:** alc (main courses £10 to £20). **Details:** 150 seats. 20 seats outside. Bar. Wheelchair access. Parking.

Symbols 

 Accommodation is available
Three courses for less than £30
 £5-off voucher scheme
Notable wine list

 Wiswell
NUMBER ONE PUB ★ TOP 50
Freemasons at Wiswell
High-impact food that's getting noticed
Cooking score: 7
Modern British | £43
8 Vicarage Fold, Wiswell, BB7 9DF
Tel no: (01254) 822218
www.freemasonswiswell.co.uk

Steve Smith's gem of a village pub exudes charm; it's hard not to be seduced from the very first steps through the door. Flagstone floors, beams, scrubbed tables and oak settles convey the feel of a present-day country pub, but venture upstairs and there's the comfort of a Victorian shooting lodge: polished tables, rich colours, plenty of taxidermy and wall-to-wall country prints. While there's no doubt that the Freemasons plays the part of a busy local perfectly, these days it is better known for its food. Steve Smith's aim is to blend traditional and contemporary, hitching tried and tested techniques to a wide-ranging, innovative approach, and basing menus on what is seasonally available. In winter there might be Carroll's heritage potatoes cooked in bacon dashi and served with a crisp hen's egg, hen of the woods and Ibérico ham, followed, perhaps, by 'very tender' maple-glazed pork belly and pork sausage with January King cabbage kim-chee, Yorkshire rhubarb, Lancashire cheese potatoes and a sauce of mead. Elsewhere, a 'sensational' deconstructed lemon meringue pie has been much praised, as have the bread rolls, 'particularly the brioche bun cooked with lamb fat and rosemary', and 'wonderful, attentive staff'. The wine list (from £15.50) inspires confidence, with a good choice from all over the world.

Chef/s: Steven Smith and Hywel Griffith. **Open:** Wed to Sat L 12 to 2.30, D 5.30 to 9 (6 to 9.30 Fri and Sat). Sun 12 to 7. **Closed:** Mon, Tue, 2 to 16 Jan. **Meals:** alc (main courses £15 to £35). Set L and early D £16. Sun L £25. Tasting menu £70. **Details:** 70 seats. 14 seats outside. Bar. Music.

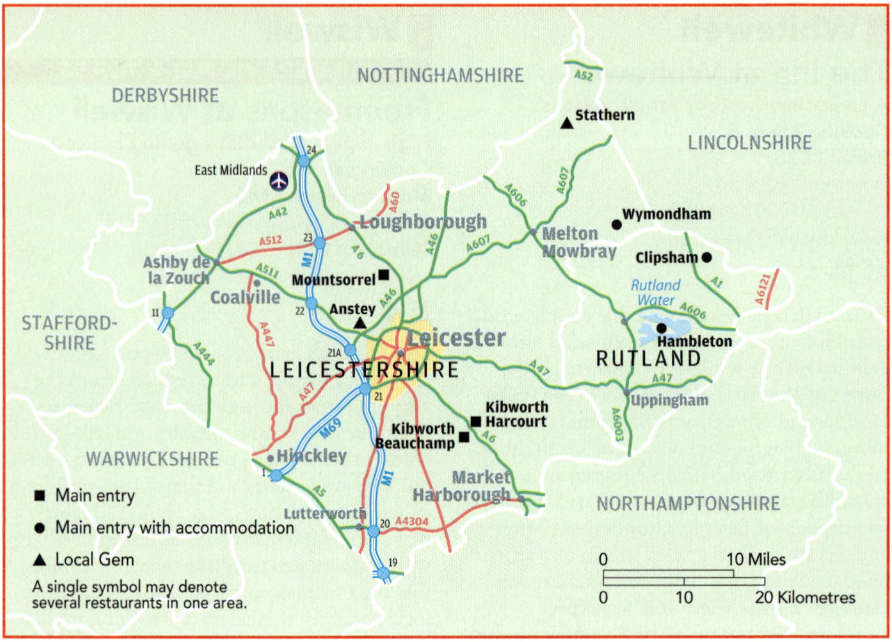

Anstey

LOCAL GEM

Sapori

Italian | £35
40 Stadon Road, Anstey, LE7 7AY
Tel no: (0116) 2368900
www.sapori-restaurant.co.uk

It may be in an 'unprepossessing suburb' with 'awful lift musak', but Sapori is a cherished local asset – the cooking clearly a cut above your average trattoria. Pasta dishes should not be missed, perhaps 'clearly homemade' scilatelli pasta sautéed with a 'more-ish' monkfish ragoût on globe artichoke cream, but reporters have also endorsed antipasti of king sea scallops with buffalo mozzarella sauce, semi-dry vine tomato tartare, basil sponge cake and bread crisp, and twice-cooked Atlantic cod fillet with gazpacho and beetroot cress. Wines from £16. Closed Mon.

Clipsham

The Olive Branch

A well-honed country-pub set-up
Cooking score: 3
Modern British | £32
Main Street, Clipsham, LE15 7SH
Tel no: (01780) 410355
www.theolivebranchpub.com

It's just a couple of miles off the thundering A1, so there's never any shortage of punters at this poshly rustic boozer-with-rooms – a stone-walled hostelry that set out its stall as a 'country pub with regional foodie credentials' back in 1999. You can figure out exactly where your lunch came from by consulting the map of local suppliers printed on the back of the menu – a lengthy compendium that covers a lot of ground from sandwiches and ploughman's to confit duck terrine with quince and pickled walnuts, hummus-crusted cod with glazed carrots and crispy bacon or a three-part tasting of pork with 'farmhouse' cabbage. Hearty helpings of vegetables are almost mandatory, while desserts (10 at the last count) range from 'white forest' gâteau with black cherry sorbet to praline parfait with caramelised pineapple. The Olive Branch also scores heavily in the drinks department, with pedigree craft ales and an imaginative choice of good-value wines from £19 (check the blackboards for bin-end bargains).

Chef/s: Sean Hope. **Open:** all week L 12 to 2 (2.30 Sat, 3 Sun), D 6.30 to 9.30 (7 to 9 Sun). **Meals:** alc (main courses £15 to £25). Set L £17 (2 courses) to £20. Set D £30. Sun L £26. **Details:** 70 seats. 30 seats outside. V menu. Bar. Wheelchair access. Music. Parking.

■ Hambleton

★ TOP 50 ★

Hambleton Hall

Cooking from a modern master

Cooking score: 7

Modern British | £68

Ketton Road, Hambleton, LE15 8TH

Tel no: (01572) 756991

www.hambleton.co.uk

Built in 1881 by the heir to a brewing fortune, Hambleton stands by the calm expanse of Rutland Water, its topiaried gardens and terraces surrounded by countryside vistas that are a tonic for the urban escapee. With lounges variously done in gentle pastels or hearty claret, and a dining room smartly turned out in layers of crisp linen and table posies, it's the full-dress country-house package. Not the least of its attractions is the long tenure of the extravagantly talented Aaron Patterson in the kitchen, now in sight of his silver jubilee here. The prettily illustrated menus don't give much away in the descriptions, but when dishes arrive, it's clear you're in the hands of an impeccably modern master. A tribute to heritage tomatoes gathers together jellies, foams, crisps and a goats' cheese croquette, before foie gras ice cream with apple purée and cinnamon biscuit weaves its picture-perfect magic. Main courses go the distance with three cuts of rabbit – rack, leg and Parma-wrapped loin – with pearl barley risotto and an intense liquorice jus, or cod in a seafood medley with prawns and razor clam, offset with smoked bacon and sauced with vermouth. Texturally compelling desserts might include praline parfait with marshmallow, rhubarb and citrus elements, or a flawlessly rendered passion fruit soufflé with sorbet of passion fruit and banana. It all comes with an authoritative wine list that has plenty of serious French merchandise, but also inspired selections in Australia and New Zealand, and a fair degree of relief at the affordable end, listed as 'Wines of the Moment'. Prices open at £22.

Chef/s: Aaron Patterson. **Open:** all week L 12 to 1.30, D 6.45 to 9.30. **Meals:** Set L £27 (2 courses) to £33. Set D £68. Tasting menu £80. Sun L £55 (3 courses). **Details:** 60 seats. V menu. Bar. Wheelchair access. Parking.

■ Kibworth Beauchamp

The Lighthouse

Bright and breezy seafood joint

Cooking score: 3

Seafood | £28

9 Station Street, Kibworth Beauchamp, LE8 0LN

Tel no: (0116) 2796260

www.lighthousekibworth.co.uk

Lino and Sarah Poli's white-painted restaurant with its woodwork picked out in blue certainly gives off a seaside vibe, but this is the pretty land-locked village of Kibworth Beauchamp, and the building used to be a violin maker's. The switch from Italian to things fishy in 2013 has given the place a new lease of life (not to mention a bright and cheerful sea-themed interior), and a menu that embraces British and global flavours. Some plates come in 'small' or 'large' sizes, so you can make Thai-style mussels your opener or your main event, or simply kick off with mackerel pâté with Melba toast. Fish and chips is a classic done very well, or go for pan-fried pollack with spicy sausage cassoulet. There are meaty alternatives (braised lamb shank, say), and desserts run to pear tarte Tatin with vanilla ice cream. The Eurocentric wine list opens at £16.50.

Chef/s: Lino Poli and Tom Wilde. **Open:** Tue to Sat D only 6 to 10. **Closed:** Sun, Mon, 25 and 26 Dec, 1 Jan, bank hols. **Meals:** alc (main courses £7 to £19). Set D £15 (2 courses) to £18. **Details:** 60 seats. Music.

Kibworth Harcourt

Boboli

Bubbly all-day Italian
Cooking score: 1
Italian | £28
88 Main Street, Kibworth Harcourt, LE8 0NQ
Tel no: (0116) 2793303
www.bobolirestaurant.co.uk

It may be better known for its Anglo-Saxon burial site (the Munt), but ancient Kibworth Harcourt also boasts an Italian surprise package. Bubbly Boboli oozes *la dolce vita* as punters munch pizzas on the Italianate piazza and sip glasses of refreshing limoncello spritz with stuzzichini snacks. Otherwise, the flexible all-day menu bristles with artisan treats, from antipasti of salt cod fritters with garlic sauce, or chicken and artichoke terrine, to rousing pastas and main courses – think spaghetti with kale and pancetta or confit rabbit wrapped in Parma ham with soft polenta. To drink, local beers compete with regional Italian wines from £15.75. Related to the Lighthouse, Kibworth Beauchamp (see entry).

Chef/s: Lino Poli and Sergio Gisbert. **Open:** all week 10 to 9.30. **Closed:** 25 and 26 Dec, 1 Jan, bank hols. **Meals:** alc (main courses £12 to £20). Set L £14 (2 courses) to £17. Sun L £14 (2 courses) to £17. **Details:** 90 seats. 28 seats outside. Bar. Wheelchair access. Music. Parking.

Mountsorrel

NEW ENTRY

John's House

Dazzling cooking, down on the farm
Cooking score: 4
British | £47
Stonehurst Farm, 139-141 Loughborough Road, Mountsorrel, LE12 7AR
Tel no: (01509) 415569
www.johnshouse.co.uk

John Duffin returned to the family farm, Stonehurst, to open his restaurant in a 17th-century cottage just before Christmas 2014. You park amid the outbuildings and old farm machinery, and enter a place whose rough-and-readiness extends to battered furniture, brick walls and drinks taken off an old suitcase. From the moment the appetisers arrive, it's clear the kitchen's orientation is in bewitching contrast to the setting, with smart precision and dazzling combinations. Seared beef fillet sliced thin as carpaccio is topped with brown shrimps and a crisp-fried quail's egg in lemon butter, while an east Asian note steals into spring onion dumplings seasoned with mint and lime, served with spring-fresh peas and broad beans. Lightly salted cod cooked in seaweed butter with cockles and yuzu is perfectly balanced for seasoning, and some of the home-grown wasabi crop electrifies rib and coffee-braised cheek of beef, and while all the boxes are ticked in a dessert of peanut-butter ice cream with bitter chocolate, banana and salty peanut brittle, the whole effect is of something much more grown-up than the norm. A taster menu runs the rule over an energetically creative repertoire. The short wine list opens at £18.

Chef/s: John Duffin. **Open:** Tue to Sat L 12 to 2, D 7 to 9. **Closed:** Sun, Mon, 24 to 27 Dec. **Meals:** Set L £24 (2 courses) to £28. Set D £42 (2 courses) £47. Tasting menu £70 (8 courses). **Details:** 30 seats. V menu. Bar. Music. Parking.

Stathern

Red Lion Inn
Modern British | £30
2 Red Lion Street, Stathern, LE14 4HS
Tel no: (01949) 860868
www.theredlioninn.co.uk

Out of the same stable as the Olive Branch, Clipsham (see entry), this is a 'really great pub to have on your doorstep' with extensive ales, bags of rustic personality and a wide-ranging repertoire based on local supplies (check the map on the back of the menu). The kitchen has a broad remit, moving from Scotch egg ploughman's, steaks and flavoursome burgers to smoked haddock and asparagus risotto or duck breast with spiced Puy lentils, braised chicory and turnip. Wines from £17. No food Sun D.

Wymondham

The Berkeley Arms
Inviting country charmer
Cooking score: 3
Modern British | £30
59 Main Street, Wymondham, LE14 2AG
Tel no: (01572) 787587
www.theberkeleyarms.co.uk

If noise, laughter and happy faces are the tell-tale signs of a restaurant in full flow, then this gentrified 16th-century inn is certainly doing all the right things. Neil and Louise Hitchen have worked wonders since moving here in 2010, transforming the Berkeley Arms into a showpiece Leicestershire hostelry with food that is bang on the money. The kitchen is driven by seasonal supplies and the owners are on first-name terms with most of their local suppliers – Ernie bags wild ducks, while Andy and Kev bring in trout from Rutland Water. Robust flavours are the order of the day, from roast partridge with red cabbage or chicken breast with pancetta and leek risotto to a tranche of halibut on the bone with spinach, gnocchi and chanterelles. Pub die-hards can feast on Lincolnshire sausages with bubble and squeak, while puds could feature caramelised blood-orange trifle. Sunday lunch is 'a joy', and the wine list promises dependable drinking from £16.
Chef/s: Neil Hitchen. **Open:** Tue to Sun L 12 to 1.45 (3 Sun), Tue to Sat D 6 to 9 (9.30 Fri and Sat). **Closed:** Mon, first 2 weeks Jan, 2 weeks summer, Tue after bank hols. **Meals:** alc (main courses £13 to £24). Set L £15 (2 courses) to £19. Set D £19 (2 courses) to £23. Sun L £20 (2 courses). **Details:** 48 seats. 24 seats outside. Bar. Wheelchair access. Parking.

Great Gonerby
Harry's Place

Homage to classic French cooking
Cooking score: 4
Modern French | £70
17 High Street, Great Gonerby, NG31 8JS
Tel no: (01476) 561780

£5 OFF

'There is definitely a time warp here, but a good warp,' was the opinion of one visitor to this long-standing, personally run restaurant. Harry and Caroline Hallam are charming, caring and very good at what they've been doing since 1988. While eating in a family's dining room surrounded by personal bits and bobs may not appeal to everyone, if you are after an intimate, traditionally cooked meal, it's just the ticket. Indeed, you have to admire how Harry has stuck to his classic guns – there are no foams, smears or squeezy bottle action – this is not cutting-edge food in any way. Dishes are well executed and presented with care, the daily changing menu offering just two choices per course, along with freshly baked bread and 'the most delicious canapés'. Start, perhaps, with a soup of locally grown celeriac, before mains of loin of spring lamb 'beautifully tender and perfectly cooked' with red cabbage, mushrooms and a red wine sauce, and finish with caramel mousse brûlée with raspberries and strawberries. Although the wine list is short it offers a good choice of styles and prices, from £26.

Chef/s: Harry Hallam. **Open:** Tue to Sat L 12.30 to 2, D 7 to 8.30. **Closed:** Sun, Mon, Christmas, 2 weeks Aug, bank hols. **Meals:** alc (main courses £40). **Details:** 10 seats. Children over 5 yrs only.

Symbols

Accommodation is available
£30 Three courses for less than £30
£5 OFF £5-off voucher scheme
Notable wine list

Join us at thegoodfoodguide.co.uk

Great Limber

★ TOP 50 PUB ★

The New Inn

Food with a strong seasonal accent
Cooking score: 4
Modern British | £30
2 High Street, Great Limber, DN37 8JL
Tel no: (01469) 569998
www.thenewinngreatlimber.co.uk

The New Inn lives up to its name now that this former village pub has been completely refurbished with a delightful garden at the back. Run by Ian and Lisa Matfin in partnership with the Brockelsby Estate – prior to opening here, Ian Matfin was head chef at Michael Caines' Restaurant at ABode Manchester (see entry) – what is on offer is an affable, cosmopolitan package of boutique bedrooms and a menu of exemplary food with a strong seasonal accent. For one reporter it's 'a significant addition of quality to eating houses in the area'. Evergreens such as traditional Sunday roasts are way above the norm, but chicken liver parfait with forced Yorkshire rhubarb, rhubarb sorbet and toasted brioche, and saddle of venison teamed with pork belly, chestnut purée, roasted root vegetables, jasmine raisins and red wine sauce are more typical of Ian's flexible approach to British and classical themes. To finish, a hot orange soufflé served with chocolate sauce and orange confit sorbet succeeds decadently at every step. The well-travelled wine list, well anotated and arranged by style, starts from £16.50.
Chef/s: Ian Matfin. **Open:** Tue to Sun L 12 to 2 (3 Sun), Mon to Sat D 6.30 to 9. **Meals:** alc (main courses from £15 to £23). Sun L £20 (2 courses) to £25. **Details:** 64 seats. 60 seats outside. Bar. Wheelchair access. Music.

Horncastle

Magpies

Quietly confident cooking
Cooking score: 5
Modern British | £47
73 East Street, Horncastle, LN9 6AA
Tel no: (01507) 527004
www.magpiesresturant.co.uk

'A lovely experience,' noted one reader after visiting Caroline and Andrew Gilbert's exemplary restaurant-with-rooms – a model of genuine warmth, good humour and dedication snuggled within a row of quaint terraced cottages. Decorated in pastel shades of pale blue and cream, the dining room's blend of low-key elegance and intimacy is a perfect match for Andrew's intelligent but never in-your-face cooking. Seasonal ingredients play their part and even his more elaborate ideas seem to work naturally on the plate, from a signature starter of smoked eel pâté with crayfish tempura, passion fruit, mango and cornbread crostini to loin of Lincolnshire venison accompanied by sweet potato and amaretti purée, Longton goats' cheese tortellini and beetroot carpaccio. Caroline not only manages front-of-house but also takes charge of desserts: her dark chocolate 'sweetshop' terrine with Dolly Mixture syrup will whisk you right back to your childhood, but she's also a dab hand at reworking the classics – witness rhubarb and ginger bread-and-butter pudding with a rhubarb and ginger-beer sorbet. The wine list is a delight, with terrific value across the board and 20 house selections from £16.35.
Chef/s: Andrew Gilbert. **Open:** Wed to Fri and Sun L 12 to 2, Wed to Sun D 7 to 9.30. **Closed:** Mon, Tue, 26 to 30 Dec, 1 to 6 Jan. **Meals:** Set L £20 (2 courses) to £25. Set D £41 (2 courses) to £47. Sun L £20 (2 courses) to £25. **Details:** 34 seats. 8 seats outside. Music.

■ Hough on the Hill

The Brownlow Arms
British | £50
Grantham Road, Hough on the Hill, NG32 2AZ
Tel no: (01400) 250234
www.thebrownlowarms.com

A blazing fire, beams, polished wood – this 17th-century inn delivers vintage charm by the bucket-load. Now operating as a country restaurant, the cooking is honest and menus aim to comfort rather than challenge. The repertoire ranges from truffle-infused herb gnocchi with porcini and thyme-creamed spinach, via whole lemon sole with caper, brown shrimp and shallot beurre noisette or saddle of Belton venison with black pudding and leek boudin blanc, to traditional Sunday roasts and desserts such as lemon posset. Wines from £17.95. Open Tue to Sat D and Sun L.

■ Lincoln
The Old Bakery
Relaxed and idiosyncratic
Cooking score: 2
Modern British | £40
26-28 Burton Road, Lincoln, LN1 3LB
Tel no: (01522) 576057
www.theold-bakery.co.uk

Eleven years on, Ivano de Serio continues to do what he does best: serving up sharply tuned flavours, with touches of new-minted Brit and some home-country Puglian sunshine. His easy-going approach is just the ticket, too, for there's a rustic feel to the 19th-century bakery located not far from the cathedral. The original oven and other features are still in place, there's a conservatory-style dining room, as well as an intimacy that endears it to locals and visitors alike. Ivano's experience at the stove is shown by a deep understanding of combinations and flavours and he's not afraid to let ingredients speak for themselves. Rum-infused roasted red onion tart with Stilton mousse and poached beetroot with spinach purée, ahead of an assured dish of pan-roasted Lincolnshire rack of lamb, served with grilled potato, peas, pancetta, Savoy cabbage and aubergine and tomato relish show the style. Wines start at £17.95.

Chef/s: Ivano de Serio. **Open:** Thur to Sun L 12 to 2, Tue to Sat D 7 to 9. **Closed:** Mon, 3 weeks Jan, 3 weeks Aug. **Meals:** alc (main courses £15 to £26). Set L £15 (2 courses) to £18. Sun L £20. Tasting menu £44. **Details:** 50 seats. Wheelchair access. Music.

■ Stamford
No. 3 The Yard

Cooking score: 2
Modern European | £29
3 Ironmonger Street, Stamford, PE9 1PL
Tel no: (01780) 756080
www.no3theyard.co.uk

The change of name gives notice that the restaurant formerly known as Jim's Yard is under new ownership, though local spies report that the transition appears to be seamless as chef Tim Luff remains in situ, now as a co-owner. He continues to oversee a simply, clearly expressed modern British menu (with occasional forays abroad) that might take in smoked sprats with pickled red cabbage and lemon and garlic mayonnaise, sea bass with tomato and saffron dauphinoise and heritage tomato salad, and poached chicken breast served with both spring vegetable fricassee and fondant potato. The result is 'the best food in town' according to one visitor, who enjoyed careful preparation, precise timing and good materials in a dish of smoked haddock chowder with queen scallops, and in slow-roast pork belly with noodles, pak choi and chilli and ginger broth. Dessert could be white chocolate and raspberry crème brûlée. Wines from £14.95.

Chef/s: Tim Luff. **Open:** Tue to Sun L 11.30 to 2.30 (12 to 3 Sun), Tue to Sat D 6 to 9.30 (10 Fri and Sat). **Closed:** Mon. **Meals:** alc (main courses £13 to £23).

Set L 15 (2 courses) to £18. Set D £20 (3 courses). Sun L £23. **Details:** 64 seats. 20 seats outside. Bar. Wheelchair access.

▌Upton

Upton Fish Shop
Seafood | £10
24 High Street, Upton, DN21 5NL
Tel no: (01427) 838607
www.uptonchippy.co.uk

This keenly priced chippy (previously a blacksmiths) is open on Friday night and Saturday lunchtime only, yet it draws folk from miles around, all prepared to queue for 30 minutes or more for what many consider to be the best fish and chips in the country. The attraction is exceptional ingredients – fresh Grimsby-landed cod or haddock, real chips, hand-cut from locally grown Lincolnshire potatoes – cooked in beef dripping on a coal-fired range dating from 1948 (possibly the only one remaining in the country). Unlicensed. Cash only. Open Fri D and Sat L, takeaway only.

▌Winteringham

Winteringham Fields
High-concept dining with mystery menus
Cooking score: 6
Modern British | £69
1 Silver Street, Winteringham, DN15 9ND
Tel no: (01724) 733096
www.winteringhamfields.co.uk

'Winteringham Fields,' writes Colin McGurran, 'has now reached that point in its evolution when the frequency of raw materials that are available to us dictates our offerings.' 'Inspires' might be a gentler way of putting it than 'dictates', but the point is that the kitchen garden is in full swing and teeming with abundance. In summer, everything on the menu comes from within one mile of this soothingly remote restaurant-with-rooms. The surprise taster formats hint at how each course will be cooked – 'roasted and confit', 'mi-cuit, green five ways' – but not what, for beguiling mystique. What may come your way are pork jowl with Morecambe shrimps, turnip purée and compressed apple in shellfish bisque, confit salmon with purple broccoli in dill oil, and fillet and cheek of beef with bone-marrow and caramelised onion. It all looks supremely creatively worked, through to the explosive impact of a pineapple and basil bomb. Wines make an energetic attempt to keep up, from £28.
Chef/s: Colin McGurran. **Open:** Tue to Sat L 12 to 2, D 7 to 9. **Closed:** Sun, Mon, Christmas, 1 week Jan, 2 weeks Aug. **Meals:** Set L £40. Sun L £45. Tasting menus £69 to £79. **Details:** 50 seats. V menu. Bar. Music. Parking.

▌Woolsthorpe by Belvoir

Chequers Inn
Sturdy food and generous hospitality
Cooking score: 1
Modern British | £27
Main Street, Woolsthorpe by Belvoir, NG32 1LU
Tel no: (01476) 870701
www.chequersinn.net

Embedded in the Vale of Belvoir, this sympathetically preserved 17th-century village inn certainly has a great deal going for it – from oak beams, heavy stone walls, log fires and real ales to a menu of sturdy dishes for modern appetites. Whether you fancy Goan fish curry, steak-frites, spicy moussaka or pie and chips, the kitchen can deliver honest sustenance to match the prevailing mood of generous hospitality. Start with beef dripping on toasted brioche with black pudding crumb, finish with strawberry Bakewell tart and malt ice cream. Wines from £16.50.
Chef/s: Andrew Lincoln. **Open:** all week L 12 to 2.30 (4 Sun), D 6 to 9.30 (8.30 Sun). **Meals:** alc (main courses £11 to £20). Set L £13 (2 courses) to £15. Set D £18. Sun L £14 (2 courses). **Details:** 150 seats. 90 seats outside. Wheelchair access. Music. Parking.

Irby
Da Piero

Bringing Sicilian sunshine to the Wirral
Cooking score: 3
Italian | £32
5 Mill Hill Road, Irby, CH61 4UB
Tel no: (0151) 6487373
www.dapiero.co.uk

£5 OFF

Piero Di Bella's neighbourhood Italian has been bringing Sicilian comfort food and sunshine to Irby for a decade now, and has acquired a band of loyal regulars. 'What he does, Piero does very well,' says one such, 'even if the menu rarely changes.' Change or no, the menus are hardly lacking in variety and appeal, all the way to a concern to look after vegetarians and vegans. Simple pasta dishes are always a win, perhaps penne with tomato sauce, fried aubergine and grated ricotta, and there are inspired renditions of osso buco, salsiccia with Umbrian lentils and pancetta (many of the ingredients are imported), or swordfish in salmoriglio dressing. A side of Parmesan mash will enhance matters no end, and ice creams variously flavoured with Amaretto, espresso, pistachio and vanilla are the alternatives to Sicilian cannoli. Half-litre carafes of house wines from £10.40.
Chef/s: Piero Di Bella. **Open:** Tue to Sat D only 6 to 11. **Closed:** Sun, Mon. **Meals:** alc (main courses £15 to £23). **Details:** 32 seats. V menu.

Liverpool

NEW ENTRY
The Art School

Ambitious, exciting newcomer
Cooking score: 5
Modern British | £29
1 Sugnall Street, Liverpool, L7 7DX
Tel no: (0151) 2308600
www.theartschoolrestaurant.co.uk

£30

It may be 'a devil to find as it doesn't seem to exist on the map and our taxi driver was none the wiser', but chef Paul Askew (ex chef-

Join us at thegoodfoodguide.co.uk

director of the London Carriage Works – see entry) has set the bar high with this gleaming, high-end eatery. The setting is beautiful, in what was once the art school's life drawing room with its vast, hall-like interior and magnificent vaulted glass ceiling. The expensive styling makes a show of the original features but also feels slick and metropolitan, with a long, glass-walled kitchen allowing a good view of the action. Askew's ambition is plain to see, and he mostly succeeds, with a 'delightful' tiramisu of crab, papaya and mango with keta caviar and a seaweed tuile out of the bag, and a 'perfectly balanced' pressed gâteau of vegetables provençale and feta cheese with asparagus, black olive dressing, Jerusalem artichoke purée and samphire that so impressed at inspection. Desserts here are a must if a 'faultless' baked Alaska with heather-honey cake crumbs, yoghurt pannacotta and lemon balm leaves is anything to go by. Service 'is some of the best I've had anywhere'. A serious wine list, overseen by an attentive sommelier, opens at £22 a bottle.

Chef/s: Paul Askew. **Open:** Tue to Sat L 12 to 2.15, D 5 to 9.15. **Closed:** Sun, Mon, 1 week Jan, 1 week Aug. **Meals:** Set L and D £23 (2 courses) to £29. Tasting menus £69 to £89. **Details:** 50 seats. V menu. Bar. Wheelchair access. Music.

Delifonseca Dockside

Informal global eatery-cum-deli
Cooking score: 2
International | £25
Brunswick Quay, Liverpool, L3 4BN
Tel no: (0151) 2550808
www.delifonseca.co.uk

'Fantastic venue' if you fancy combining a bit of deli shopping with breakfast, lunch or supper, this eatery-cum-emporium is informally done out with a mix of cosy booths, bare tables and comfy leather seating. As such, it's tailor-made for grazing and socialising over plates of charcuterie, sandwiches and salads from around the world (try the Thai beef with toasted cashews, lime and coriander, the vegan Lebanese riff or the

Brit version involving a traditional hand-raised pie). Alternatively, take the three-course route by picking from the specials board – perhaps duck and Morello cherry rillettes on toasted brioche followed by 'meltingly tender' Persian lamb with lemon, aubergine, split peas and basmati rice. After that, look for something sweet and exotic such as a coconut and lime pot with pineapple salsa. To drink, there's a fascinating choice of world beers plus a brief wine list with prices from £15.95 – or you can choose a bottle from the deli shelves (£6.50 corkage). Related to Fonseca's in Liverpool city centre (see entry).

Chef/s: Martin Cooper. **Open:** all week 12 to 9 (9.30 Fri and Sat, 5 Sun). **Closed:** 25 and 26 Dec, 1 Jan. **Meals:** alc (main courses £8 to £19). **Details:** 66 seats. 24 seats outside. Wheelchair access. Music. Parking.

Fonseca's

Relaxed, stylish, internationally inspired
Cooking score: 1
Modern European | £25
12 Stanley Street, Liverpool, L1 6AF
Tel no: (0151) 2550808
www.delifonseca.co.uk

Right in the heart of the city, Fonseca's vibrant, international cooking is good enough to stand out amid plentiful competition. A dark wine bar has salvaged theatre seats adding a touch of nostalgia, while the more modern first-floor dining room has booths, stripped-wood floors, blackboard menus and arty lighting. Asian-style flash-fried cuttlefish came with a 'powerful blast of chilli and lime', while a baked cauliflower and caramelised onion cake with fennel and orange salad proved 'fresh and wholesome', and a straight-talking chocolate mousse won a seal of approval, too. The wine list opens at £14.95.

Chef/s: Rikki Vidamour. **Open:** Mon to Sat L 12 to 2.30 (5 Fri and Sat), Mon to Sat D 5 to 9 (10 Fri and Sat). **Closed:** Sun, 25 Dec to 30 Dec, bank hols. **Meals:** alc (main courses £10 to £19). **Details:** 60 seats. Bar. Music.

The London Carriage Works

All-day eating opportunities
Cooking score: 2
Modern British | £39
Hope Street Hotel, 40 Hope Street, Liverpool,
L1 9DA
Tel no: (0151) 7093000
www.thelondoncarriageworks.co.uk

A sister to the Hope Street Hotel next door, the London Carriage Works is well located with the Philharmonic Hall and the Everyman just minutes away. Food is served all day with sharing fish and meat platters great for an informal lunch, and à la carte and excellent-value set menus showcasing local and seasonal produce. Kidderton Ash goats' cheese melting slowly over a warmed spring vegetable salad and dressed with honey and basil, excellent Claremont Farm asparagus tips with an intensely flavoured asparagus mousse, and a perfectly poached spiced pear with a velvety milk chocolate and praline sauce, vanilla ice cream and pistachio brittle were highlights at an inspection meal that also took in breast of Wirral wood pigeon with pancetta, pumpkin, crispy sage and walnut. In addition, there's an extensive and interesting wine list with some dozen by the glass and bottles starting at £17.75.
Chef/s: David Critchley. **Open:** all week L 11 to 3, D 5 to 10. **Meals:** alc (main courses £15 to £30). Set L and D £20 (2 courses) to £25. **Details:** 60 seats. Bar. Wheelchair access. Music.

Lunya

Where Spain meets Scouse
Cooking score: 2
Spanish | £19
18-20 College Lane, Liverpool One, Liverpool,
L1 3DS
Tel no: (0151) 7069770
www.lunya.co.uk

Many restaurant-cum-delis are neither one nor the other. Lunya not only functions but succeeds as both. Owners Peter and Elaine Kinsella (who are now hoping to expand Lunya's reach) also preside over another combination: at Lunya, Spain meets Scouse. This fusion takes its most literal form in the house signature, Catalan scouse, made with morcilla and chorizo, and butifarra breakfast rolls. Later in the day, tapas is 'always interesting' and features reader favourites such as chickpea stew with butternut squash, almonds and apricots. Welcoming to all-comers, the historic rough-walled space encompasses a chunk of Liverpool's oldest warehouse, and is enlivened by papier-mâché figures and a programme of events including gourmet evenings, suckling pig banquets and live music. Parents should note that the kitchen prides itself on catering flexibly for children, and there are veggie, vegan and gluten-free options too. Wines are exclusively Spanish, from £16.75.
Chef/s: Dave Upson. **Open:** Sun to Fri 10am to 9pm (9.30pm Wed and Thur, 10pm Fri, 8.30pm Sun). Sat 9am to 10pm. **Closed:** 25 Dec, 1 Jan. **Meals:** alc (tapas £5 to £8). Set L £9 (2 courses) to £11. Tapas banquet £26. **Details:** 150 seats. 30 seats outside. V menu. Bar. Wheelchair access. Music. Parking.

Join us at thegoodfoodguide.co.uk

Salt House Tapas

Lively city-centre tapas bar
Cooking score: 3
Spanish | £25
1 Hanover Street, Liverpool, L1 3DW
Tel no: (0151) 7060092
www.salthousetapas.co.uk

This lively city-centre tapas bar has a lot going for it, from a light, sleekly industrialised interior spread across two floors (sit on the mezzanine for a view of the bustle below) to 'absolutely charming' young staff serving a colourful mix of classic and modern tapas. An 'excellent-value' lunch deal brings crusty bread and three generous tapas dishes per person, but at any time of day you can expect a lot for your money. Plates of wafer-thin slices of Montoya Serrano with Manchego shavings and a drizzle of excellent olive oil, roast cauliflower with pomegranate yoghurt and dukkah, and slow-roasted, crisp-skinned belly pork with Stornoway black pudding and PX onions all delighted one reporter. Fresh, deceptively simple desserts such as sweet, fresh strawberries with basil mascarpone, honeycomb and dark chocolate, or perfect churros and chocolate sauce, are typical of the simple, gutsy style. An international selection of wines opens at £15.50.
Chef/s: Martin Renshaw. **Open:** all week 12 to 10.30. **Closed:** 25 Dec. **Meals:** alc (tapas £4 to £9). Set L £11. **Details:** 90 seats. 25 seats outside. Bar. Wheelchair access. Music.

NEW ENTRY

60 Hope Street

Town house restaurant with a wine-bar vibe
Cooking score: 1
Modern British | £37
60 Hope Street, Liverpool, L1 9BZ
Tel no: (0151) 7076060
www.60hopestreet.com

This handsome town house restaurant 'with a wine-bar vibe' has been plying its trade not far from the city centre for some 16 years, its contemporary interior sitting well with the age of the building. The food is hearty and accessible, with an emphasis on freshness and flavour. Great ingredients elevated a simple lunchtime starter of asparagus and pancetta, while typical main courses might include paprika Lancashire chicken breast with potato, tomato, chorizo and sage 'fondue', with a classic raspberry cranachan with juicy raspberries and crumbled white chocolate cookie to finish. Wines from £18.95.
Chef/s: Gary Manning. **Open:** Mon to Sat L 12 to 2.30, D 5 to 10.30. Sun 12 to 6. **Meals:** alc (main courses £19 to £32). Set L and D £20 (2 courses) to £25. **Details:** 150 seats. 15 seats outside.

Spire

Top Merseyside performer
Cooking score: 5
Modern European | £32
1 Church Road, Liverpool, L15 9EA
Tel no: (0151) 7345040
www.spirerestaurant.co.uk

Directly opposite the 'shelter in the roundabout' of Penny Lane fame, Spire lives up to its iconic location by turning out food that is so 'very special' that it merits a trip in its own right. It does so in a setting that is cosy, down to earth and buzzy: think exposed brickwork, close-packed bare-wood tables and stripped-wood floors. There's no standing to attention here – the staff bustle, the diners chat and the wine flows merrily, yet the food easily surpasses that served in many restaurants with more formal pretensions. Expect sophisticated, complex, often 'unforgettable' dishes: there's a lot going on here, but each ingredient deserves its place. Asparagus with pea purée, poached quails' eggs, broad beans, radishes and hollandaise sauce is a case in point. So too is an 'exquisite' Goosnargh chicken breast with red pepper purée, caramelised red onion and goats' cheese cake (actually a pair of feisty little croquettes), basil sauce and an artful scattering of perfectly cooked garden vegetables. A loose pannacotta, served in a Kilner jar with crumble and a scoop of raspberry sorbet, was a successful final bow. A good selection of international wines starts at £15.95.

Chef/s: Matt Locke. **Open:** Tue to Fri L 12 to 2, Mon to Sat D 6 to 9 (9.30 Fri and Sat). **Closed:** Sun, first week Jan. **Meals:** alc (main courses £14 to £22). Set L £12 (2 courses) to £16. Set D £16 (2 courses) to £19. **Details:** 70 seats. Music.

LOCAL GEM

Etsu

Japanese | £25
25 The Strand (off Brunswick Street), Liverpool, L2 0XJ
Tel no: (0151) 2367530
www.etsu-restaurant.co.uk

A Japanese venue in trendy Beetham Plaza, Etsu is a spacious, relaxing place done in light wood against a dark tiled floor. Authentic specialities are served forth by helpful staff, who are ready to guide you through a repertoire that runs from suimono clear soup with king prawns and seaweed, through yakitori skewers, donburi rice dishes and the full range of sushi, sashimi and maaki rolls. Japanese curries might incorporate panko-crumbed tuna or pork, or go for deep-fried tofu with udon noodles, wakame seaweed and spring onions. Saké and shochu supplement a short wine list from £12.95. Closed Mon and L Wed, Sat and Sun.

◼ Oxton

★ TOP 10 ★

Fraiche

Sense-tingling thrills from a Wirral wizard
Cooking score: 8
Modern French | £80
11 Rose Mount, Oxton, CH43 5SG
Tel no: (0151) 6522914
www.restaurantfraiche.com

Take one fan's advice and book well ahead if you want to experience the thrill of Fraiche – mercurial Marc Wilkinson's extraordinary little restaurant secreted away in a conservation village a few miles from Birkenhead. Eating out doesn't get any more personal than this, and the whole enterprise seems to be an ever-evolving work in progress: Marc recently refurbished the bijou dining room, created a new lounge area and continues to commission original artwork for the restaurant – note the 'moon' sculpture and the cheeky 'underpants'. He also has a new mantra: '12 months of the textures and flavours of nature'. The result is a constantly changing multi-course tasting menu that takes its inspiration from the European avant-garde and plays with flavours on the fringes of contemporary gastronomy – an audacious trip 'sans frontières' that reaps huge rewards. Dish descriptions are epigrammatic – even enigmatic – but they conceal a remarkable degree of mind-boggling skill and artistry, not to mention dogged hard work (Marc works alone in the kitchen). 'Winter tree' and 'shiitake hits' will keep you guessing, but also expect plates of scallop, avocado and pink grapefruit, venison with baby gem and celeriac or wild sea bass with smoked almond, quinoa and charred leek – all transmuted and reconfigured with cutting-edge techniques and inspired alchemy. As proceedings near their end, you will be offered something sweet – perhaps a combination of yoghurt, raspberry and rose or a dessert involving chocolate, orange and coffee. Given the size of the restaurant, it's surprising to be offered a voluminous 300-bin wine list full of treasures from around the globe, with bottles from £17.95.

Chef/s: Marc Wilkinson. **Open:** Fri to Sun L 12 to 1, Wed to Sat D 7 to 8.30. **Closed:** Mon, Tue, 25 Dec, 1 Jan, 2 weeks Aug. **Meals:** Set L £38. Set D £80 (8 courses). Sun L £38. **Details:** 10 seats. 6 seats outside. V menu. Bar. Wheelchair access. Music. Children over 8 yrs only at D.

Visit us online

To find out more about The Good Food Guide, please visit thegoodfoodguide.co.uk

Join us at thegoodfoodguide.co.uk

 Southport
Bistrot Vérité
Homely eatery with Gallic classics
Cooking score: 3
French | £28
7 Liverpool Road, Birkdale, Southport,
PR8 4AR
Tel no: (01704) 564199
www.bistrotverite.co.uk

£30

'Without doubt the most authentic French bistro for miles around,' observed one reporter after a visit to this bastion of robust Gallic food in Southport's photogenic satellite village of Birkdale. A white-fronted venue, Marc and Michaela Vérité's restaurant is dedicated to rustic French cooking. Daily changing menus offer familiar, comforting choices, from starters of fish soup with all the trimmings or crispy boudin noir with apple and mustard to mains of roasted haunch of venison, seared foie gras and pickled pear or wild sea bass with Southport shrimps, spinach and beurre noisette. Finish, perhaps, with equally classic desserts such as crêpes suzette or warm apple tart. 'Attentive but never obtrusive' service wins as many plaudits as the food, which offers more English touches during the day with traditional fish and chips among the lunch menu choices. The wine list opens with quaffable French red or white at £16.95. Carafes are also available.

Chef/s: Marc Vérité. **Open:** Tue to Sat L 12 to 1.30, D from 5.30. **Closed:** Sun, Mon, 25 and 26 Dec, 1 Jan, 1 week Feb, 1 week Aug. **Meals:** alc (main courses £13 to £27). **Details:** 45 seats. 16 seats outside. Music.

Bistro 21
Modern European | £30
21 Stanley Street, Southport, PR9 0BS
Tel no: (01704) 501414
www.bistro21.co.uk

Jan Atkinson's laid-back bistro on a town-centre backstreet is well supported by a loyal crowd. Tables are got up in their best whites, and the work of a different local artist every month adorns the walls. Dishes look smart, too, with artful presentations to the fore, and flavours ring true. Smoked haddock risotto with peas and Parmesan, venison with butternut purée, beetroot and horseradish pesto and carrot crisps, or cod with black pudding and chorizo in tomato chilli sauce, all make big emphatic statements. Finish with boozy Calvados rice pudding brûlée. Wines from £14.95. Closed Mon and Tue.

Local Gem 

Local Gems are the perfect neighbourhood venues, delivering good, freshly cooked food at great value for money.

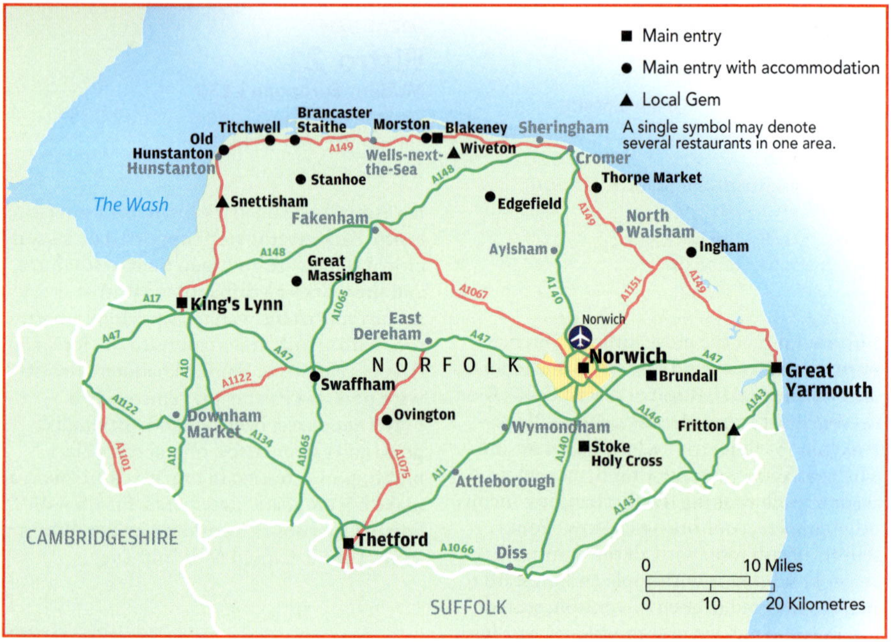

■ Blakeney
The Moorings

Endearing Norfolk bolt-hole
Cooking score: 2
Modern British | £30
High Street, Blakeney, NR25 7NA
Tel no: (01263) 740054
www.blakeney-moorings.co.uk

Muddy creeks and flint cottages, vast skies and wind farms...the iconic images of Norfolk are plentiful. Add to these fresh produce from the county's bountiful larder prepared with skill by Richard and Angela Long, and you have a recipe for joy. This little high-street eatery, a seal's bark from the quay, draws lunchtime crowds hungry for its straightforward midday offer, but ups the ante in the evening. Then, the menu offers the likes of sea-salty crab, shrimp and sorrel risotto or spicy Norfolk crab cake to start, perhaps followed by an exquisitely cooked, meaty and prettily-presented 'melange' of mussels, monkfish and scallops in an aromatic fennel broth. Roast cod with Ibérico ham, spinach and lentils would make a fine alternative, even if you push aside the lentils in favour of a spoonful of the Moorings' legendary dauphinois potatoes. A blackboard of puddings encourages a third course – maybe Angela's vivacious lemon tart. The wine list opens at £14.95.

Chef/s: Richard and Angela Long. **Open:** Tue to Sun L 10.30 to 4.30, Tue to Sat D 6 to 9. **Closed:** Mon, 1 week Dec, Jan. **Meals:** alc (main courses £15 to £22). Sun L £18. **Details:** 55 seats. Music.

Please send us your feedback

To register your opinion about any restaurant listed in this guide, or a new restaurant that you wish to bring to our attention, please visit the web address at the bottom of the page. Your feedback informs the content of the book and will be used to compile next year's reviews.

Brancaster Staithe
The White Horse

Gloriously located inn
Cooking score: 3
Modern British | £30
Brancaster Staithe, PE31 8BY
Tel no: (01485) 210262
www.whitehorsebrancaster.co.uk

General enthusiasm for this gloriously located inn remains undimmed. It is the entire package that appeals, including a lively atmosphere and the chance of alfresco eating on fine days. It's a welcoming haven – warm, enveloping, civilised – where the atmosphere is relaxed enough to cater for those who just want to pull up at the bar for a drink and a bowl of local mussels, but with a pleasant, comfortable conservatory-style dining room at the back with unrivalled views over the tidal marsh. The menus here continue to evolve, capitalising on seasonality and local supply lines, and the style of cooking is sufficiently modern to include goats' cheese cheesecake with pickled satsuma and beetroot, as well as roast loin of venison with local game hotpot, textures of parsnip, Savoy cabbage and cocoa nib. Wines from £17.50.
Chef/s: Fran Hartshorne. **Open:** all week L 12 to 2 (2.30 Sun), D 6.30 to 9. **Meals:** alc (main courses £13 to £18). **Details:** 100 seats. 100 seats outside. Bar. Wheelchair access. Music. Parking.

LOCAL GEM

The Jolly Sailors

British | £22
Brancaster Staithe, PE31 8BJ
Tel no: (01485) 210314
www.jollysailorsbrancaster.co.uk

The sheltered garden makes this traditional roadside pub reliably popular in summer, but it makes a snug setting in winter, judging by warm, contented accounts of welcoming fires, friendly, unpretentious service and good food. The bill of fare lists honest pub grub of the steak and ale pie, ham, egg and chips variety.

But there are also stone-baked pizzas to eat in or take away or bowls of excellent local mussels to be washed down with Brancaster Brewery ales or house Georges Duboeuf (£17). Open all week. Owned by the nearby White Horse, see entry.

Brundall
The Lavender House

Norfolk's foodie haven
Cooking score: 3
Modern British | £45
39 The Street, Brundall, NR13 5AA
Tel no: (01603) 712215
www.thelavenderhouse.co.uk

As an ambassador for all things gastronomic in Norfolk, Richard Hughes has fingers in several local pies – although this unassuming restaurant and cookery school not far from Norwich is his mother ship. Housed in a 16th-century thatched cottage, Lavender House may feel a tad pubby (old beams, bare brick walls), but is far removed from pints of beer – especially if you're booked in to the exclusive Opitz Room (a 'chef's theatre table' named after the famed Austrian winemaker). Meals revolve around multi-course tasting menus and, as expected, Norfolk produce sings loudly – be it whipped Binham Blue cheese (served with a winter salad, roasted plums and port) or free-range Blythburgh pork belly (perhaps accompanied by cauliflower, capers and raisins). There's a mighty local beef speciality, too, involving eight-hour cooked cheek and fillet with smoked potato, heritage carrots, prunes and Cognac, while spiced black treacle sponge with apple fritters, beer-flavoured ice cream and candied nuts is a stunning finish. Richard's auspicious wine list is a labour of love, full of fascinating selections from around the globe; prices start at £22.
Chef/s: Richard Hughes. **Open:** Sun L 12 to 3, Thur to Sat D 6.30 to 9.30. **Closed:** Mon, Tue, Wed, 26 to 30 Dec. **Meals:** Set D £45 (6 courses). Tasting menu £60 (9 courses). **Details:** 45 seats. V menu. Bar. Parking.

Edgefield
The Pigs

Gutsy food in a family-focused boozer
Cooking score: 1
British | £25
Norwich Road, Edgefield, NR24 2RL
Tel no: (01263) 587634
www.thepigs.org.uk

A 17th-century pub that has evolved into the very model of a modern country inn, the Pigs has held on to the character of the old boozer, added some boutique rooms (including some amazing spa rooms) and introduced an appealing menu that focuses on local ingredients. Top-notch kids' play is to be had inside and out. Iffits (or Norfolk 'tapas') feature Cley smoked prawns and ham hock Scotch egg, while the main menu extends to modern pub classics such as the rump burger and seasonal specials like venison faggots with roast chestnut and leek mash. Finish with a pavlova to share. Wines start at £18.
Chef/s: Ben Dawes. **Open:** Mon to Sat L 12 to 2.30, D 6 to 9. Sun 12 to 8.30. **Meals:** alc (main courses £12 to £36). **Details:** 126 seats. 72 seats outside. Bar. Parking.

Fritton

LOCAL GEM
The Fritton Arms

Modern British | £28
Church Lane, Fritton, NR31 9HA
Tel no: (01493) 484008
www.frittonarms.co.uk

This former hotel reopened in April 2014 as a pub-with-rooms but executive chef Stuart Pegg is still in the kitchen, which has gained a large wood-fired oven since the revamp. The seasonal modern British menu is underpinned by classic techniques and much of the produce is from the Somerleyton Estate. Parsnip soup with seared scallops might precede braised and glazed beef brisket, beef and oyster suet pudding, truffle mash and mushroom gravy. Wines from £16.50. Open all week.

Great Massingham

NEW ENTRY
The Dabbling Duck

A dip into a captivating village pub
Cooking score: 2
British | £28
11 Abbey Road, Great Massingham, PE32 2HN
Tel no: (01485) 520827
www.thedabblingduck.co.uk

Driving round Great Massingham can be a slow affair – on account of the ducks, in no hurry to move aside for vehicles. They do indeed 'dabble' in the (several) village ponds, and certainly pile on the charm in an already charm-overloaded place. The theme continues inside this 'dazzling gem' of a pub, mercifully saved from being turned into housing by a determined local campaign back in 2006. Swede and black pepper 'gluttony' soup deserves its soubriquet, creamy richness offset by punchy whole peppercorns and a swirl of fruity olive oil, while a scattering of radish, cucumber and brown shrimps gives texture, sea-saltiness and fresh colour to delicately seasoned plaice. Burgers are vast, cooked perfectly pink and drip with flavour, while Norfolk quail with truffles and charred baby leeks left one diner feeling 'gastronomic elation', no less. Lightly whipped rhubarb fool with a homemade garibaldi biscuit makes a fine finish. Wine from £15.95.
Chef/s: Sam Bryant. **Open:** all week L 12 to 2.30, Mon to Sat D 6.30 to 9 (6 to 9.30 Fri and Sat). **Meals:** alc (main courses £10 to £21). **Details:** 70 seats. 40 seats outside. Bar. Wheelchair access. Music. Parking.

▌ Great Yarmouth
Seafood Restaurant

Adorable seafood veteran

Cooking score: 2
Seafood | £35
85 North Quay, Great Yarmouth, NR30 1JF
Tel no: (01493) 856009
www.theseafood.co.uk

£5 OFF

Chris and Miriam Kikis run a family
restaurant of the best ilk, well established and
loyally supported by local customers, the kind
of place that's full in midweek, no matter what
the economic climate. 'Fantastic personal
service' and a 'lovely homely feel' to the former
Victorian pub's plush décor help, but it's the
'fabulous fish' that is the big draw. The
meticulously sourced local catch is treated
simply and without frills, and although the
menu barely changes, apart from a few
seasonal tweaks, its built around established
standards, which brings people back because
they know the quality won't waver from one
visit to the next. Spicy seafood soup, shellfish
platters, scampi provençale, goujons of plaice,
skate with black butter and lobster thermidor
are all present and correct, and if you're not a
fishie, try beef stroganoff or fillet steak with
pepper sauce. Cheesecake is a favourite dessert.
Wines from £16.75.

Chef/s: Christopher Kikis. **Open:** Mon to Fri L 12 to
1.45, Mon to Sat D 6.30 to 10.30. **Closed:** Sun, 2
weeks Christmas, last 2 weeks May, bank hols.
Meals: alc (main courses £13 to £36). **Details:** 42
seats. V menu. Bar. Wheelchair access. Music.
Children over 7 yrs only.

▌ Ingham
The Ingham Swan

Grown-up food in a medieval inn

Cooking score: 3
Modern European | £35
Sea Palling Road, Ingham, NR12 9GA
Tel no: (01692) 581099
www.theinghamswan.co.uk

£5 OFF 

There's something 'edge of the world' about
this part of Norfolk, but before you tumble
into the North Sea, stop here to taste Daniel
Smith's 'top-class' cooking. A crispy Cromer
crab cake, crab salad and crab claw starter
could do with a squeeze of something zesty
despite the harissa aïoli, but, as with much of
Smith's menu, it champions an iconic local
product to starry effect. The oozing
creaminess of a pan-hot beignet of local Baron
Bigod cheese is balanced by salty goats' cheese
and fruit-packed beetroot chutney, a
scattering of caramelised nuts contributing
welcome crunch. An outstanding nugget of
belly in a duo of Suffolk pork makes up for
slightly dry fillet, while monkfish and herby
prawns with just-steamed tenderstem
broccoli, sweet red peppers and peppery pea
shoots is an uplifting, spring-on-a-plate
choice. A must-taste? – the raspberry sorbet
that cuts through faultlessly-rich crème brûlée
to memorable effect. Service, 'the best in any
restaurant anywhere' for one diner, deserves
applause, as does the compact wine list (from
£20) with its useful recommendations.

Chef/s: Daniel Smith. **Open:** all week L 12 to 2 (3
Sun), D 6 to 9. **Closed:** 25 and 26 Dec. **Meals:** alc
(main courses £16 to £26). Set L £17 (2 courses) to
£19. Set D £23 (2 courses) to £28. Sun L £23. Tasting
menu £55. **Details:** 55 seats. 20 seats outside.
Music. Parking.

 King's Lynn
Market Bistro

Welcoming town-centre eatery
Cooking score: 2
Modern British | £27
11 Saturday Market Place, King's Lynn,
PE30 5DQ
Tel no: (01553) 771483
www.marketbistro.co.uk

A real sense of loyalty and affection radiates from the reports we receive about this 'true gem of a find' opposite the church in King's Lynn's historic Saturday Market Place. Occupying a quaint and crooked house with a new outside seating area facing the minster, Richard and Lucy Golding's little bistro is noted for its industriousness and dedication to Norfolk produce. Provenance and home production – including smoking fish, baking bread, curing meat and preserving – makes this an enterprising place with a genuine front-of-house warmth. The menu moves confidently from roast Jerusalem artichoke, carrot purée, parsley pesto and crushed hazelnut to Gressingham duck breast, poached rhubarb, rhubarb purée, sprouting broccoli and toasted almonds. A typical meal might end with bitter chocolate fondant, salt caramel and Kirsch ice cream. The sensibly priced wine list opens at £16.95, although it's also worth sampling one of the locally brewed Norfolk ales or quirky cocktails.
Chef/s: Richard Golding. **Open:** Tue to Sun L 12 to 2. Tue to Sat D 6 to 8.30 (9 Fri and Sat). **Closed:** Mon, 26 Dec. **Meals:** alc (main courses £11 to £23). Sun L £16. **Details:** 36 seats. 10 seats outside. Wheelchair access.

Symbols

Accommodation is available
Three courses for less than £30
£5-off voucher scheme
Notable wine list

Marriott's Warehouse

Modern British | £23
South Quay, King's Lynn, PE30 5DT
Tel no: (01553) 818500
www.marriottswarehouse.co.uk

Maritime heritage looms large at this Grade II-listed warehouse on Kings Lynn's cobbled riverside wharf by the banks of the Great Ouse. But with a cool lounge area upstairs, local artworks, great views and a diverse menu bolstered by blackboard specials, Marriott's also suits its aspirational neighbourhood to a T. Lunchtime sandwiches, small plates, sharing platters and easy mains give way to evening dishes along the lines of smoked haddock crumble, venison casserole or roast red-legged partridge on curly kale with rösti, port and redcurrant jus. Wines from £13.95. Open all week.

 Morston
Morston Hall

Classy, modern cooking near the coast
Cooking score: 5
Modern British | £66
The Street, Morston, NR25 7AA
Tel no: (01263) 741041
www.morstonhall.com

Under starter's orders by 7.30pm, diners at this tiptop coastal hotel are coaxed towards (well-spaced) tables for an 8pm start. A warm-up for Galton Blackiston's taste-bud-invigorating set seven courses might be beetroot velouté, a captivatingly crimson puddle of sweetness balanced by the salty poke of a nugget of blue cheese. An 'out of this world' fresh truffle risotto with sautéed ceps could precede a ham hock terrine, which is elevated into the realms of memorable mouthfuls by a line of foie gras and dollop of lively piccalilli. Dipping briefly at the fish stage – a small piece of wild sea bass is 'seriously underseasoned' for one diner, and the pungent promise of wild garlic doesn't quite deliver – the pace is quickly picked up with a syrupy-sweet Norfolk duckling, skin caramelised black, flesh meltingly pink. The home stretch presents a quandary: will it be the platter of British cheeses or an anticipatory taste of summer in the form of a gariguette strawberry cheesecake? A comprehensive wine list starts at £29.

Chef/s: Galton Blackiston. **Open:** Sun L 12.30 for 1 (1 sitting), Mon to Sat D 7.30 for 8 (1 sitting). **Closed:** 25 and 26 Dec, Jan. **Meals:** Set D £66 (7 courses). Sun L £36. **Details:** 40 seats. Wheelchair access. Parking.

▌ Norwich
Roger Hickman's

Clean, clear seasonal flavours
Cooking score: 5
Modern British | £44

79 Upper St Giles Street, Norwich, NR2 1AB
Tel no: (01603) 633522
www.rogerhickmansrestaurant.com

An oasis of elegant, relaxed calm in the centre of Norwich, this restaurant sees guests returning time and again. It's obvious why: Roger Hickman's cooking is first rate, his food a masterclass in how balance, restraint, seasoning and sublime ingredients can combine to delight. Puffed wild rice adds crunch to a starter of crab, its sea-saltiness sweetened by avocado and a diminutive quail's egg, while translucent curls of pickled cucumber give punchy acidity. A standout main is chicken with peppery mustard, sweetly baked onions, bitter radish and a dash of umami from mushrooms. It works a dream, especially alongside the smoky crunch of grilled Little Gem. A deeply chocolatey crémeux, happily partnered with bitter-enough coffee ice cream and a scattering of hazelnuts for substance, finishes a meal perfectly. Little extras abound, from an amuse-bouche to a memorable petit four cube of sweet-sour pineapple jelly. A compact wine list opens with Argentinian Torrontes for £24.

Chef/s: Roger Hickman. **Open:** Tue to Sat L 12 to 2.30, D 7 to 10. **Closed:** Sun, Mon, 23 Aug to 1 Sept. **Meals:** Set L £20 (2 courses) to £24. Set D £36 (2 courses) to £44. **Details:** 45 seats.

Roots

British | £28
6 Pottergate, Norwich, NR2 1DS
Tel no: (01603) 920788
www.rootsnorwich.co.uk

Whether it's for a bolstering breakfast or extravagent afternoon tea, this highly regarded bistro-cum-café covers all bases when it comes to championing Norfolk produce, including wine from a local vineyard. Set across three floors of a 300-year-old building in Norwich's Lanes area, Roots certainly impresses with starters such as apple boudin and pork Scotch egg, parsnip purée and radicchio, which might be followed by local mussels steamed with white wine, parsley and cream and served with triple-cooked chips. Wines from £19.95. Closed Sun D and Mon.

Shiki

Japanese | £20
6 Tombland, Norwich, NR3 1HE
Tel no: (01603) 619262
www.shikirestaurant.co.uk

The name means 'four seasons', and this funky come-as-you-please canteen on a leafy corner opposite Norwich Cathedral has year-round appeal for hordes of locals, students and tourists. Energetic service, honest prices and big nutritious flavours are the selling points as the open kitchen knocks out all manner of nigiri, gunkan, maki rolls and thick-cut sashimi, plus very decent renditions of the cooked classics – yakitori skewers, gyoza dumplings, tempura, katsu curries and soba noodles. Bento boxes fill the lunchtime gaps, while theatrical teppanyaki is the evening star. Drink tea, beer or saké. Closed Sun.

Old Hunstanton
The Neptune

Sought-after Norfolk destination
Cooking score: 4
Modern British | £56
85 Old Hunstanton Road, Old Hunstanton,
PE36 6HZ
Tel no: (01485) 532122
www.theneptune.co.uk

It's easy to miss on the coast road, so keep your eyes peeled for Kevin and Jackie Mangeolles' 'terrific' foliage-clad restaurant-with-rooms – a sought-after Norfolk destination noted for its warm welcome and top-notch food. Kevin deals in clear-flavoured contemporary dishes with lots of intricate detailing, and his nine-course tasting menu has yielded some seriously good stuff – from limpid 'iced tomato water' to a plate of Brancaster lobster and halibut ceviche with passion fruit and chilli that 'could have been served to applause in Lima'. Seasonal pickings also shine through on the carte – as in brill fillet with dried tomato, oyster mayonnaise, Fir Apple potatoes and wild broccoli or 'pink and perfect' loin of Norfolk lamb with sea purslane. Cleverly wrought desserts cover a lot of ground too, be it prune and Armagnac parfait with tea meringue or coconut and ginger pannacotta with banana sorbet. Jackie oversees the wine cellar and has assembled a fascinating list of out-of-the-way bottles, with plentiful house selections from £20.

Chef/s: Kevin Mangeolles. **Open:** Sun L 12 to 1.30, Tue to Sun D 7 to 9. **Closed:** Mon, 26 Dec, 3 weeks Jan, 2 weeks Nov. **Meals:** Set D £43 (2 courses) to £56. Sun L £35. Tasting menu £72 (9 courses).
Details: 22 seats. Bar. Music. Parking. Children over 10 yrs only.

Ovington
The Café at Brovey Lair

Thrilling gastro-theatre
Cooking score: 6
Global/Seafood | £53
Carbrooke Road, Ovington, IP25 6SD
Tel no: (01953) 882706
www.broveylair.com

'Unconventional' hardly does justice to Brovey Lair – Tina and Mike Pemberton's home and the setting for their 'dinner parties with paying guests'. Meals are served in the couple's ultra-glossy open-plan kitchen, and they run the show as a double act: you'll find Tina 'in her American diner gear', chatting away at the teppan grill, while Mike 'sprinkles anecdotes as an extra condiment' for the assembled company. 'Fusion seafood' is the theme, with the emphasis on very fresh fish. You're expected to discuss your likes and dislikes over the phone beforehand, and the results are always thrilling – real gastro-theatre, but up close and personal, too. You might begin with sesame-crusted scallops on a vibrantly dressed bean shoot salad, ahead of, say, spicy spinach and sweet potato soup. Fired-up centrepieces exude that 'true taste of freshness', from Cajun-spiced swordfish to seared tuna on squid-ink noodles with stir-fried shiitake mushrooms. For a worthy finale, try Moroccan-style almond and orange cake with aromatic roasted figs. Twenty apposite wines start at £19.50.

Chef/s: Tina Pemberton. **Open:** all week L 12.30 to 3, D 7.30 to 12. **Closed:** 24 to 30 Dec. **Meals:** Set L and D £53. **Details:** 20 seats. 20 seats outside. V menu. Bar. Parking. No children.

■ Snettisham

LOCAL GEM

The Rose & Crown

Modern British | £27

Old Church Road, Snettisham, PE31 7LX
Tel no: (01485) 541380
www.roseandcrownsnettisham.co.uk

Deceptively big, with 'lots of twists and turns, old beams and inglenook fireplaces', this 14th-century pub-with-rooms fits the bill if you are in the area and very hungry. It's child and dog friendly and readers report success with generous pubby offerings such as beer-battered haddock and chips and (wild boar) bangers and mash, though more involved dishes include lemongrass and chilli venison with pickled ginger and wasabi, and halibut with saffron potato and scallop bouillabaisse. Wines from £15.50. Open all week. Accom.

■ Stanhoe

The Duck Inn

Modern cooking by the village duck pond

Cooking score: 3
British | £30

Burnham Road, Stanhoe, PE31 8QD
Tel no: (01485) 518330
www.duckinn.co.uk

'It is the best, consistent, agreeable, fresh and friendly place around,' enthused one regular and others concur, praising everything from food 'of such a high standard' to the 'knowledgeable, courteous and efficient' staff. Found not far from the north Norfolk coast – 'the Burnham Market effect has certainly spread here' – this modern pub-with-rooms is an appropriate setting for Ben Handley's imaginative modern cooking. Presentation ensures that dishes look the part and local, seasonal produce features prominently – Brancaster mussels, Simon Letzer's smoked salmon, ballotine of local partridge with pancetta, porridge risotto and partridge and port jus. Hits with readers this year have been braised ox cheek doughnut ('a very brave

choice, but so worth the gamble'), goats'cheese with beetroot ('not barrier-breaking…till you taste it with tiny beetroot meringues'), the pork belly ('and assorted other parts of the pig'), Elgoods' beer-battered haddock and chips, the 'legendary' Sunday roast and pear tarte Tatin. Wines from £14.50.
Chef/s: Ben Handley. **Open:** Mon to Sat L 12 to 2.30, D 6.30 to 9. Sun 12 to 8. **Closed:** 25 Dec. **Meals:** alc (main courses £9 to £24). **Details:** 60 seats. 80 seats outside. Bar. Wheelchair access. Music. Parking.

■ Stoke Holy Cross

Stoke Mill

A slice of county heritage

Cooking score: 4
Modern British | £33

Mill Road, Stoke Holy Cross, NR14 8PA
Tel no: (01508) 493337
www.stokemill.co.uk

One of Norfolk's more head-turning destinations is the old watermill – seven centuries old – where, in 1814, Messrs Colman mixed their first mustard, a slice of county heritage indeed. With the River Tas contentedly babbling away outside, it makes a tranquil spot for a country restaurant, done up in light tones of grey on white, with simple table settings and a menu of ambitious contemporary cooking. East Anglian cheeses feature proudly in starters such as Norfolk Dapple twice-baked soufflé with chive cream, or truffled goats'cheese with a beignet of Suffolk's Bungay Brie, candied walnuts and figs. Mains might bring on Cromer crab cake as partner to sea bass in beurre blanc, or give lamb loin a Mediterranean spin with roasted red peppers, feta and smoked paprika potato cake. Finish with apple tarte Tatin for two, or a more abstemious crème brûlée with raspberry sorbet and lemonade jelly. Five house wines come at £18, or £4.65 a standard glass.
Chef/s: Andy Rudd. **Open:** Thur, Fri and Sun L 12 to 2.30, Wed to Sat D 7 to 9 (9.30 Fri, 10 Sat). **Closed:** Mon, Tue, 10 days Jan. **Meals:** alc (main courses £14

to £25). Set L £15 (2 courses) to £18. Set D £18 (2 courses) to £20. Sun L £25. **Details:** 65 seats. Bar. Music. Parking.

■ Swaffham
Strattons Hotel

Green thinking and local flavours
Cooking score: 2
Modern British | £30
4 Ash Close, Swaffham, PE37 7NH
Tel no: (01760) 723845
www.strattonshotel.com

'Recycle, reduce, reuse, recover'…the owners of this offbeat Palladian villa have always worn their eco hearts on their sleeves. Inside, green thinking meets arty, boutique design – especially in the 'semi-basement' dining room with its 'rusticated' stonework, sculpted female torso and canvases of Breckland birch trees on black walls. The kitchen follows suit, with 'true local flavours' and organic produce defining the seasonal dinner menus – think twice-baked Binham Blue soufflé, slow-cooked rabbit suet pudding with boozy raisin salsa or sea bass fillet with purple sprouting broccoli, 'stoved' new potatoes and brown shrimp butter. It's a straight-talking, unfussy approach that also yields sweet satisfaction in the shape of forced rhubarb sorbet with chilled vanilla custard or warm walnut tart with toffee sauce. Breakfast, light lunches and snacks are available in CoCoes – the hotel's all-day café-cum-deli. True to the ethos of the place, organic and biodynamic wines feature heavily on the well-annotated Corney & Barrow list; prices start at £20 (£5.25 a glass).
Chef/s: Julia Hetherton. **Open:** Sun L 12 to 2.30, all week D 6.30 to 8.30 (9.30 Fri and Sat). **Closed:** 21 to 27 Dec. **Meals:** alc (main courses £14 to £18). **Details:** 40 seats. 15 seats outside. Bar. Music. Parking.

■ Thetford
The Mulberry

Friendly, tucked-away neighbourhood treat
Cooking score: 1
Modern British | £32
11 Raymond Street, Thetford, IP24 2EA
Tel no: (01842) 824122
www.mulberrythetford.co.uk

£5
OFF

Tucked away in this unassuming Norfolk town, the Mulberry is a delicious surprise. Lively Mediterranean flavours and careful sourcing burst from the menu, tempting first with saltimbocca of wood pigeon on garlic crostini or a plate of ramacche whose crispy outside hides the savoury yumminess of southern Italian caciocavallo cheese and Parma ham. Move on to a hearty main of red wine-braised Suffolk lamb served with Parmesan-infused mash, or honey-glazed duck breast sliced pink over a roasted fennel and Gorgonzola tart. An acacia honey pannacotta with sweet poached pears and honeycomb rounds a meal off well. Wines from £15.95
Chef/s: Nathan Coleman. **Open:** Tue to Sat D only 6 to 10 (11 Fri and Sat). **Closed:** Sun, Mon, 26 Dec, 1 Jan, 1 week Aug. **Meals:** alc (main courses £11 to £23). Set D £20 (2 courses) to £25. **Details:** 45 seats. 8 seats outside. Music.

■ Thorpe Market
The Gunton Arms

Stunning location and concept
Cooking score: 3
British | £35
Cromer Road, Thorpe Market, NR11 8TZ
Tel no: (01263) 832010
www.theguntonarms.co.uk

Cooking on an open fire has become quite the foodie thing, and the vast, vaulted Elk Room (complete with high-backed pews and appropriately massive antlers over the fireplace) certainly nails the theatrical concept at this north Norfolk pub. Reports about the food have been mixed. A 'lovely' game terrine was followed by a 'mediocre' venison burger for one diner, while another found a plate of crab linguine overcooked. But a specials-board starter of lamb's sweetbreads with wild garlic and creamed spelt is deliciously sweet and nutty, and a generous Blythburgh pork chop succulent and well-seasoned. The seared skin on a fillet of hake hides the softest of flesh, a dreamy partner for buttery, garlicky seashore vegetables and Norfolk brown shrimps. Blueberry and vanilla cheesecake is the pudding choice, the tartness of the fruit a welcome foil for the creaminess of the rest. Some of the art is not for the faint hearted, service was 'so so' at inspection and the house wine comes in at £18 a bottle.

Chef/s: Stuart Tattersall. **Open:** all week L 12 to 3, D 6 to 10 (9 Sun). **Closed:** 25 Dec. **Meals:** alc (main courses £12 to £60). **Details:** 60 seats. 100 seats outside. V menu. Bar.

Titchwell
Titchwell Manor

Inventive cooking by the sea
Cooking score: 3
Modern European | £30
Titchwell, PE31 8BB
Tel no: (01485) 210221
www.titchwellmanor.com

Since arriving here in 1988, self-taught Eric Snaith and his wife have transformed Titchwell Manor into a sleek boutique hotel noted for its striking interiors and inventive cooking. Visitors looking for some casual brasserie food should seek out one of the aptly named 'eating rooms' for well-tried international staples such as fish pie with Parmesan croquettes or spiced Kansas City pork ribs, though Eric saves most of his creative energy for the carte and multi-course 'conversation' menus served in the lush conservatory overlooking the hotel's walled garden. Asian and Mediterranean themes collide as the kitchen delivers a raft of cleverly balanced, eye-catching dishes: mackerel is dressed with soy, lime, shallots and caviar; wild sea bass is given a sunny spin with

crosnes, sherry vinegar, salsify and Norfolk saffron; Houghton fallow deer sits well with celeriac ragoût, liquorice and Savoy cabbage. To finish, clove custard with honey, lemon and whisky is like spicy balm for the soul. Around 20 'selected' house wines start at £19.

Chef/s: Eric Snaith. **Open:** all week 12 to 9.30. **Meals:** alc (main courses £11 to £27). Set D £55 (5 courses) to £65 (8 courses). Sun L £29. **Details:** 100 seats. 40 seats outside. V menu. Bar. Wheelchair access. Music. Parking.

Wiveton

LOCAL GEM
Wiveton Hall Café

Modern British | £28
Wiveton Hall, Wiveton, NR25 7TE
Tel no: (01263) 740515
www.wivetonhall.co.uk

Set amid Wiveton Hall's fruitful acres (PYO in season), this offbeat café is a star for daytime refreshment, afternoon tea, light lunches and suppers. The kitchen majors on tapas-style plates inspired by Norfolk produce, from beetroot hummus or harissa-marinated Wiveton asparagus with char-grilled haloumi to Weybourne crab salad or crispy local pork belly with cumin and lemon. A new wood-fired oven also knocks out pizzas (Mon to Thur evenings during the summer hols). House wine is £14.50. Open all week Apr to end Oct (no food Sun D).

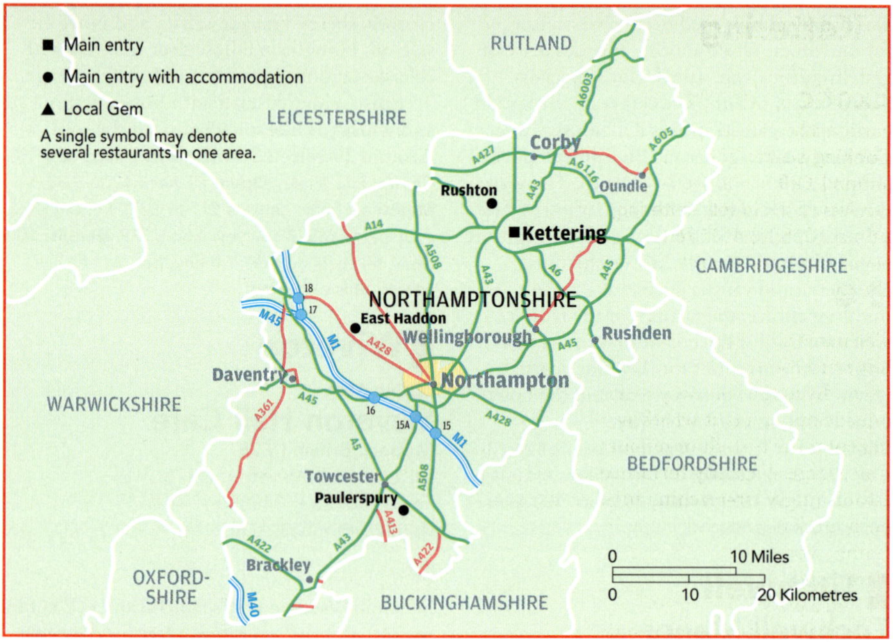

◼ East Haddon
The Red Lion

A dining destination for the area
Cooking score: 2
Modern British | £27
Main Street, East Haddon, NN6 8BU
Tel no: (01604) 770223
www.redlioneasthaddon.co.uk

Here's an updated 17th-century coaching inn of substance, though perhaps more of a restaurant than a pub these days with its spacious interior given over to dining – and best to book at busy times. It's also a nice place to stay. The kitchen casts its net wide, offering a lively hubble-bubble mix of Mediterranean and classic British flavours with a few twists from further afield (perhaps squash, pea and spinach Thai curry with sticky noodles and coriander salad). There's no going wrong with pulled salt beef (cured on site) with chunky pickles and creamed horseradish, followed by baby back ribs with beetroot coleslaw, onion rings and skin-on chips, grilled sea bream with a warm niçoise salad and poached egg or roasted chicken breast with wild garlic 'from the garden', asparagus and pearl barley risotto. Golden syrup tart with custard is as English as they come. Wines from £16.50.

Chef/s: Chloe Haycock. **Open:** Mon to Fri L 12 to 2.30, D 6 to 9 (9.30 Fri). Sat and Sun 12 to 10 (8 Sun). **Closed:** 25 Dec. **Meals:** alc (main courses £12 to £53). **Details:** 75 seats. 75 seats outside. Bar. Music. Parking.

Please send us your feedback

To register your opinion about any restaurant listed in this guide, or a new restaurant that you wish to bring to our attention, please visit the web address at the bottom of the page. Your feedback informs the content of the book and will be used to compile next year's reviews.

 Kettering

NEW ENTRY
Exotic Dining

Far-reaching Indian cuisine
Cooking score: 3
Indian | £28
3-5 Newland Street, Kettering, NN16 8JH
Tel no: (01536) 411176
www.dineexotic.co.uk

The name isn't promising and neither is the setting: a room above a Kettering shopping street. Even the takeaway menu displayed outside only hints at what's available to diners. Yet enter the first-floor restaurant and you'll find a large, elegantly furnished space and an astonishingly far-reaching menu embracing both modern and traditional Indian cookery. Game (woodcock, teal), seafood (shark, clams) and 'foreign meats' (kangaroo, camel) all find a place here, but the kitchen is no novelty act: witness such exquisitely presented dishes as moja moja rabbit (tender strips combined with mixed vegetables), followed by equally becoming murgh massalam where oval slices of breast meat arrive stuffed with minced chicken, surrounded by a tomato and yoghurt sauce bursting with the flavours of ginger, garlic and mustard. A side dish of baghara baigan (luscious, smoky baby aubergines in a thick coconut milk and poppy seed sauce) also emphasises the culinary class here. Wine from £12.95.
Chef/s: Mohammed Abadur and S. Mondol. **Open:** all week L 12 to 2.30, D 5.30 to 11 (12 Fri and Sat). **Meals:** alc (main courses £6 to £19). **Details:** 90 seats. Bar. Wheelchair access. Music.

 Paulerspury
The Vine House

Pastoral pleasantries with splendid food
Cooking score: 3
Modern British | £33
100 High Street, Paulerspury, NN12 7NA
Tel no: (01327) 811267
www.vinehousehotel.com

This pretty 300-year-old restaurant-with-rooms, run with immense pride by Marcus and Julie Springett, has been bringing a bit of pizazz to rural Northants for some 20 years. While animal-print chairs and crested bluc carpet might not be to everyone's taste, the food is far more likely to please. Excellent home-baked sourdough brings things bang up to date, and though 'Homage to a New York Deli' from the succinct modern-British menu may sound somewhat pretentious (their inverted commas, not ours), the reality is a well-executed dish where thirst for reinvention is grounded by skilful technique: heavily seasoned beef fillet, cut into wafer-thin slices – essentially a reworked bresaola – packs a punch without overpowering the beef itself. Accompaniments (mustard-pickled cauliflower, sweet dill gel, croûtons, whipped cream cheese) all earn their place on the plate. Or perhaps opt for fillet of herb-cured sea bass with braised leeks and heritage tomato chutney. Bar the odd conceptual stumble, this is food with flair. Wines from £18.50.
Chef/s: Marcus Springett. **Open:** Tue to Sat L 12 to 2, Mon to Sat D 7 to 9. **Closed:** Sun. **Meals:** Set L and D £29 (2 courses) to £33. **Details:** 33 seats. Bar. Music. Parking. Children over 8 yrs only.

The locabibe vibe

Many of us are familiar with the locavore ideal of eating foods that are grown or produced locally, but how many would extend that notion to include their favourite spirits?

At the **Foragers in Hove**, combine Blackdown Spirits' dry gin and white vermouth, both made a few miles away in the shadows of the South Downs, for the ultimate Sussex martini. And what better way to enjoy Dappa, a grappa distilled in Devon from English grape skins, than at the Seahorse on the banks of the Dart a stone's throw away?

Or how about kicking off an evening at **Lardo in Hackney** with a 'rum & coke' mixed from the East London Liquor Company's Demerara Rum and Square Root London's cola, brewed on the doorstep?

At the **Old Vicarage in Dolfor** you'll find an organic seaweed gin, produced in small batches by Dà Mhìle, an award-winning farmhouse distillery in west Wales. Seek out Sibling's triple-distilled gin at **Lumière** in their hometown of **Cheltenham**, and don't miss Victoria's Rhubarb Gin from Warner Edwards in Northamptonshire when dining at the **Red Lion in East Haddon.**

Rushton
Rushton Hall, Tresham Restaurant

Satisfying food in venerable surroundings
Cooking score: 3
Modern British | £55
Desborough Road, Rushton, NN14 1RR
Tel no: (01536) 713001
www.rushtonhall.com

£5 OFF

Deep in the Northamptonshire countryside, this magnificent listed pile was originally the seat of the Tresham family; a famous resident was Francis Tresham, a player in the Gunpowder Plot. These days it's a pristine leisure retreat with all the trappings of a grand country house, including carved stonework, tapestries, cloistered hallways and pristine grass quadrangles. Drinks are taken in the cathedral-like Great Hall before moving through to the oak-panelled restaurant, where Adrian Coulthard's cooking takes its cues from the seasons. Organic Welsh goats' cheese mousse with chicory and beetroot is a typical opener, while mains such as roasted pork loin with brawn pressing, black pudding bonbon, gnocchi, apple and crackling give a thoughtful, satisfying spin on classic flavour combinations. Finish with iced apple parfait with crumble, honeycomb, meringue and caramel gel. The weighty, all-encompassing wine list opens at £18 a bottle.
Chef/s: Adrian Coulthard. **Open:** Sun L 12 to 1 (2 Sun), all week D 7 to 9. **Meals:** Set D £55. Sun L £30.
Details: 40 seats. Bar. Wheelchair access. Music. Parking. Children over 10 yrs only at D.

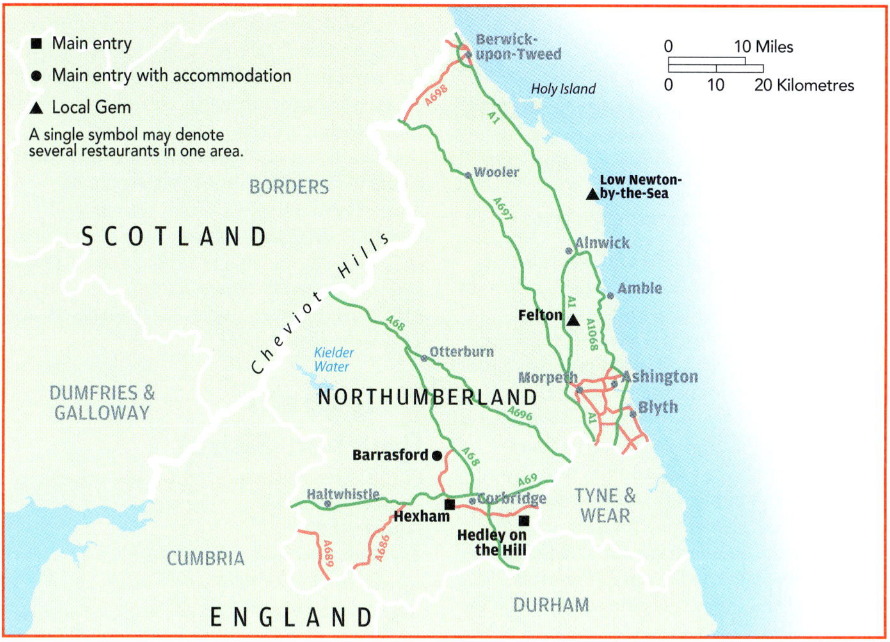

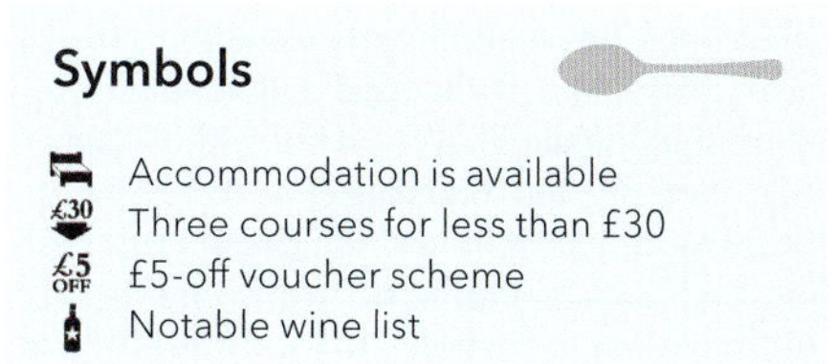

Barrasford
The Barrasford Arms

Well-run, no-frills village inn
Cooking score: 2
Modern British | £25
Barrasford, NE48 4AA
Tel no: (01434) 681237
www.barrasfordarms.co.uk

In a village north of Hexham, a stone's throw from Hadrian's Wall, Tony Binks' Victorian pub-with-rooms is well worth seeking out. An upbeat, rustic hostelry with a choice of dining areas and a superb atmosphere in the fire-warmed bar, it is a welcoming place much loved by locals and visitors. Tony's menu is built on sturdy foundations and showcases local and regional produce: at lunchtime expect a predominantly British style, say potted shrimps or 'very local' pheasant shortcrust pie with creamy mash. At dinner, however, a more European touch is revealed in the likes of twice-baked Cheddar cheese soufflé, warm crab, Parmesan and chilli tart with garlic and saffron rouille, or veal escalope with white wine and mushroom sauce. To finish, there are fine northern cheeses, while poached Yorkshire rhubarb with vanilla pannacotta and hazelnut and polenta crumb topping is a comforter with a twist. Corney & Barrow house French is £14.95.

Chef/s: Tony Binks. **Open:** Tue to Sun L 12 to 2 (2.30 Sun), Tue to Sat D 6 to 9. **Closed:** Mon, 25 and 26 Dec, bank hols. **Meals:** alc (main courses £11 to £18). Set L £13 (2 courses) to £16. Sun L £15 (2 courses) to £18. **Details:** 60 seats. 20 seats outside. Bar. Music. Parking.

Symbols

Accommodation is available
Three courses for less than £30
£5-off voucher scheme
Notable wine list

▌Felton

LOCAL GEM
The Northumberland Arms
British | £30

The Peth, West Thirston, Felton, NE65 9EE
Tel no: (01670) 787370
www.northumberlandarms-felton.co.uk

Close proximity to the A1 and an ever-so-pretty village by the River Coquet creates the right impression for visitors to this well-groomed pub. Exposed stone and real fires reinforce the mood, and in keeping with the rustic-chic surrounds, the cooking taps into the network of local producers and is served all day. Homespun English die-hards (beer-battered North Sea cod) and daytime sandwiches sit alongside more adventurous plates, perhaps asparagus tips char-grilled with Northumberland Nettle (cheese) or garlic and rosemary-flavoured flat-iron chicken with homemade chipotle sauce. Wines from £15.95. Open all week.

▌Hedley on the Hill
The Feathers Inn
Heritage cooking in a (very) old drovers' inn
Cooking score: 3
British | £25

Hedley on the Hill, NE43 7SW
Tel no: (01661) 843607
www.thefeathers.net

Perched atop Hedley's hill, with dioramic views of Northumberland all about, the Feathers began feeding and watering patrons on the old drovers' route back in the 13th century, and it has no intention of fading away through old age. The exposed beams and stonework attest eloquently enough to its years, and some of the food might not have over-startled the drovers, if they liked their roast beef rib and Yorkshire, or ox heart and mushroom pie with beef-dripping crust and creamy mash. Other items are discreetly modernised, so prepare, too, for hot-smoked mackerel with marinated beetroot and baby

gem, before braised roe deer in red wine with truffled mash. The charcuterie-board starter featuring pork rillettes, ham hock terrine and chicken liver parfait with celeriac slaw, sourdough toast and pickles is 'utter perfection', according to one reporter. Finish in the heritage cookbook with steamed gingerbread pudding. Wines start at £13.
Chef/s: Rhian Cradock. **Open:** Tue to Sun L 12 to 2 (2.30 Sat, 4.30 Sun), Tue to Sat D 6 to 8.30. **Closed:** Mon, first week Jan. **Meals:** alc (main courses £8 to £18). Sun L £14 (1 course) to £22. **Details:** 38 seats. 16 seats outside. Parking.

▌Hexham
Bouchon Bistrot
Proper French cooking at gentle prices
Cooking score: 4
French | £27

4-6 Gilesgate, Hexham, NE46 3NJ
Tel no: (01434) 609943
www.bouchonbistrot.co.uk

With a medieval abbey and historic buildings, proximity to Hadrian's Wall and the local racecourse, Hexham is a popular tourist spot. So it's worth knowing about Gregory Bureau's Bouchon Bistrot if you are in the area. Locals (and visitors) firmly believe that Hexham has nothing to rival it, both for 'proper French cooking' and value for money. Service is affably French, and helpful, and while the menu recognises the 21st century – in the shape of red onion and goats' cheese clafoutis with herb salad or Parisian gnocchi with duck egg, parsnips and kale – its heart remains in bistro fare: for example, French onion soup, chicken liver parfait, loin of venison with choux farci, red cabbage and celeriac, and crispy duck confit with gratin dauphinois. Traditions mingle in desserts, too, as profiteroles au chocolate with vanilla ice cream are juxtaposed with crème brûlée or apple tarte Tatin. The (almost) all-French wine list starts at £14.95.
Chef/s: Mark Percival. **Open:** Mon to Sat L 12 to 2, D 6 to 9 (9.30 Thur to Sat). **Closed:** Sun, 25 and 26 Dec, bank hols. **Meals:** alc (main courses £12 to

Join us at thegoodfoodguide.co.uk

£20). Set L £14 (2 courses) to £15. Pre-theatre D £15 (2 courses) to £16. **Details:** 120 seats. Wheelchair access. Music.

LOCAL GEM

The Rat Inn

British | £24

Anick, Hexham, NE46 4LN
Tel no: (01434) 602814
www.theratinn.com

£5
OFF

There's no arguing with the pubby attributes of this one-time drovers' inn overlooking the Tyne Valley. Flagstone floors, open fires, cask ales and a splendid beer garden are all present and correct, alongside a menu of hearty, no-nonsense North Country pub grub. Craster kipper rillettes and pan haggerty keep it local, likewise game terrine with fig chutney, braised beef in Allendale ale and puds such as ginger sponge with Northumbrian ice cream. Wines from £15.95. No food Sun D and Mon.

Low Newton

LOCAL GEM

The Ship Inn

British | £25

Newton Square, Low Newton, NE66 3EL
Tel no: (01665) 576262
www.shipinnnewton.co.uk

The lawn out front of the Ship Inn stops at the beach as the North Sea stretches out beyond. With its unadulterated interior of stone and wood, and even an on-site micro-brewery, there's an integrity to this place that is reflected in the simple, locally inspired menus. Walkers on the coast path will appreciate ploughman's with local cheese or hand-picked crab sandwich, while in the evening the likes of fish pie and English onion tart hit the spot. In a nod to the 21st century, cards are now accepted, but the pub recommends you take cash – the signal can be 'unreliable'. Wines from £15.95. No food D Sun to Tue.

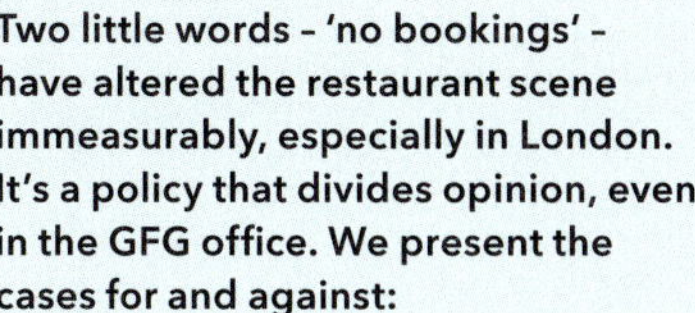

No Bookings

Two little words – 'no bookings' – have altered the restaurant scene immeasurably, especially in London. It's a policy that divides opinion, even in the GFG office. We present the cases for and against:

For...

It's spontaneous, catering for customers who can't commit to a booking, need to eat at odd times, or don't know when they're going to be seized by a need for Italian small plates.

It breaks down barriers. It doesn't matter who you are; if you wait long enough, you'll get fed. The atmosphere of triumph and relief among the recently-seated is palpable.

It's more flexible than it looks. The best front-of-house teams have been known to bend the rules for customers who are physically unable to perch on a bar stool, or stand for hours.

Against...

It's a time-sucker. You could learn the art of the perfect steamed bao bun, stacked burger or hand-pulled noodle in the time it takes to wait for one. Outside.

It's tense. Poorly-managed queues put everyone on edge. Spending 40 minutes on high alert for pushers-in, or straining to hear your name being called, sharpens the nerves rather than the appetite.

It's unpredictable. That work meeting, hot date or meal with the kids could go seamlessly, stressfully, or not at all. Who needs the jeopardy?

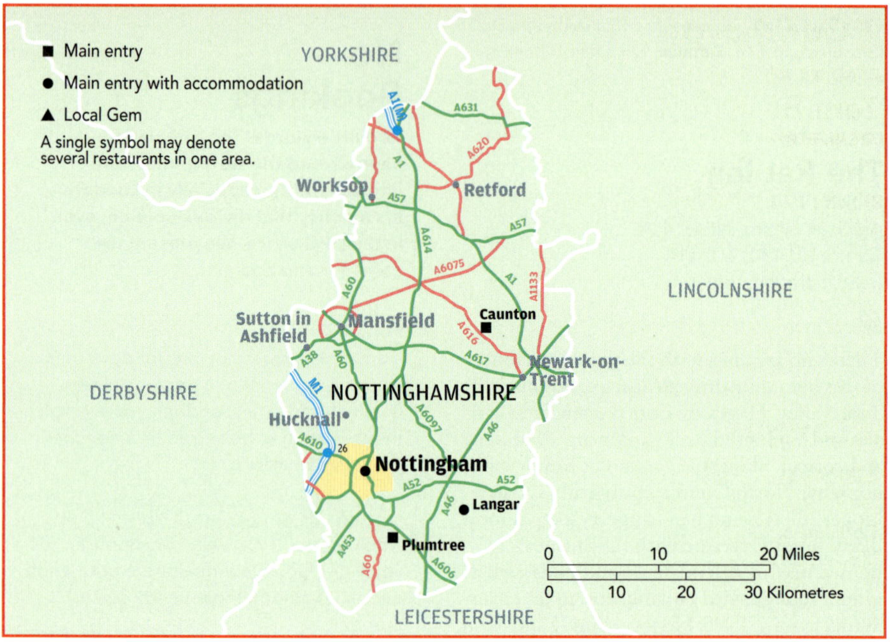

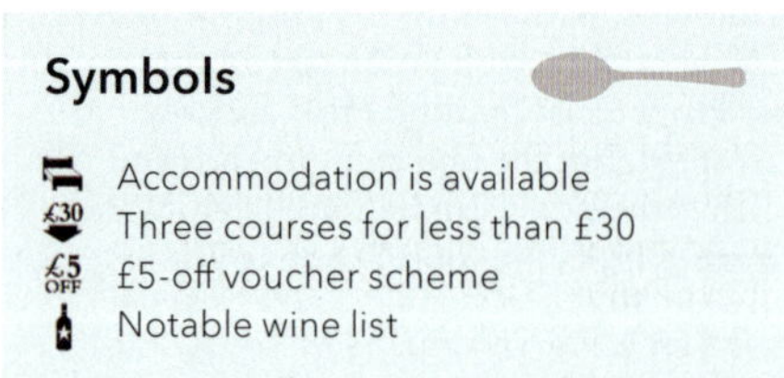

▋ Caunton
Caunton Beck

All-day treats in a rural hideaway
Cooking score: 2
Modern European | £25
Main Street, Caunton, NG23 6AB
Tel no: (01636) 636793
www.wigandmitre.com

'Never disappoints,' noted one fan who regularly makes a detour off the A1 to have breakfast at this well-liked all-day hideaway. Set in a pretty village close to the bubbling waters of Caunton Beck, it's all things to all people – café, pub, bistro, meeting house and everything in between, with beamed ceilings and open fires adding to the convivial, cottagey mood. The kitchen rolls along merrily, moving from sausage sarnies or oak-smoked salmon and scrambled eggs (with a glass of bubbly if you wish) to generous seasonal offerings such as confit Gressingham duck with candied mandarin and orange glaze, plaice meunière or locally reared beef fillet with a wild mushroom, mustard and tarragon fricassee. Nibbles and sandwiches fill any daytime gaps, while desserts might promise chilled lemon posset or hazelnut, rum and raisin semifreddo. Real ales add to the pubby vibe, and the affordably priced wine list has plenty of decent drinking from £14.95.
Chef/s: Andy Pickstop. **Open:** all week 8.30am to 10.30pm (10pm Sun). **Closed:** 25 Dec. **Meals:** alc (main courses £12 to £23). Set L and D £14 (2 courses) to £17. **Details:** 60 seats. 24 seats outside. Bar. Wheelchair access. Parking.

Symbols

Accommodation is available
Three courses for less than £30
£5-off voucher scheme
Notable wine list

Join us at thegoodfoodguide.co.uk

◼ Gunthorpe

READERS RECOMMEND

Tom Brown's Brasserie

Modern British

Trentside, Gunthorpe, NG14 7FB
Tel no: (0115) 9663642
www.tombrowns.co.uk

'The food was beautifully cooked and very pretty, and they have a particularly good selection of seafood dishes. Veggie options were interesting: I had grilled asparagus with quail's eggs as a starter; simple but delicious.'

◼ Langar

Langar Hall

Modern dining and idiosyncratic style

Cooking score: 4
Modern British | £39

Church Lane, Langar, NG13 9HG
Tel no: (01949) 860559
www.langarhall.com

The amber-fronted country house is surrounded by acres of gardens and mature parkland in the Vale of Belvoir. Decorated with idiosyncratic taste throughout, it's centred on a dining room in Georgian style with neo-classical columns and a candle-effect chandelier. Here, a modern British repertoire with strong southern European influence is the drill, with a shorter prix-fixe option mixable and matchable from the main carte. Crabmeat in both colours is partnered with pink grapefruit and avocado for a contemporary classic opener, or you might head towards chunky game terrine with cranberry and date chutney and sourdough toast. Local game shows up well in main courses, too, as also does lamb, which comes in various cuts with salt-baked turnip, mustard gnocchi and watercress, while brill hauled in from Cornwall appears with mussels and squid and a slab of potato terrine. A dessert spin on piña colada teams up rum-poached pineapple with coconut sorbet and lime granita. Wines start at £19.95.

Chef/s: Gary Booth and Ross Jeffery. **Open:** all week L 12 to 3, D 6 to 10. **Meals:** alc (main courses £14 to £27). Set L £19 (2 courses) to £24. Set D £25 (2 courses) to £30. Sun L £40. **Details:** 70 seats. 70 seats outside. Bar. Wheelchair access. Parking.

◼ Nottingham

Hart's

Professionally run and elegantly attired

Cooking score: 5
Modern British | £34

Standard Hill, Park Row, Nottingham,
NG1 6GN
Tel no: (0115) 9110666
www.hartsnottingham.co.uk

It may lack the patrician gloss of its classy 'country cousin' Hambleton Hall (see entry), but Tim Hart's Nottingham old-stager still knows how to put on the style – at prices that don't offend. It's the complete package – professionally run and elegantly attired with polished floors, partitioned booths, colourful abstract artwork and the bonus of boutique rooms in the hotel next door. The kitchen focuses on urbane food without palate-jangling gimmicks: salt cod croquettes are doused in parsley sauce, whole baby plaice is served with triple-cooked chips and there's local game pie with shortcrust pastry, too. It also takes on more ritzy ideas such as roast quail with lentils, chestnut and crispy quail's egg or line-caught pollack with spiced quinoa, pak choi and almonds before letting rip with fancy-pants desserts including poached Yorkshire rhubarb with Kaffir lime leaf pannacotta and pistachio brittle. Tim Hart's thoughtful wine list is stuffed with mouthwatering selections helpfully annotated for big spenders and everyday quaffers alike. Bottles from £21.50.

Chef/s: Daniel Burridge. **Open:** all week L 12 to 2, D 7 to 10.30 (9 Sun). **Closed:** 1 Jan. **Meals:** alc (main courses £15 to £25). Set L £16 (2 courses) to £19. Set D £24. Sun L £23. **Details:** 80 seats. Bar. Wheelchair access. Parking.

The Larder on Goosegate

Dependable city local with swagger
Cooking score: 2
Modern British | £26
16-22 Goosegate, Hockley, Nottingham,
NG1 1FE
Tel no: (0115) 9500111
www.thelarderongoosegate.co.uk

'Get a table by tall windows to watch the word go by in Hockley – Nottingham's boho quarter,' advises one reporter of this airy, mint-green restaurant, which occupies the first floor of a listed building that was once the first chemist shop of Nottingham lad Jesse Boot. Considered 'the best of its kind' in central Nottingham, the kitchen turns out some impressive modern dishes, notable for freshness of materials; fish options combine accurate timing with characterful flavouring in grilled mackerel with pickled turnip, forced rhubarb and ginger or a main course of wild Irish trout with laverbread and oatmeal cake, clams, bacon and sprouting broccoli. There's also pork loin with wild garlic, pickled pear and trotters on toast, flavourful cuts of steak (hanger, bavette, flat iron) with a choice of sauces and, to finish, treacle tart with ginger and brown-bread ice cream or excellent British cheeses. French house (£15.95) opens the wine list and rounds off with a slate of interesting beers, mainly from Nottingham. **Chef/s:** David Sneddon. **Open:** Thur to Sat L 12 to 2.30, Tue to Sat D 6 to 10. **Closed:** Sun, Mon. **Meals:** alc (main courses £13 to £22). Set L and D £14 (2 courses) to £16. **Details:** 65 seats. Music.

Please send us your feedback

To register your opinion about any restaurant listed in this guide, or a new restaurant that you wish to bring to our attention, please visit the web address at the bottom of the page. Your feedback informs the content of the book and will be used to compile next year's reviews.

Restaurant Sat Bains

An extraordinary personal endeavour
Cooking score: 9
Modern British | £85
Lenton Lane, Nottingham, NG7 2SA
Tel no: (0115) 9866566
www.restaurantsatbains.com

It's an unusual location – as we point out every year – a restaurant-with-rooms in a sylvan setting close to the mighty A52 flyover. Whether you pitch up at the chef's table, kitchen table, kitchen bench or book into the pair of monochromatic dining rooms, this place hits exactly the right note. Sat Bains isn't one to stand still, his latest on-site venture is a separate development kitchen-cum-restaurant – the accessory *du jour* of all premierleague chefs – and his free-spirited culinary intelligence continues in full flow, creating extraordinary food with strong, direct flavours and intelligently worked ideas. The bar is set high from the get-go: note the tiny but powerful horseradish ice cream sandwich accompanying an intense lovage soup that opened a summer meal. And, across the board, the search for exquisitely amalgamated, dazzling flavours is a recurring theme: in the umami hit teased out of a single scallop draped with ponzu jelly and served atop slivers of pig's trotter; in the sweetness of instantly moreish baked potato given a predictable partner, cream cheese, but also seaweed, shavings of red onion and English caviar; and a delicate construction of lamb's sweetbreads, broad beans (whole, purée, leafy shoots) set on a smear of miso. The menus are laid out in tasting format (7 or 10 courses), which means that meatiness intensifies as you proceed towards, say, a tender smoked breast of duck with feta, carrot ketchup, three varieties of pressed melon and mint jelly dotted around the plate. Finally, a lime lollipop crisply coated with multi-coloured sprinkles of aniseed and fennel and a nugget of intense miso fudge are curtain-raisers for dessert: perhaps a mini ice cream cone layered with cherry beer and sprouted wheat ice creams and topped with puffed grains, and a bar of aerated milk chocolate infused with tobacco, giving rich malted whisky notes. And it would be hard to conceive of a more comprehensive job being done in the wine department, where masterful wine service is on hand to guide diners through the impressively modern wine list, even if it is just matching a series of glasses to your meal. Bottles from £32.-

Chef/s: Sat Bains and John Freeman. **Open:** Tue to Sat L 12 to 1.30, D 6.30 to 9 (6 to 9.45 Fri and Sat). **Closed:** Sun, Mon, 2 weeks Dec to Jan, 1 week spring, 2 weeks Aug. **Meals:** Tasting menu £85 (7 courses) to £95 (10 courses). **Details:** 42 seats. V menu. Bar. Music. Parking. Children over 8 yrs only.

LOCAL GEM

Delilah

Modern European | £20
12 Victoria Street, Nottingham, NG1 2EX
Tel no: (0115) 9484461
www.delilahfinefoods.co.uk

Not only an excellent deli, but also an all-day eatery, Delilah is set in a tasteful listed bank conversion with tables in among the food displays, a central counter with bar-stools and a quieter mezzanine. Customers are a loyal bunch, drawn back time and time again to share platters of cheese, charcuterie or antipasti, or tuck into the likes of fregola pasta and haloumi salad or confit duck leg with sautéed potatoes and red cabbage. Handy for breakfast and afternoon tea, too. Wines from £13.99. Open all week.

Local Gem

Local Gems are the perfect neighbourhood venues, delivering good, freshly cooked food at great value for money.

Plumtree

Perkins

Good-value family favourite
Cooking score: 2
Modern British | £35
Station House, Station Road, Plumtree, NG12 5NA
Tel no: (0115) 9373695
www.perkinsrestaurant.co.uk

With rusty tracks outside and views of (very occasional) 'test trains' chugging past, there's still something rather nostalgic about this converted Victorian railway station – although the building has been rolling along as a family-owned restaurant since 1982. Current incumbents Jon and David Perkins have built a smokehouse, planted a herb garden and brightened up the conservatory-style dining room with pine furniture, warm lighting and a copper-topped bar. The kitchen is on top form, too, with 'updated presentation' and a raft of creative dishes reflecting the owners' rustic-meets-modern approach: roast Belvoir wood pigeon is served with red cabbage, pear and walnut salad; trimmed sirloin of beef comes with duck-fat chips, pea and horseradish purée; pot-roast pheasant keeps company with braised lentils, curly kale and parsnip crisps. Visitors have also left 'refreshed and content' after sampling excellent-value set lunches of spiced mackerel, venison rissoles and sticky bourbon pudding. Steak nights, Saturday breakfasts, afternoon teas and agreeably priced wines (from £17.25) complete a family-friendly package.

Chef/s: Sarah Newham. **Open:** all week L 12 to 2 (3 Sun), Mon to Sat D 6 to 10. **Closed:** 1 Jan. **Meals:** alc (main courses £15 to £23). Set L £14 (2 courses) to £17. Set D £17 (2 courses) to £19. Sun L £17 (2 courses) to £20. **Details:** 61 seats. 20 seats outside. Wheelchair access. Music. Parking.

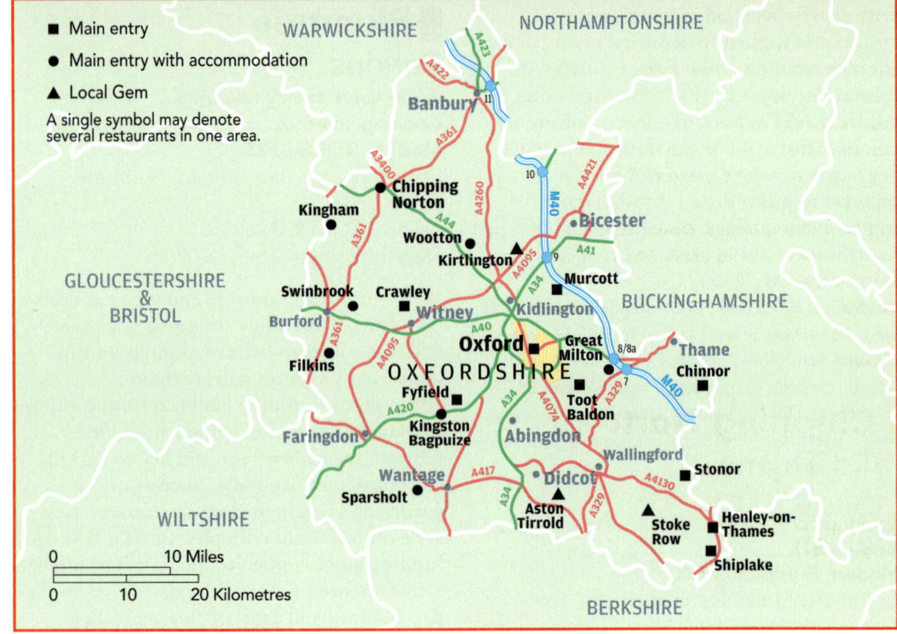

■ Aston Tirrold

LOCAL GEM

The Sweet Olive

Anglo-French | £35
Baker Street, Aston Tirrold, OX11 9DD
Tel no: (01235) 851272
www.sweet-olive.com

An old-fashioned pub with stone floors, a roaring fire in winter and a lovely garden in summer, feels reassuringly English to a T. But check the blackboard and find bourgeois French classics in among the British dishes, courtesy of the pub's two French owners. Local pheasant comes with a creamy Cognac and pepper sauce, a panaché of fish with a white wine sauce and sun-dried tomato and saffron risotto, but it's back to home turf for treacle sponge and custard. The wine list (from £19.95) is strongest in France (obvs). Closed Sun D and all Wed.

■ Chinnor

The Sir Charles Napier

Eccentric Chiltern charmer
Cooking score: 3
Modern British | £45
Sprigg's Alley, Chinnor, OX39 4BX
Tel no: (01494) 483011
www.sircharlesnapier.co.uk

This pretty flint-built pub, set in what is barely more than a hamlet, has a beautiful garden, an extensive, pagoda-covered terrace with garden views, plus an impressive sculpture collection, both inside and out. Inside is fresh and light, with charmingly mismatched furniture and original art on the walls. Expect ambitious, modern cooking that doesn't always take the most obvious route flavour-wise. After excellent breads (sweet onion brioche and good brown sourdough), a starter of asparagus with a crispy egg and a faultless hollandaise topped with toasted pine nuts hit the spot for one diner, while a main course of lamb rump with crispy belly,

Parmesan polenta, cucumber and dill showcased 'excellent ingredients'. Occasionally things get out of balance: a strawberry mille-feuille with marshmallow and 'very salt' caramel custard had been split into its constituent parts aand was 'trying to be too clever' for one reporter. A decent wine list kicks off at £19.50.
Chef/s: Anthony Skeats. **Open:** Tue to Sun L 12 to 2.30 (3.30 Sun), Tue to Sat D 7 to 10. **Closed:** Mon, first week Jan. **Meals:** alc (main courses £22 to £30). Set L and D Tue to Fri £20 (2 courses). **Details:** 70 seats. 70 seats outside. V menu. Bar. Music. Parking. Children over 6 yrs only at D.

■ Chipping Norton
Wild Thyme

Sharply defined seasonal flavours
Cooking score: 3
Modern British | £35
10 New Street, Chipping Norton, OX7 5LJ
Tel no: (01608) 645060
www.wildthymerestaurant.co.uk

Just off the main thoroughfare in Chipping Norton, Nick and Sally Pullen's restaurant-with-rooms is a cosy little number with a light, shabby-chic interior: think twinkly chandeliers, bare floorboards and distressed white furniture, with original artwork on the pale walls and a pretty courtyard garden at the rear. Nick creates dishes of some complexity using ingredients mostly drawn from local suppliers. He's an inventive cook, but never loses touch of what works well together, so expect tried-and-tested combinations, say bresaola with micro rocket, tomorosso, Parmesan, lemon juice and olive oil or free-range chicken breast and cider vinegar, leg and herb ravioli, summer greens, pancetta, truffled cauliflower, bobby beans, chanterelles, Madeira and cream. These are big-hearted, generous dishes that could leave you struggling to fit in dessert – but it's worth pushing on with the likes of a vanilla-poached pear filled with ginger ice cream, surrounded by creamy rice pudding and topped with a ribbon of peanut brittle. Wines from £15.

Chef/s: Nicholas Pullen. **Open:** Tue to Sat L 12 to 2, D 7 to 9. **Closed:** Sun, Mon. **Meals:** alc (main courses £14 to £25). Set L £18 (2 courses) to £23. **Details:** 35 seats. 10 seats outside.

■ Crawley
★ TOP 50 PUB ★

NEW ENTRY
The Lamb Inn

Refurbished pub staying true to its roots
Cooking score: 4
Modern British | £30
Steep Hill, Crawley, OX29 9TW
Tel no: (01993) 708792
www.lambcrawley.co.uk
£5 OFF

'Good cooking from a chef with a great track record,' noted a well-travelled reporter who remembers Matt Weedon's cooking at Fallowfields, Oxfordshire, and at Glenapp Castle, Scotland (see entries). Now Weedon and his wife Rachel have taken over this tastefully refurbished old pub: stone walled and low-beamed with 'little nooks scattered around' and smart, carpeted dining room. A tranche of venison liver from the specials menu, nicely seared and juicy, served on a slice of brioche with buttery girolles and girolle purée with a sunny-side-up pheasant egg, and an inspired pairing of fillet of bream on brioche toast, its plate acting as a lid for a bowl of light, frothy and creamy fish soup, show serious intent and quality produce. Worth trying, too, is seared fillet of hake piled up with wild mushrooms, crayfish tails, samphire, sprouting broccoli, mushroom purée and an almost soup-like cep sauce 'with real depth', and lemon tart with cherry purée and ripple ice cream. Wines from £17.50.
Chef/s: Matt Weedon. **Open:** Tue to Sun L 12 to 2 (2.30 Fri and Sat, 12.30 to 3.30 Sun), Tue to Sat D 6.30 to 9 (9.30 Fri and Sat). **Closed:** Mon. **Meals:** alc (main courses £17 to £23). Sun L £27. **Details:** 50 seats. 40 seats outside. V menu. Bar. Music. Parking.

Filkins

The Five Alls

Confident, classy cooking in a Cotswolds inn
Cooking score: 4
Modern British | £29
Filkins, GL7 3JQ
Tel no: (01367) 860875
www.thefiveallsfilkins.co.uk

£5 OFF

London émigrés Sebastian and Lana Snow got a taste of the Cotswold 'good life' while running the Swan at Southrop, and now they're riding high at this renovated inn-with-rooms on the Gloucesterhire/Oxfordshire border. Tweeds, Barbours and green wellies fit right in among the Five Alls' flagstone floors, auction-room furniture, chandeliers and modern artwork – but you can still enjoy a pint of Brakspear's or Sideburn cider in the bar. Sebastian's smart cooking is just the ticket, sophisticated with grown-up metropolitan flavours – no wonder readers tell us they lap up plates of beef tagliata with 'roasties', open ravioli of Loch Duart salmon with spinach and sorrel sauce or blackened cod with glass noodles, pak choi and ginger. Charcuterie boards, superfood salads and well-aged steaks appear right on cue, while desserts cover all bases from baked Alaska and rhubarb trifle to blood-orange and Campari jelly with stem ginger ice cream. Well-chosen global wines start at £17.95, and you can BYO on Monday nights (£5 corkage).
Chef/s: Sebastian Snow and Piotr Skoczew. **Open:** all week L 12 to 3, Mon to Sat D 6 to 9.30 (10 Fri and Sat). **Closed:** 25 Dec. **Meals:** alc (main courses £13 to £23). Set L and D £16 (2 courses) to £21. Sun L £23. **Details:** 100 seats. 50 seats outside. Bar. Music. Parking.

Fyfield

The White Hart

Historic hostelry in capable hands
Cooking score: 3
Modern British | £34
Main Road, Fyfield, OX13 5LW
Tel no: (01865) 390585
www.whitehart-fyfield.com

£5 OFF

Formerly owned by St John's College in Oxford, this respectfully restored 15th-century chantry house remains a favourite with the city's cognoscenti. The White Hart still boasts creaking doors, inglenooks, a soaring great hall and a minstrels' gallery, but Kay and Mark Chandler have also put this covetable slice of ecclesiastical heritage firmly on the gastronomic map. Mark has forged dependable links with the local food network, and leavens its menus with pickings from the inn's kitchen garden – as in beetroot-cured salmon with smoked salmon mousse, root vegetable slaw and thyme crisps, or slow-roast belly of Kelmscott pork with apples, carrots, celeriac purée and cider jus. Boards of mezze, seafood and antipasti are perfect for sharing, the selection of British regional cheeses is worth investigation, and desserts could include raspberry soufflé with lemon drizzle cake and condensed-milk ice cream. A list of fairly priced wines starts at £17.50.
Chef/s: Mark Chandler. **Open:** Tue to Sun L 12 to 2.30 (3.30 Sun), Tue to Sat D 6.45 to 9.30. **Closed:** Mon. **Meals:** alc (main courses £15 to £24). Set L £17 (2 courses) to £20. Sun L £23 (2 courses) to £26. **Details:** 60 seats. 50 seats outside. Music. Parking.

Great Milton

★ TOP 50 ★

Le Manoir aux Quat'Saisons

Subtle, powerful, modern French gastronomy
Cooking score: 8
Modern French | £143
Church Road, Great Milton, OX44 7PD
Tel no: (01844) 278881
www.manoir.com

The genial M. Blanc sails sedately into a fourth decade at the Manoir, one of the reference points of the most recent generation of British dining out. Where once the place stood at the forefront of nouvelle cuisine, it now trades in a more intricately worked, less programmatic and more subtly powerful modern French style, supplied as always by the glasshouses and walled garden in which guests may safely roam. The monthly-changing seasonal menus are still the mainstay, with a seven-course Découverte for the splashers. A characteristic effect is of tremendous intensity conjured from simple material and technical means: goats' cheese agnolotti with a touch of honey, black olives, artichoke and sea kale in a fine tomato essence. Fish is splendidly eloquent of itself, as when crisp-coated sea bass arrives with a plump langoustine and smoked butter mash in star anise jus. The *février* menu that proceeded from grilled mackerel with compressed apple in soy, honey, ginger and lime to a poached egg with watercress purée, Jabugo ham and hazelnuts, and then braised Jacob's Ladder of beef with pickled mushrooms and cinnamon mash, sent one customer away not just satisfied but awestruck. On the debit side, there can occasionally be a slight lack of focus to a dish, with a dessert such as the famous gariguette strawberries with mint jelly, marshmallow and biscuit crumbs retreating into the pleasant, rather than ascending to the ambrosial. There are still grouses about the service tone, with staff either stuck on 'how are we today?' mode, or else cracking on with indecent haste, in jarring defiance of the overall ambience. The magnificent wine list doesn't scruple to include a few listings from the likes of Hongrie, Liban and Arménie. Prices open at £43.

Chef/s: Raymond Blanc. **Open:** all week L 11.45 to 2.15, D 6.45 to 9.30. **Meals:** alc (main courses £42 to £54). Set L £82 (5 courses). Set D £127 (7 courses) to £159. **Details:** 90 seats. V menu. Bar. Wheelchair access. Parking.

Henley-on-Thames
Shaun Dickens at the Boathouse

Highly detailed cooking by the river
Cooking score: 3
Modern British | £40
Station Road, Henley-on-Thames, RG9 1AZ
Tel no: (01491) 577937
www.shaundickens.co.uk

'Smart restaurant, smart service and very smart food in a splendid position on the Thames riverside' is one verdict on Shaun Dickens' 'boathouse' eatery with its sought-after raised deck overlooking the water. Following some post-flood upheavals in 2014, the owners are now glad to be back on terra firma – and it's given them the chance to do some interior refurbishment too. On the food front, highly detailed, technically sound cooking is still the deal, with short menus promising the likes of sweet-and-sour torched salmon, celeriac and pickled mustard ahead of duck with confit chicory, watercress, grapefruit and potato terrine or roast lamb belly with kidney, salsify and sea vegetables. Fancy desserts bring yuzu sorbet with meringue, lime and mascarpone or a 'lovely confection' of pear financier with almond ice cream and lemon parfait. Despite the odd gripe about 'fussy' cooking, this is a restaurant 'worth extolling' – especially as it proffers some 'very complementary' food-matching wines from £21.

Chef/s: Shaun Dickens. **Open:** Wed to Sun L 12 to 2.30, D 7 to 9.30. **Closed:** Mon, Tue, 25 and 26 Dec. **Meals:** alc (main courses £19 to £24). Set L £22 (2 courses) to £26. Sun L £26. **Details:** 46 seats. 26 seats outside. V menu. Bar. Wheelchair access. Music.

Kingham

★ TOP 50 PUB ★

The Kingham Plough

A townie's rural dream
Cooking score: 4
Modern British | £35
The Green, Kingham, OX7 6YD
Tel no: (01608) 658327
www.thekinghamplough.co.uk

Despite their reputation for food, Miles and Emily Lampson (née Watkins) strive to maintain the pubbiness of their Cotswold-stone inn overlooking the village green. Drinkers and diners mingle in the spacious interior, where a large, fire-warmed bar and vaulted dining room – with exposed stone, beams, pale neutral colours and well-spaced tables – create a light, welcoming look. Trouble is taken over sourcing quality raw materials – note locally shot game, the local cheeses – and the kitchen distinguishes itself with enthusiasm and honest effort, which stretches to first-class bar snacks (hand-raised pork pie, homemade venison salami) as well as in-house-produced ice creams. The restaurant menu centres on appetising combinations: caramelised onion, sage and pearl barley risotto with Roger Crudge's Burford cheese, while purple sprouting broccoli and thyme-roasted carrots accompany loin and steamed pudding of local hogget. Among desserts, blood-orange trifle with blood-orange and sherry cream and honeycomb has impressed. Wines from £22.

Chef/s: Emily Watkins. **Open:** all week L 12 to 2 (2.30 Sat, 3 Sun), Mon to Sat D 6.30 to 9. **Meals:** alc (main courses £16 to £22). **Details:** 70 seats. V menu. Parking.

The Wild Rabbit

Classy pub food in stunning surroundings
Cooking score: 3
British | £35
Church Street, Kingham, OX7 6YA
Tel no: (01608) 658389
www.thewildrabbit.co.uk

No expense has been spared on the renovation and extension of the handsome Cotswold stone building: the bar is traditional, with exposed stonework and a magnificent open-sided fireplace, while the main dining area has meat and salamis hanging from iron hooks, a venerable old dresser bearing pewter plates, and a shiny stone floor. A glass-sided fire set in the outside wall heats the dining area and terrace simultaneously. The pub hails from the Daylesford Organics stable so ingredients are 'superb', and new chef Anthony Parkin is going great guns in the kitchen, continuing the classy but relaxed modern British cooking that first put this place on the map. Recent highlights have included a slow-cooked hen's egg with peas, ham hock and an 'intense, verdant' pea soup; and grilled Daylesford chicken breast with herby pearl barley, charred onions and fresh, tender broad beans. A lemon cream and yoghurt sorbet with a black pepper sugar crisp was an equally assured dessert. Wines from £17.50.

Chef/s: Anthony Parkin. **Open:** Tue to Sun L 12 to 2.30 (3 Sun), Tue to Sat D 7 to 9. **Closed:** Mon. **Meals:** alc (main courses £17 to £28). **Details:** 46 seats. 40 seats outside. Bar. Wheelchair access. Music. Parking.

Join us at thegoodfoodguide.co.uk

◼ Kingston Bagpuize
Fallowfields

Top-notch home-grown delights
Cooking score: 5
Modern British | £57
Faringdon Road, Kingston Bagpuize,
OX13 5BH
Tel no: (01865) 820416
www.fallowfields.com

The grounds of this spick-and-span country house hotel include not only a kitchen garden but also a farm providing everything from quails' eggs to beef and pork. Sous-chef Mark Potts has stepped up to replace Matt Weedon at the stoves, and it appears to be a smooth transition: Potts worked under Weedon for years, both here and at Lords of the Manor in Gloucestershire (see entry). The hotel's pale, fresh interior blends tradition and modernity, and the same could be said of Potts' cooking, which is fresh, light and produce-driven. Rabbit leg cannelloni with turnip and a dandelion and burdock dressing is a typical starter, while mains range from lamb rump and breast with artichoke, goats' curd and monk's beard to Cornish cod with cauliflower, glazed cheek and Muscat grapes. To finish, maybe prune and Armagnac soufflé with Earl Grey tea mousse and lavender ice cream. The commitment to sourcing shines through on the wine list, which includes organic, biodynamic, vegan and carbon neutral options. Bottles start at £22.
Chef/s: Mark Potts. **Open:** all week L 12 to 2, D 6.30 to 9.30 (9 Sun). **Meals:** alc (main courses £22 to £28). Set L £30 (2 courses) to £35. Sun L £35. Tasting menu £59. **Details:** 40 seats. 20 seats outside. V menu. Bar. Wheelchair access. Music. Parking.

Visit us online

To find out more about
The Good Food Guide, please
visit thegoodfoodguide.co.uk

◼ Kirtlington

LOCAL GEM
The Oxford Arms

Modern British | £30
Troy Lane, Kirtlington, OX5 3HA
Tel no: (01869) 350208
www.oxford-arms.co.uk

£5 OFF

Hook Norton ales, open fires, leather sofas, a pretty patio and kitchen garden – the stone-built Oxford Arms seems to have it all. This gentrified 19th-century village hostelry also does a good line in modern pub food, sourcing prime seasonal ingredients from near and far – think potted shrimps, venison burgers with triple-cooked chips, or chocolate and spiced rum mousse with blueberries, plus promising daily specials such as a warm salad of wood pigeon, Kelmscott bacon and Ramsay black pudding. Wines (from £17) are a cut above the local pub norm. No food Sun D.

◼ Murcott

★ TOP 50 PUB ★
The Nut Tree Inn

Pubby vitality and cooking with conviction
Cooking score: 5
Modern European | £39
Main Street, Murcott, OX5 2RE
Tel no: (01865) 331253
www.nuttreeinn.co.uk

With its whitewash and thatch, the Nut Tree looks like a classic country pub, although the impressive kitchen garden at the rear is a hint that it's more than just a good spot for a pint. The interior delivers exposed stonework and low beams aplenty, plus a blazing fire in the wood-burner: settle on a chesterfield for a pre-dinner drink, then move through to the dining area – a dimly lit 'romantic setting' overseen by 'excellent staff'. Expect a fair number of bells and whistles with your meal: homemade bread, a truffled shellfish bisque amuse and a 'stunning' pre-dessert of an egg shell filled with caramel and milk chocolate mousse have all been praised. The cooking style is broadly, but not rigidly British, one where Cornish lobster might be teamed with ratte potatoes, crème fraîche and a red pepper dressing or a main course of Loomswood duck 'Marco Polo' comes with pak choi, sweet-and-sour rhubarb and turnip (and offering 'flavours that sing') served with a 'delectable' smoked pomme purée. A 'perfect' pannacotta with fresh and cooked strawberries, strawberry sorbet and meringue proved a sassy spin on Eton mess. Wines from £24.

Chef/s: Michael and Mary North. **Open:** Tue to Sun L 12 to 2.30 (3 Sun), Tue to Sat D 7 to 9. **Closed:** Mon, 27 Dec to 3 Jan. **Meals:** alc (main courses £18 to £33). Set L and D £18 (2 courses). Tasting menu £55 (7 courses). **Details:** 70 seats. 30 seats outside. V menu. Bar. Music. Parking.

Oxford

Branca

Gregarious all-day Italian
Cooking score: 1
Italian | £25
111 Walton Street, Oxford, OX2 6AJ
Tel no: (01865) 556111
www.branca.co.uk

'A cheering place to be – on a cold Sunday night when all other Oxford cafés we surveyed were deserted, it was busy and welcoming', was how one visitor summed up this good-natured all-day Italian eatery. The unfussy mood is matched by competitive prices and you can get a taste of things to come from the cicchetti (small plates of, say, king prawns or salt cod crocchette) that kick-start proceedings here. Pasta and pizza are first class, while main-course dishes run to char-grilled sea bream, 28-day dry-aged ribeye, and specials such as 'top-class' guinea fowl suprême. Wines from £17.45.

Chef/s: E Blandes. **Open:** Mon to Fri 12 to 11. Sat and Sun 10am to 11pm. **Meals:** alc (main courses £10 to £23). Set L and D £14. **Details:** 110 seats. 75 seats outside. Bar. Wheelchair access. Music.

Cherwell Boathouse

Idyllic riverside favourite
Cooking score: 2
Modern British | £32
50 Bardwell Road, Oxford, OX2 6ST
Tel no: (01865) 552746
www.cherwellboathouse.co.uk

Spirit-lifting recreation and stonkingly fine wines beckon at this enchanting Oxford institution – a working Victorian boathouse down by the banks of the Cherwell, with punts for hire and a gorgeous decked terrace that comes into its own on balmy days. Bold English and French accents dominate the menu, as the kitchen glides its way through seasonal ideas such as confit and seared quail with textures of beetroot and vegetable crisps, herb-crusted black bream with a casserole of Puy lentils and Brixham cuttlefish or classic braised shoulder of Oxfordshire lamb with garlic, anchovy and dauphinois potatoes. After that, drift further afield with something like lemongrass and coconut rice pudding or mixed fruit tempura. Owner Anthony Verdin is a wine specialist who has accrued a fabulous list over the years, assembling his treasures by grape variety and bringing together some of the best stuff from great growers worldwide: France is the main player, but there are equally compelling selections from elsewhere. Mark-ups are extremely kind, with selections from the 'shortlist' opening at just £14.75 (£4.50 a glass).

Chef/s: Nick Welford. **Open:** all week L 12 to 2 (2.30 Sat and Sun), D 6 to 9.30. **Closed:** 24 to 30 Dec. **Meals:** alc (main courses £17 to £24). Set L £19 (2 courses) to £25. Set D £22 (2 courses) to £28. **Details:** 65 seats. 45 seats outside. Bar. Wheelchair access. Music. Parking.

Gee's

Oxford landmark with a flavour of the Med
Cooking score: 2
Modern European | £30
61 Banbury Road, Oxford, OX2 6PE
Tel no: (01865) 553540
www.gees-restaurant.co.uk

This listed Victorian glasshouse has come a long way since its days as a floristry business. Now an Oxford culinary landmark – it's been feeding the city for more than 30 years – it is the very model of a cool modern eatery. The kitchen's approach is to combine seasonal British produce with Mediterranean-style cooking in a relatively simple manner. Anchovy, fennel and ricotta pizzetta, various steaks with a choice of béarnaise or balsamic black pepper butter, and Gee's burger with tomato relish and chips are at the heart of the repertoire of modern brasserie dishes, while seasonal treats take in the likes of crab with chilli and dill risotto, rainbow trout with Jersey Royals and monk's beard, and grilled guinea fowl with artichokes and asparagus. If you still have room, round off with a helping of vanilla pannacotta with poached rhubarb. Wines from £19.
Chef/s: Jamie King. **Open:** all week 10am to 10.30pm. **Meals:** alc (main courses £14 to £26). Set L £14 (2 courses) to £17. **Details:** 80 seats. 40 seats outside. Bar. Wheelchair access. Music.

The Magdalen Arms

Big flavours from home and abroad
Cooking score: 2
Modern British | £29
243 Iffley Road, Oxford, OX4 1SJ
Tel no: (01865) 243159
www.magdalenarms.com

The name may be pure Oxford, but there's something decidedly cosmopolitan about this rebooted Victorian boozer on the Iffley Road. Bare floorboards, auction-room furniture and real ales in the front bar tick all the necessary boxes, while the open kitchen delivers big flavours from home and abroad. Spanish tapas

Natural & orange wine

What could be more natural than fermented grape juice? For opponents of mass-produced wines the answer, it seems, is 'quite a lot'. While there's no legal definition of natural wine, its supporters generally agree it must be made from hand-picked grapes grown with minimal intervention, that only wild yeasts are used and that little or no sulphur is added.

The resulting wines can smell and taste funky, with wide variations from bottle to bottle, so it makes sense to try them by the glass. In London, you'll find a huge selection at Terroirs and its sister restaurants Brawn and Soif. Drake's of Ripley in Surrey sells the minimal-intervention Jakot Tocai Friulano from maverick producers Radikon.

At 40 Maltby Street, Bermondsey, the all-natural list includes orange wines. These are made from white varieties, using juice that has been left in contact with the grape skins, in the style of a red wine. This gives an orange hue, hence the name. Some are made in kvevri (amphorae-like clay pots); look for Shavkapito, a Pheasant Tears wine available at Terroirs, which is made according to ancient Georgian traditions.

plates, Provençal fish soup with rouille, pork tortellini in brodo and tagliatelle nero with cuttlefish, mussels and chilli share the billing with patriotic standbys such as beer-battered hake, roast pork loin with Savoy cabbage, turnips and bacon or salt lamb shank with caper sauce, new potatoes and curly kale. Trencherman servings of cassoulet, Hereford beef rib or harissa chicken with breakfast radishes and chips are designed for sharing, while puds cover everything from lemon meringue pie to hot chocolate fondant with salted-caramel ice cream – depending on the day's menu. The wine list opens with vins de pays at £10.30 a 500ml carafe.
Chef/s: Tony Abarno. **Open:** Tue to Sun L 12 to 2.30 (3 Sun), all week D 6 to 10 (9 Sun). **Closed:** 24 to 26 Dec. **Meals:** alc (main courses £9 to £28). **Details:** 200 seats. 100 seats outside. Bar. Wheelchair access. Music.

My Sichuan

Lip-numbing Szechuan adventure
Cooking score: 3
Chinese | £20
The Old School, Gloucester Green, Oxford, OX1 2DA
Tel no: (01865) 236899
www.mysichuan.co.uk

A Grade II-listed Victorian schoolhouse is the spacious setting for what could well be the UK's largest Szechuanese restaurant. Its pilastered dark wood interior, with a sitting area in red plush, is the unlikely context for the savoury spice and fire of the southwestern Chinese specialities boldly illustrated on the bilingual menu. The level of authenticity extends to fried frog legs with Szechuan greens, braised duck tongues in black bean sauce, shredded hot tripe, and many tofu dishes, including the hearty fish stew with tofu pudding. There is no stinting on chilli or Szechuan peppercorns for the razor-sharp cutting edge associated with this fiery regional cuisine, and unusually a real effort has been made at dessert stage, with mashed taro in blueberry sauce or sweet tofu with almonds. 'If

we lived within easy reach,' sighed a reporter, 'we would go there very often.' My Sichuan prefers not to return our questionnaire, so check the website for further details.
Chef/s: Jian Juzhou. **Open:** all week 12 to 11 (12 to 12 Fri and Sat). **Closed:** 25 Dec. **Meals:** alc (main courses £7 to £19). **Details:** 260 seats.

Oli's Thai

Tiny Thai in high demand
Cooking score: 3
Thai | £18
38 Magdalen Road, Oxford, OX4 1RB
Tel no: (01865) 790223
www.olisthai.com

'Efficient, chatty, bend-over-backwards service doesn't show a flicker of the too-cool-for-school mentality that a waiting list and shambolically stripped back room might command', noted one who waited three months for a 7pm table on a Tuesday night in May. While the 20-seater 'at the wrong end of Cowley Road' has unforgiving wood on metal seating, plain white walls, orange-laminate bar and just eight bottles on the wine list, it's the food that deserves to be shouted about. On a commendably short and very reasonably priced menu there could be chunky green papaya salad, its searing heat balanced by an unusually sweet lime dressing and a neat powder of chopped peanuts; 'wizard' pink-sliced beef salad, served on fried courgettes, chilli and coriander, all bathed in a fiery pepper dressing; and Thai chicken curry of just-cooked breast meat with plenty of fresh veg in a thin but flavour-packed sauce – 'identical to the best, roadside cooked stuff I've had in Thailand'.
Chef/s: Rufus and Ladd Thurston. **Open:** Wed to Sat L 12 to 2, Tue to Sat D 5 to 9. **Closed:** Sun, Mon. **Meals:** alc (main courses £8 to £12). **Details:** 20 seats. Children at L only.

Join us at thegoodfoodguide.co.uk

The Rickety Press

Reborn Jericho boozer
Cooking score: 1
Modern British | £25
67 Cranham Street, Oxford, OX2 6DE
Tel no: (01865) 424581
www.therricketypress.com

A loyal servant of town and gown for many a year, this revitalised Jericho boozer still delivers the goods for the local drinking fraternity, while satisfying the foodie brigade with its on-trend monthly menu. Head to the conservatory-style dining room if you fancy a 'small plate' of wild mushroom, mozzarella and truffle arancini or a 'big plate' of Kelmscott Gloucester sausages with smoked mash and pickled red cabbage. Charcuterie platters, fashionable salads, dry-aged steaks and assorted burger riffs also figure prominently, while dessert might be steamed ginger and lemon pudding with custard. Around 20 wines start at £19.
Chef/s: Andrew Holland. **Open:** all week L 12 to 2.30 (3 Sun), D 6 to 9.30 (10 Fri and Sat). **Closed:** 25 and 26 Dec. **Meals:** alc (main courses £9 to £22). Sun L £14. **Details:** 110 seats. Bar. Music.

Edamame

Japanese | £18
15 Holywell Street, Oxford, OX1 3SA
Tel no: (01865) 246916
www.edamame.co.uk

Camped opposite New College, this funky Japanese canteen serves easy-priced authentic street food to hordes of students, tourists and locals who seldom baulk at its queues, no-bookings policy, cramped seating or eccentric opening hours. Lunch brings chicken kararage, pork tonkatsu, salmon teriyaki, ramen noodles in soup and other down-home classics, Thursday evening sees a sparkling fresh sushi buffet, and there are extended tapas-style suppers on Friday and Saturday nights (think octopus 'pancake balls' with

seaweed powder). Drink ice-cold Asahi beer, saké or wine (£3 a glass). Open Wed to Sun L (cash only), Thur to Sat D.

Turl Street Kitchen

Modern British | £22
16-17 Turl Street, Oxford, OX1 3DH
Tel no: (01865) 264171
www.turlstreetkitchen.co.uk

Profits from this relaxed, gently trendy eatery help power a charity situated in the same premises – a charming Georgian corner building with décor and furniture as 'plain and straightforward' as the food. 'Fresh, local, seasonal' is its mantra, the menu driven by local produce and changing daily. Wye Valley smoked salmon with duck egg, watercress and sweet mustard dressing or Cotswold pheasant with braised leg, celeriac purée, greens, bacon and cider, and rhubarb and custard tart with honey and crème fraîche are typical offerings. Wines from £15.50. Open all week.

■ Shiplake

Orwells

Menus sparkling with culinary fireworks
Cooking score: 6
Modern British | £43
Shiplake Row, Shiplake, RG9 4DP
Tel no: (01189) 403673
www.orwellsatshiplake.co.uk

'Locals have obviously latched on to this place as virtually all the other diners seemed to be repeat customers and known to the staff. How lucky they are.' So ran one enthusiastic verdict on Ryan Simpson and Liam Trotman's 'gem' of a restaurant. The white-painted former pub has been brought up to date with more than just a lick of paint and provides a suitably understated yet comfortable setting for the contemporary cooking that is Simpson and Trotman's forte – a far cry from what you might expect in the gentle Oxfordshire countryside. Much is made of local sourcing and own-grown produce, but further inspiration for dishes comes from wider-spread European roots. Reporters applaud an 'excellent, beautifully cooked and presented' starter of smoked veal sweetbreads with Périgord truffle, Parmesan and onion risotto and Xérès vinegar, and the 'clever, well-executed' guinea fowl served with egg yolk ravioli, potato, leek, turnip and carrot. Desserts have been a particular highlight for many with as much praise for the chocolate cake with caramel, peanut and vanilla as the high-quality British cheeses. Set lunches and dinners are good value, too. And wine? It's a fascinating modern list (from £20.50) with some classy organic and biodynamic wines and excellent choice by the glass.

Chef/s: Ryan Simpson and Liam Trotman. **Open:** Wed to Sun L 11.30 to 3 (3.30 Sun), Wed to Sat D 6.30 to 9.30 (10 Fri and Sat). **Closed:** Mon, Tue, first 2 weeks Jan, first week Jun, first 2 weeks Sept. **Meals:** alc (main courses £18 to £29). Set L £15 (2 courses) to £19. Set D £20 (2 courses) to £25. Sun L £30 (2 courses) to £35. Tasting menu £65. **Details:** 54 seats. 35 seats outside. Bar. Wheelchair access. Music. Parking.

Sparsholt

★ TOP 50 PUB ★

The Star Inn

Gentrified boozer with smart cooking
Cooking score: 4
Modern British | £30
Watery Lane, Sparsholt, OX12 9PL
Tel no: (01235) 751873
www.thestarsparsholt.co.uk

This smartly renovated old pub is so pristine, it almost feels new. Beyond its pretty brick frontage is a bright, whitewashed interior with bare beams dressed here and there with hops, bare-wood floors, and country pine furniture. Matt Williams now heads up the stoves and his 'intelligent, sophisticated' dishes are quickly winning fans. A starter of smoked fillet of mackerel with wasabi mayonnaise, cucumber sorbet and salad points the way, with 'fresh and feisty' flavours and 'top-notch

ingredients'. On the whole, this is proudly British cooking, with native ingredients such as foraged nettles, heritage potatoes and wild garlic making seasonal appearances. A meat-free main of thyme and juniper polenta cake with breaded goats' cheese, red onion, asparagus, caramelised onions and white wine cream really hit the spot for one reporter, impressing with its 'intelligent mix of flavours and textures'. Desserts such as a 'perfect, creamy' rice pudding with salty caramel ice cream have also won praise. Partner with wines from a list full of familiar favourites, starting at £18.

Chef/s: Matt Williams. **Open:** all week L 12 to 2.30 (3 Sat, 3.30 Sun), Mon to Sat D 6.30 to 9 (9.30 Fri and Sat). **Closed:** 5 to 12 Jan. **Meals:** alc (main courses £15 to £32). Set L and D £16 (2 courses) to £19. Sun L £17. **Details:** 65 seats. 40 seats outside. Bar. Music. Parking.

Stoke Row

LOCAL GEM

The Crooked Billet

Modern British | £35
Newlands Lane, Stoke Row, RG9 5PU
Tel no: (01491) 681048
www.thecrookedbillet.co.uk

One reader, who negotiated country lanes to reach this ancient country pub, thought the Crooked Billet resembled 'Red Riding Hood's cottage' and was charmed by the warm welcome, low beams and open fire. Good wholesome seasonal ingredients have found favour too. Chef/proprietor Paul Clerehugh rings the changes, serving everything from tuna sashimi, imam bayaldi and crispy duck to Aberdeen Angus shin of beef with winter vegetables or slow-roast suckling pig with cabbage hash, young leeks and parsley jus. Global wines from £22. Open all week.

Average price

The average price denotes the price of a three-course meal without wine.

■ Stonor
The Quince Tree
Country boozer turned foodie enclave
Cooking score: 2
Modern British | £30
Stonor, RG9 6HE
Tel no: (01491) 639039
www.thequincetree.com

Nestled in pretty Stonor among fine Chilterns countryside, the modern British Quince Tree caters to all-comers. Mid-ramble? Pop into its informal café for a sage and scrumpy sausage roll or to gather picnic supplies from the upmarket farm shop. After something more substantial? The pub offers the likes of wild garlic risotto, sea bream with samphire or decent, family-friendly roasts. Whenever you visit you'll find a genial member of staff pouring the drinks and a generosity of spirit – complimentary nibblets of, say, pork and apple Scotch eggs might greet you at the bar alongside your pint of craft pale ale. And if you've come for dinner, the kitchen bats well above average for a pub. Dishes such as gin-cured salmon on pickled cucumber spaghetti, Stonor-reared Wagyu beef and chocolate cherry palette with hazelnut crumb showcase sound cooking and inventive flourishes. Book a table in the nook for white tablecloths and a formal feel. House wines from £19.
Chef/s: Carl Jackman and Scott George. **Open:** Mon to Sun L 11.30 to 3 (12 to 5 Sun). Mon to Sat D 5 to 11. **Meals:** alc (main courses £12 to £32). Set L £25 (2 courses) to £30. Set D £26 (2 courses) to £30. Sun L £15. **Details:** 75 seats. 80 seats outside. Bar. Wheelchair access. Music. Parking.

■ Swinbrook
The Swan Inn
Idyllic village pub
Cooking score: 2
Modern British | £30
Swinbrook, OX18 4DY
Tel no: (01993) 823339
www.theswanswinbrook.co.uk

Overlooking lanes, a river and the village cricket pitch, the wisteria-clad Swan is postcard-perfect Cotswolds on a plate. So much so that David Cameron entertained François Hollande here in 2014, the crew of *Downton Abbey* descended to film Lady Sybil's elopement, and that's to say nothing of the late Dowager Duchess of Devonshire, who grew up here. All this could make the Swan a part-tourist attraction; in fact, it remains a treasured local with a roaring fire in winter and inviting suntrap garden, where regulars sup Hook Norton ales at the beamed and timbered bar and dog-walkers pop in for simple salt beef sandwiches. At its heart is a sound kitchen dealing in daily changing menus that champion carefully sourced produce. During a first-days-of-spring lunch that meant punchy mackerel fishcakes, Cotswold-reared ribeye cooked just so, moreish skinny chips, and, to end, a perky ginger and cardamom chocolate pot. Wines start at £19.
Chef/s: Matthew Laughton. **Open:** all week L 12 to 2 (2.30 Sat, 3 Sun), D 7 to 9 (6.30 to 9.30 Fri and Sat, 8.30 Sun). **Meals:** alc (main courses £14 to £19). **Details:** 70 seats. 100 seats outside.

Toot Baldon
The Mole Inn
Pubby vibes and eclectic food
Cooking score: 2
Modern British | £30
Toot Baldon, OX44 9NG
Tel no: (01865) 340001
www.themoleinn.com

An impressive CV and a couple of decades of experience gave Gary Witchalls a head start when he landed here in 2003. He's put all that to good use, pitching things 'just right' with a mix of decent ingredients, interesting flavours and flexible menus. The classy but accessible à la carte is bolstered by a keenly priced set menu and a selection of steaks. It all sits well with the homely surroundings, where little inglenooks, scuffed grey stone, distressed beams and stripped-wood floors create a setting that 'rather than seeming cluttered or over-designed, feels natural and relaxed'. The cooking combines British, European and Eastern influences: maybe Thai spiced fishcakes with aïoli, sweet chilli, crispy garlic and peanuts, then cannon of hogget with spiced lamb breast, minted pea purée and Parmesan-crumbed potatoes. Treacle tart is a classic way to finish. The international wine list opens at £18.95.

Chef/s: Gary Witchalls. **Open:** all week L 12 to 2.30 (4.30 Sun), D 7 to 9.30 (6.30 Sat, 6 to 9 Sun). **Closed:** 25 Dec. **Meals:** alc (main courses £15 to £18). Set L and D £20 (2 courses) to £25. Sun L £15. **Details:** 70 seats. 50 seats outside. Wheelchair access. Music. Parking.

Wootton
The Killingworth Castle
Born-again inn with fine food
Cooking score: 3
Modern British | £27
Glympton Road, Wootton, OX20 1EJ
Tel no: (01993) 811401
www.thekillingworthcastle.com

It's said that Sir Winston Churchill used to drive out from Blenheim Palace to take lunch in this 17th-century coaching inn – although he probably wouldn't recognise the place these days. Now run by the people from the Ebrington Arms in Gloucestershire (see entry), the Killingworth Castle has been impressively revitalised. You can drop by for a pint of ale from the owners' Yubberton Brewing Company, although most are here for plates of expertly fashioned seasonal food from the open kitchen. Chef Phil Currie and his team give the pub classics a contemporary working over – hence herb-cured salmon with watercress mousse, lemon gel and poppy seed cracker or Tidenham duck breast with a porcini dumpling, smoked Cheltenham beetroot and sprouting broccoli. To finish, how about Earl Grey pannacotta or pecan and maple tart with bacon popcorn? Aside from excellent beer, the pub has an admirable stock of terroir-led wines from independent growers, with prices from £19.

Chef/s: Phil Currie. **Open:** all week L 12 to 2.30 (3.30 Sun), D 6 to 9 (9.30 Fri and Sat, 8.30 Sun). **Closed:** 25 Dec. **Meals:** alc (main courses £14 to £22). Set L £15 (2 courses) to £19. **Details:** 68 seats. 40 seats outside. Parking.

Join us at thegoodfoodguide.co.uk

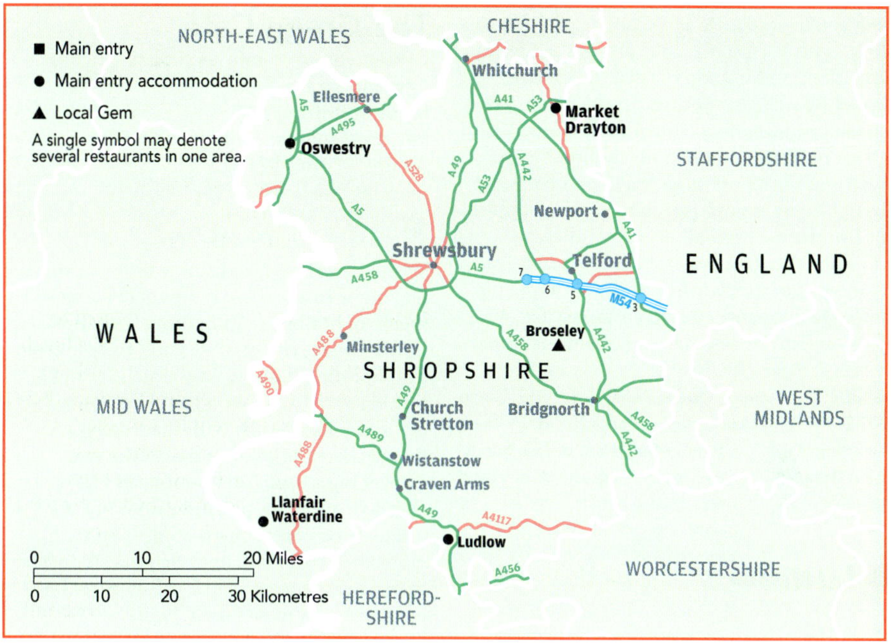

Broseley

LOCAL GEM

The King and Thai

Thai | £30
The Forester Arms, Avenue Road, Broseley, TF12 5DL
Tel no: (01952) 882004
www.thekingandthai.co.uk

'Every time we eat here we are blown away by the quality, freshness and taste of the food,' noted one regular of this welcoming Thai restaurant. Set in a smartly converted pub, it showcases Suree Coates' traditional cooking (much of it learnt from her grandmother), but even the simplest dishes are elevated with superb ingredients and careful presentation. Sesame prawn toasts come with fat whole prawns, a bright salad and a sweet-and-sour wine vinaigrette; a main of stir-fried ginger chicken packs a chilli punch and is stuffed with fresh vegetables. Desserts range from coconut pannacotta to crispy-coated deep-fried ice cream. Wines start at £20.95. Open Fri and Sat L and Tue to Sat D.

Llanfair Waterdine

The Waterdine

Foodie destination with unflashy cooking
Cooking score: 4
Modern British | £33
Llanfair Waterdine, LD7 1TU
Tel no: (01547) 528214
www.waterdine.com

Once a refuelling point on the old drovers' route between England and Wales, this 16th-century thatched longhouse has kept its time-warp looks, although it now does duty as a bookings-only foodie destination with rooms. Thick stone walls, leaded windows and an ancient inglenook testify to the building's age and the vibe is endearingly bucolic, while the food bears all the hallmarks of Ken Adams' classical training – welcome to the world of chicken liver, truffle and Cognac pâté, sea bass fillet with Vermouth sauce or pork tenderloin and black pudding on braised red cabbage. Isabel Adams cares for the productive kitchen garden and Ken makes profitable use of Welsh Black beef, mountain lamb and local game (venison with port sauce, Savoy cabbage and butter-roasted potatoes), plus regular supplies of fish from Cornwall. Sunday lunch is traditional, while desserts tread a steady path from ginger sticky toffee pudding with butterscotch sauce to iced lemon parfait with passion fruit coulis. Around 60 international wines start at £18.50.

Chef/s: Ken Adams. **Open:** Sun L 12 to 1.30, Tue to Sat D 7 to 9. **Closed:** Mon, 24 and 25 Dec, 1 week summer, 1 week autumn. **Meals:** Set D £33. Sun L £23. **Details:** 20 seats. Bar. Parking. Children over 8 yrs only at D.

Ludlow

NEW ENTRY

The Charlton Arms

Upmarket pub grub and river views
Cooking score: 1
British | £25
Ludford Bridge, Ludlow, SY8 1PJ
Tel no: (01584) 872813
www.thecharltonarms.co.uk

As riverside locations go, this one is a knockout – a hefty stone pub set high on the riverbank overlooking the picturesque Ludford bridge. It has been extended to create a classy but relaxed glass-walled restaurant with bags of terrace seating, so grab a table with a view if you can (there are plenty) and you may glimpse a kingfisher on the river below. The menu ranges from Gallic snails with garlic butter to upmarket pub classics – a retro chicken Kiev with fries and feta salad is a good way to go, maybe followed by raspberry Eton mess. Wines from £17.50.

Chef/s: Stephen Smith. **Open:** all week L 12 to 3, D 6 to 9.30 (8.30 Sun). **Meals:** alc (main courses £11 to £18). **Details:** 80 seats. 50 seats outside. Music. Parking.

The Green Café

Lovely watermill café with tasty lunches
Cooking score: 1
Modern British | £18
Mill on the Green, Ludlow, SY8 1EG
Tel no: (01584) 879872
www.thegreencafe.co.uk

Weeping willows, a gushing weir, children playing – surely there is nowhere better to spend an hour or so in Ludlow. The Green Café's simple, chalet-style end of a converted mill building has at least as much seating outside as in, so it's wonderful on sunny days, but as the menu rolls with the seasons it's worth checking in throughout the year. Expect big, rustic food with hearty flavours: a chunky courgette, pea and mint soup, for instance, or a hefty main of gnocchi with a ragù made from Italian-style pork, fennel and garlic sausage meat. Top it off with vanilla pannacotta. Wines from £19.

Chef/s: Clive Davis. **Open:** Tue to Sun L only 12 to 2.30. **Closed:** Mon, 24 Dec to 14 Feb. **Meals:** alc (main courses £7 to £13). **Details:** 30 seats. 25 seats outside. Wheelchair access.

Mr Underhill's

Bewitching waterside hideaway
Cooking score: 6
Modern British | £70
Dinham Weir, Ludlow, SY8 1EH
Tel no: (01584) 874431
www.mr-underhills.co.uk

'A real chef patron feel' pervades this magically located restaurant-with-rooms, whose dining room looks across a courtyard to the willow-hung river. Chris and Judy Bradley have been plying their trade here for over 34 years – he in the kitchen, she front-of-house – and reports indicate they remain on top form. Dishes singled out for special praise include a 'stunning' tempura of marinated salmon sushi bites with a crustless mini quiche and the duck liver custard with quince cream and red wine and coffee glaze. The main act of the lengthy

Join us at thegoodfoodguide.co.uk

tasting menu might be slow-roasted fillet of Marches beef with braised beef, potato terrine, caramelised shallot jus, spinach custard and carrot purée. To finish, there is an impressive selection of local cheeses or a further savoury option of mille-feuille of Remembered Hills Blue cheese with pear chutney and mustard ice cream as an alternative to desserts such as an Italian-style bread-and-butter pudding with mocha ice cream. The wine list (like everything here) is a labour of love, balanced between classics and more obscure discoveries. Bottles start at £26.

Chef/s: Chris Bradley. **Open:** Wed to Sun D only 7.30 to 8.15 (1 sitting). **Closed:** Mon, Tue, 25 to 31 Dec, 1 Jan, 2 weeks Jun, 1 week Oct. **Meals:** Set D £70 (9 courses). **Details:** 24 seats. 24 seats outside. V menu. Parking. Children over 6 yrs only.

Market Drayton

NEW ENTRY

Goldstone Hall

Flavour-driven food from the kitchen garden
Cooking score: 3
Modern British | £40
Market Drayton, TF9 2NA
Tel no: (01630) 661202
www.goldstonehall.com

The power driving the menu of this 'classic but never fusty' country house hotel is its vast and beautiful kitchen garden (and showpiece walled garden – worth a wander at some point during your visit). You can enjoy the view from the Victorian-style conservatory dining room or the terrace, although the oak-panelled dining room with its magnificent Arts and Crafts fireplace is another plum spot. It goes without saying that ingredients 'couldn't be bettered' and chef Chris Weatherstone has a knack for coaxing out flavour – in asparagus soup enlivened with wafer-thin slivers of raw asparagus and a scoop of crème fraîche or in a deceptively simple main of 'juicy, crisp-skinned and melt-in-the-mouth tender' Creedy Carver duck breast with an intense jus offset by a sparky combination of whole roasted carrots, slivers

of pickled carrot and 'perfectly cooked, palpably fresh' broccoli. A dessert of poached pear with pistachio pieces and white chocolate mouse lacked comparable counterpoints, but again showcased 'flavours at maximum volume'. A 'beautifully annotated' wine list opens at £20.

Chef/s: Chris Weatherstone. **Open:** all week L 12 to 3, D 7 to 10. **Meals:** alc (main courses £15 to £32). Sun L £32. **Details:** 60 seats. Bar. Wheelchair access. Music. Parking.

Oswestry

Sebastians

Bewitching setting, Gallic-tinged cooking
Cooking score: 3
French | £45
45 Willow Street, Oswestry, SY11 1AQ
Tel no: (01691) 655444
www.sebastians-hotel.co.uk

The charm offensive starts with the approach down a narrow alleyway that opens into a pretty courtyard; the restaurant itself is cave-like, glistening with fairy lights and candlelight, its low oak beams, bare floorboards and exposed stonework offset by modern furnishings and window blinds. The slightly tired French prints on the walls hint at the main thrust of the cooking (there's nothing tired about that), but besides gratins, palmiers and 'wonderful rustic French bread', there are broader influences: an exemplary onion bhaji as a canapé; wild mushroom risotto with loin of spring lamb; smoked tofu with a roasted vegetable salad. This is 'assured, eclectic cooking' noted one reporter of a meal that opened with rustic button mushroom and wild garlic Roquefort gratin, went on to corn-fed chicken breast with wild mushrooms, dauphinois potatoes and an 'intense mushroom sauce', and finished with a light, silky almond milk pannacotta, its sweetness offset by peach sorbet. Wines from £19.

Chef/s: Mark Sebastian Fisher. **Open:** Tue to Sat D only 6.30 to 9.30. **Closed:** Sun, Mon, 24 to 26 Dec, 1 Jan. **Meals:** Set D £23 (3 courses) to £45.
Details: 45 seats. 20 seats outside. Music. Parking.

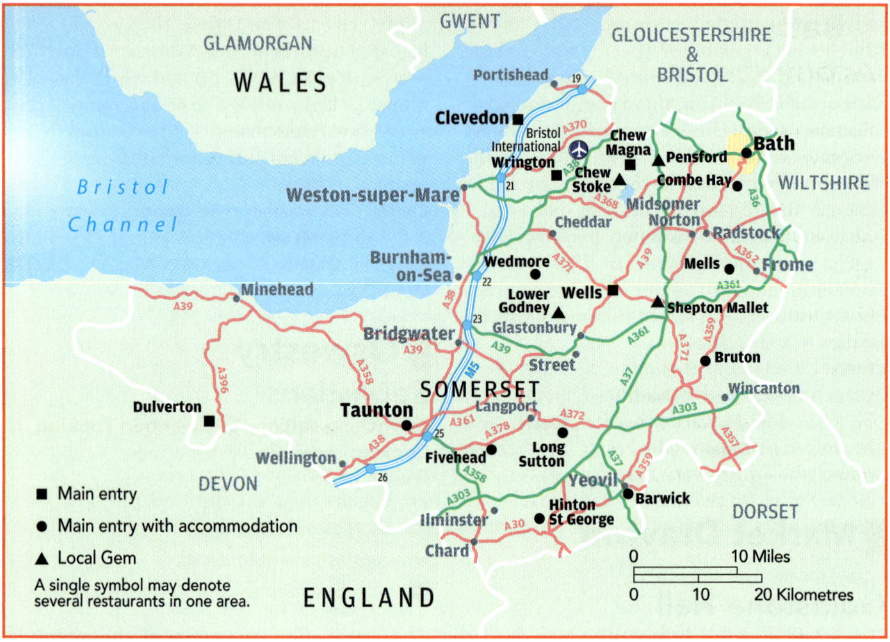

Barwick
Little Barwick House

A little English idyll
Cooking score: 5
Modern British | £48
Rexes Hollow Lane, Barwick, BA22 9TD
Tel no: (01935) 423902
www.littlebarwickhouse.co.uk

'It's the whole experience of LBH that makes it so special'; that's how one reader summed up Tim and Emma Ford's highly civilised restaurant-with-rooms. The Georgian one-time dower house is a proper English retreat, with a lush garden and smart furnishings. Tim's cooking has a timeless quality, but it's not dated – expect modern British cooking based on first-rate ingredients. Kick off with canapés in the lounge (or on the terrace) before moving to the main dining room or conservatory where a cannelloni of Cornish lobster with baby courgettes and lobster sauce (perhaps) awaits, followed by fillet of Ruby Red Devon beef (with wild mushrooms and a red wine sauce), or sea bass powered up with fennel, orange and saffron. Finish with rhubarb cheesecake. The meticulously put-together wine list has excellent options by the glass, and Le Verre de Vin system to keep them all in tip-top condition; bottles from £20.95. **Chef/s:** Tim Ford. **Open:** Wed to Sat L 12 to 2, Tue to Sat D 7 to 9. **Closed:** Sun, Mon. **Meals:** Set L £26 (2 courses) to £30. Set D £42 (2 courses) to £48. **Details:** 45 seats. 12 seats outside. Children over 5 yrs only.

Please send us your feedback

To register your opinion about any restaurant listed in this guide, or a new restaurant that you wish to bring to our attention, please visit the web address at the bottom of the page. Your feedback informs the content of the book and will be used to compile next year's reviews.

Bath
Acorn Vegetarian Kitchen
Seriously exciting contemporary veggie food
Cooking score: 3
Vegetarian | £31
2 North Parade Passage, Bath, BA1 1NX
Tel no: (01225) 446059
www.acornvegetariankitchen.co.uk

Once the home of philanthropist Ralph Allen, who reformed the British postal service, this listed Georgian building was for years the vegetarian restaurant Demuths. When it closed in 2013, chef Richard Buckley became the owner and he has kept this meat-free establishment very much on the veggie radar. Set across two floors, with wonderful rooftop views of the nearby abbey from the intimate back room, Mr Buckley's menu follows the seasons to the letter and the creative dishes champion local ingredients. At dinner, truffled broccoli with cauliflower pannacotta and pickled kohlrabi might precede a main course of smoked field mushroom with potato galette, greens and salt-baked celeriac purée. Pineapple carpaccio teamed with pine nut parfait and sultana granola makes for a light and satisfying end to a meal. A lunchtime selection of 'small plates' to share is a popular way to explore the menu further. Wine from £17.50.
Chef/s: Richard Buckley. **Open:** all week L 12 to 3 (3.30 Sat), D 5.30 to 9.30 (10 Sat). **Closed:** 25 and 26 Dec. **Meals:** alc (main courses £16). Set L £17 (2 courses) to £20. Sun L £17. **Details:** 34 seats. V menu. Music.

Symbols

Accommodation is available
Three courses for less than £30
£5-off voucher scheme
Notable wine list

Allium Brasserie
Big-city pizazz and attention-grabbing food
Cooking score: 4
Modern British | £50
Abbey Hotel, North Parade, Bath, BA1 1LF
Tel no: (01225) 461603
www.abbeyhotelbath.co.uk

There have been a few modifications to the menu of this all-day brasserie with the introduction of a burger and sharing plates to please the wide-ranging clientele of the hotel. That could be seen as a distraction, but not with an experienced chef like Chris Staines in the kitchen. In a former life, Staines was a major player on the London scene and he's been around long enough to know what people want to eat. A consommé of ham hock with fresh spring vegetables, sage and basil pesto and semi-dried tomatoes made for a remarkably light and balanced starter at inspection. It was followed by a precisely poached fillet of plaice with Jersey Royals and a rich prawn bisque studded with finely diced cucumber and fennel, while a beautifully constructed and delicate délice of gariguette strawberries with pistachio shortbread, elderflower sorbet and strawberry salad was the essence of early summer. Wines from £19.
Chef/s: Chris Staines. **Open:** all week L 12 to 3, D 5.30 to 9 (9.30 Fri and Sat). **Meals:** alc (main courses £18 to £25). Set L and D £18 (2 courses) to £24. **Details:** 60 seats. 30 seats outside. V menu. Bar. Wheelchair access. Music.

The Bath Priory
Refined contemporary food
Cooking score: 4
Modern European | £80
Weston Road, Bath, BA1 2XT
Tel no: (01225) 331922
www.thebathpriory.co.uk

Standing proud on four acres of land once owned by Bath Abbey, this many-winged Victorian pile exudes a certain sort of country-house elegance – even though it's only a mile from the city centre. Everything soothes and cossets, from the landscaped lawns to the vintage paintings, sumptuous furnishings and dutiful service in the handsome dining room, which provides a moneyed backdrop for Sam Moody's take on refined contemporary food. Expect a procession of finely honed miniatures ranging from seared scallops with St George's mushrooms, apple and hazelnuts or Longhorn beef tartare with wild garlic mayonnaise and pickled onions to a three-part 'plate of local pig' accompanied by cheesy mash, spring onions and paprika jus. The kitchen's search for rare regional delicacies might also yield goose 'ham' from Woolley Park Farm, perhaps served with gingerbread crunch and confit orange, while dessert could promise salted-caramel fondant with butterscotch and banana sorbet. A big-hitting pedigree wine list offers serious drinking from £23.

Chef/s: Sam Moody. **Open:** all week L 12.30 to 2.30, D 6.30 to 9.30. **Meals:** Set L £23 (2 courses) to £28. Set D £62 (2 courses) to £80. Tasting menu £90 (7 courses). **Details:** 42 seats. V menu. Bar. Parking. Children over 12 yrs only.

Casanis

Charming bistro with Gallic classics
Cooking score: 3
French | £35
4 Saville Row, Bath, BA1 2QP
Tel no: (01225) 780055
www.casanis.co.uk

Named after a type of pastis, this relaxed family-run bistro occupies two floors of a handsome Georgian building in a pretty pedestrianised street adjacent to the city's Assembly Rooms. Chandeliers, Provençal antiques and crisp white tablecloths accentuate a romantic and unmistakably Gallic flavour in the elegant, pastel-coloured dining room, where former film-maker Jill Couvreur runs front-of-house, while husband Laurent cooks authentic bistro classics. Casanis offers the type of honest regional French cooking you may have thought was an endangered species. A classic Provençal fish soup with rouille,

croûtons and cheese could be followed by roast ballotine of quail with chicken mousse, mushroom and herb stuffing, dauphinois potatoes, slow-roasted shallot purée, braised lentil ragoût and rosemary jus. Finish with pear and vanilla crumble with salted-caramel ice cream or choose from a board of unpasteurised French regional cheeses. Service is pleasant and the concise all-French wine list opens at £18.50.

Chef/s: Laurent Couvreur. **Open:** Tue to Sat L 12 to 1.30, D 6 to 9 (10 Fri and Sat). **Closed:** Sun, Mon, 25 and 26 Dec, first week Jan, 1 week Aug. **Meals:** alc (main courses £14 to £26). Set L £18 (2 courses) to £23. Set D £19 (2 courses) to £24. **Details:** 50 seats. 16 seats outside. Music.

The Circus Café & Restaurant

Much-loved versatile eatery
Cooking score: 3
Modern British | £32
34 Brock Street, Bath, BA1 2LN
Tel no: (01225) 466020
www.thecircuscafeandrestaurant.co.uk

£5
OFF

Over the past eight years this versatile restaurant on the street linking the Circus and the Royal Crescent has proved to be a big hit. Regulars love the conversational mood of the place, its telling blend of intimacy and bonhomie, and staff with that caring touch – although coming here is mainly about the food. Open for elevenses and light lunches, Circus ups the ante in the evening with candles and simple, ingredient-driven dishes that reveal chef/proprietor Ali Golden's deep understanding of flavour combinations, underpinned by a love of Elizabeth David and Jane Grigson. She proves her mettle with the likes of potted rabbit with carrot, radish and mustard pickle and smoked bacon jam, and Basque-style guinea fowl with peppers, olives, chorizo, wild thyme, tomatoes and sweet paprika. Elsewhere, readers have singled out 'absolutely delicious' white crabmeat on a bed of fennel and apple with a brown crabmeat mayonnaise, and a classy brioche summer pudding served with geranium cream. A wine list from small European growers starts at £17.70.

Chef/s: Alison Golden and Máté Andrasko. **Open:** Mon to Sat L 12 to 3 (3.30 Sat), D 5.30 to 10.30. **Closed:** Sun, 23 Dec for 3 weeks. **Meals:** alc (main courses £17 to £19). **Details:** 50 seats. 8 seats outside. Music. Children over 7 yrs only.

Clayton's Kitchen at The Porter

Food to suit all tastes, pockets and occasions
Cooking score: 3
Modern British | £35
The Porter, 15A George Street, Bath, BA1 2EN
Tel no: (01225) 585100
www.theporter.co.uk

Set across four floors of a Georgian town house, this cocktail bar, lounge/bar and restaurant certainly has all bases covered when it comes to feeding the masses. Whether it's affluent locals or the tourists who swarm around this part of Bath on the way to the nearby Royal Crescent, this multi-faceted operation has broad appeal. Behind the stoves of this elegantly converted former pub (think sanded bare-wood floors, distressed paint and on-trend industrial lamps with filament bulbs) is Rob Clayton, who won plaudits for his cooking at the Bath Priory (see entry) back in the day. An inspection meal opened with a light and fresh dressed Little Haven crab teamed with pickled pear and Lavosh crackers, continued with an expertly judged fillet of bream served with fregola pasta enriched with langoustine and accompanied by buttered English asparagus and a frothy fish velouté, while a deconstructed lemon meringue pie scored full marks on flavour. Wines from £18.

Chef/s: Rob Clayton. **Open:** all week L 12 to 2.30, D 6 to 9.30 (10 Sat, 8 Sun). **Closed:** 25 and 26 Dec. **Meals:** alc (main courses £14 to £24). Set L £20 (2 courses) to £25. **Details:** 140 seats. 22 seats outside. Bar. Music.

The Dower House

Contemporary cooking in an elegant setting
Cooking score: 3
Modern European | £65
Royal Crescent Hotel, 16 Royal Crescent, Bath, BA1 2LS
Tel no: (01225) 823333
www.royalcrescent.co.uk

Walk through the hotel at the centre of Bath's famous Georgian crescent and you step into a wonderfully tranquil secret garden. The greystone former dower house overlooking the immaculate landscaped gardens makes an elegant restaurant with its soft fabrics, hand-stitched silk wallpaper and French windows opening out on to the terrace. As might be expected in such an impressive setting, David Campbell's cooking is appropriately luxurious and refined, with high-quality raw materials backed up by solid technical skills, as seen in immaculately presented beetroot-cured organic salmon served with earthy beetroot salad, rich smoked roe and lime, and Anjou squab pigeon teamed with Wye Valley asparagus, veal sweetbread, morels, wild garlic and mushroom gel. Dessert choices typically include coconut parfait, Szechuan-spiced pineapple mille-feuille and compressed watermelon. 'Good without being stuffy or pretentious' was the verdict of one reporter about the knowledgeable and keen to please service. The heavyweight wine list is predictably pricey, but it opens at £27.

Chef/s: David Campbell. **Open:** all week L 12.30 to 2pm, D 6.30 to 9.30. **Meals:** alc (main courses £26 to £29). Set L £23 (2 courses) to £28. Sun L £38. **Details:** 65 seats. 110 seats outside. V menu. Bar. Wheelchair access. Music. Parking.

King William

No-nonsense cooking in a boho pub
Cooking score: 1
British | £26
36 Thomas Street, Bath, BA1 5NN
Tel no: (01225) 428096
www.kingwilliampub.com

A short walk from Bath's city centre, this more-shabby-than-chic Georgian pub is noted for its robust, no-frills approach to British comfort cooking. Whether you eat in the bar or the elegant upstairs dining room, the menu showcases conscientiously sourced seasonal ingredients, as seen in a starter of home-smoked sea trout, potato and radish salad, crispy capers, cucumber and sweet mustard dressing, and a main of rack of new-season lamb with herb-crusted, slow-cooked shoulder, carrot and rocket dumplings, spring vegetables and sauce vierge. Dessert might offer a winning combination of dark chocolate cake and white chocolate sorbet. The French-heavy wine list opens at £17.
Chef/s: Joel Lear. **Open:** all week L 12 to 2 (2.30 Sat, 3 Sun), D 6 to 9 (10 Sat). **Closed:** 25 and 26 Dec. **Meals:** alc (main courses £14 to £19). Set L £14 (2 courses) to £15. Sun L £20. **Details:** 50 seats. Bar. Music.

Menu Gordon Jones

Real innovation and surprises
Cooking score: 5
Modern British | £55
2 Wellsway, Bath, BA2 3AQ
Tel no: (01225) 480871
www.menugordonjones.co.uk

Bath foodies warn that this idiosyncratic 22-seater is currently the hardest restaurant to book in the city – and no wonder. Although the location isn't exactly auspicious and the dining room is a basic, vaguely Nordic mix of bare tables, IKEA-style blinds and rock music, Gordon Jones' fearlessly experimental cooking is making a big impact. 'Let the chef surprise you', and he certainly does just that by offering 'secret' no-choice tasting menus defined by the day's market. Expect real innovation and plenty of thrills from an eyebrow-raising line-up that might include anything from cauliflower mousse with black pudding cakes and curry oil to beetroot sorbet with pickled cucumber and kale water. In between, fish and meat often appear together: sashimi of yellowfin tuna with beef tendons and Dorset wasabi ice cream or seared red mullet with duck salami, monk's beard and swollen raisins, for example. The enlightened wine list comes courtesy of organic specialists Vintage Roots, with bottles from £22.
Chef/s: Gordon Jones. **Open:** Tue to Sat L 12.30 to 2, D 7 to 9. **Closed:** Sun, Mon. **Meals:** Set L £40 (5 courses). Set D £55 (6 courses). **Details:** 22 seats. V menu. Music. Children over 12 yrs only.

The Olive Tree

Comfort, quirks and eclectic cooking
Cooking score: 4
Modern British | £50
The Queensberry Hotel, 4-7 Russel Street, Bath, BA1 2QF
Tel no: (01225) 447928
www.olivetreebath.co.uk

Built in 1771 for the Marquis of Queensberry, this palatial Georgian town house still sells the full-on Bath heritage experience despite its lavish transformation into a modern boutique hotel. The flagship Olive Tree restaurant in the bowels of the building was due to be refurbished before the end of 2015, but chef Chris Cleghorn remains at the stoves and is on top form judging by recent reports of 'succulent, elegantly presented dishes' served by really attentive staff. His crab lasagne with mousse, bisque, basil and ginger continues to be singled out, but other classy fish dishes have included a 'beautiful' plate of halibut with leeks, shimeji mushrooms, salt-baked celeriac, Noilly Prat sauce and winter truffle. Seasonal ideas also shine through in the meat department, from braised pork belly with pumpkin purée to venison loin with quince, spiced red cabbage and Brussels sprouts. Meanwhile, exotic fruit soufflés are a fixture of the dessert menu. The smart, cosmopolitan wine list is serious but great fun, with bin ends galore, plenty by the glass and bottles from £20.

Chef/s: Chris Cleghorn. **Open:** Fri to Sun L 12 to 2, all week D 7 to 9.30 (6.30 to 10 Fri and Sat). **Meals:** alc (main courses £19 to £27). Set L £21 (2 courses) to £26. Sun L £21. **Details:** 60 seats. V menu. Bar. Music.

The White Hart Inn

Modern pub food with a walled garden
Cooking score: 2
Modern British | £33
Widcombe Hill, Widcombe, Bath, BA2 6AA
Tel no: (01225) 338053
www.whitehartbath.co.uk

In the Widcombe district of the city centre, which is to say about five minutes from Bath Spa station, the White Hart is a coaching inn originating, like most of the city, in the Georgian era, with a nicely sheltered walled garden and an ambience of clean-limbed, light-toned freshness inside. The bill of fare is modern pub food, beginning with slabs of ham hock, chorizo and white bean terrine with ciabatta toast, and barrelling on through big hunks of protein. Pork fillet is wrapped in pancetta to emphasise the point and served with celeriac gratin, while lamb is braised and cushioned with polenta in green sauce. Equally sturdy fish dishes include whole megrim with shellfish and kale, all zinging with chilli. Finish with a fashionable trio of chocolate items. Bread will pretty much come at you throughout, from nibbles to starters and side orders. Fine ales and decent wines accompany, the latter from £16.90.

Chef/s: Rupert Pitt, Steve Wesley, Kirsty Fowle and Luke Gibson. **Open:** all week L 12 to 2 (2.30 Sun), Mon to Sat D 6 to 9 (10 Thur to Sat). **Closed:** bank hols. **Meals:** alc (main courses £16 to £19). Set L £13. Sun L £22. **Details:** 50 seats. 50 seats outside. Wheelchair access. Music.

Aió Sardinia

Sardinian | £30
7 Edgar Buildings, George Street, Bath, BA1 2EE
Tel no: (01225) 443900
www.aiorestaurant.co.uk

£5 OFF

Occupying the ground floor of a Georgian town house in Bath's city centre, Aió Sardinia successfully recreates the flavours and smells of the Italian island, with an irrepressible warmth about the service that draws you in, and pavement tables a real boon in summer. Start with cuttlefish, potato and olive salad before a plate of pasta (slow-cooked hare ragû with fettuccine and oyster mushrooms, perhaps) followed by pancetta-wrapped quail stuffed with sausage meat and served with polenta. The Italian-centric wine list kicks off at £16.25. Open all week.

Yak Yeti Yak

Nepalese | £20
12 Pierrepont Street, Bath, BA1 1LA
Tel no: (01225) 442299
www.yakyetiyak.co.uk

'A great find in the centre of Bath,' noted a visitor to this cheerful, family-run Nepalese eatery located in the basement of a Georgian town house not far from Bath Abbey. It is good value and well run. Simple rooms are decorated with Nepalese artefacts and the cooking is mild with a subtle use of spices and herbs. Lightly spiced vegetable curry with 'perfect' basmati rice and 'outstanding' orange dhal has been recommended, as has a special of goat, slow-cooked with spices, ginger and cumin. Wines from £15.50. Open all week.

◼ Bruton

NEW ENTRY
Roth Bar & Grill
Combining food with contemporary art
Cooking score: 3
British | £25
Durslade Farm, Dropping Lane, Bruton,
BA10 0NL
Tel no: (01749) 814700
www.rothbarandgrill.co.uk

In a lovely spot, this unusual place is both a
working farm and a gallery, with a cocktail
bar/café/restaurant housed in a U-shaped barn
conversion strewn with eccentric art. It might
seem a difficult thing to pull off, but 'is
actually extremely enjoyable…serving simple,
reliable cooking that relies on good produce to
stand out'. From the slices of homemade
chorizo, bresaola and Parma-style ham that,
along with 'a lick of pistou, a blob of good,
mustardy remoulade and some pleasantly
chewy twists of fougasse and charred triangles
of pitta', made up one reporter's starter, via a
superb, crisp-skinned rotisserie chicken that
came with 'lashings of moderately garlicky
aïoli and a few celery leaves', to the 'good,
buttery, zesty' treacle tart with clotted cream,
it's all very appealing. Service is 'chirpy and
engaging' and the part-covered courtyard
around which the bar/restaurant is built is 'a
stunner for summer'. Excellent local artisan
beers and Somerset ciders enhance a modest
but out of the ordinary wine list (from £18).
Chef/s: Steve Horrell. **Open:** Tue to Thur and Sun L
12 to 3. Fri and Sat 12 to 11. **Closed:** Mon, 25 and
26 Dec, first week Jan. **Meals:** alc (main courses £10
to £20). **Details:** 80 seats. 60 seats outside. Bar.
Wheelchair access. Music. Parking.

◼ Chew Magna

The Pony & Trap
Pubby traditions and refined cooking
Cooking score: 6
Modern British | £35
Knowle Hill, Chew Magna, BS40 8TQ
Tel no: (01275) 332627
www.theponyandtrap.co.uk

Rural British pubs are archaic, often simple
shrines to plain walls, wood floors, and
understated paintings. Yes, we're generalising,
but we do like the way the Pony & Trap feels
like your average country pub – a distinct bar
area kept for drinkers and walk-ins, dining
split across various sections and levels of the
pub – while delivering cooking that is
ambitious and refined. In keeping with pub
tradition, Josh Eggleton does offer three
lunchtime 'pub classics' alongside his daily
changing tasting and à la carte menus. Here,
the cooking allows carefully sourced seasonal
produce to shine, from a first course of parsnip
and pear – the parsnip presented as silky
purée, crisps, pickled strips and soft cylinders
fried in crispy crumb, the pear as raw shavings,
soured purée, and pickled pieces – via a fat slab
of silky cod topped with smoky strips of
cured, fatty pork and panko crumbs, sweated
leeks studded with lardons, and surrounded
by big, juicy mussels in a light cream sauce, to
a perfectly pink rose veal rump and crisp
sweetbreads on a luxurious barley risotto
loaded with parsley butter. Service, like the
food, strikes a great balance, and the wine list
(from £15.75) is pitched just right, with
modest pricing and a huge amount of variety.
Chef/s: Josh Eggleton. **Open:** all week L 12 to 2
(3.30 Sun), D 7 to 9 (6 Fri and Sat). **Closed:** 25 Dec.
Meals: alc (main courses £10 to £23). Tasting menu
£60 (6 courses). **Details:** 65 seats. 20 seats outside.
Bar. Music. Parking.

■ Chew Stoke

LOCAL GEM

Salt & Malt

British | £20

Wally Lane, Chew Stoke, BS40 8TF
Tel no: (01275) 333345
www.saltmalt.com

For years a simple tea room overlooking
Chew Valley Lake, this new fish café is the
latest venture from chef Josh Eggleton of the
nearby Pony & Trap (see entry). The light
interior features plenty of nautical touches and
there is a separate shop for takeaways. Cream
teas are still served here but seafood is the star,
with typical dishes including chilli squid,
coriander, lemon and peanuts, monkfish tikka
masala or Cornish hake and chips. Wines from
£16. Open all week.

■ Clevedon

Murrays of Clevedon

All-day Italian enterprise

Cooking score: 2
Italian | £25

87-93 Hill Road, Clevedon, BS21 7PN
Tel no: (01275) 341555
www.murraysofclevedon.co.uk

'Clevedon is a lovely little place, free from
chain stores and seaside schmaltz – Murrays
fits in well,' noted a smitten first-time visitor.
On entering the deli you have to make your
way past boxes of tomatoes, fat Sicilian
lemons, giant red peppers and aubergines,
bowls of olives, Italian cured meats and cheeses
and ample baked goods to find the simple caffè
tucked away in a raised section above the shop.
It's popular with locals, who stop by for
breakfast, perhaps, chorizo and scrambled egg
on toast, 'very good' coffee and cakes,
lunchtime sandwiches such as hot pork with
country garden chutney or a bowl of soup, say
pea and mint. In addition, there are good
pizzas, pasta, possibly pappardelle in a light
cream sauce with plenty of asparagus and a

generous scattering of Parmesan, and such
dishes as wild Cornish sea bass with a fennel
and almond crust. Italian wines from £14.50.
Chef/s: Reuben Murray. **Open:** Tue to Sat 9 to 3.
Closed: Sun, Mon, 25 and 26 Dec. **Meals:** alc (main
courses £9 to £22). **Details:** 44 seats. 6 seats
outside. Music.

■ Combe Hay

The Wheatsheaf

Well-groomed inn with enjoyable food

Cooking score: 3
Modern British | £28

Combe Hay, BA2 7EG
Tel no: (01225) 833504
www.wheatsheafcombehay.com

'Winding, tiny roads that slope sharply
through villages and farms, a beautiful view
out across fields and woods from the pinnacle
of pretty Combe Hay…gleaming white-
painted brick walls, pale green shuttered
windows…immaculate décor.' There's no
doubt, the Wheatsheaf is an idyllic dining pub.
The food is enjoyable, too, with Eddy Rains'
menu evolving at a steady pace, picking up a
trend here and there. First up might be charred
Cornish mackerel with apple, horseradish and
watercress, with follow-ups ranging from
nicely roasted fillet of Gloucester Old Spot
pork with Parma ham, black pudding and two
crisp sage and onion croquettes, to Somerset
venison cottage pie with griottine cherries.
When it comes to dessert, warm treacle tart
with lemon curd ice cream is a great way to
finish, or look to the selection of British
cheeses. Set meal deals are keenly priced and
wines start at £16.50.
Chef/s: Eddy Rains. **Open:** Tue to Sun L 12 to 2.30,
Tue to Sat D 6.30 to 9. **Closed:** Mon, 25 and 26 Dec,
first week Jan. **Meals:** alc (main courses £13 to £25).
Set L £16 (2 courses) to £20. Set D £18 (2 courses) to
£23. Sun L £25. **Details:** 55 seats. 85 seats outside.
Music. Parking.

Dulverton

NEW ENTRY

The Exmoor Beastro

Quirky setting for unconventional dishes
Cooking score: 1
Modern British | £25
44 High Street, Dulverton, TA23 9DW
Tel no: (01398) 323712
www.theexmoorbeastro.com

'Exmoor Beastro is just utterly unexpected – like some sort of culinary hippy commune,' noted one surprised reporter. The shabby dining room is a random mix of tables and chairs, walls jump DIY-style from yellow to blue to white, ingredients are fiercely seasonal, dishes unconventional – the cooking done in a huge wood-fired oven parked in the courtyard. Run by chef Alex Nutt with 'infectious enthusiasm', the blackboard lists plates of smoked trout with watercress and horseradish, Basque chorizo with baked olives and leaves, 65-day dry-aged porterhouse steak and creamy choux buns with caramel sauce. On our visit, the absence of any wine was 'laughed off merrily' with directions to the nearby Co-op and £5 corkage charge. Note: cash only.
Chef/s: Alex Nutt. **Open:** Wed to Sun L 12 to 3, Wed to Sat D 6 to 8. Check seasonal openings. **Closed:** Mon, Tue. **Meals:** alc (main courses £12 to £45). **Details:** Cash only. 28 seats. 15 seats outside.

Fivehead

The Langford

Fresh, friendly country-house dining
Cooking score: 6
Modern British | £36
Langford Fivehead, Lower Swell, Fivehead, TA3 6PH
Tel no: (01460) 282020
www.langfordfivehead.co.uk

There's something tirelessly serene about this ancient stone-built restaurant-with-rooms set in seven acres of magnificent grounds. It dates from the 15th century and is an intimate place with period features including wood panelling, mullioned windows and stone fireplaces. Run by Olly and Rebecca Jackson (he in the kitchen, she front-of-house), who make the place memorable with their absolute untiring devotion, enthusiasm, skill and innate sense of hospitality. Where possible, ingredients are grown locally (many vegetables are grown on site), the menu is compact, with a choice of three at each course, and everybody seems to find everything delicious. There are no duff ideas here: crab and scallop is layered between thin sheets of pasta and served with chive beurre blanc and watercress, slow-cooked leg and roasted breast of pheasant is teamed with Savoy cabbage, pancetta and cauliflower purée, the selection of West Country cheeses 'some of the best we have ever experienced', and to finish a first-class vanilla pannacotta with poached rhubarb and spiced oats. Wines on the all-French list start at £22.
Chef/s: Olly Jackson. **Open:** Wed to Fri L 12.30 to 2, Tue to Sat D 7 to 9. **Closed:** Sun, Mon, 25 and 26 Dec, Jan. **Meals:** Set L £28 (2 courses) to £32. Set D £38. **Details:** 22 seats. Music. Parking. Children over 12 yrs only.

Hinton St George

The Lord Poulett Arms

Appealing village pub with seasonal food
Cooking score: 2
Modern British | £29
High Street, Hinton St George, TA17 8SE
Tel no: (01460) 73149
www.lordpoulettarms.com

A 'lovely pub in a quintessential English village', the Lord Poulett Arms is a listed Georgian building with the full complement of open fires, wood and flagstone floors and characterful old furniture. Chef Julien Handley is half French, half English and brings his French training and broad kitchen experience to bear on the Poulett's menus. Ravioli of duck with duck ham, orange coulis and truffled honey is a classy starting point,

but there are also homely options such as 'egg and beans on toast' – a duck egg with home-made baked beans, mushroom ketchup and toasted sourdough. Mains are equally eclectic, ranging from smoked lamb rump with aubergine caviar and potato fondant to tandoori chicken breast with lentil salad, tomato and onion achar and mint yoghurt. For dessert, expect a sassy take on favourites such as 'broken rocky road' – Valrhona chocolate ganache, charred marshmallow, cherry coulis and malt honeycomb. A decent, wide-ranging wine list opens at £16.
Chef/s: Julien Handley. **Open:** all week L 12 to 2.30 (3.30 Sun), D 6 to 9.15. **Closed:** 25 and 26 Dec, 1 Jan. **Meals:** alc (main courses £15 to £20). Set L and D £16 (2 courses) to £20. Sun L £22. **Details:** 65 seats. 50 seats outside. Bar. Parking.

■ Long Sutton
The Devonshire Arms

An enterprising local asset
Cooking score: 2
Modern British | £28
Cross Lane, Long Sutton, TA10 9LP
Tel no: (01458) 241271
www.thedevonshirearms.com

Over the years Phillip and Sheila Mepham have worked wonders with this old village inn-with-rooms, upgrading, revamping and reinvigorating the place. Pass through the grand entrance (it was once a hunting lodge for the Dukes of Devonshire) and find a striking mix of ancient and modern within, and you can rely on the food to be delicious. The starting point is good-quality materials, and the kitchen offers an inviting selection of contemporary pub dishes. Maybe try the home-cured salmon platter with pickled ginger, mouli, lime and wasabi, and partridge breast with pearl barley, pear and hazelnut, or comforting classics such as organic beef burger with Westcombe Cheddar and red pepper salsa, or char-grilled ribeye steak with garlic-herb butter, greens and chips. Indulge a sweet

tooth with a rich, dark chocolate and caramel tart with banana bread and homemade maple and pecan ice cream. Wines from £16.95.
Chef/s: Max Pringle. **Open:** all week L 12 to 2.30, D 7 to 9.30. **Closed:** 25 and 26 Dec. **Meals:** alc (main courses £13 to £19). **Details:** 60 seats. 60 seats outside. Bar. Music. Parking.

■ Lower Godney

LOCAL GEM
The Sheppey Inn
Modern British | £28
Lower Godney, BA5 1RZ
Tel no: (01458) 831594
www.thesheppey.co.uk

From the front it looks like a run-down village pub, the kind of place you would normally drive straight past. But once inside there's a cool, quirky interior (the owners were previously at the Wookey Hole Inn), local ciders and craft ales, occasional live music and great views over the Somerset Levels from the terrace at the back. Generous food takes in char-grilled ribeye with capsicum and smoked garlic butter and triple-cooked chips or burgers of fried chicken, spiced lamb, beef or monkfish. A real gem. Wines from £15. Closed Sun D.

■ Mells
Talbot Inn

Historic coaching inn oozing civilised charm
Cooking score: 3
British | £29
Selwood Street, Mells, BA11 3PN
Tel no: (01373) 812254
www.talbotinn.com

Overlooked by the church and manor house in one of the oldest villages in England, this gentrified 15th-century inn-with-rooms certainly puts on a convincing show. A warren of passageways revealing dining rooms with beams, timbers and roaring fires – there's no doubt, the place has an undeniable charm. Run by the same team behind the Beckford

Arms (see entry Fonthill Gifford, Wiltshire), there's an informal, relaxed vibe here. Chef Pravin Nayar and his team deliver pitch-perfect British food (with occasional Eurozone notes) on the daily changing menus; Cornish squid, laverbread, kohlrabi, lemon and sea purslane, perhaps, followed by whole roasted partridge, Parmesan polenta and chilli fried greens, or maybe a retro classic like croque-monsieur, salad and chips. Desserts include warm carrot cake and stem ginger ice cream, or you could finish with a trio of south west cheeses, including the locally made Westcombe Cheddar. Wines from £17.50.

Chef/s: Pravin Nayar. **Open:** all week L 12 to 3, D 6 to 9.30 (9 Sun). **Closed:** 25 Dec. **Meals:** alc (main courses £14 to £19). **Details:** 50 seats. 30 seats outside. Bar. Wheelchair access. Music. Parking.

▍Pensford

The Pig
British | £30
Hunstrete House, Pensford, BS39 4NS
Tel no: (01761) 490490
www.thepighotel.com

Set in 20 acres of well-manicured grounds, this elegant Georgian pile is now part of the Pig collection of boutique country house hotels. The potting-shed-inspired dining room sits a few muddy boot steps from the abundant kitchen garden that supplies seasonal ingredients on the menu. A starter of garden kale, rocket and Tor cheese salad with beetroot and shallots might be followed by slow-cooked crispy pig cheek with piccalilli and wild chive dressing. Wines from £16.50. Open all week.

Local Gem

Local Gems are the perfect neighbourhood venues, delivering good, freshly cooked food at great value for money.

▍Shepton Mallet

Blostin's
Modern British | £34
29-33 Waterloo Road, Shepton Mallet,
BA4 5HH
Tel no: (01749) 343648
www.blostins.co.uk

£5 OFF

Shepton Mallet's finest has been a feather in the Reed family's cap for 30 years now, and is strongly loved by its local constituency. There is more than a hint of French bistro to Nick Reed's cooking, though the ingredients are mostly sourced from regional farms and suppliers. Traditional fish soup with the Provençal trimmings is a case in point, and might be followed by the now classic serving of pork two ways – fillet and slow-roast belly – with apple in rich cider sauce, and then ginger meringue parfait with cappuccino cream to finish. Wines from £16.50. Open Tue to Sat D only.

▍Taunton
Augustus
Bistro cooking in a secluded courtyard
Cooking score: 5
Modern British | £28
3 The Courtyard, St James Street, Taunton,
TA1 1JR
Tel no: (01823) 324354
www.augustustaunton.co.uk

Tucked away in a little terrace not far from the Castle (see entry, Castle Bow Restaurant), from whence issued Richard Guest once upon a not-so-long-ago, Augustus is a characterful venue, the kind of place where outdoor tables in a private courtyard will fill a summer lunchtime with happiness. Guest has in recent years favoured a more nuts-and-bolts bistro style, and there's no undue modesty in offering specials such as truffled baked egg with polenta chips, or a hearty lamb stew with rosemary dumplings. That said, if you're in the market for something ritzier, Augustus can oblige with seared foie gras in celeriac soup with hazelnuts, or turbot fillet with boulangère potatoes in mushroom cream sauce. Potatoes get a thorough outing all through, whether they be paysanned, hashed, gratined or French-fried. Chips off the old pudding block come in the form of treacle tart and ginger ice cream, lemon posset or crème caramel. The big wine card is thorough in its explorations, starting at £17, with carafes and two glass sizes as well as bottles.

Chef/s: Richard Guest. **Open:** Tue to Sat 10 to 3, D 6 to 9.30. **Closed:** Sun, Mon, 1 week Christmas. **Meals:** alc (main courses £10 to £21). **Details:** 25 seats. 25 seats outside.

Castle Bow Restaurant

A special setting for outstanding dishes
Cooking score: 5
Modern British | £35
Castle Green, Taunton, TA1 1NF
Tel no: (01823) 328328
www.the-castle-hotel.com

With sizeable walls, battlements and 1,000 years of history, the imposing Castle looks like a place for a special occasion. But the Chapman family and their chef Liam Finnegan have hit on a format that suits Taunton. The Castle Bow Restaurant is stylish but informal, the food bang up to date. Liam Finnegan's passion for good ingredients underpins the whole enterprise and his cooking maintains a reassuring confidence and integrity. Making generous use of excellent material sets the tone in dishes such as ravioli of confit rabbit with broad beans, wood blewits and tarragon cream, or a sweet crab salad with heirloom tomatoes, avocado and gem lettuce, while a dish of roast turbot on a heap of leeks, spinach and samphire with mussels and a well-judged white wine cream sauce is one of many fish dishes to impress for both freshness and handling. Pimms jelly with mixed spring fruits and cucumber and mint

sorbet pleased one reporter and cheeses are the best of British. The wine list is well judged with bottles from £19.

Chef/s: Liam Finnegan. **Open:** Wed to Sat D only 6.30 to 9. **Closed:** Sun, Mon, Tue, Jan. **Meals:** alc (main courses £12 to £23). **Details:** 36 seats. Bar. Music. Parking.

The Willow Tree

Modish cooking in a low-beamed setting
Cooking score: 4
Modern British | £33
3 Tower Lane, Taunton, TA1 4AR
Tel no: (01823) 352835
www.thewillowtreerestaurant.com

Part of the draw of this restaurant in a 17th-century house hidden down a little alleyway not far from the Castle is attentive service from Rita Rambellas and her team. The intimate, rustic, country-cottage look of beams, old fireplace and candles has also met with approval. Darren Sherlock's sensible-length, modern menus offer cooking that may not be the most ambitious around, but the food is carefully prepared using good ingredients. Crowd-pleasers like the Montgomery Cheddar soufflé with a celery and walnut cream sauce (and at dessert stage bread-and-butter pudding) are never off the menu and share the stage with the likes of roasted butternut squash soup with smoked paprika oil and toasted pumpkin seed, and fillets of wild sea bass with celeriac purée and a mousse of leek and fine macaroni cheese. Bread is homemade, and desserts such as cappuccino crème brûlée finish the meal on a high note. Wines start at £18.95.

Chef/s: Darren Sherlock. **Open:** Tue, Wed, Fri and Sat D only 6.30 to 9. **Closed:** Sun, Mon, Thur, Jan, Aug. **Meals:** Set D £28 (Tue and Wed), £33 (Fri and Sat). **Details:** 25 seats. 12 seats outside. Bar. Music.

Brazz

Modern British | £28
Castle Bow, Taunton, TA1 1NF
Tel no: (01823) 252000
www.brazz.co.uk

Part of the Castle Hotel (see entry Castle Bow Restaurant), with its own entrance to one side, this contemporary, all-day eatery is run with cheerful efficiency and offers a menu of carefully wrought brasserie favourites. Flexible, seasonally aware and fairly priced, the menu casts its net wide for dishes to suit all appetites: chicken liver parfait, classic Caesar salad, steaks, burgers, roast Somerset lamb rump, roast chicken supreme with salad niçoise, and whole lemon sole with brown butter show the style. There's a short, global wine list of good-value drinking with house Sicilian at £13 a carafe. Open all week.

Wedmore
The Swan

Simple, satisfying local food
Cooking score: 2
Modern British | £28
Cheddar Road, Wedmore, BS28 4EQ
Tel no: (01934) 710337
www.theswanwedmore.com

Since this handsome old coaching inn was completely refurbished in 2011, legions of regulars have grown used to the luxury of having a consistent, welcoming hostelry at hand in Wedmore. But while the Swan has been spruced up with some style, it has not lost its atmosphere as a time-honoured English inn, complete with winter wood-burners and a summer beer garden. Just the sort of place to settle in with a newspaper and a pint of one of a host of local brews, or tuck into some proper modern British food: perhaps evergreens such as lightly spiced River Axe mussels and leeks with roast garlic aïoli, and char-grilled steak with hand-cut chips. But the kitchen can up the ante with butter-crusted cod fillet with roast salsify, barley and bordelaise sauce or Wedmore lamb chop with crispy lamb sausage, lemon and fennel, and crème caramel with blood-orange syrup and chocolate bourbon. Wines from £17.
Chef/s: Rob Smart. **Open:** all week L 12 to 3, Mon to Sat D 6 to 10. **Meals:** alc (main courses £13 to £23). Set L and D £22 (2 courses) to £28. Sun L £16.
Details: 70 seats. 50 seats outside. Bar. Wheelchair access. Music. Parking.

Wells
Goodfellows

Astute seafood cookery
Cooking score: 4
Modern British/Seafood | £36
5 Sadler Street, Wells, BA5 2RR
Tel no: (01749) 673866
www.goodfellowswells.co.uk

In the heart of England's smallest city, close to the mighty cathedral itself, Goodfellows trades on easy-going flexibility with a bustling café serving coffee and patisserie at the front, as well as a laid-back seafood-driven restaurant at the back. Up-close seating around the open kitchen on the ground floor enables diners to watch chef/patron Adam Fellows and his team at close quarters although a few tables under the atrium roof upstairs provide a more intimate setting. Either way, the results are precisely cooked and deeply satisfying dishes, from an opening seared tuna carpaccio with mustard and herbs, artichoke and olive to a main course of pan-fried scallops teamed with a crispy parcel of apple and vanilla and a light curry sauce with mussels and coriander. Poached rhubarb with strawberry ice cream and crumble biscuit makes for a memorable finale, as does the speciality tarte *du jour*. Wines from £18.
Chef/s: Adam Fellows. **Open:** Mon to Sat L 12 to 3.30, Wed to Sat D 6 to 10. **Closed:** Sun, 25 and 26 Dec, bank hols. **Meals:** alc (main courses £11 to £24). Set L £20 (2 courses) to £25. Tasting menu £48.
Details: 50 seats. 10 seats outside. Music.

The Old Spot

Unfussy fine-tuned food
Cooking score: 4
Modern British | £30
12 Sadler Street, Wells, BA5 2SE
Tel no: (01749) 689099
www.theoldspot.co.uk

'You can taste Ian Bates culinary education and lifetime of experience in every bite of his food,' wrote one who made a spring pilgrimage to this dark-wood British bistro in the centre of Wells. One major attraction is the way Mr Bates presents good materials perfectly: moules marinière 'may be boring to some' but not when the mussels are this fat, this tender, this precisely cooked, 'with lots of creamy, garlicky, parsley-loaded liquid reduced to an exacting point somewhere perfect between soup and sauce'. And where an opportunity for creativity presents itself, the kitchen is careful not to let any element of the dish suffer as a result. Onglet steak, crusty outside, pink within, Dorset snails braised to tenderness, spinach, a dollop of fiery horseradish cream, a perfect fondant potato and a single braised carrot 'that tastes of carrot' is a dish that 'that could not be improved upon'. The same can be said for crème brûlée, the engaging service 'that apparently knew every customer' and the modestly priced wine list that offers plenty of variety from £18.95.
Chef/s: Ian Bates. **Open:** Wed to Sun L 12.30 to 2.30, Tue to Sat D 7 to 9.30. **Closed:** Mon, 1 week Christmas, 1 week summer. **Meals:** alc (main courses £13 to £22). Set L £16 (2 courses) to £19. Sun L £22 (2 courses) to £25. **Details:** 50 seats.

■ Wrington
The Ethicurean

Garden-grown ingredients cooked with flair
Cooking score: 2
British | £30
Barley Wood Walled Garden, Long Lane, Wrington, BS40 5SA
Tel no: (01934) 863713
www.theethicurean.com

Terms like 'local' and 'seasonal' may have become overused menu soundbites in many establishments, but not at the Ethicurean. Located in the glasshouse of a fully-functioning restored Victorian kitchen garden on the outskirts of Bristol, you can't get much closer to your ingredients than this thriving enterprise – the chefs even make their own preserves, cider and vermouth. The ambitious kitchen utilises ethical and garden-grown ingredients with plenty of originality and panache, noted in the arresting flavours of Crown Prince squash soup with labneh, English chilli, cumin and pumpkin seed. This might be followed by Cornish hake, parsley-butter crust, swede fondant, clam sauce, black pudding and pickled charred shallots, or by slow-braised beef cheek with red cabbage purée, celeriac, fermented cucumber and samphire. Steamed quince pudding with anise sherbert, plum gel, walnut crumble and cider brandy custard is considered one satisfyingly inventive dessert. The conscientiously chosen wine list opens at £22.
Chef/s: Matthew and Iain Pennington. **Open:** Tues to Sun L 12 to 2 (2.30 Sat, 3.30 Sun), Tue to Sat D 7 to 9 (6.30 Fri and Sat). **Closed:** Mon. **Meals:** alc (main courses £17 to £22). **Details:** 60 seats. 40 seats outside. Bar. Wheelchair access. Music. Parking.

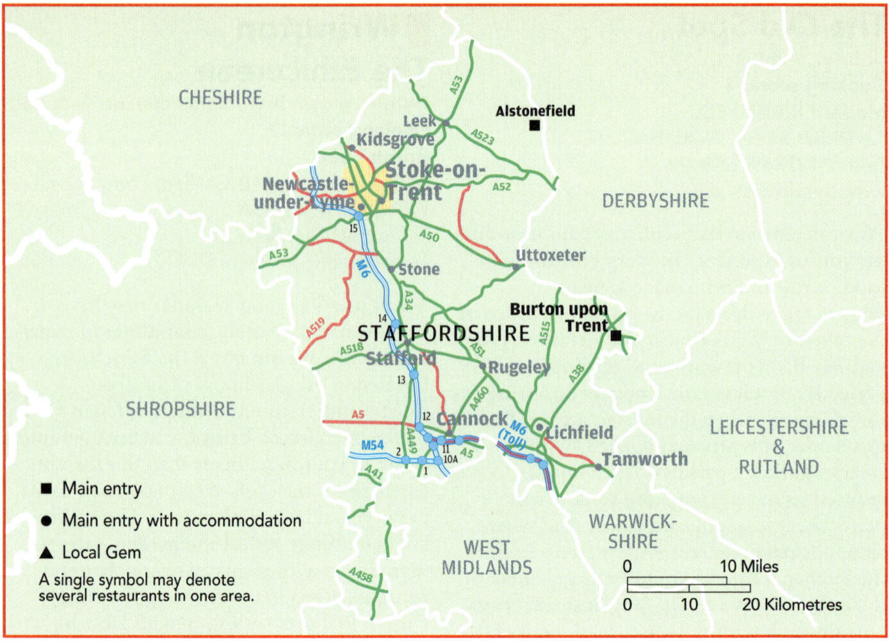

◼ Alstonefield
The George

Village local with comfort food
Cooking score: 2
Modern British | £30
Alstonefield, DE6 2FX
Tel no: (01335) 310205
www.thegeorgeatalstonefield.com

Any location scouts under instruction to find 'an idyllic English village pub' need look no further than the pretty Peakland village of Alstonefield. It's not that the George is overly chocolate-boxy, or even particularly historic or grand, it's just a cracking old stone pub that looks like it can give you a good time. And thanks to owner Emily Brighton, it can, for she has spent the last ten years getting the place into shape. The bar has rustic charm (and a little snug), and the dining room lime-plastered walls and country-style furniture. An organic garden provides for the kitchen. Start with fashionable first courses such as a salad of heritage beetroot and goats' cheese, or pig's head croquette and langoustine tail unified by a burnt apple purée. Move on to locally reared ribeye steak or Cornish cod with winter squash and gnocchi, and hit the sweet spot with vanilla bean pannacotta with honeycomb. Wines start at £18.
Chef/s: Chris Rooney. **Open:** all week L 12 to 2.30, D 6.30 to 9 (8 Sun). **Closed:** 25 Dec. **Meals:** alc (main courses £12 to £30). **Details:** 42 seats. 60 seats outside. Bar. Parking.

Please send us your feedback

To register your opinion about any restaurant listed in this guide, or a new restaurant that you wish to bring to our attention, please visit the web address at the bottom of the page. Your feedback informs the content of the book and will be used to compile next year's reviews.

Join us at thegoodfoodguide.co.uk

▋ Burton upon Trent
99 Station Street

Outstanding value from an old-town asset
Cooking score: 1
Modern British | £27
99 Station Street, Burton upon Trent,
DE14 1BT
Tel no: (01283) 516859
www.99stationstreet.com

'This place should be packed every evening,'
noted one visitor to this family-run bistro in
the shadow of Burton's famous breweries.
Owner/chef Daniel Pilkington's dedication to
the local cause shows in everything from the
unpretentious service to the straightforward
cooking of meticulously sourced ingredients.
A starter of honey-glazed ham hock salad with
sweet mustard aïoli and boiled quail's egg
might be followed by slow-braised lamb
shank with minted lamb spring roll and
rosemary, red wine and redcurrant glaze.
Bread-and-butter pudding with brandy-
soaked fruits and vanilla custard is one dessert
guaranteed to hit the sweet spot. Wines start
at £12.95.
Chef/s: Daniel Pilkington. **Open:** Thur to Sun L 12 to
2, Thur to Sat D 6.30 to 9. **Closed:** Mon, Tue, Wed.
Meals: alc (main courses £13 to £22). Set L £14 (2
courses) to £15. Sun L £17. **Details:** 40 seats.
Wheelchair access. Music.

▋ Stone

READERS RECOMMEND
Cullens

Modern British
Radford Street, Stone, ST15 8DA
Tel no: (01785) 818925
www.cullensrestaurant.co.uk
'Delicious homemade bread, appetisers and
amuse-bouche. Great attention to detail,
service friendly and efficient. Richard Cullen
is a superb chef.'

Playing Away

Chefs don't get to socialise like 'normals',
but every so often they have a trip
away from home – and they take their
knives with them. The most high-profile
relocation has seen Heston Blumenthal
move the Fat Duck to Melbourne for six
months during refurbishments in Bray. In
early 2015, René Redzepi took Noma to
Tokyo for a Japanese residency. So who
else is on the move?

Northcote's Obsession festival is the
big daddy of chef fests, turning a
quiet time for hospitality – it's usually
a week or so in late January – into a
must-go event. An impressive roster of
international and domestic chefs take
over for one night each. Ken Hom and
Phil Howard are regulars.

It's not big, but south London's Pizarro
has a mighty pull when it comes to
attracting guest chefs. Tom Kerridge,
Dan Doherty (of Duck & Waffle) and
Bocca di Lupo's Jacob Kenedy have
all cooked in José's kitchen.

Gary Usher and the Sticky Walnut
team from Cheshire are not averse to
travel, guesting at Angela Hartnett's
Murano. Gary might now be busy with
crowdfunded bistro Burnt Truffle, but
Murano will continue to host guest chefs.

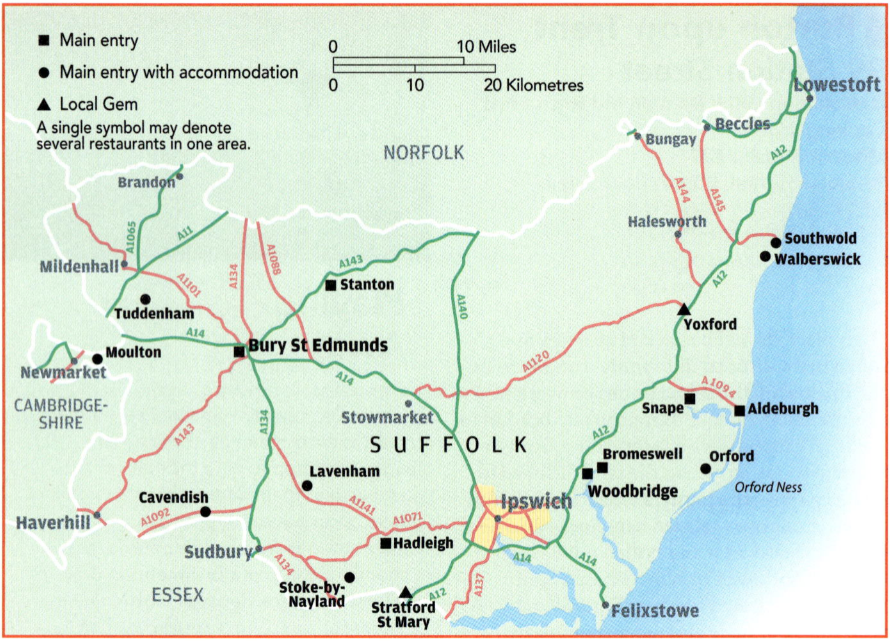

Aldeburgh
Regatta

Bright and breezy seaside brasserie
Cooking score: 1
Modern British | £28
171-173 High Street, Aldeburgh, IP15 5AN
Tel no: (01728) 452011
www.regattaaldeburgh.com

A stalwart of the Aldeburgh scene for many a year, this animated brasserie brings some welcome continental colour to a breezy Suffolk town – especially when the doors are flung open in summer. Seafood from the Aldeburgh boats plays a starring role on the menu, and Regatta is also renowned for its home-smoked delicacies – perhaps oak-smoked salmon with Thai cucumber salad or whole prawns with garlic mayo. Otherwise, the eclectic repertoire covers everything from Waldorf salad or butternut squash and sweet potato risotto to grilled Gressingham duck breast on parsnip mash with Calvados and mushroom sauce. To finish, don't miss the East Anglian cheeses. House wines from £15.
Chef/s: Robert Mabey. **Open:** all week L 12 to 2, D 6 to 10. **Closed:** 24 to 26 and 31 Dec, 1 Jan.
Meals: alc (main courses £12 to £22). Set L and early D £15 (2 courses) to £18. **Details:** 90 seats.

LOCAL GEM
The Aldeburgh Market Café

Modern British | £20
170-172 High Street, Aldeburgh, IP15 5AQ
Tel no: (01728) 452520
www.thealdeburghmarket.co.uk

Grab a pavement pew or a cosy table by the delightful deli to enjoy an eclectic fish-led menu that homes in on coastal favourites (think fish pie, smoked haddock gratin, classic fish soup with rouille and croûtons). A spirited Malaysian laksa with tiger prawns and a south Indian fish curry are among the several nods to warmer climes, while a smooth vanilla

Join us at thegoodfoodguide.co.uk

pannacotta or slice of lemon, almond and polenta cake sweetly calms any heat. Wine from £15.50. Open all week L.

Beccles

Upstairs at Baileys
Spanish
2 Hungate, Beccles, NR34 9TL
Tel no: (01502) 710609
www.upstairsatbaileys.co.uk

'The restaurant is above a delicatessen, and as the chef/owner is Spanish, so too is most of the menu, The 3-course set lunch is exceptional value and the dishes we had were all good.'

Bromeswell

NEW ENTRY
The Unruly Pig
Naughty maybe, but very nice
Cooking score: 3
Modern British | £30
Orford Road, Bromeswell, IP12 2PU
Tel no: (01394) 460310
www.theunrulypig.co.uk

Locals mourned the departure of the British Larder from this spot but have cheered vigorously the arrival of its replacement. Don't let the porcine logo's hint of menace put you off: there's a culinary treat in store. A 'something for everyone' tack means cocktails and grazing plates are offered alongside children's, sandwich and set menus, but it's à la carte that this place shines. Chef Dave Wall lets ingredients show themselves off, so a salty-sweet starter of goats' curd, beetroot and walnuts is a simple but on-the-button composition, a perfect prelude to hake fillet, which flakes softly from a pile of perfectly seasoned olive oil mash and vivid-green samphire. Share the charcoal-grilled duo of ribeye and feather-blade beef, or have a luxurious veal T-bone with muscular macaroni cheese all to yourself. The earthy flavour of a thyme pannacotta with just-poached rhubarb is a delicious pudding choice. Red wines dominate on a list that opens at £17.

Chef/s: Dave Wall. **Open:** Tue to Fri and Sun L 12 to 2.30 (3.30 Sun), Tue to Fri D 6 to 9.30. Sat 12 to 9.30. **Closed:** Mon, 1 to 14 Jan. **Meals:** alc (main courses £13 to £24). Set L £15 (2 courses) to £18. Sun L £20 (2 courses) to £25. **Details:** 90 seats. 50 seats outside. V menu. Bar. Wheelchair access. Music. Parking.

Bury St Edmunds
Maison Bleue
The freshest fish, worth seeking out
Cooking score: 4
Modern French | £43
30-31 Churchgate Street, Bury St Edmunds, IP33 1RG
Tel no: (01284) 760623
www.maisonbleue.co.uk

'Truly amazing' was all one happy diner needed to say after eating at this sleek sliver of France in the medieval heart of Bury St Edmunds. Others praise the spot-on service and the contemporary, comfortable décor – but go above all for the food. Fish is at the heart of Pascal Canevet's cooking, and he winkles out the best from the British Isles and beyond and presents it with extraordinary flair. Start with a classic fish soup or Orkney scallops – hand-dived of course – served with soft truffle meringue and egg yolk emulsion. Stick with fish for the main course and wild sea bass with Avruga caviar, ginger and tiny grelot onions, or swerve towards meat and a fillet of tender Breckland venison or rack of Suffolk lamb with salsify and a rich veal reduction. Raspberry and a coriander crème anglaise cut beautifully through an indulgent chocolate ganache. The wine list champions Gallic bottles, but is none the worse for that, and opens at a reasonable £17.95.

Chef/s: Pascal Canevet. **Open:** Tue to Sat L 12 to 2, D 7 to 9 (9.30 Sat). **Closed:** Sun, Mon, 3 weeks Jan, 2 weeks Aug. **Meals:** alc (main courses £18 to £30). Set L £20 (2 courses) to £25. Set D £34. **Details:** 60 seats. Music.

NEW ENTRY

1921

Classy cooking from a chef with pedigree
Cooking score: 3
Modern British | £33
19-21 Angel Hill, Bury St Edmunds, IP33 1UZ
Tel no: (01284) 704870
www.nineteen-twentyone.co.uk

Named after its Angel Hill address, 1921 is swiftly building a fanbase to judge by midweek lunchtime numbers. With Zack Deakins' experienced hand at the stove, maybe that's not surprising. Try his starter of hare ragù, gamey yet tender, with fittingly muscular flavours of salsify, chestnut gnocchi and pied de mouton mushrooms. A lighter option is the kaleidoscopic pink vodka-cured sea trout with golden-yolked quails' eggs on vivid-green watercress purée, topped with a flutter of baby-blue borage flowers. Gorgeous looks don't fully translate to the taste-buds, but no matter because to follow you might choose a sublime, just-cooked fillet of vanilla-scented cod that sits well with meaty oxtail and earthy white beans. Continue the fragrant theme with an orange and vanilla brûlée with orange sorbet and pain d'épices. A real draw is the exquisite canapé menu, and with a wine list opening at £15.95 it's no wonder this place is so popular.
Chef/s: Zack Deakins. **Open:** Mon to Sat L 12 to 2.15, D 6 to 9.15 (9.30 Fri and Sat). **Closed:** Sun.
Meals: alc (main courses £16 to £23). Set L £15 (2 courses) to £18. **Details:** 50 seats. Bar. Wheelchair access. Music.

Pea Porridge

Cheerily rustic neighbourhood star
Cooking score: 4
Modern British | £30
28-29 Cannon Street, Bury St Edmunds, IP33 1JR
Tel no: (01284) 700200
www.peaporridge.co.uk

Since pitching camp here in 2009, Justin and Junga Sharp have transformed this one-time village bakery into a rather special neighbourhood restaurant with its own way of doing things. You can still see the old bread ovens, and the whole place is cheerily rustic with its bare tables, crooked beams and exposed brickwork. The kitchen likes heritage ingredients, butcher's offcuts and bright Mediterranean flavours – although it also embarks on faraway forays for, say, curried sweetbreads with sweet potato and baby spinach or deep-fried pheasant kibbeh with tahini and sesame yoghurt. Pig's cheeks, ox heart and slow-braised mutton shoulder are seasonal favourites, while readers have raved about the goats' cheese salad with quince and beetroot, 'brilliantly gamey' slow-roasted leg of hare and fillet of sea bream with brown shrimps, Puy lentils and Datterini tomatoes. Desserts are a happy jumble involving anything from hot chocolate pudding and banana beignets to Pedro Ximénez sherry with vanilla ice cream. The lively wine list favours organic and boutique producers worldwide, with bottles from £16.95.
Chef/s: Justin Sharp. **Open:** Thur to Sat L 12 to 2, Tue to Sat D 6.30 to 9 (9.30 Fri and Sat). **Closed:** Sun, Mon, 2 weeks Christmas, first 2 weeks Sept.
Meals: alc (main courses £13 to £20). Set L and D £15 (2 courses) to £19. **Details:** 46 seats. Wheelchair access. Music. Babies at L only.

LOCAL GEMS

Ben's

Modern British | £26
43-45 Churchgate Street, Bury St Edmunds, IP33 1RG
Tel no: (01284) 762119
www.bensrestaurant.co.uk

Passionate farm-to-forker Ben Hutton has opened an 'excellent addition' to the Bury dining scene with this contemporary neighbourhood spot. Hutton rears much of the pork and lamb, so choose melting slow-roast pork belly or richly flavoured leg of lamb with Sunday roast trimmings. Midweek, try Ben's own bangers with black pudding bubble and squeak. Wine from £13.40. Closed Mon, Tue to Fri L and Sun D.

Join us at thegoodfoodguide.co.uk

Benson Blakes

Burgers | £20
88-89 St John's Street, Bury St Edmunds,
IP33 2AF
Tel no: (01284) 755188
www.bensonblakes.co.uk

£5 OFF

By day this high-street venue is a great burger joint popular with families – dedication to local sourcing means that the meat is almost 100% Suffolk beef, Suffolk Black bacon is the rasher of choice and buns are baked daily. At night you might want to walk on by unless you're up for live music and drinking. Reuben brisket in an onion sub roll and beerdawg (own-recipe beery bockwurst) play to the American servicemen stationed at RAF Mildenhall, there's an enthusiast's list of UK and international craft beers, and wines start at £14.95. Open all week.

■ Cavendish

NEW ENTRY
The George

Picture-perfect village eatery
Cooking score: 1
British | £30
The Green, Cavendish, CO10 8BA
Tel no: (01787) 280248
www.thecavendishgeorge.co.uk

 £5 OFF

Cavendish is a time-warp village, a place with a cared-for green, thatch aplenty, ducks on the pond and a light-filled restaurant that ices this very English cake beautifully. Wild mushrooms give a guinea fowl starter intense savouriness and broad bean, pea and Parmesan bruschetta is a flavour hit. To follow, hake with sweet potato, beetroot and spinach is as pleasing to the eye as it is tasty, while lively caper and ginger relish elevates a densely meaty cheeseburger to something special. Mango and lime offset the sweetness of a white chocolate and coconut pannacotta and pistachio crumb adds spot-on textural balance. Wine from £16.95.

Chef/s: Lewis Bennet. **Open:** all week L 12 to 3, Mon to Sat D 6 to 9.30. **Closed:** 24 to 26 and 31 Dec, 1 Jan. **Meals:** alc (main courses £10 to £22). Set L and D £13 (2 courses) £15. **Details:** 50 seats. 30 seats outside. Bar. Music. Parking.

■ Darsham

READERS RECOMMEND
Darsham Nurseries

Modern British
Main Road, Darsham, IP17 3PW
Tel no: (01728) 667022
www.darshamnurseries.co.uk
'It's heaven, a real find! Lovely plants and garden things to buy, and a fabulous café where the chef uses produce grown on site.'

■ Hadleigh
The Hadleigh Ram

Refined but relaxed market-town eatery
Cooking score: 2
Modern British | £30
5 Market Place, Hadleigh, IP7 5DL
Tel no: (01473) 822880
www.thehadleighram.co.uk

£5 OFF

All too often a splash of fashionable duck-egg paint, a bare-wood floor and some homely beams can mask a lack of foodie substance. Not so at this town-centre spot where fresh good looks frame an imaginative menu offering the likes of 'standout' tempura mussels with celeriac and caper remoulade, or a crab pannacotta with almond crumb, baby leeks and girolles to start. Taste Suffolk-reared meat in main courses that includes pan-roasted Dingley Dell pork rump and braised cheek served with a silky sweet potato purée and fittingly muscular flavours of fennel and ceps. A sweet finale could involve a lively ginger and lemon poached pear with creamy empress rice and almond crumb. There's praise for the relaxed atmosphere and 'cheerful and attentive' service. Wines from £19.20.

Chef/s: Oliver Macmillan. **Open:** all week L 12 to 2.30 (4 Sun), Mon to Sat D 6 to 9 (10 Fri and Sat). **Meals:** alc (main courses £13 to £23). Set L £16 (2 courses, Mon to Fri) to £18. Set D £16 (2 courses, Mon to Thur) to £18. **Details:** 50 seats. 20 seats outside. Wheelchair access. Music.

▋ Kessingland

READERS RECOMMEND
Waterfront
International
310 Church Road, Kessingland, NR33 7SB
Tel no: (01502) 741525
www.thewaterfrontkessingland.co.uk
'Very good value for money…a small, family run, beachside restaurant with amazing food. Fish is especially good and presentation excellent.'

▋ Lavenham

The Great House

Impressive Gallic cooking
Cooking score: 4
Modern French | £45
Market Place, Lavenham, CO10 9QZ
Tel no: (01787) 247431
www.greathouse.co.uk

Lavenham is considered to be England's best-preserved medieval village and the Great House a fine piece of Lavenham architecture (medieval encased by the 18th century), but it operates as an 'archetypal French bourgeois restaurant, immaculately done'. It's 'a real treat', too, for 30 years down the line a large part of this restaurant-with-rooms' continued appeal is cooking that keeps abreast of the times. Sweetbreads, for example, are fried in duck fat and served with glazed salsify, sautéed girolles, chicken broth and truffle oil emulsion, and main courses pile on the ingredients in happy profusion: roasted monkfish tail arrives with red onion and walnut marmalade, Roquefort cheese all fired up with espelette chilli, and glazed Williams pear balls; or there could be roast saddle of English lamb with garden peas

flan, fondant potatoes, lemongrass and oregano jus. To finish, both the warm dark chocolate fondant and a superlative plate-load from the French cheese trolley are hard to trump. The French-leaning wine list opens at £17.95.
Chef/s: Régis Crépy. **Open:** Wed to Sun L 12 to 2.30, Tue to Sat D 7 to 9 (9.30 Fri and Sat). **Closed:** Mon, Jan, 2 weeks summer. **Meals:** alc (main courses £20 to £30). Set L £20 (2 courses) to £25. Set D £35. Sun L £35. **Details:** 50 seats. 20 seats outside. Music.

▋ Moulton

The Packhorse Inn

Thoroughbred cooking in swanky surrounds
Cooking score: 3
Modern British | £30
Bridge Street, Moulton, CB8 8SP
Tel no: (01638) 751818
www.thepackhorseinn.com

Smartly refurbished, this one-time local drinking den in a village not far from Newmarket is now a thoroughbred in the pub-dining stakes – and a 'great place to stay', too. Food is 'way above expectations' – and terrific fun too. There are tricks and treats at every turn, from cups of partridge tea and a rabbit 'BLT' involving bacon jelly, loin and confit tomato to loin of Suffolk venison with braised shin, salsify and char-grilled broccoli or a take on scampi and chips with braised lettuce and minted peas. To finish, nibble on some 'mini afters' (doughnuts, fruit pastilles etc.) or try the clever-clever 'banana and custard' presented in a 'quilted jar' along with toffee fudge, banana bread and tempura banana. Service is professional, relaxed and chatty. Well-chosen 'affordable' wines from £17.50, with around 20 by the glass.
Chef/s: Phil Skinner. **Open:** all week L 12 to 2.30, D 7 to 9.30. **Meals:** alc (main courses £15 to £20). Set L £18 (2 courses) to £24. **Details:** 80 seats. 25 seats outside. Bar. Wheelchair access. Music. Parking.

Orford
Trinity, Crown & Castle
Anglo-Italian flavours in a magical setting
Cooking score: 3
Modern British | £35
Orford, IP12 2LJ
Tel no: (01394) 450205
www.crownandcastle.co.uk

An arrow's ping from medieval Orford Castle is this much-loved coastal restaurant. There's an unpretentious confidence about the place and a menu that is as appealing as the fire-warmed bar area is cosy. Starters such as a plate of Pinney's smoked salmon with brown bread and butter, or partridge from nearby Blaxhall with roast garlic and celeriac risotto, make the most of Suffolk's rich larder. A skate wing (landed at Orford of course) is golden-buttery, and while a scattering of capers doesn't quite give enough edge, the fish is substantially, satisfyingly flaky. Powerful Italian flavours dominate elsewhere – a dish of creamy seafood risotto wouldn't win any beauty contests but makes up for it with the salty sea-ness of the brown shrimps, langoustines and mussels. A meringue and apricot sundae is strictly for the sweet-toothed, finishing a meal roundly, especially when followed by an espresso that would please the pickiest of Italian guests. The wine list, its offer opening at £18.50, is a pleasure to browse.
Chef/s: Charlene Gavazzi and Ruth Watson. **Open:** all week L 12.15 to 2.15, D 6.30 to 9.15. **Meals:** alc (main courses £16 to £25). **Details:** 50 seats. 30 seats outside. V menu. Bar. Wheelchair access. Children over 8 yrs only at D.

Snape Maltings
The Plough & Sail
Making its mark by the Maltings
Cooking score: 1
Modern British | £25
Snape Maltings, IP17 1SR
Tel no: (01728) 688413
www.theploughandsailsnape.com

Set hard by the Snape Maltings, the Plough & Sail reels in the crowds with its rustic-chic good looks, Adnams ales and menus that make the most of local ingredients. The food strikes many chords, from pub classics of ploughman's and fish and chips, to carefully worked contemporary ideas such as a well-reported smoked duck salad with ginger, rhubarb and orange, and a 'superb' brown-sugar tart with crème fraîche sorbet and almond crumble. For mains, try breast of Gressingham duck, Parmentier potatoes and thyme jus. Wines from £15.50.
Chef/s: Oliver Burnside. **Open:** all week L 12 to 2.30 (3 Sat and Sun), D 6 to 9. **Meals:** alc (main courses £12 to £17). Set D £15 (2 courses) to £19.
Details: 80 seats. 50 seats outside. Bar. Wheelchair access. Music. Parking.

Southwold
Sutherland House
Oak-beamed heritage and low food miles
Cooking score: 2
Modern British | £30
56 High Street, Southwold, IP18 6DN
Tel no: (01502) 724544
www.sutherlandhouse.co.uk

There's much to praise about Andy and Kinga Rudd's restaurant-with-rooms: the setting in a 15th-century building (the oldest in Southwold); the dedication to seasonality and local sourcing; the charming service. Jed Tejada's robust cooking more than lives up to the occasion and he makes good use of fish, seafood and meats available from local markets. Fish dominates, and meals could

Symbols

 Accommodation is available
£30 Three courses for less than £30
£5 OFF £5-off voucher scheme
Notable wine list

open with well-flavoured garlic prawns with vegetable noodles, aïoli and lime, or tender salt-and-pepper battered squid teamed with chorizo, 'which worked well'. Beautifully fresh and well-timed roasted North Sea cod loin could follow, with bacon, root vegetable noodles and lyonnaise potatoes or, for those in the mood for meat, slow-braised belly of Blythburgh pork with mash, apple fondant, creamed cabbage and own-made black pudding. Among straightforward posh comfort desserts, a wonderful bread-and-butter pudding with an orange marmalade ice cream stands out. Wines from a short list start at £17.50.

Chef/s: Jed Tejada. **Open:** Tue to Sun L 12 to 2, D 7 to 9. **Closed:** Mon, 2 weeks Jan. **Meals:** alc (main courses £15 to £24). **Details:** 40 seats. 40 seats outside. Wheelchair access. Music.

LOCAL GEM

Southwold Smokehouse
Seafood | £20
Shed 22e, Blackshore, Southwold, IP18 6ND
Tel no: (01502) 724241
www.solebayfishco.co.uk

Readers delight in the rustic brick and wood surrounds, mismatched wooden furniture, the odd plates waiting on the tables along with cutlery in a jar and kitchen towel, but it's the family friendliness and good value that draws them back to this harbourside smokehouse and fish restaurant. The big selling point is plainly served, locally landed seafood: 'delicious fresh and battered oysters with an apparently homemade mayonnaise', say, or battered cod, lemon sole, sea bass or lobster, all served with excellent chips and salad. Seafood platters are popular, as is hot-roast smoked salmon, and there's a short, well-priced wine list from £16. Open daytime all week.

Stanton
The Leaping Hare
Charming vineyard eatery
Cooking score: 3
Modern British | £30
Wyken Vineyards, Stanton, IP31 2DW
Tel no: (01359) 250287
www.wykenvineyards.co.uk

£5
OFF

A devotee who has frequented the Leaping Hare for 15 years confirms that it's one of the area's more dependable culinary assets and a real charmer to boot: 'lovely place to eat, manages to be relaxed and stylish in a country sort of way'. It's not hard to see why the place is a local favourite – who could resist the impressively timbered, 400-year-old barn conversion and ever-courteous staff, not to mention the prospect of some cracking food. Wyken Estate game, perhaps in a terrine or a venison fillet with braised cabbage and beetroot tart Tatin, is an outright winner, but the kitchen also rolls out salmon, hot-smoked over vine prunings, and calf's liver with creamed potato, Savoy cabbage and crispy Suffolk bacon. Finish with a plate of local cheeses or something sweet – perhaps vanilla pannacotta, poached rhubarb and ginger madeleine. Try the fish-friendly Madeleine Angevine from Wyken Vineyards for £20, or a bottle of house red from Spain.

Chef/s: Simon Woodlow. **Open:** all week L 12 to 2.15, Fri and Sat D 7 to 9.15. **Closed:** 24 Dec to 6 Jan. **Meals:** alc (main courses £14 to £22). Set L £19 (2 courses) to £21. **Details:** 50 seats. 30 seats outside. Wheelchair access. Parking.

Stoke by Nayland

NEW ENTRY

The Angel Inn

Welcoming village pub back on foodie form
Cooking score: 2
Modern British | £28
Polstead Street, Stoke by Nayland, CO6 4SA
Tel no: (01206) 263245
www.angelinnsuffolk.co.uk

Stoke by Nayland is surely one of the prettiest places you could wish to visit. More importantly, it boasts a fine foodie pub. The reputation of the once-lauded Angel Inn has been restored by the skill of chef Mark Allen and the management team that run this and two other nearby places. Ham hock terrine is no stranger to posh pub menus, but Mark's is muscular and meaningful, the saltiness of the meat offset by densely sweet red onion marmalade. Follow it with sublime, crisp-skinned fillet of sea bass on spinach linguine, served with lip-lickingly buttery, garlicky prawns, or a trio of local venison (marinated loin, mini cottage pie, crispy terrine) with homely swede mash and glazed carrots. Just-poached rhubarb brings a welcome edge to an over-sweet rhubarb parfait. A thoughtful wine list opens at £15.95.
Chef/s: Mark Allen. **Open:** all week L 12 to 2.30 (3 Sat, 4 Sun), D 6 to 9.30 (9 Sun). **Meals:** alc (main courses £12 to £20). Set L £15 (2 courses, exc Sun) to £18. **Details:** 70 seats. 20 seats outside. Bar. Music. Parking.

Stratford St Mary

LOCAL GEM

The Swan

British | £28
Lower Street, Stratford St Mary, CO7 6JR
Tel no: (01206) 321244
www.stratfordswan.com

What joy when a pub manages to marry location, menu, drinks and service! This 16th-century former coaching inn on a pretty bend of the River Stour does just that. Follow a simple starter of pickled mackerel, dill mayonnaise and salted cucumber with a generous sharing platter of rare-breed meats, including local Red Poll beef. This is a haven for non-drivers with every dish thoughtfully paired with an interesting beer and wine. Brooklyn Black Chocolate Stout with white chocolate and vanilla ice cream anyone? Wine from £15.50. No food Mon and Tue.

Tuddenham
Tuddenham Mill

Appealing cooking in seductive setting
Cooking score: 5
Modern British | £40
High Street, Tuddenham, IP28 6SQ
Tel no: (01638) 713552
www.tuddenhammill.co.uk

As a boutique-style hotel, Tuddenham Mill has always been seen as a refreshingly stylish contrast to its olde-worlde setting. The former watermill, in 'gorgeous' countryside, is now an appealing, beautifully renovated building that mixes beams with bare black tables and stark, modern downlights. But there's substance as well as style, thanks to Lee Bye's contemporary cooking that fizzes and pops with bright ideas. Set menus are startlingly good value: spinach soup with blue cheese and crispy kale, and salmon with peperonata, whitebait and sea cabbage are both intricate enough to belie such kind pricing. Ingredients, too, are out of the top drawer – Goosnargh duck with Spanish squash, smoked paprika, feta and kale, for example, or Angus bavette steak with roasted bone marrow, chips, garlic and watercress both showcase British meat. For dessert, bitter chocolate mousse with walnuts, coriander and a zingy Calamansi lime ice cream is a particular delight. Wines from £18.95.
Chef/s: Lee Bye. **Open:** all week L 12 to 2.15, D 6.30 to 9.15. **Meals:** alc (main courses £17 to £25). Set L £16 (2 courses) to £25. Set D £25. Sun L £20 (2 courses) to £25. **Details:** 50 seats. 40 seats outside. V menu. Bar. Music. Parking.

Walberswick
The Anchor
Country-pub cooking of seasonal freshness
Cooking score: 3
Modern British | £30
The Street, Walberswick, IP18 6UA
Tel no: (01502) 722112
www.anchoratwalberswick.com

Look for the sky-blue frontage of the village pub across the footbridge from Southwold, where three expansive lawn areas can accommodate no fewer than 200 outdoor diners – practically enough for a rave. Sophie Dorber continues to cook inspired country-pub food with the accent on seasonal freshness. Seafood is highly reliable, as was discovered by a reporter regaled with 'an extremely generous helping' of mussels and leeks in cream sauce. Cod is either roasted and doused in Asian broth, or else beer-battered and dressed in tartare fired up with jalapeño, while ribeye steaks and duck confit with spiced red cabbage and mash take care of meat business. A Sunday party had the 'beautifully pink' roast lamb with a mound of roasties: 'portion sizes are designed for country walkers, and rather outfaced the weedier among us'. Had they been able to tackle puddings, treacle tart and clotted cream ice cream could have gone down a treat. Speciality beers are a strong suit. Wines from £15.95.
Chef/s: Sophie Dorber and Jason Bright. **Open:** all week L 12 to 3, D 6 to 9 (10 Sun). **Closed:** 25 Dec. **Meals:** alc (main courses £14 to £19). **Details:** 90 seats. 200 seats outside. Bar. Wheelchair access. Parking.

Local Gem

Local Gems are the perfect neighbourhood venues, delivering good, freshly cooked food at great value for money.

Woodbridge
The Riverside
Meals and movies by the river
Cooking score: 1
Modern British | £30
Quay Street, Woodbridge, IP12 1BH
Tel no: (01394) 382174
www.theriverside.co.uk

£5 OFF

A restaurant, theatre and cinema, The Riverside is the entertainment hub of this thriving Suffolk town, where you can catch a movie and tuck into some classy modern British grub. The glass-fronted restaurant overlooks the road – not the river – and makes a cheery spot for the likes of seared pigeon with braised lentils and pancetta, moules marinière and pan-roasted cod with pearl barley and black truffle granola. Finish with passion fruit and orange tart. Wines from £15.
Chef/s: Dan Jones. **Open:** all week L 12 to 2.15 (2.30 Sun), Mon to Sat D 6 to 9.30 (10.15 Fri and Sat). **Closed:** 25 and 26 Dec. **Meals:** alc (main courses £12 to £20). **Details:** 40 seats. 18 seats outside. Bar. Wheelchair access. Music.

Yoxford
LOCAL GEM
Main's
Modern British | £27
High Street, Yoxford, IP17 3EU
Tel no: (01728) 668882
www.mainsrestaurant.co.uk

Bread-making classes and great-value 'pauper's nights' add to the bubbly vibe in Nancy Main's self-named restaurant – a local asset occupying a converted draper's shop. Seasonal Suffolk ingredients get top billing on a regularly updated menu that might run from wild sea bass with spinach velouté and parsnip purée to roast pheasant with braised leeks, lemon and white wine gravy. After that, Seville orange tart with porcini ice cream sounds particularly intriguing. Wines from £14.50. Open Thur to Sat D.

Join us at thegoodfoodguide.co.uk

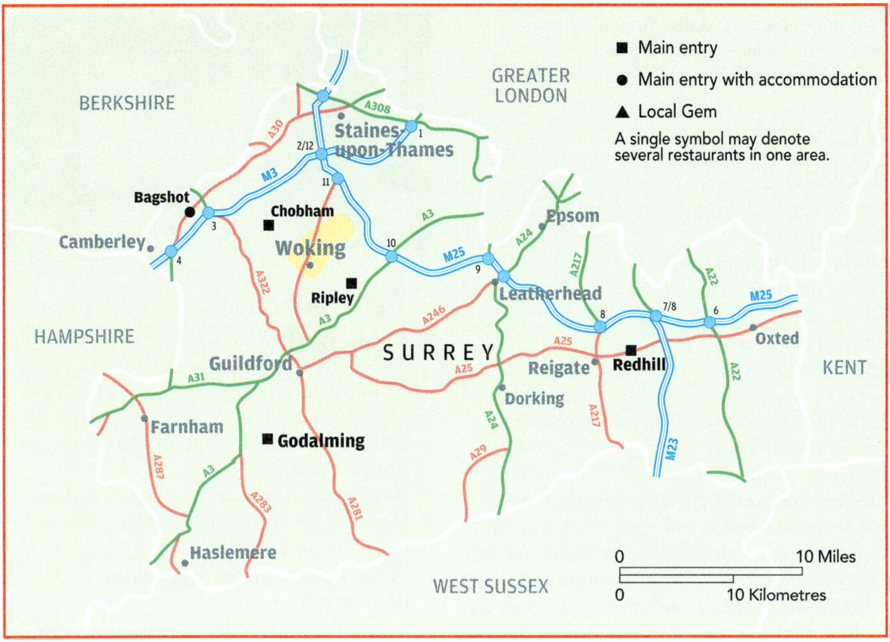

Bagshot

Michael Wignall at the Latymer

Bold, creative, risk-taking chef
Cooking score: 6
Modern European | £88
Pennyhill Park Hotel, London Road, Bagshot,
GU19 5EU
Tel no: (01276) 486150
pennyhillpark.co.uk

The olde-worlde styling of this luxury hotel can feel a little concocted, as it's clear that some parts are relatively new, but the heart of the place dates back to 1609. It's hard to tell where old ends and new begins, particularly in the restaurant, where beamed ceilings, wood panelling, tapestry panels and leaded windows crank up the antique charm. Michael Wignall's cooking is not the most obvious match for such a traditional setting. The bold, creative chef knows how to take risks and pulls in ingredients from far and wide – especially Japan – and the results can be stunning: the 'balanced, intricate flavours' of langoustine ceviche with octopus presse, avocado, smoked roe taramasalata, Belgian oscietra caviar and pickled mooli, or a 'thrilling' intermediate course of clam cassoulet with cuttlefish gnocchi. A main course featuring poached and roasted turbot, oriental cabbage, silken tofu, teriyaki shimeji mushrooms and spring onion with sesame and coconut dressing also garnered praise, but Wignall's spirit of invention can stretch too far for some: a pre-dessert of violet ice cream with white chocolate 'Aero', crumbled ginger cake, chocolate 'rocks' and yoghurt gel left one diner unconvinced, although a fresh pairing of compressed pineapple with mint, sweet cicely ice cream and a coconut biscuit got the thumbs-up. The wine list is hefty, with prices to match. Be prepared to spend £49 and over.

Chef/s: Michael Wignall. **Open:** Wed to Fri L 12 to 1.45, Tue to Sat D 6.30 to 8.45 (7 Wed to Fri). **Closed:** Sun, Mon, first 2 weeks Jan. **Meals:** Set L £38 (3 courses). Set D £88 (3 courses). Tasting menu

£105 (10 courses). **Details:** 50 seats. V menu. Bar. Wheelchair access. Parking. Children over 12 yrs only.

Chobham

Stovell's

Ambitious cooking in leafy commuter-land
Cooking score: 6
Modern European | £42
125 Windsor Road, Chobham, GU24 8QS
Tel no: (01276) 858000
www.stovells.com

£5 OFF

'A true find,' enthused a first-time visitor to this venerable Tudor farmhouse, now a well-bred and handsome restaurant. The half-timbered building still drips heritage, but modern furnishings and bold wallpaper lend some zest to the antiquated, beamed interior. Fernando and Kristy Stovell's ambitious, sometimes complex, cookery – 'a far cry from the standard fare available at outlets in the Chobham, Woking, Weybridge area' – deals in seasonal ingredients that are worked up into precisely timed, imaginative dishes packed with accessible flavours. Reporters not only applaud the breadth of the menu, but also highlight their favourites, from a carpaccio of roe deer teamed with jalapeño, mushrooms, tahoon (cress) and ponzu dashi, to mains of sensitively handled halibut poached in olive oil and served with pickled pear, parsnips, salsify and razor clams, and a côte de boeuf (for two) from the wood-fired grill. There has been praise, too, for the homemade bread, the 'exquisite' pata negra aged ham carved at the table, and for a 'divine' rhubarb pannacotta with hibiscus jelly, yoghurt fool and granola. A well-thought-out wine list opens at £22.
Chef/s: Fernando and Kristy Stovell. **Open:** Tue to Fri and Sun L 12 to 2.30 (3 Sun), Tue to Sat D 6 to 10.
Closed: Mon, first 2 weeks Jan. **Meals:** Set L £17 (2 courses) to £21. Set D £35 (2 courses) to £42.
Details: 74 seats. 20 seats outside. Bar. Music. Parking.

Fernando Stovell

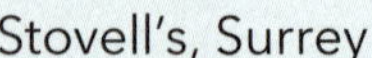

Stovell's, Surrey

What do you enjoy the most about being a chef?
Seeing fresh produce arrive each day and dealing with passionate suppliers.

What's your newest ingredient discovery?
Wood, I never stop learning about it. Fire offers an amazing spectrum of flavour, it can be very addictive. It's a very primal element that's instinctively human.

At the end of a long day, what do you like to cook?
Fresh crab sandwich with brown and white meat, chilli and lots of mayonnaise.

Is there a particular dish that evokes strong memories for you?
Victor Arguinzoniz from Asador Etxebarri's lightly grilled oscietra caviar, that says it all. Simplicity, skill and quality of ingredients.

Tell us something about yourself that will surprise your diners.
I was an officer in the Mexican army many years ago.

Join us at thegoodfoodguide.co.uk

Godalming

La Luna

Smart Italian blend of classic and new
Cooking score: 4
Italian | £32
10-14 Wharf Street, Godalming, GU7 1NN
Tel no: (01483) 414155
www.lalunarestaurant.co.uk
£5
OFF

The sleek contemporary décor of charcoal-grey and blond wood distinguishes La Luna from the run of Italian trattorie. It's a smart location for some vividly seasoned, fresh regional dishes and standards, cooked with flair and energy by Valentino Gentile. If you can tear yourself away from the antipasti platters of cured meats and fritti, there are grilled mackerel with puntarelle in anchovy dressing, or smoked mozzarella with dried tomatoes and aubergine, to start. Main courses reach back through the centuries for surprising ways with fish – crusting a skate wing in orange zest and fennel – or wrapping pork fillet in Sardinian ham and pairing it with caponata. Pasta, gnocchi and risotto options are all present and correct at primi stage for those with the appetite, and the desserts are hard to resist, too, when tiramisu is further pepped up with orange and chocolate, and an apple, sultana and pine nut torta comes with crème brûlée ice cream and caramel sauce. An authoritative tour of Italy's wine regions opens in Sicily at £15.95.
Chef/s: Valentino Gentile. **Open:** Tue to Sat L 12 to 2, D 7 to 10 (6.30 Sat). **Closed:** Sun, Mon, 25 and 26 Dec, Easter, bank hols. **Meals:** alc (main courses £12 to £22). Tasting menu £85 (7 courses). **Details:** 58 seats. Music.

Redhill

The Pendleton

Innovative, modern, Brit-Med cooking
Cooking score: 3
Modern British | £37
26 Pendleton Road, St Johns, Redhill, RH1 6QF
Tel no: (01737) 760212
www.thependleton.co.uk
£5
OFF

With its pretty back terrace, pared-down interior (think plain tables and neutral colours) and excellent front of house, this restaurant in a former pub is just the ticket for Redhill's locals. It's also a destination for those living further afield, for Jon Coomb, who last appeared in the Guide in 2012 at the Westerly in Reigate, has a loyal following in these parts. He puts much effort into sourcing and the cooking is innovative in a modern British-cum-Mediterranean way, with occasional global forays such as the 'stunning' ceviche of scallops (thick chunks) in a sauce zingy with lime, coriander, chilli and cool avocado mojo that so impressed at inspection. Carefully crafted dishes follow the seasons – in April that could mean English asparagus with soft boiled egg and dukkah, and confit of duck landaise with watercress and blood-orange salad and al forno potatoes. Rhubarb topped with a glazed Sauternes custard is a brilliant final flourish. Wines from £16.
Chef/s: Jon Coomb. **Open:** Wed to Sun L 12 to 2.30 (3.30 Sun), Wed to Sat D 7 to 10. **Closed:** Mon, Tue (for food), 24 to 26 Dec. **Meals:** alc (main courses £14 to £23). **Details:** 42 seats. 40 seats outside. Bar. Music. Parking.

▌Ripley
The Anchor
Inviting dining pub with a touch of class
Cooking score: 3
Modern British | £35
High Street, Ripley, GU23 6AE
Tel no: (01483) 211866
www.ripleyanchor.co.uk
£5
OFF

Found on Ripley's high street, across the road from its big-brother fine diner, Drakes (see entry), this 16th-century pub is a cut above your average village watering hole. Inside it is smart and sassy, with original features offset by simple modern furnishings, slate floors and understated imagery (which pays tribute to Ripley's heritage as a one-time cycling mecca). Mike Wall-Palmer's commendably short, seasonal menus are bursting with good ideas, perhaps rabbit ravioli with mushrooms and chestnut sauce or slow-cooked duck leg with mash, Savoy cabbage and liquorice sauce. Fish also shows up strongly, as in well-timed hake teamed with Jerusalem artichoke, broccoli, almond and crispy oyster. There's also no dipping when it comes to desserts such as frozen chocolate mousse with peanut biscotti and orange ice cream. Bar snacks and the excellent-value set lunch also get the thumbs-up, and the short, wide-ranging wine list starts at £18.
Chef/s: Michael Wall-Palmer. **Open:** Tue to Sun L 12 to 2.30 (4 Sun), Tue to Sat D 6 to 9.30. **Closed:** Mon, 25 Dec. **Meals:** alc (main courses £12 to £19). Set L £15 (2 courses) to £19. **Details:** 40 seats. 20 seats outside. Bar. Wheelchair access. Music. Parking. No children after 7.30

Drake's Restaurant
Picture-perfect modern food
Cooking score: 5
Modern British | £60
The Clock House, High Street, Ripley, GU23 6AQ
Tel no: (01483) 224777
www.drakesrestaurant.co.uk
£5
OFF

The dapper Georgian building in a village that dates back to Norman times is home to a restaurant with 21st-century vivacity. Not the setting so much – which is simply chic and soothing – but what appears on the plate, for Steve Drake is a chef with the measure of contemporary ways when it comes to making an impact. Via tasting menus named 'Flavour Journey' and 'Flavour Discovery', and now a fixed-price carte that affords a choice (back by popular demand, perhaps, and not available Saturday night), the kitchen delivers inspired dishes such as Norfolk quail with a sherry glaze, langoustine and swede spiked with cumin. Flavours are judged just so and every dish is a looker: roast halibut with girolles purée and miso and red wine emulsion, say, and a dessert that creatively combines lavender, blueberry and ginger as parfait, compote and ice cream. The serious wine list starts at £18 and gives good options by the glass.
Chef/s: Steve Drake. **Open:** Wed to Sat L 12 to 2, Tue to Sun D 7 to 9.30. **Closed:** Mon, 1 week Jan, 1 week Easter, 2 weeks Aug. **Meals:** Set L £28 (3 courses). Tasting menu £60 (6 courses) to £80. **Details:** 40 seats. V menu. Bar.

Brighton
The Chilli Pickle

Quirky modern Indian
Cooking score: 2
Indian | £26
17 Jubilee Street, Brighton, BN1 1GE
Tel no: (01273) 900383
www.thechillipickle.com
£30

'I haven't had such a good Indian since my last time in India!' Chilli Pickle's zingy, confident take on the subcontinent's culinary traditions has drawn the crowds since opening in 2008. Brighton readers are enthusiastic about this modern and colourful Indian joint. The diverse repertoire avoids bog-standard curry house fare. Staying true to traditional Indian methods yet veering off on creative tangents, the extensive menu covers myriad bases, from Kerala to Hyderabad, via the Himalayas and beyond. Daytime offerings include thalis, a veritable cornucopia of goodies: a platter of vibrant curries, rice, bread, dal, raita, vegetables, chutney and pickle. Pungent Kathi rolls, roti and dosa, and street-food inspired bites feature, too. For dinner, more substantial fare is on the cards: tandoori chicken, kebabs, curries and biryanis. Wines from £18.
Chef/s: Alun Sperring. **Open:** all week L 12 to 3, D 6 to 10.30 (10 Sun). **Meals:** alc (main courses £11 to £16). Set D £25 (2 courses) to £29. **Details:** 115 seats. 16 seats outside. Wheelchair access. Music.

Food For Friends

Eclectic veggie favourite
Cooking score: 1
Vegetarian | £24
17-18 Prince Albert Street, The Lanes, Brighton, BN1 1HF
Tel no: (01273) 202310
www.foodforfriends.com

£30

As a veggie vanguard since 1981, Food For Friends may have started off as an old-school wholefood stopover, but for over a decade now it's been at the sharp end of contemporary vegetarian dining. The corner spot with its curvy windows and sleek woody interior is the setting for meze-style sharing plates and refined-looking dishes of Med-, Middle Eastern- and North African-inspired food. Share ricotta and shallot dumplings with creamy caraway-flavoured Savoy cabbage (or go solo), and move on to main-course curry platter or twice-baked goats' cheese soufflé with hazelnut and parsley pesto. Finish with a vegan chocolate truffle torte. Wines from £18. **Chef/s:** Tomas Kowalski. **Open:** all week 12 to 10 (10.30 Fri and Sat). **Closed:** 25 and 26 Dec. **Meals:** alc (main courses £11 to £13). Set L and D (3 courses) £22. **Details:** 70 seats. 20 seats outside. V menu. Wheelchair access. Music.

The Gingerman

Jam-packed foodie hot spot
Cooking score: 3
Modern European | £37
21a Norfolk Square, Brighton, BN1 2PD
Tel no: (01273) 326688
www.gingermanrestaurants.com

As the Gingerman approached a landmark birthday (18 in the summer of 2016), refurbishment introduced a more casual look, introducing exposed brickwork and plain brown leather banquettes to the relatively small space. It's hardly a sea change, but the new-found neutrality and extra edge seems entirely in keeping with both Brighton and current trends. The fixed-price carte (a proper bargain at lunch) serves up perky modern dishes that impress with their creativity and execution. Get going with red cabbage gazpacho with crispy goats' cheese or pigeon breast with a maple glaze and cauliflower purée, before cod (au naturel and smoked) arrives with a trendy charred leek and buttermilk dressing. Veggies get a fab duck egg curry. Among desserts, popcorn pannacotta with peanut butter, powder and banana crisp plays to the gallery, while rhubarb soufflé delivers classic refinement. Wines from £16.

Chef/s: Ben McKellar and Mark Charker. **Open:** Tue to Sun L 12.30 to 2, D 7 to 10. **Closed:** Mon, first 2 weeks Jan. **Meals:** Set L £15 (2 courses) to £18. Set D £32 (2 courses) to £37. Sun L £24. **Details:** 32 seats. Music.

The Jolly Poacher

Easy-going pub with fashionable food
Cooking score: 2
Modern European | £30
100 Ditchling Road, Brighton, BN1 4SG
Tel no: (01273) 683967
www.thejollypoacher.com

£5 OFF

Set up by the team behind the Jolly Sportsman at East Chiltington (see entry), this revitalised town boozer sits well in food-obsessed Brighton. Drinkers have just enough room to sup real ales amid the rough wooden tables, but most attention focuses on the blackboard menu and the output of the open-to-view kitchen. Modern nibbles of Manchego and quince or bread with dukkah start things off, and the menu is littered with equally fashionable ideas ranging from baked duck egg with chorizo on toast or pan-fried scallops with 'dong po' pork to crispy calves' brains or confit pumpkin and wild mushroom arancini with artichoke hearts and smoked aubergine dressing. Char-grilled steaks and beer-battered cod naturally come with triple-cooked chips, sides include black cabbage, and wholesome desserts might feature walnut, ginger and apricot pudding with Muscovado sauce and whipped cream. A tidy 30-bin wine list has house selections from £11.50 a carafe (£5.75 a glass).

Chef/s: Anthony Burns. **Open:** Tue to Sun L 12 to 2.30 (10 to 3 Sat and Sun), Tue to Sat D 6 to 9.30 (10 Fri and Sat). **Closed:** Mon. **Meals:** alc (main courses £15 to £23). Set L £10 (2 courses) to £14. Set D £14 (2 courses) to £17. Sun L £20 (2 courses). **Details:** 60 seats. 16 seats outside. Music.

The Restaurant at Drakes

Fine dining at a classy boutique hotel
Cooking score: 4
Modern European | £40
43-44 Marine Parade, Brighton, BN2 1PE
Tel no: (01273) 696934
www.therestaurantatdrakes.co.uk

The expression 'boutique hotel' was first coined in the USA in 1984 (apparently, according to Wikipedia), and it's fair to say that Drakes is the personification of the style in a city that is particularly suited to the genre. This Georgian pearl overlooking the sea has a cocktail bar with watery views and a basement restaurant that aims to bring a bit of refinement to the seafront. The fine-dining gloss extends to a menu that is interspersed with freebie courses such as an excellent salmon ballotine to get you going. There are no fireworks or histrionics, simply classically minded modern European options from maple-glazed quail breast with faro 'risotto' to a spring vegetable salad of seasonal stuff presented in a pretty pile. Guinea fowl and sweetbreads come in a main course with macho Umbrian lentils, and local sea trout with a shy sorrel sauce, while Brillat-Savarin brings a satisfying hit to a cheesecake. Wines start at £25.
Chef/s: Andrew MacKenzie. **Open:** all week L 12.30 to 1.45, D 7 to 9.30. **Meals:** alc (main courses £20 to £25). Set L £20 (2 courses) to £25. Set D £30 (2 courses) to £40. Sun L £30. Tasting menu £55.
Details: 42 seats. Bar. Music.

The Salt Room

Big, bold and seafood-focused
Cooking score: 2
Modern British | £36
106 Kings Road, Brighton, BN1 2FN
Tel no: (01273) 929488
www.saltroom-restaurant.co.uk

Occupying a corner of the Hilton Metropole Hotel, with views over the skeletal remains of the West Pier and the new i360, the Salt Room is a seafood-focused restaurant that is just as happy to whack a Black Angus ribeye steak as a whole sea bass in its Josper oven. Related to the Coal Shed (see entry), it's big, bold and full of beans. The terrace has those views over the traffic to the sea, while indoors an army of waiting staff await in the large, throbbing dining room. They make a big deal of sustainability and like the idea of you sharing with a friend (that sea bass maybe). Keep a starter such as octopus with heritage tomatoes all to yourself, or check out the oysters. Main-course South Indian fish burger reflects the casual ethos, with red meat represented by those steaks or rump of lamb. Lemongrass mousse with jelly, sherbet and a sorbet made from local sparkling wine is a modern finish. Needed extra side dishes can bump up the cost. Wines start at £17.
Chef/s: Dave Mothersill. **Open:** all week L 12 to 4, D 6 to 10 (10.30 Fri and Sat). **Meals:** alc (main courses £14 to £24). Set L and early D £15 (2 courses) to £18.
Details: 84 seats. 55 seats outside. Bar.

Sam's of Brighton

Bistro classics in the heart of Kemptown
Cooking score: 3
Modern European | £30
1 Paston Place, Kemptown, Brighton, BN2 1HA
Tel no: (01273) 676222
www.samsofbrighton.co.uk

Sam Metcalfe's restaurant, right in the heart of Kemptown between the Royal Sussex Hospital and the sea, received an injection of Gallic va-va-voom when he went into partnership with Frenchman Ollie Couillaud in 2014. They're both talented chefs and the word is 'exciting new ventures are planned'. Lucky Brighton. An easy-going attitude pervades front-of-house, where blackboards display daily specials and photos of Sam's family dominate the rear wall. If the setting is unpretentious and classically inspired, so too is the menu, with Ollie turning out flavour-packed, generously sized dishes of vim and vigour. Galician-style octopus, fired up with smoky paprika, is as tender as can be in a warm salad, with main courses showing a light touch (wild sea bass steamed to perfection) and providing forceful flavours (pink and tender duck breast with candied beetroot and port jus). Finish with a cracking rhubarb crumble. The wine list has plenty of choice by the glass and carafe; bottle prices start at £17.

Chef/s: Ollie Couillaud. **Open:** Tue to Sun L 12 to 4, D 6 to 10 (10.30 Sat, 9 Sun). **Closed:** Mon, 25 and 26 Dec. **Meals:** alc (main courses £14 to £22). Set L £15 (2 courses) to £16. Set D £28 (3 courses). Sun L £24. **Details:** 50 seats. Music.

The Set

Boho set-up with on-trend menus
Cooking score: 2
Modern British | £30
Artist Residence, 33 Regency Square,
Brighton, BN1 2GG
Tel no: (01273) 324302
www.thesetrestaurant.com

The city's newest landmark is the i360, a 163-metre viewing tower (imagine a doughnut sliding up and down a pole), and the Artist Residence boutique hotel has a prime position overlooking the action (or building works as we go to press). This hip hotel has an equally boho restaurant called the Set, where the young chefs work from an open kitchen creating plates of food that could hardly be more on-trend. Choose one of three set menus (one of them veggie) and prepare for some creative combos that (mostly) work a treat. Excellent produce is central to the conceit, like the ace tomatoes placed in a salad with red and white strawberries, olives and sheets of white balsamic gel, or a smoky number that combines BBQ hake with charred chicory, pulled ham and smoked aïoli. Mackerel comes with vindaloo bacon, the white chocolate for dessert is smoked, and even the music is smoking hot. Wines start at £18.

Chef/s: Dan Kenny and Semone Bonner. **Open:** Tue to Sat L 12.30 to 3, D 6 to 9.30. **Closed:** Mon, Sun. **Meals:** Set L and D £29 to £35. **Details:** 20 seats. V menu.

Silo

Principled and passionate
Cooking score: 3
Modern British | £28
39 Upper Gardner Street, Brighton, BN1 4AN
Tel no: (01273) 674259
www.silobrighton.com

When you hear about the 'pre-industrial food system', the zero waste philosophy (that's Bertha, the compost machine on the way in) and catch a glimpse of the chipboard walls and chairs, you might be thinking you'll be eating mung bean casserole, so how about ox heart with ugly onions and horseradish mash? Douglas McMaster has created a bakery, café and restaurant in a chunky warehouse in the North Lanes, where old and new techniques collide to create a menu that places provenance and flavour above all else. From the open kitchen come heirloom tomatoes grown in the county, tasting like actual tomatoes (so rare these days), with smoked quinoa and lovage, a generous pile of asparagus served simply with a runny egg, followed by that ox heart, a dish full of heart (and soul), or a fishy number such as locally landed plaice with seaweed salad. Whey sorbet with pickled petals is icy and aromatic. Drink locally brewed beers (from jam jars), cocktails and wines from £22.

Chef/s: Douglas McMaster. **Open:** Mon to Sat 9 to 8.30 (5 Mon). Sun 10 to 5. **Meals:** alc (main courses £9 to £14). **Details:** 55 seats. Wheelchair access. Music.

64 Degrees

Loud, packed and a lot of fun
Cooking score: 4
Modern British | £30
53 Meeting House Lane, Brighton, BN1 1HB
Tel no: (01273) 767914
www.64degrees.co.uk

With its sister restaurant opening in London in 2014, Michael Bremner's 64 Degrees continues to ride the small plate zeitgeist. Here where it all began (and that was only in 2013), the spirit and vitality of the place brings in the hordes to sit at the counter by the open kitchen, or at one of the few simple wooden tables (which you might have to share). It's urban, intimate, loud and exciting. There are four dishes in each section of the menu – meat, fish, veg, dessert – and you might well want them all. Hits this year include alexander buds stuffed with cheese and served with hollandaise dipping sauce ('a revelation') and the slow-cooked beef rib. The chicken wings fired up with kim-chee and Barkham Blue cheese remain a fixture, as does the 'positively intoxicating' rum bear jelly dessert. The staff keep on top of the fast-paced activity. Drink English artisan beer, Welsh cider or something from the concise wine list (from £21).

Chef/s: Michael Bremner. **Open:** all week L 12 to 3, D 6 to 9.45 (10.30 Sat and Sun). **Closed:** 25 and 26 Dec, 1 Jan. **Meals:** alc (small plates £6 to £13). **Details:** 24 seats. Music. No children after 7.30.

Terre à Terre

Quirky vegetarian favourite
Cooking score: 3
Vegetarian | £30
71 East Street, Brighton, BN1 1HQ
Tel no: (01273) 729051
www.terreaterre.co.uk

Philip Taylor and Amanda Powley opened their pioneering vegetarian restaurant in 1993 and have proved to a generation that meat-free food can be stimulating and exciting. The menu leads with jokey titles such as 'better batter and lemony Yemeni relish' and 'fancy nancy', but what arrives are seriously well-constructed, creative dishes with punchy flavours. The global larder is raided for inspiration: steamed rice buns are stuffed with haloumi flavoured with Szechuan spices, for example, and come with pickles and miso-chilli sauce (this one is called 'peeking buns'), while 'easy-peasy Calabrese' is a satisfying Med-inspired number. Desserts are as equally imaginative, with gluten-free and vegan options highlighted on the menu. Drink organic wines (from £19).

Chef/s: Matty Bowling. **Open:** all week 12 to 10.30 (11 Sat). **Closed:** 25 and 26 Dec. **Meals:** alc (main courses £14 to £15). Set L and D £28 to £30. **Details:** 100 seats. 15 seats outside. V menu. Wheelchair access. Music.

Twenty Four St Georges

Ambitious cooking in the modern vein
Cooking score: 3
Modern European | £33
24-25 St George's Road, Brighton, BN2 1ED
Tel no: (01273) 626060
www.24stgeorges.co.uk

Dean Heselden and Jamie Everton-Jones opened up on St George's Road in the city's Kemptown area at the back end of 2009 and have built a reputation as a contemporary dining destination. This is a world where pretty plates are dressed with artful swipes and foaming sauces, where beetroot gets smoked in hay and pears pickled, and at the root of it all is good quality regional ingredients. This is a celebration sort of place, so maybe go the whole hog with the tasting menu and tuck into the likes of smoked salmon with truffled scrambled egg, plaice with lobster tortellini, and a feisty mojito sorbet. Next up, the meat courses (venison carpaccio followed by an assiette of winter birds), before Sussex cheeses and an impressive mulled pear dessert. Wines start at £19.

Chef/s: Dean Heselden. **Open:** Tue to Fri D only 5.30 to 9.30. Sat 12.30 to 9.30. **Closed:** Sun, Mon. **Meals:** alc (main courses £13 to £24). Set D £20 (2 courses) to £23. Tasting menu £59 (7 courses). **Details:** 52 seats. Music. Children before 6.30 only.

LOCAL GEMS

The Coal Shed

British | £40
8 Boyces Street, Brighton, BN1 1AN
Tel no: (01273) 322998
www.coalshed-restaurant.co.uk

Steaks and seafood cooked over charcoal in a Josper oven is a simple enough proposition and draws in the punters to this boisterous joint (it's loud) at one end of a narrow twitten.

Choose between the likes of ribeye, porterhouse, prime rib, black bream and lobster (and more), pick a weight (and consider the cost!). Start with cured mackerel or some Jersey rock oysters. The wine list offers advice on what red best suits your cut of meat. Wines start at £18. Open all week.

Curry Leaf Cafe

Indian | £23

60 Ship Street, Brighton, BN1 1AE
Tel no: (01273) 207070
www.curryleafcafe.com

Judging by the tightly packed throng, the considerable appetite in Brighton for Indian street food has not been sated by the Chilli Pickle (from whence the chef here came). It's casual, colourful and loud, with a menu that deals in South Indian classics such as medu vadas and Keralan-style Alleppey chicken. The tandoor turns out breads and spiced-up whole sea bream, and, to drink, the choice of IPAs and lagers is craft nirvana. House wine is £17. Open all week.

East Chiltington
The Jolly Sportsman

Country-style pub-restaurant
Cooking score: 2
Modern British | £30

Chapel Lane, East Chiltington, BN7 3BA
Tel no: (01273) 890400
www.thejollysportsman.com

A country pub of the dining kind, the diminutive bar (it's tiny, really) at the Jolly Sportsman still manages to dispense local beers straight from the barrel and stock bottled brews from hither and yon. Sitting outside in the lushly planted garden it feels every inch the country pub. Indoors, though, the smart wooden tables are laid up for dining and the walls are hung with local artworks you can purchase if you like the look of them. There's a fabulous covered (and heated) terrace. The menu reflects British and broader European styles, so smoked haddock comes with crispy goose egg and asparagus, and beetroot

carpaccio with a mousse of the same and some granola. Not everything hits the mark, but satisfying main courses include roast gurnard with flavour-packed gnocchi and wood pigeon in the classic company of Agen prunes and port sauce. The wine list has good options by the glass and carafe, with bottle prices from £17.50.

Chef/s: Bruce Wass. **Open:** Tue to Sun L 12 to 2.30 (3.30 Sun), Tue to Sat D 6 to 9.30. **Closed:** Mon, 25 Dec, 1 Jan. **Meals:** alc (main courses £14 to £20). Set L £16 (2 courses). Set D £20. Sun L £20. **Details:** 80 seats. 60 seats outside. Wheelchair access. Parking.

Eastbourne
The Mirabelle

Assured cooking in a vintage setting
Cooking score: 5
Modern European | £44

The Grand Hotel, King Edward's Parade, Eastbourne, BN21 4EQ
Tel no: (01323) 412345
www.grandeastbourne.com

Eastbourne's landmark Grand Hotel is a multi-tiered architectural wedding cake that still flaunts its bygone-era charms to a mature crowd of locals and holidaymakers. The BBC Palm Court orchestra once played here, and it still feels like yesteryear in the lavish dining room (jacket and tie please, gentlemen). That said, long-serving chef Gerald Röser tempers the underlying mood of luxurious flamboyance with a sure hand and a free-spirited sensibility when it comes to flavours and ingredients. Reworked Larousse classics such as leek and saffron velouté or 'mother-in-law's' pavlova with Champagne rhubarb are manna for the old guard, but dig a little deeper and you'll also discover cod with butter-bean purée and garlic crisps or a thoroughly modern, eclectic assemblage of char-grilled lamb cutlets with morcilla tortilla, aubergine rolls, slow-roasted peppers and romesco sauce. The patrician wine list is a suitably grand affair with exhaustive French coverage at the top end, but bargains aplenty elsewhere; prices from £27 (£7.25 a glass).

Chef/s: Gerald Röser. **Open:** Tue to Sat L 12.30 to 2, D 7 to 10. **Closed:** Sun, Mon, first 2 weeks Jan. **Meals:** Set L £22 (2 courses) to £26. Set D £37 (2 courses) to £44. Tasting menu £63 (7 courses). **Details:** 50 seats. Bar. Wheelchair access. Music. Parking.

Fletching
The Griffin Inn

Rural inn for food and views
Cooking score: 3
Modern British | £32
Fletching, TN22 3SS
Tel no: (01825) 722890
www.thegriffininn.co.uk

The Pullen family's unalloyed rural idyll sits at the heart of an ancient village, set in its own gardens overlooking one of Sussex's most seductive landscapes. With its full quota of beams, roaring winter fires, local real ales and smart accommodation, the Griffin has all the appeal of a traditional village inn, but seasonal food makes a big impact here, with the kitchen rolling out a repertoire of big, bold food with uncluttered flavours. Some of our best native ingredients are showcased with a few Mediterranean flourishes: Peasmarsh wild boar ragù, for example, served with pappardelle and pecorino romano; Romney Marsh lamb rump, which arrives with fondant potato and hazelnut purée; and reporters have been equally content with half a dozen Maldon oysters dressed in cucumber and gin jelly and a dab of caviar. Excellent local artisan (what else?) cheeses with red onion marmalade are the savoury alternative to warm plum frangipane with clotted cream and plum compote. Growers are carefully selected on the good, well-annotated wine list (from £15.50), the choice as inspiring in the New World as the Old.

Chef/s: Matthew Starkey. **Open:** all week L 12 to 2.30 (3 Sat and Sun), Mon to Sat D 7 to 10. **Closed:** 25 Dec. **Meals:** alc (main courses £14 to £25). Sun L £25 (2 courses) to £30. **Details:** 60 seats. 25 seats outside. Bar. Wheelchair access. Parking.

Hove
The Foragers

Corner boozer with a local flavour
Cooking score: 3
Modern British | £27
3 Stirling Place, Hove, BN3 3YU
Tel no: (01273) 733134
www.theforagerspub.co.uk

Regulars are clearly delighted to have Paul Hutchinson's airy, light pub close to home. Found in a quiet backstreet in Hove it's fun, relaxed and run with positive enthusiasm. There are local ales for drinkers, while diners are drawn by the heavy commitment to local, seasonal produce, generous portions and good pricing. The regularly changing menu is peppered with ideas that attempt to please all palates, perhaps in the form of BBQ-cured salmon with char-grilled orange, chilli dressing and squid-ink crackers or cod fillet with Toulouse sausage and white bean cassoulet. Elsewhere, there could be beef stew cobbler with leek and onion cheese scones or ribeye steak with hand-cut chips. To finish, there's pineapple sponge with rum and raisin parfait and pineapple gel. A compact, global wine list starts at £15.50. .

Chef/s: Danny Frape. **Open:** all week L 12 to 3 (4 Sat, 6 Sun), Mon to Sat D 6 to 10. **Meals:** alc (main courses £12 to £20). Set L and D £15 (2 courses) to £20. **Details:** 90 seats. 90 seats outside. Bar. Music.

The Ginger Pig

All-rounder with punchy flavours
Cooking score: 3
Modern British | £30
3 Hove Street, Hove, BN3 2TR
Tel no: (01273) 736123
www.thegingerpigpub.com

An accomplished spin on modern British cooking may grace its tables, but the Gingerman group's big, solid corner pub just minutes from the beach has kept itself at the heart of Hove life. Locals still sup real ales in the front bar, a patio garden is among its attractions and there's a warm, easy-going vibe to the whole operation. The brasserie looks the part – all wood, leather and polish – and is a genuinely unaffected eatery that runs on dedication, charm and integrity. There's a breezy, modern feel to menus where inspiration comes from near and far: baked Parmesan custard with broccoli and pine nut brittle or roast rump of lamb and dukkah crumb accompanied by lamb offal pie and caramelised cauliflower and kale sit happily beside homespun English diehards such as beef and oxtail pie; while desserts range from a trio of rhubarb to chilled chocolate fondant with praline and cherry sorbet. Wines from £16.
Chef/s: Steve Sanger. **Open:** all week L 12 to 2 (12.30 to 4 Sun), D 6.30 to 10 (6 Sat, 6 to 9 Sun). **Closed:** 25 Dec. **Meals:** alc (main courses £14 to £21). Set L £13 (2 courses). Set D £13 (2 courses). **Details:** 80 seats. 30 seats outside. Bar. Music.

The Little Fish Market

Classy seafood cookery in a former fish shop
Cooking score: 4
Seafood | £50
10 Upper Market Street, Hove, BN3 1AS
Tel no: (01273) 722213
www.thelittlefishmarket.co.uk

£5 OFF

Duncan Ray's restaurant off the main drag through Hove, by the old fish market, shines out as a beacon of individuality in a world of corporate blandness. He works alone in the basement kitchen (hence arrivals are staggered), the menu is a five-course tasting job, there's a solo waiter and it's cash only. It's not always easy securing a booking, with no one there half the time to answer the phone, but persistence is rewarded with a menu of stellar seafood dishes that show off Mr Ray's considerable skills. With experience at high-end places, not least the Fat Duck, the chef/patron turns out impressive plates of local and sustainable seafood such as tea-smoked salmon with crispy quail's egg, beetroot and horseradish, followed by crab risotto, lemon sole with shallots and thyme, and the staggeringly good monkfish with pork belly. Dessert might be the enigmatically titled rhubarb and custard. The wine list starts at £23.
Chef/s: Duncan Ray. **Open:** Sat L 12 to 2, Tue to Sat D 7 to 9.30. **Closed:** Sun, Mon, 1 week Apr, 2 weeks Sept, 1 week Dec. **Meals:** Set L £20 (2 courses) to £25. Tasting menu £50. **Details:** Cash only. 22 seats. Music.

Rye

Landgate Bistro

Landmark bistro that champions local food
Cooking score: 3
Modern British | £31
5-6 Landgate, Rye, TN31 7LH
Tel no: (01797) 222829
www.landgatebistro.co.uk

Martin Peacock took over an already successful restaurant in 2005 and has maintained Landgate's position as the prominent place to eat in Rye. The unassuming restaurant occupies a pair of Georgian cottages/former shops set in a long terrace that overlooks the impressive 14th-century Landgate. While much is made of local sourcing, dishes come from wider-spread European roots. Readers have applauded a 'standout' soup of pea and mint that was 'fresh and wonderful to taste', as well as spiced pigeon breast with a port reduction, breast and confit leg of Gressingham duck with Puy lentils, spinach and gratin potato, and the 'cooked to perfection' rib, cheek and belly of pork, served with apple ketchup, potato and apple balls and purple sprouting broccoli. Desserts are a particular highlight, and prune in Armagnac crème brûlée garners as much praise as the British artisan cheeses. Wines from £17.80.

Chef/s: Martin Peacock. **Open:** Sat and Sun L 12 to 2.15, Wed to Sat D 7 to 9 (6.30 to 9.15 Sat). Sun D 7 to 9 (bank hols only). **Closed:** Mon, Tue, 23 to 25 Dec, 1 week Jun. **Meals:** alc (main courses £14 to £20). Set L £16 (2 courses) to £19. Set D £19 (2 courses) to £22 (Wed and Thur). **Details:** 32 seats. Bar. Music.

Westfield

The Wild Mushroom

Civilised country restaurant
Cooking score: 2
Modern British | £30
Woodgate House, Westfield Lane, Westfield, TN35 4SB
Tel no: (01424) 751137
www.webbesrestaurants.co.uk

£5
OFF

Long-established and very much part of the local dining scene, the Webbes' late-Victorian farmhouse not far from Hastings delivers 'very good value for money' in a comfortable, formal setting. There's a small garden or conservatory for pre-meal drinks, a dining room with a light spacious feel and a seasonally changing menu based on local supplies. A winter lunch may bring skate cheek salad with sauce gribiche, and a main course of slow-braised Jacob's Ladder with mustard mash and claret jus. At dinner, the carte may produce twice-cooked goats' cheese soufflé with apple and walnut salad, followed by Rye Bay turbot with Fleurie sauce, lardons, caramelised onion and Savoy cabbage. Wines from £17.95.

Chef/s: Chris Weddle. **Open:** Wed to Sun L 12 to 2, Wed to Sat D 7 to 10. **Closed:** Mon, Tue. **Meals:** alc (main courses £14 to £22). Set L £18 (2 courses) to £22. Sun L £25. Tasting menu £35. **Details:** 40 seats. Bar. Wheelchair access. Music. Parking.

Withyham

LOCAL GEM

The Dorset Arms

British | £28
Buckhurst Park, Withyham, TN7 4BD
Tel no: (01892) 770278
www.dorset-arms.co.uk

£5
OFF

If it sounds a long way from home that's because this 18th-century pub on the Sussex Weald is part of the Buckhurst Estate which has been home to earls and dukes of Dorset. It's a proper pub with a bar replete with darts, real ales and water bowl for Rover, and a separate dining area that offers up prawn cocktail or crab brûlée to start, and sausage and mash or venison steak to follow. Wines start at £18. No food Sun D.

Albourne
The Ginger Fox
Country pub with urban roots
Cooking score: 3
Modern British | £36
Muddleswood Road, Albourne, BN6 9EA
Tel no: (01273) 857888
www.gingermanrestaurants.com

The Ginger stable has several bases covered in Brighton and Hove via a couple of dining pubs and a restaurant (see entries for two of them – 'Pig' and 'Man'), plus this smart thatched country inn standing all on its own near Albourne. There may be a pretty garden, a superior ploughman's and views over the Downs, not to mention real ales at the pumps, but really and truly it's the sort of place you come to dine. The opened-up interior has a somewhat contemporary finish. The kitchen doesn't shy away from big flavours, putting saddle, shoulder and offal of hogget together with goats' cheese and a Med-style medley of veg, while another main course might be the more genteel sea bass with oyster beignet and parsley root purée. Vegetarians get their own tasting plate. Desserts are a sophisticated bunch; pistachio cake, say, with chocolate sorbet and crystallised pistachios. Wines start at £16.

Chef/s: James Dearden and Ben McKellar. **Open:** all week L 12 to 2 (3 Sat, 4 Sun), D 6 to 10 (6.30 Sat, 9 Sun). **Closed:** 25 Dec. **Meals:** alc (main courses £14 to £21). **Details:** 62 seats. 90 seats outside. Bar. Music. Parking.

Angmering
READERS RECOMMEND
The Lamb
Modern British
The Square, Angmering, BN16 4EQ
Tel no: (01903) 774300
www.thelamb-angmering.com
'Everything about the establishment has the mark of quality and care. We sampled the roast duck, the guinea fowl, the Provençal vegetarian tart and the roast turbot.'

 Arundel
The Town House
Resembling a classy Parisian brasserie
Cooking score: 3
Modern British | £30
65 High Street, Arundel, BN18 9AJ
Tel no: (01903) 883847
www.thetownhouse.co.uk

Arundel isn't short of period buildings and this Georgian Grade II-listed number can hold its own in some esteemed company, helped by the fact it's in possession of a 16th-century Florentine ceiling that brings its shimmering magnificence to the otherwise gently contemporary dining room. Lee and Kate Williams' restaurant-with-rooms provides the town with the sort of restaurant that is elegant enough to suit special occasions yet affable enough to fit the bill the rest of the time. The food is as similarly equitable, with its roots in rich classical cooking and interjections from the modern era carefully moderated. Warm confit salmon is a fashionable preparation these days, and here it arrives with artichoke purée and pea shoots, while main courses might offer up roasted local partridge (game chips et al), a special of Dover sole 'cooked simply' or a 'really good' veal chop. Accurate, careful cooking continues to the end, where pear frangipane tart may well be waiting. Wines start at £18.

Chef/s: Lee Williams. **Open:** Tue to Sat L 12 to 2.30, D 7 to 9.30. **Closed:** Sun, Mon, 25 to 27 Dec, 1 to 3 Jan, 2 weeks Easter, 2 weeks Oct. **Meals:** Set L £18 (2 courses) to £22. Set D £26 (2 courses) to £30. **Details:** 24 seats. V menu. Music.

 Cuckfield
Ockenden Manor
Confident cooking with panache
Cooking score: 5
Modern French | £60
Ockenden Lane, Cuckfield, RH17 5LD
Tel no: (01444) 416111
www.hshotels.co.uk

A show of Elizabethan wealth in a village on the edge of the Weald, with glorious views to the south towards Brighton, the rather grand Ockenden Manor offers hospitality of the old-school. That's not to say it is stuck in the past – not entirely – not with a deluxe spa in a modern building further down the drive. The old manor has all the real fires, wonky walls and rich furnishings you might imagine, plus a restaurant headed up by Stephen Crane that offers an appropriate level of refinement. Fine produce is sourced in the region and turned into attractive plates of classically inspired dishes such as the Selsey crab that arrives in a richly satisfying lasagne, or the home-smoked duck that comes with a crispy samosa and foie gras boudin. The luxe preparations continue into main courses – wood pigeon enriched with more of that foie gras, monkfish wrapped in Parma ham – and well-being is assured to the end when warm gooseberry Bakewell with crème fraîche ice cream arrives. Wines start at £26.

Chef/s: Stephen Crane. **Open:** all week L 12 to 2, D 7 to 9 (6.30 Fri and Sat). **Meals:** Set L £20 (2 courses) to £26. Set D £60. Sun L £37. **Details:** 80 seats. Bar. Parking.

East Grinstead
Gravetye Manor
Enchanting Elizabethan charmer
Cooking score: 5
Modern British | £65
Vowels Lane, East Grinstead, RH19 4LJ
Tel no: (01342) 810567
www.gravetyemanor.co.uk

Gravetye Manor is the very image of soft-focus country house opulence, one where a mile-long drive winds through woods and sudden valleys and deposits you at a many gabled Elizabethan manor that's all dark panelling, blazing fires and ornate plaster mouldings. Add George Blogg's expressive cooking and the faultless front-of-house team to the mix and you'll want to eat here 'again and again'. George has quickly put his stamp on the menu, fleshing out his network of dedicated suppliers and plundering the walled kitchen garden for seasonal pickings – how about a pretty plate of winter garden salad with confit hen's yolk, crisp brassicas and vegetables, or tartar of smoked local venison with corned venison, horn of plenty, ale-pickled onions and horseradish cream? Elsewhere South Coast sea bass arrives with baked spaghetti squash, Jerusalem artichoke risotto and English black truffle, and dessert brings a passion fruit soufflé and coulis with coconut ice cream and Thai basil. The well-collated wine list features an even-handed selection of countries beside France, from £32.

Chef/s: George Blogg. **Open:** all week L 12 to 2, D 6.30 to 9. **Meals:** alc (main courses £29 to £34). Set L £25 (2 courses) to £30. Set D £40. Sun L £35. Tasting menu £85. **Details:** 30 seats. V menu. Bar. Wheelchair access. Music. Parking. Children over 7 yrs only.

East Lavant
The Royal Oak Inn
Country inn focused on food
Cooking score: 2
Modern British | £32
Pook Lane, East Lavant, PO18 0AX
Tel no: (01243) 527434
www.royaloakeastlavant.co.uk

This may look like a pub, with real ales tapped from the cask, low beams, mismatched furniture and an open fire, but these days the Royal Oak operates more effectively as a restaurant-with-rooms. Food is taken seriously: local suppliers provide most of the raw materials, the menu changes frequently and fish is delivered daily from the South Coast. In addition to the carte, daily specials are chalked up on a board. At lunch there are pub classics – 'small plates' might include garlic mushrooms or Thai-spiced fishcakes, or there could be comfort-inducing O'Hagan's Italian sausage with mash or cod and chips. In the evening the kitchen pulls out the stops with scallops, bacon jam, parsnip purée, confit chicken wings, then breast of guinea fowl with rösti potatoes, wilted greens with pancetta and wild mushroom jus, and chocolate fondant with salted-caramel ice cream to finish. Wines from £18.

Chef/s: James Dean. **Open:** all week L 12 to 2.30 (3 Sun), D 6 to 9 (9.30 Sat, 6.30 Sun). **Meals:** alc (main courses £15 to £28). **Details:** 50 seats. 30 seats outside. Music. Parking.

East Wittering

Samphire

Laid-back by the beach
Cooking score: 1
Modern British | £30
57 Shore Road, East Wittering, PO20 8DY
Tel no: (01243) 672754
www.samphireeastwittering.co.uk

David's Skinner's restaurant grew in 2015 to make room for another dozen or so seasiders at each sitting. With its outside tables and relaxed attitude, the holiday vibe is maintained. The beach is only 50 yards away so you might expect a decent showing of seafood and the pick of the bunch has to be the South Coast fish stew (sea bass, Selsey crab, mussels, cockles and brown shrimps, plus a scattering of samphire). There's a modern ring to a starter of tandoori chicken terrine with golden sultana purée, while a meaty main might be wild mallard with an orange and honey jus. Wines start at £15.50.
Chef/s: David Skinner and Liam Duke Hasted. **Open:** Mon to Sun L 12 to 2 (4 Sun), Mon to Sat D 6 to 9. **Closed:** 25 and 26 Dec, 2 weeks Jan. **Meals:** alc (main courses £13 to £22). Set L £13 (2 courses) to £16. Set D £17 (2 courses) to £22. Sun L £14. **Details:** 40 seats. 10 seats outside. Music.

Fernhurst

★ TOP 50 PUB ★

The Duke of Cumberland Arms

Archetypal country pub with high aspirations
Cooking score: 4
Modern British | £37
Henley, Fernhurst, GU27 3HQ
Tel no: (01428) 652280
www.dukeofcumberland.com

There's much to praise about Simon Goodman's upbeat and modishly rustic hostelry in the South Downs National Park and it's well worth seeking out. Lovely gardens and terraces deliver the perfect alfresco experience, a heavily beamed, fire-warmed bar with cask-drawn ales sets the tone inside, while a modern dining room extension gives notice that food is taken very seriously here. Simon's menu showcases local (and home-grown) produce and reveals realistic ambition: his clear focus is greatly appreciated. Smoked haddock and smoked salmon fish-cakes with tartare sauce, followed by eight-hour braised lamb shank with roasted garlic mash, green beans and mint jus typifies the predominantly British style, although elsewhere there might be salt-and-pepper squid with saffron mayonnaise, pickled samphire and wasabi nut crumble or pea, prawn and crayfish risotto. There's a good selection of British cheeses if puddings such as strawberry and vanilla crème brûlée with homemade doughnuts don't appeal. Wines from £15.10.
Chef/s: Simon Goodman. **Open:** all week L 12 to 2, Tue to Sat D 7 to 9. **Closed:** 26 Dec. **Meals:** alc (main courses £14 to £30). **Details:** 70 seats. 100 seats outside. Bar. Wheelchair access. Music. Parking.

Funtington

Hallidays

Local produce in an ancient setting
Cooking score: 2
Modern British | £37
Watery Lane, Funtington, PO18 9LF
Tel no: (01243) 575331
www.hallidays.info

Housed in a row of thatched medieval cottages at the foot of the South Downs, Andrew Stephenson's personally run restaurant might look picture-postcard pretty, but there's nothing twee about his sterling efforts in the kitchen. He works hard at the stove, respects seasonal ingredients and knows his home patch when it comes to supplies – from Selsey crab and fish from the South Coast day boats to Blackmoor venison and locally shot pigeon. The result is a thoughtful, weekly changing menu that might involve pan-fried scallops with Jerusalem artichokes and hazelnuts, honey-roast guinea fowl or slow-braised oxtail in red wine with horseradish mash and crispy onions. Aged sirloin steaks are served the old way with cream, brandy and peppercorn sauce, while desserts span everything from warm French chocolate torte with crème fraîche ice cream to iced mango and lime parfait with pineapple salad. A well-spread wine list opens with house selections from £19.50.

Chef/s: Andrew Stephenson. **Open:** Wed, Thur and Sun L 12 to 2, Wed, Thur and Sat D 7 to 9.30. Fri 12 to 9.30. **Closed:** Mon, Tue, 1 week Mar, 1 week Aug. **Meals:** alc (main courses £18 to £22). Set L £16 (2 courses) to £23. Set D £21 (2 courses) to £28. Sun L £24. **Details:** 26 seats. Bar. Wheelchair access. Parking.

■ Haywards Heath

Jeremy's Restaurant

Modern dining on a classic English estate
Cooking score: 4
Modern European | £40

Borde Hill Garden, Balcombe Road, Haywards Heath, RH16 1XP
Tel no: (01444) 441102
www.jeremysrestaurant.co.uk

£5 OFF

Borde Hill Garden is 200 acres of England's finest, and Jeremy Ashpool was able to nab the former stable block on the estate back in 1998 and turn it into a restaurant that fits beautifully into the setting. Terrace tables overlooking the Victorian walled garden are a hot ticket in warm weather, although it's perfectly sunny on the inside, too, where a refurbishment in 2015 has gone for a more contemporary look and ditched the linen tablecloths. Jeremy's cooking spans British and European modes, with regional ingredients steadfastly providing a sense of place. Salt-baked heritage carrots with black beans and Sussex Slipcote (a soft, creamy sheep's cheese) makes an impression from the off, followed perhaps by loin and sweetbread of Ryeland hogget or loin and meatball of Balcombe Estate venison with Hispi cabbage and chocolate sauce. Rhubarb and ginger are

happy bedfellows, here found in a mille-feuille with candied fennel and blood-orange sorbet. Wines from £18.

Chef/s: Jimmy Gray. **Open:** Tue to Sat L 12 to 3 (3.30 Sun), Tue to Sat D 7 to 9.30. **Closed:** Mon, first 2 weeks Jan. **Meals:** alc (main courses £15 to £26). Set L and D £18 (2 courses) to £22. Sun L £26 (2 courses) to £32. **Details:** 55 seats. 45 seats outside. Bar. Wheelchair access. Music. Parking.

■ Horsham

Restaurant Tristan

Outstanding cooking at moderate prices
Cooking score: 6
Modern British | £45

3 Stans Way, Horsham, RH12 1HU
Tel no: (01403) 255688
www.restauranttristan.co.uk

'We've been eating at Tristan's since it first opened several years ago and the food just keeps on getting better', is one of many endorsements for Tristan Mason's classy restaurant in Horsham's old town. It's on the first floor of a 16th-century building (above the all-day bar-café), a smart, heavily beamed room that's quite the special-occasion restaurant, though one needn't save it for best, given that the three-course lunch menu is £25. Whether eating from the carte or the tasting menu, dishes exhibit a fine-tuned precision, with three-dimensional flavours and juxtapositions that make sense. Smoked venison tartare with cucumber and wasabi is a statement starter, or there may be a modish foie gras with mango, honeycomb and hazelnuts, before main courses explore the resonances to be teased from pork belly, squid and marmalade toast or beef, oyster and beetroot. For a fashionable sweet/savoury finish try butternut pannacotta with wattleseed and sorrel. The wine list skims the vinous world's surface, netting some fine growers. Bottles from £24.

Chef/s: Tristan Mason. **Open:** Tue to Sat L 12 to 2.30, D 6.30 to 9.30. **Closed:** Sun, Mon. **Meals:** Set L £25 (3 courses) to £30. Set D £45 (4 courses). Tasting Menu £65 (6 courses) to £80. **Details:** 42 seats. V menu. Bar. Music. Children over 10 yrs only.

Horsted Keynes
The Crown Inn

Proper pub, proper cooking
Cooking score: 2
Modern British | £40
The Green, Horsted Keynes, RH17 7AW
Tel no: (01825) 791609
www.thecrown-horstedkeynes.co.uk

The Crown backs on to the cricket ground and is spot-on for an alfresco lunch on the terrace, but, then again, when flames flicker in the hearths in the cooler months, it's hard to tear yourself away from one of the fireplaces (the smaller bar has a stonker). Doing the business since the first half of the 16th century, the pub has been run by seasoned chef Mark Raffan since early 2013. He's had the good sense to maintain proper spaces for drinkers, and it still looks and feels like a pub, but as you head on through you'll find tables ready and waiting for dining. Beer-battered cod shows the kitchen is willing to do populist things (and do them well), and the menu extends to a brasserie-style repertoire of confit rabbit terrine with celeriac remoulade and fillet of sea bass with cockles, prawns and spring onion mash. Finish with winter berry and apple crumble. Wines from £18.50.
Chef/s: Mark Raffan. **Open:** all week L 12 to 2 (2.30 Fri and Sat, 4 Sun), Mon to Sat D 6 to 9 (9.30 Fri and Sat). **Closed:** 25 Dec. **Meals:** alc (main courses £13 to £25). **Details:** 60 seats. 60 seats outside. Bar. Wheelchair access. Parking. No children after 8.

Lavant
The Earl of March

Contemporary dining in a posh pub
Cooking score: 3
Modern British | £34
Lavant Road, Lavant, PO18 0BQ
Tel no: (01243) 533993
www.theearlofmarch.com

The story goes that William Blake wrote the words to 'Jerusalem' gazing out over the South Downs from this coaching inn back in 1803. The view won't have changed (grab a table on the terrace if you can), but since falling into the hands of former Ritz man Giles Thompson in 2007, the pub has made its mark as a dining destination. The main culinary business takes place in the smart restaurant, where pictures of fast cars and Spitfires are reminders of the area's racy past and present. The kitchen is capable of delivering punchy flavours and a good degree of refinement in dishes such as whole roast sardine with smoked tomato and red pepper ragoût, and braised pork belly interspersed with black pudding and finished with a slick of flavoursome jus. Sticky toffee pudding failed to convey the same level of attention to detail at inspection. Wines start at £18.
Chef/s: Adam Hawden. **Open:** all week L 12 to 2.30 (3 Sun), D 5.30 to 9 (9.30 Fri and Sat, 6 Sun). **Meals:** alc (main courses £16 to £23). Set L and D £20 (2 courses) to £22. **Details:** 70 seats. 60 seats outside. V menu. Bar. Wheelchair access. Music. Parking.

Lickfold

★ TOP 10 PUB ★

BEST NEW PUB ENTRY

NEW ENTRY

The Lickfold Inn

A destination above a real pub

Cooking score: 6

Modern British | £45

Highstead Lane, Lickfold, GU28 9EY

Tel no: (01789) 532535

www.thelickfoldinn.co.uk

A dazzlingly creative restaurant above a rural pub in lush Sussex countryside – what's the story? Taken over by Tom Sellers at the back end of 2014, the Lickfold Inn is the country cousin of Restaurant Story in Bermondsey (see entry), with Mr Sellers' trusted sous-chef, Graham Squire, at the stove. The handsome Tudor pub offers up real ales, exciting snacks and a roaring fire downstairs, not to mention views over the glassed-in state-of-the-art kitchen. Head upstairs to the simply dapper beamed dining room where inspiring culinary adventures await. Warm sourdough bread arrives with ethereally light whipped chicken butter, followed by 'snacks' and a divine amuse-bouche of almond cream with asparagus. The à la carte follows suit with stunningly well-constructed dishes such as smoked eel with richly flavoured tomatoes and little blobs of zesty, fruity emulsion, or a main course of halibut with cauliflower and sloes that delivers deep satisfaction. The technical dexterity shown by the kitchen is impressive, with spikes of sweetness and acidity here and there, and flavour combinations hit the heights when bitter chocolate, passion fruit and lavender combine in an exceedingly pretty finale. The wine list kicks off at £19 and heads north quickly.

Chef/s: Graham Squire. **Open:** Tue to Sun L 12 to 2.30 (4 Sun), Tue to Sat D 6 to 9. **Closed:** Mon, 24 and 25 Dec. **Meals:** alc (main courses £19 to £32). Set L £19 (2 courses) to £25. **Details:** 40 seats. 20 seats outside. V menu. Bar. Parking.

Lower Beeding

The Crabtree

A genuine hostelry with sound culinary talent

Cooking score: 2

Modern British | £32

Brighton Road, Lower Beeding, RH13 6PT

Tel no: (01403) 892666

www.crabtreesussex.co.uk

Real ales, winter fires, a glorious garden and pub food with big city flavours reward visitors to this gentrified 16th-century inn. It's a tribute to owner Simon Hope's vision that he has managed to preserve the Crabtree as an honest-to-goodness country hostelry. It feels just right, so easy is the atmosphere. The kitchen's aim is to combine first-rate materials with uncomplicated modern cooking to produce a menu with broad appeal. Simple classics have a please-all quality – for example, the well-reported twice-baked Cheddar soufflé served with wild mushrooms, charred broccoli and truffle cream – but the kitchen also turns out starters of cured salmon with burnt apple, beetroot and crispy quinoa, and mains of suckling pig with apple, creamed potato, black pudding and red kale. There's applause, too, for the bar menu of fish and chips and ribeye steak, the knowledge and friendliness of the staff, and the well-put-together wine list, which opens at £18.

Chef/s: Gary Hewitt. **Open:** Mon to Sat L 12 to 3, D 6 to 9.30. Sun 12 to 7. **Meals:** alc (main courses £13 to £21). Set L £15 (2 courses) to £18. Sun L £22. **Details:** 70 seats. 120 seats outside. Wheelchair access. Music. Parking.

Symbols

Accommodation is available

Three courses for less than £30

£5-off voucher scheme

Notable wine list

The Pass

First-rate food in close-up
Cooking score: 6
Modern British | £65
South Lodge Hotel, Brighton Road, Lower
Beeding, RH13 6PS
Tel no: (01403) 891711
www.southlodgehotel.co.uk

As befits a grand, immaculately kept 19th-century mansion, décor is formal with much in the way of drapes, panelling and chandeliers. By contrast, the Pass avoids all these country-house clichés: to eat here means eating in the startlingly modern kitchen watching the chefs demystify the use of blow-torch, piping bag and squeezy bottle. For foodies, this is as central a location as they could wish for. Armchair-style stools at high tables are comfortable, screens show Matt Gillan and his team in close-up, and tasting menu small plates are the only way to go. Contemporary crossover dishes such as wild mushrooms on truffle toast, covered with a fine mushroom and chocolate jelly ('lovely umami flavours') or an 'inspired combination' of veal with sweetbread, morels and blueberries reveal plenty of original ideas. Equally, a beguiling pre-dessert of violet custard with rhubarb ice, and a finale of strawberry mousse, strawberries, beer meringue and buttermilk simply dazzle. Materials are first rate, there's 'superb' bread and the whole place is run with exceptional professionalism. The cosmopolitan wine list starts at £25.50.
Chef/s: Matt Gillan. **Open:** Wed to Sun L 12 to 1.30 (12.30 Sun), D 7 to 8.30. **Closed:** Mon, Tue, 25 Dec, first 2 weeks Jan. **Meals:** Set L £28 (4 courses) to £38. Set D £65 (6 courses) to £75. **Details:** 26 seats. V menu. Wheelchair access. Parking. Children over 12 years only.

Petworth
The Leconfield

Smart cooking in classy surroundings
Cooking score: 3
Modern British | £50
New Street, Petworth, GU28 0AS
Tel no: (01798) 345111
www.theleconfield.co.uk

With Petworth House (NT) just round the corner and smart boutiques all around, the Leconfield is exactly what you might expect to find in such a classy setting (but rarely do). Occupying a prettily restored 17th-century building with pastel shades and contemporary comforts as well as original beams and floorboards, the Leconfield is a demure Sussex bolt-hole complete with a light-drenched 'orangery' and a smartly appointed dining room. Brittany-born Pascal Proyart from One-O-One, Knightsbridge, has been drafted in as consultant chef, and the kitchen deals in sophisticated seasonal dishes in the modern mould (at central London prices) – think roast cod loin and prawns 'a la plancha' with truffled cocoa bean cassoulet and bisque. Selsey crabs and lobsters are a speciality, while meat and game tend to receive classic treatment – from steak tartare with hand-cut chips to peppered venison 'Grand Veneur' with wild cranberry and celeriac gratin. 'Bites y pinchos' are served in the adjoining cocktail bar, and France is the main player on the well-considered wine list. Prices start at £21 (£6.25 a glass).
Chef/s: David Lewis. **Open:** Tue to Sun L 12 to 3, Tue to Sat D 6 to 9. **Closed:** Mon, 25 and 26 Dec. **Meals:** alc (main courses £19 to £30). Set L and D £25 (2 courses) to £29. Sun L £25 (2 courses) to £30. **Details:** 75 seats. 28 seats outside. Bar. Music.

 Sidlesham
The Crab & Lobster
Sussex produce in a harbourside inn
Cooking score: 3
Modern European | £39
Mill Lane, Sidlesham, PO20 7NB
Tel no: (01243) 641233
www.crab-lobster.co.uk

Hard by the marshes and mudflats of Pagham Harbour Nature Reserve, this 350-year-old whitewashed inn is not only a rallying point for 'twitchers' but also attracts plenty of food-loving locals and tourists with its offer of Sussex seafood and more besides. Sit outside (weather permitting) or decamp to the gently modernised low-beamed bar and dining room for capable cooking with strong Anglo-European accents – think soft-poached duck egg with smoked duck breast, cauliflower velouté and watercress or Southdown lamb cutlets with Jersey Royals, wild garlic and tarragon butter. The catch of the day is presented simply, but the kitchen can also handle more ambitious fish dishes ranging from fillet of turbot served on Selsey crab and tarragon risotto to stone bass with mussels, brown shrimps, potato and leek chowder. Sandwiches and salads are available most lunchtimes, while dessert might bring warm honey, apricot and almond rice pudding with sea buckthorn ice cream. Wines start at £16.85. **Chef/s:** Clyde Hollett. **Open:** Mon to Fri L 12 to 2.30, D 6 to 9.30 (10 Fri). Sat and Sun 12 to 10 (9 Sun). **Meals:** alc (main courses £17 to £29). Set L £22 (2 courses) to £26. **Details:** 48 seats. 48 seats outside. Wheelchair access. Music. Parking.

Visit us online

To find out more about The Good Food Guide, please visit thegoodfoodguide.co.uk

 Singleton

The Partridge Inn
British | £26
Grove Road, Singleton, PO18 0EY
Tel no: (01243) 811251
www.thepartridgeinn.co.uk

£5 OFF

A sister pub to the Earl of March (see entry, Lavant), this 16th-century coaching inn on the Goodwood Estate has all the rustic accoutrements you'd expect given its vintage (inglenook fireplace, dark-wood beams), a pretty garden and a menu that sticks to pub territory. That means sandwiches at lunchtime, plus a menu of old favourites done well: potted shrimps, whole tail scampi, steak, mushroom and ale pie, or the more racy slow-roast pork belly with chilli and apple relish. Wines start at £16. Open all week.

 Tangmere
Cassons
Small restaurant run with passion
Cooking score: 3
Modern British | £39
Arundel Road, Tangmere, PO18 0DU
Tel no: (01243) 773294
www.cassonsrestaurant.co.uk

£5 OFF

'I was impressed with the quality of the cooking and the value for money of the set lunch menu,' concluded one reporter after visiting Vivian and 'Cass' Casson's unassuming restaurant on the south side of the A27, some two miles east of Chichester. They run a tight ship, both front-of-house, where Cass is in charge, and behind the scenes, where a blend of the traditional and contemporary is Vivian's modus operandi. Starters may include Selsey crab with sweetcorn mousse, lime mayonnaise, potato glass and lemon gel, with mains taking in venison (fillet and sausage croquette) served with wild mushrooms, celeriac purée, red cabbage, broccoli, fondant potato and game jus, or suckling pig (loin, belly, confit leg, crackling) with potato mille-feuilles, parsnip velouté and a cider reduction. Textures of chocolate with salted-caramel ice cream makes a fine finish. The wine list (from £21) takes a quick, reasonably priced spin round the winemaking globe.

Chef/s: Vivian Casson. **Open:** Wed to Sun L 12 to 2, Tue to Sat D 7 to 9.30. **Closed:** Mon, 25 to 30 Dec. **Meals:** Set L £17 (2 courses) to £20. Set D £31 (2 courses) to £39. Sun L £23 (2 courses) to £28. **Details:** 36 seats. 16 seats outside. Bar. Music. Parking.

◼ Tillington

The Horse Guards Inn

Best kind of independently owned village inn
Cooking score: 2
British | £28
Upperton Road, Tillington, GU28 9AF
Tel no: (01798) 342332
www.thehorseguardsinn.co.uk

'Country pub perfection' is how one doting regular described the rustic charms of this 350-year-old inn. It certainly has everything you might expect: an auspicious village location (not far from Petworth House); all the ancient beams, worn bricks, nooks, fireplaces and low ceilings you could wish for; the quirkiest collection of knick-knacks and vintage finds; real ales on tap. A pretty garden with contented hens and a little allotment growing herbs and vegetables for the kitchen gives notice that much rests on the produce used. Home-cured salmon gravadlax served with crème fraîche, beetroot, shallot and parsley salad start things off with a zing, while mains might offer South Downs pigeon breast with curly kale, potato gratin, beetroot and red wine gravy or a bouillabaisse with rouille and croûte. For pudding, an old-fashioned marmalade sponge with Drambuie custard keeps the comfort factor high. Staff are 'warm and chummy' and the wine list opens at £17.
Chef/s: Mark Robinson. **Open:** all week L 12 to 2.30 (3 Sat, 3.30 Sun), D 6.30 to 9 (9.30 Fri and Sat). **Closed:** 25 and 26 Dec. **Meals:** alc (main meals £10 to £22). **Details:** 55 seats. 50 seats outside. Music.

◼ West Ashling

The Richmond Arms

Globetrotting, free-spirited food
Cooking score: 4
Modern British | £31
Mill Road, West Ashling, PO18 8EA
Tel no: (01243) 572046
www.therichmondarms.co.uk

In a pretty village just north of Chichester, which just sneaks into the boundaries of the South Downs National Park, you'll find the Richmond Arms close to the large millpond. William and Emma Jack injected a touch of 21st-century pizazz into the place in 2011, and now the village has an inn (there are a couple of classy bedrooms) that pulls in punters for its canny globally inspired menu. There's a fresh contemporary finish to the traditional spaces, and even a rustic bar (called WoodFire) in the old skittle alley where wood-fired pizzas are dispensed from an old Citroën van – very hipster! The main eating, though, is done indoors in the restaurant where you might start with BBQ octopus with sobrasada Ibérico (a Mallorcan sausage) with crispy chickpeas and move on to charcoal-grilled local pheasant or 'hot, molten and spicy' Selsey crab Kiev. Finish with the alcohol-fuelled 'B52' or blood-orange posset with toasted pistachio-flavoured meringues. Beer is local and wines start at £16.
Chef/s: William Jack. **Open:** Wed to Sun L 12 to 2 (3 Sun), Wed to Sat D 6 to 9. **Closed:** Mon, Tue. **Meals:** alc (main courses £15 to £27). **Details:** 40 seats. 40 seats outside. Bar. Music. Parking.

Symbols

▬	Accommodation is available
£30	Three courses for less than £30
£5 OFF	£5-off voucher scheme
▮	Notable wine list

West Hoathly
The Cat Inn

A cracking village pub
Cooking score: 2
Modern British | £29
Queen's Square, West Hoathly, RH19 4PP
Tel no: (01342) 810369
www.catinn.co.uk

Wander through the churchyard opposite this 16th-century tile-hung pub and you'll discover you're actually high up on the Sussex Weald with great views across open countryside. That's if you can tear yourself away from the bar. The Cat is a proper local with real ales and fish and chips, hops hanging from the beams and real fires, but there's genuine pedigree here, too. The informal dining area opens on to a terrace garden. The menu and blackboard specials aim to please with classic options and some more à la mode stuff: a fashionable salt-baked beetroot and goats' curd starter, say, followed by a classy burger or steak, ale and mushroom pie, or the more Eurocentric guinea fowl with Puy lentils and pancetta. Not everything hits the heights, like an overly zealous potted crab. Finish with a slice of Bakewell tart or poshed-up chocolate brownie. The wine list includes local Sussex options; prices start at £16.
Chef/s: Alex Jacquemin. **Open:** all week L 12 to 2 (2.30 Fri to Sun), Mon to Sat D 6 to 9 (Fri and Sat 9.30). **Closed:** 25 Dec. **Meals:** alc (main courses £10 to £23). **Details:** 80 seats. 40 seats outside. Wheelchair access. Parking. Children over 7 yrs only.

Please send us your feedback

To register your opinion about any restaurant listed in this guide, or a new restaurant that you wish to bring to our attention, please visit the web address at the bottom of the page. Your feedback informs the content of the book and will be used to compile next year's reviews.

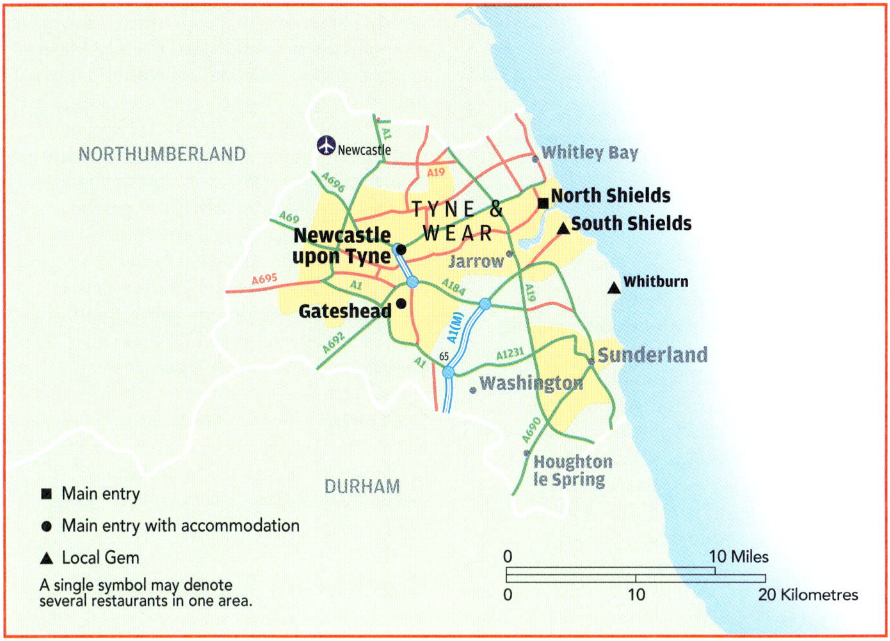

Gateshead
Eslington Villa

Galvanising modern cooking
Cooking score: 2
Modern British | £29
8 Station Road, Low Fell, Gateshead, NE9 6DR
Tel no: (0191) 4876017
www.eslingtonvilla.co.uk

Double sets of steps lead up to the handsome Victorian brick villa that overlooks the Team Valley, standing in a couple of acres of impressive landscaped gardens. Tables turned out in their best whites sit in the glassed extension to the front, all set for some galvanising modern cooking that strikes many a harmonious chord. Panko-crumbed pig's cheeks could hardly be more on-trend, their vadouvan sauce sealing the deal, while smoked mackerel has the sharpening notes of confit tomatoes, pickled shallots and olive crème fraîche. For main, cod from the newly replenished North Sea is earthily served by wild mushroom risotto dressed in white truffle oil. Slow cooking produces resonantly memorable results in duck-fat-crusted beef shin with spinach, pancetta and mash. Breton butter cake is one of France's less familiar ancestral dishes, served here with rhubarb compote and orange pannacotta. House wines from Emilia-Romagna are £17.50 (£4.50 a glass).

Chef/s: Jamie Walsh. **Open:** Mon to Sat L 12 to 2 (3 Sat), D 5.30 to 10 (6.30 Sat). Sun 12 to 9.30. **Closed:** 25 and 26 Dec, 1 Jan. **Meals:** Set L £15 (2 courses) to £18. Set D £25 (2 courses) to £29. Sun L £21. **Details:** 90 seats. 30 seats outside. Bar. Wheelchair access. Music. Parking.

Symbols

Accommodation is available
Three courses for less than £30
£5-off voucher scheme
Notable wine list

Six

Modern British | £38

Baltic Centre for Contemporary Art, South
Shore Road, Gateshead Quays, Gateshead,
NE8 3BA
Tel no: (0191) 4404948
www.sixbaltic.com

On the top floor of the Baltic Centre for
Contemporary Art, with floor-to-ceiling
glass windows providing panoramic views of
the city, Six is a celebration place – with
window tables much in demand. Décor is
sleek, minimalist and 'appropriate for an arty
venue', and the food suits the place, too:
'simple, reasonably seasonal and pretty
populist'. Hand-dived scallops with Cullen
skink, smoked haddock and parsley oil, and
lamb rump with fondant potato, baby turnips,
courgettes, spring onions and green sauce are
typical of the style. Wines from £17.50. Closed
Sun D.

■ Newcastle upon Tyne

Artisan

Clearly wedded to seasonality
Cooking score: 3
Modern British | £32

The Biscuit Factory, Stoddart Street, Newcastle
upon Tyne, NE2 1AN
Tel no: (0191) 2605411
www.artisannewcastle.com

Andrew Wilkinson has arrived at this
converted Victorian biscuit factory with
something of a reputation to uphold – and
there seems to be plenty of local support for
this enterprising chef. Located on the ground
floor of a contemporary art gallery visible
through a floor-to-ceiling glass wall lined
with shelves of ceramics and *objets d'art*, Artisan
lives up to its 'where food is art' tagline, with
meticulously presented modern dishes singing
with seasonal flavours. Wilkinson is clearly

wedded to seasonality, grows herbs and leaves
on kitchen windowsills and in early May his
menu 'featured everything I would hope to
find – lots of wild garlic, peas, asparagus,
broad beans, sea trout'. A test meal opened
with a 'suprisingly light' pea cream with fresh
crab, fennel and apple, went on to a 'faultless'
seared fillet of sea trout with intensely
flavoured wild garlic croquette and lightly
cooked asparagus, peas and broad beans, and
ended with a not too rich Brillat-Savarin
cheesecake with an intense apricot sorbet and
roasted apricot in ginger. Wines from £16.50.
Chef/s: Andrew Wilkinson. **Open:** all week L 12 to 2
(3 Sun), Mon to Sat D 5.30 to 9 (9.30 Fri, 6 to 9.30
Sat). **Closed:** bank hols. **Meals:** alc (main courses
£14 to £24). Set L £15 (2 courses) to £20. Set D £20
(2 courses) to £24. Sun L £16. **Details:** 80 seats. 16
seats outside. V menu. Bar. Wheelchair access.
Music. Parking.

Blackfriars Restaurant

Modern food where medieval monks dined
Cooking score: 3
British | £30

Friars Street, Newcastle upon Tyne, NE1 4XN
Tel no: (0191) 2615945
www.blackfriarsrestaurant.co.uk

Much of the 13th-century Blackfriars
building, established as a Dominican friary, is
still intact and 'exudes history and mystery',
yet the former refectory comes across as a
'warm and cosy rustic restaurant', especially
on a freezing January night. The premises may
be eight centuries old, but there's nothing
archaic about the 'inviting' and 'memorable'
proper British food on offer. Sourcing is key
to the kitchen's efforts, and it 'delivers on all
levels' whether a pressed Durham ham terrine
with pease pudding and pickled vegetables or
braised Northumbrian beef with horseradish
dumplings. North Sea fish and shellfish pie is a
winner, while others have devoured slow-
roasted belly pork with colcannon mash,
crackling and cider jus, and there is a well-
reported spiced plum pithiviers with candied

almonds and nutmeg ice cream to finish, as well as English cheeses. Prices are very reasonable, and wines start at £18.
Chef/s: Christopher Wardale. **Open:** all week L 12 to 2.30 (4 Sun), Mon to Sat D 5.30 to 10. **Closed:** 25 and 26 Dec, 1 Jan, bank hols. **Meals:** alc (main courses £12 to £25). Set L and D £15 (2 courses) to £18. Sun L £18. **Details:** 72 seats. 30 seats outside. Music.

The Broad Chare

Big-boned British pub food
Cooking score: 4
Modern British | £27
25 Broad Chare, Newcastle upon Tyne, NE1 3DQ
Tel no: (0191) 2112144
www.thebroadchare.co.uk

In a side street adjacent to the city's quayside law courts, this stylishly restored three-storey building is a happy mix of Dickensian tavern and rustic French auberge. Downstairs, the mantra is all about proper beer from local breweries soaked up with bar snacks of black pudding rissoles, while the upstairs dining room combines chophouse with brasserie via window shutters, bare wooden boards, tarnished mirrors and tan leather button-back banquettes. The food draws comparisons with London nose-to-tail establishments but the polished service and presentation gives it broad appeal. A deep bowl of full-flavoured spring pea, ham and lettuce soup was an impressive start to an inspection meal, followed by exemplary fishcakes, tartare sauce and chips served with a well-dressed and unadvertised salad. Gooseberry crumble and custard and apricot turnover with vanilla ice cream are typical of the seasonal desserts. If you can drag yourself away from the formidable beer list, wines start at £16.95.
Chef/s: Christopher Eagle. **Open:** all week L 12 to 2.30 (5 Sun), Mon to Sat D 5.30 to 10. **Closed:** 25 and 26 Dec, 1 Jan. **Meals:** alc (main courses £13 to £20). **Details:** 60 seats. Bar. Music.

Café 21

Stylish quayside favourite
Cooking score: 4
Modern British | £39
Trinity Gardens, Quayside, Newcastle upon Tyne, NE1 2HH
Tel no: (0191) 2220755
www.cafetwentyone.co.uk

Local food hero Terry Laybourne's stylish flagship brasserie is a fixture of Newcastle's Quayside and a firm favourite with the city's restaurant-goers, who appreciate the vitality of the place, the well-informed service and the chic, cosmopolitan dining room with its polished woodwork, leather banquettes and smart grey-and-citrus tones. They're also sold on chef Chris Dobson's classy food, which shows off his open-minded approach to things: terrine of Northumberland venison, plates of Lindisfarne oysters and fishcakes with parsley cream and chips doff their cap to the North Country, while Ibérico ham with toasted tomato bread, crab lasagne, and confit duck with lyonnaise potatoes are proof of a well-stamped gastronomic passport. Beef from the Glenarm Estate is aged in Himalayan salt, fish from the East Coast ports might be simply grilled, and desserts add a final flourish in the shape of, say, warm kumquat and ginger pudding with custard. An intelligent wine list offers house selections from £13.50 a carafe (£18.90 a bottle).
Chef/s: Chris Dobson. **Open:** Mon to Sat L 12 to 2.30 (3 Sat), D 5.30 to 10.30. Sun 12 to 8. **Closed:** 25 and 26 Dec, 1 Jan, Easter Mon. **Meals:** alc (main courses £16 to £30). Set L £18 (2 courses) to £21. Set D £19 (2 courses) to £22. Sun L £22. **Details:** 130 seats. V menu. Bar. Wheelchair access. Music.

Visit us online

To find out more about The Good Food Guide, please visit thegoodfoodguide.co.uk

House of Tides

Finely tuned concept-dining on the Quayside
Cooking score: 5
Modern British | £45
28-30 The Close, Newcastle upon Tyne,
NE1 3RF
Tel no: (0191) 2303720
www.houseoftides.co.uk

Parts of this Grade I-listed former merchant's house date from the 12th century but these days House of Tides is home to chef Kenny Atkinson. Rusting steel girders, mullioned windows and exposed stone walls in the downstairs bar are a reminder of the building's heritage, as is the lopsided, bipartite first-floor dining room with its sloping polished boards, gnarled pillars and mustard-coloured chairs and banquettes. Atkinson's tersely written tasting menus conceal finely tuned dishes that challenge as well as titillate – notably a fascinating blend of king crab, pink grapefruit, sourdough croûtons, sea fennel and apple blossom. Seasonal ingredients receive purposeful, robust treatment, from a standout dish of Wye Valley asparagus, pheasant egg, hollandaise, garden peas and tomato to Goosnargh chicken breast, Hispi cabbage, apple, spring turnip, smoked bacon and wild mushrooms. A fascinating dandelion and burdock crème brûlée is a clever take on the classic dessert. Excellent warm breads (sourdough and rosemary and tomato focaccia), followed by meltingly soft cheese sablé and 'a variety of home-smoked and salted nuts' have impressed, as has the 'faultless service'. Wines start at £22.

Chef/s: Kenny Atkinson. **Open:** Wed to Sat L 12 to 1.30 Tue to Sat D 6 to 10 (5 Fri and Sat). **Closed:** Sun, Mon, 21 Dec to 8 Jan, 30 Mar to 5 Apr, 27 Jul to 2 Aug. **Meals:** Set L £25 (2 courses) to £30. Set D £38 (2 courses) to £45. Tasting menu £65.
Details: 50 seats. V menu. Bar. Wheelchair access. Music. Parking. Children over 9 yrs only.

Jesmond Dene House

Pretty plates of smart, metropolitan food
Cooking score: 4
Modern European | £50
Jesmond Dene Road, Newcastle upon Tyne,
NE2 2EY
Tel no: (0191) 2123000
www.jesmonddenehouse.co.uk

Set among leafy gardens, this lavishly converted Arts and Crafts house feels a world away from the bustle of Newcastle but is only a short drive from the city centre. An imposing gothic stone mansion, it's as close to a self-appointed country house hotel as you will find and diners can eat at well-spaced tables in the sedate former music room or the conservatory. North Country ingredients are given a refined spin in precise dishes with no-holds-barred flavours. An inspection visit got off to a flying start with a plump raviolo of native lobster and Ibérico ham teamed with a rich bisque and samphire. It was followed by a full-flavoured fillet of Belted Galloway beef that came with a salt beef croquette, swede, charred leeks and a little jug of seriously rich jus. 'Eye-popping presentation' marked out a 'faultless' baked vanilla custard with poached rhubarb, salted crumb and rhubarb sorbet. Wines from £21.

Chef/s: Michael Penaluna. **Open:** all week L 12 to 2.30 (3 Sun), D 7 to 9.30 (6.30 Sat, 7 Sun). **Meals:** alc (main courses £20 to £35). Set L £22 (2 courses) to £25. Set D £25 (2 courses) to £31. Sun L £25.
Details: 60 seats. 20 seats outside. V menu. Bar. Wheelchair access. Music. Parking.

Peace & Loaf

Quirky restaurant with ambition
Cooking score: 4
Modern British | £34
217 Jesmond Road, Newcastle upon Tyne,
NE2 1LA
Tel no: (0191) 2815222
www.peaceandloaf.co.uk

Lauded as one of Newcastle's most exciting
new openings, Peace & Loaf is 'a genuine
experience' according to one reporter. Set
across three floors in a row of shops, its
unexpectedly off-centre location is matched
by the quirkily contemporary décor. The
relaxed and informal service is spot-on and
Dave Coulson's food regularly reaches the
high notes. Seasonal flavours hit you head on
whether you order from the good-value set
menu or the carte. An exemplary starter of
'almost spreadable' chicken and wild garlic
terrine with quail's egg and sourdough
croûtons punched well above its weight. Main
courses are equally as full-flavoured, as
demonstrated by hake, brown shrimp, purple
sprouting broccoli and fondant potato
anointed with a silky hollandaise. A dessert of
mango, ginger and pink Champagne – in the
form of gel, sponge and sorbet – was artfully
presented and displayed a light touch. A
thoughtful wine list opens at £17.95.
Chef/s: David Coulson. **Open:** all week L 12 to 2.30
(2 Sat, 3.30 Sun), Mon to Sat D 5.30 to 9.30. **Closed:**
25 and 26 Dec, 1 Jan. **Meals:** alc (main courses £15
to £24). Set L £16 (2 courses) to £20. Set D £20 (2
courses) to £25. Sun L £21. Tasting menu £70 (10
courses). **Details:** 55 seats. Wheelchair access.
Music. Parking.

Local Gem

Local Gems are the perfect
neighbourhood venues, delivering
good, freshly cooked food at great
value for money.

Caffè Vivo

Italian | £28
29 Broad Chare, Newcastle upon Tyne,
NE1 3DQ
Tel no: (0191) 2321331
www.caffevivo.co.uk

'Non-cliché modern Italian at a fair price,'
thought one reporter of Terry Laybourne's
charismatic and artfully simple warehouse
enoteca near the Tyne. It offers everything
from snacks and sharing platters to gutsy
three-course meals – perhaps char-grilled
calamari with lemon, chilli and rocket, ahead
of chicken alla diavola with sweet bell peppers,
then Florentine 'donuts' with lemon curd and
whipped cream. The almost exclusively Italian
wine list offers plenty by the glass, with
bottles starting at £16. Closed Sun.

North Shields

Irvins Brasserie

Cherished all-day brasserie with serious food
Cooking score: 3
Modern British | £28
Union Road, The Fish Quay, North Shields,
NE30 1HJ
Tel no: (0191) 2963238
www.irvinsbrasserie.co.uk

'The cooking is accomplished and the setting
slick,' was the verdict from one roving reporter
on this expansive, all-day brasserie set in a
listed trawlerman's building on North Shields
fish quay. Chef/proprietor Graeme Cuthell's
food bristles with modern-day resolve. Local
and regional sourcing is at the heart of his
fiercely seasonal menu, whether it's dressed
North Shields crab, Craster kipper salad with a
poached egg, or haunch of Yorkshire roe deer
with Jerusalem artichoke. Simple but alluring
combinations they may be, but the result is
cooking that sings with flavour. There's been
praise, too, for perfectly timed roast cod
teamed with Puy lentils and olive vinaigrette,
and for the homemade bread, while pear,

almond and demerara sponge with vanilla ice cream appeals solely on the grounds of deliciousness. Prices are modest – many dishes come in small or large portions – and there's a good-value set lunch. The short wine list opens at £16.95.

Chef/s: Graeme Cuthell. **Open:** Wed to Sun 12 to 9.30 (10.30 Fri and Sat, 7.30 Sun). **Closed:** Mon, Tue. **Meals:** alc (main courses £9 to £21). Set L and D £12 (2 courses) to £16. Sun L £18 (2 courses) to £20. **Details:** 76 seats. Bar. Wheelchair access. Music.

LOCAL GEM

The Staith House

Modern British | £26

57 Low Lights, Fish Quay, North Shields, NE30 1JA
Tel no: (0191) 2708441
www.thestaithhouse.co.uk

John Calton had his moment as a finalist on *MasterChef: The Professionals*, before winding up at this reclaimed boozer overlooking North Shields' fish quay. Ship's charts, portholes and maritime knick-knacks add to the quirky vibe, while the menu makes much of locally sourced produce. Fish and chips is a bestseller, but also expect anything from grilled hake with black pudding, chorizo and aïoli to saddle of fallow deer with glazed chicory, braised cabbage and roast plums. Wines from £15.50. No food Sun D.

▐ South Shields

LOCAL GEM

Colmans

Seafood | £20

182-186 Ocean Road, South Shields, NE33 2JQ
Tel no: (0191) 4561202
www.colmansfishandchips.com

Little changes at this unreservedly British institution. Fans applaud the way Colmans (established 1926) remains true to its original fish and chip shop character, despite taking things upmarket with a smart restaurant and

short wine list. The good-value menu is unashamedly and uncompromisingly old-school, offering generous portions of high-quality, very fresh fish cooked in 'light and crisp' batter with 'mouthwateringly good' chips. Crab salad, seafood platters and local lobster extend the repertoire, service is excellent and house Chilean is £13.50. Open daytime all week.

▐ Whitburn

LOCAL GEM

Latimer's

Seafood | £30

Shell Hill, Bents Road, Whitburn, SR6 7NT
Tel no: (0191) 5292200
www.latimers.com

'It's a simple café noted for its wonderful seafood,' notes a visitor to Robert Latimer's popular and well-run seaside café, which incorporates a fishmonger and smokery too. Fabulous views over the beach and the decked sitting area are crowd-pullers, as are crab sandwiches, seafood platters, 'naked' fish and chips, and proper homemade fruit and cheese scones and cakes (try the carrot cake). No booking means it's first come, first served. There's no licence either, but corkage is a reasonable £3. Open daytime Tue to Sun.

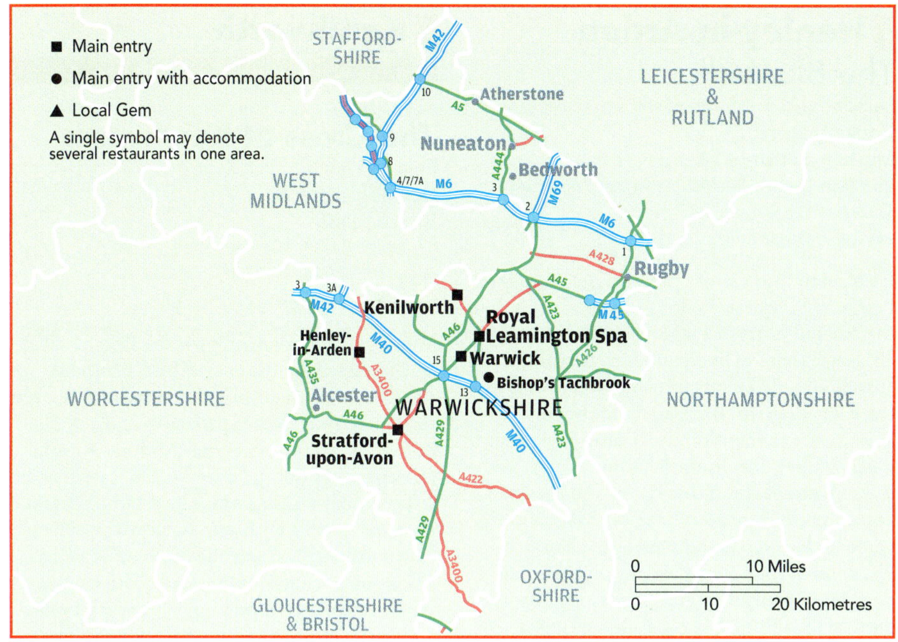

Bishop's Tachbrook
The Dining Room at Mallory Court

Pedigree package with perky food
Cooking score: 5
Modern British | £65
Harbury Lane, Bishop's Tachbrook, CV33 9QB
Tel no: (01926) 330214
www.mallory.co.uk

£5 OFF

It's all about pedigree at Mallory Court – a well-bred Lutyens-style country mansion set in ten acres of landscaped grounds just three miles from Royal Leamington Spa. This studious haven for Shires tourists and the wealthy denizens of Middle England might seem an unlikely home for a chef with youthful zing in his blood, but Paul Foster (ex-Tuddenham Mill, see entry) is making quite an impact here. Mallory's ornate Dining Room (all oak panelling, starched cloths and deep-pile carpets) now entertains bright, clean flavours, foraged pickings and plates of artfully jumbled ingredients – from charred leeks with onion, black garlic and brown shrimp to poached apple with toasted oat parfait and yeast caramel. In between, there are concessions to the old-money setting in the shape of brill fillet with potato agnolotti, gem lettuce and roast chicken sauce, or Ibérico pork loin with quince terrine, glazed parsnip and sprouting broccoli. The aristocratic global wine list speaks a similar language, with prices from £23 (£6.75 a glass).
Chef/s: Paul Foster. **Open:** Sun to Fri L 12 to 1.30, all week D 6.30 to 9. **Meals:** Set L £35. Set D £48. Tasting menu £70 (5 courses). Sun L £40. **Details:** 60 seats. 25 seats outside. V menu. Bar. Wheelchair access. Music. Parking.

Average price

The average price denotes the price of a three-course meal without wine.

Henley-in-Arden
The Bluebell

Upbeat and modishly rustic hostelry
Cooking score: 3
Modern British | £34
93 High Street, Henley-in-Arden, B95 5AT
Tel no: (01564) 793049
www.bluebellhenley.co.uk

It's hard to find a more picturesque place than Leigh and Duncan Taylor's Elizabethan pub in the ancient heart of Henley-in-Arden, although there's a lively modern personality in among the old beams: blue neon lighting in the bar; colourful furniture and mirrors galore; not to mention the dining alcove with black leather panelling that's more *Fifty Shades* than Shakespeare. A decade on and the food continues to impress – tasty crab tart with spinach, Parmesan and asparagus; ham hock spiced up with pineapple chutney and quail's egg. Main courses might include Lighthorne lamb with a tomato-ey accompanying shepherd's pie or a wonderfully rich, crispy chicken with silky golden mash, broad beans and tarragon cream. Desserts delight, too, whether chocolate and olive oil ganache, or cardamom crème brûlée. Wines cover all the main bases with most bottles above £25, and 15 by the glass, and a chintzy cup selection ensures the perfect cup of tea.

Open: Tue to Sun L 12 to 2.30 (3.30 Sun), Tue to Sat D 6 to 9.30. **Closed:** Mon. **Meals:** alc (main courses £14 to £25). Sun L £25. **Details:** 50 seats. 40 seats outside. Bar. Music. Parking. Children over 12 yrs only at D.

Visit us online

To find out more about
The Good Food Guide, please
visit thegoodfoodguide.co.uk

Kenilworth

★ TOP 50 PUB ★

NEW ENTRY
The Cross at Kenilworth

One to watch...
Cooking score: 5
British | £42
16 New Street, Kenilworth, CV8 2EZ
Tel no: (01926) 853840
www.thecrosskenilworth.co.uk

When not away battling for the Bocuse d'Or (the culinary equivalent of the Olympics), chef Adam Bennett plies his trade at this large renovated pub – an expensive Farrow & Ball reboot by Simpson's owner Andreas Antona (see entry). A test meal found intricate starters to be 'worth waiting for' – beef tartare 'looked fantastic' served with wasabi atop a geometric flower of radish alongside quinoa for a 'slight (welcome) crunch', while crispy duck egg and white asparagus came with super-rich potato and garlic mousse and a truffle poultry jus that begged to be mopped up by the accompanying sourdough. Main courses kept up the pace, with discs of colourful winter vegetables accompanying lightly charred squab pigeon, duck liver and rich truffle broth; its counterpart was a 'beautifully presented' pollack on a coral-style fan of blood orange, endives and lentils. Front-of-house doesn't quite match the kitchen's finesse, caught between pub casual and fine-dining stools, but overall there's more to come here, and reporters say 'it's one to watch'. Wine from £20 a bottle.

Chef/s: Adam Bennett. **Open:** all week L 12 to 2 (2.30 Sat, 4 Sun), Mon to Sat D 6.30 to 10 (6 Fri and Sat). **Meals:** alc (main courses £20 to £36). Set L £20 (2 courses) to £25. Tasting menu £65. **Details:** 80 seats. 20 seats outside. V menu. Bar. Wheelchair access. Music. Parking.

Leamington Spa
Restaurant 23

Serious food fizzing with bright ideas

Cooking score: 4

Modern European | £45

34 Hamilton Terrace, Leamington Spa,
CV32 4LY
Tel no: (01926) 422422
www.restaurant23.co.uk

£5 OFF

'Definitely dress up for Peter Knibb's super-smart, gorgeous Georgian restaurant', enthused one visitor, 'as it's all cocktails in the stylish upstairs bar before descending to the fantastic dining room with its high ceilings, parquet floor and candlelight bouncing off white linen — we felt extremely cosseted.' Equally good looking is the succinct menu of 'sublime' dishes, starting, perhaps, with seared scallops with a tasty pig croquette, apple and caper purée or a Cornish crab salad spiced up with curry oil and mango, before pork with pancetta terrine or halibut with almond and truffle pesto. Dessert, such as a mini banana and passion fruit soufflé with lime leaf ice cream, is fancifully delivered. As an overall experience it's hard to beat, 'a good special-occasion restaurant' with 'exceptional service which happens around you without you ever really noticing'. Wines start around the £25 mark, but are generally above £30.

Chef/s: Peter Knibb. **Open:** Tue to Sat L 12 to 2, D 3 to 9.15. **Closed:** Mon, Sun, 25 and 26 Dec, 1 Jan. **Meals:** Set L £20 (2 courses) to £25. Set D £40 (2 courses) to £45. Tasting menu £70. **Details:** 55 seats. 25 seats outside. V menu. Bar. Wheelchair access. Music.

Called to the Bar

We're not saying tables are going out of fashion, but when a restaurant is officially full - or even when it's not - eating at the bar is a no-nonsense, sociable and spontaneous way to find out what the kitchen's up to. Here are some of our favourite perches.

Polpetto, London

In a small, often oversubscribed restaurant (it must be the cavolo nero with anchovy and burnt butter bread) the handful of bar seats are first come, first served.

Hawksmoor, Manchester

The tiled dining room is light and bright, but for moodier moments the northernmost Hawksmoor boasts a handsome and capacious bar, with plenty of proper tables, in atmospheric near-darkness. You can order à la carte, but the bar snacks are pretty good.

Zoilo, London

Space is at a premium throughout this buzzy Argentinian double-decker, so you might as well pull up a bar stool. Downstairs, you'll be up close to the chefs as they turn out garlicky chips and grilled lamb sweetbreads; upstairs it's all about the wine.

Stratford-upon-Avon
No 9 Church St

Capable food and keen prices
Cooking score: 1
Modern British | £35
9 Church Street, Stratford-upon-Avon,
CV34 6HB
Tel no: (01789) 415522
www.no9churchst.com

With William Shakespeare's old school across the road and reminders of the Bard round every corner, it's no wonder this pleasing restaurant in a quaint 400-year-old town house is a boon for theatre buffs, tourists and locals looking for capable food at keen prices. No-nonsense lunches and early-evening deals are greatly appreciated, but chef/proprietor Wayne Thomson can dish up more fancy stuff too: his tasting menu is 'unforgettable', while the carte might offer flashy ideas such as warm quail salad with pickled wild mushrooms, quince, Scotch egg and shallot purée or baked pollack with leeks, orzo, mussels and smoked haddock sauce. Clever desserts close the show, and wines start at £15.50.
Chef/s: Wayne Thomson. **Open:** Mon to Sat L 12 to 2, D 5 to 9.30. **Closed:** Sun, 25 and 26 Dec. **Meals:** alc (main courses £13 to £24). Set L £14 (2 courses) to £18. Tasting menu £60 (9 courses). **Details:** 40 seats. Bar. Music.

Warwick
Tailors

Fantastic service and contemporary food
Cooking score: 3
Modern British | £40
22 Market Place, Warwick, CV34 4SL
Tel no: (01926) 410590
www.tailorsrestaurant.co.uk

'A snug fit!', exclaimed a reporter who 'really enjoyed' his meal at this 28-seater ex-outfitter's on Warwick's Market Place (do book ahead). It's a pleasant room with wood floors, contemporary wallpaper and an exposed brick wall, with 'fantastic service' from co-owner/co-chef Mark Fry – 'out front and in a suit, and obviously really enjoying himself'. In the kitchen Dan Cavell fashions modern British dishes with flair – a de-constructed corned beef sandwich with pickled red onions and HP sauce is as 'tongue 'n' cheek' as beef fillet with ox cheek and tongue salt beef (paired with beetroot terrine, pickles and cream cheese). Elsewhere, smoked almonds have provided a salty bite to pan-roasted sea trout, also served with new potato and green bean salad, while dessert might be treacle tart with homemade brown-toast ice cream. Wines are arranged by style rather than geography, with plenty in the £20 to £30 range. It is all good value, with the set lunch menu, in particular, ensuring this 'friendly neighbourhood restaurant has it all sewn up'.
Chef/s: Dan Cavell and Mark Fry. **Open:** Tue to Sat L 12 to 1.30, D 6.30 to 8.45. **Closed:** Sun, Mon, 23 Dec to 3 Jan. **Meals:** Set L £17 (2 courses) to £22. Set D £29 (2 courses) to £40. **Details:** 28 seats. V menu. Music. Children over 12 yrs only at D.

Join us at thegoodfoodguide.co.uk

Birmingham

★ TOP 50 ★

Adam's

Utterly brilliant eatery on the move
Cooking score: 7
Modern British | £50
21a Bennetts Hill, Birmingham, B2 5QP
Tel no: (0121) 6433745
www.adamsrestaurant.co.uk

Sitting tight to the pavement, less than five minutes' walk from Birmingham New Street station, Adam's is held in high affection. There is nothing unduly ostentatious about the place, but then this bijou dining room has been a temporary home for two years. At some point in the life of this guide, Adam's will move to larger premises round the corner with a bar, chef's table and development kitchen planned (check the restaurant's website for details). But much depends on the food and that is what Adam Stokes is about – he is capable of great things. First and foremost clarity and freshness go hand in hand, in a beautifully balanced dish of salt-baked carrots with thin slices of deeply flavoured pork jowl and hen of the woods mushrooms or perfectly timed halibut with leek purée, flavourful brown shrimps and purslane leaves. Elsewhere, earthier influences come into play. Loin of venison is pointed up with dots of apple purée, accompanying slices of Jersey Royals getting a kick-start from lime zest. On trend themes resurface in desserts: lemon verbena teamed with apricot, pistachio and Sauternes jelly; a tiny triangle of rich, sweet dark chocolate mousse on a crisp base, offset by slightly bitter lovage ice cream and dotted with sorrel leaves. British cheeses and homemade bread are up to the mark, and the wine list is a well-judged collection with prices from £24.

Chef/s: Adam Stokes. **Open:** Tue to Sat L 12 to 2, D 7 to 9.30. **Closed:** Sun, Mon, 2 weeks Dec to Jan, 2 weeks summer. **Meals:** Set L £32 (3 courses). Tasting menu £50 (5 courses) to £80 (9 courses). **Details:** 26 seats. V menu. Wheelchair access. Music.

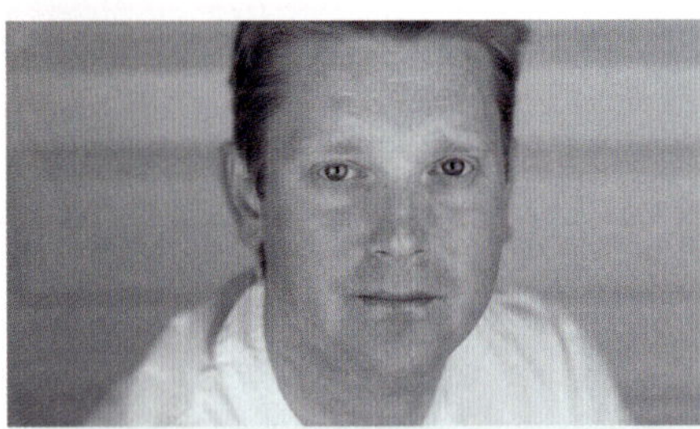

Adam Stokes 

Adam's, Birmingham

What do you enjoy the most about being a chef?

I enjoy cooking and eating the best foods, whether it be scallops or a piece of broccoli; when something is perfect, it is a joy to eat.

What is your favourite time of year for food?

Winter, for the game season. It takes a well-trained chef to treat game birds with the respect that they deserve. When that happens, the results are magical.

Do you have a guilty foodie pleasure?

A really well-made kebab in a naan is a thing of beauty – but it has to be good. We are spoilt in Birmingham for quality ones.

What food could you not live without?

Bacon – it is amazing. Everyone likes bacon.

Is there a particular ingredient that evokes strong memories for you?

Broad beans – while I was growing up my father used to grow them in his allotment; every year when the first crop was harvested we had a 'broad bean party'.

Carters of Moseley

Food to capture the imagination

Cooking score: 5

Modern British | £45

2c Wake Green Road, Moseley, Birmingham, B13 9EZ

Tel no: (0121) 4498885

www.cartersofmoseley.co.uk

£5 OFF

'Far exceeded our expectations,' commented one happy visitor to this classy yet informal restaurant in a parade of shops not far from the centre of Moseley. The first solo venture from chef Brad Carter and Holly Jackson, it offers some seriously focused, clean and inventive cooking that uses quality, mainly seasonal British ingredients in imaginative ways. There's unanimous praise for 'fantastic bread' and 'absolutely yummy' pigs' butter (made from the fat of Tamworth pigs, with hints of salt and onion), and reports of 'excellent' plates of food have included Devon crab dumpling with a brown crab broth, and 'so tender' 35-day aged ribeye with turnips and horseradish buttermilk. Other clever pairings, among them Cornish mackerel with Yorkshire rhubarb; sheep's milk yoghurt with beets and blackcurrant; and roast red deer with kabocha squash and quince, have been praised for robust flavours and just the right amount of refinement. For dessert, try a 'refreshing' buttermilk mousse with strawberries, and then coffee with 'divine' homemade cardamom chocolate. Service, led by Holly, is 'friendly and very knowledgeable'. Plenty of thought has gone into the nicely annotated wine list, which starts at £19.95.

Chef/s: Brad Carter. **Open:** Wed to Sun L 12 to 1.45 (2.30 Sun), D 6.30 to 9.30. **Closed:** Mon, Tue, 2 weeks Jan, 2 weeks Aug. **Meals:** Set L £28 (4 courses). Set D £49 (5 courses). Sun L £32. Sun D £32 (5 courses). **Details:** 32 seats. V menu. Wheelchair access. Music. Parking. Children over 8 yrs only.

Imran's

Pakistani Lord of the Ladypool Road
Cooking score: 3
Indian | £20
262-266 Ladypool Road, Birmingham,
B12 8JU
Tel no: (0121) 4491370
www.imrans.com

A major presence in Balsall Heath's Pakistani restaurant enclave since opening in 1971, Imran's has expanded and marched upmarket over the years – yet stayed true to its Punjabi roots. Behind the sweet counter and the open kitchen (where the charcoal grill resides), the dining area stretches back far, with its white-robed chairs and pointed Islamic archways. The menu, too, has expanded since the early days, embracing the standard kormas and bhunas as well as the baltis for which the area is famed. Breads and tandoori food are particular strengths, so perhaps start with a robustly spiced seekh kebab or tandoori fish, seared to succulent perfection and ideal with a shared roti. Next, devotees of Punjabi food might try the orgery, strips of lamb tripe in a rich masala sauce, though on-the-bone chicken karahi is equally suffused with flavour, and the thick tarka dhal is delectable. Unlicensed: corkage, no charge.
Open: all week 12 to 11. **Meals:** alc (main courses £7 to £12). **Details:** 250 seats.

Lasan

Delightful contemporary Indian cuisine
Cooking score: 4
Indian | £41
3-4 Dakota Buildings, James Street, St Paul's Square, Birmingham, B3 1SD
Tel no: (0121) 2123664
www.lasan.co.uk

'A really enjoyable visit, the warm and friendly service really helps but the food has moved up a few notches over the years,' noted a regular visitor to this smart Indian restaurant found on an unassuming side street a short walk from the city centre. Lasan offers a menu of innovative and contemporary dishes and at a test meal the vegetarian tikki and the mahi machli (marinated salmon) were found to be 'superb', both starters showing a lightness of touch with the accompanying spices. Mains followed suit with the overnight-braised Elaichi beef (served with bone-marrow pakora and tandoori sweetbread in a black cardamom-spiced gravy) delivering a knockout punch. Finish with kheer (rice pudding with plums). Although more expensive than your standard Indian eatery, the prices reflect the quality of ingredients and skill in the kitchen. Service is excellent with staff friendly and attentive throughout. A decent wine list starts at £19 a bottle.
Chef/s: Aktar Islam. **Open:** Mon to Fri L 12 to 2.30, D 6 to 11. Sat and Sun 12 to 9. **Closed:** 25 and 26 Dec, 1 Jan. **Meals:** alc (main courses £16 to £25). Set D £33 to £37. **Details:** 72 seats. V menu. Bar. Wheelchair access. Music.

Opus

Bullish Brummie brasserie
Cooking score: 2
Modern British | £37
54 Cornwall Street, Birmingham, B3 2DE
Tel no: (0121) 2002323
www.opusrestaurant.co.uk

Glimpsed behind a vast expanse of glass, this upmarket brasserie has occupied its commercial district site for more than a decade and remains as well turned out as its clientele. And a decade on the approach to food remains consistent – namely vibrant modern British dishes based on fresh, seasonal produce, delivered by confident staff. Instantly appealing food is the deal, with reporters praising simple grilled lobster, leek and smoked haddock fishcakes with a poached egg and butter sauce, John Dory served on spiced chickpeas with a heritage potato farl and cardamom and cumin fragranced yoghurt, and dry-aged beef fillet with crisp hand-cut chips and peppercorn sauce. Desserts are given the full contemporary treatment, with poached Yorkshire rhubarb served with a white chocolate mille-feuille and Granny Smith apple sorbet guaranteeing a happy ending. The set lunch is excellent value and the well-spread wine list kicks off at a reasonable £18.95.

Chef/s: Ben Ternent. **Open:** Mon to Fri and Sun L 12 to 2.15 (3 Sun), Mon to Sat D 6 to 9.30. **Closed:** 24 Dec to 2 Jan, bank hols. **Meals:** alc (main courses £13 to £26). Set L and D £14 (2 courses) to £16. Sun L £25. **Details:** 85 seats. Bar. Wheelchair access. Music.

Purnell's

No-holds barred approach to cooking
Cooking score: 5
Modern British | £65
55 Cornwall Street, Birmingham, B3 2DH
Tel no: (0121) 2129799
www.purnellsrestaurant.com

For many years Purnell's has been seen as an exciting foodie venue: 'brilliant service'; 'food excellent'; 'flavours I have never tasted before' – just some of the praise heaped on Glynn Purnell's spacious, modern flagship in Brum's financial district. Dazzling reports have highlighted a seemingly simple crab salad of flaked white meat topped with a little crab bisque, a sumac wafer lending lemony citrus notes, while part two of the dish delivers a single 'perfectly cooked' scallop dressed with an almond satay and a dash of ponzu sauce. Or consider the 'good cooking' of a small fillet of red mullet, a little pommes dauphine and red wine sauce, rose veal cheek, long cooked and flavour-packed, with sesame and treacle, and a 'crumble' of lemon posset, dates, pine nuts and Bourneville honey. But while Purnell undoubtedly possesses the skill and intelligence to pull off avant-garde cooking with aplomb, others have found 'Reminisce', Purnell's back catalogue of dishes, a bit hit and miss, leaving diners with the impression that while the chef's standards have not changed, others have surpassed him. On the resounding

plus side, there's a substantial wine list that's enhanced by the 'knowledge and enthusiasm of the sommelier'; bottles from £23.95.

Chef/s: Glynn Purnell. **Open:** Tue to Sat L 12 to 1.30, Tue to Fri D 7 to 9 (Sat 6.30 to 9.30). **Closed:** Sun, Mon, 2 weeks Christmas, 1 week Easter, 2 weeks Aug. **Meals:** Set L £32 (3 courses) to £42. Tasting menu £65 (6 courses) to £85. **Details:** 45 seats. Bar. Wheelchair access. Music. Children over 10 yrs only.

Purnell's Bistro

Glynn Purnell's own brand of bistro
Cooking score: 2
Modern British | £30
11 Newhall Street, Birmingham, B3 3NY
Tel no: (0121) 2001588
www.purnellsbistro-gingers.com

Glynn Purnell's second gaff (see entry, Purnell's) has quite a swagger. Big windows give lots of light and street views, and those lured into the spacious, lively bar and pair of bistro-style dining rooms at the back don't leave disappointed. There's an elegant 1930s feel to Ginger's bar, which is custom-built for the local crowd with its enterprising cocktail list and bar snacks of hot dogs, burgers or hand-cut chips with curry sauce, while in the bistro the big attraction is good-value menus that aim to please all-comers. Classic dishes are cooked with brio and flair, whether it's game terrine, honey-glazed duck confit with spiced red cabbage, pork belly with choucroute, smoked bacon, braised carrot and onion purée, or risotto of wild mushroom. To finish, there's warm madeleine with pear fool or passion fruit crème brûlée with coconut sorbet. The wine list is a modern global affair with prices from £17.95.

Chef/s: Micheal Dipple. **Open:** Sun to Fri L 12 to 1.45 (2.45 Sat, 3.45 Sun), Mon to Sat D 6.30 to 9.30 (5 Sat). **Closed:** 25 to 31 Dec, 1 Jan. **Meals:** alc (main courses £15 to £26). Set L and D £16 (2 courses) to £20. Sun L £18. **Details:** 85 seats. Bar. Wheelchair access. Music.

Saffron

Creative Indian cookery, with glitz
Cooking score: 1
Indian | £22
909 Wolverhampton Road, Oldbury,
Birmingham, B69 4RR
Tel no: (0121) 5521752
www.saffron-online.co.uk

Dressed to please, Saffron attracts local
(mostly non-Asian) families with well-spaced
tables, a soundtrack of soft Western pop,
sparkling glass light fittings and comfortable
beige seating. Likewise, food is expertly
presented, ranging from curry-house
ubiquities to unusual beef dishes and
interesting modern Indian inventions such as a
starter of tender, warming rabbit varuval.
Spicing is generally meek, and at inspection an
aubergine side dish seemed bland.
Nevertheless, fall-off-the-bone lamb shank
came in flavoursome gravy, the naan was first
rate and an East–West fusion dessert of apple,
banana and chocolate spring rolls made a
satisfying ending. Wines (listed by style)
from £11.95.
Chef/s: Avijit Mondal. **Open:** all week L 12 to 2.30,
D 5.30 to 10.30 (11 Fri and Sat, 10 Sun). **Meals:** alc
(main courses £8 to £22). **Details:** 92 seats. Bar.
Wheelchair access. Music. Parking.

Simpsons

A memorable gastronomic experience
Cooking score: 6
Modern British | £55
20 Highfield Road, Edgbaston, Birmingham,
B15 3DU
Tel no: (0121) 4543434
www.simpsonsrestaurant.co.uk

On the edge of the leafy suburb of Edgbaston
and a world away from the hustle and bustle of
the nearby city, Simpsons still delights with its
brand of refined yet flavoursome cooking:
'Still in my view the best in Birmingham,' as
one regular noted. The combination of a carte,
tasting menu (both meat and vegetarian) and a

fixed-price lunch, which includes a half-
bottle of wine, is worthy of note and certainly
gives the kitchen a lot to do. Luke Tipping
takes a thoughtful and refined approach to
modern British cooking, serving appealing
combinations such as 'a sensational dish' of
deep-fried duck egg with salsify, watercress,
hazelnut and truffle pesto and trompettes, an
excellent roasted squab pigeon 'Pierre Orsi'
with jus gras, and Cornish lamb with
pomegranate, cracked wheat, cumin,
aubergine and goats' cheese. Standing out
among desserts was a 'light-as-air' caramelised
speculoos biscuit soufflé. Wines start at £28 a
bottle. Note: an extensive refurbishment to
extend the main dining area and update the
décor is due to be completed after the Guide
goes to press.
Chef/s: Luke Tipping. **Open:** all week L 12 to 2
(12.30 to 2.30 Sun), Mon to Sat D 7 to 9 (9.30 Fri and
Sat). **Closed:** 25 and 26 Dec, bank hols. **Meals:** alc
(main courses £24 to £35). Set L £40. Tasting menu
£85. **Details:** 75 seats. V menu. Wheelchair access.
Parking.

Turners Restaurant

An ambitious culinary journey
Cooking score: 5
Modern British | £55
69 High Street, Harborne, Birmingham,
B17 9NS
Tel no: (0121) 4264440
www.turnersrestaurantbirmingham.co.uk

An established member of Birmingham's
vibrant dining scene, Richard Turner delivers
creative cooking with a great deal of technical
skill. The 10-minute ride from the city centre
to a location in an ordinary row of shops
might surprise, but once through the door this
is a restaurant that 'is anything but ordinary'.
Small, maybe, but the mirrored walls and
well-spaced tables mean you certainly won't
feel cramped, 'although the barcode-patterned
carpet takes getting used to'. The food isn't
cheap, but a menu of Turner's classics offers
more reasonable options at lunchtime and on
Tuesday evenings. At a test meal, scallop

ceviche teamed with beetroot, apple, yoghurt and horseradish, sea bass with lobster tortellini, and a main of Longhorn beef sirloin with crispy cheek showed a sure touch. Dessert was also on form with a moreish Yorkshire rhubarb crumble soufflé with custard ice cream making a good finale. Service could relax a little; serious food doesn't need over-serious staff to serve it. Wines start at £27.

Chef/s: Richard Turner. **Open:** Fri and Sat L 12 to 2, Tue to Sat D 7 to 9.30. **Closed:** Sun, Mon, 25 and 26 Dec, first week Jan. **Meals:** Set L £35 (3 courses). Set D £55 (3 courses) to £85. Tasting menu £90. **Details:** 26 seats. Wheelchair access. Music. Children over 12 yrs only.

Café Opus at Ikon

Modern British | £19

1 Oozells Square, Brindleyplace, Birmingham, B1 2HS
Tel no: (0121) 2483226
www.cafeopus.co.uk

A few minutes' walk from the city centre, on the ground floor of the Ikon Gallery, Café Opus provides an ideal opportunity to watch the world go by. As well as offering a selection of homemade cakes (try the 'fabulous' coffee and walnut cake), the all-day menu delivers fresh carrot soup, a generous portion of chicken thighs on a bed of garlic potatoes and greens or lightly battered monkfish cheeks if you just fancy a snack. Set menus offer excellent value for money. A limited wine list starts at £16.50. Closed D Sun to Wed.

Dorridge
The Forest

Local destination with easy-going food
Cooking score: 3
Modern European | £29
25 Station Approach, Dorridge, B93 8JA
Tel no: (01564) 772120
www.forest-hotel.com

Once Dorridge's railway hotel, the Forest now does a grand job as an all-comers' destination for travellers and locals in search of brasserie-style food and personable hospitality. Long-serving chef Dean Grubb's kitchen is fuelled by supplies of top-notch produce for a globetrotting menu that delivers everything from sticky BBQ beef doughnuts with pickled vegetables to curried monkfish with dhal, vegetable bhaji and mint yoghurt. Along the way, readers have also dined well on scallops with celeriac, apple and walnut, 'perfectly cooked' duck Wellington and lamb cutlets with sautéed kidney, sweetbreads and 'excellent meaty gravy', although desserts have been reported as 'less accomplished'. Family favourites such as burgers, fish and chips or chicken and mushroom pie chime with the chintzy dining room's polished tables, standard lamps and foliage-patterned décor, and trendy deli sandwiches also feature at lunchtime. Service is friendly, prices are fair and the wine list offers dependable drinking from £16.25.

Chef/s: Dean Grubb. **Open:** all week L 12 to 2.30 (4 Sun), Mon to Sat D 6.30 to 9.30. **Closed:** 25 Dec. **Meals:** alc (main courses £14 to £21). Set L and D £14 (2 courses) to £16. Sun L £22. **Details:** 65 seats. 45 seats outside. Bar. Wheelchair access. Music. Parking.

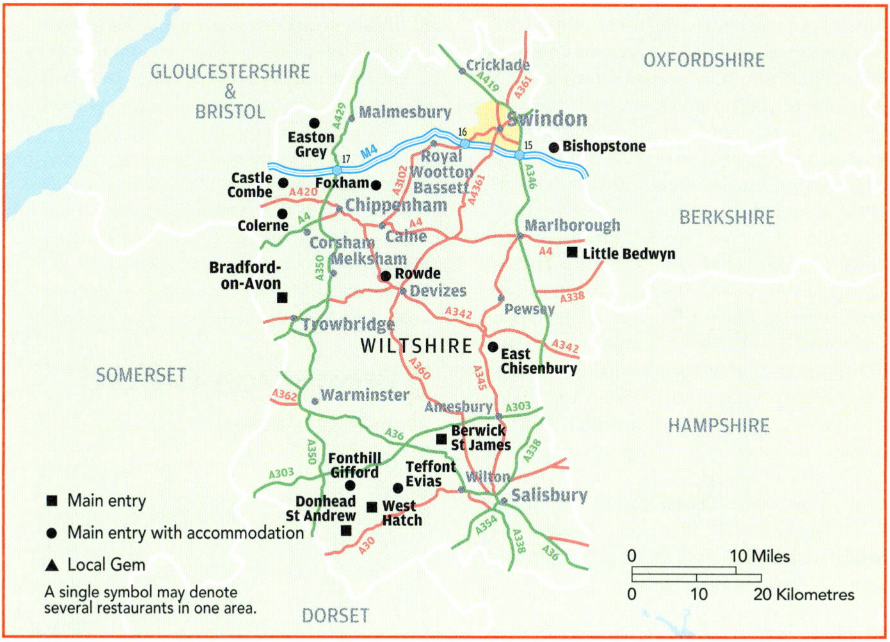

Berwick St James

The Boot Inn

Appealing pub with home cooking
Cooking score: 1
British | £24
High Street, Berwick St James, SP3 4TN
Tel no: (01722) 790243
www.theboot.pub

'Outstanding for its food, service, value for money and overall warm and friendly atmosphere,' enthused one visitor to Giles and Cathy Dickinson's much-loved village pub, which cherishes locals and visitors alike and stands out for many reporters 'as a brilliant example of what every British pub should aspire to be'. Expect not only a great bar, winter fire and garden when sunny, but also a blackboard menu that delivers good, honest home cooking, from 'delicious' bread and lunchtime classics (beef burgers, mutton cottage pie), to slow-roast duck with caramelised orange and watercress salad and wonderful sticky toffee pudding. Wines from £16.90.
Chef/s: Giles Dickinson. **Open:** Tue to Sun L 12 to 2.15 (2.30 Sun), Tue to Sat D 6.30 to 9.15 (9.30 Sat). **Closed:** Mon, 25 Dec, 1 to 13 Feb. **Meals:** alc (main courses £10 to £16). **Details:** 34 seats. 24 seats outside. Music. Parking.

Bishopstone

Helen Browning at the Royal Oak

Cheery organic pub-cum-B&B
Cooking score: 3
British | £29
Cues Lane, Bishopstone, SN6 8PP
Tel no: (01793) 790481
www.helenbrowningorganics.co.uk

Helen Browning OBE is Director of the Soil Association and an organic farmer of some repute, which means the roasted Eastbrook

(that's her farm) pork loin and belly, with mash and seasonal veg, is doubtless worth a punt. There's no standing on ceremony at her pub, where you'll find three ales at the pumps, a passion for sustainability, and a menu rich with produce from the farm and broader local community. Eastbrook air-dried ham is a great opener (proper stuff this), or go for mushrooms stuffed with Oxford Blue cheese, before a beef burger (yep…from the farm again) with skinny fries and salad. It's hearty stuff, with haddock fillet with green tapenade and tomato sauce about as dainty as it gets (although even that comes with mash). Sweet risotto rice pudding with orange marmalade and dark chocolate is a top finisher. The organic wines come by the glass, carafe and bottle, the latter starting at £19.
Chef/s: Paul Winch. **Open:** Mon to Sat L 12 to 3 (3.30 Sat), D 6 to 9.30. Sun 12 to 8. **Closed:** 25 Dec. **Meals:** alc (main courses £12 to £25). **Details:** 50 seats. 60 seats outside. Parking.

■ Bradford-on-Avon
The Three Gables

Resurrected charmer with a French accent
Cooking score: 3
Modern European | £35
St Margaret's Street, Bradford-on-Avon, BA15 1DA
Tel no: (01225) 781666
www.thethreegables.com

£5 OFF

An agreeable feeling of pastoral prosperity characterises this lovingly resurrected, listed stone building, which sits just across from the River Avon in the centre of town. The place runs smoothly under the watchful eye of Vito Scaduto, while in the kitchen Marc Salmon adds some French and Mediterranean nuances to fastidiously sourced West Country ingredients. An assured dish of cured Creedy Carver duck breast with confit leg and gizzard with beetroot, orange, sprout and hazelnut salad shows the style, and there's also a seasonal edge to roasted loin of Skrei cod served with greens, sweet carrot, brown shrimp and parsley butter. Desserts move into the realms of praline moelleux with white coffee ice cream. The set lunches are popular, the very good value encouraging regulars to splash out on the well-written, well-researched wine list, which is built on interest and appeal – and kicks off with good recommendations by the glass. Bottles start at £17.50.
Chef/s: Marc Salmon. **Open:** Tue to Sat L 12 to 2, D 6 to 10. **Closed:** Sun, Mon, first 2 weeks Jan. **Meals:** alc (main courses from £19 to £26). Set L £14 (2 courses) to £18. Set D £32. **Details:** 50 seats. 25 seats outside. Bar. Wheelchair access. Music.

■ Broughton Gifford

READERS RECOMMEND
The Fox

British
Broughton Gifford, SN12 8PN
Tel no: (01225) 782949
www.thefox-broughtongifford.co.uk
'The food was perfectly executed… the staff are warm, welcoming and really friendly and the wine list and well stocked bar make this an amazing country pub. An absolute must.'

■ Castle Combe
The Manor House Hotel, Bybrook Restaurant

Modern food in heritage surroundings
Cooking score: 5
Modern British | £62
Castle Combe, SN14 7HR
Tel no: (01249) 782206
www.manorhouse.co.uk

£5 OFF

When Steven Spielberg filmed *War Horse* in the unspoilt village of Castle Combe, he said it was as if 'Hollywood built it', a statement that could be applied to the imposing 14th-century Manor House too. Surrounded by 365 acres of parkland, with the River Bybrook running through the beautiful Italianate gardens, it pushes all the right buttons when it comes to Cotswold charm. Richard Davies' contemporary cooking is defined by clear flavours, inventiveness and pin-sharp

Join us at thegoodfoodguide.co.uk

accuracy, as displayed in an opener of silky ravioli filled with free-range chicken and teamed with the lightest Montgomery Cheddar velouté, crispy shallots and Trealy Farm ham. Pan-fried fillet of Cornish turbot, cèpe, celeriac and pancetta fricassee is a sure-footed main, while an overly grainy mandarin gel with an intensely flavoured tonka bean brûlée and bitter chocolate sorbet was a rare misfire in an otherwise successful test meal. A heavyweight wine list with serious prices opens at £25.

Chef/s: Richard Davies. **Open:** Wed to Sun L 12.30 to 2, all week D 6.30 to 9. **Meals:** Set L £25 (2 courses) to £30. Set D £62 (3 courses). Sun L £35. Tasting menu £74 (7 courses). **Details:** 65 seats. V menu. Bar. Wheelchair access. Parking. Children over 11 yrs only.

Colerne

Lucknam Park

British cooking of delicacy and depth
Cooking score: 5
Modern British | £80
Colerne, SN14 8AZ
Tel no: (01225) 742777
www.lucknampark.co.uk

Lucknam Park has some history to live down, the estate having been successively financed over the years with revenues from tobacco importation and slave labour, but pumping iron in the fitness suite, you can set all that aside. It's a majestic 17th-century manor, reached by a mile-long drive, in which the Park dining room awaits with chandeliers and boudoir drapes. Hywel Jones produces an extensive repertoire of modern British food full of bright ideas and things you've never come across, adding potato mousse and Exmoor caviar to langoustines and gribiche, chamomile jelly and pickled peach to duck foie gras. There's delicacy as well as depth in main dishes like braised turbot on iceberg lettuce with crab and truffle-buttered macaroni, and a firm hand on the tiller when it comes to bold assertive dessert flavours. Passion fruit cream, lemongrass sorbet and

mango jelly comes as welcome relief to more salted caramel. The wine list is full of enterprise and connoisseurial zest, with go-to producers all over the show, and affordable gems for those prepared to forage. Prices open at £25. Glasses are the small measure though.

Chef/s: Hywel Jones. **Open:** Sun L 12 to 2.30, Tue to Sat D 6.30 to 9.30. **Closed:** Mon. **Meals:** Set D £80. Sun L £39. Gourmet menu £105. **Details:** 64 seats. V menu. Wheelchair access. Parking.

Donhead St Andrew

The Forester

Well-tended country boozer
Cooking score: 2
Modern British | £29
Lower Street, Donhead St Andrew, SP7 9EE
Tel no: (01747) 828038
www.theforesterdonheadstandrew.co.uk

Thatched roof, log fires, beams, leather sofas…the Forester is a smart country pub and no mistake, with the Australian owners – Chris and Lizzie Matthews – showing a genuine commitment to the traditions of the village tavern. When it comes to culinary matters, the kitchen's output is rooted in the region's produce, with fresh seafood shipped up from Devon and Cornwall, and much of everything else sourced from the surrounding area. It's relatively simple, robust stuff, pitched to satisfy and sustain. Freshwater crayfish find their way into a terrine with crab and leeks, served with a sauce vierge, while the kitchen shows its mettle by home-curing its own bresaola from Donhead Estate venison. That venison turns up in burger form among the 'pub classics', too, or go for Brixham lemon sole grilled on the bone. Lunchtime sandwiches arrive on homemade bread, and, for dessert, Seville orange tart comes with a nifty fennel sorbet. Wines start at £19.

Chef/s: Andrew Kilburn. **Open:** Tue to Sun L 12 to 2, Tue to Sat D 6.30 to 9. **Closed:** Mon. **Meals:** alc (main courses £14 to £22). Set L and D £19 (2 courses) to £23. Sun L £17. **Details:** 60 seats. 40 seats outside. V menu. Bar. Music. Parking.

East Chisenbury

★ TOP 10 PUB ★

The Red Lion

Much more than your average free house
Cooking score: 6
Modern British | £35
East Chisenbury, SN9 6AQ
Tel no: (01980) 671124
www.redlionfreehouse.com

Reporters are in no doubt that Guy and Brittany Manning's bucolic village inn is a serious foodie beacon, praising the 'delicious seasonal food', 'great service' and 'cosy local pub atmosphere', and convinced it leads the way for dining pubs in Wiltshire, if not nationally. The menu may be short, but it never fails to set pulses racing judging by reports of 'wonderfully tender and tasty guinea fowl leg, quite delicious baked cod, pork belly to die for and splendid burgers for the kids'. Guy's food hits you with big assertive flavours and his confidence is palpable: consider a risotto of slow-cooked octopus and Sandridge Farm bacon with red wine and crispy pigs' ears that so impressed one February diner, or note the definite seasonal edge to roast Skrei cod with cep purée, fondant potato, purple sprouting broccoli and sauce almondine, while beer and peanut layer cake with milk chocolate custard and malt ice cream is 'a fitting way to bring the curtain down'. There are good local ales, too, and a large proportion of the short, wide-ranging wine list is available by the glass; bottles from £17.50.
Chef/s: Guy Manning. **Open:** all week L 12 to 2.30 (3 Sun), D 6 to 9 (8 Sun). **Meals:** alc (main courses £15 to £30). Set L £18 (2 courses) to £24. **Details:** 45 seats. 20 seats outside. Music. Parking.

Visit us online

To find out more about The Good Food Guide, please visit thegoodfoodguide.co.uk

Easton Grey

★ TOP 50 ★

Whatley Manor, The Dining Room

Extravagantly talented cooking
Cooking score: 8
Modern French | £110
Easton Grey, SN16 0RB
Tel no: (01666) 822888
www.whatleymanor.com

Whatley Manor is a beautifully restored Georgian manor house near Malmesbury, all soft-focus charm from the climbing ivy outside to the nut-brown panelling within. A Canadian owner in the 1920s, who was a big noise in the Beaufort Hunt, added the wing that now houses the Dining Room, where striped upholstery, an uncovered floor and neutral cream walls constitute a fashionably mute backdrop for the extravagantly talented Martin Burge. He's now dispensed with the à la carte approach in favour of a trio of seven-course tasting menus, one of which is vegetarian. Burge cooks in three dimensions, with dishes that exercise powerful appeal to the senses and achieve stunning depths of complex flavour. The poached and roasted foie gras, dressed with compressed pear and ginger, is luxuriously rich, down to its unctuous Sauternes sauce. Innovative approaches to pasta include oyster and lime cannelloni with steamed turbot in Champagne and caviar, while main meats might be veal fillet, cooked two ways again, sauced in Madeira, alongside its braised cheek and caramelised sweetbread, and textures of hazelnut. Reverse the fish and meat order for stuffed quail with morteau, then John Dory with deep-fried cod cheeks in bouillabaisse consommé. Following a play on clementine with mandarin sorbet and juniper foam, prepare to be bowled a spherical dessert: Kirsch-laced pistachio mousse in a white chocolate case with cherry compote. A line-up of tremendous wines has been arranged to go with it, each country divided into its regions, from Austria's Wachau to Washington

State and South Australia's Eden Valley. Ten wines by the glass start at £5.70, bottles at £26.

Chef/s: Martin Burge. **Open:** Wed to Sun D only 7 to 10. **Closed:** Mon, Tue. **Meals:** Tasting menu £110 (7 courses) to £175. **Details:** 40 seats. Bar. Wheelchair access. Music. Parking. Children over 12 yrs only.

Fonthill Gifford

★ TOP 50 PUB ★

Beckford Arms

Upper-crust rural inn
Cooking score: 3
British | £36
Fonthill Gifford, SP3 6PX
Tel no: (01747) 870385
www.beckfordarms.com

In a remote setting on the Fonthill Estate, this handsome, ivy-clad building stands at a country crossroads and is both 'beautifully styled and homely'. There's a choice of dining rooms: the wood-panelled bar with its inglenook fireplace; a country-house-style sitting room; and the slightly more formal dining room, which opens on to the garden and terrace. It's all equally inviting, whether you opt for a warm sausage roll, hand cut at the bar, and a pint of local ale, or a full-blown three-course dinner. Potted Brixham crab with celery and pea shoot salad, 'meltingly soft' veal brisket with a punchy dressing of mustard and shallot, and a fabulous ribeye steak with bone marrow and chips are typical choices, and there's a short list of pub classics, from ploughman's to fish and chips. Desserts are either deeply comforting (steamed quince and stem ginger pudding with custard), or rich and decadent (chocolate and Amaretto torte with caramelised chestnuts). Wines from £17.50.

Chef/s: Nigel Everett. **Open:** all week L 12 to 3 (3.30 Sun), D 6 to 9 (9.30 Fri and Sat). **Closed:** 25 Dec. **Meals:** alc (main courses £14 to £22). **Details:** 75 seats. 38 seats outside. Bar. Music. Parking.

Foxham

The Foxham Inn

Family-run village pub
Cooking score: 1
Modern British | £28
Foxham, SN15 4NQ
Tel no: (01249) 740665
www.thefoxhaminn.co.uk

Tucked away and hard to find, Sarah and Neil Cooper's red-brick village pub-with-rooms has a timeless charm, 'complete with a red phone box next to a lean-to shelter at the front'. It continues to impress reporters who note the 'excellent ambience' and 'high standard' of food. It's a traditional, unpretentious place with a warming wood-burner in the bar and light and modern dining room, while the solid, confident and generous cooking is based on local ingredients. There's a mix of pub classics and more imaginative ideas, say Dorset snails, Marlborough mushrooms and wild garlic ragoût, followed by gilthead bream, spinach and creamy Devon crab risotto. Wines from £16.75.

Chef/s: Neil Cooper. **Open:** Tue to Sun L 12 to 2, D 7 to 9.30 (9 Sun). **Closed:** first week Jan, 1 week Oct. **Meals:** alc (main courses £12 to £18). Set L £18 (2 courses) to £24. Set D £22 (2 courses) to £28. Sun L £12. **Details:** 60 seats. 30 seats outside. Wheelchair access. Music. Parking.

Little Bedwyn

The Harrow at Little Bedwyn

Real food and extraordinary wines
Cooking score: 6
Modern British | £55
High Street, Little Bedwyn, SN8 3JP
Tel no: (01672) 870871
www.theharrowatlittlebedwyn.com

'If there is a better value wine list in Britain than this one I would like to see it', commented a visitor to Sue and Roger Jones's

tiny dining room, in what was once Little Bedwyn's only pub. The food is not far behind. The kitchen buys really unique, high quality produce and then offers a master class in simplicity. A tranche of turbot, for example, is lightly grilled and perched on an ethereally creamy dollop of truffle-packed risotto; lamb is two thick, ruby-red slices of loin, a little kofta-style mince of shoulder, with semi-dried tomatoes, couscous and a little shot of mint sauce. Everything is distinct, clutter free and tastes exactly of what it is. Even when strong flavours are used, as when chilli, ginger, coriander and garlic accompany a Pembrokeshire lobster tail, nothing gets lost. It's hard to resist a little shot of clementine and passion fruit parfait, followed by a strawberry soufflé, but the cheese selection is 'a triumph', too. The knowledge, forethought and money that have been poured in to Roger Jones' cellar is mindboggling but prices (from £28) are reasonable given the fabulous credentials.
Chef/s: Roger Jones and John Brown. **Open:** Wed to Sat L 12 to 2, D 7 to 9. **Closed:** Sun, Mon, Tue, 25 Dec to 4 Jan. **Meals:** alc (main courses £30). Set L £40. Set D £50. Tasting menu £75. **Details:** 34 seats. 24 seats outside. V menu. Music.

■ Rowde
The George & Dragon

Proper local with top-notch seafood
Cooking score: 3
Modern British | £30
High Street, Rowde, SN10 2PN
Tel no: (01380) 723053
www.thegeorgeanddragonrowde.co.uk

£5 OFF

'An excellent, value-for-money experience,' said one reader of this proper, 'no nonsense' village local deep in landlocked Wiltshire. Carved Tudor roses adorn the beams of the centuries-old coaching inn, there's a secret tunnel under the building and CAMRA supporters sit by the fire, supping pints of Butcombe Bitter and guest ales. However, one look at the blackboard will tell you that this pub is also serious about food: fish comes up from St Mawes and the day's line-up might

run from succulent sardines, 'happily unadorned' megrim or gilthead bream to skilfully rendered plates of seared scallops with artichoke purée and crispy Parma ham, beer-battered whiting or roast salmon with wilted spinach and creamed sweetcorn. Alternatively, open with coronation chicken or twice-baked cheese soufflé before tackling 'granny's' steak and kidney pie or a char-grilled ribeye steak with wild mushroom sauce. Organic house red is £10.95 a carafe.
Chef/s: Christopher Day and Tom Bryant. **Open:** all week L 12 to 3 (4 Sat and Sun), Mon to Sat D 6.30 to 10 (11 Fri and Sat). **Meals:** alc (main courses £9 to £21). Set L and D £17 (2 courses) to £20. Sun L £20.
Details: 40 seats. 36 seats outside. V menu. Bar. Wheelchair access. Music. Parking.

■ Teffont Evias
Howard's House Hotel

Country comforts and quietly confident food
Cooking score: 3
Modern European | £45
Teffont Evias, SP3 5RJ
Tel no: (01722) 716392
www.howardshousehotel.co.uk

£5 OFF

'There is a genuine wow-factor,' thought one visitor to this 17th-century dower house in one of Wiltshire's prettiest villages. Howard's House is found down a winding country lane alongside a tiny stream, surrounded by attractive gardens in a lush and hidden valley – 'an impossibly lovely location matched by the smartly traditional interior'. The kitchen makes good use of the abundant local produce, as well as fish delivered from the south coast, and on the whole dishes are grounded in tradition and confident cooking. At inspection a warm salad of crispy breast of lamb with a punchy caper and shallot dressing, and a precisely cooked fillet of wild turbot with ratte potato purée, sweet and briny brown shrimps, spinach and a rich crab bisque 'clearly made from good stock' both impressed, and a perfectly risen passion fruit soufflé with chilli-poached pineapple, coconut crisp and Malibu ice cream got a big thumbs-up. Wines from £18.

Chef/s: Nick Wentworth. **Open:** all week L 12 to 2, D 7 to 9. **Closed:** 23 to 26 Dec. **Meals:** alc (£36 2 courses, £45 3 courses). Set L and D Mon to Sat £25 (2 courses) to £30. Tasting menu £65. **Details:** 40 seats. 24 seats outside. V menu. Music. Parking.

■ West Hatch
Pythouse Kitchen Garden Shop and Café

Gorgeous garden café
Cooking score: 2
British | £20
West Hatch, SP3 6PA
Tel no: (01747) 870444
www.pythouse-farm.co.uk

You'd be hard-pressed to better the bucolic scene at this former potting shed, a long glasshouse that overlooks a Victorian walled garden, nursery and the fields beyond. Pythouse Kitchen Garden café, on the Pythouse Estate, deftly walks the line between elegant and rustic with a bare-brick backdrop and mismatched furniture, and it plies its wares, too, selling garden produce alongside deli treats. Tea and homemade cake is on offer throughout the day, but it's also a lovely spot for lunch. The concise menu, to which the garden contributes, offers all kinds of things you want to eat: from substantial options such as the Pythouse burger or whole plaice with herb crust to lighter dishes along the lines of pretty-as-a-picture baba ganoush with baby vegetable crudités, or cod croquettes with a peppy caponata. Those with a sweet tooth will be happy with the selection of cakes on the Welsh dresser. Wines from £16.95.

Chef/s: Peter Buckey. **Open:** all week L 12 to 2.30, Fri D 7 to 11. **Closed:** 25 and 26 Dec, 1 Jan. **Meals:** alc (main courses £10 to £14). Set D (Fri only) £25. **Details:** 60 seats. 62 seats outside. V menu. Wheelchair access.

Nathan Outlaw

Restaurant Nathan Outlaw, Cornwall

What do you enjoy the most about being a chef?

I enjoy everything about being a chef. Cooking, creating, being able to use fantastic local produce, working with my team, the list goes on... However, what I like least are the days when I can't get into the kitchen to cook because of paperwork!

What's your newest ingredient discovery?

I'm using a lot of different seaweeds at present. Not really new because the Irish and the Japanese have been using them for years. I'm lucky that The Cornish Seaweed Company is right on my doorstep and they supply it ready-prepared.

What food could you not live without?

Fish - obviously! I really like mackerel because it is so versatile. Also cheese - oh, and cake; life wouldn't be worth living without it!

Tell us something about yourself that will surprise your diners.

Until I began cooking professionally, I wouldn't eat any fish other than fish fingers!

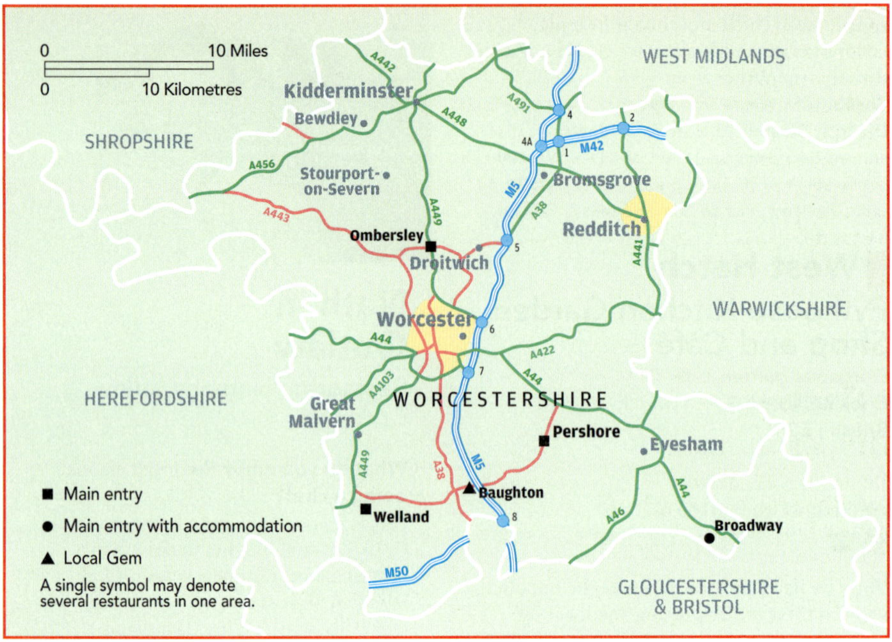

Baughton

LOCAL GEM

The Jockey Inn

Modern European | £28
Pershore Road, Baughton, WR8 9DQ
Tel no: (01684) 592153
www.thejockeyinn.co.uk

Closed for more than three years, this tucked-away village inn reopened early in 2015 after a multi-million pound renovation. Now a food-driven pub with a hard-to-miss horse and jockey theme, which some think 'borders on overkill', it delivers solid and competent cooking. Sharing boards and a range of char-grilled local steaks jostle for attention with wild English cod and Var salmon fishcakes, and free-range 'Cotswold White' chicken breast with dauphinois potatoes, baby leeks, wild mushrooms and chive cream. There's apple and almond tart to finish. Wines from £14.95. Open all week.

Broadway

Russell's

Prime boutique spot with local flavour
Cooking score: 4
Modern British | £35
20 High Street, Broadway, WR12 7DT
Tel no: (01386) 853555
www.russellsofbroadway.co.uk

Andrew and Gaynor Riley opened their restaurant-with-rooms in the former workshop of renowned furniture designer, Sir Gordon Russell, in 2004 and have created a divertingly handsome spot for eating, drinking and sleeping. They've kept the heart and soul of the old place, introduced a little 21st-century style, and looked to the nearby landscape to provide much of the food for the table. Neil Clarke changes his menu every day depending on what's hot and what's not, and puts together winning combinations that are modern without being over the top. Start with quail Kiev, for example, served with its stuffed

leg and Russian salad, or three hand-dived scallops that arrive with celeriac in various textures. Artichoke and truffle risotto is simple and refined, while stone bass gets a Med spin with its Parmesan polenta, caponata and basil espuma. There are steaks, too, and desserts run to mirabelle plum soufflé with Earl Grey pannacotta. Wines start at £19.50.
Chef/s: Neil Clarke. **Open:** all week L 12 to 2.15 (2.30 Sun), Mon to Sat D 6 to 9.15. **Closed:** 1 Jan, bank hols. **Meals:** alc (main courses £16 to £28). Set L and D £17 (2 courses) to £24. Sun L £25.
Details: 50 seats. 20 seats outside. Music.

■ Ombersley
The Venture In
Gently modernised food
Cooking score: 4
Modern European | £40
Main Road, Ombersley, WR9 0EW
Tel no: (01905) 620552
www.theventurein.co.uk

From its external whitewash and beams to its homely interior, Toby Fletcher's well-established little restaurant maxes out on cottagey charm. There's nothing overly styled about the place: primrose walls, an inglenook fireplace and bare beams give it all the character it needs. In contrast, Fletcher's cooking has clearly moved with the times, striking the sweet spot between familiarity and gentle invention. After 'superb' home-made breads, a 'perfectly risen, intensely cheesy' Roquefort soufflé with rocket and poached pears impressed one reporter, while Fletcher's passion for seafood shines in a main course of market-fresh plaice with a fricassee of asparagus, prawn and mussels that 'simply shone with flavour.' The same could be said of a silken vanilla and rum pannacotta served with nicely sweet/tart rhubarb. Service is charming and knowledgeable, but be prepared for the occasional wait. The wine list includes lots of favourites at accessible prices. Bottles start at £18.

Chef/s: Toby Fletcher. **Open:** Tue to Sun L 12 to 2, Tue to Sat D 7 to 9. **Closed:** Mon, 1 week Christmas, 1 week Mar, 1 week Jun, 2 weeks Aug,. **Meals:** Set L £26 (2 courses) to £30. Set D £40. Sun L £30.
Details: 32 seats. Music. Children over 10 yrs only.

■ Pershore
Belle House
Value as well as contentment
Cooking score: 3
Modern European | £30
5 Bridge Street, Pershore, WR10 1AJ
Tel no: (01386) 555055
www.belle-house.co.uk

Belle House's high ceilings, vintage cream walls and huge windows (once doorways for fire engines at this former fire station) emphasise the feeling of space and light. It feels classic yet modern, the extravagant plasterwork offset by contemporary art, bare oak floors and simple wood tables with Lloyd Loom chairs. Both service and cooking rise to the occasion nicely: expect modern European dishes with a hint of invention. An amuse of heritage tomatoes with pesto and bocconcini makes a sprightly forerunner to a silky broccoli soup poured over toasted almond potato croquettes, and a main course of pink, tender picanha of beef with Anna potatoes, wild mushrooms and an intense claret jus. Desserts include a classy riff on Eton mess comprising yoghurt ice cream and strawberry jelly as well as the expected meringues, strawberries and cream. When you've finished, it's worth popping into the adjoining deli – part of the same business – for take-home treats. Wines from £19.50.
Chef/s: Steve Waites. **Open:** Tue to Sat L 12 to 2, D 7 to 9.30. **Closed:** Sun, Mon, 25 to 30 Dec, first 2 weeks Jan. **Meals:** Set L £18 (2 courses) to £24. Set D £27 (2 courses) to £35. **Details:** 70 seats. Bar. Wheelchair access. Music.

Welland

The Inn at Welland

Cleverly reinvigorated country inn
Cooking score: 3
Modern British | £28
Hook Bank, Drake Street, Welland, WR13 6LN
Tel no: (01684) 592317
www.theinnatwelland.co.uk

'The area needs more like this!' exclaimed one reader after visiting David and Gillian Pinchbeck's cleverly reinvigorated country pub in the shadow of the Malvern Hills. The stone-floored interior looks a treat and the owners have also improved their outdoor dining area, while chef Chris Exley has devised a wide-ranging menu that suits his customers down to a T. Fans of 'pub classics' can get stuck into steak, sandwiches, corned beef hash, pies or beer-battered fish and chips, while those with slightly more adventurous palates might be drawn to seasonal plates of pan-seared scallops with baby spinach, chorizo and herb oil or roast loin of venison with sweet potato, caramelised chestnuts, Savoy cabbage and rich port reduction. There are top Sunday roasts, the British cheese slate features some terrific regional names and desserts play the comfort card – think pear Bakewell tart or chocolate and hazelnut torte. Wines from £14.95.

Chef/s: Chris Exley. **Open:** Tue to Sun L 12 to 2.30, Tue to Sat D 6 to 9.30. **Closed:** Mon, 25 and 26 Dec, bank hols. **Meals:** alc (main courses £13 to £22). Sun L £22 (2 courses) to £26. **Details:** 60 seats. 40 seats outside. Wheelchair access. Music. Parking.

Symbols

Accommodation is available
Three courses for less than £30
£5-off voucher scheme
Notable wine list

Main entry
Main entry with accommodation
Local Gem
A single symbol may denote several restaurants in one area.
DURHAM
CUMBRIA
LANCASHIRE
GREATER MANCHESTER
DERBYSHIRE
NOTTINGHAM-SHIRE
LINCOLNSHIRE
YORKSHIRE
Richmond
Middleton Tyas
Staddlebridge
Osmotherley
Northallerton
Leyburn
Hawes
West Witton
Bedale
Maunby
Masham
Scawton
Helmsley
Harome
Thirsk
Oldstead
Sawdon
Pickering
Scarborough
Filey
Ramsgill
Ripon
Boroughbridge
Malton
Flamborough Head
Bridlington
Bridlington Bay
Settle
Grassington
Hetton
Bolton Abbey
Ferrensby
Knaresborough
Harrogate
Newton-on-Ouse
York
A166
Driffield
Skipton
Ilkley
Wetherby
Tadcaster
A1079
Market Weighton
South Dalton
Sancton
Hornsea
Withernwick
Beverley
Keighley
Leeds/Bradford
Leeds
Selby
A613
Hull
Bradford
Morley
Castleford
Goole
Withernsea
Todmorden
Halifax
Drighlington
Shibden
Wakefield
Pontefract
Thorne
Humber
Sowerby Bridge
Lindley
Honley
Huddersfield
Barnsley
Bentley
Doncaster
Robin Hood
Spurn Head
Holmfirth
Stocksbridge
Chapeltown
Rotherham
Bawtry
Maltby
Sheffield
Goldsborough
Whitby
57
56
51
50
49
47
46
45
44
43/48
42
41
40
39
38
37
36
35
34
33
32
31
3
1
26
27
23
6
5
4
2/35
7/35
1
38
37
36
A66
A172
A174
A171
A169
A171
A167
A1
A684
A684
A167
A168
A170
A64
A170
A6108
A165
A168
A19
A61
A65
A629
A658
A59
A1(M)
A64
A63
A614
A165
A164
A1034
A614
A62
A1041
M62
A63
A1
A19
A638
A635
M1
M18
A57
A625
A1033
20 Miles
30 Kilometres
0 10 20
0 10 20 30
ENGLAND | YORKSHIRE

◼ Beverley
Whites

Creative, dynamic tasting-menus
Cooking score: 4
Modern British | £25
12a North Bar Without, Beverley, HU17 7AB
Tel no: (01482) 866121
www.whitesrestaurant.co.uk

Best known for its minster, Beverley has another ace up its sleeve in the shape of John Robinson's restaurant. Situated in a three-storey town house on the intriguingly named North Bar Without (it sounds best when said in a Yorkshire accent), it's only little – just 20 covers – with four bedrooms upstairs and a rooftop terrace. Via two tasting menus, the shorter of which is only available midweek, the chef/patron delivers a series of dynamic modern plates. His creative mind and grasp of contemporary cooking techniques are best explored on the full-on nine-course menu, where you might go from hand-dived scallop ceviche with cider jelly and semi-cooked onion, to garden-herb dumplings with lemon foam. Flavour, texture and temperature all play their part. Slow-cooked ox cheek gets a hit of blue cheese from its accompanying foam, while the sweet courses are as equally well constructed; cherry cannelloni, say, with lemon curd and nutmeg pannacotta. Wines start at £18.50.

Chef/s: John Robinson. **Open:** Sat L 12 to 1.30, Tue to Sat D 6.45 to 8.30. **Closed:** Sun, Mon, 2 weeks Christmas, 1 week Aug. **Meals:** Set L £20. Tasting menus £25 (4 courses, Tue to Thur only) to £50 (9 courses). **Details:** 20 seats. Wheelchair access. Music.

◼ Bolton Abbey
The Burlington at the Devonshire Arms

Inventive cooking in 30,000 acres
Cooking score: 5
Modern French | £65
Bolton Abbey, BD23 6AJ
Tel no: (01756) 710441
www.burlingtonrestaurant.co.uk

The Devonshire Arms may sound like a comfy old boozer, but is in fact a Jacobean country house that has been part of the Duke's Bolton Abbey Estate since 1753. Sitting in 30,000 acres, it's obviously got a bit more than a beer garden, and the Burlington dining room extends from a flesh-pink room hung with landscape paintings into a lovely conservatory, from which you can view the real thing. Adam Smith produces a vigorous rendition of modernist cooking, with the option of a multi-course taster, and dishes are impressive in their emphatic precision. A marinated scallop arrives with blobs of avocado, radish and pig brawn croquettes, to be followed by Hereford beef rib with braised cheek, salt-baked turnip and mushroom purée, and then perhaps a poached apricot with lavender parfait, honey ice cream and almonds. The tasting journey might embark from smoked tongue in jellied tomato consommé with horseradish and fennel, arriving eight stops later at strawberries in buttermilk with Champagne sorbet. A magisterial wine list is fully in keeping, opening with Spanish house wines at £17, and tramping exhaustively through the classic regions.

Chef/s: Adam Smith. **Open:** Tue to Sun D only 6.30 to 9.30. **Closed:** Mon, 25, 26 and 31 Dec, 1 Jan. **Meals:** Set D £65. Tasting menu £75. **Details:** 60 seats. V menu. Bar. Wheelchair access. Parking. Children over 7 yrs only.

Join us at thegoodfoodguide.co.uk

The Devonshire Brasserie

Ducal eatery with a metropolitan edge
Cooking score: 2
Modern British | £32
Bolton Abbey, BD23 6AJ
Tel no: (01756) 710710
www.devonshirebrasserie.co.uk

Many of the Devonshire Brasserie's hardcore supporters have been coming to this chic country bolt-hole for more than a decade, lured by its vibrant, sunny disposition, open-minded menus and easy prices. The Devonshire Arms' second restaurant (see entry, The Burlington), most agree that it still delivers the goods. It makes quite a statement with its dazzling colours and contemporary canvases, and the kitchen remit spreads over the modern British repertoire with plenty of input from Yorkshire produce. This could mean new-season pea soup with goats' curd, salted almonds and olive oil, or English asparagus with crisp duck egg, hollandaise and watercress, followed by herb-fed chicken pie with bacon, sprouting broccoli and buttered ratte potatoes. A wodge of rhubarb crumble with pastry cream and roasted almond ice cream makes a great finale. Wine from £16.
Chef/s: Sean Pleasants. **Open:** all week L 12 to 2.30 (4 Sun), D 6 to 9.30 (9 Sun). **Meals:** alc (main courses £16 to £28). **Details:** 70 seats. 40 seats outside.

Boroughbridge
The Dining Room

Welcoming family-run restaurant
Cooking score: 2
Modern British | £30
20 St James Square, Boroughbridge, YO51 9AR
Tel no: (01423) 326426
www.thediningroomonline.co.uk

£5 OFF

A fixture on Boroughbridge's attractive Georgian square for 16 years, Lisa and Chris Astley's restaurant welcomes with a comfortable dining room and well-drilled but pleasant service. Pre-dinner drinks are taken upstairs in the well-upholstered lounge (dining happens downstairs), while the cooking takes a sensible, broadly modern British line, offering smoked haddock risotto with shaved Parmesan and pea shoots or ham hock terrine with piccalilli. While there's nothing too revolutionary, ingredients are sound and results have pleased across the board. Free-range chicken breast with a white wine and tarragon sauce or fillets of sea bass with a dressing of sweet peppers and basil are typical main courses, and desserts have included warm chocolate brownie with vanilla ice cream and chocolate sauce or rhubarb and Prosecco jelly. Wines are pitched to meet the requirements of interest and affordability, with bottles from £19.80.
Chef/s: Chris Astley. **Open:** Sun L 12 to 2, Tue to Sat D 6 to 9.15. **Closed:** Mon, 26 Dec, 1 Jan, bank hols. **Meals:** alc (main courses £13 to £26). **Details:** 32 seats. 20 seats outside. Bar. Music.

Drighlington
Prashad

Delicate vegetarian flavours
Cooking score: 2
Indian Vegetarian | £24
137 Whitehall Road, Drighlington, BD11 1AT
Tel no: (0113) 2852037
www.prashad.co.uk

Like so many aspiring Indian restaurateurs, the Patel family started out peddling savoury snacks and sweetmeats in a backstreet café, but fast-forward some 22 years and they're now riding high in a converted three-storey pub between Leeds and Bradford. Following a serious makeover, the cavernous high-ceilinged rooms positively shimmer with vibrant colours and ethnic designs from the owners' native Gujarat – perfect for dishes that celebrate the vegetarian cooking of the region. As expected, delicately flavoured snacks get top billing – from kachoris and pani puri to hara bara kebab (mashed pea and cauliflower), steamed idli and fluffy uttapam (rice pancakes). Also look for the range of dosas, bhajis with garlic naan and familiar regional specialities ranging from Bombay bataka (potatoes with mustard seeds, tomatoes and tamarind) to mattar paneer, tarka dhal and chole (chickpeas spiked with cumin seeds). Breads, rice and sides such as masala chips are spot-on, too. Drink Mongozo mango beer or house wine (£13.95). **Chef/s:** Minal Patel. **Open:** Fri to Sun L 12 to 5, Tue to Sun D 5 to 11. **Closed:** Mon, 25 Dec. **Meals:** alc (main courses £8 to £12). **Details:** 70 seats. V menu. Wheelchair access. Music. Parking.

■ Ferrensby

★ TOP 50 PUB ★

The General Tarleton
Much-admired inn, close to the A1
Cooking score: 4
Modern British | £35
Boroughbridge Road, Ferrensby, HG5 0PZ
Tel no: (01423) 340284
www.generaltarleton.co.uk

Brick and beams are warmed up with log fires and Yorkshire tweeds at John Topham's smart restaurant-with-rooms, conveniently close to the A1 at Ferrensby. 'Food with Yorkshire Roots' is the title of the à la carte with dishes that take you from a starter of Wensleydale soufflé, followed by locally reared suckling pig with black pudding and dauphinoise potatoes, finishing with a plate of Yorkshire rhubarb, all accurately cooked and artfully presented. Two favourites go back to Topham's days at the Angel at Hetton (see entry) where, in the early 1980s under Denis Watkins, he helped pioneer what became known as Britain's first gastropub: fish soup with rouille, croûtons and Gruyère cheese; and seafood 'moneybags' in filo pastry with lobster sauce – two dishes that have never been off the menu at either establishment, as popular as ever. Wines from £20, £3.65 a glass.

Chef/s: John Topham and Marc Williams. **Open:** all week L 12 to 2, D 6 to 9 (9.15 Sat, 8.30 Sun). **Meals:** alc (main courses £14 to £24). Set L and D £16 (2 courses) to £20. Sun L £23 to £27. **Details:** 120 seats. 60 seats outside. Parking.

■ Goldsborough

The Fox & Hounds
Serious food in a pint-sized hideaway
Cooking score: 5
Modern European | £36
Goldsborough, YO21 3RX
Tel no: (01947) 893372

It's devilishly hard to find, out in the wild country between Sandsend and Runswick Bay, but Sue and Jason Davies' pint-sized gastronomic hideaway is well worth the trek. Restricted opening times, limited space and a necessarily brief menu may not work in its favour, but there's no arguing with the results on the plate: 'understated excellence' sums it up, and Jason has the knack of keeping things simple while creating finely honed dishes based on locally sourced produce (much of it organic). The North Sea is just a stroll away, so 'supper' always features some spanking fresh fish – perhaps a salad of skate, capers and parsley with anchovy and garlic dressing or fillet of wild sea bass accompanied by braised fennel, spinach and lemon oil. There's generally a dry-aged steak, too, before Neal's Yard cheeses and a trio of crafty desserts such as dark chocolate truffle cake with espresso mascarpone cream. A snappy little wine list matches the food to a T, with prices from £20. **Chef/s:** Jason Davies. **Open:** Wed to Sat D only 6.30 to 8.30. **Closed:** Sun, Mon, Tue, Christmas, bank hols. **Meals:** alc (main courses £18 to £30). **Details:** 18 seats. Parking. No children.

Grassington
Grassington House Hotel
Impressive field-to-fork food
Cooking score: 3
Modern British | £35
5 The Square, Grassington, BD23 5AQ
Tel no: (01756) 752406
www.grassingtonhousehotel.co.uk

'I've never been disappointed by the attention to quality or by the presentation of the food' is a typical report on John and Sue Rudden's chic and stylish Georgian town house overlooking Grassington's cobbled square, with the majestic Yorkshire Dales on all sides. In the No. 5 restaurant you can taste produce from this stunning landscape: John might cook up pan-fried Grassington moor lamb loin, braised breast and fillet with lamb fat potatoes, cumin, pumpkin and lamb juices, or 28-day aged Pateley Bridge beef fillet, pan-fried and served with onion rings, peppercorn sauce, tomato, mushrooms and hand-cut chips. Either side of these hearty mains might be Goosnargh corn-fed chicken liver pâté, and sticky toffee pudding with butterscotch sauce, or impressive English cheeses. Wines from £16.
Chef/s: John Rudden. **Open:** all week L 12 to 2.30 (4 Sat and Sun), D 6 to 9.30 (8.30 Sun). **Meals:** alc (main courses £13 to £26). **Details:** 44 seats. 46 seats outside. V menu. Bar. Wheelchair access. Music. Parking.

Halifax
Ricci's Place
Full-flavoured versions of Med classics
Cooking score: 2
Mediterranean | £23
4 Crossley House, Crossley Street, Halifax, HX1 1UG
Tel no: (01422) 646422
www.riccisplace.co.uk

Michael Ricci continues his advance on Halifax – his smart 'tapas and cicchetti' outfit is to be found at Dean Clough along with a popular cocktail lounge (53 Degrees North) – and here's Ricci's Place in the town centre. It occupies a listed building, a light, airy space with a vaulted brick ceiling, drop lights, scrubbed-wood floors and white leather banquettes, with 'groovy tunes' nicely in the background. Expect deeply flavoured versions of rustic Mediterranean classics – crispy baby squid served with rocket, chilli, lemon and allioli, sea bass ravioli in a creamy tomato and crab sauce, and confit shoulder of lamb in a broth of peas, capers, mint and trofie pasta – and the odd exquisite Asian dish, perhaps tuna sashimi in rice-paper rolls. Opening all day, breakfast through dinner, is quite a hard trick to pull off, but they do it well here. Service is lovely and it's all good value for money; house wine is £12.
Chef/s: John Ferris and Mark Mattock. **Open:** Mon to Sat 9am to 11pm (midnight Fri and Sat). **Closed:** Sun, 25 and 26 Dec, 1 Jan. **Meals:** alc (main courses £8 to £18). **Details:** 60 seats. Music.

Harome
The Pheasant Hotel
Smart rural package with modern food
Cooking score: 4
Modern British | £36
Mill Street, Harome, YO62 5JG
Tel no: (01439) 771241
www.thepheasanthotel.com

This elegant and comforting venue is a classy rural package from head to toe, with hunting-lodge overtones and a lovely wisteria-garlanded terrace, plus an airy conservatory and smart dining room for those with food on their minds. The kitchen garners seasonal ingredients from the region and beyond for a rolling menu packed with appetising modern ideas – from tartare of organic Scottish salmon with piccalilli, apple and samphire or poached eggs (from the hotel's brood) with charred leeks, potato and aged ham to salted-butterscotch cream with spiced apple, chestnut and lemon thyme. In between, roast breast of mallard might be served with confit leg fritter, roasted foie gras, kale and wood blewits, while 'village-reared' sirloin and braised cheek could be matched with beetroot, potato and blackberries. An admirable wine list offers serious choice at prices that won't offend, with a page of house selections from £11 a carafe (£5 a glass).

Chef/s: Peter Neville. **Open:** all week L 12 to 2, D 6.30 to 9.30 (9 Sun). **Meals:** alc (main courses £20 to £26). Set D £36. Sun L £29 (2 courses) to £34. Tasting menu £55 (6 courses). **Details:** 70 seats. 40 seats outside. Bar. Wheelchair access. Parking.

★ TOP 50 PUB ★

The Star Inn

Refined modern food with a Yorkshire accent
Cooking score: 5
Modern British | £45
High Street, Harome, YO62 5JE
Tel no: (01439) 770397
www.thestaratharome.co.uk

A couple of miles from Helmsley on the edge of the North York Moors, the Star shines brightly whichever way you come at it. 'Welcoming, warm and professional' staff are half the battle, and the 14th-century thatched inn itself works a little magic with its kitchen garden, strutting hens and smartly appointed dining room. Andrew Pern styles his food as 'modern Yorkshire', and if ingredients occasionally come from a little further afield, as with the Norfolk quail in an osso buco with beetroot, haggis and salsify, its juices boosted with whisky and orange, it's the free and easy way with them that counts. Foie gras might suggest airs and graces, but partner it with black pudding, watercress and a reduction of scrumpy and it soon finds its northern accent. Vintage elderberry vinegar is the medium for grilled cod with garlic snails and caramelised onion, and nobody is going to leave Yorkshire these days without a taste of rhubarb, perhaps in a gingerbread-based cheesecake, served with a shot of rhubarb schnapps. Wines are a well-chosen jumble that inspire confidence, from £5 glasses of Valdivieso Chilean varietals to Vega Sicilia's Ribera del Duero. Bottles open at £19.50.

Chef/s: Andrew Pern and Steve Smith. **Open:** Tue to Sun L 12 to 2 (6 Sun), Mon to Sat D 6.30 to 9.30. **Meals:** alc (main courses £19 to £36). Set L and D £20 (2 courses) to £25. Sun L £19. **Details:** 76 seats. 60 seats outside. V menu. Bar. Music. Parking.

Harrogate

NEW ENTRY

Norse

Daytime café turns Scandi-style by night
Cooking score: 3
Scandinavian | £31
22 Oxford Street (at Baltzersen's), Harrogate, HG1 1PU
Tel no: (01423) 202363
www.norserestaurant.co.uk

The white-tiled daytime café Baltzersen's morphs into a Scandi-inspired restaurant at night, offering a list of eight small, medium or large plates. The menu presents predominantly northern-climate ingredients like mackerel, bass, mussels and kale, liberally sprinkled with more esoteric finds of grelot onions, monk's beard, wild leek and maitake, all eagerly explained by a youthful, check-shirted team. A small plate of crab, Jersey Royal terrine, puffed bulgur wheat and sweet cicely pleased, as did a larger one of saddle of lamb with duck-fat carrot, charred courgette, sea spinach, oxalis root and Jack-by-the-hedge. Not everything clicked. 'Charred tartare of mackerel' was more warmed over than charred or tartare. A dense pine kernel cake was lifted by a quirky mix of artichoke ice cream, malted cream, cinnamon and parsnip. Good bread, delicious smoked butter, an exemplary beer list, and some interesting wines (from £19) as well as cocktails and countless gins.

Chef/s: Murray Wilson. **Open:** Tue to Sat D only 6 to 9. **Closed:** Sun, Mon, 25 and 26 Dec. **Meals:** alc (main courses £7 to £14). Tasting menu £39 (6 courses). **Details:** Music.

Orchid

Well-liked pan-Asian stalwart
Cooking score: 2
Pan-Asian | £30
Studley Hotel, 28 Swan Road, Harrogate,
HG1 2SE
Tel no: (01423) 560425
www.orchidrestaurant.co.uk

Lacquered mango-wood, Japanese lattice screens, bare tables and intimate alcoves create just the right mood in this pan-Asian stalwart within Harrogate's Studley Hotel. Flavours may be slightly toned down for local palates, but the kitchen makes a good fist of things and the back-packing menu has all-round appeal — whether you're in the mood for crispy lemon chicken (a Hong Kong classic), Thai red duck curry, steamed sea bass with birdseye chillies, lemon and spring onion or a plate of Malaysian chow quey tiew noodles with beef. Starters also cover a lot of territory, from well-made Korean steamed dumplings and Japanese wasabi prawns to duck spring rolls, Szechuan bang-bang chicken and crispy soft-shell crab. There are special family buffets on Sundays, while banquet-style set menus offer a whistle-stop tour of the regions. To drink, opt for a bottle of Asian beer or a spice-friendly Gewürztraminer; otherwise, Chilean house wine is £19.40.
Chef/s: Kenneth Poon. **Open:** Mon to Fri and Sun L 12 to 2, all week D 6 to 10. **Closed:** 25 and 26 Dec. **Meals:** alc (main courses £12 to £21). Set L £11 (2 courses) to £14. Sun L £17. **Details:** 100 seats. 24 seats outside. Bar. Music. Parking.

Please send us your feedback

To register your opinion about any restaurant listed in this guide, or a new restaurant that you wish to bring to our attention, please visit the web address at the bottom of the page. Your feedback informs the content of the book and will be used to compile next year's reviews.

Sasso

Distinctive regional Italian cooking
Cooking score: 3
Italian | £32
8-10 Princes Square, Harrogate, HG1 1LX
Tel no: (01423) 508838
www.sassorestaurant.co.uk

This cheerful basement restaurant in the centre of Harrogate is smartly decked out in fresh white linen with original art on the walls and impeccable service. It has a tendency to over-elaborate with its combinations, but when simply done, Sasso is a cut above most Italians around. Start with crab cakes and a caramelised lemon and garlic sauce, followed by potato and rosemary gnocchi in a speck, courgette and cream sauce or one of their excellent handmade pasta dishes like tortellini with roasted red pepper and goats' cheese in a tomato and basil sauce. You might follow with fish of the day or ribeye steak given a herb and garlic crust, then a dessert of homemade ice cream. Lunch and pre-theatre dinners deliver remarkable value. Italian wines predominate the list starting with a Trebbiano and a Sangiovese at £13.95 rising into the hundreds for a top Piemonte Gaja.
Chef/s: Stefano Lancellotti. **Open:** Mon to Sat L 12 to 2 (2.30 Sat), D 5.45 to 10 (10.30 Fri and Sat). **Closed:** Sun, 25 and 26 Dec, 1 Jan. **Meals:** alc (main courses £11 to £23). Set L and early D £10 (2 courses) to £14. **Details:** 90 seats. 25 seats outside. Music.

Van Zeller

A chef firing on all cylinders
Cooking score: 6
Modern British | £50
8 Montpellier Street, Harrogate, HG1 2TQ
Tel no: (01423) 508762
www.vanzellerrestaurants.co.uk

'Superb flavoursome cooking, artistically presented' is one succinct appraisal; 'go for the experience of 21st-century culinary art,' urges another. The beauty and rhythm of each composition will certainly give you pause, but crucially, it's also wonderful to eat – so wonderful that you'll quickly forget this restaurant boasts 'about 20 tables crammed into a space for half that number'. The clinically cool interior design ('interrogation lights, geometric layouts') emphasises the art-school leanings of Tom Van Zeller's kitchen, turning out tasting menus of varying length and complexity, alongside an engaging three-courser. To start, pigeon is teamed with beets and ketchup while smoked eel sports chervil, cucumber, apple and goats' curd. Next up, maybe fillet and braised shin of beef with horseradish, violet potatoes and kale. To finish, there are northern delights including local rhubarb and ginger or blood orange with caramelised white chocolate and parkin. The wide-ranging wine list offers plenty of classics, starting at £21.

Chef/s: Tom Van Zeller. **Open:** Tue to Sat L 12 to 2, D 6 to 10. **Closed:** Sun, Mon, first week Jan. **Meals:** Set L £35 (3 courses). Set D £50. Tasting menu £60 (6 courses) to £85. **Details:** 30 seats. V menu. Music.

La Feria

Mediterranean | £18
1 Royal Parade, Harrogate, HG1 2SZ
Tel no: (01423) 538181
www.laferiarestaurants.co.uk

They've roughed up the interior of this 25-seater restaurant since its days as an elegant antique shop. Now the zinc tables, vintage café chairs and industrial lighting come with a whiff of sherry, an Andalusian vibe and a menu that offers a whole, half or quarter chicken marinated in lemon juice, rubbed with cumin and smoked paprika, and spit-roasted to be served with fries and aïoli. 'Posh chicken and chips' owner Jez Verity calls it, though there is more to it than that, with starters of authentic Ibérico ham, chorizo cooked in sherry and Moroccan orange and lemon cake to finish. Wines from £22. Closed L Mon and Tue.

Stuzzi

Italian | £25
46b Kings Road, Harrogate, HG1 5JW
Tel no: (01423) 705852

A café and deli by day, a restaurant and bar by night, Stuzzi is the story of how four lads from Salvo's (see entry, Leeds) gave in their notice and took off with tents and sleeping bags on a food odyssey around Italy, learning about provenance and signing up suppliers. Back in Harrogate they furnished this brash, noisy, buzzy joint with eBay finds, and now serve robust Italian dishes like trofie with tomato and pesto, seafood linguine and gelato with Amaretto sauce, with a fine line in wines, beers and soft drinks, all inspired by their travels. Open Tue to Sat.

Helmsley

The Vine House Café

British | £15
Helmsley Walled Garden, Cleveland Way, Helmsley, YO62 5AH
Tel no: (01439) 771427
www.helmsleywalledgarden.org.uk

Created in 1994 by a local woman who saw gardening as therapy, the charitable Helmsley Walled Garden is a tranquil retreat. To add to its charm, William Mowbray (ex-Moro, see entry, London) runs a café in one of the old greenhouses. Besides exceedingly good cakes, he serves the likes of gnocchi with pesto, pine nuts and ricotta, an all-nighter pork sandwich cooked in his 'big green egg' barbecue, and salads of smoky baba ganoush, beetroot with smoked onion powder, grilled courgette and artichoke salad. Bi-monthly themed dinners are served in the Orchid House. A deserved gem. Open all week April to Oct.

▌Hetton
The Angel Inn

Pioneering Yorkshire inn
Cooking score: 2
Modern British | £30
Hetton, BD23 6LT
Tel no: (01756) 730263
www.angelhetton.co.uk

Run by members of the Watkins family since
1983, this swish Dales inn pioneered the
notion of upmarket pub food and still puts its
faith in honest-to-goodness regional produce.
Readers tend to prefer the low-ceilinged bar/
brasserie, which has the added virtues of real
ales, open fires and a gentrified pubby vibe –
plus a menu that moves from Yorkshire tapas
(aka Yapas) and sandwiches of pastrami on rye
to devilled lamb's kidneys, game and ale stew
or pork fillet with homemade black pudding,
butternut squash purée, roast potatoes and
pig's head fritter. However, if you prefer
Champagne aperitifs, dressed-up service and
higher prices, head to the restaurant for the
likes of sea bass fillet with Jerusalem artichoke
cream, crispy kale and crayfish beignet
followed by lemon meringue pie with lime
sorbet. The connoisseur's wine list is a treasure
trove of fine drinking from France and
beyond, with some 20 selections by the glass
for those who want to explore. Bottles start
at £17.25.
Chef/s: Bruce Elsworth. **Open:** all week L 12 to 2.15
(2.30 Sun), D 6 to 9.30. **Closed:** 11 to 15 Jan.
Meals: alc (main courses £13 to £27). Set L and D
£15 (2 courses) to £19. Sun L £28. **Details:** 100
seats. 40 seats outside. Bar. Wheelchair access.
Parking.

▌Holmfirth
The Spiced Pear

Single-minded class on a Yorkshire hillside
Cooking score: 2
British | £40
Sheffield Road, Holmfirth, HD9 7TP
Tel no: (01484) 683775
www.thespicedpearhepworth.co.uk

The setting, on a hillside looking out 'on
unending green fields studded with sheep', is
beautiful, and the walk from the car park 'amid
bubbling waterfalls and climbing shrubbery'
makes a rustic contrast to the modern interior.
Offering the choice of a cocktail bar, vintage
tea room or smart, tartan-carpeted restaurant,
it's no wonder that chef/proprietor Tim
Bilton's Spiced Pear is considered unique to
the area. Reporters eat very well here, with
one singling out first courses for special
mention, especially the pear and onion tarte
Tatin. A dedication to seasonal flavours sets the
culinary tone, and the menu is loaded with
intriguing possibilities: scallops and a crisp
cheek of Gloucester Old Spot pig teamed with
apple purée, Waldorf salad, puffed skin and a
soy and pork reduction, perhaps, followed by a
marinated venison haunch steak teamed with
a crisp venison cigar, parsley root purée and
Pontefract liquorice sauce. Good-value
lunches and afternoon tea are well reported,
and wines start at £18.
Chef/s: Timothy Bilton. **Open:** Wed to Sun L 12 to 2
(4 Sun), Wed to Sat D 6 to 9.30. **Closed:** Mon, Tue.
Meals: alc (main courses £17 to £32). Set L £21 (2
courses) to £25. Sun L £29. **Details:** 97 seats. 21
seats outside. V menu. Bar. Music. Parking.

■ Honley
Mustard & Punch
Industrious local favourite
Cooking score: 3
British | £30
6 Westgate, Honley, HD9 6AA
Tel no: (01484) 662066
www.mustardandpunch.co.uk

It's almost 20 years since Richard Dunn and Wayne Roddis took charge of this charming, unpretentious bistro in Honley, a handsome stone village an olive stone's throw from the fleshpots of Huddersfield, and their staff still manage 'one of the warmest and most genuine welcomes I've encountered in a while'. They might call it bistro food, but we think it's more sophisticated than that. Dunn's thoughtful, considered approach to cooking results in starters like a 'faultless' cured ham, queen scallops, pea pannacotta and herb-crusted soft egg, with mains ranging from a perfectly presented pan-roast beef fillet, treacle-braised ox cheek and braised shallots to oven-roast spring lamb, lamb and potato pie, glazed goats' cheese, yellow pepper purée and lamb sauce – a deeply flavoured and unusual combo 'that worked really well'. Others praise the outstanding winter game dishes and the 'accessible and affordable' wine list, which opens at £18.
Chef/s: Richard Dunn. **Open:** Tue to Sat D only 5.30 to 9 (9.30 Fri and Sat). **Closed:** Sun, Mon. **Meals:** alc (main courses £16 to £22). Set D £23 (2 courses) to £25. **Details:** 55 seats. V menu. Music. Parking.

■ Hull

NEW ENTRY
1884 Dock Street Kitchen
Manhattan style with a Yorkshire heart
Cooking score: 2
British | £45
Humber Dock Street, Hull, HU1 1TB
Tel no: (01482) 222260
www.1884dockstreetkitchen.co.uk

Converted from a dockside warehouse into a light and spacious restaurant, 'it feels more like Manhattan than East Yorkshire' thought one visitor. 1884 Dock Street Kitchen has quickly become a destination venue (given the crowd there on our visit), serving 'really good food' in a lively and buzzing atmosphere. From the à la carte come starters of chestnut mushrooms on toast with scrambled egg – pronounced excellent – and risotto of North Sea lobster with spinach and Mrs Kirkham's Lancashire cheese, while from the grill, Hambleton beer-fed ribeye (served with béarnaise and beef-dripping chips) may not have been 'at Hawksmoor levels, but was one of the best steaks eaten outside London'. The cheese course offers a good selection, but service can let the side down. Bargain lunch and evening market menus are worth noting. An innovative wine list offers choices to suit all pockets, from £16 a bottle.
Chef/s: James Allcock. **Open:** Tue to Sun L 12 to 2 (3 Sun), Tue to Sat D 6 to 9.30. **Closed:** Mon.
Meals: alc (main courses £19 to £32). Set L £14 (2 courses) to £18. Set D £22 (Tue to Thur).
Details: 110 seats.

Join us at thegoodfoodguide.co.uk

■ Ilkley
The Box Tree

One of Yorkshire's finest
Cooking score: 6
Anglo-French | £65
35-37 Church Street, Ilkley, LS29 9DR
Tel no: (01943) 608484
www.theboxtree.co.uk

A homing beacon for food lovers since the 1960s, the Box Tree has a grand reputation to uphold, but chef/proprietor Simon Gueller made a shrewd move back in 2013 when he recruited Lawrence Yates from Cambridge's Midsummer House (see entry) as his right-hand man. The two have proved something of a dream team, revitalising cooking that already had a reputation for great skill and refinement. While the food has moved forward, the interior of this handsome Yorkshire house remains stately and resolutely traditional, from its gilt-framed oil paintings to its antique furniture. An amuse of caramelised onion foam with a Gruyère cheese straw kicks off a meal as serious as the surroundings. After that, maybe Cornish crab and haddock brandade with a crispy Arlington hen's egg, then Scottish loin of venison with braised red cabbage, roasted sprout leaves and Cumberland sauce, and the classic Box Tree lemon tart with yoghurt ice cream to finish. The wine list is a magnificent tome, its wide global reach throwing up countless interesting finds as well as weighty classics: you'll find the greatest vintages from the greatest terroirs here, but you'll also get something impressive for just £19.
Chef/s: Simon Gueller and Lawrence Yates. **Open:** Fri to Sun L 12 to 2, Tue to Sat D 7 to 9.30. **Closed:** Mon, 26 to 30 Dec, 1 to 8 Jan. **Meals:** Set L £30. Set D £60. Sun L £35. Gourmand menu £75 (6 courses). **Details:** 60 seats. V menu. Bar. Music. Children over 10 yrs only at D.

■ Leeds
Brasserie Forty 4

Simple brasserie fare on the Aire
Cooking score: 2
Modern European | £30
44 The Calls, Leeds, LS2 7EW
Tel no: (0113) 2343232
www.brasserie44.com

The Brasserie celebrates a little of Leeds' industrial heritage in its 200-year-old red-brick cornmill on the River Aire, a setting where outdoor tables make the most of the sunshine and indoors is a bustling hive of activity. Not many places offer the use of a free lunchtime chauffeur service for those who like to make an entrance. However you arrive, it's robust, simply constituted brasserie fare you'll be after, seen in the likes of well-wrought smoked haddock risotto with mascarpone and chives to start, followed by lamb rump with quinoa, roast peppers and black olives in sherry vinaigrette, or a fish special such as cod with spinach and tomato in saffron cream. Crumbles, brûlées and brownies make the right noises on the pudding list, as does a moistly tempting blueberry frangipane tart with lemon curd ice cream. Wines are varietally grouped, the bidding opening with Chilean Chardonnay and Merlot at £17.50.
Chef/s: David Robson. **Open:** Tue to Sat L 12 to 2 (1 to 3 Sat), D 6 to 9.30 (5 to 10 Sat). **Closed:** Sun, Mon, 25 and 26 Dec, bank hols (exc Good Friday). **Meals:** alc (main courses £13 to £24). Set L and D £20. **Details:** 120 seats. 18 seats outside. Bar. Wheelchair access. Children over 2 yrs only.

Crafthouse

Slick, stylish cosmopolitan eatery
Cooking score: 3
Modern British | £37
Level 5, Trinity Leeds, 70 Boar Lane, Leeds, LS1 6HW
Tel no: (0113) 8970444
www.crafthouse-restaurant.com

In a lofty spot above Leeds' still-shiny Trinity shopping centre, Crafthouse sees restaurant group D&D London looking north. It might sound rustic, but homespun and horny-handed Crafthouse is not: the interior consists of a sleek bar, sleek dining room and sleek terrace (though if you want something more casual, little sister Angelica can be found on the floor above). Service can lack flexibility, but reporters rate the set lunch for value and a 'wonderfully fresh' mackerel tartare with cucumber salad and coriander and ginger flatbread. Main courses might be a pair of baby Dover soles with steamed Pink Fir potatoes and seasonal greens or devilled veal kidneys with tagliatelle, and a Josper grill produces pleasingly charred prime cuts including Denby Dale lamb chops. Puddings include guava mousse with green tea and hibiscus. An extensive wine list (more serious than the food, perhaps) starts at £18.

Chef/s: Lee Bennett. **Open:** Tue to Sat L 12 to 2.45, Mon to Sat D 5 to 11. Sun 12 to 10. **Meals:** alc (mains £15 to £26). Set L £19 (2 courses) to £23. Tasting menu £65. **Details:** 120 seats. 20 seats outside.

NEW ENTRY

The Man Behind the Curtain

Culinary wizardry in West Yorkshire
Cooking score: 6
Modern British
68-78 Vicar Lane, Leeds, LS1 7JH
Tel no: (0113) 2432376
www.themanbehindthecurtain.co.uk

We're off to see the wizard (a.k.a. the man behind the curtain of *Wizard of Oz* fame) once you locate him on the top floor above Flannels clothes shop – 'which means a doorman has to greet you and take you upstairs as the shop closes at 5pm'. Worth the journey according to many – 'Leeds has not seen a restaurant like this for some time.' Exemplary cooking skills, innovative ideas, impeccable ingredients and an element of excitement, the man behind the curtain (Michael O'Hare, last seen cooking at the late Blind Swine in York) has all of these elements. O'Hare aims to provide a creative exploration of flavours, textures, ingredients and techniques via a 12-course (no choice

except lunch) tasting menu in a large minimalist space that's bright in daylight and dimly lit in the evening. Highlights include 'really exceptional' langoustine tails, served almost raw, covered with a wafer-thin film made from lardo, and a sprinkle of powdered lavender; crispy-skinned John Dory on a small mound of orzo risotto with a delicate smoky chorizo flavour; a perfectly pink slice of duck with roasted pineapple; veal sweetbreads 'lovely – soft and yielding with a crisp coating'; a spoonful of Stinking Bishop and pickled tomato paving the way for a fennel lollipop that in turn clears the palate for sweet mouthfuls of gariguette strawberries with Parmesan ice cream, balsamic vinegar, basil and raspberry crumb. Wines from £22.00.

Chef/s: Michael O'Hare. **Open:** Fri and Sat L 12.30 to 3, Wed to Sat D 6.30 to 9.30. **Closed:** Sun, Mon, Tue. **Meals:** Tasting menu £65

The Reliance

Modern British deliciousness
Cooking score: 3
Modern British | £23
76-78 North Street, Leeds, LS2 7PN
Tel no: (0113) 2956060
www.the-reliance.co.uk

The Reliance is a Yorkshire cloth mill, reconceived for a bar and restaurant crowd drawn to indie food festivals and quality junk food, to name just two of the alliances it has forged on the Leeds gastronomic scene. An in-house cinema for bespoke screenings of your own guilty-movie pleasures while you eat is a neat idea. Tom Hunter stepped up from sous-chef in early 2015 to head up a kitchen that puts out sharing boards of home-cured charcuterie, as well as big and little plates of modern British deliciousness. A bowl of mussels and chorizo simmered in tomato and fino sherry might lead to fashionable mutton shoulder with root veg dauphinois and caper sauce, or perhaps skrei cod with tomatoes, olives and saffron mash. Yorkshire rhubarb naturally receives its place in the sun (or the spring frosts, as may be), turning up with Muscovado meringues and cream. House Italian is £14.95, or £3.90 a glass.

Chef/s: Tom Hunter. **Open:** Mon to Sat L 12 to 5, D 5.30 to 10 (10.30 Thur to Sat). Sun 12 to 8.30. **Closed:** 25 and 26 Dec, bank hols. **Meals:** alc (main courses £10 to £15). Pre-theatre D £15 (2 courses) to £19. **Details:** 128 seats. 6 seats outside. Bar. Music.

Salvo's

Fantastic pizzas and budget prices
Cooking score: 2
Italian | £28
115 Otley Road, Headingley, Leeds, LS6 3PX
Tel no: (0113) 2755017
www.salvos.co.uk

'Good old Salvo's – probably the best bet on a Sunday evening in Leeds,' noted one reporter. 'Within walking distance of cricket and rugby ground so very convenient for post-match meal,' noted another, happy to have found the Dammone family's one-of-a-kind Italian eatery in the suburban student habitat of Headingley. It's a Leeds stalwart, celebrating 40 years in 2016, but with its clean contemporary lines doesn't show its age and is still a crowd-puller – which testifies to the consistency and quality of the food, service and plentiful choice. Pizza and pasta are the lead items, the latter – such as tagliatelle al ragù and lasagne – sticking closer to tradition than the pizzas, which might include 'pizza Kiev' (a folded pizza stuffed with chicken, ham, garlic butter and cheese). Otherwise, there might be specials of, say, swordfish with agrodolce vegetables, sultanas, pine nuts and new potatoes and 'a delightfully tart chocolate ganache with proper vanilla ice cream' to finish. Wines from £16.95.

Chef/s: Gip Dammone. **Open:** Mon to Sat L 12 to 2, D 6 to 10.30 (5.30 to 11 Fri and Sat). Sun 12 to 9. **Closed:** 25 and 26 Dec, 1 Jan. **Meals:** alc (main courses £9 to £23). Set L £12. Set D £15 (2 courses) to £18. Sun L £15. **Details:** 88 seats. 20 seats outside. Bar. Wheelchair access. Music.

Friends of Ham

Modern European | £20
4-8 New Station Street, Leeds, LS1 5DL
Tel no: (0113) 2420275
www.friendsofham.com

Barely any of the food at this bustling bar-cum-charcuteria (just metres from the train station) is actually cooked. The star attraction is its selection of specialist cured meats, which takes in everything from Italian fennel seed salami to Spanish cured beef and Cornish chorizo – all of it expertly stored and sliced by young and enthusiastic staff. There's an impressive list of British and European cheeses, too, some of which are deftly paired with cured meat. Not a friend of ham? You'll find a small selection of classic tapas dishes, including marinated anchovies and a duck and walnut ballotine. The snappy wine list starts at £17 and there's a huge and daily changing craft beer selection. Open all week.

Hansa's

Indian Vegetarian | £20
72-74 North Street, Leeds, LS2 7PN
Tel no: (0113) 2444408
www.hansasrestaurant.com

According to one Leeds regular, this long-standing restaurant just off the city centre is a good budget option in the area. Hansa Dashi specialises in Gujarati vegetarian cooking, and flavours span a broad range, from chilli paneer and masala dhosa (lightly spiced vegetables wrapped in a rice pancake) to ondhiya (a traditional mixed vegetable curry cooked with fenugreek koftas) and bhagat muthiya (a spiced curry of chickpea koftas and potatoes). Comforting dhals also feature. Finish with fruit shrikhand. Wines from £15.95. Open Sun L and Mon to Sat D.

Zucco

Italian | £28
603 Meanwood Road, Leeds, LS6 4AY
Tel no: (0113) 2249679
www.zucco.co.uk

If the menu of Italian dishes for sharing and the décor – bare filament lightbulbs, white subway tiles, high stools – ring bells of Soho's Polpo, that could be because the owner Michael Leggiero was their general manager and took it as his inspiration for this main-road bacaro in Meanwood. His brother Rosario (ex Salvo's) cooks nifty dishes of octopus with pickled vegetables, rabbit stew, spaghetti with razor clams and deep fried courgettes, eschewing pizza/pasta standards. Pleasing food and a thoughtful wine list. Closed Mon.

■ Leyburn
The Sandpiper Inn

Highly polished Dales inn
Cooking score: 3
Modern British | £33
Market Place, Leyburn, DL8 5AT
Tel no: (01969) 622206
www.sandpiperinn.co.uk

Jonathan and Janine Harrison have done Leyburn proud during their 17 years' residence at this handsome, centuries-old stone inn. They have cleverly balanced all the virtues of a well-heeled pub, thanks to genuine hospitality, real ales and good food. Many locals and visiting diners are here simply for the comforting familiarity of crowd-pleasing classics like fish and chips, sausage and mash, steak burgers and Yorkshire rarebit, but it is worth exploring the 'menu of the day' for dishes such as pressed Dales lamb with dauphinois potatoes, Swinton Park venison with chorizo, fried potatoes and chestnut mushrooms or roasted sea trout on a spaghetti of courgette and smoked salmon. The chocolate desserts will win friends, but there might be sticky toffee pudding with butterscotch sauce and English apple ice

cream. The wine list of some 30-plus bins is well considered and good value, starting with Italian red or white for £15.95.
Chef/s: Jonathan Harrison. **Open:** Tue to Sun L 12 to 2.30, D 6.30 to 9 (6 to 9.30 Sat, 6 to 8 Sun). **Closed:** Mon, Tue (winter), 2 weeks Jan. **Meals:** alc (main courses £15 to £22). **Details:** 60 seats. 20 seats outside. Bar. Music. Parking.

■ Lindley
Eric's

Exotic flavours and a warm welcome
Cooking score: 3
Modern British | £38
73-75 Lidget Street, Lindley, HD3 3JP
Tel no: (01484) 646416
www.ericsrestaurant.co.uk

Sandwiched among a row of terraced shops in an affluent suburb of Huddersfield, Eric's doesn't sound the most glamorous of places – but one glance at the dining room and the menu tells a very different story. Local artwork, oak floors and stone walls set the scene, while the food is ablaze with colour, warmth and exotic flavours. Energetic chef/proprietor Eric Paxman honed his craft with Aussie star Bill Granger down under – and it shows: charred tandoori salmon appears with cardamom-pickled carrots, dill raita and coriander, while pan-fried Scarborough woof is dressed with salt-baked beetroot, samphire and capers. Away from the sea, there's also plenty to pique the palate, from braised ox cheek with wild mushroom and celeriac risotto to poached pear and almond cake with chocolate gnocchi and Sauternes sabayon. Eric also pulls in the crowds with his full vegetarian menu, lunchtime sandwiches and monthly G&T afternoon teas. There's a creditable wine list, too, with prices from £17.25.
Chef/s: Eric Paxman and James Thompson. **Open:** Tue to Fri and Sun L 12 to 2 (4 Sun), Tue to Sat D 6 to 10 (5.30 Fri and Sat). **Closed:** Mon. **Meals:** alc (main courses £17 to £28). Set L £16 (2 courses) to £19. Set D £20 (2 courses) to £25. Sun L £20 (2 courses) to £25. **Details:** 70 seats. V menu. Bar. Music.

■ Lower Dunsforth

READERS RECOMMEND

The Dunsforth

British

Lower Dunsforth, YO26 9SA
Tel no: (01423) 320700
www.thedunsforth.co.uk

'Modern, imaginative and exciting. I had wood pigeon, pearl barley, roast beetroot and asparagus for a starter, [then] fillet of beef with burnt onion textures. This place is such a breath of fresh air.'

■ Masham

Samuel's at Swinton Park

Stately cooking in a stately setting

Cooking score: 4
Modern British | £55
Swinton Park, Masham, HG4 4JH
Tel no: (01765) 680900
www.swintonpark.com

They run Downton at Swinton weekends here complete with black tie dinners and Scottish country dancing. You can see why when you sweep up to this castellated country pile with its endless carpeted corridors, opulent public rooms and the gilded Samuel's restaurant with views over 20,000 acres of parkland. Chef Simon Crannage celebrates the best of local produce and Swinton's walled garden in his menus of three and seven courses at dinner and weekend lunches. At inspection, Sunday lunch provided two praiseworthy roasts: generous cuts of pork and beef, both with featherweight Yorkshire pudding and gravy, accompanied by a flavoursome cauliflower cheese. Starters of mackerel fillet with cucumber, grapefruit and radish garnish and confit of smoked trout in an asparagus velouté were pleasing, too, though the caramelised goats' cheese on couscous failed to impress, as did a rather overdone poached fillet of halibut. Back on form, desserts brought a classic sticky toffee pudding and a delightful gariguette

strawberry mousse and strawberry sorbet wrapped in chocolate. A substantial wine list starts at £27.

Chef/s: Simon Crannage. **Open:** Sat and Sun L 12.30 to 2, all week D 7 to 9.30. **Meals:** Set L £22 (2 courses) to £30 (Sat only). Sun L £28. Set D £58. Tasting menu £70. **Details:** 60 seats. Bar. Wheelchair access. Music. Parking. Children over 8 yrs only at D.

Vennell's

Confident cooking in delightful Masham

Cooking score: 5
Modern British | £28
7 Silver Street, Masham, HG4 4DX
Tel no: (01765) 689000
www.vennellsrestaurant.co.uk

It's ten years since Jon and Laura Vennell opened in Silver Street just off Masham's majestic market square. The redesign in 2012 is holding up well with its smart aubergine theme upstairs and downstairs, and they celebrated in style with a week that presented a six-course tasting menu featuring the Vennell's long-time favourite of venison carpaccio with soused julienned vegetables, shaved Parmesan and truffle oil. This was followed by an excellent trio of beef, rare beef Wellington, brisket and sirloin, and a pitch-perfect vanilla pannacotta with a touch of orange and Grand Marnier. At other times of year a special menu might feature game or lobster, otherwise the à la carte offers a worthy choice with the likes of roast monkfish cheek followed by Dales lamb, grilled Dover sole or squab pigeon with pork confit, mustard mash and sherry sauce. If a tad familiar, Jon Vennell's technique is exact and dependable. A trusty wine list begins at £19.50.

Chef/s: Jon Vennell. **Open:** Sun L 12 to 4, Tue to Sat D 7.30 to 11. **Closed:** Mon, first 2 weeks Jan, 1 week Easter, last week Aug. **Meals:** Set L £21 (2 courses) to £26. Set D £25 (2 courses) to £28. Sun L £21. **Details:** 30 seats. Bar. Music.

Maunby
The Buck Inn

Extraordinary cooking in an ordinary pub
Cooking score: 2
British | £30
Maunby, YO7 4HD
Tel no: (01845) 587777
www.thebuckinnmaunby.co.uk

This rambling village pub between Thirsk and Northallerton continues to build on its reputation for good food under chef/owner Matthew Roath and his efficient front-of-house partner Sammy Clark. Sandwiches, fish cakes and burgers are served in the beamed bar. In the dining room, a test meal opened with potted shrimps with Roath's toasted rye bread and seared wood pigeon and black pudding pimped up with a couple of pickled grapes. An inspired main course featured hake and oxtail, the delicate fish a foil for the tender, glutinous, slow-cooked oxtail served with the smoothest celeriac purée and a miniature pan of greens and mint butter. An immaculate treacle tart and a crème brûlée with Yorkshire rhubarb passed the pudding test and cheeses majored on a selection from Shepherd's Purse, the excellent local cheesemaker three miles down the road. A serviceable wine list opening at £15.95 covers the usual bases.
Chef/s: Matthew Roath. **Open:** Tue to Sun L 12 to 2 (4 Sun), Tue to Sat D 5 to 9.30 (6 Sat). **Closed:** Mon, 26 Dec, 1 Jan, 1 week Jan. **Meals:** alc (main courses £13 to £49). Set L and early D £15 (2 courses) to £18. Sun L £15 (2 courses) to £18. **Details:** 40 seats. 6 seats outside. Bar. Music. Parking.

Middleton Tyas

NEW ENTRY
The Coach House at Middleton Lodge

Cooking score: 3
Modern British | £32
Kneeton Lane, Middleton Tyas, DL10 6NJ
Tel no: (01325) 377977
www.middletonlodge.co.uk

Reporters have written enthusiastically about the £2m conversion of the coach house and stables of John Carr's 18th-century Middleton Lodge: 'Understated but absolutely beautiful' was how one described the 2,000 square foot dining room furnished in simple country-kitchen style with tweed banquettes, rough wooden tables, tongue-and-groove panelling and distressed plasterwork. The food by chef Gareth Rayner has been met with similar approval, with praise ranging from 'out of this world' to 'food outstanding', while one fervent diner reckoned the slow-roast belly pork was a 'Game. Changer. Baby.' Hyperbole apart, we were impressed by blowtorched mackerel with rhubarb garnish, and asparagus with black pudding and soft egg yolk. Sea bream with Israeli couscous and crab beignet delivered again, while the saddle and slow-cooked shoulder of lamb accompanied by crisp-coated smoked Ribblesdale cheese and smoked garlic gnocchi was excellent. A solid wine list begins at £17.
Chef/s: Gareth Rayner. **Open:** Wed to Sun L 12 to 2 (4 Sun), D 6 to 9 (7 to 9 Sun). **Closed:** Mon, Tue. **Meals:** alc (mean courses £12 to £24). **Details:** 80 seats. V menu. Bar. Wheelchair access. Music. Parking.

Newton-on-Ouse
The Dawnay Arms
Brit cooking with verve and gusto
Cooking score: 3
Modern British | £35
Moor Lane, Newton-on-Ouse, YO30 2BR
Tel no: (01347) 848345
www.thedawnayatnewton.co.uk

The garden out back of this three-storey Georgian coaching inn meets the mostly benign River Ouse to create an idyllic spot to nurse a pint of beer or a glass of English sparkling rosé. The requisite beams, flagstones and open fires confirm the antiquity of the place (built in 1779), but the finish within adds a touch of contemporary style in the bar and dining room (natural wooden tables, colours from the fashionable neutral palette and posh chairs). Chef/patron Martel Smith's menus show an inclination towards classic combinations and his spiffy new eco-kitchen proves a commitment to doing things the right way. Black pudding is made on the premises and is served with crispy pig's head and apple chutney, to be followed by a chunk of smoked Whitby cod with sauté potatoes and sauce mousseline, or pork three ways. Dry-aged steaks are cooked a la plancha, and, to finish, warm chocolate fondant comes with pistachio ice cream. Wines start at £15.
Chef/s: Martel Smith. **Open:** Tue to Sun L 12 to 2.30 (6 Sun), Tue to Sat D 6 to 9.30. **Closed:** Mon, 1 Jan. **Meals:** alc (main courses £15 to £19). Set L £13 (2 courses) to £18. Set D £14 (2 courses) to £19. Sun L £15 (2 courses) to £19. **Details:** 60 seats. 40 seats outside. V menu. Bar. Wheelchair access. Music. Parking.

Oldstead
The Black Swan
Home-grown produce takes centre stage
Cooking score: 6
Modern British | £55
Oldstead, YO61 4BL
Tel no: (01347) 868387
www.blackswanoldstead.co.uk

There are plenty of restaurants digging up a plot and growing their own fruit and veg, but for chef Tommy Banks, at the family-run Black Swan, the creation of an allotment on a two and a half acre sloping hillside has significantly raised his cooking in flavour and signature. Flowers, fruit and vegetables are celebrated at every stage. A nasturtium flower stuffed with a morsel of mushroom is one of a series of original pre-dinner 'snacks'. A dish of young vegetables brings miniature cooked and raw carrot, turnip, hazelnut and sheep's milk yoghurt, typifying the primacy of freshly picked produce. Delicately poached trout and fried squid smoothly incorporate both radish and radish broth. Chicken is given a rich leek and wild mushroom sauce. Segue into dessert with three 'lollipops' of graduated sweetness from mushroom through fennel to sweet apple. Finally, honey sorbet is sharpened with a dash of vinegar and served with honeycomb, viola flowers and viola jam. It's a dazzling performance. The à la carte has been ditched in place of three-, five- or nine-course tasting menus plus complete vegetarian and pescatarian menus. The wine list, from Serbia to Santorini, is intriguingly original (with bottles from £24).
Chef/s: Tommy Banks. **Open:** Sat and Sun L 12 to 2, all week D 6 to 9. **Closed:** 1 week Jan. **Meals:** Set weekend L £32. Tasting menus £55 (5 courses) to £80. **Details:** 40 seats. 10 seats outside. V menu. Bar. Wheelchair access. Music. Parking.

Osmotherley
Golden Lion
Warm-hearted watering hole
Cooking score: 2
Anglo-European | £29
6 West End, Osmotherley, DL6 3AA
Tel no: (01609) 883526
www.goldenlionosmotherley.co.uk

Very little – if anything – has changed in decades at this wonderfully welcoming village pub. It will have had a lick of paint, for sure, but the stone flagged floors, wood stoves and burnished dark-wood bar remain the same. The menu hasn't altered much either, but who cares when there's barbecue ribs and homemade chicken Kiev on offer? Slow-roast daube of beef, sea bass milanese risotto and calf's liver and onions hint at the style here – this is comfort food at its best. But the kitchen can be subtle, too: grilled aubergine with ratatouille is presented with delicacy, and the flavours sing. Salmon fishcake, chive beurre blanc and spinach is 'packed with flavour' and 'lusciously tender' steak and kidney with suet crust makes the perfect rib-sticker on a chilly day. Desserts are old-school, so pace yourself if you fancy steamed treacle sponge with custard. Wines from £16.95.
Chef/s: Christopher Wright. **Open:** Wed to Sun L 12 to 2.30 (3 Sun), all week D 6 to 9. **Closed:** 25 Dec. **Meals:** alc (main courses £11 to £22). **Details:** 63 seats. 16 seats outside. Wheelchair access. Music.

Pickering
The White Swan Inn
Big-hearted Yorkshire hospitality
Cooking score: 3
British | £36
Market Place, Pickering, YO18 7AA
Tel no: (01751) 472288
www.white-swan.co.uk

A long time has passed since stagecoaches stopped here while working the route between York and Whitby, and you're much more likely to see a Jag out back these days than a horse, but the 16th-century White Swan still possesses much of its old character. With real fires, beams and cosy corners as touchstones to its past, the finish is actually rather contemporary. The kitchen team's output also neatly slips between past and present – they make just about everything themselves (bread, chutneys and so on) – with the likes of smoked Whitby fishcakes and fish and chips showing their willingness to play the comfort card. But there's much more besides: grilled Lowna goats' cheese, for example, with beetroot relish and pecan and Cheddar biscuit, or a main course that matches roast rump of Levisham lamb with caper sauce. A charcoal grill works its magic on meats supplied by Ginger Pig. Finish with rich chocolate tart. Wines start at £18.
Chef/s: Darren Clemmit. **Open:** all week L 12 to 2, D 6.45 to 9. **Meals:** alc (main courses £14 to £26). **Details:** 65 seats. 25 seats outside. Bar. Parking. No children after 8 in restaurant.

Ramsgill
★ TOP 50 ★
The Yorke Arms
In harmony with the seasons
Cooking score: 6
Modern British | £65
Ramsgill, HG3 5RL
Tel no: (01423) 755243
www.yorke-arms.co.uk

It began life as a Georgian shooting lodge but now, bashfully hidden in climbing ivy, the Yorke makes an alluring country inn on the grandish scale. That said, there's nothing bombastic about the main dining room, where unclothed tables and simple settings make a relaxing backdrop to cooking that celebrates the seasons, and has a confident feel for modern combinations. Seared tuna and shrimp come with puffed anchovy grains, beetroot, blood orange and hummus in a compendious starter, with perhaps loin and kidney of newly fashionable hare and black pudding to follow, along with cavolo nero and caramelised onion. There is a lively thread of imagination running through dishes that might add lychee and sprout skins to smoked duck, or match bacon gnocchi, caramelised swede and girolles to turbot in miso with a scallop, while dessert might juxtapose Szechuan-peppered coconut bavarois with passion fruit jelly, ginger meringue and macadamia crumble. A modest amount of quality ground is covered in each of the wine list's regions, with prices from £25.

Chef/s: Frances Atkins. **Open:** all week L 12 to 2, D 7 to 9 (Sun D residents only). **Meals:** alc (main courses £35 to £39). Set L £40. Sun L £50. Tasting menu £85. **Details:** 40 seats. 20 seats outside.

■ Ripon
Lockwoods

Café-restaurant that aims to please
Cooking score: 1
Modern British | £29
83 North Street, Ripon, HG4 1DP
Tel no: (01765) 607555
www.lockwoodsrestaurant.co.uk

£30

'Their food is the equal of anything we had in five months travelling through France,' notes one fan of Matthew Lockwood's thriving café-bar and restaurant. A short wander from Ripon's market square, it's a period building with a modern finish (zinc-topped bar, bold paintwork, semi-open kitchen). There's no standing on ceremony here – and that extends to the cooking, which is hearty, fun and wholesome: by day there are big brunches, sandwiches and colourful choices such as Asian noodle salad. The menu morphs into full restaurant mode in the evening, offering familiar fare – maybe tempura squid and king prawns with sweet chilli sauce – alongside attractive inventions such as roast beetroot risotto with Swaledale blue cheese, baby spinach and Brazil nut crumble. To finish, try sticky marmalade sponge with vanilla custard and candied orange. The wine list is full of favourites, and includes plenty by the glass. Bottles start at £15.95.

Chef/s: Louie Miller. **Open:** Tue to Sun L 12 to 2.30 (4 Sun), D 5 to 9.30 (10 Fri and Sat). **Closed:** Mon. **Meals:** alc (main courses £11 to £24). Set early D £14 (2 courses) to £17. **Details:** 60 seats. V menu. Bar. Wheelchair access. Music.

■ Sancton

The Star at Sancton

A champion of Yorkshire produce
Cooking score: 4
Modern British | £32
King Street, Sancton, YO43 4QP
Tel no: (01430) 827269
www.thestaratsancton.co.uk

Not only a boon for cyclists and hikers trudging through the Yorkshire Wolds, this smartly upholstered roadside hostelry also stakes its claim as a destination for serious foodies. The hardier among us can repair to the bar for a pint from the Great Newsome Brewery plus a reviving plate of bangers and root vegetable mash, otherwise attention focuses on the menus served in the dining room. Yorkshire ingredients are name-checked in loving detail, and the kitchen also garners produce from village allotments – as well as the pub's own garden and orchard. The result is a gutsy and immensely appealing repertoire that might run from pan-roast pigeon with heritage beetroot, Lisman's black pudding fritters, celeriac coleslaw and quince jam to turbot with Stockbridge vine tomatoes, gnocchi, baby leeks, Greedy Little Pig pancetta and lemon thyme dressing. To finish, rhubarb clafoutis with custard ice cream is a must. 'Yorkshire lunches' are terrific value and the well-spread global wine list also keeps its prices in check, with bottles from £15.95.

Chef/s: Ben Cox. **Open:** Tue to Sun L 12 to 2 (3 Sun), D 6 to 9.30 (8 Sun). **Closed:** Mon, bank hols. **Meals:** alc (main courses £15 to £25). Set L £17 (2 courses) to £19. **Details:** 80 seats. 30 seats outside. V menu. Bar. Wheelchair access. Music. Parking.

 Sawdon
The Anvil Inn

Satisfying food in a former smithy
Cooking score: 2
Modern European | £29
Main Street, Sawdon, YO13 9DY
Tel no: (01723) 859896
www.theanvilinnsawdon.co.uk

In the pretty village of Sawdon, on the edge of the North York Moors National Park, the 200-year-old stone building that makes up the Anvil Inn was once the village forge, but now its business is that of a stylish dining pub-with-rooms. The look is rustic with the original furnace a feature of the bar, along with roughcast stone walls, beamed ceilings and polished wooden tables. The atmosphere is relaxed, but one is left in no doubt that this is a serious operation. A simple lunch menu brings roast Yorkshire beef open sandwich or honey-roast air-cured ham, free-range eggs and chips, while in the evening diners might be treated to smoked salmon and crab with pickled cucumber and capers and Bloody Mary coulis, followed perhaps by Moroccan spiced lamb tagine with steamed Kashmir Gold saffron rice, then black cherry Bakewell with pistachio ice cream. Breads are homemade, and the wine list opens at £17.50.
Chef/s: Mark Wilson. **Open:** Sat and Sun L 12 to 2 (2.30 Sun), Wed to Sun D 6.30 to 9 (6 to 8 Sun). **Closed:** Mon, Tue. **Meals:** alc (main courses £13 to £26). **Details:** 36 seats. 12 seats outside. Bar. Music. Parking.

Please send us your feedback

To register your opinion about any restaurant listed in this guide, or a new restaurant that you wish to bring to our attention, please visit the web address at the bottom of the page. Your feedback informs the content of the book and will be used to compile next year's reviews.

Scarborough
Lanterna

A proper Piedmontese ristorante
Cooking score: 3
Italian | £37
33 Queen Street, Scarborough, YO11 1HQ
Tel no: (01723) 363616
www.lanterna-ristorante.co.uk

Giorgio and Rachel Alessio's ristorante, not far from the Stephen Joseph Theatre, is a cherished fixture of Scarborough's dining scene. The owners hail from Piedmont and native traditions prevail on the menu: white truffles from Moncalvo make their treasured seasonal appearance and fish is also a forte: Giorgio gets up at the crack of dawn most days to procure the best from the town's market (try the red mullet stew, grilled shark or a risotto with locally landed sea trout). Pasta is always a good shout (venison, Parmesan and spinach ravioli, for example), and it's worth checking out intriguing daily specials such as osso buco with porcini, orange juice and tomato sauce or marinated ox cheeks dressed with a scattering of turnip crisps. To finish, don't miss the creamy 'torta' layered with Gorgonzola, mascarpone and walnuts. The wine list is a fine repository of directly imported bottles from Italian regional vineyards, with prices from £15.95.
Chef/s: Giorgio Alessio. **Open:** Mon to Sat D only 7 to 9.30. **Closed:** Sun, 25 and 26 Dec, 1 Jan, last 2 weeks Oct. **Meals:** alc (main courses £16 to £49). **Details:** 35 seats. Music.

Eat Me Café

Modern British | £10
2 Hanover Road, Scarborough, YO11 1LS
Tel no: (07445) 475328
www.eatmecafe.com

Regulars vouch for the 'delicious food at amazingly low prices' at this bright, unpretentious café located behind Scarborough's acclaimed Stephen Joseph Theatre. Drop in for breakfast, pick from the user-friendly daytime menu (served 10.30–7)

Join us at thegoodfoodguide.co.uk

or nip in for coffee and cake. Lunch brings some eclectic flavours to the table – generally a hearty soup or a ramen noodle bowl, salads and sandwiches alongside a well-reported Thai green chicken curry, chilli, mac 'n' cheese, and various burgers. Unlicensed. Closed Sun. Note: cash only.

Scawton
The Hare Inn

Adventurous food in country setting
Cooking score: 4
Modern British | £40
Scawton, YO7 2HG
Tel no: (01845) 597769
www.thehare-inn.com

It's a high-wire act offering a no-choice, highly sophisticated, uncompromising four-, six- or eight-course menu in what is essentially a country pub where passing visitors might usually expect a pie and a pint. But Paul Jackson's three menus prove to be not only cracking value but also 'top class' and 'consistently superb'. The four-courser begins with local Dexter beef served raw and chopped, combined with watercress, macadamia nuts, smoked oil and grated bone marrow – 'it was outstanding'. Next a sea trout fillet, cured and slow-cooked, served with asparagus and a touch of hollandaise. Venison is smoothly paired with beetroot, blueberry, goats' cheese and walnut and a hint of liquorice. Strawberry, buttermilk mousse, green tea and lemongrass feature in a light, fresh plate at dessert and excellent petits fours finish off an exciting and notably generous lunch. There are wine pairings with each menu or £20 from the list.
Chef/s: Paul Jackson. **Open:** Wed to Sun L 12 to 2.30 (4 Sun), Wed to Sat D 6 to 9. **Closed:** Mon, Tue. **Meals:** Tasting menus £30 (4 courses) to £60. **Details:** 36 seats. 10 seats outside. V menu.

Sheffield
Rafters

New-found confidence and ambition
Cooking score: 3
Modern British | £39
220 Oakbrook Road, Nether Green, Sheffield, S11 7ED
Tel no: (0114) 2304819
www.raftersrestaurant.co.uk

An unexpected gem above a suburban shopping parade, Rafters has been on the foodie radar for years but shifted up a gear in 2013 when Alastair Myers and Thomas Lawson took over. As the name suggests, the interior makes a show of the original rafters, but you'll spend more time looking at your plate thanks to Thomas's ambitious and creative modern British cooking. Never one to cut corners, he churns his own butter, bakes his own bread and makes his own chocolates. In between might be seared scallops with Jerusalem artichoke and Ibérico ham; roasted squab pigeon with confit legs, rösti potato and salt-baked beetroot; and nutmeg brûlée with forced Yorkshire rhubarb and gingerbread. On-going front-of-house improvements mean the ambience gets 'better and better', while service, led by Alastair, is 'friendly and attentive without being too much'. Wine pairings are suggested on the great value tasting menu, and a decent global list, with plenty under £30, begins at £16.50.
Chef/s: Thomas Lawson. **Open:** Sun L 12 to 2, Wed to Sun D 7 to 8.30 (9 Fri and Sat, 8 Sun). **Closed:** Mon, Tue, 1 week Jan, 1 week Aug. **Meals:** Set L £35. Set D £42. Sun L £28 (2 courses) to £34. Tasting menu £58. **Details:** 36 seats. V menu. Music. Children over 12 yrs only.

Lokanta

Turkish | £26
478-480 Glossop Road, Sheffield, S10 2QA
Tel no: (0114) 2666444
www.lokanta.co.uk

'Amazing food, super atmosphere,' notes one report of this smart, modern Turkish restaurant, which everyone seems to agree stands head and shoulders above the rest. The 'delightful owners' used to run a beachfront restaurant in Turkey and still employ Turkish-trained chefs, who make everything from scratch. The pan-fried lamb's liver served with fresh onion and sumac seafood comes highly recommended, as do meze dishes such as courgette fritters, grilled haloumi and homemade bread. Baked tahini pudding is a good way to finish. Turkish wines start at £16.

Shibden

Shibden Mill Inn

Captivating inn with solid cooking
Cooking score: 3
Modern British | £30
Shibden Mill Fold, Shibden, HX3 7UL
Tel no: (01422) 365840
www.shibdenmillinn.com

You can see why this country inn is popular. A sympathetically restored 16th-century mill hidden within the folds of the Shibden Valley, it's the kind of hostelry we'd all crave as our local, with open fires and beams galore; its easy-going approach is just the ticket, too, allowing options of just drinking, or snacking, or eating a big, hearty meal. The traditional-looking ground-floor dining area (polished wooden tables, evening candles), contrasts with the intimate, formal look of the Grill Room upstairs, which has its own char-grill menu. Otherwise, the extensive menu is a wide-ranging affair, offering hand-picked East Coast crab with beetroot or partridge and chestnut pie, then fish pie stuffed with halibut, smoked cheese, clams and prawns or rump and cutlet of lamb with Jerusalem artichokes and pearl barley risotto. It's all backed up by good-value set menus, an impressive Yorkshire cheeseboard, and a sound global wine list (from £17.35).
Chef/s: Darren Parkinson. **Open:** Mon to Sat L 12 to 2 (2.30 Fri and Sat), D 5.30 to 9 (9.30 Fri, 6 to 9.30 Sat). Sun 12 to 7.30. **Closed:** 25 and 26 Dec. **Meals:** alc (main courses £12 to £19). Set L and D £14 (2 courses) to £17. Sun L £14. **Details:** 130 seats. 70 seats outside. V menu. Bar. Music. Parking.

South Dalton

The Pipe and Glass Inn

Pubby virtues and refined food
Cooking score: 5
Modern British | £35
West End, South Dalton, HU17 7PN
Tel no: (01430) 810246
www.pipeandglass.co.uk

Since arriving at this whitewashed Wolds hostelry in 2006, James and Kate Mackenzie have transformed it into something rather marvellous – a minor miracle of pubby virtues and refined cooking with a big dollop of good humour thrown in. The kitchen may have sky-high culinary aspirations, but you can still sup pints of Yorkshire ale at the bar and gorge on plates of braised faggots as the fire crackles. Alternatively, partake of some more worldly sustenance in the commodious, conservatory-style dining room, where the food is all about generous satisfaction and seasonal oomph. Flavours are full-on but finely judged – from home-cured duck bresaola with a confit rissole, blood orange and celery to goats' cheesecake with beetroot macaroon and candied walnuts. The kitchen also shows its muscular side, fashioning plates of parkin-crusted venison or beef fillet with ox cheek fritter, horseradish hollandaise and chips before knocking 'em dead with its boozy hot chocolate pudding laced with juniper and sloe gin. The knowledgeably chosen wine list

is a drinker's delight with fascinating food-matching suggestions, gentle mark-ups and a splendid choice by the glass; bottles start at £17.
Chef/s: James Mackenzie. **Open:** Tue to Sun L 12 to 2 (4 Sun), Tue to Sat D 6 to 9.30. **Closed:** Mon (exc bank hols), 1 week Jan. **Meals:** alc (main courses £11 to £29). **Details:** 100 seats. 60 seats outside. V menu. Bar. Wheelchair access. Music. Parking.

■ Sowerby Bridge
Gimbals

Modern British food with personality
Cooking score: 4
Modern British | £30
76 Wharf Street, Sowerby Bridge, HX6 2AF
Tel no: (01422) 839329
www.gimbals.co.uk

£5 OFF

The Bakers' village venue in winsome Sowerby Bridge is not one for blushing understatement. A battlefield-sized Union flag and an original Blackpool illumination are among the decorative features at a place that fairly overflows with personality. Simon Baker draws inspiration from all over the known world, and many of his raw materials from the wilds of Yorkshire, to craft an idiosyncratic version of modern British style. Slow-baked portobellos filled with chopped leek, feta and raisins with honeyed kale is a gutsy way to begin, while the seafood option may be king crab and shrimps in lemon mayo with shaved fennel in pink grapefruit and caper vinaigrette. Spine-tingling spice lights up a main dish of Persian-style lamb chops with rose-pickled shallots, chickpeas, raita and chilli jam, while afters could be pineapple, irresistibly roasted in molasses, with chocolate peanut brittle. The short wine list opens with eight house wines in all three colours at £17.
Chef/s: Simon Baker. **Open:** Tue to Sat D only 6.30 to 9.15. **Closed:** Sun, Mon, 24 to 27 Dec. **Meals:** alc (main courses £14 to £22). Set D £17 (2 courses) to £20. Tasting menu £25 (5 courses). **Details:** 60 seats. V menu. Music.

■ Staddlebridge
The Cleveland Tontine

Glammed-up Yorkshire hospitality
Cooking score: 3
French | £35
Staddlebridge, DL6 3JB
Tel no: (01609) 882671
www.theclevelandtontine.co.uk

Synonymous with the eccentric McCoy brothers for more than three decades, this vintage slice of glammed-up Yorkshire hospitality is now rolling along nicely with a new team on board. Dating from 1804, the Tontine looks much as it did during the McCoy's stewardship – particularly the idiosyncratic basement dining room with its fabulously ornate ceiling, original fireplace, flickering candles, huge mirrors and gleaming silver. The food is much the same too – a confident, gutsy mix of reworked bourgeois favourites with the odd nod to Yorkshire and faraway lands. Seafood pancakes thermidor is a Tontine classic, but also look for pan-fried Dover sole fillets with herb purée and frog's legs Kiev or a cutlet of 'grand reserve' lamb with a mini hotpot and pickled cabbage. Locally reared steaks are served the old way, while dessert might herald a ginger-spiked terrine of rhubarb from the 'Yorkshire triangle' with rhubarb sorbet and lemon shortcake slice. The wine list is a grand globetrotter with bottles from £18.50.
Chef/s: James Cooper. **Open:** all week L 12 to 2.30, D 6.30 to 9. **Meals:** alc (main courses £14 to £33). Set L £17 (2 courses) to £20. Early set D (Sun to Thur) £17 (2 courses) to £20. Sun L £22 (2 courses) to £25. **Details:** 100 seats. Bar. Music. Parking.

Visit us online

To find out more about The Good Food Guide, please visit thegoodfoodguide.co.uk

 Todmorden

NEW ENTRY

Blackbird

Tapas in Todmorden

Cooking score: 2
International | £25
23 Water Street, Todmorden, OL14 5AB
Tel no: (01706) 813038
www.blackbirdbar.co.uk

£30

Todmorden's often considered to be Hebden Bridge's plainer sister, but it's rapidly becoming a foodie mecca. Find Blackbird on an atmospheric cobbled street opposite the Greek Revival Town Hall where 'you can imagine yourself in the Med if it wasn't for the horizontal rain'. It's also 'very Manc Northern Quarter, without the nose-bleeding prices'. Come for coffee and cake (and alcohol) during the day, small plates later on. Although the kitchen takes a rather generous approach to portion control (needing 'either smaller plates or bigger tables'), the cooking is sophisticated, marrying local with seasonal. Expect organic beetroot carpaccio, Tuscan meatballs, Yorkshire smoked salmon and a dark, sticky game stew. There's a well-thought-through wine list (from £17), craft beers and a good range of cocktails – and of course, chilled tunes in a friendly, laid-back environment.
Chef/s: Ian Kendall and Kerry Hardman. **Open:** all week 12 to 11 (D 4 to 9). **Meals:** alc (tapas £4 to £7). **Details:** Music.

Wakefield

LOCAL GEM

Iris

Modern British | £27
12 Bull Ring, Wakefield, WF1 1HA
Tel no: (01924) 367683
www.iris-restaurant.com

 £5 OFF

'Coping well with its rising popularity,' says a fan of this enthusiastically run neighbourhood restaurant close to Wakefield's Bull Ring fountains. Local boy Liam Duffy named the place after his grandmother, but there's nothing twee or homespun about his excellent-value, seasonally accented menus – witness salt-baked beetroot with truffled goats' cheese and spiced pumpkin seeds or hake with chorizo gnocchi and curly kale. There are well-aged steaks from a Wakefield butcher, too, while puds include 'blissful' Yorkshire parkin with honeycomb. Wines from £14.95. Closed Sun D.

West Witton

The Wensleydale Heifer

Seafood-centred menu in the Dales
Cooking score: 3
Seafood | £40
Main Street, West Witton, DL8 4LS
Tel no: (01969) 622322
www.wensleydaleheifer.co.uk

£5 OFF 

A white-fronted country pub not far from Hawes in the Yorkshire Dales, otherwise known as Wensleydale Central, the Heifer has been reborn as boutique hotel, fish bar and restaurant. Relax in the beamed whisky lounge, before moving on to the sandy-hued dining room, or the garden tables when West Witton is bathed in sunshine. The seafood-centred menu covers a lot of ground for both range and culinary inspiration, setting king prawn pakora with lentil dhal and raita, and chicken Caesar salad with bacon and anchovies, alongside beer-battered fish and goose-fat chips, traditional fish pie, and daily specials that dare to stray beyond the comfort zone, such as Moroccan-spiced sea bass with lemon couscous, apricots and sultanas. Lobster dishes and grilled steaks provide old-fashioned temptation, as do sweet treats such as raspberry cheesecake, or a Knickerbockered version of tiramisu. The wine list is styled like an old news sheet, and opens with an international spread of house selections at £21.50.

Chef/s: David Moss. **Open:** all week L 12 to 2, D 6 to 9.30. **Meals:** alc (main courses £16 to £44). Set L and D £20 (2 courses) to £22. Sun L £22. **Details:** 80 seats. 40 seats outside. V menu. Bar. Wheelchair access. Music. Parking.

◼ Wetherby

Mango Vegetarian

Indian | £20

12-14 Bank Street, Wetherby, LS22 6NQ
Tel no: (01937) 585755
www.mangovegetarian.com

'My new favourite place to eat' was the verdict of one reporter of this much-loved family-run restaurant in the Wetherby district of Leeds, which specialises in vegetarian and gluten-free dishes. Southern Indian specialities along the lines of authentic masala dosa filled with spiced potato, leeks, cauliflower and onions sit happily alongside traditional Gujarati dishes such as vatana ringhan (peas and potatoes in tomato sauce with mustard, cumin and fenugreek) and Kashmiri-style mushroom korma. In-the-know locals order the four-course thalis. Wines from £13.50. Closed Sun and Mon.

◼ Whitby

Bridge Cottage Bistro

Endearing eatery by the sea

Cooking score: 2
Modern British | £28

On the bridge, Sandsend, Whitby, YO21 3SU
Tel no: (01947) 893438
www.bridgecottagebistro.com

You can't get much nearer the sea than this charming café-by-day/restaurant-by-night venue in pretty Sandsend. The general consensus is that Alex Perkins 'really seems to have hit his stride here'. The interior has been refreshed, and while it still feels sea-sidey, don't expect tacky painted driftwood; it's now much more stylish, with Verner Panton chairs, scratched silvered mirrors and stag's antler lights. The evening menu reflects Perkins' love of all things fishy, featuring the likes of hake tempura (with borlotti beans, pancetta and tomato making 'a very good beany broth'), potted shrimps 'with a nice kick' and 'exemplary' sea trout with samphire and hollandaise. It's not all fish, though: ricotta gnocchi with sage butter is a great plate of food and the burger is good, too. During the day find a place on the pretty patio and rejoice in the selection of cakes – the lemon and pistachio is particularly good – and the view of the ocean. Wines from £16.

Chef/s: Alexander Perkins. **Open:** Tue, Wed and Sun 10 to 5, Thur to Sat 10 to 9. **Closed:** Mon. **Meals:** alc (main courses £12 to £22). **Details:** 30 seats. 30 seats outside. Bar. Music. Parking.

Magpie Café

Seafood | £25

14 Pier Road, Whitby, YO21 3PU
Tel no: (01947) 602058
www.magpiecafe.co.uk

'I've been eating here for years and the food never fails to amaze me: fresh seafood at its best,' enthused one regular of this evergreen seafood restaurant. Indeed, the tea room atmosphere doesn't prepare you for the level of sourcing and skill that goes into the food here. If you want fish and chips, you're in the right place, but they also do a 'hard to beat' pan-fried hake with shellfish in a creamy basil sauce, served with potatoes, bacon and onion – followed, perhaps, by a lemon meringue pot. Wines start at £14.95. Open all week.

Symbols

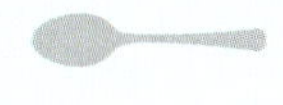

🛏	Accommodation is available
£30	Three courses for less than £30
£5 OFF	£5-off voucher scheme
🍾	Notable wine list

Withernwick

★ **TOP 50 PUB** ★

NEW ENTRY

The Falcon Inn

Superior pub classics in a welcoming inn
Cooking score: 4
British | £33
Main Street, Withernwick, HU11 4TA
Tel no: (01964) 527925
www.thefalconatwithernwick.co.uk

Richard and Lindsey Johns ran the much acclaimed Artisan at Hessle for almost a decade before taking everyone by surprise and selling up for a new challenge. It came in the form of a run-down village pub in one of the quieter corners of the East Riding. Now fully refurbished, the dining room proves that Richard Johns has made the transition from a fine-dining restaurant to a superior pub menu without missing a beat, as has Lindsay Johns' assiduous front-of-house hosting. Local ham comes with celeriac remoulade and a warm and perfect quail Scotch egg. Johns' own treacle-cured salmon is served with a delicate mango and chilli salsa; and sea bass with a fulsome pea and lemon risotto. Roasts and desserts follow pub-classic routes with crème brûlée, sticky toffee pudding – 'the very best I've ever had' from one reader – rising to a standout passion fruit jelly and coconut ice cream. Wine standards begin at £13.95.
Chef/s: Richard Johns. **Open:** Fri to Sat L 12 to 2 (2.30 Sat, 1 to 5 Sun), Tue to Sat D 6 to 9 (6.30 to 8.30 Tue). **Closed:** Mon. **Meals:** alc (main courses £14 to £27). **Details:** 30 seats. 6 seats outside. Bar. Wheelchair access. Music. Parking.

York

NEW ENTRY

Le Cochon Aveugle

Compact and adventurous French bistro
Cooking score: 4
French | £35
37 Walmgate, York, YO1 9TX
Tel no: (01904) 640222
www.lecochonaveugleyork.com

When the recherché Blind Swine relocated to Leeds and renamed itself The Man Behind the Curtain (see entry), it left behind its little French cousin Cochon Aveugle. This proved no problem for head chef Josh Overington (ex-Waterside Inn, Hand & Flowers, Le Langhe) who took his chance and made the quirky little bistro his own. With his partner Victoria Roberts supervising front-of-house, they offer a no-choice, fortnightly changing, keenly priced six-course menu: it's a tour de force. Since when did an amuse-gueule involve a burnt celeriac consommé with miso and passion fruit, a jam jar of warm marinated goats' cheese and a dish of pickled trompette mushrooms? The autumn menu proper offers a rich potage of Brie de Meaux and Jerusalem artichoke with morsels of lamb's tongue tucked beneath a truffle crumble. A rice-less 'risotto' is made from minutely diced squid and cauliflower in a 'prawn-head broth' followed by 12-hour beef and soft black pudding. The pre-dessert of warm canelés (little fluted cakes) and rum and banana milk is followed by crème brûlée, blood-orange purée and chocolate ice cream, the least thrilling dish in a remarkably sophisticated menu, which is fast flying the Tricolour as one of the best in town. The short wine list is predominantly, French starting at £17.
Chef/s: Joshua Overington. **Open:** Tue to Sat D only 6 to 9. **Closed:** 3 weeks Jan. **Meals:** Set D only £35 (6 courses). **Details:** 18 seats. V menu. Music.

Le Langhe

Much-admired modern Italian
Cooking score: 5
Italian | £33
The Old Coach House, Peasholme Green,
York, YO1 7PW
Tel no: (01904) 622584
www.lelanghe.co.uk

£5 OFF 🍷

'I could eat here every week,' enthused one fan. 'Amazing,' exclaimed another about Otto Bocca's handmade pappardelle and wild boar ragù, one of a list of superb pasta dishes in this much-admired café/restaurant. Lunch might begin with a richly flavoured porcini and Parmesan soup followed by that pappardelle, moving on to pork belly or calves' liver with a tarte Tatin to finish. There are cheese and meat boards created from Le Langhe's well-stocked deli (the only source of fresh truffles in the city) and superior salads. The menu expands on Friday and Saturday evenings with tuna tartare, avocado and lime or hare, polenta and bitter chocolate. A pasta course might feature Italian black truffle, followed by veal or pheasant. There are artisan cheeses and simple desserts. Upstairs and downstairs the shelves are stuffed with a vast and impressive range of regional Italian wines that start at £17 and rise stratospherically.

Chef/s: Ottavio Bocca. **Open:** Mon to Sat L 12 to 3, Fri and Sat D 6.45 to 10. **Closed:** Sun, 25 to 27 Dec, first two weeks Jan, Easter. **Meals:** alc (main courses £15 to £28). Tasting menu L £25, D £39. **Details:** 55 seats. 25 seats outside. Wheelchair access. Music.

Melton's

Top-class cooking at fair prices
Cooking score: 5
Modern British | £35
7 Scarcroft Road, York, YO23 1ND
Tel no: (01904) 634341
www.meltonsrestaurant.co.uk

£5 OFF

'Just the sort of place that should be well up in *The Good Food Guide*'s estimation,' reported one regular after a tasting menu with 'no duds

in five courses'. The recipe for Michael and Lucy Hjort's long-running success sounds simple: intelligent and interesting dishes using the best local ingredients, yet few places maintain such consistency over two and a half decades. Situated 'out of the limelight of the city but by an interesting high street of independent shops and cafes', the interior of this Victorian building has a weathered charm, the close-packed tables adding to the mood of quirky intimacy. A selection of appetisers (lamb kofta, taramasalata) or an amuse of carrot and orange soup with 'delicious breads', may precede the likes of 'beautifully presented' mille-feuille of spiced butternut squash or beetroot blini. A 'very tasty' sea bream could follow, teamed with chorizo and Puy lentils, with rhubarb and ginger misu, rhubarb sorbet and shortbread to finish. The weighty wine list offers an impressive range of Old and New World wines, with France covered by region. Prices are very reasonable, kicking off at £18 a bottle.

Chef/s: Michael Hjort and Calvin Miller. **Open:** Tue to Sat L 12 to 2, D 5.30 to 10. **Closed:** Sun, Mon, 2 weeks Dec. **Meals:** alc (main courses £17 to £23). Set L £23 (2 courses) to £26. Tasting menu £40. **Details:** 42 seats. Music.

The Park

Precise cooking in town-house hotel
Cooking score: 3
British | £48
Marmadukes Town House Hotel, 4-5 St Peter's Grove, York, YO30 6AQ
Tel no: (01904) 540903
www.theparkrestaurant.co.uk

Last year Adam Jackson was running his own ship at Sutton Park after a star-studded period at the Black Swan at Oldstead (see entry). This year he's moved again, to operate independently at the restaurant in the boutique Marmadukes Hotel. In a smart, modern glass-roofed extension Jackson has retained his no-choice tasting menu, reducing it from eight to six courses and transferring some of the same dishes – like his enjoyable plate of broccoli, goats' cheese and almond. Of the six courses tried at inspection, the beef fillet with ricotta and watercress stood out, and we liked the chocolate mango and coconut, though found it rather large for a pre-dessert. While there's no doubting Jackson's technical skill and painstaking presentation, some might wish for more thrills on the plate. A short and well-balanced wine list rises progressively from £25.

Chef/s: Adam Jackson. **Open:** Tue to Sat D only 7 to 9. **Closed:** Sun, Mon, 2 weeks Jan, 2 weeks summer. **Meals:** Set D (6 courses) £48. **Details:** 14 seats. V menu. Wheelchair access. Music. Parking.

The Star Inn the City
All-day riverside venue
Cooking score: 2
British | £35
Lendal Engine House, Museum Street, York, YO1 7DR
Tel no: (01904) 619208
www.starinnthecity.co.uk

The city offspring of Harome's Star Inn (see entry) has the best of medieval York's heritage going for it. Sited in the old engine house on the edge of the Museum Gardens, between the Minster and the Lendal Bridge over the Ouse, it's open all day from eggs Florentine and bacon butties onwards. There's an awful lot going on in the main menus, much of it with heartening appeal. A smoked haddock 'cassoulet' with white beans and Wensleydale herb crumb might yield to citrus-stuffed duck breast with anise-scented carrot purée and rhubarb, the latter firmly endorsed by a reporter who was less enamoured with an almost entirely white dish of cod with mussels on garlic mash. The odd dish shows poor timing, suggesting still that the kitchen is spinning too many plates at once, but a rhubarb version of knickerbocker glory with crumbled parkin topping will send you off happy. Wines start at £18.

Chef/s: Matthew Hunter. **Open:** all week 8.30am to 10pm (9am Sun). **Meals:** alc (main courses £12 to £32). Set L £17 (2 courses) to £22. Sun L £19. **Details:** 120 seats. 80 seats outside. Bar. Wheelchair access. Music.

Walmgate Ale House
Real-ale bar and relaxed bistro
Cooking score: 2
British | £25
25 Walmgate, York, YO1 9TX
Tel no: (01904) 629222
www.walmgateale.co.uk

Restyled and renamed, Melton's Too was transformed this year into the Walmgate Ale House. Reprising its days as Ellerker's rope and saddle makers, there are skeins of ropes hanging from the hooks and beams, while the cosy bar area downstairs features a raft of Yorkshire real ales and ciders and snacks of fat sausage rolls, pork pies and cheeses. Upstairs the bistro is simpler than before but continues to celebrate foods local and seasonal, a signature of owners Michael and Lucy Hjort (see Melton's). An autumn menu offered stone bass with mussels and crushed new potatoes and a pork plate featured shoulder, pulled pork, chorizo and black pudding. A vanilla pannacotta served with berries and shortbread impressed at inspection, and both food and service are consistently praised by readers, as are the good-value lunches and early doors deals. A solid wine list with house at £14.95.

Chef/s: Michael Hjort and Calvin Goddard. **Open:** all week 12 to 10.30 (10am Sat and Sun). **Closed:** 25 and 26 Dec, 1 Jan. **Meals:** alc (main courses £12 to £19). Set L and D £13 (2 courses) to £16. Sun L £13. **Details:** 100 seats. Bar. Wheelchair access. Music.

Please send us your feedback

To register your opinion about any restaurant listed in this guide, or a new restaurant that you wish to bring to our attention, please visit the web address at the bottom of the page. Your feedback informs the content of the book and will be used to compile next year's reviews.

SCOTLAND

Borders, Dumfries & Galloway,
Lothians (inc. Edinburgh),
Strathclyde (inc. Glasgow), Central, Fife,
Tayside, Grampian, Highlands & Islands

■ Ancrum

NEW ENTRY

The Ancrum Cross Keys

Essence of country pub
Cooking score: 6
Modern British | £30
Ancrum, TD8 6XH
Tel no: (01835) 830242
www.ancrumcrosskeys.com

£5
OFF

A stone pub overlooking the village green, cheery locals propping the bar – so far, so traditional. The Ancrum Cross Keys could just be a great rural, dog-friendly, real ale haunt if it weren't for the unusual ambition, innovation and sheer quality of its food. Here, even the crisps are hand-fried heritage potatoes with dried balsamic salt, and porky scratchings transcend into home-cured pancetta. Beyond the bar snacks, the more spacious dining room with its open pass and busy white-clad chefs confirms this goes way beyond pub grub. The locally foraged and sourced menu adopts a sparse modern style only hinting at the complexities beneath. White asparagus, for example, is partnered by soft-yolked breaded pheasant egg, brown-buttered fungi and an aromatic tarragon coulis; larch-cured halibut arrives as sashimi offset by a distilled cucumber essence, crunchy black radish and emerald cubes of sorrel jelly; while a dish of spring lamb with artichoke, nettle, sweetbread and curd draws you to the surrounding meadowland. This is a kitchen happy to experiment and not afraid of less familiar combinations such as a dessert of rhubarb and rose custard. Prices are reasonable, the wine list starts at £16 and the ale comes direct from the micro-brewery that belongs to the restaurant's owner.

Chef/s: David Malcolm. **Open:** Fri to Sun L 12 to 3, Wed to Sun D 6 to 9. **Closed:** Mon, Tue. **Meals:** alc (main courses £15 to £21). **Details:** 40 seats. 54 seats outside. Bar. Wheelchair access. Parking.

▌Ednam
Edenwater House

Personally run borderland retreat
Cooking score: 4
Modern British | £40
Ednam, TD5 7QL
Tel no: (01573) 224070
www.edenwaterhouse.co.uk

From its three country-style en-suite B&B rooms, to the simple charms of its diminutive dining room, Edenwater House (an old manse) makes a charmingly traditional stopover in a wee hamlet in the Upper Tweed Valley. Jeff and Jacqui Kelly run the place with hands-on enthusiasm, offering up a four-course set dinner four evenings a week (non-residents are very welcome). If it all sounds low-key, rest assured Jacqui's cooking is pretty feisty, with considered combinations of first-class ingredients. It starts with a soup — mussel and leek broth flavoured with Pernod, say — and might move on to roast quail on a savoury granola cake, dressed with a white port jus, before a pesto-crusted halibut with tomato salsa and basil beurre blanc. Finish with raspberry-poached pears with an intriguing avocado ice cream. Wines from £20.
Chef/s: Jacqui Kelly. **Open:** Thur to Sat D only 6 to 10. **Closed:** Sun to Wed, Dec to Mar. **Meals:** Set D £40. **Details:** 16 seats. Parking.

▌Jedburgh
The Caddy Mann

Quirky local restaurant
Cooking score: 2
Modern British | £25
Mounthooly, Jedburgh, TD8 6TJ
Tel no: (01835) 850787
www.caddymann.com

'Food here is always terrific, and has been over the four years we have been visiting,' noted one reader of this idiosyncratic restaurant formed from three old crofters' cottages. 'The atmosphere and ambience still make one think of a roadside café,' she adds — but don't expect café food. Chef/owner Ross Horrocks honed his skills at Gleneagles and has a passion for sourcing the best local ingredients, especially game; even squirrel gets a look in on his endlessly inventive menus, which are keenly priced for food this labour-intensive. Try seared pigeon with truffled spelt risotto and roe deer that has been home-smoked over juniper, heather and gorse; and 18-hour slow-baked Borders lamb on pan-fried rumbledethumps (a Borders dish of potato, cabbage and onion) with crab apple and wild rowanberry jus. However, the separate vegetarian menu, offering treats such as goats' cheese soufflé or arancini, may tempt. Roasted caramelised pears with warm toffee apple cake and ginger wine syrup is one way to finish. Wines start at £14.50.
Chef/s: Ross Horrocks. **Open:** all week L 12 to 2, Fri and Sat D 7 to 12. **Closed:** 25 and 26 Dec, 1 to 3 Jan. **Meals:** alc (main courses £11 to £19). **Details:** 50 seats. 20 seats outside. V menu. Wheelchair access. Parking.

▌Kelso
The Cobbles

Local beer and victuals
Cooking score: 1
Modern British | £25
7 Bowmont Street, Kelso, TD5 7JH
Tel no: (01573) 223548
www.thecobbleskelso.co.uk

'Its micro-brewery is booming and so, too, is the restaurant,' reports one visitor to Gavin and Annika Meiklejohn's updated Victorian coaching inn. Another has praised a bar lunch of 'beautiful mussels, lovely burger', but restaurant meals, too, are notable for high-quality ingredients. West Coast scallops teamed with chicken and tarragon ravioli, mushroom consommé and pak choi could be followed by venison haunch with skirlie mash (potatoes, oats, onions), bourguignon sauce and black pudding, while desserts include a sticky date pudding with butterscotch sauce and Earl Grey ice cream. You can sample the full range of Tempest ales here, and wines start at £14.95.

Chef/s: Daniel Norcliffe. **Open:** Mon to Sat L 12 to 2.30, D 5.45 to 9 (9.15 Fri and Sat). Sun 12 to 8. **Closed:** 25 Dec. **Meals:** alc (main courses £10 to £21). Sun L £20. **Details:** 35 seats. 16 seats outside. Bar. Music.

 Melrose

Burt's Hotel

Culinary satisfaction in a grand old inn
Cooking score: 2
Modern British | £38
Market Square, Melrose, TD6 9PL
Tel no: (01896) 822285
www.burtshotel.co.uk

Burt's has been putting up passing travellers and satisfying the sybaritic needs of locals since the 18th century. It's got a prime position on the Market Square and looks particularly spruce when the hanging baskets are in bloom. For the last 45 years or so it has been under the stewardship of the Henderson family. The Bistro Bar doles out real ales and rather more than your average pub grub (pressed ham hock with peach compote to start, say, followed by classy fish and chips), or head into the traditionally adorned restaurant for the full fine-dining experience (pristine linen et al). Haggis croquette with turnip purée and parsley and whisky sauce provides time-honoured flavours dressed up for our times, followed perhaps by duck breast with boulangère potatoes. Finish with an apple-fest including crumble and sponge pudding. Wines from £18.

Chef/s: Trevor Williams. **Open:** Sat and Sun L 12 to 2, all week D 7 to 9 (9.30 Sun). **Closed:** 4 to 11 Jan. **Meals:** alc (main courses £15 to £26). **Details:** 50 seats. 10 seats outside. Bar. Parking. Children over 8 yrs only.

 Peebles

Osso

Light by day and smart by night
Cooking score: 2
Modern British | £27
Innerleithen Road, Peebles, EH45 8BA
Tel no: (01721) 724477
www.ossorestaurant.com

£30

Conveniently located by the Eastgate Arts Centre, Osso has a casual daytime café vibe, hosting shoppers and day-trippers to brunch, lunch and teas. Thursday to Saturday evenings, the soups, scones and pushchairs give way to a classier experience. While retaining the friendly informality of service, soft candles now accent the dark wood and mirrored finishes to set a more subtle stage for modern British bistro cooking. Home-soused mackerel with pickled cucumber and a wasabi-sesame finish or crab fishcake in a lightly curried coriander broth show a chef prepared to incorporate global inspirations. More local Borders' heritage and ingredients are not overlooked with mains of crispy rolled spring lamb breast with a velvety carrot purée or handmade steak burger with bone marrow and proper beef dripping chips (so wrong they have to be right!). Desserts richly reflect the Scottish love affair with sugar. House wine £17.25.

Chef/s: Ally McGrath and Stuart Smith. **Open:** all week 10 to 4.30, Thur to Sat D 6 to 9. **Closed:** 25 Dec, 1 Jan. **Meals:** alc (main courses £12 to £18). **Details:** 38 seats. 6 seats outside. Wheelchair access. Music.

◼ Moffat

The Limetree

Reassuring food in amiable surroundings
Cooking score: 4
Modern British | £29
Hartfell House, Hartfell Crescent, Moffat,
DG10 9AL
Tel no: (01683) 220153
www.hartfellhouse.co.uk

Locals may remember it on Moffat's high street, but since 2008 the Limetree has been happily ensconced within Hartfell House – a grand-looking Grade B-listed guesthouse on the edge of town. Nothing much changes in the cosy, old-fashioned dining room (note the distinctive wood graining), although chef Matt Seddon continues to ring the changes on his short, fixed-price dinner menu. He cooks alone, rustling up dishes that he 'likes to eat' – perhaps smoked haddock and brown shrimp risotto or grilled pork belly with Chinese spices, cucumber salad and soy dressing followed by rump of Barony venison with root vegetables, thyme and shallot sauce or a sunny Med-inspired combo of ling fillet in tomato and pepper sauce with Spanish potatoes, cumin-roast aubergine and fennel à la grecque. It's all very safe, sound and reassuring, right down to desserts such as pannacotta with brandied prune compote. As always, service is 'gracious, attentive and unhurried, with discreet well-judged pauses between courses'. Two-dozen wines start at £16.

Chef/s: Matt Seddon. **Open:** Tue to Sat D only 6.30 to 8.30. **Closed:** Sun, Mon, 24 to 30 Dec, 1 to 14 Jan, 10 days Oct. **Meals:** Set L £21 (2 courses) to £24. Set D £24 (2 courses) to £29. **Details:** 24 seats. Wheelchair access.

◼ Portpatrick

Knockinaam Lodge

Sedate luxury and refined food
Cooking score: 5
Modern British | £68
Portpatrick, DG9 9AD
Tel no: (01776) 810471
www.knockinaamlodge.com

When Churchill and Eisenhower wanted somewhere suitably remote for a private meeting during the Second World War, they chose this singular Victorian hunting lodge surrounded by wooded glens and rugged cliffs, with a secret cove overlooking the Irish Sea. It's no surprise that this landscape also inspired John Buchan's thriller *The Thirty-Nine Steps*, but nowadays Knockinaam Lodge is better known for its comforting blend of sedate luxury and refined food with Scottish nuances. No-choice, fixed-price dinners follow the well-tried country-house format to the letter: steamed Luce Bay turbot dressed with Champagne and chive butter sauce; a sip or two of soup (perhaps a cappuccino of celeriac, parsley and blue cheese); a meat or game centrepiece (slow-roast fillet of Speyside beef with braised shallots, truffle and port reduction), then something fruity to finish – say a tuile basket filled with coconut ice cream and seasonal berries. Owner David Ibbotson's gently evolving 'wine collection' is stuffed with impeccable vintages and growers from every corner of the globe, with scores of half-bottles to encourage sampling. House selections from £23.

Chef/s: Tony Pierce. **Open:** all week L 12 to 1.15, D 7 to 9. **Meals:** Set L £40 (4 courses). Set D £68 (5 courses). Sun L £33 (4 courses). **Details:** 20 seats. Bar. Music. Parking. Children over 12 yrs only at D.

 Sanquhar

Blackaddie House Hotel

Foodie oasis in the borderlands
Cooking score: 4
Modern British | £55
Blackaddie Road, Sanquhar, DG4 6JJ
Tel no: (01659) 50270
www.blackaddiehotel.co.uk

£5 OFF

Ian McAndrew is a talented chef of long standing, first featuring in the Guide in the early 1980s. Since pitching camp at this stone manse by the River Nith in 2007, he has gained a reputation as an excellent host, although food is the main attraction in the dining room. Ian's kitchen takes its cue from Scotland's regional larder, seasonal sourcing is at a premium and meals are interspersed with 'wonderful' extras. Precise cooking with lots of intricate detailing and fancy presentation is the house style – from a salad of cured duck with rhubarb chutney to warm cinnamon doughnuts with banana milkshake, toffee sauce and coconut sorbet. In between, there's satisfaction to be had from monkfish with black rice, mussels and girolles, 'a tasting of seriously aged beef' or loin of roe deer with a fashionable melange of acidulated chocolate, pickled raspberries, braised walnuts and sticky venison ragoût. Service is all smiles and charm, and the wine list starts at £22.50.
Chef/s: Ian McAndrew. **Open:** all week L 12.30 to 1.30 (min 1 day notice), D 6.30 to 9. **Meals:** Set L £22 (1 course) to £36. Set D £55 (4 courses).
Details: 22 seats. Bar. Wheelchair access. Music. Parking.

Time for tea

Forget the hipster coffee revolution – it's the teas that will get you twiddling your 'tache at many of the UK's leading restaurants.

At **Restaurant Gordon Ramsay** there's a choice of ten different brews including teas and tisanes (herbal teas). Your order is measured and timed according to the variety of tea, and straining is a no-no because it removes flavour. Glass teapots are used 'for purity'.

Alongside a selection of tisanes, the **Cinnamon Club** majors on perfumed teas including whole rosebud and jasmine pearls. Also on offer are smoky, organic bohea tea and the famous silver-needle white tea, which is made from leaf shoots gathered in the Fujian province of China.

At **Restaurant Story**, head sommelier Seamus Sharkey curates the tea menu in collaboration with Lalani & Co, an importer of artisanal teas from small gardens across the world. These are imported in small batches, so the selection is always changing.

Jing teas are the focus at **Dinner by Heston Blumenthal**. The tea is infused at 90 degrees celsius and the infusion time for each tea varies. The tea menu has tasting notes on each variety.

◼ Dunbar
The Creel

Spanking-fresh seafood and keen prices
Cooking score: 2
Modern British | £28
25 Lamer Street, Dunbar, EH42 1HJ
Tel no: (01368) 863279
www.creelrestaurant.co.uk

Trim, shipshape and nautically themed, Logan
Thorburn's modest eatery near Dunbar's
harbour and castle ruins delivers the goods in a
plain setting of wood floors, Formica tables
and maritime knick-knacks. There's always
plenty of fresh seafood on the menu and
Thorburn cares about sustainable sourcing (he
earned his stripes with Rick Stein, among
others): bowls of shellfish soup, Maryland crab
cakes, steamed crevettes with homemade
mayo and Belhaven beer-battered fish
(perhaps sea bass) are joined by slightly more
ambitious ideas such as grilled Eyemouth hake
fillet with onion and tarragon salsa, fried
potatoes and sour cream. If fish isn't your bag,
you can pick something suitable from the line-
up of seared Aberdeen Angus steaks,
vegetarian pasta dishes and local novelties such
as meatloaf with crushed potatoes, apple and
onion gravy, before rounding off with a
homely fruit crumble, pannacotta or
cardamom-scented farola (milk pudding)
with caramelised oranges. Exceedingly
friendly pricing also extends to the wine list,
which kicks off at £16.95 (£4.50 a glass).
Chef/s: Logan Thorburn. **Open:** Thur to Sun L 12 to
2.30, Wed to Sat D 6.30 to 9. **Closed:** Mon, Tue.
Meals: Set L £17 (2 courses) to £20. Set D £25 (2
courses) to £28. Sun L £20 (2 courses) to £25.
Details: 36 seats. Wheelchair access. Music. No
children after 7.

Average price

The average price denotes the price
of a three-course meal without wine.

◼ Edinburgh
Angels with Bagpipes

Uptown meets Old Town
Cooking score: 3
Modern European | £30
343 High Street, Royal Mile, Edinburgh,
EH1 1PW
Tel no: (0131) 2201111
www.angelswithbagpipes.co.uk

It may be on the Royal Mile but this ain't no
tourist trap. Not a bit of it. Ambling past
Angels with Bagpipes' 17th-century town
house with its two pavement tables out front
you would be forgiven for thinking it was just
another place to refuel before trudging
onwards. Big mistake. The place is much
bigger than it looks from the front, with a
slick contemporary finish and a modern menu
that owes something to Scottish and broader
European traditions. To begin, the humble
mackerel gets the trendy charring treatment
and a hit of curry flavour, while main courses
bring together pollack with pickled mussels
and beurre noisette, and rump and belly of
lamb with spiced lentils and aubergine. The
evident passion for contemporary cooking
techniques continues into desserts such as
chocolate brownie with miso ice cream. Wines
start at £21.
Chef/s: Fraser Smith. **Open:** all week 12 to 9.30.
Meals: alc (main courses £15 to £31). Set L £15 (2
courses) to £19. **Details:** 70 seats. 16 seats outside.
Wheelchair access. Music.

Café St Honoré

Scottish produce in a Parisian setting
Cooking score: 3
French | £35
34 North West Thistle Street Lane, Edinburgh,
EH2 1EA
Tel no: (0131) 2262211
www.cafesthonore.com

Dripping with *fin de siècle* nostalgia, Café St
Honoré makes its case with distressed mirrors,
black-and-white tiled floors, candlelight and

Join us at thegoodfoodguide.co.uk

soft jazz. So far, so retro, but chef/patron Neil Forbes lives in the present: he's a member of the Slow Food Chef Alliance, championing organic produce and sustainability – a recently installed low-energy kitchen proves the point. He also takes time and pays attention to the culinary details, whether it's Douglas fir-smoked pigeon served with organic Pippin apple, celery and walnut salad and a dollop of Katy Rodger's crème fraîche or Orkney 'beremeal' bannocks offered with Highland crowdie and Mellis honey. Otherwise, his bright seasonal line-up runs from braised Scottish pork belly with buttered mash, kale and local organic salami to North Sea hake with Shetland blue-shell mussel chowder. As for pud, expect lemon tart (organic, of course) or a mousse made of Original Beans 'Beni wild harvest' chocolate. The same ethos applies to the free-ranging terroir-led wine list; bottles from £18.90.
Chef/s: Neil Forbes. **Open:** all week L 12 to 2, D 5.15 to 10 (6 Sat and Sun). **Closed:** 24 to 26 Dec, 1 Jan. **Meals:** alc (main courses £15 to £22). Set L £15 (2 courses) to £19. Set D £18 (2 courses) to £24. **Details:** 45 seats. Music.

Castle Terrace

'From nature to plate'
Cooking score: 6
Modern British | £60
33-35 Castle Terrace, Edinburgh, EH1 2EL
Tel no: (0131) 2291222
www.castleterracerestaurant.com

Secreted in an elegant town house under the gaze of Edinburgh Castle, this understated, contemporary dining room runs with the same themes as its elder sibling The Kitchin (see entry). Uncluttered design, warm brown tones and flashes of colour from the French-designed Elitis wallpaper set the scene for some superlative modern cooking: 'from nature to plate' is the mantra, and chef/proprietor Dominic Jack means what he says. Thrilling, high-impact dishes abound, from roast North Sea monkfish wrapped in Ayrshire ham with sweet pepper marmalade and Pink Fir Apple potatoes to saddle of Stobo Estate roe deer accompanied by celery, celeriac, apple and caramelised walnuts. Elsewhere, Shetland salmon is fashioned into sushi and 'hampe' of Scotch beef is given the 'bourguignon' treatment with the addition of ox tongue and polenta. Tasting menus offer 'surprises from land and sea', while desserts show off the kitchen's technical prowess – witness a mille-feuille of Cox's Orange Pippin and vanilla with hibiscus sorbet. The long list of global wines is stuffed with pedigree growers large and small. Sixteen house selections start at £22.50 (£6.50 a glass).
Chef/s: Dominic Jack. **Open:** Tue to Sat L 12 to 2.15, D 6.30 to 10. **Closed:** Sun, Mon, 20 Dec to 19 Jan. **Meals:** alc (main courses £27 to £42). Set L £29. Tasting menu £75 (6 courses). **Details:** 65 seats. V menu. Bar. Wheelchair access. Music. Children over 5 yrs only.

David Bann

Globetrotting contemporary veggie
Cooking score: 2
Vegetarian | £23
56-58 St Mary's Street, Edinburgh, EH1 1SX
Tel no: (0131) 5565888
www.davidbann.co.uk

The seductive décor of mood lighting and rich, warm colours puts paid to any thoughts of vegetarianism of the old school, for David Bann's joint is of the new wave, where the globetrotting, meat-free menu fizzes with good ideas. Just off the Royal Mile, it's open all day for creative veggie tucker such as Thai fritters with home-smoked tofu and the kick of green chilli and ginger (served with banana chutney and plum dressing), or the more Euro-centric ravioli filled with artichoke, chickpeas and basil. And that's just for starters. Move on to a risotto of mushrooms and celeriac, or a spiced aduki bean and cashew nut pie. Brunch is up for grabs at the weekends. For dessert, whisky pannacotta arrives in the company of a warm pear, and the dark

chocolate soufflé with homemade vanilla ice cream. The vegetarian wine list has vegan options; bottles from £16.
Chef/s: David Bann. **Open:** all week 12 to 10 (11am Sat and Sun). **Closed:** 25 and 26 Dec, 1 Jan. **Meals:** alc (main courses £11 to £13). Set L £17 to £22. **Details:** 80 seats. V menu.

NEW ENTRY
Field
Scottish ingredients with contemporary verve
Cooking score: 2
Modern British | £27
41 West Nicolson Street, Edinburgh, EH8 9DB
Tel no: (0131) 6677010
www.fieldrestaurant.co.uk

Three impressive talents are behind this engaging small restaurant in the heart of Edinburgh's student quarter. Gordon Craig (chef) and Richard and Rachel Conway (maître d' and operations manager respectively) come with an impressive pedigree – Waterside Inn, Peat Inn, the Wee Restaurant and the Plumed Horse – but they have made this their own, showcasing Scottish seasonal ingredients with contemporary verve. A test meal showed off mackerel with chorizo, apple purée and cashew nuts followed by chicken breast, Puy lentils and a stellar black pudding Scotch egg. On a short menu, vegetarians are imaginatively catered for with cauliflower beignets and curried crème fraîche with a rum, raisin, mango and chilli salsa followed by a comforting potato and dill ravioli with crisp balls of vegetarian haggis (nuts, barley, carrots and oatmeal). At dessert, pear crumble was paired with a zingy ginger-beer sorbet. Lunch and pre-theatre dinners are cracking value. A thoughtful wine list starts at £17. It's cool and it's tiny, so best to book.
Chef/s: Gordon Craig. **Open:** Tue to Sun L 12 to 2, D 5.30 to 9. **Closed:** Mon. **Meals:** alc (main courses £11 to £23). Set L and early D £12 (2 courses) to £15. **Details:** 22 seats. Music. Children over 5 yrs only.

Fishers in Leith
Quirky seafood bistro
Cooking score: 1
Seafood | £30
1 The Shore, Leith, Edinburgh, EH6 6QW
Tel no: (0131) 5545666
www.fishersrestaurantgroup.co.uk

Set in a 17th-century watchtower overlooking the Leith waterfront, this well-appointed, long-standing seafood bistro knows what it does best. Plates of oysters, queenie scallops with pesto butter, and langoustine tails in garlic butter are star turns, fishcakes have plenty of takers and the choice might stretch to a chilled seafood platter, whole megrim sole or monkfish, mussel, coley, squid and chorizo paella. The menu also presses the comfort button, offering Aberdeen Angus steaks and mutton, pork and pickle pie for those in the mood for meat. Sticky toffee pudding is the way to end. Wines from £15.90.
Chef/s: Andrew Bird. **Open:** all week 12 to 10.30 (12.30 Sun). **Closed:** 25 and 26 Dec, 1 Jan. **Meals:** alc (main courses £11 to £26). Set L £14 (2 courses) to £17. **Details:** 44 seats. 16 seats outside. V menu. Bar. Music.

Galvin Brasserie de Luxe
France meets London in Scotland
Cooking score: 3
French | £34
The Caledonian, Princes Street, Edinburgh, EH1 2AB
Tel no: (0131) 2228988
www.galvinbrasseriedeluxe.com

When does a brasserie serve haggis? When it's a Galvin brasserie, and it's in Edinburgh. The haggis starter is not entirely typical of the brothers' Scottish output: escargots à la bourguignonne and steak tartare are also offered at this Edinburgh reimagining of their bustling London original. The classics are served in a plainish room that needs people to soften it; no problem when Orkney scallops and langoustine come hot off the grill with garlic butter and there's Old Spot pork cheeks with choucroute or duck breast with boudin noir and lyonnaise salad. A set seasonal menu at £20 for three courses has obvious appeal. To finish, it's got to be rum baba or Valrhona mousse with caramelised banana and peanut brittle. For even more luxe at the same address, the Galvins also operate The Pompadour (see separate entry). Wines are mainly French, from £25.

Chef/s: Jamie Knox. **Open:** all week L 12 to 2.30 (12.30 to 3 Sun), D 6 to 10. **Meals:** alc (main courses £14 to £31). Set L and D £17 (2 courses) to £20. Sun L £15. **Details:** 130 seats. V menu. Bar. Wheelchair access. Music. Parking.

The Gardener's Cottage
Inventive cooking in World Heritage park
Cooking score: 2
British | £35
1 Royal Terrace Gardens, London Road, Edinburgh, EH7 5DX
Tel no: (0131) 5581221
www.thegardenerscottage.co

The battered blackboard menu in the garden gives notice of a different kind of venue to the big-city norm. It really was once home to the gardener who looked after the Royal Terrace lawns, now part of the World Heritage Site park. Long communal tables create a refectory air as a congenial setting for inventive, locally sourced food, which comes in simple but powerfully appealing guises. Barbecued squid with apple, bacon and crisp-fried kale might presage a main dish of roast pork with Savoy cabbage, onion, roasties and rowan jelly. The seven-course set dinner menu (including a cheese course) is an absolute steal, perhaps built around mallard with salt-baked turnip, apple and macerated gin sloes, bookending that cheese with a pair of desserts – rhubarb with alexanders and ricotta, and sea buckthorn curd sponge with hazelnut meringue and yoghurt sorbet. The tiny wine list starts with a Salento Primitivo at £18.90, or £4.40 a glass.

Chef/s: Dale Mailley and Edward Murray. **Open:** Thur to Mon L 12 to 2.30, D 5 to 9.30. **Closed:** Tue, Wed, 2 weeks Christmas. **Meals:** alc (main courses £15 to £18, L only). Tasting menu £35 (7 courses). **Details:** 30 seats. 12 seats outside. Music.

La Garrigue
A taste of the Midi off the Royal Mile
Cooking score: 3
French | £35
31 Jeffrey Street, Edinburgh, EH1 1DH
Tel no: (0131) 5573032
www.lagarrigue.co.uk

£5
OFF

Taking its name from the scrubby vegetation of his native Languedoc, Jean-Michel Gauffre's brightly decorated bistro brings a taste of the Midi to the heart of Auld Reekie. Vivid Provençal colours and paintings of sunnier climes set the mood, while the bilingual menu is stuffed with seasonal flavours and specialities that have become synonymous with the region – from soupe de poissons with saffron-tinged rouille to 'le cassoulet languedocien' accompanied by a walnut salad. The kitchen also ventures forth, picking up deep-rooted ideas from elsewhere – perhaps scallops with chicory, black pudding and orange butter sauce, pot-au-feu or roast and confit pheasant with apples, grapes and chestnuts. After that, it's back to Gauffre's home patch for traditional lavender crème brûlée or apple turnovers with cinnamon ice cream. The wine list is a treasure trove from the Languedoc and neighbouring regions, with honourable mentions for Le Mas de Daumas Glassac and Le Domaine de Clovallon. Vins de Pays d'Oc start at £16.50.

Chef/s: Jean-Michel Gauffre. **Open:** all week L 12 to 2, D 6 to 9.30. **Meals:** Set L £15 (2 courses) to £18. Set D £28 (2 courses) to £35. Sun L £15. **Details:** 45 seats. V menu. Wheelchair access.

★ TOP 50 ★

The Kitchin

Star player on the waterfront
Cooking score: 7
Modern European | £70
78 Commercial Quay, Leith, Edinburgh,
EH6 6LX
Tel no: (0131) 5551755
www.thekitchin.com

The location on Leith's waterfront, opposite the offices of the Scottish Government, may not 'look much from the outside' but, within the one-time bonded whisky warehouse, looks newly minted following a major refurb – 'elegant, graciously appointed and actually quite calm despite the busy-ness of the place'. Having acquired the premises next door, there's now space for a private dining room, whisky snug and temperature-controlled wine cellar, while the main restaurant has been laced with heritage touches (tartans, sheepskins, silver birch) and diners can watch the culinary action 'at full pace' through a window into the kitchen. 'From nature to plate' is still Tom Kitchin's culinary mantra – 'guests are given a little rolled-up coloured map of Scotland showing the exact locations from whence the various ingredients were sourced' – and Kitchin proves the point with signature dishes of Isle of Barra 'spoots' (razor clams) cooked to order with wild herbs, chorizo and diced vegetables or yoghurt pannacotta with apple sorbet, and East Lothian sea buckthorn consommé. Elsewhere the chef marries Scottish seasonality with the precision-tuned technical know-how of French haute cuisine: boned and rolled pig's head is served with roasted Tobermory langoustine and a crispy ear salad, while boudin of Inverurie ox tongue is accompanied by braised ox shin, bone-marrow potato and Parisienne carrots (from Vallum Farm). Applause, too, for a delectable 'rock pool' of local shellfish and sea vegetables, the crispy veal sweetbreads served with Jerusalem artichoke and pearl barley risotto, and the 'exquisite' Perthshire plum and ginger soufflé

with stem ginger ice cream. The intelligent, impeccably sourced wine list is a distillation of modern viticulture, with fascinating seasonal selections – although you'll struggle to find much below £35.

Chef/s: Tom Kitchin. **Open:** Tue to Sat L 12.15 to 2.30, D 6.30 to 10. **Closed:** Sun, Mon, Christmas and New Year. **Meals:** alc (main courses £29 to £40). Set L £29. Tasting menu £75 (7 courses). **Details:** 75 seats. 20 seats outside. V menu. Bar. Wheelchair access. Music. Children over 5 yrs only.

Number One

Dynamic cooking in landmark surroundings
Cooking score: 6
Modern European | £70
The Balmoral, 1 Princes Street, Edinburgh,
EH2 2EQ
Tel no: (0131) 5576727
www.restaurantnumberone.com

Opened as a railway hotel in 1902, the grand old Balmoral is now an iconic Edinburgh landmark – all imperial pomp and marble-hued magnificence. By contrast, the capacious Number One restaurant in the windowless basement is a vision of Olga Polizzi opulence complete with solid timber floors, golden banquettes, black-framed contemporary artworks and red lacquered walls. Long-serving executive chef Jeff Bland has shuffled his kitchen team, but the food has lost none of its patrician class or creative dynamism – witness a dish of Orkney beef fillet with baby aubergine, baba ganoush and braised oxtail. Seasonal Scottish ingredients are name-checked throughout the menu, from hand-dived Dingwall scallop with Puy lentils, parsnip and pig's trotter to anise-tinged Whitmuir organic pork with onion purée and apricot ketchup. The kitchen never stints on the luxuries of gastronomic life, while saving much of its flamboyant artistry for desserts such as green apple parfait with cinnamon doughnut, caramel and fromage-blanc ice cream. Informed, professional service extends

to the heavyweight wine list, a compendium of aristocratic treasures and big-name bottles with a strong French bias. Prices start at £30.
Chef/s: Brian Grigor and Jeff Bland. **Open:** all week D only 6.30 to 10 (6 Fri to Sun). **Closed:** 2 weeks Jan. **Meals:** Set D £70. Tasting menu £79 (7 courses) to £110 (10 courses). **Details:** 65 seats. V menu. Bar. Wheelchair access. Music.

Ondine

Sustainable seafood favourite
Cooking score: 4
Seafood | £40
2 George IV Bridge, Edinburgh, EH1 1AD
Tel no: (0131) 2261888
www.ondinerestaurant.co.uk

Suave, classy and a perennial hit with Edinburgh's fish-loving foodies, Ondine is perched above the Royal Mile – with full-height windows providing panoramic vistas over George IV Bridge. The cool, contemporary vibe, funky art and baroque mirrors in the eye-catching dining room are a good fit for cooking that promises sophistication as well as fish and chips – all underpinned by a commitment to sustainable sourcing. The kitchen casts its net wide, offering a haul of 'elegantly presented' dishes ranging from dressed brown crab with quail's egg, 'first-class' fish soup or salt-and-pepper squid tempura with Vietnamese dressing to monkfish curry, grilled lemon sole with cockles, chorizo and croquetas or classic lobster thermidor. Meat eaters fare best by ordering from the set menu, while pud might bring orange and almond cake. Alternatively, park up at the all-glass crustacean bar and watch as staff expertly shuck oysters and assemble spectacular fruits de mer. Zingy aperitifs pique the palate, and the thoughtful fish-friendly wine list starts at £20.50.
Chef/s: Roy Brett. **Open:** Mon to Sat L 12 to 2.30, D 5.30 to 9.30. **Closed:** Sun, 24 to 26 Dec. **Meals:** alc (main courses £17 to £45). Set L and D £17 (2 courses) to £20. **Details:** 75 seats. Wheelchair access. Music.

Plumed Horse

Impeccable dishes and service to match
Cooking score: 5
Modern European | £55
50-54 Henderson Street, Edinburgh, EH6 6DE
Tel no: (0131) 5545556
www.plumedhorse.co.uk

The sober dining room at this well-established Leith restaurant is enlivened by vibrant modern art and an ultra-professional team front-of-house which even extends to donning white gloves to place the cutlery. Choose from a substantial eight-course tasting menu or three-course à la carte, though this one throws in plenty of extras like clever canapés and a delicate fish mousseline amuse-bouche. Move on to a generous soup of oyster, scallop and plaice, with a broth that brings in the fresh flavours of ginger, apple and herbs. At mains, slow-braised ox cheek and slow beef fillet marginally won the day over roast halibut with caramelised celeriac purée, Jerusalem artichoke and white and green asparagus. A pre-dessert is followed by a white chocolate marquise that was skilful and prettily presented without quite lifting off, while good coffee and petits fours round off an impressive dinner. A notable wine list starts at £21.
Chef/s: Tony Borthwick and William Grubb. **Open:** Tue to Sat L 12.30 to 2, D 7 to 9 (9.30 Sat). **Closed:** Sun, Mon, Christmas, 2 weeks summer, 1 week Easter, 1 week autumn. **Meals:** Set L £25. Set D £55. Tasting menu £69. **Details:** 40 seats. Wheelchair access. Music. No children after 8.

Visit us online

To find out more about The Good Food Guide, please visit thegoodfoodguide.co.uk

The Pompadour by Galvin

Big-ticket luxury and French flavours
Cooking score: 5
French | £55

The Caledonian, Princes Street, Edinburgh,
EH1 2AB
Tel no: (0131) 2228975
www.thepompadourbygalvin.com

The reincarnation of this former railway-hotel
dining room put the Pompadour back in the
limelight. Now, four years down the line, the
ornate, tastefully pale, first-floor restaurant is
the special-occasion venue to beat all others,
thanks to Chris and Jeff Galvin's reputation for
flawless, fine-tuned French cooking. Fraser
Allan interprets the Galvin style perfectly, his
confident, refined dishes are as light and smart
as the surroundings, built around top-notch
ingredients with balance and depth of flavour
a given. From a beguiling opener of lasagne of
Berwick lobster with shellfish emulsion and
sea purslane (something of a Galvin signature
dish) to a tagine of Bresse pigeon with
couscous, confit lemon and harissa sauce, he
continues to keep the place in the first
division. Desserts embrace the classic: try
apple tarte Tatin or a baked egg custard tart
with Yorkshire rhubarb. Professional service
and a masterly wine list (from £19) add allure.
Chef/s: Fraser Allan. **Open:** Wed to Sat D only 6 to
10. **Closed:** Sun, Mon, Tue, 3 weeks Jan. **Meals:** alc
(main courses £25 to £35). Set seasonal D £24 (2
courses) to £29. Menu gourmand £68. **Details:** 60
seats. V menu. Bar. Wheelchair access. Music.
Parking.

Purslane

Basement eatery with big ideas
Cooking score: 2
Modern British | £30

33a St Stephen Street, Stockbridge,
Edinburgh, EH3 5AH
Tel no: (0131) 2263500
www.purslanerestaurant.co.uk

Perfectly suited to its trendy Stockbridge
location, Purslane is just the thing for a classy
lunch or a meander through the seven-course
tasting menu. The setting doesn't let its hair
down quite enough to deliver the 'rustic,
casual fine dining' promised on the restaurant's
website, but it is attractive nonetheless.
'Informal metropolitan' might be a better
description, while the cooking is informed by
chef/proprietor Paul Gunning's time spent
under high-flyng chef Jeff Bland (see entry
Number One at the Balmoral Hotel). Expect
classic cooking at competitive prices. Pan-
fried scallops with orange marmalade and
carrot foam is a typical starter, while
Gressingham duck breast with braised
chicory, Savoy cabbage, confit leg and red
wine jus is a characteristically comfortable
main. In a similar vein, desserts offer classic
techniques and sensible flavour combinations,
such as vanilla pannacotta with poached
rhubarb and ginger jam, or dark chocolate
mousse with caramel ice cream. A decent,
global selection of wines kicks off at a
reasonable £15.95.
Chef/s: Paul Gunning. **Open:** Tue to Sun L 12 to 2, D
6 to 10. **Closed:** Mon. **Meals:** Set L £15 (2 courses)
to £18. Set D £25 (2 courses) to £30. Sun L £15.
Details: 22 seats. Music. Children over 6 yrs only.

Restaurant Mark Greenaway

Harmonious food in elegant surrounds
Cooking score: 4
Modern British | £43
69 North Castle Street, Edinburgh, EH2 3LJ
Tel no: (0131) 2261155
www.markgreenaway.com

Since January 2013, this Georgian building near Queen Street Gardens has been home to Mark Greenaway's 'fantastically well-run' restaurant, the kind of place that people write to us copiously about. Greenaway's style is all about concentrating the essence of fine ingredients in novel preparations, described with a minimum of flourish on the tersely written menus. His dishes are defined by their 'look at me' artistry: Loch Fyne crab cannelloni, for example, gains hugely from its busy, highly worked approach and combination of smoked cauliflower custard, lemon pearls, herb butter and baby coriander. Equally deft is the utterly memorable, 'melt-in-the-mouth' slow-roasted pork belly, served with pork cheek 'pie', blackened fillet, sweetcorn and a toffee apple jus 'that was an unusual, but very tasty accompaniment'. Desserts are clever and innovative, with 'knot' chocolate tart (as seen on BBC Two's *Great British Menu*) considered a complete winner. Prices (from £21) are fair on the cosmopolitan wine list.

Chef/s: Mark Greenaway. **Open:** Tue to Sat L 12 to 2.30, D 5.30 to 10. **Closed:** Sun, Mon, 25 and 26 Dec, 1 and 2 Jan. **Meals:** alc (main courses £22 to £32). Set L and early D £17 (2 courses) to £22. Tasting menu £66 (8 courses). **Details:** 66 seats. Music.

Symbols

 Accommodation is available
£30 Three courses for less than £30
£5 OFF £5-off voucher scheme
 Notable wine list

Restaurant Martin Wishart

Inspired cooking from a Caledonian star
Cooking score: 7
Modern French | £70
54 The Shore, Leith, Edinburgh, EH6 6RA
Tel no: (0131) 5533557
www.martin-wishart.co.uk

'Absolutely fantastic, and a delight from start to finish,' is how one reporter summed up a visit to Martin's Wishart's flagship overlooking Leith's waterfront. The mood in the urbane low-key dining room is formal – polite staff attend to every detail – while the kitchen shows its class with a clutch of tasting menus and a stripped-back carte offering just three choices at each stage. The result is a finely honed repertoire of complex, intelligent and inspired creations with a noticeable French accent but loyalty to prime Scottish produce. It's food that makes a gentle impact – witness Wishart's signature Orkney scallop and black truffle with Jerusalem artichoke, sweet potato and hazelnut or a fabulous combination of Scottish cod, celeriac, endive and apple with Sauternes and curry sauce. Mellow seasonal flavours are never far away either, from game *tourte* with braised Savoy cabbage, wild mushrooms and truffle jus to Borders roe deer with braised lettuce, carrot, date and BBQ winter onion. And then there are the exquisitely artistic desserts – say Valrhona Dulcey chocolate with caramelised pecans, chocolate sablé and exotic sorbet. But that's not all: from anticipatory amuse-bouches to a cascade of petits fours and dainty homemade chocolates, the kitchen delivers brilliance at every turn, while the superlative modern wine list is a spot-on match for the food. Vintage classics and big hitters sit alongside bottles from lesser-known artisan producers, with prices starting at £26.

Chef/s: Martin Wishart. **Open:** Tue to Sat L 12 to 2, D 7 to 9 (6.30 to 9.30 Fri and Sat). **Closed:** Sun, Mon, 25 and 26 Dec, first 3 weeks Jan, 10 days Jul.

Meals: Set L £29. Set D £70. Tasting menu £75 (6 courses). **Details:** 50 seats. V menu. Wheelchair access. Music.

Rhubarb at Prestonfield

Unrestrained opulence and luxurious food
Cooking score: 4
Modern British | £55
Prestonfield House, Priestfield Road,
Edinburgh, EH16 5UT
Tel no: (0131) 2251333
www.prestonfield.com

With its ravishing gardens, curly gables, baroque extravagance, oil paintings and opulent antiques, this lavishly modernised 17th-century pile is Scotland at its most splendiferous. Palatial Prestonfield now does duty as a boutique hotel for very special occasions, while Regency-style Rhubarb puts on an equally grand show with its gold-trimmed drapes, dusky colour schemes and exotic fabrics. Given the flouncy baronial setting, it's no surprise that the kitchen deals in elaborately worked contemporary food involving native Scottish produce: smoked Tweeddale lamb in a salade niçoise with crispy tongue, red onion and olive confit; Arbroath smokies paired with smoked haddock velouté, amande clams and wild garlic from the garden; flame-grilled loin of roe deer alongside heritage carrots cooked in salt clay, pickled ginger, glazed turnips and sauce poivrade. Rhubarb was famously cultivated at Prestonfield during the 18th century and it regularly crops up among the desserts – perhaps in a crumble with blackcurrant purée, frozen orange yoghurt, tarragon and sauce anglaise. The mighty wine list opens with 14 house selections from £23.
Chef/s: John MacMahon. **Open:** all week L 12 to 2 (3 Sat, 12.30 to 3 Sun), D 6 to 10 (11 Fri and Sat).
Meals: Set L 20 (2 courses) to £25. Set D £35. Sun L £20. **Details:** 120 seats. 40 seats outside. Wheelchair access. Music. Parking. No children after 7pm.

The Scran & Scallie

Messrs Kitchin and Jack's lively dining pub
Cooking score: 3
Modern British | £28
1 Comely Bank Road, Edinburgh, EH4 1DT
Tel no: (0131) 3326281
www.scranandscallie.com

£30

A pub as envisioned through the eyes of a couple of top-flight chefs (Messrs Kitchin and Jack – see entries for The Kitchin and Castle Terrace respectively), Scran & Scallie is not your average boozer. There may well be cask ales on tap – Broken Dial from the Harviestoun Brewery, say – but really and truly it's a dining pub with a designer rustic interior with a Scottish/Scandinavian flavour. Sticking to the 'from nature to plate' philosophy of the founding fathers, the menu impresses with its mix of old (or updated old) and new, so you might start with beef tartare and bone marrow on toast and move on to fish and chips with chunky tartare sauce or Jerusalem artichoke and pearl barley risotto. There's a Robert Burns vibe to the menu with 'Yer Starters' and 'Yer Puddins', with the latter including treacle tart with crème fraîche. The focused wine list has good options by the glass; bottle prices start at £18.50.
Chef/s: James Chapman. **Open:** Mon to Fri L 12 to 3, D 6 to 10. Sat and Sun 12 to 10. **Closed:** 25 Dec.
Meals: alc (main courses £6 to £22). Set L £15 (Mon to Fri). **Details:** 100 seats. Bar. Wheelchair access. Music.

Timberyard

Nordic-inspired food in a rustic setting
Cooking score: 4
Modern British | £43
10 Lady Lawson Street, Edinburgh, EH3 9DS
Tel no: (0131) 2211222
www.timberyard.co

If the term 'family-run restaurant' conjures up images of sedate dining rooms and traditional menus, think again, for the Radford family's Timberyard is anything but. Behind large garage doors lurks an expansive industrial-style space (a one-time wood merchants), which, for some, is somewhat poorly lit at dinner, where the Radfords stick to sustainable and ecological principles to deliver food that is creative and of our times (think Noma). The ingredients lead the way, arriving from local artisan producers, growers and foragers (plus stuff from their own veg patch in the courtyard garden). Choose from 'bite', 'small' or 'large' plates, or dive into the eight-course tasting menu, and expect ingredients such as spelt, curd, whey and scurvy grass (all in the same dish as it happens, with beetroot and kohlrabi). Smoked beef stars in a 'large' plate with an array of veggie textures and flavours, and bass with cockles and clams includes the Jerusalem artichoke-like knotroot. Sweet courses are equally thrilling. The drinks list includes some seriously creative cocktails (check out the Filthy Pig), with wines from £22.

Chef/s: Ben Radford. **Open:** Tue to Sat L 12 to 2, D 5.30 to 9.30. **Closed:** Sun, Mon, 24 to 26 Dec, 1 week Apr, 1 week Oct. **Meals:** alc (main course £21 to £26). Set L and D £23 (2 courses) to £30. Set D £65 (8 courses). **Details:** 72 seats. 30 seats outside. Wheelchair access. Music. Children over 5 yrs only.

21212

Artful, offbeat food in gorgeous town house
Cooking score: 6
Modern French | £42
3 Royal Terrace, Edinburgh, EH7 5AB
Tel no: (0131) 5231030
www.21212restaurant.co.uk

Paul Kitching cannot be accused of going with the flow. Having made his name and reputation in Altrincham, he and his partner (and front-of-house dynamo) Katie O'Brien settled in this gorgeous Georgian town house in Royal Terrace. It makes an engaging restaurant-with-rooms with four luxe modern bedrooms and a swish dining room where Paul lets rip with his brand of dynamic, thrilling and slightly bonkers contemporary cooking. The five-course menu includes a soup and cheese course, and if that makes it

sound dated, it really, really isn't (really). There's bold adventure in the likes of 'summer truffle blanquette' with abalone, gigli and fregola pasta (and more besides), and fun in the naming of 10cc (corn-fed chicken with another nine 'c' ingredients including cashews, chips and curry). Modern cooking techniques and creative presentations make for a memorable experience. Finish with a sweet course such as the wildly creative 'ginger nuts' with its blackberry brûlée and 'crème stem'. The wine list is put together with the same level of passion and intelligence; bottles start at £32.

Chef/s: Paul Kitching. **Open:** Tue to Sat L 12 to 1.45, D 6.45 to 9.30. **Closed:** Sun, Mon. **Meals:** Set L £22 (2 courses) to £53 (5 courses). Set D Tue to Fri £55 (3 courses) to £70 (5 courses). Sat D £70. **Details:** 38 seats.

Valvona & Crolla Caffè Bar

Edinburgh's favourite Italian wine caffè
Cooking score: 3
Italian | £22
19 Elm Row, Edinburgh, EH7 4AA
Tel no: (0131) 5566066
www.valvonacrolla.co.uk

The Caffè arm of Edinburgh's favourite Italian wine merchants – press on towards the back of the deli and wine shop – has been running for nearly 20 years, keeping a loyal constituency of regulars from far and wide well supplied with traditional Italian home-cooking from the regions. Single or sharing platters of antipasti loaded with salumi, bruschetta, mozzarella di bufala and roasted vegetables glistening with oil are the best way to kick things off. Thus appetised, you might proceed to plentiful fritto misto with sharply dressed saladings, a grilled sea bass in lemon butter with griddled fennel and sautéed greens, or a whole roast quail, delicately swaddled in pancetta and served with rosemary potatoes. A slice of Sicilian torta di limone with crème fraîche will just about seal the deal, except that it remains to mention the wines. Pick up a bottle from one of the 800 in the shop, add £8 to the retail price, and you've bought into one of the most authoritative Italian wine listings in the country. Bottles from the digested Caffè listing start at £16.95.

Chef/s: Mary Contini and Pina Trano. **Open:** all week L 11.45 to 5 (Sun 10 to 4.30). **Closed:** 25 and 26 Dec, 1 and 2 Jan. **Meals:** alc (main courses £10 to £17). Set L £16 (2 courses) to £19. Set D £19 (2 courses) to £23. Sun L £19. **Details:** 60 seats. Wheelchair access. Music. Parking.

Victor and Carina Contini Ristorante

Lively all-day Italian eatery
Cooking score: 1
Italian | £35
103 George Street, Edinburgh, EH2 3ES
Tel no: (0131) 2251550
www.contini.com

Formerly Centotre, nothing else has changed, for Victor and Carina Contini continue to court the Edinburgh foodie throngs with an atmosphere of warm informality, suave good looks and menus that allow for nibbling as much as three-coursing it. Pasta is a dependable shout (try orecchiette with fresh Italian piccante sausage, cremini mushrooms, and cream) but the rolling menu takes in everything from mozzarella di bufala and pizza to medium-rare Scottish ribeye. It's a handy spot for breakfast, mid-morning pastries and there's great in-house gelati. Wine is taken seriously, too: the list offers one of the most comprehensive selections of Italian wines in Scotland; bottles from £19.50.

Chef/s: Prisco Ferrigno. **Open:** all week 7.30am to midnight (9am Sat and Sun; 8pm Sun). **Meals:** alc (main courses £14 to £20). Set L £16 (2 courses) to £19. **Details:** 80 seats. 30 seats outside. Wheelchair access. Music.

Average price

The average price denotes the price of a three-course meal without wine.

Tanjore
Indian | £15
6-8 Clerk Street, Edinburgh, EH8 9HX
Tel no: (0131) 4786518
www.tanjore.co.uk

Named after an ancient city in what is now the southern Indian state of Tamil Nadu, the menu at Boon Ganeshram's restaurant has an authenticity that is as refreshing as a mango lassi (which can be yours for £2.70 a glass). Dry-cooked chicken chuka, Chennai fish curry, stuffed baby aubergine and cracking dosa such as a green lentil version show clear spicing and full-on flavours. Veggies fare very well indeed. It's great value and even more so with the BYO policy. Open all week.

▮ Gullane
Chez Roux
Golfing mecca with French food
Cooking score: 4
French | £40
Greywalls Hotel, Muirfield, Gullane, EH31 2EG
Tel no: (01620) 842144
www.greywalls.co.uk

£5 OFF 🛏

Built by Sir Edwin Lutyens in 1901, Greywalls is an impressive country hotel set in extensive gardens (laid out by Gertrude Jekyll), overlooking Muirfield golf course and the Firth of Forth. Furnishings are in keeping with the period and set the tone. Albert Roux's fingerprints may be all over the bilingual menu but the famous Roux style is interpreted on a day-to-day basis by chef Mark Saddler who, since arriving in the summer of 2014, has impressed locals and visitors alike with his cooking. The food is not about surprise or innovation, although there are some fairly modern dishes, but it is about comfort, precision and indulgence: seen in soufflé suissesse, in quenelle de brochet with sauce nantua, or in a dish of roast saddle and slow-cooked leg of hare with Puy lentil purée,

crosnes, baked celeriac and bitter chocolate jus. The wine list leans towards France and is well chosen, with prices from £24.
Chef/s: Mark Saddler. **Open:** all week L 12 to 2, D 6.30 to 10. **Meals:** alc (main courses £16 to £23). Set L £30. Set D £32. Sun L £30. **Details:** 60 seats. 16 seats outside. V menu. Bar. Parking.

La Potinière

A cavalcade of immensely pleasurable food
Cooking score: 6
Modern British | £38
34 Main Street, Gullane, EH31 2AA
Tel no: (01620) 843214
www.lapotiniere.co.uk

'Easily the best restaurant in East Lothian and one of the best in Scotland,' is one reporter's verdict of this 'attractive, airy, colourfully decorated, sunlit restaurant' occupying 'what amounts to the front room of a bungalow'. Chefs Keith Marley and Mary Runciman run the kitchen and front-of-house between them, apparently with no assistance, and diners love everything from the 'gracious, attentive' service to the 'exceptional-value' food. Expect a cavalcade of excellent ingredients from name-checked local suppliers, all cooked with pin-sharp precision. Twice-baked smoked haddock soufflé with smoked haddock and horseradish sauce and tomato compote is a fitting overture to poached and seared Scotch beef fillet with dauphinois potatoes, seasonal vegetables, shallot, bacon and wild mushroom sauce. A warm pear and ginger tart with ginger-scented caramel and chocolate ice cream typifies the kitchen's flair for comforting, intelligent flavour combinations. The international wine list includes plenty by the glass or half-bottle, and opens at £17.
Chef/s: Mary Runciman and Keith Marley. **Open:** Wed to Sun L 12.30 to 1.30, Wed to Sat D 7 to 8.30. **Closed:** Mon, Tue, 3 weeks Jan, 1 week Oct. **Meals:** Set L £20 (2 courses) to £26. Set D £38 (3 courses) to £43. Sun L £26. **Details:** 24 seats. Wheelchair access. Parking.

The diffusion line

Temples of gastronomy might be fabulous, but sometimes something more relaxed, accessible and, yes, cheaper is what's called for. In food as in fashion, many big names have diffusion lines where the high-profile chef is a rare sight but the food upholds their reputation. Here are some of our favourites.

The Star Inn the City: **Andrew Pern**'s York outpost opens at breakfast time and keeps on serving sterling local ingredients, from a pun-rich menu, all day long. The Museum Gardens setting is almost as bewitching as the rural mothership, The Star Inn, in Harome.

Outlaw's Fish Kitchen: **Nathan Outlaw** must be Cornwall's (and London's) busiest restaurateur. In Port Isaac there are two Outlaw options: the flagship, and this cosy, whitewashed bistro with its delectable small plates and harbour views.

The Pompadour by **Galvin**: Casual it ain't, but why should Londoners get all the Galvin? Chris and Jeff's presence in Edinburgh (represented by chef Fraser Allan) is felt in the form of cleverly updated French classics and belle époque luxury.

■ Annbank

Enterkine House

Splendour, charm and sophisticated cooking
Cooking score: 4
Modern European | £38
Enterkine Estate, Annbank, KA6 5AL
Tel no: (01292) 520580
www.enterkine.com

Built in the 1930s for a P&O shipping magnate, this 'very, very fine establishment' sits in 300 acres of grounds with magical views over the River Ayr. The interior radiates baronial splendour, but the pine floors and bare tables of the dining room hint at a more modern style of dining. Paul Moffat's mould-breaking, imaginative dishes combine European influences and Scottish ingredients to stunning effect. A starter of smoked Cheddar soufflé with red pepper and Meaux mustard sauce is 'light and perfect in execution', while an 'excellent' celery root velouté with caramelised walnuts, Arbroath smokie and parsley oil has also garnered praise. Moffat doesn't miss a beat with subsequent courses, either: perhaps a fillet of Orkney Gold beef with haggis, Jerusalem artichoke, spinach and winter chanterelles, and then a bold and vibrant dessert of tonka bean pavé with passion fruit cream and Grand Marnier ice cream. The service is 'impeccable – friendly and efficient'. A respectable selection of international wines opens at £21.95.

Chef/s: Paul Moffat. **Open:** all week L 12 to 2, D 6.30 to 9.30. **Meals:** alc (main courses £15 to £25). Set L £17 (2 courses) to £19. Set D £25 (2 courses) to £38. Sun L £19. **Details:** 40 seats. 20 seats outside.

Symbols

Accommodation is available
£30 Three courses for less than £30
£5 OFF £5-off voucher scheme
Notable wine list

■ Ballantrae
Glenapp Castle

Formidable cooking at a top-notch hotel
Cooking score: 6
Modern British | £65
Ballantrae, KA26 0NZ
Tel no: (01465) 831212
www.glenappcastle.com

Now here's a place to play the Scottish laird: through the discreet, buzzer-entry gate, a winding drive climbs through carefully tended woodland. A sudden twist of the road and the castle appears, a feast of turrets and battlements in soft grey stone. Everything here is on a grand scale, from the formal but friendly welcome to the polished antiques, capacious sofas and sumptuous hallways of the interior. It takes something special to live up to all this endearing pomp, but chef Tyron Ellul is bedding in nicely, producing 'excellent cooking with wonderful presentation'. A seven-course dinner might open with sweetcorn velouté with pancetta and ras el hanout dressing, and then supreme of wood pigeon with its confit leg and roast potatoes. Local ingredients take centre stage in roast cauliflower and Isle of Mull Cheddar risotto with smoked haddock, and in pan-roasted fillet of aged Scotch beef with garden rosemary potato gratin. Wind down with hazelnut pannacotta with a hazelnut financier, and then coffee with petits fours. A lengthy international selection of wines, including a fair number of half-bottles, opens at £34.
Chef/s: Tyron Ellul. **Open:** all week L 12.30 to 2, D 6.30 to 9.30. **Closed:** 22 to 27 Dec, 3 Jan, late Mar. **Meals:** Set L £40. Set D £65. Sun L £30. **Details:** 40 seats. V menu. Wheelchair access. Parking. Children over 3 yrs only.

Average price

The average price denotes the price of a three-course meal without wine.

■ Carradale
Dunvalanree

Enchanting views and a local flavour
Cooking score: 2
Modern British | £29
Port Righ, Carradale, PA28 6SE
Tel no: (01583) 431226
www.dunvalanree.com

The view across Kilbrannan Sound to the Isle of Arran is reward enough for undertaking the journey to Dunvalanree on the wild and peaceful eastern side of Kintyre. But there's a 'real treat' in store when it comes to the more sybaritic opportunities here, too, for Alan and Alyson Milstead's restaurant-with-rooms is a wee oasis. She's the hand at the stove, and her focus is very much on the bounty from hereabouts, delivered via a table d'hôte menu that is sensibly concise and 'the most incredible value'. Settle down in the smart dining room and tuck into seared Kilbrannan scallops with roasted fennel and balsamic reduction, and move on to fillet of sole stuffed with prawns and wrapped in pancetta, or honey-roast duck breast with rhubarb compote and orange sauce. It's simple and honest stuff. Finish with a crème brûlée made from their own eggs. Wines start at £17.
Chef/s: Alyson Milstead. **Open:** all week D only 7.30 (1 sitting). **Closed:** Christmas. **Meals:** Set D £25 (2 courses) to £29. **Details:** 24 seats. V menu. Music.

■ Dalry
Braidwoods

Long-standing consistency
Cooking score: 5
Modern British | £46
Drumastle Mill Cottage, Dalry, KA24 4LN
Tel no: (01294) 833544
www.braidwoods.co.uk

Following the country lane to the converted whitewashed cottages that have been home to Keith and Nicola Braidwood's restaurant for over 20 years feels like stepping into a simpler world. The two small rooms hold just half a dozen tables and the concise daily changing menu allows dishes to reflect that day's produce, weather or mood. This is all about quality ingredients and classic delivery, not fancy tricks or techniques. A starter of confit canard is deboned and its richness offset with pomegranate and watermelon, while a wobbling custardy Parmesan tart demonstrates a deft touch with pastry. Main courses such as pink-roasted quail breasts with slow-cooked leg and Jerusalem artichoke purée demonstrate that careful preparation and attention to detail can coax out real complexity of flavour. Desserts again reflect seasonality and locality – with the tayberry coulis and raspberry jellies accompanying a pecan parfait evoking late summer fruit-picking excursions. A focused wine list starts at £23.95.

Chef/s: Keith Braidwood. **Open:** Wed to Sun L 12 to 1.30, Tue to Sat D 7 to 9. **Closed:** Mon, 25 Dec to 25 Jan, first 2 weeks Sept. **Meals:** Set L £26 (2 courses) to £29. Set D £46 (3 courses) to £50. Sun L £32. **Details:** 24 seats. V menu. Parking. Children over 5 yrs only at L and 12 yrs only at D.

◼ Glasgow
Brian Maule at Chardon d'Or

Scottish ingredients with a Gallic touch
Cooking score: 5
French | £50
176 West Regent Street, Glasgow, G2 4RL
Tel no: (0141) 2483801
www.brianmaule.com

Ornate white plaster cornicing and starched linen bring to mind a traditionally iced wedding cake; intricate and rich with a touch of occasion. 'Chardon d'Or' is French for 'golden thistle' and the cooking reflects that 'auld alliance' between Scotland and France. Elegant yes, but it remains familiar and friendly. A clever amuse-bouche of beef croustillant is carefully presented with 'personal compliments from Brian'. Combinations are thoughtful and their

delivery assured. A perfectly set goats' cheese pannacotta with beetroot variations and almonds balances sweetness, acidity and texture. Main courses showcase their key ingredient, so grilled sea bream is simply presented alongside an indulgent ingot of truffled polenta, seasonal asparagus tips and a fragrant chicken jus. Desserts are light touch, and an iced coconut parfait with mango and basil refreshes the palate while still delivering a certain indulgence. The accessible wine list showcases the classics but also reflects seasonal variety and starts at a very reasonable £19.75 a bottle.

Chef/s: Brian Maule. **Open:** Mon to Sat L 12 to 2.30, D 5 to 9. **Closed:** Sun. **Meals:** alc (main courses £26 to £29). Set L and early D £21 (2 courses) to £24. **Details:** 140 seats. V menu.

Cail Bruich

Fine dining, delivered affordably
Cooking score: 4
Modern British | £36
725 Great Western Road, Glasgow, G12 8QX
Tel no: (0141) 3346265
www.cailbruich.co.uk

Recent investment has opened up this well-established family operation near the Botanic Gardens on the Great Western Road to allow the engaging front-of-house team to broker a closer relationship between kitchen and diners. The enhanced surroundings have inspired chef/patron Chris Charalambous to build creatively on his already sound technical competence 'mixing flavours and textures to awaken taste-buds you didn't know existed'. Local sourcing is showcased through a 'straight-talking' menu that demonstrates both integrity and depth. A deceptively simple starter of crisp spring vegetables with cèpe and hazelnut is a sensory work of art – its airy delicacy contrasting the earthy nuttiness. Dornoch lamb, rare and tender, is served with fresh goats' curd, milky sweetbread and char-grilled lettuce, epitomising spring on a plate. A la carte and table d'hôte offerings are

Join us at thegoodfoodguide.co.uk

supplemented by a bargain six-course tasting menu with the vegetarian version proving equally interesting. House wines start at £18. **Chef/s:** Chris Charalambous. **Open:** Tue to Sun L 12 to 2.30 (12.30 to 3 Sun), all week D 5.30 to 9.30 (10 Sat, 8 Sun). **Closed:** 26 and 27 Dec, 1 and 2 Jan. **Meals:** alc (main courses £18 to 24). Set L £16 (2 courses) to £21. Set D £19 (2 courses) to £25. Tasting menu £49. **Details:** 48 seats. V menu. Music. Children before 8pm only.

Crabshakk

Cracking shellfish spot
Cooking score: 3
Seafood | £44
1114 Argyle Street, Glasgow, G3 8TD
Tel no: (0141) 3346127
www.crabshakk.com

Tuck your elbows in, order wisely and hope for the space to operate a seafood pick; Crabshakk is small and popular. But the close quarters mean there's no lack of atmosphere at this Finnieston pioneer, which runs a twice-daily changing specials board in conjunction with a seafood-powered menu (the non-fish options are rump and chips or risotto). The house bisque, seared scallops with anchovies or tempura squid with soy and coriander dipping sauce could be followed by a full or 'wee' fish supper, lobster cold or grilled, or a big plate of crab cakes. Add bread and butter, garlic or lemon mayo, chips or a green salad as you wish; the no-frills menu may put you in mind of a piscine St John (see entry, London). Desserts are available, but not the point. Crabshakk's Table 11 oyster bar is down the street (at no 1132), providing a wraparound sherry and shellfish experience. Wines are from £19.95.
Chef/s: David Scott. **Open:** Tue to Sun 12 to 12. **Closed:** Mon. **Meals:** alc (main courses £9 to £27). **Details:** 53 seats. 6 seats outside. Wheelchair access. Music.

Gamba

Unashamedly pescetarian
Cooking score: 3
Seafood | £38
225a West George Street, Glasgow, G2 2ND
Tel no: (0141) 5720899
www.gamba.co.uk
£5
OFF

Stepping down from pavement level past fishy murals and twinkling lights feels like diving under the sea, and the surprisingly airy basement delivers calm isolation from the city's bustle. The décor juxtaposes neutral tones with splashes of turquoise, jade and silver, like mackerel in the wake of a boat, but then chef/patron Derek Marshall's culinary passion is all about fish. Dishes are not over-fussy: the signature soup is generous on gingered crab with tiny prawn dumplings; pearlescent Gigha halibut with creamed leeks, mussels and a briny hit of pancetta is instant comfort; while chunky roast Shetland cod mixes it up with a well-judged lentil banana curry. Scotland's freshest seafood, sustainably sourced and simply showcased, has drawn well-heeled couples, work colleagues and other 'a-fish-ionados' to Gamba for 17 years. There are meat and vegetarian choices for landlubbers. Desserts such as warm cherry and coconut Bakewell tart ensure a homely finish.
Chef/s: Derek Marshall. **Open:** Mon to Sat L 12 to 2.30, all week D 5 to 10 (9 Sun). **Closed:** first week Jan. **Meals:** alc (main courses £12 to £32). Set L and D £19 (2 courses) to £22. **Details:** 60 seats. Bar. Music.

Stravaigin

Scottish ingredients, global flavours
Cooking score: 2
Global | £35
28 Gibson Street, Glasgow, G12 8NX
Tel no: (0141) 3342665
www.stravaigin.co.uk
£5
OFF

The name translates roughly as 'wandering about', and this Glasgow renegade has been on the food trail since 1994, filling its backpack

with wild ideas and exotic tit-bits. Stravaigin's mantra ('think global, eat local') may have been hijacked along the way, but the kitchen stays true to its principles, buying prime seasonal ingredients from trusted Scottish producers and transforming them into a compendium of vivid dishes ablaze with colour and intensity. The challenges come thick and fast and the menu pays no heed to national borders or traditions: masala chicken livers are paired with chickpea and coriander polenta, neep relish and tamarind chutney, while slow-cooked lamb shoulder keeps company with pistachio, apricot and freekeh salad, baba ganoush, spinach labneh and wilted lettuce – you get the picture. Sides of black-salt potatoes dusted with amchur (dried mango powder) tell a similar story, then it's back on the road for coconut bread-and-butter pudding with passion fruit ice cream. Wines (from £18.75) are an eclectic bunch, too.
Chef/s: Kenny Mackay. **Open:** all week 9am to 11pm (11am Sat and Sun). **Closed:** 25 Dec, 1 Jan. **Meals:** alc (main courses £13 to £24). **Details:** 62 seats. Bar. Music.

Ubiquitous Chip

Glasgow icon
Cooking score: 4
Modern British | £40
12 Ashton Lane, Glasgow, G12 8SJ
Tel no: (0141) 3345007
www.ubiquitouschip.co.uk

It's more than 40 years since the Ubiquitous Chip made its home in Glasgow's bohemian West End. And while nowadays patriotic flavours are no longer rare on Scottish menus, the Chip remains a top choice for favourites such as homemade haggis with champit tatties, carrot crisp and neep cream, which has been on the menu since 1971. A versatile space set around a Victorian mews and glass-roofed courtyard, it includes a popular bar, and brasserie or restaurant dining. You'll find a profusion of wild things on the menu, from seared Islay scallops with pumpkin fondant,

malt crumble and seaweed butter to Galloway roe deer haunch with char-grilled celeriac, hazelnut spelt, beetroot and mushrooms. For dessert, the hazelnut and olive oil cake with hazelnut brittle and strawberry ice cream comes highly recommended. The Chip is rightly renowned for its wine list, which covers France in detail then strikes out to places as diverse as Argentina, Lebanon and Turkey. Bottles start at £18.95.
Chef/s: Andrew Mitchell. **Open:** all week 11 to 11. **Closed:** 25 Dec, 1 Jan. **Meals:** alc (main courses £16 to £35). Set L and early D £16 (2 courses) to £20. Sun L £20. **Details:** 100 seats. V menu. Bar. Wheelchair access. Music.

LOCAL GEM
Number 16

Modern British | £30
16 Byres Road, Glasgow, G11 5JY
Tel no: (0141) 3392544
www.number16.co.uk

Number 16's confident blending of Scottish ingredients with Asian and Mediterranean influences has generated an enthusiastic local following. The split-level mid-terrace restaurant is small and closely seated but broader ambitions characterise its tiny kitchen. An earthy beetroot and truffled leek tartlet, lifted by salty/sweet crumbled feta and pecan brittle, works well ahead of slow-cooked pork belly with creamy korma, onion bhaji and pickles that nods cheekily towards Glasgow's love of Indian food.

■ Isle of Colonsay

LOCAL GEM
The Colonsay

Modern British | £28
Scalasaig, Isle of Colonsay, PA61 7YT
Tel no: (01951) 200316
www.colonsayestate.co.uk

Teeming with wildlife, littered with archaeological remains and blessed with glorious sandy beaches, the Isle of Colonsay is also home to this reinvigorated Georgian inn – a godsend for visitors and islanders alike. Locally brewed beer and bar lunches do their job, while dinner is a no-frills showcase for home-grown and island produce – think Cullen skink, seared scallops with leek and celeriac purée or confit Colonsay lamb with green beans, tapenade, mushroom and tarragon sauce. To finish, Scottish cheeses and homemade honey ice cream are standouts. Wines from £12.50. Closed Nov to Mar.

▌Isle of Eriska

Isle of Eriska
Secluded island hideaway
Cooking score: 5
British | £55
Benderloch, Isle of Eriska, PA37 1SD
Tel no: (01631) 720371
www.eriska-hotel.co.uk

Just ten miles north of Oban, a short bridge and apparent time zone separate the mainland and the private Isle of Eriska. Rampant rhododendrons and striking Scottish baronial architecture provide a dramatic backdrop for the ambitious cooking of Ross Stovold. Despite the secluded location fostering a sense of other-worldliness, the set four-course dinner menu (24 hours' notice for non-residents) is grounded firmly in the local and the seasonal. Oysters and salmon come from Loch Creran, which laps the island's shores, and foraged fruits are transformed into chutneys and jellies. A cauliflower, blood sausage and lobster starter is a rich velouté revealing hidden treasure of sweet lobster and earthy black pudding. Sweet Mallaig turbot, crisp on the outside and flaking perfectly, is offset by a well-balanced onion and pine vinegar sauce. If the chocolate caramel parfait with clotted cream ice cream proves too rich then a justifiably reputed alternative is the Celtic cheeseboard with around 40 UK farmhouse cheeses and its own specialist fromagier to guide selection. The extensive wine list reflects the distinctive personal recommendations and interests of both owner and sommelier and suits a wide range of tastes and budgets with house wine starting at £20. **Chef/s:** Ross Stovold. **Open:** all week D only 7.30 to 9. **Closed:** Jan. **Meals:** Set D £55 (4 courses). Tasting menu £85. **Details:** 50 seats. Wheelchair access. Parking.

▌Isle of Mull
Café Fish
Ozone-fresh Scottish seafood
Cooking score: 3
Seafood | £30
The Pier, Main Street, Tobermory, Isle of Mull, PA75 6NU
Tel no: (01688) 301253
www.thecafefish.com

'The only things frozen are our fishermen,' says a note on the menu at fiercely independent Café Fish – a no-frills eatery perched on the top floor of the old CalMac ferry building overlooking Tobermory harbour. Daily supplies of seafood from the owners' boat dictate what's on the regularly updated menu, a sprightly line-up that bristles with clear ozone-fresh flavours. Keep it simple with a 'wee' bowl of moules marinière or a plate of cracked Mull crab claws with yuzu mayo; otherwise, splash out on a mighty roast shellfish platter or something more exotic – perhaps Tuscan seafood stew with gremolata or seared scallops with Malaysian coconut and turmeric laksa. Traditionalists can have their fish grilled (haddock, sea bass, hake etc.), while those who fancy swimming against the tide might plump for a Glenorm ribeye steak, Lebanese-style chicken or dengaku nasu (miso-glazed aubergine, mushroom and haloumi with wasabi-dressed salad and crispy noodles). After that, Pavlova and warm Belgian waffles await. Wines from £16.50. **Chef/s:** Liz McGougan. **Open:** all week L 12 to 3, D 5.30 to 10. **Closed:** Nov to Mar. **Meals:** alc (main courses £15 to £30). **Details:** 32 seats. 60 seats outside. Music. No children under 3 yrs at D.

Ninth Wave

Fine cooking in a converted bothy
Cooking score: 4
Modern British | £46
Bruach Mhor, Fionnphort, Isle of Mull, PA66 6BL
Tel no: (01681) 700757
www.ninthwaverestaurant.co.uk

The name references obscure Celtic mythology, but there's nothing otherworldly about John and Carla Lamont's lovingly converted, off-the-beaten-track granite bothy. They are fully grounded when it comes to procuring ingredients, growing much of their own produce on a seven-acre croft or buying from island producers; John also fishes for lobsters and crabs. Carla is an extraordinary talent, her dinner menu designed to show off daring combinations, such as her crab and smoked cheddar cheesecake ('more like a soufflé, hot and airy'), on a fine biscuit base and accompanied by a succulent fresh crab claw. Or there could be fillet of Mull codling with caper and duck egg salsa verde, steamed langoustine and garden nasturtium butter or a surprising Middle Eastern dish of roast quail marinated in Persian pomegranate alongside 'jewelled' blueberry rice, candied walnuts and spinach 'booraniyeh' (a yoghurt dip). After that, try a scoop or two of Carla's sweet woodruff and toasted pecan ice cream. Wines from £16.75.
Chef/s: Carla Lamont. **Open:** Wed to Sun D only 7 to 11. **Closed:** Mon, Tue, Nov to mid Apr. **Meals:** Set D £46 to £64 (5 courses). **Details:** 18 seats. V menu. Wheelchair access. Parking. Children over 12 yrs only.

Symbols

 Accommodation is available
 Three courses for less than £30
£5 OFF £5-off voucher scheme
Notable wine list

■ Kilberry
The Kilberry Inn

Seafood-led cooking on a remote peninsula
Cooking score: 3
Modern British | £35
Kilberry Road, Kilberry, PA29 6YD
Tel no: (01880) 770223
www.kilberryinn.com

Out on an Argyll peninsula, 16 miles along a one-track road with otters and seals frolicking on the beaches, the Kilberry is a single-storeyed whitewashed inn with a corrugated roof of red tin and roses growing out front. Exposed stone walls inside make a rustic setting for Clare Johnson's seafood-led menus. The house version of Provençal fish soup with rouille and croûtons is a reliable standby, or you could start with squid braised in red wine with chilli, fennel and orange, served with fennel and dill flatbread. Then may come majestic roasted monkfish from Jura, with tomatoes, chickpeas, chorizo and spinach, or perhaps a ribeye steak in Café de Paris butter. The deal closes with nutty Amaretto cake and malted chocolate ice cream. Wines start at £18.
Chef/s: Clare Johnson. **Open:** Thur to Sun L 12 to 2, Tue to Sun D 6.30 to 10. **Closed:** Mon, 1 Jan to mid Mar. **Meals:** alc (main courses £15 to £22).
Details: 30 seats. 10 seats outside. Wheelchair access. Music. Parking.

■ Loch Lomond
Martin Wishart at Loch Lomond

A Scottish maestro's country retreat
Cooking score: 6
Modern French | £75
Loch Lomond, G83 8QZ
Tel no: (01389) 722504
www.martinwishartlochlomond.co.uk

A grand lochside baronial mansion is the stately country retreat of one of Scotland's highest-flying chefs, and a neat counterpoint to the comparatively compact headquarters in Leith (see Restaurant Martin Wishart, Edinburgh). Here, Graeme Cheevers produces a beautifully balanced menu that's well pitched to its audience, with absolute consistency in presentation, attention to detail and exactitude, some of the dishes having been adapted for the journey from city to countryside. Taster menus of six and eight courses supplement the abbreviated carte, which might offer roast quail in mushroom bouillon with sweetcorn purée, wild mushroom tortellini and foie gras, followed by Scrabster turbot fillet in a seafood medley with squid, oyster and baby leeks. Otherwise, expect the unexpected, as for langoustine with ricotta gnudi in lemon verbena, or else luxuriously redefined classicism, as in veal sweetbread with caramelised onion and a mousseline of Yukon Gold potato and Comté, or the finale of dark Valrhona soufflé with pistachio ice cream. A broadly based wine list opens at £27 for a Mendoza Viognier.

Chef/s: Graeme Cheevers. **Open:** Sat and Sun L 12 to 2.30, Wed to Sun D 6.30 to 10 (7 Sun). **Closed:** Mon, Tue, first 2 weeks Jan. **Meals:** Set L £29 (2 courses). Set D £65 (2 courses) to £75. Sun L £29. Tasting menu £75 (6 courses) to £95. **Details:** 45 seats. V menu. Bar. Wheelchair access. Music. Parking.

▊ Oban

Waterfront Fishouse

Minimal frills, super-fresh seafood
Cooking score: 1
Seafood | £22
1 Railway Pier, Oban, PA34 4LW
Tel no: (01631) 563110
www.waterfrontoban.co.uk

Recently refurbished and relaunched following storm damage during winter 2014, this versatile restaurant on the first floor of an old fishermen's mission is still in the business of dispensing wholesome nourishment – although its target audience is very different. Chef/proprietor Alex Needham buys his fish from the Oban boats, but leavens his seasonal menus with vivid, exotic flavours – from scallop and black pudding salad with saffron and lime dressing to lobster ravioli or cod with giant couscous, chorizo and sweet potato. Bivalves from the nearby Caledonian Oyster Co are a speciality, and there are a few meaty items too – char-grilled pork T-bone with Dijon mustard sauce, say. Wines from £14.99.

Chef/s: Alex Needham. **Open:** all week L 12 to 2, D 5.30 to 9.30. **Closed:** 25 Dec. **Meals:** alc (main courses £10 to £22). Set L and D £13 (2 courses) to £16. **Details:** 75 seats. Bar. Music.

LOCAL GEM

Ee-Usk

Seafood | £32
North Pier, Oban, PA34 5QD
Tel no: (01631) 565666
www.eeusk.com

On the pier at Oban, Ee-Usk is a glassy modern construction with a prized view over the water. Given the proximity to the source material, it is not surprising that seafood is the order of the day, served up in a bright, contemporary room without undue fuss. Whole dressed crab is a winner, or start with salmon mousse served with toast, and move on to langoustines and lobster with a choice of accompanying sauces. Haddock and chips, seafood pasta and Thai fishcakes play their part, too. Wines start at £17. Open all week.

■ Balquhidder
Monachyle Mhor

Family enterprise with a foodie heart
Cooking score: 5
Modern British | £57
Balquhidder, FK19 8PQ
Tel no: (01877) 384622
www.mhor.net

Follow the narrow winding track that snakes along the shores of Loch Voil to reach remote Monachyle Mhor – a pink-washed Trossachs farmhouse that is also the beating heart of the Lewis family's foodie portfolio. 'Farm to table' is the ethos, and everything is grounded in the local landscape: the owners maintain a smallholding, rear their own livestock, bake bread, go foraging and do just about everything in the name of good food. Light lunches are a warm-up, but chef/patron Tom Lewis saves his best endeavours for dinner, when fixed-price menus show off his artistry and 'immense respect for ingredients'. Clear, natural flavours shine through across the board, from plates of Perthshire Blackface lamb with Colleen potatoes, navets and gribiche dressing or home-reared Tamworth pork with smoked pancetta cassoulet and curly kale, to Gigha halibut with a bone-marrow bonbon, celeriac and Savoy cabbage. To finish, pickings from the garden make a seasonal impact in desserts ranging from rhubarb bavarois to sage pannacotta with macerated blueberries. Gold-standard vintages, 'oddballs' and quirky regional varietals pepper the authoritative but highly distinctive wine list; prices start at £22.

Chef/s: Tom Lewis and Marysia Paszkowska. **Open:** all week L 12 to 1.45, D 7 to 8.45. **Meals:** Set L £24 (2 courses) to £30. Set D £57. Sun L £30. **Details:** 34 seats. 10 seats outside. V menu. Music. Parking.

Average price

The average price denotes the price of a three-course meal without wine.

Join us at thegoodfoodguide.co.uk

▌**Strathyre**
Creagan House
Delightful farmhouse with standout food
Cooking score: 4
Modern European | £38
Strathyre, FK18 8ND
Tel no: (01877) 384638
www.creaganhouse.co.uk

Visitors looking for a dreamy Highland location with strong Rob Roy connections often beat a retreat to this lovingly maintained 17th-century farmhouse, not far from Loch Lomond and the Trossachs National Park. Since arriving in 1986, Gordon and Cherry Gunn have turned Creagan House into an immensely pleasurable haven complete with a lavish baronial dining room – medieval tapestries, stone fireplaces, vaulted ceilings and all. However, the cooking is a world away from conservative country-house clichés as Gordon adds some haute French finery and European accessories to carefully sourced Scottish produce. Pancetta-wrapped monkfish is served with lentils, breast of local grouse appears on celeriac fondant with a worcesterberry, beetroot and heather-honey sauce, while Gigha halibut is partnered by a 'double-dived' Sligachan scallop, sultana ragoût and coral sauce. Others will appreciate aged Aberdeen Angus steaks 'served in your favourite way', as well as fine Scottish cheeses and desserts such as Edinburgh tart with Drambuie ice cream. Cherry Gunn's expertly curated wine list opens with house selections from £20.65.

Chef/s: Gordon Gunn. **Open:** Fri to Tue D only 7.15 for 8 (1 sitting). **Closed:** Wed, Thur, 1 Jan to 17 Mar, 26 Oct to 31 Dec. **Meals:** Set D £38. **Details:** 14 seats. Bar. Wheelchair access. Parking. Children over 10 yrs only.

Tyron Ellul
Glenapp Castle, Ballantrae

What do you enjoy the most about being a chef?
I really enjoy the fact that you can be creative and that gives me great job satisfaction.

What inspired you to become a chef?
I was always curious and interested in knowing how food is produced, then I joined catering college which is where it all began for me.

What is your favourite time of year for food?
I like autumn for the game birds and wild mushrooms.

At the end of a long day, what do you like to cook?
It's not very often that I want to cook when I get home, but when I do, it's usually something quick and easy like an oven-ready pizza or a ham and cheese toastie.

What food could you not live without?
Cheese and biscuits, I could live on them alone!

Is there a particular dish that evokes strong memories for you?
My mum's chicken broth, it brings back memories of my childhood back home.

∎ Anstruther
The Cellar
Fresh flavours and technical precision
Cooking score: 6
Modern British | £42
Anstruther, KY10 3AA
Tel no: (01333) 310378
www.thecellaranstruther.co.uk

'It feels like a well-kept secret,' remarked a visitor to this long-standing restaurant located behind the Fisheries Museum and reached 'via a hidden alley and courtyard'. Once found, it's a charming place, a 17th-century former smokery and cooperage with rough stone walls, low beams, candles and wood-burning stoves, now in the capable hands of local lad Billy Boyter – his first solo venture after seven years at Edinburgh's Number One (see entry). His set-price menu may be concise – only three choices per course – but it's highly enticing. The food's simple and direct appeal is a product of good raw materials and intelligent handling – for example, in a loin of lamb with shallot purée and roasted turnips – and its hallmark is clear flavours. Elsewhere, hake with cockles, curried couscous and red pepper has been praised, as have first courses of crab with salt-baked celeriac, almond and olive, and scallops with chorizo, pickled apple and hazelnut. Desserts are on a par, judging by a crème fraîche custard tart with green apple sorbet. Wines from £16.
Chef/s: Billy Boyter. **Open:** Thur to Sun L 12.30 to 1.45, Wed to Sun D 6 to 9. **Closed:** Mon, Tue, 24 to 26 Dec, 1 and 2 Jan, 1 week Mar, 1 week Oct.
Meals: Set L £24 (3 courses). Set D £42 (3 courses).
Details: 28 seats. Bar. Music.

LOCAL GEM
Anstruther Fish Bar
Seafood | £15
42-44 Shore Street, Anstruther, KY10 3AQ
Tel no: (01333) 310518
www.anstrutherfishbar.co.uk

This spruce fish and chip restaurant overlooks the harbour, where the fishermen land lobsters and crabs. The owners clearly take real pride in their business, for they have been here for more than a dozen years. The obvious choice is cooked-to-order haddock either crisp-battered or bread-crumbed, but there's also lemon sole or dressed local crab (in season) and lovely homemade ice cream for afters. If you want the fish, but not the full monty in the restaurant, a takeaway from the fryer should do the trick. Wine is £9. Open all week.

∎ Cupar
Ostlers Close
Gently persuasive cooking from a local hero
Cooking score: 5
Modern British | £42
25 Bonnygate, Cupar, KY15 4BU
Tel no: (01334) 655574
www.ostlersclose.co.uk

Resilient local heroes Jimmy and Amanda Graham are well into their fourth decade at Ostlers Close – a cottagey eatery housed in what was once the scullery of a temperance hotel. These days, an air of thoughtful dedication and domesticity wafts through the place with its country-pine furniture, freshly picked flowers and handwritten menus. Amanda is always welcoming and 'full of cheer' out front, while Jimmy is a highly talented chef who knows how to tease out the best from scrupulously sourced ingredients. He buys directly from local producers, plunders Fife farmers' market, forages for wild mushrooms and also maintains a thriving vegetable garden (complete with weather-resistant polytunnels). Everything comes together on a short daily menu full of gently persuasive dishes – perhaps fillet of wild turbot with Pardina lentils and crispy Serrano ham or a warming wintry salvo of roast duck breast with potato and confit duck terrine, roast sweet potatoes and seasonal greens. To conclude, toasted oat meringues might be enlivened with salted-caramel ice cream, caramelised bananas and raspberry sauce. The highly personal wine list promises fascinating drinking from around £20.

Chef/s: Jimmy Graham. **Open:** Tue to Sat D only 7 to 9.30. **Closed:** Sun, Mon, 25 and 26 Dec, 1 and 2 Jan. **Meals:** alc (main courses £23 to £26). **Details:** 26 seats. Children over 6 yrs only.

▌Elie
Sangster's
Modern Scottish village bistro cooking
Cooking score: 4
Modern British | £40
51 High Street, Elie, KY9 1BZ
Tel no: (01333) 331001
www.sangsters.co.uk

Bruce and Jackie Sangster's village restaurant stands proud on the high street, a welcome redoubt in a tight-knit community. It feels smart but comfortably domestic inside, with framed seascapes on the white walls and tables dressed in their best. Bruce cooks what could be characterised as modern Scottish bistro food, full of rewarding flavours and a gentle tendency to richness, but maintaining an essential appealing simplicity. Seared scallops with tomato and chilli jam, or open ravioli of pigeon and mushroom ragoût in Marsala are the openers to fortifying main dishes built around substantial offerings of protein in alcohol-fuelled sauces: fillet and cheek of beef in red wine, breast and thigh of guinea fowl with cabbage and pancetta in port, or seared hake with spinach-topped potato gratin. Finish with luxurious dark chocolate pavé with white chocolate ice cream and vanilla sauce. A painstakingly annotated wine list opens at £21.50, or £6.50 a glass.

Chef/s: Bruce Sangster. **Open:** Sun L 12.30 to 1.30, Tue to Sat D 7 to 8.30. **Closed:** Mon, Jan, first week of November. **Meals:** Set D £34 (2 courses) to £48. Sun L £29.50. **Details:** 28 seats. Children over 12 yrs only.

Scotland on a budget

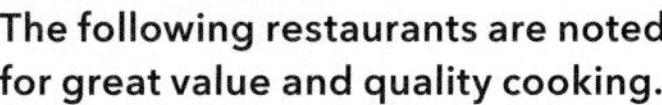

The following restaurants are noted for great value and quality cooking.

Anstruther Fish Bar, Anstruther
Spruce fish-and-chip restaurant overlooking the harbour; the long-standing owners take real pride in their business.

Creelers of Skye, Isle of Skye
Long-honoured for a robust delivery of Skye's seafood catch in a paper-tablecloth caff setting.

Mountain Café, Aviemore
Simple café with views over the Cairngorms and few pretensions beyond providing substantial, homely, well-cooked dishes.

The Creel, Dunbar
A modest eatery near Dunbar's harbour and castle ruins with plenty of fresh seafood on the menu.

Tanjore, Edinburgh
With an authenticity that is as refreshing as a mango lassi, this southern Indian restaurant is great value – even more so with the BYO policy.

▮ North Queensferry
The Wee Restaurant
A diamond under the Forth Bridge
Cooking score: 3
Modern European | £36
17 Main Street, North Queensferry, KY11 1JG
Tel no: (01383) 616263
www.theweerestaurant.co.uk

If you want to see the Forth Bridge up close, head for North Queensferry. If you want a good dinner, head round the corner for Craig and Vikki Wood's Wee Restaurant. Not all that wee as it turns out, with nigh on 40 covers over two levels, but the simple whitewashed walls, woven willow lamps and a splash of original art make for an attractive local restaurant. Begin with Anstruther hot-smoked salmon served with a dill, honey and mustard dressing or a salad of crisp baked artichokes. The excellent mussels, bacon, basil, pine nuts and Parmesan cream is so popular it pops up on the mains as well, along with smoked haddock, poached egg and mustard beurre blanc and a tender rabbit confit with tagliatelle, peas, pancetta and truffle velouté. Steak comes with gratin dauphinois and sea bass with creamed leeks, all of which points to a near surfeit of richness. Wines start at £17.50 with half a dozen by the glass.
Chef/s: Craig Wood. **Open:** Tue to Sun L 12 to 2, D 6.30 to 9. **Closed:** Mon, 25 and 26 Dec. **Meals:** Set L £18 (2 courses) to £22. Set D £29 (2 courses) to £36. **Details:** 40 seats. Music.

Please send us your feedback

To register your opinion about any restaurant listed in this guide, or a new restaurant that you wish to bring to our attention, please visit the web address at the bottom of the page. Your feedback informs the content of the book and will be used to compile next year's reviews.

▮ Peat Inn
★ TOP 50 ★
The Peat Inn
Blue-chip dining destination
Cooking score: 7
Modern European | £55
Peat Inn, KY15 5LH
Tel no: (01334) 840206
www.thepeatinn.co.uk

'This restaurant goes from strength to strength', was one seasoned reporter's verdict on the Smeddles' elegant 18th-century coaching inn. It's been a beacon of Scottish haute cuisine for a decade, run with a consummate professionalism often praised by readers. Now a highly civilised restaurant-with-rooms, the Peat Inn is soothing on the eye and ear – the fire-warmed sitting room and three interlinked dining rooms are gently lit and softly furnished. However, it's the food that really lifts the senses, and Geoffrey Smeddle knows how to impress without resorting to gimmicks. His focus is rather more French than British, although the boundaries are increasingly fluid. Skilled craftsmanship and intense flavours are a given, ranging from a 'beautifully presented' St Andrews Bay lobster with a light seaweed butter sauce to Scottish grouse, served with cocotte potatoes, Savoy cabbage and bacon, damson compote and Madeira jus that was proclaimed 'the best I have ever tasted'. 'Beautifully tender' wild Cairngorm venison also has its say, the accompanying truffled potato beignets, crushed root vegetables, Puy lentils, celeriac and walnut purée and juniper sauce 'very effectively adding to the overall flavours and creativity of the dish'. As for dessert, dark Amedei chocolate ganache, coconut ice cream, chocolate and coconut streusel and salted-caramel sauce is clever and innovative. Service is beyond reproach, particularly when demystifying the astutely assembled wine list that spreads itself geographically as well as economically. Prices start at £19.

Join us at thegoodfoodguide.co.uk

Chef/s: Geoffrey Smeddle. **Open:** Tue to Sat L 12.15 to 1.45, D 6.30 to 9.30. **Closed:** Sun, Mon, 24 to 26 Dec, first week Jan. **Meals:** alc (main courses L £15 to £18, D £22 to £28). Set L £19. Set D £45. Tasting menu £65 (6 courses). **Details:** 50 seats. V menu. Bar. Wheelchair access. Music. Parking.

◼ St Andrews
The Seafood Restaurant

Sustainable seafood in a spectacular setting
Cooking score: 3
Seafood | £49
The Scores, Bruce Embankment, St Andrews, KY16 9AB
Tel no: (01334) 479475
www.theseafoodrestaurant.com

Jutting out over the seawall, the view changing depending on whether the tide is in or out (and the weather, which is as unpredictable as ever), this sharply modern building has floor-to-ceiling glass so no one misses out on the view. With its prime position and all that prime seafood to draw on it's still a dependable address to enjoy the fruits of the sea. Despite the contemporary setting, it's actually more formal than you might imagine. The modern output means that among starters East Neuk crab finds its way into a bonbon and velouté, and hand-dived scallops get a black pudding crumb (plus some honey-pickled cucumber). Lunchtime might provide moules marinière with hand-cut chips, and the evening fillet of monkfish in the robust company of Puy lentils and smoked pancetta. Desserts are a sophisticated bunch like Valrhona chocolate ganache with mandarin sorbet and white chocolate snow. Wines start at £20.
Chef/s: Serge Savickis. **Open:** all week L 12 to 2.30 (12.30 to 3 Sun), Mon to Sat D 6 to 10. **Meals:** Set L £22 (2 courses) to £26. Set D £40 (2 courses) to £49.
Details: 50 seats. 20 seats outside. Wheelchair access. Music. Parking.

◼ St Monans
Craig Millar @ 16 West End

Dynamic modern Scottish seafood cookery
Cooking score: 4
Modern British | £42
16 West End, St Monans, KY10 2BX
Tel no: (01333) 730327
www.16westend.com

£5
OFF

Be they ever so humble, little fishermen's cottages often come with sumptuous views, this one commanding a wide sweep of the Firth of Forth with the Bass Rock and Isle of May in the middle distance. Craig Millar settled here in 2011, and set about supplying the harbour village of St Monans with dynamic, seafood-based modern Scottish cooking. Techniques are as voguishly pernickety as you like, the sea trout simmered at 44°C in oyster soup garnished with miso caramel, pickled cucumber and passion-fruit. Sticking with the fish theme might lead you to scallops as a main, the inevitable cauliflower purée boosted with Catalan butifarra sausage and gnocchi in curry oil, a productive mixture of messages, while meat could be aromatic mutton loin with salt-baked celeriac, pickled turnip and puréed shallots. Nor does the inventive energy flag in desserts such as pannacotta with black olive caramel, puffed candy, apple purée and blackberry sorbet. House wines start at £20 for an IGP Viognier.
Chef/s: Craig Millar. **Open:** Wed to Sun L 12.30 to 2, D 6.30 to 9. **Closed:** Mon, Tue, 24 to 26 Dec, 1 Jan, 2 weeks Jan, 1 week Sept. **Meals:** Set L £22 (2 courses) to £26. Set D £42. Tasting menu £60.
Details: 40 seats. 20 seats outside. Bar. Wheelchair access. Parking. Children over 12 yrs only at D.

■ Auchterarder

★ TOP 50 ★

Andrew Fairlie at Gleneagles

One of Scotland's modern masters
Cooking score: 8
Modern French | £95
Auchterarder, PH3 1NF
Tel no: (01764) 694267
www.andrewfairlie.co.uk

At the heart of the Gleneagles golfing resort, set amid the rarefied purity of rural Tayside, Andrew Fairlie's autonomous restaurant is the kind of dining for which the term 'experience' might have been minted. You enter an entirely hermetic, spacious black grotto, where spotlit modern portraits shimmer in the tenebrous dusk and staff glide silently about as though on well-oiled rails. Fairlie is one of Scotland's modern masters, a forceful presence in a self-effacing space, whose culinary spells are cast without the fashionable need for putting the kitchen on display. What emerges is delicately constructed food built from potently impressive materials, hardly more eloquent than in the signature smoked lobster starter with its pin-sharp lime herb butter. Opening dishes have much of the intensity of mains, when caramelised veal sweetbreads appear with Jerusalem artichokes in madeira jus, and yet the principal dishes themselves move up another gear for red deer loin with spelt risotto and a smoked bonbon in wildly aromatic game jus, or the matchless grilled sea bass with bacon and sea flora and a circlet of crushed celeriac. Old-fashioned technique is as dazzling as the new, when a perfectly risen apple and quince soufflé anointed with butterscotch and cinnamon ice cream turns up, or there are concentrated alcohol-driven mousses of Cointreau or Poire William, the latter with chestnut sablé and pear sorbet. First-division wines for the deep of pocket start at £35 (£9 for a small glass).

Chef/s: Andrew Fairlie and Stephen McLaughlin. **Open:** Mon to Sat D only 6.30 to 10. **Closed:** Sun, 3 weeks Jan. **Meals:** alc (main courses £46). Set D £95 (6 courses) to £125 (8 courses). **Details:** Cash only. 50 seats. V menu. Wheelchair access. Music. Parking.

■ Blairgowrie
Kinloch House Hotel

Grand Scottish hospitality
Cooking score: 5
Modern British | £53
Dunkeld Road, Blairgowrie, PH10 6SG
Tel no: (01250) 884237
www.kinlochhouse.com

In a 'superb setting' – with 25 acres of prime Perthshire countryside all to itself – Kinloch House majors in traditional comforts including 'excellent, not overly formal' service. Hefty, handsome and creeper-clad, it sports all the country house essentials: a real fire, wood panelling, antique furniture and stern portraits in oils. The kitchen is capable of complexity, but also knows when to step back and let the ingredients work their own wonders, as in 'simple, enjoyable' starters of oak-smoked salmon with shallots and capers or creel-caught langoustine tails with herb mayonnaise. Game is a regular feature, perhaps roast breast of mallard duck with wild mushroom sausage, creamed spelt, roast red onions, prune and apple sauce. For dessert the 'beautifully presented' dark chocolate truffle tart with milk ice cream comes highly recommended. The weighty wine list offers particularly good coverage of France, and starts at a reasonable £16.50.
Chef/s: Steve MacCallum. **Open:** all week L 12.30 to 2, D 7 to 8.30. **Closed:** 12 to 29 Dec. **Meals:** Set L £20 (2 courses) to £26. Set D £53 (3 courses). Sun L £30. **Details:** 34 seats. Bar. Wheelchair access. Parking. Children over 5 yrs only at D.

Little's Restaurant

Known for its fresh and varied fish
Cooking score: 2
Modern British | £35
4 Wellmeadow, Blairgowrie, PH10 6ND
Tel no: (01250) 875358
www.littlesrestaurant.co.uk

'A real find in Blairgowrie,' thought one visitor to William Little's plain and simple restaurant in the middle of town; local spies say it is necessary to book ahead these days. While there are meat options – sirloin or fillet steak, venison rump with red cabbage, black pudding and red wine sauce – and pizzas, too, it's the fish and shellfish that draw folk from miles around. High standards are a given, from the fastidiously sourced produce to the personable service and passionate dedication of the owner. Lobster bisque, mussels in a lightly spiced gumbo sauce with smoked bacon, or an outstanding smoked haddock in a pastry case with a poached egg are the way to start, followed by a classic sole véronique, say, or loin of cod in an Arbroath smokie chowder with mashed potato. Finish with pecan tart with Drambuie ice cream. The global wine list opens at £14.95.
Chef/s: William Little. **Open:** Fri and Sat L 12 to 2.30, Tue to Sat D 4 to 9.30 (6 to 9.30 Fri and Sat). **Closed:** Sun, Mon, first 2 weeks Nov. **Meals:** Set L and D £18.95. **Details:** 48 seats. Wheelchair access. Music.

■ Inverkeilor
Gordon's

Precision cooking in a coastal village
Cooking score: 5
Modern British | £55
Main Street, Inverkeilor, DD11 5RN
Tel no: (01241) 830364
www.gordonsrestaurant.co.uk

The Watsons' family enterprise hits all the right notes for a coastal village retreat. Set in an Angus village by Lunan Bay, it's a bracing location, and the place itself has been done in restful contemporary style, with exposed stone and tartan upholstery in the dining room. Gordon's name may still be on the venue, but it's Watson *fils*, namely Garry, who is gradually taking over the culinary reins, and a masterful job he is doing too. Dishes are timed and presented with precision, and register strongly with reporters. Loch Duart salmon with an honour guard of smoked mussels is a bold curtain-raiser to a meal that might continue with breast and confit leg of Gressingham duck with purple cabbage, celeriac gnocchi and glazed apple in a peppery honey jus. An intermediate of Jerusalem artichoke velouté with pancetta is no mere makeweight, and careful combining at dessert stage produces chocolate fondant served chilled alongside red wine, pear and chocolate sorbet. The helpfully annotated wines start at £19.95 (£6.50 a glass).
Chef/s: Gordon and Garry Watson. **Open:** Wed to Fri and Sun L 12 to 2 (12.30 Sun), Tue to Sun D 7 to 9. **Closed:** Mon, 3 weeks Jan. **Meals:** Set L £34. Set D £55. **Details:** 24 seats. Wheelchair access. Parking. Children over 12 yrs only.

■ Killiecrankie
Killiecrankie House

Personally run Victorian retreat
Cooking score: 2
Modern British | £42
Killiecrankie, PH16 5LG
Tel no: (01796) 473220
www.killiecrankiehotel.co.uk

This traditional whitewashed country house hotel three miles north of Pitlochry has been under the watchful eye of owner Henrietta Fergusson for over 15 years with her chef Mark Easton similarly in post. Perhaps unsurprising then that the menu and cooking is more old-school than cutting edge with starters of king scallops and pea purée, carrot and coriander soup and a rather over-rich avocado, Stilton and walnut tart. Mains offered a choice of sea bream, lamb, duck and risotto. The sea bream had been accurately cooked but the couscous

and cherry tomatoes needed more garlic butter sauce. Lamb stuffed with red onion mousse and wrapped in pancetta served with Stornoway black pudding, rosti potato, red cabbage, cauliflower and Madeira jus left one of our inspectors too stuffed for the white chocolate brûlée with Grand Marnier cream and shortbread, or the warm financier and poached pear, let alone the Scottish cheese course. Coffee and chocolates complete a full-blown £42 set dinner. Wines start at £20.
Chef/s: Mark Easton. **Open:** all week L 12.30 to 2, D 6.30 to 8.30. **Closed:** 3 Jan to 17 Mar. **Meals:** alc (main courses £12 to £18). Set D £42 (4 courses). **Details:** 35 seats. Bar. Parking.

▌ Muthill
Barley Bree

Scottish inn with French connections
Cooking score: 3
Anglo-French | £42
6 Willoughby Street, Muthill, PH5 2AB
Tel no: (01764) 681451
www.barleybree.com

The warm and welcoming dining room at this restaurant-with-rooms in rural Perthshire belies its plain exterior. Stone walls and painted panelling, rough wooden tables alongside polished mahogany create a welcoming interior, a good match for Fabrice Bouteloup's thoughtful Fench/Scottish menu – say pressed beef on a wild garlic leaf served with spiced fig purée and an orange reduction or delicately smoked salmon with grapefruit slices and a grapefruit and fennel salad and crispy kombu. At a test meal, sea bream arrived with orso pasta, sun-dried tomatoes and modest harissa, while a pheasant breast special was somewhat overdone, yet the Savoy cabbage with pancetta and creamy mash was spot on. Excellent bread; service from young staff is 'very attentive', and a strong wine list covers Old and New World wines from £19, with plenty by the glass and carafe.

Chef/s: Fabrice Bouteloup. **Open:** Wed to Sun L 12 to 2 (5.30 Sun), Wed to Sat D 6.45 to 9. **Closed:** Mon, Tue, 25 and 26 Dec. **Meals:** alc (main courses £22 to £24). **Details:** 35 seats. 12 seats outside. V menu. Parking.

▌ Perth
Deans

Eclectic food from a local favourite
Cooking score: 3
Modern British | £31
77-79 Kinnoull Street, Perth, PH3 1LU
Tel no: (01738) 643377
www.letseatperth.co.uk

Willie and Margo Deans have dropped the tagline 'Let's Eat', but the informal invitation still stands at their well-liked restaurant near the centre of Perth. Occupying what was the town's original Theatre Royal (circa 1822), Deans now sports a new 'theatre bar' for cocktails and snacks – although the recently refurbished dining room continues to play to full houses with its offer of lively eclectic food based on the likes of Shetland scallops, Loch Etive trout, Stornoway black pudding and plenty of well-aged Orkney beef. Also present and correct are more unusual ideas ranging from a peanut raviolo of slow-cooked pork with miso caramel to venison loin with baked Rooster potato-skin mash, vegetable tagliatelle, carbonara cream and liquorice sauce. Desserts throw down the gauntlet, too, be it a mini fudge Pavlova or iced mango and lime terrine with a pear and toffee filo parcel. The wine list opens with a page of house selections from £16.
Chef/s: Willie Deans. **Open:** Tue to Sat L 12 to 2.30 (2 Sat), D 6 to 9 (9.30 Fri and Sat). **Closed:** Sun, Mon, 2 weeks Jan, 1 week Nov. **Meals:** alc (main courses £14 to £26). Set L £13 (2 courses) to £18. Set D £20 (2 courses) to £25. **Details:** 65 seats. Wheelchair access. Music.

■ Pitlochry

NEW ENTRY
Sandemans
A marriage of modern and traditional
Cooking score: 5
Modern British | £50
Fonab Castle Hotel, Foss Road, Pitlochry,
PH16 5ND
Tel no: (01796) 470140
www.fonabcastlehotel.com

Baronial sandstone turrets blend smoothly into contemporary glass-walled pavilions in this recently developed castle hotel. Floor-to-ceiling loch and mountain vistas in the lounge and brasserie give way to the opulent dark-panelled formal dining room with its riffs on tweeds and tartans. The tasting menus in Sandemans mirror this easy juxtaposition of the established and the innovative. While lead ingredients such as scallop, lobster, turbot and beef fillet might feel like a predictable roll call of the Scottish classics, they are presented with a precision and assurance that allows innovative interpretation. A seared scallop is sweetly matched with parsnip velouté and finished with intense drops of star anise pork belly broth and powdered coral. Rare beef fillet is grounded in the woody flavours of morels and Madeira and then lifted with crisp new-season asparagus tips and a tiny crunchy beignet of slow-cooked shoulder. The sweet and savoury salad with toasted macadamia nuts successfully segues the 'traditional cheese course' into dessert. A skilled sommelier oversees the wine list and brings some fresh insight to established areas. As the former home of the Sandemans port dynasty, fortified wines are well represented as well as an extensive range of single malts and artisan gins. Wine prices cover a wide range but start at a reasonable £23.50.

Chef/s: Paul Burns. **Open:** Wed to Sat D only 7 to 9. **Closed:** Sun, Mon, Tue. **Meals:** Set D £50 (5 courses) to £70. **Details:** 25 seats. Bar. Wheelchair access. Parking.

No-choice menus

The best chefs and ingredients are more fetishised than ever, and no-choice menus are designed to showcase both. In the spirit of Noma and the Fat Duck, the no-choice menu can be long and complex or short and sweet. It's never going to suit the terminally fussy, but try it and you'll find:

It's foolproof: You don't have to choose. Someone else creates a sequence of dishes fitting seamlessly together; no accidental repeats, no clumsy ordering.

It's seasonal: At Casamia in Bristol, the five set courses are built around ingredients currently at their best. When something's too good to miss, you won't miss it.

It's generous: At Hunan, you tell the waiter what you eat before the parade of up to 18 Taiwan-influenced dishes begins. Sometimes, they ask if you want more.

It's manageable: The price won't vary, making it easier to deal with the bill and budget for wine.

It's creative: Chefs like Mikael Jonsson at Hedone serve their most offbeat dishes, knowing they'll be eaten rather than languishing, ignored, on the à la carte.

■ Aberdeen
Silver Darling
Redoubtable seafood veteran
Cooking score: 3
Seafood | £48
Pocra Quay, North Pier, Aberdeen, AB11 5DQ
Tel no: (01224) 576229
www.thesilverdarling.co.uk

It seems fitting that this redoubtable seafood veteran should take its title from the old Scottish nickname for herring; it also seems apt that the Silver Darling should go about its business in a conservatory dining room in Aberdeen's old Customs House, with inviting views of the harbour and the boats adding an extra briny fillip to proceedings. Chef/proprietor Didier Dejean's French roots help to anchor the kitchen, although the food soaks up influences from far and wide – from mussels in coconut, curry and chilli broth to fillet of sea bream with a ratatouille croquette, green tapenade and confit fennel. The 'catch of the moment' is worth a punt, and Didier also respects the seasons by offering occasional meat and game dishes such as loin of Highland venison with chestnut gnocchi, glazed celeriac and beetroot purée. After that, pick exotic lime pannacotta with mango salsa or keep it homely with sticky toffee pudding. The sharp wine list includes some 'brilliant' bottles from £20.

Chef/s: Didier Dejean. **Open:** Mon to Fri L 12 to 1.45, Mon to Sat D 6.30 to 9.30. **Closed:** Sun, 2 weeks in Dec and Jan. **Meals:** alc (main courses £17 to £27). Set L £20 (2 courses) to £25. **Details:** 50 seats. Music. No children after 8pm.

Symbols

🛏 Accommodation is available
£30 Three courses for less than £30
£5 OFF £5-off voucher scheme
🍾 Notable wine list

▍Banchory
Cow Shed Restaurant
Robustly seasonal, sharply contemporary
Cooking score: 2
Modern British | £30
Raemoir Road, Banchory, AB31 5QB
Tel no: (01330) 820813
www.cowshedrestaurant.co.uk

£5
OFF

Amid the rolling fields a cowshed is exactly what you'd expect to find, so to happen upon this vast, modern restaurant is a surprise. It takes its name from an adjacent shed, but there is nothing rustic about this interior: sleek chrome and wood furniture, an extravagant glass-walled wine cellar and a sparkling kitchen all suggest it has teleported from the metropolis – although the views through tall windows keep you grounded. Classic and patriotic influences lead the way in the kitchen: a starter of sausages, celeriac and potato purée comes with Scottish oatcake, while roasted Aberdeen Angus rump cap is teamed with potatoes, salted onion marmalade and natural gravy. Occasional forays further afield might result in Scottish lamb chump being teamed with couscous, pancetta, garlic confit and lime pickle crème fraîche. For dessert, expect old favourites like sticky toffee pudding or lemon tart. The wine list opens at £19.
Chef/s: Graham Buchan. **Open:** Sat and Sun L 12 to 2, Wed to Sat D 6 to 9.30. **Closed:** Mon, Tue, 25 to 30 Dec, 1 to 8 Jan. **Meals:** alc (main courses £14 to £30). **Details:** 50 seats. Wheelchair access. Music. Parking.

▍Udny Green
Eat on the Green
Convivial village restaurant
Cooking score: 2
Modern European | £44
Udny Green, AB41 7RS
Tel no: (01651) 842337
www.eatonthegreen.co.uk

Chef/proprietor Craig Wilson (aka the kilted chef) has a passion for Scottish ingredients, which are brought in from across the country and turned into posh plates of fine-dining fare. It all takes place in a robust stone building that used to be the village post office and may well look like a pub from the outside, but is in fact a smart restaurant with comfy lounge area and a private dining space called the Tasting Room. A starter called 'Little Taste of Eat on the Green' shows off the kitchen's ambition neatly – haggis and beef formed into a kofta, a parsnip and sweet potato soup, confit duck with apple and ginger, plus a goats' cheese salad. Follow on with baked sea bass with scallops and winter greens fired up with lemon and capers, dressed with a Champagne sauce, or fillet of Aberdeenshire beef. Finish with an assiette of sweet stuff including lemon posset. Wines start at £25.
Chef/s: Craig Wilson. **Open:** Wed to Fri and Sun L 12 to 2, Wed to Sun D 6 to 9 (5.30 to 9.30 Sat, 8 Sun). **Closed:** Mon, Tue, first week Jan. **Meals:** alc (main courses £24 to £32). Set L £24 (2 courses) to £27. Sun L £30 (2 courses) to £35. Tasting menu £80. **Details:** 80 seats. Bar. Music. Parking.

■ Auldearn
Boath House
Exacting country-house cooking
Cooking score: 4
Modern European | £45
Auldearn, IV12 5TE
Tel no: (01667) 454896
www.boath-house.com

Diners are cosseted from the moment they cross the threshold of this impressive Georgian mansion, from the pre-dinner drinks in the plush drawing room to the no-choice, three- or six- course menu taken in the elegant dining room, where floor-to-ceiling windows overlook the ornamental lake. Antiques and polished parquet are complemented by contemporary oak tables and original art. A spring menu brought cured then poached salmon on wafer-thin beetroot slices with beetroot purée, beetroot jelly and a soft-boiled quail's egg followed by sous-vide duck breast with crisp, crumbled skin and carrot and orange purée, a whole poached carrot and a carrot curl. A rich vanilla rice pudding with puréed mango and passion fruit and a sesame biscuit ended the three courses and while all dishes were eloquent and exacting they did not shout joie de vivre – 'another element or two on the plate would have raised Boath House from the austerely impressive'. An imaginative wine list starts at £29.

Chef/s: Charlie Lockley. **Open:** all week L 12 to 1.15, D 7 to 7.30. **Meals:** Set L £24 (2 courses) to £30. Set D £45 (3 courses) to £70. **Details:** 28 seats. V menu. Wheelchair access. Parking. Children over 8 yrs only.

Symbols

Accommodation is available
£30 Three courses for less than £30
£5 OFF £5-off voucher scheme
Notable wine list

 Aviemore
Mountain Café

A jewel in the midst of Aviemore
Cooking score: 1
British | £24
111 Grampian Road, Aviemore, PH22 1RH
Tel no: (01479) 812473
www.mountaincafe-aviemore.co.uk

£30

This Aviemore café with views over the Cairngorms has few pretensions beyond providing substantial, homely, well-cooked dishes and it consistently delivers on all points. This is colourful, eclectic cooking from New Zealander Kirsten Gilmour, spanning comfort food (all-day breakfast with local butchers' sausages and free-range eggs; an excellent beef burger), international flavours, as in Kiwi sweetcorn fritter stack and Asian-style smoked chicken salad, and lighter snacks such as soups, salads and baguettes with imaginative fillings. There are some exceedingly good cakes, too. It's hugely popular, so be prepared to queue and expect first-class, friendly service. Wines from £15.
Chef/s: Kirsten Gilmour. **Open:** all week 8.30 to 5.30. **Closed:** 25 and 26 Dec, 31 Dec, 1 Jan.
Meals: alc (main courses from £8 to £12).
Details: 52 seats. 12 seats outside. V menu. Music. Parking.

Delny
The Birch Tree

Country restaurant with confident food
Cooking score: 3
Anglo-French | £30
Delny Riding Centre, Delny, IV18 0NP
Tel no: (01349) 853549
www.the-birch-tree.com

Single-track roads lead to this cosy, simply decorated restaurant that chef/proprietor Barry Hartshorne created from a stable block at his parents' riding centre, just off the A9 near Invergordon. 'This is what all small restaurants should aspire to be like' noted one satisfied visitor, who went on to praise the distant

views to Cromarty Firth, the well-spaced tables, the fiercely seasonal and sensibly compact menu, and the warmth of the welcome. Butter-poached quail with truffle custard, chestnut and mushroom consommé, or langoustine, scallop and crab boudin with langoustine bisque and sea vegetables are typical of Mr Hartshorne's Anglo-French treatments, while duck breast with duck crackling, potato terrine and carrot purée is all about great ingredients and great flavours. Puddings are a delight, whether a chocolate and raisin financier offset by fennel ice cream and chocolate soil or an impressive mango soufflé with coconut sorbet and mango soup. A relatively concise, serviceable wine list opens at £15.95.
Chef/s: Barry Hartshorne. **Open:** Wed to Sun L 12 to 2, Wed to Sat D 6 to 10. **Closed:** Mon, Tue.
Meals: alc (main courses £13 to £20). Set L £15 (2 courses) to £18. Set D £25 (2 courses) to £30.
Details: 32 seats. V menu. Wheelchair access. Music. Parking.

Fort William
Crannog

Fun fish restaurant on the pier
Cooking score: 1
Seafood | £35
Town Pier, Fort William, PH33 6DB
Tel no: (01397) 705589
www.crannog.net

It's hard to miss Crannog with its prized position out on the pier and bright red roof. A beacon for lovers of stunning local seafood prepared without fuss for over 25 years, the place also serves up idyllic views over Loch Linnhe. A log-burner makes sure it's all snug in the cooler months (which is quite a few of them, it has to be said). Start with hot and cold smoked salmon or Mallaig crab and spinach tart with a fancy crab emulsion, followed by baked cod or some shellfish as nature intended. There are meat and veggie options too. Wines start at £18.

Chef/s: Stewart MacLachlan. **Open:** all week L 12 to 2, D 6 to 9. **Closed:** 25 Dec, 1 Jan. **Meals:** alc (main courses £15 to £22). Set L £15 (2 courses) to £19. **Details:** 50 seats. Wheelchair access. Music.

Inverlochy Castle
Baronial pile with contemporary food
Cooking score: 5
Modern British | £67
Torlundy, Fort William, PH33 6SN
Tel no: (01397) 702177
www.inverlochycastlehotel.com

Dining at Inverlochy Castle hotel comes with all the grandeur and opulence you expect of a 19th-century tycoon's Gothic mansion that once hosted Queen Victoria. Pre-dinner drinks are taken in the Great Hall or one of the sumptuous sitting rooms with views to Ben Nevis. Lunch is in the Red Dining Room, rich with brocades and heavily carved furniture. A modest inspection meal began with accurately cooked pigeon and foie gras given a beetroot garnish and curry-dusted West Coast scallops with cauliflower and julienne of apple. To follow: Parmesan-crusted beef with slow-cooked shoulder, fondant potato topped with quail's egg, and a crisp-skinned cod accompanied by Jersey Royal potatoes, asparagus, wild garlic and a beurre blanc. The price and the endeavour rack up at dinner with more elaborate dishes and a dress code that requests jacket and tie. Wines start at £35 and progress stratospherically into the thousands.
Chef/s: Philip Carnegie. **Open:** all week L 12.30 to 1.30, D 6 to 10. **Meals:** Set L £28 (2 courses) to £38. Set D £67. Tasting menus £85. **Details:** 40 seats. Parking.

Lochleven Seafood Café
Fun-packed lochside gem
Cooking score: 2
Seafood | £35
Onich, Fort William, PH33 6SA
Tel no: (01855) 821048
www.lochlevenseafoodcafe.co.uk

More than a lobster shack or even a café, this lochside gem was born out of a demand for the shellfish landed here by the Lochleven Shellfish Company. It's in a purpose-built add-on to its shop and export operation and save for a couple of metal sculptures the room is spare, bright and clattery. High ceilings, tiled floors, formica tables and generally happy diners create the clamour. An efficient front-of-house team has you briskly bibbed and seated for a menu that showcases the best of Scotland's West Coast seafood. The kitchen then delivers with a clear understanding of how to exploit freshness with a smack. Tuck in to a shellfish platter – hot or cold, surf clams with ham and sherry, palourdes in garlic butter, oysters, mussels in cider, diver-caught scallops, razor clams with almonds and Oloroso, lobster mayonnaise or terrific bowls of roasted langoustine with lemon and herb butter with more of that ilk on the daily specials board. There is steak if you must, but must you? Eat on the terrace or lochside on clement days. The wine list is commendably strong on good-value European whites, opening at £15.50.
Chef/s: Scott Fraser and Marcel Vindka. **Open:** all week L 12 to 3, D 6 to 9. Seasonal opening hours apply. **Meals:** alc (main courses £14 to £23). **Details:** 40 seats. 20 seats outside. Wheelchair access. Parking.

Join us at thegoodfoodguide.co.uk

 Inverness
Rocpool

Eye-catching riverside restaurant
Cooking score: 2
Modern European | £35
1 Ness Walk, Inverness, IV3 5NE
Tel no: (01463) 717274
www.rocpoolrestaurant.com

£5 OFF

With its abstract artwork, bare surfaces and flashy glass frontage providing great views of the river, Rocpool brings some sparkle to the chilly environs of Inverness. Utterly charming staff play their part, while the kitchen adds plenty of global pep to a larder full of carefully sourced Scottish ingredients: grilled West Coast langoustines are served on giant pearl couscous with roasted red peppers and minted yoghurt, while roast fillet of Rothesay smoked cod appears on a chorizo and butter-bean cassoulet. There are some nifty meat dishes, too, such as roast rump of lamb with rose harissa, spiced pilaf and cucumber tzatziki. For dessert, consider bread-and-butter pudding with rum and pineapple. Set menus offer commendable value and the wine list promises decent drinking from £16.90.
Chef/s: Steven Devlin. **Open:** Mon to Sat L 12 to 2.30, D 5.45 to 10. **Closed:** Sun, 25 and 26 Dec, 1 to 3 Jan. **Meals:** alc (main courses £13 to £25). Set L £16 (2 courses). Set D £18 (2 courses). **Details:** 55 seats. Wheelchair access. Music.

 Isle of Harris
Scarista House

Gorgeous getaway showcasing island bounty
Cooking score: 2
Modern British | £44
Scarista, Isle of Harris, HS3 3HX
Tel no: (01859) 550238
www.scaristahouse.com

Appreciative visitors give thanks for the graciousness of the service and the unpretentious elegance of this handsome old manse overlooking three miles of sandy Harris beaches. The two lovingly put together dining rooms make a pleasant setting for a three-course dinner at 8 o'clock. Like many remote Scottish hotels, the menu here is fixed price and no choice, with Tim and Patricia Martin making intelligent use of whatever comes there way, be it locally or own-grown vegetables, local game, meat or seafood. The overall style can be gauged from a meal of Uist peat- and hot-smoked salmon with a Parmesan tuile, pink grapefruit and Campari vinaigrette, then roast pigeon squab with giblet gravy, bread sauce, olive oil mash and spiced red cabbage. The wine list focuses on France and opens at £20.
Chef/s: Tim and Patricia Martin. **Open:** all week D only 8 (1 sitting). **Closed:** Dec to Feb. **Meals:** Set D £34 (2 courses) to £44. **Details:** 20 seats. V menu. Parking. Children over 8 yrs only.

 Isle of Skye
Creelers of Skye

Robust seafood dishes with a French accent
Cooking score: 2
French | £28
Broadford, Isle of Skye, IV49 9AQ
Tel no: (01471) 822281
www.skye-seafood-restaurant.co.uk

£5 OFF **£30**

Long honoured for robust delivery of Skye's seafood catch in a paper-tablecloth caff setting, David Wilson's cheerful Creelers continues to pack them in with bourgeois French cooking and general bonhomie. You can opt for the daube d'agneau, vegetable curry or chicken jambalaya, but fish and seafood are the treat here. Begin with mussels à la Landaise, in butter, garlic and white wine, follow up with monkfish tail served on the bone in a soy and Pernod reduction or Wilson's take on the classic Marseillaise bouillabaisse for two. He casts his nets beyond France with seafood gumbo and Cajun haddock, then sails back home with Skye-sourced razor clams, cockles and palourdes in a creamy broth or hand-dived king scallops and the local speciality, squat lobster tails: sweet, fragile, tiny morsels sautéed in sherry and heaped high in, yes, a rich cream sauce. Wines from £18.

Chef/s: David Wilson. **Open:** Mon to Sat 12 to 9. **Closed:** Sun, Nov to Feb. **Meals:** alc (main courses £15 to £19). **Details:** 26 seats. Wheelchair access. Music. Parking.

Kinloch Lodge

Breathtaking views, contemporary dishes
Cooking score: 5
Modern British | £70
Sleat, Isle of Skye, IV43 8QY
Tel no: (01471) 833214
www.kinloch-lodge.co.uk

Beautifully situated overlooking the Sound of Sleat, Kinloch Lodge is the family home of Lady Claire Macdonald, best known after four decades at the helm of this country house hotel, for her cookery books, cookery school and in 2014 an OBE for services to the hospitality industry. She has handed kitchen duties on to Marcello Tully who presents five-course dinner and three-course lunch menus of skilled contemporary dishes with a pronounced Scottish accent that sustains Kinloch's high reputation. Start with a foaming cup of delicate tomato and red pepper soup, move on to a warm crab mousse and seared scallops in a rich seafood sauce. Mains include Speyside beef fillet topped with Strathdon Blue cheese mousse with shallots, wild mushrooms and courgettes and a rich brandy sauce. To finish: vanilla crème fraîche pannacotta with blackcurrent sorbet. A substantial and impressive wine list starts at £33 and rises, with plenty by the glass and half bottle. Praised by one reader for its 'convivial country-house charm' – we concur.

Chef/s: Marcello Tully. **Open:** all week L 12 to 2, D 6 to 9.30. **Meals:** Set L £33 (2 courses) to £38. Set D £70 (5 courses) to £80 (7 courses). Sun L £33.
Details: 50 seats. V menu. Bar. Wheelchair access. Music. Parking. Children at L and early D only.

Loch Bay

Homely seafood specialist in beautiful setting
Cooking score: 2
Seafood | £35
1-2 Macleod Terrace, Stein, Isle of Skye, IV55 8GA
Tel no: (01470) 592235
www.lochbay-seafood-restaurant.co.uk

This cheerful one-room restaurant in a row of whitewashed cottages in the conservation village of Stein is run with verve and energy by Alison and David Wilkinson and on a busy Saturday night they keep all the plates spinning while making the best of local seafood in a time-honoured fashion. A three course set menu might offer oysters – straight or baked with Parmesan and garlic or Sconsor scallops with local Orbost coriander, both of Skye provenance. Follow up with cod, halibut, wild Esk sea trout or a fulsome shellfish platter of mussels, prawns, squat lobster tails, oysters, king prawns and lobster. There are five desserts on offer ranging from Scottish cloutie dumpling to a delicate pannacotta. A regular wine list starts at £18 a bottle.

Chef/s: David Wilkinson. **Open:** Wed to Sat D only 6 to 9. **Closed:** Sun, Mon, Tue, mid Oct to Easter. **Meals:** Set D £35. **Details:** 24 seats. 8 seats outside. Music. Parking. Children over 8 yrs only.

The Three Chimneys

Original food and matchless hospitality
new chef/no score
Modern British | £65
Colbost, Isle of Skye, IV55 8ZT
Tel no: (01470) 511258
www.threechimneys.co.uk

After 30 continuous years in the Guide, it's all change at the iconic Three Chimneys in the far corner of Skye. Chef/director Michael Smith has departed after 11 years, along with head chef Kevin McLean, replaced by *MasterChef: The Professionals* (2013) finalist Scott Davies. Davies was not in place when we visited in

May, so our report reflects the old regime. However, since Eddie and Shirley Spear have been doling out matchless hospitality for three decades, and the Three Chimneys' reputation for highly original cooking is inspired by the island's seasonal larder, we hope the change signals nothing more than a steady continuation of the style. One where Black Isle ox cheek and tongue are teamed with pickled walnuts, cauliflower and a purée of local herbs; seared wood pigeon is nicely paired with miniature 'tattie scones', rhubarb, crowdie and gingerbread; and the deservedly renowned seafood platter, sourced within a few miles, could be preceded by an original take on Cullen skink – a tiny lidded glass dish filled with smoked haddock and marag dubh (aka Stornaway black pudding) and topped off with soft egg yolk. To finish, the famous hot marmalade pudding soufflé with Drambuie syrup remains (we hope) an immovable feature of the dessert menu. The wine list is a globe-spanning labour of love, with bottles from £26 and a top-drawer selection by the glass. Check out the Scottish gins, too.
Chef/s: Scott Davies. **Open:** all week L 12 to 2, D 6 to 9.30. **Closed:** 1 Dec to 23 Jan. **Meals:** Set L £38. Set D £65 (5 courses). Tasting menu £90 (8 courses). **Details:** 36 seats. 6 seats outside. Bar. Wheelchair access. Parking. Children over 5 yrs only at L, over 8 yrs at D.

◾ Kingussie
The Cross
Assured cooking in a peaceful setting
Cooking score: 4
Modern British | £55
Ardbroilach Road, Kingussie, PH21 1LB
Tel no: (01540) 661166
www.thecross.co.uk

'I suspect it is the best eating in the area,' remarks a visitor to this converted, late 19th-century tweed mill, which stands in four acres of riverside grounds in the heart of the Cairngorms National Park. Now in their third year, Derek and Celia Kitchingman have continued to upgrade the hotel and a new chef has settled in the kitchen since the last edition of the Guide. David Skigg's food is modern, ingredients-led from best regional supply lines, and follows comfortably on the heels of his predecessor, Ross Sutherland, according to loyal returnees. A Gressingham duck trio is a show stopper, turning up on a winter tasting menu in the form of smoked breast, confit leg and excellent parfait on toasted brioche. Loin of lamb with hotpot potatoes, young vegetables and jus gras has also been praised, as has the generous selection of mainly Scottish cheeses; a chocolate bar with honeycomb, caramel and vanilla ice cream is another highpoint. When it comes to wine, the Cross's first love is France but high standards are maintained for the rest of the world on a thoughtfully compiled list. Prices from £22.
Chef/s: David Skiggs. **Open:** All week L 12 to 2, D 7 to 8.30. **Closed:** 24 to 27 Dec, 4 Jan to mid Feb. **Meals:** Set L £25. Set D £55. Tasting menu £60 (6 courses). **Details:** 26 seats. 10 seats outside. Wheelchair access. Parking.

Auld Alliance
French
East Terrace, Kingussie, PH21 1JS
Tel no: (01540) 661506
www.auld-alliance.com
'Outstanding…a hidden gem that deserves greater recognition. The two meals we had there recently were superb, including breast of duck and a Black Isle potato terrine.'

◾ Lochaline
The Whitehouse
Creative dining with seafood aplenty
Cooking score: 3
Modern British | £35
Lochaline, PA80 5XT
Tel no: (01967) 421777
www.thewhitehouserestaurant.co.uk

Arriving by ferry from Mull whets the appetite wonderfully for the seafood specialities that are Mike Burgoyne's stock-in-trade at this atmospherically remote west coast destination within sight of the ruined castle. In such a location, regionalism is a virtue made from happy necessity, and the menus offer an appealing mix of traditional favourites like partan bree (crab soup), lobster ravioli, and langoustines with mayonnaise, and ideas from the modernist repertoire. There are pedigree meats too, pork belly slow-roasted for 12 hours and dressed with apple and plum chutney, or the signature liver and kidneys of Ardtornish venison, sauced with Tomatin single malt. Scottish cheeses with homemade chutneys, oatcakes and a cheeky dram are the alternative to creative desserts like autumn squash brûlée with orange and ginger shortbread, or chilled condé with poached blackberries. The wine list comes with helpful advice for matching bottles to dishes. Prices start at £18.95.

Chef/s: Mike Burgoyne. **Open:** Tue to Sat L 12 to 2.30, D 6 to 10. **Closed:** Sun, Mon, Nov to Easter. **Meals:** alc (main courses £7 to £30). Set L £20 (2 courses) to £23. **Details:** 26 seats. 10 seats outside. Wheelchair access.

■ Lochinver
Albannach

Solace, sustenance and fine hospitality
Cooking score: 6
Modern British | £70
Baddidarroch, Lochinver, IV27 4LP
Tel no: (01571) 844407
www.thealbannach.co.uk

Colin Craig and Lesley Crosfield have featured in the Guide for 16 years and know a thing or two about hospitality – no wonder readers are quick to applaud the attention given at their Victorian house. The setting is a plus, too, with spectacular views across the bay to the Assynt mountains. Seasonal food makes a big impact here, and they source the best local materials – the sweetest Lochinver langoustine, a tart of local wild mushrooms, roast hill-fed Highland hogget – which are worked into a no-choice, five-course dinner menu served at a single sitting. Seafood is a dominant theme and reporters have praised a

dish of scallops and roast monkfish teamed with charred fennel, white and green asparagus, celeriac cream and Champagne sauce. And at dessert a perfectly executed hot citrus soufflé with a bitter chocolate ice cream has also impressed. Wines from £21. Note: a new venture, the Caberfeidh, a dining pub in nearby Lochinver serving game and locally landed seafood, offers a more informal dining option.

Chef/s: Colin Craig and Lesley Crosfield. **Open:** Tue to Sun D only 8 (1 sitting). **Closed:** Mon, Mon to Wed (Nov to Dec), Jan to mid Mar. **Meals:** Set D £70 (5 courses). **Details:** 20 seats. V menu. Parking. Children over 12 yrs only.

■ Orkney Islands
The Creel

Orcadian oasis dedicated to island produce
Cooking score: 6
Modern British | £40
Front Road, St Margaret's Hope, Orkney Islands, KW17 2SL
Tel no: (01856) 831311
www.thecreel.co.uk

Alan and Joyce Craigie's Orcadian oasis has been quietly going about its business since 1985, seducing tourists with an irresistible blend of congenial hospitality, harmonious cooking and peerless views over St Margaret's Bay (magical sunsets included). It's humble and homely in the best sense, a tribute to tranquillity and single-minded persistence defined by Alan's unembellished approach to Orkney produce. Here you will find the freshest langoustines (creel-caught, naturally) and seaweed-fed mutton from North Ronaldsay as well as a host of seasonal ingredients – all showcased on a modest three-course dinner menu that maximises flavour and value. Crab salad is sensitively dressed with avocado salsa, pickled cucumber and apple mayonnaise, while slow-cooked Aberdeen Angus brisket brings richness, depth and generosity to the table in company with Scotch mince, buttered carrots, roast beetroots and gravy. To finish, guests can

choose dessert (perhaps chocolate mousse with raspberries, strawberries and a brandy-snap) or a selection of artisan cheeses. A minimal list of cherry-picked global wines opens with house selections from £19.50 (£5.80 a glass).
Chef/s: Alan Craigie. **Open:** Tue to Sat D only 6 to 8. **Closed:** Sun, Mon, Oct to Apr. **Meals:** Set D £40. **Details:** 16 seats. Wheelchair access. Parking.

■ Plockton
Plockton Inn

All-purpose inn with a liking for fish
Cooking score: 2
Seafood | £23
Innes Street, Plockton, IV52 8TW
Tel no: (01599) 544222
www.plocktoninn.co.uk

It was a profitable homecoming when siblings Mary and Kenny Gollan returned to Plockton in 1997, bought the old manse and set about transforming it into an unassuming, all-purpose inn. The fondness for fish is understandable with the harbour and Loch Carron just a stroll away. Day boats land much of the catch seen on the menu and Kenny even has his own smokehouse at the back of the inn – so quality and freshness are guaranteed. The menu changes with the haul, but some items are constants – notably the famous creel-caught 'Plockton prawns' (aka langoustines), served hot or cold with crusty bread. Home-smoked salmon is also a good call, likewise moules marinière, haddock and chips or skate with foaming black butter. Otherwise, hefty seafood platters offer a bit of everything from the boats and smokehouse. Not in the mood for fish? Then there's Provençal lamb shank, and haggis with clapshot. Wines start at £14.95 and there are myriad malt whiskies too.
Chef/s: Mary Gollan. **Open:** all week L 12 to 2.15, D 6 to 9. **Closed:** 25 and 26 Dec. **Meals:** alc (main courses £10 to £19). **Details:** 70 seats. 20 seats outside. Wheelchair access. Music. Parking.

■ Port Appin
Airds Hotel

Former ferry inn full of delights
new chef/no score
Modern British | £55
Port Appin, PA38 4DF
Tel no: (01631) 730236
www.airds-hotel.com

The restaurant has been refurbished to create a slightly more relaxed atmosphere, but otherwise it's business as usual at this immaculate gastronomic outpost in one of Scotland's loveliest corners. The garden – an incongruously well-tended jewel amid the wilds – overlooks loch, castle and mountains; you'll get these views from the restaurant, too. Jordan Annabi has left to work in Abu Dhabi, and Chris Stanley was appointed too late for the Guide to arrange an inspection, but the style of complex, imaginative cooking using the best ingredients from the region looks to be continuing unchanged. In the past this has included West Coast langoustine, pan-seared foie gras, guava gel, morels, nori sponge, Cointreau and shellfish butter sauce, and fillet of Gressingham duck with poached sweetbreads, Gruyère gratin, kale, baby navets (turnips), baby carrot, pistachio sponge and blood orange jus. The wide-reaching wine list offers plenty under £40, and opens at £23.50.
Chef/s: Chris Stanley. **Open:** all week L 12 to 2.30, D 7.15 to 9.15. **Closed:** first 2 weeks Dec. **Meals:** Set D £55. **Details:** 36 seats. 20 seats outside. V menu. Bar. Music. Parking. Children over 8 yrs only.

Symbols

Accommodation is available

Three courses for less than £30

£5-off voucher scheme

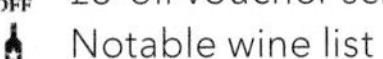

Notable wine list

▌Scrabster
The Captain's Galley

Terrific harbourside eatery
Cooking score: 3
Seafood | £49
The Harbour, Scrabster, KW14 7UJ
Tel no: (01847) 894999
www.captainsgalley.co.uk

Built as a salmon store and barrel-vaulted ice house more than two centuries ago, this fascinating piece of Scottish history keeps faith with its maritime roots – although the emphasis is now on spanking-fresh local seafood from sustainable stocks. Former fish trader Jim Cowie heads down to Scrabster's quayside market each day, buys what he needs and cooks it with considerable acumen in the kitchen of this cracking little place. There's no holding back when it comes to uncompromising global flavours, although the results are never muddled or overworked: crab is pointed up with daikon salad and jalapeño vinaigrette, turbot is paired with 'Asian oxtail', and John Dory comes embellished with roasted peppers, pearl couscous and kale pesto. Desserts such as ginger crème brûlée with toffee doughnut maintain the kitchen's creative momentum, or you could nibble some artisan Highland cheeses with oatcakes. The restaurant is also proud of its 'quality takeaways'. Around two dozen fish-friendly wines start at £17.95 (£4.50 a glass).
Chef/s: Jim Cowie. **Open:** Tue to Sat L 12 to 3, D 6.30 to 9. **Closed:** Sun, Mon, 25 and 26 Dec, 1 and 2 Jan. **Meals:** Set L £20 (2 courses) to £28. Set D £37 (2 courses) to £49. **Details:** 25 seats. 25 seats outside. Bar. Wheelchair access. Music. Parking.

▌Strontian
Kilcamb Lodge

Welcoming retreat of the best Highland kind
Cooking score: 4
Modern British | £35
Strontian, PH36 4HY
Tel no: (01967) 402257
www.kilcamblodge.co.uk

The house dates from the 18th century, but much of what you see today is the work of some industrious Victorians. What hasn't changed is the spectacular location a short stroll from the lapping waters of Loch Sunart, and the surrounding 22 acres of woodland and meadows. The interior doesn't attempt to distort the rural idyll, but enhances it with its soothingly traditional (and smart) country décor, with log fires and views out to the loch. The formal, floral and elegant restaurant and more contemporary brasserie offer the same menu, making much of the local seafood without ignoring what the land can provide. Start with a platter of langoustines, crab and more, and move on to an Aberdeen Angus steak with wild mushroom and sherry sauce or sea bass with tomato and olive tart. Among desserts, vanilla pannacotta with orange and star anise sorbet brings a touch of foreign sunshine to the table. Wines start at £21.
Chef/s: Gary Phillips. **Open:** all week L 12 to 2 (3 Sun), D 5.30 to 10. **Closed:** Jan. **Meals:** alc (main courses £11 to 28). Set D £52. Sun L £20. **Details:** 36 seats. 10 seats outside. V menu. Bar. Music. Parking. Children over 5 yrs only in restaurant.

WALES

Glamorgan, Gwent, Mid–Wales, North–East Wales, North–West Wales, West Wales

Barry
The Gallery

Big hearted, great value food
Cooking score: 4
Modern British | £27
2 Broad Street, Barry, CF62 7AA
Tel no: (01446) 735300
www.the-gallery-restaurant.co.uk

'A fabulous independent restaurant run by an enthusiastic and passionate team.' So runs one glowing report, catching the tone of this bar-restaurant combo. The ground-floor bar sports a log-burner, exposed brickwork and dispenses cocktails, beers and bistro-style dishes, but the main attraction is upstairs where chef/owner Barnaby Hibbert can be seen producing imaginative dishes made with locally sourced ingredients in an open kitchen. The setting is a happy collision of vintage (chandeliers, ornate wallpaper, stripped floors) and cool modern styling, the chunky tables set comfortably apart. At a test meal, pan-roasted pigeon with game gala pie and pickled cauliflower was right on the money, flavours zinging. A main of 'juicy and tender' seared venison, home-smoked venison faggots, braised red cabbage and potato and swede mash also impressed, as did the bara brith bread-and-butter pudding with rum and prune ice cream. 'Wonderful' breads get special mention, too. A modest wine list starts at £15.
Chef/s: Barnaby Hibbert. **Open:** Fri to Sun L 12 to 2.30 (3.30 Sun), Thur to Sat D 6 to 9 (9.30 Fri and Sat). **Closed:** Mon, Tue, Wed, 26 Dec, 1 Jan. **Meals:** Set L £17 (2 courses) to £20. Set D £23 (2 courses) to £27. Sun L £16. **Details:** 50 seats. 30 seats outside. Bar. Music.

Symbols

Accommodation is available
£30 Three courses for less than £30
£5 OFF £5-off voucher scheme
Notable wine list

Cardiff

Arbennig

Fresh is the word
Cooking score: 4
Modern British | £30
6-10 Romilly Crescent, Cardiff, CF11 9NR
Tel no: (029) 2034 1264
www.arbennig.co.uk

John and Ceri Cook have done a grand job here, reimagining what was local favourite Oscar's as a stylish suburban eatery done out with bistro furnishings and richly coloured walls. Visitors have found the welcome 'warm' and the food 'first class', with locally sourced ingredients adding some extra cred to the menu – the restaurant's name means 'fresh' in Welsh, so you know where the owners' priorities lie. Recommended dishes such as crab and avocado with 'pico de gallo' salsa or wild sea bass with smoked prawn and basil butter show the kitchen's fondness for fish, but the eclectic seasonal repertoire also runs from Welsh lamb tagine with saffron risotto, salsa verde, fried garlic and shallots to Huntsham Court pork 'three ways' or a steak burger with Cajun brisket, ale mustard, triple-cooked chips and coleslaw. To conclude, you might consider yoghurt pannacotta with honey-roasted figs or apple and cinnamon crumble with pistachio ice cream. 'Excellent' house wine selections from £15.95.
Chef/s: John Cook. **Open:** Tue to Sun L 11.30 to 2.30 (4 Sun), Tue to Sat D 6 to 9.30 (10 Sat). **Closed:** Mon. **Meals:** alc (main courses £13 to £24). Set L £13 (2 courses) to £16. Sun L £14 (2 courses) to £16. **Details:** 60 seats. Wheelchair access. Music. Parking.

Bully's

Powerful French allegiances
Cooking score: 2
Modern French | £35
5 Romilly Crescent, Cardiff, CF11 9NP
Tel no: (029) 2022 1905
www.bullysrestaurant.co.uk

'The quirky atmosphere always gives you something to talk about no matter how dull your dinner date,' asserted one reporter of this homely neighbourhood restaurant, whose walls are decorated with an eclectic assortment of family memorabilia. There's a new team in the kitchen, headed by chef Christie Matthews, and word is that they are turning out 'fantastic food, which over the last few months has gone from strength to strength'. Classically-based but full of fresh ideas, the food showcases top-tier ingredients with pan-fried foie gras with ginger and hazelnut crumb and mango purée, char-grilled Welsh beef fillet with dauphinois potatoes, wild garlic, yellow chanterelles and Madagascan peppercorn sauce, and vanilla pannacotta with bitter orange and basil sorbet typical offerings. The wine list includes a keenly priced selection of the owner's favourites, plus a 'prestige selection' of mostly European finds priced with a 'simple cash margin' to bring guests the best value. House wine is £18.
Chef/s: Christie Matthews. **Open:** all week L 12 to 2 (3.30 Sun), Mon to Sat D 6.30 to 9 (6 to 10 Sat). **Meals:** alc (main courses £14 to £26). Set L £14 (2 courses) to £16. Set D £15 (2 courses) to £20. **Details:** 40 seats. Music.

Casanova

Charming, authentic city-centre Italian
Cooking score: 1
Italian | £30
13 Quay Street, Cardiff, CF10 1EA
Tel no: (029) 2034 4044
www.casanovacardiff.com

Now into its tenth year, this homely little Italian is as charming and seductive as the man who inspired its name. Casanova is run by three friends who have brought an authentic slice of Italy to a part of Cardiff dominated by chain restaurants. Keenly priced set lunch and dinner menus offer a roll call of rustic regional dishes, perhaps diver-caught scallops with chilli, black pudding, pumpkin purée and spicy tomato jam, followed with venison and pork ragù. Pannacotta and blackberry jam is one traditional way to finish. Wines, from the unashamedly all-Italian wine list, start at £17.50.

Chef/s: Antonio Cersosimo. **Open:** Mon to Sat L 12 to 2.30, D 5.30 to 10. **Closed:** Sun, 25 and 26 Dec, 31 Dec, 1 Jan, bank hols. **Meals:** Set L £15 (2 courses) to £20. Set D £25 (2 courses) to £30. **Details:** 35 seats. Music.

Chapel 1877

Classic flavours in a unique setting
Cooking score: 2
Modern British | £34
Churchill Way, Cardiff, CF10 2WF
Tel no: (029) 2022 2020
www.chapel1877.com

Perfect for people-watching, this striking Methodist chapel has been lovingly restored to create a swanky and singular eating/drinking venue. Downstairs is a lively bar, but restaurant diners should head for the tranquil mezzanine floor with its view of the bustle below. If you prefer a bit of romantic seclusion, ask to be seated in one of the booths. The menu is a truly wide-ranging affair, with choices ranging from salmon sashimi with crispy slaw and sesame, soy, chilli, ginger and lime salsa to roast loin of Breconshire venison with prosciutto, beetroot and goats' cheese gnocchi, curly kale and porcini mushroom jus. To finish, maybe flourless blood-orange and almond cake, Jersey crème fraîche, rosewater and cardamom. Previous issues with service appear to have been ironed out, with one reporter commenting on 'remarkably brisk, pleasant and attentive service' on a busy night. The substantial wine list (from £18) offers helpful notes on wine/food pairings.
Chef/s: Kieran Harry. **Open:** all week L 12 to 2.30 (3 Fri and Sat, 5.30 Sun), Mon to Sat D 5.30 to 10. **Closed:** 25 and 26 Dec, 1 Jan. **Meals:** alc (main courses £12 to £30). Set L £13 (2 courses). Sun L £19. **Details:** 125 seats. 22 seats outside. Bar. Music. No children under 16 yrs after 9.

Fish at 85

Marine life fresh from the fishmonger
Cooking score: 3
Seafood | £35
85 Pontcanna Street, Cardiff, CF11 9HS
Tel no: (029) 2002 0212
www.fishat85.co.uk

It seems like a simple enough proposition (although some have found it 'bewildering'): pick out the fish you want at the counter, select a cooking method and choose a sauce. And so it will come to pass. This enterprising fishmonger's has a counter loaded with locally landed stuff in tiptop condition and a cheery no-frills décor with white the dominating theme (walls, tables, chairs). There is a menu, from which you might go for a starter of crispy calamari, or a soft-boiled duck egg with smoked salmon and asparagus, and move on to roasted monkfish wrapped in Parma ham with Mediterranean vegetables and sauce vierge. If you do go for the catch of the day option (the lemon sole with tarragon and tomato beurre blanc has received good notices), don't be shy of asking how much it will cost. Side dishes include fat or skinny chips, samphire and heritage carrots. Wines start at £16.95.
Chef/s: Dom Powell. **Open:** Tue to Sat L 12 to 2.30, D 6 to 9 (8.30 Tue and Wed). **Closed:** Sun, Mon, 25 Dec to 2 Jan. **Meals:** alc (main courses £22 to £32). Set L £13 (2 courses) to £16. **Details:** 32 seats. 8 seats outside. V menu. Music.

Mint and Mustard

Contemporary and classic Indian food
Cooking score: 2
Indian | £25
134 Whitchurch Road, Cardiff, CF14 3LZ
Tel no: (029) 2062 0333
www.mintandmustard.com

Mint and Mustard is a great bet for anything from a comforting chicken tikka masala to interesting modern Indian dishes. A long-reigning star of the Cardiff dining scene (now with offshoots in Taunton, Penarth and

Weston-Super-Mare), it is a smart, modern space that conjures a sense of occasion while also cultivating a relaxed, cheery buzz. Bright images of India fill the walls and the service is equally sunny. To begin, choose from familiar classics (onion palak pakora, Bombay chat) or less predictable options such as a venison trio (tikka, kebab and samosa). The main influence here is the fresh, light and healthy food of Kerala, so main courses focus on regional dishes such as Nadan chicken curry (with coconut milk, tomatoes and spices); a festive pineapple Kalan; and Malabar lamb shank, marinated in Keralan spices and cooked in the tandoor. To finish, try the tandoori pineapple with pistachio ice cream. A decent wine list, with bottles graded by style, opens at £15.95.

Chef/s: Santhosh Nair. **Open:** all week L 12 to 2, D 5 to 11. **Closed:** 25 and 26 Dec. **Meals:** alc (main courses £8 to £16). Set L £15 (2 courses) to £20. Tasting menu £40. **Details:** 100 seats. Bar. Wheelchair access. Music.

The Potted Pig

Generous cooking and a lively atmosphere
Cooking score: 2
Modern British | £40
27 High Street, Cardiff, CF10 1PU
Tel no: (029) 2022 4817
www.thepottedpig.com

The discreet doorway in Cardiff's city centre gives no clue to the size of this subterranean restaurant. Set in a former bank vault, its bare brickwork, low lighting and industrial piping conjure an air of underground cool, while the menu delivers a trendy take on British favourites – especially pigs. They may come potted with toast or in a sharing dish of whole mustard-glazed ham hock with coleslaw, cauliflower and new potatoes. Gin, the perfect partner, is offered in countless guises. The patriotic theme sometimes takes an unexpected turn, as in a starter of sprout flowers with charred sprout tops, Stilton and breadcrumbs. Other dishes, such as pan-roasted hake with cockle, laverbread and bacon cake, cavolo nero, cauliflower purée and mussel broth, have a distinctly Welsh flavour.

To finish, try good old sticky toffee pudding with spiced raisin ice cream. If gin is not your thing, there is a decent international wine selection starting at £18.

Chef/s: Gwyn Myring and Tom Furlong. **Open:** Tue to Sun L 12 to 2, Tue to Sat D 7 to 9 (6.30 to 9.30 Fri and Sat). **Closed:** Mon. **Meals:** alc (main courses £13 to £28). Set L £12 (2 courses) to £16. Sun L £15. **Details:** 85 seats. Wheelchair access. Music. Children over 14 yrs only at D.

Purple Poppadom

Indian invention and surprises
Cooking score: 3
Indian | £35
Upper Floor, 185a Cowbridge Road East, Cardiff, CF11 9AJ
Tel no: (029) 2022 0026
www.purplepoppadom.com

There's no fanfare to announce this Cardiff starlet: blink and you'll miss its entrance on a busy city thoroughfare. The first-floor dining room is equally unsurprising – mellow lighting, rich shades of purple – yet a buzz of happy diners create a relaxed, unpretentious mood that belies the ambition of the cooking. Anand George made his name at Mint and Mustard (see entry) but really excels here, combining fresh local ingredients and vivid Indian flavours in dishes that reference both classic European and regional Indian traditions. How about 'tiffin cup' hake, pan-seared on a bed of tapioca mash, served in classic toddy-shop style, soused in roasted coconut and smoked tamarind sauce, with a 'petite' naan bread? Or Nawabi chicken – tandoor-cooked breast marinated with cardamom and mace, pickled chicken legs, sautéed turnip, black cabbage and quail's egg? To finish, try tandoori pineapple with coconut ice cream. Wines from £15.95.

Chef/s: Anand George. **Open:** Tue to Sat L 12 to 2, D 5.30 to 11. Sun 1 to 9. **Closed:** Mon, 25 and 26 Dec, 1 Jan. **Meals:** alc (main courses £9 to £18). Set L and early D £15. Tasting menu £38 (5 courses) to £48. **Details:** 70 seats. Music.

Cowbridge

Bar 44

Enjoyable, cheery tapas joint
Cooking score: 2
Spanish | £18
44c High Street, Cowbridge, CF71 7AG
Tel no: (01446) 776488
www.bar44.co.uk

 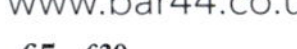

The Morgan boys' passion for Spanish culinary culture has resulted in two restaurants thus far (number two being Bar 44 in Penarth), and it's a winning formula borne out of a genuine affection for the adopted motherland. Inside, the tiles and mellow colours look the part – think Med sunshine rather than South Wales drizzle – and the deli means you can take some goodies home if you want. Blackboards reveal what cured meats are up for grabs (freshly carved jamón Ibérico, lomo, cecina), while tapas range from simple boquerones and tortilla to compelling options such as white crab tostadas, spiced slow-roasted duck with cauliflower and pomegranate, and sautéed chicken livers fired up with Pedro Ximénez. Finish with vanilla, turrón and blackberry cheesecake. Sherry gets the attention it deserves on a list including spanish wines, cocktails, beers and ciders (it's a bar after all). Wines start at £15.
Chef/s: Chris Edwards. **Open:** all week 12 to 9 (5 Mon, 10 Fri and Sat). **Meals:** Tapas (£4 to £8). Set L £10 (Mon to Fri). **Details:** 55 seats. Music.

Oscars of Cowbridge

Accommodating all-day eatery
Cooking score: 1
International | £25
65 High Street, Cowbridge, CF71 7AF
Tel no: (01446) 771984
www.oscarsofcowbridge.com

Recently refurbished 'in line with freshness, fashion and trends' (according to the owners), this accommodating all-day eatery covers all bases – from morning coffee out on the pavement to bargain lunches, early-bird deals and full-blown suppers. The busy kitchen rustles up open sandwiches, mac 'n' cheese, salads and burgers for the daytime crowd, before raising its game in the evening: expect anything from sticky baby back ribs with pomegranate molasses to Welsh rarebit with wild mushrooms on brioche, or slow-cooked maple-glazed pulled pork with mustard mash. Wines start at £15.95.
Chef/s: Gareth Chivell. **Open:** Mon to Sat 12 to 9.30 (10 Fri and Sat). **Closed:** Sun, 25 Dec. **Meals:** alc (main courses £10 to £18). **Details:** 50 seats. 25 seats outside. Bar. Wheelchair access. Music. Parking.

Mumbles

Munch of Mumbles

Skilled cooking at gentle prices
Cooking score: 2
British | £30
650 Mumbles Road, Mumbles, SA3 4EA
Tel no: (01792) 362244
www.munchofmumbles.com

An upmarket fishing village at Swansea's western edge, Mumbles has more than its fair share of boutiques, lunching mums and restaurants. Munch is not only one of the best, but also one of the cheapest, thanks to snappy set menus and a BYO policy. The rather drab interior used to be readers' only gripe, but a refurbishment at the end of 2014 ushered in new colours, new furniture and a profusion of artwork from local artists. Chef/proprietor Ben Griffiths continues to cook the unpretentious, gently creative food that first put Munch on the map, with local ingredients very much to the fore. Venison boudin with Gower swede, orange and cranberry, Gower sea bass with Oxwich Point lobster ravioli, samphire and bisque emulsion, and chocolate crémeux with milk crumb and malt ice cream are typical of the approach. While you are encouraged to bring your own wine, there is a modest selection of bottles from £12.50.

Chef/s: Ben Griffiths. **Open:** Wed to Sun L 12 to 2.30, Wed to Sat D 6 to 9.30. **Closed:** Mon, Tue, 24 to 26 Dec, 1 week Feb, 1 week Jul, 3 weeks Oct. **Meals:** Set L £16 (2 courses) to £20. Set D £25 (2 courses) to £30. Sun L £16 (2 courses) to £20. **Details:** 40 seats. Music.

▌Penarth
The Fig Tree

Panoramic views and seasonal food
Cooking score: 3
Modern British | £29
The Esplanade, Penarth, CF64 3AU
Tel no: (029) 2070 2512
www.thefigtreepenarth.co.uk

A beautifully restored Victorian beach shelter, with grandstand views across the Bristol Channel to Weston-super-Mare in Somerset from the dining room, verandah and roof terrace, this is a restaurant of high local repute. Chef-proprietor Mike Caplan-Hill has a crusading attitude to local produce – as much as possible is sourced within a 30-mile radius – that he turns into fresh, light, modern dishes of strong appeal. A March menu yielded home-smoked Cornish mackerel served with pickled samphire and horseradish cream, and Goosnargh duck hash topped with a fried duck egg, and went on to slow-cooked Vale of Glamorgan pork belly with spring greens, honey mustard mash and cider and sage sauce, and crab linguine with lemongrass, chilli and garlic. Favoured desserts include a Thai-style rice pudding with mango sorbet, and chocolate tart teamed with white chocolate ice cream. Wines start at £14.

Chef/s: Mike Caplan-Hill. **Open:** Tue to Sun L 12 to 3 (3.30 Sat, 4 Sun), Tue to Sat D 6 to 9.30. **Closed:** Mon, 25 and 26 Dec, 1 Jan. **Meals:** alc (main courses £12 to £20). Set L £11 (2 courses) to £14. Sun L £16 (2 courses) to £20. **Details:** 50 seats. 28 seats outside. Wheelchair access. Music.

Restaurant James Sommerin

Modern cooking with classical foundations
Cooking score: 7
Modern British | £65
The Esplanade, Penarth, CF64 3AU
Tel no: (029) 2070 6559
www.jamessommerinrestaurant.co.uk

The dedicated reporters who arrived on the Penarth seafront amid relentless drizzle and howling winds could have been forgiven for wishing they'd stayed at home, until James Sommerin's seven-course tasting menu had its way with them. From the moment the first little pasta dish, a 'silk slip' of raviolo bursting with fresh peas under Parmesan foam, gave way to the succeeding risotto of Jerusalem artichoke with a sous-vide egg yolk and shaved truffle, they didn't much care what the weather was doing. Sommerin's bright, understated modern restaurant, with its tiled walls and letterbox-slot window into the kitchen, is the nerve centre of some of the most dynamic cooking in South Wales. Dishes have the all-important contemporary look to them, chic and neat little bundles of ingredients in which detonations of mesmerising flavours lurk, but the foundation is more classical than it might look. Fish could be a crisp-skinned fillet of sea bass in smoked butter sauce dotted with caviar, served, if you please, with fish knives ('I could happily pretend I was in an Agatha Christie novel'), while meat might be exquisitely tender guinea fowl with sweetcorn, sprouts and bacon. At the sweet end of things, well-thought-out combinations produce vanilla-scented cream cheese with rhubarb and a sprinkling of toasted oat crumble, or a composition of figs and nougatine in Grand Marnier. Wines offer an abbreviated account of each region, opening at £29 (£6 a glass).

Chef/s: James Sommerin. **Open:** Tue to Sun L 12 to 2.30, D 7 to 9.30 (9 Sun). **Closed:** Mon, 1 to 8 Jan. **Meals:** Set L £28 (2 courses) to £32. Tasting menu £55 (5 courses) to £85. **Details:** 70 seats. V menu. Wheelchair access. Music.

▌ Pontlliw
Rasoi

Lively Indian creations
Cooking score: 2
Indian | £19
Bryntirion Road, Pontlliw, SA4 9DY
Tel no: (01792) 882409
www.rasoiwales.co.uk

The time when this out-of-town venue was a regular pub is now a distant memory: Rasoi has earned its place on the map as one of the region's most distinctive Indian restaurants, and at the time of going to press there were whispers of a second branch coming to Swansea's trendy SA1 dockland area. Meanwhile, it's very much business as usual here in Pontlliw. A vast, artfully styled restaurant with moody lighting, lots of booth seating and a spicy colour scheme, it copes easily with everything from romantic twosomes to merry groups. The menu checks off regional specialities like aloo tikki, fish Amritsari and Goan fish curry, and throws in stalwarts such as chicken tikka masala or tandoori chicken. The naan breads, cooked in a part-open kitchen, are a must. Decent dessert options include gulab jaman and ice cream; and Shirikhand cheesecake with tamarind glaze. A snappy wine list, with helpful tasting notes, begins at just £13.95.
Chef/s: Kunwar Singh. **Open:** Mon to Thur L 12 to 2.30, D 5.30 to 10.30. Fri to Sun 12 to 11.30. **Closed:** 25 Dec. **Meals:** alc (mains £8 to £18). Set L £9 (2 courses) to £11. **Details:** 200 seats. 80 seats outside. V menu. Wheelchair access. Music. Parking.

James Sommerin

Restaurant James Sommerin, Penarth

What do you enjoy the most and least about being a chef?

I enjoy creating dishes and seeing our diners' reactions to them. There's nothing I don't enjoy; all of the challenges are what makes the job interesting and fun.

What would you be if you weren't a chef?

I don't know, being a chef is all I have ever wanted to be, I can't imagine being anything else.

What's your newest ingredient discovery?

White sprouting broccoli.

Do you have a guilty foodie pleasure?

I love corned beef hash and lasagne, you can't beat them.

At the end of a long day, what do you like to cook?

If it is for myself? It would probably have to be cheese on toast.

Tell us something about yourself that will surprise your diners.

I love simple, home-cooked food.

Pontypridd

★ TOP 50 PUB ★

Bunch of Grapes

Hostelry that does the neighbourhood proud
Cooking score: 4
Modern British | £29
Ynysangharad Road, Pontypridd, CF37 4DA
Tel no: (01443) 402934
www.bunchofgrapes.org.uk

It has been described as a 'community pub' and this talented all-rounder run by the owner of the Otley Brewing Company has a proper, dark, traditionally attired bar where real ales and wines are taken seriously – and offers hearty pub grub of the ploughman's/burger and chips variety. To really see what the kitchen can do, turn to the restaurant, which spreads over several artfully rustic rooms into a bright conservatory. Chef Sebastien Vanoni knows a thing or two about flavour, and doesn't stint on the details, delivering devilled lamb's kidneys on toasted focaccia, then perhaps pan-roasted breast of Cefnllan Farm duck with glazed heritage carrots, turnips and 'sensational' potatoes dauphinois. Toasted bara brith with Penderyn whisky ice cream is a suitably patriotic endnote. Wonderful breads and chutneys are made on site and can be bought in the pub's own deli. An impressive selection of wines opens at £15.90.
Chef/s: Sebastien Vanoni. **Open:** all week L 12 to 3 (4 Sat and Sun), Mon to Sat D 6 to 9.30 (10 Fri and Sat). **Meals:** alc (main courses £10 to £26). **Details:** 66 seats. 24 seats outside. Bar. Wheelchair access. Music. Parking.

Symbols

 Accommodation is available
£30 Three courses for less than £30
£5 OFF £5-off voucher scheme
🍾 Notable wine list

Reynoldston

Fairyhill

Smart hotel with clear-flavoured cooking
Cooking score: 4
Modern British | £45
Reynoldston, SA3 1BS
Tel no: (01792) 390139
www.fairyhill.net

Seasons change, the years roll by, but Andrew Hetherington and Paul Davies' country house hotel endures undimmed. Rambling through several immaculate rooms, mostly with garden views, it offers just the right level of friendliness, with 'lovely service from young waitresses'. Chef David Whitecross has been here since 2013, serving up classically based cooking with zealous enthusiasm. Try deep-fried and 'wonderfully truffly' Perl Wen cheese say, spilling from its crisp shell to join a 'lovely rich slick' of earthy cauliflower purée, and then pearly lemon sole, its skin cooked to brittle perfection, enlivened by the play of verjus with sweet carrot purée, sultanas and fragrant fennel. Desserts such as sticky toffee pudding with a good, darkly caramelised sauce don't quite match the deft creativity of the preceding courses, but they still deserve attention – as does the truly global wine list, which opens at £21.50.
Chef/s: David Whitecross. **Open:** all week L 12 to 2 (3 Sun), D 7 to 9. **Closed:** 26 Dec, 3 weeks Jan. **Meals:** Set L £20 (2 courses) to £25. Set D £35 (2 courses) to £45. Sun L £28. **Details:** 60 seats. 30 seats outside. V menu. Bar. Music. Parking.

Swansea

Didier & Stephanie

Tasteful French cuisine
Cooking score: 4
French | £30
56 St Helen's Road, Swansea, SA1 4BE
Tel no: (01792) 655603

'Polished perfection' could be the mantra of this Swansea stalwart, which has been serving tiptop French food to its loyal followers for over a decade. In recent years it has acquired a slick new look that suggests a coming of age: soft greys, with pops of berry red and Art Deco-inspired lighting, all smack of luxury and good taste. The cooking keeps pace, making the familiar seem remarkable with the sheer quality of ingredients and precision of delivery. First off there are plump, crusty, oven-fresh rolls ('it's impossible to imagine how these could be improved'). Then, perhaps a goats' cheese tart comprising an airy layer of puff pastry topped with caramelised onions and a pearly disc of melting chèvre. Beautiful ingredients are the making of a straight-talking main of sea bass with beurre blanc and garden vegetables, while a generous dessert of white chocolate, coconut and Malibu mousse delighted with its melting richness. An ample wine list with plenty from France opens at £15.90.

Chef/s: Didier Suvé. **Open:** Tue to Sat L 12.30 to 2.30, D 7 to 10.30. **Closed:** Sun, Mon, Christmas to New Year, 2 weeks summer. **Meals:** alc (main courses £17 to £20). **Details:** 20 seats. Music.

Hanson at the Chelsea

Unfussy but sophisticated bistro
Cooking score: 4
Modern European | £30
17 St Mary Street, Swansea, SA1 3LH
Tel no: (01792) 464068
www.hansonatthechelsea.co.uk

In the warm embrace of this homely Swansea stalwart, the shouts of nearby Wind Street (the city's rumbustious pub quarter) fade away. Andrew Hanson's cooking has gained lustre and creativity over the years. Never one to stint on portions, his current offerings include a duck Scotch egg of kingly proportions, sliced in two so its slick, sunny yolk spills on to tender asparagus and velvety hollandaise. Expect global influences including plenty from Europe – maybe monkfish with fat ribbons of homemade pappardelle, plump mussels and clams in a delicate parsley and Parmesan cream sauce. Desserts are always a strength, so try to squeeze one in, say brioche bread-and-butter pudding served with a

luscious honey and whisky cream. Service is charming and prompt, but the mellow lighting and simple wood-floored interior invite you to linger over a bottle from the above par international list, especially as prices start at £13.95.

Chef/s: Andrew Hanson. **Open:** Mon to Sat L 12 to 2, D 7 to 9.30. **Closed:** Sun. **Meals:** alc (main courses £12 to £22). Set L £14 (2 courses) to £18. Set D £20. **Details:** 40 seats. V menu. Music.

NEW ENTRY
Slice

Flourishing Swansea star
Cooking score: 4
Modern British | £35
73-75 Eversley Road, Swansea, SA2 9DE
Tel no: (01792) 290929
www.sliceswansea.co.uk

Slice has been a star of the Swansea dining scene for years, but it turned over a new leaf in May 2014 when chef/owners Adam Bannister and Chris Harris took the reins. Both have impressive CVs, including time spent at the Hardwick near Abergavenny (see entry), and they diplomatically take turns front-of-house and in the kitchen. The interior is as before, with seating upstairs for just 16, while pale wood, stripped floors and simple wood furnishings create a cool, Scandi-tinged interior. The cooking echoes this homely-yet-streamlined vibe: the homemade focaccia is delectably salty and oily; an amuse of roasted cauliflower soup impresses with its 'intense, rounded flavours'; crayfish bisque poured over a fat crayfish ravioli is equally potent; while a main of pan-fried halibut with broccoli purée, purple sprouting broccoli and lentils 'showcases fresh, flawless ingredients'. As a finale, the silky/crunchy deconstructed caramelised pineapple and honeycomb cheesecake is a clever, texture-rich dessert. Wines from £16.

Chef/s: Chris Harris and Adam Bannister. **Open:** Fri to Sun L 12 to 2, Wed to Sun D 6.30 to 9. **Closed:** Mon, Tue. **Meals:** Set L £26 (2 courses) to £30. Set D £35. **Details:** 16 seats. V menu. Music.

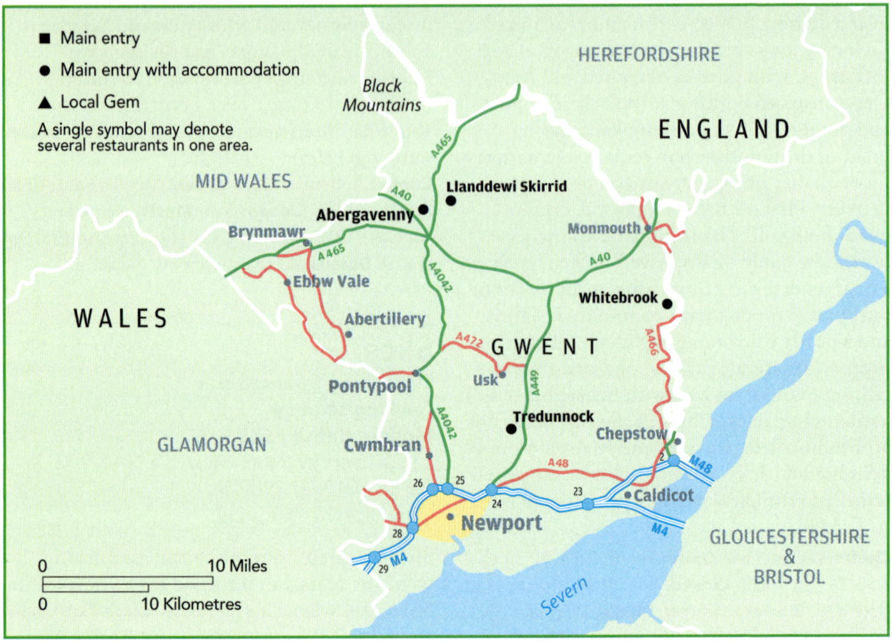

Abergavenny

★ TOP 50 PUB ★

The Hardwick

An all-round Welsh winner
Cooking score: 5
Modern British | £40
Old Raglan Road, Abergavenny, NP7 9AA
Tel no: (01873) 854220
www.thehardwick.co.uk

An unflashy rural haven with affluent metropolitan sensibilities, this instantly likeable all-rounder strikes just the right note for a modern inn — not bad for a chef who earned his stripes in the kitchen of Le Gavroche (see entry). Since pitching camp here in 2005, Welsh-born Stephen Terry has won friends with his big cosmopolitan flavours and lack of pomposity: one minute you're in Italy, sampling panzanella and puntarelle salad or shoulder of Brecon lamb with deep-fried polenta and salsa verde, the next you're holed up in a US diner scoffing plates of 'HFC' chicken breast with sweet potato fries, char-grilled onion and slaw. Even homespun ideas are given an unexpected kick (baked lemon gel with salmon fishcakes, for example), while fans of high-protein should sign up for the dry-aged delights of the 'Johnny Morris beef box'. The cheeseboard is a true Welsh patriot, Terry's ice creams are legendary and it's also worth sampling the crunchy homage to his mum's lemon meringue pie. Just add a classy, modern and democratic wine list, with prices from £19.
Chef/s: Stephen Terry and Lee Evans. **Open:** all week L 12 to 3, D 6.30 to 10. **Closed:** 25 Dec.
Meals: alc (main courses £17 to £34). Set L and D £21 (2 courses) to £26. Sun L £22 (2 courses) to £28.
Details: 80 seats. 20 seats outside. Bar. Wheelchair access. Music. Parking.

Restaurant 1861

Homely roadside restaurant
Cooking score: 3
Modern British | £40
Cross Ash, Abergavenny, NP7 8PB
Tel no: (01873) 821297
www.18-61.co.uk

Snug beside a snaking road in deepest, greenest Monmouthshire, this pretty, cosily traditional black-and-white restaurant is a family affair, run by chef Simon King and his wife Kate. Simon makes the most of the excellent produce available locally, including fresh vegetables from his father-in-law's nursery in Nant-y-derry. Having notched up years of experience in some heavyweight kitchens (notably the Waterside Inn at Bray), Simon pulls no punches with his classically inspired menu, which might offer fish soup and rouille with garlic croûtons ahead of seared skirt of beef marinated in red wine and herbs and served with mushroom coulis. From the lengthy dessert menu there's a fine banana soufflé with chocolate sauce, but interesting alternatives include a savoury offering in the form of cider and Stilton rarebit with a poached egg. A fairly lengthy international wine list offers plenty under £25 with prices from £17.50.
Chef/s: Simon King. **Open:** Tue to Sun L 12 to 1.45, Tue to Sat D 7 to 8.45. **Closed:** Mon, 26 Dec to 10 Jan. **Meals:** alc (main courses £20 to £24). Set L £22 (2 courses) to £25. Set D £35. Sun L £25. Tasting menu £55. **Details:** 35 seats. Music. Parking.

Llanddewi Skirrid

The Walnut Tree

Re-energised Welsh icon
Cooking score: 6
Modern British | £45
Llanddewi Skirrid, NP7 8AW
Tel no: (01873) 852797
www.thewalnuttreeinn.com

It is hard to believe that one could find such a hidden gem in the foothills of the Black Mountains, but the much-acclaimed Walnut Tree certainly ticks all the right epicurean boxes. There's no disputing there's acute talent in the kitchen and Shaun Hill has certainly given this former pub – long regarded as a British culinary institution – restored status since taking over in 2007. The food is deceptively simple, with no unnecessary fuss or trimmings, just high-quality ingredients lightly and confidently handled. Expansive, yet very appealing menus blend the traditional, say veal kidneys with bacon and mustard sauce or saddle of venison with its own hash, with modern touches in such dishes as pollack with salt cod brandade, broccoli and olives. Typically, start with 'mind-blowing' veal sweetbreads with sauerkraut and warm dressing, and finish with pear and raspberry streusel tart. The set-lunch menu gets the thumbs-up – 'the most delicious food' – and the wine list is no less delightful: well chosen and keenly priced, divided into 'essential', 'core' and 'classic' choices. Bottles from £20.
Chef/s: Shaun Hill and Roger Brook. **Open:** Tue to Sat L 12 to 2.30, D 6.30 to 9.30. **Closed:** Sun, Mon, 1 week Christmas. **Meals:** alc (main courses £16 to £30). Set L £25 (2 courses) to £30. **Details:** 50 seats. 12 seats outside. Bar. Wheelchair access. Parking.

Tredunnock

NEW ENTRY

Newbridge on Usk

Riverside charmer with imaginative food
Cooking score: 3
Modern British | £36
Tredunnock, NP15 1LY
Tel no: (01633) 451000
www.celtic-manor.com

This former pub – now an outpost of Newport's Celtic Manor Resort – channels country gent and woolly hipster in equal measure. There are oriental rugs on quarry-tiled floors, leather chairs by the log-burner and terracotta plant pots on the tables. Candles flicker in vintage china cups and the chips come (naturally) in white-and-blue enamel camping mugs. It's a winning formula, and the service is pitched nicely between formal and relaxed. Expect homely but often imaginative food that bursts with flavour: crisp-coated lamb breast with curried sweetbreads, celeriac remoulade and Puy lentil vinaigrette was an 'exceptional' starter, while 28-day matured pan-roasted Welsh beef with roasted garlic mash, bone marrow, wild mushrooms and oxtail jus proved 'rich and satisfying'. A dessert of coconut rice pudding overpowered by pineapple was the only uncomfortable pairing in an otherwise assured inspection meal. A decent list of international wines and beers kicks off at £17.50.

Chef/s: Adam Whittle. **Open:** all week L 12 to 2.30 (4 Sun), D 6.30 to 9.30. **Meals:** alc (main courses £16 to £28). Set L £16 (2 courses) to £20. **Details:** 65 seats. 40 seats outside. Bar. Music. Parking.

▌ **Whitebrook**
The Whitebrook

Cooking in tune with the times
Cooking score: 5
Modern British | £54
Whitebrook, NP25 4TX
Tel no: (01600) 860254
www.thewhitebrook.co.uk

They may question the name change, but regulars agree that chef/proprietor Chris Harrod has started 'another fine chapter' for this delightful restaurant-with-rooms hunkered down on a steep hillside in a straggly village not far from the River Wye. Everywhere has been redecorated: 'the dining room and bar area are lighter and more comfortable, tables are in three areas (you don't feel isolated if some are not occupied) and are, praise be, a sensible size with room for bottles, glasses, cutlery, fashionably large plates and even elbows'. Harrod's food is serious stuff and he's in tune with the times, leavening his seasonal menus with 'elements foraged from the valley' – especially good has been scallops with chicory, orange, aromatic nuts and seeds; halibut with parsley root, nasturtium tubers, ham and celandine; and a 'memorable' suckling pig with caramelised celeriac. Elsewhere, venison from 'the valley'

might be dramatically presented with walnuts, Brussels tops, quince and semi-dried grape, while desserts go back to nature – think blackcurrant, chamomile and sorrel or rhubarb with Jersey milk, walnut crunch and medlar syrup. There's a 'very fine cheeseboard with a strong Welsh presence', excellent service and an enlightened wine list that favours small growers, organic producers and lesser-known grape varieties; also note the bottles from Ancre Hill Estate in Monmouthshire. Fifteen cracking house selections start at £23 (£5.50 a glass).

Chef/s: Chris Harrod. **Open:** Tue to Sun L 12 to 2, D 7 to 9. **Closed:** Mon, first 2 weeks Jan. **Meals:** Set L £25 (2 courses) to £29. Set D £54. Sun L £35. Tasting Menu £67 (7 courses). **Details:** 32 seats. V menu. Music. Parking.

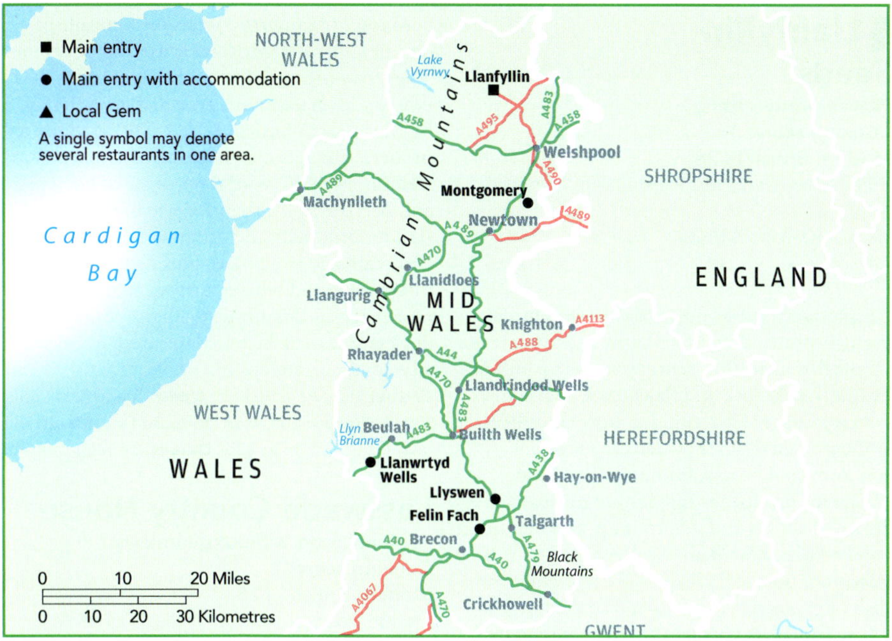

■ Felin Fach

★ TOP 50 PUB ★

The Felin Fach Griffin

A beacon of Brecon hospitality

Cooking score: 4
Modern British | £33
Felin Fach, LD3 0UB
Tel no: (01874) 620111
www.eatdrinksleep.ltd.uk

'The welcome, the service, the food, the wine list… impeccable,' is the verdict of a devotee who has been supporting Charles and Edmund Inkin's smart rural inn from the start. The convivial way the place is run is a great draw, thanks in part to a careful balance of pubby approachability, and to a kitchen that focuses squarely on unpretentious but clever modern cooking. Own-grown or knowledgeably sourced local and regional produce is the jumping-off point for forthright seasonal dishes such as roast pheasant breast with a pheasant and black pudding pie, slow-cooked belly of pork, or pollack fillet teamed with chorizo, mussel, clam, chickpea and tomato ragù. Lamb pastilla with Jerusalem artichoke or home-cured salmon with fennel, tarragon and beetroot start things off well; top desserts have included a chocolate brownie with peanut crunch and chocolate ice cream; or you may want to look to the well-chosen wine list (from £17.50) for something to accompany the impressive selection of British cheeses.

Chef/s: Max Wilson. **Open:** all week L 12 to 2.30, D 6 to 9 (9.30 Fri and Sat). **Closed:** 4 days mid Jan. **Meals:** alc (main courses £8 to £20). Set L £18 (2 courses) to £21. Set D £23 (2 courses) to £29. Sun L £20 (2 courses) to £25. **Details:** 65 seats. 35 seats outside. Bar. Wheelchair access. Music. Parking.

Average price

The average price denotes the price of a three-course meal without wine.

 Llanfyllin
Seeds

Picture-pretty setting
Cooking score: 1
Modern British | £28
5 Penybryn Cottages, High Street, Llanfyllin,
SY22 5AP
Tel no: (01691) 648604

£30

Restaurant settings don't come much more picture-pretty than this. Right in the heart of Llanfyllin, this 16th-century cottage is full of beams, brickwork and flagstones. Mark and Felicity Seager have run the show since 1991, and between them they deliver a warm welcome and hearty, unpretentious food. Excellent produce is apparent in dishes such as cream of rocket and potato soup, and in tender chicken breast with an excellent, full-flavoured port and cream sauce and generous dish of perfectly cooked veg. For dessert, the white chocolate cheesecake with caramel sauce is a good way to finish. Wines from £16.
Chef/s: Mark Seager. **Open:** Thur to Sat L 11 to 2, Tue to Sat D 6.30 to 10. **Closed:** Mon, (Mon, Tue and Wed winter), 2 weeks Jan. **Meals:** alc (main courses £10 to £19). Set D £24 (2 courses) to £28. **Details:** 20 seats. 6 seats outside.

 Llanwrtyd Wells
Carlton Riverside

Smart yet homely riverside retreat
Cooking score: 5
Modern British | £37
Irfon Crescent, Llanwrtyd Wells, LD5 4SP
Tel no: (01591) 610248
www.carltonriverside.com

£5 OFF

Close to the river in the smallest town in Wales, this handsome grey-stone building has a lot going for it: upmarket guest rooms, a locals' bar in the basement serving all-day pizzas, and a homely restaurant offering everything from Welsh ribeye with chips to five-course chef's tasting menus. The chef in question is Mary Ann Gilchrist, who's been cooking in Llanwrtyd Wells for a couple of decades – first at Carlton House and now here. There's an intimate feel to the restaurant, which is overseen with polished proficiency by Mary Ann's husband Alan. The food has a modern European feel: beetroot-cured salmon, perhaps, with remoulade of beet, port and beetroot jelly, then assiette of pork (tenderloin, belly and croquette) with stir-fried cabbage and potato purée, while orange marmalade and whisky tart with oranges marinated in Drambuie is a hard-to-skip dessert. Alan can be relied upon for good wine advice; the list opens at £16.95.
Chef/s: Mary Ann Gilchrist. **Open:** Tue to Sat D only 7 to 9. **Closed:** Sun, Mon, 15 to 30 Dec. **Meals:** alc (main courses £16 to £25). **Details:** 16 seats. Music.

Lasswade Country House

Seasonal food without gimmickry
Cooking score: 2
Modern British | £28
Station Road, Llanwrtyd Wells, LD5 4RW
Tel no: (01591) 610515
www.lasswadehotel.co.uk

 £30

Boutique hotels and their cannily styled interiors – with knowing winks towards tradition – are the norm these days, but this country house hotel is endearingly of the old school. The majestic early 1900s house with spectacular country views and a genuinely traditional interior delivers peachy carpets, polished tables and patterned wallpaper in the dining room. Roger and Emma Stevens are the driving force, offering a genuinely warm welcome and plenty of friendly attention. Roger's cooking draws on the locality, including lamb from local hill farms and vegetables from his nearby cottage garden. A test meal produced brandade of Cardigan Bay mackerel with a pea purée ahead of a 'perfectly pitched' main course of seared breast of Gressingham duck with compote of beetroot and pears, fennel and a sweet potato purée, and the bar stayed high for dessert: a zingy baked lemon tart with fresh raspberries. A short but interesting wine list kicks off at a very reasonable £13.95.

Chef/s: Roger Stevens. **Open:** all week D only 7.30 to 9. **Closed:** 25 and 26 Dec. **Meals:** Set D £28. **Details:** 20 seats.

Llyswen

★ TOP 50 ★

NEW ENTRY
Llangoed Hall

Bold cooking in a stunning country mansion
Cooking score: 7
Modern British | £65
Llyswen, LD3 0YP
Tel no: (01874) 754525
www.llangoedhall.co.uk

'The best outside the West End,' says one reporter of this gorgeous Edwardian mansion whose grounds include an extensive kitchen garden and smokehouse. Chef Nick Brodie's influence is clear inside, too: settle in the lounge, with its polished floorboards, fascinating art collection and cavernous fireplace, and two lads from the kitchen will bring your canapés and advise on the menu. Those canapés are delightful: at a test meal the spread included (among others) a pork scratching with ham hock; elderberry meringue with a foie gras filling; and a celeriac crisp with duck truffle egg. They set the tone for something special. Brodie's food – served in a quietly dreamlike, pastel blue dining room – is smart, sophisticated and complex, each flavour leading to the next with exact precision. Truffle-poached celeriac with mushroom, crème fraîche, walnuts, Ibérico ham and a mushroom velouté combine in a starter full of nuances and textural contrasts. A main course of butternut 'cannelloni', goats' cheese shavings, pumpkin textures, parsnip and cheese is equally complex, its sweet, earthy vegetable tones a revelation. Brodie is clever enough to innovate successfully, but

also knows the power of the familiar: a stylised apple 'strudel' for dessert is crisp and clever but also comforting.

Chef/s: Nick J. Brodie. **Open:** all week L 12 to 2, D 6.30 to 9.30. **Meals:** alc (main courses £32 to £39). Set L £20 (2 courses) to £30. Set D £40 (2 courses) to £65. Tasting menus £65 to £115. **Details:** 50 seats. 20 seats outside. V menu. Bar. Wheelchair access. Music.

Montgomery
The Checkers

Classical French food in the Welsh borders
Cooking score: 6
French | £50
Broad Street, Montgomery, SY15 6PN
Tel no: (01686) 669822
www.thecheckersmontgomery.co.uk

Not far from the border between Shropshire and old Montgomeryshire, the Checkers is a renovated coaching inn, now transformed into a rustic-chic restaurant-with-rooms by a French chef/patron from Agen, via the Waterside Inn and Le Manoir. Though there are certainly some modern grace-notes to Stéphane Borie's repertoire – scallops and smoked bacon dressed in honey and clementine, roasted monkfish with onion tartlet in port and olive sauce – the core is very much in the classical French idiom. Swirling Périgord truffle cream into a bowl of Jerusalem artichoke velouté, adding a touch of his own culinary heritage in Agen prune chutney to foie gras ballotine, and balancing a stuffed leg of hare on braised lentils in thyme and garlic jus all give plenty evidence of that. A seven-course tasting menu is the high-rolling option, culminating with Grand Marnier soufflé. Wales gets a look-in among the cheeses, and wines are by no means limited to France, starting at £16 for Chilean Cabernet.

Chef/s: Stéphane Borie. **Open:** Fri and Sat L 12 to 1.45, Tue to Sat D 6 to 9. **Closed:** Sun, Mon, 2 weeks Jan, 1 week summer. **Meals:** alc (main courses £18 to £29). Tasting menu £75 (7 courses). **Details:** 50 seats. Children over 8 yrs only at D.

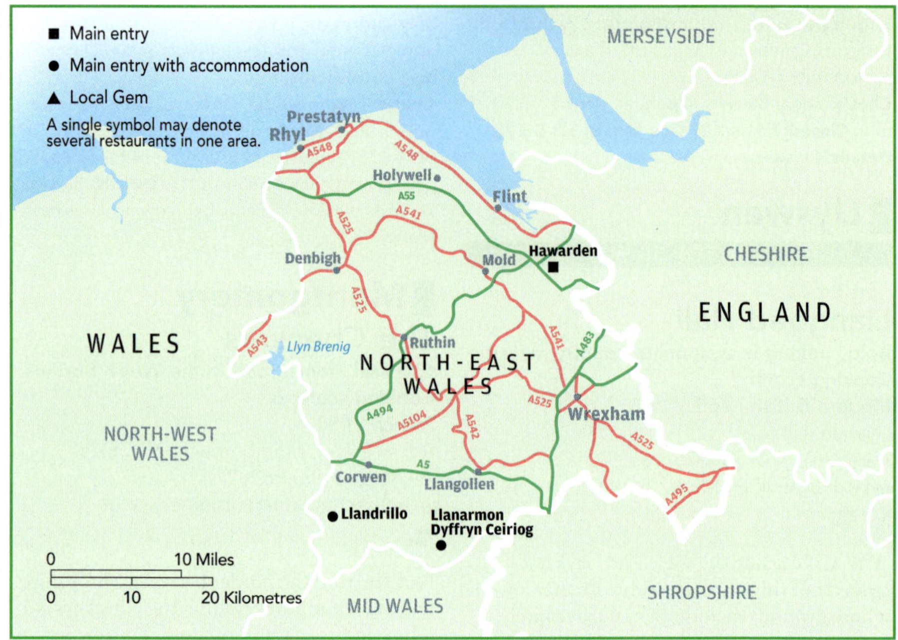

■ Hawarden

NEW ENTRY

The Glynne Arms

Cool village inn serving big-hearted food

Cooking score: 3
British | £30
3 Glynne Way, Hawarden, CH5 3NS
Tel no: (01244) 569988
www.theglynnearms.co.uk

Interesting that this village pub is owned by the Gladstones, who run the posh online shop Pedlars: their taste is evident in the interior design, which channels hipster and heritage style in equal measure. A one-armed bandit, mounted antlers aplenty, chairs that look like they've been salvaged from a village hall – it's a charming mash-up of vintage flavours. Fed by sister business The Hawarden Estate Farm Shop, the kitchen turns out dishes as eclectic as the interior: sticky honey-glazed ribs or a magnificent burger are a nod across the pond, but there are also playful takes on Brit classics, such as the 'ham, egg and chips' starter combining poached egg, a ham shank croquette and a gargantuan rosti-style 'chip'. A main of salt cod, pearl barley, tenderstem broccoli and verjus was 'perfectly executed, with clear, balanced flavours', while a dessert of vanilla rice pudding topped with jam proved 'simple and faultless'. This is big, heartwarming food that will fill you up – though there are also lighter options, from Scotch eggs to sandwiches. Wash it down with interesting ales or wines priced from £16. **Chef/s:** Adam Stanley. **Open:** all week 12 to 9 (9.30 Fri and Sat, 8 Sun). **Meals:** alc (main courses £12 to £19). **Details:** 70 seats. 36 seats outside. Bar. Parking.

Symbols

▭ Accommodation is available
£30 Three courses for less than £30
£5 OFF £5-off voucher scheme
🍾 Notable wine list

Llanarmon Dyffryn Ceiriog

The West Arms

Pleasing food in characterful inn
Cooking score: 2
Modern British | £28
Llanarmon Dyffryn Ceiriog, LL20 7LD
Tel no: (01691) 600665
www.thewestarms.co.uk

Nestled in the foothills of the Berwyn Mountains, this well-preserved 16th-century drovers' inn now does duty as a charming, characterful hostelry praised for its roaring fires, lovely antique furniture, welcoming staff and personal hospitality. Owners Geoff and Gill Leigh-Ford aim to please, offering extended Sunday lunches, sandwiches and afternoon tea right through the day, as well as a fully rounded menu of dishes old and new. Snuggle by the mighty inglenook in the lounge or trade up to the 'well-polished' restaurant for food that caters to all palates and preferences – from 'perfect' cottage pie, whole Ceiriog trout with almonds, or gammon, pineapple and chips to pheasant cassoulet with celeriac purée or pan-fried Anglesey sea bass with seared scallops, herb gnocchi and saffron butter sauce. Starters might include chestnut and vegetable arancini or beetroot-wrapped salmon mousse, while pud could be local damson and hazelnut tart with salt-caramel ice cream. A wide-ranging wine list opens with Tanners house selections from £16.95.
Chef/s: Grant Williams. **Open:** all week L 12 to 2.30 (6 Sun), D 6.30 to 9.30. **Meals:** alc (main courses £13 to £22). **Details:** 72 seats. 40 seats outside. Bar. Wheelchair access. Music. Parking.

Visit us online

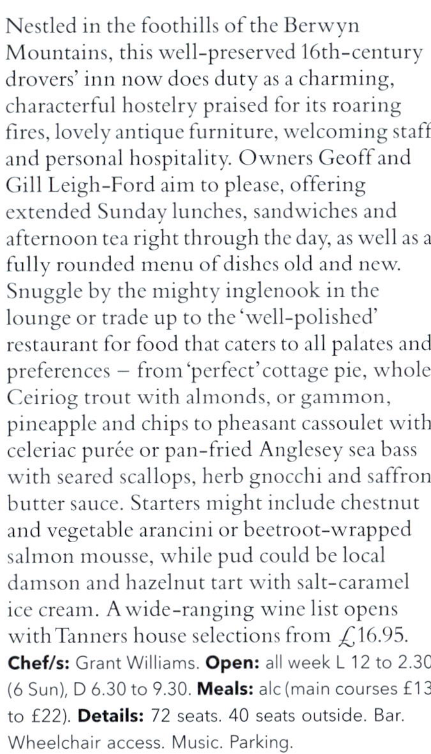

To find out more about The Good Food Guide, please visit thegoodfoodguide.co.uk

Llandrillo

Tyddyn Llan

Cooking with great panache
Cooking score: 6
Modern British | £57
Llandrillo, LL21 0ST
Tel no: (01490) 440264
www.tyddynllan.co.uk

Formerly the Duke of Westminster's shooting lodge, this grey-stone Georgian house has found its niche as a serious-minded but approachable restaurant-with-rooms deep in the Denbighshire countryside. Since 2002, it's been home to Bryan and Susan Webb, who run Tyddyn Llan with great panache, warmth and good humour. Bryan has Welsh blood in his veins and tips his hat to the homeland when it comes to sourcing – although his highly accomplished seasonal cooking has strong European inflections. Traditionalists can take comfort from clear-flavoured renditions of leek and winter truffle risotto, Cefnllan Farm duck breast with cider and apples or wild sea bass with laverbread butter sauce, but the kitchen also springs a few surprises – witness crubeens (stuffed pig's trotter) with piccalilli, watercress and chicory salad or red mullet with creamed aubergine, chilli and garlic oil. Desserts often add some Mediterranean sunshine to proceedings, as in frozen zabaglione or pannacotta with blood orange and grappa. The exceptional, ever-evolving, global wine list is a labour of love, with kind mark-ups at both ends of the spectrum – 'a couple of absolute bargains!' – imaginative selections across the range, and meaningful, concise notes. The list includes 20 by the glass or carafe. Bottles from £27.
Chef/s: Bryan Webb. **Open:** Fri to Sun L 12.30 to 2, all week D 7 to 9. **Closed:** last 2 weeks Jan.
Meals: alc L (main courses £24 to £30). Set L £25 (2 courses) to £30. Set D £47 (2 courses) to £57. Sun L £30. Tasting menu £70 (6 courses) to £85 (9 courses). **Details:** 40 seats. 8 seats outside. V menu. Bar. Wheelchair access. Parking.

▮ Abergele

The Kinmel Arms

Revitalised inn with fulfilling Welsh food
Cooking score: 4
Modern British | £32
St George, Abergele, LL22 9BP
Tel no: (01745) 832207
www.thekinmelarms.co.uk

'Excellent beers, an enthusiastic front-of-house and above average pub grub' pretty much sums up what you'll get at this 17th-century sandstone inn set in a lovely woodland estate. It may be all mullioned windows and carriage lamps on the outside, but the interior wears a contemporary look, including paintings by co-proprietor Tim Watson, who has a studio and gallery here. Chef Chad Huges has been in the kitchen since 2011, but recently stepped up to become head chef. His cooking draws on the best local produce, including home-grown herbs and salads. Partridge breast and crispy leg with Alsace cabbage, pickled pear and caramelised walnut is typical of the modern British style, followed perhaps by slow-cooked roe deer haunch with port-braised red cabbage, fondant potato, chestnut, pancetta and sprouts and juniper jus. Finish with gianduja fondant, Bavarian custard and hazelnut ice cream. A decent, wide-ranging wine list includes plenty by the glass; bottles start at £17.50.
Chef/s: Chad Huges. **Open:** Tue to Sat L 12 to 2, D 6 to 9.30. **Closed:** Sun, Mon, 25 Dec, 1 Jan, bank hols. **Meals:** alc (main courses £17 to £23). Set early D £15 (2 courses) to £19. Set D £27 (2 courses) to £32. **Details:** 70 seats. 28 seats outside. V menu. Bar. Wheelchair access. Music. Parking.

Visit us online

To find out more about The Good Food Guide, please visit thegoodfoodguide.co.uk

Abersoch
Porth Tocyn Hotel

Bayside modern cooking at a family-run hotel
Cooking score: 3
Modern British | £46
Bwlch Tocyn, Abersoch, LL53 7BU
Tel no: (01758) 713303
www.porthtocynhotel.co.uk

The Fletcher-Brewers have been running Porth Tocyn since it was hewn from a cluster of lead-miners' cottages in 1948. Perched above Cardigan Bay overlooking Snowdonia, it's a hot bet for an escapist holiday, and its delightful gardens and simply appointed dining room are part of the allure. The menus offer a confidently expressed tour of the modern British style. Start with a sardine baked en paupiette with roast ratatouille and pesto-dressed salad before shifting up a gear for mains such as prosciutto-wrapped hake on samphire with saffron potatoes in lemon dressing, or fine Welsh beef fillet on thyme rösti in redcurrant glaze. Finishing treats include Belgian chocolate tart offset with kumquat compote and mint syrup. A wine list full of useful descriptions starts at £17.95.
Chef/s: Louise Fletcher-Brewer and Ian Frost. **Open:** all week L 12 to 2.30, D 7 to 9. **Closed:** early Nov to week before Easter. **Meals:** Set D £39 (2 courses) to £46. Sun L £27. **Details:** 50 seats. 25 seats outside. Parking. No children at D.

Bangor

LOCAL GEM
Blue Sky Café

British | £15
Ambassador Hall, 236 High Street, Bangor, LL57 1PA
Tel no: (01248) 355444
www.blueskybangor.co.uk

Blue Sky Café certainly appeals to Bangor's residents, who regard the former Second World War dance hall as a 'local gem'. The bustling interior with its laid-back vibe and warming wood-burner is testament to its popularity. Flexible menus include Welsh rarebit, warm lentil, chorizo and sausage salad, the ever-popular handmade burger made with Welsh beef, and sweet things such as pistachio meringue with Welsh cream. Wines from £11.75. Closed Sun and D.

Barmouth
Bistro Bermo

Pint-sized local bistro
Cooking score: 2
Modern British | £30
6 Church Street, Barmouth, LL42 1EW
Tel no: (01341) 281284
www.bistrobarmouth.co.uk

£5
OFF

Emma and Paul Ryder are a great double act: they run pretty much everything here themselves – he conjuring up assured seasonal dishes, she running front-of-house. Their 'tastefully decorated' little gem of a bistro certainly brightens up Barmouth's main street – stop by for crab tian followed by slow-cooked pork belly with a black pudding fritter and pork gravy. This is comfortably familiar, modern British food built on carefully sourced ingredients. For dessert, expect classics such as sticky toffee pudding or crème brûlée. Wines start at £16.50.
Chef/s: Paul Ryder. **Open:** Tue to Sat D only 6 to 9. **Closed:** Sun, Mon. **Meals:** alc (main courses £15 to £24). **Details:** 18 seats. Music.

Beaumaris
Loft Restaurant

Contemporary food in a grand old inn
Cooking score: 5
Modern British | £48
Ye Olde Bull's Head Inn, Castle Street, Beaumaris, LL58 8AP
Tel no: (01248) 810329
www.bullsheadinn.co.uk

A bull with pedigree, this grand old inn was built in 1472 and 'improved' in 1617 – hence the deliberately archaic name tag. Set in the shadow of majestic Beaumaris Castle, it has played host to literati, politicians and a parade of famous faces – although today's visitors are mostly hungry tourists. Easy-going food is served in the conservatory-style brasserie, but those in the know book for the dressed-up Loft Restaurant – an eye-catching eyrie squeezed into the eaves of the original inn. With its skewed ceiling, circular mirrors and arty partitions, it provides a striking backdrop for Hefin Roberts' highly worked contemporary cooking. Welsh ingredients have their say, and the kitchen is tuned into current trends – think blowtorched pork belly with garlic cream, blanched leeks and gin-soaked raisins, or roast cannon and salt-baked shoulder of lamb or turbot fillet with fermented cabbage, brown shrimps, celeriac purée and purple watercress pesto. To conclude there might be apple and lime cheesecake with dehydrated apple sponge and basil ice cream. Shrewdly chosen French wines take pole position on the serious wine list, with bottles from £22.

Chef/s: Hefin Roberts. **Open:** Tue to Sat D only 7 to 9.30 (6.30 Fri and Sat). **Closed:** Sun, Mon, 25 and 26 Dec. **Meals:** Set D £48 (3 courses). **Details:** 45 seats. Bar. Parking. Children over 7 yrs only.

▌Betws-y-Coed

LOCAL GEM

Bistro Betws-y-Coed

British | £25
Holyhead Road, Betws-y-Coed, LL24 0AY
Tel no: (01690) 710328
www.bistrobetws-y-coed.co.uk

£5
OFF

A touristy honeypot in summer, Betws-y-Coed was a sensible place for Gerwyn Williams to set up shop, but his bistro is not just a fair-weather friend – his generous, varied menus are a pleasing prospect throughout the year. Williams' classical foundations were laid down in such places as Odette's in London (see entry), and here combine well with local flavours. Sautéed breast of wild wood pigeon with blueberry

pancakes, crispy bacon and a rich red wine and chocolate sauce, then smoked haddock with a Welsh rarebit topping, leek mash and mustard sauce, and homemade meringue nest with Baileys custard, toffee nut sauce, vanilla ice cream and berry compote are typical offerings. Wines start at £14.50.

▌Caernarfon

NEW ENTRY

Blas

Generous, wholesome food
Cooking score: 1
Modern British | £30
23-25 Hole in the Wall Street, Caernarfon, LL55 1RF
Tel no: (01286) 677707
www.blascaernarfon.co.uk

£5
OFF

'Blas' translates as 'taste', and you can expect vibrant flavours at this pretty little eatery tucked down a narrow street in Caernarfon's old town. Vintage combines with modern art to create an endearingly homely space overseen by 'genuinely friendly' staff. By day a café offering everything from burgers to pan-fried sea trout with a salad of new potatoes, dill, pea shoots and green beans, things shift up a gear in the evening when there are tasting menus as well as conventional à la carte offerings of, say, fillet steak with béarnaise butter. Desserts deliver a 'show-stopping' glazed lemon tart with pistachio (ice cream and meringue) and lemon (curd and sherbet). Wines from £14.95.

Chef/s: Daniel ap Geraint. **Open:** Tue to Sun L 10.30 to 3 (10 Sun), Tue to Sat D 6 to 9. **Closed:** Mon. **Meals:** alc (main courses £13 to £23). Sun L £14 (2 courses) to £18. Tasting menu £40. **Details:** 42 seats. 12 seats outside. Music.

Average price

The average price denotes the price of a three-course meal without wine.

■ Colwyn Bay

LOCAL GEM
Hayloft
Modern British | £30
Bodnant Welsh Food, Furnace Farm, Tal-y-Cafn, Colwyn Bay, LL28 5RP
Tel no: (01492) 651100
www.bodnant-welshfood.co.uk

A gastronomic beacon in the Conwy Valley, the Bodnant Welsh Food Centre is a bountiful repository for local produce from the farm and surrounding countryside. Buy from the shop or sample the patriotic wares on offer in the vaulted Hayloft restaurant, where the seasonal menu delivers everything from gravadlax with beetroot dressing and laverbread biscuits to home-reared lamb casserole with smoked garlic or stir-fried Welsh Black beef with leeks. House wines from £13.50. Closed Sun D. Also check out the Furnace Tearoom in the old stables.

■ Conwy
Dawsons at the Castle Hotel
Designer décor and local produce
Cooking score: 2
Modern British | £30
High Street, Conwy, LL32 8DB
Tel no: (01492) 582800
www.castlewales.co.uk

£5 OFF

With its handsome frontage of local granite and Ruabon brick, the Castle Hotel is quite the looker. It owes its present-day appearance to the Victorians, but its history goes back, in parts, to the 15th century. In recent years the restaurant has enjoyed a swanky 'boutique'-style makeover, but not at the expense of the Shakespearian paintings by Victorian illustrator John Dawson-Watson, which still adorn the walls. It has been said that the kitchen tries to be 'all things to all customers' – but fortunately it does those things well. It made a 'good job' of a classic prawn cocktail for one reporter, who also enjoyed a 'faultless'

griddled pork chop with a stew of butter beans, chorizo and tomato, a cake of mashed potato mixed with a little pulled pork and a 'lovely strip of crackling'. Sticky toffee pudding with butterscotch sauce and locally sourced ice cream is a typically diplomatic dessert. There is an impressive selection of international wines by the glass, with bottles starting at £16.50.
Chef/s: Andrew Nelson. **Open:** all week 12 to 9.30. **Closed:** 25 and 31 Dec. **Meals:** alc (main courses £16 to £23). **Details:** 80 seats. 40 seats outside. Bar. Music. Parking.

■ Dolgellau
Mawddach
Mediterranean flavours on a family farm
Cooking score: 2
Modern British | £32
Llanelltyd, Dolgellau, LL40 2TA
Tel no: (01341) 421752
www.mawddach.com

Diversification is the watchword for British farmers these days and here it's been done in style: Ifan Dunn's sophisticated restaurant brings diners right into the heart of the family farm where the lamb for his modern British menu is raised. The 17th-century barn-conversion restaurant has a contemporary swagger but also a reverence for its past. Floor-to-ceiling windows allow 'outstanding views' and a small farm shop in the corner of the bar offers homemade chutneys, bread, Welsh cheeses, wines and more. Welsh and European ingredients sit comfortably together on the menu: try Severn & Wye smoked salmon with salt-baked beetroot, shallot, sherry vinegar and home-made salad cream, and then the home-reared lamb in a 'shepherd's pie' with Arborio rice, root vegetables and celeriac sauce. Douglas fir pine custard slice on toffee apple pudding with honey ice cream and brown-sugar crumble is a showpiece dessert. The international wine list includes a good selection of Welsh finds, and opens at £15.50.
Chef/s: Ifan Dunn. **Open:** Wed to Sun L 12 to 2.30, Thur to Sat D 6.30 to 9. **Closed:** Mon, Tue, (Wed in winter) 26 Dec to 1 Jan, 1 week spring, 2 weeks Nov.

Meals: alc (main courses £14 to £21). Sun L £24.
Details: 70 seats. 40 seats outside. Bar. Wheelchair access. Music. Parking.

Harlech

Castle Cottage

Proudly regional cooking below the Castle
Cooking score: 2
Modern British | £40
Y Llech, Harlech, LL46 2YL
Tel no: (01766) 780479
www.castlecottageharlech.co.uk

Just off the high street, compactly occupying a pair of old stone-built cottages, the Roberts' restaurant-with-rooms is overlooked at point-blank range by the stolid fastness of Harlech Castle, adding a sense of centuries-long security to the hospitable cheer with which the place is managed. Welsh oak tables are got up in their best whites for Glyn Roberts' seasonal Welsh cooking, which takes the fashionable multifarious approach to main ingredients. So salmon comes three ways – hot-smoked, cold-smoked and gravadlax – and then lamb does too, with roast rack, sautéed loin and confit shoulder served alongside bubble and squeak and buttered carrots in red wine and shallot sauce. Even sea bass fished off Barmouth has king prawns for company, as well as fine beans in a creamy sauce of white wine and basil. Finish in irreproachable local style with crempogs: buttery Welsh pancakes served with wimberry compote and clotted cream ice cream. Wines start at £19.
Chef/s: Glyn Roberts. **Open:** all week D only 7 to 9 (8 Sun). **Closed:** 3 weeks Nov. **Meals:** Set D £35 (2 courses) to £40. Tasting menu £45 (5 courses).
Details: 35 seats. Bar. Music. Parking.

Local Gem

Local Gems are the perfect neighbourhood venues, delivering good, freshly cooked food at great value for money.

Llanberis

LOCAL GEM

The Peak

Modern British | £28
86 High Street, Llanberis, LL55 4SU
Tel no: (01286) 872777
www.peakrestaurant.co.uk

It's a long way from Soho's Groucho Club to the foothills of Snowdonia, but one-time big-city chef Angela Dwyer is now feeding the throngs of walkers, climbers and tourists who flock to this mountainous neighbourhood. Her monthly dinner menus have an international flavour, moving from sticky spare ribs or deep-fried cod goujons with guacamole to pie and mash, Welsh ribeye steak or duck breast with Tuscan bean and curly kale stew. Wines from £14.95. Open Wed to Sun D only.

Llandudno

Jaya

Lovingly cooked north Indian food
Cooking score: 2
Indian | £25
36 Church Walks, Llandudno, LL30 2HN
Tel no: (01492) 818198
www.jayarestaurant.co.uk

Head off-piste into a residential area and you'll be rewarded with an excellent curry. Jaya is not your everyday sort of Indian restaurant. It's in a 19th-century town house B&B for a start and neatly avoids curry-house cliché in favour of a slick, contemporary look of cream-coloured walls, bright modern art and glass-topped tables. Indian music sets the mood and you can kick off with a cocktail in the lounge bar. Amid all this modernity, Sunita Katoch turns out north Indian food of authenticity and heart, with an East African influence along the way. Start with fish pakora, jeera chicken or Kenyan-style chilli mogo (casava with chilli and garlic), before palak chicken with its thick spinach sauce, masala fish, karai lamb or a vegetarian dish such as aloo anday (boiled eggs and potato in a rich north Indian sauce). Wines start at £13.95.

Chef/s: Sunita Katoch. **Open:** Thur to Sat D only 6 to 10. **Closed:** Sun to Wed, 3 weeks Dec/Jan. **Meals:** alc (main courses £10 to £13). **Details:** 20 seats. Bar. Music. Parking.

Llanfaethlu
The Black Lion Inn

Simple food in a lovely 18th-century pub
Cooking score: 1
Modern British | £27
Llanfaethlu, LL65 4NL
Tel no: (01407) 730718
www.blacklionanglesey.com

A long-derelict pub rescued by local couple Leigh and Mary Faulkner in 2012, the Black Lion offers a happy blend of old and new: you can eat in the traditional bar with its wood-burners and slate floors, or in the newly extended dining room whose French doors open on to a patio with views across Anglesey to craggy Snowdonia. The kitchen handles pub stalwarts like fish and chips with aplomb, but also turns out more ambitious dishes such as seared scallops with textures of apple, glazed with roe butter, or braised lamb shoulder with a root vegetable rösti and a thyme reduction sauce. To finish, try classic Eton mess. A snappy wine list starts at £15.95.

Chef/s: Wayne Roberts. **Open:** Thur, Fri and Sun L 12 to 2.30 (3 Sun), Wed to Fri D 6 to 8 (9 Fri). Sat 12 to 9. **Closed:** Mon, Tue, 6 to 16 Jan. **Meals:** alc (main courses £13 to £19). Sun L £12 (1 course) to £19. **Details:** 78 seats. 20 seats outside. Wheelchair access. Music. Parking.

Menai Bridge
Sosban and the Old Butcher's

Surprises all the way
Cooking score: 4
Modern British | £44
Trinity House, 1 High Street, Menai Bridge, LL59 5EE
Tel no: (01248) 208131
www.sosbanandtheoldbutchers.com

'From start to finish, the experience exceeded all expectations,' confessed a visitor to this idiosyncratic charmer run by chef Stephen Stevens and his wife Bethan. Open just three evenings a week and serving a six-course no-choice tasting menu only, it smacks of the couple doing things their own way, but diners are happy to go along for the ride. The setting combines the creature comforts of a smart modern restaurant with original features of the old butcher's shop including slate slabs and an original tiled frieze. The menu features 'the best produce the surrounding area has to offer' coupled with some stonking finds from further afield – maybe Scottish salmon (with apple, celeriac, cucumber), and Coed y Brenin venison (with pear, Savoy cabbage, parsnip and celery). Elsewhere, 'beautiful is an understatement' is one description of a deconstructed rhubarb cheesecake. A nicely annotated international wine list opens at £15.60.

Chef/s: Stephen Stevens. **Open:** Thur to Sat D only 7 to 11. **Closed:** Sun to Wed, 23 Dec to mid Feb. **Meals:** Tasting menu £44 (6 courses). **Details:** 16 seats. V menu. Children over 12 yrs only.

▌Newborough

NEW ENTRY
The Marram Grass Café
Surprising, creative campsite restaurant
Cooking score: 2
British | £23
White Lodge, Penlon, Newborough, LL61 6RS
Tel no: (01248) 440077
www.themarramgrass.com

There's charm from the off at this interesting yet earthy restaurant in what is effectively 'a lovely shed' on a campsite. Under a low corrugated-iron roof is a grotto-like interior, with funky lime green walls, lots of exposed wood, twinkly with candlelight and full of cosy corners. The food is gutsy yet ambitious, and more sophisticated than the rustic presentation might suggest. After a 'stunning' amuse of feisty heritage tomato gazpacho, a starter of disappointingly small mussels was the only gripe for one reporter, who was 'bowled over' by a main course of pearly-fresh sea bass with roasted new potatoes, watercress and several different takes on Jerusalem artichoke (purée, crisps and pickled). Equally delightful was a deconstructed bara brith: tea-poached dried fruit topped with luscious vanilla rice pudding and brown-sugar jelly, with thick bara brith ice cream on the side. A mostly European selection of wines begins at £14.25.
Chef/s: Ellis Barrie. **Open:** all week L 12 to 2.30, D 6 to 9. **Meals:** alc (main courses £14 to £17). Set D £19 (2 courses) to £22. Sun L £15. **Details:** 45 seats. 45 seats outside. Bar. Music. Parking.

▌Penmaenpool
Penmaenuchaf Hall
Old-fashioned elegance and modern menus
Cooking score: 2
Modern British | £45
Penmaenpool, LL40 1YB
Tel no: (01341) 422129
www.penhall.co.uk

A gabled Victorian mansion in the foothills of the Cader Idris range, Pen Hall is all about old-fashioned elegance, so expect antiques, big leather sofas and wood panelling aplenty. Smartly attired staff oversee the conservatory dining room, which has wonderful views across the gardens to the Mawddach estuary, and the menu is perfectly in tune with the surrounding landscape. Confit of Rhug Estate organic pork belly with bacon compote and balsamic glaze, then roasted loin of wild venison with braised red cabbage, fondant potato and dark chocolate sauce are typical of the kitchen's approach. For dessert, expect an upmarket take on classics such as croissant bread-and-butter pudding with dark chocolate sauce and vanilla ice cream. The outstanding wine list speaks of real passion and expertise, and offers great value for money. Bottles start at £21, and are available to take home at retail prices.
Chef/s: Justin Pilkington. **Open:** all week L 12 to 2, D 7 to 9.30 (9 Sun). **Closed:** 13 to 21 Dec, 4 to 19 Jan. **Meals:** alc (main courses £27 to £32). Set L £19 (2 courses) to £21. Set D £25 (2 courses) to £28. Sun L £21. **Details:** 36 seats. 20 seats outside. Bar. Wheelchair access. Music. Parking. Children over 6 yrs only.

Pwllheli

Plas Bodegroes

Landmark hotel with impressive food
Cooking score: 5
Modern British | £49
Efailnewydd, Pwllheli, LL53 5TH
Tel no: (01758) 612363
www.bodegroes.co.uk

A boutique restaurant-with-rooms since well before the phrase was actually coined, Chris and Gunna Chown's alluring Georgian house in a bucolic setting has been one of Wales' premium dining addresses since 1986. There are five acres of grounds through which to wander and the sea is only a mile away. The dining room is surprisingly contemporary, although gently so, and the kitchen follows suit with an output based around regional ingredients (which are a passion here; evidently matched only by a love of art). Pork and morcilla haslet (or meatloaf) gets a pineapple chutney to cut through its meatiness, and roast loin of monkfish comes with a fashionable ox cheek bonbon and beurre rouge to beef it up even more. Welsh Black beef and mountain lamb will likely figure among main courses, the latter with an onion cake and rosemary jus, and, to finish, cherry frangipane tart is matched with pistachio ice cream. The wine list is a treasure trove of little gems opening at £19.50.
Chef/s: Chris Chown and Hugh Bracegirdle. **Open:** Sun L 12 to 2.30, Tue to Sat D 7 to 9.30. **Closed:** Mon, 1 Dec to 28 Feb. **Meals:** Set D £49. Sun L £25. **Details:** 40 seats. V menu. Bar. Wheelchair access. Parking.

Rhosneigr

The Oyster Catcher

Eco-friendly social enterprise
Cooking score: 1
Modern British | £27
Rhosneigr, LL64 5JP
Tel no: (01407) 812829
www.oystercatcheranglesey.co.uk

Taking inspiration from Jamie Oliver's Fifteen (see entries), John and Alex Timpson (of shoe repairs fame) set up the Oyster Catcher as a social enterprise and local food initiative dedicated to training up disadvantaged youngsters. Occupying a German-designed eco-friendly building overlooking Anglesey's shifting sands, this outgoing venture offers a casual seasonal menu with something for everyone – from local mussels in cider, Thai fishcakes or roast hake on red wine risotto to burgers, pasta and braised lamb shank with colcannon. The restaurant's self-proclaimed culinary 'cadets' also help to create lunchtime charcuterie boards and puds such as hazelnut meringue with praline cream. Wines from £16.50.
Chef/s: Claire Lara. **Open:** Mon to Fri L 12 to 2.30, D 6 to 9. Sat and Sun 12 to 9 (8 Sun). **Meals:** alc (main courses £11 to £22). **Details:** 129 seats. 100 seats outside. Bar. Wheelchair access. Music. Parking.

■ Aberaeron
Harbourmaster
Sleek harbourside hotel
Cooking score: 2
Modern British | £30
Pen Cei, Aberaeron, SA46 0BT
Tel no: (01545) 570755
www.harbour-master.com

One of Wales' best-known boutique hotels, the Harbourmaster is quite the looker, occupying a plum spot near the mouth of Aberaeron's gorgeous harbour. Its smartly styled interior splits into two parts: a modern-rustic locals' bar (crammed with people enjoying fish and chips on our visit); and the more refined restaurant, calming in shades of pale sea blue, with industrial lighting, wood floors, paintings by local artists and harbour views. The menu is built on fresh local ingredients, including excellent seafood such as the 'crunchy' crab fritters in a slick of ginger mayonnaise dotted with cubes of melon that

made a 'fresh and enjoyable' starter at inspection. This was followed by two crisp-skinned sea bass fillets, a heap of samphire, new potatoes sprinkled with cockles and a chicken vinaigrette. A thick, creamy white chocolate pot with strawberry compote and black pepper shortbread made a 'perfectly pitched' dessert. Wines from £15.
Chef/s: Ludo Dieumegard. **Open:** all week L 12 to 2.30, D 6.30 to 9. **Closed:** 25 Dec. **Meals:** alc (main courses £18 to £25). Set D £25 (2 courses) to £30. Sun L £19 (2 courses) to £25. **Details:** 95 seats. 15 seats outside. Bar. Wheelchair access. Parking.

Symbols

Accommodation is available
£30 Three courses for less than £30
£5 OFF £5-off voucher scheme
Notable wine list

■ Aberystwyth

Ultracomida
Well-stocked deli and tapas joint
Cooking score: 2
Spanish | £19
31 Pier Street, Aberystwyth, SY23 2LN
Tel no: (01970) 630686
www.ultracomida.co.uk

The Ultracomida name encompasses an online deli and wine merchant plus two delicatessens that double as wine shops, cafés and tapas joints. This Aberystwyth branch, just off the promendade, is where it all began in 2001 and its raison d'être is simple: to sell the very best Spanish produce and show it off in vibrant tapas dishes such as meatballs in a tomato sofrito sauce, Iberian pig's cheeks cooked in Pedro Ximénez, king prawns in garlic butter and garlic mushrooms with cream and sherry. There are also cheeses with membrillo, charcuterie platters and children's plates of ham, Manchego, bread and olives. Desserts focus on café classics such as carrot cake, rocky road and chocolate brownies. The wonderful Spanish wine list includes a map pinpointing the style and origin of each wine, with bottles starting at just £11.95. Another branch is at 7 High Street, Narberth; tel: (01834) 861491.
Chef/s: Joaquim Garrido and Ian Davies. **Open:** Mon to Sat 10 to 9 (4.30 Mon). Sun L 12 to 3.30. **Closed:** 25 and 26 Dec, 1 Jan. **Meals:** alc (tapas £3 to £10). **Details:** 30 seats. V menu. Wheelchair access. Music.

Treehouse
British | £15
14 Baker Street, Aberystwyth, SY23 2BJ
Tel no: (01970) 615791
www.treehousewales.co.uk

When it opened above a wholefood-organic shop in the centre of town, Treehouse was a place with a mission – providing good, wholesome food made from fresh local and organic produce at reasonable prices. Almost ten years down the line, this humble all-day eatery still goes down well, known for filling soups, perhaps spicy split pea, served with a homemade roll; burgers (both veggie and chicken) with garlic mayo and homemade relish; Dexter beef spaghetti bolognese; and excellent home-baked scones and cakes. Wines from £11. Closed Sun.

■ Broad Haven

The Druidstone
Global | £30
Broad Haven, SA62 3NE
Tel no: (01437) 781221
www.druidstone.co.uk

If you're drawn by the hippyish flavour of its name, Druidstone will not disappoint. If you want a slick boutique hotel, best go elsewhere. A homespun, eccentric country house perched near a cliff edge, it gets busy on sunny days with people keen to enjoy the view. Soak it up from an outdoor picnic table or take a window seat in the quirky restaurant, which is strung with bunting and fairy lights. Surfy young staff will serve you rustic home-cooked dishes such as Moroccan lamb and chickpea soup, local dressed crab with Marie Rose sauce and salad, and banoffee pie. Wines start at £15 a bottle. Open all week.

■ Eglwysfach

★ TOP 50 ★

Ynyshir Hall
Cooking that's moving into top gear
Cooking score: 7
Modern British | £80
Eglwysfach, SY20 8TA
Tel no: (01654) 781209
www.ynyshirhall.co.uk

Joan and Rob Reen's luxurious and gorgeously arty country house hotel has long been a destination for serious eating, but under chef Gareth Ward's tenure the bar has been raised to vertiginous new heights. He's a chef admirably in tune with his surroundings – and what magnificent surroundings they are: the graceful whitewashed building overlooks gardens originally planted for Queen Victoria, who kept this as her country retreat. Beyond all the colour and velveteen lawns is a vast RSPB reserve – perfect for lengthy rambles – and the whole scene is cradled by mountains. Rob Reen's paintings in the turquoise-hued dining room immortalise the sheep that roam this landscape, while Ward showcases everything from local hogget to Welsh Wagyu beef on his epic tasting menus (there is no à la carte here, nor should there be – you're in safe hands). Fruit, vegetables, herbs and salads are plucked from the kitchen garden or from the surrounding woods and marshes. Standout dishes have included the 'not French onion soup' – an umami feast of miso onions with a dashi stock; gently warmed mackerel with a vivid sweet-and-sour sauce; and pork belly with charcoal, seaweed, shallot and soy. Salt-baked Welsh Hill Speckled Face hogget is full-flavoured, meltingly tender and served with succulent marshland vegetables, while a thoroughly modern, deconstructed tiramisu is an intensified, transcendent version of an old favourite. The extensive wine list offers everything from classics to rare treats, starting at £24 a bottle.

Chef/s: Gareth Ward. **Open:** all week L 12 to 2, D 7 to 9. **Meals:** Set L £35 (5 courses) to £80. Set D £80 (7 courses) to £90. Sun L £35. **Details:** 35 seats. V menu. Bar. Wheelchair access. Music. Parking. Children over 9 yrs only at D.

■ Laugharne
The Cors

Tucked-away restaurant-with-rooms
Cooking score: 3
Modern British | £35
Newbridge Road, Laugharne, SA33 4SH
Tel no: (01994) 427219
www.thecors.co.uk

This enchanting Victorian residence, set in an exotically leafy, otherworldly bog garden decorated with sculptures, is run as a restaurant-with-rooms and is as idiosyncratic as it is romantic. The rambling interior has a raffish, bohemian air, there's a candlelit, ruby-red grotto of a dining room, and chef/proprietor Nick Priestland delivers generous portions of unpretentious food unhampered by fads or trends. The short handwritten menu makes full use of local and seasonal produce and the cooking draws regulars from afar with its well-executed straightforwardness. Dinner might begin with a bruschetta of grilled local goats' cheese and roasted red peppers or a signature starter of smoked haddock 'crème brûlée'. Main dishes are in the same vein, perhaps roasted rack of local Welsh spring lamb with a rosemary garlic crust and caramelised onion gravy or char-grilled smoked salmon with new-season asparagus, roasted cherry tomato sauce and salsa verde. The compact global wine list starts at £16.50.

Chef/s: Nick Priestland. **Open:** Thur to Sat D only 7 (1 sitting). **Closed:** Sun to Wed, first 2 weeks Nov. **Meals:** alc (main courses £16 to £26). **Details:** 24 seats. 10 seats outside. Children over 12 yrs only.

Join us at thegoodfoodguide.co.uk

■ Llanarthne
Wright's Food Emporium
Gutsy favourites at a cheerful deli/café
Cooking score: 3
Modern British | £20
Golden Grove Arms, Llanarthne, SA32 8JU
Tel no: (01558) 668929
www.wrightsfood.co.uk

One of the coolest, most devastatingly delicious things happening in West Wales at present, Wright's is a food store-cum-restaurant for the passionate – in the process of upping an already powerful game by adding a cheese and charcuterie room. A former coaching inn stripped back and lightened in typically trendy-rustic style, its rooms include a wine store, deli and a hotchpotch of furniture, with blackboard menus listing the day's creations. The kitchen takes what's in store, plus what's available from local suppliers, and runs with it – gleefully, generously and without wasting time on prissy presentation. Highlights from the daytime menu include a salad of faro, radish, pistachios and sultanas and a pork belly cubano. In the evening you could chow down on rare roast beef tonnato; porchetta with cavolo nero; and baked sultana and nutmeg cheesecake. The in-house wine shop means there are plenty of bottles to choose, starting from a bargain price of £12.

Chef/s: Maryann Wright, Tom Mason, Phoebe Powell and Charlotte Pasetti. **Open:** Sun to Tue 11 to 7 (5 Sun). Wed to Sat 9 to 7 (9 Fri and Sat). **Closed:** 25 and 26 Dec. **Meals:** alc (main courses £7 to £13). **Details:** 70 seats. 30 seats outside. Wheelchair access. Music. Parking.

■ Llandybie
Valans
Personable local restaurant
Cooking score: 2
Modern European | £23
29 High Street, Llandybie, SA18 3HX
Tel no: (01269) 851288
www.valans.co.uk

Dave and Remy Vale have a decade on the clock and counting in their personable high-street village restaurant, once a florist's shop. The son of a Welsh farming family, Dave's career path has brought him logically to the business of celebrating fine regional produce, which he does on a lengthy, resourceful menu of seasonal dishes that are described in detail and deliver on the plate. Duck smoked over hickory and beechwood with honey makes the sophisticated centrepiece for a starter salad with orange and mozzarella, all dressed in balsamic, while scallops are voguishly teamed with black pudding and apple. For main, there's thoroughbred Carmarthenshire beef, slow-cooked for six hours and served in peppercorn sauce with decent chips, or else sea bream with mussels in white wine sauce. Cockle-warming desserts include banana and caramel trifle scattered with toasted almonds, or a crème brûlée laced with Merlyn cream liqueur. Chilean house wines are £15, or £3.95 a standard glass.

Chef/s: Dave Vale. **Open:** Tue to Sat L 12 to 3, D 7 to 11. **Closed:** Sun, Mon, 27 Dec to 4 Jan, 30 May to 5 Jun. **Meals:** alc (main courses £16 to £23). Set L £13 (2 courses) to £17. Sat D £20 (2 courses) to £23. **Details:** 35 seats. V menu. Wheelchair access. Music.

■ Llanelli
Sosban

Slick dockside contender
Cooking score: 3
French | £30
North Dock, Llanelli, SA15 2LF
Tel no: (01554) 270020
www.bwytysosban.com

£5 OFF

A former pump house on Llanelli's Millennium Coastal Path was given an open-wallet conversion to create Sosban. Several years later, it's a reputable fixture on the local dining scene. From its vaulted ceilings to slate floors, the building radiates an air of relaxed, post-industrial cool. It's a vast space, with a well-stocked bar and a lively buzz at busy times. Chefs Sian Rees and Ian Wood echo the building's modern aesthetic, creating streamlined dishes built around sprightly local ingredients. Try Penclawdd shellfish gratin or a Welsh charcuterie board with piccalilli to start, then perhaps tagine of Gower salt marsh lamb or Carmarthen Bay sea bass with curly kale and laverbread sauce. There are plenty of classics here, especially at dessert, when you could round off a meal with chocolate and coffee gâteau and chocolate mousse or a simple crème brûlée. A respectable, helpfully annotated wine list opens at £17.
Chef/s: Sian Rees and Ian Wood. **Open:** all week L 12 to 2.30, Mon to Sat D 5.30 to 9 (9.30 Fri and Sat). **Closed:** 25 Dec, 1 week Jan. **Meals:** alc (main courses £15 to £28). Set L and D £16 (2 courses) to £19. **Details:** 100 seats. 80 seats outside. Wheelchair access. Music. Parking.

■ Nantgaredig
Y Polyn

Broad-shouldered regional cooking
Cooking score: 4
Modern British | £35
Capel Dewi, Nantgaredig, SA32 7LH
Tel no: (01267) 290000
www.ypolyn.co.uk

With its black-and-white timbered façade, wood-burners and sturdy wood tables within, this 200-year-old former tollhouse may feel like a bucolic watering hole, but these days it does duty as a charmingly rustic restaurant and serious foodie destination (booking recommended) known for its love of invigorated British flavours. Mark and Susan Manson have carved out their own niche here, matching cordial hospitality with a straightforward approach to food that suits the current vogue for keeping things simple and fresh, with produce almost entirely locally or regionally sourced. Their regularly changing menu might turn up anything from a well-reported duck ragù with pappardelle to roast rump of Machynlleth hogget teamed with confit lamb breast, celeriac purée and onion soubise, and a dessert of rhubarb and custard Knickerbocker glory. Lovely bread, Welsh cheeses and a snappy, well-annotated wine list (from £16) are equally typical.
Chef/s: Susan Manson. **Open:** Tue to Sun L 12 to 2 (2.30 Sat and Sun), Tue to Sat D 7 to 9 (6.30 to 9.30 Fri and Sat). **Closed:** Mon. **Meals:** alc (main courses £16 to £19). Set L £14 (2 courses) to £17. Set D £28 (2 courses) to £35. Sun L £20 (2 courses) to £25. **Details:** 50 seats. 20 seats outside. Bar. Wheelchair access. Music. Parking.

◼ Narberth
The Grove

Sought-after gastronomic getaway
Cooking score: 5
Modern British | £54
Molleston, Narberth, SA67 8BX
Tel no: (01834) 860915
www.thegrove-narberth.co.uk

'Bliss', proclaimed one reader after a sojourn at the Grove – a highly sought-after boutique hotel and gastronomic getaway snuggled in a Pembrokeshire valley with the Preseli Mountains looming in the distance. There are enticing glimpses of the bountiful garden from the traditional wood-panelled dining room – a reminder that this is a kitchen that likes to leaven its cooking with local snippets and seasonal pickings. The result is an ever-changing menu peppered with modish inflections and influences – a crispy Burford Brown hen's egg with celeriac textures, pear and chicken skin, for example. You might seek warming wintry solace with a plate of slow-cooked beef rib and ox cheek, smoked beetroot, cabbage and shallots, while springtime could herald rump and heart of Preseli Bluestone lamb with asparagus, broad beans and wild garlic or a celebratory warm salad of young vegetables with mustard beignet and lemon beurre blanc. Afterwards, keep it seasonal with cherry fondant or 'early harvest' rhubarb with buttermilk, thyme and candied almonds. The prestigious 300-bin wine list is loaded with peerless vintages and little-known treasures from growers worldwide. Prices from £21 (£6 a glass).
Chef/s: Peter Whaley. **Open:** all week L 12 to 2.30, D 6 to 9.30. **Meals:** Set L £21 (2 courses) to £28. Set D £54. Sun L £28. Tasting menu £78 (7 courses).
Details: 70 seats. 50 seats outside. V menu. Bar. Wheelchair access. Music. Parking.

◼ Newport
Cnapan

Home from home with excellent ingredients
Cooking score: 2
Modern British | £32
East Street, Newport, SA42 0SY
Tel no: (01239) 820575
www.cnapan.co.uk

It's largely one of Cnapan's strengths that you feel as though you're dining in someone's home – albeit the very pretty home of a passionate cook. From the smart, comfortably domestic lounge with its pale walls, wood-burner and big sofas to the dining room sporting seascapes and a Welsh dresser, it feels like the family-run affair it is. The cooking sits well with this: in an age of cheffy blowtorch and squeezy bottle action, it has a refreshingly homespun edge. A starter of pear and goats' cheese tart with a walnut crust and colourful salad is big, wholesome and vibrant, while a main of fillet of venison with crispy pancetta and a cranberry and juniper jus enriched with dark chocolate arrives with 'pots and pots of wonderful vegetables', from baked beetroot with horseradish to potatoes dauphinois. The generosity extends to desserts such as raspberry, lemon and ginger syllabub. The wine list offers plenty by the glass or carafe; bottles start at £16.50.
Chef/s: Judith Cooper. **Open:** Wed to Mon D only 6.30 to 10. **Closed:** Tue, 19 Dec to 17 Mar.
Meals: Set D £26 (2 courses) to £32. **Details:** 36 seats. V menu. Bar. Wheelchair access. Music. Parking.

Porthgain
The Shed
Homespun seafood cookery by the harbour
Cooking score: 1
Seafood | £25
Porthgain, SA62 5BN
Tel no: (01348) 831518
www.theshedporthgain.co.uk

A stone's throw from the water's edge, the Shed is all about fresh fish cooked up in batter with chips or, more creatively, drawing on a broad palette of flavours. A quirky, homespun quayside building with much of its seating on the first floor, it's perfectly placed as the end of a walk around this fascinating village with its old quarry buildings and harbour. Cardigan Bay scallops simply pan-fried with garlic butter, grey mullet with a tomato and chilli broth and egg noodles, and homemade marmalade cake are typical offerings, but there are also decent vegetarian options and steak and chips. Wines start at £15.50.
Chef/s: Matt Cox and Brian Mullins. **Open:** all week L 12 to 3, D 5.30 to 9. **Meals:** alc (main courses £7 to £15). **Details:** 50 seats. 50 seats outside. Music. Parking.

St David's

Cwtch
Modern British | £30
22 High Street, St David's, SA62 6SD
Tel no: (01437) 720491
www.cwtchrestaurant.co.uk

Cwtch's new owners really excel front-of-house, offering a genuine welcome and smooth service. The setting retains the same rustic charm as before, with whitewashed stonework, exposed beams and shelves crammed with foodie books. The kitchen keeps things local and regional in dishes that are accurately cooked, if a bit timid flavour-wise. Courgette, pea and fennel soup with a Parmesan tuile, fillet of sewin with red pepper and butter-bean sauce and aïoli, and bara brith sticky toffee pudding are typical offerings. The wine list opens at £19. Open all week D and Sun L.

Saundersfoot
Coast
Assured cooking in a breathtaking location
Cooking score: 4
Modern British | £38
Coppet Hall Beach, Saundersfoot, SA69 9AJ
Tel no: (01834) 810800
www.coastsaundersfoot.co.uk

When the owners of the Grove at Narberth (see entry) were looking for a second string to their bow, they hit upon this eco-friendly, cedar-clad new build overlooking Coppet Hall Beach and Carmarthen Bay – check out the views from the huge suntrap terrace. They also drafted in chef Will Holland (ex-La Bécasse in Ludlow) to head up the kitchen, and the result is a relaxed, family-friendly venue with high culinary aspirations, but a flexible approach to food and drink. Fresh seafood from the bay takes pole position on the seasonal menu, so expect anything from grown-up 'fish fingers' to seared scallops with Jerusalem artichokes, truffle and honey dressing or grilled lobster with herb butter and Cajun potatoes. Elsewhere, char-grilled Welsh beef and plates of air-dried Carmarthen ham with crispy egg and lentils strike a patriotic note, while dessert might promise sticky ginger pudding with marinated pineapple and mango cream. Astutely chosen global wines start at £17 (£4.50 a glass).
Chef/s: Will Holland. **Open:** all week L 12 to 2.30, D 6 to 9.30. **Meals:** alc (main courses £15 to £26). Set L and D £18 (2 courses) to £24. Tasting menu £59 (6 courses). **Details:** 60 seats. 50 seats outside. V menu. Bar. Wheelchair access. Music. Parking.

CHANNEL ISLANDS

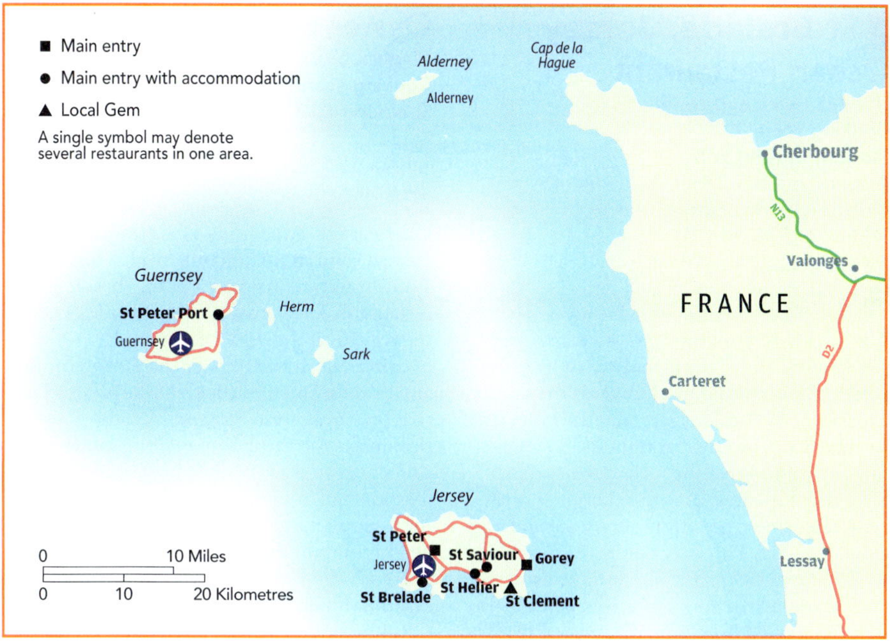

Gorey, Jersey
Sumas

Easy-going seaside eatery
Cooking score: 2
Modern British | £35
Gorey Hill, St Martin, Gorey, Jersey, JE3 6ET
Tel no: (01534) 853291
www.sumasrestaurant.com

£5 OFF

There's no question that Gorey Hill is an enchanting spot, with gorgeous views over the stone-walled, palm-fronded harbour and centuries-old Mont Orgeuil castle from the terrace of this easy-going seaside eatery. Inside, Sumas' cute but classy dining room sets out its stall with a big glass frontage, whitewashed walls and wooden floors, while the kitchen makes profitable use of Jersey produce – especially fish from the local boats. Organically reared Royal Bay oysters are a must, but the menu also takes in everything from pan-fried squid with pickled carrot, fennel and radish to fillet of lemon sole and salmon mousse 'en paupiette' with vegetable couscous and tomato compote. Meat and game are generally given more classic treatment, as in fillet of Angus beef with celeriac purée, dauphinois potato and Vichy carrots or roast loin of venison with sweet potato, roast turnip and sweet-and-sour cabbage. To finish, try tangerine pannacotta or the signature lime tart with brown-sugar reduction. Wines start at £17.50.
Chef/s: Patrice Bouffaut. **Open:** all week L 12 to 2.30 (12.30 to 3.30 Sun), Mon to Sat D 6 to 9.30. **Closed:** 21 Dec to mid Jan. **Meals:** alc (main courses £15 to £26). Set L and D £18 (2 courses) to £20. Sun L £23. **Details:** 35 seats. 20 seats outside. V menu. Music.

Visit us online

To find out more about
The Good Food Guide, please
visit thegoodfoodguide.co.uk

■ St Brelade, Jersey
Ocean Restaurant
Holiday views and serious food
Cooking score: 4
Modern British | £65
Atlantic Hotel, Le Mont de la Pulente, St Brelade, Jersey, JE3 8HE
Tel no: (01534) 744101
www.theatlantichotel.com

The setting is wonderful, with views across the Atlantic Hotel's immaculate lawns, palm trees and swimming pool towards the sandy expanse of St Brelade's Bay, and the hotel itself is relaxed and breezy throughout. So it's a surprise to find that the Ocean Restaurant offers the full-dress dining experience with crisp table linen, gleaming glassware and stiff, formal service. This may be the thoroughbred world of contemporary European cuisine, but chef Mark Jordan does stay close to home for supplies, taking his cue from land and sea. The journey might embark with lobster – a split tail, a tempura of claw – with potato salad, mango and a few dots of caviar. To follow, perhaps a piece of turbot topped with crisp potato scales and set on softened leeks with a mussel cream or fillet of roe deer with vegetable dauphinois and vanilla jus, while desserts might take in glazed banana with vanilla cream, toffee popcorn and caramel ice cream. Some 17 wines by the glass open a pedigree list featuring peerless growers and top vintages; bottles from £23.
Chef/s: Mark Jordan. **Open:** all week L 12.30 to 2.30, D 6.30 to 10. **Closed:** 4 Jan to 4 Feb. **Meals:** Set L £20 (2 courses) to £25. Set D £55. Sun L £30. Tasting menu £80. **Details:** 60 seats. V menu. Bar. Music. Parking.

Local Gem

Local Gems are the perfect neighbourhood venues, delivering good, freshly cooked food at great value for money.

Oyster Box
Magical beachside haven
Cooking score: 3
Seafood | £30
Route de la Baie, St Brelade, Jersey, JE3 8EF
Tel no: (01534) 850888
www.oysterbox.co.uk

Chef Patrick Tweedie and his crew have created something quite magical at this stunning, contemporary on-the-beach restaurant. The views over St Brelade's Bay are unrivalled, and there's a distinctly Mediterranean feel to both the dining room and the alluring terrace. It's no surprise, either, that bracingly fresh fish and seafood dominates the menu, though one can choose calf's liver or slow-cooked beef shoulder too. The kitchen buys diligently from a network of local suppliers and transforms the haul into a bright, vibrant modern British menu with an acute seasonal edge. Begin with seared tuna sashimi or perhaps hand-picked Jersey Chancre crab, before mains such as John Dory with seared scallops, French beans and Chantenay carrots or Champagne-poached lobster tail pappardelle, while desserts run to pistachio crème brûlée with raspberry sorbet and pear tarte Tatin with ginger ice cream. Jersey wines appear on a global list that starts at £17.50.
Chef/s: Patrick Tweedie. **Open:** Tue to Sun L 12 to 2.30 (3 Sun), all week D 6 to 9 (9.30 Fri and Sat). **Closed:** 25 and 26 Dec, 1 Jan. **Meals:** alc (main courses £14 to £30). Set L and D £19 (2 courses) to £24. **Details:** 90 seats. 60 seats outside. Bar. Wheelchair access. Music.

■ St Clement, Jersey

LOCAL GEM
Green Island Restaurant
Mediterranean | £35
Green Island, St Clement, Jersey, JE2 6LS
Tel no: (01534) 857787
www.greenisland.je

Billed as the 'most southerly restaurant in the British Isles', Green Island wows the tourists with its splendid sea views, sought-after

Join us at thegoodfoodguide.co.uk

alfresco tables and dreamy location atop the slipway. The kitchen casts its net across the Mediterranean (and beyond), but locally landed fish is always a sound bet – try brill fillet with Parmesan polenta and char-grilled vegetables. Otherwise expect a mixed bag, from vine leaves with lamb kofta or chicken breast with gnocchi to baked Alaska and local ice creams. Wines from £16.50. Closed Sun D and Mon.

St Helier, Jersey

★ TOP 50 ★

Bohemia

Knockout contemporary cooking
Cooking score: 7
Modern European | £59
The Club Hotel & Spa, Green Street, St Helier, Jersey, JE2 4UH
Tel no: (01534) 880588
www.bohemiajersey.com

£5 OFF

This hotel dining room is a Jersey institution that Steve Smith has quietly made his own since arriving in 2013 – the relentlessly inventive chef delivering 'knockout cooking that alone justifies a flight to Jersey'. Smith brings balance and a lightness of touch to his remarkably consistent output, perhaps in a re-imagined Waldorf salad that so impressed one visitor: a vivid celery pannacotta teamed with celery, walnuts, macerated grapes, compressed apples, 'the smoothest, firmest' apple sorbet and golden raisins, or when pineapple is turned into a cannelloni-wrapper for pristine white crabmeat and framed by dots of brown meat espuma, horseradish cream and yuzu gel. Other courses focus on luxury ingredients more than wizard technique. Two fat, sweet langoustines, for example, set on toasted hazelnuts and diced claw meat with smoked butter, sea herbs and a smooth parsnip purée, or a thick slice of turbot draped in lardo and paired with nuggets of braised oxtail and Jerusalem artichoke and purée. Squab pigeon – the bird shared between two diners – arrives as confit legs (crisped, smoked and served on hay), liver parfait on toast beneath tiny char-grilled fillets, the breast paired with beetroot (baked, purée, remoulade) and an intense sauce with a hint of liquorish. The common thread running through all this is food that fully exploits contrasting flavours and textures. Desserts are equally focused, whether clementine sorbet and jelly with spiced biscuit and spiced gel or an intricate, layered chocolate bar spiked with whisky and topped with malt ice cream. On the wine front, bottles start at £18 and you can drink very well in the £30 to £40 range.
Chef/s: Steve Smith. **Open:** Mon to Sat L 12 to 2.30, D 6.30 to 10. **Closed:** Sun, 25 to 30 Dec. **Meals:** Set L £20 (2 courses) to £25. Set D £50 (2 courses) to £59. Tasting menus £49 (6 courses) to £85.
Details: 54 seats. V menu. Bar. Wheelchair access. Music. Parking.

Ormer

High-spec dining with brasserie-style buzz
Cooking score: 5
Modern French | £55
Don Street, St Helier, Jersey, JE2 4TQ
Tel no: (01534) 725100
www.ormerjersey.com

£5 OFF

'Ormer is as it was on opening,' noted a returnee, approving the 'accurate cooking, excellent ingredients, highly professional staff, and a cool, casual vibe that stems from the immeasurably slick, brasserie-style interior'. If you can get past the bar ('mustard-yellow leather stools, velvet banquettes and beautiful, faded copper bar top') and some of the 'best oysters I have ever eaten', you can expect Shaun Rankin's trademark interpretations of contemporary French cuisine. Perhaps a single lobster raviolo, its tail meat set in a scallop mousse, in a tomato and crab bisque and topped by spring onions, puffed black rice and coriander shoots, or go for slices of barely seared tuna and wafers of raw scallop with a sweet cucumber sorbet and distinctly fiery Bloody Mary jelly tempered by guacamole. A simply conceived pine nut-crusted fillet of turbot was a hit at inspection, its accompaniments just raw cauliflower, cauliflower purée and all sorts of sea herbs, while an intense chocolate delice studded with little shards of feuilletine and accompanied by an excellent parsnip ice cream made a fine finale. The extensive wine list opens at £22. **Chef/s:** Shaun Rankin. **Open:** Mon to Sat L 12 to 2.30, D 6.30 to 10. **Closed:** Sun, 25 and 26 Dec. **Meals:** alc (main meals £27 to £32). Set L £19 (2 courses) to £25. Tasting menu £75. **Details:** 52 seats. 20 seats outside. V menu. Bar. Music.

Tassili

Headline restaurant at a luxury spa hotel
new chef/no score
Modern European | £49
Grand Jersey, The Esplanade, St Helier, Jersey, JE2 3QA
Tel no: (01534) 722301
www.grandjersey.com

Sipping Champagne on the terrace is a favourite pastime at this luxe Jersey Hotel overlooking St Aubin's Bay, although some guests prefer to be pampered in the spa. There's also serious food to be had in the Tassili restaurant – a soothing space done out in shades of peach and white. Chef Richard Allen has decamped to Rockliffe Hall, but his replacement Nicolas Valmagna is no slouch – earning his stripes with Raymond Blanc, before cooking in top-end kitchens around the world. As a result, his style fuses haute French technique with global flavours and a liking for local produce: Jersey Chancre crab might appear with yuzu gel, bisque dressing and crab espuma, while turbot might be paired with mushroom and saffron risotto, cockles, sea vegetables and tapioca crisp. Elsewhere, expect Nantes foie gras, Anjou pigeon and milk-fed Pyrénean lamb as well as 'Classic Herd' pork with boudin noir and compressed apple. For afters, perhaps try poached rhubarb with ginger foam and Jersey black-butter ice cream. Well-chosen wines from £18.50.

Chef/s: Nicolas Valmagna. **Open:** Fri and Sat L 12 to 1.45, Tue to Sat D 7 to 10. **Closed:** Sun, Mon, first 2 weeks Jan. **Meals:** Set L £19 (2 courses) to £25. Set D £52. Tasting menu £67 (7 courses). **Details:** 28 seats. V menu.

The Green Olive

Mediterranean | £25
1 Anley Street, St Helier, Jersey, JE2 3QE
Tel no: (01534) 728198
www.greenoliverestaurant.co.uk

Chef/proprietor Paul Le Brocq gives fresh fish and vegetarian dishes top billing at this funky little first-floor eatery overlooking St Helier's town square. Seasonal menus might feature Jersey scallops with vanilla-scented carrot and ginger purée or spinach, pea and asparagus risotto served with feta crumble. Asian flavours also have their moment (Thai red curry with tofu or slow-cooked pork belly with teriyaki glaze, say), while puds might include raspberry meringue roulade. House wine is £16.95. Closed Sat L, Sun and Mon.

St Peter Port, Guernsey

La Frégate

Stunning seascapes and complex cooking
Cooking score: 4
Modern British | £40
Beauregard Lane, Les Cotils, St Peter Port, Guernsey, GY1 1UT
Tel no: (01481) 724624
www.lafregatehotel.com

Sitting high on a hill overlooking the narrow streets of St Peter Port, this elegantly extended 18th-century manor house makes the most of its harbour views and tantalising glimpses of ancient Castle Cornet. There are panoramic vistas, too, from the arched windows of the white-walled dining room. Long-serving chef Neil Maginnis is in the business of creating highly intricate, pretty-looking

seasonal dishes based on locally sourced meat and fresh fish from the island boats: Rocquiane Bay oysters are grilled with garlic butter and chorizo, pistachio-crusted brill is presented with curly kale, mussels and saffron broth, while thyme-roasted lamb fillet comes with Mediterranean vegetables, salsa verde and Parmesan gnocchi. Maginnis also likes to toss in a few oriental riffs here and there, from curry-scented scallops with cauliflower tempura to confit duck spring rolls with kumquat reduction. Plain grills please the traditionalists, as do 'lovely' crêpes Suzette, flambéed at the table with much theatrical brio. Wines from France dominate the old-school list, with prices from £22.
Chef/s: Neil Maginnis. **Open:** all week L 12 to 1.30, D 7 to 9.30. **Meals:** alc (main courses £19 to £24). Set L £18 (2 courses) to £24. Set D £35. Sun L £24. **Details:** 70 seats. 20 seats outside. V menu. Bar. Music. Parking.

Da Nello
Italian | £40

46 Lower Pollet, St Peter Port, Guernsey, GY1 1WF
Tel no: (01481) 721552
www.danello.gg

A Guernsey institution since it first opened its doors in 1978, Da Nello may occupy a building more than 500 years old, but this robust Italian trattoria has moved with the times, making good use of local fish and shellfish, as well as showcasing the island's veal. Signature dishes include a starter of gratinated open mushroom with local crab, garlic butter and Parmesan, followed by a main of medallions of beef with Barolo sauce. Open all week.

Fermain Beach Café
Italian | £30

Fermain Lane, St Peter Port, Guernsey, GY1 1ZZ
Tel no: (01481) 238636

A charming ambience and simple food has won many friends at this all-day beach café specialising in seafood. Many come for sunny chill-outs at rough tables by the sea – with blankets and outdoor heating for less favourable weather (though there is an indoor eating area). Most reporters have stumbled on the place while on a cliff walk and stopped for well-filled crab sandwiches, prawn sandwiches, marinated steak ciabattas and some very good cakes. Wine from £14.95. Open all week in season.

St Peter, Jersey
Mark Jordan at the Beach
Crowd-pleasing brasserie dishes
Cooking score: 3
Modern British | £36

La Plage, La Route de la Haule, St Peter, Jersey, JE3 7YD
Tel no: (01534) 780180
www.markjordanatthebeach.com

Opened as a crowd-pleasing foil to Mark Jordan's cooking at the more upmarket Ocean Restaurant at the Atlantic Hotel (see entry), this laid-back, brasserie-style restaurant is right across the road from the beach. Service is warm and friendly, appropriate to the casual seaside setting, while the exterior, with Mark Jordan's signature emblazoned on a pink-red entrance canopy, offers great alfresco opportunities in fine weather. The cooking is suitaby uncomplicated, too, along the lines of fish soup with a good rouille, or poached oysters with a beurre blanc and a warm dice of cucumber – 'about as good as this Jersey classic gets' – and sea bass on a cylinder of potato crushed with crabmeat and ringed by mussels in cream sauce. For one reporter, the highlight was a dessert of rich, 'almost caramel' poached pear on a just-set cinnamon pannacotta with meringue shards and a good pear sorbet. Wines from £16.
Chef/s: Mark Jordan and Tamas Varsanyi. **Open:** all week L 12 to 2.30, D 6 to 9.30. **Closed:** Mon (winter), 9 to 23 Nov. **Meals:** alc (main courses £15 to £29). Set L £20 (2 courses) to £25. Set D £28. Sun L £28. **Details:** 50 seats. 30 seats outside. Bar. Music. Parking.

St Saviour, Jersey
Longueville Manor

Special-occasion dining and seamless service
Cooking score: 5
Modern British | £60
St Saviour, Jersey, JE2 7WF
Tel no: (01534) 725501
www.longuevillemanor.com

This 'hidden gem' of a medieval manor promises polish, serenity and seamless, genuinely committed service. Long-serving chef Andrew Baird remains a key figure, his cooking a who's-who of Jersey produce served in intricate yet not over the top dishes. Consider white crabmeat, guacamole and a crisp, tempura crab claw with citrusy mayo dotted with cucumber, caviar and watermelon, or lobster tail and lobster won ton with caviar, a spaghetti of vegetables, a light ginger dressing and 'a quality bisque poured at the table'. A single lamb chop, perfectly pink, arrives 'rolled in bright green crumbs and mustard', and teamed with artichokes, aubergine purée, dauphinois and a subtle lamb sauce. For dessert there's a neat play on pina colada – light coconut mousse and sorbet, pineapple pieces and purée – ahead of a baked apple terrine with a light bavarois flavoured with black butter (a local delicacy) and a superb calvados ice cream. And there's real breadth to the wine list (from £28); for many years the owners have bought directly from the vineyards – the Bordeaux section, for example, really is something special.
Chef/s: Andrew Baird. **Open:** all week L 12 to 2, D 6 to 10. **Meals:** Set L £25 (2 courses) to £30. Set D £53 (2 courses) to £60. Sun L £40. Tasting menu £80. **Details:** 90 seats. 35 seats outside. V menu. Bar. Music. Parking.

Shaun Rankin

Ormer, St Helier, Jersey

What inspired you to become a chef?
I grew up in North Yorkshire and I inherited my initial love of food and cooking from my mother. I am now very fortunate to have worked with some of the greatest chefs in the world and travelled to the most incredible places. The best thing about cooking is that it's pretty much a language in itself. No matter where you travel, you can communicate through the skills you have learned and apply them to a range of cuisines.

What food trends are you spotting at the moment?
Foraging from the sealine and woodlands is a really exciting gastronomic trend and I use a variety of sea herbs in the dishes at Ormer.

What would you be if you weren't a chef?
A fisherman! I try to get out on the sea as often as possible but with all the businesses now under the SR brand it really is a rare treat. If I weren't a chef I'd love to be out there in the boat sourcing our fantastic local seafood and making sure it's delivered sustainably and ethically.

NORTHERN IRELAND

Armagh, Co Armagh
Uluru Bar & Grill
Aussie tucker in Armagh

Cooking score: 2
Australian | £30

3-5 Market Street, Armagh, Co Armagh,
BT61 7BX
Tel no: (028) 3751 8051
www.ulurubistro.com

Having shifted a few metres down the road to new premises, Uluru (aka Ayers Rock) has lighting that changes through the day in homage to the daily visual transformation undertaken by the massive sandstone rock formation it's named after. This Aussie-run bar and eatery is vibrant, fun and lively, with a Josper grill fired up to dish out BBQ-style stuff such as the Bondi burger (the owners met on Bondi Beach), pulled pork with coleslaw and tobacco onions, or char-grilled kangaroo loin with kumera chips (sweet potato). Steaks also get a good workout on the grill (T-bone, ribeye etc.) and rustic pizzette include a version topped with honey-glazed ham, pineapple and local Cheddar. Wine from £13.
Chef/s: Dean Coppard. **Open:** all week 9 to 4 (12 to 4 Sun), D 4 to late. **Closed:** 25 and 26 Dec, 1 Jan. **Meals:** alc (main courses £13 to £23). Set L £16. Set early D £16 (2 courses) to £19. **Details:** 70 seats. 12 seats outside. V menu. Bar. Wheelchair access.

Bangor, Co Down
The Boat House
Cooking with big ambitions

Cooking score: 6
Modern British | £33

1a Seacliff Road, Bangor, Co Down, BT20 5HA
Tel no: (028) 9146 9253
www.theboathouseni.co.uk

£5
OFF

This is the story of two Dutch brothers who have created one of Northern Ireland's most dynamic restaurants. The action all takes place down at the marina in Bangor – in the former harbourmaster's office no less – and it's a very modern tale. Joery Castel cooks, his brother Jasper does the rest, and they're most definitely the A-team. The solid old building has a neutral contemporary finish within and nothing detracts from the sharply modern culinary goings-on. Fabulous Irish ingredients (and more) are subjected to some cutting-edge cooking techniques, with evidence of sound judgement and serious dedication to the craft. Kick off with smoked Irish scallops, which arrive with compressed apple, pickled turnips and pepper foam (plus a nifty scallop roe cracker), and move on to Atlantic cod with some Asian flavours, or a richly satisfying guinea fowl suprême with a goats' cheese and onion 'pizza' and some fashionable charred cauliflower. Desserts maintain the pace, Dutch-style blue cheese soufflé, say, and the intelligently gathered wine list starts at £19.

Chef/s: Joery Castel. **Open:** Wed to Sun L 12.30 to 2.30 (1 Sun), D 5.30 to 9.30 (8 Sun). **Closed:** Mon, Tue. **Meals:** Set L £18 (2 courses) to £24. Set D £27 (2 courses) to £33. **Details:** 32 seats. 6 seats outside. Bar. Music. Parking.

█ Belfast, Co Antrim

Eipic

Compelling modern cooking chez Deane
Cooking score: 4
Modern European | £30
28-40 Howard Street, Belfast, Co Antrim, BT1 6PF
Tel no: (028) 9033 1134
www.michaeldeane.co.uk

There's a lot going down on Howard Street thanks to the regional culinary powerhouse that is Michael Deane. The choice between the easy-going Love Fish or the beefy Meat Locker may well cause relationship issues if you can't decide between one or t'other, but there's always agreement to be found in Eipic's divertingly contemporary offering. Eipic is only open one lunchtime and four evenings a week, so book a table when you can and settle into the slick dining room with its swish contemporary finish. The kitchen is headed up by Danni Barry, who is among Ireland's

leading female chefs, turning out savvy tasting menus that might begin with oak-smoked haddock with duck yolk and move on to Strangford crab with barbecued cabbage heart, salted peanuts and buttermilk. It's very of the moment, with chicken wings turning up with caramelised cauliflower and a roast chicken and sherry vinegar emulsion, and burnt white chocolate and sour cherries partnering a chocolate caramel mousse among sweet courses. Wines start at £20.

Chef/s: Danni Barry. **Open:** Fri L 12 to 3, Wed to Sat D 5.30 to 10. **Closed:** Sun, Mon, Tue, 25 and 26 Dec, 1 Jan, Jul. **Meals:** Set L and D £30. Tasting menu £40 (4 courses) to £60. **Details:** 30 seats. V menu. Bar. Wheelchair access. Music.

Hadskis

Brasserie classics in an old iron foundry
Cooking score: 3
Modern European | £30
33 Donegall Street, Belfast, Co Antrim, BT1 2NB
Tel no: (028) 9032 5444
www.hadskis.co.uk

Secreted along a little cobbled alley not far from St Anne's Cathedral, Hadskis takes its name from a man who once made pots and pans here in an iron foundry established in the 1760s. It all looks utterly urban-chic now of course, with a discreet dark-grey frontage and a long stylish bar inside, as well as a row of unclothed little tables in a contemporary brasserie atmosphere. The food suits the mood, with continental classics aplenty, from charcuterie plates and mushroom arancini in truffled mayo, to big belting mains such as osso buco with orzo and gremolata, tomahawk pork chop with crushed sweet potato, and steaks from the charcoal grill. Fish luxuries include a whole salt-baked sea-bream, and it all climaxes with pineapple Tatin and yoghurt sorbet, or blackberry-topped vanilla cheesecake. House Spanish is £16.

Chef/s: David Scott. **Open:** all week 12 to 10.30 (11am Sat and Sun). **Meals:** alc (main courses £11 to £23). **Details:** 40 seats. 10 seats outside. Bar. Wheelchair access. Music.

Il Pirata

Casual 'small plates' Italian
Cooking score: 3
Italian | £18
279-281 Upper Newtownards Road,
Ballyhackamore, Belfast, Co Antrim, BT4 3JF
Tel no: (028) 9067 3421
www.ilpiratabelfast.com

With its white-tiled walls, chunky wooden tables and sharing-plate concept, Il Pirata is riding a contemporary wave. Those small plates are cicchetti and pizzetta and the vibe is energetic and engaging. A taste of Italy in east Belfast seems to be just the ticket, judging by the crowds, and they come for feisty plates of full-flavoured stuff like sliced pork and fennel slider, polenta fritters with roast pepper salsa, and chilli and rocket pizzetta. If sharing just isn't your thing, keep duck ragù with gnocchi and spinach all to yourself. Pasta is a good bet – squid-ink linguine or tagliatelle carbonara made with smoked pancetta – and finish with a classic dessert such as tiramisu or Amaretto pannacotta with fruit compote. Wines from £17.50.
Chef/s: Jonny Phillips. **Open:** all week 12 to 10 (11pm Fri and Sat). **Closed:** 25 and 26 Dec. **Meals:** alc (main courses £10 to £14). **Details:** 80 seats. Bar. Wheelchair access. Music. Parking.

James Street South

Serious cooking at accessible prices
Cooking score: 6
Modern European | £35
21 James Street South, Belfast, Co Antrim,
BT2 7GA
Tel no: (028) 9043 4310
www.jamesstreetsouth.co.uk

Niall McKenna has a lot on his plate. The mainstay of his empire is first and foremost his flagship restaurant that opened in 2003 and quickly assumed a place at the city's top table. The Bar & Grill, in the same eponymous street, is a fiery spot with a Josper oven, and there is also Hadskis (see entry). David Gillmore leads the brigade at James Street South, producing pin-sharp, French-inflected contemporary food in the McKenna mould. It all takes place in a smart, understated dining room with prime Irish ingredients finding their way into the kitchen and out to your table. The mostly 'outstanding' output – offered via carte, tasting and set lunch/pre-theatre menus – might see you kicking off with chilled Portavogie crab lasagne, with a rich and fragrant lemongrass and brown crab bisque, followed by suckling pig's belly with scallop cannelloni, or wild sea bass with a racy squid and chorizo bolognese. Presentation is creative and eye-catching, down to a dessert of smoked chocolate clafoutis. Wines start at £18.
Chef/s: David Gillmore. **Open:** Tue to Sat L 12 to 2.45, Mon to Sat D 5.30 to 10.45. **Closed:** Sun, 25 and 26 Dec, 1 Jan, Easter Sun and Mon, 11 and 12 Jul. **Meals:** alc (main courses £16 to £25). Set L and D £16 (2 courses) to £19. **Details:** 65 seats. V menu. Wheelchair access. Music.

Mourne Seafood Bar

Local seafood hero
Cooking score: 3
Seafood | £25
34-36 Bank Street, Belfast, Co Antrim, BT1 1HL
Tel no: (028) 9024 8544
www.mourneseafood.com

Next door to Belfast's boozing legend Kelly's Cellars, this local seafood hero majors on cockles, mussels and oysters from the owners' beds in Carlingford Lough and daily consignments of fish from Annalong and Kilkeel. Inside, Mourne's is totally traditional (all dark wood and exposed brickwork), with an on-site fishmonger and cookery school ramming home the piscophile message. In addition the repertoire comprises a mixed bag of seafood classics and upbeat contemporary ideas ranging from pan-fried crab claws, fish fingers and lobster with chips to salt-and-chilli squid, scallop ceviche or roast fillet of cod. Char-grilled Irish ribeye steaks are the only sop to meat eaters. Note that the full restaurant menu is also served in the street-level oyster bar, although neither takes

bookings for lunch. Wines from £16.25. The original Mourne's is on Main Street, Dundrum, BT33 0LU; tel: (028) 4375 1377.
Chef/s: Andy Rea. **Open:** Mon to Thur 12 to 9.30. Fri and Sat L 12 to 4, D 5 to 10.30. Sun 1 to 6.
Meals: alc (main courses £8 to £20). **Details:** 80 seats. V menu. Bar. Wheelchair access.

★ TOP 50 ★

RESTAURANT OF THE YEAR

OX

Creative, ingredients-led, seasonal food
Cooking score: 6
Modern European | £33
1 Oxford Street, Belfast, Co Antrim, BT1 3LA
Tel no: (028) 9031 4121
www.oxbelfast.com

Packing a major punch in Belfast, chef Stephen Toman and Alain Kerloch's high-achieving restaurant offers some exciting contemporary cooking. The dining room sports a simple look – open-to-view kitchen, hard surfaces (wall, floor, table tops, chairs), with natural light from a full-height shop window – but is filled with laughter and life by folk enjoying themselves. Stephen Toman uses modern techniques in an unobstrusive fashion, delivering light, modern, colourful plates driven by seasonality and a focus on vegetables over animal protein. The common thread running through all this is food that fully exploits contrasting flavours and textures, as seen in a textural riff on cauliflower, almond, nasturtium and maple with richness from a tiny lobe of foie gras. Elsewhere, an undeniably fresh, beautifully cooked piece of brill is teamed with sea lettuce, vin jaune, confit leek and a little pile of sweet, briny crab, or chateaubriand, served perfectly rare, arrives with shallot, horseradish, wild garlic and potato. Equally, a beguiling combination of Jerusalem artichoke with pecan, banana and caramel simply dazzles. The well-considered wine list is

sourced with an eager eye for little known gems and quality drinking, with prices from £18.
Chef/s: Stephen Toman. **Open:** Tue to Sat L 12 to 2.30, D 6 to 10. **Closed:** Sun, Mon, 24 to 31 Dec, 7 to 14 Apr, 11 to 28 Jul. **Meals:** alc (main courses £16 to £22). Set L £14 (2 courses) to £18. Tasting menu £45 (5 courses). **Details:** 40 seats. V menu. Bar. Wheelchair access. Music.

The Potted Hen

Lively contemporary bistro
Cooking score: 3
Modern European | £25
11 Edward Street, Belfast, Co Antrim, BT37 0BQ
Tel no: (028) 9023 4554
www.thepottedhen.co.uk

If the pristine colonnaded exterior in a posh square gives off an air of exclusivity, you'll find that inside is all thrusting exuberance with exposed internal ducting and a vibrant, brasserie-style menu. Terrace tables increase the continental vibe. Salt-and-chilli prawns is a suitably hot number, with Asian slaw and its own potent dip, while another starter has rare beef in a salad with pickled shallots and Cashel Blue mayo (mayo, slaw...abbreviations rule). Follow on with roast rump of new season lamb with Moroccan-spiced couscous, or grilled salmon with smoked red pepper purée, and end on a sweet note with cappuccino semifreddo with homemade doughnuts (or 'donuts'). Drink cocktails, or wines from £17.95.
Chef/s: Dermot Regan. **Open:** Mon to Sat L 12 to 3, D 5 to 9.30 (10 Fri and Sat). Sun 12 to 9. **Closed:** 24 to 26 Dec, 1 and 2 Jan, 12 and 13 Jul. **Meals:** alc (main courses £11 to £23). Set D £16 (2 courses) to £18. Sun L £19 (2 courses) to £22. **Details:** 170 seats. 30 seats outside. V menu. Music.

NEW ENTRY

Shu

Cementing a fine reputation

Cooking score: 4
Modern British | £32
253 Lisburn Road, Belfast, Co Antrim,
BT9 7EN
Tel no: (028) 9038 1655
www.shu-restaurant.com

It's only recently that those beyond Belfast have taken note of what locals have been saying for years, that – funny name aside (the Egyptian god of the atmosphere) – Shu is a winner with its basement cocktail bar, ground-floor restaurant with open-to-view kitchen, and first-floor private dining room. Opened in 2000 in a Victorian terrace on the Lisburn Road (south of the city centre), Brian McCann took over as head chef in 2004. Over the last decade he has cemented Shu's fine reputation with unpretentious, technically assured cooking that makes the most of the local larder but is not afraid to make clever use of flavours from further afield: an approach typified by starters like foie gras and chicken liver parfait served with apple and chilli jelly, and by mains such as turbot teamed with black rice, lemon, chilli, coriander seeds, fennel, beetroot. Wines from £17.25.
Chef/s: Brian McGann. **Open:** Mon to Sat L 12 to 2.30, D 5.30 to 9.30. **Closed:** Sun, 24 to 26 Dec, 1 Jan. **Meals:** alc (main courses £13 to £23). Set L £13 (2 courses) to £19. Set D £23 (2 courses) to £28.
Details: 76 seats. Bar. Music. Parking.

LOCAL GEM

The Ginger Bistro

Modern European | £35
7-8 Hope Street, Belfast, Co Antrim, BT12 5EE
Tel no: (028) 9024 4421
www.gingerbistro.com

Simon McCance's easy-going bistro is bright and breezy with bare-wood floors and simple furnishings. The kitchen has a wide-ranging outlook – dishes range from tempura of asparagus with Asian salad and a pineapple and pickled ginger dressing, through to local fillet of cod roasted with caper, brown shrimp and leek butter with a potato and wholegrain mustard gratin – and diners report an 'exquisite dining experience' with palpably fresh ingredients. Finish with banana tarte Tatin or classic crème brûlée. Wines from £17.50. Closed Mon.

Comber, Co Down

The Old Schoolhouse Inn

Honest intent and highly personal style

Cooking score: 4
Modern British | £30
100 Ballydrain Road, Comber, Co Down,
BT23 6EA
Tel no: (028) 9754 1182
www.theoldschoolhouseinn.com

A humble B&B on the outskirts of Comber, located in what was once the local primary school, has undergone a transformation in recent years. In 2012, after time spent in London with Philip Howard at the Square, and at Bruce Poole and Nigel Platts-Martin's the Glasshouse (see entries), Will Brown returned home and set about turning his family's Old Schoolhouse Inn into an immaculate restaurant with rooms. Menus make use of local game, beef and poultry, seafood from nearby Strangford Lough, foraged herbs, fungi, marine plants from Mahee Island, and produce grown in the inn's own kitchen garden. There's something immensely appealing about Brown's honest intent and highly personal style. His 'bistro' menu offers takes on accessible classics such as mussels cooked in Farmageddon ale with shallot, pearl barley, garlic and parsley, fish and chips with garden pea purée, and beef bourguignon with creamed potatoes, foraged mushrooms and bordelaise sauce, there's the option of a five-course tasting menu, and good value set lunch and dinner deals. Wines from £21.

Chef/s: Will Brown. **Open:** Tue to Sat 12 to 10.30.
Sun 12 to 8. **Meals:** alc (main courses £12 to £23).
Set L and D £10 (2 courses) to £14. Sun L £19.
Details: 60 seats. 50 seats outside. V menu. Bar.
Wheelchair access. Music. Parking.

Donaghadee, Co Down

The Governor Rocks
Fantastic fish and seafood
Cooking score: 3
Seafood | £20
27 The Parade, Donaghadee, Co Down,
BT21 0HE
Tel no: (028) 9188 4817
www.thegovernorrocks.com

A change of hands and the arrival of a new chef
have not put this seafront charmer off its
stride: you can still expect 'incredibly
reasonably priced ocean wonders' plus a decent
showing from field and turf. The shabby-chic
interior (antique mirrors, mismatched
furniture, nautical bric-à-brac) sets an
informal tone that is reflected in the
unpretentious cooking. Mussels from the
harbour in a 'white wine sauce worthy of
Escoffier' come highly recommended, as does
the 'lazy lobster', a keenly priced half, served
with cheese, garlic oil and an optional and
surprisingly mild Tabasco dressing. Typical
meaty options include pork belly fritter with
baby leaf salad and celeriac remoulade. To
finish, maybe a chocolate fondant. Wines
from £12.95.
Chef/s: James Luke Cummins. **Open:** Mon to Sat L
12 to 3, D 5 to 9.30. Sun 12 to 9. **Meals:** alc (main
courses £8 to £27). **Details:** 140 seats. V menu.
Wheelchair access. Music.

Average price

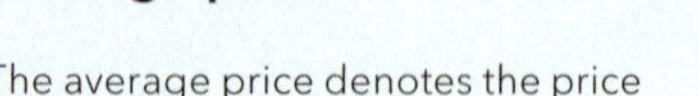

The average price denotes the price
of a three-course meal without wine.

Holywood, Co Down

LOCAL GEM
The Bay Tree
Modern British | £25
118 High Street, Holywood, Co Down,
BT18 9HW
Tel no: (028) 9042 1419
www.baytreeholywood.co.uk

The Farmers' all-day venue is as homely as can
be, with café tables, a slate-tiled floor and local
art going on behind the stripy curtains. Start
the day here with a sausage soda bread
sandwich, drop in for a lunch of aubergine, red
pepper and goats' cheese terrine, followed by
spiced chicken salad with coconut and mango
in lime and coriander dressing, or book in
advance for Friday night dinner, when sole
véronique or duck breast in apricot, ginger
and coriander may be the order of the evening.
Dessert could be dark chocolate and hazelnut
meringue with poached pear and raspberry
sorbet. Wines from £15. Open daytime all
week and Fri D.

Killinchy, Co Down
Balloo House
Classy old coaching inn
Cooking score: 2
Modern British | £27
1 Comber Road, Killinchy, Co Down,
BT23 6PA
Tel no: (028) 9754 1210
www.balloohouse.com

There are plenty of places in rural Northern
Ireland that are warmly welcoming, but
readers find the quality, ambience and
friendliness at this 400-year-old former
farmhouse to be of the highest, and they all
complement the modern Irish bistro cooking.
Polished flagstones, stone walls, plus a blazing
range in winter, provide the perfect backdrop
for robust, gutsy dishes – think starters of
smoked bacon and Glebe Brethan cheese tart
with salsa verde and green bean salad or

smoked salmon and potato pancake with dressed crab and avocado purée, and main courses of slow-cooked Dexter beef blade with herb-crusted confit potatoes, truffled celeriac purée and wild mushrooms or pan-fried cod with spring pea and Strangford prawn risotto. Classics of fish and chips and steak and Farmageddon stout pie are on hand too, and there's a fine chocolate and hazelnut tart with salt-caramel sauce and hazelnut ice cream to finish. Wines from £16.45.

Chef/s: Danny Millar and Grainne Donnelly. **Open:** all week 12 to 9 (8.30 Sun and Mon, 9.30 Fri and Sat). **Closed:** 25 Dec. **Meals:** alc (main courses £10 to £23). Set L and D £15 (2 courses) to £19. Set D £15 (2 courses) to £19. Sun L £23. **Details:** 80 seats. 10 seats outside. Bar. Wheelchair access. Music. Parking.

Newcastle, Co Down
Vanilla

Colourful surrounds, colourful food

Cooking score: 3
Modern British | £33
67 Main Street, Newcastle, Co Down,
BT33 0AE
Tel no: (028) 4372 2268
www.vanillarestaurant.co.uk

The atmosphere is lively with cheerful, informal service at this reinvigorated local restaurant where proprietor Darren Ireland continues to draw the Newcastle crowds, who treat Vanilla as a place to sup or to celebrate – various menus and set deals cater for both. In general, the cooking style is at the sophisticated end of the comfort food spectrum, with dishes ranging from chicken liver parfait with fig jam and onion marmalade to Indian-curried monkfish with sticky coconut rice, mango chutney and onion relish. Main courses are more likely to appear with classic flavour combinations: cod with truffled polenta chips, bacon and peas, say, or Old Spot pork belly with roast apple and black pudding mash. Lunch brings sandwiches and wraps, steaks and burgers. Wines from £14.95.

Chef/s: Colin Birtles. **Open:** Mon to Sat L 12 to 3.30, D 5 to 9 (9.30 Fri and Sat). Sun 12 to 9. **Meals:** alc (main courses £16 to £23). Set L and D £16 (2 courses) to £20. **Details:** 36 seats. 8 seats outside. Wheelchair access. Music.

Portstewart, Londonderry

NEW ENTRY
Harry's Shack

Accomplished comfort food

Cooking score: 4
Seafood | £30
116 Strand Road, Portstewart, Londonderry,
BT55 7PG
Tel no: 028 7083 1783

Occupying a National Trust-owned beachside shed on the north coast, overlooking the Atlantic, Harry's Shack has made quite a splash since opening in August 2014. The setting is special, in possession of a rugged calm when the sun comes out, but offering a brutal beauty on stormy days, and it makes a perfect pit stop before or after a visit to the Giant's Causeway. But that alone doesn't explain why reservations are at a premium throughout the year. Derek Creagh, who back in the day worked for Heston Blumenthal, oversees the menu both here and at Harry's Restaurant on the other side of the border at Bridgend, where two acres provide fruit and vegetables for both outposts. He delivers accomplished comfort food with an understandable emphasis on seafood, from whitebait dusted with paprika and served with Marie Rose for dipping, via buttermilk-battered haddock with chips and mushy peas, to megrim soul fried in butter with roast cauliflower, brown shrimps, capers and cucumber. Currently unlicensed, so BYO, corkage £3.

Chef/s: Derek Creagh. **Open:** Summer all week 10.30 to 4, D 5 to 9. Call for winter openings. **Meals:** alc (main courses £11 to £15). **Details:** 65 seats. 30 seats outside. V menu. Wheelchair access.

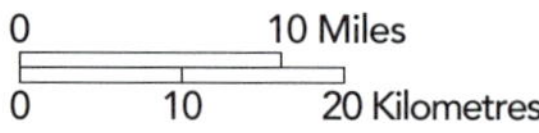

MAP 7

- ■ Main entry
- ● Main entry with accommodation
- ▲ Local Gem

A single symbol may denote
several restaurants in one area.

```
0                10 Miles
0      10        20 Kilometres
```

Note: Maps 1 to 6 can be found at the front
of the London section

Isles of Scilly
Same scale as main map

10
8
Bristol Channel
Weston-super-Mare
Wrington
21
Cheddar
Burnham-on-Sea
Wedmore
22
Lower Godney
A371
Glastonbury
23
Bridgwater
Street
A39
A38
SOMERSET
Langport
Taunton
25
Long Sutton
A361
Ilfracombe
Lynton
Minehead
A39
Fivehead
A358
Braunton
A361
A39
Dulverton
Wellington
26
M5
Hinton St George
Barnstaple
Knowstone
A303
Ilminster
Bideford
South Molton
A361
27
A358
Great Torrington
Kings Nympton
Tiverton
28
A30
Chard
Crewkerne
A39
A386
A3072
A396
A373
A358
Beaminster
Hatherleigh
A3072
Crediton
Honiton
Axminster
A377
Clyst Hydon
A388
A3072
DEVON
Exeter
Newton Poppleford
A3052
Bridport
Ashwater
Okehampton
A30
Exeter
30
29
Topsham
Sidford
Seaton
Lyme Regis
Drewsteignton
Sidmouth
Lyme Bay
Exmouth
A382
31
A379
A376
Lewdown
A386
Dartmoor
Bovey Tracey
Dawlish
Lifton
A380
Teignmouth
Treburley
Shaldon
Gulworthy
Ashburton
A38
Newton Abbot
A390
Tavistock
Buckfastleigh
Torquay
Yelverton
South Brent
A385
Totnes
Paignton
A388
Ivybridge
Saltash
Sparkwell
A38
Brixham
Plymouth
Dittisham
Millbrook
A381
Dartmouth
A379
Kingsbridge
Bigbury-on-Sea
South Pool
Salcombe
Start Point

Channel Islands
Not to same scale
Alderney
Alderney
Guernsey
St Peter Port
Herm
Guernsey
Sark
Jersey
St Peter
St Saviour
Jersey
Gorey
St Brelade
St Clement
St Helier

11
MAP 8
Main entry
Main entry with accommodation
Local Gem
A single symbol may denote
several restaurants in one area.
0   10 Miles
0   10   20 Kilometres
10
Felin Fach
2 M50
Tewkesbury
Eldersfield   Corse   9
Lawn   10   Winchcombe
A449   Stow-on-
the-Wold
4   A417   Cheltenham   Upper
Slaughter
Ross-on-   Gloucester   11A   11   Hills
A4136   Wye   GLOUCESTERSHIRE   A40
Cinderford   Cotswold   Northleach
Arlingham   A46   A417   A429
13   A419   Barnsley
A38   Stroud   A429   Cirencester
A48   A419
Severn   Nailsworth   A4135   Cricklade
M5   Dursley   Tetbury
26 25   Thornbury   A433   Swindon
A470   A468   23   24   A4135   Malmesbury   16
Pontypridd   Caldicot   1   Easton   A3102   Royal
Caerphilly 28   22   21   Grey   Wootton
Newport   16   Chipping   M4   Bassett
32   17   20/15   Sodbury   17   A4361
29   Avonmouth   18A   Bristol Filton   A46   Castle Combe Foxham   A4
34 33   19   Portishead   19   18   Colerne   Chippenham
Cardiff   Long Ashton   3   1   A420   Corsham   Calne   WILTSHI
Clevedon   Bristol   Chew   A4   Bath   Melksham
Penarth   Bristol   Magna   Pensford   Bradford-   A350   Rowde
International   Chew   Combe Hay   on-Avon   Devizes
Barry   Stoke   A36   A342
Cardiff   Weston-   21   Wrington   Midsomer   A367   Trowbridge   Pewsey
super-Mare   Norton   A36   East
Cheddar   A368   Radstock   Chisenbury
A371   A39   Frome   Warminster   A345
Burnham-   Mells   A361   A360
on-Sea   Wedmore   Wells   A362   Amesbury
22   Lower   A361   A36
Godney   Shepton Mallet   A359   Berwick
23   Glastonbury   A371   St James
Bridgwater   Street   A37   Bruton   A303   Fonthill   Teffont   Wilton
A39   A39   Gifford   Evias   Salisbury
A358   SOMERSET   A37   Wincanton   West Hatch   A30
Taunton   Langport   Long   Shaftesbury   Donhead
25   A361   Sutton   A372   A357   St Andrew
Wellington   Fivehead   A350
A38   26 M5   A358   Yeovil   Sherborne   Sturminster
27   A303   Hinton   Barwick   Newton   Stuckton
A38   Ilminster   St George   A352   A357   A354   A338
7   Chard   A30   Crewkerne   Blandford   Ringwood
28   A356   Forum   Wimborne   A31
Clyst   A373   A358   DORSET   Minster   A350
Hydon   Honiton   A3066   Beaminster   A354   Bournemouth
Axminster   A37   A35   A31
A30   Bridport   A35   Christchurch
A3052   Lyme   Dorchester   A35
Sidford   Regis   Wareham   Poole
Newton   Sidmouth   Seaton   A354   A352   Bournemouth
Poppleford   Burton   A353   A351   Poole
Bradstock   Bay
Lyme Bay   Weymouth   Studland
Fortuneswell   St Alban's   Swanage
Head
Easton
Bill of Portland

12
9
9
Moreton-in-Marsh
Chipping Norton
Kingham
Wootton
Kirtlington
Swinbrook
Crawley
Murcott
Easington
Dinton
Aylesbury
BUCKINGHAMSHIRE
Bicester
Dunstable
Leighton Buzzard
Luton
London Luton
Willian
Hitchin
Stevenage
Welwyn Garden City
HERTFORDSHIRE
Hemel Hempstead
Chiltern Hills
OXFORDSHIRE
Kidlington
Witney
Burford
Filkins
Oxford
Fyfield
Great Milton
Toot Baldon
Thame
Chinnor
Great Missenden
Amersham
St Albans
Northaw
Watford
Chandler's Cross
Bushey
Kingston Bagpuize
Abingdon
Didcot
Wallingford
High Wycombe
GREATER
Wembley
Harrow
Faringdon
Wantage
Sparsholt
Aston Tirrold
Stonor
Stoke Row
Henley-on-Thames
Goring
Shiplake
Marlow
Burchett's Green
Cookham
Taplow
Bray
Slough
Windsor
Holyport
Paley Street
Maidenhead
White Waltham
London
LONDON
Richmond
Bishopstone
BERKSHIRE
Woodspeen
Marlborough
Hungerford
Little Bedwyn
Newbury
Thatcham
Shinfield
Reading
Wokingham
Bracknell
Staines-upon-Thames
London Heathrow
Epsom
Baughurst
Camberley
Bagshot
Chobham
Woking
Ripley
Leatherhead
Old Basing
Fleet
Farnborough
Guildford
SURREY
Redhill
Reigate
Basingstoke
Aldershot
Farnham
Dorking
Andover
Longparish
Preston Candover
Alton
Godalming
London Gatwick
Crawley
Stockbridge
Sparsholt
HAMPSHIRE
Alresford
Liphook
Haslemere
Horsham
Winchester
West Meon
Petersfield
Fernhurst
Lickfold
Petworth
Billingshurst
Lower Beeding
Cuckfield
Tillington
Midhurst
WEST SUSSEX
Burgess Hill
Romsey
Eastleigh
Southampton
Droxford
Albourne
M27
Southampton
Waterlooville
West Ashling
Singleton
Lavant
East Lavant
Arundel
Hove
Brighton
Woodlands
Lyndhurst
Hythe
Fareham
Funtington
Emsworth
Chichester
Tangmere
Worthing
Brockenhurst
Beaulieu
Gosport
Havant
Southsea
Bognor Regis
Littlehampton
New Milton
Lymington
Cowes
Portsmouth
East Wittering
Sidlesham
Barton on Sea
Yarmouth
Ryde
Newport
Freshwater
ISLE OF WIGHT
St Helens
Selsey Bill
Sandown
Isle of Wight
Ventnor
Bonchurch
Shanklin

12
8
8
8
Banbury
Brackley
Milton Keynes
BEDFORDSHIRE
Royston
A1
A505
A10
Buckingham
Bletchley
Woburn
Letchworth
Baldock
A507
Hitchin
Willian
Buntingford
Stevenage
Chipping Norton
Bicester
BUCKINGHAMSHIRE
Leighton Buzzard
Dunstable
Luton
London Luton
A602
Hunsdon
Wootton
Kirtlington
A41
Welwyn Garden City
Hertford
Crawley
Aylesbury
Easington
Dinton
Hemel Hempstead
HERTFORDSHIRE
OXFORDSHIRE
Murcott
Kidlington
Thame
St Albans
Northaw
Witney
Oxford
Great Milton
Chinnor
Great Missenden
Watford
Bushey
Enfield
Kingston Bagpuize
Fyfield
Toot Baldon
Amersham
Chandler's Cross
Faringdon
Abingdon
High Wycombe
Harrow
GREATER
Wantage
Didcot
Wallingford
Stonor
Marlow
Burchett's Green
Cookham
Taplow
London
LONDON
Sparsholt
Aston Tirrold
Stoke Row
Henley-on-Thames
Goring
Maidenhead
Bray
Slough
Wembley
Richmond
Shiplake
White Waltham
Holyport
Windsor
Bromley
BERKSHIRE
Paley Street
Bracknell
London Heathrow
Croydon
Woodspeen
Reading
Wokingham
Staines-upon Thames
Epsom
Hungerford
Newbury
Shinfield
Bagshot
Chobham
Woking
Leatherhead
Thatcham
Camberley
Farnborough
Ripley
SURREY
Oxted
Baughurst
Old Basing
Fleet
Guildford
Reigate
Redhill
Basingstoke
Aldershot
Farnham
Dorking
East Grinstead
Andover
Preston Candover
Godalming
London Gatwick
Longparish
Alton
HAMPSHIRE
Liphook
Haslemere
Horsham
Crawley
West Hoathly
Stockbridge
Alresford
Fernhurst
Lickfold
Billingshurst
Lower Beeding
Horsted Keynes
Haywards Heath
Sparsholt
Winchester
West Meon
Petersfield
Tillington
Petworth
Cuckfield
Burgess Hill
Romsey
Eastleigh
Droxford
Midhurst
WEST SUSSEX
Albourne
East Chiltington
Southampton
Southampton
Waterlooville
West Ashling
Singleton
Lavant
East Lavant
Arundel
Brighton
Woodlands
Hythe
Havant
Funtington
Tangmere
Worthing
Hove
Lyndhurst
Brockenhurst
Fareham
Gosport
Emsworth
East Wittering
Chichester
Littlehampton
Beaulieu
Southsea
Bognor Regis
Lymington
Cowes
Portsmouth
Sidlesham
Yarmouth
Ryde
St Helens
Newport
Sandown
Freshwater
ISLE OF WIGHT
Shanklin
Isle of Wight
Ventnor
Bonchurch
English

12
Saffron Walden
Gestingthorpe
Stoke-by-Nayland
Stratford St Mary
Felixstowe
Halstead
Dedham
Mistley
Harwich
London Stansted
Braintree
The Naze
Bishop's Stortford
Great Dunmow
Fuller Street
Colchester
Clacton-on-Sea
ESSEX
Witham
West Mersea
Mersea Island
Harlow
Maldon
Chelmsford
Stock
Burnham-on-Crouch
Brentwood
Rayleigh
London Southend
Basildon
Southend-on-Sea
Barking Romford
Horndon on the Hill
Canvey Island
Thames
Woolwich
Grays
Tilbury
Sheerness
Herne Bay
Margate
London City
Dartford
Gravesend
Rochester
Manston
Manston
Broadstairs
Locksbottom
Chatham
Gillingham
Whitstable
Minster
Ramsgate
Oare
Faversham
Canterbury
Sandwich
Maidstone
Sittingbourne
Stalisfield Green
Deal
Sevenoaks
KENT
Crundale
Lower Hardres
Tonbridge
Ashford
Tunbridge Wells
Biddenden
Dover
Withyham
Tenterden
Hythe
Folkestone
Channel Tunnel
Crowborough
New Romney
Strait of Dover
Fletching
Rye
Lydd (London Ashford)
EAST SUSSEX
Westfield
Battle
Lewes
Hailsham
Hastings
Newhaven
Bexhill
Seaford
Eastbourne
Channel
MAP 9
Main entry
Main entry with accommodation
Local Gem
A single symbol may denote several restaurants in one area.
0   10 Miles
0   10   20 Kilometres

11
MAP 10
Main entry
Main entry with accommodation
Local Gem
A single symbol may denote
several restaurants in one area.
0   10 Miles
0   10   20 Kilometres
Cardigan
Bay
Tywyn
Aberdovey
A493
Machynlleth
Eglwysfach
Talybont
A44
Aberystwyth
Devil's
Bridge
A4120
A487
Aberaeron
Tregaron
New Quay
A485
A486
Lampeter
Cambrian
A475
A482
Cardigan
A484
Newcastle
Emlyn
WEST
WALES
A483
A487
A484
Llandovery
Llanwrda
A485
A484
A40
A4069
Fishguard
Newport
Porthgain
A487
A40
Nantgaredig
Llandeilo
St David's
Carmarthen
Llanarthne
A40
A48
Llandybie
Haverfordwest
Narberth
St Clears
Ammanford
A4067
A4076
A477
A484
A483
A474
Broad Haven
Milford
Haven
Pendine
Laugharne
Kidwelly
A476
49
Pontardawe
Pembroke
Dock
Saundersfoot
48
Pontlliw
Neath
Llanelli
M4
45
Pembroke
A4139
Tenby
Gorseinon
47
Swansea
43
42
A4107
Carmarthen
Reynoldston
Port
Talbot
40
Bay
A4118
Mumbles
Port Eynon
Bristol
Channel
Lynton
Ilfracombe
A361
A39
Lundy
7

11
Mountains
Montgomery
Newtown
Minsterley
SHROPSHIRE
Broseley
Wolverhampton
A41
A458
A442
Dudley
Halesowen
Stourbridge
A489
A490
A488
A489
Church Stretton
Bridgnorth
A458
A491
A448
Llanidloes
Llangurig
MID WALES
Llanfair Waterdine
Wistanstow
Craven Arms
A49
Kidderminster
Bewdley
A4117
Ludlow
Stourport-on-Severn
A4110
A456
A443
Bromsgrove
M5
Rhayader
A488
Knighton
A4113
A44
Ombersley
Droitwich
Worcester
WORCESTER-SHIRE
A422
Beulah
Builth Wells
Llandrindod Wells
A483
Titley
Pembridge
Leominster
A44
Kington
A4112
A49
Bromyard
A44
Great Malvern
A4103
Baughton
Pershore
Welland
A38
M5
Llanwrtyd Wells
A438
Hay-on-Wye
A438
HEREFORDSHIRE
Hereford
A438
Ledbury
Tewkesbury
Eldersfield
Corse Lawn
M50
A417
Llyswen
A470
Talgarth
Felin Fach
A479
A465
A49
Ross-on-Wye
A40
Brecon
A40
Glasbury-on-Wye
M50
Walford
Cheltenham
Gloucester
GLOUCESTERSHIRE
11A
Crickhowell
Llanddewi Skirrid
Abergavenny
Brynmawr
A465
Monmouth
A40
Cinderford
A4136
Arlingham
Stroud
A4109
Merthyr Tydfil
Ebbw Vale
Whitebrook
GWENT
A466
A48
A38
Nailsworth
Dursley
A4135
Tetbury
A429
A465
Aberdare
Abertillery
A472
Pontypool
Usk
A449
Chepstow
Severn
M5
Malmesbury
Treorchy
A4059
Bargoed
A469
Cwmbran
Tredunnock
M48
Thornbury
A433
Easton Grey
GLAMORGAN
A472
A468
Caerphilly
Newport
Caldicot
Chipping Sodbury
Castle Combe
M4
Maesteg
Pontypridd
A470
28
Bristol Filton
18
Chippenham
Pyle
Llantrisant
A4119
32
29
Avonmouth
Colerne
Corsham
Bridgend
Cardiff
Clevedon
Long Ashton
Bristol
Bath
Melksham
Porthcawl
A48
Cowbridge
Penarth
Bristol International
Chew Magna
Pensford
Bradford-on-Avon
A350
Barry
Cardiff
Weston-super-Mare
Chew Stoke
Combe Hay
A367
A36
Trowbridge
Wrington
A38
A368
Midsomer Norton
Radstock
Frome
Warminster
Burnham-on-Sea
Cheddar
A371
A39
Mells
A361
A362
Minehead
A39
Wedmore
Lower Godney
Wells
Shepton Mallet
A359
Bridgwater
Glastonbury
A361
8
9

13
MERSE
Amlwch
A5025
Llanfaethlu
Anglesey
Holyhead
Holy Island
A55
Menai
Bridge
Beaumaris
A4080
Rhosneigr
Newborough
Caernarfon
A4086
Llanberis
A5
Bangor
Great Ormes
Head
Llandudno
Conwy
Colwyn
Bay
Abergele
A55
A548
A470
Prestatyn
Rhyl
A548
Dee
Holywell
A55
A548
Denbigh
A525
A541
Ruthin
A525
NORTH-
WAL
Caernarfon
Bay
A4085
A499
A498
A470
Capel
Curig
Betws-
y-coed
Llanrwst
A543
Llyn Brenig
Pentrefoelas
A5
A5104
A542
Beddgelert
A487
NORTH-WEST
WALES
Blaenau Ffestiniog
Corwen
Llangollen
Nefyn
Criccieth
A497
Porthmadog
A499
Pwllheli
A4212
Llandrillo
Bala
Llyn Tegid
Llanarmon
Dyffryn Ceiriog
Abersoch
Tremadog
Bay
Harlech
Llanbedr
A496
Llyn
Trawsfynydd
A470
A494
Lake
Vyrnwy
Llanfyllin
Bardsey
Island
Barmouth
Penmaenpool
A493
Dolgellau
A470
Dinas
Mawddwy
A487
A489
A458
Mountains
A495
Tywyn
Aberdovey
A493
Machynlleth
A470
Montgomery
A489
Newtown
Eglwysfach
A487
Cardigan
Talybont
A487
Llangurig
A470
Llanidloes
A483
Aberystwyth
A44
MID WALES
Bay
A4120
Devil's
Bridge
Cambrian
WEST
WALES
Rhayader
A44
A488
A470
Llandrindod Wells
A483
Tregaron
A485
Llyn
Brianne
Beulah
Builth
Wells
A482
A483
Llanwrtyd
Wells
Glasbury-
on-Wye
Llyswen
Llandovery
Llanwrda
Felin Fach
Talgarth

MAP 11

■ Main entry
● Main entry with accommodation
▲ Local Gem

A single symbol may denote
several restaurants in one area.

0   10 Miles
0   10   20 Kilometres

10

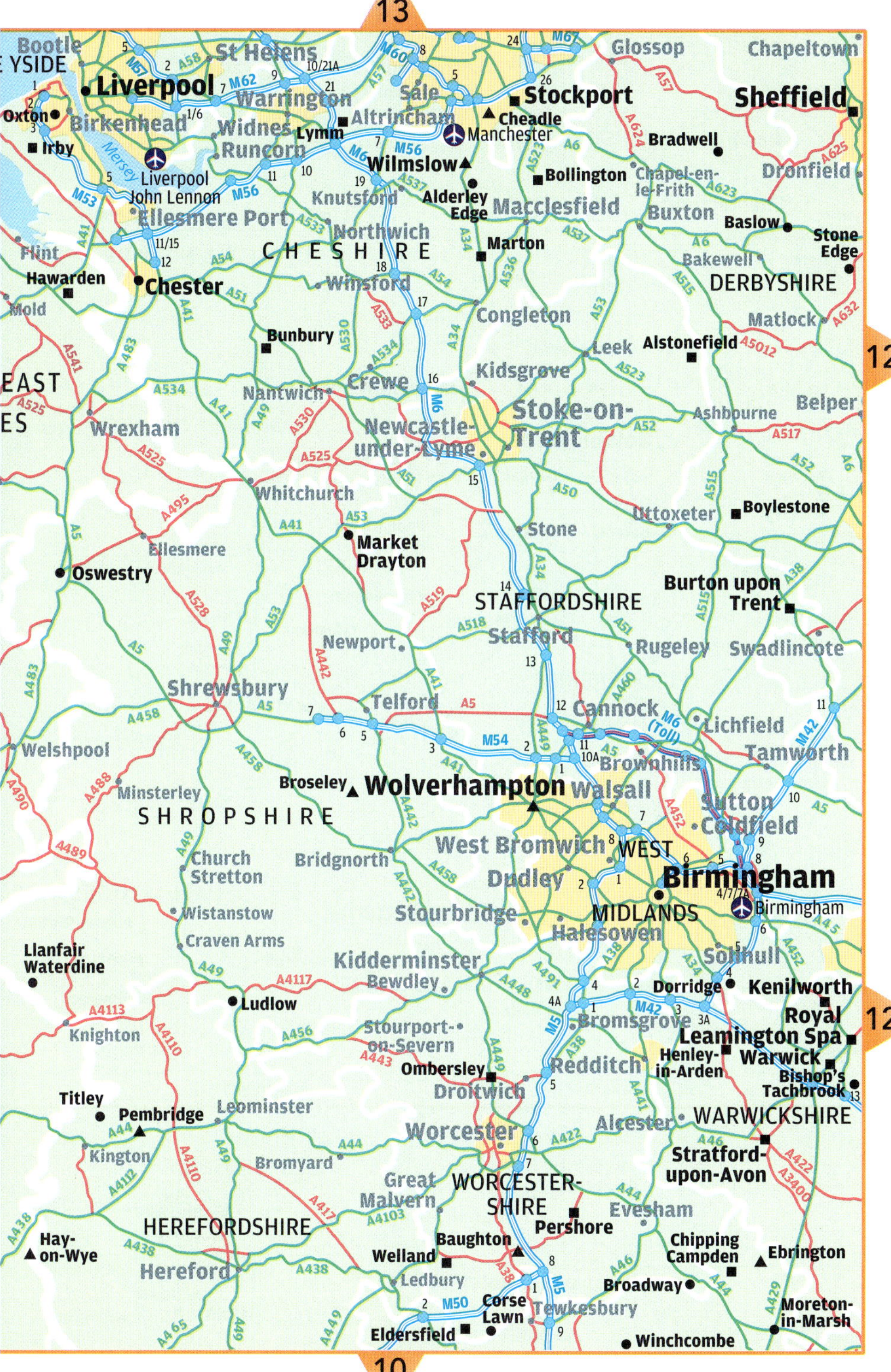

13
12
12
10
Bootle
YSIDE
Oxton
Irby
Liverpool
Birkenhead
Widnes
Runcorn
Flint
Hawarden
Mold
Chester
St Helens
Warrington
Altrincham
Lymm
Liverpool John Lennon
Ellesmere Port
Winsford
CHESHIRE
Sale
Wilmslow
Knutsford
Northwich
Bunbury
Nantwich
Crewe
Sale
Stockport
Cheadle
Manchester
Alderley Edge
Macclesfield
Marton
Congleton
Leek
Kidsgrove
Stoke-on-Trent
Newcastle-under-Lyme
Glossop
Bradwell
Bollington
Chapel-en-le-Frith
Buxton
Bakewell
Alstonefield
Ashbourne
Chapeltown
Sheffield
Dronfield
Baslow
Stone Edge
DERBYSHIRE
Matlock
Belper
Boylestone
EAST
ES
Wrexham
Whitchurch
Ellesmere
Oswestry
Market Drayton
STAFFORDSHIRE
Stafford
Stone
Uttoxeter
Burton upon Trent
Rugeley
Swadlincote
Welshpool
Shrewsbury
Newport
Telford
Cannock
Lichfield
Tamworth
Minsterley
SHROPSHIRE
Broseley
Wolverhampton
Walsall
Brownhills
Sutton Coldfield
Llanfair Waterdine
Church Stretton
Bridgnorth
West Bromwich
WEST
Birmingham
Wistanstow
Craven Arms
Dudley
Stourbridge
Halesowen
MIDLANDS
Birmingham
Solihull
Kidderminster
Bewdley
Dorridge
Kenilworth
Ludlow
Bromsgrove
Royal Leamington Spa
Knighton
Stourport-on-Severn
Henley-in-Arden
Warwick
Titley
Pembridge
Leominster
Ombersley
Redditch
Droitwich
Alcester
Bishop's Tachbrook
WARWICKSHIRE
Kington
Bromyard
Worcester
Stratford-upon-Avon
HEREFORDSHIRE
Great Malvern
WORCESTER-SHIRE
Pershore
Evesham
Chipping Campden
Ebrington
Hay-on-Wye
Hereford
Welland
Baughton
Ledbury
Corse Lawn
Tewkesbury
Broadway
Winchcombe
Moreton-in-Marsh
Eldersfield

14
11 
11
9

A61
Rotherham
34 33 32
Maltby
Bawtry
A631
Gainsborough
Upton
Market Rasen
Louth
Sheffield
31
A18
M18
A57
A1
A620
A156
A1500
A46
A157
A153
A16
Ridgeway
Worksop
Retford
30
Dronfield
A57
A158
Chesterfield
A619
A632
A614
A6075
Lincoln
Horncastle
Partney
DERBYSHIRE
A1
A1133
LINCOLNSHIRE
A155
Stone Edge
29
Sutton in Ashfield
Mansfield
A616
A617
Caunton
Newark-on-Trent
A17
A607
A153
A619
A632
A61
Alfreton
28
NOTTINGHAMSHIRE
A46
Hough on the Hill
Sleaford
A1121
Boston
Hucknall
A38
A60
A6097
Belper
A610
A153
Heanor
A6
Ilkeston
26
Nottingham
A52
Great Gonerby
A52
Darley Abbey
A52
Langar
A52
Grantham
Derby
25
Long Eaton
A453
A60
Plumtree
Stathern
A1
Woolsthorpe by Belvoir
Spalding
A151
A50
A42
24
A607
A151
Holbeach
East Midlands
Wymondham
Ashby de la Zouch
A512
23
Loughborough
A46
A607
Melton Mowbray
Clipsham
Bourne
A6121
Market Deeping
A16
Mountsorrel
A511
M1
A6
Coalville
22
LEICESTERSHIRE
Rutland Water
A606
Stamford
A47
11
A444
Anstey
Oakham
Hambleton
A444
A447
21A
Leicester
A47
RUTLAND
Peterborough
Atherstone
A447
21
Wigston
Uppingham
A6003
A605
Whittlesey
March
M69
Kibworth Harcourt
A1
A141
Hinckley
Kibworth Beauchamp
Corby
17
A605
Chatteris
Nuneaton
1
M1
A6
Market Harborough
A6116
Oundle
16
A10(M)
3
Bedworth
Lutterworth
20
Rushton
A43
CAMBRIDGESHIRE
2
M6
A4304
A14
Kettering
A43
14
Abbots Ripton
Coventry
19
A508
Keyston
A14
Huntingdon
A45
Rugby
A43
NORTHAMPTONSHIRE
A6
St Ives
18
Hemingford Grey
Royal Leamington Spa
17
East Haddon
A45
Rushden
Grafham Water
A14
Warwick
Wellingborough
A1
St Neots
14
Bishop's Tachbrook
Daventry
A428
Northampton
Bolnhurst
13
M40
A425
A45
Bedford
12
WARWICKSHIRE
A361
16
15A
15
A428
BEDFORDSHIRE
A1198
A603
A10
A423
A5
A508
A509
M1
A422
A421
A600
A505
A4422
A422
Towcester
A509
A422
A6
Biggleswade
Royston
Paulerspury
A421
A1
Banbury
A422
Brackley
Milton Keynes
14
A507
Letchworth
Baldock
11
Buckingham
Bletchley
Woburn
13
Hitchin
Willian
9
Buntingford
A361
A4421
A422
A421
A5
M1
A4012
A505
Stevenage
Chipping Norton
10
BUCKINGHAMSHIRE
A4146
Leighton Buzzard
12
A505
8
A4422

MAP 12
Main entry
Main entry with accommodation
Also recommended
A single symbol may denote several restaurants in one area.
0 10 Miles
0 10 20 Kilometres
Mablethorpe
A52
A158
Skegness
A52
The Wash
Old Hunstanton
Hunstanton
Titchwell
A149
Brancaster Staithe
Morston
Blakeney
Wells-next-the-Sea
Wiveton
Sheringham
Cromer
Stanhoe
Snettisham
Thorpe Market
A149
Edgefield
North Walsham
Fakenham
A148
Aylsham
Ingham
A148
A1065
Great Massingham
A1067
A140
A1151
A149
A17
King's Lynn
East Dereham
A47
A47
Norwich
Great Yarmouth
A1101
A47
NORFOLK
Norwich
Wisbech
A10
A1122
Swaffham
Brundall
A47
A143
Downham Market
A1122
Ovington
Wymondham
A146
Fritton
A1101
A134
A1065
A11
Stoke Holy Cross
A140
Lowestoft
A1075
Attleborough
Littleport
A10
Brandon
Thetford
A1066
Diss
A143
Bungay
Beccles
A144
A145
A12
Ely
A142
Mildenhall
A11
Halesworth
Southwold
A142
A1101
A1088
A143
Walberswick
A1123
A134
Stanton
A140
Yoxford
Tuddenham
A14
Bury St Edmunds
A1120
Newmarket
Moulton
A14
Woodditton
SUFFOLK
Snape
Aldeburgh
Cambridge
A11
Little Wilbraham
A143
Stowmarket
A12
Bromeswell
Orford
Woodbridge
Orford Ness
A1307
Cavendish
A134
Lavenham
A1141
Ipswich
A1071
Haverhill
A1092
Sudbury
Stoke-by-Nayland
Hadleigh
Stratford St Mary
A14
Felixstowe
9A
9
Gestingthorpe
A134
Saffron Walden
M11
A1017
A131
Dedham
A12
Mistley
Harwich
ESSEX
Halstead
A137
The Naze
Braintree
A120
Colchester
A120

MAP 13

■ Main entry
● Main entry with accommodation
▲ Local Gem

A single symbol may denote several restaurants in one area.

0   10 Miles
0   10   20 Kilometres

15
Redcar
Bishop Auckland
Aycliffe
STOCKTON-on-Tees
Middlesbrough
Goldsborough
Summerhouse
Guisborough
Barnard Castle
Winston
Darlington
A688
A67
A66
A1(M)
59
58
57
Brough
Hutton Magna
A66
56
Durham Tees Valley
A171
A174
Kirkby Stephen
Hurworth-on-Tees
A167
A172
Richmond
Middleton Tyas
Staddlebridge
A169
A1
Osmotherley
Northallerton
A684
Leyburn
A684
51
Bedale
Maunby
Scawton
Helmsley
Pickering
Hawes
13
A684
A167
Thirsk
Harome
A170
A170
West Witton
A6108
Masham
A168
Oldstead
50
Ramsgill
Ripon
49
Malton
A64
YORKSHIRE
A19
Settle
Grassington
Boroughbridge
A166
A65
Hetton
Ferrensby
Newton-on-Ouse
A658
Knaresborough
47
A59
Bolton Abbey
A59
Harrogate
A661
York
Skipton
A629
Ilkley
A65
Wetherby
46
45
A1079
Keighley
A658
Leeds/Bradford
Tadcaster
A1(M)
A64
A682
Grindleton
A1079
A613
Downham
44
A6068
A59
A614
Fence
Nelson
Bradford
Leeds
43/48
Selby
Wiswell
Burnley
A6033
A629
3
46
A63
A62
6
Accrington
1
42
A1041
M62
Todmorden
Shibden
Drighlington
Morley
30
Castleford
Goole
A646
Halifax
26 27
Wakefield
41
33
37
Rawtenstall
Sowerby Bridge
Batley
29
Pontefract
34
36
Ramsbottom
23
Dewsbury
40
A638
7/35
Thorne
A161
M66
Norden
Lindley
Huddersfield
39
A628
6
A18
Bury
Birtle
Honley
38
A1
5
1
Rochdale
A629
Bentley
A614
A58
2
M62
20
Oldham
38
A635
A161
2
Holmfirth
37
Doncaster
A624
Lydgate
Barnsley
37
4
15
M60
18
19
M60
22
36
36
2/35
A1(M)
Robin Hood
Worsley
Ashton-under-Lyne
A628
35
Bawtry
Manchester
Stocksbridge
Chapeltown
Rotherham
A159
Salford
24
Glossop
A61
1
A631
8
Sale
26
M67
34
Maltby
Gainsborough
Altrincham
A57
33 32
M18
A620
A156
Stockport
Sheffield
A57
A1
7
Cheadle
Ridgeway
31
Worksop
Retford
Manchester
A6
Bradwell
30
NOTTINGHAMSHIRE
M56
Wilmslow
Chapel-en-le-Frith
Dronfield
Knutsford
Bollington
A623
A619
Alderley Edge
A619
Chesterfield
A614
A57
Macclesfield
Buxton
Baslow
A6075
Marton
A34
Bakewell
A619
A632
A1
Stone Edge
29
A60
Congleton
A54
A537
A6
29
M1
A616
Caunton
18
A536
A53
A515
DERBYSHIRE
A61
A632
Mansfield
A1133
17
Matlock
11

MAP 14

■ Main entry
● Main entry with accommodation
▲ Also recommended

A single symbol may denote
several restaurants in one area.

0   10 Miles
0   10   20 Kilometres

Whitby
A171
Sawdon
Scarborough
Filey
A64
A165
Flamborough Head
A614
Bridlington
Driffield
A164
A165
Bridlington Bay
South Dalton
A1035
Hornsea
Market Weighton
Beverley
Withernwick
A1034
Sancton
A164
Hull
A63
Withernsea
A1033
Barton-upon-Humber
Humber
Winteringham
A1077
A15
A1077
Immingham
A180
Spurn Head
Scunthorpe
5
A 18
Great Limber
Grimsby
3
Humberside
Cleethorpes
4
M180
Brigg
A1173
A46
A18
A16
A1031
Caistor
A631
A631
Louth
Mablethorpe
Upton
Market Rasen
A15
A46
A157
A153
A16
A52
A1500
A158
A1028
Lincoln
Horncastle
Partney
LINCOLNSHIRE
A158
Skegness
A155

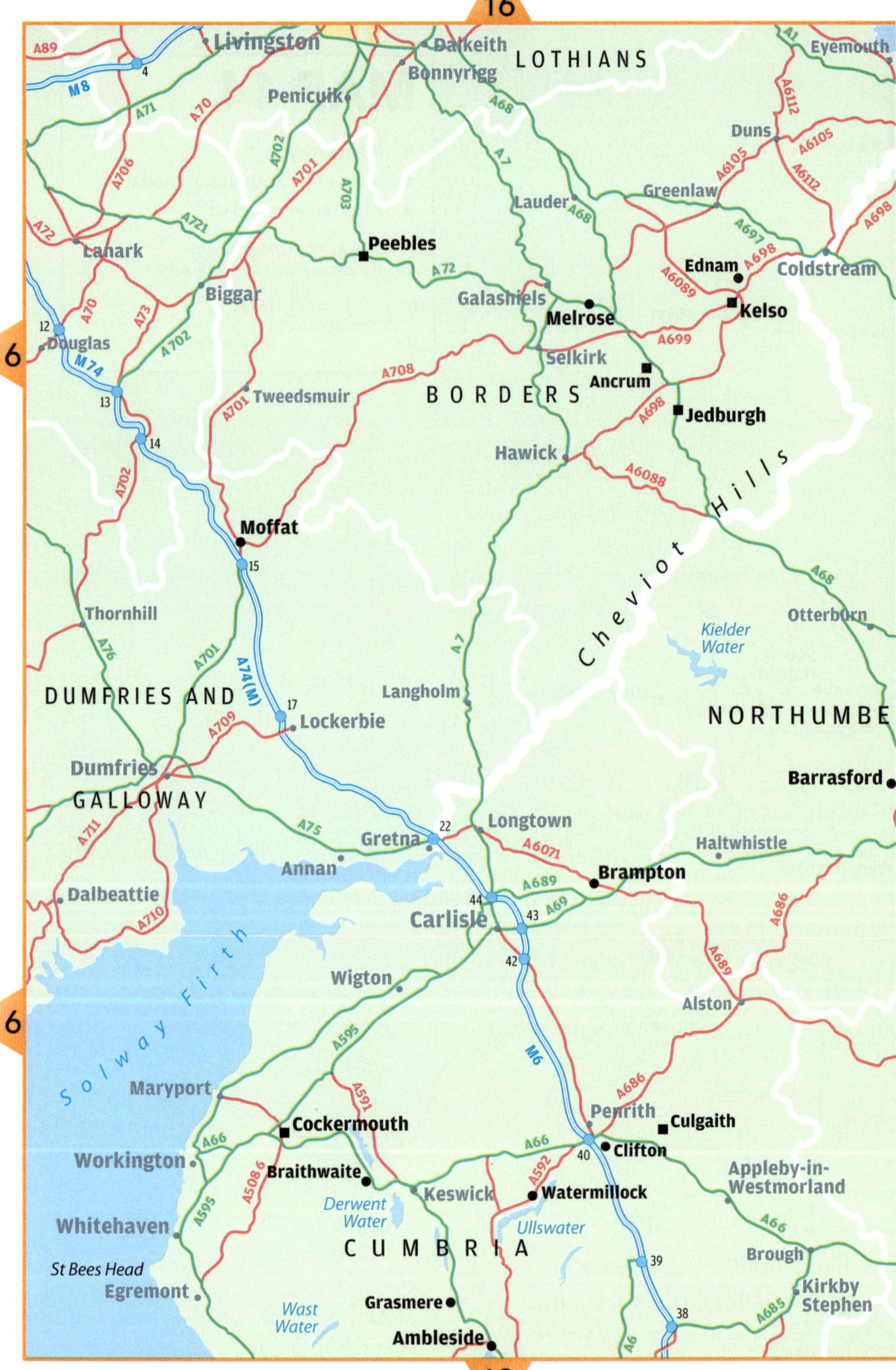

16
16
16
16
13
A89
M8
4
A71
A70
A706
A702
A701
A703
Livingston
Dalkeith
Bonnyrigg
LOTHIANS
Eyemouth
A1
Penicuik
A68
Duns
A6112
A72
A721
A6105
A6112
Lanark
A70
A73
A702
Biggar
Peebles
A72
Lauder
A68
Greenlaw
A6105
A697
A698
Douglas
12
A701
Tweedsmuir
A708
Galashiels
Melrose
Selkirk
BORDERS
Ancrum
Ednam
A6089
Kelso
Coldstream
A698
A699
Jedburgh
A698
M74
13
14
A702
Hawick
A6088
Cheviot Hills
Moffat
15
Kielder
Water
Otterborn
A68
Thornhill
A76
A701
A74(M)
A7
Langholm
NORTHUMBE
Lockerbie
17
A709
DUMFRIES AND
Dumfries
GALLOWAY
A711
A75
Gretna
22
Longtown
A6071
Barrasford
Annan
A689
Brampton
Haltwhistle
Dalbeattie
A710
44
43
A69
Carlisle
A586
42
A689
Wigton
Alston
Solway Firth
A595
M6
A686
Maryport
Penrith
Culgaith
A66
Cockermouth
A66
Clifton
40
Appleby-in-
Westmorland
Workington
A508.6
A595
Braithwaite
Keswick
A592
Watermillock
A66
Derwent
Water
Ullswater
Brough
Whitehaven
CUMBRIA
39
St Bees Head
Egremont
Wast
Water
Grasmere
A6
38
A685
Kirkby
Stephen
Ambleside

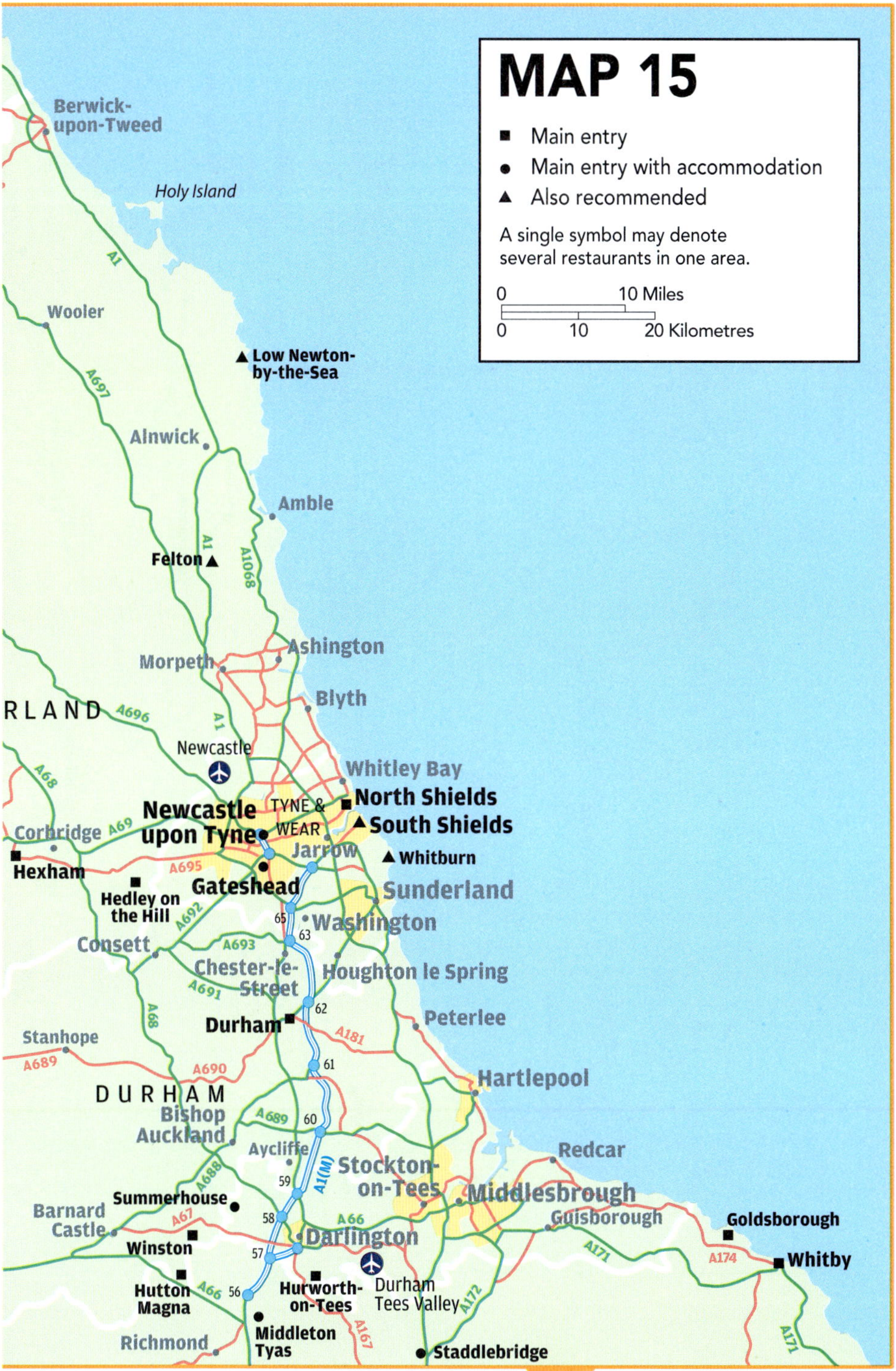
MAP 15
Main entry
Main entry with accommodation
Also recommended
A single symbol may denote several restaurants in one area.
0 10 Miles
0 10 20 Kilometres
Berwick-upon-Tweed
Holy Island
Wooler
Low Newton-by-the-Sea
Alnwick
Amble
Felton
Ashington
Morpeth
Blyth
RLAND
Newcastle
Whitley Bay
North Shields
South Shields
Newcastle upon Tyne
TYNE & WEAR
Jarrow
Whitburn
Corbridge
Hexham
Gateshead
Sunderland
Hedley on the Hill
Washington
Consett
Chester-le-Street
Houghton le Spring
Durham
Peterlee
Stanhope
Hartlepool
DURHAM
Bishop Auckland
Aycliffe
Redcar
Stockton-on-Tees
Middlesbrough
Summerhouse
Guisborough
Goldsborough
Barnard Castle
Darlington
Whitby
Winston
Hutton Magna
Hurworth-on-Tees
Durham Tees Valley
Middleton Tyas
Richmond
Staddlebridge
A1
A697
A1068
A696
A68
A69
A695
A692
A693
A691
A181
A689
A690
A688
A1(M)
A67
A66
A167
A172
A171
A174
56
57
58
59
60
61
62
63
65

14

Mainland
Finstown
Shapinsay
Kirkwall
Kirkwall
Stromness
Scapa Flow
Orkney Islands
Hoy
St Margaret's Hope
South Ronaldsay
Burwick
Pentland Firth
Dunnet Head
Island of Stroma
Duncansby Head
John o'Groats
Shetland Islands
Not to same scale
Herma Ness
Haroldswick
Gutcher
Unst
Belmont
Fetlar
Cape Wrath
Whiten Head
Durness
Scrabster
Thurso
Melvich
North Roe
Yell
Shetland Islands
Butt of Lewis
Port of Ness
Loch Hope
Tongue
Noss Head
Wick
Esha Ness
Hillswick
St Magnus Bay
Ulsta
Whalsay
Outer Hebrides
Barvas
Tolsta Head
Scourie
Loch Naver
Altnaharra
Kinbrace
Latheron
Papa Stour
Sandness
Mainland
Callanish
Stornoway
Point of Stoer
Lochinver
Inchnadamph
Helmsdale
Scalloway
Lerwick
Bressay
Isle of Lewis
Kebock Head
Rubha Coigeach
Elphin
Loch Shin
Lairg
Brora
Sumburgh
Sumburgh
Sumburgh Head
Tarbert
Cailleach Head
Ullapool
Bonar Bridge
Sgarasta Bheag
Harris
Leverburgh
Laide
HIGHLANDS AND ISLANDS
Dornoch
Tain
Moray Firth
Gairloch
Loch Maree
Delny
Alness
Invergordon
Cromarty
Lossiemouth
Portknockie
Buckie
Macduff
Fraserburgh
Lochmaddy
Kinlochewe
Garve
Dingwall
Fortrose
Nairn
Forres
Elgin
Banff
Aberchirder
Turriff
Rattray Head
Mintlaw
Uig
Achnasheen
Inverness
Tore
Auldearn
Craigellachie
Keith
Huntly
North Uist
Stein
Shieldaig
Inverness
Peterhead
Benbecula
Colbost
Dunvegan
Portree
Loch Monar
Beauly
Inverness
Dufftown
Raasay
Plockton
Cannich
Grantown-on-Spey
Rhynie
Oldmeldrum
Ellon
Sconser
Scalpay
Stromeferry
Drumnadrochit
Loch Ness
Carrbridge
GRAMPIAN
Udny Green
Skye
Shiel Bridge
Loch Affric
Invermoriston
Aviemore
Alford
Inverurie
Dyce
South Uist
Broadford
Kyle of Lochalsh
Fort Augustus
Aberdeen
Lochboisdale
Sleat
Newtonmore
Kingussie
Grampian Mountains
Ballater
Banchory
Aberdeen
Eriskay
Armadale
Invergarry
Stonehaven
Canna
Kinloch
Mallaig
Loch Quoich
Loch Arkaig
Loch Lochy
Spean Bridge
Braemar
Barra
Castlebay
Rhum
Eigg
Glenfinnan
Dalwhinnie
Inverbervie
Mingulay
Muck
Galmisdale
Loch Ericht
Blair Atholl
Kilchoan
Arinagour
Coll
Tobermory
Strontian
Loch Shiel
Fort William
Blackwater Reservoir
Ballachulish
Loch Rannoch
Loch Tummel
Killiecrankie
Pitlochry
Kirriemuir
Brechin
Montrose
Kilchoan
Aberfeldy
Loch Laidon
TAYSIDE
Forfar
Inverkeillor
Red Head
The Minch
The Little Minch
Sea of the Hebrides
Hebrides

MAP 16
Main entry
Main entry with accommodation
Local Gem
A single symbol may denote
several restaurants in one area.
0 40 50 Miles
0 80 Kms
15
13
North Sea
NORTHUMBERLAND
Masham
Felton
Amble
Morpeth
Otterburn
Low Newton-by-the-Sea
Berwick-upon-Tweed
Alnwick
Wooler
Holy Island
Eyemouth
Coldstream
Ednam
Kelso
Ancrum
Jedburgh
Duns
Lauder
Galashiels
Melrose
Selkirk
Hawick
Peebles
BORDERS
Tweedsmuir
Moffat
Langholm
Sanquhar
Thornhill
DUMFRIES AND GALLOWAY
Dumfries
Dalbeattie
Castle Douglas
Kirkcudbright
New Galloway
Newton Stewart
Wigtown
Whithorn
Burrow Head
Maryport
Workington
Whitehaven
Egremont
Seascale
Broughton in Furness
Bowland Bridge
St Bees Head
Abbey Head
Solway Firth
Drummore
Mull of Galloway
Point of Ayre
Isle of Man
Ramsey
Ramsey Bay
Glenluce
Stranraer
Kirkcolm
Portpatrick
Ballantrae
Girvan
Ailsa Craig
Maybole
Ayr
Annbank
Prestwick
Troon
Irvine
Kilmarnock
Mauchline
Cumnock
Dalmellington
Loch Doon
Douglas
Lanark
Motherwell
Livingston
Edinburgh
LOTHIANS
Linlithgow
Falkirk
Penicuik
North Queensferry
Dunfermline
Stirling
Glasgow
STRATHCLYDE
Greenock
Wemyss Bay
Largs
Dalry
Ardrossan
Lochranza
Arran
Brodick
Lamlash
Campbeltown
Carradale
Tayinloan
Gigha
Kilberry
Ardlussa
Jura
Islay
Port Askaig
Port Ellen
Mull of Oa
Portnahaven
Colonsay
Scalasaig
Fionnphort
Iona
Tiree
Scarinish
Mull
Lochaline
Eriska
Oban
Port Appin
Connel
Lismore
Firth of Lorn
Crianlarich
Inveraray
Lochgilphead
Tarbert
Portavadie
Rothesay
Kennacraig
Claonaig
Dunoon
Strachur
Killin
Balquhidder
Strathyre
Callander
Muthill
Crieff
Lochearnhead
Loch Tay
Loch Earn
Loch Katrine
Loch Lomond
Loch Awe
Loch Etive
Dunkeld
Blairgowrie
Perth
Auchterarder
Dunblane
CENTRAL
Loch Lomond
Cupar
FIFE
Glenrothes
Kirkcaldy
Gullane
North Berwick
Dunbar
Firth of Forth
St Andrews
Peat Inn
Anstruther
St Monans
Elie
Arbroath
Carnoustie
Dundee
Coupar Angus
Kielder Water
Cheviot Hills
North Channel
Firth of Clyde
Inner Hebrides
Portstewart
Coleraine
Portrush
Bushmills
Ballycastle
Cushendall
Carnlough
Larne
Ballymoney
Ballymena
Antrim
Belfast International
Lough Neagh
Belfast
Belfast City
Newtownabbey
Carrickfergus
Bangor
Holywood
Donaghadee
Newtownards
Comber
Killinchy
Portaferry
Strangford Lough
Portavogie
Downpatrick
St John's Point
Newcastle
Banbridge
Ballynahinch
Dromore
Lisburn
Lurgan
Portadown
Craigavon
Tandragee
Armagh
Dungannon
Cookstown
Moneymore
Magherafelt
Maghera
Dungiven
Limavady
Londonderry
City of Derry
Lough Foyle
Moville
Inishowen Head
Malin Head
Fanad Head
Strabane
Lifford
Newtownstewart
Omagh
Irvinestown
Enniskillen
Lisnaskea
Upper Lough Erne
Rathlin Island

Note: The INDEX BY TOWN does not include London entries.

Join us at thegoodfoodguide.co.uk

Join us at thegoodfoodguide.co.uk

Join us at thegoodfoodguide.co.uk

Join us at thegoodfoodguide.co.uk

Join us at thegoodfoodguide.co.uk

Join us at thegoodfoodguide.co.uk

Join us at thegoodfoodguide.co.uk

Join us at thegoodfoodguide.co.uk

Thank you

This book couldn't have happened without a cast of thousands.
Our thanks are due to the following contributors,
among many others.

Francesca Abbott
Rod Abbott
Tammy Aberdeen
Anthony Abrahams
Roy Ackerman
Chris Ackroyd
Alasdair Adam
Judith Adam
Christine Adams
Elizabeth Adams
Gillian Adams
Julia Adams
Richard Adams
Emily Adlam
Maggie Agamemnonos
James Agnew
Chris Agombar
Mark Ahern
Iqbal Ahmed
Liz Ahmed
Holly Ainsworth
John Aird
Lynda Albutt
Jessica Alcock
Diane Alderton
David Alexander
Helen Alexander
Rachel Alexander
Minera Alfaray
Jane Alflat
Martin Allan
Chris Allen
Jane Allen
Jill Allen
Peter Allen
Roger Allen
Rachael Allen-Wilkinson
Tessa Allingham
George Allison
Sue Allison
Emma Allum
M Altun
David Ambrose
John Amoore
Linda Amos
Berenice Anderson
Frank Anderson
Eva Anderton
Lucy Andrew
Stefanie Andrew
Camilla Andrews
Joanne Andrews
Giedre Andriusaityte
Steven Andurby
Laura Aney
Sarah Ansey
Sebastian Anstey
Lucy Anstrie
Karine Antinoro
Dan Appleby
Andrew Ardern
Gabrielle Argent
Jenny Arkell
Kate Armes
Caledenia Armstrong
Hilary Armstrong
John Armstrong
Rachel Armstrong
Marjorie Arnison
James Arthur
Donald Ashburn

Kenneth Ashken
Christopher Ashley
Deborah Ashley
Geoffrey Ashley
Samantha Ashton
Tia Aspinall
Paul Astley
Margaret Atherton
Shelley Atia
Paul Atkins
Veronica Atkins
Evelyn Atkinson
James Atkinson
Frank Attwood
Wayne Austin
Charlie Austin-Brown
Ester Avagliano
Barbara Avern
Rick Awdas
Xinhui Awyong
Melanie Ayers
Tony Ayers
Melanie Ayling
David Babb
James Bache
Rebecca Backwell
Chris P Bacon
Lucy Bacon
Jane Badstevener
Claudine Baele
Kevin Bage
Jane Bagshaw
Christopher Baigent
John Bailey
Lynette Bailey
Michael Bailey
Olivia Bailey
Chris Bailey-Green
Rebecca
Jason Bain
Alan Bainbridge
Rebecca Bains
James Baird
Bob Bairstow
Debbie Baker
Katie Baker
Polly Baker
Maggie Balding
Julie Balfour
Nicola Balfour
Andrew Ball
Ben Ball
Diane Ball
Garry Ball
Harriet Ball
Lesley Ball
Philip Ball
David Balls
John Balmont
Fraser Band
Hannah Banks
Joanna Banks
Rebecca Banwell-
  Moore
Galina Barakova-Pares
Sophie Barberini
David Barclay
Iain Barker
Niamh Barker
Craig Barlow
Joanne Barlow

Keith Barlow
Richard Barnard
Nicholas Barnes
Robert Barnes
Steve Barnes
Angus Barnett
Calum Barnett
Gail Barnett
Jake Barnett
Alex Barns
Andrew Barnset
Sarah Baron
Cheryl Barr
Penny Barr
Cheryl Barraclough
Patricia Barrett
Kirsty Barsby
Sally Bartlett
Ryan Bartley
Natasha Bartman
Tracy Barton
Axel Bartz
Francesca Bashall
Daniel Bateman
Penny Bateman
Graham Bates
Jackie Bates
Jonathan Bates
Kelly Bates
Thomas Bates
Adam Batley
Gill Batsman
Aurelia Battista
Tim Battle
Tina Bauld
Steohen Baxter
Martin Baylis
Katrina Baynes
Charlie Bazzant
Arabella Beacham
Georgette Beacham
Alan Beard
Hannah Bearder
Peter Beddow
Victoria Bedford
Christian Beech
Alice Beese
Rebecca Beesley
Shoki Begum
Valerie Beint
F Belhassine
Darren Bell
David Bell
Graham Bell
James Bell
Nicola Bell
Peter Bell
Sandra Bellas
Dan Belt
Tommy Bendall
Denise Bending
Frank Benfield
Darrell Benge
Sally Benley
David Bennest
Julie Bentall
Christine Bentham
Joy Bentley
Philip Berridge
Emma Berry
Gordon Berry

Karan Berry
Sandra Berti
Julie Best
W J Best
Rory Bett
Vivien Betts
Emma Bevan
Bob Biddle
Jenny Biddle
Clare Biggs
Paul Bignell
Diane Bilbrough
Wendy Bile
Robert Bingley
John Binnie
Chris Birch
Richard Birchall
Sarah Birchall
Rose Birches
Sarah Bird
Stephen Bird
Sarah Birrell
Virginia Birtles
John Birtwell
Adam Bishop
Rob Bishop
Mark Bixter
Val Blackmore
Gary Blake
Rachel Blake
Georgina Blanco
Patm Blandamer
Neville Blech
Stephanie Bliss
Phil Bloomfield
Jeff Blumsom
John Blundell
Jane Blunt
Daniel Blyth
Harriet Boardman
Julie Boardman
Andy Boase
Jon Bocking
Laura Boddy
Paula Boddy
Bethan Boden
Sandra Boellinger-Aine
Lara Boglione
Karen Bognall
John Boham-Cook
Laura Boles
Matthew Bolton
Amanda Bond
Maddalena Bonino
Sonia Bonney
Neil Bonsall
Neil Bontoft
David Booker
Ben Booth
Daniel Booth
Sara Booth
Karen Boothby
Claire Boother
Becky Boothman
Giedre Booyle
Hannahfaye Borley
Carole Boros
Francine Bosomworth
Ruth Botterill
Caroline Bottomley
Ruth Botwright

Grace Bovil
Andrew Bovingdon
Elin Bowden
Sophie Bowen
Hazel Bowers
Felix Bowers-Brown
Nicky Bowes
Claire Bowley
Pamela Bowling
Barbara Bowman
Liz Bowyer-Jones
Gabriel Boxall
Lynne Boyd
Francis Boyes
Cliona Boyle
Michael Boyle
Tom Boyle
Gill Bracey
Katie Bradbred
Anthony Bradbury
Nicola Braddock
Chantelle Bradley
Kate Bradley
Jane Bradley-Kidd
Lenore Bradshaw
Graham Bragg
Martin Brailsford
Michael Bramall
Lisa Brannan
Clare Brass
Thomas Bray
Amanda Brebner
Alison Breese
Danielle Brennan
Vicki Brennan
Sue Brett-Droman
Lilian Brewis
Pamela Brick
Gemma Bridge
Geoffrey Bridge
Jo Bridges
Emily Bridgewater
Kevin Brierley
Mike Briffett
Celia Brigstocke
Tim Brigstocke
Kevin Brindley
Fay Brinscrom
Joyce Brisby
Nicholas Briston
Julian Britton
Simon Broad
Alex Broadbent
Jan Brockmeijer
Andrew Brodie
Claire Brodie
Paul Brook
Sarah Brookes
Andy Brooks
Patricia Brooks
Amy Broomfield
Mavis Broomfield
Michaela Brosnan
Neil Brotherhood
Carole Brothertan
Jasper Browell
Callum Brown
Caroline Brown
David Brown
Gillian Brown
Hannah Brown

James Brown
Janet Brown
Kerry Brown
Mike Brown
Moira Brown
Sandra Brown
Sarah Brown
Shirely Brown
Catherine Bruce
James Bruce
AnneLouise Brufford-
  Rape
Anne Brusatte
Sharon Brushnen
Antonia Bryans
Jayne Bryant
John Bryant
Stephanie Bryant
Iain Bryne
Rebecca Buchanan
Kathryn Buckman
Michael Buckman
Geraldine Buffery
Anne Bulfin
Glenda Bullock
Kathy Bullough
Naomi Bullus
James Bunsen
Stephen Burcham
Jess Burchell
Ivan Burdfield
Connor Burford
Matthew Burge
Gillian Burgess
James Burgess
Jenni Burgess
Jonathan Burgess
Brenda Burling
Jackie Burnham
Lynne Burns
Martin Burns
Michael Burns
Sonia Burns
Laura Burnside
Ady Burr
Michael Burrows
Alan Burton
Andy Burton
Annie Burton
Karen Burton
Phillip Burton
Trudi Burton
Hannah Burwell
Diane Bushell
Mark Butler
Rob Butler
Helen Butterworth
Samuel Butterworth
Melainie Byrne
Katie Byrne-Perkins
Glyn Byrnes
Stephen Bywater
Carol Cadden
Maureen Cadden
Rob Cadwell
Mathiev Cagna
Brian Cairns
Susan Cairns
Harriet Calder
Debbie Calderbank
Tim Caley

John Call
Maureen Callaghan
Emma Callington
Imogen Cameron
Katy Camidge
Donald Campbell
Gillian Campbell
Margaret Campbell
Marie Campbell
Thomas Candex
Kris Cannon
Mary Cannon
Chris Capel
Nuria Cardenas
Angie Carr
Geoffrey Carr
Sylvia Carr
Ann Carroll
Heidi Carroll
Audrey Carson
David Carter
Richard Carter
Tim Carter
Georgina Cartledge
Jane Cartledge
Nicola Cartwright
Jenny Carver
June Carver
Mike Carwithen
Dorothy Casey
Janine Casey
Mark Casey
Matthew Cashin
Vicci Caslin
Alexandra Cassar
Carole Cassells
Emma Cassidy Gray
Gillian Cast
Natalia Castillejo
Dawn Castle
Ciriaw Castro
Laim Caufield
Clare Caulfield
Laura Caun
Tim Ceete
Colleen Ceplice
Maria Ceraldi
Hollie Chadderton
Lawrence Chadwick
Mangalkumar
  Chakkasserilgopi
Tony Chalmers
Sebastian Chamberlain
Tom Chamberlain
Yohan Chan
Christopher Chang
Charlotte Chapman
Erica Chapman
Jen Chapman
Richard Chapman
Robert Chapman
Victoria Charalambous
Abigail Charkham
Jo Charles
Steven Charles
Chris Charlton
Lynda Charlton
Chloe Charlwood
John Charman
Richard Charman
Esme Charters
Pauline Charters
Richard Chase
Robyn Chase
Louise Chater
Kate Cheasman
Lesley Checker
Sue Cheeseman
Dave Chepstow
Anastasia Chernobay
Anastasiya Chernobay
Brett Chester
Sue Chesterman
Meryl Chetwood
Dean Chick
Mary Child
Sorcha Chipperfield
Caroline Chiu
Nicholas Chiu
James Christensen
Claire Christie
Stuart Christie
Andrew Church
Juliette Churchill
Diane Circuit
Robert Circuit
Johan Claesen
Margaret Clancy
Sarah Clancy
John Clare

David Clark
Deborah Clark
Jonathan Clark
Maria Clark
Miles Clark
Sally Clark
Sammy Clark
Steve Clark
Allen Clarke
Bob Clarke
Chenice Clarke
Chris Clarke
Claire Clarke
Diane Clarke
John Clarke
Pauline Clarke
Stacey Clarke
Steven Clarke
Ted Clarkson
Jenny Clay
Mark Clayson
Cherie Clegg
Alison Clejanie
Dawn Cleland
Emma Clements
Richard Clements
Paul Cliff
Chris Clifford
Joanna Clifford
Pamela Clifford
Jacqui Close
Mike Closey
Charles Clough
Gillian Cloughton
Kirsty Clowes
Helen Coates
Sue Coates
David Cockburn
Hayley Cockburn
Simon Coddington
Helen Coddlington
Peter Coen
Paul Cohen
Shelagh Cohen
Karen Colcayne
Deborah Coldwell
Ian Cole
Neil Coleman
Peter Coles
Rikki Coles
Wilf Coles
Susan Collier
Maria Collins
Martha Collins
Mary Collins
Nicola Collins
Graham Collis
Anne Collison
Annemelodie
  Comandre
Alan Comerton
Bridget Comiskey
Darren Conlon
Penny Connelly
Derek Connery
Andrew Connolly
Emily Connolly
Wynne Connolly
Carl Connor
Chris Connor
Andrew Consil
Ann Constable
Liam Convie
Jim Cook
Brian Cooke
Carol Cooke
Joanna Cooke
Sheila Cooke
Sue Cooke
Ruth Coombs
Alexandra Cooper
Alinda Cooper
Carey Cooper
Clare Cooper
Gaynor Cooper
Graham Cooper
Sue Cooper
Suzanne Cooper
Bill Cope
Juliet Cope
Joseph Copeland
Barry Corner
Jessica Corney
Karen Cornthwaite
Cristina Correa
Sally Corrie
Kayleigh Cosgrove
Michele Cossu
Carole Cotterell
Sue Cotton

Mary Coughlin
Francins Coulson
Ollie Courtney
Robert Couttie
Olive Coverton
Jane Cox
Nicholas Cox
Danny Coyne
Joshua Cracknell
Kellie Craig
Charlotte Craudace
Laura Crawley
Lynette Creasey
Suzanne Creedan
Richard Crees
Rachel Cresswell
Joe Cripps
Paul Cripps
Caraline Crocker
Queen Croft
Mark Crompton
Sarah Cronin
Beth Crook
Richard Crosby
Antony Cross
Graham Cross
Lorraine Cross
Shelley Crossland
Clare Crowther
Carole Crudgington
Greig Cruickshank
Andrea Cruise
Rosie Crump
Pamela Crutchley
Martin Cudworth
Pete Culley
Cass Cullum
Matt Cunliffe
Frank Cunnane
Scott Cunningham
Suzanne Curley
Edward Curnow
Carol Curran
Keith Curran
Nick Curran
Maggie Currie
Audrey Curry
Catherine Curry
Paul Curtin
Mel Cutcliffe
Terry Cutler
Philppa Dacosta
Rachel Dacre
Alison Dagg
Sadhna Dahya
Lisa Dainty
Anthony Dale
Amber Dalton
Anthony Dalton
Michael Dalton
Stuart Dalton
William Dalton
Charles Dalton Holmes
Jessica Dames
Faye Danby
Abby Dance
Leon Daniels
Rebecca Danner
Margaret Danson
Victoria Darby
Celia Darbyshire
Malcolm Darbyshire
Andrew Darley
Louise Darling
Anne Darracroft
Marcel Darroch Davies
Jacky Darville
Clare Datson
Shree Datta
Jackie Davenport
Clement Davey
Catherine Davidson
Alice Davies
Alun Davies
Amy Davies
Ben Davies
Charlotte Davies
David Davies
Gemma Davies
Hilary Davies
Jen Davies
Jeremy Davies
Kate Davies
Kathryn Davies
Momotha Davies
Nigel Davies
Stephen Davies
Richard Davis
Frankie Davison
Joel Davison

Mary Davison
Robert Davitt
Garry Daw
Pauline Dawes
Bernard Dawson
Debbie Dawson
Hannah Dawson
Deborah Day
Derek Day
Elaine Day
Richard Day
Sian Day
Natasha Dayaramani
Claire Daymall
Lauren Deadman
Alison Dean
Ben Dean
Joan Dean
Belan Debo
Helen Dee
Nicholas Dee
Hannah Deeral
Matthieu Degottal
Jonathan Dellord-Lyle
Gilbert Delord
Michael Deman
Claire Demery
Mark Denby
Jennifer Denhin
Belinda Dennis
Fiona Dennis
Andrea Denson
Emilie Denyer
Maggie Depledge
Ann Derham
Tim Desborough
Zoe Desilva
Greg Devine
Christina Devlin
Mark Devlin
Dora Dewhurst
Carolyn Dexter
Lauren Dexter
Caroline Diacon
Maria Diaz
Linda Dicken
Leana Dickie
Charleh Dickinson
Emma Dickinson
Lauren Dickinson
Mark Dickinson
Sarah Dickinson
Brian Dicks
Angela Dillon
Rachel Dillon
Mark Dimond
Maiden Distress
Avril Dixon
Alan Doak
Kerry Dobbin
Emily Dobbs
Jacqueline Dobinson
Ann Dobson
Graham Dobson
Jo Dodd
Martin Dodd
Pam Dodd
Isabella Dodge
Marian Dods
Gonul Dogay
Antonia Doggart
Brian Doig
Katie Don
Natalie Donald
Andrew Donaldson
Rebecca Donaldson
Terry Donaldson
Gregory Dones
Roy Donovan
Anastasia Dontsova
Stephen Doran
Tom Doran
Kay Dorman
Simon Dorman
Philip Dorrell
Ann Dougan
Kelly Douglas
Hamish Dow
Mark Dowse
Kat Doyle
Alan Drabble
Dick Drain
Joan Drain
Dudley Drayson
Hannah Drew
Kate Driver
Katie Drouet
John Ducker
Julien Ducret
Allison Duffy

Conor Duffy
Paul Duffy
James Duggan
W P Duggan
Mark Duggett
Louise Dunbar
S Dunbar
James Duncan
Aaron Dunleavy
Alan Dunn
Kate Dunning
Karen Dunstan
Margaret Durance
Beatrice Durant
Leigh Durn
Elaine Dutta
Angela Dyche-Lock
Elzbietaellie Dyduch
Lucy Dymond
Claire Dyson
R S Eades
Susan Earnshaw
Laurence East
Mick Easthope
Kath Easthops
Rachel Eastley
Rachael Eaton
Laura Eaves
Bethany Ebanks
Anne-Marie Eden
Chris Edgal
Annette Edgar
Craig Edmunds
Sandra Edmunds
Bethan Edwards
Brianna Edwards
John Edwards
Kate Edwards
Kelly Edwards
Mark Edwards
Matthew Edwards
Natalie Edwards
Roy Edwards
Vanessa Edwards
Helen Egan
Gary Elflett
Juliet Elias
Marie Elias
Gordon Elks
Shirley Elliot
Camilla Elliott
Derrick Elliott
Joanna Elliott
Michael Elliott
Paul Elliott
Steve Elliott
Sue Elliott
Jane Elliott Toncic
Sian Elliott-Williams
Elizabeth Ellis
Mark Ellis
Rob Ellis
Martin Ellison
Rupert Ellwood
Peter Elwin
Henry Elworthy
Annes Elwy
Georgia Emerson
Susan Emmens
Anna Emmison
Joanne Enough
Jessica Enright
Eve Entwisle
Lisa Eriksson
Mark Errington
William Etherington
Andy Evans
Chris Evans
Huw Evans
Julia Evans
Karen Evans
Lynnette Evans
Marie Evans
Mark Evans
Megan Evans
Paul Evans
Margaret Evelyn
Claire Evennett
Andrew Everard
Emma Everett
Shelley Everitt
Michael Evison
Sally Ewart
Henrietta Eyre
Nicole Fabre
Robert Fagan
Tom Fahey
Jacob Falcon
Eugenio Falconer
Tina Falone

Jennie Farmer
Rhonda Farr
Alison Farrell
Gillian Farren
Alice Farrington
Jira Faulkenborg
Catherine Faulkner
Michele Fawns
Danielle Fear
Josephine Fear
Andrea Fearne
Victoria Fearnley
Jenny Feasey
Laura Feeham
Justin Feinberg
Jamie Fellows
Pauline Felstead
Wendy Fender
Lucy Fenn
Kathryn Fenner
Andrea Ferguson
John Ferguson
Katie Ferguson
Leila Ferguson
Linda Ferguson
Louise Ferguson
Rachel Ferla
Shirley Fern
Nada Ferns
Roger Ferraby
Karen Fesenko
Terry Fesenko
Carla Fiadeiro
Sarah Fiedosiuk
Ellie Field
Jon Fielding
Neville Filar
Sebastian Finch
Andrea Finlay
Eric Finney
Joana Fioueirido
Sadie Fisher
Alison Fishpool
Thomas Fitch
Gary Fitzpatrick
Kathryn Flanagan
David Flanaghan
Scott Flaw
Tom Fleetham
Vicky Fleetwood
Charleswillis Fleming
Jordan Fleming
Karen Fletcher
Steven Fletcher
Callum Flett
Jhona Flett
Callum Flint
David Flint
Craig Floate
Charlotte Flood
Louise Foers
Dominic Foley
Vernice Foong
Carrie Ford
Howard Ford
Mapela Forde
Jo Forel
Doreen Forsyth
Martina Fortunato
Lisa Forward
Roger Forward
Jill Foster
Mandy Foster
Shelagh Foster
Susan Foster
Christine Foulds
Debbie Foulkes
Tom Foulkes
Paula Foulser
John & Annabel
  Foulston
Alison Fountain
John Fowler
Chris Fowles
Adele Fox
Brenda Fox
James Fox
Julia Fox
Chris Foxton
Marilyn Foyle
Ann Frain
Jonathon Francis
Silvana Franco
Amanda Frangleton
Nick Frankgate
Faye Franklin
Francesca Franklin
Neil Franklin
Julian Frankum
Fiona Fraser

John Fraser
Moira Fraser
Peter Fraser
Kelly Frears
Peter Freeman
Sam Freeman
Sally French
Patrick Frew
Bryony Frewer
Jane Friedmann
Margaret Fright
Attila Frolich
Matt Frost
Dorothee Fry
Elizabeth Fry
Daniel Fryer
Hannah Fuellenkemper
Katie Fullagar
Chris Fuller
Lauren Fumish
Adam Funston
Jessica Gabriel
Helena Gailey
Stephen Gaimster
Emily Galasso-Farsey
Edwardarthur Gale
Vanessa Galic
Sarah Gall
Sylvie Gallon
Jill Galvin
Ken & Hazel Gamble
Ashley Game
Mary Ganapatsingh
Ciara Ganly
Anthony Gannon
Janine Gantley
Oscar Garcia
Tonacio Garcia
Anita Gardener
Anna Gardiner
Elizabeth Gardner
Jim Gardner
Karen Gardner
Kevin Gardner
Francis Garner
Ann Garnham
Alex Garrett
John Garside
Chris Gartside
Jo Garwood
Joan Garwood
Amy Gastman
Alan Gates
Toni Gaventa
Natalie Gay
Irene Gelsler
Tony Gelsthorpe
Dana Gendler
Shaw Geo
Seamus Geoghegan
Glyn George
Lorraine George
Nicky Gerrard
Stephen Gerrard
Neil Gershon
Caterina Giannotti
Angela Gibbs
Ashley Gibbs
Philip Gibbs
Brian Gibson
Jennifer Gibson
Palova Gil
Sarah Gilbank
Belinda Gilbert
Carol Gilbert
Helen Gilbert
Julia Gilbert
Paul Gilbert
Karl Gilby
Judy Giles
Ally Gill
Leanne Gill
Field Gillian
Richard Gillis
Craig Gilmour
Gill Gilworth
Shrikant Giri
Alessandro Giudici
Catherine Gladwyn
Gill Glass
Andrina Glen
Shelley Goacher
Christopher Godber
Sophie Godwin
Georgina Gold
Joyce Gold
Kathryn Golding
Sarah Golding
Adrian Goldsborough
Sergei Golubev

Adam Gooch
Tim Goodacre
Jan Goodenough
Hannah Gooding
Abigail Goodland
Claire Goodman
Pauline Goodson
Rachel Goodwin
Sophie Goodwin
Michael Gordge
Joanne Gordon
Jodie Gordon
Nicola Gore
Adriand Gori
Adriano Gori
Mike Goulding
Andrea Graham
Andrew Graham
Greg Graham
William Graham
Becky Grant
Jessica Grant
Milly Grant
Carla Grassy
Karla Graves
Alison Gray
Anna Gray
Aynsley Gray
Eliza Gray
James Gray
Jennifer Gray
Valerie Gray
Rachel Grean
Lawrence Greasley
Julia Greaves
Sheila Greaves
Lauren Green
Peter Green
Jonathan Greenbank
Kirsty Greener
John Greenhalgh
Alicia Greenwood
Carley Greenwood
Leigh Greenwood
Rachael Greenwood
Hannah Gregory
Ian Gregory
John Gregory
Rachel Gregory
Hilary Griffin
David Griffiths
Sian Griffiths
Morene Griggs
Jeanette Grimley
Alan Grimwade
Nigel Grimwood
Martin Grinold
Gemma Groom
Jenny Groom
Caroline Grove
Jim Grover
Claire Groves
Nikki Grundy
Anna Gryer
Alison Guenaoui
Christopher Guest
Lee Guest
Tiboude Guin
Clare Guinan
Mike Gulland
Nicola Gulland
Philip Gunn
Jerusalen Gunning
Jen Gurney
Ipek Gursu
Helen Gustard
Tim Gutch
Jane Guy
Josephine Guy
Konrad Guza
Eleanor Gvahann
Alex Hacton
Tom Hadfield
Jane Haggarty
Lucy Haggis
Michelle Haigh
Vicky Haining
Astrid Hakaldsen
Liz Hale
Anna Hales
Bob Hall
Brenda Hall
Charles Hall
Emilie Hall
Jody Hall
John Hall
Kathryn Hall
Nigel Hall
Pauline Hall
Rachael Hall

Rebecca Hall
Steve Halligan
Vincent Hambleton-Grey
Mike Hambling
Gemma Hames
Maisie Hamilton
Ann Hamlin
Phil Hammond
Charlotte Hampson
Shelley Hampson
Nicola Hampton
Sam Han
Alice Hancock
Andrew Hancock
David Hancock
Bruno Handley
Lynn Handley
Juliet Hanka
Charlotte Hanks
Christina Hansen
Richard Hanstock
Harrie Haran
Malcolm Harbour
Jess Harbutt
Gordon Harby
Kate Harcus
Cathie Hardey
Charlotte Harding
Sean Hardon
Amanda Hare
Melanie Hare
Dawn Harget
Alessandra Hargrave
Nicole Harker
Donald Harley
Sandra Harley
Amanda Harman
Helen Harmer
Sam Harmes
Paul Harnedy
Laura Harnon
Ian Harper
Ken Harper
Ben Harris
Daniel Harris
Jeanette Harris
Jordan Harris
Liam Harris
Paul Harris
Phil Harris
Rodney Harris
Sian Harris
Wanda Harris
Will Harris
Chris Harrison
Christopher Harrison
Derek Harrison
Gillian Harrison
Jade Harrison
Pearl Harrison
Susan Harrison
Teresa Harrison
Phil Harriss
John Harrop
Jenna Hart
John Hart
Joanne Hartley
John Hartley
Juliet Hartridge
Eunice Hartstone
Miles Hartwell
Ben Harvey
Lily Harvey
Richard Harvey
Michael Haskell
Chris Haskett
Emine Hassan
Nooshin Hassan
Kevin Hassett
Linda Haste
Rachel Hatfield
John Hawes
Colin Hawgood
Tracey Hawker
Victoria Hawksfield
Eloise Haworth
Jacqueline Hayes
Julia Hayes
Natalie Hayes
Rosie Hayes
Stpehanie Hayter
Janine Haytere
Sally Hayward
Richard Hayward-Pring
Jodie Haywood
Stanley Haywood
Alice Hazard
Daniele Hazzan
Leah Head

Jeanne Heald
Ema Healey
Jo Healey
Nicola Healey
Joanna Heard
Louise Heard
Sarah Hearne
Aby Heath
Amanda Heath
David Heather
Mark Heaton
Enno Hebbelmann
Jan Hedges
Andrea Hedlund
Sheila Heffernan
June Hellewell
Mathew Helm
Louise Hembury
David Hemingray
Clare Hemmer
Katrina Hempstead
Mark Hempstock
Fiona Henderson
Julie Henderson
Kate Henderson
Lucy Henderson
Micheal Henderson
Thomas Henderson
Steve Henley
Liz Henry
Judith Henshaw
Wendy Henton
Alison Hepworth
David Herman
Barry Heron
Robert Herring
Helen Hesford
Kris Heslop
Kaura Hesseler
Malcolm Heughan
Gad Heuman
Jenny Hewett
Alex Heyward-Jones
Katherine Hibbert
John Hickman
Elizabeth Hicks
Rebecca Higg
Sally Highes-Gabb
Louise Hignett
Ashley Hildebrandt
Celeste Hiley
Andrea Hill
Bob Hill
Emily Hill
Jane Hill
John Hill
Martin Hill
Rebekah Hill
Richard Hill
William Hill
Jeremy Hill-Baker
Jenn Hillie
Andy Hilton
Paul Hilton
Mark Hindle
Brenda Hines
David Hinojosa
Gwen Hinton
Clare Hipkin
Emily Hirschmann
Chris Hirst
Elaine Hirst
Hannah Hirst
Freddie Hitchcock
Julie Hitchcock
Julian Hitchman
Olivia Hithersay
Laurel Hixon
Hayley Hobbs
Judith Hobbs
Melanie Hobson
Margaret Hodge
Jerry Hodgkinson
Victoria Hodsman
Elaine Hogan-Hughes
Gill Hoggard
Helen Hoggarth
Johnny Holden
Lorraine Holden
Richard Holden
Susan Holdon
Stacey Holdsworth
Alex Holland
John Holland
Kim Holland
Richard Holland
Mo Hollier
Shane Holloway
Amy Holmes
Joy Holmes

Maia Holmes
Tamsyn Holmes
Tom Holmes
Alexander Holsgrove
David Holt
Jo Honigmann
Michael Hook
Ryan Hook
Elaine Hookem
Deborah Hooker
Jo Hookway
Linda Hopes
Janet Hopkins
Matthew Hopkins
Mark Hopkinson
Debbie Hore
Ellie Horner
Simon Horner
Sophy Horner
Sara Horrell
Stephen Horrocks
Fern Horsburgh
Richard Horsley
Alan Horton
Daphne Hossle
Graham Hotchkiss
Joanne Hotham
Pam Houghton
Scott Houghton
S Houlder
Nikki Hounsell
Steven Hourston
Natasha Howard
Andrew Howden
Elizabeth Howden
Amanda Howell
Pete Howell
Carol Howitt
Nigel Howitt
Tammy Howland
Alison Hoy
Lawrence Hoy
Joe Hoyles
Andrea Huber
Joanna Huddart
David Hudson
Donald Hudson
Jackie Hudson
Mark Hughan
Brian Hughes
David Hughes
Delyth Hughes
Gavin Hughes
Katherine Hughes
Margaret Hughes
Simon Hughes
Tom Hughes
Ann Huitson
Sandra Hulme
James Hume
Anne Humphreys
Julia Humphreys
Maureen Humphreys
Marcus Humphries
Christine Hunt
Evelyn Hunt
Louise Hunt
Martin Hunt
Patsy Hunt
Pauline Hunt
Aaron Hunter
Graham Hunter
Leif Hunter
Nino Hunter
Angela Hurlstone
Lauren Hurst
Stef Hurst
Tracey Hurst
Racheal Husband
David Huse
Linda Hutcheon
Caro Hutchings
Tanya Hutchings
Andy Hutchinson
Jade Hutchinson
Joy Hutchinson
Lindy Hutchinson
Owen Hutchinson
Carol Hutt
Anne Hydon
Veronica Hydon
Thea Iffland
Peter Iles
Stuart Illingworth
Angelus Illran
Jane Ingleman
David Inkster
Louise Inman
Rosanna Innes
Richard Invine

Jackie Ireland
Margaret Ireland
Jen Irvine
Ibi Issolah
Emma Isteed
Rijan Itani
Mary Jack
Daniel Jackson
Lorna Jackson
Paul Jackson
Simon Jackson
Tania Jackson
Tara Jackson
Zoe Jackson
Barbara Jacobs
Archie James
Christian James
Jenn James
Julie James
Jacqueline Jamieson
Robert Jamieson
Jess Janas
Jonathan Jannaway
Francesca Jarrett
Roy Jawaheer
Jenny Jefferies
Gill Jeffery
Emma Jeffrey
Tina Jenkin
Joanne Jenkins
Joely Jenkins
Steven Jenkins
Julie Jenkins-Wigley
John Jenner
Kate Jenner
Cara Jennings
Helen Jennings
Christine Jensen
Matty Jensen
Fiona Jerome
Chloe Jessup
Jane Jewison
Pam Jibson
Emma Johansen
Alann Johnson
Andy Johnson
Ben Johnson
Ian Johnson
Janey Johnson
Jean Johnson
Louise Johnson
Nicola Johnson
Ryan Johnson
Sophie Johnson
Suzanne Johnson
Daniel Johnston
David Johnston
Liz Jolly
Rosemary Jolly
Anna Jones
Anne Jones
Annette Jones
Beryl Jones
Declan Jones
Delyth Jones
Emily Jones
Emyr Jones
Hannah Jones
Ian Jones
Jill Jones
Katie Jones
Ken Jones
Lisa Jones
Lisbeth Jones
Nathan Jones
Nesta Jones
Paul Jones
Robert Jones
Sam Jones
Susan Jones
Travis Jones
Trefor Jones
Samara Jones-Hall
Jess Jose
Russell Joseph
Phil Joubert
Leslye Jourdan
Dan Joyce
Samantha Joyce
Lisa Joynes
Finbarr Joynson
Anya Jump
Martyn Jupp
Kris Jury
Salah Kadisz
Anne Kaiser
Ridhi Kalaria
Rumy Kapadia
Neil Kapoor
Lauren Kauser

Eileen Kavanagh
Laura Kavanagh
Emily Kavanaugh
Izabela Kawecka
Francesca Kay
Shannon Kay
Tom Kay
Julia Keddie
Lucy Kedge
Katie Keeling
Rob Keller
Samantha Kellock
Alison Kelly
Deborah Kelly
Graham Kelly
Mark Kelly
Sue Kelly
Vanessa Kelly
Eilen Kelsey
Hannah Kelsey
Joanna Kelsey
Heidi Kemble
Cassie Kemp
Samuel Kendall
Linda Kennedy
Peter Kennedy
Trish Kennedy
Stephen Kenny
James Kent
Jessica Keny
Ian Kenyon
Richard Kenyon
Sean Kerlin
Felicity Kerr
Lynne Kerr
Emily Kerrigan
Shelby Kessell
Rebecca Kew
Julie Keylock
John Kidston
Susan Kilburn
Jo Kilgour
Romy Killick
Mark Killing
Collette King
Laura King
Nick King
Sue Kingdon
Paul Kingston
Adam Kipling
Denise Kirby
Arran Kirk
Barbara Kirk
John Kirk
Mark Kirkbride
Christine Kirkham
Becky Kissel
Bethany Knibb
Adrienne Knight
Alexito Knight
Christine Knight
Dan Knight
Hannah Knight
Jon Knight
Olga Knight
Patricia Knight
Jan Knighties
Rebecca Knox
Greg Komada
Katarina Kovacova
Agnieszka Kozubek
Christine Kraina
Hollie Kutchinsky
Sophie Kuzniar
Shona Kyle
Peter Lacey
Kim Lacey-Smith
Nicole Lackenby
Dina Lad
Fiona Laing
Owen Lake
Dean Lakey
Deepak Lal
Sophie Lalor
Jackie Lambert
Megan Lambert
Nicole Lambert
Richard Lambie
Emma Lamble
Izzy Lamble
Peter Lane
Deborah Langford
Kirsty Langley
Lara Lapikens
Sharon Larcombe
Barbara Large
Joanne Last
Kate Latham
Rosie Latham

Natasha Lauder
Alexandra Laverick
Sara Laverick
Carolyn Law
Steve Law
Andrew Lawler
Bernadette Lawley
Del Lawrence
Haydon Lawrence
Tony Lawrence
Lizzie Lawrie
Linda Laws
Matthew Lawson
Maurice Lay
Kevin Layson
Andrew Lazarus
Lucinda Lea
Warren Lea
Warwick Lea
Steve Leacock
Alan Leading
Alan Leaman
Jen Lebutt
Claire Leckie
Beth Lecrone
Jackie Lee
Katherine Lee
Lucy Lee
Saffie Lee
Vicky Leech Prateos
Andrew Lees
Steven Lees
Marlyn Leese
Tammy Leggetter
Franz Leibenfrost
Mary Leigh
David Lemasurier
Awie Lemzotre
Helen L'Enfant
Sophie Lennon
Victoria Lenygon
Katie Leon
Paola Leon
Sian Leonard
Cheryl Lepoidevin
Jeremy Lepoidevin
Jenny Lerescu
Teodor Lerescu
Susan Leslie
Holly Lester
Deborah Letts
Estelle Levacher
Andy Levers
Marilyn Levi
Deanna Levoff
Joe Lewandowski
Jennifer Lewington
Andrew Lewis
Christine Lewis
Damian Lewis
Dan Lewis
David Lewis
Gillian Lewis
Hazel Lewis
Helen Lewis
Jenny Lewis
Junior Lewis
Justin Lewis
Keith Lewis
Mark Lewis
Mike Lewis
Richard Lewis
Steff Lewis
Tony Lewis
Elisabeth Lewis-Jones
Christina Li
Leonard Licht
Angelica Liddell
Alison Lidderdale
Dean Light
Cindy Lillard
John Lilley
Roisin Lilley
Paul Lilly
Eric Lindo
Katherine Lindop
Roy Lindop
Jan Lindsay
Janice Lindsay
Martin Lindsay
Rebecca Ling
Jeanne Linscott
Penelope Lintin-
  Constable
Carolyn Linton
Robert Lishman
Lisa Lister
Nicki Little
Helen Littleover

Helen Littlewood
Heather Liversidge
Deborah Livesey
Kate Livesey
Chum Liyang
Leanne Llewellyn
Eric Lloyd
Jo Lloyd
John Lloyd
Sarah Lloyd
Michael Loch
Sam Locke
Jackie Lockwood
Stephen Lodge
Laura Lodwick
Patrick Logan
David Lomas
Juliet Lomas
Amy Lonsdale
Gareth Lonsdale
Juliette Losq
Mel Lottse
Emma Louise
Linda Lovegrove
Crad Lowe
Susan Lowe
Jo Lowery
Adrian Lucas
Amanda Lucas
Kristie Lucas-Taylor
Henry Luce
Samantha Luckhurst
Richard Ludlow
Catherine Ludman
Unamoy Lue
Stella Lumb
Phil Lumsden
Dianne Lunt
Jane Lushey
Gary Lynch
Leila Lynch
Margare Lynch
Jean Lynn
Val Lyon
Gary Lyons
Jackie Lyons
Stella Lyssa
Jean Lyster
David Mabey
Claire MacAllister
Chris Macaskill
Joanna MacDonald
Dean Mace
Jen Mace
Ashleigh Macfarlane
Ross Macfarlane
Andrew Mackay
Alastair Mackenzie
Jamie Mackenzie
Karla Mackenzie
Peter Mackenzie-
  Williams
Andy Mackie
Hugh Mackintosh CBE
Christine Macleod
Cieran Macleod
Isla Macleod
Anna MacMillan
Fiona Macneill
Andrew Macpherson
Katrina Macrae
Edward Madden
Tara Magan
Catherine Magee
Kristin Magnuson
Tom Mahon
Steve Main
Vincent Maiolini
David Mair
Sundeep Makkar
Alan Malcolm
Katie Malcolmson
Rafael Maldonado
Calum Maliver
Clive Mallender
Andrew Mallett
Paul Malpass
Gemma Manchett
Daniel Manell
Stelle Manell
Alexandra Mangan
Alison Mann
Anne Mann
Hannah Mann
Stella Mann
Jocelyn Manners-
  Armstrong
Alex Manning
David Manning

Lynsey Mannion
Giuseppe Marasco
Beverley Marchant
Lucie Marciano
Sashini Mariathasan
Dadies Marinc
Valentine Mark Phillips
Adrian Markley
Sharon Marks
Charles Markus
Gavin Markwick
Mary Marmion
Rob Marsden
Rosemary Marsh
Jackie Marshall
Lucy Marshall
Lydia Marshall
Lynsey Marshall
Valerie Marshall
Zoe Marshman
Stjohn Marston
Aideen Martin
Basil Martin
Catherine Martin
Claire Martin
Colin Martin
Graham Martin
James Martin
Lily Martin
Nigel Martin
Scott Martin
Valerie Martin
Chloe Martine
Lesley Mashiter
Charlotte Maslen
Charlotte Mason
Cicely Mason
Emily Mason
Sandra Mass
Dorothy Massey
Jane Masters
Ritchie Maston
Simon Mathers
Donald Matheson
Alexandra Mathie
Paul Mathieu
Janette Matthews
Olivia Matthews
Owen Matthews
Gill Mattinson
Andrzej Matyla
Georgina Maud
Jum Mawby
Richard Mawer
Guy Maxwell
Anna May
Bridie May
Jonny May
Louise May
Michael May
Philip May
Samuel May
Jen Mayer
Christopher Mayes
Adele Maynard
Richard Mayor
Liliane Maziere
Hazel McAteer
Kathy McAteer
Debbie McCabe
Clare McCafferty
Fiona McCandless-
  Sugg
Erica McCann
Tony McCarthy
Louis McCesker
Carol McCloud
Stephanie McClure
Shaun McClurg
Mary McCluskie
Nicola McCord
Dean McCormack
Donya McCormick
Chris McCreesh
Anne McCue
Ann McCutcheon
Catherine McDermott
Nicholas McDermott
Karen McEnaney
Kelly McFarland
Catherine McFie
Heather McGarrigle
Tracy McGarva
Michael J McGauley
Julia McGee
Richard McGillan
Eleanor McGhee
Thomas McGillen
Colleen McGleenon

Dale McGleenon
Liz McGgoldrick
Fionan McGrath
Jamie McGuffog
Victoria McGuigan
Fiona McHardy
Andrew McIvor
Alison McKay
Nicola McKee
Bruce McKellar
Frank McKenna
Calum McKenzie
Iain McKenzie
Rose McKernan
Lisa McKinlay
Robert McKnight
Caroline McLaren
Jayde McLean
Nina McLeish
Georgina McLeod
Lucy McLeod
Patricia McManus
Ruth McNab
Shirley McNally
Frank McNichol
Sinead McNicholl
John McNulty
Karin Mear
Alex Medrecki
Alex Meiklejohn
Ryan Meldrum Hall
Kathy Mellish
Clare Mellor
Susanne Melrose
Kristan Menard
Ash Menon
Joe Mercer
Lyn Merrell
Stephen Merrell
Jonathan Merritt
Anna Merton
Nadia Meska
Salvo Messina
Marjorie Mewish
Andrea Meynick
Fahmida Miah
Shakes Miah
Daniel Micallef
Ellie Michell
Patricia Michie
Judith Middlemiss
Peter Middleton
Rebecca Middleton
Loreta Mikulyte
Peter Miles
Richard Milford
Adam Miller
Ben Miller
Jonathan Miller
Lee Miller
Lucy Miller
Stephen Miller
Alex Mills
Bernard Mills
Hayley Mills
Louise Mills
Sylvia Mills
Susan Millward
Michael Milne
Sally Milne
Kevin Milward
Kate Mingay
Keith Minshull
Rachel Mitchell
Suzanne Mitchell
Alison Mitton
Rosemary Mitzhener
John Mochan
Riswana Mohamed
Sophie Moinon
Vicki Molineux
Julie Molt
Andrew Moncrieff
Charles Mondahl
Mardi Monello
Kate Montague
Francesca Montero
Stephen Montgomery
Grace Moore
Holly Moore
Kerry Moore
Mhairi Moore
Rebbecca Moore
Somerset Moore
Rodney Morant
Robert More
Mariac Moreno
Rogelio Moreno
Alexandra Moreton

Chantelle Morgan
Debbie Morgan
Lynn Morgan
Sara Morgan
Valerie Morghese
Colin Morison
Brett Morrell
Adriana Morris
Andrew Morris
Debbie Morris
Kate Morris
Marjorie Morris
Nicola Morris
Iain Morrison
Rita Morrison
Julie Mortimer
Karen Morton
Melanie Morton
Ashley Mosdell
Laura Moses
Janet Moss
Stephanie Moss
Vaughan Moss
Emile Moucarry
Fiona Moucq
Lindy Moulton
Fiona Mowbray
Peter Mowlds
Adrienne Moyce
Ray Mudie
Martin Muers
Ian Muir
Laura Muir
Linzi Muir
Sharon Muir
Stewart Muir
Daniel Mules
Jan Mulholland
Shelly Munro
Chris Murphy
Frith Murphy
Tania Murphy
Adrian Murray
Ann Murray
Barbara Murray
Irene Murray
Judith Murray
Kate Murray
Lu Murray
Thomas Murray
Sheila Musgrove
Sarah Mushrow
Julie Musk
Johanna Muszynski
Sarah Mutton
Sara Muzio
Oliver Myers
Natalie Myler
Guy Myram
Jane Nathan
Adam Naylor
Amanda Neal
James Neal
Roger Neale
Laura Nellist
John Newcomb
Victoria Newland
Kevin Newman
Sheila Newman
Philip Newport-Black
Jeffrey Ng
Andy Niblock
Karen Nice
Luke Nicholes
Alan Nicholls
Louise Nicholls
Bill Nicholson
Maggie Nicholson
Tessa Nicholson-Smith
Anne Nickless
Laura Nickoll
Mary Niclub
Bob Nicol
Jennie Nicol
Charlotte Nield
Nicki Nigh
Ariel Nimba
Georgina Nixon
Lesley Norman
Michael North
Carolyn Northover
Anne Norton
Kerrie Norton
Tony Norton
Kira Novak
Adele Nozedar
Emily Nudd
Nathan Nurton
Ian Nuttall

Neville Nuttall
Jayne Nutting
Charles Nyereyegona
Katy Nyman
Alison Oakervee
David Oakes
Nigel Oakes
James Oakley
Ryan Oates
Alan O'Brien
Claire O'Brien
Helen O'Brien
Whitney O'Carroll
Sarah O'Connor
Truuske Odde
Donya Odonnell
Geraldine Odonnell
Geraldine O'Donnell
Marietherese
    Odonohue
Therese O'Donohue
Jennifer O'Dwyer
Lily O'Farrell
Hannah Ogden
Colin Ogier
Richard Ogier
Richard O'Hare
Calum Oliver
Kevin O'Mahoney
Dermod O'Malley
Aoife O'Meara
Halli O'Neil
Tony O'Neill
Ciara O'Reilly
Jessica O'Reilly
Kirsty O'Reilly
Laura O'Reilly
Meg O'Reilly
Julia Orford
Geoff Ormrod
Jojo Orrissey
Michelle Osborn
Chris Osborne
Claire Osborne
Eleanor Osborne
Jack Osborne
Robert Osborne
Michelle Osbourne
Gustauo Oseda
Janet O'Shaughnessy
Madeleine Ostling
Amy O'Sullivan
Susan Oswell
Riona Overend
Conrad Owen
Jolene Owen
Jude Owens
Ann Owston
Eve Oxley
Caitriona Oxx
Joanne Pace
Anne Page
Joanne Paisner
Christine Palfreyman
Harriet Palfreyman
Sam Palfreyman
Alejandro Palma
Desmond Palmer
Jack Palmer
Rachel Palmer
Sue Palmer
Bev Paris
Emily Parish
Anthony Park
James Park
Penny Park
Marian Parke
Alex Parker
Benedict Parker
Joan Parker
Samantha Parker
Simon Parker
Joel Parkes
Carl-Cedric Parkin
Penny Parkin
Alan Parkinson
Carl Parkinson
Charlotte Parkinson
Becky Parr
Heather Parry
Steve Parry
Phil Parsonage
Joan Parsons
Rick Parsons
Robert Parsons
Vivienne Parsons
Clifford Partridge
Lionel Partridge
Alan Pascoe
Emma Pascoe

Becky Paskin
Kathee Pass
Kirsty Pass
Anish Patel
Beverley Paterson
David Paterson
Stuart Paterson
Teea Pato
Carol Patrick
Sam Patrick
Neville Patten
Karen Patterson
Lauren Patterson
Donall Patton
Jack Paull
Peter Pawsey
Alex Payne
Kate Payne
Massimiliano Pazzaglia
Steve Peach
Tamara Peach
Megan Peacock
Wiliam Peacock
Debbie Pearce
Steven Pearce
Annette Pearson
Katy Pearson
Nicky Pearson
James Peddle
Andrea Peers
Sophie Pegg
Hilary Pegum
John Peirce
Chris Pemberton
Neil Pendleton
Paul Penman
Eve Pennant-Jones
Jackie Penney
Kevin Penney
Eric Pennington
Margaret Pennington
Simon Pennington
Ilaria Pepponi
Peter Perchard
Matthew Percival
Karen Pereira
Julia Perez
Joy Perkins
Sophie Perres
Diane Perrin
Nick Pescod
Carrie Pester
Amanda Peters
Karen Pettemerides
Brian Pettifer
Nicola Pettit
Cheryl Pettitt
Tej Phadnis
Linda Phelan
Hannah Philipps
Fiona Phillips
Harriette Phillips
Iain Phillips
Louise Phillips
Sally Phillips
Becky Phillpot
Maureen Philpot
Bob Pickering
Helen Pickford
George Pickvance
Anthony Pidden
Bill Pidden
Karen Piggott
Francoine Pigut
Tara Pilcher
Milly Pilston
Victoria Pinchbeck
Catherine Pinder
Alexandre Pinheiro-
    Torres
Ed Pink
Alessandro Pinna
John Pinschof
Paul Pissarro
Laura Pitts
Issie Place
Tony Platt
Jane Plumb
Ann Pnden
Jackie Poate
Stan Pochron
Hannah Pocock
Julia Pointer
Tom Polashicz
Linda Pollard
Joy Poole
Y Pope
Emma Porter
Geraldine Porter
Nicola Porter

Daniel Potter
Jacob Potter
John Potter
Sarah Potterton
Oliver Potts
Stuart Potts
Dimitra Pouli
Jessica Powderly
Snoo Powell
An Powes
Rebecca Powler
Sinead Poxon
Nick Poyner
Charlotte Pratt
Kevin Pratt
Robert Pratt
Jann Preen
Katrine Preen
Julie Pressey
Kala Preston
Luke Preston
Danielle Price
Derek Price
Joe Price
Clare Priddy
Susan Priestley
Virginia Priestley
Jane Prinsley
Anthea Pritchard
Tim Pritchard
George Prole
Kevin Protheroe
Martin Prout
Joanna Pryjda
Gale Pryor
John Pudduck
David Pulley
Marie Purt
Hilary Puxley
Natalie Pye
C Pyle
Darren Queen
Kathryn Quick
Kim Quick
Debbie Quinn
Liam Quinn
Sean Quinn
Gary Quinney
Estefania Quintana
Rebekah
    Quixanohenriques
George Rab
James Raeburn
Sheila Ragg
June Raines
Alan Rainford
Anita Rakauskaite
Geeta Ral
Gemma Ralph
Derek Ramage
Ashley Ramsden
Sarah Ramsey
Leeann Rana
Sue Randall
T.A. Rankin
Ronald Rankine
Lesley Ratcliffe
Oscar Ratcliffe
Nadine Ratzel
Elizabeth Ravereclt
Amanda Rawson
Phillip Ray
Bruce Raybould
Brett Raynes
Marcus Raynor
David Raynsford-Dyer
Dom Rea
Madeline Read
Katie Ready
Peggy Reardon
Michael Redfern
Stephen Redmond
Alan Reed
Andrew Reed
Louise Reed
Emma Rees
Gemma Rees
Laura Rees
Sian Reeslloyd
Jeni Reeve
Penny Reeves
Alison Reid
Annabel Reid
John Reid
Paul Reilly
Peter Reilly
Leigh Rengger
Julie Reveillere
Guy Reynolds
Neil Reynolds

Elli Rhodes
Paul Ricce
Nick Rice
Ollie Rice
Thomas Richard
    Hughes
Anita Richards
Christopher Richards
Gill Richards
Jason Richards
Jo Richards
Savannah Richards
Anna Richardson
Cjohn Richardson
Dawn Richardson
Katy Richardson
Johanna Riches
Peter Richmond
Antje Rickowski
David Rickwood
Anne Ridgway
Pam Ridley
Richard Rigby
Florence Riley
Martin Riley
Gill Riseley
Gemma Ritchie
Nicola Ritchie
Suzi Rixon
Richard Robbins
Abi Roberts
Anne Roberts
Charlotte Roberts
Enid Roberts
Hannah Roberts
John Roberts
Marlene Roberts
Sarah Roberts
Victoria Roberts
Maryjane Roberts-
    Fishwick
Judy Robertshaw
Iain Robertson
John Robertson
Lee Robertson
Sarah Robertson
Lucie Robin
Philip Robins
Tim Robins
Caroline Robinson
Hen Robinson
Jay Robinson
Julie Robinson
Katie Robinson
Paul Robinson
Peter Robinson
Rosemary Robinson
Sheila Robinson
Zoe Robinson
Ann Robson
Anne Robson
Dave Robson
Lucy Robson
Mary Robson
Ronald Robson
Adam Roche
Maria Rochelle
Georgia Roderick
Lena Rodson
Catherine Rogers
Elaine Rogers
Gregory Rogers
Karen Rogers
Katherine Rogers
Madeleine Rogers
Maureen Rogers
Tricia Rogers
Jane Rollinson
Tom Ronayne
Elaine Root
James Rose
Linde Rose
David Roshier
Alex Ross
Amy Ross
Martine Ross
Raymond Rouse
Francesca Rowden-
    Jones
Clayton Rowe
Josie Rowe
Margaret Rowe
Zara Rowe
John Rowell
Sarah Rowland
Elin Rowlands
John Rowlands
Lisa Rowles
Emma Roy
Tanya Royer

Sasha Rudes
Nicola Rudland
Sharon Ruff
Georgia Rule
Fran Rumbelow
Sarah Rushton
Barbara Russell
Emma Russell
Esmee Russell
Philip Russell
Laurence Ruston
Naomi Rutherford
Amber Rutter
James Ryan
Phoebe Ryan
Madeleine Ryder
Madeline Ryder
Alexandra Ryman
Ewa Rzadkow
Christine Sachs
Sharea Sackey
Amar Sadarancand
Magdalena Sadlo
Amy Sainsbury
Alex Salgueropineyro
Anna Sallows
Sue Salman
Jean Salter
Keith Salway
Isabella Samengo-
    Turner
Marianne Sampson
Jen Samson
John Samson
Jayne Samuel-Walker
Harvey Samways
Rick Sana
Nadia Sanche
Alexis Sanches
Matthew Sanders
Simran Sandru
John Sankey
Emma Sansom
Savien Sarga
Lee Sargeant
Margaret Sargent
Deborah Sarginson
Hannah Saunders
John Saunders
Mal Saunders
Clair Saunders-Grant
Chris Savage
Sar Sawe
Simon Schiff
Samantha Scholes
Dan Schrieber
Dee Schrier
Ronald Schwarz
Sue Scotland
Alastair Scott
Amy Scott
Charles Scott
Denise Scott
Helen Scott
Marvyn Scott
Phillip Scott
Rebecca Scott
Trisha Scott
Joe Scowen
Chris Scrimgour
Atia Scrivens
Barbara Scullard
Emma Scurr
Gabriella Seage
John Searby
Jo Seddon
Sam Seejay
David Sefton
Edwin Self
Henry Semple
Tom Setterfield
Koshni Shah
Julia Shailes
Mike Shakespeare
Tora Shand
David Shapiro
Sai Sharma
Katie Sharman
Nancyruth Sharp
Richard Sharp
Yvonne Sharp
Alexa Shaw
Hilary Shaw
Nicola Shaw
Robert Shaw
Skeine Shaw
Ilan Sheady
Linda Sheard
Mark Sheargold
Lesley Shearman

James Sheath
Clare Sheeran
Monica Shelley
Lorraine Shelsher
Conor Shepherd
Ralph Shepherd
Venetia Sheppard
Roy Sheridan
Claire Sherriff
Louise Sherrington
Jyoti Shetty
Clive Shiach
Jasmine Shill
Sue Shipley
Kate Shone
Laura Shooter
Gilbert Short
Jos Short
Julie Shoudley
Valeria Shukdauda
Jessica Shum
Theresa Sibbett
Maureen Sibley
Stephen Sides
Liea Sierina
Pilar Sifas
Stewart Sim
Dianne Simcock
Louisa Simcox-Maclean
Lucie Simic
Rebecca Simmonds
Sally Simmons
Sam Simmons
Martin Simons
Adam Simpson
Christopher Simpson
Deborah Simpson
Gary Simpson
Isaac Simpson
J Simpson
John Simpson
Loo Simpson
Mary Simpson
Mhairi Simpson
Sarah Simpson
Eva Sinclair
James Sinclair
Adam Singer
William Sitwell
Gillian Skene
Peter Slape
Brian Slater
Julie Slater
Linda Slater
Pamela Slater
Sally Slater
Ivor Slee
Alan Slomson
Margaret Slughter
Lorna Smalley
Elsje Smart
Robert Smedley
Alison Smile
Alister Smith
Amy Smith
Ashleigh Smith
Brad Smith
Brian Smith
Chloe Smith
Chrisde Smith
Craig Smith
Danielle Smith
Esther Smith
Frank Smith
Gemma Smith
Gillian Smith
Jackie Smith
Jacqui Smith
Jj Smith
Joanne Smith
Joseph Smith
Kevin Smith
Lindsey Smith
Lisa Smith
Lydia Smith
Mark Smith
Mary Smith
Morven Smith
Natalie Smith
Neil Smith
Oliver Smith
Rachel Smith
Richard Smith
Rose Smith
Sally Smith
Stacey Smith
Stephen Smith
Stuart Smith
Susan Smith
Gordon Smyth

Mark Smyth
Betty Smythe
Emma Snaith
Elizabeth Sneath
Morgana Sneddon
Dave Snow
Helen Snowden
Margaret So
Amanda Sofocleous
Sarah Somers
Richard Somerville
Brian Songhurst
Mia Sonny
Raul Souca
Tim Soudain
Helen Soutar
Gary South
Tracy Southam
Michael Southward
David Spackman
Joanne Spackman
Darryl Spain
Carol Spanner
Viviana Spantucci
Jane Sparrow
Steven Speed
Virginia Speed
Guy Speir
John Speller
Harold Spencer
Catriona Spickernell
Jess Spragg
David Sprague
Alan Spring Wallis
David Springer
Kirsty Squire
Karen Stafford
Dee Stagles
Julian Stamford
Victoria Stang
Annabel Stannard
Clare Stanton
Fiona Stark
Jennie Staunton
Julie Stead
Wendy Steadman-
   Callander
Mark Steel
Jennifer Steele
Chloe Steers
Silvia Stefancikova
Simon Steggles
Paula Stei
Barbara Stenhouse
Heidi Stenhouse
Lisa Stephens
Daniel Stephenson
Rebecca Stephenson
Richard Stephenson
Ilene Sterns
Becky Stevens
Deborah Stevens
Jan Stevens
Jenny Stevens
Lloyd Stevens
John Stevenson
Tom Steward
Beryl Stewart
John Stewart
Kevin Stewart
Robin Stewart
Valerie Stewart
Hilary Stickland
Allen Stidwill
Jo Stiff
Sarah Stimpson
Bill Stimson
Vivienne Stobo
Chris Stock
Debbie Stock
Nozan Stoker
Lyndon Stokes
Lesley Stone
Sonia Stone
Sandra Stonehouse
Sue Stott
Laura Stowe
Camilla Straker
Karenrose Strathmore
Lorna Stroupnilsson
Alastair Struthers
Iain Stuart
Joyce Stuart
Sophie Stubbles
Peter Stubbs
Neil Stuke
Ruth Sturdy
Emma Sturgess
Jade Styan

Liz Styles
Jennifer Sualez
Lyndsey Such
Anna Sudbury
Stephen Suggitt
Scott Sullivan
Alex Sumray
Yuan Sun
Lyn Sunyard
Helen Super
Robin Surtees
Wakefield
Susan Susskind
Amy Sutcliffe
Diane Sutcliffe
Michael Sutcliffe
Daniel Sutherland
Heather Sutton
Paul Sutton
Sharon Sutton
Hilary Swallow
Georgina Swan
Gill Swayne-Jones
Kate Sweetapple
Roger Sweetapple
Swtest Swtest
Alison Sykes
Christine Sykes
Sabrina Sykes
Lorna Sylvester
Sandra Sylvester
Joanne Synel
Lidia Szmid
Yvan Taillandier
Dharmesh Tailor
Emily Talbot
Charlotte Talbotrice
Douglas Talintyre
Peter Tallon
Kayleigh Talton
Linda Tame
Richard Tame
Nicholas Tan
Justina Tanonyit
Mark Tapley
Daniel Tapper
Kelly Tary
Alex Tasker
Sarah Tate-Smith
Mark Taubert
Alex Taylor
Andrew Taylor
Eric Taylor
Geoff Taylor
George Taylor
Jayne Taylor
Jean Taylor
Jodi Taylor
Julia Taylor
Karl Taylor
Kathy Taylor
Ken Taylor
Lesley Taylor
Louise Taylor
Mark Taylor
Mia Taylor
Sue Taylor
Susie Taylor
Trina Taylor
Victoria Tehrani
Catia Teixeir
Nish Tej
Jane Tejer
Penny Telford
Graeme Temple
Joan Tennant
Simon Tennet
Eileen Teo
Helen Terrington
Patricia Terry
Marjorie Thacker
Sara Thackray
Sofia Theologitis
Lisa Thirkettle
Adam Thomas
Angela Thomas
Chelsea Thomas
Christopher Thomas
Heulwen Thomas
Jason Thomas
Karen Thomas
Kelly Thomas
Rebecca Thomas
Richard Thomas
Shelley Thomas
Sue Thomas
Brenda Thompson
Clive Thompson
Izzy Thompson

James Thompson
Jane Thompson
Jenny Thompson
Lesley Thompson
Lorraine Thompson
Lucy Thompson
Max Thompson
Millie Thompson
Rachel Thompson
Sarah Thompson
Tina Thompson
Jacqui Thoms
Caitlin Thomson
Charlotte Thomson
Eddie Thomson
Greta Thornbory
Jenny Thorndycraft
Jack Thorne
Charlotte Thorney
Charlotte Thorneycroft
Maggie Thornton
Keil Thorup
Michelle Throssell
Chirstopher Thwaites
Emrys Tindal
Lindsay Tindal
Barbara Tinsley
Margaret Tinsley
Aaron Tippett
Helen Tipping
Giles Tirant
Julia Tod
Juliette Toft
David Tombleson
Michael Tomlinson
Gary Toner
James Tonkin
Gabriella Tonlolo
Rebecca Toole
Paul Toomer
Maria Jesus Torres
Ray Totty
Ivory Towers
Kate Towers
Melanie Towershesketh
Chris Townsend
Jody Townsend
Lady Townsend
Neil Townshend
Marie Tracey
Peter Tracey
Linh Tran
Kevin Travis
Steve Trayler
Dei Treanor
Lauren Treasure
Tery Tredget
Louise Tripp
Kate Triscott
Sarah Trollope
Sandra Troughton
Steve Trueman
Charlotte Tucker
Karl Tucker
Martin Tucker
Anita Tuddenham
A Tuke
Caroline Tulloch
Richard Tulz
Sheena Tunney
Scooby Turley
Michael Turnbull
Emma Turner
Glen Turner
Jill Turner
John Turner
Sarah Turner
Tyler Turner
Jill Turton
Andy Turvil
Kirstie Tuzinkiewicz
Tina Tweed
Deborah Twist
Jean Twomey
Andrew Tye
Claire Tyler
Laura Tyler
Charles Tyndall
Philip Tyres
Kylie Tyszyk
Chi Ugoala
Isabella Underhill
Rachel Unicomb
Jessica Valenghi
Lisa Valentino
Aidan Valters
Steven Vandewalle
Andre Vandierendonck
Gemma Vanrooyen

Rachael Vanroy
Jonathan Varey
Bob Vaughan
Richard Veal
Darah Veale
Rebecca Veazey
Sara Vegarosas
Lorna Venn
Tania Ver-Burgos
Alan Vere
Chris Vickery
Elmor Victor
Antonio Vigorito
Pere Villegs
Katie Vincent
Kevin Vincent
Janet Vinter
Isobel Virevfa
Mandy Voyse
Clara Wade
David Wade
Dave Wagstaff
Simon Wagstaff
Mark Wagstaffe
Jason Wain
Kerry Wainman
Wendy Waite
David Wakefield
Susanne Wakefield
Jennifer Wakerley
Verity Wakley
Helen Walden
Karen Walden
Christine Walder
Charlotte Walker
Fran Walker
Jessica Walker
Katie Walker
Katy Walker
Kevin Walker
Matthew Walker
Nigel Walker
Sharon Walker
Stephen Walker
Stuart Walker
Tess Walker
Richard Wall
John Wallace
Mike Wallace
Nicola Wallace
Tom Wallace
Derek Waller
Diana Waller
Karen Waller
David Wallis
Dominic Wallis
Allison Walls
Chris Walmer
Mary Walmsley
Olivia Walmsley
Aimi Walsh
Emma Walsh
Louisa Walters
Sophie Walters
Jackie Walton
Richard Walton
Stuart Walton
Pat Warbrid
Caroline Warburton
Cyril Ward
Deborah Ward
Glynne Ward
Jennifer Ward
John Ward
Michelle Wardingley
Gary Wardle
Katie Wardman
Samantha Wardman
Alex Warner
Alisom Warner
Alison Warner
Tara Warner
Claire Waters
Danielle Watkins
David Watkins
Caroline Watson
Frances Watson
John Watson
Lindsay Watson
Miriam Watson
Patrick Watson

Stuart Watson
Sarah Watson-Fisher
Pauline Watt
Helen Watters
Lorraine Watters
Georgia Watts
Stacey Watts
Emma Wayland
Stephanie Weager
Jackie Weare
Lee Weaver
Zoe Weaver
Ahsen Webb
Christian Webb
Dianne Weeks
Julie Welch
Katherine Welch
Katherine Welch
Charlotte Welham
Mathew Welham
Claire Weller
Vicky Wells
Jo Wernham
Anthony West
Samantha West
Tessa West
Patricia Wharry
Richard Wheatley
Cassandra Wheeldon
Christina Wheeler
John Wheeler
Renee Wheeler
Ryan Whelan
John Whetsel
Martin Whirehouse
Benjamin White
Jemma White
Jenny White
Jess White
Paul White
Philppac White
Rita White
Roger White
Sue White
AnneMarie Whitehead
Peter Whitehead
Lisa Whitehouse
Gillian Whiteley
Johnscott Whiteley
Meredith Whitely
Micheal Whitfield
Meredith Whitley
Richard Whitley
Emma Whittaker
John Whittaker
Simon Whitting
Darren Whittington
Lindsay Whittle
Sophie Whittle
Jessie Whitworth
Catherine Whyle
Julie Whysall
Ali Wickerson
Gail Wicks
Sonia Wiebe
Anika Wightman
Mandy Wilcock
Mandy Wilcock Moore
Emma Wilcox
Ena Wilcz
Eileen Wilde
Jade Wilkes
Jan Wilkins
Roy Wilkins
Darren Wilkinson
Helen Wilkinson
Irene Wilkinson
Miles Wilkinson
Pamela Wilkinson
Pat Wilkinson
Sue Wilkinson
Allan Willetts
Charlie Williams
Debbie Williams
Dominic Williams
Edwyn Williams
Gemma Williams
Giovanni Williams
Hayley Williams
Jane Williams
John Williams
Julia Williams
Kerry Williams
Lucy Williams
Mike Williams
Nicki Williams
Nicola Williams

Owen Williams
Peter Williams
Raymond Williams
Seven Williams
Sunita Williams
Suzanne Williams
Lisa Williamsellis
Allison Williamson
Debbie Williamson
George Williamson
Hubert Williamson
Liz Williamson
Martin Williamson
Ella Willis
Katherine Willis
Sophie Willis
Antony Willman
Shelley Wills
Carole Wilson
Clare Wilson
Eileen Wilson
Helen Wilson
Henry Wilson
Jean Wilson
Ken Wilson
Kerry Wilson
Malcolm Wilson
Melissa Wilson
Nigel Wilson
Phil Wilson
Primrose Wilson
Rob Wilson
Sarah Wilson
Stuart Wilson
Lucy Winch
George Windsor
Kate Winfield
Phillipa Winfield
Roy Winfield
Trevor Wing
Lesley Winship
Jason Winstanley
Philiplouis
   Winterbottom
Sam Winterson
Paul Withers
Alan Wood
Carol Wood
Don Wood
Jacqueline Wood
Karl Wood
Linda Wood
Lisa Wood
Rosamund Wood
Steve Wood
Trevor Wood
Jane Woodford
Paulene Woodhead
Alina Woodhouse
Tracy Woods
Jim Woodward
June Woofdield
Joe Woohey
Simon Woollacott
Shakira Wooloff
Joanna Worthington
Frances Wotton
Amanda Wragg
Jenny Wrest
Amanda Wright
Jennifer Wright
Jo Wright
John Wright
Julie Wright
Nick Wright
Sue Wright
Diana Wyatt
Amanda Wyeth
Gordon Wykes
Joseph Wylie
Gavin Yam
John Yates
Kevin Yates
Nadia Yates
Mariam Yazdian
Catherine Young
Hattie Young
Oswald Young
Sally Young
Stephen Young
Aycan Yumusak
Jessica Zeun
Yvonne Zukawski